Movie Awards

A *Variety* Book

MOVIE AWARDS

The Ultimate, Unofficial Guide to the Oscars®, Golden Globes®, Critics, Guild & Indie Honors

Tom O'Neil

Foreword by Peter Bart, Editor in Chief, *Variety*

A PERIGEE BOOK

A Perigee Book
Published by The Berkley Publishing Group
A division of Penguin Putnam Inc.
375 Hudson Street
New York, New York 10014

First edition: January 2001

Published simultaneously in Canada.

The Penguin Putnam Inc. World Wide Web site address is
http://www.penguinputnam.com

Library of Congress Cataloging-in-Publication Data

O'Neil, Tom
Movie awards : the ultimate, unoffical guide to the Oscars, Golden Globes, critics, guild
and indie honors / Tom O'Neil ; foreword by Peter Bart, editor in chief.
p. cm.
Includes index.
ISBN 0-399-52651-X
1. Motion picture—Awards. I. Title
PN1993.92.053 2001
791.43'079—dc21   00-049202

Printed in the United States of America

10 9 8 7 6 5 4 3

To Frank and Marge O'Neil,
true superstars

Contents

Acknowledgments

Salutes and cheers go to the team at Perigee Books—John Duff, Tess Bresnan and Craig Burke—and the savvy crew at *Variety*, who championed this project: Peter Bart, Charlie Koones, Henry Shapiro, Peter Cowie, Madelyn Hammond, Elizabeth Guider, Bruce Brosnan, Bashirah Muttalib and Dan Edelson.

Research was headed up by two expert sleuths—George Figueroa and Michele Mavissakalian, who unearthed invaluable nuggets while prospecting for old awards gold in the haunted Hollywood hills. Many thanks, too, to Stephen Garrett, who provided key research on the New York Film Critics Circle, and to Sherie Van Sanford, Steve Hernandez and Victor Barreiro, who pitched in on library duty.

Dennis and Diane Gregory toiled tirelessly to help compile the immense listings. I was tempted to sneak their names into that section of this book, rather than here, to emphasize what winners they are.

The whole gang at the Oscars' Margaret Herrick Library in Los Angeles was helpful and fun to work with (except that chap who yelled at me for accidentally exceeding the number of pages permitted to photocopy—sorry!). Other thanks are owed to John Pavlik and Scott Miller at the Oscars; Chantal Dinnage and Helmut Voss at the Golden Globes; Liz Weiss at the National Society of Film Critics; Godfrey Cheshire at the New York Film Critics Circle; Jean Oppenheimer at the Los Angeles Film Critics Association; Joey Berlin at the Broadcast Film Critics Association; Greg Krizman at the Screen Actors Guild; Chuck Warn, Laraine Savelle and Darrell Hope at the Directors Guild of America; Sherrie Newman, Angela Wales Kirgo, Karen Pederson, Richard Stayton and Barbara Ditlow at the Writers Guild of America; Vance Van Petten, Erica Pruety and Ken Ross at the Producers Guild of America; Josh Welsh at the Independent Spirits; and Annette Insodorf and Lois Ballon at the National Board of Review. A number of film crix helped out with key info: Kevin Thomas, Kenneth Turan, Henry Sheehan, Peter Rainer, John Simon, Jerry Roberts, Len Klady, David Sterritt and Thelma Adams.

A slew of other folks also deserve huzzahs: Dick Kagan, Sue Karlin, Gordon Clapp, John Mack Carter, Curtiss Anderson, Brad Pomerance, Audrey Clark, Susan King, Tariq Kahn, Steve Hanson at USC and dear, sweet Claire at Eddie Brandt's Saturday Matinee in North Hollywood.

Also, a bow goes to that Extraordinary gang at E!: John Rieber, Antonio Ruiz, Gary Snegaroff, Eddie Delbridge, Joan and Melissa Rivers, Edward Zarcoff, Peggy Jo Abraham, Sean Reid, Art Lovell, Linda Grasso, Corie Hirschtick, Steve Kmetko, Jules Asner, Todd Newton, Suzanne Sena, Dave Adelson, Patrick Stinson, Michael Castner, Dagny Hultgreen, Christine Hsia, Gerry Johnston, Jennifer Colbert, Cassandra Costa, Tim Gibbs, Tiffany Meyers, Kristi Horgan, Fred Mendes, James "Big Boy" Medlin, Tom McNamara, John Wood, Eliza Cost, Colin McLean, Shannon Keenan, Lynn Helmsteadt, Lisa DiGiovone, Steve Root and Scott Robson.

Some other media pals also deserve hailing for their enthusiastic kudos coverage: Brad Bessey at *Entertainment Tonight;* Lynn Lester at CNN; Bill McCuddy, Dave Brown, Patrick McLaughlin, Stacy Shapiro, Paula Zahn and Bill O'Reilly at Fox News Channel; Sam Rubin and Jamie Grossman at KTLA; Bill Diehl of ABC Radio; Bill Moran of Business Network Radio; and Natalie Batos and John Gambling and gang at WOR radio.

My deepest bow, though, goes to Caroline White, who once took a flier on this awards-crazed writer and published his first books. Look, Caroline—they're still soaring!

Foreword

There are too many awards and too many award shows—just about everyone agrees on that. Everyone understands as well that this proliferation does not stem from an outpouring of magnanimity. While kudos extended by professional groups are designed to reward genuine achievement, the raison d'être for most awards is that they make money for people. The Academy Awards, the godfather of all award shows, brings millions not only to the Academy but also to the film companies that win the Oscars and to the performers as well. A star like Jodie Foster may say, "Whenever I win an award, I can't stop laughing," but in point of fact she's laughing all the way to the bank.

According to *Variety,* there were 3,182 awards given last year just in the entertainment business alone. Imagine all the "I would like to thank"'s that they generated. Think, also, of all the dollars that changed hands in the process.

Though it's all too easy to be dismissive of awards, the fact remains that people love to bestow them, and other people—especially performers—positively relish receiving them. No matter how many "aw shucks" attitudes an actor may assume, no matter how many "I don't deserve this" speeches he may make, actors positively bask in the aura of awards ceremonies. I have attended a myriad of awards shows and have had ample opportunity to observe the delight, the excitement, the sheer narcissistic glow that's exuded when his name is announced. And when "the other guy" wins, I'm amazed at how the runner-up can produce that broad smile and clap his hands enthusiastically, all the while muttering, "That creep doesn't deserve it, I deserve it."

As delicious as it is to win awards, it is extraordinarily difficult to decide how to bestow them. As Tom O'Neil skillfully spells out, organizations that give awards often are wracked by the most intense debates. The complexity of this decision-making process is evidenced by the fact that, as O'Neil points out, the New York and Los Angeles film critics groups have been in agreement only eight times in twenty-five years on the Best Picture category. The Oscars, meanwhile, usually march to an entirely different drummer.

No one has studied awards processes more diligently than O'Neil, nor been more cognizant of the political and economic forces at work. And while he really delights in awards shows—the wonderful thing about him is that he remains, first and foremost, a fan—he also can point up their occasionally arch motivations. He reminds us that the Academy of Motion Picture Arts and Sciences was really created to help crunch film workers wage demands and, along the way, decided that dispensing kudos would lend itself a more enlightened aura. The original moguls felt comfortable with the Oscars, as originally constituted, because they knew they could control the voting. They simply instructed all their employees how to vote. The present day anarchy that marks the Academy voting no doubt would drive them crazy.

The bottom line, however, is that the Oscars usually reward outstanding achievements. Other awards, too, strive to encourage excellence and, through the wide range of their choices, to stimulate a healthy diversity as well. And if someone happens to make a few bucks along the way, well, oddly, it's all in a good cause, as Tom O'Neil would enthusiastically testify.

Peter Bart
Editor in Chief
Variety

Introduction
Hollywood's Gold Derby

There is no such thing as a Best Picture of the Year.

In fact, there are dozens of films declared the best in any given year by such informed folks as critics, scholars and showbiz pros belonging to guilds, circles, societies, trade organizations and the Academy of Motion Picture Arts and Sciences. At this point, there are so many kudos that someone should create a Best Picture Award Award so that we mere mortals can have it settled once and for all which voice-from-the-mountaintop we should be listening to.

But in Hollywood schmoozespeak, everything's "the best"—"the best Scorsese pic yet," "the best restaurant in Beverly Hills"—and one is forced to accept the illogic of it if one wants to discover the shining examples of a celluloid art form renowned for its embarrassment of riches. Underneath it all, everyone knows that those statuettes are merely gold-*plated*.

In the 25 years of their coexistence, the Los Angeles and New York critics' groups have agreed on Best Picture only eight times: *Kramer vs. Kramer* (1979), *Terms of Endearment* (1983), *Hannah and Her Sisters* (1986), *GoodFellas* (1990), *Schindler's List* (1993), *Leaving Las Vegas* (1995), *L.A. Confidential* (1997) and *Saving Private Ryan* (1998). The Oscars concurred on only three of those choices: *Kramer, Terms* and *Schindler*. The National Society of Film Critics, which often strays in favor of international pix, has agreed with the N.Y. and L.A. groups only three times—*GoodFellas, Schindler's List* and *L.A. Confidential*—which means that the only U.S. movie that's received backing from all three crix orgs and the Oscars was *Schindler's List*. Since *Schindler* also reaped the Golden Globe in 1993 plus accolades from the National Board of Review and the producers', directors' and writers' guilds, it reigns as the only

Schindler's List is the only film in recent showbiz history to sweep all of the top Best Picture awards.

pic in recent showbiz history to achieve a cross-kudos consensus.

That's how elusive Hollywood's holy grail can be. But still there will always be a naysayer, of course. In 1993, just when Hollywood had finally made up its collective mind at long last, the rest of the country piped up and the People's Choice Award went to a different Spielberg pic: *Jurassic Park*.

Back before the recent proliferation of film awards—and the subsequent, inevitable competition between them—harmony reigned far more frequently. The Oscars and New York Film Critics agreed on Best Picture only once in the first nine years of the crix group's existence (*The Life of Emile Zola* in 1937), but then, suddenly, the two kudos got noticeably chummy and concurred on 18 of their next 24 top pics. During the first 23 years of the Globe's existence, its voters concurred with members of the motion picture academy and the Gotham crix group 13 times (the National Board of Review strayed 9 times). In 1966, all four kudos lined up behind *A Man for All Seasons,* but that was the same year that the contrary-minded National Society of Film Critics was formed, which up-ended everything by picking *Blow-Up,* and nothing's been the same since.

Mark Twain's Pudd'nhead Wilson once said, "It's not best that we should all think alike or else there'd be no point to horse races," and a horse race is exactly what all the top movie awards are.

As long ago as the 1930s, *Variety* began referring to the Oscar race as a "derby" and employed the metaphor frequently and playfully to declare who was out front, falling back or totally out of the running. When the film critics, the showbiz guilds and the foreign press saw how much fun the contest was, they launched their own kudos and positioned theirs ahead of the Oscar race so they could decide the early front-runners. Pretty soon the many award match-ups composed one big overall derby stretching on the calendar (or two calendars) from mid-December to late March or early April, and all of the kudos orgs were aggressive about pushing their horses out of the gate.

The big derby begins every year at the Sundance Film Festival. Two winners of its Special Jury Prize (docus *The Times of Harvey Milk* and *When We Were Kings*) have made it the distance to the Oscars. No fest Grand Jury Prize winner has done so yet, but a few have been nominated. *Tumbleweeds* won the fest's Filmmaker's Trophy in 1998, then bagged a Golden Globe award and Oscar nom for star Janet McTeer a year later. Audience Award champ *Hoop Dreams* swept the crix trifecta (L.A., New York and National Society of Film Critics) even though it was shut out of the Oscars.

After Sundance, other fests then pipe in—Cannes, Toronto, Venice and Berlin—and often contribute impressive contenders

The Oscar is the most accurate award, according to AFI.

such as eventual Oscar Best Picture champs *Marty* and *Chariots of Fire.* At that point, everything's left to America's critics.

There are many crix kudos bestowed by groups in Boston, Chicago, San Francisco and elsewhere, but the New York Film Critics Circle, the Los Angeles Film Critics Association and the National Society of Film Critics make up the holy trinity (it's too early to pass judgment on the respectability and impact of the relatively new Broadcast Film Critics Association). Winning crix kudos can give an honoree legitimacy—or even "snob appeal," to quote what Kathleen Turner once said when she accepted a L.A. crix award. After that, around the next bend are the foreign press awards (Golden Globes). Winning one of those means you've got real pop culture appeal, since the Globes often shamelessly do what the Oscars so far have refused to—give acting awards to Madonna, Sharon Stone, Brad Pitt, Jim Carrey, John Travolta and Tom Cruise.

Then come the guild prizes, which sometimes look more like club indoctrinations. But because these are peer-group awards just like the Oscars—and they share many of the same voters—the results can be tip-offs on who'll win the Academy Awards later.

The finish line is the stage at the Oscar ceremony.

Overall, here are the scores on how the various groups performed opposite the Oscars. The National Society of Film Critics has agreed only three times in its 34 years on Best Picture. The Gotham crix named the same Best Picture as the Oscars 27 times over 65 years. The L.A. crix concurred only seven times in 25 years (a period of time during which the Gotham crix and Oscars agreed eight times). The Globes have two Best Picture awards (drama and comedy/musical). The Oscars chose one of them 41 times in 57 years.

En route to Oscar's finish line, many of the groups back many different horses for the overall derby. At rare times many of them root for the same Best Pictures, such as *On the Waterfront, Around the World in 80 Days* and *Terms of Endearment*, or for thesps such as Sissy Spacek (*Coal Miner's Daughter*), Sally Field (*Norma Rae*), Meryl Streep (*Sophie's Choice*), Jack Nicholson (*Terms of Endearment*), Emma Thompson (*Howards End*), Holly Hunter (*The Piano*) and Nicolas Cage (*Leaving Las Vegas*)—who are the only stars to sweep all the top races (Oscars, Golden Globes, National Board of Review and the crix trifecta). Jane Fonda (*Klute*), Martin Landau (*Ed Wood*) and Dianne Wiest (*Bullets over Broadway*) reaped all of the same kudos except the National Board of Review, a prize many award watchers discount because it's not actually a crix kudo (call it an Enlightened People's Choice Award since it's determined by New York teachers, editors, lawyers, and other sophisticated film fans).

At other times the competing kudos split into two rival camps on Best Picture, as happened in 1982 when the L.A. crix and Golden Globes backed *E.T.* and the New York crix and Oscars cheered on *Gandhi*. Usually, however, the groups—just like horse breeders everywhere—prefer to sponsor their own fillies, as happened in 1969 when the foreign press backed *Anne of the Thousand Days*, the crix hopped on *Z* and Oscar voters rode *Midnight Cowboy*.

Watching how the contenders pace on the big track is the fun part and the interplay between the races can be fascinating. *Driving Miss Daisy, Dances with Wolves, Forrest Gump* and *American Beauty* were all examples of pix that were cited early on in the year's derby by the National Board of Review, but then fell behind when the crix tripped them up. All of those pix later rallied at the Golden Globes and finally made it across Oscar's finish line.

At other times the crix will launch a horse early on, such as *Annie Hall, The Deer Hunter, Gandhi* or *The Silence of the Lambs*, but it will stumble at the Golden Globes, then catch up at the guild kudos and pull ahead. Some dark horses such as *Midnight Cowboy, Braveheart* and *The Godfather, Part II* don't show up until the last leg.

When Hilary Swank came sailing over the finish line at the 1999 Oscars, such a dramatic victory by an unknown thesp must've left more than just a few observers wondering: Where'd she come from? But they would have known if they'd been paying attention to the whole overall derby earlier, when the little-known ex-star of *Beverly Hills 90210* broke out of the pack and made a graceful, impressive—and suspenseful—romp toward the Oscars. Her eventual victory would turn out to be historic: Never before had a screen newbie won a lead Academy Award for an indie pic.

Swank's derby run was so dramatic that it would make a good Hollywood movie. She was first discovered by crix whose job it is to sit in empty art-house theaters and watch gritty pix produced, in the case of Swank's *Boys Don't Cry*, by downtown Manhattan lesbians with a political message. The New York and L.A. crix were so impressed by what they saw that they made the brave decision to give their Best Actress trophies to a movie that no one had ever heard of. The National Society of Film Critics released its vote results two weeks later and disagreed,

Meryl Streep (Best Actress Oscar, *Sophie's Choice*, 1982) is one of seven thesps who won all of the top kudos in one year.

pushing its own rival—Reese Witherspoon, star of another then-obscure indie, *Election*. Both Swank and Witherspoon remained out front for only a brief time. As they came around the bend and faced the Golden Globes a few weeks later, there they ran smack into some formidable established competish—two old pros who'd gotten a head start thanks to their previous track record. They included past Oscar and Globe nominee Annette Bening, who starred in the film destined to win Best Picture at the Globes and Oscars (*American Beauty*). Also there was Julia Roberts, a past multiple-Globe champ who gave one of the most winning perfs of her career in a movie that was one of the biggest grossers of 1999 (*Notting Hill*). When sizing up that race, all bets were off.

The victors turned out to be shockers. Swank snagged the Best Drama Actress laurels, while the Globe for Best Comedy/Musical Actress was snatched by a surprising dark horse: Janet McTeer (*Tumbleweeds*), who'd previously been cited only by the National Board of Review. Of the two winners, Swank clearly became the media favorite afterward as she was cheered on in magazine and newspaper articles written by the same crix who had originally sponsored her. As the Screen Actors Guild prizes approached, the suspense was gripping because the stakes were high: the winner of that trophy usually claims the Oscar next. If Swank prevailed again, it would mean she was a cinch to cop a prize that had seemed, just months earlier, far out of her grasp. But this was where the inevitable Hollywood plot complication occurred. Swank was suddenly overtaken by Annette Bening, who pulled off a dazzling comeback after her Golden Globe loss to Swank. Bening now looked invincible because she had it all: not only the next Best Picture on her side, but Warren Beatty on her arm and their newest baby in her ballooning belly, which she showed off proudly all over Hollywood as she campaigned tirelessly to win.

The holy trinity of crix kudos: N.Y., L.A. and the national society.

As Swank and Bening headed down that last stretch toward the finish line, they appeared to be neck and neck. Certainly, the media couldn't decide who was ahead. *Entertainment Weekly*, Las Vegas oddsmakers, E! Online and *The Chicago Sun-Times*'s Roger Ebert said Bening was out front; *TV Guide* and the *L.A. Times* insisted Swank would win. At the Academy Awards, when Swank sprinted ahead and finally was declared triumphant, she arrived on stage so breathless and flustered that, in the long list of people she mentioned at the podium, she forgot to name her husband.

Trying to predict who's going to end up in the winner's circle can be a foolhardy exercise. In December 1986, after all the major pix were viewed and the L.A. and New York Film critics had agreed on *Hannah and Her Sisters* as Best Picture, the *L.A. Herald Examiner* insisted that "*Hannah* now has to be considered the year's front-runner for any and all available laurels" and predicted that director/writer Woody Allen would soon pull off the same kind of kudos sweep he'd accomplished in 1977 with *Annie Hall*. Two weeks later, however, the National Society of Film Critics disagreed and bestowed a record-tying number of laurels on *Blue Velvet*. Then America's movie-goers piped in, along with the national noncritical media, and trumpeted *Platoon*, which was suddenly sparking a firestorm of public debate over its honestly ugly portrayal of the Vietnam war. The Golden Globes became the first to declare *Platoon* a winner. After that, *Platoon* was considered an obvious cinch to take Oscar's highest honor next. And it did, leaving *Hannah* to settle for two consolation statuettes: Best Supporting Actress (Dianne Wiest) and Original Screenplay (Allen).

Even when *The Wall Street Journal* polled 6 percent of the academy's membership while trying to predict the 1999 winners, it still got Best Actor wrong: *Hurricane*'s Denzel Washington ended up losing to *American Beauty*'s Kevin Spacey.

The *Journal* should've learned from *Variety*'s past experience. *Variety* polled roughly 15 percent of the academy's 1,700 members for eight years spanning the 1947 to 1954 award races, then finally heeded complaints from academy leaders and backed off. For the next three years, it continued its poll, but not by snooping among Oscar voters. From 1955 to 1957, editors mailed out surveys to 2,250 Hollywood film pros and 250 exhibitors nationwide and were pleased to discover that the results had roughly the same batting average as the earlier polling method. *Variety* finally killed off the poll anyway, though, because too many people complained that it was spoiling all of the fun.

Over all, both polls scored a combined batting average of .868, "which might be deemed fair in most leagues," the paper said after the last race in 1957. But *Variety* scored 100 percent only four times (1949, 1950, 1954 and 1955). When it was wrong, the goofs were doozies—three bad calls in the top Best Picture races. *Variety* picked *Johnny Belinda* in 1948 (*Hamlet* won), *A Place in the Sun* in 1951 (*An American in Paris* danced off with the trophy) and *High Noon* in 1952 (*The Greatest Show on Earth* proved how truly great it was). *Variety* was so certain that *High Noon* would prevail in 1952 that it had called it "a cinch" to win. The paper should've known what trouble it was getting into the very first year when it predicted that Rosalind Russell would win Best Actress in 1947 for *Mourning Becomes Electra*. The nominee who *Variety* said was in fourth place—Loretta Young (*The Farmer's Daughter*)—pulled off a jaw-dropper.

How do all of the showbiz awards differ? What distinguishes each prize?

The Oscars will always be the Kentucky Derby—nay, the Super Bowl—of showbiz kudos because they're prizes bestowed by the winners' peers. And since approval is everything in Hollywood, those will always matter most. After that, history must be kept in mind and that's where the film crix come in. They—presumably—make choices that will still look good years later when film fans open books like this one in order to set-

tle arguments rising up in colleges, offices and saloons. Which group of voters is most correct? If we leave the answer to an impartial judge, the American Film Institute, then the surprising conclusion is—the Oscars. That's the award that had the most Best Pictures listed on the rostrum of the 100 Best Movies Ever Made when the institute polled 1,500 film pros in 1996. The Oscars, begun in 1928, had 33 pics on the list; the New York Film Critics, formed in 1935, had 20.

Oscar voters seem to like their Best Pictures big—and long. They generally don't like the year's top grossers, but they will embrace a popcorn pic such as *Titanic* now and again just to prove that they're still in the groove with the movie-going public. The crix like big pix, too, but only the L.A. Film Critics Association—never its New

Rosalind Russell (*Gypsy*, 1962) never won an Oscar or New York film crix kudo, but she's the biggest champ among actresses at the Golden Globes (5 wins) where she never lost a race.

York counterpart nor the national society—has the guts to honor the same movies that make the most coin (*Star Wars, E.T.*). The Oscars and all of the crix awards like to send a political message ("Vietnam was a mistake" = *The Deer Hunter*; "Gay is OK" = *Boys Don't Cry*). All of the kudos honor adaptations of Broadway plays (*Who's Afraid of Virginia Woolf?, Children of a Lesser God*), costume dramas (*Lawrence of Arabia*) and sometimes both (*A Man for All Seasons, The Lion in Winter*). They love anything English. The winners' lists of all groups are full of actors with British accents (Laurence Olivier, Glenda Jackson, Judi Dench) and Best Pictures filmed somewhere in an empire where once the sun never set (*The English Patient, Tom Jones*).

Many of the kudos, curiously, share the same all-time champ among thesps, too—Jack Nicholson. He is the biggest winner of awards from the Gotham crix (seven), national society (five) and National Board of Review (five). He has the most among the male thesps at the Oscars (tied with Walter Brennan, who both have one less than Katharine Hepburn), Globes (five, tied for the most overall with Rosalind Russell), and L.A. film crix (four, one less than Meryl Streep).

Other names are high-ranking champs on most of the award rosters, too, including Billy Wilder, Woody Allen and Steven Spielberg. Even the Independent Spirits borrow heavily from other kudos. A huge number of their top contenders have been past Sundance Film Festival honorees, or else they were swiped from the derby track as they ran by grasping for Oscars, Globes and crix and guild laurels. *Fargo, Leaving Las Vegas, Platoon* and *Pulp Fiction* are among the Spirits' biggest winners.

How the Oscars differ from the crix awards is interesting. It's rare for a small indie pic to do well at the Oscars, although occasionally the feisty voters make a point of cheering on a *Chariots of Fire* (which

Tom Cruise, John Travolta and Jim Carrey won Globes, but not Oscars.

was originally hailed by Roger Ebert and a band of fellow Yankee crix attending the Cannes Film Festival). But the critics embrace indies all the time and often even seem to make a point of doing so, no doubt to demonstrate how much smarter they are by picking more highbrow or less accessible fare such as *Nashville*. The critics' groups sometimes even like to one-up the Oscars by reminding everyone that their Best Pictures aren't merely limited to Hollywood. If the Oscar voters *really, really like* Sally Field, then the crix *really, really adore* Sweden's Ingmar Bergman. Three of his pix were named the best by the national society.

The crix kudos and Golden Globes seem to have more of a sense of humor than the Oscars. Academy voters usually frown on comedies, but the crix sometimes surprise award watchers with Best Picture picks such as *Babe, Tootsie* and *Hannah and Her Sisters*. The Globes, which have that separate category for comedies and musicals, hail laffers such as *Mrs. Doubtfire, Working Girl* and *Arthur* all the time. Whenever the Oscars summon up the guts to pick a howler for Best Picture, it's usually because the crix and/or Globes gave them permission ahead of time to laugh: *The Apartment, Tom Jones, Annie Hall* and *Terms of Endearment*. Both the national society and Gotham crix named Steve Martin Best Actor of 1984 for *All of Me*, but he didn't even get Oscar nommed. The Globes have pushed Jim Carrey twice (*The Truman Show, Man on the Moon*) in recent years, but the academy doesn't get the joke. Robin Williams scored three Globes (*Mrs. Doubtfire; The Fisher King; Good Morning, Vietnam*) before he finally snagged an Oscar for getting serious in *Good Will Hunting*.

All of the awards are starstruck. Actors win outside their categories all the time. Emma Thompson, Billy Bob Thornton, Ben Affleck and Matt Damon have screenplay Oscars. The writers' guild gave kudos to Thompson and Thornton, but snubbed

Affleck and Damon (who did receive nominations). The Globes honored Thompson, Affleck and Damon in the writing category, but didn't nominate Thornton. Thompson swept the N.Y., L.A. and broadcast crix kudos for scripts.

Clint Eastwood, Robert Redford, Warren Beatty, Mel Gibson and Kevin Costner have golden boys for directing. All of those male heartthrob stars—plus Paul Newman—have reaped helmers' trophies from the crix, directors' guild and/or Globes, too.

The directors' guild rarely strays from the pix suggested by the earlier crix prizes and Golden Globes, but when it did, the winners were notable because most of them went on to claim Oscars, too—Oliver Stone (*Born on the Fourth of July*), George Roy Hill (*The Sting*), George Stevens (*Giant*) and Joseph L. Mankiewicz (*A Letter to Three Wives*). What's odd, though, is that only one of those four movies won Best Picture, too: *The Sting*. Other guild choices that strayed from the pack turned out to be dead ends: Ron Howard (*Apollo 13*) and Steven Spielberg (*The Color Purple*).

There are vast differences in the varying voting methods used by all the awards. When voters determine the nominees for Oscars and guild kudos (directors, writers and actors), they list five choices on a paper ballot, but only the directors' guild and the Oscars use a weighted system, having voters rank their five choices in descending order (only three choices are listed by Oscar voters in some crafts categories). All guild members vote in all categories for nominees and winners. At the Oscars, voters are restricted to voting only in their peer-group categories and Best Picture during the nomination polling, then all academy members determine winners in all races except foreign pix, documentaries and short subjects (members must attend screenings to vote for those).

The National Society of Film Critics and

Variety's Oscar poll scored a batting average of .868 percent.

the New York Film Critics Circle use virtually the same system. Voters list just one choice on the first round. If no candidate wins a majority, a second round ensues using a weighted ballot on which voters list their top three choices in descending order (three points go to the leading candidate). Winners must not only achieve the highest point score, but their names must appear on at least half of the ballots. The only major difference between the two orgs' systems is that Gotham circle voting is secret. When ballots are counted up at the society, the name of each critic is read off as his or her ballot results are announced and tallied. At the L.A. group, crix utter their own votes aloud, citing their top three picks, ranked preferentially, in each category.

All of the kudos hold parties to dispense their prizes, except one: the national society did hold galas in its first few years, but then ran low on cash, scrapped them and never celebrated again. Scrolls are now mailed to the winners.

The many awards can be pretty rough on each other. The Oscars look down on all of the competish, but probably have the right. The crix can be brutal toward their rivals. The National Board of Review is the crix's favorite punching bag for a number of reasons: the public often confuses the board with being a crix org; the board claims legitimacy by virtue of its history, but won't reveal who its members are; and, most of all, because the board usually jumps ahead of the crix to announces its winners first. The crix also love to rough up the foreign press who decide the Golden Globes, dismissing them as part-time journos who don't have credibility. But those same Yankee crix, interestingly enough, refrain from taking aim at their peers in the Los Angeles Film Critics Association, even though far less than half of that group's members review pix full time for leading media.

Hollywood spends aplenty to woo all of the kudos. *Variety* has only attempted to calculate expenditures for the Oscar race, but pegs the total at $50 million spent on trade ads, special screenings and videotape campaigns every year—an outrageous sum if one considers that the 55 statuettes that the marketers are trying to buy cost only $18,000 to manufacture. If that $50 million total is divided by the 5,600 Oscar voters, it comes out to $8,928 per person. One studio exec once told *Variety*, "You could get a lot more value for your money by just bribing these people."

That sum-per-voter has soared in recent years. In 1979, Roger Ebert estimated that the studios spent $500 for each one of the academy's 3,600 voters—or $1.8 million total.

But the investment is worth it because the payoff can be immense. *Annie Hall* doubled its b.o. as a result of its Oscar Best Picture victory. *Shakespeare in Love* grossed an additional $100 million worldwide after being nominated for, and winning, the top trophy. If the sum that *Titanic* earned once it steered into Oscar waters is divided by its record-tying 11 wins, the amount comes out to $24 million per statuette. But not all champs hit the jackpot. *Braveheart* scored only an additional 3 percent gross domestically (from $68 million to $70 million), probably because the film earned most of its money when it was released in May 1995, then reissued in December in order to create Oscar buzz. By the time the Academy Awards came around in March 1996, most interested movie-goers had already seen it.

"If money could buy an Oscar, I'd have had a real one long ago!" Bob Hope told *Variety*'s Army Archerd in 1970, but the notorious joker must have been kidding. The reason that Marlon Brando was the only cast member of *A Streetcar Named Desire* not to win an Oscar was probably because he refused to campaign. A wily Humphrey Bogart saw his chance that year, blitzed *Variety* with ads ballyhooing his best reviews, bought lots of rounds of drinks at Romanoff's and claimed the purse for *The*

Jack Nicholson is most awards' top male winner.

African Queen. Paul Newman had a frustrating long wait for his Oscar, suffering six defeats before the academy finally tossed him a bone for *The Color of Money*. But Newman not only refused to campaign himself, he ordered the studios not to lobby on his behalf. Joan Crawford, on the other hand, finally won her golden boy for *Mildred Pierce* in 1945 when she hired a savvy PR man to do shameless tub-thumping for her. Olivia de Havilland, furious over having lost to her sister Joan Fontaine in 1941, hired the same chap in 1946 and won, too (*To Each His Own*). The chap didn't earn his paycheck from Rosalind Russell, though. She hired him away from de Havilland one year later and somehow managed to lose—even though every pundit in Hollywood (including, of course, *Variety*) had her pegged as a shoo-in for *Mourning Becomes Electra*.

Where did it all start?

The first showbiz kudo was launched in the late 1920s with the Academy Award of Merit, which was created as a fluke—a desperate afterthought of a group looking for a reason to exist when it failed at its first mission.

The Oscar was created by the Academy of Motion Picture Arts and Sciences, which was founded by MGM topper Louis B. Mayer for the purpose of being an independent cross-industry union that could settle such hot-button issues as wages, benefits and royalties. The original idea for the academy was doomed from the start. Moguls such as Mayer clearly had their stranglehold on the group, but its existence seemed like a good idea at first, so lots of Hollywood's leading lights joined. Since everyone was also interested in something more pressing than industry problem solving—that is, making money from their collective hard work—they created awards to trumpet some of the titles that movie-goers might miss if they weren't reading the reviews penned by newspaper critics. Even better: if the crix were dead wrong about a pic, academy members got to pipe in with their own opinion about what's good.

It was clear that the original academy's mission was a failure by the mid-1930s. That's when writers and directors bolted in order to form their own separate guilds that could do a far better job negotiating with the studios, but the Oscars were up and running by then and were such an unqualified hit that they seemed like enough of a reason all by themselves to keep the academy doors open.

Meantime, out in rival New York City— still a booming movie-making town—strongly opinionated film aficionados wanted to speak up with their own choices for the best pix and thesps of the year.

First came the National Board of Review. Its awards were created—just like the Oscars—by an organization looking for a reason to exist. The board had been created as a censorship panel when it was established in 1909 by community leaders who signed up to be cinema's moral watchdogs in order to stop New York's mayor from doing the job himself. By the late 1920s and early 1930s, the Hays Office officially took over the role as Hollywood's censor, so the board evolved into a film-appreciation society of brainy citizens (lawyers, editors, teachers) who published a lofty movie journal (*Films in Review*) and frequent lists of recommended movies. It started publishing lists of the year's top 10 films in 1929. Three years later, it listed one pic on top, followed by the remaining nine. When the results were published in the Gotham newspapers, they infuriated those papers' film critics, who had previously been accustomed to getting the last word on movie quality.

In the mid-1930s, New York's drama and film critics started to band together into professional societies after they witnessed their colleagues do so in London. The New York Film Critics ("Circle" was added to its title in 1973) formed in 1935

> ## "To put it bluntly," the Gotham crix's voting sessions have been "nigh unto brawls."

and thereafter declared its anointed as if unveiling the winners from atop Mount Olympus. More than a few people noticed, however, that when the choices were examined closely, it was quite clear that the crix sometimes swiped their ideas from the list issued two weeks earlier by the National Board of Review. The crix denied it, but the copycatting occurred so often in the early years (*The Informer, Mr. Deeds Goes to Town, The Citadel, In Which We Serve*) that it couldn't be mere coincidence.

But the film crix's award list was nonetheless respected and often—very often—Oscar voters stole *their* ideas from the Gothamites. The two groups have agreed on Best Picture only 27 times in 65 years, but the Gotham crix can probably take credit for at least 13 Oscar Best Pictures, from *The Lost Weekend* and *Gentleman's Agreement* in the 1940s to *Terms of Endearment* in the 1980s and *The Silence of the Lambs* in the 1990s.

One of the guilds jumped into the kudos game soon after being formed in the 1930s, but it had trouble getting its awards just right. The Screen Actors Guild went overboard at first and started bestowing kudos for the Best Actor and Actress of the Month. Initially, Hollywood stars went along and got all gussied up for the presentation galas held every 30 days at fancy hotels, but that soon got boring, even in Tinsel Town where nobody had ever before tired of donning fine silk, popping champagne corks and slapping each other on the back. But the kudos soon got scrapped and didn't return until 1994, when they would be introduced as annual honors.

Meantime, other journalists—the ones working for foreign newspapers—wanted in on the act, too, so they created the Golden Globes in 1943. The Globes didn't have much clout, though, until they started to appear on TV, first locally in L.A. in the late 1950s, then nationally in the 1960s. In 1972,

HFPA leaders wisely moved the ceremony from February to the end of January so it would land close to the time when Oscar nomination ballots are due in, and suddenly the Globes' impact became obvious.

In 1948, the writers' and directors' guilds decided to give awards a try. Their kudos presentations were not televised—they weren't even packed with stars—but they were hot tickets coveted from the start because of the credentials of the electorate. Pretty soon it was clear that Oscar voters were doing more than just paying attention to their choices. It looked as if they were just rubber-stamping them. Oscar and DGA voters have agreed on Best Director 92 percent of the time; 54 percent of all Oscar screenplay winners since 1948 were honored with WGA prizes a few weeks earlier.

After the guild kudos and Globes joined the Oscars, the crix awards and the National Board of Review in the year's kudos derby, the overall race remained more or less the same for about two decades—from the 1940s till the 1960s—when everything changed after a war broke out between film critics in New York City. The Gotham crix group had always been a newspaper-only club, but when a citywide newspaper strike hit in 1962, the shutdown killed off a few dailies and the 16-member group lost three crix by the time it got back down to awards business in 1963. It finally admitted a magazine scribe—*Time*'s Bruce Williamson—to the December 1965 voting conclave, but by then it was too late. Other magazine scribes who'd been rejected by the Gotham group started conspiring to form their own rival org, which debuted in 1966. They even had the gumption to up the ante and call their group the National Society of Film Critics, even though virtually all of their members lived in Gotham. What's more: foreign pix were no longer brushed off into a lesser, secondary category. They got to compete with Yankee fare for the big Best Picture prize and the group promised to impose loftier standards on every one of its awardees.

From the start, the national society made a point of showing how smart it was by picking highbrow pix. In its first year, it cited Michelangelo Antonioni's Italian-British indie *Blow-Up* as Best Picture. The next two years it made its first venture to non-English shores, to Sweden, picking Ingmar Bergman's *Persona* (1967) and *Shame* (1968). The New York Film Critics across town stuck to its guns at first and kept embracing the same kind of fare it usually preferred—costume dramas based on stage plays (*A Man for All Seasons, The Lion in Winter*) or pix with an important social message (*The Defiant Ones*)—but it fought the society head to head on one front. The Gotham group suddenly welcomed a stampede of national society members into its ranks, no doubt hoping to put the society out of business. By 1973, 19 crix belonged to both the 22-member Gotham circle and the 23-member national society. There were murmurings of a merger between the orgs, but the society decided to stick to its separate path while inviting crix from outlying cities such as Chicago and Los Angeles to join.

The influx of new blood into the Gotham group caused it to choose edgier Best Pictures such as *Five Easy Pieces* (1970) and *A Clockwork Orange* (1971), but it also caused it to follow the national society overseas. The Gothamites embraced foreign-lingo pix such as Ingmar Bergman's *Cries and Whispers* (1972) and even some of the same ones the society named, such as *Z* (1969) and *Day for Night* (1973). When the membership overlap between the two groups reached its height in 1973, they agreed on an unprecedented six categories overall. The overlap diminished somewhat afterward while the society added more members from distant cities, but it remained considerable enough to lead to frequent agreement on Best Picture—*Nashville* (1975), *All the President's Men* (1976), *Annie Hall* (1977) and *Kramer vs. Kramer* (1979)—until the 1980s, when the two groups finally went their separate ways. There's still a significant overlap in membership. Today 18 crix in the 31-member New York Film Critics Circle are also members of the 52-member national society, while the 53-member L.A. group shares 11 members with the national org.

The Los Angeles Film Critics Association jumped into the derby in 1975. It started backing mainstream movies (*One Flew over the Cuckoo's Nest, Rocky*) that were obviously being embraced next by the Oscars, which must have made the New Yorkers downright nostalgic for their old Oscar clout, which they had abandoned ever since they started aping the national society's lofty tastes. The Gothamites soon hot-footed it right back to Yankee shores and endorsed pix that average Americans could actually see at their local shopping malls.

Since then, the New York group has still remained especially attentive to small pix, but it's obvious that one of its primary missions is to launch its ponies toward the Oscars. The L.A. crix don't take it lying down, though, and a fight now often ensues between the two orgs as the lofty czars of American pop culture suddenly get down and dirty in a game of leapfrog with the National Board of Review while they all try to be the first one on the calendar to name their bests.

In the 25 years since the L.A. crix org came on the scene, the New Yorkers have managed to jump ahead of the Left Coasters, announcing their own winners first, six times. During the same period, the National Society of Film Critics outmanuevered both rival crix groups twice. Since the society was formed in 1966, it has sneaked ahead of the Gothamites three times.

In the 65 years since the New York Film Critics was formed, here's who has managed to start off the year's derby by making their announcements first: National Board of Review (47 times), L.A. crix (11), Gotham crix (7) and the national society (0).

Of all the top film kudos, the most mysterious by far are the crix's honors, probably because they're decided behind closed doors by journalists who are pros at keeping their mouths shut about source information. Theirs are schizophrenic kudos, benefiting in reputation on one hand from the crix's exalted status as cultural gurus, but they're also tarnished by the crix's sour rep.

The most dramatic evidence of how revered the crix kudos are came from George C. Scott, who was not shy about deriding the Oscar in public in 1970, but graciously accepted his Best Actor prize from the New York Film Critics for *Patton*. He didn't show up personally to claim it at the party, but he dispatched his wife, Colleen Dewhurst, who told the crowd, "George thinks this is the only film award worth having."

Scott valued his plaque because it came from such an esteemed group, but not every showbiz titan thinks the crix deserve the respect. Director Frank Capra once denounced the average critic as "a legless man who teaches running." Some crix even agree with Capra. Kenneth Turan of the *L.A. Times* says crix are "people who know the way, but can't drive the car."

The public doesn't seem to hold the crix in high regard. Crix reaped only a 28 percent thumbs-up endorsement in a recent national poll by MarketCast, and the following negative comments received surprisingly high responses: "Critics can't relate to normal audiences" (57 percent) and "I ignore what critics say about a movie" (61 percent).

The winners chosen by the crix are often suspect when it's clear that the voters had a personal agenda. Sometimes their votes are really messages directed at the studios. Back in 1980, Universal had planned to re-edit and retitle *Melvin and Howard* when it fared poorly in a few cities during limited release, but studio suits were stopped cold by the national society, which named the original version Best Picture. The L.A. crix named an unreleased film, *Brazil*, as Best Picture in 1985 as a way of forcing Universal to take it off the shelf.

Their messages can sometimes be directed at each other, too. In 1976, during the second year of the L.A. crix group's existence, the New Yorkers were still preoccupied with aping the esoteric Best Picture choices being made by the national society, even picking such foreign-lingo pix as *Cries and Whispers, Day for Night* and *Amarcord* in the early 1970s. The Left Coasters decided to get the Gothamites' attention by throwing a shrewd low punch. They named Sly Stallone's lowbrow crowd-pleaser *Rocky* as Best Picture and, months later, when Stallone vaulted up onto the Oscar stage to claim the heavyweight belt for top pic, everyone was stunned, including *Rocky*'s director. John G. Avildsen confessed to the press, "I had no idea *Rocky* would be such a hit. I thought it was going to be the second half of a double bill at a drive-in."

Something else possibly clouds the decisions made by all the crix groups, too, including the case of *Rocky*—testosterone. Men compose 84 percent of the Gotham circle, 82 percent of the national society and 87 percent of the L.A. group. In 1989, when the New Yorkers passed by Jessica Tandy (*Driving Miss Daisy*) for Best Actress in favor of Michelle Pfeiffer in *The Fabulous Baker Boys* (in which Pfeiffer dons a slinky red dress and wiggles on a pianotop), a few female members of the group publicly slammed the outcome as a "testosterone vote." They—and many others—leveled the same charge in 1998 when the same group picked Cameron Diaz (*There's Something about Mary*) over Fernanda Montenegro (*Central Station*).

The women may have a point. A pattern of machismo is fairly clear just from citing some of the notable times that various crix groups departed from the Oscars on Best Picture. In the years when Oscar voters (a dual-gender group) endorsed *The Greatest Show on Earth, Hamlet, Gigi, Out of Africa, The English Patient, Ordinary People, Titanic, Forrest Gump* and *Shakespeare in Love*, some crix groups backed *High Noon, The Treasure of the Sierra Madre, The Defiant Ones, Prizzi's Honor, Fargo, Raging Bull, L.A. Confidential, Pulp Fiction* and *Saving Private Ryan*. If the sexist charge is true, it might help to explain Janet Maslin's bafflement over *Pulp Fiction* in 1994. She praised the pic in the *N.Y. Times*, but, in her review's lead paragraph, she referred to how her male peers were fawning so fanatically over the movie. She said that the gushing, in historical terms, was "bound to look suspect from afar."

All of their testosterone has certainly given the crix all kinds of trouble internally. George Bernard Shaw once said, "Clearly a critic should not belong to a club at all. He should not know anybody. His hand should be against every man, and every man's hand against his." But when crix do get together in clubs, those hands often fly. The most shocking thing to be learned from a study of the crix's voting conclaves is how violent and mean-spirited they have been—and not just occasionally. The outbursts occurred routinely over decades among the Gotham crix and members of the national society. (The L.A. group has been admirably decorous, by comparison.)

Longtime Gotham circle member Bosley Crowther of the *New York Times* once wrote, "To put it bluntly, the voting sessions of the critics have sometimes been nigh unto brawls." The earliest meetings of the Gotham group were described as being full of "screams of dissenters" and "fierce laments."

"And some of the horse trading that went on in such sessions!" Leo Mishkin of the *Morning-Telegraph* once gasped. " 'You vote for my actress, I'll vote for your director and let's get out of here fast!' . . . were real eye-openers." Frank S. Nugent described the 1939 voting conclave in the *New York Times*, saying, "The log-rolling, lobbying and vote-trading that went on in the traditional smoke-filled room were shameful and very funny."

Mishkin once described a hilariously hypocritical outburst that occurred when a critic stood up during a voting session, denounced awards-giving as a corruption of the crix's ethics, resigned and stormed out of the room. She returned a few minutes later, looking a bit sheepish. "She had forgotten all the Christmas presents she had received from the film companies, which she had carried into the meeting that day," Mishkin observed.

But most of the outbursts were nothing

One critic had a heart attack during a "combative" NSFC voting conclave.

to chuckle over. Carrie Rickey of *The Chicago Tribune* once reported on the national society, "Arthur Schlesinger, Jr., joined our group just in time to witness the famous blow-up between Manny Farber and John Simon, an eruption, Schlesinger insists, that surpasses anything he experienced in the Kennedy inner sanctum during the Cuban Missile Crisis."

The Gotham circle tried to demonstrate how progressive it was by admitting a scribe from the Communist *Daily Worker* in 1936, a man who would end up fleeing for his life when he quit in 1951. The incident occurred at a particularly stressful eight-hour voting session that climaxed at 4 A.M. when his peers had him pinned against a wall while accusing him of being a Russian stooge. He slipped from their grasps and bolted, never to return.

Things had calmed down in the circle by the mid-1970s when Kathleen Carroll of the *Daily News* said, sighing with regret, "I remember the good old days when the group behaved more as if it were an Apache war party having a powwow. (Now) there is no bloodshed. There are no violent explosions of temper."

That wasn't true at the national society. Things got so bad during that same period that *The Chicago Tribune*'s Rickey noted, "In 1975, during another combative meeting, then–*New York Times* critic Roger Greenspun felt his arm go numb, left and went to the hospital where he was diagnosed as having had a heart attack." As late as 1988, Rickey reported that "rancor often flavors the annual proceedings." Rickey surmised as to one of the contributing problems: "Most of the 40-plus members down more than one cocktail while voting, which may account for the obstreperous opinionation of the proceedings."

Liquor had been responsible for so many nasty meetings in the early days of the Gotham circle (usually when the scotch ran out and members wanted to go home) that the group decided to meet in the morning hours by the mid-1950s. The switcheroo helped, but not completely. A decade later Bosley Crowther left an especially "vitriolic" voting session and confessed to his readers in the *Times*, "This never-despairing participant holds his peers in varying degrees of low regard."

Several things finally occurred to improve the proceedings: liquor and debating were banned and the voting rules were changed in order to decide winners sooner. Now relative peace reigns at all three groups, but that hasn't stopped the fighting.

Much of it goes on behind the scenes before the meetings even occur. Throughout the histories of both the Gotham circle and national society, they both had prominent members who controlled large blocs of votes. Bosley Crowther is credited with being the mightiest manipulator during the circle's early years, but, it turns out, looking back, that his influence has been greatly exaggerated. He may have been the group's topper for many years and may have slammed through *In the Heat of the Night* over front-runner *Bonnie and Clyde* in 1967, but, in fact, most of his Best Picture choices did not win during his 27-year reign (1940–1967).

After Crowther left the group, Judith Crist of *New York Magazine* and NBC's *Today Show* wielded considerable influence in both orgs (among her coups was *Amarcord*'s victory at the New York Film Critics Circle in 1974), but nothing matched the power blocs that formed behind Pauline Kael of *The New Yorker* and Andrew Sarris of *The Village Voice*. Both crix belonged to the Gotham circle and national society and were accused of working the phones like Bronx political bosses in order to line up votes before meetings. During the 1970s and 1980s, they each had plenty of followers they could count on. (*Voice* critic Geor-

Best-pic prizes to *Brazil* and *Melvin and Howard* were messages aimed at the studios.

gia Brown once wrote of Kael, "One regularly hears that she has been breeding for posterity—cultivating acolytes and placing them in jobs." Richard Schickel of *Life* called Kael an "almost demonically possessed little woman, who was usually brutal with those who stood outside her charmed circle.") Kael's and Sarris's troops were known as the "Paulettes" and the "Sarrisites" and they frequently clashed like crusaders and infidels maneuvering to take a hill in the Holy Land. Kael won the most battles overall and, when she finally retired from *The New Yorker*, she left behind a legacy of Best Pictures such as *Nashville*, which won the top prize from both crix groups in 1975.

The voting system used by the circle and national society seems to encourage the formation of rival camps that often can't claim victory. The Gotham crix named *Wuthering Heights* Best Picture of 1939 simply because it couldn't decide between *Gone With the Wind* and *Mr. Smith Goes to Washington. My Left Foot* won in 1989 because voters couldn't decide between *Do the Right Thing* and *Enemies, A Love Story. Quiz Show* didn't receive a single vote during the first-round balloting for Best Picture of 1994, but it won when the camps backing *Forrest Gump* and *Pulp Fiction* surrendered.

The crix put forth so many compromise choices and so many movies wrapped in a message when they announce their winners that one must wonder: Are they really picking the best film work of the year? But the crix, on the other hand, have named so many superlative choices Best Picture overall—*The Grapes of Wrath, A Streetcar Named Desire, The Lion in Winter, Atlantic City, The Player* and *Being John Malkovich*, all of which failed to win the top Oscar—that they must be taken seriously, and sometimes even be admired. In 1941, the chutzpah of the Gotham crix displayed itself in a courageous choice: they embraced as Best Picture the movie that the American Film Institute poll would later decree to be the greatest movie of all time—*Citizen Kane*—while Academy Award voters that year opted for *How Green Was My Valley*, a film that would hold the dubious distinction one

day of being the last Oscar Best Picture champ to be released on VHS tape.

The crix have also hailed great talents who never won an Oscar, including thesps Tallulah Bankhead, Ralph Richardson, Liv Ullmann and Ralph Fiennes in addition to directors Alfred Hitchcock, Ingmar Bergman, Stanley Kubrick, Paul Mazursky and Martin Scorsese. Where the crix and Oscars have both made oversights, the Golden Globes embraced such Best Pictures as *Sunset Boulevard*, legendary directors such as Cecil B. de Mille and megawatt stars such as Rosalind Russell, Angela Lansbury and Julia Roberts. In the end, the deficiencies of any one award are, happily, often redressed by the generosity of another. The annual derby to snag them all may be composed of wild horses and may often be ruthless ("Why don't you put that award where your heart should be?" Margot Channing barked in *All about Eve*), but at least it spreads around more laurels to lots of worthy champs.

"Whenever I win an award, I can't stop laughing!" Jodie Foster once said and perhaps that cavalier attitude is healthy, but there's still something monumentally tragic about the fact that Greta Garbo went to her grave without an Oscar, even if she always wanted to be left alone. Comfort and consolation can be had from knowing that the New York crix honored her twice. She was so grateful to them that the notoriously shy star even tried to attend one of their kudos parties a few years after her dual victories for *Anna Karenina* and *Camille*. In 1940, Garbo got as far as the Rainbow Room's elevators when she ran into a flock of autograph fans—and fled.

Past Oscar Best Actress champ Anne Bancroft warns that winning isn't all it's cracked up to be. Moments after she handed Sidney Poitier his Oscar for *Lilies of the Field* in 1963, she whispered to him in a conspiratorial tone, "Live it up, chum. It doesn't last long."

But winning a kudo can be an exhilarating experience, giving honorees that rare chance to feel an inner explosion of total joy. Martin Landau perhaps described it best when he accepted his Oscar for Best Supporting Actor for *Ed Wood* in 1994, exclaiming, "My God! What a night! What a life! What a moment! What everything!"

This book makes liberal use of *Variety*'s playful "slanguage," which can be daunting to the uninitiated, but it's employed here in order to tell an inside-showbiz story in the words of showbiz insiders. Following long-standing industry protocol, virtually all years cited in the text refer to a film's award year, not when the actual kudos ceremony occurred in the next calendar year. Actual ceremony dates and times when winners were announced are given in the listings sections, which are arranged chronologically according to when the winners were proclaimed, not when the kudos were bestowed. Dates noted for the announcement of the crix awards reflect when their voting conclaves occurred. Often the results were not officially unveiled until printed in newspapers the next day, but word of who and what won always spread fast as soon as those blabbermouth journalists hit the door—so that certainly qualifies as an announcement. Every effort was made to include complete info. The crix's voting records, however, were sometimes incomplete or, worse,

proved to be no longer extant. The state of record keeping by those orgs, in fact, is consistently sloppy. Even today the New York Film Critics Circle does not maintain an archive of its past voting tallies. The Los Angeles Film Critics Association says that it might, but no member seems to know where it is. The National Society of Film Critics did not keep records for its first eight years. Americans aren't the only award-bestowing journalists who've been flip or negligent about preserving old paperwork. A few years ago the Hollywood Foreign Press Association made a heroic effort to organize archival material, but it found that the first 20 years of Golden Globe nominations were missing. Apparently, these same journalists who toil on the job to record history as it unfolds around them do not have much historical regard for their own goings-on. Happily, a lot of the vanished info is printed here thanks to this book's tireless researchers, George Figueroa and Michele Mavis-sakalian, who doggedly sleuthed through dusty files, out-of-print books and microfilm of long-dead publications at many libraries and archives—but, alas, they could not find everything.

When Hollywood's future golden boy was still just a golden infant, he wasn't known as Oscar yet, but as an "Academy Award of Merit"— and he failed to get top billing in *Variety*. In fact, the tradepaper reported his debut on page seven, burying the news of Oscar's first winners under an article considered much more important at the time. Its banner headline warned "TALKER PATENT WAR LOOMS" when *Variety* reported that secret new sound equipment was tampered with during a movie theater break-in.

News of the first Oscar winners was buried on *Variety*'s page seven. Statuettes were bestowed three months later.

Three months later, when the first statuettes were bestowed, the whole presentation took only five minutes, which would turn out to be one-half minute less than it would take Greer Garson to accept one 14 years later. But the event marked the start of something amazing when 300 members of America's new film royalty gathered at Hollywood's Roosevelt Hotel for that first shameless ritual of crowning themselves.

A hotel journal described the scene: "The Blossom Room was a gorgeous sight, with its soft lantern lights shedding rays and shadows on the brilliant gowns and gay blooms. Thirty-six tables, with their scintillating glassware and long tapers, each table bearing a replica in waxed candy of the bronze and gold statuette award, filled the entire floor space of the room." Such romantic luxury came at a bargain price: five dollars per ticket.

Academy president Douglas Fairbanks presided and entertainment was provided in part by Al Jolson, who amused the crowd, *Variety* noted, when he "expressed his indignation that an actor should be asked to sing." But he crooned for his peers nonetheless and made the best joke of the night when he mused about the new golden statuettes and confessed, *Variety* said, that "for the life of him he couldn't conceive what Jack Warner could do with one of them."

"It couldn't say 'yes,' " Jolson wisecracked.

Jolson's *The Jazz Singer* had recently become the first film to blast through the medium's sound barrier, but it was declared ineligible for the competitive awards because the motion picture academy thought it might have an unfair advantage. Instead, it reaped a special prize as "the pioneer outstanding talking picture, which has revolutionized the industry."

The academy actually named several outstanding films of the year spanning August 1, 1927, to July 31, 1928. Perhaps sensing that award judges might be seduced by commercial success over creative excellence when picking the winner of the Best Picture prize, academy leaders minted a separate category for Best Unique and Artistic Film—even though one movie could theoretically win both races. The first accolade went to a b.o. blockbuster, *Wings*, which thrilled throngs of theater-goers with World War I aerial battles described by *Variety* as buzzing with "bombing machines, captive balloons, smashes and crashes of all types." Although *Wings* was a silent film, its prize was accepted by Paramount's absent prexy Adolph Zukor, who appeared in a sound film produced earlier in New York and unspooled, after much fanfare, before the Oscar celebrants. *Variety* reported that the mogul "extended his company's thanks and addressed the Academy as if he were present in person."

The year's best artistic movie was supposed to be *The Crowd*, King Vidor's realistic portrayal of an average New York couple's struggle with daily hardships. Most critics loved it; so did the award's Central Board of Judges, who were appointed by academy founder Louis B. Mayer. But Mayer feared a backlash if the MGM hit won, so he kept the judges awake till dawn until he persuaded them to pick the Fox studio's *Sunrise. Variety* had marveled at *Sunrise* in its review, citing its "artistry" and "dramatic power" in depicting the tragic twists of a sordid love triangle.

Sunrise was one of three hit films, including *7th Heaven* and *Street Angel*, that made Janet Gaynor the year's breakout star and a popular choice for the first Best Actress honor. The wide-eyed 22-year-old claimed the statuette with a simple "Thank you" and a demure smile. Years later she wrote in the academy's official history, "Had I known then what (the award) would come to mean in the next few years, I'm sure I would have been overwhelmed." At the time, she considered the real thrill of the evening to be her "chance to meet the dashing Douglas Fairbanks!"

Even though the winners were given three months' advance notice, Best Actor Emil Jannings (*The Last Command, The Way of All Flesh*) became the first honoree to be absent on awards night. The oft-proclaimed "world's greatest actor" had a sauerkraut-thick German accent that he knew would doom him in the new talking pictures, so when his contract expired with Paramount, the Brooklyn-born actor fled to Germany, where he had once reigned as a silent-film idol. He arrived in Berlin on Oscar night and sent the banquet revelers a telegram expressing his "heartfelt thanks" for the honor that "I shall cherish all my life as a kind of remembrance in recognition of my artistic activities in U.S.A." Soon thereafter he starred in numerous Nazi propaganda flicks and his career eventually ended in disgrace.

The first year's award nominees were determined by a group of 20 industry leaders, while the winners were chosen by the academy's Central Board of Judges, which was composed of five producers handpicked by academy founder Louis B. Mayer. The judges refused to embrace Hollywood rebel Charlie Chaplin in any of the three categories in which he was up—directing, acting and writing—and even nullified his nominations. Later they feared that the snubs might cause an outcry, so they created a special award to give him "for versatility and genius in writing, acting, directing and producing *The Circus*." Chaplin snubbed them in return by refusing to show up to accept it. On awards night, the crowd was told, "Mr. Chaplin is not here due to cold feet, but he has wired his high appreciation of the honor."

In its next-day coverage, *The Los Angeles Times* declared the new kudos gala a real winner, adding, "The awards banquet, it is hoped by members of the academy, will become an annual event and one of the impressive film ceremonies of the year."

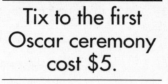

Tix to the first Oscar ceremony cost $5.

▪ 1927–28 ▪

ACADEMY AWARDS

The awards' eligibility period spanned August 1, 1927, to July 31, 1928. Winners were announced on February 17, 1929. The awards were presented on May 16 at the Hollywood Roosevelt Hotel.

BEST PICTURE

- *Wings*
The Last Command
The Racket
7th Heaven
The Way of All Flesh

BEST UNIQUE AND ARTISTIC PICTURE

- *Sunrise*
Chang
The Crowd

BEST DIRECTOR, DRAMATIC PICTURE

- Frank Borzage, *7th Heaven*
Herbert Brenon, *Sorrell and Son*
King Vidor, *The Crowd*

BEST DIRECTOR, COMEDY PICTURE

- Lewis Milestone, *Two Arabian Knights*
Charles Chaplin, *The Circus**
Ted Wilde, *Speedy*

BEST ACTOR

- Emil Jannings, *The Last Command, The Way of All Flesh*
Richard Barthelmess, *The Noose, The Patent Leather Kid*
Charles Chaplin, *The Circus**

BEST ACTRESS

- Janet Gaynor, *7th Heaven, Street Angel, Sunrise*
Louise Dresser, *A Ship Comes In*
Gloria Swanson, *Sadie Thompson*

BEST WRITING (ADAPTATION)

- Benjamin Glazer, *7th Heaven*
Alfred Cohn, *The Jazz Singer*
Anthony Coldeway, *Glorious Betsy*

BEST WRITING (ORIGINAL STORY)

- Ben Hecht, *Underworld*
Lajos Biro, *The Last Command*
Charles Chaplin, *The Circus**

---

*Charles Chaplin's three nominations were nullified
after they were announced, and he was given a
special award.

Janet Gaynor received her Best Actress Oscar from the emcee of the first ceremony, Douglas Fairbanks.

BEST WRITING (TITLE WRITING)

- Joseph Farnham, *Telling the World; The Fair Co-Ed; Laugh, Clown, Laugh*
Gerald Duffy, *The Private Life of Helen of Troy*
George Marion, Jr., *Oh Kay!*

Winners

BEST CINEMATOGRAPHY

- Charles Rosher, Karl Struss, *Sunrise*
- Karl Struss, *Sunrise*

BEST ENGINEERING EFFECTS

- Roy Pomeroy, *Wings*

BEST INTERIOR DIRECTION

- William Cameron Menzies, *The Dove, The Tempest*

SPECIAL AWARDS

- Charles Chaplin, *The Circus*
- Warner Bros., *The Jazz Singer*

▪ 1928–29 ▪

Oscar talks!

"WALL STREET LAYS AN EGG," *Variety* proclaimed when the stock market crashed five months after the first Oscar revelers, oblivious to looming economic disaster, feasted merrily on filet of sole sauté au buerre while dressed in silk gowns and tuxedoes. Little did they know then, too, that the very thing they had barred from their first competitive awards—the talking pictures that so terrified studio moguls who made their riches from silent celluloid—would soon save them from financial ruin.

In 1929, *Variety* reported, "Sound didn't do any more to the industry than turn it upside down and shake the entire bag of tricks from its pocket." Sound also filled industry pockets with lots of new coin. At the second Oscar derby, the studios listened up. One day after the Wall Street crash, Oscar leaders announced their second set of nominations, which were dominated by sound movies released between August 1, 1928, and July 31, 1929. Listed in the Best Picture race was what Fox lauded as "the first 100 percent all-talking drama filmed outdoors," *In Old Arizona*, described by *Variety* as "a Western with a climax twist." Also cited was *The Broadway Melody*, which MGM ballyhooed as "100 Percent All Talking! 100 Percent All Singing! 100 Percent All Dancing!" *Variety* cheered "the excellent bits of sound workmanship" in "the first screen musical," which followed the plot twists of two sisters who fall for the same song-and-dance man in a Broadway revue.

The ceremony was held at the Ambassador Hotel, where celebrants sat under the nodding palms in the Cocoanut Grove while a local radio station broadcast the festivities to film fans beyond. The awards gala promised new drama, since winners would be revealed during the ceremony instead of three months earlier.

The Broadway Melody was not only the first talkie to win Oscar's Best Picture prize, it was "100 Percent All Singing! 100 Percent All Dancing!"

Mary Pickford was in the Best Actress running for portraying a feckless Southern flirt in *Coquette*, which survived damning reviews thanks to hoards of theater-goers curious to hear "America's Sweetheart" speak for the first time and to behold her new short, shingled hairdo. Desperate to prove the critics wrong, Pickford pined for an Academy Award as proof that she'd survived the transition to talkies, and she set out to woo the five members of Oscar's Central Board of Judges shamelessly. She invited them over to her estate, Pickfair, for tea and thereby entered the history books as the first nominee to campaign openly for an Oscar. She won, beating two contenders that many movie critics considered more worthy: Ruth Chatterton (*Madame X*) and the recently deceased Jeanne Eagels (*The Letter*). At the podium, Pickford set another Oscar precedent by being the first winner to cry as she confessed, "I've forgotten my prepared speech!"

In Old Arizona's buff star Warner Baxter won Best Actor easily for what *Variety* hailed as his "great screen performance" as the guitar-strumming Mexican outlaw Cisco Kid, who became a pop cult hero. He topped unsympathetic thug roles by Chester Morris (*Alibi*) and George Bancroft (*Thunderbolt*) and silent-screen turns by Lewis Stone (*The Patriot*) and Paul Muni (*The Valiant*).

In Old Arizona had the most noms— five—along with *The Patriot*, a movie with "a valid claim to greatness," said *Variety*, for its portrayal of 18th-century court intrigues surrounding "Czar Paul, the insane emperor of all the Russians, idiot-monster of Nero-like proportions." The five Oscar judges, all producers, preferred the year's top-grossing musical extravaganza, *The Broadway Melody*, which cost only $500,000 to make but earned a record $4 million when throngs of theater-goers paid as much as an unprecedented $2 per ticket. Its

"Sound turned Hollywood upside down," said *Variety*.

victory caused an outcry, since it had been produced by academy founder Louis B. Mayer, who appointed the judges to their jobs.

Other top winners raised suspicions, too: Best Director Frank Lloyd (*The Divine Lady*) was one of the academy's founding charter members; so was Mary Pickford, who was married to the academy's first president, Douglas Fairbanks. The award for interior decoration went to the same man who designed the Academy Award statuette, Cedric Gibbons (*The Bridge of San Luis Rey*).

Soon after the ceremony, critics cried foul and, six days later, *Variety* announced the "scrapping of the complicated machinery by which achievements for awards by the Academy are judged. Awards for 1929–30 will be made by vote of the entire Academy membership." The 300 film professionals would be entrusted with deciding both nominees and winners, a move that finally defined the industry's highest prize as showbiz's first peer-group trophy.

▪ 1928–29 ▪

ACADEMY AWARDS

The awards' eligibility period spanned August 1, 1928, to July 31, 1929. Nominations were announced on October 31. Awards were presented on April 30, 1930, at the Cocoanut Grove of the Ambassador Hotel in Los Angeles.

BEST PICTURE
▪ *The Broadway Melody*
Alibi
Hollywood Revue
In Old Arizona
The Patriot

BEST DIRECTOR
▪ Frank Lloyd, *The Divine Lady*
Lionel Barrymore, *Madame X*

Harry Beaumont, *The Broadway Melody*
Irving Cummings, *In Old Arizona*
Frank Lloyd, *Drag**
Frank Lloyd, *Weary River*
Ernst Lubitsch, *The Patriot*

BEST ACTOR
▪ Warner Baxter, *In Old Arizona*
George Bancroft, *Thunderbolt*
Lewis Stone, *The Patriot*
Chester Morris, *Alibi*
Paul Muni, *The Valiant*

---

*Official documents of the Academy of Motion Picture Arts and Sciences disagree over whether these listees were nominated.

BEST ACTRESS
- Mary Pickford, *Coquette*
Ruth Chatterton, *Madame X*
Betty Compson, *The Barker*
Jeanne Eagels, *The Letter*
Corinne Griffith, *The Divine Lady*
Bessie Love, *The Broadway Melody*

BEST WRITING
- Hans Kraly, *The Patriot*
Tom Barry, *In Old Arizona*
Tom Barry, *The Valiant*
Hans Kraly, *The Last of Mrs. Cheyney*
Josephine Lovett, *Our Dancing Daughters*
Bess Meredyth, *A Woman of Affairs*
Bess Meredyth, *Wonder of Women*

Winners

BEST CINEMATOGRAPHY
- Clyde DeVinna, *White Shadows in the South Seas*

BEST INTERIOR DECORATION
- Cedric Gibbons, *The Bridge of San Luis Rey*

NATIONAL BOARD OF REVIEW

The board's top 10 American films and 5 favorite foreign movies of 1929 were arranged alphabetically. The vote results were announced in late December 1929.

BEST PICTURES
- *Applause*
- *Broadway*
- *Bulldog Drummond*

Mary Pickford's hairdo in *Coquette* sparked a national craze and was more memorable, said crix, than her Oscar-winning perf.

- *The Case of Lena Smith*
- *Disraeli*
- *Hallelujah!*
- *The Letter*
- *The Love Parade*
- *Paris Bound*
- *The Valiant*

BEST FOREIGN FILMS
- *Arsenal*
- *Homecoming*
- *The Passion of Joan of Arc*
- *Piccadilly*
- *Ten Days That Shook the World*

▪ 1929–30 ▪

Membership Rules

"**W**hat do you expect? She sleeps with the boss!" Joan Crawford harrumphed when Norma Shearer, wife of MGM wunderkind Irving J. Thalberg, won Best Actress. But *Variety* said Shearer was "excellent" in *The Divorcée*, which came close to being axed by censors because of its blatant depiction of the lead character's trysts before winning back her husband. *Variety* failed to get excited by MGM's frenzied "Garbo Talks!" campaign and was merely respectful when its reviewer first heard the brusque Nordic accent of fellow nominee Greta Garbo in *Anna Christie*. And when Oscar rival and silent-screen icon Gloria Swanson finally spoke up—and sang—in *The Trespasser*, the tradepaper merely applauded her "clear diction which does not grate."

Of the three movies, only *The Divorcée* was up for Best Picture, but the nomination was only a formality. The winner was a foregone conclusion: *All Quiet on the Western Front*, the $1.2 million anti-war saga that hit worldwide cinemas like a grenade going off. American patriots denounced its sympathetic portrayal of German soldiers in World War I, while the pic was banned from theaters in Germany until the 1960s because of its horrific portrayal of a war blamed on the Fatherland. *Variety* called it "a harrowing, gruesome, morbid tale of war, compelling in its realism, bigness and repulsiveness," but the paper agreed with the critical consensus that *All Quiet* was a masterpiece.

Academy founder Louis B. Mayer presented the Best Picture prize to producer Carl Laemmle, who "acknowledged Mr. Mayer's tribute by stating that next to the fact that he recently became a grandfather, nothing had thrilled him as much as the award," *Variety* reported. "He added that with Mayer's daughter also recently married, the MGM executive can probably appreciate that."

There was no suspense on Oscar night over who'd win in any category. *Variety* published the vote results in that morning's edition. Best thesps George Arliss and Norma Shearer obviously knew even earlier, since they posed for a photo with their statuettes two days before the ceremony.

> There was no suspense. *Variety* published the vote results in that morning's edition.

Despite such advance word, Arliss was not present on awards night to be lauded by his peers for his portrayal of the wily British prime minister Benjamin Disraeli in *Disraeli*, which was also up for Best Picture and the writing kudos. "Acting and characterization are a continuous delight," *Variety* said in its review. "*Disraeli* without George Arliss is to shudder." Arliss knew the role well: he originally performed it on the British stage in 1911, then again in a 1921 silent film before he became widely known as "The First Gentleman of the Talking Screen."

After the abolition of Louis B. Mayer's Central Board of Judges last year, academy members now determined the award winners.

ACADEMY AWARDS

The awards' eligibility period spanned August 1, 1929, to July 31, 1930. Nominations were announced on September 19. Awards were presented on November 5 at the Fiesta Room of the Ambassador Hotel in Los Angeles.

BEST PICTURE

▪ *All Quiet on the Western Front*
The Big House
Disraeli
The Divorcée
The Love Parade

BEST DIRECTOR

▪ Lewis Milestone, *All Quiet on the Western Front*
Clarence Brown, *Anna Christie*
Clarence Brown, *Romance*
Robert Leonard, *The Divorcée*
Ernst Lubitsch, *The Love Parade*
King Vidor, *Hallelujah*

BEST ACTOR

▪ George Arliss, *Disraeli*
George Arliss, *The Green Goddess*
Wallace Beery, *The Big House*
Maurice Chevalier, *The Big Pond*
Maurice Chevalier, *The Love Parade*
Ronald Colman, *Bulldog Drummond*
Ronald Colman, *Condemned*
Lawrence Tibbett, *The Rogue Song*

BEST ACTRESS

▪ Norma Shearer, *The Divorcée*
Nancy Carroll, *The Devil's Holiday*
Ruth Chatterton, *Sarah and Son*
Greta Garbo, *Anna Christie*
Greta Garbo, *Romance*
Norma Shearer, *Their Own Desire*
Gloria Swanson, *The Trespasser*

BEST WRITING

▪ Frances Marion, *The Big House*
George Abbott, Maxwell Anderson, Del Andrews, *All Quiet on the Western Front*
Howard Estabrook, *Street of Chance*
Julian Josephson, *Disraeli*
John Meehan, *The Divorcée*

Winners

BEST CINEMATOGRAPHY

▪ Joseph T. Rucker, Willard Van Der Veer, *With Byrd at the South Pole*

BEST INTERIOR DIRECTION

▪ Herman Rosse, *King of Jazz*

BEST SOUND RECORDING

▪ Douglas Shearer, *The Big House*

NATIONAL BOARD OF REVIEW

The board's top 10 American films and 5 favorite foreign movies of 1930 were arranged alphabetically. The vote results

Variety called Best Picture *All Quiet on the Western Front* a "harrowing" and "compelling" portrayal of World War I.

were announced in late December 1930.

BEST PICTURES

- *All Quiet on the Western Front*
- *Holiday*
- *Laughter*
- *The Man from Blankely's*
- *Men without Women*
- *Morocco*
- *Outward Bound*
- *Romance*
- *The Street of Chance*
- *Tol'able David*

BEST FOREIGN FILMS

- *High Treason* (Germany)
- *Old and New* (*The General Line*) (U.S.S.R.)
- *Soil* (U.S.S.R.)
- *Storm over Asia* (U.S.S.R.)
- *Zwei Herzen im ¾ Takt (*Two Hearts in ¾ Time) (Germany)

MGM salutes Norma Shearer for her Best Actress victory (*The Divorcée*) in one of the first Oscar ads published in *Variety*.

· 1930–31 ·

Size Matters

"**C**imarron seems strongly favored because of its bigness," *Variety* reported early on Oscar day about the award chances of the epic about the Oklahoma land rush of 1888 that had swept the nominations with a record tally of seven, including bids in all of the top categories. Its two lead thesps were up for honors, too, but were not expected to win: silent-film star Richard Dix and recent Broadway import Irene Dunne. *Variety* foresaw that its director might be far luckier, since voters "seem to favor *Cimarron* unofficially, with *Skippy* runner-up and then *A Free Soul, The Front Page* and *Morocco*."

Cimarron's toughest competish for best pic was *The Front Page*, an adaptation of the Broadway exposé of sleazy Chicago newspapermen that earned a Best Actor bid for Adolphe Menjou. *Cimarron* prevailed, however, nabbing three awards, including kudos for writing and interior decoration.

The director's laurels were nabbed in an upset by Norman Taurog, who proved equally gutsy when filming *Skippy*: He'd bullied its star, his 10-year-old nephew Jackie Cooper, into crying on cue by threatening to shoot the boy's dog. The child star seemed unruffled by his intimidating uncle on Oscar night and unfazed by the awards hubbub around him, even though he competed as a Best Actor nominee. The trophies were bestowed after midnight, way past his bedtime, so he snoozed through most of the festivities with his head on the arm of Marie Dressler.

Secret Balloting on Academy Awards Favors Dressler, Barrymore, 'Cimarron'

Variety's earliest Oscar predictions proved prescient, scoring 100 percent despite "secret balloting kept q.t."

> ## 10-year-old Best Actor rival Jackie Cooper slept on Marie Dressler's arm.

Dressler was a leading contender for Best Actress, being the year's most popular film star, an unlikely rank for the frumpy, self-professed ugly duckling. The 63-year-old thesp had a breakout year as the gin-swilling, husband-slugging proprietress of a waterfront boardinghouse in MGM's top grosser *Min and Bill*. In the Oscar contest, she slugged it out against one proven champ, last year's winner Norma Shearer, who had her biggest b.o. hit yet in *A Free Soul*. Also formidable was the saucy German star of *The Blue Angel* and *Morocco*, Marlene Dietrich, who had recently arrived in America greeted by brassy media fanfare.

Variety sized up the actress race as truly dramatic: "The characterizations are so varied that this will be one of the closest competitions, although Miss Dressler's *Min* looks strong."

When Dressler won, she transferred the snoozing Jackie Cooper into his mother's lap, then made her way, stunned, to the podium. *Variety* observed that she felt "so grand and happy—her frank tears of joy fully attested to that." She said, accepting the statuette, "I have always believed that our lives should be governed by simplicity. But tonight I feel very important."

Variety forecast that Cooper, despite his

diminutive size when compared to his five adult rivals, actually towered above four of them: "In the male acting division the voting will not be as close, according to comment among Academy members, with Lionel Barrymore's *Free Soul* performance mentioned No. 1 and Jackie Cooper's Skippy No. 2." One of the other contenders was Fredric March, who was nominated for his hambone portrayal of Lionel's brother John in *The Royal Family of Broadway*, a sassy parody of the whole Barrymore clan. Since Lionel had been nominated for Best Director last year for *Madame X*, he was the first person to score bids in two different categories.

When the Best Actor contenders were read off, nobody woke up Jackie Cooper, which turned out to be a good thing since Lionel Barrymore prevailed for portraying a firebrand, booze-guzzling lawyer who saves Clark Gable's neck, then must defend his son-in-law for killing Gable. *Variety* reported that Barrymore accepted the laurel "inarticulately but appropriately."

Just like Cooper, *Variety* thought that Oscar night was a snooze, calling it "a dull evening of a nature which will repel many a Hollywoodian next year (unless memories dim and time makes 'em forget)." The proceedings were broadcast on radio across the West Coast.

One month after the November 11, 1931, Academy Awards night, the National Board of Review cited two Oscar honorees among its list of the year's 10 best—*Cimarron* and *The Front Page*—but not more, no doubt because the board's awards eligibility period, which ended in mid-December, overlapped only part of the Oscars' eligibility span, which cut off in July.

▪ 1930–31 ▪

ACADEMY AWARDS

The awards' eligibility period spanned August 1, 1930, to July 31, 1931. Nominations were announced on October 5. Awards were presented on November 10 at the Biltmore Hotel in Los Angeles.

BEST PICTURE
▪ *Cimarron*
East Lynne
The Front Page
Skippy
Trader Horn

BEST DIRECTOR
▪ Norman Taurog, *Skippy*
Clarence Brown, *A Free Soul*
Lewis Milestone, *The Front Page*
Wesley Ruggles, *Cimarron*
Josef Von Sternberg, *Morocco*

BEST ACTOR
▪ Lionel Barrymore, *A Free Soul*
Jackie Cooper, *Skippy*

Richard Dix, *Cimarron*
Fredric March, *The Royal Family of Broadway*
Adolphe Menjou, *The Front Page*

BEST ACTRESS
▪ Marie Dressler, *Min and Bill*
Marlene Dietrich, *Morocco*

Cimarron led with a record tally of seven noms and won three: Best Picture, Writing and Interior Decoration.

Irene Dunne, *Cimarron*
Ann Harding, *Holiday*
Norma Shearer, *A Free Soul*

BEST WRITING (ADAPTATION)
- Howard Estabrook, *Cimarron*
Horace Jackson, *Holiday*
Francis Faragoh, Robert N. Lee, *Little Caesar*
Joseph L. Mankiewicz, Sam Mintz, *Skippy*
Seton I. Miller, Fred Niblo, Jr., *The Criminal Code*

BEST WRITING (ORIGINAL STORY)
- John Monk Saunders, *The Dawn Patrol*
John Bright, Kubec Glasmon, *The Public Enemy*
Rowland Brown, *The Doorway to Hell*
Harry D'Abbadie D'Arrast, Douglas Doty, Donald Ogden Stewart, *Laughter*
Lucien Hubbard, Joseph Jackson, *Smart Money*

Winners

BEST CINEMATOGRAPHY
- Floyd Crosby, *Tabu*

BEST INTERIOR DECORATION
- Max Ree, *Cimarron*

BEST SOUND RECORDING
- Paramount Publix Studio Sound Department

SCIENTIFIC OR TECHNICAL AWARDS
Class I (Statuette)
- DuPont Film Manufacturing, Eastman Kodak

- Electrical Research Products, RCA-Photophone, RKO Radio Pictures
Class II (Certificate)
- Fox Film Corp.
Class III (Honorable Mention)
- Electrical Research Products
- RCA-Photophone
- RKO Radio Pictures

NATIONAL BOARD OF REVIEW

The board's top 10 American films and 5 favorite foreign movies of 1931 were arranged alphabetically. The vote results were announced in late December 1931.

BEST PICTURES
- *Cimarron*
- *City Lights*
- *City Streets*
- *Dishonored*
- *The Front Page*
- *The Guardsman*
- *Quick Millions*
- *Rango*
- *Surrender*
- *Tabu*

BEST FOREIGN FILMS
- *Die Dreigroschenoper (The Threepenny Opera)* (Germany)
- *Das Lied von Leben (The Song of Life)* (Germany)
- *Le Million* (France)
- *Sous les Toits de Paris (Under the Roofs of Paris)* (France)
- *Vier vom der Infantrie (Comrades of 1918)* (Germany)

· 1931–32 ·

A Kudos First: Two Best Pictures

"JUST A GUESS" said a small headline on *Variety*'s front page. It appeared over a boxed-off article citing "probable winners of the Academy Awards at the banquet at the Ambassador Hotel tonight."

Nobody could've really foreseen what would happen in the race for Best Actor, though. *Variety* predicted that the prize would go to Wallace Beery in *The Champ*, which the paper called "a good talker" thanks to "a studied, adult" performance by Beery as "a broken-down ex-heavyweight champ training for a comeback" in between bouts with dice, the bottle and his frisky son, played by Jackie Cooper.

But when Norma Shearer revealed the champ on Oscar night, she named Fredric March for *Dr. Jekyll and Mr. Hyde* (his cinematic transformation "into the bestial, apelike monster Hyde carries a terrific punch," cheered *Variety* in its review). Accepting the honor, March thanked his makeup artist Wally Westmore, who crafted the monstrous touches during three hours of careful work each day of filming.

After that, the Oscar ceremony moved on to other categories while judges continued to count and shuffle ballots. Suddenly, one of them caused a stir and summoned academy president Conrad Nagel, who listened intently, then turned to the audience to ask Wallace Beery to join him on stage. When the two men met at the podium, Nagel declared, "Mr. Beery, it is my pleasure to announce that you have tied with Mr. March for the best male performance of the year for your splendid portrayal in *The Champ*."

The next day *Variety* reported "dissension among Academy members, some of whom claim that Conrad overstepped his authority in making such a presentation." March had beaten Beery by one vote. Last year's rules declared that "the candidate or

Grand Hotel pulled off an upset over *Arrowsmith* as Oscar's Best Picture thanks to its "bigness," said the *L.A. Times.*

candidates who are within three votes of a tie shall be given an award."

"When the rules were written for this year, however, such a clause was omitted," *Variety* noted. Academy leaders weighed the controversy, but rather than ask Beery to return his statuette, they announced that he could keep it.

March didn't seem to mind sharing the honor. On Oscar night, he made an infamous wisecrack after noting that both he and Beery had recently adopted children: "Under the circumstances, it seems a little odd that Wally and I were both given awards for the best male performance of the year."

Variety correctly predicted who'd win the Best Actress accolade: Helen Hayes, the Broadway thesp who recently moved to L.A. to be with her scriptwriter husband Charles MacArthur and agreed to make films only after being bullied by Irving Thalberg. The reluctant film star became a sudden superstar when her early pics became hits. She won Best Actress for *The Sin of Madelon Claudet*, a tearjerker about a Parisian woman who sinks to the lowest social depths and becomes a prostitute so her bastard son can have a good life. Several months before the Oscars it had been cited as the Most Touching Film at the Venice Film Festival and also earned Hayes a prize for Favorite Actress.

While accepting her Academy Award, Hayes equated winning to the thrill of giving birth to her daughter: "The only other time in my life when I really felt great or superb, all I could think to say was 'Gosh, isn't she red?!' I hope I do better the second time, but I doubt it."

Hayes beat another notable stage thesp, Lynn Fontanne, whose husband Alfred Lunt was nominated in the actor's race for the same pic, *The Guardsman*.

Hayes's other standout film of the year—*Arrowsmith*, based on the Sinclair Lewis book—was *Variety*'s choice to win Best Picture. Rivals included *The Champ*, Josef von Sternberg's *Shanghai Express* (starring Marlene Dietrich as rebel mistress Shanghai Lily), and two Maurice Chevalier operettas: *One Hour with You* (costarring Jeanette MacDonald) and *The Smiling Lieutenant* (with Claudette Colbert). Also in the race were a surprise b.o. hit with no major stars—*Bad Girl*—and a new kind of

> *Variety* reported "dissension" over the Best Actor tie between Beery and March.

composite film filled with cameos by maxistars in lots of mini stories: *Grand Hotel*. Booked into the posh Berlin lodging "where nothing ever happens" were Joan Crawford, Wallace Beery, two Barrymores (John and Lionel), and a world-weary Greta Garbo, who declared "I vant to be alone" three times.

None of its stars, nor director Edmund Goulding, nabbed noms. Nonetheless, when it triumphed as Best Picture, a disappointed *L.A. Times* harrumphed, "*Grand Hotel* filled, it appeared, the requirements of bigness."

Consolation kudos went to *Bad Girl*, whose helmer Frank Borzage was named Best Director, a prize he had won at the first Oscar ceremony for *7th Heaven* in 1927–28.

In past years, the National Board of Review had merely listed its top 10 choices for best films of the year without citing a solo favorite. This year the board boldly proclaimed a single Best Picture, opting for a film released late in the year after the July 31 cutoff for Oscar eligibility. In its review of the movie, *Variety* gave it a vote of confidence, too: "*I Am a Fugitive from a Chain Gang* is a picture with guts." The tale of an innocent man brutalized by the criminal justice system "packs lots of punch," the paper added. *Fugitive* would be considered a heavyweight contender for Best Picture at next year's Oscars and its star, Paul Muni, would break out early as the favorite to win Best Actor.

▪ 1931–32 ▪

ACADEMY AWARDS

The awards' eligibility period spanned August 1, 1931, to July 31, 1932. Nominations were announced on October 12. Awards were presented on November 18 at the Ambassador Hotel in Los Angeles.

BEST PICTURE
▪ *Grand Hotel*
Arrowsmith
Bad Girl
The Champ
Five Star Final
One Hour with You
Shanghai Express
The Smiling Lieutenant

BEST DIRECTOR
- Frank Borzage, *Bad Girl*

Josef von Sternberg, *Shanghai Express*

King Vidor, *The Champ*

BEST ACTOR (TIE)
- Wallace Beery, *The Champ*
- Fredric March, *Dr. Jekyll and Mr. Hyde*

Alfred Lunt, *The Guardsman*

BEST ACTRESS
- Helen Hayes, *The Sin of Madelon Claudet*

Marie Dressler, *Emma*

Lynn Fontanne, *The Guardsman*

BEST WRITING (ADAPTATION)
- Edwin Burke, *Bad Girl*

Percy Heath, Samuel Hoffenstein, *Dr. Jekyll and Mr. Hyde*

Sidney Howard, *Arrowsmith*

BEST WRITING (ORIGINAL STORY)
- Frances Marion, *The Champ*

Lucien Hubbard, *The Star Witness*

Grover Jones, William Slavens McNutt, *Lady and Gent*

Jane Murfin, Adela Rogers St. Johns, *What Price Hollywood?*

Winners

BEST CINEMATOGRAPHY
- Lee Garmes, *Shanghai Express*

BEST INTERIOR DECORATION
- Gordon Wiles, *Transatlantic*

BEST SHORT SUBJECT
(CARTOON)
- *Flowers and Trees*

(COMEDY)
- *The Music Box*

(NOVELTY)
- *Wrestling Swordfish*

The National Board of Review named a single Best Picture for the first time ever: *I Am a Fugitive from a Chain Gang*, which was a film "with guts," *Variety* said.

BEST SOUND RECORDING
- Paramount Publix Studio Sound Department

SCIENTIFIC OR TECHNICAL AWARDS
Class II (Plaque)
- Technicolor Motion Picture Corp.

Class III (Certificate)
- Eastman Kodak

SPECIAL AWARD
- Walt Disney

NATIONAL BOARD OF REVIEW

The board declared a single best U.S. and foreign film of 1932, then listed its remaining favorites alphabetically. The vote results were announced on December 22, 1932.

BEST PICTURE
- *I Am a Fugitive from a Chain Gang*

A Bill of Divorcement

A Farewell to Arms

As You Desire Me

Madame Racketeer

Payment Deferred

Scarface

Tarzan

Trouble in Paradise

Two Seconds

BEST FOREIGN FILM

- *A Nous la Liberté* (France)
Der Andere (Germany)
The Battle of Gallipoli (U.K.)
Golden Mountains (U.S.S.R.)
Kameradschaft (Germany)

Mädchen in Uniform (Germany)
Der Raub der Mona Lisa
  (Germany)
Reserved for Ladies (U.K.)
Road to Life (U.S.S.R.)
Zwei Menschen (Germany)

▪ 1932–33 ▪

British Sovereigns

The movie academy may have been founded in part to arbitrate Hollywood labor crises, but when its leaders endorsed a studio-led call for a 50 percent pay cut by all employees during the bleak Depression days, hundreds of actors and writers quit and regrouped under the banners of the Screen Actors Guild and the Screen Writers Guild. Remaining Oscar voters would echo that same spirit of defiance against the studios in a loud way on awards night.

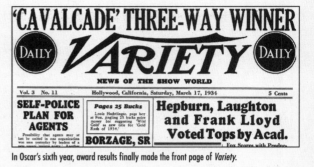

In Oscar's sixth year, award results finally made the front page of *Variety*.

Variety revealed early rumblings four days before the ceremony when it reported that the studios' top contenders—*Little Women, State Fair, I Am a Fugitive from a Chain Gang* and *A Farewell to Arms*—weren't the front-runners for Best Picture. The paper cited *Cavalcade*, which was produced by Fox on Yankee soil, but was considered a foreign film because it featured a British cast in Noel Coward's veddy English tale of a family's ordeals spanning the Boer War, the sinking of the *Titanic* and World War I. Even more surprising: *Variety* claimed that the best bet for Best Actor was Brit Charles Laughton for *The Private Life of Henry VIII*, which had been filmed in the U.K. Earlier, in its review, *Variety* declared that the rotund Laughton was "unquestionably the perfect pick for the part of the corpulent ruler" prone to beheading his wives and belching at the banquet table. Prior to *Variety*'s forecast, the assumption around Hollywood was that Paul Muni would take the prize for his critically hailed role as an innocent runaway in *I Am a Fugitive from a Chain Gang.*

When *Cavalcade* premiered in New York City, the audience stood and cheered. When it won Best Picture on the West Coast on Oscar night, industry leaders greeted the news with respectful applause. The audience response was far less enthusiastic when the Best Actor choice turned out to be Laughton, who was, happily, in his homeland far away from the limp acknowledgment of his win.

Variety—like most other Hollywood watchers—believed that May Robson would win Best Actress as the gruff apple vendor–turned–society swan in Frank Capra's *Lady for a Day*, also up for Best Picture. The paper did cite Katharine Hepburn as a "close runner-up," however, after having heralded her "strong performance" in *Morning Glory* "as an innocent country girl who comes to Broadway seeking footlight fame" only to become a "bedraggled Cinderella." In real life, Hepburn had come to Hollywood less than two years earlier after a star turn on Broadway in *A Bill of Divorcement*, which she repeated on celluloid, followed by a film rendition of Louisa May Alcott's novel *Little Women*, which was up for Best Picture this year. Hepburn quickly became bedraggled by rumors that she was a haughty film diva, though, so she headed back to Broadway, where she was cut down to size by savage crix shortly before Oscar night. When she won the Academy Award, *The L.A. Times* was shocked because the absent champ wasn't "a particularly popular choice around the film colony."

Variety considered Frank Capra the best bet for Best Director, perhaps contributing to his embarrassment when another winner was actually announced at the Fiesta Room of the Ambassador Hotel. The gala's host, hayseed humorist Will Rogers, said after he opened the envelope, "It couldn't have happened to a nicer guy. Come up and get it, Frank!" Capra leapt up and raced toward the stage. So did rival and actual winner Frank Lloyd, who'd won the same award three years earlier for *The Divine Lady* and now was bathed in the spotlight as he strutted forward to claim a new statuette for *Cavalcade*. Capra caught his mistake before he reached the stage, halted, spun around and began "the longest, saddest, most shattering walk in my life" back to his table, he recalled later in his memoirs. He'd soon be called to the podium for real, however. Victory would be his next year, and twice more during his career, thereby giving him one trophy more than Lloyd.

Capra could take some solace in learning that he came in second for the helmer's laurels when this year's vote results were disclosed later. In the Best Picture race, *Cavalcade* topped second-placed *A Farewell to Arms* and third-placed *Little Women* by hefty margins. "Miss Hepburn had 20 percent more votes than the runner-up May Robson," *Variety* reported on the actress race, citing *Cavalcade*'s Diana Wynyard in third place. Laughton "had a leeway of 10 percent of the votes over Paul Muni (in sec-

ond place) and Leslie Howard (in third)." The night's real landslide champ was Walt Disney, who reaped 80 percent of the ballots deciding Best Cartoon. As Disney accepted the trophy for *The Three Little Pigs*, he expressed his thanks for winning an "Oscar." Disney's use of the term on March 16, 1934, is considered to be the earliest known public reference in showbiz history.

The awards gala at the Ambassador Hotel was crowded this year. *Variety* reported, "Although reservations were supposed to be closed at 750, at least 200 more than this number were accommodated at the banquet, necessitating a last minute rearrangement of dining seats. Duke Ellington's band produced hot music, but it was a general bunny hug all 'round. Will Rogers wisecracked his way through the master of ceremonies act and handed the winners their various statuette awards."

Walt Disney made the first public mention of an "Oscar."

The eligibility period for this year's prizes spanned August 1, 1932, to December 31, 1933. In the future, the awards would convert to a calendar-year basis.

The National Board of Review remained, for the most part, on a calendar basis. Its eligibility cutoff for best film of 1933 was actually in mid-December, which meant that the year's big Yuletide release would not be considered until next year's vote by the board's Committee on Exceptional Photoplays. Despite the differences between the board's and Oscar's timespans, their two lists of Best Picture contenders for most of 1933 included some agreement, including *Little Women, State Fair, She Done Him Wrong* and *Cavalcade*. The board opted to give its top laurel to a movie overlooked by Oscar, however: *Topaze*, which featured John Barrymore in a stellar perf as an innocent schoolteacher duped by a scheming tycoon.

NATIONAL BOARD OF REVIEW

The board declared a best film of 1933, then listed its remaining favorites alphabetically. The vote results were announced on December 29, 1933.

BEST PICTURE
- *Topaze*
Berkeley Square
Cavalcade
Little Women
Mama Loves Papa
The Pied Piper (cartoon)
She Done Him Wrong
State Fair
Three-Cornered Moon
Zoo in Budapest

BEST FOREIGN FILM
- *Hertha's Erwachen* (Germany)
Ivan (U.S.S.R.)
M (Germany)
Morgenrot (Germany)
Niemandsland (Germany)
Poil de Carotte (France)
The Private Life of Henry VIII (U.K.)
Quatorze Juillet (France)
Rome Express (U.K.)
Le Sang d'un Poete (*Blood of a Poet*) (France)

ACADEMY AWARDS

The awards' eligibility period spanned August 1, 1932, to December 31, 1933. Nominations were announced on February 26, 1934. Awards were presented on March 16 at the Ambassador Hotel in Los Angeles.

BEST PICTURE
- *Cavalcade*
A Farewell to Arms
42nd Street
I Am a Fugitive from a Chain Gang
Lady for a Day
Little Women
The Private Life of Henry VIII
She Done Him Wrong
Smilin' Through
State Fair

BEST DIRECTOR
- Frank Lloyd, *Cavalcade*
Frank Capra, *Lady for a Day*
George Cukor, *Little Women*

BEST ACTOR
- Charles Laughton, *The Private Life of Henry VIII*
Leslie Howard, *Berkeley Square*
Paul Muni, *I Am a Fugitive from a Chain Gang*

Variety correctly predicted that a Brit, Charles Laughton (*The Private Life of Henry VIII*), would beat Hollywood front-runner Paul Muni.

BEST ACTRESS
- Katharine Hepburn, *Morning Glory*

May Robson, *Lady for a Day*

Diana Wynyard, *Cavalcade*

BEST WRITING (ADAPTATION)
- Victor Heerman, Sarah Y. Mason, *Little Women*

Paul Green, Sonya Levien, *State Fair*

Robert Riskin, *Lady for a Day*

BEST WRITING (ORIGINAL STORY)
- Robert Lord, *One Way Passage*

Charles MacArthur, *Rasputin and the Empress*

Frances Marion, *The Prizefighter and the Lady*

Winners

BEST ASSISTANT DIRECTORS
- William Tummel, Charles Dorian, Charles Barton, Dewey Starkey, Fred Fox, Scott Beal, Gordon Hollingshead

BEST CINEMATOGRAPHY
- Charles Bryant Lang, Jr., *A Farewell to Arms*

BEST INTERIOR DECORATION
- William S. Darling, *Cavalcade*

BEST SHORT SUBJECT
(CARTOON)
- *The Three Little Pigs*

(COMEDY)
- *So This Is Harris*

(NOVELTY)
- *Krakatoa*

BEST SOUND RECORDING
- Harold C. Lewis, *A Farewell to Arms*

SCIENTIFIC OR TECHNICAL AWARDS
Class II (Plaque)
- Electrical Research Products
- RCA-Victor

Class III (Certificate)
- Fox Film Corp.; Fred Jackman, Warner Bros.; Sidney Sanders, RKO Studios

· 1934 ·

First Screwball Comedy Gets the Last Laugh

Who knew that the rigidly upright golden boy—Oscar—had a secret sense of humor?

Only once in the award's six-year history had Best Picture gone to something light (*The Broadway Melody*, a musical), and voters had *never* opted for a comedy. This year it was another tuner that led the race with the most bids (six): *One Night of Love*, starring Best Actress nominee Grace Moore as an opera ingenue who falls for her mentor. Other top contenders included *The Thin Man* (with William Powell nominated for Best Actor as the martini-swilling detective Nick Charles) and *The Barretts of Wimpole Street* (Norma Shearer earned a bid as doomed poet Elizabeth Barrett Browning), plus three Claudette Colbert starrers: Cecil B. DeMille's epic *Cleopatra*, racial soaper *Imitation of Life* and Hollywood's first "screwball comedy" *It Happened One Night*, which the National Board of Review had named Best Picture two months prior to Oscar night. Colbert was nominated for her role as a runaway heiress who falls for a wisecracking reporter in *One Night*, a part she originally turned down, then begrudgingly agreed to do when Columbia offered her $50,000 for 30 days' work. She was also given MGM's matinee idol Clark Gable as a costar. *Variety* cheered "the deft direction of Frank Capra and the spirited and good-humored acting of the stars."

When *It Happened One Night* made an unpredecented sweep of the top awards (Best Picture, Director, Actor, Actress, Screenplay), *Variety* reported it in an unprecedented way, giving the movie award its first banner headline on page one: "COLUMBIA MOPS UP!" The article noted that the pic's five victories, "nearly all of them in the important classifications, comprise a record which may never be surpassed." In future years, two other films would pull off sweeps

It Happened One Night pulled off a historic sweep, including Oscars for Clark Gable and Claudette Colbert, but a clueless Colbert asked, "What's the award?"

of the top five categories, *One Flew over the Cuckoo's Nest* in 1975 and *Silence of the Lambs* in 1991.

When the votes for Best Picture of 1934 were counted, *Variety* noted that *It Happened One Night* won by "a wide margin over the Metro entry *Barretts of Wimpole Street*, while the other Columbia picture, *One Night of Love*, ran third."

Comedian Irvin S. Cobb hosted the ceremony and announced the winner of Best Director by slyly using the same words that had humiliated Frank Capra last year when Capra *thought* he won, but really lost to Frank Lloyd. This time Capra froze when he heard, "Come on up and get it, Frank!" Capra finally headed to the stage when his nearby friends and colleagues assured him that he had really won.

When Clark Gable first heard that he was

nominated, he was shocked. When he heard that he'd won, he was flabbergasted. While up at the podium, he was at a loss for words until an old friend shouted from the audience, "How do you feel, Clark?"

"As happy as a kid and a little bit foolish that they picked me," Gable replied, snapping out of it. "It's a grand and glorious feeling, but I'll be wearing the same size hat tomorrow."

When this year's nominations were announced, *The Hollywood Citizen-News* reflected industrywide outrage over who was missing from the Best Actress race: "Everyone in the profession is expressing amazement that Bette Davis is not even mentioned." Critics had swooned over Davis as a Cockney strumpet in W. Somerset Maugham's *Of Human Bondage*, but when she failed to nab an Oscar bid, Davis accused Jack Warner of pressuring Warner Bros. employees not to vote for her since she'd been out on loan to RKO. The movie academy responded to the controversy by announcing that, for the first time ever, write-in candidates would be permitted.

> ## Colbert was yanked off a train and whisked to the Oscar gala via police escort.

"It seemed inevitable that I would receive the coveted award," Davis wrote in her memoirs years later. "The press, the public and the members of the academy who did the voting were sure I would!" Not all the press, actually. *Variety* reported on Oscar day: "Indications are that the plan this year to throw the voting into a free-for-all, by allowing members to write in choices, will not affect the original nominees. Indications are that Clark Gable and Claudette Colbert will poll such a heavy vote for *It Happened One Night* that they cannot be knocked out of top rating."

Curiously, on the same page was a short item noting that the overworked Colbert was leaving town that night for a five-week vacation to New York. Colbert apparently

didn't know about the relatively new movie awards and was boarding a train just at the moment when she was called up to the podium to receive one. Friends raced to the station to fetch her.

Variety reported, "Claudette Colbert was yanked off the Chief a few minutes before it was to pull out and rushed back to the Biltmore to receive her trophy, preceded by special police escort. Emotion overwhelmed the girl and she dissolved into an hysterical cataract of tears. 'What's it about? What's the award?' she fumbled (on the level, too) amid the lachrymose shower."

Meanwhile, the train was held at the station until Colbert returned a short while later. Colbert didn't stick around the Biltmore Hotel long enough to hear Cobb read off the vote tallies. Clark Gable beat Frank Morgan by a close vote. No write-in candidates surpassed the three male nominees, even though two had been considered strong candidates: John Barrymore (*Twentieth Century*) and Fredric March (*The Barretts of Wimpole Street*).

Reporting on the Best Actress race, Cobb claimed that Norma Shearer came in second place, followed by Grace Moore. The academy's official history claims that he was wrong, however, insisting that Bette Davis actually edged Moore in third place.

On Oscar day, a brief article appeared in *Variety* on the same page as the pieces on who might win and who might be missing (Colbert). It said: "Warner Bros. is dickering with a New York legit producer for the rights to *Jezebel*. Studio may bring Ruth Chatterton back to the lot to play it."

That flamboyant role of a headstrong Southern belle would end up being swiped by Bette Davis, who'd win an Oscar for it, her second. Her first Oscar would come next year after she set out to avenge this year's snub.

NATIONAL BOARD OF REVIEW

The board declared a best film of 1934, then listed its remaining favorites alphabetically. The vote results were announced on December 20, 1934.

BEST PICTURE

▪ *It Happened One Night*
The Count of Monte Cristo
Crime without Passion
Eskimo
The First World War
The Lost Patrol
Lot in Sodom (nontheatrical short)
No Greater Glory
The Thin Man
Viva Villa!

BEST FOREIGN FILM

▪ *Man of Aran* (U.K.)
The Blue Light (Germany)
Catherine the Great (U.K.)
The Constant Nymph (U.K.)
Madame Bovary (France)

ACADEMY AWARDS

Nominations were announced on February 5, 1935. Awards were presented on February 27 at the Biltmore Hotel in Los Angeles.

BEST PICTURE

▪ *It Happened One Night*
The Barretts of Wimpole Street
Cleopatra
Flirtation Walk
The Gay Divorcée
Here Comes the Navy
The House of Rothschild
Imitation of Life
One Night of Love
The Thin Man
Viva Villa!
The White Parade

BEST DIRECTOR

▪ Frank Capra, *It Happened One Night*
Victor Schertzinger, *One Night of Love*
W. S. Van Dyke, *The Thin Man*

BEST ASSISTANT DIRECTOR

▪ John Waters, *Viva Villa!*
Scott Beal, *Imitation of Life*
Cullen Tate, *Cleopatra*

BEST ACTOR

▪ Clark Gable, *It Happened One Night*
Frank Morgan, *The Affairs of Cellini*
William Powell, *The Thin Man*

BEST ACTRESS

▪ Claudette Colbert, *It Happened One Night*
Grace Moore, *One Night of Love*
Norma Shearer, *The Barretts of Wimpole Street*

BEST WRITING (ADAPTATION)

▪ Robert Riskin, *It Happened One Night*
Frances Goodrich, Albert Hackett, *The Thin Man*
Ben Hecht, *Viva Villa!*

After being humiliated at last year's Oscar ceremony, Frank Capra (right) finally received the Best Director award from comic Irvin S. Cobb.

L.A. Herald

BEST WRITING (ORIGINAL STORY)

- Arthur Caesar, *Manhattan Melodrama*

Mauri Grashin, *Hide-Out*

Norman Krasna, *The Richest Girl in the World*

BEST SONG

- "The Continental," *The Gay Divorcée*, Con Conrad, Herb Magidson

"Carioca," *Flying down to Rio*, Edward Eliscu, Gus Kahn

"Love in Bloom," *She Loves Me Not*, Ralph Rainger, Leo Robin

Winners

BEST CINEMATOGRAPHY

- Victor Milner, *Cleopatra*

BEST FILM EDITING

- Conrade Nervig, *Eskimo*

BEST INTERIOR DECORATION

- Cedric Gibbons, Frederic Hope, *The Merry Widow*

BEST MUSIC SCORE

- Victor Schertzinger, Gus Kahn, Louis Silvers, *One Night of Love*

BEST SHORT SUBJECT

(CARTOON)

- *The Tortoise and the Hare*

(COMEDY)

- *La Cucaracha*

(NOVELTY)

- *City of Wax*

BEST SOUND RECORDING

- Paul Neal, *One Night of Love*

SCIENTIFIC OR TECHNICAL AWARDS

Class II (Plaque)

- Electrical Research Products

Class III (Certificate)

- Columbia Pictures
- Bell and Howell

SPECIAL AWARD

- Shirley Temple

· 1935 ·

Mutiny in Gotham

New York film critics were tired of criticizing the choices made by Oscar voters. The East Coasters now set up their own rival kudos and, so that they might inform those West Coasters what the best pictures really were, they went first.

The results were fearlessly defiant of Hollywood ballyhoo, which this year trumpeted *Mutiny on the Bounty*, MGM's $2 million blockbuster that would reap a bounty of Oscar bids—a record-setting eight—but, strangely, only one statuette. It was the big one, though: Best Picture.

The contrary-minded critics went with *The Informer*, a b.o. flop about a drunken thug who betrays his best friend for coin during the Irish revolt of 1922. They endorsed it with a unanimous vote, which would occur only one more time in the crix org's future—when choosing Olivia de Havilland as the Best Actress of 1948 for *The Snake Pit*.

The crix later claimed credit for *The Informer*'s success at the Academy Awards when it took statuettes for Best Director (John Ford), adapted screenplay and musical score. After the triple Oscar triumph, *The New York Times* crowed, "It was conceded in the industry that the picture had little chance of winning, but with all the disturbance caused by the Broadway lads, the picture could not be ignored." Perhaps the crix could also take ultimate credit for *The Informer*'s financial success, too. After it earned so many kudos, the movie was rereleased to theaters and finally earned back the $243,000 it cost to film over 18 days, thus becoming the first movie to benefit noticeably from winning awards.

But the New York laddies weren't the first to hail *The Informer* as the year's best. That happened two weeks earlier across town at the National Board of Review,

The Gotham crix's first Best Picture *The Informer* starred Oscar's Best Actor Victor McLaglen (left).

which was so defiant of mainstream views that it also dared to name the Bolshevik propaganda flick *Chapayev* as Best Foreign Film.

And the crix didn't totally mutiny against MGM. They gave their Best Actor scroll to *Mutiny on the Bounty*'s Charles Laughton, who gave "a faithful portrayal," said *Variety*, of Captain Bligh, "as despicable a character as has ever heavied across a screen." Laughton beat *Informer* star Victor McLaglen by a 10-to-1 vote on the first ballot. McLaglen would earn a golden consolation prize, though: the Oscar, which he'd win when three costars (Laughton, Clark Gable and Franchot Tone) split the votes by *Mutiny* fans.

But the New York Film Critics' decisions had obvious integrity. They hailed Greta Garbo for *Anna Karenina* even though the reclusive icon was certain to snub their inaugural gala set to debut two months later at the New York Ritz-Carlton Hotel. She didn't win until the second round of voting, though. The crix almost agreed with Bette Davis, who said that Katharine Hepburn gave the year's best perf in *Alice Adams*. Garbo only edged Hepburn by a single vote on the first ballot, then trounced her on the second.

The New York Film Critics gala was hosted by playwright and former *Vanity Fair, Post* and *Herald* staffer Robert Sherwood, who said that this was the first time that "any group of critics has ever invited its victims to a cocktail party." In attendance were such film luminaries as William Wyler, Ernst Lubitsch, Ilka Chase and Kitty Carlyle. Missing were all of the award winners. Charles Laughton was in England making a movie (British Consul-General Gerald Campbell accepted his scroll); Greta Garbo claimed to be back in her homeland (Swedish Consul-General Martin Kas-tengren took her bow). The *Times* noted, however, that "radio saved the day." As part of its coast-to-coast broadcast, NBC piped in several winners from the coast. *The Informer*'s John Ford expressed his thanks for the director's prize, and three members of its cast (Victor McLaglen, Margot Graham and Preston Foster) performed three scenes from the film.

The *Times* also noted, "Criticizing the critics was the favorite sport of the afternoon—that and raiding the cocktail bar. Samuel Goldwyn was heard saying, 'I think you're all wrong!' and Douglas Fairbanks Jr. made a mock attempt to throttle one reviewer. Anyhow, the party seemed to be a success—so the hat-check girl said."

Meantime, across the U.S.A., the crix weren't the only ones taking on Hollywood. So were the unions and studio bosses. The actors', writers' and directors' guilds no longer trusted the motion picture academy to negotiate their employment terms with the studios, and they pressed their members to boycott the Oscars. Academy member-

---

New York critics jumped into the kudos derby.

---

ship plunged from 600 to 40. The studios also gave up on the academy as a labor liaison and yanked their funding. Desperate to keep the Oscar show going, the academy's new prexy, Frank Capra, came up with a shrewd idea to lure the Hollywood faithful: he announced that the gala would salute an industry legend, D. W. Griffith, who agreed to be feted by the same showbiz leaders who had refused to give him funding for any new films in recent years.

Variety described the Oscar gala: "There was not the galaxy of stars and celebs in director and writer groups which distinguished awards banquets of recent years. Banquet tickets had been liberally distributed to secretaries and others on the various lots." Missing was Best Director champ John Ford. On hand, however, was the thesp voted the year's Best Actor despite *Variety*'s early report claiming that "Charles Laughton is expected to nose out Victor McLaglen." When he won, McLaglen clutched his award heartily.

When the Gotham crix's Best Actress champ Greta Garbo failed to score an Oscar bid, *Variety* said, "Checkup of voters shows that Bette Davis (*Dangerous*) and Elisabeth Bergner (*Escape Me Never*) are due to wage a hot battle. Academy members are likely to hand honors to Bette Davis this year, in view of freeze-out of the player from nominations last year for *Of Human Bondage*."

Davis's performance as a love-spurned Broadway has-been was "fine on the whole despite a few imperfect moments," *Variety* said in its *Dangerous* review, adding that there are scenes "when a lighter acting mood would be opportune." Later in life, Davis would ultimately denounce the film as "maudlin and mawkish," but when it brought her an Oscar, *Variety* caught her "clasping the award in both arms and holding it tight as tears of joy ran down her cheeks."

Variety spied other tears on awards night when it came time for "the big smack of the evening"—bestowing the special honor upon D. W. Griffith. "Griffith was overcome with reception accorded him as he accepted the distinguished token," *Variety* reported. "He went into the history of the picture business from its beginnings, telling how he opened a cigar box to make the first fadeout. . . . He became more and more dramatic, bringing tears to the eyes of many of the old timers and himself gulping his final sentence that the picture business is the most wonderful in the world."

Informer scribe Dudley Nichols was the first winner to refuse an Oscar. As a writers' guild cofounder, he was part of the "revolt" against the film academy.

Scribe Dudley Nichols had a different opinion of the Oscars, refusing to touch his award for penning *The Informer*. "NICHOLS JILTS ACAD. DOLL," *Variety* proclaimed in a page-one banner headline. The article noted, "It's the first instance in eight years of Academy voting that a winner in the balloting refused to accept an award." Nichols reminded the academy leadership by letter that he was "one of the founders of the Screen Writers Guild, which was conceived in revolt against the Academy and was born out of disappointment with the way it functioned against employed talent in any emergency."

"Academy says it will not change the award," *Variety* reported, "but will keep the doll and, if Nichols wants it at any time, it's his."

Mutiny on the Bounty may have been 1935's b.o. champ and an example of "Hollywood at its very best," according to *Variety*, but the tradepaper didn't spy it as the early Oscar favorite for the top prize: "Four pictures are closely bunched in the drive for best production of the year out of the dozen nominated. *The Informer* holds strategic position over the others because of various awards already made for that picture, but it will have plenty of competition from *David Copperfield, Bengal Lancer* and *Mutiny*."

Later, when the final vote counts were revealed, *Variety* reported that *Mutiny* "led by a wide margin" over second-placed *Informer* and third-ranked *Captain Blood*, while "John Ford romped home ahead of the field to draw the statuette for the best direction" over Henry Hathaway (*The Lives of a Bengal Lancer*). Katharine Hepburn was Bette Davis's closest rival, followed by Elisabeth Bergner (*Escape Me Never*).

The tally of votes for the Best Actor race was truly shocking: none of the *Mutiny* actors came in second place. "Very surprising was the write-in of Paul Muni's name on the ballot for *Black Fury*. He was within narrowest margin of sneaking into first place past McLaglen. Charles Laughton, who was figured as chief contender against McLaglen for first honors, was a trailer in third position."

Muni was pushed by studio chief Jack Warner, who pressed his employees to ignore all of the academy's nominees and back the company's talent. It worked for Hal Mohr, cinematographer of *A Midsummer Night's Dream*, who became—and remains—the only person to win an Oscar due to a write-in campaign.

MGM was aggressive in its Oscar drive, too, becoming the first studio to campaign for Oscar votes in the tradepapers. The ads touted *Ah, Wilderness!* starring Wallace Beery and Lionel Barrymore, but they failed to score a single nomination.

NATIONAL BOARD OF REVIEW

The board declared a best film of the year, then listed its remaining favorites alphabetically. The vote results were announced on December 16, 1935.

BEST PICTURE
■ *The Informer*
Alice Adams
Anna Karenina
David Copperfield
The Gilded Lily
The Lives of a Bengal Lancer
Les Misérables
Mutiny on the Bounty
Ruggles of Red Gap
Who Killed Cock Robin? (cartoon)

BEST FOREIGN FILM
■ *Chapayev* (U.S.S.R.)
Crime et Chatiment (Crime and Punishment) (France)
Le Dernier Milliardaire (France)
The Man Who Knew Too Much (U.K.)
Marie Chapdelaine (France)
La Maternelle (France)
The New Gulliver (U.S.S.R.)
Peasants (U.S.S.R.)
Thunder in the East (France)
The Youth of Maxim (The Childhood of Maxim Gorky) (U.S.S.R.)

NEW YORK FILM CRITICS

Winners were announced on January 2, 1936. Awards were presented on March 2 at the Ritz-Carlton Hotel in New York. The ceremony was broadcast live nationwide by NBC radio.

BEST PICTURE
■ *The Informer*

BEST DIRECTOR
■ John Ford, *The Informer*

BEST ACTOR
■ Charles Laughton, *Mutiny on the Bounty, Ruggles of Red Gap*

BEST ACTRESS
■ Greta Garbo, *Anna Karenina*

ACADEMY AWARDS

Nominations were announced on February 7, 1936. Awards were presented on March 5 at the Biltmore Hotel in Los Angeles.

BEST PICTURE
■ *Mutiny on the Bounty*
Alice Adams
Broadway Melody of 1936
Captain Blood
David Copperfield
The Informer
The Lives of a Bengal Lancer
A Midsummer Night's Dream
Les Misérables
Naughty Marietta
Ruggles of Red Gap
Top Hat

BEST DIRECTOR
■ John Ford, *The Informer*
Michael Curtiz, *Captain Blood**
Henry Hathaway, *The Lives of a Bengal Lancer*
Frank Lloyd, *Mutiny on the Bounty*

BEST ASSISTANT DIRECTOR
■ Clem Beauchamp, Paul Wing, *The Lives of a Bengal Lancer*
Joseph Newman, *David Copperfield*
Sherry Shourds, *A Midsummer Night's Dream**
Eric Stacey, *Les Misérables*

BEST ACTOR
■ Victor McLaglen, *The Informer*
Clark Gable, *Mutiny on the Bounty*
Charles Laughton, *Mutiny on the Bounty*
Franchot Tone, *Mutiny on the Bounty*
Paul Muni, *Black Fury**

*Official documents of the Academy of Motion Picture Arts and Sciences disagree on whether or not these listees were nominees.

BEST ACTRESS
- Bette Davis, *Dangerous*

Elisabeth Bergner, *Escape Me Never*

Claudette Colbert, *Private Worlds*

Katharine Hepburn, *Alice Adams*

Miriam Hopkins, *Becky Sharp*

Merle Oberon, *The Dark Angel*

BEST WRITING (ORIGINAL STORY)
- Ben Hecht, Charles MacArthur, *The Scoundrel*

Stephen Avery, Don Hartman, *The Gay Deception*

Moss Hart, *Broadway Melody of 1936*

Gregory Rogers, *G-Men**

BEST WRITING (SCREENPLAY)
- Dudley Nichols, *The Informer*

Achmed Abdullah, John L. Balderston, Grover Jones, William Slavens McNutt, Waldemar Young, *The Lives of a Bengal Lancer*

Jules Furthman, Talbot Jennings, Carey Wilson, *Mutiny on the Bounty*

Casey Robinson, *Captain Blood**

BEST SONG
- "Lullaby of Broadway," *Gold Diggers of 1935*, Harry Warren, Al Dubin

"Cheek to Cheek," *Top Hat*, Irving Berlin

"Lovely to Look At," *Roberta*, Jerome Kern, Dorothy Fields, Jimmy McHugh

Winners

BEST CINEMATOGRAPHY
- Hal Mohr, *A Midsummer Night's Dream*

BEST FILM EDITING
- Ralph Dawson, *A Midsummer Night's Dream*

BEST DANCE DIRECTION
- David Gould, *Broadway Melody of 1936, Folies-Bergère*

BEST INTERIOR DECORATION
- Richard Day, *The Dark Angel*

BEST MUSIC SCORE
- Max Steiner, *The Informer*

BEST SHORT SUBJECT
(CARTOON)
- *Three Orphan Kittens*

(COMEDY)
- *How to Sleep*

(NOVELTY)
- *Wings over Mt. Everest*

BEST SOUND RECORDING
- Douglas Shearer, *Naughty Marietta*

SCIENTIFIC OR TECHNICAL AWARDS
Class II (Plaque)
- Agfa Ansco Corp.
- Eastman Kodak Co.

Class III (Certificate)
- MGM Studio
- William A. Mueller, Warner Bros.
- Mole-Richardson
- Douglas Shearer, MGM Sound Department
- Electrical Research Products
- Paramount Productions
- Nathan Levinson, Warner Bros.–First National Studio

SPECIAL AWARD
- David Wark Griffith

Bette Davis was snubbed last year for *Of Human Bondage*, but finally snagged an Oscar for *Dangerous*.

Warner Bros.

▪ 1936 ▪

Great Deeds and Ziegfeld

The best performances of the year were surely given by the 18 usually stodgy New York film critics huddled behind a locked door at the Hotel Victoria on January 4, 1937, while choosing their anointed. The *World-Telegram* reported "screams of dissenters" and "fierce laments," but the outbursts may not have been fully fueled by rational debate. The *New York Post* noted that the voters "were predominantly drinkers of scotch, the supply of which was soon exhausted. The rye and brandy held up very well."

When a Best Picture—*Mr. Deeds Goes to Town*—was chosen on the second ballot, the crusaders behind the defeated alternative, Fritz Lang's *Fury*, expressed fury of their own or else echoed the lament of *Daily News* scribe Kate Cameron, who sighed, "I could cry."

Grief over the recent death of MGM producer Irving Thalberg was expected to propel his widow Norma Shearer through all the year's film kudos for *Romeo and Juliet*, but she didn't survive the first round of the crix's vote. The *Post* reported: "At first Ruth Chatterton (*Dodsworth*) was running ahead of Luise Rainer (*The Great Ziegfeld*). On the second ballot she had 8 votes to 5 for Rainer. Someone suggested that Miss Chatterton's shock upon learning that she had won might kill her. This seemed so appealing to some of her violent opponents that she almost won. But at the last moment a powerful Rainer faction by dint of strenuous log-rolling won the day."

It took five ballots for *Dodsworth* star Walter Huston to win Best Actor. "Spencer Tracy adherents died hard," the *Post* noted. "The epic battle over Best Director ended with Rouben Mamoulian (*The Gay Desper-*

Wednesday, March 3, 1937   **PICTURES**   *VARIETY*   5

SHEARER, MUNI--ACAD TOPS?

Variety correctly forecasted Paul Muni as Oscar's Best Actor, but wrongly thought that the "winnahs" would include Thalberg's widow Norma Shearer.

ado) winning over Fritz Lang after 10 ballots in which the lead was first with one and then with the other." Neither would be nominated at the Oscars two months later. The award would go to motion picture academy president Frank Capra for *Mr. Deeds*, which lost Best Picture to *The Great Ziegfeld*. The only award the two groups would agree on was Best Actress.

But once again the critics agreed completely with the National Board of Review's choices, which were announced two weeks before the crix's summit at the Hotel Victoria. The crix even copied the board by adding a category for Best Foreign Film and gave it to the same film—*La Kermesse Heroique (Carnival in Flanders)*, described by *Variety* as "the biggest French production since talkers began." But the movie was also everybody's foreign favorite of 1935. When it played in New York City, it was not shown in a small downtown art house but in RKO's 42 theaters throughout the metro area.

This year the board broke with its past tradition of listing its favorite films alphabetically after flagging its pick for the single best. Now its Top 10 list was arranged according to the votes each film received from the members of the board's Committee on Exceptional Photoplays. No records survive of what was said at those pow-wows—or how much scotch was imbibed—and the board did not yet stage a fete to toast its choices publicly.

The media scribes, however, were not

media shy. Aiming to upstage the Oscars, the crix moved their fete up six weeks, to January 24, and their locale headed in the same direction. The cocktail soirée was held atop Rockefeller Center in the fog-choked Rainbow Room. On hand, according to *The New York Daily Mirror*, were "300 guests and 100 crashers" who included director Fritz Lang and star Gloria Swanson, "who wore the cutest hat, making her appear like a Tibetan sorceress."

The gala was hosted by one of the group's founders, Richard Watts, Jr., of *The New York Herald Tribune*, who had recently quit the film desk for the Broadway beat. Walter Huston was the only winner present, but other honorees were piped in via NBC's international radio hookup. Again, like last year, the stars recreated scenes from their movies: from Hollywood came the voices of Gary Cooper and Jean Arthur (*Mr. Deeds*), Luise Rainer (*The Great Ziegfeld*) and, from equally foggy London, Francoise Rosay (*La Kermesse Heroique*). To bring *Dodsworth* to life before the Rainbow Room crowd, Walter Huston ditched his film partner Ruth Chatterton in favor of his wife, who'd performed the role opposite him on Broadway.

United Artists' *Dodsworth* and Columbia's *Mr. Deeds Goes to Town* were both up for Oscar's Best Picture prize, but *Variety* believed that an MGM film would prevail since the studio's employees composed the largest bloc of academy voters. Unfortunately, it bet on the wrong MGM pic, saying, "Outstanding production will undoubtedly go to Metro, with indications that *San Francisco* will grab the honor. Pic has been most sensational money-getter of the year and unless studio switches vote to *Great Ziegfeld*, this one will rate tops."

But voters chose *The Great Ziegfeld* as

Booze-fueled screaming plagued the Gotham crix voting conclave.

tops, the $2 million biopic of Broadway impresario Florenz Ziegfeld that made a sudden star out of recent Austrian import Rainer as the producer's jilted first wife. The notoriously shy 26-year-old did not care to swoon over Oscar voters, however, and stayed home on awards night, no doubt assuming, like everyone else, that the Best Actress prize would go to Thalberg's widow. But *Variety* did hold out some hope for Rainer in its faulty early forecast: "For best performance of actresses, indications are that Norma Shearer will get the statuette for *Romeo and Juliet* unless the studio group has a last-minute change of heart and tosses its ballots toward Luise Rainer, also Metro."

When word leaked out early on awards night that Rainer won, MGM execs telephoned her immediately and ordered her to the gala at the Biltmore Hotel in time to accept the statuette.

Variety did a better job sizing up the Best Actor race, which it believed would go to the same thesp who claimed the Volpi Cup at the Venice Film Festival in August: "Indications point toward Paul Muni in *The Story of Louis Pasteur* (Warner Bros.). It was figured that Spencer Tracy might be a close contestant for top honors with his performance in *San Francisco* (MGM), but it is believed that Muni will get sufficient outside support (beyond WB) to carry him over the line."

Some film historians believe that some of the heftiest support for the Warner Bros. star actually came from a rival studio as a result of Louis B. Mayer's continuing efforts to manipulate the vote even though winners were no longer chosen by his hand-picked judges. Rumor had it that Mayer and Jack Warner made a back-room deal: the lion studio agreed to throw its loyal bloc votes behind Muni in exchange for Warner Bros. supporting *The Great Ziegfeld* for Best Picture and Actress.

The Oscars added new prizes (plaques, not golden boys) for supporting stars. *Variety* correctly foresaw who'd nab the first one for men, claiming Walter Brennan (*Come and Get It*) "looks like a cinch, with closest candidate being Akim Tamiroff in *General Died at Dawn*." The tradepaper hedged on the equivalent female kudos, though: "Performance by actress for best supporting role award lies between Maria Ouspenskaya in *Dodsworth* and Gale Sondergaard in *Anthony Adverse*, with the chances about even." Rookie thesp Sondergaard prevailed for Warner Brothers' costliest production *Anthony Adverse*, marking the first time that a nominee won for a debut film role. *Adverse* also scored the most total Oscars (four), including kudos for film editing, cinematography and musical score.

Variety handicapped the directors' derby thus: "William Wyler, for direction of *Dodsworth*, appears to be outstanding candidate, with Robert Z. Leonard for handling of *Great Ziegfeld* and Frank Capra for *Mr. Deeds Goes to Town*, both close runners-up. Possibility is that either might cross the winning barrier." Capra made it.

The awards banquet began at 8 P.M. in the hotel's Biltmore Bowl room and was presided over by George Jessel, who referred to the recent abdication of England's King Edward while imploring winners to keep their thank-yous short: "Remember, a fellow gave up the British Empire in two minutes."

Price Waterhouse accountants didn't count the votes until the polls closed at 5 P.M. The results were supposed to be kept secret until winners were announced after 11 P.M., but word leaked out early when reporters downstairs in the press room were tipped off so they could meet their East Coast deadlines. Upstairs, lips were no doubt loosened by the unprecedented serving of California champagne during the Depression-era dinner, which proved, said *Variety*, that "prosperity is back to stay."

Among Jessel's duties, once the winners were announced, was to reveal how the nominees ranked in the vote outcome. Carole Lombard (*My Man Godfrey*) and Norma Shearer came in second and third place, respectively, in the actress race; Gary Cooper placed for Best Actor behind winner Paul Muni (*The Story of Louis Pasteur*). Best Director Frank Capra (*Mr. Deeds Comes to Town*) got his toughest competish from W. S. Van Dyke (*San Francisco*). *The Great Ziegfeld* won Best Picture by only a few votes over *The Story of Louis Pasteur*.

Jessel made a bold gaffe when he bestowed the Best Actress award to Rainer. He upstaged last year's recipient Bette Davis, who was supposed to do the honor. A furious Davis cornered him after the ceremony. He blamed last year's winner Victor McLaglen, who botched the introduction of Muni by babbling too much before handing him the Best Actor award, then interrupting his acceptance speech.

Widow Shearer made her first public appearance since the loss of her husband only to lose her Oscar bid, but she received a notable consolation prize: academy president Frank Capra ended the Oscar ceremony by announcing the creation of the new Irving G. Thalberg Award to honor venerable producers. The news was greeted by a rousing ovation and a roomful of wet eyes turned toward Shearer as she bowed her head.

This year's nominations were chosen by a committee of 50 people who shamelessly chose themselves—including Carole Lombard and directors Frank Capra, W. S. Van Dyke and Robert A. Leonard. The system was scrapped after the outcry it caused this year and the voting was returned to the academy's membership.

▪ 1936 ▪

NATIONAL BOARD OF REVIEW

The board declared a best film of the year, then listed its remaining favorites according to highest scores. The vote results were announced on December 18, 1936.

BEST PICTURE

- ▪ *Mr. Deeds Goes to Town*
- *The Story of Louis Pasteur*
- *Modern Times*
- *Fury*
- *Winterset*
- *The Devil Is a Sissy*
- *Ceiling Zero*
- *Romeo and Juliet*
- *The Prisoner of Shark Island*
- *The Green Pastures*

BEST FOREIGN FILM

- ▪ *La Kermesse Heroique (Carnival in Flanders)* (France)
- *The New Earth* (Netherlands)
- *Rembrandt** (U.K.)
- *The Ghost Goes West* (U.K.)
- *Nine Days a Queen* (U.K.)
- *We Are from Kronstadt* (U.S.S.R.)
- *Son of Mongolia* (U.S.S.R.)
- *The Yellow Cruise* (France)
- *Les Misérables* (France)
- *The Secret Agent* (U.K.)

NEW YORK FILM CRITICS

Winners were announced on January 4, 1937. Awards were presented on January 24 at the Rainbow Room in New York. The ceremony was broadcast live nationwide by NBC radio.

BEST PICTURE

- ▪ *Mr. Deeds Goes to Town*

BEST DIRECTOR

- ▪ Rouben Mamoulian, *The Gay Desperado*

BEST ACTOR

- ▫ Walter Huston, *Dodsworth*

*Also appears on 1937 list.

BEST ACTRESS

- ▪ Luise Rainer, *The Great Ziegfeld*

BEST FOREIGN FILM

- ▪ *La Kermesse Heroique (Carnival in Flanders)* (France)

ACADEMY AWARDS

Nominations were announced on February 7, 1937. Awards were presented on March 4 at the Biltmore Hotel in Los Angeles.

BEST PICTURE

- ▪ *The Great Ziegfeld*
- *Anthony Adverse*
- *Dodsworth*
- *Libeled Lady*
- *Mr. Deeds Goes to Town*
- *Romeo and Juliet*
- *San Francisco*
- *The Story of Louis Pasteur*
- *A Tale of Two Cities*
- *Three Smart Girls*

BEST DIRECTOR

- ▪ Frank Capra, *Mr. Deeds Goes to Town*
- Gregory La Cava, *My Man Godfrey*
- Robert Z. Leonard, *The Great Ziegfeld*
- W. S. Van Dyke, *San Francisco*
- William Wyler, *Dodsworth*

BEST ASSISTANT DIRECTOR

- ▪ Jack Sullivan, *The Charge of the Light Brigade*

Word leaked out early that Paul Muni (left), Luise Rainer and Frank Capra won Oscars. Rainer heard the news at home and rushed to the ceremony.

Clem Beauchamp, *The Last of the Mohicans*
William Cannon, *Anthony Adverse*
Joseph Newman, *San Francisco*
Eric G. Stacey, *The Garden of Allah*

BEST ACTOR

- Paul Muni, *The Story of Louis Pasteur*
Gary Cooper, *Mr. Deeds Goes to Town*
Walter Huston, *Dodsworth*
William Powell, *My Man Godfrey*
Spencer Tracy, *San Francisco*

BEST ACTRESS

- Luise Rainer, *The Great Ziegfeld*
Irene Dunne, *Theodora Goes Wild*
Gladys George, *Valiant Is the Word for Carrie*
Carole Lombard, *My Man Godfrey*
Norma Shearer, *Romeo and Juliet*

BEST SUPPORTING ACTOR

- Walter Brennan, *Come and Get It*
Mischa Auer, *My Man Godfrey*
Stuart Erwin, *Pigskin Parade*
Basil Rathbone, *Romeo and Juliet*
Akim Tamiroff, *The General Died at Dawn*

BEST SUPPORTING ACTRESS

- Gale Sondergaard, *Anthony Adverse*
Beulah Bondi, *The Gorgeous Hussy*
Alice Brady, *My Man Godfrey*
Bonita Granville, *These Three*
Maria Ouspenskaya, *Dodsworth*

BEST WRITING (ORIGINAL STORY)

- Pierre Collings, Sheridan Gibney, *The Story of Louis Pasteur*
Adele Comandini, *Three Smart Girls*
Robert Hopkins, *San Francisco*
Norman Krasna, *Fury*
William Anthony McGuire, *The Great Ziegfeld*

BEST WRITING (SCREENPLAY)

- Pierre Collings, Sheridan Gibney, *The Story of Louis Pasteur*
Frances Goodrich, Albert Hackett, *After the Thin Man*
Eric Hatch, Morris Ryskind, *My Man Godfrey*

Sidney Howard, *Dodsworth*
Robert Riskin, *Mr. Deeds Goes to Town*

BEST SONG

- "The Way You Look Tonight," *Swing Time*, Jerome Kern, Dorothy Fields
"Did I Remember," *Suzy*, Walter Donaldson, Harold Adamson
"I've Got You under My Skin," *Born to Dance*, Cole Porter
"A Melody from the Sky," *Trail of the Lonesome Pine*, Louis Alter, Sidney Mitchell
"Pennies from Heaven," *Pennies from Heaven*, Arthur Johnston, Johnny Burke
"When Did You Leave Heaven," *Sing Baby Sing*, Richard A. Whiting, Walter Bullock

Winners

BEST CINEMATOGRAPHY

- Gaetano Gaudio, *Anthony Adverse*

BEST FILM EDITING

- Ralph Dawson, *Anthony Adverse*

BEST DANCE DIRECTION

- Seymour Felix, "A Pretty Girl Is Like a Melody," *The Great Ziegfeld*

BEST INTERIOR DECORATION

- Richard Day, *Dodsworth*

BEST MUSIC SCORE

- Erich Wolfgang Korngold, Leo Forbstein, *Anthony Adverse*

BEST SHORT SUBJECT

(CARTOON)
- *Country Cousin*
(ONE REEL)
- *Bored of Education*
(TWO REEL)
- *The Public Pays*
(COLOR)
- *Give Me Liberty*

BEST SOUND RECORDING

- Douglas Shearer, *San Francisco*

SCIENTIFIC OR TECHNICAL AWARDS

Class I (Statuette)
- Douglas Shearer, MGM Sound Department

Class II (Plaque)
- E. C. Wente, Bell Telephone Laboratories

Class III (Certificate)
- RCA Manufacturing
- Electrical Research Products
- United Artists

SPECIAL AWARDS
- *March of Time*
- W. Howard Greene, Harold Rosson

· 1937 ·

Huzzahs for Zola

The National Board of Review's choices wowed *Time* magazine: "Of 1937's pretentious crop, it found unpretentious *Night Must Fall* the best." The b.o. dud was cheered by critics, but shunned by movie-goers because it featured matinee idol Robert Montgomery as a psychotic killer. New this year from the board was a list of top-10 acting performances, which included Montgomery's, and it impressed *Time* because of the addition of "the French Harry Bauer in the Prague-made *The Golem* and Soviet Nikolai Cherkassov (*Baltic Deputy*). Hollywood's 14-year-old Jackie Cooper made the list; the industry's 1937 darling, Mr. Paul Muni, did not." Also missing was one of the two eventual winners of the top trophies at the Oscars: Spencer Tracy.

Camille earned Greta Garbo her second award from the New York crix in three years. She was considered a shoo-in for the Oscar next, but lost.

Partisans of Muni (*The Life of Emile Zola*) and Tracy (*Captains Courageous*) squared off in a testy clash over the New York Film Critics kudos, which were decided the day before the National Board of Review announced its picks, so the crix were unaffected by them. Again the scribes met at the Hotel Victoria, this time ordering up crackers, salami and cheese to offset the effects of scotch. "The real fun began when the cinema defenders tried to decide on the best male performance," *The New York World-Telegram* reported. The *Post* added that the voting "brought dissension, deadlock, attempts to trade votes, political maneuvers, cheating and charges of silliness."

After eight ballots failed to produce the two-thirds vote needed to name a winner, the critics put that polling on hold, then moved on to the Best Actress front. "This didn't get off to any better start," the *World-Telegram* observed, "but on the fifth ballot Greta Garbo (*Camille*) received 12 votes, Katharine Hepburn (*Stage Door*) 2 and Car-

ole Lombard (*Nothing Sacred, True Confessions*) and Deanna Durbin (*100 Men and a Girl, Three Smart Girls*) 1 each, and the critics went back to the best male performance. This went on indefinitely with nobody really voting for anyone, but always against someone."

Exasperated, the group finally agreed to suspend the rule of secrecy and have a show-of-hands tally on the 11th ballot, which revealed a curious gender bias, the women leaning toward Tracy. "The next, final and 12th vote was Muni 11 and Tracy 5," the *Post* reported. "This was met with expressions of extreme disgust from the dauntless 5 who would have voted for Spencer Tracy, long may he be wonderful, all night long."

The other categories were decided easily. Only one vote was needed to pick the year's Best Director: Gregory La Cava for *Stage Door*. The biggest battle of all—Best Picture—was decided amicably in favor of *The Life of Emile Zola* after only two rounds.

Civility reigned at the Rainbow Room on January 11 when the honors (a gold medal for Best Picture, illuminated scrolls for others) were bestowed at the cocktail party attended by 300 luminaries, including Mary Pickford "slim and pretty in black and mink" and Ethel Merman "stunning in silver fox," noted the *Post*.

New Yorker drama critic Robert Benchley presided as emcee over the event, which included a 30-minute NBC radio broadcast. Piped in from Hollywood was the voice of Jack Warner, who accepted the top prize for *Zola* by asserting that the critics' kudos would encourage the production of more historical and biographical movies.

The New York Times added, "Mr. Muni, vacationing in Europe, was hooked in from Budapest and said, briefly, that he was to share his distinction with all who had worked on the picture." The elusive Garbo was absent, reputedly in Sweden, so Benchley suggested an absence of sound—"a period of silence"—to honor her.

Scenes from *Zola* were dramatized by its stars Erin O'Brien-Moore and Morris Carnovsky, but the *Post* noticed that the radio program was drowned out by rude cocktail chitchatting. The paper's reporter spied one notorious reveler noticeably on the wagon: "John Barrymore doesn't like big parties these days. When the time came to leave, he said, 'Thank you—and thank God!' But we think he had a good time on ginger ale anyway!"

Afterward, the critics' honorees were considered Oscar's front-runners. *Zola* led with the most nominations—a record-setting 10, including one for Muni, who was expected to grab the actor's gold again—and Garbo was considered a shoo-in for her overdue Best Actress crown.

Disaster, however, struck early when a flash flood caused the ceremony to be postponed by one week. Perhaps Muni and Garbo foresaw the further dark clouds

A hoaxer snatched Alice Brady's Oscar— and was never caught.

ahead. Neither one showed up for the rescheduled fete.

Others were missing, too. Host George Jessel got sick, so comedian Bob "Bazooka" Burns was called in to substitute. Spencer Tracy was hospitalized with appendicitis. Supporting actress contender Alice Brady was favored to win for her portrayal of cow owner Mrs. O'Leary in *In Old Chicago*, but she was laid up with a broken ankle. Supporting actor nominee Joseph Schildkraut (*The Life of Emile Zola*) stayed home because his agent told him he wouldn't win. Once again Luise Rainer (*The Good Earth*) stayed home, too, no doubt believing what Paul Muni had told Jack Warner before scooting off to Europe: "Nobody wins two years in a row."

Then mayhem broke loose when the winners were revealed at the ceremony and the studio bosses looked around for their shining stars.

Schildkraut was roused from sleep and summoned. Paul Muni wasn't missed. The winner turned out to be Spencer Tracy, who was excused for not attending due to being in Good Samaritan Hospital, but the irascible star got so irked by all the congratulatory calls after the announcement that he unhooked the phone. Lucky for him, he didn't see the statuette the academy had waiting for him when he checked out. It was accidentally inscribed to "Dick Tracy," but the mistake was caught and corrected before Tracy saw it.

At 8:30 P.M. soon after the 1,200 Oscar guests sat down to sup on boneless squab and peas, word leaked out on who would soon claim the golden boys. Frantic MGM execs called Rainer at home and ordered her to the Biltmore Hotel pronto. "Miss Rainer hurriedly dressed in a long-sleeved pink crepe gown and long black velvet cape," *Variety* reported. "She did not bother with make-up or pause to more than comb her hair. She was the last of the celebs to arrive."

Homebound Alice Brady seemed to

have the possibility of winning covered when a man accepted the golden boy on her behalf, then left the room. "Messenger carried Miss Brady's trophy to her home," *Variety* noted, but soon had to retract that report. The statuette vanished and the mysterious thief was never identified. A week and a half later, the academy gave the star a substitute award.

Again the Oscar prizes and noms hailed Hollywood's biggest pictures. *The Good Earth* (produced for $2.8 million) and *Camille* ($1 million) were high-profile legacies of the late Irving Thalberg. *Captains Courageous* cost $1 million, too, but paid back handsomely as MGM's top grosser. *Zola* made the most money for Warner Bros. and won Best Picture easily. Seven thousand members of the directors', writers' and actors' guilds joined academy members in voting for the nominees and winners. Fifteen thousand acting extras were permitted to vote for winners, too, a right they would keep until 1944.

The first recipient of the new Irving G. Thalberg Memorial Award was Twentieth Century-Fox mogul Darryl F. Zanuck (*In Old Chicago, 7th Heaven, Wee Willie Winkie*), who beat out Samuel Goldwyn and David O. Selznick.

Not all of Hollywood's champs stayed lucky—or in Hollywood. Soon after becoming the first star to win back-to-back best-acting trophies, Luise Rainer quit the film biz. Later in life, she blamed bad scripts that she refused to perform, the breakup of her marriage to dramatist Clifford Odets and her own immaturity for her failure to cope with the sudden stardom and Oscar glory she basked in at age 27.

"One was acclaimed now; therefore one's doings, one's motives, one's every utterance seemed to have greater dimension and therefore suddenly became suspect," she wrote years later. "It seemed harder to continue one's work quietly. Shortly later I left Hollywood."

▪ 1937 ▪

NATIONAL BOARD OF REVIEW

The board declared a best film of the year, then listed its remaining favorites according to highest scores. Winners of the new Best Acting awards were listed alphabetically. The vote results were announced on December 30, 1937.

BEST PICTURE
▪ *Night Must Fall*
The Life of Emile Zola
Black Legion
Camille
Make Way for Tomorrow
The Good Earth
They Won't Forget
Captains Courageous
A Star Is Born
Stage Door

BEST ACTING
▪ Harry Baur, *The Golem*

▪ Humphrey Bogart, *Black Legion*
▪ Charles Boyer, *Conquest*
▪ Nikolai Cherkassov, *Baltic Deputy*
▪ Danielle Darrieux, *Mayerling*
▪ Greta Garbo, *Camille*
▪ Robert Montgomery, *Night Must Fall*
▪ Maria Ouspenskaya, *Conquest*
▪ Luise Rainer, *The Good Earth*
▪ Joseph Schildkraut, *The Life of Emile Zola*
▪ Dame May Whitty, *Night Must Fall*
▪ Mathias Wieman, *The Eternal Mask*

BEST FOREIGN FILM
▪ *The Eternal Mask* (Austria/Switzerland)
The Lower Depths (France)
Baltic Deputy (U.S.S.R.)
Mayerling (France)
The Spanish Earth (Spain)
Golgotha (France)
Elephant Boy (U.K.)
Rembrandt (U.K.)
Janosik (Czechoslovakia)
The Wedding of Palo (Greenland/Denmark)

NEW YORK FILM CRITICS

Winners were announced on December 30, 1937. Awards were presented on January 9, 1938, at the Rainbow Room in New York. The ceremony was broadcast live nationwide by NBC radio.

BEST PICTURE
- *The Life of Emile Zola*

BEST DIRECTOR
- Gregory La Cava, *Stage Door*

BEST ACTOR
- Paul Muni, *The Life of Emile Zola*

BEST ACTRESS
- Greta Garbo, *Camille*

BEST FOREIGN FILM
- *Mayerling* (France)

ACADEMY AWARDS

Nominations were announced on February 6, 1938. Awards were presented on March 10 at the Biltmore Hotel in Los Angeles.

BEST PICTURE
- *The Life of Emile Zola*
The Awful Truth
Captains Courageous
Dead End
The Good Earth
In Old Chicago
Lost Horizon
One Hundred Men and a Girl
Stage Door
A Star Is Born

BEST DIRECTOR
- Leo McCarey, *The Awful Truth*
William Dieterle, *The Life of Emile Zola*
Sidney Franklin, *The Good Earth*
Gregory La Cava, *Stage Door*
William A. Wellman, *A Star Is Born*

DAILY VARIETY DAILY
NEWS OF THE SHOW WORLD
Vol. 19 No. 5 Hollywood, California, Friday, March 11, 1938 5 Cents

'ZOLA,' ZANUCK, TRACY, RAINER AND McCAREY

FULL LIST OF WINNERS

Irving Thalberg Memorial Award
Darryl F. Zanuck, 20th-Fox, for his contribution to the screen through 'In Old Chicago,' 'Ali Baba Goes to Town,' 'Happy Landing' and 'Love and Hisses.'

Best Performance

Production
'The Life of Emile Zola,' Warners.

Actor
Spencer Tracy, Metro, 'Captains Courageous.'
Actress
Luise Rainer, Metro, 'The Good Earth.'
Supporting Actor
Joseph Schildkraut in 'The Life of Emile Zola.'
Supporting Actress
Alice Brady in 'In Old Chicago.'

Direction
Leo McCarey for Columbia's 'The Awful Truth.'
Original Story
William Wellman and Robert Carson, Selznick—
◆ Continued on page 22 ◆

MG Gets 5 Firsts
WB, Col 3 Each

In gala mood and dress, and feeling justly proud of its distinguished 1937 production achievements, the motion picture industry last night held its self-congratulatory celebration at the 10th annual awards dinner of the Academy of Motion Picture Arts and Sciences at Biltmore Bowl. Some 1,400 persons, representing every branch of the industry, paraded, dined, listened to laudatory speeches and congratulated the winners as they received the symbols of highest excellence in performance, production, direction, writing and the various picture arts and technical contributions. Warners got the best picture award for 'The Life of Emile Zola.' Metro, scoring highest numerically, walked away with five firsts, while Warners and Columbia shared the runner up honors with three each, and 20th-Fox took two, plus the special Irving Thalberg Memorial

INDIES WIN DUAL SUIT—

Philadelphia, Penn., March 10.—
Courts today again upheld Indie ex-

For the first time yet, Oscars voters agreed with the Gotham crix on Best Picture.

BEST ASSISTANT DIRECTOR
- Robert Webb, *In Old Chicago*
C. C. Coleman, Jr., *Lost Horizon*
Russ Saunders, *The Life of Emile Zola*
Eric Stacey, *A Star Is Born*
Hal Walker, *Souls at Sea*

BEST ACTOR
- Spencer Tracy, *Captains Courageous*
Charles Boyer, *Conquest*
Fredric March, *A Star Is Born*
Robert Montgomery, *Night Must Fall*
Paul Muni, *The Life of Emile Zola*

BEST ACTRESS
- Luise Rainer, *The Good Earth*
Irene Dunne, *The Awful Truth*
Greta Garbo, *Camille*
Janet Gaynor, *A Star Is Born*
Barbara Stanwyck, *Stella Dallas*

BEST SUPPORTING ACTOR
- Joseph Schildkraut, *The Life of Emile Zola*
Ralph Bellamy, *The Awful Truth*
Thomas Mitchell, *The Hurricane*
H. B. Warner, *Lost Horizon*
Roland Young, *Topper*

BEST SUPPORTING ACTRESS
- Alice Brady, *In Old Chicago*
Andrea Leeds, *Stage Door*

Anne Shirley, *Stella Dallas*
Claire Trevor, *Dead End*
Dame May Whitty, *Night Must Fall*

BEST WRITING ORIGINAL STORY)
- Robert Carson, William A. Wellman, *A Star Is Born*

Niven Busch, *In Old Chicago*
Heinz Herald, Geza Herczeg, *The Life of Emile Zola*
Hans Kraly, *One Hundred Men and a Girl*
Robert Lord, *Black Legion*

BEST WRITING (SCREENPLAY)
- Heinz Herald, Geza Herczeg, Norman Reilly Raine, *The Life of Emile Zola*

Alan Campbell, Robert Carson, Dorothy Parker, *A Star Is Born*
Marc Connelly, John Lee Mahin, Dale Van Every, *Captains Courageous*
Vina Delmar, *The Awful Truth*
Morris Ryskind, Anthony Veiller, *Stage Door*

BEST SONG
- "Sweet Leilani," *Waikiki Wedding*, Harry Owens

"Remember Me," *Mr. Dodd Takes the Air*, Harry Warren, Al Dubin
"That Old Feeling," *Vogues of 1938*, Sammy Fain, Lew Brown
"They Can't Take That Away from Me," *Shall We Dance*, George Gershwin, Ira Gershwin
"Whispers in the Dark," *Artists and Models*, Frederick Hollander, Leo Robin

Winners

BEST CINEMATOGRAPHY
- Karl Freund, *The Good Earth*

BEST FILM EDITING
- Gene Havlick, Gene Milford, *Lost Horizon*

BEST DANCE DIRECTION
- Hermes Pan, *Damsel in Distress*

BEST ART DIRECTION
- Stephen Goosson, *Lost Horizon*

BEST MUSIC SCORE
- (No composer credit), Charles Previn, *One Hundred Men and a Girl*

BEST SHORT SUBJECT
(CARTOON)
- *The Old Mill*

(ONE REEL)
- *Private Life of the Gannets*

(TWO REEL)
- *Torture Money*

(COLOR)
- *Penny Wisdom*

BEST SOUND RECORDING
- Thomas Moulton, *The Hurricane*

SCIENTIFIC OR TECHNICAL AWARDS
Class I (Statuette)
- Agfa Ansco Corp.

Class II (Plaque)
- Walt Disney Productions
- Eastman Kodak
- Farciot Edouart, Paramount Pictures
- Douglas Shearer, MGM Sound Department

Class III (Certificate)
- John Arnold, MGM Camera Department
- John Livadary
- Thomas T. Moulton, United Artists Sound Department
- RCA Manufacturing
- Joseph E. Robbins, Paramount Pictures
- Douglas Shearer, MGM Sound Department

IRVING G. THALBERG MEMORIAL AWARD
- Darryl F. Zanuck

SPECIAL AWARDS
- Mack Sennett
- Edgar Bergen
- Museum of Modern Art Film Library
- W. Howard Greene

· 1938 ·

Mighty Citadel

One year after the fickle New York critics and Los Angeles Oscar voters finally got together on a Best Picture choice, they split up.

But both Manhattan kudos groups—the crix and the National Board of Review—were back in sync, snubbing Hollywood in favor of two of their own Gotham stars and a film from across the Atlantic.

Their joint choice for Best Picture, *The Citadel*, was considered a British movie even though it was produced in part by MGM. In order to make it eligible for its top honor, the National Board of Review bunched U.S. and U.K. fare together into a new category for English-speaking films. A majority of Brits composed the board's list of the year's top 10 thesps, too: Ralph Richardson, Robert Donat, Will Fyffe, Wendy Hiller, Charles Laughton and Robert Morley. Also hailed were the two New Yorkers who the critics would declare best thesps: Broadway vet Margaret Sullavan (*Three Comrades*) and New Yorker James Cagney (*Angels with Dirty Faces*), who was enjoying a career comeback. The board made a particularly gutsy snub: Hollywood diva Bette Davis (*Jezebel*) wasn't listed, although she'd later wreak her revenge and seize a hefty consolation prize.

Davis had little support when the critics voted 19 days after the board released its picks, too. England's Wendy Hiller (*Pygmalion*) led on the first ballot, then Yankee Sullavan came on strong and pulled out a win on the fourth round. *The Citadel* led with eight votes on the first tally for Best Picture; the U.K.'s *To the Victor* was runner-up with three. *The Citadel* finally towered above all others on its fourth try.

"There were valiant challengers in each competitive class and the log-rolling, lobbying and vote-trading that went on in the tra-

Past Oscar champs Spencer Tracy (left) and Bette Davis struck gold again when statuettes were presented by Cedric Hardwicke.

ditional smoke-filled room were shameful and very funny," *The New York Times* reported. "Mr. William Boehnel of the *World-Telegram* fought his annual losing battle for Katharine Hepburn and sneered that Miss Sullavan had won only because she had a consumptive's death scene to do in *Three Comrades*. (Garbo's *Camille* had won the year before.) Mr. B. R. Crisler of the *Times* was white-faced and thin-voiced pleading for Will Fyffe."

Britain's Fyffe (*To the Victor*) actually led on the first four ballots. Spencer Tracy (*Boys Town*) posed a serious challenge, but Cagney looked weak at first: the slugger from Manhattan's Lower East Side only had a single vote on the first ballot, but then muscled up increasingly more support to knock out all others in the ninth round.

"The Cagney selection was perhaps the most surprising of the lot," the *Times* said, "but it was time the critics placed a wreath at the feet of the screen's best public enemy." Not everyone agreed. *The Brooklyn Eagle*'s Herbert Cohn was among the dissident critics who groused in print afterward that the award was a sham because Cagney was playing himself.

There was no quarrel over who got the

laurels for Best Director. Brit Alfred Hitchcock (*The Lady Vanishes*) snagged them on the first ballot. *Grand Illusion* was always the top vote-getter for the new award for Best Foreign Film, but it took seven pollings before it received the required two-thirds majority needed to fend off *Professor Mamlock* and *Ballerina*.

The oft-snobby crix refused to let the year's cartoon blockbuster, *Snow White and the Seven Dwarfs*, compete for Best Picture. "Mr. Howard Barnes of the *Herald-Tribune* was crushed," reported the *Times*, but Barnes was the gang's president and he prevailed on them to give *Snow White* a special new award as a consolation.

The scrolls and bronze plaque (for Best Picture) again were bestowed at a cocktail party at the Rainbow Room atop Rockefeller Center, where Dudley Nichols, president of the Screen Writers Guild, presided as host. At 7 P.M., he began his opening remarks, which were carried live over NBC's national hookup, then the broadcast cut to Paris where *Grand Illusion* director/producer Jean Renoir thanked the crix for his prize.

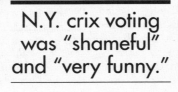

N.Y. crix voting was "shameful" and "very funny."

Next, the program cut to London, where Hitchcock and *Citadel* star Robert Donat had the jitters, according to the *Times*: "Hitch took his wife and small daughter along to the BBC headquarters to support him through the broadcast. Donat, who broadcast from his own home, pulled himself together on coffee and resolutely refused supper. His script, written out in longhand and laboriously pasted together from the family glue-pot, was spread out on cushions from the dining-room sofa. In the privacy of his study in the Chilterns, he tore off collar and tie and went into that speech from *The Citadel*. . . . It was one of England's wildest January nights and the short waves were crackling with static."

When Donat finished, the program returned to New York, where Cagney performed a scene from *Angels*, then tossed out

to Hollywood, where Margaret Sullavan recreated *Three Comrades* and Walt Disney accepted his consolation kudos with the words, "All I can say is thanks a lot." A musical medley from *Snow White* wrapped up the 30-minute show.

Sullavan faced a formidable challenge when Oscar time came. She received a nomination, but she was up against Bette Davis, who may have been snubbed by the newspaper scribes, but *Time* magazine's editors had just put her on their cover and Davis's dutiful fans were flocking to theaters to see her as a foxy Southern belle in *Jezebel*. It was no coincidence that the role seemed similar to the lead in the much-hyped *Gone With the Wind*, then in production. Hollywood wags wisecracked that, when Davis failed to get the part of Scarlett O'Hara, she bullied Jack Warner into finding her a part just like it—and made him get the film out first. At the 1938 Oscar derby, she was a dark horse pulling up fast and she arrived at the Biltmore gala with Sullavan's ex, *Jezebel* director William Wyler, on her arm.

In order to nab her second golden boy, Davis also needed to surpass past Oscar champ Norma Shearer, who was rebounding from hubby Irving Thalberg's death with the $1.8 million *Marie Antoinette*, which netted her the best notices of her career and the Volpi Cup as Best Actress at the Venice Film Festival in June 1938.

"Big campaign was waged by friends to give Norma Shearer the award," *Variety* reported about her Oscar drive, but added that the race seemed to be "between the Metro star Bette Davis in *Jezebel* and Fay Bainter in *White Banners*. Latter also was nominated for best performance by a supporting actress for acting in *Jezebel*," thereby becoming the first performer to score two Oscar noms in one year. Bainter had Hollywood sentiment on her side, since she'd recently returned to her hometown after shining for two decades as one of Broadway's brightest stars.

Also nominated was the second-highest vote-getter among the New York critics, Wendy Hiller, who'd recently became an overnight star when stage icon George Bernard Shaw selected her to play the lead in his film adaptation of *Pygmalion*, which would earn Shaw the scriptwriter's Oscar.

Meantime, in the Best Actor race, Spencer Tracy was hoping to pull off what Luise Rainer did last year—a second consecutive win. He was up against the fiesty and suddenly respectable James Cagney, *The Citadel*'s Robert Donat, *Pygmalion*'s Leslie Howard (Best Actor champ at the Venice film fest) and Charles Boyer, who was seducing film lovers with his immortal invitation "Come with me to the Casbah" in *Algiers*.

Variety sized up the male race: "James Cagney, who climbed back into popular favor through his performance in *Angels with Dirty Faces* is reported to have had a big lead in early voting. General belief is that the winner lies between Cagney and Spencer Tracy."

Davis and Tracy were not to be denied. Both prevailed. When Tracy got his second trophy, the academy made a copy of it for the real Boystown compound in Nebraska.

Supporting actor nominee Walter Brennan (*Kentucky*) also scored his second Oscar, which was attributed to strong support from the thousands of extras permitted to vote. "They carry the balance of power," *Variety* warned the day before the Oscar gala, adding the reminder, "Brennan worked as a $5 extra for some time before given a picture break by Samuel Goldwyn."

Despite her loss in the lead actress category, Fay Bainter prevailed for her supporting role in *Jezebel*.

"Frank Capra is popular with actors, writers and directors and is certain to finish among the leaders" on Oscar night, *Variety* said about the helmer race before the awards ceremony. "If Capra fails to take directorial honors, it is believed award will go to Michael Curtiz, who drew nominations for *Angels with Dirty Faces* as well as *Four Daughters*." Capra snagged the laurel easily, garnering his third career Oscar for his screen rendition of *You Can't Take It with*

You Can't Take It with You was one of the rare laffers to win Oscar's Best Picture prize.

You, the Pulitzer champ, still running on Broadway, about a young woman who must introduce her beau's conventional parents to her wacky family. The recently elected prexy of the directors' guild was also triumphant on awards night for recently having faced down the producers' guild, which had refused to recognize Capra's group as the agents empowered to negotiate on behalf of Hollywood's helmers. Capra, still president of the motion picture academy, too, threatened an industry-wide directors' strike and a boycott of the Oscars. The producers caved.

Being a comedy, *You Can't Take It with You* was handicapped in the race for Best Picture and confronted formidable foes: *Jezebel, Pygmalion*, the Gotham crix's top pic *The Citadel*, MGM's top grosser *Boys Town* and the first foreign-language film to compete in the category, *Grand Illusion*, Jean Renoir's art house hit that appealed to America's pacifist leanings while Hitler bullied Europe. One day before the Oscars, *Variety* cited three films as front-runners—*You Can't Take It with You, Alexander's Ragtime Band* and *Jezebel*—and declared that Capra's laffer was "crowding" the competish. When the winner was revealed, Capra's *You Can't Take It with You* had the last laugh.

Just like at the New York Film Critics

kudos, *Snow White and the Seven Dwarfs* wasn't permitted to compete for Best Picture, but again Walt Disney was given a special award. This one was specially designed, too—the figure of Oscar was surrounded by seven dwarfed clones—and it was bestowed by the diminutive Shirley Temple.

"I'm so proud of it I'm going to burst!" the studio exec beamed.

"Oh, don't do that, Mr. Disney!" Shirley said. The audience howled.

There was no official ceremony host. Most of the top acting awards were presented by Tyrone Power and Cedric Hardwicke. Again the nominees and winners were chosen by members of the motion picture academy and all of the primary Hollywood guilds. When the movie extras were also allowed to check off ballots, the electorate swelled. "Approximately 12,000 ballots for the final voting will be mailed by the Academy on Feb. 10 with voting to close Feb. 20," *Variety* reported. The studios were shameless in courting the favor of the huge bloc of extras. *Variety* observed: "For three days Central Casting was overwhelmed with demands for atmosphere players. In that time there were more than 6,000 urgent invitations to work, recalling the simple days when political candidates wept on the shoulders of the workingmen along about the first Tuesday after the first Monday in November."

▪ 1938 ▪

NATIONAL BOARD OF REVIEW

The board declared a best film of the year, then listed its remaining favorites according to highest scores. Winners of the Best Acting awards were listed alphabetically. The vote results were announced on December 15, 1938.

BEST PICTURE
▪ *The Citadel*
Snow White and the Seven Dwarfs
The Beachcomber
To the Victor
Sing, You Sinners
The Edge of the World
Of Human Hearts
Jezebel
South Riding
Three Comrades

BEST ACTING
▪ Lew Ayres, *Holiday, Young Dr. Kildare*
▪ Pierre Blanchar, Harry Baur, Louis Jouvet, Raimu, *Un Carnet de Bal*
▪ James Cagney, *Angels with Dirty Faces*
▪ Joseph Calleia, *Algiers*
▪ Chico, *The Adventures of Chico*
▪ Robert Donat, *The Citadel*
▪ Pierre Fresnay, Jean Gabin, Dita Parlo, Eric von Stroheim, *Grand Illusion*

▪ Will Fyffe, *To the Victor*
▪ John Garfield, *Four Daughters*
▪ Wendy Hiller, *Pygmalion*
▪ Charles Laughton, Elsa Lanchester, *The Beachcomber*
▪ Robert Morley, *Marie Antoinette*
▪ Ralph Richardson, *South Riding, The Citadel*
▪ Margaret Sullavan, *Three Comrades*
▪ Spencer Tracy, *Boys Town*

BEST FOREIGN FILM
▪ *Grand Illusion* (France)
Ballerina
Un Carnet de Bal (France)
Generals without Buttons (France)
Peter the First (U.S.S.R.)
Professor Mamlock

NEW YORK FILM CRITICS

Winners were announced on January 3, 1939. Awards were presented on January 8 at the Rainbow Room in New York. The ceremony was broadcast live by NBC radio.

BEST PICTURE
▪ *The Citadel*

BEST DIRECTOR
▪ Alfred Hitchcock, *The Lady Vanishes*

BEST ACTOR
- James Cagney, *Angels with Dirty Faces*

BEST ACTRESS
- Margaret Sullavan, *Three Comrades*

BEST FOREIGN FILM
- *Grand Illusion* (France)

SPECIAL AWARD
- *Snow White and the Seven Dwarfs*

ACADEMY AWARDS

Nominations were announced on February 5, 1939. Awards were presented on February 23 at the Biltmore Hotel in Los Angeles.

BEST PICTURE
- *You Can't Take It with You*

The Adventures of Robin Hood
Alexander's Ragtime Band
Boys Town
The Citadel
Four Daughters
Grand Illusion
Jezebel
Pygmalion
Test Pilot

BEST DIRECTOR
- Frank Capra, *You Can't Take It with You*

Michael Curtiz, *Angels with Dirty Faces*
Michael Curtiz, *Four Daughters*
Norman Taurog, *Boys Town*
King Vidor, *The Citadel*

BEST ACTOR
- Spencer Tracy, *Boys Town*

Charles Boyer, *Algiers*
James Cagney, *Angels with Dirty Faces*
Robert Donat, *The Citadel*
Leslie Howard, *Pygmalion*

BEST ACTRESS
- Bette Davis, *Jezebel*

Fay Bainter, *White Banners*
Wendy Hiller, *Pygmalion*
Norma Shearer, *Marie Antoinette*
Margaret Sullavan, *Three Comrades*

BEST SUPPORTING ACTOR
- Walter Brennan, *Kentucky*

John Garfield, *Four Daughters*
Gene Lockhart, *Algiers*
Robert Morley, *Marie Antoinette*
Basil Rathbone, *If I Were King*

BEST SUPPORTING ACTRESS
- Fay Bainter, *Jezebel*

Beulah Bondi, *Of Human Hearts*
Billie Burke, *Merrily We Live*
Spring Byington, *You Can't Take It with You*
Miliza Korjus, *The Great Waltz*

BEST WRITING (ORIGINAL STORY)
- Eleanore Griffin, Dore Schary, *Boys Town*

Irving Berlin, *Alexander's Ragtime Band*
Rowland Brown, *Angels with Dirty Faces*
Marcella Burke, Frederick Kohner, *Mad about Music*
John Howard Lawson, *Blockade*
Frank Wead, *Test Pilot*

BEST WRITING (SCREENPLAY)
- Ian Dalrymple, Cecil Lewis, W. P. Lipscomb, George Bernard Shaw, *Pygmalion*

Lenore Coffee, Julius J. Epstein, *Four Daughters*
Ian Dalrymple, Elizabeth Hill, Frank Wead, *The Citadel*
John Meehan, Dore Schary, *Boys Town*
Robert Riskin, *You Can't Take It with You*

BEST SONG
- "Thanks for the Memory," *The Big Broadcast of 1938*, Ralph Rainger, Leo Robin

"Always and Always," *Mannequin*, Chet Forrest, Edward Ward, Bob Wright
"Change Partners and Dance with Me," *Carefree*, Irving Berlin
"The Cowboy and the Lady," *The Cowboy and the Lady*, Lionel Newman, Arthur Quenzer
"Dust," *Under Western Stars*, Johnny Marvin
"Jeepers Creepers," *Going Places*, Johnny Mercer, Harry Warren
"Merrily We Live," *Merrily We Live*, Phil Charig, Arthur Quenzer

"A Mist over the Moon," *The Lady Objects*, Oscar Hammerstein II, Ben Oakland
"My Own," *That Certain Age*, Harold Adamson, Jimmy McHugh
"Now It Can Be Told," *Alexander's Ragtime Band*, Irving Berlin

Winners

BEST ART DIRECTION
- Carl J. Weyl, *The Adventures of Robin Hood*

BEST CINEMATOGRAPHY
- Joseph Ruttenberg, *The Great Waltz*

BEST FILM EDITING
- Ralph Dawson, *The Adventures of Robin Hood*

BEST MUSIC
(ORIGINAL SCORE)
- Erich Wolfgang Korngold, *The Adventures of Robin Hood*

(SCORING)
- Alfred Newman, *Alexander's Ragtime Band*

BEST SHORT SUBJECT
(CARTOON)
- *Ferdinand the Bull*

(ONE REEL)
- *That Mother Might Live*

(TWO REEL)
- *Declaration of Independence*

BEST SOUND RECORDING
- Thomas Moulton, *The Cowboy and the Lady*

SCIENTIFIC OR TECHNICAL AWARDS
Class III (Certificate)
- John Aalberg, RKO Radio Studio Sound Department
- Byron Hasken, Warner Bros. Special Effects Department

IRVING G. THALBERG MEMORIAL AWARD
- Hal B. Wallis

SPECIAL AWARDS
- J. Arthur Ball
- Walt Disney
- Deanna Durbin
- Gordon Jennings
- Oliver Marsh, Allen Davey
- Mickey Rooney
- Harry M. Warner

▪ 1939 ▪

A *"Civil War" over* Gone With the Wind

Because of its insistence upon being the first film kudos, the National Board of Review missed the biggest movie of the year. The board's cutoff date for award eligibility was December 15, just a few days before the hugely hyped and long-awaited *Gone With the Wind* finally swept across America's silver screens.

Instead, the board courageously picked a movie that would be overlooked by the New York Film Critics and Oscar voters: *Confessions of a Nazi Spy*, starring Paul Lukas as a member of the Gestapo's "fifth column" operating in the United States. It was a brave selection for another reason, too. *Confessions* infuriated isolationists of the day who accused Hollywood of trying to push America into Europe's war. The House Un-American Activities Committee investigated the film for being "prematurely anti-fascist."

There were other surprising omissions on the board's lists as well. The second biggest movie of the year, *Mr. Smith Goes to Washington*, was hailed as one of its 10 best, but star Jimmy Stewart wasn't on the board's separate roster of best actors. Also absent: MGM's new British matinee idol Robert Donat (*Goodbye, Mr. Chips*), who would play a dramatic role at the Oscars— and almost at the New York Film Critics.

The crix also missed picking the year's blockbuster—but on purpose after a fierce battle broke out among the pundits who met on December 27 in the directors' room of *The New York Times* just a few yards away from the two Times Square theaters where *Gone With the Wind*'s opening was causing a whirlwind of excitement.

"You would have thought the Civil War was being fought all over again," William Boehnel of the *World-Telegram* wrote of the crix's clash while trying to pick a Best Picture, "with *Gone With the Wind* in the role of

Gotham crix voted *Wuthering Heights* (starring Laurence Olivier and Merle Oberon) Best Picture on the 14th ballot after being deadlocked between *Gone With the Wind* and *Mr. Smith Goes to Washington*.

Johnny Reb and *Mr. Smith Goes to Washington* and *Wuthering Heights* playing the Damned Yankees. Although the *Gone With the Wind* bloc fought furiously and gamely, the struggle, like that of the Confederacy, was doomed from the beginning. It lashed out heroically, when on several ballots it jumped from six to nine votes and threatened the opposition much as Lee gave the North the willies when he advanced as far as Gettysburg. But it gasped its last on the fourteenth ballot and had to surrender.

"Although *Wuthering Heights* was always in the running, it wasn't until after it appeared as if a deadlock between *Mr. Smith* and *Gone With the Wind* had been reached, along about the ninth ballot, that it began to come into its own." Then *Wuthering Heights* finally scored the necessary 13 votes, or two-thirds majority, needed among the 17 crix.

The *World-Telegram* noted that "a temporary truce" was called while the group turned to the task of choosing the acting and directing kudos, which by comparison "was like eating pumpkin pie. There was never any doubt that Miss (Vivien) Leigh would win the feminine honors," which she did on the second ballot. Jimmy Stewart ran second to Robert Donat during the first two tallies, but snatched victory from him on the third. Naming John Ford Best Director for *Stagecoach* "was never in any doubt," the paper added. "His only serious contender was Ernst Lubitsch (*Ninotchka*)."

When an armistice was declared after the voting, a new clash erupted when the crix asked Mayor Fiorello LaGuardia to emcee their January 7 awards ceremony, which was to include NBC's usual half-hour radio broadcast until a network exec heard who was skedded to host. The exec said that the network was "sick and tired of LaGuardia horning in on the movies, theater and everything else for political reasons" and threatened to ax the show. Furious, the crix made alternative broadcast plans with CBS, which were nixed as soon as NBC's chief David Sarnoff got an irate phone call from LaGuardia. The peacock's show went on as planned.

Mayhem nonetheless reigned on awards night when the revolving dance floor at the Rainbow Room "whirled around so briskly that numerous distinguished guests had to hang on to the bar for support," reported the *Herald-Tribune*. The dizzy glitterati included Joan Crawford, Van Heflin, Jean Hersholt, Shirley Booth and Walter Huston.

Also present was *Wuthering Heights* producer Samuel Goldwyn, who accepted the crix's bronze plaque for Best Picture, but grew weary of holding it up for photographers. The *Times* reported that Goldwyn complained "in a tone almost of petulance: 'It's heavy!' "

The Hollywood portion of the radio show included remarks from *Wuthering Heights* director William Wyler, a performance of one of its scenes by stars Laurence Olivier and Merle Oberon, and a speech from *Mr. Smith Goes to Washington* by Jimmy Stewart. All went smoothly until LaGuardia forgot to mention the recipient of Best Foreign Film, and the U.S. distributor of France's *Harvest* stormed out. The next day hizzoner apologized to the snubbed party in his typically glib fashion: "There is simply no excuse for my stupidity, just as there is no excuse for your getting excited about it." The distributor "announced his satisfaction," the *Times* announced.

At the Oscars seven weeks later, the national frenzy over *Gone With the Wind* was reaching hurricane pitch. When David O. Selznick's $4 million Civil War epic breezed through the Oscar nominations, it swept up an unprecedented 13.

Having won the New York Film Critics' scroll, British import Vivien Leigh was the favorite to win the actress Oscar, but there was also noticeable support behind two-time past champ Bette Davis (*Dark Victory*), who was America's second most popular female star after Shirley Temple. Upsets were also possible from Marlene Dietrich, who was riding a comeback via stagecoach in the western *Destry Rides Again*, and the Oscar-overdue Garbo, who was also seen in an unlikely new vehicle—a comedy, *Ninotchka*.

> "Hallelujah!" Hattie McDaniel cried upon winning the Oscar.

It was assumed that Clark Gable, being "the King" of Hollywood, would claim the actor's crown, but there were two possible usurpers in the wings: Jimmy Stewart and Robert Donat. Nonetheless, Gable and the rest of the *Gone With the Wind* contenders arrived at the Cocoanut Grove like royal conquerors—Vivien Leigh "covered with long ermine robe," noted *Variety*, as she entered on Selznick's arm. Her appearance "was a signal for a near riot of admirers who rushed to view the star," the paper added. Not far behind, "bedecked in orchids," followed costar and supporting nominee Hattie McDaniel, who "was given a great ovation" and responded "flashing a smiling recognition of the tribute."

Bette Davis's entrance, by comparison, merely "called for sustained applause by crowd," *Variety* noticed.

Inside, all the rivals were greeted by true, new Oscar royalty: first-time emcee Bob Hope, who would go on to reign as the kudos' favorite host 18 times in all (11 solo, seven as cohost). Introduced as the "Rhett Butler of the air," the then-radio star welcomed the 1,200 guests saying, "What a wonderful thing, this benefit for David Selznick." Selznick strode to the podium twice that night. The first time was to accept the helmer's gold for Victor Fleming, the director he had bullied into a nervous breakdown. Selznick claimed Fleming was "ill" on Oscar night and "heaped much praise on (him) for his hard work in making *Gone With the Wind* an artistic success," noted *Variety*. As Selznick approached the podium for the second time, Hope joshed, "David, you should have brought roller skates."

Soon after the Oscar banquet began at 8:30 P.M., there was no mystery who would claim honors. "*The Los Angeles Times* jumped the gun in releasing winners in the 8:45 P.M. edition, although sheet was pledged not to published them until 11 o'clock" when the awards were skedded to be presented, *Variety* reported. There were no gasps heard when the absent Donat beat Gable for Best Actor, and Bette Davis got over the news of her loss in time to put on a cherry show while congratulating Leigh at Selznick's table. Later, when the full vote tallies were revealed, it turned out that Davis came close to beating Leigh and that Gable was a mere also-ran behind Donat and Jimmy Stewart.

Another *Wind* star prevailed in the category of Best Supporting Actor, but not for the Civil War drama in which he played Scarlett O'Hara's father. Thomas Mitchell accepted the award for *Stagecoach*, saying, "I didn't think I was that good." "Mitchell begged off any speech-making, saying he was too 'incoherent,' " *Variety* said.

Wind claimed a record tally of eight golden boys in all and set another precedent when the screenwriter's gold went to Sidney Howard: it was the first time an award was bestowed posthumously. Howard had died a few months earlier when he was crushed by a tractor on his Massachusetts farm.

Another breakthrough occurred when the award was handed out for Best Supporting Actress. Last year's victor Fay Bainter presented the honor with a grand flourish and words that betrayed she knew who the winner was. "This is more than an occasion," she announced. "It is a tribute to a country where people are free to honor noteworthy achievements regardless of creed, race or color."

The award went to Hattie McDaniel as *Wind*'s effusive black maid, who shrieked "Hallelujah!" when she heard the news and raced to the podium. "This is the happiest moment of my life," she said, but then "emotion overcame her," *Variety* observed, as "she declared she would always try to be a credit to her race and the motion picture industry. Speech was broken off abruptly with a choked 'thank you.' "

Variety noted, "Not only was she the first of her race to receive an award, but she was also the first Negro ever to sit at an Academy banquet." After winning, the grateful champ "rushed from the stand," *Variety* added, and she returned to her seat—at a table in the back of the room.

▪ 1939 ▪

NATIONAL BOARD OF REVIEW

The board declared a best film of the year, then listed its remaining favorites according to highest scores. Winners of the Best Acting awards were listed alphabetically. The vote results were announced on December 24, 1939.

BEST PICTURE
▪ *Confessions of a Nazi Spy*
Wuthering Heights
Stagecoach

Ninotchka
Young Mr. Lincoln
Crisis
Goodbye, Mr. Chips
Mr. Smith Goes to Washington
The Roaring Twenties
U-Boat 29

BEST ACTING

- James Cagney, *Roaring Twenties*
- Bette Davis, *Dark Victory, The Old Maid*
- Geraldine Fitzgerald, *Dark Victory, Wuthering Heights*
- Henry Fonda, *Young Mr. Lincoln*
- Jean Gabin, *Port of Shadows*
- Greta Garbo, *Ninotchka*
- Francis Lederer, *Confessions of a Nazi Spy*
- Paul Lukas, *Confessions of a Nazi Spy*
- Thomas Mitchell, *Stagecoach*
- Laurence Olivier, *Wuthering Heights*
- Flora Robson, *We Are Not Alone*
- Michel Simon, *Port of Shadows, The End of a Day*

BEST FOREIGN FILM

- *Port of Shadows* (France)
Alexander Nevsky (U.S.S.R.)
The End of a Day (France)
Harvest (France)
Robert Koch (Germany)

NEW YORK FILM CRITICS

Winners were announced on December 27, 1939. Awards were presented on January 7, 1940, at the Rainbow Room in New York. The ceremony was broadcast live by NBC radio.

BEST PICTURE
- *Wuthering Heights*

BEST DIRECTOR
- John Ford, *Stagecoach*

BEST ACTOR
- James Stewart, *Mr. Smith Goes to Washington*

BEST ACTRESS
- Vivien Leigh, *Gone With the Wind*

BEST FOREIGN FILM
- *Harvest* (France)

ACADEMY AWARDS

Nominations were announced on February 11, 1940. Awards were presented on February 29 at the Cocoanut Grove of the Ambassador Hotel in Los Angeles.

BEST PICTURE
- *Gone With the Wind*
Dark Victory
Goodbye, Mr. Chips
Love Affair
Mr. Smith Goes to Washington
Ninotchka
Of Mice and Men
Stagecoach
The Wizard of Oz
Wuthering Heights

BEST DIRECTOR
- Victor Fleming, *Gone With the Wind*
Frank Capra, *Mr. Smith Goes to Washington*
John Ford, *Stagecoach*
Sam Wood, *Goodbye, Mr. Chips*
William Wyler, *Wuthering Heights*

Gone With the Wind scored a record-setting eight Oscars, including one for Vivien Leigh (left), but not for Clark Gable or Olivia de Havilland.

BEST ACTOR
- Robert Donat, *Goodbye, Mr. Chips*

Clark Gable, *Gone With the Wind*

Laurence Olivier, *Wuthering Heights*

Mickey Rooney, *Babes in Arms*

James Stewart, *Mr. Smith Goes to Washington*

BEST ACTRESS
- Vivien Leigh, *Gone With the Wind*

Bette Davis, *Dark Victory*

Irene Dunne, *Love Affair*

Greta Garbo, *Ninotchka*

Greer Garson, *Goodbye, Mr. Chips*

BEST SUPPORTING ACTOR
- Thomas Mitchell, *Stagecoach*

Brian Aherne, *Juarez*

Harry Carey, *Mr. Smith Goes to Washington*

Brian Donlevy, *Beau Geste*

Claude Rains, *Mr. Smith Goes to Washington*

BEST SUPPORTING ACTRESS
- Hattie McDaniel, *Gone With the Wind*

Olivia de Havilland, *Gone With the Wind*

Geraldine Fitzgerald, *Wuthering Heights*

Edna May Oliver, *Drums along the Mohawk*

Maria Ouspenskaya, *Love Affair*

BEST WRITING (ORIGINAL STORY)
- Lewis R. Foster, *Mr. Smith Goes to Washington*

Mildred Cram, Leo McCarey, *Love Affair*

Felix Jackson, *Bachelor Mother*

Melchior Lengyel, *Ninotchka*

Lamar Trotti, *Young Mr. Lincoln*

BEST WRITING (SCREENPLAY)
- Sidney Howard, *Gone With the Wind*

Charles Brackett, Walter Reisch, Billy Wilder, *Ninotchka*

Sidney Buchman, *Mr. Smith Goes to Washington*

Ben Hecht, Charles MacArthur, *Wuthering Heights*

Eric Maschwitz, R. C. Sherriff, Claudine West, *Goodbye, Mr. Chips*

BEST SONG
- "Over the Rainbow," *The Wizard of Oz*, Harold Arlen, E. Y. Harburg

"Faithful Forever," *Gulliver's Travels*, Ralph Rainger, Leo Robin

"I Poured My Heart into a Song," *Second Fiddle*, Irving Berlin

"Wishing," *Love Affair*, Buddy De Sylva

Winners

BEST ART DIRECTION
- Lyle Wheeler, *Gone With the Wind*

BEST CINEMATOGRAPHY
(BLACK AND WHITE)
- Gregg Toland, *Wuthering Heights*

(COLOR)
- Ernest Haller, Ray Rennahan, *Gone With the Wind*

BEST FILM EDITING
- Hal C. Kern, James E. Newcom, *Gone With the Wind*

BEST MUSIC
(ORIGINAL SCORE)
- Herbert Stothart, *The Wizard of Oz*

(SCORING)
- Richard Hageman, Frank Harling, John Leipold, Leo Shuken, *Stagecoach*

BEST SHORT SUBJECT
(CARTOON)
- *The Ugly Duckling*

(ONE REEL)
- *Busy Little Bears*

(TWO REEL)
- *Sons of Liberty*

BEST SOUND RECORDING
- Bernard B. Brown, *When Tomorrow Comes*

BEST SPECIAL EFFECTS
- E. H. Hansen, Fred Sersen, *The Rains Came*

SCIENTIFIC OR TECHNICAL AWARDS
Class III (Certificate)
- George Anderson
- John Arnold
- Thomas T. Moulton, Fred Albin, Goldwyn Studio Sound Department
- Farciot Edouart, Joseph E. Robbins, William Rudoph, Paramount Pictures

- Emery Huse, Ralph B. Atkinson
- Harold Nye
- A. J. Tondreau
- F. R. Abbott, Haller Belt, Alan Cook, Bausch & Lomb
- Mitchell Camera
- Mole-Richardson
- Charles Handley, David Joy, National Carbon
- Winton Hoch, Technicolor Motion Pictures
- Don Musgrave, Selznick International Pictures

IRVING G. THALBERG MEMORIAL AWARD
- David O. Selznick

SPECIAL AWARDS
- Douglas Fairbanks
- Motion Picture Relief Fund
- Judy Garland
- William Cameron Menzies
- Technicolor Co.

· 1940 ·

Chaplin's Wrath

Three days before Christmas, the National Board of Review gave producer Darryl Zanuck a fine present—its Best Picture bow to *The Grapes of Wrath*—and the defunct U.S. Film Service earned the board's first prize for Best Documentary (*The Fight for Life*).

A week later the New York Film Critics toasted *Grapes*, too, but when they tried to give their actor's scroll to comedian Charlie Chaplin for his parody of Hitler in *The Great Dictator*, it was no laughing matter: he refused.

Chaplin was furious that many of the crix initially panned his performance in their newspapers, but then, after being deadlocked for 22 ballots while trying to pick a Best Actor, chose him because crix chief Bosley Crowther of *The New York Times* promised "he'll be a swell free attraction for us" at the Rainbow Room kudos ceremony, it was revealed by *The New York Mirror*. After Chaplin read the report, he fired off a telegram to Crowther, saying that he had respect for "most" members of the group, but he denounced their "process of electioneering, (because) such a procedure is, in my humble opinion, far afield from sound critical appraisal." His wording mirrored the *Mirror* article, which described the "electioneering and swapping of votes that incongruously took place in the dignified setting of the executive directors' room of the conservative *New York Times*."

It had been a contentious voting session. The crix took 20 rounds to name a Best Director and finally gave the laurel to their old favorite John Ford (*The Grapes of Wrath, The Long Voyage Home*) for a third time in six years. Ford's films were the two leading contenders for Best Picture, with *Grapes* squashing *Voyage* after seven votes.

The *Mirror* reported that Katharine Hepburn prevailed as Best Actress in *The*

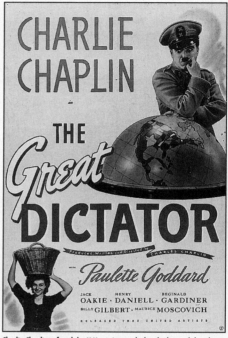

Charlie Chaplin refused the N.Y. crix's award when he learned that they chose him because he could be "a swell free attraction" at their party.

Philadelphia Story only after the *World-Telegram* critic bullied his peers into voting for her. The *Times*, however, claimed that "Hepburn came through almost undisputed after an absence of two years from the screen." Hepburn had been dismissed as "box office poison" by the prexy of the Independent Theater Owners of America, but now the crix heralded her dramatic career rebound. Hepburn told them she was "hysterically happy" to win when she accepted the honor via a two-way NBC radio hookup from Dallas, where she was performing *The Philadelphia Story* on stage. When her voice was piped into the crix's gala, she performed a scene from the film for the kudos crowd.

The crowd included showbiz's fanciest: Joan Crawford, Rosalind Russell, Jean Renoir and Gale Sondergaard among them. It also *almost* included the elusive Greta Garbo, "who had been invited to the party and came as far as the lobby of the RCA building, but fled when she saw the mob of autograph seekers," reported the *Times*. "She went back to the Ritz Towers where the autograph hounds have posted a 24-hour sentry service to guard against the escape of one Clara Brown, registered," added the *World-Telegram*.

Darryl Zanuck was the only award recipient present at the gala. A scene from his *Grapes of Wrath* was performed on the radio by Henry Fonda, who managed the task blindfolded from Hollywood, where he was recovering from eye surgery.

When the party was over, the critics noticed that somebody had stolen Katharine Hepburn's scroll for Best Actress. "Oddly enough, no one made a pass for the scroll which Charlie Chaplin refused to accept," the *Times* noticed.

All of the crix's picks made it into the Oscar derby, which was the most suspenseful ever. Sealed envelopes were used for the first time to conceal the names of winners, which were leaked early last year by *The Los Angeles Times*. At the Biltmore Hotel on Oscar night, "There was considerable betting at each table on the winners," *Variety* reported.

Ten films jockeyed for Best Picture, most of them by three directors: two by John Ford (*The Grapes of Wrath, The Long Voyage Home*), a duo by recent British import Alfred Hitchcock (*Rebecca, Foreign Correspondent*), a pair by Sam Wood (*Our Town, Kitty Foyle*), plus Charlie Chaplin's *The Great Dictator*, George Cukor's *The Philadelphia Story*, William Wyler's *The Letter* and Anatole Litvak's *All This, and Heaven Too*. Throughout 1940, *The Grapes of Wrath* was considered the early front-runner, but by Oscar voting time it was a year old and vulnerable.

"This is what old-fashioned bookies would call an open race," *Variety* reported. "There is no Man o' War on the track. . . . Odds of 8 to 5 are being offered that the winner of this year's Best Production Award will be decided between *Rebecca, Grapes of Wrath* and *Our Town*."

The acting races were also cliffhangers. Bette Davis had a stellar year with *All This, and Heaven Too* and *The Letter*, reaping a bid for the latter role, which previously earned Jeanne Eagels an Oscar nomination for the 1928 screen version. The year's two breakout new stars were up: Joan Fontaine (*Rebecca*) and Martha Scott (*Our Town*). Hepburn's career comeback and her embrace by the New York Film Critics made her a sexy choice. Also formidable was Hepburn's ex-colleague and occasional rival at RKO, Ginger Rogers, who had recently hung up her dance shoes to show off her strengths as a serious actress. *Variety* cheered Rogers for giving a "strong dramatic portrayal" in *Kitty Foyle*, and RKO flagged such notices while campaigning aggressively for her in tradepaper ads.

When Chaplin was nominated for Best Actor, he did not refuse the bid even though he was thereby "acknowledging the fact that actors are competing with each other," which he'd railed against at the crix's kudos. Most oddsmakers considered the race between former Hollywood roommates Henry Fonda and Jimmy Stewart, who both had strong career years. Fonda showed off his chops as a serious thesp in *The Grapes of Wrath* and his hambone gifts in Preston Sturges's *The Lady Eve*, which was doing boffo b.o. just when Oscar ballots were being inked. Stewart really had just a supporting role in *The Philadelphia Story*, but he had three factors in his Oscar favor: rival *Grapes* was year-old vintage, *Philadelphia* was fresh and many Hollywood watchers thought Stewart should've won last year for *Mr. Smith Goes to Washington*.

When Oscar night came, the high drama was underscored by a dramatic opening

> # Garbo *almost* attended the Gotham crix gala, but lost her nerve and fled.

number: a radio address from President Franklin Roosevelt, who thanked Hollywood leaders for championing "the American way of life." When that seriousness was over and the fun part of the awards show began, emcee Bob Hope spied the table full of Oscars about to be bestowed and asked, "What's the matter? Did Selznick bring them back?"

Last year Selznick walked off with an unprecedented eight awards for *Gone With the Wind*. This year he actually came back for more, mounting a vigorous campaign for *Rebecca*, which resulted in the year's most noms (11). *Variety* cheered *Rebecca* for capturing "all the sombreness and dramatic tragedy of the book" by Daphne du Maurier. When Selznick prevailed, he became the first producer to win consecutive golden boys for Best Picture. The only other award the film won, however, was for cinematography.

Variety's review hailed Alfred Hitchcock for the "inspired direction" of his debut American film, but he lost the race for Best Director to previous champ John Ford, who was so cavalier about the current showdown that he snubbed the Oscar gala to go fishing with Henry Fonda.

Jimmy Stewart was the only Best Actor nominee present. When he won, he "presented a bashful picture as he came to the fore" of the crowded room, *Variety* noted, where he expressed his "satisfaction, pride and most of all gratefulness," adding, "With all my heart I thank you." After the ceremony, Stewart gave the Oscar to his father, who put it on display at his hardware store in Indiana, Pennsylvania.

When Ginger Rogers pulled off a shocking upset for Best Actress, she brought her mother with her to the podium and "cried,

Laurence Olivier and Joan Fontaine starred in Best Picture *Rebecca*, which failed to reap an Oscar for director Alfred Hitchcock.

in sheer delight and emotion, as she took the prized Oscar," observed *Variety*. She then thanked her mother for being "the one who has stood by me faithfully."

Best Supporting Actor champ was old Oscar favorite Walter Brennan (*The Westerner*). He owed his third career trophy to the large voting bloc of movie extras, who considered him one of their own.

Currently unemployed star Jane Darwell (*The Grapes of Wrath*) won Best Supporting Actress and risked the wrath of studio bosses by griping in her acceptance speech: "Awards are nice, but I'd much rather have a job." The next day *Variety* reported—in a prominent page-one box—that Darwell "has worked only five weeks since appearing in this picture and has been unemployed for the past seven months." Soon afterward, Twentieth Century-Fox put her back in front of the cameras.

▪ 1940 ▪

NATIONAL BOARD OF REVIEW

The board declared a best film of the year, then listed its remaining favorites according to highest scores. Winners of the Best Acting awards were listed alphabetically. The vote results were announced on December 22, 1940.

BEST PICTURE
- *The Grapes of Wrath*
The Great Dictator
Of Mice and Men

Our Town
Fantasia
The Long Voyage Home
Foreign Correspondent
The Biscuit Eater
Gone With the Wind
Rebecca

BEST ACTING
- Jane Bryan, *We Are Not Alone*
- Charles Chaplin, *The Great Dictator*
- Jane Darwell, *The Grapes of Wrath*
- Betty Field, *Of Mice and Men*
- Henry Fonda, *The Grapes of Wrath, The Return of Frank James*
- Joan Fontaine, *Rebecca*
- Greer Garson, *Pride and Prejudice*
- William Holden, *Our Town*
- Vivien Leigh, *Gone With the Wind, Waterloo Bridge*
- Thomas Mitchell, *The Long Voyage Home*
- Raimu, *The Baker's Wife*
- Ralph Richardson, *The Fugitive*
- Flora Robson, *We Are Not Alone*
- Ginger Rogers, *The Primrose Path*
- George Sanders, *Rebecca*
- Martha Scott, *Our Town*
- James Stewart, *The Shop around the Corner*
- Conrad Veidt, *Escape*

BEST FOREIGN FILM
- *The Baker's Wife* (France)

BEST DOCUMENTARY
- *The Fight for Life*

NEW YORK FILM CRITICS

Winners were announced on December 30, 1940. Awards were presented on January 5, 1941, at the Rainbow Room in New York. NBC radio broadcast 15 minutes of the ceremony live nationwide.

BEST PICTURE
- *The Grapes of Wrath*

BEST DIRECTOR
- John Ford, *The Grapes of Wrath, The Long Voyage Home*

BEST ACTOR
- Charles Chaplin, *The Great Dictator*

BEST ACTRESS
- Katharine Hepburn, *The Philadelphia Story*

BEST FOREIGN FILM
- *The Baker's Wife* (France)

SPECIAL AWARD
- *Fantasia*

ACADEMY AWARDS

Nominations were announced on February 10, 1941. Awards were presented on February 27 at the Biltmore Hotel in Los Angeles.

BEST PICTURE
- *Rebecca*
All This, and Heaven Too
Foreign Correspondent
The Grapes of Wrath
The Great Dictator
Kitty Foyle
The Letter
The Long Voyage Home
The Philadelphia Story
Our Town

BEST DIRECTOR
- John Ford, *The Grapes of Wrath*
George Cukor, *The Philadelphia Story*
Alfred Hitchcock, *Rebecca*
Sam Wood, *Kitty Foyle*
William Wyler, *The Letter*

BEST ACTOR
- James Stewart, *The Philadelphia Story*
Charles Chaplin, *The Great Dictator*
Henry Fonda, *The Grapes of Wrath*
Raymond Massey, *Abe Lincoln in Illinois*
Laurence Olivier, *Rebecca*

BEST ACTRESS
- Ginger Rogers, *Kitty Foyle*
Bette Davis, *The Letter*
Joan Fontaine, *Rebecca*
Katharine Hepburn, *The Philadelphia Story*
Martha Scott, *Our Town*

BEST SUPPORTING ACTOR

- Walter Brennan, *The Westerner*

Albert Basserman, *Foreign Correspondent*

William Gargan, *They Knew What They Wanted*

Jack Oakie, *The Great Dictator*

James Stephenson, *The Letter*

BEST SUPPORTING ACTRESS

- Jane Darwell, *The Grapes of Wrath*

Judith Anderson, *Rebecca*

Ruth Hussey, *The Philadelphia Story*

Barbara O'Neil, *All This, and Heaven Too*

Marjorie Rambeau, *The Primrose Path*

BEST WRITING (ORIGINAL STORY)

- Benjamin Glazer, John S. Toldy, *Arise, My Love*

Hugo Butler, Dore Schary, *Edison, The Man*

Stuart N. Lake, *The Westerner*

Leo McCarey, Bella Spewack, Samuel Spewack, *My Favorite Wife*

Walter Reisch, *Comrade X*

BEST WRITING (SCREENPLAY)

- Donald Ogden Stewart, *The Philadelphia Story*

Joan Harrison, Robert E. Sherwood, *Rebecca*

Nunnally Johnson, *The Grapes of Wrath*

Dudley Nichols, *The Long Voyage Home*

Dalton Trumbo, *Kitty Foyle*

BEST SONG

- "When You Wish Upon a Star," *Pinocchio*, Leigh Harline, Ned Washington

"Down Argentine Way," *Down Argentine Way*, Mack Gordon, Harry Warren

"I'd Know You Anywhere," *You'll Find Out*, Jimmy McHugh, Johnny Mercer

"It's a Blue World," *Music in My Heart*, Chet Forrest, Bob Wright

"Only Forever," *Rhythm on the River*, John Burke, James Monaco

"Our Love Affair," *Strike Up the Band*, Roger Edens, Arthur Freed

"Love of My Life," *Second Chorus*, Johnny Mercer, Artie Shaw

"Waltzing in the Clouds," *Spring Parade*, Gus Kahn, Robert Stolz

---

A Real Picture

Jane Darwell, who received the award last night for the best performance for supporting actress for her work in 'The Grapes of Wrath,' has worked only five weeks since appearing in this picture and has been unemployed for the past seven months.

The day after the Oscars, *Variety* reported on winner Jane Darwell's chronic unemployment. Twentieth Century-Fox quickly recast her.

"Who Am I?," *Hit Parade of 1941*, Walter Bullock, Jule Styne

Winners

BEST ART DIRECTION
(BLACK AND WHITE)
- Cedric Gibbons, Paul Groesse, *Pride and Prejudice*

(COLOR)
- Vincent Korda, *The Thief of Bagdad*

BEST CINEMATOGRAPHY
(BLACK AND WHITE)
- George Barnes, *Rebecca*

(COLOR)
- Georges Perinal, *The Thief of Bagdad*

BEST FILM EDITING
- Anne Bauchens, *North West Mounted Police*

BEST MUSIC
(ORIGINAL SCORE)
- Leigh Harline, Paul J. Smith, Ned Washington, *Pinocchio*

(SCORE)
- Alfred Newman, *Tin Pan Alley*

BEST SHORT SUBJECT
(CARTOON)
- *The Milky Way*

(ONE REEL)
- *Quicker 'n a Wink*

(TWO REEL)

- *Teddy, the Rough Rider*

BEST SOUND RECORDING

- Douglas Shearer, *Strike up the Band*

SCIENTIFIC OR TECHNICAL AWARDS

Class I (Statuette)

- Daniel Clark, Grover Laube, Charles Miller, Robert W. Stevens, Twentieth Century-Fox Film Corp.

Class III (Certificate)

- Anton Grot, Warner Bros. Studio Art Department

SPECIAL AWARDS

- Bob Hope
- Nathan Levinson

· 1941 ·

Kane *Peaks,* Then Valley

In 1996, the American Film Institute asked 1,500 film pros and critics to name the best picture ever made.

The overwhelming answer: *Citizen Kane.*

Considering the view of future hindsight, it's curious to note how *Citizen Kane* fared for the kudos declaring the Best Picture of its release year. The National Board of Review was the first to hail it as tops of 1941, a courageous choice considering the board received more than $1,500 a year in funding from MGM, which was in financial cahoots with the media mogul the film skewered—William Randolph Hearst. In fact, MGM topper Louis B. Mayer offered RKO $800,000 to kill the picture and Hearst successfully bullied Warner's, Paramount's and Loew's theaters into refusing to unspool it.

A few newspaper columnists applauded the board's result, but expressed surprise that *Sergeant York* wasn't on the Committee on Exceptional Photoplay's list of 10 best flicks. Not only was the Gary Cooper starrer about the Tennessee backwoodsman–turned–World War I hero the year's top-grossing film, but it should've been a patriotic favorite since it entered the annual kudos battle just weeks after the United States entered World War II. The board's choice for Best Foreign Film was *Pepe le Moko*, an art house hit from France about a criminal who hides from police in the Casbah region of Algiers.

The New York Film Critics eliminated their category for foreign films due to the limited number of offshore movies being shown in the United States during the war years. For their overall Best Picture prize, they proved gutsy by embracing *Citizen Kane* even though one of their members, Rose Pelswick, worked at Hearst's *Journal-American* (no record survives of how she voted). Afterward, Howard Barnes of the *Herald-Tribune* crowed a bit: "The mere

Despite being heckled in public, the N.Y. crix joined the National Board of Review in naming *Citizen Kane* Best Picture.

fact that a dozen people have heckled me about our choice . . . makes me believe that we are exercising an important function."

Admittedly, support for the pic among the crix had to build during their voting, which occurred "with a dispatch which baffled belief," observed *The New York Times. Sergeant York* led on the first ballot, then tied *Citizen Kane* on the second. Suddenly and mysteriously, *Sergeant York*'s troops then retreated while *How Green Was My Valley* rose to take on *Citizen Kane*, which finally won on the sixth tally. The clash between them would've continued if winners were still chosen the way they used to be. The *Times* added: "Perhaps a new voting procedure, whereby the choice in each instance went to the candidate polling a plurality on the sixth ballot (if it hadn't won a two-thirds vote before), accounted in a large measure for the speed with which the preferences were named."

The new procedure also resolved a growing stalemate between director candidates. John Ford (*How Green Was My Valley*) and the ferocious young turk behind *Citizen Kane*, Orson Welles. A majority vote of 10 to 8 upon the sixth ballot gave the kudos to Ford for the third consecutive year and a fourth time in the crix group's seven-year history.

The acting races were decided easily using the old voting system since the crix didn't reach a sixth ballot. Gary Cooper prevailed on the first round. "Joan Fontaine (*Suspicion*) was selected by a two-thirds majority on the fifth," the *Times* observed. "But we also admired tremendously the work of Olivia de Havilland in *Hold Back the Dawn* and were pleased that Miss de Havilland should have vied as heatedly with her sister as she did for the award."

In past years the awards (a bronze plaque for best film, scrolls for the others) were bestowed at a cocktail party held either at the Rainbow Room or the Ritz-Carlton Hotel. This year the crix decided they wanted a full banquet like the Oscars had, so the gala was moved to Leone's restaurant on West 48th Street, smack in the Broadway theater district. John Ford came up from Washington, D.C., for the occasion, but other winners had to be piped in during NBC's 15-minute radio broadcast. Orson Welles and Joan Fontaine performed scenes from their films from Hollywood. *Sergeant York*'s Gary Cooper was a shameless deserter. His scroll was accepted by a Warner Bros. exec.

Just when the crix decided to give themselves a full-course gala, the Oscars feared to do the same, since it might look self-indulgent at a time when self-sacrifice was called for as America went to war. Motion picture academy topper Bette Davis suggested that the banquet be scrapped and the ceremony be moved to a theater where seats

> "Of course we fight," Olivia de Havilland said about her sister Joan Fontaine.

could be set aside for the public, but when she was voted down, she stepped down as prexy and, still furious weeks later, snubbed the Oscar show despite her nomination for *The Little Foxes*.

But PR-conscious Oscar leaders did snuff some of the fun and dim the glitter by banning dancing at the dinner and encouraging stars to dress down. *Variety* reported, "Result was the biggest attendance in its history, mostly in workaday clothes, with a sprinkling of soldiers and sailors and part-time military-naval-film execs in their resplendent uniforms." *Variety* noticed that even the cost of admission was cut back: "Tops at $10, instead of the customary $25."

The race for the gold statuettes was left to provide the drama—and it did.

"Major interest in this year's event centers around Orson Welles and his *Citizen Kane*," *Variety* said. "If he gets the play from extras on best production, and as Best Actor, he may make a clean sweep of events. On the other hand, he will have to get sizeable block of these votes to overcome popularity of his competitors and vote trading that is already under way. There is considerable jealousy over acclaim his picture has received throughout the country, which makes it difficult for advance prediction as to the final outcome of main events."

Variety braved predictions nonetheless and claimed that Welles would lose Best Picture and Best Actor, but would probably take the prize for Best Original Screenplay. The paper also believed that *Citizen Kane* "should have a walkaway" for best black-and-white cinematography, adding, "Race for the best achievement in directing is strictly between Welles and John Ford for *How Green Was My Valley*."

Welles didn't attend the Oscar derby, claiming that he was tied up filming *The Magnificent Ambersons*. In reality, he was at home in Hollywood on awards night. His absence turned out not to matter much.

Although he did earn the scribe's prize (triggering expected boos from the roomful of studio execs—but also lots of cheers), *Valley* peaked early during the evening, claiming the awards for interior decoration and then the big prize for Best Director, giving John Ford his third victory in the category. *Valley* also pulled off an upset for cinematography and dealt a blow to *Here Comes Mr. Jordan*, whose James Gleason, *Variety* had claimed, looked "like a cinch for best performance by a supporting actor." Accepting the statuette, veteran thesp Donald Crisp encouraged film producers and Oscar voters to remember other "old timers" in the future.

Gossip watchers spied the actress showdown most closely, since columnists had sized it up as a catfight between sisters Olivia de Havilland and Joan Fontaine, who had squared off at the New York film crix vote.

"Of course we fight. What sisters don't battle?" Olivia de Havilland admitted to Louella Parsons, who flagged the quote in all of her Hearst newspaper columns. By the time the siblings arrived at the Oscar ceremony, "1,600 sets of eyes shifted curiously" back and forth between them, noted columnist Harold Heffernan, as "the two girls faced each other, chatting and smiling with forced gaiety and nonchalance." The two were considered far-out front-runners for the prize, with a slight edge given to Joan Fontaine since she had lost last year despite starring in Best Picture champ *Rebecca*. "Only entry that stands chance of upset is Barbara Stanwyck in *Ball of Fire*," *Variety* said.

When Fontaine won, she accepted the statuette tearfully from Ginger Rogers and returned to her table where her good-sport sister greeted her, smiling, and shook her

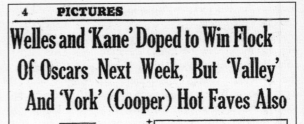

4 PICTURES

Welles and 'Kane' Doped to Win Flock Of Oscars Next Week, But 'Valley' And 'York' (Cooper) Hot Faves Also

Hollywood, Feb. 17.

Unbiased opinion gives Orson Welles an excellent chance to cop first money in at least two events and possibly more Academy awards at the annual dinner a week from Thursday (Feb 26). Welles' fate, however, is pretty much in the hands of 6,000 extras who hold the balance of power. If he gets a substantial block of extra votes, he may make a clean sweep of the field.

His 'Citizen Kane' holds No. 2 post in nominations for the most outstanding production, but in this event he's believed to stand less of a chance than in others where it qualified. It's generally believed to be a race between 20th-Fox's 'How Green Was My Valley' and Warners' 'Sergeant York,' with smart money going on 'Valley' to finish first.

Welles is also up for the best performance by an actor, but will have to overcome the popularity of Gary Cooper and his performance in 'Sergeant York,' or Robert Montgomery's work in 'Here Comes Mr. Jordan.' It

Alien Registration

Washington, Feb. 14.

Editor, 'Variety':

As you undoubtedly know, the Department of Justice is requiring all aliens of German, Japanese or Italian nationality to file applications for Certificates of Identification at their nearest postoffices.

The identification program is already concluded in eight western states and will be completed elsewhere in the United States on Feb. 28.

Through the medium of your publication you can do a great deal to help us acquaint your readers with the requirements. Although most of your readers are citizens, a number of them may have alien friends or relatives who are subject to the requirements of the identification program.

Earl G. Harrison,
(Special Asst. to Attorney Gen'l)
(Department of Justice)

Contrary to popular belief today, *Citizen Kane* was considered a serious Oscar contender in 1941. It won only one golden boy, though: Best Screenplay.

hand. Fontaine thus became the only thesp ever to win an Oscar for a Hitchcock film.

There was less suspense in the actors' derby. "It looks like Cooper, with (Robert) Montgomery (*Here Comes Mr. Jordan*) standing an outside chance," *Variety* had forecasted. When Gary Cooper prevailed for *Sergeant York*, he credited the real-life hero he portrayed, saying, "It was Sergeant Alvin York who won this award."

York's Margaret Wycherly and *Valley*'s Sara Allgood both lost the race for Best Supporting Actress to veteran trouper Mary Astor, just as *Variety* had foreseen when it reported earlier: "It looks like Mary Astor (although) Sara Allgood may nose out a win." In its review of *The Great Lie*, *Variety* had said Astor "scores notably as the case-hardened concert artist whose ambitions transcend motherly and wifely attributes of womanhood." Astor thanked her costar Bette Davis.

Many Oscar oddsmakers believed

Sergeant York, having the most nominations (11) and benefiting from wartime patriotism, would win Best Picture. *How Green Was My Valley*, with 10 bids, had late-breaking momentum, however, since producer Darryl Zanuck mounted a shrewd campaign that included opening the film on the last day of Oscar eligibility so it'd be fresh in voters' minds. *Valley* also had *Variety* on its side: "It's generally believed to be a race between 20th-Fox's *How Green Was My Valley* and Warners' *Sergeant York*, with smart money going on *Valley* to finish first."

At the end of Oscar night, veteran director Cecil B. DeMille announced the winner: *How Green Was My Valley*.

A few days later, *Variety* sized up the derby's overall results: "The biggest enigma of the voting and Oscaring was the near washout of Orson Welles. That most of the 6,000 extras who voted scuttled his chances is foregone. The mob prefers a regular guy to a genius.... Across the length and breadth of Hollywood there are none to quarrel with the prevailing opinion that the extras took care of him."

▪ 1941 ▪

NATIONAL BOARD OF REVIEW

The board declared a best film of the year, then listed its remaining favorites according to highest scores. Winners of the Best Acting awards were listed alphabetically. The vote results were announced on December 20, 1941.

BEST PICTURE

▪ *Citizen Kane*
How Green Was My Valley
The Little Foxes
The Stars Look Down
Dumbo
High Sierra
Here Comes Mr. Jordan
Tom, Dick and Harry
The Road to Zanzibar
The Lady Eve

BEST ACTING

▪ Sara Algood, *How Green Was My Valley*
▪ Mary Astor, *The Great Lie, The Maltese Falcon*
▪ Ingrid Bergman, *Rage in Heaven*
▪ Humphrey Bogart, *High Sierra, The Maltese Falcon*
▪ Patricia Collinge, *The Little Foxes*
▪ Gary Cooper, *Sergeant York*
▪ George Coulouris, *Citizen Kane*
▪ Donald Crisp, *How Green Was My Valley*
▪ Bing Crosby, *The Road to Zanzibar, Birth of the Blues*

▪ Bette Davis, *The Little Foxes*
▪ Isabel Elsom, *Ladies in Retirement*
▪ Joan Fontaine, *Suspicion*
▪ Greta Garbo, *The Two-Faced Woman*
▪ James Gleason, *Meet John Doe, Here Comes Mr. Jordan*
▪ Walter Huston, *All That Money Can Buy*
▪ Ida Lupino, *High Sierra, Ladies in Retirement*
▪ Roddy MacDowell, *How Green Was My Valley*
▪ Robert Montgomery, *Rage in Heaven, Here Comes Mr. Jordan*
▪ Ginger Rogers, *Kitty Foyle; Tom, Dick and Harry*
▪ James Stephenson, *The Letter, Shining Victory*
▪ Orson Welles, *Citizen Kane*

Oscar's four honored thesps: Gary Cooper, Joan Fontaine, Mary Astor and Donald Crisp. Crisp's victory was the only upset.

BEST FOREIGN FILM
- *Pepe le Moko* (France)

BEST DOCUMENTARY
- *Target for Tonight*

NEW YORK FILM CRITICS

Winners were announced on December 31, 1941. Awards were presented on January 10, 1942, at Leone's restaurant in New York. NBC radio broadcast 15 minutes of the ceremony live nationwide.

BEST PICTURE
- *Citizen Kane*

BEST DIRECTOR
- John Ford, *How Green Was My Valley*

BEST ACTOR
- Gary Cooper, *Sergeant York*

BEST ACTRESS
- Joan Fontaine, *Suspicion*

ACADEMY AWARDS

Nominations were announced on February 3, 1942. Awards were presented on February 26 at the Biltmore Hotel in Los Angeles.

BEST PICTURE
- *How Green Was My Valley*
Blossoms in the Dust
Citizen Kane
Here Comes Mr. Jordan
Hold Back the Dawn
The Little Foxes
The Maltese Falcon
One Foot in Heaven
Sergeant York
Suspicion

BEST DIRECTOR
- John Ford, *How Green Was My Valley*
Alexander Hall, *Here Comes Mr. Jordan*
Howard Hawks, *Sergeant York*
Orson Welles, *Citizen Kane*
William Wyler, *The Little Foxes*

BEST ACTOR
- Gary Cooper, *Sergeant York*
Cary Grant, *Penny Serenade*
Walter Huston, *All That Money Can Buy*
Robert Montgomery, *Here Comes Mr. Jordan*
Orson Welles, *Citizen Kane*

BEST ACTRESS
- Joan Fontaine, *Suspicion*
Bette Davis, *The Little Foxes*
Olivia de Havilland, *Hold Back the Dawn*
Greer Garson, *Blossoms in the Dust*
Barbara Stanwyck, *Ball of Fire*

BEST SUPPORTING ACTOR
- Donald Crisp, *How Green Was My Valley*
Walter Brennan, *Sergeant York*
Charles Coburn, *The Devil and Miss Jones*
James Gleason, *Here Comes Mr. Jordan*
Sydney Greenstreet, *The Maltese Falcon*

BEST SUPPORTING ACTRESS
- Mary Astor, *The Great Lie*
Sara Allgood, *How Green Was My Valley*
Patricia Collinge, *The Little Foxes*
Teresa Wright, *The Little Foxes*
Margaret Wycherly, *Sergeant York*

BEST WRITING (ORIGINAL STORY)
- Harry Segall, *Here Comes Mr. Jordan*
Richard Connell, Robert Presnell, *Meet John Doe*
Monckton Hoffe, *The Lady Eve*
Thomas Monroe, Billy Wilder, *Ball of Fire*
Gordon Wellesley, *Night Train*

BEST WRITING (ORIGINAL SCREENPLAY)
- Herman J. Mankiewicz, Orson Welles, *Citizen Kane*
Harry Chandlee, Abem Finkel, John Huston, Howard Koch, *Sergeant York*
Paul Jarrico, *Tom, Dick and Harry*
Norman Krasna, *The Devil and Miss Jones*
Karl Tunberg, Darrell Ware, *Tall, Dark and Handsome*

BEST WRITING (SCREENPLAY)
- Sidney Buchman, Seton I. Miller, *Here Comes Mr. Jordan*

Charles Brackett, Billy Wilder, *Hold Back the Dawn*
Philip Dunne, *How Green Was My Valley*
Lillian Hellman, *The Little Foxes*
John Huston, *The Maltese Falcon*

BEST MUSIC (SONG)
- "The Last Time I Saw Paris," *Lady Be Good*, Oscar Hammerstein II, Jerome Kern
- "Baby Mine," *Dumbo*, Frank Churchill, Ned Washington
- "Be Honest with Me," *Ridin' on a Rainbow*, Gene Autry, Fred Rose
- "Blues in the Night," *Blues in the Night*, Harold Arlen, Johnny Mercer
- "Boogie Woogie Bugle Boy of Company B," *Buck Privates*, Hugh Prince, Don Raye
- "Chattanooga Choo Choo," *Sun Valley Serenade*, Mack Gordon, Harry Warren
- "Dolores," *Las Vegas Nights*, Lou Alter, Frank Loesser
- "Out of the Silence," *All-American Co-Ed*, Lloyd B. Norlind
- "Since I Kissed My Baby Goodbye," *You'll Never Get Rich*, Cole Porter

Winners

BEST ART DIRECTION
(BLACK AND WHITE)
- Richard Day, Nathan Juran, *How Green Was My Valley*

(COLOR)
- Cedric Gibbons, Urie McCleary, *Blossoms in the Dust*

BEST CINEMATOGRAPHY
(BLACK AND WHITE)
- Arthur Miller, *How Green Was My Valley*

(COLOR)
- Ernest Palmer, Ray Rennahan, *Blood and Sand*

BEST FILM EDITING
- William Holmes, *Sergeant York*

BEST DOCUMENTARY (SHORT SUBJECT)
- *Churchill's Island*, National Film Board of Canada

BEST INTERIOR DECORATION
(BLACK AND WHITE)
- Thomas Little, *How Green Was My Valley*

(COLOR)
- Edwin B. Willis, *Blossoms in the Dust*

BEST MUSIC
(SCORING OF A MUSICAL PICTURE)
- Frank Churchill, Oliver Wallace, *Dumbo*

(SCORING OF A DRAMATIC PICTURE)
- Bernard Herrmann, *All That Money Can Buy*

BEST SHORT SUBJECT
(CARTOON)
- *Lend a Paw*

(ONE REEL)
- *Of Pups and Puzzles*

(TWO REEL)
- *Main Street on the March!*

BEST SOUND RECORDING
- Jack Whitney, *That Hamilton Woman*

BEST SPECIAL EFFECTS
- Farciot Edouart, Gordon Jennings, Louis Mesenkop, *I Wanted Wings*

SCIENTIFIC OR TECHNICAL AWARDS
Class II (Plaque)
- RCA Manufacturing, Western Electric Research Products Division

Class III (Certificate)
- Ray Wilkinson, Paramount Studio Laboratory; Charles Lootens, Republic Studio Sound Department; Wilbur Silvertooth, Paramount Studio Engineering Department; Paramount Pictures, Twentieth Century-Fox Film Corp.; Douglas Shearer, MGM Studio Sound Department, Loren Ryder, Paramount Studio Sound Department

IRVING G. THALBERG MEMORIAL AWARD
- Walt Disney

SPECIAL AWARDS
- William Garity, John N. A. Hawkins, Walt Disney, RCA Manufacturing Co.
- Rey Scott
- British Ministry of Information
- Leopold Stokowski

· 1942 ·

Salutes for War-Themed Pix

"There are rumors that a truly great motion picture is about to hit New York," reported *The New York Herald Tribune*, referring to the hype surrounding the opening of the debut film by Broadway and London stage darling Noel Coward. Full-page ads in the city's dailies promised "EXCITED WHISPERS . . . that will become a nationwide roar of acclaim!" The celebrated actor, writer, director, songsmith and showbiz gadfly had had his theater works turned into movies in the past—*Cavalcade* had won Best Picture at the Oscars a decade ago—but now Coward held all the celluloid reins for the first time ever. He produced his film about the battles of a British destroyer in the early days of World War II, composed its musical score, co-directed it with David Lean and starred in the lead role as the ship's stiff-upper-lipped captain.

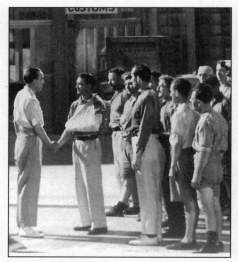

The N.Y. Times called In Which We Serve *"one of the finest films ever made." The Gotham crix and National Board of Review proclaimed it Best Picture, but the Oscars snubbed it due to a sked snafu.*

When the *Herald Tribune* critic Howard Barnes finally saw the film, he called the rumors "triumphantly confirmed" and boldly heralded *In Which We Serve* as "a masterpiece of film making." The *Times* called it "one of the finest films ever made."

The National Board of Review became the first to pin a medal on it as the year's best pic. A few days later came one more endorsement.

"There was no question in my mind about the best film of 1942. My vote was cast aggressively on this matter," the *Herald Tribune*'s Barnes reported when the New York Film Critics met to ink ballots at the Algonquin Hotel. Bosley Crowther echoed this same opinion when describing the crix's conclave in the *Times* same-day edition: "In this writer's mind there was no question. *In Which We Serve* was the year's best film by so wide a margin that competition was to us incomprehensible."

Crowther's prose, widely noted for being

purple, overstated his case as usual. In reality, *In Which We Serve* had such serious competition that it didn't win Best Picture until the sixth ballot, when a two-thirds vote of the 18 crix was no longer needed and it finally prevailed over *Wake Island* by a tally of 11 to 7. The latter pic, a war drama about the U.S. Marines' defense of a remote Pacific outpost, earned John Farrow the helmer's accolade as a consolation prize, however, "and thereby the law of compensation took its invariable due," griped the *Times*, which had been rooting for Coward and Lean.

The crix's patriotism and love of Gotham stage stars showed itself in their choice for Best Actor—a thesp previously known chiefly for gangster roles who now surprised many film aficionados by playing a vaudeville crooner and hoofer born on the Fourth of July. "It was eminently fitting that

James Cagney's performance in *Yankee Doodle Dandy* was selected," said the *Herald Tribune*. Cagney had started out in showbiz as a vaudeville song-and-dance man, and he was personally chosen by Cohan to play the part on celluloid. When the crix endorsed him, too, they did so by a resounding 13-to-2 score on the first ballot, a stark contrast to the heated nine-round vote that preceded their decision to honor him in 1938 for *Angels with Dirty Faces*.

Cagney's role was also among the staggeringly long list of 31 perfs cited as the year's best by the National Board of Review; the crix's single choice for Best Actress was also included among the generous listings.

"I must admit that I was a bit startled by the critics' vote" for female thesp, confessed the *Herald Tribune*'s Barnes. "Agnes Moorehead gave a brilliant and thoughtful portrayal in the somber and murky Orson Welles picture *The Magnificent Ambersons* (but) I definitely preferred Greer Garson's modulated performance in *Mrs. Miniver*." The *Times*'s Crowther agreed: "The failure of Miss Garson to clean up was probably the one big surprise in the awards, for certainly her *Mrs. Miniver* had been the most-talked-of role of the year. We won't even try to explain it." Garson actually led on the first ballot with 7 votes compared to 3 each for Moorehead and Katharine Hepburn (*Woman of the Year*), but she lost on the sixth round by an 11-to-7 score.

Variety described *Mrs. Miniver* as "a story of the joys and sorrows, the humor and pathos of middle-class family life in wartime England," adding, "*Mrs. Miniver* truly brings the war into one's own family." The hit film also brought lots of coin into MGM coffers—$6 million—and made Garson a superstar. It failed to snag even a single vote, however, when the 18 crix chose their Best Picture.

War frenzy so gripped the crix that they

Greer Garson gave the longest acceptance speech in Oscar history.

created a new award—Best War Fact Film, which would never be bestowed again—to give out when they gathered at the Berkshire Hotel on East 52nd Street. The trophy went to the same pic hailed by the National Board of Review as Best Documentary—*Moscow Strikes Back*, which recounted how the Soviets repelled the 1941 Nazi attack on their capital city.

"Conflicting work schedules and wartime travel restrictions prevented the Hollywood award winners from being present at the buffet supper," reported the *Times*, although Jimmy Cagney "reenacted scenes in the film from Hollywood" via NBC's Blue Network radio while his sister Jeanne accepted his scroll in person. "A scheduled broadcast from London with Noel Coward had to be canceled because he was 'on tour of duty somewhere in England,'" added the *Times*.

Coward may have been temporarily out of touch, but he soon got word of shocking news: *In Which We Serve* wasn't eligible for the Oscars. Film academy leaders had recently moved up Oscar's eligibility cutoff date from January 12 to December 31, giving United Artists only three weeks' notice to move up the pic's Los Angeles premiere. When panicked execs couldn't find an open theater, the film got shut out. Anticipating an outcry, the academy declared that Noel Coward would receive a special award "for outstanding production achievement in *In Which We Serve*." He would not show up to accept it.

The year's other top British war pic—*Mrs. Miniver*—became the Oscar frontrunner with 12 nominations, one short of the record held by *Gone With the Wind*. It competed for Best Picture against Greer Garson's other standout film of 1942—*Random Harvest*, in which she fell for Ronald Colman as a "prosperous Briton who loses his memory as a result of shellshock in the First World War," said *Variety*, which declared Garson "more charming and seductive than ever." *Variety* added about the two pics' chances: "Those on the inside were touting Metro to have the inside rail for a bevy of Oscars with its productions *Mrs. Miniver* and *Random Harvest.*"

Harvest reaped seven noms. The other top contenders were patriotic American fare: they focused on U.S. war battles (*Wake Island*), waved the stars and stripes (*Yankee Doodle Dandy*) and cheered the national pastime of baseball (*The Pride of the Yankees*—"a stirring epitaph on Lou Gehrig," said *Variety*). The biggest surprise in the Best Picture lineup was the inclusion of *The Magnificent Ambersons*, Orson Welles's somber adaptation of Booth Tarkington's novel about a spoiled upper-crust family. RKO certainly didn't think the film was so magnificent—the studio had seized control from Welles late in production, chopped an hour out of its two-and-a-half-hour running time and released it on a double bill with *Mexican Spitfire Sees a Ghost* starring Lupe Velez.

Mrs. Miniver was the easy winner, giving academy founder Louis B. Mayer his sixth Best Picture victory in the Oscars' 15 years.

In its review of *Mrs. Miniver, Variety* insisted, "It's impossible to praise too highly William Wyler's direction," adding that he was "clearly the understanding heart" of the film. Oscar voters agreed. Wyler's wife accepted the award for him while the lieutenant colonel was in Germany.

In the Best Actress showdown, Greer Garson faced two-time past champ Bette Davis in *Now, Voyager* ("one of her superlative acting roles," cheered *Variety*), previous victor Katharine Hepburn in *Woman of the Year* (her first comic partnership with Spencer Tracy), rookie contender Rosalind Russell in *My Sister Eileen* and Garson's *Mrs. Miniver* costar Teresa Wright, who was nominated in the lead lineup as Mrs. Lou Gehrig in *The Pride of the Yankees.*

Garson's victory was widely expected, but she admitted at the podium, "I am practically unprepared," then proceeded to ramble for so long that some wags claimed her acceptance speech was longer than her performance in *Mrs. Miniver*. A few witnesses reported that she prattled on for a half hour. Later in life Garson insisted that she talked only for five and a half minutes. "I admit I do have a gift for gab," she confessed in the academy's official history, "and it seems to have gotten me in hot water that time." Her remarks became the notorious epitome of acceptance-speech verbosity and they haunted her for the rest of her career.

Walter Pidgeon, who played Mr. Miniver, faced formidable foes for Best Actor, including Gary Cooper as Gehrig in *The Pride of the Yankees*, Ronald Colman in *Random Harvest* and James Cagney in *Yankee Doodle Dandy*. Cagney was clearly the frontrunner. He was president of the Screen Actors Guild and *Variety* reported that the studios' extras campaigned vigorously on his behalf. When he won, Cagney's victory marked the first time that an Oscar went to a song-and-dance role. Accepting it, he said, "An actor is only as good or as bad as people think he is. I am glad so many people think I was good." Cagney wrapped up by echoing Cohan's famous send-off: "My mother thanks you, my father thanks you, my sister thanks you and I thank you."

The New York Film Critics' choice for Best Actress, Agnes Moorehead, was nominated in the supporting category at the Academy Awards. She had little chance against sudden star Teresa Wright, who had been Oscar nominated last year for *The Little Foxes* and now had two bids, including one for her triumpant turn as Garson's widowed daughter-in-law in *Mrs. Miniver*. When she accepted the latter prize, she burst into tears and had to be led off stage.

The winner of Best Supporting Actor was Van Heflin, the 32-year-old former Broadway star who prevailed for his second film. *Variety* declared that Heflin was "outstanding . . . as the perpetually soused companion of (Robert) Taylor" in *Johnny Eager*, the tale of a gangster who chases Lana Turner and plots to open a dog track.

In real life, Heflin was an Air Force lieutenant, one of many men in uniform present on Oscar night. *Variety* noted that the "annual awards banquet had a decided military flavor." The gala began when "the industry service flag was unfurled by Tyrone Power and Alan Ladd, disclosing a total of 27,677 members of the industry in the service." A letter was read from President Franklin Roosevelt that "commended the film industry for its part in sustaining the war effort and holding up morale of the public," added *Variety*. Jeanette MacDonald then sang the national anthem.

"After the final award, all the winners were called before the mike for brief hello to the American boys on the various fighting fronts," *Variety* concluded. "Their cheering words were shortwaved to all fighting fronts. As the guests filed out of the (Ambassador) hotel, the general consensus of opinion was that the 15th annual awards dinner was the most successful of all predecessors and that the achievement Oscars went to those most deserving them."

▪ 1942 ▪

NATIONAL BOARD OF REVIEW

The board declared a best film of the year, then listed its remaining favorites according to highest scores. No award was bestowed for foreign films. Winners of the Best Acting awards were listed alphabetically. The vote results were announced on December 24, 1942.

BEST PICTURE
▪ *In Which We Serve*
One of Our Aircraft Is Missing
Mrs. Miniver
Journey for Margaret
Wake Island
The Male Animal
The Major and the Minor
Sullivan's Travels
The Moon and Sixpence
The Pied Piper

BEST ACTING
▪ Ernest Anderson, *This Our Life*
▪ Florence Bates, *The Moon and Sixpence*
▪ James Cagney, *Yankee Doodle Dandy*
▪ Jack Carson, *The Male Animal*
▪ Charles Coburn, *H. M. Pulham, Esq.; In This Our Life; Kings Row*
▪ Greer Garson, *Mrs. Miniver, Random Harvest*
▪ Sidney Greenstreet, *Across the Pacific*
▪ William Holden, *The Remarkable Andrew*
▪ Tim Holt, *The Magnificent Ambersons*
▪ Glynis Johns, *The Invaders*
▪ Gene Kelly, *For Me and My Gal*
▪ Ida Lupino, *Moontide*

▪ Diana Lynn, *The Major and the Minor*
▪ Hattie McDaniel, *In This Our Life*
▪ Bernard Miles, *In Which We Serve*
▪ John Mills, *In Which We Serve*
▪ Thomas Mitchell, *Moontide*
▪ Agnes Moorehead, *The Magnificent Ambersons*
▪ Margaret O'Brien, *Journey for Margaret*
▪ Susan Peters, *Random Harvest*
▪ Edward G. Robinson, *Tales of Manhattan*
▪ Ginger Rogers, *Roxy Hart, The Major and the Minor*
▪ George Sanders, *The Moon and Sixpence*
▪ William Severn, *Journey for Margaret*
▪ Ann Sheridan, *Kings Row*
▪ Rudy Vallee, *The Palm Beach Story*
▪ Anton Walbrook, *The Invaders*
▪ Googie Withers, *One of Our Aircraft Is Missing*
▪ Monty Woolley, *The Pied Piper*
▪ Teresa Wright, *Mrs. Miniver*
▪ Robert Young, *H. M. Pulham, Esq.; Joe Smith, American; Journey for Margaret*

BEST DOCUMENTARY
▪ *Moscow Strikes Back*

NEW YORK FILM CRITICS

Winners were announced on December 26, 1942. Awards were presented on January 3, 1943, at the Barberry Room of the Berkshire Hotel in New York. NBC radio broadcast 15 minutes of the ceremony live nationwide.

BEST PICTURE
▪ *In Which We Serve*

BEST DIRECTOR
- John Farrow, *Wake Island*

BEST ACTOR
- James Cagney, *Yankee Doodle Dandy*

BEST ACTRESS
- Agnes Moorehead, *The Magnificent Ambersons*

BEST WAR FACT FILM
- *Moscow Strikes Back*

ACADEMY AWARDS

Nominations were announced on February 8, 1943. Awards were presented on March 4 at the Cocoanut Grove of the Ambassador Hotel in Los Angeles.

BEST PICTURE
- *Mrs. Miniver*
The Invaders
Kings Row
The Magnificent Ambersons
The Pied Piper
The Pride of the Yankees
Random Harvest
The Talk of the Town
Wake Island
Yankee Doodle Dandy

BEST DIRECTOR
- William Wyler, *Mrs. Miniver*
Michael Curtiz, *Yankee Doodle Dandy*
John Farrow, *Wake Island*
Mervyn LeRoy, *Random Harvest*
Sam Wood, *Kings Row*

BEST ACTOR
- James Cagney, *Yankee Doodle Dandy*
Ronald Colman, *Random Harvest*
Gary Cooper, *The Pride of the Yankees*
Walter Pidgeon, *Mrs. Miniver*
Monty Woolley, *The Pied Piper*

BEST ACTRESS
- Greer Garson, *Mrs. Miniver*
Bette Davis, *Now, Voyager*
Katharine Hepburn, *Woman of the Year*
Rosalind Russell, *My Sister Eileen*
Teresa Wright, *The Pride of the Yankees*

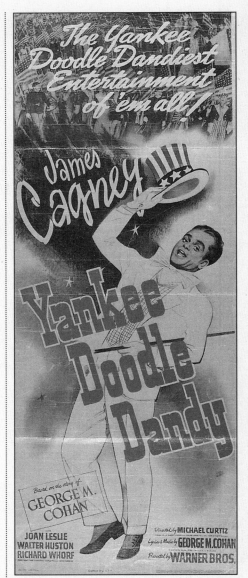

Ex-vaudeville star and SAG prexy Jimmy Cagney was voted Best Actor by the Gotham crix and Oscars for portraying George M. Cohan.

BEST SUPPORTING ACTOR
- Van Heflin, *Johnny Eager*
William Bendix, *Wake Island*
Walter Huston, *Yankee Doodle Dandy*
Frank Morgan, *Tortilla Flat*
Henry Travers, *Mrs. Miniver*

BEST SUPPORTING ACTRESS
- Teresa Wright, *Mrs. Miniver*

Gladys Cooper, *Now, Voyager*

Agnes Moorehead, *The Magnificent Ambersons*

Susan Peters, *Random Harvest*

Dame May Whitty, *Mrs. Miniver*

BEST WRITING (ORIGINAL STORY)
- Emeric Pressburger, *The Invaders*

Irving Berlin, *Holiday Inn*

Robert Buckner, *Yankee Doodle Dandy*

Paul Gallico, *The Pride of the Yankees*

Sidney Harmon, *The Talk of the Town*

BEST WRITING (ORIGINAL SCREENPLAY)
- Michael Kanin, Ring Lardner, Jr., *Woman of the Year*

W. R. Burnett, Frank Butler, *Wake Island*

Frank Butler, Don Hartman, *The Road to Morocco*

George Oppenheimer, *The War against Mrs. Hadley*

Michael Powell, Emeric Pressburger, *One of Our Aircraft Is Missing*

BEST WRITING (SCREENPLAY)
- George Froeschel, James Hilton, Claudine West, Arthur Wimperis, *Mrs. Miniver*

Rodney Ackland, Emeric Pressburger, *The Invaders*

Sidney Buchman, Irwin Shaw, *The Talk of the Town*

George Froeschel, Claudine West, Arthur Wimperis, *Random Harvest*

Herman J. Mankiewicz, Jo Swerling, *The Pride of the Yankees*

BEST SONG
- "White Christmas," *Holiday Inn*, Irving Berlin

"Always in My Heart," *Always in My Heart*, Kim Gannon, Ernesto Lecuona

"Dearly Beloved," *You Were Never Lovelier*, Jerome Kern, Johnny Mercer

"How about You?" *Babes on Broadway*, Ralph Freed, Burton Lane

"It Seems I Heard That Song Before," *Youth on Parade*, Sammy Cahn, Jule Styne

"I've Got a Gal in Kalamazoo," *Orchestra Wives*, Mack Gordon, Harry Warren

"Love Is a Song," *Bambi*, Frank Churchill, Larry Morey

"Pennies for Peppino," *Flying with Music*, Chet Forrest, Edward Ward, Bob Wright

"Pig Foot Pete," *Hellzapoppin'*, Gene De Paul, Don Raye

"There's a Breeze on Lake Louise," *The Mayor of 44th Street*, Mort Greene, Harry Revel

Winners

BEST ART DIRECTION
(BLACK AND WHITE)
- Richard Day, Joseph Wright, Thomas Little, *This Above All*

(COLOR)
- Richard Day, Joseph Wright, Thomas Little, *My Gal Sal*

BEST CINEMATOGRAPHY
(BLACK AND WHITE)
- Joseph Ruttenberg, *Mrs. Miniver*

(COLOR)
- Leon Shamroy, *The Black Swan*

BEST DOCUMENTARIES
- *Kokoda Front Line!*, Australian News and Information Bureau
- *Moscow Strikes Back*, Artkino, U.S.S.R.
- *Prelude to War*, U.S. Army Special Services
- *The Battle of Midway*, U.S. Navy Twentieth Century-Fox

BEST FILM EDITING
- Daniel Mandell, *The Pride of the Yankees*

BEST MUSIC
(SCORING OF A DRAMATIC OR COMEDY PICTURE)
- Max Steiner, *Now, Voyager*

(SCORING OF A MUSICAL PICTURE)
- Ray Heindorf, Heinz Roemheld, *Yankee Doodle Dandy*

BEST SHORT SUBJECT
(CARTOON)
- *Der Fuehrer's Face*

(ONE REEL)
- *Speaking of Animals and Their Families*

(TWO REEL)
- *Beyond the Line of Duty*

BEST SOUND RECORDING
- Nathan Levinson, *Yankee Doodle Dandy*

BEST SPECIAL EFFECTS
- Farciot Edouart, Gordon Jennings, Louis Mesenkop, William L. Pereira, *Reap the Wild Wind*

SCIENTIFIC OR TECHNICAL AWARDS
Class II (Plaque)
- Daniel B. Clark, Twentieth Century-Fox; Carroll Clark, F. Thomas Thompson, RKO Studio Miniature Department

Class III (Certificate)
- Daniel J. Bloomberg, Republic Studio Sound Department; Robert Henderson, Paramount Studio Engineering and Transparency Departments

IRVING G. THALBERG MEMORIAL AWARD
- Sidney Franklin

SPECIAL AWARDS
- Charles Boyer
- *In Which We Serve*, Noel Coward
- MGM

· 1943 ·

A New Golden Globe Shines

There was such fierce disagreement over declaring 1943's best movie that the four top award groups picked four different pics, a split that would not occur so disparately again until 1965.

The National Board of Review chose director William A. Wellman's drama about a Nevada lynch mob, *The Ox-Bow Incident*, while the New York Film Critics opted for the celluloid rendition of Lillian Hellman's play *Watch on the Rhine*, which had previously been lauded as the best of Broadway by the New York Drama Critics Circle in 1941.

As scripted for the screen by Hellman's lover Dashiell Hammett, *Watch on the Rhine* was, said *Variety*, "even better than its powerful original stage version," with Paul Lukas reprising his theatrical role as a German pursued by Nazi agents in the United States. Nabbing four votes on the crix's first ballot, it tied *The Human Comedy*, director Clarence Brown's adaptation of William Saroyan's story of a small American town during wartime. *Watch* prevailed on the sixth round by a score of 11 to 6, with Lukas winning Best Actor easily on the first tally with 15 votes.

The crix's prexy Bosley Crowther of *The New York Times* called the voting "surprisingly pacific for such a usually tempestuous affair," noting that "the conclave was so peaceful that an old-time dissenter" like himself "blushed for shame." He offered two possibilities for the sudden good will: his colleagues might believe that "disputation over pictures would be childish and vain" compared to the tragic war raging around the world, or else "it may also be that everybody was so lukewarm toward most of last year's fare that mental and physical violence seemed a foolish and useless waste." Crowther concluded: "In this voter's private reflections, the latter was frankly the case."

Casablanca shocked Oscar pundits by nabbing Best Picture over *Song of Bernadette* and *For Whom the Bell Tolls*.

While *The Ox-Bow Incident* failed to receive any votes for Best Picture, William A. Wellman ran neck-and-neck with Fritz Lang (*Hangmen Also Die*) on the first four ballots in the race for Best Director. Neither turned out to be the winner: distant dark horse George Stevens (*The More the Merrier*) suddenly leapt from behind to tie Wellman on the fifth and sixth rounds, then beat him on the seventh.

An upset also occurred in the Best Actress race after it looked, on the first ballot, to be a showdown between Katina Paxinou (*For Whom the Bell Tolls*) and Joan Fontaine (*The Constant Nymph*). Ida Lupino (*The Hard Way*) ended up trouncing Paxinou on the sixth ballot by an 11-to-6 score for her role as a headstrong woman who pushes her sister onto the Broadway stage. The *Times* denounced Lupino's victory as "one of those strange deviations which we don't even pretend to understand," while the *Herald Tribune* insisted that Lupino "amply deserved her laurels." The Oscars would agree with the *Times* and fail to nominate her.

A new film award was introduced this year that would disagree with both the crix and the National Board of Review by giving its prizes for Best Picture and Best Actress to a film overlooked by them both. Formed in 1940, the Hollywood Foreign Correspondents Association now joined the annual film-awards derby with its own kudos, the Golden Globe. The offshore scribes gave their first Best Picture prize to *The Song of Bernadette*, described by *Variety* as "an absorbing, emotional and dramatic picturization" of the real-life story of an 18th-century peasant girl who claimed she saw the Virgin Mary at Lourdes, France. Best Actress champ was *Bernadette* star Jennifer Jones, who, *Variety* said, "delivers an inspirationally sensitive and arresting performance." Paul Lukas was the Globes' first Best Actor. Winners were presented with scrolls at an informal ceremony held at the Twentieth Century-Fox studio.

> ## Song of Bernadette won the first Golden Globe and led the Oscar race.

Fox producer Darryl Zanuck positioned *The Song of Bernadette* for prominent Oscar consideration by opening it in Los Angeles on Christmas Day 1943, so the film could gain late-breaking momentum as he trumpeted it as a "masterpiece" in glossy trade ads. Zanuck restricted its showings to a few limited theaters and charged high ticket prices in order to give the pic a lofty aura. Paramount countered by debuting its chief Oscar candidate, *For Whom the Bell Tolls*, in a similar fashion, selling seats on a reserved basis only, then withdrawing the movie for broader release later. Both strategies worked for the first round of Oscar voting: *The Song of Bernadette* led with the most nominations—12—followed by 9 for *For Whom the Bell Tolls*. Variety cheered the latter as "one of the important pictures of all time, although almost three hours of running time can overdo a good thing." The two films were considered the front-runners for Best Picture, with a slight edge given to *Bernadette*.

Being sensitive to wartime calls for frugality, Oscar leaders scrapped dinner plans, moved the ceremony to Grauman's Chinese Theater, added entertainment acts and passed out 200 tickets to members of the U.S. military. "All of the colorfulness of previous Academy Awards that took place in hotels was gone and the 16th annual award was just one of those things," *Variety* sighed.

Organizers overlooked one logistical matter. There were "no parking attendants to handle the cars, (causing) much delay and lateness in getting into the theater," *Variety* reported. "Many of the stars found themselves pushed around by minions of the law and expressed their chagrin. All the glamour that is Hollywood was still in evidence, despite wartime restrictions. Bleachers seating several hundred stargazers were jammed to capacity and the night in front of Grauman's Chinese Theater was filled with ovations of varying intensity as the film names arrived."

The Oscars, as they're widely known today, were thus born.

Inside the theater, the ceremony was presided over by Jack Benny, who said, "I'm here through the courtesy of Bob Hope's having a bad cold." He then groused about the lack of dinner, adding, "Not even chop suey—and they call this place Grauman's Chinese?"

In the Best Actor race, Paul Lukas faced serious competish from Humphrey Bogart (*Casablanca*) and Gary Cooper (*For Whom the Bell Tolls*). When Lukas nonetheless pulled off a victory, *Variety* described him as looking "excited and genuinely moved" as he looked at his plaster trophy (all metals were being hoarded for war needs) and said,

"Oscar, it's called a symbol of achievement, something every actor hopes to win," then thanked Broadway playwright Lillian Hellman and stage producer Herman Shumlin.

The front-runner for Best Actress was Ingrid Bergman, who had two celebrated roles this year—in *Casablanca* and *For Whom the Bell Tolls*, the latter earning her an Oscar bid. When Jennifer Jones pulled off an upset, *Variety* described the winner as looking "flustered" and noted that the occasion also marked her 25th birthday. Jones expressed her gratitude to showbiz mogul David O. Selznick, who'd discovered her, plus the film's creative team, then uttered "thank you" twice. Backstage later, Jones apologized to Bergman for beating her, but Bergman graciously assured the champ that voters had made the right choice. Soon after the Oscars, gossip scribes revealed that Jones and Selznick were romantically involved, and later the two were married.

One nominee for Best Supporting Actor was clearly a popular favorite based upon the rousing reception he received when arriving at the theater. *Variety* reported "a tremendous hand from the star-gazers" greeting Charles Coburn, who portrayed a wily matchmaker in *The More the Merrier*. When Oscar voters endorsed him, too, *Variety* noted that his win was welcomed with "heart-warming applause" and added that the veteran 67-year-old thesp "brought the house down" when he said in his acceptance speech, "I hope that, at the end of another 50 years of service in the theater, your children and children's children have courage enough to vote for me again."

After being cited as one of the year's top performers by the National Board of Review and narrowly losing the New York film critics' laurels for Best Actress, Greek stage star Katina Paxinou won the consolation Oscar as Best Supporting Actress for her role as a gypsy rebel in *For Whom the Bell Tolls*. "Gracious Katina Paxinou was so visibly moved at receiving the nod that her words did not carry to many of the audience," *Variety* observed. Her words of thanks were actually addressed to friends far beyond the gathered crowd—to her colleagues back at the Royal Theatre in war-torn Athens. "I hope they are still alive," she said, "but I doubt it."

Considering the good luck of Jennifer Jones, *The Song of Bernadette* seemed poised to claim most of the other top trophies, too, but there was an early upset in the match-up for best screenplay, which went to *Casablanca*. Another shocker followed when the statuette for Best Director went to *Casablanca*'s Michael Curtiz, who'd previously lost Oscar bouts in 1938 and 1942 and now accepted his elusive award saying that he'd expected to lose again.

The reason: *Casablanca* was old news as of awards night—March 2, 1944—having opened in New York in December 1942 and in L.A. one month later. When it won Best Picture, *Variety* reported that *Casablanca*'s victory "brought forth a long, loud burst of applause—also a big laugh when Jack Benny tried frantically to find someone to accept it, ignoring Jack L. Warner fighting his way to the stage."

In its post-Oscars coverage, *Variety* credited *Casablanca*'s success to the faulty campaign strategies behind *The Song of Bernadette* and *For Whom the Bell Tolls*, both of which failed to take into account thousands of Oscar voters. *Variety*'s poll revealed that only 25 percent of Hollywood's acting extras had seen either film due to high ticket prices or limited showings.

▪ 1943 ▪

NATIONAL BOARD OF REVIEW

The board declared a best film and documentary of the year, then listed its remaining favorites according to highest scores.

No award was bestowed for foreign films. Winners of the Best Acting awards were listed alphabetically. The vote results were announced on December 23, 1943.

BEST PICTURE

- *The Ox-Bow Incident*
Watch on the Rhine
Air Force
Holy Matrimony
The Hard Way
Casablanca
Lassie Come Home
Bataan
The Moon Is Down
The Next of Kin

BEST ACTING

- Gracie Fields, *Holy Matrimony*
- Cedric Hardwicke, *The Moon Is Down, The Cross of Lorraine*
- Paul Lukas, *Watch on the Rhine*
- Henry Morgan, *The Ox-Bow Incident, Happy Land*
- Katina Paxinou, *For Whom the Bell Tolls*
- Teresa Wright, *Shadow of a Doubt*

BEST DOCUMENTARY

- *Desert Victory*
Battle of Russia (*Why We Fight* series)
Prelude to War (*Why We Fight* series)
Saludos Amigos
The Silent Voyage

NEW YORK FILM CRITICS

Winners were announced on December 28, 1943.

BEST PICTURE

- *Watch on the Rhine*

BEST DIRECTOR

- George Stevens, *The More the Merrier*

BEST ACTOR

- Paul Lukas, *Watch on the Rhine*

BEST ACTRESS

- Ida Lupino, *The Hard Way*

SPECIAL AWARD

- *Why We Fight* series and *Report from the Aleutians* (Army Signal Corps)

GOLDEN GLOBES

Winners announced in late January 1944. Awards were presented later at the Twentieth Century-Fox studio.

BEST PICTURE

- *The Song of Bernadette*

BEST ACTOR

- Paul Lukas, *Watch on the Rhine*

BEST ACTRESS

- Jennifer Jones, *The Song of Bernadette*

BEST SUPPORTING ACTOR

- Akim Tamiroff, *For Whom the Bell Tolls*

BEST SUPPORTING ACTRESS

- Katina Paxinou, *For Whom the Bell Tolls*

ACADEMY AWARDS

Nominations were announced on February 6, 1944. Awards were presented on March 2 at Grauman's Chinese Theater in Hollywood.

BEST PICTURE

- *Casablanca*
For Whom the Bell Tolls
Heaven Can Wait
The Human Comedy
In Which We Serve
Madame Curie
The More the Merrier
The Ox-Bow Incident
The Song of Bernadette
Watch on the Rhine

A quartet of Oscar's best thesps, from left: Paul Lucas, Jennifer Jones, Katina Paxinou and Charles Coburn.

BEST DIRECTOR
- Michael Curtiz, *Casablanca*

Clarence Brown, *The Human Comedy*
Henry King, *The Song of Bernadette*
Ernst Lubitsch, *Heaven Can Wait*
George Stevens, *The More the Merrier*

BEST ACTOR
- Paul Lukas, *Watch on the Rhine*

Humphrey Bogart, *Casablanca*
Gary Cooper, *For Whom the Bell Tolls*
Walter Pidgeon, *Madame Curie*
Mickey Rooney, *The Human Comedy*

BEST ACTRESS
- Jennifer Jones, *The Song of Bernadette*

Jean Arthur, *The More the Merrier*
Ingrid Bergman, *For Whom the Bell Tolls*
Joan Fontaine, *The Constant Nymph*
Greer Garson, *Madame Curie*

BEST SUPPORTING ACTOR
- Charles Coburn, *The More the Merrier*

Charles Bickford, *The Song of Bernadette*
J. Carrol Naish, *Sahara*
Claude Rains, *Casablanca*
Akim Tamiroff, *For Whom the Bell Tolls*

BEST SUPPORTING ACTRESS
- Katina Paxinou, *For Whom the Bell Tolls*

Gladys Cooper, *The Song of Bernadette*
Paulette Goddard, *So Proudly We Hail!*
Anne Revere, *The Song of Bernadette*
Lucile Watson, *Watch on the Rhine*

BEST WRITING (ORIGINAL STORY)
- William Saroyan, *The Human Comedy*

Steve Fisher, *Destination Tokyo*
Guy Gilpatric, *Action in the North Atlantic*
Gordon McDonell, *Shadow of a Doubt*
Frank Ross, Robert Russell, *The More the Merrier*

BEST WRITING (ORIGINAL SCREENPLAY)
- Norman Krasna, *Princess O'Rourke*

Noel Coward, *In Which We Serve*
Lillian Hellman, *The North Star*
Dudley Nichols, *Air Force*
Allan Scott, *So Proudly We Hail!*

BEST WRITING (SCREENPLAY)
- Julius J. Epstein, Philip G. Epstein, Howard Koch, *Casablanca*

Richard Flournoy, Lewis R. Foster, Frank Ross, Robert Russell, *The More the Merrier*
Dashiell Hammett, *Watch on the Rhine*
Nunnally Johnson, *Holy Matrimony*
George Seaton, *The Song of Bernadette*

BEST SONG
- "You'll Never Know," *Hello, Frisco, Hello*, Mack Gordon, Harry Warren

"Black Magic," *Star Spangled Rhythm*, Harold Arlen, Johnny Mercer
"A Change of Heart," *Hit Parade of 1943*, Harold Adamson, Jule Styne
"Happiness Is a Thing Called Joe," *Cabin in the Sky*, Harold Arlen, E. Y. Harburg
"My Shining Hour," *The Sky's the Limit*, Harold Arlen, Johnny Mercer
"Saludos Amigos," *Saludos Amigos*, Ned Washington, Charles Wolcott
"Say a Pray'r for the Boys over There," *Hers to Hold*, Jimmy McHugh, Herb Magidson
"They're Either Too Young or Too Old," *Thank Your Lucky Stars*, Frank Loesser, Arthur Schwartz
"We Mustn't Say Goodbye," *Stage Door Canteen*, Al Dubin, James Monaco
"You'd Be So Nice to Come Home To," *Something to Shout About*, Cole Porter

Winners

BEST ART DIRECTION/INTERIOR DECORATION
(BLACK AND WHITE)
- James Basevi, William Darling, Thomas Little, *The Song of Bernadette*

(COLOR)
- Alexander Golitzen, John B. Goodman, Russell A. Gausman, Ira S. Webb, *The Phantom of the Opera*

BEST CINEMATOGRAPHY
(BLACK AND WHITE)
- Arthur Miller, *The Song of Bernadette*

(COLOR)
- W. Howard Greene, Hal Mohr, *The Phantom of the Opera*

BEST DOCUMENTARY
(FEATURE)
- *Desert Victory*, British Ministry of Information

(SHORT SUBJECT)
- *December 7th*, U.S. Navy

BEST FILM EDITING
- George Amy, *Air Force*

BEST MUSIC
(SCORING OF A DRAMATIC OR COMEDY PICTURE)
- Alfred Newman, *The Song of Bernadette*

(SCORING OF A MUSICAL PICTURE)
- Ray Heindorf, *This Is the Army*

BEST SHORT SUBJECT
(CARTOON)
- *Yankee Doodle Mouse*

(ONE REEL)
- *Amphibious Fighters*

(TWO REEL)
- *Heavenly Music*

BEST SOUND RECORDING
- Stephen Dunn, *This Land Is Mine*

BEST SPECIAL EFFECTS
- Roger Heman, Fred Sersen, *Crash Dive*

SCIENTIFIC OR TECHNICAL AWARDS
Class II (Plaque)
- E. I. DuPont De Nemours, Photo Products Department; Farciot Edouart, Earle Morgan, Barton Thompson, Paramount Studio Engineering Department, Paramount Studio Transparency Department

Class III (Certificate)
- Daniel J. Bloomberg, Republic Studio Sound Department; Charles Galloway Clarke, Twentieth Century-Fox Studio Camera Department; Farciot Edouart, Paramount Studio Transparency Department; Willard H. Turner, RKO Radio Studio Sound Department

IRVING G. THALBERG MEMORIAL AWARD
- Hal B. Wallis

SPECIAL AWARD
- George Pal

· 1944 ·

Going My Way *Goes All the Way*

Rarely has there been harmonious agreement over naming the year's Best Picture, but now a sentimental tuner about Irish Catholic priests heard a chorus of hosannas from those usually cynical New York film crix and the devilish Hollywood crowd. In fact, 1944 marked the first time since 1937 that the crix and Oscar voters embraced the same pic.

Going My Way had almost everything going its way: it was heralded as the year's best by the editors of *Photoplay* and the readers of *Film Daily* and *Screen Guild Magazine*. The National Board of Review sounded the only discordant note, picking *None But the Lonely Heart* as its top choice, followed by *Going My Way* in second place. During the Gotham critics' voting, *Going My Way* was "the favorite from the start," reported *The New York Times*, although three ballots were needed before the pic claimed the necessary two-thirds majority over *Hail the Conquering Hero* and *Wilson*.

Some critics reported later that they pressed for *Hail the Conquering Hero* because the farce about a small-town man mistaken for a war hero was one of two great works released this year by writer/director Preston Sturges, who also earned the crix's cheers for *The Miracle of Morgan's Creek*. *Wilson* was a patriotic paean to America's 26th president produced by Twentieth Century-Fox chief Darryl F. Zanuck, who lobbied aggressively for award honors in an ad campaign ballyhooing his handiwork as "the most important event in 50 years of motion pictures." *Variety* appreciated *Wilson*'s "authority, warmth, idealism" and even its ambitious scope, saying, "The production is said to cost over $3 million and looks it," but *Variety*'s reviewers nonetheless preferred *Going My Way* as "topnotch entertainment."

Going My Way (starring Bing Crosby, Jean Heather and Barry Fitzgerald) nabbed Best Picture kudos from the Oscars, Globes and New York crix. The three awards remained in sync for three more years.

The crix gave their nod for Best Director to *Going My Way*'s helmer and scribe Leo McCarey over Sturges by a narrow seven-to-five vote on the sixth ballot, when only a simple majority vote was needed instead of the two-thirds tally earlier. What's curious is which of the pic's two stars the crix embraced as Best Actor: Barry Fitzgerald, who portrayed a crusty pastor of a church strapped for cash. "Here was as fine a characterization as has ever been put upon the screen—full-bodied, deep and comprehending, with such humor, humility and strength," gushed the *Times*. Fitzgerald won by a landslide on the first ballot with 11 votes out of the 16 crix present, topping Alexander Knox as Woodrow Wilson (2 votes), Fred MacMurray as a conniving insurance salesman in *Double Indemnity* (1 vote) and Fitzgerald's costar Bing Crosby (2 votes).

Crosby, who'd been known chiefly as America's best-selling crooner despite occasional film roles, really had the pic's lead role. He played an amiable young priest who battles the curmudgeonly Fitzgerald, turns a gang of local thugs into choirboys, saves the church and sings three songs, including a tune that would become one of his signature hits—"Swinging on a Star." Golden Globe voters wouldn't be confused over the two stars' pecking order—the foreign journalists would give Fitzgerald their Best Supporting Actor's prize—but the controversy would result in a split decision at the Oscars when Fitzgerald became the only thesp to earn nominations in both the lead and supporting categories.

For their Best Actress choice, the New York crix embraced a veteran Broadway thesp who'd been overlooked by the National Board of Review and would soon be snubbed by the Golden Globes and Oscars, too: Tallulah Bankhead. The *Herald Tribune* critic praised Bankhead for giving an "extraordinarily versatile performance" as the survivor of a U-boat attack in Alfred Hitchcock's *Lifeboat*. Bankhead won on the sixth ballot with 10 votes, topping Ingrid Bergman in *Gaslight* (5 votes) and Barbara Stanwyck in *Double Indemnity* (1 vote).

Fitzgerald and Crosby split the crix and Oscar Best Actor awards.

Voters of the new Golden Globes agreed that *Going My Way* was the year's Best Picture, but they disagreed on who were the year's best thesps, citing *Wilson*'s Alexander Knox and *Gaslight*'s Ingrid Bergman. They toasted the victors at their first awards ceremony, which was held at the Beverly Hills Hotel. Bill Mooring, prexy of the Hollywood Foreign Correspondents Association, recalled the event years later to *TV Guide*: "The group was so short of money that we all kicked in together. We had no flowers for the hotel dining-room tables. But I knew a gardener who worked for Joan Bennett and Walter Wanger. He got us some blossoms from their garden and brought them to the hotel. They were very nice."

Bergman entered the Academy Award race as the front-runner for her celebrated role in *Gaslight*, which was based on the Broadway thriller *Angel Street* about a naive heiress duped into marrying a jewel thief who murdered her aunt. Bergman was up against three past champs—Claudette Colbert (*Since You Went Away*), Bette Davis (*Mr. Skeffington*) and Greer Garson (*Mrs. Parkington*) plus the Oscar-overdue Barbara Stanwyck (*Double Indemnity*)—but she was the sentimental favorite since she lost the award last year in an upset by Jennifer Jones.

To dramatize that there was no ill will between the former foes, Bergman arrived at the ceremony with Jones on her arm and was greeted by "cheering from 1,700 bleacherites across the street" from Grauman's Chinese Theater, reported *Variety*. *Going My Way* and *Wilson* entered the night's races tied for the most nominations: 10. *Variety* added, "All seats were sold for $10, plus $2 federal tax, and when studios bought seats they paid $15 extra to help the academy defray expenses of the affair," which totaled $30,000. The tradepaper added: "It cost the academy $600 to set up the bleachers adjacent to the forecourts and across the street. The first bleacher grabbers arrived in place shortly before 3 P.M.," which was five hours before the start of the show.

Bing Crosby was up for Best Actor, but he believed that Alexander Knox would win, so he planned to skip the ceremony. Two hours before the gala, however, Paramount's PR men discovered him at a local golf course and coaxed him into attending after they connected him on the phone with his mother, who ordered him to go. Crosby buckled, but dreaded going because the night's emcee was his comic costar of three *Road* pictures, Bob Hope, who was sure to give him the raspberries whether he got the Oscar or not.

Indeed, *Variety* reported that there was "long drawn-out razzing" of Crosby all night by Hope—except when Crosby prevailed as champ. *Variety* added, "There was no kidding on Bob's part, for Bing's victory was something that touched him deeply. There was no doubt about his sincerity as he congratulated the King of Croon."

Crosby accepted the honor saying, "I couldn't be more surprised if I won the Kentucky Derby. Can you imagine the jokes Hope's going to write about this in his radio show? This will give him 12 straight weeks of material."

Hope couldn't wait till his next radio broadcast. Later that night, after the solemnity of his friend's victory passed, he compared the oddity of Crosby winning an Oscar to the unlikely possibility of film mogul Samuel Goldwyn ever lecturing at Oxford.

When Crosby's costar Barry Fitzgerald won Best Supporting Actor, *Variety* noted that the former star of Dublin's Abbey Theater "was the popular choice of the audience," drawing "a round of applause such as greeted no other victory. And when it came time to making his speech, he was just a kindly bashful priest he portrayed in *Going My Way*." The same film continued its awards juggernaut by claiming the director's laurels for Leo McCarey, who'd previously won the same honor in 1937 for *The Awful Truth*. When McCarey also claimed the statuette for Best Original Story, *Variety* noted that "he set a new record for Academy winners—two full-sized Oscars in one evening. No other person in the 17 years of the award ever has accomplished it." The prize for Best Supporting Actress went to veteran stage star Ethel Barrymore as a cancer-stricken Cockney shopkeeper and mother of Cary Grant (nominated for Best Actor) in *None but the Lonely Heart*, her first new film in 12 years. She was not present to accept it.

The Best Actress award was bestowed by last year's victor, Jennifer Jones, who acknowledged this year's champ, Ingrid Bergman, saying, "Your artistry has won our vote and your graciousness has won our hearts." Bergman accepted the honor, saying, "Tomorrow I go work in a picture with Bing and Mr. McCarey (*The Bells of St. Mary's*, a sequel to *Going My Way*) and I'm afraid if I didn't have an Oscar, too, they wouldn't speak to me."

"The Bergman triumph was unofficially forecast by the crowds outside the theatre long before the actual announcement of the award," *Variety* said in its post-Oscars coverage, noting that the star had been "applauded enthusiastically by the assembled fans as she entered the showhouse and there was no question that the choice of the judges was a popular one."

Variety declared that "the most dramatic happening" of the night occurred when the widow of Irving Thalberg, Norma Shearer, "a slender, gracious and beautiful blonde personality, mounted the steps" and bestowed the Thalberg Award to the producer of *Wilson*, Darryl Zanuck. Zanuck's *Wilson* may have lost the top Oscars, but it nonetheless scored a total of five victories—for original screenplay, color cinematography, color art direction, editing and sound.

The night's big winner—including Best Picture—turned out to be *Going My Way*, which nabbed seven prizes, including honors for screenplay and song ("Swinging on a Star") plus the kudos for Crosby, Fitzgerald and the two statuettes scored by McCarey.

In its post-Oscar coverage, *Variety* reported, "It was practically a betless derby. For weeks everybody had been picking the winners and there wasn't a bookie in town reckless enough to cover a bet on the favorites. When Bing Crosby, Barry Fitzgerald, Ingrid Bergman, Ethel Barrymore and *Going My Way* romped home on the bit, Joe Public threw out his chest and said, 'Didn't I tell you?' "

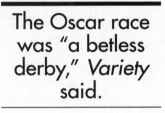

The Oscar race was "a betless derby," Variety said.

NATIONAL BOARD OF REVIEW

The board declared a best film and documentary of the year, then listed its remaining favorites according to highest scores. No award was bestowed for foreign films. Winners of the Best Acting awards were listed alphabetically. The vote results were announced on December 23, 1944.

BEST PICTURE
- *None but the Lonely Heart*
Going My Way
The Miracle of Morgan's Creek
Hail the Conquering Hero
The Song of Bernadette
Wilson
Meet Me in St. Louis
Thirty Seconds over Tokyo
Thunder Rock
Lifeboat

BEST ACTING
- Ethel Barrymore, *None but the Lonely Heart*
- Ingrid Bergman, *Gaslight*
- Humphrey Bogart, *To Have and Have Not*
- Eddie Bracken, *Hail the Conquering Hero*
- Bing Crosby, *Going My Way*
- June Duprez, *None but the Lonely Heart*
- Betty Hutton, *The Miracle of Morgan's Creek*
- Margaret O'Brien, *Meet Me in St. Louis*
- Franklin Pangborn, *Hail the Conquering Hero*

BEST DOCUMENTARY
- *Memphis Belle*
Attack! The Battle for New Britain
With the Marines at Tarawa
Battle for the Marianas
Tunisian Victory

NEW YORK FILM CRITICS

Winners were announced on December 27, 1944.

Golden Globe champ Ingrid Bergman (*Gaslight*) was the Oscar fave after having lost the previous year year to Jennifer Jones.

BEST PICTURE
- *Going My Way*

BEST DIRECTOR
- Leo McCarey, *Going My Way*

BEST ACTOR
- Barry Fitzgerald, *Going My Way*

BEST ACTRESS
- Tallulah Bankhead, *Lifeboat*

GOLDEN GLOBES

Winners were announced in late January 1945. Awards were presented later at the Beverly Hills Hotel.

BEST PICTURE
- *Going My Way*

BEST DIRECTOR
- Leo McCarey, *Going My Way*

BEST ACTOR
- Alexander Knox, *Wilson*

BEST ACTRESS
- Ingrid Bergman, *Gaslight*

BEST SUPPORTING ACTOR
- Barry Fitzgerald, *Going My Way*

BEST SUPPORTING ACTRESS
- Agnes Moorehead, *Mrs. Parkington*

ACADEMY AWARDS

Nominations were announced on February 3, 1945. Awards were presented on March 15 at Grauman's Chinese Theater in Hollywood. The ceremony was broadcast by ABC radio.

BEST PICTURE
- *Going My Way*
Double Indemnity
Gaslight
Since You Went Away
Wilson

BEST DIRECTOR
- Leo McCarey, *Going My Way*
Alfred Hitchcock, *Lifeboat*
Henry King, *Wilson*
Otto Preminger, *Laura*
Billy Wilder, *Double Indemnity*

BEST ACTOR
- Bing Crosby, *Going My Way*
Charles Boyer, *Gaslight*
Barry Fitzgerald, *Going My Way*
Cary Grant, *None but the Lonely Heart*
Alexander Knox, *Wilson*

BEST ACTRESS
- Ingrid Bergman, *Gaslight*
Claudette Colbert, *Since You Went Away*
Bette Davis, *Mr. Skeffington*
Greer Garson, *Mrs. Parkington*
Barbara Stanwyck, *Double Indemnity*

BEST SUPPORTING ACTOR
- Barry Fitzgerald, *Going My Way*
Hume Cronyn, *The Seventh Cross*
Claude Rains, *Mr. Skeffington*
Clifton Webb, *Laura*
Monty Woolley, *Since You Went Away*

BEST SUPPORTING ACTRESS
- Ethel Barrymore, *None but the Lonely Heart*

Jennifer Jones, *Since You Went Away*
Angela Lansbury, *Gaslight*
Aline MacMahon, *Dragon Seed*
Agnes Moorehead, *Mrs. Parkington*

BEST WRITING (ORIGINAL STORY)
- Leo McCarey, *Going My Way*
David Boehm, Chandler Sprague, *A Guy Named Joe*
Edward Doherty, Jules Schermer, *The Sullivans*
Alfred Neumann, Joseph Than, *None Shall Escape*
John Steinbeck, *Lifeboat*

BEST WRITING (ORIGINAL SCREENPLAY)
- Lamar Trotti, *Wilson*
Jerome Cady, *Wing and a Prayer*
Richard Connell, Gladys Lehman, *Two Girls and a Sailor*
Preston Sturges, *Hail the Conquering Hero*
Preston Sturges, *The Miracle of Morgan's Creek*

BEST WRITING (SCREENPLAY)
- Frank Butler, Frank Cavett, *Going My Way*
John L. Balderston, Walter Reisch, John Van Druten, *Gaslight*
Irving Brecher, Fred F. Finkelhoffe, *Meet Me in St. Louis*
Raymond Chandler, Billy Wilder, *Double Indemnity*
Jay Dratler, Samuel Hoffenstein, Betty Reinhardt, *Laura*

BEST SONG
- "Swinging on a Star," *Going My Way*, Johnny Burke, James Van Heusen
"I Couldn't Sleep a Wink Last Night," *Higher and Higher*, Harold Adamson, Jimmy McHugh
"I'll Walk Alone," *Follow the Boys*, Sammy Cahn, Jule Styne
"I'm Making Believe," *Sweet and Lowdown*, Mack Gordon, James V. Monaco
"Long Ago and Far Away," *Cover Girl*, Ira Gershwin, Jerome Kern
"Now I Know," *Up in Arms*, Harold Arlen, Ted Koehler
"Rio de Janeiro," *Brazil*, Ary Barroso, Ned Washington

"Too Much in Love," *Song of the Open Road*, Kim Gannon, Walter Kent

"The Trolley Song," *Meet Me in St. Louis*, Ralph Blane, Hugh Martin

"Remember Me to Carolina," *Minstrel Man*, Harry Revel, Paul Webster

"Silver Shadows and Golden Dreams," *Lady, Let's Dance*, Charles Newman, Lew Pollack

"Sweet Dreams Sweetheart," *Hollywood Canteen*, M. K. Jerome, Ted Koehler

Winners

BEST ART DIRECTION/ INTERIOR DECORATION
(BLACK AND WHITE)
- William Ferrari, Cedric Gibbons, Paul Huldschinsky, Edwin B. Willis, *Gaslight*

(COLOR)
- Wiard Ihnen, Thomas Little, *Wilson*

BEST CINEMATOGRAPHY
(BLACK AND WHITE)
- Joseph LaShelle, *Laura*

(COLOR)
- Leon Shamroy, *Wilson*

BEST DOCUMENTARY
(FEATURE)
- *The Fighting Lady*, U.S. Navy

(SHORT SUBJECT)
- *With the Marines at Tarawa*, U.S. Marine Corps

BEST FILM EDITING
- Barbara McLean, *Wilson*

BEST MUSIC
(SCORING OF A DRAMATIC OR COMEDY PICTURE)
- Max Steiner, *Since You Went Away*

(SCORING OF A MUSICAL PICTURE)
- Carmen Dragon, Morris Stoloff, *Cover Girl*

SCIENTIFIC OR TECHNICAL AWARDS
Class II (Plaque)
- Stephen Dunn, RCA, RKO Radio Studio Sound Department

Class III (Certificate)
- Linwood Dunn, Cecil Love, Acme Tool Manufacturing; Grover Laube, Twentieth Century-Fox Studio Camera Department; Western Electric; Russell Brown, Ray Hinsdale, Joseph E. Robbins; Gordon Jennings; RCA, RKO Radio Studio Sound Department; Daniel J. Bloomberg, Republic Studio Sound Department; Bernard B. Brown, John P. Livadary; Paul Zeff, S. J. Twining, George Seid; Paul Lerpae

BEST SHORT SUBJECT
(CARTOON)
- *Mouse Trouble*

(ONE REEL)
- *Who's Who in Animal Land*

(TWO REEL)
- *I Won't Play*

BEST SOUND RECORDING
- E. H. Hansen, Twentieth Century-Fox Studio Sound Department, *Wilson*

BEST SPECIAL EFFECTS
- A. Arnold Gillespie, Donald Jahraus, Warren Newcombe, Douglas Shearer, *Thirty Seconds over Tokyo*

IRVING G. THALBERG MEMORIAL AWARD
- Darryl F. Zanuck

SPECIAL AWARDS
- Bob Hope
- Margaret O'Brien

· 1945 ·

Lost—*Winner*

After the Depression and World War II, Hollywood was in a sober mood and ready to confront the personal conflicts dramatized in *The Lost Weekend*, Billy Wilder's haunting glimpse into the life of an alcoholic that *Variety* hailed as "intense, morbid—and thrilling."

"The filming by Paramount of *The Lost Weekend* marks a particularly outstanding achievement," announced *Variety* in its review, lauding the movie's honest treatment of a subject often handled flippantly by Hollywood. "At no time can there be even a suggestion of levity to the part Ray Milland plays" as a wanna-be writer so desperate for a drink that he pawns his typewriter, *Variety* said. The tradepaper added, "Ray Milland has certainly given no better performance in his career," which spanned 14 years of mostly B-grade movies.

The National Board of Review was the first to acclaim Milland as the year's Best Actor. Next came the normally contentious New York film critics, who picked him easily. "Milland was the only winner to achieve the two-thirds majority necessary to win an award before the sixth ballot," reported *The New York Herald Tribune*. "He won over Robert Mitchum in *The Story of G.I. Joe* on the fourth ballot by a vote of 13 to 4."

Despite its title, *The Story of G.I. Joe* was really director William Wellman's tale of war correspondent Ernie Pyle. It put up a valiant fight for Best Picture and the director's laurels, but *The Lost Weekend* ultimately claimed both honors by the same score: nine to eight on the sixth ballot, when a mere majority vote was needed.

"Considering the final year of the war, the critics were wise," surmised the *Herald Tribune*'s Howard Barnes when praising his peers for bestowing special awards on two war documentaries. One of them, *The True Glory*, was compiled from newsreels super-

The Lost Weekend scored a rare triple header as Best Picture: Oscars, Golden Globes and New York Film Critics.

vised by General Dwight D. Eisenhower, and it was described by Barnes as "one of the most powerful war pictures ever filmed." Apparently, the National Board of Review thought so, too: the group surprised many award watchers by naming *The True Glory* Best Picture and ranking *The Lost Weekend* in second place.

The board also raised eyebrows with one of its acting honors. *Variety* cited "the eye-opening selection of Joan Crawford as best actress of the year" in *Mildred Pierce*. Crawford hadn't had a hit film since *The Women* in 1939 and hadn't had a praising review since quitting MGM for Warner Brothers in 1942. In *Mildred Pierce*, *Variety* said, "Joan Crawford reaches a peak of her acting career in this pic (about) a woman's sacrifices for a no-good daughter." Crawford sensed a potential comeback and pressed her private publicist to tout her for film awards.

Crawford's name suddenly popped up in lots of newspaper columns, but her overt campaign didn't help her with the New York newspaper critics. Crawford did nab endorsements from 3 of the 17 voters, but she lost to Ingrid Bergman on the sixth ballot. "Unquestionably, Bergman was the year's top actress," insisted the *Times*, citing the latter's superior work as a psychiatrist in Hitchcock's *Spellbound* and her role as a "Sister Superior" in *The Bells of St. Mary's*, a sequel to last year's awards sweeper *Going My Way*. "We would settle for the *Spellbound* performance alone," the *Times* added.

But it was a scene and song from *The Bells of St. Mary's* that the crix asked Bergman to perform when they gathered with 175 guests to bestow their honors during an afternoon reception at the Stork Club. Bergman did so from Los Angeles via ABC radio, which carried the ceremony on its *Philco Radio Hall of Fame*. She was joined out west by *Lost Weekend*'s Ray Milland, director/co-writer Billy Wilder and producer/co-writer Charles Brackett.

The same honorees would soon hook up again at a party held in Los Angeles for a relatively new film kudos bestowed by the Hollywood Foreign Correspondents association. The journalists announced their winners one day before the Oscars, then held their presentation ceremony three weeks later. Champs were Bergman (Best Actress), Milland (Best Actor), Wilder (Best Director), Brackett (producer of Best Picture) plus best supporting thesps Angela Lansbury (*The Picture of Dorian Gray*) and J. Carrol Naish (*A Medal for Benny*). All of the honorees attended the awards luncheon at the Hollywood Knickerbocker Club, where they were joined by Frank Sinatra, who accepted the new prize for Best Picture Promoting International Understanding, which went to *The House I Live In*, a short subject preaching social and religious tolerance that featured Ol' Blue Eyes crooning two popular tunes.

A few days before the Oscars, *Variety* spied its crystal ball and boldly proclaimed its predictions on page one: "*The Lost Weekend* looks like the money horse . . . the

standout favorite for Best Picture, with *Mildred Pierce* and *The Bells of St. Mary's* being the only entries capable of furnishing the opposition." *The Bells of St. Mary's* was a formidable foe. Not only was it a spin-off of last year's Oscar champ *Going My Way*, but it was this year's top-grossing hit and it led the current awards derby with the most noms—eight. *The Lost Weekend* was in second place with seven. *Mildred Pierce* had six chances.

Last year Billy Wilder (*Double Indemnity*) lost the race for Best Director to Leo McCarey (*Going My Way*), but this year he wreaked revenge over his rival, who was now up for *The Bells of St. Mary's*. The *Lost Weekend* also prevailed as Best Picture, just as *Variety* had foreseen, although the paper wrongly guessed that McCarey would win the helmer's gold again.

Oscar co-host Bob Hope snidely sized up the Best Actor showdown as a saloon slugfest, telling the audience, "It's Four Roses against Old Granddad." The former was a reference to Milland and the latter an affectionate swipe at his pal and past costar of several *Road* movies—Bing Crosby, last year's Best Actor winner who was now back in the race with *The Bells of St. Mary's*. But Crosby was not present on Oscar night, even though he was skedded to perform two songs. His absence didn't matter in the actor's race. Ray Milland won. The champ had ample forewarning—*Variety* predicted the category correctly ahead of time—but Milland nonetheless seemed unprepared, or overwhelmed, upon winning and was speechless at the podium.

"Joan Crawford is expected to place an easy winner in the Best Actress class," *Variety* said prior to the awards showdown in which she competed against Ingrid Bergman (*The Bells of St. Mary's*), Greer Garson (*The Valley of Decision*), Jennifer Jones (*Love Letters*) and Gene Tierney (*Leave Her to Heaven*). Crawford was so nervous over the matchup that she stayed away from Grau-

> # Ray Milland swept all four Best Actor awards.

man's Chinese Theater, professing to be sick. *Variety* appeared to fall for her story, reporting that Crawford was homebound "wrestling with a flock of flu germs." What Crawford was really doing at home was sipping cocktails while lounging on her bed and listening to the ceremony on ABC radio. Years later she confessed to author Roy Newquist that she was "hopeful, scared, apprehensive, almost hoping I wouldn't get it, but wanting it so badly . . . (so) I fortified myself, probably a little too much."

When the winner was announced, *Variety* reported "an explosion of applause" from the crowd at Grauman's. Crawford seemed to explode, too, as she suddenly forgot her "illness" and bounded out of bed to telephone the ceremony to express her thanks. Meantime, her assistants fussed frantically with Crawford's hair and makeup as her house staff fended off reporters and cameramen at the front door. The media was finally permitted entry later on, only after *Mildred Pierce* director Michael Curtiz arrived to deliver Crawford's Oscar to her at bedside. By then the film diva was back in between the sheets, giving the best performance of her career as she appeared to fend off fever spells while bravely expressing her thanks to peers and fans worldwide. "This is the greatest moment of my life," she said, eyes fluttering weakly. "My tears speak for me." Photos of the *Camille*-like scene filled the front pages of America's newspapers the next day.

> "Seasoned thesps galloped home to win the Oscar derby," *Variety* noted.

Variety may have fared well when predicting the top categories, but its editors bombed when sizing up the supporting races. In the male contest, they said, "It looks like a standoff between J. Carrol Naish for *A Medal for Benny* and Michael Chekhov for *Spellbound*." The victor turned out to be veteran Hollywood thesp James Dunn for his portrayal of a slap-happy drunk in *A Tree Grows in Brooklyn*. In the supporting actress category, *Variety* guessed that Ann Blythe (*Mildred Pierce*) or Angela Lansbury (*The Picture of Dorian Gray*) would win. Instead, the laurels were snagged by another showbiz trouper, Anne Revere, who portrayed Elizabeth Taylor's mother in *National Velvet*.

Weighing all the acting champs later, *Variety* declared that it was "Old Home Week," adding, "In other words, the seasoned thespians galloped home in front by several lengths to win the Oscar derby."

In its wrap-up coverage, *Variety* noted that the "first Oscar function in peacetime since Pearl Harbor brought out the boys in their black ties while the gals arrayed themselves in formal exposure. With searchlights wandering all over the California skies and no enemy airplanes in sight, the film fans who couldn't get into Sid Grauman's Chinese theater not only filled the 5,000 bleacher seats but impeded traffic on Hollywood Boulevard from 6 P.M. until after midnight. The show outside the house was better than the one inside."

▪ 1945 ▪

NATIONAL BOARD OF REVIEW

The board declared a best film of the year, then listed its remaining favorites according to highest scores. No award was bestowed for foreign films. The vote results were announced on December 21, 1945.

BEST PICTURE
- ▪ *The True Glory*
- *The Lost Weekend*
- *The Southerner*
- *The Story of G.I. Joe*
- *The Last Chance*
- *The Life and Death of Colonel Blimp*
- *A Tree Grows in Brooklyn*

The Fighting Lady
The Way Ahead
The Clock

BEST DIRECTOR
- Jean Renoir, *The Southerner*

BEST ACTOR
- Ray Milland, *The Lost Weekend*

BEST ACTRESS
- Joan Crawford, *Mildred Pierce*

NEW YORK FILM CRITICS

Winners were announced on January 1, 1946. Awards were presented on January 20 at the Stork Club in New York. The ceremony was broadcast by ABC radio on the *Philco Radio Hall of Fame* program.

BEST PICTURE
- *The Lost Weekend*

BEST DIRECTOR
- Billy Wilder, *The Lost Weekend*

BEST ACTOR
- Ray Milland, *The Lost Weekend*

BEST ACTRESS
- Ingrid Bergman, *The Bells of St. Mary's, Spellbound*

SPECIAL AWARDS: BEST DOCUMENTARY
- *The True Glory*
- *The Fighting Lady*

GOLDEN GLOBES

Winners were announced on March 6, 1946. Awards were presented on March 30 at the Hollywood Knickerbocker Club.

BEST PICTURE
- *The Lost Weekend*

BEST PICTURE PROMOTING INTERNATIONAL UNDERSTANDING
- *The House I Live In*

BEST DIRECTOR
- Billy Wilder, *The Lost Weekend*

BEST ACTOR
- Ray Milland, *The Lost Weekend*

BEST ACTRESS
- Ingrid Bergman, *The Bells of St. Mary's*

BEST SUPPORTING ACTOR
- J. Carrol Naish, *A Medal For Benny*

BEST SUPPORTING ACTRESS
- Angela Lansbury, *The Picture of Dorian Gray*

ACADEMY AWARDS

Nominations were announced on January 27, 1946. Awards were presented on March 7 at Grauman's Chinese Theater in Hollywood. The ceremony was broadcast by ABC radio.

BEST PICTURE
- *The Lost Weekend*
Anchors Aweigh

Variety called Joan Crawford's National Board of Review victory for *Mildred Pierce* "eye-opening." Oscar voters spotted her next.

The Bells of St. Mary's
Mildred Pierce
Spellbound

BEST DIRECTOR
- Billy Wilder, *The Lost Weekend*
Clarence Brown, *National Velvet*
Alfred Hitchcock, *Spellbound*
Leo McCarey, *The Bells of St. Mary's*
Jean Renoir, *The Southerner*

BEST ACTOR
- Ray Milland, *The Lost Weekend*
Bing Crosby, *The Bells of St. Mary's*
Gene Kelly, *Anchors Aweigh*
Gregory Peck, *The Keys of the Kingdom*
Cornel Wilde, *A Song to Remember*

BEST ACTRESS
- Joan Crawford, *Mildred Pierce*
Ingrid Bergman, *The Bells of St. Mary's*
Greer Garson, *The Valley of Decision*
Jennifer Jones, *Love Letters*
Gene Tierney, *Leave Her to Heaven*

BEST SUPPORTING ACTOR
- James Dunn, *A Tree Grows in Brooklyn*
Michael Chekhov, *Spellbound*
John Dall, *The Corn Is Green*
Robert Mitchum, *The Story of G.I. Joe*
J. Carrol Naish, *A Medal for Benny*

BEST SUPPORTING ACTRESS
- Anne Revere, *National Velvet*
Eve Arden, *Mildred Pierce*
Ann Blyth, *Mildred Pierce*
Angela Lansbury, *The Picture of Dorian Gray*
Joan Loring, *The Corn Is Green*

BEST WRITING (ORIGINAL STORY)
- Charles G. Booth, *The House on 92nd Street*
Alvah Bessie, *Objective, Burma!*
Laszlo Gorog, Thomas Monroe, *The Affairs of Susan*
Ernst Marischka, *A Song to Remember*
John Steinbeck, Jack Wagner, *A Medal for Benny*

BEST WRITING (ORIGINAL SCREENPLAY)
- Richard Schweizer, *Marie-Louise*
Myles Connolly, *Music for Millions*
Milton Holmes, *Salty O'Rourke*

Harry Kurnitz, *What Next, Corporal Hargrove?*
Philip Yordan, *Dillinger*

BEST WRITING (SCREENPLAY)
- Charles Brackett, Billy Wilder, *The Lost Weekend*
Leopold Atlas, Guy Endore, Philip Stevenson, *The Story of G.I. Joe*
Frank Davis, Tess Slesinger, *A Tree Grows in Brooklyn*
Ranald MacDougall, *Mildred Pierce*
Albert Maltz, *Pride of the Marines*

BEST SONG
- "It Might as Well Be Spring," *State Fair*, Oscar Hammerstein II, Richard Rodgers
"Accentuate the Positive," *Here Come the Waves*, Harold Arlen, Johnny Mercer
"Anywhere," *Tonight and Every Night*, Sammy Cahn, Jule Styne
"Aren't You Glad You're You?" *The Bells of St. Mary's*, Johnny Burke, James Van Heusen
"The Cat and the Canary," *Why Girls Leave Home*, Ray Evans, Jay Livingston
"Endlessly," *Earl Carroll Vanities*, Kim Gannon, Walter Kent
"I Fall in Love Too Easily," *Anchors Aweigh*, Sammy Cahn, Jule Styne
"I'll Buy That Dream," *Sing Your Way Home*, Herb Magidson, Allie Wrubel
"Linda," *The Story of G.I. Joe*, Ann Ronell
"Love Letters," *Love Letters*, Eddie Heyman, Victor Young
"More and More," *Can't Help Singing*, E. Y. Harburg, Jerome Kern
"Sleighride in July," *Belle of the Yukon*, Johnny Burke, James Van Heusen
"So in Love," *Wonder Man*, Leo Robin, David Rose
"Some Sunday Morning," *San Antonio*, Ray Heindorf, M. K. Jerome, Ted Koehler

Winners

BEST ART DIRECTION/ INTERIOR DECORATION
(BLACK AND WHITE)
- Wiard Ihnen, A. Roland Fields, *Blood on the Sun*

(COLOR)
- Hans Dreier, Ernst Fegte, Sam Comer, *Frenchman's Creek*

BEST CINEMATOGRAPHY
(BLACK AND WHITE)
- Harry Stradling, *The Picture of Dorian Gray*

(COLOR)
- Leon Shamroy, *Leave Her to Heaven*

BEST DOCUMENTARY
(FEATURE)
- *The True Glory*

(SHORT SUBJECT)
- *Hitler Lives?*

BEST FILM EDITING
- Robert J. Kern, *National Velvet*

BEST MUSIC
(SCORING OF A DRAMATIC OR COMEDY PICTURE)
- Miklos Rozsa, *Spellbound*

(SCORING OF A MUSICAL PICTURE)
- Georgie Stoll, *Anchors Aweigh*

SCIENTIFIC OR TECHNICAL AWARDS
Class III (Certificate)
- Loren L. Ryder, Charles R. Daily, Paramount Studio Sound Department;

Michael S. Leshing, Benjamin C. Robinson, Arthur B. Chatelain, Robert C. Stevens, John G. Capstaff, Twentieth Century-Fox

BEST SHORT SUBJECT
(CARTOON)
- *Quiet Please!*

(ONE REEL)
- *Stairway to Light*

(TWO REEL)
- *Star in the Night*

BEST SOUND RECORDING
- Stephen Dunn, *The Bells of St. Mary's*

BEST SPECIAL EFFECTS
- John Fulton, Arthur W. Johns, *Wonder Man*

SPECIAL AWARDS
- Daniel J. Bloomberg, Republic Studio, Republic Studio Sound Department
- Peggy Ann Garner
- *The House I Live In*
- Walter Wanger

· 1946 ·

Yankee Best Beats Brit "Threat"

Suddenly after World War II, America was invaded by a barrage of high-caliber movies from overseas. *The New York Times* critic Bosley Crowther warned, "Films now coming from Europe have such quality and class as to render them serious competition to the products of Hollywood. Let not the Hollywood brethren be indifferent to this phenomenon or be confused by their own conceits." A *Variety* headline declared that the Oscars and other film kudos faced a "BIG THREAT" from foreign fare.

Chief among the imports was Laurence Olivier's ambitious mounting of Shakespeare's *Henry V*. In its review, *Variety* said, "Production cost ran to about $2 million and every cent of it is evident on the screen. The color, the sets, the expanse and the imaginative quality of the filming are unexcelled." In addition to directing it, Olivier starred as England's 15th-century warrior king who defeated the French at Agincourt; Crowther was among the many crix who proclaimed Olivier the year's reigning thesp. *Henry V* turned out to be an unlikely b.o. hit, just like a British import from Noel Coward, whose writings had been the basis for Oscar's Best Picture of 1932–33, *Cavalcade*, and whose directorial debut, *In Which We Serve*, was voted top film of 1942 by the New York Film Critics. Crowther was among the Gotham crix who now claimed that Coward's latest pic, starring Trevor Howard and Celia Johnson in an ill-starred romance, even surpassed his earlier screen work, saying, *"Brief Encounter* does more for Noel Coward's reputation as a skilled film producer than *In Which We Serve."* Another standout of 1946 was *Open City*, described by *Variety* as director Roberto Rossellini's "human, credible story of the fine behavior of the 'little people' during the German occupation of Rome."

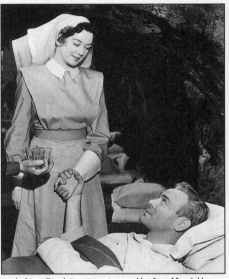

Rosalind Russell (with Dean Jagger) snagged her first of five Golden Globes for *Sister Kenny*.

Henry V and *Open City* premiered in the spring of 1946; *Brief Encounter* debuted in early September. The latter two pics gained early awards notice when they were hailed at the new Cannes Film Festival, which was launched on the French Riviera in late September. Both pics were included among the 11 films sharing the fest's first top laurel, the Grand Prix (later renamed the Palme d'Or in 1954).

By now Hollywood producers were well aware that movies released late in the year had the best chance for U.S. kudos. In the final five weeks of 1946, they unveiled their biggest guns—and this year their volleys behind the pics would become the most ferocious in Hollywood history. MGM put its weight behind *The Yearling*, described by *Variety* as a "heart-warming story" about a boy and his pet fawn that had "impressive underlying power." RKO premiered *It's a*

Wonderful Life, starring Jimmy Stewart as a wanna-be suicide whose guardian angel shows him what the world would be like without him. *Variety* called it "tender" and "flawless." Twentieth Century-Fox sliced through the competish with *The Razor's Edge*; "a moving picture that moves," said *Variety* about the screen adaptation of W. Somerset Maugham's bestseller, starring Tyrone Power and Gene Tierney, in a "romance more than slightly on the sizzling side."

But the most formidable drive was mounted by *The Best Years of Our Lives*, Samuel Goldwyn's gripping three-hour drama about three World War II veterans struggling to adjust to civilian life in peacetime America. The *Times*'s Crowther called it "an eminently outstanding picture in anybody's league," adding, "As a matter of fact, all the other pictures which Hollywood showed us last year were plainly inferior to it."

But when the first set of film kudos were bestowed for 1946, *Variety* announced in a bold, all-cap headline: "CRITICS SLAP HOLLYWOOD BY PICKING FOREIGN PIX IN THEIR 10 BEST OF THE YEAR."

Variety was referring to the choices made by the National Board of Review, which declared *Henry V* the year's finest, followed by *Open City* in second place and *The Best Years of Our Lives* in third. Laurence Olivier was named Best Actor. Best Actress was *Open City*'s Anna Magnani, who *Variety* said gave a "top performance" as the girlfriend of the film's rebel hero.

Twelve days after the board announced its prizes, the 18 New York film crix gathered at the newspaper guild's offices in a conclave described by the *Times*'s Crowther as "without blows." Crowther reported that the crix "voted sentiments which will not be admired in Hollywood," adding, "They showed a decided disposition toward foreign personalities and films" when determining the acting honors. "Mr. Olivier was

> ## Olivier's *Henry V* posed a strong, early threat to *Best Years of Our Lives*.

quickly accepted by a two-thirds majority as the year's Best Actor," Crowther said, noting that six votes nonetheless went to Fredric March (*The Best Years of Our Lives*) as a former army sergeant disillusioned by his dull bank job after the war. Olivier topped him with 12 votes, however, on the second ballot.

In their initial vote for Best Actress, the crix favored Olivia de Havilland in *To Each His Own*, a soaper about an unwed mother. De Havilland led with seven votes on the first ballot—four more than her nearest rival—but then lost on the sixth tally to *Brief Encounter*'s Celia Johnson, who *Variety* said was "terrific as the small-town mother whose brief encounter with a doctor, encumbered with a wife and kids, plunges into a love affair from which she struggles vainly to escape." The critics got patriotic with their other choices. Crowther noted, "They were heartily in favor of *The Best Years of Our Lives* as the year's best film—and of William Wyler, its director," who won on the first ballot. *The Best Years of Our Lives* prevailed on the second round of voting when it trounced *Henry V* by a score of 12 to 6. This year both the crix and the National Board of Review reinstated prizes for best Foreign Film—and they gave the accolades to the same film: *Open City*.

By contrast, the foreign journalists in Hollywood voted a straight American ticket. *The Best Years of Our Lives* won the award for Best Picture, but otherwise the Golden Globes went to recipients overlooked by earlier film honors. The awards banquet, emceed by Douglas Fairbanks, Jr., took place at the same place where his father once presided over the first Oscar banquet in 1929: the Hollywood Roosevelt Hotel.

Gregory Peck was named Best Actor for his role as a doting backwoodsman dad in *The Yearling*, while Best Actress went to Rosalind Russell as an Australian nurse fighting infantile paralysis in *Sister Kenny*. Neither star showed up to claim his or her award, although all other winners were present. Those included the Globes' Best Director Frank Capra (*It's a Wonderful Life*) and two stars of *The Razor's Edge* who took the prizes for supporting thesps: Clifton Webb and Anne Baxter.

Another supporting star played a lead role at the Globes when he received a special award for Most Natural Performance: Harold Russell, a real-life wartime amputee who starred in *The Best Years of Our Lives* as a sailor who lost his hands during battle. Douglas Fairbanks, Jr., told Russell that the prize was like receiving "the highest compliment" because "the art of acting is not to be natural—that would be to appear boring—but to create the illusion of being natural, which is a very difficult thing to do."

Oscars leaders prepared a special award for Russell, too, even though he was also nominated for Best Supporting Actor. They apparently believed that the real-life nonactor would lose to such seasoned showbiz pros as Clifton Webb (*The Razor's Edge*) or Claude Rains (*Notorious*) and so they didn't want to miss the chance to acknowledge the most notable film newcomer of the year.

Oscar leaders also announced a special award for Laurence Olivier, no doubt believing that, given the anti-British bias rampant throughout Hollywood, he and his *Henry V* would lose their bids for Best Actor and Best Picture. Obviously, Olivier thought so, too—he snubbed the awards ceremony and stayed home in Britain, not even bothering to show up for his guaranteed special statuette.

Over the past nine years, voting was done by nearly 10,000 members of the actors', directors' and writers' guilds in addition to members of the film academy. This year balloting was limited to academy members only, which resulted in membership booming from 700 to 1,600. *Variety*

and other showbiz tradepapers were suddenly booming, too—bursting with a record number of campaign ads targeted at those 1,600 judges.

The ads paid off well for independent producer Samuel Goldwyn when *The Best Years of Our Lives* nabbed eight nominations. Scoring seven bids was *The Yearling*, which MGM backed up with print ads plus what *Variety* called "the most ambitious policy in publicizing a motion picture locally via radio." *Variety* surmised that the race for Best Picture was narrowed between those two, although *It's a Wonderful Life* and *The Razor's Edge* joined *Henry V* in the lineup. British films were not considered the frontrunners in any major categories, although they scored an impressive 11 nominations overall, mostly for *Henry V* (four bids) and *Brief Encounter* (three chances).

> With eight Oscar noms, *Best Years* lost only one race.

Among the five contenders for Best Actress, Rosalind Russell (*Sister Kenny*) clearly spent the most on trade ads, but her overall campaign was not as encompassing or strategic as one plotted by a rival.

Olivia de Havilland hadn't worked for two years while she sued her old bosses at Warner Bros. Soon after she won the court case—and her professional freedom—she made two hit films: one for Universal, a thriller called *The Dark Mirror*, and the other a tearjerker for Paramount called *To Each His Own*, which earned her a scroll from the New York Film Critics. De Havilland was desperate to win an Oscar next, not only because it would signal that her career comeback was complete, but because she was still sore about losing the Best Actress trophy to her sister Joan Fontaine in 1941. Late in 1946, de Havilland planned to concentrate on pushing just one of her two new pics, deciding on *To Each His Own* because it featured her in a more sympathetic role. Then she made her shrewdest move of all: she hired the same publicist who finagled the Oscar last year for Joan Crawford.

When de Havilland arrived at the awards gala, she "was easily the belle of the occasion," said *Variety*, "when she swept in on the arm of her new husband, Marcus Goodrich—cane and all—in a bouffant dress of pale blue marquisette over taffeta with a wreath of flowers painted down the side." The gushing reporter added that "she looked like a sweetheart in it, even if (her producer) Charlie Brackett did spill gravy on it at dinner."

The awards venue was switched this year to the Shrine Auditorium, which had 6,000 seats—enough to permit the sale of tickets to the general public for the first time ever. Outside, a crowd of 5,000 onlookers gathered as searchlights swept the sky like "pillars of fire by night," said *Variety*. "Bobby soxer percentage in the street audience was high and the cheers and ovations were almost pure scream. In fact, by the time big name figures began arriving, the audience response was tremolo of tattered tonsils."

Once the ceremony began indoors, host Jack Benny and Oscar leaders began by bestowing the special awards, including the statuette to Harold Russell, who clutched it gratefully in one of the hooks that subbed for his hands. Soon afterward, the gathered crowd was stunned to learn that Russell was also the recipient of the Oscar for Best Supporting Actor. When the audience heard the news, *Variety* reported a rousing ovation that "came from the heart" and noted that the winner was obviously touched deeply, too: "This time the young man was so overcome that he broke down and cried."

Throughout the rest of the night, *The Best Years of Our Lives* continued to sweep, suffering only a single loss—for sound. It claimed kudos for screenplay, music scoring

and editing—plus the director's prize for William Wyler, who'd reaped the same honor for *Mrs. Miniver* in 1942. Another past Oscar champ was honored again when the Best Actor was revealed to be Frederic March, who'd previously won the same award in 1931–32 for *Dr. Jekyll and Mr. Hyde*. The former matinee idol, now 49 years old, was not present to accept it.

The film's producer was certainly on hand to accept his own laurels, though, which included the prizes for Best Picture and the Irving Thalberg Award. *Variety* declared that the success of *The Best Years of Our Lives* resulted in "the best night in all the years of Sam Goldwyn's life."

In the race for Best Supporting Actress, *Variety* reported that "youth won over experience" when Frank Lloyd Wright's 23-year-old granddaughter "finished out in front of four elder entries." It was recent

Large Oscar pix bumped text reports off the front page when *Variety* added photography to its pages during the mid-1940s.

Golden Globe champ Anne Baxter, who was hailed for her role as a wanton drunk in *The Razor's Edge.*

Variety wondered if March's and Baxter's victories might be part of a trend: "Male stars who portrayed souses romped home with top honors. Ray Milland and Jimmie Dunn last year and Fredric March this year. Women tosspots get under the wire such as Anne Baxter."

Variety also wondered, like many other award watchers, about the sad aftermath of the Best Actress race.

Joan Fontaine was asked to present the Best Actor award this year. After dispatching her duties, she waited backstage to congratulate her sister in case she won Best Actress.

Variety reported what happened after Olivia de Havilland prevailed and headed back toward the press room: "In the dark, Olivia didn't seem to recognize her sister and stuck out her hands. When she saw who it was, Olivia drew back, retreated hurriedly, and, turning to her very personal press agent, said, 'I don't know why she does that when she knows how I feel.' The docile flack escorted her into the room where the photographers were waiting. Joan stood looking after her with a bewildered expression and then shrugged her shoulders and walked off."

Post-Oscar coverage the next day was filled with fiery tales of the spat between the sisters.

▪ 1946 ▪

NATIONAL BOARD OF REVIEW

The board declared a best film of the year, then listed its remaining favorites according to highest scores. The vote results were announced on December 18, 1946.

BEST PICTURE
▪ *Henry V*
The Best Years of Our Lives
Brief Encounter
A Walk in the Sun
It Happened at the Inn
My Darling Clementine
The Diary of a Chambermaid
The Killers
Anna and the King of Siam

BEST DIRECTOR
▪ William Wyler, *The Best Years of Our Lives*

BEST ACTOR
▪ Laurence Olivier, *Henry V*

BEST ACTRESS
▪ Anna Magnani, *Open City*

BEST FOREIGN-LANGUAGE FILM
▪ *Open City* (Italy)

NEW YORK FILM CRITICS

Winners were announced on December 30, 1946. Awards were presented on January 9, 1947, at Leone's restaurant in New York. The ceremony was broadcast by ABC radio.

BEST PICTURE
▪ *The Best Years of Our Lives*

BEST DIRECTOR
▪ William Wyler, *The Best Years of Our Lives*

BEST ACTOR
▪ Laurence Olivier, *Henry V*

BEST ACTRESS
▪ Celia Johnson, *Brief Encounter*

BEST FOREIGN FILM
▪ *Open City* (Italy)

GOLDEN GLOBES

Awards were presented on February 26, 1947, at the Hollywood Roosevelt Hotel.

BEST PICTURE
▪ *The Best Years of Our Lives*

BEST PICTURE PROMOTING INTERNATIONAL UNDERSTANDING
- *The Last Chance* (Switzerland)

BEST DIRECTOR
- Frank Capra, *It's a Wonderful Life*

BEST ACTOR
- Gregory Peck, *The Yearling*

BEST ACTRESS
- Rosalind Russell, *Sister Kenny*

BEST SUPPORTING ACTOR
- Clifton Webb, *The Razor's Edge*

BEST SUPPORTING ACTRESS
- Anne Baxter, *The Razor's Edge*

SPECIAL ACHIEVEMENT AWARD
- Harold Russell, *The Best Years of Our Lives* (Most Natural Performance)

ACADEMY AWARDS

Nominations were announced on February 9, 1947. Awards were presented on March 13 at the Shrine Auditorium in Los Angeles. The ceremony was broadcast by ABC radio.

BEST PICTURE
- *The Best Years of Our Lives*
Henry V
It's a Wonderful Life
The Razor's Edge
The Yearling

BEST DIRECTOR
- William Wyler, *The Best Years of Our Lives*
Clarence Brown, *The Yearling*
Frank Capra, *It's a Wonderful Life*
David Lean, *Brief Encounter*
Robert Siodmak, *The Killers*

BEST ACTOR
- Fredric March, *The Best Years of Our Lives*
Laurence Olivier, *Henry V*
Larry Parks, *The Jolson Story*
Gregory Peck, *The Yearling*
James Stewart, *It's a Wonderful Life*

BEST ACTRESS
- Olivia de Havilland, *To Each His Own*
Celia Johnson, *Brief Encounter*
Jennifer Jones, *Duel in the Sun*
Rosalind Russell, *Sister Kenny*
Jane Wyman, *The Yearling*

BEST SUPPORTING ACTOR
- Harold Russell, *The Best Years of Our Lives*
Charles Coburn, *The Green Years*
William Demarest, *The Jolson Story*
Claude Rains, *Notorious*
Clifton Webb, *The Razor's Edge*

BEST SUPPORTING ACTRESS
- Anne Baxter, *The Razor's Edge*
Ethel Barrymore, *The Spiral Staircase*
Lillian Gish, *Duel in the Sun*
Flora Robson, *Saratoga Trunk*
Gale Sondergaard, *Anna and the King of Siam*

BEST WRITING (ORIGINAL STORY)
- Clemence Dane, *Vacation from Marriage*
Charles Brackett, *To Each His Own*
Jack Patrick, *The Strange Love of Martha Ivers*
Vladimir Pozner, *The Dark Mirror*
Victor Trivas, *The Stranger*

BEST WRITING (ORIGINAL SCREENPLAY)
- Muriel Box, Sydney Box, *The Seventh Veil*
Raymond Chandler, *The Blue Dahlia*
Melvin Frank, Norman Panama, *Road to Utopia*
Ben Hecht, *Notorious*
Jacques Prevert, *Children of Paradise*

BEST WRITING (SCREENPLAY)
- Robert E. Sherwood, *The Best Years of Our Lives*
Sergio Amidei, Federico Fellini, *Open City*
Sally Benson, Talbot Jennings, *Anna and the King of Siam*
Anthony Havelock-Allan, David Lean, Ronald Neame, *Brief Encounter*
Anthony Veiller, *The Killers*

BEST SONG
- "On the Atchison, Topeka and the Santa Fe," *The Harvey Girls*, Johnny Mercer, Harry Warren

"All Through the Day," *Centennial Summer*, Oscar Hammerstein II, Jerome Kern
"I Can't Begin to Tell You," *The Dolly Sisters*, Mack Gordon, James Monaco
"Ole Buttermilk Sky," *Canyon Passage*, Jack Brooks, Hoagy Carmichael
"You Keep Coming Back Like a Song," *Blue Skies*, Irving Berlin

Winners

BEST ART DIRECTION/ INTERIOR DECORATION
(BLACK AND WHITE)
- William Darling, Lyle Wheeler, Thomas Little, Frank E. Hughes, *Anna and the King of Siam*

(COLOR)
- Cedric Gibbons, Paul Groesse, Edwin B. Willis, *The Yearling*

BEST CINEMATOGRAPHY
(BLACK AND WHITE)
- Arthur Miller, *Anna and the King of Siam*

(COLOR)
- Arthur Arling, Charles Rosher, Leonard Smith, *The Yearling*

BEST DOCUMENTARY (SHORT SUBJECT)
- *Seeds of Destiny*, U.S. Department of War

BEST FILM EDITING
- Daniel Mandell, *The Best Years of Our Lives*

BEST MUSIC
(SCORING OF A DRAMATIC OR COMEDY PICTURE)
- Hugo Friedhofer, *The Best Years of Our Lives*

(SCORING OF A MUSICAL PICTURE)
- Morris Stoloff, *The Jolson Story*

SCIENTIFIC OR TECHNICAL AWARDS
Class III (Certificate)
- Harlan L. Baumbach, Paramount West Coast Laboratory; Herbert E. Britt; Burton F. Miller, Warner Bros. Studio Sound Department; Carl Faulkner, Twentieth Century-Fox; Mole-Richardson Co.; Arthur F. Blinn, Robert O. Cook, C. O. Slyfield, Walt Disney Studio Sound Dept.; Burton F. Miller, Warner Bros. Studio Sound Dept.; Marty Martin, Hal Adkins, RKO Radio Studio Miniature Department; Harold Nye, Warner Bros. Studio Electrical Department

BEST SHORT SUBJECT
(CARTOON)
- *The Cat Concerto*

(ONE REEL)
- *Facing Your Danger*

(TWO REEL)
- *A Boy and His Dog*

BEST SOUND RECORDING
- John Livadary, *The Jolson Story*

BEST SPECIAL EFFECTS
- Thomas Howard, *Blithe Spirit*

IRVING G. THALBERG MEMORIAL AWARD
- Samuel Goldwyn

SPECIAL AWARDS
- Claude Jarman, Jr.
- Ernst Lubitsch
- Laurence Olivier, *Henry V*
- Harold Russell, *The Best Years of Our Lives*

· 1947 ·

Three Kudos Agree on Gentleman's Agreement

The rebellious National Board of Review continued its snub of Hollywood studio pix that began in 1945 and would continue until 1950. The group declared 1947's Best Picture to be *Monsieur Verdoux*, Charlie Chaplin's b.o. bomb about "a modern Parisian Bluebeard who has been driven to marrying and murdering middling mesdames in order to provide for his ailing wife and their son of 10 years' marriage," said *Variety*. The board eschewed Yankee stars, too, preferring British thesps in screen adaptations of stage hits: Best Actor Michael Redgrave in Eugene O'Neill's *Mourning Becomes Electra* and Best Actress Celia Johnson in Noel Coward's *This Happy Breed*.

Variety called N.Y. crix, Globe and Oscar Best Picture *Gentleman's Agreement* a "vital and stirring film."

The board released four lists of the year's Top 10 movies: choices made by its student committee, local movie councils nationwide, its review panel and its Committee on Exceptional Motion Pictures. Only one pic appeared on all four lists: director David Lean's retelling of the Charles Dickens classic *Great Expectations*, which *New York Times* critic Bosley Crowther hailed as one of the truly great films of all time. "We can't think of many pictures much better than *Great Expectations* that have been made," Crowther crowed.

But after this year's conclave of the New York Film Critics, Crowther pouted shamelessly in the pages of the *Times* when reporting that *Great Expectations* lost Best Picture "by the slim margin of two votes"— a score of nine to seven on the sixth ballot. It was defeated by *Gentleman's Agreement*, which *Variety* praised as a "vital and stirring" film about "a writer who poses as a Jew to write a magazine series on anti-Semitism." Elia Kazan won Best Director for both *Gentleman's Agreement* and *Boomerang!*, a thriller about a man wrongly accused of murdering a minister. Kazan triumphed on the sixth round by a tally of 11 to 3 over Edward Dymtryk, director of *Crossfire*, another Hollywood pic exposing anti-Semitism and a recent co-winner of the Grand Prix prize at the Cannes Film Festival. *Crossfire*'s chances for further kudos would be resurrected at the Oscars where it would become a cause célèbre.

The critics needed a half-dozen ballots to decide on Best Actor, too. William Powell (*Life with Father, The Senator Was Indiscreet*) led during the first election with six votes, followed by three each for Gregory Peck (*Gentleman's Agreement, The Yearling*), Robert Ryan (*Crossfire*) and John Garfield (*Body and Soul, Gentleman's Agreement*). When Powell finally nabbed endorsements from 10 of 16 crix present, his only remaining rival was Garfield.

Civility reigned among the journos when deciding the equivalent palms for lead female thesp. The *Times*'s Crowther proudly proclaimed that he was part of "the overwhelming vote for Deborah Kerr as the year's Best Actress for her performances in the British pictures *Black Narcissus* and *The Adventuress*." He reported that she "swept to victory" by reaping the necessary two-thirds vote on the second polling when 12 crix embraced her. All other award races this year, by comparison, were dragged out to the sixth ballot, when a simple majority vote could break previous deadlocks.

Although Kerr was such a popular and easy choice for the critics, the British-born star would soon be passed over by the foreign journalists voting on Hollywood's Golden Globes—and she wouldn't be nominated at the Oscars.

For the most part the foreign press again preferred American fare. *Gentleman's Agreement* took the Globes for Best Picture, Best Director Elia Kazan and Best Supporting Actress Celeste Holm. New prizes were added for Most Promising Newcomer, Male (Richard Widmark, "an acting sensation as a dim-wit, blood-lusty killer" in *Kiss of Death*, said *Variety*) and female (Canadian-born Lois Maxwell, who would soon leave Hollywood after starring in only six films, including the critically panned *That Hagen Girl*, but return triumphantly later in life as Miss Moneypenny in 13 James Bond pics).

Two Brits managed to reap honors nonetheless. The laurels for Best Supporting Actor went to a former stage thesp discovered by playwright George Bernard Shaw, Edmund Gwenn, who became a breakout screen star this year when he went all the way to the U.S. Supreme Court to prove that he was Santa Claus in *Miracle on 34th Street*. Hedda Hopper certainly believed in him: she touted him heavily in her column for an Oscar.

The Globes' Best Actor was a 56-year-old, British-born performer who was not among the six candidates considered by the New York Film Critics for their equivalent accolade. Ronald Colman wasn't easy to overlook: he was celebrating his 25th year in showbiz and capped it off with a Golden Globe for *A Double Life*, in which he portrayed an actor playing Othello who goes mad while confusing real life with his stage

life. *Variety* heralded his perf as "flawless—a histrionic gem of unusual versatility."

Last year's Best Actress champ returned for another Globe: Rosalind Russell (*Mourning Becomes Electra*), who joined Colman and *Gentleman's Agreement* producer Darryl F. Zanuck at the Hollywood Roosevelt Hotel 10 days before the Oscars. Last year Russell outspent all other nominees when buying "For Your Consideration" ads in the trades for the Academy Awards race—then lost to Olivia de Havilland. This year she mounted an even more aggressive ad push and hired the same publicist who had handled the successful Oscar campaigns of de Havilland and, the year before that, Joan Crawford.

Prospects looked excellent for Russell when Oscar night came, at least according to a controversial new straw poll *Variety* conducted that canvassed 13 percent of the academy's membership. The results ("obtained by reporters in days of painstaking work," the paper boasted) sized up the Best Actress race thus: Russell was far ahead in first place, followed by Dorothy McGuire (*Gentleman's Agreement*), Susan Hayward (*Smash Up*), Loretta Young (*The Farmer's Daughter*) and Joan Crawford (*Possessed*). At least one Las Vegas casino was betting on Russell, too.

Young was probably aware of *Variety*'s forecast that she was going to lose, but the veteran Hollywood trouper proved to be a good sport as she hobnobbed in front of the Shrine Auditorium before the ceremony with front-runner Russell. The two of them braved freezing winds in their low-slung gowns as they warmed up the spirits of thousands of ogling fans, many shivering under shared blankets. "The color that goes with this top Hollywood event was strictly chilblain purple," said *Variety*, but Loretta Young wore a green taffeta dress, which inspired one bystander to shout to another, "There goes her chances for an award. Green is an unlucky color!' "

> ## Great Expectations lost the crix's top prize by just two votes.

Most everyone agreed that Oscar night would prove to be lucky for *Gentleman's Agreement*. It led with the most noms (eight) and *Variety* pegged it to win top pic, director and supporting actress (Celeste Holm). Producer Darryl F. Zanuck had left nothing to chance this time, after having lost his previous Oscar bouts for *Wilson* in 1944 and *The Razor's Edge* in 1946. He premiered *Gentleman's Agreement* in November in New York, gathered up the best reviews, plastered endorsement quotes ("Expect this masterpiece to win the Academy Oscar," said *The New York Mirror*) all over ads in *Variety* and *The Los Angeles Times*, and then—after one month of unflagging buildup—unveiled the pic at Christmastime in Hollywood.

Gentleman's Agreement competed for Best Picture against *Great Expectations* (three nominations), *The Bishop's Wife* (toplined by Loretta Young—five bids) and *Miracle on 34th Street* (three chances). *Miracle's* Edmund Gwenn was set to win Best Supporting Actor, according to *Variety's* poll, which also predicted a great night for Ronald Colman.

Loretta Young's "dazzling" Oscar upset took *Variety* by surprise.

Among the nominations that shocked some award watchers were the deuce for *Crossfire*—to Adrian Scott as producer of the Best Picture contender, and to helmer Edward Dmytryk. Both men were suspected of being Communists and recently had been denounced in Congress for refusing to testify before the House Un-American Activities Committee. A few days afterward, the 2 members of the Hollywood 10 were fired by the RKO studio. Eleven weeks later, they got encouraging votes of support from their peers when they were nommed for Oscars, which they'd lose.

The Oscar for Best Picture went, as predicted, to *Gentleman's Agreement*, although producer Zanuck was considered less than a gentleman for the way he accepted the honor. He started off graciously enough, thanking the movie's creative team, then, as *Variety* put it, "created something of a sen-

sation" when he "assured the audience that he is 'still trying' and that 'this award will make up for previous disappointments,' specifically recalling that they had failed to give him an Oscar for *Wilson*."

Gentleman's Agreement's Best Director Elia Kazan played his scene humbly, saying, "I guess, being a comparative newcomer to the industry, I'm more grateful than most for the help that I needed and received."

Best Supporting Actress champ Celeste Holm was also a relative newcomer, having come, just like Kazan, from the New York theater scene. *Gentleman's Agreement* was only her third film after having gained fame for her legit role as Ado Annie in *Oklahoma!* In her acceptance speech, she said, "I'm happy to be part of an industry that can create so much understanding in a world that needs it so much."

In the race for Best Supporting Actor, *Variety* reported, "Christmas, a bit late, came to Edmund Gwenn in the form of a non-whiskered Oscar for ringing the jingle bells in *Miracle on 34th Street*. Amid applause that could be heard from here to Macy's, Edmund admitted that he believed in Santa Claus. The jolly old rascal." The Santa star turned out to be a popular choice with female Oscar attendees. Hours after the ceremony, a *Variety* reporter noticed that the domed-topped thesp had six flame-red lipstick prints smeared on his bald head.

All of *Variety*'s early award predictions appeared to be coming true throughout the night, even its risky call that Ronald Colman would surpass the hugely popular Gregory Peck (*Gentleman's Agreement*) and finally catch up with the Oscar he lost in 1929–30 for *Bulldog Drummond* and *Condemned* and in 1942 for *Random Harvest*. When Colman finally held the statuette in his grasp, he said, "I am very happy and very proud and very lucky."

"Right up to the final Oscar hand-out everything went pretty much according to the best-authenticated advance predictions," *Variety* observed. "Then came the quick switch. They put a surprise ending on the Academy Award Show."

Last year's Best Actor champ prepared to reveal the winner of the last award of the night when, *Variety* added, "In the rear rows, some of the attendees were beginning to file, not too quietly, toward the nearest exit as March ripped open the envelope containing the name of the Best Actress. As he shouted, 'The winner is . . . ' there was no halt in the exodus. Then the name came through . . . 'Loretta Young.'

"It was a right blustery, windy night outside, but the gasp that arose from the audience when Miss Young's name was read by Fredric March just about matched the heaviest gusts whipping around the Shrine Auditorium. Up to the moment when she was announced and headed for the stage to accept the Oscar, consensus of opinion had had Rosalind Russell set for the honor on the strength of her role in *Mourning Becomes Electra.*" Given the hefty dramatic weight of Russell's role, it seemed doubly shocking that she was defeated by Young's light and breezy turn as a Minnesota country girl who starts out as a Congressman's maid and ends up as a member of Congress. In its review of *The Farmer's Daughter, Variety* had cheered Young's work with one qualification: "Difficulty with the Swedish accent, which occasionally collapses into straight Americanese, is the only flaw in Young's performance."

When Young got to the Oscar stage, she examined the winner's envelope to make sure that there hadn't been a mistake.

The 34-year-old native of Salt Lake City had been making movies for 20 years and now obviously appreciated her belated acknowledgment. "Up to now, this occasion has been for me a spectator sport," she said. "When I first came to Hollywood 150 years ago, I wanted one of these."

After she took her bow, *Variety* noticed,

Oscar champs (from left) Darryl F. Zanuck, Edmund Gwenn, Lorretta Young, Ronald Colman and Celeste Holm pose together for photos backstage at the Shrine Auditorium.

"The blood was racing so wildly when she walked off the stage with the unexpected Oscar in her hands, the diamond necklace around her throat was moving up and down in a trinkling sort of rhythm."

Onlookers were also rattled by the biggest upset in Oscar's 20-year history. *Variety* added: "The wise boys were jolted out of their seats when Loretta was announced as the winnah and the new champeen. To hear their post-mortems, it was something like a 100-to-1 shot running away with a Hunnert Grand."

But how did she do it? Many post-Oscar pundits said that it was the handiwork of RKO's new production chief Dore Schary, who threw the studio's considerable weight behind Young since *The Farmer's Daughter* was produced during his new tenure. RKO's *Mourning Becomes Electra* was snubbed because it was overseen by the previous corporate regime.

Variety called Young's victory "a dazzling climax to an otherwise unexciting show" and refused to apologize for calling the actress category incorrectly: "It wasn't as pure as Ivory Soap, but *Daily Variety*'s poll on the six leading Academy Awards proved 83 one-third percent correct."

NATIONAL BOARD OF REVIEW

The board declared a best film of the year, then listed its remaining favorites according to highest scores. No award was bestowed for foreign films. The vote results were announced on December 19, 1947.

BEST PICTURE
■ *Monsieur Verdoux*
Great Expectations
Shoeshine
Crossfire
Boomerang!
Odd Man Out
Gentleman's Agreement
To Live in Peace
It's a Wonderful Life
The Overlanders

BEST DIRECTOR
■ Elia Kazan, *Gentleman's Agreement, Boomerang!*

BEST ACTOR
■ Michael Redgrave, *Mourning Becomes Electra*

BEST ACTRESS
■ Celia Johnson, *This Happy Breed*

NEW YORK FILM CRITICS

Winners were announced on December 29, 1947. Awards were presented on January 19, 1948, at Leone's restaurant in New York.

BEST PICTURE
■ *Gentleman's Agreement*

BEST DIRECTOR
■ Elia Kazan, *Gentleman's Agreement, Boomerang!*

BEST ACTOR
■ William Powell, *Life with Father, The Senator Was Indiscreet*

BEST ACTRESS
■ Deborah Kerr, *Black Narcissus, The Adventuress*

BEST FOREIGN FILM
■ *To Live in Peace* (Italy)

GOLDEN GLOBES

Awards were presented on March 10, 1948, at the Hollywood Roosevelt Hotel.

BEST PICTURE
■ *Gentleman's Agreement*

BEST DIRECTOR
■ Elia Kazan, *Gentleman's Agreement*

BEST ACTOR
■ Ronald Colman, *A Double Life*

BEST ACTRESS
■ Rosalind Russell, *Mourning Becomes Electra*

BEST SUPPORTING ACTOR
■ Edmund Gwenn, *Miracle on 34th Street*

BEST SUPPORTING ACTRESS
■ Celeste Holm, *Gentleman's Agreement*

NEW MALE STAR OF THE YEAR
■ Richard Widmark, *Kiss of Death*

NEW FEMALE STAR OF THE YEAR
■ Lois Maxwell, *That Hagen Girl*

BEST SCREENPLAY
■ George Seaton, *Miracle on 34th Street*

BEST CINEMATOGRAPHY
■ Jack Cardiff, *Black Narcissus*

BEST MUSIC SCORE
■ Max Steiner, *Life with Father*

SPECIAL ACHIEVEMENT AWARDS
■ Walt Disney (Hindustani version of *Bambi*)
■ Dean Stockwell, *Gentleman's Agreement* (Best Juvenile)

ACADEMY AWARDS

Nominations were announced on February 15, 1948. Awards were presented on March 20 at the Shrine Auditorium in Los Angeles. The ceremony was broadcast by ABC radio.

BEST PICTURE
- *Gentleman's Agreement*
The Bishop's Wife
Crossfire
Great Expectations
Miracle on 34th Street

BEST DIRECTOR
- Elia Kazan, *Gentleman's Agreement*
George Cukor, *A Double Life*
Edward Dmytryk, *Crossfire*
Henry Koster, *The Bishop's Wife*
David Lean, *Great Expectations*

BEST ACTOR
- Ronald Colman, *A Double Life*
John Garfield, *Body and Soul*
Gregory Peck, *Gentleman's Agreement*
William Powell, *Life with Father*
Michael Redgrave, *Mourning Becomes Electra*

BEST ACTRESS
- Loretta Young, *The Farmer's Daughter*
Joan Crawford, *Possessed*
Susan Hayward, *Smash-Up*
Dorothy McGuire, *Gentleman's Agreement*
Rosalind Russell, *Mourning Becomes Electra*

BEST SUPPORTING ACTOR
- Edmund Gwenn, *Miracle on 34th Street*
Charles Bickford, *The Farmer's Daughter*
Thomas Gomez, *Ride the Pink Horse*
Robert Ryan, *Crossfire*
Richard Widmark, *Kiss of Death*

BEST SUPPORTING ACTRESS
- Celeste Holm, *Gentleman's Agreement*
Ethel Barrymore, *The Paradine Case*
Gloria Grahame, *Crossfire*
Marjorie Main, *The Egg and I*
Anne Revere, *Gentleman's Agreement*

BEST WRITING (ORIGINAL STORY)
- Valentine Davies, *Miracle on 34th Street*
Frank Cavett, Dorothy Parker, *Smash-Up*
Georges Chaperot, Rene Wheeler, *A Cage of Nightingales*
Herbert Clyde Lewis, Frederick Stephani, *It Happened on Fifth Avenue*
Eleazar Lipsky, *Kiss of Death*

BEST WRITING (ORIGINAL SCREENPLAY)
- Sidney Sheldon, *The Bachelor and the Bobby-Soxer*
Sergio Amidei, Adolfo Franci, C. G. Viola, Cesare Zavattini, *Shoe-Shine*
Charles Chaplin, *Monsieur Verdoux*
Ruth Gordon, Garson Kanin, *A Double Life*
Abraham Polonsky, *Body and Soul*

BEST WRITING (SCREENPLAY)
- George Seaton, *Miracle on 34th Street*
Moss Hart, *Gentleman's Agreement*
Anthony Havelock-Allan, David Lean, Ronald Neame, *Great Expectations*
Richard Murphy, *Boomerang!*
John Paxton, *Crossfire*

BEST SONG
- "Zip-A-Dee-Doo-Dah," *Song of the South*, Ray Gilbert, Allie Wrubel
"A Gal in Calico," *The Time, the Place and the Girl*, Leo Robin, Arthur Schwartz
"I Wish I Didn't Love You So," *The Perils of Pauline*, Frank Loesser
"Pass That Peace Pipe," *Good News*, Ralph Blane, Roger Edens, Hugh Martin
"You Do," *Mother Wore Tights*, Mack Gordon, Josef Myrow

Winners

BEST ART DIRECTION/SET DECORATION
(BLACK AND WHITE)
- John Bryan, Wilfred Shingleton, *Great Expectations*
(COLOR)
- Alfred Junge, *Black Narcissus*

BEST CINEMATOGRAPHY
(BLACK AND WHITE)
- Guy Green, *Great Expectations*

(COLOR)
- Jack Cardiff, *Black Narcissus*

BEST DOCUMENTARY
(FEATURE)
- *Design for Death,* Richard O. Fleischer, Sid Rogell, Theron Warth

(SHORT SUBJECT)
- *First Steps,* United Nations Division of Films and Visual Information

BEST FILM EDITING
- Francis Lyon, Robert Parrish, *Body and Soul*

BEST MUSIC
(SCORING OF A DRAMATIC OR COMEDY PICTURE)
- Dr. Miklos Rozsa, *A Double Life*

(SCORING OF A MUSICAL PICTURE)
- Alfred Newman, *Mother Wore Tights*

SCIENTIFIC OR TECHNICAL AWARDS
Class II (Plaque)
- C. R. Daily, Paramount Studio Film Laboratory; C. C. Davis, Western Electric

Class III (Certificate)
- Nathan Levinson, Warner Bros. Studio Sound Department; Farciot Edouart, C. R. Daily, Hal Corl, H. G. Cartwright, Paramount Studio Transparency and Engineering Departments; Fred Ponedel, Warner Bros. Studio Sound Department; Kurt Singer, RCA-Victor; James Gibbons, Warner Bros. Studio

BEST SHORT SUBJECT
(CARTOON)
- *Tweetie Pie*

(ONE REEL)
- *Good-Bye Miss Turlock*

(TWO REEL)
- *Climbing the Matterhorn*

BEST SOUND RECORDING
- Gordon Sawyer, *The Bishop's Wife*

BEST SPECIAL EFFECTS
- A. Arnold Gillespie, Warren Newcombe, Douglas Shearer, Michael Steinore, *Green Dolphin Street*

SPECIAL AWARDS
- James Baskett
- *Bill and Coo*
- *Shoe-Shine*
- Col. William N. Selig, Albert E. Smith, Thomas Armat, George K. Spoor

To Be Best Picture or Not to Be

Yankee and British troops teamed up to rout the Nazis from Italy in Roberto Rossellini's *Paisan*, the National Board of Review's surprising choice for Best Picture. The win wasn't startling because the Italian art house hit was unworthy—the New York Film Critics would soon name it Best Foreign Film—but because its victory in a category once ruled by U.S. fare was one more volley in an off-shore assault on Hollywood that would not stop there.

At the awards showdowns to follow, the U.K. and U.S. would square off against each other, pitting a lofty Shakespeare classic against a scruffy Yankee oater. Over the past two years, the New York Film Critics, Golden Globes and Oscars all agreed on one U.S. pic as the year's best. This year the Anglo-Yankee tension would cause a split vote.

England's $2 million production of *Hamlet* was an unlikely b.o. smash in the United States, but with good reason. "This is picture-making at its best," *Variety* cheered. "Star-producer-director Laurence Olivier was the driving force behind the whole venture." It competed against a b.o. flop, *The Treasure of the Sierra Madre*, which *Variety* hailed as a "standout film" starring Humphrey Bogart, Tim Holt and Walter Huston as "gold prospectors who start out for pay dirt in the Mexican mountains as buddies, but wind up in a murderous tangle."

When the two films tangled at the New York Film Critics powwow held at the newspaper guild's office off Times Square in late December, *Hamlet* led *Treasure* eight votes to five, but needed a two-thirds majority in order to be named Best Picture by the 18 crix present. After five rounds, the rivals were tied with eight endorsements each. *The Snake Pit* held the other two. On the

N.Y. crix's surprising choice for best pic, *Treasure of the Sierra Madre,* starred Humphrey Bogart (center) and Walter Huston (right).

sixth tally a winner could finally be declared by one film claiming the most votes, and it was then that *Hamlet* suffered a tragic end and *Treasure* hit the jackpot.

Treasure's John Huston also edged *Hamlet*'s Olivier for Best Director, but Olivier fended off Huston's father Walter for the Best Actor laurel, an honor the latter had snagged earlier from the National Board of Review. "Although Walter Huston's performance is a rare and flavored piece of character acting, it isn't quite up to the Olivier job," *The New York Times* insisted. Both voting groups honored the same Best Actress: Olivia de Havilland. "The esteem in which the critics held Miss de Havilland's performance as the mentally disturbed heroine of *The Snake Pit* was evidenced by the actress' unanimous victory on the first ballot," reported the *Times*. Only once before had all the crix backed one candidate on the first voting round—*The Informer*, Best Picture champ of 1935.

Otis L. Guernsey, Jr., of the *Herald Tribune* groused later in print about a star overlooked for Best Actress: "Not mentioned in this unanimous opinion was Jane Wyman's sensitive achievement as the deaf and dumb girl in *Johnny Belinda*. It was equal in artistry with Miss de Havilland's performance, but the role did not demand quite so much volume and variety of its star." Eight months later, de Havilland would claim the additional laurel of Best Actress at the Venice film fest.

"New York's movie critics went Hollywood" this year, said the *Herald Tribune*. "Not only did they make the affair a public one for the first time, but they held it in Radio City Music Hall, largest movie house in the country." Hundreds of the hall's reserved seats sold out a week earlier so that film fans could "see, hear and applaud celebrities and tolerate critics," added the paper. Winners Olivia de Havilland, John and Walter Huston and Roberto Rossellini were present, but Olivier was not. "His crisp, British expression of gratitude came by way of a London broadcast recording and was distributed through the theater's loudspeaker system," observed the *Herald Tribune*.

In recent years, members of the Hollywood Foreign Correspondents Association showed strong preferences for American work when bestowing the Golden Globes. That occurred again when Shakespeare's tale of the Prince of Denmark reigned only in the actor category. Proof that the film wasn't a contender for Best Picture came when *The Treasure of the Sierra Madre* tied with *Johnny Belinda*, Warner Brothers' top grosser of the year. *Belinda* star Jane Wyman pulled off an upset in the actress race, too, for a perf *Variety* called "a socko demonstration that an artist can shape a mood and sway an audience through projected emotions without a spoken word."

Wyman was on hand to accept her Golden Globe statuette, while Douglas Fairbanks, Jr., stood in for the absent Laurence Olivier when 150 celebrants met at the Hollywood Roosevelt Hotel one week before the Academy Awards.

The Globes turned into a family affair when both Hustons prevailed: John for best megger and Walter for best supporting thesp. Everyone wondered: could they do it again at the Oscars?

At the Oscars, *Variety* reported "many expressions of distaste for British films" because of a general belief that "English film tycoons have hurt the foreign market for American pictures." That wasn't evidenced in the nominations. *Hamlet* entered the awards battle for Best Picture grandly astride a British ally—the ballet fable *The Red Shoes*, which competed against *Johnny Belinda*, *The Snake Pit* and *The Treasure of the Sierra Madre*.

Execs from three studios (Columbia, Republic and Universal) were so outraged by Britain's hefty showing that they withdrew their usual funding from the Oscar show and stayed home on awards night. Having less money to spend, Oscar leaders couldn't afford the 6,000-seat Shrine Auditorium. They moved the ceremony to the smallish Academy Theatre ("The audience was a mere 950," observed *Variety*) and seemed unruffled by the threat that Britannia might actually rule. After all, *Johnny Belinda* had a comfortable lead with 12 noms, twice the number of *Hamlet*, and *Variety*'s poll predicted it would win Best Picture. Any upset was expected to come from *Treasure* mining Oscar gold on the sly.

Yankee optimism prevailed early on during awards night when the Johnny Green Orchestra opened the gala with a rousing rendition of "The Star-Spangled Banner."

Treasure did well throughout the night, with John Huston claiming the 18-karat statuettes for directing and writing, just as *Variety* forecast. When his father won Best

> ## The Golden Globes were a family affair for the Hustons.

Supporting Actor for his role as a feisty sourdough, *Variety* observed, "The crowd seemed excessively delighted that father and son had scored so heavily."

While accepting the honor, the senior Huston said, "Many years ago, I raised a son and I said to him, 'If you ever become a writer or a director, please find a good part for your ole man.'"

Variety was right on that count, too, as it also was when Claire Trevor was honored for her supporting role as a boozy floozy in *Key Largo*. Proving that she's a savvy thesp in reality, she "topped Huston the elder," *Variety* claimed, when she said at the podium, "I have three boys and I hope they grow up to be writers or directors so that they can give their old lady a part."

"Interest this year will rest primarily in the Best Actress award," *Variety* promised prior to awards night. Olivia de Havilland might have won the New York Film Critics vote unanimously on the first ballot, but she faced a strong challenge at the Oscars from Jane Wyman, who could count on a strong sympathy vote after her divorce from Ronald Reagan and the death of their premature baby. When Wyman won for portraying a deaf mute, she said, "I accept this very gratefully for keeping my mouth shut for once. I think I will do it again."

"Olivier appears to be tops among the candidates for Best Actor," *Variety* foresaw, but when his name was announced as winner on awards night, he was in far-off London appearing on stage with his Oscar-winning wife, Vivien Leigh, in *The School for Scandal.*

In all, *Hamlet* claimed four Oscars, including kudos for art direction, costume design and the final trophy that gave the night what *Variety* called its "surprise ending."

When presenter Ethel Barrymore revealed that *Hamlet* had won Best Picture, *Variety* reported, "The gasp that went up

The directors' and writers' guilds debuted their own awards.

was very similar to the one that greeted Loretta Young, last year's dark horse."

The Red Shoes nabbed two crafts trophies, giving the U.K. more total prizes than any Hollywood studio. "So the British ran away with the most awards," *Variety* shrugged afterward. Even though the trade-paper called the top award wrong, it was still pleased that it did "not need to join Gallup, Roper and Crossley at the weeping wall . . . Anyhow, you can't go broke picking six of seven winners."

Two months after the Academy Awards, the Screen Directors Guild of America unveiled its own peer-group awards. The helmer's group had named quarterly winners throughout the past year and now met to proclaim the year's top megger in the same place where the Oscars held its first awards gala: the Hollywood Roosevelt Hotel.

On hand were such studio chiefs as Twentieth Century-Fox's Darryl F. Zanuck. ("Louis B. Mayer reported ill with virus infection," said the *L.A. Times.*) Contemporary press reports disagree on the actual prize—one says "a large medallion," while another describes a gold plaque—which was bestowed by group prexy George Marshall to Joseph L. Mankiewicz (elected vice-president after the dinner) for *A Letter to Three Wives,* released in early 1949 and topping such 1948 pics as Fred Zinnemann's *The Search.* The late release of Mankiewicz's pic made it eligible for next year's Oscar derby—where it would run a deft race.

One month later, the Screen Writers Guild of America followed suit, inaugurating a new award, too. The initial prizes went to the scribes behind *Easter Parade* (Best Musical), *The Treasure of the Sierra Madre* (Best Western) and *The Snake Pit* (Best Written Drama and kudos for being the Screenplay Dealing Most Ably with Problems of the American Scene). Presiding over the event as "chairman of the day" was the president of the Academy of Motion

Picture Arts and Sciences, Charles Brackett, who was also a writer nominated three times for the new guild honors (for *Miss Tatlock's Millions, A Foreign Affair* and *The Emperor Waltz*). *Variety* noted that in his speech, Brackett "described the lack of press and public recognition for the literary craft, blaming it in part on the writers themselves for making jokes about their profession."

The tradepaper described the gala: "Affair had a garden-party air as the awards were handed out at the edge of the Bel-Air blue oval swimming pool while attending writers and their guests small-talked, sipped cocktails and nibbled hors d'oeuvres. The social aspects of the affair often intruded on the more dignified presentations and made it difficult for the guest speakers to be audible to those interested in the awards."

▪ 1948 ▪

NATIONAL BOARD OF REVIEW

The board declared a best film of the year, then listed its remaining favorites according to highest scores. No award was bestowed for foreign films. The vote results were announced on December 21, 1948.

BEST PICTURE
- *Paisan*
Day of Wrath
The Search
The Treasure of the Sierra Madre
Louisiana Story
Hamlet
The Snake Pit
Johnny Belinda
Joan of Arc
The Red Shoes

BEST DIRECTOR
- Roberto Rossellini, *Paisan*

BEST ACTOR
- Walter Huston, *The Treasure of the Sierra Madre*

BEST ACTRESS
- Olivia de Havilland, *The Snake Pit*

BEST SCREENPLAY
- John Huston, *The Treasure of the Sierra Madre*

NEW YORK FILM CRITICS

Winners were announced on December 28, 1948. Awards were presented on January 21, 1949, at Radio City Music Hall in New York.

BEST PICTURE
- *The Treasure of the Sierra Madre*

BEST DIRECTOR
- John Huston, *The Treasure of the Sierra Madre*

BEST ACTOR
- Laurence Olivier, *Hamlet*

BEST ACTRESS
- Olivia de Havilland, *The Snake Pit*

BEST FOREIGN FILM
- *Paisan* (Italy)

GOLDEN GLOBES

Awards were presented on March 16, 1949, at the Hollywood Roosevelt Hotel.

BEST PICTURE (TIE)
- *Johnny Belinda*
- *The Treasure of the Sierra Madre*

BEST PICTURE PROMOTING INTERNATIONAL UNDERSTANDING
- *The Search*

BEST DIRECTOR
- John Huston, *The Treasure of the Sierra Madre*

BEST ACTOR
- Laurence Olivier, *Hamlet*

BEST ACTRESS
- Jane Wyman, *Johnny Belinda*

BEST SUPPORTING ACTOR
- Walter Huston, *The Treasure of the Sierra Madre*

BEST SUPPORTING ACTRESS
- Ellen Corby, *I Remember Mama*

BEST SCREENPLAY
- Richard Schweizer, *The Search*

BEST CINEMATOGRAPHY
- Gabriel Figueroa, *The Pearl*

BEST ORIGINAL SCORE
- Brian Easdale, *The Red Shoes*

SPECIAL ACHIEVEMENT AWARD
- Ivan Jandl, *The Search* (Best Juvenile)

ACADEMY AWARDS

Nominations were announced on February 10, 1949. Awards were presented on March 24 at the Academy Theater in Hollywood.

BEST PICTURE
- *Hamlet*
Johnny Belinda
The Red Shoes
The Snake Pit
The Treasure of the Sierra Madre

BEST DIRECTOR
- John Huston, *The Treasure of the Sierra Madre*
Anatole Litvak, *The Snake Pit*
Jean Negulesco, *Johnny Belinda*
Laurence Olivier, *Hamlet*
Fred Zinnemann, *The Search*

BEST ACTOR
- Laurence Olivier, *Hamlet*
Lew Ayres, *Johnny Belinda*
Montgomery Clift, *The Search*
Dan Dailey, *When My Baby Smiles at Me*
Clifton Webb, *Sitting Pretty*

BEST ACTRESS
- Jane Wyman, *Johnny Belinda*

Ingrid Bergman, *Joan of Arc*
Olivia de Havilland, *The Snake Pit*
Irene Dunne, *I Remember Mama*
Barbara Stanwyck, *Sorry, Wrong Number*

BEST SUPPORTING ACTOR
- Walter Huston, *The Treasure of the Sierra Madre*
Charles Bickford, *Johnny Belinda*
José Ferrer, *Joan of Arc*
Oscar Homolka, *I Remember Mama*
Cecil Kellaway, *The Luck of the Irish*

BEST SUPPORTING ACTRESS
- Claire Trevor, *Key Largo*
Barbara Bel Geddes, *I Remember Mama*
Ellen Corby, *I Remember Mama*
Agnes Moorehead, *Johnny Belinda*
Jean Simmons, *Hamlet*

BEST WRITING (STORY)
- Richard Schweizer, David Wechsler, *The Search*

Laurence Olivier's *Hamlet* lost a close vote at the N.Y. crix, but rallied with an upset victory at the Oscars.

Borden Chase, *Red River*
Frances Flaherty, Robert Flaherty,
   Louisiana Story
Emeric Pressburger, *The Red Shoes*
Malvin Wald, *The Naked City*

BEST WRITING (SCREENPLAY)
- John Huston, *The Treasure of the Sierra Madre*

Charles Brackett, Richard L. Breen, Billy
   Wilder, *A Foreign Affair*
Millen Brand, Frank Partos, *The Snake Pit*
Richard Schweizer, David Wechsler, *The Search*
Allen Vincent, Irmgard Von Cube, *Johnny Belinda*

BEST SONG
- "Buttons and Bows," *The Paleface*, Ray Evans, Jay Livingston

"For Every Man There's a Woman,"
   Casbah, Harold Arlen, Leo Robin
"It's Magic," *Romance on the High Seas*,
   Sammy Cahn, Jule Styne
"This Is the Moment," *That Lady in Ermine*, Frederick Hollander, Leo Robin
"The Woody Woodpecker Song," *Wet Blanket Policy*, Ramey Idriss, George Tibbles

Winners

BEST ART DIRECTION/SET DECORATION
(BLACK AND WHITE)
- Roger K. Furse, Carmen Dillon, *Hamlet*

(COLOR)
- Hein Heckroth, Arthur Lawson, *The Red Shoes*

BEST CINEMATOGRAPHY
(BLACK AND WHITE)
- William Daniels, *The Naked City*

(COLOR)
- Winton Hoch, William V. Skall, Joseph Valentine, *Joan of Arc*

BEST COSTUME DESIGN
(BLACK AND WHITE)
- Roger K. Furse, *Hamlet*

(COLOR)
- Dorothy Jeakins, Barbara Karinska, *Joan of Arc*

First directors' guild champ Joseph L. Mankiewicz spoke at the first writers' guild kudos bash.

BEST DOCUMENTARY
(FEATURE)
- *The Secret Land*

(SHORT SUBJECT)
- *Toward Independence*

BEST FILM EDITING
- Paul Weatherwax, *The Naked City*

BEST MUSIC
(SCORING OF A DRAMATIC OR COMEDY PICTURE)
- Brian Easdale, *The Red Shoes*

(SCORING OF A MUSICAL PICTURE)
- Roger Edens, Johnny Green, *Easter Parade*

SCIENTIFIC OR TECHNICAL AWARDS
Class II (Plaque)
- Maurice Ayers, Victor Caccialanza, Paramount Studio Set Construction Department; Nick Kalten, Louis J. Witti, Twentieth Century-Fox Studio Mechanical Effects Department

Class III (Certificate)

- Jack Lannon, Marty Martin, Russell Shearman, RKO Radio Studio Special Effects Department; A. J. Moran, Warner Bros. Studio Electrical Department

BEST SHORT SUBJECT
(CARTOON)
- *The Little Orphan*
(ONE REEL)
- *Symphony of a City*
(TWO REEL)
- *Seal Island*

BEST SOUND RECORDING
- Thomas T. Moulton, Twentieth Century-Fox Studio Sound Department, *The Snake Pit*

BEST SPECIAL EFFECTS
- Paul Eagler, Charles Freeman, J. McMillan Johnson, Russell Shearman, Clarence Slifer, James G. Stewart, *Portrait of Jennie*

SPECIAL FOREIGN-LANGUAGE FILM AWARD
- *Monsieur Vincent* (France)

IRVING G. THALBERG MEMORIAL AWARD
- Jerry Wald

SPECIAL AWARDS
- Sid Grauman
- Adolph Zukor
- Walter Wanger, *Joan of Arc*
- Ivan Jandl, *The Search*

SCREEN DIRECTORS GUILD OF AMERICA

Nominees were all winners of the guild's quarterly awards. A separate award was bestowed for best director of the year on May 22, 1949, at a dinner ceremony held at the Hollywood Roosevelt Hotel and broadcast by local radio station KLAC.

BEST DIRECTOR
- Joseph L. Mankiewicz, *A Letter to Three Wives*

Howard Hawks, *Red River*

Anatole Litvak, *The Snake Pit*
Fred Zinnemann, *The Search*

SPECIAL AWARD
- George Stevens

SCREEN WRITERS GUILD OF AMERICA

Awards were presented on June 23, 1949, at the Bel-Air Hotel in Los Angeles.

BEST WRITTEN DRAMA
- *The Snake Pit*, Frank Partos, Millen Brand, based on the novel by Mary Jane Ward

All My Sons, Chester Erskine, based on the play by Arthur Miller

Another Part of the Forest, Vladimir Pozner, based on the play by Lillian Hellman

Berlin Express, Harold Medford, Curt Siodmak

Call Northside 777, Jerome Cady, Jay Dratler, based on articles by James P. McGuire, adapted by Leonard Hoffman and Quentin Reynolds

Command Decision, William Laidlaw, George Froeschel, based on the play by William Wister Haines

I Remember Mama, DeWitt Bodeen, based on the play by John Van Druten, based on the book *Mama's Bank Account* by Kathryn Forbes

Johnny Belinda, Irmgard von Cube, Allen Vincent, based on the play by Elmer Harris

Key Largo, Richard Brooks, John Huston, based on the play by Maxwell Anderson

The Naked City, Albert Maltz, Malvin Wald

Sorry, Wrong Number, Lucille Fletcher, based on her radio play

The Treasure of the Sierra Madre, John Huston, based on the novel by B. Traven

BEST WRITTEN COMEDY
- *Sitting Pretty*, F. Hugh Herbert, based on the novel by Gwen Davenport

Apartment for Peggy, George Seaton, based on a short story by Faith Baldwin

A Foreign Affair, Charles Brackett, Billy

Wilder, Richard Breen, based on a story by David Shaw, adapted by Robert Harari

I Remember Mama, DeWitt Bodeen, from the play by John Van Druten, based on the book *Mama's Bank Account* by Kathryn Forbes

June Bride, Ranald MacDougall, from the play *Feature for June* by Eileen Tighe and Graeme Lorimer

The Mating of Millie, Louella MacFarlane, St. Clair McKelway, Adele Comandini

Miss Tatlock's Millions, Charles Brackett, Richard L. Breen, based on the play *Oh, Brother!*, by Jacques Deval

Mr. Blandings Builds His Dream House, Norman Panama, Melvin Frank, based on the novel by Eric Hodgins

No Minor Vices, Arnold Manoff

The Paleface, Edmund Hartmann, Frank Tashlin, Jack Rose

BEST WRITTEN MUSICAL

■ *Easter Parade*, Sidney Sheldon, Frances Goodrich, Albert Hackett

The Emperor Waltz, Charles Brackett, Billy Wilder

Luxury Liner, Gladys Lehman, Richard Connell, based on the story *Daddy Is a Wolf* by Ferenc Molnar

On an Island with You, Dorothy Kingsley, Dorothy Cooper, Charles Martin, Hans Wilhelm

That Lady in Ermine, Samson Raphaelson

When My Baby Smiles at Me, Lamar Trotti, based on an adaptation by Elizabeth Reinhardt of *Burlesque*, a play by George Manker Watters and Arthur Hopkins

You Were Meant for Me, Elick Moll, Valentine Davies

BEST SCREENPLAY DEALING MOST ABLY WITH PROBLEMS OF THE AMERICAN SCENE

■ *The Snake Pit*, Frank Partos, Millen Brand, based on the novel by Mary Jane Ward

All My Sons, Chester Erskine, based on the play by Arthur Miller

Another Part of the Forest, Vladimir Pozner, based on the play by Lillian Hellman

Apartment for Peggy, George Seaton, based on a short story by Faith Baldwin

Call Northside 777, Jerome Cady, Jay Dratler, based on articles by James P. McGuire, adapted by Leonard Hoffman and Quentin Reynolds

Command Decision, William Laidlaw, George Froeschel, based on the play by William Wister Haines

Cry of the City, Richard Murphy, based on *The Choir for Martin Rome*, a novel by Henry Edward Helseth

I Remember Mama, DeWitt Bodeen, adapted from the play by John Van Druten, based on the book *Mama's Bank Account* by Kathryn Forbes

The Louisiana Story, Frances Flaherty, Robert Flaherty

The Naked City, Albert Maltz, Malvin Wald

The Street with No Name, Harry Kleiner

BEST WRITTEN WESTERN

■ *The Treasure of the Sierra Madre*, John Huston, from the novel by N. Traven

Fort Apache, Frank Nugent, based on the story "Massacre" by James Warner Bellah

Four Faces West, Graham Baker, Teddi Sherman, based on the novel *Paso por Aqui* by Eugene Manlove Rhodes, as adapted by William and Milarde Brent

Fury at Furnace Creek, Charles G. Booth, Winston Miller, based on the novel *Four Men and a Prayer* by David Garth

Green Grass of Wyoming, Martin Berkeley, based on the novel by Mary O'Hara

The Man from Colorado, Robert D. Andrews, Ben Maddow, Borden Chase

The Paleface, Edmund Hartmann, Frank Tashlin, Jack Rose

Rachel and the Stranger, Waldo Salt, based by the short story "Rachel" by Howard Fast

Red River, Borden Chase, Charles Schnee

Station West, Frank Fenton, Winston Miller, based on the novel by Luke Short

ROBERT MELTZER AWARD

■ Frank Partos, Millen Brand, *Snake Pit*

▪ 1949 ▪

All the King's Men *Pulls Off a Coup*

Once again the National Board of Review went off on one of its foreign jaunts, this time riding Italy's *The Bicycle Thief*, which *Variety* called "a pure exercise in directorial virtuosity" by Vittorio De Sica. The New York Film Critics and Golden Globes would soon follow with awards for Best Foreign Film, while the Oscars, which didn't yet have a category for offshore fare, would give *The Bicycle Thief* a special trophy.

Otherwise, at this year's awards derby, the crix, Globes and Oscars—for the first and last time in their mutual history—would all agree on the same Yankee pix for Best Picture, Actor and Actress. Despite such harmony in the three races, all three kudos would disagree on Best Director—and the film they would embrace as the year's finest was not included anywhere on the National Board of Review's list of 1949's Top 10.

Film-derby handicappers were initially baffled over what to bet on. None of 1949's top grossers seemed like typical gold-purse grabbers: *Jolson Sings Again, Pinky, I Was a Male War Bride, The Stratton Story* and *Mr. Belvedere Goes to College.* Three war pics were considered the heaviest guns: *Battleground* ("extraordinary celluloid achievement," said *Variety), Twelve O'Clock High* ("the picture to beat" for the Oscar, insisted Louella Parsons) and *Iwo Jima* ("the best of the war pictures!" wailed Walter Winchell).

Then the New York film crix gathered for their annual December conclave at the newspaper guild's office near Times Square. The group now huddled early in the day—at 10:30 A.M.—no doubt wishing to avoid what used to occur at their evening sessions when much scotch and bourbon flowed, lubricating vicious tongues.

No talking was permitted anymore before the tally was taken for Best Picture.

Lamberto Maggiorani and Enzo Staiola (right) in Vittorio Di Sica's *The Bicycle Thief*, which was named Best Picture by the National Board of Review and won other kudos from the Oscars, Gotham crix and Globes.

Therefore, no one heralded the emergence of the dark horse that suddenly broke loose when the votes were counted on the first ballot.

Out of the 17 crix polled, "*All the King's Men* received 7 votes right off the bat," reported a stunned *Herald Tribune.* "Since no discussion precedes this ballot at critics' meetings, this clear-cut expression of opinion was unusual. *Intruder in the Dust* received three votes and *The Fallen Idol* 2." The balance were scattered among five other films.

"In the course of the voting, *All the King's Men* won going away," the *Herald Tribune* added, "picking up 2 more votes to make it 9 against 5 for *Intruder in the Dust* and 3 for *The Fallen Idol* on the last ballot. This gradual altering of the original score is the result of changes to second choices as the losers drop out, and thus is a group opinion formed."

The successes of *All the King's Men, Intruder in the Dust* and *The Fallen Idol* were shocking. Initially, all three were box-office flops with no-name stars. In fact, when director, writer and indie producer Robert Rossen convinced his distributor, Columbia, to release *All the King's Men* at Christmastime, studio chief Harry Cohn made it clear he thought the political pic had no Oscar chances and refused to help Rossen pay for an ad campaign.

All the King's Men starred veteran B-movie thesp Broderick Crawford in a film adaptation of Robert Penn Warren's Pulitzer Prize–winning novel. "The rise and fall of a backwoods political messiah"—based transparently on Louisiana Governor Huey Long—"is given graphic celluloid treatment," said *Variety*. "Crawford delivers one of the most dynamic character studies the screen has ever glimpsed. The most compelling of the femme players is Mercedes McCambridge, the mistress to the great man."

All the King's Men had been a box-office bomb.

Intruder in the Dust was director Clarence Brown's screen translation of William Faulkner's novel about a Southern mob that wants to lynch a black man accused of murder. For *The Fallen Idol*, lensed by Carol Reed, British writer Graham Greene wrote the screenplay adaptation of his short story about a boy who worships a butler suspected of murder.

Carol Reed, Clarence Brown and Robert Rossen all reaped four votes each on the first vote for Best Director. The race was then narrowed down to Reed and Rossen, with the former winning on the sixth ballot by an 11-to-6 score.

When it came time to decide the acting honors, the crix embraced another b.o. dud—*The Heiress*, director William Wyler's adaptation of Henry James's novella *Washington Square* about a homely woman, portrayed by Olivia de Havilland, who plots revenge on a fortune hunter who dupes her into marrying him.

Ralph Richardson had been hailed as the year's best actor by the National Board of Review for his joint roles as de Havilland's cruel father in *The Heiress* and the mysterious butler in *The Fallen Idol*. When the crix decided the male thesp's race on the sixth ballot, Richardson received five votes compared to three for Juano Hernandez as the black mob victim in *Intruder*. Both candidates were topped, however, by *All the King's Men*'s Broderick Crawford, who nabbed nine.

In the actress contest, the *Herald Tribune* reported that "joy and admiration" reigned: "Miss de Havilland's portrait of a cheated and vengeful heiress stood out clearly with 10 votes on the first go-round and took the prize on the fifth ballot with a two-thirds majority of 12 against 5 for Edith Evans in *Dolwyn*. Miss de Havilland has the further distinction of becoming the first artist ever to win a critics' award two years in succession. She won last year for *The Snake Pit* and it is a pleasure to repeat the applause."

De Havilland and Broderick Crawford were present to accept their scrolls when the critics gathered for an afternoon gala at the Rainbow Room at Rockefeller Center. Missing was Carol Reed, whose helmer's scroll was accepted by noted thesp Sir Cedric Hardwicke. The *Herald Tribune* reported: "Prior to the reception, the presentation ceremony was filmed by Paramount News and by NBC for television."

A week before the Golden Globe awards, the Hollywood Foreign Correspondents Association released a list of nominees, but there was little suspense over who'd win. *All the King's Men* claimed all the prizes for Best Picture, Director and Actor—and two for Mercedes McCambridge, who was named Best Supporting Actress in addition to being cited as the best new female star of the year. Its total tally set a new record for winning the most Golden Globes in a year (four—*Kings*'s award for new star doesn't count toward a film's tally, according to kudos scorekeeping protocol).

Olivia de Havilland was the easy winner of Best Actress and accepted the statuette before 500 people at the Ambassador Hotel, saying, "This golden replica of the world is romantic. It covers places and cities that I would like to visit but where so far only my shadow has been."

Most of the champs were present at the ceremony, which was presided over by Gene Kelly as emcee and recorded for later broadcast by the Armed Forces Radio Service. Among the other celebs on hand was Best Supporting Actor James Whitmore (*Battleground*), who "marched to the platform," noted *The Hollywood Citizen-News*, "and paid tribute to the soldiers who fought the Battle of the Bulge in December, 1944."

A few weeks before the Globes were doled out, *All the King's Men* picked up two more kudos when the Screen Writers Guild revealed its choices for Best Drama and Best Screenplay Dealing Most Ably with Problems of the American Scene. (The latter prize was also known as the Robert Meltzer Award, named after a film scribe killed in World War II.) The event at the Beverly Hills Hotel was attended by 672 people who paid $5.50 per ticket for dinner and entertainment, which included Phil Silvers as emcee and writer Ben Hecht playing fiddle with the Marx Brothers.

The guild's trophy for Best Comedy went to the same pic that won the Screen Directors Guild's first award, which was bestowed nine months earlier: *A Letter to Three Wives*, written and directed by Joseph L. Mankiewicz. The new prize suddenly reawakened interest in *Three Wives*, which now gained Oscar buzz despite having had no ad campaign in the trade press. In its review, *Variety* had described the pic as "a standout in every respect," including its script, which the paper called "nifty" for its twisted tale of three suburban women who get letters from a stranger who claims to have run off with one of their husbands.

As it headed into the Oscars, *A Letter to Three Wives* had three noms—for Best Picture, Director and Screenplay. Two war movies fought it out for top film, too: *Battleground* with six noms and *Twelve O'Clock High* with four bids. Another rival, *All the King's Men*, had seven chances, and *The Heiress* reigned with the most nominations—eight.

This year academy leaders convinced the studios to reinstate their financial backing of the gala, which gave them the funds needed to move the ceremony to L.A.'s reigning movie palace, the 2,800-seat RKO Pantages Theater, where it would remain for the next 11 years. Again the kudofest was held on a chilly day, which did not discourage thousands of film fans from hovering outside and storming the bleachers "almost before the technicians tightened the last bolt," *Variety* noted. The tradepaper described "almost continuous bedlam as the sleek new sedans, station wagons and convertibles rolled up in front of the theater in an almost steady flow" and as 120 L.A. policemen and 30 studio guards tried to contain the throngs that pressed against the sidewalk ropes.

"By 7:45, the crowd was beginning to get anxious," *Variety* observed. "Olivia de Havilland, obviously the popular choice to win the award as Best Actress, had not yet put in an appearance. There were repeated cries of 'Livvy, we want Livvy!'" Soon after the ceremony began at 8 P.M., she finally arrived and rushed into the theater, her white ermine cape billowing behind her.

In the Best Actress race, de Havilland also had the backing of *Variety*'s straw poll, which predicted she'd triumph over past proven champ Loretta Young (*Come to the Stable*), Oscar-overdue Susan Hayward (*My Foolish Heart*), Jeanne Crain (*Pinky*) and the New York crix's 1947 choice for Best Actress, Deborah Kerr (*Edward, My Son*), who finally earned her first Academy Award bid. When de Havilland won her second Oscar in four years, she said, "Your award

Variety claimed a "clean sweep!" when its Oscar poll scored 100 percent.

for *To Each His Own* I took as an incentive to venture forward. Thank you for this very generous assurance that I have not failed to do so."

By comparison, the winner of the Best Actor trophy, Broderick Crawford (*All the King's Men*), seemed flustered when he prevailed, just as *Variety* predicted, against John Wayne (*Sands of Iwo Jima*) and Gregory Peck (*Twelve O'Clock High*).

Twelve O'Clock High rallied when it claimed the prize for Best Supporting Actor for Dean Jagger, who may have been a seasoned showbiz trouper, but he revealed to the kudos audience, "I feel as emotional as the dickens."

In the supporting actress race, two movies competed with two contenders each—*Come to the Stable* (Celeste Holm, Elsa Lanchester) and *Pinky* (Ethel Barrymore, Ethel Waters)—thereby splitting the vote to give an easy win to the fifth nominee. Mercedes McCambridge won for *All the King's Men*, which marked her screen debut after toiling for years in TV, theater and radio. She addressed other struggling thesps in her acceptance speech: "I just want to say to all beginning actresses—never get discouraged. Hold on. Just look what can happen!"

All the King's Men earned nominations for Best Screenplay and Best Director for Robert Rossen, but *Variety*'s straw poll predicted that both kudos would be claimed by Joseph L. Mankiewicz (*A Letter to Three Wives*). When Mankiewicz scored his double triumph as forecasted, he headed backstage to show them off to the press. As he clutched each naked statuette around the middle with a fist, he said gleefully, "I'm glad they're both boys!"

Variety nonetheless predicted that *All the King's Men* would rebound by nabbing the night's top prize—Best Picture. When its crystal ball was proven correct, Rossen said at the podium, "It's been a long evening. I just can't talk."

Variety crowed loudly the next day: "It's a clean sweep!" After being humiliated last year by failing to foresee *Hamlet*'s upset for Best Picture, the tradepaper now felt vindicated and shamelessly thumped its chest, adding, "All of the favorites in the Oscar derby romped into the winners' circle! The *Daily Variety* poll galloped home ahead with all the hoofs beating a winning tune. It was a gallop—not a Gallup."

Two months later, Rossen's peers would make up for his Oscar loss as Best Director by giving him the equivalent laurel for *All the King's Men* at the next awards ceremony held by the Screen Directors Guild, which was presided over by George Jessel at the Beverly Hills Hotel. Last year's champ, Joseph L. Mankiewicz, was not nommed this year.

▪ 1949 ▪

NATIONAL BOARD OF REVIEW

The board declared a best film of the year, then listed its remaining favorites according to highest scores. No awards were bestowed for best actress or foreign films. The vote results were announced on December 18, 1949.

BEST PICTURE
▪ *The Bicycle Thief*
The Quiet One
Intruder in the Dust
The Heiress
Devil in the Flesh
Quartet
Germany, Year Zero
Home of the Brave
A Letter to Three Wives
The Fallen Idol

BEST DIRECTOR
▪ Vittorio De Sica, *The Bicycle Thief*

BEST ACTOR
▪ Ralph Richardson, *The Heiress, The Fallen Idol*

BEST SCREENPLAY

- Graham Greene, *The Fallen Idol**

NEW YORK FILM CRITICS

Winners were announced on December 27, 1949. Awards were presented on February 5, 1950, at the Rainbow Room in New York.

BEST PICTURE

- *All the King's Men*

BEST DIRECTOR

- Carol Reed, *The Fallen Idol*

BEST ACTOR

- Broderick Crawford, *All the King's Men*

BEST ACTRESS

- Olivia de Havilland, *The Heiress*

BEST FOREIGN FILM

- *The Bicycle Thief* (Italy)

SCREEN WRITERS GUILD OF AMERICA

Awards were presented on February 5, 1950, at the Beverly Hills Hotel in Los Angeles.

BEST WRITTEN DRAMA

- *All the King's Men*, Robert Rossen, based on the novel by Robert Penn Warren
Battleground, Robert Pirosh
Champion, Carl Foreman, based on a short story by Ring Lardner
The Hasty Heart, Ranald MacDougall, based on the play by John Patrick
The Heiress, Ruth Goetz, Augustus Goetz, adapted from their play based on the novel *Washington Square* by Henry James
Intruder in the Dust, Ben Maddow, based on the novel by William Faulkner
The Window, Mel Dineli, based on the novelette *The Boy Cried Murder* by Cornell Woolrich

---

*Lesley Storm and William Templeton also share screenplay credit, but they were not cited by the board for this award.

BEST WRITTEN COMEDY

- *A Letter to Three Wives*, Joseph L. Mankiewicz, based on Vera Caspary's adaptation of the novel by John Klempner
Adam's Rib, Ruth Gordon, Garson Kanin
Come to the Stable, Oscar Millard, Sally Benson, Clare Booth Luce
Every Girl Should Be Married, Stephen Morehouse Avery, Don Hartman, Eleanor Harris
I Was a Male War Bride, Charles Lederer, Leonard Spigelgass, Hagar Wilde, based on a story by Henri Rochard
It Happens Every Spring, Valentine Davies, Shirley Smith

BEST WRITTEN MUSICAL

- *On the Town*, Betty Comden, Adolph Green, adapted from their musical play, based on an idea by Jerome Robbins
The Barkleys of Broadway, Betty Comden, Adolph Green
In the Good Old Summertime, Frances Goodrich, Albert Hackett, Ivan Tors, based on a screenplay by Samson Raphaelson and the play *Perfumerie* by Miklos Laszlo
Jolson Sings Again, Sidney Buchman
Take Me out to the Ball Game, Harry Tugend, George Wells, Gene Kelly, Stanley Donen
You're My Everything, Lamar Trotti, Will Hays, Jr., from the short story "I'm the Star" by George Jessel

"All of the favorites in the Oscar derby romped into the winners' circle!" *Variety* said. From left: Mercedes McCambridge, Broderick Crawford, Olivia de Havilland and Dean Jagger.

BEST SCREENPLAY DEALING MOST ABLY WITH PROBLEMS OF THE AMERICAN SCENE

- *All the King's Men*, Robert Rossen, based on the novel by Robert Penn Warren
Home of the Brave, Carl Foreman, based on the play by Arthur Laurents
Intruder in the Dust, Ben Maddow, based on the novel by William Faulkner
Lost Boundaries, Virginia Shaler, Eugene Ling, based on Charles Palmer's adaptation of nonfiction by William L. White
Pinky, Philip Dunne, Dudley Nichols, based on the novel by Cid Ricketts Sumner

BEST WRITTEN WESTERN

- *Yellow Sky*, Lamar Trotti, W. R. Burnett
The Gal Who Took the West, William Bowers, Oscar Brodney
She Wore a Yellow Ribbon, Frank Nugent, Lawrence Stallings, based on the stories "The Big Hunt" and "War Party" by James Warner Bellah
Streets of Laredo, Charles Marquis Warren, Louis Stevens, Elizabeth Hill
Whispering Smith, Frank Butler, Karl Kamb, based on the novel by Frank H. Spearman

ROBERT MELTZER AWARD

- Robert Rossen, *All the King's Men*

GOLDEN GLOBES

Nominations were announced on February 14, 1950. Awards were presented on February 23 at the Ambassador Hotel in Los Angeles.

BEST PICTURE

- *All the King's Men*
Come to the Stable

BEST PICTURE PROMOTING INTERNATIONAL UNDERSTANDING

- *The Hasty Heart*
Monsieur Vincent

BEST DIRECTOR

- Robert Rossen, *All the King's Men*
William Wyler, *The Heiress*

BEST ACTOR

- Broderick Crawford, *All the King's Men*
Richard Todd, *The Hasty Heart*

BEST ACTRESS

- Olivia de Havilland, *The Heiress*
Deborah Kerr, *Edward, My Son*

BEST SUPPORTING ACTOR

- James Whitmore, *Battleground*
David Brian, *Intruder in the Dust*

BEST SUPPORTING ACTRESS

- Mercedes McCambridge, *All the King's Men*
Miriam Hopkins, *The Heiress*

BEST NEW ACTOR

- Richard Todd, *The Hasty Heart*
Juano Hernandez, *Intruder in the Dust*

BEST NEW ACTRESS

- Mercedes McCambridge, *All the King's Men*
Ruth Roman, *Champion*

BEST SCREENPLAY

- Robert Pirosh, *Battleground*
Walter Doniger, John Paxton, *Rope of Sand*

BEST FOREIGN FILM

- *The Bicycle Thief* (Italy)
The Fallen Idol (U.K.)

Winners

BEST CINEMATOGRAPHY, BLACK AND WHITE

- Frank Planer, *Champion*

BEST CINEMATOGRAPHY, COLOR

- Walt Disney Studios, *The Adventures of Ichabod and Mr. Toad*

BEST PHOTOGRAPHY

- *All the King's Men*

BEST ORIGINAL SCORE

- Johnny Green, *The Inspector General*

ACADEMY AWARDS

Nominations were announced on February 12, 1950. Awards were presented on March

23 at the RKO Pantages Theatre in Hollywood.

BEST PICTURE
- *All the King's Men*
- *Battleground*
- *The Heiress*
- *A Letter to Three Wives*
- *Twelve O'Clock High*

BEST DIRECTOR
- Joseph L. Mankiewicz, *A Letter to Three Wives*

Carol Reed, *The Fallen Idol*
Robert Rossen, *All the King's Men*
William A. Wellman, *Battleground*
William Wyler, *The Heiress*

BEST ACTOR
- Broderick Crawford, *All the King's Men*

Kirk Douglas, *Champion*
Gregory Peck, *Twelve O'Clock High*
Richard Todd, *The Hasty Heart*
John Wayne, *Sands of Iwo Jima*

BEST ACTRESS
- Olivia de Havilland, *The Heiress*

Jeanne Crain, *Pinky*
Susan Hayward, *My Foolish Heart*
Deborah Kerr, *Edward, My Son*
Loretta Young, *Come to the Stable*

BEST SUPPORTING ACTOR
- Dean Jagger, *Twelve O'Clock High*

John Ireland, *All the King's Men*
Arthur Kennedy, *Champion*
Ralph Richardson, *The Heiress*
James Whitmore, *Battleground*

BEST SUPPORTING ACTRESS
- Mercedes McCambridge, *All the King's Men*

Ethel Barrymore, *Pinky*
Celeste Holm, *Come to the Stable*
Elsa Lanchester, *Come to the Stable*
Ethel Waters, *Pinky*

BEST WRITING (STORY)
- Douglas Morrow, *The Stratton Story*

Clare Boothe Luce, *Come to the Stable*

Harry Brown, *Sands of Iwo Jima*
Valentine Davies, Shirley W. Smith, *It Happens Every Spring*
Virginia Kellogg, *White Heat*

BEST WRITING (SCREENPLAY)
- Joseph L. Mankiewicz, *A Letter to Three Wives*

Carl Foreman, *Champion*
Graham Greene, *The Fallen Idol*
Robert Rossen, *All the King's Men*
Cesare Zavattini, *The Bicycle Thief*

BEST WRITING (STORY AND SCREENPLAY)
- Robert Pirosh, *Battleground*

Sergio Amidei, Federico Fellini, Alfred Hayes, Marcello Pagliero, Roberto Rossellini, *Paisan*
Sidney Buchman, *Jolson Sings Again*
T. E. B. Clarke, *Passport to Pimlico*
Helen Levitt, Janice Loeb, Sidney Meyers, *The Quiet One*

BEST SONG
- "Baby, It's Cold Outside," *Neptune's Daughter*, Frank Loesser

"It's a Great Feeling," *It's a Great Feeling*, Sammy Cahn, Jule Styne
"Lavender Blue," *So Dear to My Heart*, Eliot Daniel, Larry Morey
"My Foolish Heart," *My Foolish Heart*, Ned Washington, Victor Young
"Through a Long and Sleepless Night," *Come to the Stable*, Mack Gordon, Alfred Newman

Winners

BEST ART DIRECTION/SET DECORATION
(BLACK AND WHITE)
- Harry Horner, John Meehan, Emile Kuri, *The Heiress*

(COLOR)
- Cedric Gibbons, Paul Groesse, Jack D. Moore, Edwin B. Willis, *Little Women*

BEST CINEMATOGRAPHY
(BLACK AND WHITE)
- Paul C. Vogel, *Battleground*

(COLOR)
- Winton Hoch, *She Wore a Yellow Ribbon*

BEST COSTUME DESIGN
(BLACK AND WHITE)
- Edith Head, Gile Steele, *The Heiress*

(COLOR)
- Leah Rhodes, Travilla and Marjorie Best, *The Adventures of Don Juan*

BEST DOCUMENTARY
(FEATURE)
- *Daybreak in Udi*

(SHORT SUBJECT)
- *A Chance to Live*
- *So Much for So Little*

BEST FILM EDITING
- Harry Gerstad, *Champion*

BEST MUSIC
(SCORING OF A DRAMATIC OR COMEDY PICTURE)
- Aaron Copland, *The Heiress*

(SCORING OF A MUSICAL PICTURE)
- Roger Edens, Lennie Hayton, *On the Town*

SCIENTIFIC OR TECHNICAL AWARDS
Class I (Statuette)
- Eastman Kodak

Class III (Certificate)
- Loren L. Ryder, Bruce H. Denney, Robert Carr, Paramount Studio Sound Department; M. B. Paul; Herbert Britt; Andre Coutant, Jacques Mathot; Charles R. Daily, Steve Csillag, Paramount Studio Engineering, Editorial and Music Departments; International Projector Corp.; Alexander Velcoff

BEST SHORT SUBJECT
(CARTOON)
- *For Scent-Imental Reasons*

(ONE REEL)
- *Aquatic House-Party*

(TWO REEL)
- *Van Gogh*

BEST SOUND RECORDING
- Thomas T. Moulton, *Twelve O'Clock High*

BEST SPECIAL EFFECTS
- Cooper, RKO Productions, *Mighty Joe Young*

SPECIAL AWARDS
- *The Bicycle Thief* (Italy)
- Fred Astaire
- Cecil B. DeMille
- Bobby Driscoll
- Jean Hersholt

SCREEN DIRECTORS GUILD OF AMERICA

Nominees were all winners of the guild's quarterly awards. A separate award was bestowed for best director of the year on May 28, 1950, at the Beverly Hills Hotel.

BEST DIRECTOR
- Robert Rossen, *All the King's Men*

Carol Reed, *The Third Man*

Mark Robson, *Champion*

Alfred Werker, *Lost Boundaries*

All About Showbiz

Two movies spotlighting ferocious showbiz divas—one a dethroned silent-film queen, the other a has-been Broadway hellcat—were poised at each other, claws outstretched.

As they scratched it out for the year's top awards, each would grab a few, but, in the end and just like one of the films' plot lines, a sneaky ingenue would upstage them both.

This year's awards derby was all about showbiz because it pitted *All about Eve* against *Sunset Boulevard.* Both were brutally dark depictions of what happens when great stars dim. *Eve* featured Bette Davis as an embittered, overripe stage thesp, who, *Variety* noted, did "not spare herself, makeup wise, in the aging star assignment." *Sunset* showcased a fallen Hollywood tragedienne mugging to the max. "Gloria Swanson, returning to the screen after a very long absence, socks hard with a silent-day technique to put over the decaying star," *Variety* cheered.

The National Board of Review chose *Sunset Boulevard* for its top honor and Swanson for Best Actress, but passed over its director-writer Billy Wilder for the helmer's prize. That went to John Huston for lensing his sympathetic portrayal of jewel thieves in *The Asphalt Jungle.*

The New York Film Critics preferred Hollywood's send-up of the New York stage scene when they met at the newspaper guild's offices on West 44th Street. Again a two-thirds vote was needed to win on the first five ballots, a simple majority after that.

"*All About Eve* romped away with the Best Picture award, winning on the first ballot by 11 votes to 3 over its closest rival, *Sunset Boulevard,*" reported *The New York Times.* Director Joseph L. Mankiewicz had a tougher time, needing four ballots to claim victory in his race.

"The sharpest contest was in the Best

Anne Baxter and Bette Davis squared off in *All About Eve,* hailed by the N.Y. crix, Oscars and guilds.

Actress category," the *Times* added, noting that Bette Davis had to thrash it out till the final, sixth round before prevailing. The Best Actor fight also turned out to be prickly. It took Gregory Peck the same half-dozen tallies before he was saluted for his role as an air force general in *Twelve O'Clock High,* a role that had earned him an Oscar nomination last year (when it was released in Los Angeles prior to its New York premiere), although he lost to Broderick Crawford.

For the first time ever, all of the U.S. films hailed by the Gotham crix turned out to be from one studio, Twentieth Century-Fox, but that caused no furor. Instead, there was an uproar over the group's choice of Best Foreign Film—and one so violent that it ended up squashing the crix's gala awards ceremony, skedded to be staged grandly at Radio City Music Hall for a second year in a row.

The hubbub began when the honored film, a trilogy of three small works jointly called *Ways of Love,* was denounced as "blasphemous" by New York's Cardinal Spellman when it opened a month earlier.

The offending segment was Roberto Rosselini's *The Miracle*, which depicted a devout Italian peasant who thinks she's become pregnant by God. Gotham censors forced the Paris Theatre to pull it from the picture and threatened to revoke the license of any other film house that showed it. Local crix rallied to the movie's defense and sent the mayor a telegram denouncing the city's "suppressive action" as "dangerous censorship," but the censors had their way.

One month later, just when the hullabaloo died down, it flared up again when the crix announced that *Ways of Love* would receive a scroll at their Radio City Music Hall fete. Local religious leaders immediately threatened to call a boycott and to storm the hall with picketers.

The crix were forced to cancel their show at the music hall, but they refused to back down altogether. They moved their awards presentation to the Rainbow Room and gave *Ways of Love*'s scroll to its U.S. distributor. The exec called the honor "a tribute to the integrity of people who really care about films."

Also on hand to receive their honors were best thesps Gregory Peck and Bette Davis. Peck thanked his director Henry King and Davis thanked helmer Mankiewicz, adding, "We all followed him blindly. This is Joe's night."

"Speculation concerning the real-life identity of the stage star portrayed in the film by Miss Davis had been lively, with the name Tallulah Bankhead mentioned most frequently," *The New York Times* reported. "In his acceptance remarks, Mr. Mankiewicz sought to settle the matter by saying, 'It might be fitting to disclose that the woman who was in my thoughts, who always has interested me, was none other than Peg Woffington of the Old Drury Lane.'"

When the Screen Writers Guild of America announced the recipients of its top prizes a week later, *Sunset Boulevard* and *All about Eve*, nominated in different categories, both emerged winners—for, respectively, Best Written Drama and Best Written Comedy. Stars from both casts (Bette Davis and Gary Merrill from *Eve*, William Holden and Nancy Olsen from *Sunset*) performed scenes parodying the pics at the festivities held at the Ambassador Hotel. The surprise highlight of the night's gridiron-style entertainment turned out to be a spoof of the TV show *You Bet Your Life* in which host Groucho Marx quizzed Jerry Wald and Norman Krasna about what they did for a living. *Variety* quoted the skit:

Groucho: You say you make pictures. Do you write them?

Jerry: Oh, no. We hire writers for that.

Groucho: Then you direct them?

Norman: No, we hire directors.

Groucho: Then you act in them?

Jerry: No, we hire actors.

Groucho: Do you sell the pictures on the road?

Norman: We have a selling organization for that.

Groucho: Let's see now. You fellows don't write, you don't act, you don't direct, you don't sell the pictures—I can't figure out your job. Oh, yes, now I get it. You fellows are producers!

"Hollywood was still chuckling" over the guild show a week later, *Variety* said, nothing that "another laugh-getter was George Jessel, in a beard, doing a takeoff on the national's oldest living exhibitor demonstrating to Hollywood its lack of knowledge of the economics of the business." Jessel also hosted the gala.

Jessel served as host of the Golden Globes at Ciro's restaurant, too, where members of the Hollywood Foreign Correspondents Association demonstrated that they preferred the movie about old Hollywood over its rival about faraway Broadway. *Sunset Boulevard* claimed four honors: Best Picture, Best Music Score, Best Direc-

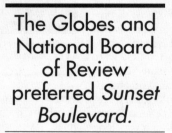

The Globes and National Board of Review preferred *Sunset Boulevard*.

tor (Billy Wilder) and Best Actress (Gloria Swanson). The prize for Best Picture was claimed by *Sunset* producer and co-writer Charles Brackett, who also happened to be prexy of the motion picture academy, which bestows the Oscar. (His film's success at the Globes would seem ironic considering how *Sunset* would later fare at his own kudos.) Swanson accepted her honor via telephone from New York, saying, "Please send me my Golden Globe air mail. If you had waited as long as I have for this award, you would understand my desire for speed."

All about Eve's only consolation prize turned out to be the screenplay award for Joseph L. Mankiewicz.

The Globes created separate acting accolades for comedy/musical movies, but did not classify *All about Eve* as humorous, which the Screen Writers Guild had done. Therefore, Bette Davis wasn't listed in the new Best Actress category (she got trounced by Swanson in the drama showdown). The new kudos went to Judy Holliday as the dimwitted mistress of a junkyard tycoon in *Born Yesterday*, a role she originated on Broadway and then got to play on film when Rita Hayworth ditched the project at the last minute to get hitched to Sheik Aly Khan. Although *Born Yesterday*, was only her third film, Holliday wasn't an Oscar long shot: Columbia Pictures was desperate to earn back the huge sum it paid for the Broadway show's screen rights, so it pushed Holliday hard for kudos. The campaign worked.

Holliday also nabbed a Globe nomination for Best Supporting Actress in *Adam's Rib*, but lost that honor to Josephine Hull, who reprised her Broadway role in *Harvey*.

The new Globe for best actor in a comedy/musical pic went to Fred Astaire for his fleet-footed portrayal of songsmith Bert Kalmar in *Three Little Words*. The Globe for Best Drama Actor went to the star who lobbied hardest for awards recognition: José Ferrer, who was honored for the screen adaptation of his Broadway role in *Cyrano*

de Bergerac ("an outstanding achievement in histrionics, quick with humor and sadness," said *Variety*).

Back in 1948, Ferrer was nominated for Best Supporting Actor for *Joan of Arc*, but now he courted a chance at best lead thesp with a blitz of ads in the tradepapers. His brashness paid off with a bid, but his chances of winning were soon jeopardized when he was accused of Communist sympathies and called to testify before the House Un-American Activities Committee. Ferrer ran new ads professing his patriotism, a move cheered by *Variety*: "He is taking much of the steam out of the irresponsible accusations filed against him."

When the Oscar nominations were announced, the biggest surprise was the dual success of *All about Eve*—scoring 14 nominations, the most ever—and *Sunset Boulevard* with 11. *Variety* added: "*Eve* also has the unique distinction of being the first picture in Acad history to qualify two femme stars for the Oscar run-off" for Best

> **All About Eve nabbed the most Oscar noms ever: 14.**

Actress. Ironically, Bette Davis was matched up against Anne Baxter, the actress who schemed to upstage her in *Eve*. They both faced the two recent Globe champs, Gloria Swanson and Judy Holliday, in one of the most heated Oscar bouts in years.

All about Eve competed for Best Picture against *Born Yesterday, Father of the Bride, King Solomon's Mines* and *Sunset Boulevard*. Nominees were determined by 12,050 members of the film industry; winners would be chosen by the 1,850 members of the movie academy.

Excitement over who'd win was evident from the frenzy outside the awards gala, which was hosted by Fred Astaire, who proved to be a good sport even though the Golden Globe champ didn't score an Oscar bid. "It looked like a World Series on Hollywood Boulevard, with the bleachers filled hours before the game started," *Variety* observed. "The bleachers were in two sections and right field section was crowded before the workmen started putting up the left field seats."

The top players were missing, though. "It was like watching the oldtime Yanks in a World Series with Ruth, Gehrig, Dickey, Coombs, etc., somewhere out in the sticks playing exhibition games," *Variety* added. "Among the absentees were Judy Holliday, Bette Davis, Gloria Swanson, José Ferrer, Spencer Tracy and Louis Calbern, all heavy-hitting candidates in the thesping awards."

Swanson and Ferrer couldn't be present because they were performing on Broadway in *Twentieth Century*, but they got together on Oscar night to celebrate Swanson's 52nd birthday, which actually took place two days earlier. The New York party seemed like so much more fun that the staid Hollywood fete that fellow nominees Judy Holliday, George Cukor and Sam Jaffe joined them at Lazombra restaurant. So did ABC radio, hooking the gang up to the West Coast gala, fearful of missing the real party, whichever coast it would turn out to be on.

Variety predicted that the top two acting champs would be among the New York revelers. Revealing the results of its latest straw poll, the paper reported, "In the Best Actor class, while José Ferrer of *Cyrano de Bergerac* is ahead, William Holden (*Sunset Boulevard*) showed up very strong on some of the pollsters' tabulations."

In New York, Holliday and Swanson sat on either side of Ferrer as Helen Hayes read the award results at the Los Angeles Pantages Theatre. When she said, "The best actor of the year, José Ferrer!" the women both hugged and kissed him madly. The recently reaffirmed patriot then addressed America on the radio hookup. *Variety* noted, "Ferrer's voice came in strong and clear over the open circuit from N.Y. Ferrer thanked his coworkers on *Cyrano* and then said, 'It is more than an honor to an actor's performance—I consider it an act of faith and vote

of confidence. All of you who voted for me know what I mean. And, believe me, I will not let you down."

Weeks before the awards bash, *Variety* columnist Bob Thomas promised, "It's still a wide-open race, particularly among the fillies and it's continuing right down to the wire." On awards day, however, the paper's straw poll narrowed the race down to just one horse: Judy Holliday.

Since Holliday's costar in *Born Yesterday*, Broderick Crawford, was last year's Best Actor champ, he had the pleasure of revealing her as the victor. When the partiers in New York heard the news, the room exploded with excitement and Swanson, proving to be a true showbiz trouper, hugged Holliday, smiled and said playfully, "Darling, why couldn't you have waited till next year?"

Variety reported that Holliday faced a tech problem when she tried to accept the honor via radio: "Her mouth opened for her speech, but the mike was dead." Ethel Barrymore took over in L.A. and thanked the crowd on Holliday's behalf.

Variety sized up the other male acting race thus: "While George Sanders (*All about Eve*) is out in front in the supporting thesp race, Jeff Chandler of *Broken Arrow* is crowding him for top honors." George Sanders may have portrayed a crusty drama critic in *Eve*, but when he won the Oscar, *Variety* noted that he "hurried up to pick up" the statuette, then dashed backstage and cried.

Variety foresaw no rival to Josephine Hull as Best Supporting Actress and was proven right. When the star of *Harvey* headed to the Pantages stage to accept the

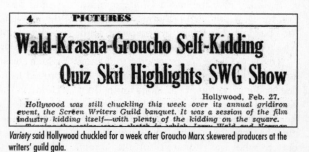

Variety said Hollywood chuckled for a week after Groucho Marx skewered producers at the writers' guild gala.

prize, she pretended to be escorted by the film's title character, an imaginary, human-size rabbit. She said, "I must thank you all and that wonderful six-and-a-half-foot Harvey. He has brought happiness to me in Hollywood."

The rest of Oscar night proceeded exactly as *Variety* had prophesized, too. "It's a walkaway for *All about Eve* in the Best Picture and Screenplay races," the paper had promised. Both came true—just like its call for Best Director.

When Joseph L. Mankiewicz picked up both the helmer's and scribe's tributes, it marked the only time in Oscar history that both awards were claimed by the same person two years in a row.

Variety thought he should've scored more, too: "Joe Mankiewicz deserved a spe-cial Oscar for knowing all about Eve. Adam didn't."

All about Eve's big loser—Bette Davis—was in Britain filming *Another Man's Poison* on Oscar night. She and the film's crew listened to the awards ceremony via radio. When she heard the news of her defeat, Davis exclaimed, "Good! A new-comer won. I couldn't be more pleased."

Six months later she'd receive two con-solation prizes when she'd be voted Best Actress at the Cannes Film Festival and *All about Eve* would reap a special jury prize.

One month after the Oscars, Mankiewicz retired as the prexy of the Screen Directors Guild, but nonetheless won its top trophy for a second time in the award's three-year history.

▪ 1950 ▪

NATIONAL BOARD OF REVIEW

The board declared a best picture and for-eign film of the year, then listed its remain-ing favorites according to highest scores. The vote results were announced on December 20, 1950.

BEST PICTURE
- ▪ *Sunset Boulevard*
- *All about Eve*
- *The Asphalt Jungle*
- *The Men*
- *Edge of Doom*
- *Twelve O'Clock High*
- *Panic in the Streets*
- *Cyrano de Bergerac*
- *No Way Out*
- *Stage Fright*

BEST DIRECTOR
- ▪ John Huston, *The Asphalt Jungle*

BEST ACTOR
- ▪ Alec Guinness, *Kind Hearts and Coronets*

BEST ACTRESS
- ▪ Gloria Swanson, *Sunset Boulevard*

BEST FOREIGN FILM
- ▪ *The Titan—The Story of Michelangelo* (Italy)
- *Tight Little Island (Whiskey Galore)* (U.K.)
- *The Third Man* (U.K.)
- *Kind Hearts and Coronets* (U.K.)
- *Paris, 1900* (France)

NEW YORK FILM CRITICS

Winners were announced on December 27, 1950. Awards were presented on January 28, 1951, at the Rainbow Room in New York.

BEST PICTURE
- ▪ *All about Eve*

BEST DIRECTOR
- ▪ Joseph L. Mankiewicz, *All about Eve*

BEST ACTOR
- ▪ Gregory Peck, *Twelve O'Clock High*

BEST ACTRESS
- ▪ Bette Davis, *All about Eve*

BEST FOREIGN FILM
- ▪ *The Ways of Love* (France/Italy)

SCREEN WRITERS GUILD OF AMERICA

Awards were presented on February 20, 1951, at the Ambassador Hotel in Los Angeles. The ceremony was broadcast by NBC radio.

BEST WRITTEN DRAMA

- *Sunset Boulevard*, Charles Brackett, Billy Wilder, D. M. Marshman, Jr.

All about Eve, Joseph L. Mankiewicz

The Asphalt Jungle, Ben Maddow, John Huston, based on a novel by W. R. Burnett

The Men, Carl Foreman

Panic in the Streets, Richard Murphy, from a story by Edward and Edna Anhalt, adapted by Daniel Fuchs

BEST WRITTEN COMEDY

- *All about Eve*, Joseph L. Mankiewicz

Adam's Rib, Ruth Gordon, Garson Kanin (screenplay also nominated in 1949)

Born Yesterday, Albert Mannheimer, based on the play by Garson Kanin

Father of the Bride, Frances Goodrich, Albert Hackett, based on the novel by Edward Streeter

The Jackpot, Phoebe and Henry Ephron, based on a *New Yorker Magazine* article by John McNulty

BEST WRITTEN MUSICAL

- *Annie Get Your Gun*, Sidney Sheldon, based on the musical play by Herbert and Dorothy Fields with music and lyrics by Irving Berlin

My Blue Heaven, Lamar Trotti, Claude Binyon, S. K. Lauren

Summer Stock, George Wells, Sy Gomberg

Three Little Words, George Wells

The West Point Story, John Monks, Jr., Charles Hoffman, Irving Wallace

BEST SCREENPLAY DEALING MOST ABLY WITH PROBLEMS OF THE AMERICAN SCENE

- *The Men*, Carl Foreman

The Asphalt Jungle, Ben Maddow, John Huston, based on a novel by W. R. Burnett

Broken Arrow, Michael Blankfort, based on *Blood Brother*, a novel by Elliott Arnold

Judy Holliday (left) and José Ferrer heard the news of their Oscar victories via radio while at a Gotham eatery. Loser Gloria Swanson (right) failed to hide her disappointment.

No Way Out, Joseph L. Mankiewicz, Lesser Samuels

Panic in the Streets, Richard Murphy, from a story by Edward and Edna Anhalt, adapted by Daniel Fuchs

BEST WRITTEN WESTERN

- *Broken Arrow*,* Michael Blankfort, based on *Blood Brother*, a novel by Elliott Arnold

Devil's Doorway, Guy Trosper

The Gunfighter, William Bowers, William Sellers, Andre de Toth

Rio Grande, James Kevin McGuinness, based on the story "Mission with No Record" by James Warner Bellah

A Ticket to Tomahawk, Mary Loos, Richard Sale

Winchester .73, Robert L. Richards, Borden Chase, based on a story by Stuart L. Lake

ROBERT MELTZER AWARD

- Carl Foreman, *The Men*

GOLDEN GLOBES

Nominations were announced on February 9, 1951. Awards were presented on February 28 at Ciro's nightclub in Los Angeles.

BEST PICTURE

- *Sunset Boulevard*

All about Eve

---

*In 1991, the Guild acknowledged scribe Albert Maltz, posthumously, as the actual winner.

Born Yesterday
Cyrano de Bergerac
Harvey

BEST PICTURE PROMOTING INTERNATIONAL UNDERSTANDING
- *Broken Arrow*
The Big Lift
The Next Voice You Hear

BEST DIRECTOR
- Billy Wilder, *Sunset Boulevard*
George Cukor, *Born Yesterday*
John Huston, *The Asphalt Jungle*
Joseph L. Mankiewicz, *All about Eve*

BEST ACTOR, DRAMA
- José Ferrer, *Cyrano de Bergerac*
Louis Calhurn, *Magnificent Yankee*
James Stewart, *Harvey*

BEST ACTRESS, DRAMA
- Gloria Swanson, *Sunset Boulevard*
Bette Davis, *All about Eve*
Judy Holliday, *Born Yesterday*

BEST ACTOR, COMEDY OR MUSICAL
- Fred Astaire, *Three Little Words*
Dan Dailey, *When Willie Comes Marching Home*
Harold Lloyd, *Mad Wednesday*

BEST ACTRESS, COMEDY OR MUSICAL
- Judy Holliday, *Born Yesterday*
Spring Byington, *Louisa*
Betty Hutton, *Annie Get Your Gun*

BEST SUPPORTING ACTOR
- Edmund Gwenn, *Mister 880*
George Sanders, *All about Eve*
Erich von Stroheim, *Sunset Boulevard*

BEST SUPPORTING ACTRESS
- Josephine Hull, *Harvey*
Judy Holliday, *Adam's Rib*
Thelma Ritter, *All about Eve*

MOST PROMISING NEWCOMER
- Gene Nelson, *Tea for Two*
Mala Powers
Debbie Reynolds

BEST SCREENPLAY
- *All about Eve*, Joseph L. Mankiewicz
The Asphalt Jungle, John Huston, Ben Maddow
Sunset Boulevard, Charles Brackett, D. M. Marshman., Jr., Billy Wilder

Winners

BEST CINEMATOGRAPHY, BLACK AND WHITE
- Frank Planer, *Cyrano de Bergerac*

BEST CINEMATOGRAPHY, COLOR
- Robert Surtees, *King Solomon's Mines*

BEST ORIGINAL SCORE
- Franz Waxman, *Sunset Boulevard*

WORLD FILM FAVORITES
- Gregory Peck
- Jane Wyman

ACADEMY AWARDS

Nominations were announced on February 12, 1951. Awards were presented on March 29 at the RKO Pantages Theatre in Hollywood.

BEST PICTURE
- *All about Eve*
Born Yesterday
Father of the Bride
King Solomon's Mines
Sunset Boulevard

BEST DIRECTOR
- Joseph L. Mankiewicz, *All about Eve*
George Cukor, *Born Yesterday*
John Huston, *The Asphalt Jungle*
Carol Reed, *The Third Man*
Billy Wilder, *Sunset Boulevard*

BEST ACTOR
- José Ferrer, *Cyrano de Bergerac*
Louis Calhern, *The Magnificent Yankee*
William Holden, *Sunset Boulevard*
James Stewart, *Harvey*
Spencer Tracy, *Father of the Bride*

BEST ACTRESS
- Judy Holliday, *Born Yesterday*
Anne Baxter, *All about Eve*

Bette Davis, *All about Eve*
Eleanor Parker, *Caged*
Gloria Swanson, *Sunset Boulevard*

BEST SUPPORTING ACTOR

■ George Sanders, *All about Eve*
Jeff Chandler, *Broken Arrow*
Edmund Gwenn, *Mister 880*
Sam Jaffe, *The Asphalt Jungle*
Erich von Stroheim, *Sunset Boulevard*

BEST SUPPORTING ACTRESS

■ Josephine Hull, *Harvey*
Hope Emerson, *Caged*
Celeste Holm, *All about Eve*
Nancy Olson, *Sunset Boulevard*
Thelma Ritter, *All about Eve*

BEST WRITING (STORY)

Edna Anhalt, Edward Anhalt, *Panic in the Streets*
William Bowers, Andre de Toth, *The Gunfighter*
Giuseppe de Santis, Carlo Lizzani, *Bitter Rice*
Sy Gomberg, *When Willie Comes Marching Home*
Leonard Spigelgass, *Mystery Street*

BEST WRITING (SCREENPLAY)

■ Joseph L. Mankiewicz, *All about Eve*
Micheal Blankfort, *Father of the Bride*
Albert Hackett, Frances Goodrich, *Father of the Bride*
John Huston, Ben Maddow, *The Asphalt Jungle*
Albert Maltz, *Broken Arrow*
Albert Mannheimer, *Born Yesterday*

BEST WRITING (STORY AND SCREENPLAY)

■ Charles Brackett, D. M. Marshman, Jr., Billy Wilder, *Sunset Boulevard*
Carl Foreman, *The Men*
Ruth Gordon, Garson Kanin, *Adam's Rib*
Virginia Kellogg, Bernard C. Schoenfeld, *Caged*
Joseph L. Mankiewicz, Lesser Samuels, *No Way Out*

BEST SONG

■ "Mona Lisa," *Captain Carey, U.S.A.*, Ray Evans, Jay Livingston

"Be My Love," *The Toast of New Orleans*, Nicholas Brodszky, Sammy Cahn
"Bibbidi-Bobbidi-Boo," *Cinderella*, Mack David, Al Hoffman, Jerry Livingston
"Mule Train," *Singing Guns*, Fred Glickman, Hy Heath, Johnny Lange
"Wilhelmina," *Wabash Avenue*, Mack Gordon, Josef Myrow

Winners

BEST ART DIRECTION /SET DECORATION
(BLACK AND WHITE)
■ Hans Dreier, John Meehan, Sam Comer, Ray Moyer, *Sunset Boulevard*
(COLOR)
■ Hans Dreier, Walter Tyler, Sam Comer, Ray Moyer, *Samson and Delilah*

BEST CINEMATOGRAPHY
(BLACK AND WHITE)
■ Robert Krasker, *The Third Man*
(COLOR)
■ Robert Surtees, *King Solomon's Mines*

BEST COSTUME DESIGN
(BLACK AND WHITE)
■ Edith Head, Charles Lemaire, *All about Eve*
(COLOR)
■ Edith Head, Dorothy Jeakins, Elois Jenssen, Gile Steele, Gwen Wakeling, *Samson and Delilah*

BEST DOCUMENTARY
(FEATURE)
■ *The Titan—Story of Michelangelo*
(SHORT SUBJECT)
■ *Why Korea?* Twentieth Century-Fox Movietone

BEST FILM EDITING
■ Conrad A. Nervig, Ralph E. Winters, *King Solomon's Mines*

BEST MUSIC
(SCORING OF A DRAMATIC OR COMEDY PICTURE)
■ Franz Waxman, *Sunset Boulevard*
(SCORING OF A MUSICAL PICTURE)
■ Adolph Deutsch, Roger Edens, *Annie Get Your Gun*

SCIENTIFIC OR TECHNICAL AWARDS

Class II (Plaque)

- James B. Gordon, Twentieth Century-Fox Studio Camera Dept.; John Paul Livadary, Floyd Campbell, L. W. Russell, Columbia Studio Sound Department; Loren L. Ryder, Paramount Studio Sound Dept.

BEST SHORT SUBJECT

(CARTOON)

- *Gerald McBoing-Boing*, UPA, Columbia

(ONE REEL)

- *Grandad of Races,* Warner Bros.

(TWO REEL)

- *In Beaver Valley*, Disney, RKO Radio

BEST SOUND RECORDING

- Thomas T. Moulton, Twentieth Century-Fox Sound Department, *All about Eve*

BEST SPECIAL EFFECTS

- George Pal, Eagle-Lion, *Destination Moon*

HONORARY FOREIGN-LANGUAGE FILM AWARD

- *The Walls of Malapaga* (France/Italy)

IRVING G. THALBERG MEMORIAL AWARD

- Darryl F. Zanuck

SPECIAL AWARDS

- Louis B. Mayer
- George Murphy

SCREEN DIRECTORS GUILD OF AMERICA

Nominees were all winners of the guild's quarterly awards. A separate award was bestowed for best director of the year on May 27, 1951, at the Beverly Hills Hotel. The ceremony was broadcast by NBC radio.

BEST DIRECTOR

- Joseph L. Mankiewicz, *All about Eve*

John Huston, *The Asphalt Jungle*

Vincente Minnelli, *Father's Little Dividend*

Billy Wilder, *Sunset Boulevard*

▪ 1951 ▪

Streetcar *Derailed*

There seemed to be only two serious contenders for the year's trophies for top pic, both of them dramatizing doomed love triangles. The National Board of Review declared one of them Best Picture first: *A Place in the Sun*, hailed by *Variety* for its "wonderfully shaded and poignant performances" by Montgomery Clift, Shelley Winters and Elizabeth Taylor. *Variety* also applauded the acting in the rival movie, *A Streetcar Named Desire*, an adaptation of Tennessee Williams's stage sensation chosen as Best Picture by the New York Film Critics four years after it was voted best Broadway play by the New York Drama Critics Circle. The tradepaper said Vivien Leigh was "compelling," Kim Hunter "excellent" and Marlon Brando "strong," but groused that the latter's perf was "marked by frequent garbling of his dialog."

The National Board of Review snubbed all of the above stars for its acting honors, however, preferring Richard Basehart as a desperate man on a skyscraper ledge in *Fourteen Hours* and Jan Sterling as the uncaring wife of a man trapped in an Indian cave in *The Big Carnival* (originally released as *An Ace in the Hole*). The board continued its recent romance with foreign films by voting Akira Kurosawa Best Director for the Japanese art house hit *Rashomon*, which also earned its laurels for Best Foreign Film after winning the Grand Prize at the Venice Film Festival.

But the board's Best Picture *A Place in the Sun* was not a top contender among the New York film crix. Toughest competish came from a movie overlooked earlier by the board and, later, the Oscars: *The River*, director Jean Renoir's "distinctive story of adolescent love with a philosophy that life flows on just as the Ganges River in West Bengal," according to *Variety*. Among the 15 crix voting, *Streetcar* nabbed five votes

A Streetcar Named Desire swept the N.Y. crix kudos, but then appeared to crash at the Globes and guilds' awards.

to *River*'s four on the first ballot and finally won on the sixth round by the narrow edge of eight to seven.

Streetcar easily claimed the Best Actress accolade for Vivien Leigh, who'd recently received the same honor at the Venice fest. The pic's helmer, Elia Kazan, also reaped the scroll for Best Director. Brando led on the first ballot for Best Actor, tying Arthur Kennedy, who portrayed a blinded war veteran in *Bright Victory*. Brando's support never built beyond 5 votes, though, so Kennedy finally claimed ultimate victory on the third tally with 10 crix behind him. For a second time in three years, Italian helmer Vittorio De Sica won Best Foreign Film, this time for what he called his "fantastic comedy," *Miracle in Milan*, which beat *Rashomon* by the same 10–5 score.

When the crix gathered to bestow their four scrolls and single bronze plaque, *Streetcar*, winner of most of them, arrived at the Algonquin Hotel with all its champs aboard. They were greeted in the Rose Room by stars sipping bourbon old-fashioneds and scotches and soda, reported the *Morning Telegraph*, while Jackie Cooper "stood at the corner of the bar looking over the crowd with great interest (and) Henry Fonda sat on one of the leather settees along the entrance trying to keep his feet out of the way."

When everyone else took their seats for the formal ceremony, crix topper Bosley Crowther of the *Times* turned the crowd's attention to "the gentleman sitting at Miss Vivien Leigh's side," noted the *Morning Telegraph*, "a handsome, heavy-lidded English actor who also happens to be her husband."

"We are particularly fortunate in having Sir Laurence with us at this time," Crowther said, "so that we may now convey to him in person our felicitations and congratulations for having also won an award from the New York Film Critics two years ago for his portrayal of *Hamlet*. Now perhaps Sir Laurence and Lady Olivier will be able to hang these two scrolls on opposite walls of their living room, one marked 'his' and the other marked 'hers.' " The *Morning Telegraph* observed, "Sir Laurence had a thoughtful look on his face as if it might not be a bad idea."

When calling attention to Vivien Leigh, Crowther praised her beauty and suggested that her Dixie character in *Streetcar* could possibly be the great-granddaughter of her character in *Gone With the Wind*, a film that had earned Leigh a crix's scroll 12 twelve years earlier.

Elia Kazan was also present to accept his scroll for directing *Streetcar* while producer Charles Feldman claimed the weighty bronze plaque for Best Picture. Missing were Arthur Kennedy (his pal Jane Wyatt stood

in) and Vittorio de Sica (*Miracle*'s U.S. distributor took his bow). Once the awards were bestowed, the rest of the ceremony was broadcast on Ed Sullivan's CBS variety show *Toast of the Town*.

A few weeks later, the Golden Globes ceremony, hosted by Dick Powell at Ciro's restaurant, took on a somber tone when it inaugurated a special new prize to be bestowed annually "to the most outstanding motion picture personality." Ronald Reagan bestowed the first Cecil B. DeMille Award to DeMille himself, who accepted it by thanking "you foreign correspondents, to whom no part of the free world is really foreign. You are promoting a medium that is truly a universal language, the motion picture."

A Place in the Sun triumphed as best drama picture, but, strangely, it received no other awards. The tally champ was *Death of a Salesman*, earning four. "The vise-like grip with which *Death of a Salesman* held Broadway theatergoers for almost two years continues undiminished," *Variety* said of the film version. "Fredric March, in the part created on the New York stage by Lee Cobb, gives perhaps the greatest performance of his career. Kevin McCarthy, as Biff, is a film newcomer who entrenches himself strongly in the role." Globes went to Best Actor March, New Male Artist of the Year McCarthy, top helmer Laslo Benedek and the pic's cinematographer. March wasn't present at Ciro's restaurant to receive the honor, but he telephoned his acceptance speech from Washington, D.C. Seven months later, March would reap another top accolade for his perf: the Volpi Cup as Best Actor at the Venice Film Festival.

Although *Streetcar*'s Kim Hunter prevailed as Best Supporting Actress, a shocker occurred in the race for best female thesp when Broadway darling Vivien Leigh was edged by Jane Wyman as a World War I widow who devotes her life to helping children in *The Blue Veil*.

Streetcar lost to A Place in the Sun at the Golden Globes.

In the races for best comedy or musical thesps, June Allyson prevailed for *Too Young to Kiss*, a choice applauded by *The Hollywood Citizen-News* because the star, pretending to be a child prodigy, "enacted both a young lady and a teen-ager, a difficult assignment that she managed with great skill and finesse." Best Actor went to Danny Kaye, who also portrayed dual roles—as an entertainer and French war hero in *On the Riviera*. Wyman and Allyson were present to accept their laurels, but Jack Benny stood in for Danny Kaye.

Neither *Too Young to Kiss* nor *On the Riviera* took the new award for Best Comedy or Musical Picture, which went, as expected, to blockbuster *An American in Paris*, "one of the most imaginative musical confections turned out by Hollywood," raved *Variety*.

The tuner also claimed the accolade as Best Written Musical from the Screen Writers Guild, although the group "took the edge off the excitement" of this year's kudos, said *Variety*, by informing winners of their victories one week before they received plaques before 1,200 of their peers gathering at the Hollywood Palladium. The plaque for Best Written Drama was shared by *A Place in the Sun*'s Michael Wilson, who was recently blacklisted in Hollywood after taking the Fifth Amendment and refusing to reveal to the House Committee on Un-American Activities whether he was a Communist.

On the eve of the Oscars, *Variety* polled 15 percent of the academy's 1,700 members and predicted that *A Streetcar Named Desire* and *A Place in the Sun* would split the top awards this year, with the former taking the four acting trophies and *Place* prevailing for Best Picture ("by a comfortable poll margin") and Director (George Stevens "walked away with the award in the poll"). Both pics had head starts. *Streetcar* led with 12 noms, followed by nine for *Place* and eight each for MGM's two big screeners *Quo Vadis* and *An American in Paris*. Between the latter

two, new MGM chief Dore Schary was rooting for *Quo Vadis?* so he could recoup his $7 million investment in the soaper about ancient Rome that *Variety* said suffered from aesthetic "shortcomings."

On awards night, most of *Variety*'s prophesies came true. *A Place in the Sun*'s George Stevens received the helmer's laurels just as he'd reaped the equivalent kudo from the directors' guild a few weeks earlier. *Streetcar*'s supporting stars triumphed, too. Ex–New Yorker Karl Malden was the only *Streetcar* winner present, however, and he broadcast his appreciation for Oscar's golden welcome gift when he accepted it, saying, "I haven't been out here very long, but I can tell you how I feel—great!"

Meantime, Kim Hunter was in Malden's hometown rehearsing a new Broadway play when she got word that she had won the statuette for Best Supporting Actress, which was accepted for her by Bette Davis. Vivien Leigh was already performing on Broadway and couldn't break away for a trip to the coast to claim the second Oscar everyone knew she'd win—and did. That would've meant maneuvering past the throngs of fans storming the Ziegfeld Theater where she and her knighted lover starred, on alternate nights, in George Bernard Shaw's *Caesar and Cleopatra* and Shakepeare's *Antony and Cleopatra*. "Two on the Nile" was what local wags called the biggest Broadway event in years, which earned Leigh, for the first time ever, better reviews than Olivier.

Streetcar's Marlon Brando was also missing on Oscar night, even though the aloof star was expected to be honored for the role he initiated on Broadway. Brando was so detached from all the Oscar hubbub that he hadn't even bothered to campaign. By contrast, Humphrey Bogart invested in extensive trade advertising and hired a publicist to hype his role in *The African Queen* as a scruffy captain of a riverboat carrying a haughty Katharine Hepburn. As of Oscar

> The Oscar audience gasped when *An American in Paris* won Best Picture.

night, Bogart's chances had improved considerably. *Variety* reported, "Brando's lead is comparatively slim and Arthur Kennedy, Humphrey Bogart and Fredric March are all bunched closely together behind him. A last-minute surge for any of the other three leading contenders could end Brando's chance to win an award with his second film appearance."

It was Greer Garson's job this year to bestow the prize. *Variety* observed: "There was a pause as she opened the envelope and stared, almost unbelievingly for a second, before announcing triumphantly, 'Humphrey Bogart!' The crowded house came to life almost for the first time, giving Bogart an ovation as he strode down the aisle."

"It's a very long way from the heart of the Belgian Congo to the stage of the Pantages Theater," he said. "But I'm here. And I want to thank John Huston and Katharine Hepburn, who helped make it possible." *Variety* columnist Army Archerd reported that, after Bogart won, the whiskey-loving skipper "anchored at Romanoff's restaurant bar for a week."

Bogie's upset would turn out to be one of several shockers on awards night. Another occurred when *A Place in the Sun* scribe Michael Wilson earned screenwriters' honor from academy voters, who were thought to be far more conservative than members of the Screen Writers Guild.

But the biggest jaw-dropper on Oscar night occurred just as "some of the audience had begun to file out silently" before the last award was bestowed, *Variety* said. "The retreating crowd was stunned into a momentary silence" when the winner was revealed: *An American in Paris*. "The audible gasp from every section of the house was quickly replaced by applause."

Instead of gasps of surprise, the next day's newspapers were filled with cries of outrage from highbrow film critics who suddenly forgot that they had sung the tuner's praises when it opened the previous summer.

The film's producing studio countered by roaring proudly but humbly in the pages of *Variety*. It ran an ad that depicted the MGM lion looking slyly at his Oscar, saying, "Honestly, I was just standing *In the Sun* waiting for *A Streetcar*."

The high-stepping *An American in Paris* carried off the lion's share of Oscars (six), including trophies for best screenplay, music score, color cinematography, color art direction and color costume design. Neither star-choreographer Gene Kelly nor scribe Alan Jay Lerner was present to step up to the podium and accept his honors.

"It was a night of stand-ins with few principals present," noted columnist Sheilah Graham, who headed backstage after the kudofest and caught sight of Bette Davis dashing about, waving Kim Hunter's statuette and shrieking, "It's great! It's great! But it isn't mine. I won mine a long time ago!"

"Yeah, about 25 years!" Bogart snarled.

"Bette bounced out," *Variety* observed.

▪ 1951 ▪

NATIONAL BOARD OF REVIEW

The board declared a best picture and foreign film of the year, then listed its remaining favorites according to highest scores. The vote results were announced on December 17, 1951.

BEST PICTURE

▪ *A Place in the Sun*
The Red Badge of Courage
An American in Paris
Death of a Salesman
Detective Story
A Streetcar Named Desire
Decision before Dawn
Strangers on a Train
Quo Vadis?
Fourteen Hours

BEST DIRECTOR
- Akira Kurosawa, *Rashomon*

BEST ACTOR
- Richard Basehart, *Fourteen Hours*

BEST ACTRESS
- Jan Sterling, *The Big Carnival* (*Ace in the Hole*)

BEST SCREENPLAY
- T. E. B. Clarke, *The Lavender Hill Mob*

BEST FOREIGN FILM
- *Rashomon* (Japan)
The River (India)
Miracle in Milan (Italy)
Kon-Tiki (Norway/Sweden)
The Browning Version (U.K.)

NEW YORK FILM CRITICS

Winners were announced on December 27, 1951. Awards were presented on January 20, 1952, at the Algonquin Hotel in New York. Part of the ceremony was broadcast on Ed Sullivan's CBS TV program *Toast of the Town*.

BEST PICTURE
- *A Streetcar Named Desire*

BEST DIRECTOR
- Elia Kazan, *A Streetcar Named Desire*

BEST ACTOR
- Arthur Kennedy, *Bright Victory*

BEST ACTRESS
- Vivien Leigh, *A Streetcar Named Desire*

BEST FOREIGN FILM
- *Miracle in Milan* (Italy)

SCREEN DIRECTORS GUILD OF AMERICA

Only three quarterly awards were bestowed because the prize for best director of the year was presented on January 27, 1952, which was earlier in the calendar than last year. The quarterly winners were the final

nominees for the annual award; other directors listed were nominees for the quarterly honors.

BEST DIRECTOR
- George Stevens, *A Place in the Sun* (also quarterly winner)
Laslo Benedek, *Death of a Salesman*
Michael Gordon, *Cyrano de Bergerac*
Alfred Hitchcock, *Strangers on a Train* (quarterly winner)
Elia Kazan, *A Streetcar Named Desire*
Henry King, *David and Bathsheba*
Mervyn LeRoy, *Quo Vadis?*
Anatole Litvak, *Decision before Dawn*
Vicente Minneli, *An American in Paris* (quarterly winner)
George Sidney, *Showboat*
Richard Thorpe, *The Great Caruso*
William Wyler, *Detective Story*

GOLDEN GLOBES

Nominations were announced on January 31, 1952. Awards were presented on February 21 at Ciro's restaurant in Los Angeles. (*Note:* Only a partial list survives of nominees and winners.)

Humphrey Bogart (with Katharine Hepburn in *The African Queen*) pulled off an upset for the Best Actor Oscar when Marlon Brando refused to campaign.

BEST DRAMA PICTURE
- *A Place in the Sun*
Bright Victory
Detective Story
Quo Vadis?
A Streetcar Named Desire

BEST COMEDY OR MUSICAL PICTURE
- *An American in Paris*

BEST PICTURE PROMOTING INTERNATIONAL UNDERSTANDING
- *The Day the Earth Stood Still*

BEST DIRECTOR
- Laslo Benedek, *Death of a Salesman*
George Stevens, *A Place in the Sun*
Mervyn Leroy, *An American in Paris*

BEST ACTOR, DRAMA
- Fredric March, *Death of a Salesman*
Kirk Douglas, *Detective Story*
Arthur Kennedy, *Bright Victory*

BEST ACTRESS, DRAMA
- Jane Wyman, *The Blue Veil*
Shelley Winters, *A Place in the Sun*
Vivien Leigh, *A Streetcar Named Desire*

BEST ACTOR, COMEDY OR MUSICAL
- Danny Kaye, *On the Riviera*
Bing Crosby, *Here Comes the Groom*
Gene Kelly, *An American in Paris*

BEST ACTRESS, COMEDY OR MUSICAL
- June Allyson, *Too Young to Kiss*

BEST SUPPORTING ACTOR
- Peter Ustinov, *Quo Vadis*

BEST SUPPORTING ACTRESS
- Kim Hunter, *A Streetcar Named Desire*
Lee Grant, *Detective Story*
Thelma Ritter, *The Mating Season*

MOST PROMISING NEWCOMER—MALE
- Kevin McCarthy, *Death of a Salesman*

MOST PROMISING NEWCOMER—FEMALE
- Pier Angeli, *Teresa*

Winners

BEST CINEMATOGRAPHY, BLACK AND WHITE
- Frank Planer, *Death of a Salesman*

BEST CINEMATOGRAPHY, COLOR
- William V. Skall, *Quo Vadis?*
- Robert Surtees, *Quo Vadis?*

BEST ORIGINAL SCORE
- Victor Young, *A September Affair*

BEST SCREENPLAY
- Robert Buckner, *Bright Victory*

SPECIAL ACHIEVEMENT AWARD
- Esther Williams, *Henrietta* (Most Popular Actress)

CECIL B. DEMILLE AWARD
- Cecil B. DeMille

SCREEN WRITERS GUILD OF AMERICA

Winners were announced on February 18, 1951. Awards were presented on February 25 at the Hollywood Palladium.

BEST WRITTEN DRAMA
- *A Place in the Sun*, Michael Wilson, Harry Brown, based on the novel *An American Tragedy* by Theodore Dreiser and the play adapted by Patrick Kearney
Death of a Salesman, Stanley Roberts, based on the play by Arthur Miller
Detective Story, Philip Yordan, Robert Wyler, based on the play by Sidney Kingsley
Fourteen Hours, John Paxton, Joel Sayre
A Streetcar Named Desire, Tennessee Williams, based on his play as adapted by Oscar Saul

BEST WRITTEN COMEDY
- *Father's Little Dividend*, Frances Goodrich, Albert Hackett
People Will Talk, Joseph L. Mankiewicz, based on the play *Dr. Praetorius* by Curt Goetz
That's My Boy, Cy Howard
You're in the Navy Now, Richard Murphy,

based on a *New Yorker Magazine* article by John W. Hazard

BEST WRITTEN MUSICAL

- *An American in Paris*, Alan Jay Lerner
The Great Caruso, Sonya Levien, William Ludwig
Here Comes the Groom, Virginia Van Upp, Liam O'Brien, Myles Connolly, Robert Riskin
On the Riviera, Valentine Davies, Phoebe Ephron, Henry Ephron, based on the play by Rudolph Lothar and Hans Adler, adapted by Jessie Ernst
Show Boat, John Lee Mahin, adapted from the musical play by Jerome Kern and Oscar Hammerstein II, based on the novel by Edna Ferber

BEST SCREENPLAY DEALING MOST ABLY WITH PROBLEMS OF THE AMERICAN SCENE

- *Bright Victory*, Robert Buckner, based on the novel *Lights Out* by Baynard Kendrick
Death of a Salesman, Stanley Roberts, based on the play by Arthur Miller
A Place in the Sun, Michael Wilson, Harry Brown, based on the novel *An American Tragedy* by Theodore Dreiser and the play adapted by Patrick Kearney
Saturday's Hero, Millard Lampell, Sidney Buchman, based on the novel *The Hero* by Millard Lampell
The Well, Russell Rouse, Clarence Greene

BEST WRITTEN LOW-BUDGET FILM

- *The Steel Helmet*, Samuel Fuller
The First Legion, Emmet Lavery
Five, Arch Oboler
Little Big Horn, Charles Marquis Warren, Harold Shumate
Pick-Up, Hugo Haas, Arnold Phillips, based on the novel by Joseph Kopta

ROBERT MELTZER AWARD

- Robert Buckner, *Bright Victory*

ACADEMY AWARDS

Nominations were announced on February 11, 1952. Awards were presented on March 20 at the RKO Pantages Theatre in Hollywood.

BEST PICTURE

- *An American in Paris*
Decision before Dawn
A Place in the Sun
Quo Vadis?
A Streetcar Named Desire

BEST DIRECTOR

- George Stevens, *A Place in the Sun?*
John Huston, *The African Queen*
Elia Kazan, *A Streetcar Named Desire*
Vincente Minnelli, *An American in Paris*
William Wyler, *Detective Story*

BEST ACTOR

- Humphrey Bogart, *The African Queen*
Marlon Brando, *A Streetcar Named Desire*
Montgomery Clift, *A Place in the Sun*
Arthur Kennedy, *Bright Victory*
Fredric March, *Death of a Salesman*

BEST ACTRESS

- Vivien Leigh, *A Streetcar Named Desire*
Katharine Hepburn, *The African Queen*
Eleanor Parker, *Detective Story*
Shelley Winters, *A Place in the Sun*
Jane Wyman, *The Blue Veil*

BEST SUPPORTING ACTOR

- Karl Malden, *A Streetcar Named Desire*
Leo Genn, *Quo Vadis?*
Kevin McCarthy, *Death of a Salesman*
Peter Ustinov, *Quo Vadis?*
Gig Young, *Come Fill the Cup*

BEST SUPPORTING ACTRESS

- Kim Hunter, *A Streetcar Named Desire*
Joan Blondell, *The Blue Veil*
Mildred Dunnock, *Death of a Salesman*
Lee Grant, *Detective Story*
Thelma Ritter, *The Mating Season*

BEST WRITING (STORY)

- James Bernard, Paul Dehn, *Seven Days to Noon*
Budd Boetticher, Ray Nazarro, *Bullfighter and the Lady*
Alfred Hayes, Stewart Stern, *Teresa*
Oscar Millard, *The Frogmen*

Liam O'Brien, Robert Riskin, *Here Comes the Groom*

BEST WRITING (SCREENPLAY)
- Harry Brown, Michael Wilson, *A Place in the Sun*

James Agee, John Huston, *The African Queen*

Jacques Natanson, Max Ophuls, *La Ronde*

Tennessee Williams, *A Streetcar Named Desire*

Robert Wyler, Philip Yordan, *Detective Story*

BEST WRITING (STORY AND SCREENPLAY)
- Alan Jay Lerner, *An American in Paris*

Philip Dunne, *David and Bathsheba*

Clarence Greene, Russell Rouse, *The Well*

Walter Newman, Lesser Samuels, Billy Wilder, *The Big Carnival*

Robert Pirosh, *Go for Broke!*

BEST SONG
- "In the Cool, Cool, Cool of the Evening," *Here Comes the Groom*, Hoagy Carmichael, Johnny Mercer

"A Kiss to Build a Dream On," *The Strip*, Oscar Hammerstein II, Bert Kalmar, Harry Ruby

"Too Late Now," *Royal Wedding*, Burton Lane, Alan Jay Lerner

"Never," *Golden Girl*, Eliot Daniel, Lionel Newman

"Wonder Why," *Rich, Young and Pretty*, Nicholas Brodszky, Sammy Cahn

Winners

BEST ART DIRECTION/SET DECORATION
(BLACK AND WHITE)
- Richard Day, George James Hopkins, *A Streetcar Named Desire*

(COLOR)
- Preston Ames, Cedric Gibbons, Keogh Gleason, Edwin B. Willis, *An American in Paris*

BEST CINEMATOGRAPHY
(BLACK AND WHITE)
- William C. Mellor, *A Place in the Sun*

(COLOR)
- John Alton, Alfred Gilks, *An American in Paris*

BEST COSTUME DESIGN
(BLACK AND WHITE)
- Edith Head, *A Place in the Sun*

(COLOR)
- Orry-Kelly, Walter Plunkett, Irene Sharaff, *An American in Paris*

BEST DOCUMENTARY
(FEATURE)
- *Kon-Tiki*

(SHORT SUBJECT)
- *Benjy*

BEST FILM EDITING
- William Hornbeck, *A Place in the Sun*

BEST MUSIC
(SCORING OF A DRAMATIC OR COMEDY PICTURE)
- Franz Waxman, *A Place in the Sun*

(SCORING OF A MUSICAL PICTURE)
- Saul Chaplin, Johnny Green, *An American in Paris*

SCIENTIFIC OR TECHNICAL AWARDS
Class II (Plaque)
- Olin L. Dupy, MGM Studio; Gordon Jennings, S. L. Stancliffe, Paramount Studio Special Photographic and Engineering Departments; RCA Victor Division

Class III (Certificate)
- Richard M. Haff, Frank P. Herrnfeld, Garland C. Misener, Ansco Film Division of General Aniline and Film Corp.; Fred Ponedel, Ralph Ayres, George Brown, Warner Bros.; Glen Robinson, Jack Gaylord, MGM Construction Dept.; Carols Rivas, MGM

BEST SHORT SUBJECT
(CARTOON)
- *Two Mouseketeers*

(ONE REEL)
- *World of Kids*

(TWO REEL)
- *Nature's Half Acre*

BEST SOUND RECORDING
- Douglas Shearer, *The Great Caruso*

BEST SPECIAL EFFECTS
- Paramount, *When Worlds Collide*

HONORARY FOREIGN-LANGUAGE FILM AWARD
- *Rashomon* (Japan)

IRVING G. THALBERG MEMORIAL AWARD
- Arthur Freed

HONORARY AWARD
- Gene Kelly

High Noon *Shoot-Out*

For the first time ever, the National Board of Review and the New York Film Critics agreed on the same Best Actor and Actress of the year.

Their leading male thesp was the star of *Breaking the Sound Barrier*, Ralph Richardson, who gave, said *The New York Times*, "a restrained portrayal of a mentally harried plant manufacturer who essays to build a supersonic aircraft in the British-made feature." Richardson also gave Charlie Chaplin a serious fight for this award. The crix got caught giving Chaplin an insincere palm in 1940, but now many of them thought they owed him a real one and considered honoring him for his role in *Limelight*, which eerily mirrored Chaplin's real life as an aging clown. The onetime Little Tramp led Richardson on the crix's first ballot by a score of five to two, but then Richardson rallied to claim the necessary two-thirds vote on the fifth ballot, winning 10 to 5.

Although *The African Queen* competed at last year's Oscars, its late release in New York City pushed it into consideration for this year's crix kudos. Its star Katharine Hepburn didn't really get much consideration, in the end, however; Shirley Booth won Best Actress easily on the second ballot by a tally of 12 to 3 for her brave portrayal of an alcoholic's groveling wife in *Come Back, Little Sheba*. "Shirley Booth has the remarkable gift of never appearing to be acting," *Variety* praised her in its review. But Booth had originally honed the part to perfection while performing it hundreds of times on Broadway, earning a Tony Award in 1950. More kudos would follow. After sweeping the board and crix's votes for her film rendition next, Booth would go on to claim a Golden Globe and Oscar, too. Only once before had one star claimed all four U.S. film prizes in a single year: Ray Milland for *The Lost Weekend* in 1945. Both

New York crix's and National Board of Review's Best Actor Ralph Richardson (*Breaking the Sound Barrier*) was not nommed at the Globes or Oscars.

Milland and Booth also received offshore laurels at Cannes.

The African Queen also figured into the crix's election for Best Picture, earning three votes on the first ballot, which put it in second place behind *High Noon*, with five. Thereafter the two pics squared off in a fierce duel that lasted six rounds, with *High Noon* finally emerging victorious, 10 to 5, once the smoke cleared.

High Noon was one of the year's high points in film, both critically and commercially. It starred Gary Cooper as a retiring frontier marshal who's compelled by conscience to linger in his job long enough to take on a mad gunman without any help from cowering townspeople. "*High Noon* is a stinging comprehension of courage and cowardice, done with directness and momentum in a familiar Western frame," cheered *The New York Times*'s Bosley Crowther. "It bears a close relation to things that are happening in the world today, where people are being terrorized by bullies and surrendering their freedoms out of senselessness and fear." Crowther was referring to Washington D.C.'s recent attack on Hollywood leftists, including *High Noon*'s scribe Carl Foreman, who, Crowther added, "is virtually an enforced exile from Hollywood where he finds doors shut to his talents. He is now living abroad."

The crix gave *High Noon*'s megger Fred Zinnemann the two-thirds vote he needed to win Best Director on the second ballot after he towered over six rivals on the first. Missing among the contenders, curiously, was the crix's fave choice in the past, four-time champ John Ford, who had a triumphant year helming his first romantic drama, *The Quiet Man*, starring John Wayne as a boxer who returns to his Irish homeland and falls in love with a spunky Maureen O'Hara. Ford would receive a valued consolation prize from his peers by reaping the top award "at the Screen Directors Guild of America's annual dinner at the Biltmore Bowl before an SRO crowd of 800," noted *Variety*. *The Quiet Man* was also the National Board of Review's choice for Best Picture and it was voted the year's best-penned comedy by the Screen Writers Guild; *High Noon* copped the scribes' kudos for dramas.

To receive his plaque from the crix for Best Picture, *High Noon*'s producer Stanley Kramer joined them at the famed showbiz eatery Sardi's, which would remain the chief venue for the kudos' presentation for decades to come. Also on hand were Best Director Zinnemann and Best Actress Booth. Missing was Richardson, who was back in his native Britain touring in a new

play, but he sent his thanks on audiotape. "Before the ceremonies, the winners participated in an afternoon program telecast by NBC TV, including scenes from the films, that was repeated over the NBC radio network at 11:30 P.M.," the *Times* reported. The peacock web was becoming America's top kudos telecaster since it also aired the Oscar show.

High Noon would soon claim honors from the foreign press in Hollywood, too, but the accolades would come from *two* groups, not one. A faction of the Hollywood Foreign Correspondents Association had recently broken away and set up rival showbiz awards. The Foreign Press Association's presentation, emceed by Vincent Price, was held in Palm Springs; the HFCA ceremony, presided over by David Wayne, was held at the Ambassador Hotel in Los Angeles.

"Of the two dinners, the FPA's with their Henriettas ran the faster show," said *Variety* columnist Frank Scully. "The HFCA's with their Golden Globes showed more glamour." Both groups named Susan Hayward Best Actress for *With a Song in My Heart*. She claimed the Globe for best perf in a comedy or musical, while the Globe for drama thesp went to Shirley Booth. The Henrietta Award for Best Actor was bestowed upon John Wayne for *The Quiet Man*, while the two male Globes went to Gary Cooper for *High Noon* (best drama actor) and Donald O'Connor for *Singin' in the Rain* (best actor in a comedy or musical). O'Connor told the HFCA that the Globe was the first award he'd ever won, and he accepted it at the black-tie affair while dressed in a herringbone business suit. *Variety*'s Scully said that O'Connor "explained that he was trying out a new formal attire in the shade of midnight gray. He easily could have blown up in his lines, but he came through as the magnificent trouper he is."

Singin' in the Rain was considered a front-runner for the Best Picture Globe bestowed on a comedy or musical, but the

John Ford's *Quiet Man* was a quiet, but tough rival.

laurel was snatched by *With a Song in My Heart*, the biopic of songbird Jane Froman described by *Variety* as "heartening drama . . . deftly handled" by the Globes' Best Actress Hayward.

The biggest upset occurred in the race for Best Drama Picture when *High Noon* lost to the year's top b.o. hit—*The Greatest Show on Earth* by legendary movie ringmaster Cecil B. DeMille, who was voted Best Director. In its review, *Variety* said the pic, at least in terms of cinema spectacle, was a truly great show: "This is the circus with more entertainment, more thrills, more spangles and as much Big Top atmosphere as Ringling Bros. and Barnum & Bailey itself can offer."

Three weeks later, on Oscar night, *High Noon* seemed to be riding high once again. It tied *The Quiet Man* and *Moulin Rouge* with the most noms—seven. *The Greatest Show on Earth* followed with five. Furthermore, *High Noon* was expected to have a great night, according to *Variety*'s straw poll, which so far had batted .910 over five past Oscar games. "*High Noon* may become the year's most honored film, winning 4 and possibly 5 of the top 8 Academy Awards," *Variety* said this year. "*High Noon* is a cinch to win the trophy as Best Picture of the year and gain added glory through the victories of Gary Cooper as Best Actor, the title tune as Best Song and the script by Carl Foreman as the Best Screenplay." The fifth possible victory was for director Fred Zinnemann, although the poll believed that *The Quiet Man*'s John Ford had a slight edge in the "neck and neck" race.

All of the Oscar races were almost called off this year, however, when the film studios yanked their financial support of the awards gala, just as they had in 1948. This time they blamed their declining profits thanks to

DAILY *VARIETY* **DAILY**

Vol. 79   No. 11,   Hollywood (28) California, Friday, March 20, 1953   Ten Cents

METRO SHADES UA AND PAR IN SILVER ANNI OSCAR DERBY

'GREATEST', BOOTH, COOPER, GRAHAME, QUINN AND FORD

METRO for a second successive year pushed to the front in this year's Oscar Derby, with a total of 10 wins, but United Artists breathed hard down its neck with eight golden statuettes. Two of Metro's Awards included recognition in the Scientific and Technical classification, which gave it the edge over the distribution company.

Paramount, second last year, was third in the Academy's Silver Anniversary sweepstakes, with five, including Best Picture, Best Performance by an Actress and the coveted Irving Thalberg Award, which went to veteran producer Cecil B. DeMille. In the also-ran category, 20th-Fox won three Oscars, Republic and RKO each two, Universal-International, one. The Culver lot's lead was due to "The Bad And The Beautiful" copping six awards, including Best Performance By A Supporting Actress, Screenplay, Cinematography, Art Direction, Set Decoration and Costume Design.

United Artists climbed up to its second position on the strength of

(Continued on Page 2)

GARY COOPER
Best Actor

SHIRLEY BOOTH
Best Actress

Variety correctly foresaw Oscars for Gary Cooper and Shirley Booth, but said *High Noon* was "a cinch" for Best Picture. *Greatest Show* proved how truly great it was.

competish from TV. What could Oscar leaders do? They turned to TV execs, who paid them a license fee of $100,000 to broadcast the star-studded event. Even better: kudocast producers decided to split the gala into *two* ceremonies, one held at L.A.'s Pantages Theatre, the other at New York's NBC Century Theater. The program would be a "simulcast" that would cut back and forth between the two locales—a daring feat attempted years before satellite technology would make such camera zigzagging commonplace.

The gamble began ominously. "There were plenty of stars at the Pantages Theatre, but none in the sky," *Variety* reported. "The rain dampened some of the clothes, but not the spirit of the crowd." Celebrity gawkers still crowded the front of the theater, though, just as they did out in New York, where Oscar fans also braved a wet night. Former film academy president Conrad

Nagel hosted in Gotham. In Los Angeles, producers tapped Bob Hope, who hadn't been invited back to host the gala since 1946 because of his recent ventures into TV.

The next day, *Variety* hailed the outcome: "Oscar turned 25 last night and an estimated 91 million people via TV and radio helped him celebrate with a party that for drama, thrills, showmanship and nostalgia was as good as anything in the history of the Academy of Motion Picture Arts & Sciences. And the film industry's cousin-by-marriage, and currently its chief competitor for the entertainment time of American audiences, made much of the excitement possible with a dazzling display of electronic ingenuity. The $12 pew-holders didn't have as good a seat as the home set-siders."

What home viewers saw was Bob Hope at the top of his game as he "gagged and quipped through most of his emceeing and even took a turn at hoofing," noted *Variety*. His best joke was borrowed from studio topper Jack Warner, who once described TV as "the piece of furniture that stares back at you."

The actual awards packed lots of drama, too—especially when several upsets dealt *Variety* its worst score ever as a forecaster.

Among the tradepaper's bold pronouncements was its insistence that 45-year-old veteran thesp Shirley Booth, who first appeared on stage at age 18, was "certain" to win the Best Actress trophy for her film debut. She competed against Globe champ Susan Hayward, who was recently decreed Most Popular Actress by a poll of the nation's moviegoers conducted by *Photoplay* magazine. Booth and Hayward faced off against two past Oscar champs: Joan Crawford (*Sudden Fear*) and Bette Davis, whose bid for *The Star* extended her record tally of nominations to nine. Norma Shearer was in second place with six.

But when *Variety* was proved right, Shirley Booth was so excited to hear her name called that she dashed up to the stage

of the International Theater in New York, fell down on one knee, picked herself up and scrambled to the podium. Once there, she said, "I am a very lucky girl. I guess this is the peak. The view has been wonderful all along the way. And I can only say, to my new friends, thanks for their hope. To my old friends, thanks for their faith. And to everybody, thanks for their charity."

Sheilah Graham gushed in her *Variety* column the next day: "Shirley Booth fell upstairs to get her Oscar, and wasn't her acceptance speech wonderful?"

Ralph Richardson, who'd been hailed earlier in the year as Best Actor by both the National Board of Review and the Gotham film crix, wasn't nominated in the Oscar lineup. Instead, the category included Marlon Brando (who'd win Best Actor at Cannes for *Viva Zapata!* in September), Kirk Douglas (*The Bad and the Beautiful*), José Ferrer (*Moulin Rouge*) and Alec Guinness (*The Lavender Hill Mob*). They were all pitted against Globe champ Gary Cooper (*High Noon*), who'd previously won an Oscar in 1941 for *Sergeant York* but hadn't had a hit film since *Saratoga Trunk* in 1946.

> ## Shirley Booth became the first star since Ray Milland to sweep all top awards.

Variety called this showdown correctly, too, but Cooper wasn't present to accept his latest golden boy, being in Mexico shooting a new movie with supporting Oscar nominee Anthony Quinn. The statuette was accepted for him by a jaunty John Wayne, who called Cooper "one of the nicest fellows I know" and told Oscar watchers that he and Cooper "fell off horses together and into pictures."

Duke Wayne was also called to the stage to collect an Oscar for another colleague, his boss on the set of *The Quiet Man*—John Ford. *Variety* reported, "He promised to take the Oscar to Ford's home and put it 'alongside his five previous Oscars.' Wayne miscalculated. Ford had won only three Oscars previously, for *The Informer, Grapes of Wrath* and *How Green Was My Valley.*"

Variety said Gloria Grahame had "a commanding lead" in the race for Best Supporting Actress. She was nominated for her portrayal of a leggy Southern belle in *The Bad and the Beautiful*, but also starred as a flaky assistant to an elephant trainer in Best Picture nominee *The Greatest Show on Earth*. She was presented with the statuette by Edmund Gwenn, who won Best Supporting Actor in 1947 for playing Santa Claus in *Miracle on 34th Street*. He introduced *The Bad and the Beautiful* star to Oscar watchers by saying, "She's the beautiful."

Variety was also correct about what would win Best Song: "Do Not Forsake Me, Oh My Darlin' " from *High Noon*. But beyond that, the rest of picks proved to be duds.

The writer of *The Bad and the Beautiful*, Charles Schnee, topped blacklisted writer Carl Foreman (*High Noon*) for the screenplay prize. The tradepaper picked the Golden Globes' Best New Male Star of the Year, Richard Burton, to win Best Supporting Actor. ("He creates a strong impression in the role of a love-torn, suspicious man," *Variety* said in its review of *My Cousin Rachel*.) The paper did warn, though, that Burton was "being closely pressed by Anthony Quinn, selected for his work in *Viva Zapata!* and the latter may be one of the upset victors at the awards ceremony." Quinn proved to be the category's spoiler. In his absence, the statuette was claimed by his wife Katherine, who said, "I know he'll be a happy man."

Katherine Quinn was the daughter of Cecil B. DeMille, who would turn out to be the other big spoiler on Oscar night—at least in terms of *Variety*'s claim that *High Noon* would win Best Picture.

Mary Pickford revealed that the category's actual champ was DeMille's *The Greatest Show on Earth*. The news triggered the second biggest ovation of the night as the producer/director accepted the prize thanking "the thousands of stars, elec-

tricians, circus people and others" who made the film. "I am only a little link in the chain that produced the picture," he added, humbly.

The greatest ovation of the night came just a few minutes later, when DeMille was declared the winner of the Irving Thalberg Award, which was presented to him by a fellow Hollywood titan who'd won it three times—Darryl F. Zanuck.

"He has kept pace," Zanuck said of the showbiz pioneer, "and he has forged ahead." DeMille had kept pace since the days of silent black-and-white films, when he "came to Hollywood to make movies among the orange groves," *Variety* said. Now he stood center stage at an event honoring talking color pictures while television cameras beamed the proceedings to more than 90 million viewers throughout the United States and Canada. Underestimating his audience size by nearly half, he addressed home viewers, saying, "I understand there are 50 million people watching. I want to thank them for the way they have received the motion picture industry as an art, the way they have stood by us. They respond to good work and they chastise us for bad work by staying away. I thank them for their part in (the) dreams that have brought me this award, which I shall keep close to me all of my life." He would die less than six years later at age 77.

"On that fitting note," *Variety* said, "the orch slid into the strains of 'No Business Like Show Business'—and the academy reluctantly but triumphantly ended its Silver Anniversary birthday celebration."

Variety had little to celebrate the next day when it acknowledged that its straw poll had suffered its worst performance ever by "accurately forecasting only 5 of the 8 top awards . . . a batting average of .615." The poll's six-year score now dragged the overall batting average down from .910 to .847—"which still ranks with the best in poll-taking anywhere," the paper insisted.

NATIONAL BOARD OF REVIEW

The board declared a best picture and foreign film of the year, then listed its remaining favorites according to highest scores. The vote results were announced on December 29, 1952.

BEST PICTURE
■ *The Quiet Man*
High Noon
Limelight
Five Fingers
The Snows of Kilimanjaro
The Thief
The Bad and the Beautiful
Singin' in the Rain
Above and Beyond
My Son John

BEST DIRECTOR
■ David Lean, *Breaking the Sound Barrier*

BEST ACTOR
■ Ralph Richardson, *Breaking the Sound Barrier*

BEST ACTRESS
■ Shirley Booth, *Come Back, Little Sheba*

BEST FOREIGN FILM
■ *Breaking the Sound Barrier* (U.K.)
The Man in the White Suit (U.K.)
Forbidden Games (*Jeux Interdits*) (France)
Beauty and the Devil (Italy/France)
Ivory Hunter (U.K.)

NEW YORK FILM CRITICS

Winners were announced on December 29, 1952. Awards were presented on January 17, 1953, at Sardi's restaurant in New York.

BEST PICTURE
■ *High Noon*

BEST DIRECTOR
■ Fred Zinnemann, *High Noon*

BEST ACTOR
■ Ralph Richardson, *Breaking the Sound Barrier*

BEST ACTRESS
■ Shirley Booth, *Come Back, Little Sheba*

BEST FOREIGN FILM
■ *Forbidden Games* (*Jeux Interdits*) (France)

SCREEN DIRECTORS GUILD OF AMERICA

Four quarterly winners were named throughout the year. A separate award was bestowed for best director of the year on February 1, 1953, at the Biltmore Bowl in Los Angeles. The quarterly winners were the final nominees for the annual award; other directors listed were nominees for the quarterly honors.

BEST DIRECTOR
■ John Ford, *The Quiet Man* (also quarterly winner)
Charles Crichton, *The Lavender Hill Mob* (quarterly winner)
George Cukor, *Pat and Mike*
Michael Curtiz, *I'll See You in My Dreams*
Cecil B. DeMille, *The Greatest Show on Earth*
Stanley Donen, Gene Kelly, *Singin' in the Rain*

Cecil B. DeMille (left, with Elliott Dexter and Bob Hope) relished the Best Picture Oscar upset scored by his *Greatest Show on Earth*.

L.A. Herald

Hugo Fregonese, *My Six Convicts*
Howard Hawks, *The Big Sky*
Elia Kazan, *Viva Zapata!*
Henry King, *The Snows of Kilimanjaro*
Akira Kurosawa, *Rashomom*
Albert Lewin, *Pandora and the Flying Dutchman*
Joseph L. Mankiewicz, *Five Fingers* (quarterly winner)
Vincente Minnelli, *The Bad and the Beautiful*
George Sidney, *Scaramouche*
Richard Thorpe, *Ivanhoe*
Charles Vidor, *Hans Christian Andersen*
Fred Zinnemann, *High Noon* (quarterly winner)

SCREEN WRITERS GUILD OF AMERICA

Awards were presented on February 25, 1953, at the Hollywood Palladium.

BEST WRITTEN DRAMA
- *High Noon*, Carl Foreman, based on the magazine story "The Tin Star" by John W. Cunningham

The Bad and the Beautiful, Charles Schnee, based on the short stories "Memorial to a Bad Man" and "Of Good and Evil" by George Bradshaw
Come Back, Little Sheba, Ketti Frings, based on the play by William Inge
Five Fingers, Michael Wilson, based on the book *Operation Cicero* by L. C. Moyzisch
Moulin Rouge, Anthony Veiller, John Huston, based on the novel by Pierre LaMure

BEST WRITTEN COMEDY
- *The Quiet Man*, Frank S. Nugent, based on the short story "Green Rushes" by Maurice Walsh

The Happy Time, Earl Felton, based on the novel by Robert Louis Fontaine and the play by Samuel A. Taylor
The Marrying Kind, Ruth Gordon, Garson Kanin
Pat and Mike, Ruth Gordon, Garson Kanin
Room for One More, Melville Shavelson, Jack Rose

BEST WRITTEN MUSICAL
- *Singin' in the Rain*, Betty Comden, Adolph Green

Hans Christian Andersen, Moss Hart, Myles Connolly
I'll See You in My Dreams, Jack Rose, Melville Shavelson
Where's Charley? John Monks, Jr., based on the musical play by George Abbott and Frank Loesser
With a Song in My Heart, Lamar Trotti

LAUREL AWARD
- Sonya Levien

GOLDEN GLOBES

Nominations were announced on February 4, 1953. Awards were presented on February 26 at the Ambassador Hotel in Los Angeles.

BEST DRAMA PICTURE
- *The Greatest Show on Earth*

Come Back, Little Sheba
Happy Time
High Noon
The Thief

BEST COMEDY OR MUSICAL PICTURE
- *With a Song in My Heart*

Hans Christian Andersen
I'll See You in My Dreams
Singin' in the Rain
Stars and Stripes Forever

BEST PICTURE PROMOTING INTERNATIONAL UNDERSTANDING
- *Anything Can Happen*

Assignment in Paris
Ivanhoe

BEST DIRECTOR
- Cecil B. DeMille, *The Greatest Show on Earth*

Richard Fleischer, *The Narrow Margin*
John Ford, *The Quiet Man*

BEST ACTOR, DRAMA
- Gary Cooper, *High Noon*

Charles Boyer, *The Happy Time*
Ray Milland, *The Thief*

BEST ACTRESS, DRAMA
- Shirley Booth, *Come Back Little Sheba*

Joan Crawford, *Sudden Fear*

Olivia de Havilland, *My Cousin Rachel*

BEST ACTOR, COMEDY OR MUSICAL
- Donald O'Connor, *Singin' in the Rain*

Danny Kaye, *Hans Christian Andersen*

Clifton Webb, *Dreamboat*

BEST ACTRESS, COMEDY OR MUSICAL
- Susan Hayward, *With a Song in My Heart*

Katharine Hepburn, *Pat and Mike*

Ginger Rogers, *Monkey Business*

BEST SUPPORTING ACTOR
- Millard Mitchell, *My Six Convicts*

Kurt Kasznar, *The Happy Time*

Gilbert Roland, *The Bad and the Beautiful*

BEST SUPPORTING ACTRESS
- Katy Jurado, *High Noon*

Mildred Dunnock, *Viva Zapata!*

Gloria Grahame, *The Bad and the Beautiful*

BEST SCREENPLAY
- Michael Wilson, *Five Fingers*

Carl Foreman, *High Noon*

Russell Rouse, Clarence Greene, *The Thief*

Winners

BEST ORIGINAL SCORE
- Dimitri Tiomkin, *High Noon*

MOST PROMISING NEWCOMER—MALE
- Richard Burton, *My Cousin Rachel*

MOST PROMISING NEWCOMER—FEMALE
- Colette Marchand, *Moulin Rouge*

WORLD FILM FAVORITES
- Susan Hayward
- John Wayne

BEST CINEMATOGRAPHY, BLACK AND WHITE
- Floyd Crosby, *High Noon*

BEST CINEMATOGRAPHY, COLOR
- George Barnes, Peverell Marley, *The Greatest Show on Earth*

CECIL B. DEMILLE AWARD
- Walt Disney

SPECIAL ACHIEVEMENT AWARDS
- Brandon De Wilde, *The Member of the Wedding* (Best Juvenile)
- Francis Kee Teller, *Navajo* (Best Juvenile)

ACADEMY AWARDS

Nominations were announced on February 9, 1953. Awards were presented on March 19 at the RKO Pantages Theater in Hollywood and the NBC Century Theater in New York. The ceremony was broadcast by NBC TV and radio.

BEST PICTURE
- *The Greatest Show on Earth*

High Noon

Ivanhoe

Moulin Rouge

The Quiet Man

BEST DIRECTOR
- John Ford, *The Quiet Man*

Cecil B. DeMille, *The Greatest Show on Earth*

John Huston, *Moulin Rouge*

Joseph L. Mankiewicz, *Five Fingers*

Fred Zinnemann, *High Noon*

BEST ACTOR
- Gary Cooper, *High Noon*

Marlon Brando, *Viva Zapata!*

Kirk Douglas, *The Bad and the Beautiful*

José Ferrer, *Moulin Rouge*

Alec Guinness, *The Lavender Hill Mob*

BEST ACTRESS
- Shirley Booth, *Come Back, Little Sheba*

Joan Crawford, *Sudden Fear*

Bette Davis, *The Star*

Julie Harris, *The Member of the Wedding*

Susan Hayward, *With a Song in My Heart*

BEST SUPPORTING ACTOR
- Anthony Quinn, *Viva Zapata!*

Richard Burton, *My Cousin Rachel*

Arthur Hunnicutt, *The Big Sky*

Victor McLaglen, *The Quiet Man*

Jack Palance, *Sudden Fear*

BEST SUPPORTING ACTRESS

- Gloria Grahame, *The Bad and the Beautiful*

Jean Hagen, *Singin' in the Rain*

Colette Marchand, *Moulin Rouge*

Terry Moore, *Come Back, Little Sheba*

Thelma Ritter, *With a Song in My Heart*

BEST WRITING (STORY)

- Frank Cavett, Frederic M. Frank, Theodore St. John, *The Greatest Show on Earth*

Edna Anhalt, Edward Anhalt, *The Sniper*

Martin Goldsmith, Jack Leonard, *The Narrow Margin*

Leo McCarey, *My Son John*

Guy Trosper, *The Pride of St. Louis*

BEST WRITING (SCREENPLAY)

- Charles Schnee, *The Bad and the Beautiful*

John Dighton, Roger MacDougall, Alexander MacKendrick, *The Man in the White Suit*

Carl Foreman, *High Noon*

Frank S. Nugent, *The Quiet Man*

Michael Wilson, *Five Fingers*

BEST WRITING (STORY AND SCREENPLAY)

- T. E. B. Clarke, *The Lavender Hill Mob*

Sydney Boehm, *The Atomic City*

Ruth Gordon, Garson Kanin, *Pat and Mike*

Terence Rattigan, *Breaking the Sound Barrier*

John Steinbeck, *Viva Zapata!*

BEST SONG

- "High Noon (Do Not Forsake Me, Oh My Darlin')," *High Noon*, Dimitri Tiomkin, Ned Washington

"Am I in Love," *Son of Paleface*, Jack Brooks

"Because You're Mine," *Because You're Mine*, Nicholas Brodszky, Sammy Cahn

"Thumbelina," *Hans Christian Andersen*, Frank Loesser

"Zing a Little Zong," *Just for You*, Leo Robin, Harry Warren

Winners

BEST ART DIRECTION/SET DECORATION

(BLACK AND WHITE)

- Edward Carfagno, Cedric Gibbons, Keogh Gleason, Edwin B. Willis, *The Bad and the Beautiful*

(COLOR)

- Paul Sheriff, Marcel Vertes, *Moulin Rouge*

BEST CINEMATOGRAPHY

(BLACK AND WHITE)

- Robert Surtees, *The Bad and the Beautiful*

(COLOR)

- Winton C. Hoch, Archie Stout, *The Quiet Man*

BEST COSTUME DESIGN

(BLACK AND WHITE)

- Helen Rose, *The Bad and the Beautiful*

(COLOR)

- Marcel Vertes, *Moulin Rouge*

BEST DOCUMENTARY

(FEATURE)

- *The Sea around Us*

(SHORT SUBJECT)

- *Neighbours*

BEST FILM EDITING

- Harry Gerstad, Elmo Williams, *High Noon*

BEST MUSIC

(SCORING OF A DRAMATIC OR COMEDY PICTURE)

- Dimitri Tiomkin, *High Noon*

(SCORING OF A MUSICAL PICTURE)

- Alfred Newman, *With a Song in My Heart*

SCIENTIFIC OR TECHNICAL AWARDS

Class I (Statuette)

- Eastman Kodak, General Aniline and Film Corp., Ansco Film Division

Class II (Plaque)

- Technicolor Motion Picture Corp.

Class III (Certificate)

- Projection, Still Photographic and Development Engineering Departments of MGM; John G. Frayne, R. R. Scoville,

Westrex Corp.; Photo Research Corp.;
Gustav Jirouch; Carlos Rivas, MGM

BEST SHORT SUBJECT
(CARTOON)
- *Johann Mouse*

(ONE REEL)
- *Light in the Window: The Art of Vermeer*

(TWO REEL)
- *Water Birds*

BEST SOUND RECORDING
- London Film Sound Department,
  Breaking the Sound Barrier

HONORARY FOREIGN FILM AWARD
- *Forbidden Games* (France)

IRVING G. THALBERG MEMORIAL AWARD
- Cecil B. DeMille

HONORARY AWARDS
- Merian C. Cooper
- Bob Hope
- Harold Lloyd
- George Alfred Mitchell
- Joseph M. Schenck

· 1953 ·

Eternity: *From Crix Kudos to Oscars*

The fight over Best Picture kudos pitted the Sacred versus the Profane versus the revered Bard.

The Bard prevailed at the outset when the National Board of Review hailed *Julius Caesar*, starring what *Variety* called "one of the finest casts assembled for a film. Any fears about Marlon Brando appearing in Shakespeare are dispelled by his compelling portrayal as the revengeful Mark Antony. James Mason, as the noble, honorable Brutus, is excellent." The board gave its Best Actor trophy to Mason for *Caesar* plus several other pics—*Face to Face, The Desert Rats* and *The Man Between*. Jean Simmons was named Best Actress for three films—*Young Bess, The Actress* and the "sacred" pic that was, if not the year's best, then at least its highest grosser: *The Robe*.

The Robe was also the most expensive movie of the year, costing $4.5 million to produce. "It is a big picture in every sense of the word," *Variety* said. *The Robe* was the first film shown in CinemaScope, a novelty designed to lure Americans from their small TV sets at home to wide-screen theaters where they could be overwhelmed by the debonair new British star Richard Burton as a Roman centurion who sets out to crucify Christ, but ends up converting to Christianity. *New York Daily News* critic Kate Cameron was one of the pic's devout disciples. Employing her usual four-star rating, she gave *The Robe* eight: four stars for the film, four more for the divine new CinemaScope.

But Cameron was *The Robe*'s only supporter when the 14 New York film critics met at the newspaper guild's office on West 44th Street to choose their anointed. *The Robe* got only one vote for Best Picture. Nine votes went to director Fred Zinnemann's profane drama about servicemen's hedonistic life in Hawaii on the eve of Pearl Harbor. *From Here to Eternity* claimed vic-

Crix and Oscar Best Picture *From Here to Eternity* starred crooner Frank Sinatra (left, with Montgomery Clift) in a break-out role. *Variety* noted that his "bones shook" when he accepted his Oscar.

tory as Best Picture on the second ballot with 11 votes, thereby reaping the necessary two-thirds tally long before a simple majority would have decided the winner on the sixth round. *From Here to Eternity*'s only real competish came from the documentary *The Conquest of Everest*, which was given a special award as a consolation prize.

"This year's balloting was unusual in that none of the polling was carried through to the final vote," observed *The New York Times*. Zinnemann repeated his triumph of last year by topping George Stevens (*Shane*) for Best Director on the second ballot by an easy 10–3 score. The *Times* noted that *Eternity*'s lead actor had similar good luck: "Burt Lancaster's portrayal of the tough first sergeant won out over James Mason's Brutus and Sir John Gielgud's Cassius in *Julius Caesar*, Spencer Tracy's father in *The Actress* and William Holden's suspected prisoner of war in *Stalag 17*." Lancaster nabbed seven votes on the first ballot, compared to one for Gielgud and two each for

Mason, Holden and Tracy. Lancaster finally won on the fifth round with 11.

The Robe's Jean Simmons received only a single endorsement for Best Actress. The contest was really between Audrey Hepburn in *Roman Holiday* (seven votes on the first ballot) and Ava Gardner in *Mogambo*) three votes). Hepburn prevailed on the third tally by an 11-to-3 count, winning for her debut film role as a perky princess who runs off to discover Rome as a private citizen. When *The New York Herald Tribune* reported her victory, the paper reminded its readers that Hepburn "was remembered locally for her stage performance in *Gigi*."

Hepburn was just then preparing to star on Broadway as a water sprite in *Ondine*, so she was in New York to accept her scroll when the crix gathered at Sardi's restaurant. The other champs weren't on hand, though: Elia Kazan accepted for Fred Zinnemann and Deborah Kerr stood in for her *Eternity* costar Burt Lancaster.

Many of the year's top kudos contenders were out in California at the Golden Globes banquet, which was presided over by Walter Pidgeon and promised to be the most harmonious gala ever.

The reason: the two rival groups of offshore journos—the Hollywood Foreign Correspondents Association and the Foreign Press Association of Hollywood—finally merged and bestowed one set of awards. But when they actually hooked up at the Club Del Mar, "there weren't adequate seating arrangements," *Variety* reported. "Some left in a huff and a few in Cadillacs. Of those who stayed, the monocled Scandinavian twin correspondents, Gustaf and Bertil Unger, were the most noticeable. They exchanged blows with another set of twins. The Unger twins were distinguished by the fact that one wears a monocle in the right eye and the other wears a monocle in the left eye. When they departed at the end of the evening, one of them also was sporting a black eye."

Some of the winners repeated previous kudos honorees: Best Actress Audrey Hepburn and top helmer Zinnemann. Surprises included victories by Spencer Tracy as Best Drama Actor for *The Actress*, David Niven as Best Actor in a Comedy or Musical for *The Moon Is Blue*, Ethel Merman as Best Actress in a Comedy or Musical for *Call Me Madam* and—most newsworthy—Frank Sinatra as Best Supporting Actor in *From Here to Eternity*.

Sinatra's career had been in a slump since the late 1940s, when he reigned as America's top crooner with a devoted fan base of squealing bobby-soxers. He now pined for a showbiz comeback—one as an actor this time—and he lobbied Columbia Pictures hard for the part of a likable G.I. with a short fuse and fast fists in the much-anticipated film adaptation of the James Jones bestseller. When his pleadings failed, he finally got the part thanks to the intervention of his wife, Ava Gardner, who persuaded studio chief Harry Cohn to give him a chance.

Sinatra's award was only one of two Globe victories for *Eternity*. The greatest upset on awards night occurred when it lost Best Drama Picture to *The Robe*. (No award was bestowed for Best Comedy or Musical Picture.)

Eternity rebounded over the next few weeks, however, Zinnemann claimed the palm from the Screen Directors Guild and scripter Daniel Taradash was given the accolade for best drama from the Screen Writers Guild. The prize for best comedy went to *Roman Holiday*'s Ian McLellan Hunter and John Dighton. Hunter was fronting for his friend Dalton Trumbo, a blacklisted scribe who'd created the film's plot. Soon afterward, Hunter would be listed solo at the Oscars in the screenplay story category—and would win again despite being on the lam in Mexico, where he was dodging a subpoena from the House Un-American Activities Committee. Trumbo would not receive his rightful due

> *Roman Holiday* was really penned by blacklisted scribe Dalton Trumbo.

until after his death, when the film academy acknowledged him posthumously.

Excitement over the 1953 Oscars seemed diminished, considering the sparse crowd waiting for stars outside the Pantages Theater on awards night. "Here's something else they can blame on television," *Variety* griped. "By 6:30 P.M., the street bleachers were unfilled." The poor turnout couldn't be pinned on the weather. *Variety* noted that this year "marked the first time in three years the Derby was run on a dry track."

But the small group of fans gathered out front cheered lustily for their favorite stars. "When Frank Sinatra arrived, the crowd gave him one of the biggest ovations of the evening," *Variety* said. The tradepaper was also rooting for him. Its seventh annual straw poll, which surveyed 15 percent of the movie academy's membership, picked him to win. "Sinatra pulled almost twice as many votes as his competitors," *Variety* noted.

From Here to Eternity was way out in front in many categories, according to the paper. While it was up against *The Robe, Julius Caesar, Roman Holiday* and *Shane* for Best Picture, *Variety* predicted an "easy victory" since *Eternity* "polled almost three times as many votes as its four competitors combined for the biggest landslide in Straw Poll history." Many Oscar watchers were skeptical, however, since last year the poll had declared that *High Noon* was "a cinch" to take the top prize, which was actually claimed by *The Greatest Show on Earth*. *Eternity* led this year with the most nominations—13 (one shy of the record set by *All about Eve*)—and *Variety* proclaimed that it would nail at least five of the top eight categories.

Once again NBC aired the two-hour show as a simulcast, with Donald O'Connor hosting in Hollywood and Fredric March emceeing in New York. Soon after the

2 SETS OF TWINS SQUARE OFF, GIVE AWARDS PARTY INT'L INCIDENT FLAVOR

Two pair and a full house produced fisticuffs at the Club Del Mar, Santa Monica, Friday night when the rival factions of Hollywood's foreign press corps got together for one big Awards Banquet. Folk balladeer Burl Ives and thesp Gilbert Roland acted as peacemakers so that the program could proceed on schedule.

Difficulty began when many of the guests discovered that there weren't adequate seating arrangements. Some left in a huff and a few in Cadillacs. Of those who stayed, the monocled Scandinavian twin correspondents, Gustave and Bertil Unger, were the most noticeable. They exchanged blows with another set of twins, Aly and Amad Sadick, cotton brokers, over who had whose seats. The Unger twins are distinguished by the fact that one wears a monacle in the right eye and the other wears a monocle in the left eye. When they departed at the end of the evening, one of them also was sporting a black eye.

Pat Medina Vis-a-Vis Montgomery In 'Tripoli'

Patricia Medina, who arrives back in NY tomorrow after her overseas co-star stint with Alan Ladd in "The Black Knight," has been signed by Sam Katzman for the femme lead opposite George Montgomery in "Pirates of Tripoli." Film rolls Feb. 16 at Columbia under direction of Felix Feist.

Montgomery, incidentally, originally was signed for duo of Katzman westerns, "Indian Scout" and "Bat Masterson, Badman," but will do "Pirates" first.

Harmony should've reigned after the two rival foreign press orgs merged, but fists flew at the Golden Globes ceremony when a seat shortage occurred.

awards show began, it was apparent early on that *From Here to Eternity* was on the march. The World War II drama first seized tech prizes for editing, sound and black-and-white cinematography, then the gold for best screenplay—followed by a blitz of the supporting thesp categories.

Sinatra's victory seemed to overwhelm the usually cocky star. *Variety* noted that his victory "touched off an ovation that lifted Sinatra all the way down the aisle and onto the stage where he stood, nervously clutching the Oscar." Columnist Army Archerd noticed the same thing: "Even cool Frank Sinatra's bones shook as his hand was clasped after he got his award."

In his acceptance speech, Sinatra referred to the night's musical entertainment, which included performances of the Best Song contenders. He said, "You know, they're doing a lot of singing here, but nobody asked me to sing." Sinatra didn't mention that Oscar leaders asked him to sing at the 1946 ceremony, but he refused. *Variety* did note that host Donald O'Connor "started a move to get 'the voice' warbling, but Sinatra grinned his way offstage and the program moved on to a cafe scene in which Dean Martin sang Best Song nominee 'That's Amore.' "

Variety predicted that Sinatra's costar Donna Reed would take the supporting actress category. The wholesome star had shocked movie-goers when she was cast against type as a hooker. She seemed shocked herself—and excited—when she heard that she was Oscared for it. She raced up to the stage from her seat far back in the Pantages and said, nearly out of breath, "It's a long walk and I didn't think I'd make it. I'm very proud and very grateful. It was a wonderful road *From Here to Eternity*, but it was even more wonderful from *Eternity* to here."

Afterward, *Variety*'s Army Archerd noted, "Donna Reed nearly collapsed as she came offstage with her award."

Costars Burt Lancaster and Montgomery Clift were both up for Best Actor, which led many pundits to think they'd lose after splitting the *Eternity* vote. *Variety* was less certain, although it was betting that the accolade would go to William Holden for portraying a Yankee POW suspected of being a Nazi spy in *Stalag 17*. "Based on a percentage breakdown of the total votes, Holden appears to be assured of winning the coveted trophy," *Variety* maintained. "A last-minute shift of sentiment, however, could give the award to Lancaster."

After he won, *Variety* observed, "Bill Holden got the biggest hand of the evening. His speech was also popular. He said, 'Thank you, thank you.' Brief and to the point." Ceremony emcee O'Connor told the audience that Holden was too excited to say more.

Eternity's Deborah Kerr and *Mogambo*'s Ava Gardner were in the lineup for Best Actress, but *Variety* said that Audrey Hepburn was a "shoo-in" since she polled "as many votes as all of her competitors put together."

On Oscar night, Hepburn was in New York starring in her Broadway show, but, as soon as it was over, she jumped into her limo and was given a police escort so she could make it to the Gotham Oscar ceremony in time for her category to be announced.

She made it, although *Variety* noticed that she was still in her stage character's makeup as a water sprite as last year's Oscar champ, Shirley Booth, read off the nominees from a remote TV hookup in Philadelphia. When Hepburn won, she thanked "everybody in the past few months and years who helped me so much."

The rest of the top honors were claimed, as predicted, by *From Here to Eternity*. When Zinnemann won Best Director, he thanked "the entire Pacific Command of the U.S. Army."

When *Eternity* won the last big trophy of the night—Best Picture—it tied the Oscars record for most wins set by *Gone With the Wind* (eight). Its 13 bids left it one shy of *All About Eve's* noms record.

Variety was thrilled. After sticking its neck out in eight races, the paper called only one category incorrectly—Best Song. It backed "That's Amore" from *The Caddy*, but warned of a possible upset by "Secret Love" from *Calamity Jane*. *Calamity* indeed struck—and "Secret Love" won—but *Variety* was nonplussed, noting that the poll "came within inches of its third perfect score." Its cumulative batting average was .851 over seven years.

▪ 1953 ▪

NATIONAL BOARD OF REVIEW

The board declared a best picture and foreign film of the year, then listed its remaining favorites according to highest scores. The vote results were announced in late December 1953.

BEST PICTURE
▪ *Julius Caesar*
Shane
From Here to Eternity
Martin Luther
Lili
Roman Holiday
Stalag 17

The Little Fugitive
Mogambo
The Robe

BEST DIRECTOR
- George Stevens, *Shane*

BEST ACTOR
- James Mason, *Face to Face, The Desert Rats, The Man Between, Julius Caesar*

BEST ACTRESS
- Jean Simmons, *Young Bess, The Robe, The Actress*

BEST FOREIGN FILM
- *A Queen Is Crowned* (U.K.)
Moulin Rouge (U.K.)
The Little World of Don Camillo (France/Italy)
Strange Deception (Italy)
The Conquest of Everest (U.K.)

NEW YORK FILM CRITICS

Winners were announced on December 28, 1953. Awards were presented on January 23, 1954, at Sardi's restaurant in New York.

BEST PICTURE
- *From Here to Eternity*

BEST DIRECTOR
- Fred Zinnemann, *From Here to Eternity*

BEST ACTOR
- Burt Lancaster, *From Here to Eternity*

BEST ACTRESS
- Audrey Hepburn, *Roman Holiday*

BEST FOREIGN FILM
- *Justice Is Done* (France)

GOLDEN GLOBES

Awards were presented on January 22, 1954, at the Club Del Mar in Santa Monica. Nominee information was unavailable.

BEST DRAMA PICTURE
- *The Robe*

Fred Zinnemann (right) received his directors' guild plaque for *Eternity* from George Sidney.

BEST MOTION PICTURE PROMOTING INTERNATIONAL UNDERSTANDING
- *Little Boy Lost*

BEST ACTOR, DRAMA
- Spencer Tracy, *The Actress*

BEST ACTRESS, DRAMA
- Audrey Hepburn, *Roman Holiday*

BEST ACTOR, COMEDY OR MUSICAL
- David Niven, *The Moon Is Blue*

BEST ACTRESS, COMEDY OR MUSICAL
- Ethel Merman, *Call Me Madam*

BEST SUPPORTING ACTOR
- Frank Sinatra, *From Here to Eternity*

BEST SUPPORTING ACTRESS
- Grace Kelly, *Mogambo*

MOST PROMISING NEWCOMER—MALE
- Richard Egan
- Steve Forrest
- Hugh O'Brian

MOST PROMISING NEWCOMER—FEMALE
- Pat Crowley
- Bella Darvi
- Barbara Rush

BEST SCREENPLAY
- Helen Deutsch, *Lili*

WORLD FILM FAVORITES

- Alan Ladd
- Marilyn Monroe
- Robert Taylor

CECIL B. DEMILLE AWARD

- Darryl F. Zanuck

SPECIAL ACHIEVEMENT AWARDS

- Jack Cummings
- Walt Disney, *The Living Desert*
- Guy Madison

SCREEN DIRECTORS GUILD OF AMERICA

Four quarterly winners were named throughout the year. A separate award was bestowed for best director of the year on January 24, 1954, at the Biltmore Hotel in Los Angeles. The quarterly winners were the final nominees for the annual award; other directors listed were nominees for the quarterly honors.

BEST DIRECTOR

- **Fred Zinnemann, *From Here to Eternity***
- Melvin Frank, Norman Panama, *Above and Beyond*
- Henry Koster, *The Robe*
- Walter Lang, *Call Me Madam*
- Joseph L. Mankiewicz, *Julius Caesar*
- Daniel Mann, *Come Back, Little Sheba*
- Jean Negulesco, *Titanic*
- George Sidney, *Young Bess*
- George Stevens, *Shane* (quarterly winner)
- Charles Walters, *Lili* (quarterly winner)
- Billy Wilder, *Stalag 17* (quarterly winner)
- William Wyler, *Roman Holiday* (quarterly winner)

SPECIAL D. W. GRIFFITH AWARD

- Cecil B. DeMille

SCREEN WRITERS GUILD OF AMERICA

Awards were presented on February 25, 1954, at the Beverly Hills Hotel in Los Angeles.

The Robe, the top-grossing pic of 1953, earned the top Globe plus the NBR's Best Actress laurel for Jean Simmons (left).

BEST WRITTEN DRAMA

- ***From Here to Eternity***, Daniel Taradash, based on the novel by James Jones
- *Above and Beyond*, Melvin Frank, Norman Panama, Beirne Lay, Jr.
- *Little Fugitive*, Ray Ashley, Ruth Orkin, Morris Engel
- *Martin Luther*, Allan Sloane, Lothar Wolff
- *Shane*, A. B. Guthrie, Jr., Jack Sher, based on the novel by Jack Schaefer

BEST WRITTEN COMEDY

- ***Roman Holiday*** (Award was originally bestowed to Ian McLellan Hunter and John Dighton, although the script was actually written by blacklisted scribe Dalton Trumbo, who received official credit from the guild posthumously in 1991.)
- *The Actress*, Ruth Gordon, based on her play *Years Ago*
- *How to Marry a Millionaire*, Nunnally Johnson, based on two plays, *The Greeks Had a Word for It* by Zoe Akins and *Loco* by Dale Eunson and Katherine Albert
- *The Moon Is Blue*, F. Hugh Herbert
- *Stalag 17*, Billy Wilder, Edwin Blum, based on the play by Donald Bevan and Edmund Trzcinski

BEST WRITTEN MUSICAL

- ***Lili***, Helen Deutsch, based on a short story by Paul Gallico

The Band Wagon, Betty Comden, Adolph Green

Call Me Madam, Arthur Sheekman, based on the musical comedy by Howard Lindsay and Russell Crouse

Gentlemen Prefer Blondes, Charles Lederer, based on the musical book by Joseph Fields and Anita Loos

LAUREL AWARD
■ Dudley Nichols

ACADEMY AWARDS

Nominations were announced on February 15, 1954. Awards were presented on March 24 at the RKO Pantages Theater in Hollywood and the NBC Century Theater in New York. The ceremony was broadcast by NBC TV and radio.

BEST PICTURE
■ *From Here to Eternity*
Julius Caesar
The Robe
Roman Holiday
Shane

BEST DIRECTOR
■ Fred Zinnemann, *From Here to Eternity*
George Stevens, *Shane*
Charles Walters, *Lili*
Billy Wilder, *Stalag 17*
William Wyler, *Roman Holiday*

BEST ACTOR
■ William Holden, *Stalag 17*
Marlon Brando, *Julius Caesar*
Richard Burton, *The Robe*
Montgomery Clift, *From Here to Eternity*
Burt Lancaster, *From Here to Eternity*

BEST ACTRESS
■ Audrey Hepburn, *Roman Holiday*
Leslie Caron, *Lili*
Ava Gardner, *Mogambo*
Deborah Kerr, *From Here to Eternity*
Maggie McNamara, *The Moon Is Blue*

BEST SUPPORTING ACTOR
■ Frank Sinatra, *From Here to Eternity*
Eddie Albert, *Roman Holiday*

Brandon De Wilde, *Shane*
Jack Palance, *Shane*
Robert Strauss, *Stalag 17*

BEST SUPPORTING ACTRESS
■ Donna Reed, *From Here to Eternity*
Grace Kelly, *Mogambo*
Geraldine Page, *Hondo*
Marjorie Rambeau, *Torch Song*
Thelma Ritter, *Pickup on South Street*

BEST WRITING (STORY)
■ Dalton Trumbo, *Roman Holiday* (originally awarded to Ian McLellan Hunter)
Ray Ashley, Morris Engel, Ruth Orkin, *Little Fugitive*
Alec Coppel, *The Captain's Paradise*
Louis L'Amour, *Hondo*
Beirne Lay, Jr., *Above and Beyond*

BEST WRITING (SCREENPLAY)
■ Daniel Taradash, *From Here to Eternity*
Eric Ambler, *The Cruel Sea*
Helen Deutsch, *Lili*
John Dighton, Ian McLellan Hunter, *Roman Holiday*
A. B. Guthrie, Jr., *Shane*

BEST WRITING (STORY AND SCREENPLAY)
■ Charles Brackett, Richard Breen, Walter Reisch, *Titanic*
Harold Jack Bloom, Sam Rolfe, *The Naked Spur*
Betty Comden, Adolph Green, *The Band Wagon*
Millard Kaufman, *Take the High Ground*
Richard Murphy, *The Desert Rats*

BEST SONG
"My Flaming Heart," *Small Town Girl*, Nicholas Brodszky, Leo Robin
"The Moon Is Blue," *The Moon Is Blue*, Sylvia Fine, Herschel Burke Gilbert
"Sadie Thompson's Song (Blue Pacific Blues)," *Miss Sadie Thompson*, Lester Lee, Ned Washington
"Secret Love," *Calamity Jane*, Sammy Fain, Paul Francis Webster
"That's Amore," *The Caddy*, Jack Brooks, Harry Warren

Winners

BEST ART DIRECTION/SET DECORATION
(BLACK AND WHITE)
- Edward Carfagno, Cedric Gibbons, Hugh Hunt, *Julius Caesar*

(COLOR)
- George W. Davis, Lyle Wheeler, Paul S. Fox, Walter M. Scott, *The Robe*

BEST CINEMATOGRAPHY
(BLACK AND WHITE)
- Burnett Guffey, *From Here to Eternity*

(COLOR)
- Loyal Griggs, *Shane*

BEST COSTUME DESIGN
(BLACK AND WHITE)
- Edith Head, *Roman Holiday*

(COLOR)
- Charles LeMaire, Emile Santiago, *The Robe*

BEST DOCUMENTARY
(FEATURE)
- *The Living Desert*

(SHORT SUBJECT)
- *The Alaskan Eskimo*

BEST FILM EDITING
- William Lyon, *From Here to Eternity*

BEST MUSIC
(SCORING OF A DRAMATIC OR COMEDY PICTURE)
- Bronislau Kaper, *Lili*

(SCORING OF A MUSICAL PICTURE)
- Alfred Newman, *Call Me Madam*

SCIENTIFIC OR TECHNICAL AWARDS
Class I (Statuette)
- Herbert Bragg, Henri Chretien, Carl Faulkner, Lorin Grignon, Sol Halprin, Earl Sponable, Twentieth Century-Fox Studio; Fred Waller

Class II (Plaque)
- Reeves Soundcraft Corp.

Class III (Certificate)
- Westrex Corp.

BEST SHORT SUBJECT
(CARTOON)
- *Toot, Whistle, Plunk and Boom*

(ONE REEL)
- *The Merry Wives of Windsor Overture*

(TWO REEL)
- *Bear Country*

BEST SOUND RECORDING
- John P. Livadary, *From Here to Eternity*

BEST SPECIAL EFFECTS
- Pal, Paramount Studio, *The War of the Worlds*

IRVING G. THALBERG MEMORIAL AWARD
- George Stevens

HONORARY AWARDS
- Bell and Howell
- Joseph I. Breen
- Pete Smith
- Twentieth Century-Fox

· 1954 ·

On the Waterfront *on All Fronts*

For the first time ever, the Oscars, the Golden Globes, the New York Film Critics and the National Board of Review all agreed on one Best Picture. Even more amazing: the directors' and writers' guilds lined up, too.

On the Waterfront was an obvious winner when it premiered on the screen, but when it was still just an idea being pitched to the Hollywood studios, the suits all turned it down.

"From Darryl Zanuck at 20th Century, from Jack Warner, from MGM and Universal and finally from Harry Cohn's imperiously dominated Columbia, we had tasted indigestible rejection," scribe Budd Schulberg wrote years later in *Variety*. He based his screenplay on a Pulitzer Prize–winning series of newspaper articles about union racketeering at New Jersey's shipping docks, and he spent two years investigating the drama himself. His screenplay became a personal crusade to clean up waterfront corruption, but when Zanuck looked at Schulberg's script, he barked, "All you've got is a lot of sweaty longshoremen!" Schulberg was close to giving up when independent producer Sam Spiegel knocked on his hotel room door one night and invited him to a party across the hall. Schulberg went—and sold Spiegel the pitch over much champagne.

Under the inspired direction of Elia Kazan, with a career-crowning perf by Marlon Brando and with a budget of only $820,000, *On the Waterfront* became a masterpiece that would one day be ranked tenth on the American Film Institute's list of the greatest movies ever made. "Marlon Brando puts on a spectacular show," *Variety* cheered in its review, "giving a fascinating, multifaceted performance as the uneducated dock walloper and former pug, who is basically a softie with a special affection for his

Judy Garland accepted an Oscar in *A Star Is Born*, but lost in real life. She and costar James Mason did reap Golden Globes.

rooftop covey of pigeons and a neighborhood girl back from school."

On the Waterfront was a summer release, but its importance was still felt in December when the New York Film Critics gathered to vote. "Their hasty and happy agreement was almost unprecedented," Bosley Crowther wrote in *The New York Times*. "So far as this member can recall, the ladies and gentlemen of the scribe tribe have never been in a sweeter harmony."

Waterfront claimed the kudos for Best Picture, Director and Actor on the first ballots, thereby nabbing two-thirds of the votes from the 16 crix. It failed to pull off a complete sweep when its lead female thesp, screen newcomer Eva Marie Saint, reaped only 2 votes for Best Actress. Far ahead was Grace Kelly, who led with 9 endorsements on the first tally and then won on the second canvass with 12. "Although she was named for portrayals in three features—*The Country Girl, Dial M for Murder* and *Rear Window*—most of the ballots cited her delineation of Bing Crosby's harassed wife in *The Country Girl* as outstanding," noted the *Times*.

Over the previous six years at the Screen Directors Guild of America Awards, Elia Kazan had lost two bids as Best Director (*A Streetcar Named Desire, Viva Zapata!*). He finally prevailed this year, but he was not on hand to accept the honor, so last year's champ Fred Zinnemann stood in for him before the 980 showbiz leaders gathered at the Biltmore Bowl. The star attraction turned out to be Walt Disney, who gave a heartfelt and often humorous speech when he was honored with a lifetime guild membership. Musical entertainment was provided by the Les Brown Orchestra and Jeanette MacDonald, who sang "The Star-Spangled Banner."

The entertainment was particularly lively at the kudos gala for the Screen Writers Guild of America and would end up inspiring an historic writerly partnership. The gridiron sketches included the first performance of a skit that would become an oft-repeated standard in the future. Originally titled "Two Writers," it was penned by I. A. L. Diamond and "featured Danny Dayton and Danny Arnold as collaborators stuck for a descriptive adverb" to relate how an actor should pronounce a line of dia-

logue, reported *Variety*. The skit would eventually be retitled "Quizzically" after the adverb the writers start with—and then end up with, quite happily, 10 agonizing minutes later when they forget that they'd rejected it earlier. When Billy Wilder saw the skit, he admired it so much that he asked Diamond to become his writing partner.

Budd Schulberg was present to receive his trophy for Best Written Drama, but Robert Riskin (*It Happened One Night, Mr. Deeds Goes to Town*) was too ill to accept his special Laurel Award honoring his full career achievement. His wife, actress Fay Wray, stood in.

This was the second year that the Hollywood Foreign Correspondents Association and the Foreign Press Association of Hollywood got together to bestow their Golden Globe and Henrietta Awards.

Waterfront was the first unanimous Best Picture choice.

"It was by far the most lavish, and most successful gala," reported *The Hollywood Citizen-News*, "and proves that the policy of staging the awards jointly is wise."

Among the Henriettas to be bestowed were the prizes for World Film Favorites, which were decided by polls of moviegoers in 40 nations. Recipients were Gregory Peck, who was present to accept his trophy, and Audrey Hepburn, who sent a recorded message from London thanking the foreign scribes for the award she called "a passport of international good will."

"Unusual was the fact that Brando appeared to accept his award," the *L.A. Times* observed.

"Marlon Brando showed up at the banquet wearing impeccably tailored dinner clothes and a charming smile," the *Mirror-News* added. "In fact, he was so downright human that one old hand cracked, 'What happened to all his false reserve?' "

Brando had refused to participate in award campaigns or ceremonies in the past and lost three Oscar and Golden Globe bouts in a row. This year he switched strategies and was honored by the offshore press with one of four Globes for *Waterfront*. The other three honors were Best Picture, Director and Cinematography.

The foreign journalists endorsed one more choice made earlier by the New York newspaper crix, too: they hailed Grace Kelly as Best Actress, although she was not present to accept.

A Star Is Born had been positioned as the top tuner of the year, but when it failed to score boffo b.o., Warner Bros. spent no money on a kudos campaign. *Carmen Jones* pulled off a Globe upset as Best Comedy/Musical Picture, but Judy Garland and James Mason rallied to claim Best Comedy/Musical Actress and Actor. *Star* was Garland's first film since being fired from MGM in 1950. It may not have been a financial hit at the outset, but it heralded her career comeback ("Judy Garland glitters with stardust!" *Variety* cheered in its review). Visibly pregnant, she gushed gratefully as she accepted the Golden Globe before the crowd of 1,000 at Cocoanut Grove, while Mason missed his tribute because he was "busy on TV," said the *L.A. Times*.

Mason agreed to be a presenter on Oscar night, but he skipped town and headed to San Francisco at the last minute without informing the telecast producers. He later told *Variety* columnist Army Archerd, "I'm thinking about doing a TV series up there," but the Best Actor nominee also admitted that, even if he'd stayed in Hollywood, "I would have ducked the awards." Archerd added, "Sez he's too shy about appearing at big functions."

Best Actor rival Bing Crosby told Archerd that he planned on attending the Oscars: "You bet I'll be there, but Brando will win it." Crosby starred in the top-grossing film of the year, *White Christmas*, and earned a Best Actor trophy from the National Board of Review for *The Country Girl*, but he was so sure that he would lose the Oscar to Brando that he bet Jerry Lewis $50 on it.

> "Revenge was sweet," Budd Shulberg wrote in *Variety*.

On the Waterfront certainly looked unbeatable when the Oscar bids came out, nabbing 12—thereby tying *Mrs. Miniver* and *Gone With the Wind* as the third-most nominated film ever. (*All about Eve*) led with 14 noms, followed by 13 for *From Here to Eternity*). It also tied *Mrs. Miniver, All about Eve* and *From Here to Eternity* for having the most acing bids: five. The noms were chosen by 13,438 members of the film industry; 1,700 academy members would pick the winners.

Variety's straw poll of the members confirmed the pic's front-runner status: "*On the Waterfront* should dominate the Oscar derby, winning 4 of the top 8 awards. *Waterfront* garnered more votes for Best Picture than all of its competition combined. Brando scored an even bigger vote over his competition in the Best Actor category. Kazan swamped his opposition in the Best Director race in the poll." *Variety* also predicted a win for Best Story and Screenplay, but didn't size up its lead.

Brando was obviously the public's fave as he arrived at the Pantages Theatre in Los Angeles. "A roar from the fans greeted the arrival of Marlon Brando—looking somewhat bewildered," *Variety* reported. The star may have been worried about the family members he had in tow. Archerd observed, "Brando was frantic when his poppa was lost in the throng."

It was so obvious that Oscar night belonged to *Waterfront* that, once the ceremony began, Brando was tapped to bestow the prize for Best Director. His helmer Kazan accepted it on the New York half of the simulcast, saying, "A director doesn't make a picture. A whole lot of people do."

Brando was jubilant when he was declared Best Actor. He "almost leaped to the stage to get the award for which he had been nominated three times previously," *Variety* reported. "He fondled the statuette for a second before turning to the audience, 'It's much heavier than I imagined. I cannot ever remember anything in my life for which so many people were responsible. This is a wonderful moment and I'm certainly indebted.'

"Brando was unnerved as he walked offstage, clutching the Oscar, and muttering, 'It must be made of gold! It *must* be!' "

His costar Eva Marie Saint wasn't nominated for Best Actress because producer Sam Spiegel didn't want the screen rookie competing against the heavyweights in that lineup. Instead, she was nommed for Best Supporting Actress, which she claimed easily. The pregnant star accepted the honor in New York, bouncing with excitement, saying, "I may have my baby right here!"

Judy Garland gave birth to her baby two days before the Oscarcast, but she was still recovering. "NBC erected a platform outside her hospital room, 20 feet above the ground, where (she could lift) the blinds for a quick 'thank you' " if she won, Archerd reported. Meantime, Garland planned to watch the ceremony on a small TV set that producer/husband Sid Luft brought to her room.

Garland's Oscar chances appeared to dim right before Oscar night. *Variety* reported on its straw poll results: "Grace Kelly and Judy Garland appeared to be on even ground with Academy voters until the final week, when Miss Kelly racked up a respectable margin over her rival."

Variety noted that the race included noteworthy contender: "Nomination of Dorothy Danbridge in the Best Actress category marks the first time that a colored actress has ever won this distinction, although Hattie McDaniels (sic) won an Oscar for Best Supporting Actress in *Gone With the Wind*."

When Grace Kelly won, *Variety* described her voice as "emotion-packed" as she said, "The thrill of this moment keeps me from saying what I really feel. Thanks to all who made it possible." As she retreated off stage, "Grace Kelly folded and broke into tears as she went into the wings," Archerd observed.

Garland shed no tears over her loss. She told reporters, "It's OK. I have my own live Oscar," referring to her new son, Joey.

"Garland has received 1,000 wires from

Grace Kelly (with William Holden) "broke into tears as she went into the wings" after winning an Oscar for *The Country Girl*, *Variety* reported.

L.A. Herald

all over the world congratulating and 'consoling' her," Archerd reported afterward. Among them was a telegram from Groucho Marx: "Dear Judy, This is the biggest robbery since Brink's!"

In the race for Best Supporting Actor, *Variety* endorsed Edmond O'Brien, who played a bombastic press agent in *The Barefoot Contessa*, but warned, "His edge over Lee J. Cobb (*On the Waterfront*) was not a great one."

When O'Brien won, *Variety* noted, "The burly actor rushed to the stage to accept the award and declared, 'The calendar says March 30, but it can't be right—this must be March 17,' referring to St. Patrick's Day."

Contessa's writer/director Joseph L. Mankiewicz sent O'Brien a congratulatory telegram the next day: "And you did it on the first take!"

O'Brien topped three *Waterfront* nominees in his category, but the pic rebounded to claim the kudos for Best Story and Screenplay over *The Barefoot Contessa*.

"Schulberg noted that the trophy had an 'added kick' for him as the son of B. P. Schulberg, former Paramount production chief, who won the first Academy Award in 1928 for *Wings*," *Variety* said.

Waterfront also claimed honors for cinematography, art direction and film editing, bringing its total tally to eight. It tied *From Here to Eternity* and *Gone With the Wind* as the biggest champ in Oscar history.

"Yes, revenge was sweet," Schulberg wrote years later in *Variety*, "but we had taken too much from Zanuck and Cohn to lie down with the lions. Call us petty and unforgiving, but we weren't about to attend the Governors Ball and make nice with the insufferable suits who had punished us every step of the three-year climb. Instead, we held our own defiant fiesta at a midtown Chinese restaurant, the House of Chan.

"On a table in the middle of the restaurant, we lined up our Oscars. Our almost-nine-months-pregnant ingenue, the saintly Eva Marie Saint—winning for her very first time on screen—danced with one of the five ex-heavyweight contenders who played the goons. After tying the then all-time record for Oscars—which should have included one more for Leonard Bernstein's classic score—we couldn't foresee the centipede legs of our film or know that it was headed for a Top 10 list in the company of *Citizen Kane* and *Gone With the Wind.*"

▪ 1954 ▪

NATIONAL BOARD OF REVIEW

The board declared a best picture and foreign film of the year, then listed its remaining favorites according to highest scores. The vote results were announced on December 20, 1954.

BEST PICTURE
▪ *On the Waterfront*
Seven Brides for Seven Brothers
The Country Girl
A Star Is Born
Executive Suite
The Vanishing Prairie
Sabrina
20,000 Leagues under the Sea
The Unconquered
Beat the Devil

BEST DIRECTOR
▪ Renato Castellani, *Romeo and Juliet*

BEST ACTOR
▪ Bing Crosby, *The Country Girl*

BEST ACTRESS
▪ Grace Kelly, *The Country Girl, Dial M for Murder, Rear Window*

BEST SUPPORTING ACTOR
▪ John Williams, *Sabrina, Dial M for Murder*

BEST SUPPORTING ACTRESS
▪ Nina Foch, *Executive Suite*

BEST FOREIGN FILM
▪ *Romeo and Juliet* (U.K., Italy)
The Heart of the Matter (U.K.)
Gate of Hell (Japan)
Diary of a Country Priest (France)
The Little Kidnappers (U.K.)
Genevieve (U.K.)
Beauties of the Night (France/Italy)
Mr. Hulot's Holiday (France)
The Detective (U.K.)
Bread, Love and Dreams (Italy)

In its eighth and last year, *Variety's* film-academy poll scored its third perfect score.

SPECIAL AWARDS

- For the choreography of Michael Kidd in *Seven Brides for Seven Brothers*
- For the modernization of traditional Japanese acting by Machiko Kyo in *Ugetsu* and *Gate of Hell*
- For the new methods of moving puppets in *Hansel and Gretel*

NEW YORK FILM CRITICS

Winners were announced on December 28, 1954.

BEST PICTURE

- *On the Waterfront*

BEST DIRECTOR

- Elia Kazan, *On the Waterfront*

BEST ACTOR

- Marlon Brando, *On the Waterfront*

BEST ACTRESS

- Grace Kelly, *The Country Girl, Rear Window, Dial M for Murder*

BEST FOREIGN FILM

- *Gate of Hell* (Japan)

SCREEN DIRECTORS GUILD OF AMERICA

Four quarterly winners were named throughout the year. A separate award was bestowed for best director of the year on February 13, 1955, at the Biltmore Hotel in Los Angeles. The quarterly winners were the final nominees for the annual award; other directors listed were nominees for the quarterly honors.

BEST DIRECTOR

- Elia Kazan, *On the Waterfront*
George Cukor, *A Star Is Born*
Edward Dmytryk, *The Caine Mutiny*
Stanley Donen, *Seven Brides for Seven Brothers*
Melvin Frank, Norman Panama, *Knock on Wood*
Samuel Fuller, *Hell and High Water*
Alfred Hitchcock, *Dial M for Murder*

Alfred Hitchcock, *Rear Window* (quarterly winner)
Henry King, *King of the Khyber Rifles*
Anthony Mann, *The Glenn Miller Story*
Jean Negulesco, *Three Coins in the Fountain*
George Seaton, *The Country Girl* (quarterly winner)
Don Siegel, *Riot in Cell Block 11*
William Wellman, *The High and the Mighty* (quarterly winner)
Billy Wilder, *Sabrina* (quarterly winner)
Robert E. Wise, *Executive Suite*

HONORARY LIFETIME MEMBER

- Walt Disney

GOLDEN GLOBES

Awards were presented on February 24, 1955 at the Cocoanut Grove in the Ambassador Hotel in Los Angeles. Nominee information was unavailable.

BEST DRAMA PICTURE

- *On the Waterfront*

BEST COMEDY OR MUSICAL PICTURE

- *Carmen Jones*

BEST MOTION PICTURE PROMOTING INTERNATIONAL UNDERSTANDING

- *Broken Lance*

BEST DIRECTOR

- Elia Kazan, *On the Waterfront*

BEST ACTOR, DRAMA

- Marlon Brando, *On the Waterfront*

BEST ACTRESS, DRAMA

- Grace Kelly, *The Country Girl*

BEST ACTOR, COMEDY OR MUSICAL

- James Mason, *A Star Is Born*

BEST ACTRESS, COMEDY OR MUSICAL

- Judy Garland, *A Star Is Born*

BEST SUPPORTING ACTOR

- Edmond O'Brien, *The Barefoot Contessa*

BEST SUPPORTING ACTRESS
- Jan Sterling, *The High and the Mighty*

MOST PROMISING NEWCOMER—MALE
- Jeff Richards

MOST PROMISING NEWCOMER—FEMALE
- Shirley MacLaine
- Kim Novak
- Karen Sharpe

BEST SCREENPLAY
- Billy Wilder, Ernest Lehman, Samuel Taylor, *Sabrina*

BEST FOREIGN-LANGUAGE FILMS
- *Genevieve* (England)
- *La Mujer de las Camelias* (Argentina)
- *No Way Back* (Germany)
- *Twenty-Four Eyes* (Japan)

WORLD FILM FAVORITES
- Audrey Hepburn
- Gregory Peck

BEST CINEMATOGRAPHY, BLACK AND WHITE
- Boris Kaufman, *On the Waterfront*

BEST CINEMATOGRAPHY, COLOR
- Joseph Ruttenberg, *Brigadoon*

SPECIAL ACHIEVEMENT AWARDS
- Dimitri Tiomkin
- *Anywhere in Our Time* (Germany)

CECIL B. DEMILLE AWARD
- Jean Hersholt

PIONEER AWARD
- John Ford

SCREEN WRITERS GUILD OF AMERICA

Awards were presented on February 28, 1955, at the Moulin Rouge in Los Angeles.

BEST WRITTEN DRAMA
- *On the Waterfront*, Budd Schulberg, based on articles by Malcolm Johnson
The Barefoot Contessa, Joseph L. Mankiewicz

The Country Girl, George Seaton, based on the play Clifford Odets
Executive Suite, Ernest Lehman, based on the novel by Cameron Hawley
Rear Window, John Michael Hayes, based on a story by Cornell Woolrich

BEST WRITTEN COMEDY
- *Sabrina*, Billy Wilder, Samuel Taylor, Ernest Lehman, based on the play *Sabrina Fair* by Samuel Taylor
It Should Happen to You, Garson Kanin
Knock on Wood, Norman Panama, Melvin Frank
The Long, Long Trailer, Frances Goodrich, Albert Hackett, based on the novel by Clinton Twiss
Susan Slept Here, Alex Gottlieb, based on the play *Susan* by Steve Fisher and Alex Gottlieb

BEST WRITTEN MUSICAL
- *Seven Brides for Seven Brothers*, Albert Hackett, Frances Goodrich, Dorothy Kingsley, based on the story "The Sobbin" by Stephen Vincent Benet
Carmen Jones, Harry Kleiner, based on the musical play with book and lyrics by Oscar Hammerstein II
The Glenn Miller Story, Valentine Davies, Oscar Brodney
A Star Is Born, Moss Hart, based on the 1937 screenplay by Dorothy Parker, Alan Campbell and Robert Carson, adapted from a story by William A. Wellman and Robert Carson
There's No Business Like Show Business, Phoebe Ephron, Henry Ephron, Lamar Trotti

LAUREL AWARD
- Robert Riskin

ACADEMY AWARDS

Nominations were announced on February 12, 1955. Awards were presented on March 30 at the RKO Pantages Theater in Hollywood and the NBC Century Theater in New York. The ceremony was broadcast by NBC TV and radio.

BEST PICTURE

- *On the Waterfront*
The Caine Mutiny
The Country Girl
Seven Brides for Seven Brothers
Three Coins in the Fountain

BEST DIRECTOR

- Elia Kazan, *On the Waterfront*
Alfred Hitchcock, *Rear Window*
George Seaton, *The Country Girl*
William Wellman, *The High and the Mighty*
Billy Wilder, *Sabrina*

BEST ACTOR

- Marlon Brando, *On the Waterfront*
Humphrey Bogart, *The Caine Mutiny*
Bing Crosby, *The Country Girl*
James Mason, *A Star Is Born*
Dan O'Herlihy, *Adventures of Robinson Crusoe*

BEST ACTRESS

- Grace Kelly, *The Country Girl*
Dorothy Dandridge, *Carmen Jones*
Judy Garland, *A Star Is Born*
Audrey Hepburn, *Sabrina*
Jane Wyman, *Magnificent Obsession*

BEST SUPPORTING ACTOR

- Edmond O'Brien, *The Barefoot Contessa*
Lee J. Cobb, *On the Waterfront*
Karl Malden, *On the Waterfront*
Rod Steiger, *On the Waterfront*
Tom Tully, *The Caine Mutiny*

BEST SUPPORTING ACTRESS

- Eva Marie Saint, *On the Waterfront*
Nina Foch, *Executive Suite*
Katy Jurado, *Broken Lance*
Jan Sterling, *The High and the Mighty*
Claire Trevor, *The High and the Mighty*

BEST WRITING (MOTION PICTURE STORY)

- Philip Yordan, *Broken Lance*
François Boyer, *Forbidden Games*
Jed Harris, Tom Reed, *Night People*
Ettore Margadonna, *Bread, Love and Dreams*
Lamar Trotti, *There's No Business Like Show Business*

BEST WRITING (SCREENPLAY)

- George Seaton, *The Country Girl*
Frances Goodrich, Albert Hackett, Dorothy Kingsley, *Seven Brides for Seven Brothers*
John Michael Hayes, *Rear Window*
Stanley Roberts, *The Caine Mutiny*
Ernest Lehman, Samuel Taylor, Billy Wilder, *Sabrina*

BEST WRITING (STORY AND SCREENPLAY)

- Budd Schulberg, *On the Waterfront*
Oscar Brodney, Valentine Davies, *The Glenn Miller Story*
Melvin Frank, Norman Panama, *Knock on Wood*
Joseph L. Mankiewicz, *The Barefoot Contessa*
William Rose, *Genevieve*

BEST SONG

- "Count Your Blessings Instead of Sheep," *White Christmas*, Irving Berlin
"The High and the Mighty," *The High and the Mighty*, Dimitri Tiomkin, Ned Washington
"Hold My Hand," *Susan Slept Here*, Jack Lawrence, Richard Myers
"The Man That Got Away," *A Star Is Born*, Harold Arlen, Ira Gershwin
"Three Coins in the Fountain," *Three Coins in the Fountain*, Sammy Cahn, Jule Styne

Winners

BEST ART DIRECTION/SET DECORATION
(BLACK AND WHITE)
- Richard Day, *On the Waterfront*
(COLOR)
- John Meehan, Emile Juri, *20,000 Leagues under the Sea*

BEST CINEMATOGRAPHY
(BLACK AND WHITE)
- Boris Kaufman, *On the Waterfront*
(COLOR)
- Milton Krasner, *Three Coins in the Fountain*

BEST COSTUME DESIGN
(BLACK AND WHITE)
- Edith Head, *Sabrina*

(COLOR)
- Sanzo Wada, *Gate of Hell*

BEST DOCUMENTARY
(FEATURE)
- *The Vanishing Prairie*

(SHORT SUBJECT)
- *Thursday's Children*

BEST FILM EDITING
- Gene Milford, *On the Waterfront*

BEST MUSIC
(SCORING OF A DRAMATIC OR COMEDY PICTURE)
- Dimitri Tiomkin, *The High and the Mighty*

(SCORING OF A MUSICAL PICTURE)
- Saul Chaplin, Adolph Deutsch, *Seven Brides for Seven Brothers*

SCIENTIFIC OR TECHNICAL AWARDS
Class I (Statuette)
- John R. Bishop, Paramount Pictures, Loren L. Ryder

Class III (Certificate)
- Columbia Studio Sound Department, Frank Crandell, Orien Ernest, Karl Freund, K. M. Frierson, Max Goeppinger, Samuel Goldwyn Studio Sound Department, David S. Horsley, Fred Knoth, John P. Livadary, Magnascope Corp., MGM Studio Projection Department, MGM Studio Sound Department, Roland Miller,

Wesley C. Miller, Photo Research Corp., Carlos Rivas, Lloyd Russell, G. M. Sprague, J. W. Stafford, Universal-International Studio Special Photographic Department, Universal-International Studio Technical Department, Fred Wilson, P. C. Young

BEST SHORT SUBJECT
(CARTOON)
- *When Magoo Flew*

(ONE REEL)
- *This Mechanical Age*

(TWO REEL)
- *A Time out of War*

BEST SOUND RECORDING
- Leslie I. Carey, *The Glenn Miller Story*

BEST SPECIAL EFFECTS
- Walt Disney Studios, *20,000 Leagues under the Sea*

HONORARY FOREIGN-LANGUAGE FILM AWARD
- *Gate of Hell* (Japan)

HONORARY AWARDS
- Bausch & Lomb Optical Co.

Greta Garbo
Danny Kaye
Kemp R. Niver
Jon Whiteley
Vincent Winter

· 1955 ·

Little Marty *Hits It Big*

Film awards—not critics or regular movie-goers—were the first to spot *Marty* as a real winner.

Initially, the idea of lensing *Marty* as a feature film was dismissed by most studio execs because it had already been produced for TV as part of NBC's *Goodyear Playhouse* in May 1953. Independent producers Burt Lancaster and Harold Hecht finally found an uneasy distribution partner in United Artists and they proceeded to offer its original star, Rod Steiger, the chance to reprise the title role. Steiger, however, balked at the terms offered. ("Burt wanted me to sign my life over to him," Steiger fumed years later, "but I told him, 'Hey, *I* decide who I sleep with!' ") The part of the fumbling Bronx butcher who falls for a spinster schoolteacher ended up going to Ernest Borgnine, a bit player previously known for playing villains. *Variety* cheered the remake, calling *Marty* "warm, human and enjoyable," adding, "Studio story editors better spend more time at home looking at television."

But United Artists' execs didn't pay much attention to *Marty* at first. The pic had been filmed cheaply on black-and-white stock in a mere 16 days. With no marquee names toplining it, *Marty* was forced to play small indie theaters while the studio delayed releasing it to the main chains. Desperate to get the film some attention, Lancaster and Hecht took it to the French Riviera in late summer 1955, and there *Marty* became the first American movie to win the Palme d'Or at the Cannes Film Festival. Borgnine shared the Best Actor prize with Spencer Tracy (*Bad Day at Black Rock*) and his costar Betsy Blair, who assumed the role originally played by Nancy Marchand, was voted Best Actress.

When *Marty* came back to the United States to take on the domestic market, Lan-

After winning Best Actor at Cannes, Ernest Borgnine claimed all four U.S. trophies (Oscar, Globe, crix and NBR) for *Marty*.

caster and Hecht invested heavily to get it further awards notice. They thus became the only producers in showbiz history to spend more on a film's awards campaign ($400,000) than they did on making the movie ($343,000).

The National Board of Review and the New York Film Critics both followed suit by casting their votes for *Marty* as the year's Best Picture. *Marty* snagged the crix's award by the necessary two-thirds tally when 12 out the 16 critics backed it on the second ballot. "The competition was virtually token," reported *The New York Times*, noting that *Mister Roberts* was the runner-up with the other four votes. "Mr. Borgnine had more hurdles than his vehicle," observed the *Herald-Tribune*. "He was tied with Frank Sinatra (*The Man with the Golden Arm*) at 4 votes each on the first ballot." Borgnine finally prevailed with nine endorsements in the sixth round, when a only a majority vote was needed to determine the champ. At that point, Sinatra still had four votes, Alec Guinness (*The Prisoner*) three.

The board and crix also concurred Best Actress. "The great Anna Magnani ran away with the vote" among the crix, said the *Times*, recording her landslide (13 votes) on the first ballot over Katharine Hepburn (two votes for *Summertime*) and Jennifer Jones (one for *Love Is a Many-Splendored Thing*). Magnani was cited for her role as a feisty seamstress who rebounds from widowhood in *The Rose Tattoo*, a part originally tailored for her as a stage role by Tennessee Williams. But Italy's top film star refused to do the part when it was offered as a Broadway play, fearing that her English wasn't good enough. Williams finally prevailed on her to do the screen version and *Variety* hailed her perf as "spellbinding."

Curiously, neither the board nor the crix gave the director's prize to *Marty*'s helmer, probably because it was his first feature film. Delbert Mann was no rookie, though: he'd lensed the original production plus scores of other acclaimed TV programs. Instead, the National Board of Review chose William Wyler for *The Desperate Hours*, a tense tale of three escaped convicts who hold a suburban family hostage. The Gotham crix disagreed, giving Wyler only a single vote on their first polling. They picked David Lean on the sixth ballot for *Summertime*, which starred Katharine Hepburn as an American tourist who falls in love—after falling in a dirty canal—in Venice.

Delbert Mann's dual defeats were avenged a few weeks later when "the young television director walked off with the top honors from the Screen Directors Guild of America," reported *The New York Times*, which emphasized his greenness by adding, "He will celebrate his 36th birthday tomorrow." *The Los Angeles Times* noted that the victory of a young TV director "sets a most

The directors' guild avenged previous snubs by hailing *Marty*'s helmer.

unusual precedent for the guild." *Variety* reported that the banquet was so popular this year that guild leaders panicked trying to cope with an overflow crowd of 300 extra attendees.

Throughout his distinguished career, the noted TV scribe Paddy Chayefsky never won an Emmy Award for his celebrated works such as *Marty*, but this year his peers who belonged to the Screen Writers Guild of America honored him with their Best Written Drama Award for his celluloid adaptation of his teleplay.

Marty was less appreciated when 800 stars and foreign journalists gathered for the Golden Globe Awards. "Every star who could manage it crowded into the Cocoanut Grove," observed *The Los Angeles Mirror-News*. The glitterati included Elizabeth Taylor, Dean Martin, Jack Benny, Ernie Kovacs and Zsa Zsa Gabor, who all served as presenters. "Many of those who were called to the mike played to Frank Sinatra, who was seated at a ringside table," the *Mirror-News* observed.

The only Globe that *Marty* won went to Best Drama Actor Ernest Borgnine. The little movie was usurped for Best Drama Picture by director Elia Kazan's blockbuster *East of Eden*, based on John Steinbeck's novel about two brothers feuding for their father's love. One of the brothers was portrayed by teen idol James Dean, who died in a car crash five months before the Globes ceremony and now was the focus of a national cult following. The Globes revered him, too, with a posthumous trophy for Best Drama Actor.

Anna Magnani continued her awards juggernaut by claiming, in absentia, the Globe for Best Drama Actress. Marisa Pavan, who portrayed her love-smitten daughter in *The Rose Tattoo*, took a bow in the supporting category.

Two of the golden orbs for comedy/musical movies went to *Guys and Dolls*, Joseph L. Mankiewicz's screen rendition of the hit Broadway tuner about Times Square misfits. It was voted Best Picture and star Jean Simmons was hailed as Best Actress for her smart comic turn as a Salvation Army crusader.

East of Eden may have earned more than $5 million at the b.o. plus the admiration of the press (*Variety* called it "a tour-de-force"), but it wasn't nominated for Best Picture at the Oscars. Instead, the top lineup included *Picnic* (with a total of six noms), *Mister Roberts* (three noms) and three films with eight bids each: *The Rose Tattoo, Love Is a Many-Splendored Thing*—and *Marty*. Nominations were determined by 14,834 film industry pros, while winners were picked by the academy's 1,710 members.

This year *Variety* heeded continuing pleas from the AMPAS leadership to stop asking academy members how they voted. The paper scrapped its usual straw poll in favor of canvassing the industry in general, mailing out 2,250 ballots to movie pros and 250 to exhibitors. Winners were projected by counting up the 1,327 ballots (60 percent) that were returned.

On Oscar day, *Variety* flagged the results at the top of page one: *Marty* led in four major races—picture, actor, director and writer. "Last year the straw poll hit 100 percent for the third time in its eight-year career, giving it a lifetime batting average of .870—a figure virtually without precedent in the records of straw polls on any subject," the tradepaper boasted. But privately its editors wondered: can the results of the new polling technique be trusted?

Once again NBC aired the ceremony as a simulcast originating from L.A.'s Pantages Theatre and New York's Century Theater, and once again noted Chrysler spokesman Bob Hope wasn't asked to emcee since the kudocast was being underwritten by $350,000 from Oldsmobile. Jerry Lewis took over the host's job and had "a triumphant evening of high carnival," said *Variety*.

Cost to film Best Picture *Marty*: $353,000. Oscar campaign: $400,000.

Marty's Joe Mantell was a candidate for Best Supporting Actor along with *Rebel without a Cause* heartthrob Sal Mineo, but *Variety* wagered on Jack Lemmon, who really had a lead role as a wacky ensign aboard a navy cargo ship in *Mister Roberts*. Lemmon was a jittery about the race, according to *Variety* columnist Army Archerd: "Jack Lemmon was so nervous he forgot to take his theater tix and, when he arrived, put his hand in a bucket of paint!" When the 32-year-old thesp won, *Variety* described him as "the excited and emotional young actor." He paid tribute to the "highest professionals with whom I've had the good fortune of working ever since I got into this business."

The Best Supporting Actress lineup included recent Globe champ Marisa Pavan (*The Rose Tattoo*), *Marty's* Betsy Blair, songbird Peggy Lee giving a dramatic perf in *Pete Kelly's Blues* and Natalie Wood as James Dean's girlfriend in *Rebel without a Cause*. *Variety* bet correctly on the fifth candidate: Jo Van Fleet as James Dean's mother in *East of Eden*. Van Fleet was a veteran Broadway actress who had recently starred in two other major pics—*I'll Cry Tomorrow* and *The Rose Tattoo*. She refused to mount an Oscar campaign, even though "some reporters warned me that if I didn't advertise, I had no chance of winning," she later told the film academy. When she won, *Variety* described her as "fighting back tears" as she thanked "Elia Kazan, who directed her in the film and was himself an unsuccessful candidate for directorial honors."

Kazan was one of three Best Director candidates whose films were not up for Best Picture. The split between the categories may have helped Delbert Mann earn the accolade he failed to receive from the New York Film Critics, the National Board of Review, the Golden Globes and even the judges at Cannes. *Variety* reported his ultimate Oscar victory: "Mann, in NY for the ceremonies, said merely 'Thank you! Thank you very much!' "

Also at the New York ceremony was another winner who seemed strangely at a loss for words when his victory was announced: the author of the words for *Marty*—Paddy Chayefsky. When he accepted the Best Screenplay trophy from Claudette Colbert, he merely said, "I'm just very proud right now. Thank you—very much."

Oscar producers used a film clip to make it look as if the screenplay winner had been revealed by Best Actress contender Anna Magnani, who was shown reading off the nominees and opening an envelope while standing beside a fountain in Rome. At that point, Colbert piped in to report that the statuette went to Chayefsky, then handed it to him when he met her on stage. In fact, Magnani was asleep in Italy at that moment. She dozed until a reporter called later on to tell her that she had just won the Best Actress award. The notoriously hotheaded, gruff-acting thesp barked at him, "If you are kidding, I will get up right away and kill you wherever you are!"

But Magnani did win and her trophy was accepted for her in Hollywood by costar Marisa Pavan, "who stuttered that she had prepared a speech but had forgotten it," *Variety* reported.

Best Actor contender Ernest Borgnine was so excited about his film's many award chances that he had been the first nominee to arrive for the ceremony. When he won as best male thesp, he gave what *Variety* called "one of the most poignant 'thank you' speeches in Oscar history." He saluted his recently deceased mother "for giving me the idea and encouragement for going into this wonderful business, my pop for being steadfast and my lovely wife for helping."

The award was bestowed by last year's Best Actress champ Grace Kelly, who was lingering in Hollywood only long enough to dispatch the duty. She planned to leave town the next morning to marry Prince Rainier of Monaco.

Before Oscar night was over, a little pauper of a movie, *Marty*, would end up reigning as Best Picture.

Producer Harold Hecht accepted the trophy, saying, "We are very fortunate to live in a country where any man, no matter how humble his origin, can become president—and in an industry where any picture, no matter how low its budget, can win an Oscar."

Marty's co-producer was much less somber. *Variety* columnist Army Archerd noted: "Nomination for the most excited man in the theater went to Burt Lancaster, who nearly did a full flip each time a *Marty* winner was announced."

The next day, *Variety*'s banner headline proclaimed, "ALL OSCAR FAVORITES WIN." Inside, an article crowed, "For the fourth time the poll racked up a perfect score. The result gives the poll a lifetime batting average of .887."

▪ 1955 ▪

NATIONAL BOARD OF REVIEW

The board declared a best picture and foreign film of the year, then listed its remaining favorites according to highest scores. The vote results were announced on December 20, 1955.

BEST PICTURE
▪ *Marty*
East of Eden

Mister Roberts
Bad Day at Black Rock
Summertime
The Rose Tattoo
A Man Called Peter
Not as a Stranger
Picnic
The African Lion

BEST DIRECTOR
▪ William Wyler, *The Desperate Hours*

BEST ACTOR
- Ernest Borgnine, *Marty*

BEST ACTRESS
- Anna Magnani, *The Rose Tattoo*

BEST SUPPORTING ACTOR
- Charles Bickford, *Not as a Stranger*

BEST SUPPORTING ACTRESS
- Marjorie Rambeau, *A Man Called Peter,*
  The View from Pompey's Head

BEST FOREIGN FILM
- *The Prisoner* (Italy)
The Great Adventure (Sweden)
The Divided Heart (U.K.)
Les Diaboliques (France)
The End of the Affair (U.K.)

SPECIAL CITATION
- For aerial photography in *Strategic Air Command*

NEW YORK FILM CRITICS

Winners were announced on December 27, 1955. Awards were presented on January 21, 1956, at Sardi's restaurant in New York.

BEST PICTURE
- *Marty*

BEST DIRECTOR
- David Lean, *Summertime*

BEST ACTOR
- Ernest Borgnine, *Marty*

BEST ACTRESS
- Anna Magnani, *The Rose Tattoo*

BEST FOREIGN FILM (TIE)
- *Les Diaboliques*
- *Umberto D*

SCREEN DIRECTORS GUILD OF AMERICA

Four quarterly winners were named throughout the year. A separate award was bestowed for best director of the year on January 29,

Just like Borgnine, Anna Magnani (*The Rose Tattoo*, with Burt Lancaster) swept all four top kudos.

1956. The quarterly winners were the final nominees for the annual award; other directors listed were nominees for the quarterly honors.

BEST DIRECTOR
- Delbert Mann, *Marty*
Richard Brooks, *Blackboard Jungle*
John Ford, *The Long Gray Line*
John Ford, Mervyn LeRoy, *Mister Roberts*
  (quarterly winners)
Elia Kazan, *East of Eden* (quarterly
  winner)
Henry Koster, *A Man Called Peter*
Joshua Logan, *Picnic* (quarterly winner)
Daniel Mann, *The Rose Tattoo*
Mark Robson, *The Bridges of Toko-Ri*
John Sturges, *Bad Day at Black Rock*
  (quarterly winner)
Charles Vidor, *Love Me or Leave Me*
Billy Wilder, *The Seven-Year Itch*

SPECIAL D. W. GRIFFITH AWARD
- Henry King

HONORARY LIFETIME MEMBER
- Donald Crisp

GOLDEN GLOBES

Awards were presented on February 23, 1956, at the Cocoanut Grove in the Ambassador Hotel in Los Angeles. Nominee information was unavailable.

BEST DRAMA PICTURE
- *East of Eden*

BEST COMEDY OR MUSICAL PICTURE
- *Guys and Dolls*

BEST OUTDOOR DRAMA PICTURE
- *Wichita*

BEST MOTION PICTURE PROMOTING INTERNATIONAL UNDERSTANDING
- *Love Is a Many Splendored Thing*

BEST DIRECTOR
- Joshua Logan, *Picnic*

BEST ACTOR, DRAMA
- Ernest Borgnine, *Marty*

BEST ACTRESS, DRAMA
- Anna Magnani, *The Rose Tattoo*

BEST ACTOR, COMEDY OR MUSICAL
- Tom Ewell, *The Seven-Year Itch*

BEST ACTRESS, COMEDY OR MUSICAL
- Jean Simmons, *Guys and Dolls*

BEST SUPPORTING ACTOR
- Arthur Kennedy, *Trial*

BEST SUPPORTING ACTRESS
- Marisa Pavan, *The Rose Tattoo*

MOST PROMISING NEWCOMER—MALE
- Ray Danton
- Russ Tamblyn

MOST PROMISING NEWCOMER—FEMALE
- Victoria Shaw
- Anita Ekberg
- Dana Wynter

BEST FOREIGN-LANGUAGE FILMS
- *Dangerous Curves* (England)
- *Eyes of Children* (Japan)
- *Ordet* (Denmark)
- *Sons, Mothers and a General* (Germany)
- *Stella* (Greece)

Winners

WORLD FILM FAVORITES
- Marlon Brando
- Grace Kelly

SPECIAL POSTHUMOUS AWARD FOR BEST DRAMATIC ACTOR
- James Dean

HOLLYWOOD CITIZENSHIP AWARD
- Esther Williams

CECIL B. DEMILLE AWARD
- Jack Warner

SCREEN WRITERS GUILD OF AMERICA

Awards were presented on March 8, 1956, at the Beverly Hilton Hotel.

BEST WRITTEN DRAMA
- *Marty*, Paddy Chayefsky

Bad Day at Black Rock, Millard Kaufman, Don McGuire, from the short story "Bad Times at Hondo" by Howard Breslin

Blackboard Jungle, Richard Brooks, based on the novel by Evan Hunter

East of Eden, Paul Osborn, based on the book by John Steinbeck

Picnic, Daniel Taradash, based on the play by William Inge

BEST WRITTEN COMEDY
- *Mister Roberts*, Frank Nugent, Joshua Logan, adapted from the play by Thomas Heggen and Joshua Logan, based on the novel by Thomas Heggen

Phfft, George Axelrod

The Seven-Year Itch, Billy Wilder, George Axelrod, based on the play by George Axelrod

The Tender Trap, Julius J. Epstein, based on the play by Max Schulman and Robert Paul Smith

To Catch a Thief, John Michael Hayes, based on the novel by David Dodge

BEST WRITTEN MUSICAL
- *Love Me or Leave Me*, Daniel Fuchs, Isobel Lennart, Daniel Fuchs
Daddy Long Legs, Phoebe Ephron, Henry Ephron, based on the novel by Jean Webster
Guys and Dolls, Joseph L. Mankiewicz, adapted from the play by Jo Swerling and Abe Burrows, based on a story by Damon Runyon
It's Always Fair Weather, Betty Comden, Adolph Green
Oklahoma!, Sonya Levien, William Ludwig

LAUREL AWARD
- Julius and Philip Epstein, Albert Hackett, Frances Goodrich

ACADEMY AWARDS

Nominations were announced on February 18, 1956. Awards were presented on March 21 at the RKO Pantages Theater in Hollywood and the NBC Century Theater in New York. The ceremony was broadcast by NBC TV and radio.

BEST PICTURE
- *Marty*
Love Is a Many-Splendored Thing
Mister Roberts
Picnic
The Rose Tattoo

BEST DIRECTOR
- Delbert Mann, *Marty*
Elia Kazan, *East of Eden*
David Lean, *Summertime*
Joshua Logan, *Picnic*
John Sturges, *Bad Day at Black Rock*

BEST ACTOR
- Ernest Borgnine, *Marty*
James Cagney, *Love Me or Leave Me*
James Dean, *East of Eden*
Frank Sinatra, *The Man with the Golden Arm*
Spencer Tracy, *Bad Day at Black Rock*

BEST ACTRESS
- Susan Hayward, *I'll Cry Tomorrow*
Katharine Hepburn, *Summertime*
Jennifer Jones, *Love Is a Many-Splendored Thing*

Anna Magnani, *The Rose Tattoo*
Eleanor Parker, *Interrupted Melody*

BEST SUPPORTING ACTOR
- Jack Lemmon, *Mister Roberts*
Arthur Kennedy, *Trial*
Joe Mantell, *Marty*
Sal Mineo, *Rebel without a Cause*
Arthur O'Connell, *Picnic*

BEST SUPPORTING ACTRESS
- Jo Van Fleet, *East of Eden*
Betsy Blair, *Marty*
Peggy Lee, *Pete Kelly's Blues*
Marisa Pavan, *The Rose Tattoo*
Natalie Wood, *Rebel without a Cause*

BEST WRITING (MOTION PICTURE STORY)
- Daniel Fuchs, *Love Me or Leave Me*
Joe Connelly, Bob Mosher, *The Private War of Major Benson*
Beirne Lay, Jr., *Strategic Air Command*
Jean Marsan, Jacques Perret, Raoul Ploquin, Henry Troyat, Henri Verneuil, *The Sheep Has Five Legs*
Nicholas Ray, *Rebel without a Cause*

BEST WRITING (SCREENPLAY)
- Paddy Chayefsky, *Marty*
Richard Brooks, *Blackboard Jungle*
Daniel Fuchs, Isobel Lennart, *Love Me or Leave Me*
Millard Kaufman, *Bad Day at Black Rock*
Paul Osborn, *East of Eden*

BEST WRITING (STORY AND SCREENPLAY)
- Sonya Levien, William Ludwig, *Interrupted Melody*
Betty Comden, Adolph Green, *It's Always Fair Weather*
Emmet Lavery, Milton Sperling, *The Court-Martial of Billy Mitchell*
Henri Marquet, Jacques Tati, *Mr. Hulot's Holiday*
Jack Rose, Melville Shavelson, *The Seven Little Foys*

BEST SONG
- "Love Is a Many-Splendored Thing," *Love Is a Many-Splendored Thing*, Sammy Fain, Paul Francis Webster
"I'll Never Stop Loving You," *Love Me or Leave Me*, Nicholas Brodszky, Sammy Cahn

"(Love Is) The Tender Trap,"
The Tender Trap, Sammy
Cahn, James Van Heusen
"Something's Gotta Give,"
Daddy Long Legs, Johnny
Mercer
"Unchained Melody,"
Unchained, Alex North,
Hy Zaret

DAILY VARIETY DAILY

No. 12   Hollywood (28), California, Wednesday, March 21, 1956   Ten Cents

Daily Variety Poll:

MARTY', MAGNANI, BORGNINE, D.MANN, VAN FLEET AND LEMMON

Variety polled industry pros instead of Oscar voters and again scored 100 percent.

Winners

BEST ART DIRECTION/SET DECORATION
(BLACK AND WHITE)
- Tambi Larsen, Hal Pereira, Sam Comer, Arthur Krams, *The Rose Tattoo*

(COLOR)
- William Flannery, Jo Mielziner, Robert Priestly, *Picnic*

BEST CINEMATOGRAPHY
(BLACK AND WHITE)
- James Wong Howe, *The Rose Tattoo*

(COLOR)
- Robert Burks, *To Catch a Thief*

BEST COSTUME DESIGN
(BLACK AND WHITE)
- Helen Rose, *I'll Cry Tomorrow*

(COLOR)
- Charles Lemaire, *Love Is a Many-Splendored Thing*

BEST DOCUMENTARY
(FEATURE)
- *Helen Keller in Her Story*, Nancy Hamilton

(SHORT SUBJECT)
- *Men against the Arctic*, Walt Disney

BEST FILM EDITING
- William A. Lyon, Charles Nelson, *Picnic*

HONORARY FOREIGN FILM AWARD
- Samurai, *The Legend of Musashi* (Japan)

BEST MUSIC
(SCORING OF A DRAMATIC OR COMEDY PICTURE)
- Alfred Newman, *Love Is a Many-Splendored Thing*

(SCORING OF A MUSICAL PICTURE)
- Robert Russell Bennett, Jay Blackton, Adolph Deutsch, *Oklahoma!*

SCIENTIFIC OR TECHNICAL AWARDS
Class I (Statuette)
- National Carbon Company

Class II (Plague)
- Eastman Kodak Company; Farciot Edouart, Hal Corl, Paramount Studio Transparency Department

Class III (Certificate)
- Dave Anderson, Bausch & Lomb Company, Hal Corl, Farciot Edouart, Henry Fracker, Walter Jolley, Steve Krilanovich, Maurice Larson, Paramount Studio, Paramount Studio Transparency Department, Loren L. Ryder, R.H. Spies, Twentieth Century-Fox Studio, Charles West

BEST SHORT SUBJECT
(CARTOON)
- *Speedy Gonzales*

(ONE REEL)
- *Survival City*

(TWO REEL)
- *The Face of Lincoln*

BEST SOUND RECORDING
- Fred Hynes, *Oklahoma!*

BEST SPECIAL EFFECT
- Paramount Studio, *The Bridges at Toko-Ri*

▪ 1956 ▪

4 Best-Pic Prizes for 80 Days

O ver the past several years, small to medium-sized black-and-white pics—*Marty, On the Waterfront, From Here to Eternity*—claimed the top film kudos. Now, suddenly, big-money, wide-lensed, color extravaganzas vied for the gleaming golden tributes.

"It's all on the screen, every penny of the $5–6 million that went into the making of *Around the World in 80 Days*," observed *Variety* in its awestruck review of the blockbuster adaptation of the Jules Verne classic about an Englishman who bets he can circle the globe in a hurry. It was produced by Broadway impresario Mike Todd, who set out to dazzle movie-goers with his first film. "There's rarely been a picture that can boast of so many star names in bit parts," *Variety* marveled, citing cameo bows by Shirley MacLaine, Marlene Dietrich, Frank Sinatra and Red Skelton. Theaters positioned the pic as a special event, selling seats on a reserved basis, distributing programs and shutting down the popcorn concession. *Variety* hailed the celluloid result for its "taste, imagination, ingenuity and splendor" and applauded the "wondrous effects" of its widescreen "Todd-AO" cinematography. The National Board of Review was the first to declare it Best Picture of the year.

The other top films of 1956 were also epic eyefuls, including what *Variety* called Cecil B. DeMille's "super spectacular"—*The Ten Commandments*, which cost $13.5 million and employed 25,000 extras. Director King Vidor spent $6 million weaving Tolstoy's *War and Peace* into what *Variety* described as "three-and-a-half hours of vivid cinematic magic" starring Audrey Hepburn, Henry Fonda and 6,000 extras. John Huston doled out $5 million to lens his ambitious retelling of Herman Melville's *Moby Dick*. In *Giant, Variety* noted that producers "spent freely to capture the mood of

"I've gone from saint to whore and back to saint again," Ingrid Bergman mused after she received her N.Y. crix prize for *Anastasia*.

the Edna Ferber novel (about) the vastness and mental narrowness . . . that make up Texas." Even the film translation of Broadway tuner *The King and I* achieved what *Variety* called "full glory" as a "truly blockbuster presentation" thanks largely to Cinemascope.

When the 16 members of the New York Film Critics met at the offices of the newspaper guild to decide their award winners, they considered only one "little" pic as an alternative to *80 Days*—*Lust for Life*, the Vincent Van Gogh bio starring Kirk Douglas—for the top prize. The first round's score was: *Around the World in 80 Days* (10 votes), *Giant* (three), *The King and I* (one), *Lust for Life* (one) and *Moby Dick* (one). On the second tally, *Around the World* claimed 13 votes, thereby reaping the two-thirds majority it needed for victory.

The outcome was ground-breaking, noted *The New York Times*: "It is the first time a color picture has received the critics' top award." The movie also scored the crix's new prize for screenplays, but failed to take the kudos for best direction. Helmer Michael Anderson received only a single vote on the first ballot, compared to six for John Huston (*Moby Dick*) and three for Elia Kazan (*Baby Doll*). Huston beat Kazan on the third tally by an 11-to-5 score. One week earlier, Huston had won the same kudos from the National Board of Review.

Kirk Douglas (*Lust for Life*) needed three ballots before he eclipsed Laurence Olivier (*Richard III*) and Yul Brynner (*The King and I*), who was the National Board of Review's choice for Best Actor. The winner of the actress race, noted the *Times*, "ran away with the honors," surpassing Deborah Kerr (*The King and I*) and Audrey Hepburn (*War and Peace*) on the third ballot. It was the second time that the crix honored Ingrid Bergman, and her latest victory marked a triumphant career—and personal—comeback.

The star of *Joan of Arc, Notorious* and *Casablanca* had become a martyr to love a few years earlier when she fell for the fiery charms of her Italian director, Roberto Rossellini, during the filming of *Terra di Dio*. When she bore his love child out of wedlock in 1950, 38,000 newspaper articles covered the scandal, the Federal Council of Churches blamed the couple for "the moral decay of the West" and Bergman was denounced in the U.S. Congress as "a powerful influence for evil." The duo eventually married and had two more children. By mid-decade, movie mogul Darryl Zanuck thought the stage was set and timing just right for a Hollywood-Bergman reconciliation.

He cast her in *Anastasia*—an adaptation of a French play about a street derelict who purports to be the surviving child of Russia's murdered czar—and filmed it in Paris. *Variety* lauded the result as "a wonderfully moving and entertaining motion picture from start to finish, and the major credit inevitably must go to Ingrid Bergman, who turns in a great performance."

When the crix gathered at Sardi's restaurant in New York for their awards ceremony, Bergman made her first trip to America in seven years to accept her scroll. She had been in Paris appearing on stage in *Tea and Sympathy*, but Twentieth Century-Fox bought out three performances so she could make the trip, which turned out to be a dramatic homecoming heralded by cheering mobs and fawning paparazzi. Years later she marveled at the scandal's extraordinary swings, writing, "I've gone from saint to whore and back to saint again all in one lifetime."

One month later, Bergman was also acknowledged with a Golden Globe, but she was in no hurry to return to Hollywood. The awards ceremony went on without her at the Cocoanut Grove and it was still a media event, receiving "the largest radio-TV coverage in its 14-year history," *Variety* reported. NBC, CBS, MGM and Universal all sent newsreel cameras and the gala was broadcast on the radio by L.A. station KPOL, Voice of America and the Armed Forces Radio Service.

Around the World in 80 Days won Best Drama Picture over *Giant, Lust for Life, The Rainmaker* and *War and Peace*, but award watchers were mystified by the movie's contradictory classifications. One of its stars, Mexican comic Cantinflas (Mario Moreno), won Best Actor in a Comedy or Musical.

The Teahouse of the August Moon led with the most overall noms (five), but lost the Globe for Best Comedy or Musical Picture to *The King and I*, which also claimed kudos for star Deborah Kerr. For Best

The feisty writers' guild gave a kudo to blacklistee Michael Wilson.

Drama Actor, the Globes agreed with the Gotham crix and hailed Kirk Douglas's portrait of Van Gogh in *Lust for Life*.

While the crix and the National Board of Review both endorsed John Huston as the year's top megger, the Globes opted for Elia Kazan, whom *Variety* praised for "expertly nurturing a feeling of decay" when directing Tennessee Williams's naughty tale of a nymphet bride in *Baby Doll*.

The Screen Directors Guild of America didn't nominate Kazan, however. Huston made the long list of 18 contenders, but, just like *80 Days*'s Michael Anderson, he failed to make the cut as a finalist. The top prize—a large gold medallion—ended up going to George Stevens for *Giant*, which he also co-produced. Anderson was among the nominees who received silver medallions as consolation, but he wasn't on hand to accept it. He was across town at the wedding of his 50-year-old boss Mike Todd, who was getting hitched to 25-year-old Elizabeth Taylor.

This year's disagreement over the year's best director was nothing compared to the uproar that would ensue between the kudos over writers.

The first hubbub erupted over *Friendly Persuasion*, director William Wyler's adaptation of a book by Jessamyn West about a Quaker family's struggles during the Civil War. The script was penned by Michael Wilson, who was blacklisted in 1951 when he invoked the Fifth Amendment before the House Committee on Un-American Activities. Wyler and the pic's distributor, Allied Artists, denied Wilson's claim of authorship, but the scribe was backed up by a ruling of the Writers Guild of America. The endorsement turned out to be a hollow victory, however, since the distributor still legally snubbed Wilson when the pic was released in 1956. *The New York Times* noted, "The company took advantage of a clause in the basic contract with the guild which permits a producer to delete the name

Oscar leaders officially barred suspected Commies from winning awards.

of a writer who declines to clear himself of Communist accusations."

Twelve days before Oscar bids were to be announced, movie academy leaders panicked. Wilson had embarrassed them five years earlier when he won a screenplay statuette soon after being blacklisted. Fearing that a Wilson film would be nominated again, the Board of Governors held what *Variety* called "a highly secretive meeting" at which they passed a new rule permitting the pic to be cited, but, the paper added, "disbarring anyone from receiving an award if he or she has admitted membership in the Communist Party and has not renounced such membership, or has refused to testify before a Congressional Committee, or has refused to respond to a subpoena." The new rule would be axed in 1959 as "unworkable," but in the meantime *Friendly Persuasion* did earn a bid. Its listing was flagged with the notation: "Achievement nominated but writer ineligible for an award under Academy bylaws."

The writers' guild publicly condemned the ruling, but the academy held firm. Two weeks later the guild staged its own awards presentation at the Moulin Rouge restaurant and, in an act of defiance, gave Wilson its prize for Best Written Drama. The solemnity of the occasion was lightened by Groucho Marx, who claimed that *The Ten Commandments* faced similar political problems: "The producers were forced to keep Moses' name off the writing credits because they found out he had once crossed the Red Sea."

Among the guild's other honorees were two scribes denied credit for writing *Around the World in 80 Days* when the New York Film Critics bestowed its screenplay prize earlier this year. Producer Mike Todd claimed that S. J. Perelman did the job alone, but five days before its awards ceremony, the guild ruled that James Poe and John Farrow should also be cited. Soon thereafter the group hailed all three scribes with its prize for the year's Best Written Comedy.

The Oscars conceded the guild's ruling and included Poe and Farrow as contenders for Best Adapted Screenplay, but an embarrassing gaffe surfaced in another writing race. "Surprise of the nominations was the selection of *High Society* for the best motion picture story classification," *Variety* reported under the headline "BIGGEST BOO-BOO IN ACAD ANNALS." Voters no doubt thought they were backing John Patrick's adaptation of *The Philadelphia Story* starring Bing Crosby, Grace Kelly and Frank Sinatra. In fact, they endorsed a Bowery Boys pic of the same name. The nominees conceded the confusion and withdrew their names.

Another, bigger boo-boo also lurked in the same category—a nomination for nonexistent Robert Rich as the author of *The Brave One*. Worse, "Rich" would go on to win the Oscar and turn out to be blacklisted writer Dalton Trumbo, a member of the Hollywood 10 who had previously duped the film academy in 1953 when he hid behind frontman Ian McLellan Hunter and won a screenplay prize for *Roman Holiday*. Years later the academy would finally and officially recognize Trumbo just before his death in 1976.

Controversies engulfed Oscar's acting categories, too, when some stars tried to duplicate Jack Lemmon's success of 1955 by downplaying their lead status so they could compete for best supporting thesps. The strategy paid off in noms for four contenders: Mickey Rooney (*The Bold and the Brave*), Don Murray (*Bus Stop*) and *Written on the Wind*'s Robert Stack and Dorothy Malone.

But while Hollywood insiders howled over the lower contests, America watched one lead race closely and wondered: Would the town renowned for casual morals finally forgive sexual exile Ingrid Bergman?

Bergman refused to chance rejection and stayed away on Oscar night. She may have been a proven past winner for 1944's *Gaslight*, but now she faced tough competish, including *Baby Doll* star Carroll

L.A. Herald

Mexican comic Cantinflas shows off his Golden Globe to Elizabeth Taylor and *80 Days* producer Michael Todd.

Baker as a nymphet bride, Nancy Kelly as the mother of an evil moppet in *The Bad Seed*, and two-time Oscar bridesmaid Deborah Kerr as an English schoolteacher in Siam in *The King and I*. All of them took on headstrong past champ Katharine Hepburn as the ugly duckling who finally finds love in *The Rainmaker*.

Kirk Douglas (*Lust for Life*) was considered the early front-runner for Best Actor, having won the equivalent kudos from the Gotham film crix and Golden Globes, but he was up against sudden star Yul Brynner, who had a banner year as a pharaoh in *The Ten Commandments*, a con man in *Anastasia* and the monarch who matches wits with Deborah Kerr in in *The King and I*. His Oscar bid as a leading man was a notable kudos promotion: after originating the same role on Broadway, Brynner won a Tony Award five years earlier as a secondary, featured player.

Both actors faced formidable opposition for the top Oscar from the late James Dean (*Giant*), who not only had sentiment behind him, but Hedda Hopper's tireless cheerleading in her syndicated newspaper column. Other rivals were *Giant* costar Rock Hudson and Sir Laurence Olivier, whose performance in *Richard III* was first shown on NBC television, then distributed to moviehouses.

Showbiz buzz may have favored Douglas in the actors' race, but *Variety* discovered a different front-runner after it mailed out 2,250 ballots to Hollywood film pros and 250 exhibitors nationwide (1,504 were returned). Its poll revealed that Brynner was actually ahead, along with Ingrid Bergman, Dorothy Malone, Robert Stack, George Stevens (Best Director), *The Bold and the Brave* (original screenplay), *The Brave One* (original story) and *Friendly Persuasion*'s "Thee I Sing" (song). The tradepaper trumpeted the results with cocky confidence: "The *Daily Variety* poll in its previous nine tabulations has achieved the unprecedented lifetime polling average of .887. For the last two years (and in 1949 and 1950) the poll was 100% accurate. On three other occasions it had only one category wrong." This year, however, *Variety* would be greatly humbled by missing the mark three out of nine times.

Various union and guild members composed many of the 16,721 voters who determined this year's nominees; winners were chosen by the academy's 1,770 members. The five best picture contenders led with the most bids: *Giant* (10), *The King and I* (nine), *Around the World in 80 Days* (eight), *The Ten Commandments* (seven) and *Friendly Persuasion* (six). *Variety* declared that Best Picture champ would be *Around the World in 80 Days*.

Most of *Variety*'s blunders came early on Oscar night and, in the case of the race for best original screenplay, the paper shared its embarrassment with the academy: the victor turned out to be *The Red Balloon*, a film with no dialogue. While *Variety* predicted a win for *Friendly Persuasion*'s "Thee I Love" as best song, it warned that the vote was so close that "Whatever Will Be, Will Be" from *The Man Who Knew Too Much* could pull of an upset. *Variety* was right on the latter score.

But nobody foresaw the jaw-dropper coming in the contest for Best Supporting Actor. Thanks to their weighty, leading-man perfs, Robert Stack, Mickey Rooney and Don Murray were believed to be the front-runners, but *Variety* reported that "the Pantages audience gasped in surprise" when the champ turned out to be the same spoiler who'd pulled off an upset over Richard Burton in 1952: Anthony Quinn. This time

---

No Oscar Chance

Michael Wilson's Writers Guild Award for the screenplay of "Friendly Persuasion" cued conjecture yesterday as to the writer's chances in the Academy Awards, even though his nomination was disqualified by the Academy because of his taking the Fifth Amendment before the Red probers. There was speculation yesterday that Wilson might amass a certain amount of write-in votes for the Oscar for Best Screenplay, Adapted.

However, Academy prexy George Seaton pointed out yesterday that there is absolutely no possibility that Wilson can win an Oscar since write-in votes are never counted in Academy balloting.

Variety reported that an Oscar write-in campaign couldn't help blacklistee Michael Wilson, who was snubbed despite *Friendly Persuasion* being nommed.

Quinn's victory was all the more stunning because he was hailed for a mere nine-minute portrayal of artist Paul Gauguin in *Lust for Life*.

"Quinn wasted no time getting to the stage to receive his Oscar," *Variety* reported on his exuberant response to winning. Once there, Quinn said, "Acting has never been a matter of competition to me. I was only competing against myself, and I thank you for letting me win that fight with myself."

As *Variety* predicted, the statuette for Best Supporting Actress went to Dorothy Malone as the spoiled rich girl who lusts for Rock Hudson in *Written on the Wind*. *Variety* called her victory "a popular choice and not unexpected. Miss Malone raced breathlessly to the stage to grab the Oscar. She then went into a long thank-you speech in which she even kudosed (Universal Studios') board of directors." Oscarcast emcee Jerry Lewis ultimately intervened, "frantically waving a stopwatch in front of her as she finally stopped with the audience much amused," *Variety* added.

The winner of Best Actor was equally excited. *Variety* noted that Yul Brynner "bounded on stage to clutch his trophy, declaring, 'I hope this is not a mistake because I wouldn't give it back for anything in the world.' "

There are conflicting historic accounts of what Ingrid Bergman was doing in Paris when her *Notorious* costar Cary Grant opened an envelope at the Pantages Theatre and revealed that she had won Best Actress. Bergman once claimed that she was lounging casually in the bathtub while listening to the Oscar broadcast on the radio. Another account reports that she was so nervous about the award's outcome that she had to be sedated and was sleeping.

Producer Mike Todd could've used a sedative when *Around the World in 80 Days*

won Best Picture. He vaulted out of his seat, dashed toward the stage, stopped, raced back to hug Elizabeth Taylor, then headed up toward the podium. "The most priceless picture of the year was Mike Todd, quickly composing himself as he reached the stage, trying to act unruffled and dignified as he was about to accept the Oscar," *Variety* columnist Army Archerd wrote.

"I'd like to thank you on behalf of the 60-odd thousand people who worked on this show," Todd said joyously once up on stage. "I am especially thrilled. This is my first time at bat." It would also be his last time at Oscar bat. His new, widescreen cinematography process Todd-AO would win a golden boy next year, but its bawdy champion, who so impressed Hollywood with his exuberant love of life, would not be alive to accept it.

▪ 1956 ▪

NATIONAL BOARD OF REVIEW

The board declared a best picture and foreign film of the year, then listed its remaining favorites according to highest scores. The vote results were announced on December 20, 1956.

BEST PICTURE
- *Around the World in 80 Days*
Moby Dick
The King and I
Lust for Life
Friendly Persuasion
Somebody up There Likes Me
The Catered Affair
Anastasia
The Man Who Never Was
Bus Stop

BEST DIRECTOR
- John Huston, *Moby Dick*

BEST ACTOR
- Yul Brynner, *The King and I, Anastasia, The Ten Commandments*

BEST ACTRESS
- Dorothy McGuire, *Friendly Persuasion*

BEST SUPPORTING ACTOR
- Richard Basehart, *Moby Dick*

BEST SUPPORTING ACTRESS
- Debbie Reynolds, *The Catered Affair*

BEST FOREIGN FILM
- *The Silent World* (France)
War and Peace (U.S./Italy)
Richard III (U.K.)
La Strada (Italy)
Rififi (France)

NEW YORK FILM CRITICS

Winners were announced on December 27, 1956. Awards were presented on January 19, 1957, at Sardi's restaurant in New York.

BEST PICTURE
- *Around the World in 80 Days*

BEST DIRECTOR
- John Huston, *Moby Dick*

BEST ACTOR
- Kirk Douglas, *Lust for Life*

BEST ACTRESS
- Ingrid Bergman, *Anastasia*

BEST SCREENPLAY
- S. J. Perelman,* *Around the World in 80 Days*

BEST FOREIGN FILM
- *La Strada* (Italy)

SCREEN DIRECTORS GUILD OF AMERICA

The initial list of nominees was narrowed down to a group of finalists who competed for the Best Director award, bestowed on February 3, 1957, at the Biltmore Hotel in Los Angeles.

BEST DIRECTOR
- George Stevens, *Giant*
  Michael Anderson, *Around the World in 80 Days*
  John Ford, *The Searchers* (finalist)
  Alfred Hitchcock, *The Man Who Knew Too Much* (finalist)
  Alfred Hitchcock, *The Trouble with Harry* (finalist)
  John Huston, *Moby Dick*
  Nunnally Johnson, *The Man in the Gray Flannel Suit* (finalist)
  Henry King, *Carousel* (finalist)
  Walter Lang, *The King and I* (finalist)
  Joshua Logan, *Bus Stop*
  Daniel Mann, *The Teahouse of the August Moon*
  Carol Reed, *Trapeze* (finalist)
  Robert Rossen, *Alexander the Great* (finalist)
  Roy Rowland, *Meet Me in Las Vegas* (finalist)
  George Sidney, *The Eddy Duchin Story* (finalist)
  King Vidor, *War and Peace*

---

*The Writers Guild of America claimed that James Poe and John Farrow also deserved credit.

Robert E. Wise, *Somebody up There Likes Me*
William Wyler, *Friendly Persuasion*

SPECIAL D. W. GRIFFITH AWARD
- King Vidor

GOLDEN GLOBES

Nominations were announced on January 20, 1957. Awards were presented on February 28 at the Cocoanut Grove in the Ambassador Hotel in Los Angeles.

BEST DRAMA PICTURE
- *Around the World in 80 Days*
  Giant
  Lust for Life
  The Rainmaker
  War and Peace

BEST COMEDY OR MUSICAL PICTURE
- *The King and I*
  Bus Stop
  The Opposite Sex
  The Solid Gold Cadillac
  The Teahouse of the August Moon

BEST MOTION PICTURE PROMOTING INTERNATIONAL UNDERSTANDING
- *Battle Hymn*
  The Brave One
  Friendly Persuasion
  The King and I
  The Teahouse of the August Moon

BEST DIRECTOR
- Elia Kazan, *Baby Doll*
  Michael Anderson, *Around the World in 80 Days*
  Vincente Minnelli, *Lust for Life*
  George Stevens, *Giant*
  King Vidor, *War and Peace*

BEST ACTOR, DRAMA
- Kirk Douglas, *Lust for Life*
  Gary Cooper, *Friendly Persuasion*
  Charlton Heston, *The Ten Commandments*
  Burt Lancaster, *The Rainmaker*
  Karl Malden, *Baby Doll*

BEST ACTRESS, DRAMA
- Ingrid Bergman, *Anastasia*
- Carroll Baker, *Baby Doll*
- Helen Hayes, *Anastasia*
- Audrey Hepburn, *War and Peace*
- Katharine Hepburn, *The Rainmaker*

BEST ACTOR, COMEDY OR MUSICAL
- Cantinflas, *Around the World in 80 Days*
- Marlon Brando, *The Teahouse of the August Moon*
- Yul Brynner, *The King and I*
- Glenn Ford, *The Teahouse of the August Moon*
- Danny Kaye, *The Court Jester*

BEST ACTRESS, COMEDY OR MUSICAL
- Deborah Kerr, *The King and I*
- Judy Holliday, *The Solid Gold Cadillac*
- Machiko Kyo, *The Teahouse of the August Moon*
- Marilyn Monroe, *Bus Stop*
- Debbie Reynolds, *Bundle of Joy*

BEST SUPPORTING ACTOR
- Earl Holliman, *The Rainmaker*
- Eddie Albert, *The Teahouse of the August Moon*
- Oscar Homolka, *War and Peace*
- Anthony Quinn, *Lust for Life*
- Eli Wallach, *Baby Doll*

BEST SUPPORTING ACTRESS
- Eileen Heckart, *The Bad Seed*
- Mildred Dunnock, *Baby Doll*
- Marjorie Main, *Friendly Persuasion*
- Dorothy Malone, *Written on the Wind*
- Patti McCormack, *The Bad Seed*

Winners

BEST FOREIGN-LANGUAGE FILMS
- *Before Sundown* (Germany)
- *The Girls in Black* (Greece)
- *Richard III* (English language)
- *Roses on the Arm* (Japan)
- *War and Peace* (Italy)
- *The White Reindeer* (Finland)

MOST PROMISING NEWCOMER—MALE
- John Kerr
- Paul Newman
- Anthony Perkins

MOST PROMISING NEWCOMER—FEMALE
- Carroll Baker
- Jayne Mansfield
- Natalie Wood

BEST MALE FOREIGN NEWCOMER AWARD
- Jacques Bergerac (France)

BEST FEMALE FOREIGN NEWCOMER AWARD
- Taina Elg (Finland)

WORLD FILM FAVORITES
- James Dean
- Kim Novak

BEST ORIGINAL SCORE
- Dimitri Tiomkin, *Friendly Persuasion*

HOLLYWOOD CITIZENSHIP AWARD
- Ronald Reagan

CECIL B. DEMILLE AWARD
- Mervyn LeRoy

SPECIAL ACHIEVEMENT AWARDS
- Elizabeth Taylor
- Edwin Schallert

WRITERS GUILD OF AMERICA

Awards were presented on March 7, 1957, at the Moulin Rouge restaurant in Los Angeles.

BEST WRITTEN DRAMA
- *Friendly Persuasion*, Michael Wilson, based on the book by Jessamyn West

Baby Doll, Tennessee Williams

Giant, Fred Guiol, Ivan Moffat, based on the novel by Edna Ferber

The Rainmaker, N. Richard Nash

Somebody up There Likes Me, Ernest Lehman, based on the autobiography of Rocky Graziano

BEST WRITTEN COMEDY
- *Around the World in 80 Days*, James Poe, John Farrow, S. J. Perelman, based on the novel by Jules Verne

Bus Stop, George Axelrod, based on the play by William Inge

Full of Life, John Fante
The Solid Gold Cadillac, Abe Burrows, based on the play by George S. Kaufman and Howard Teichman
The Teahouse of the August Moon, John Patrick, based on the book by Verne J. Sneider

BEST WRITTEN MUSICAL

- *The King and I*, Ernest Lehman, from the Rodgers and Hammerstein musical, based on the book *Anna and the King of Siam* by Margaret Landon
Carousel, Phoebe Ephron, Henry Ephron, from the musical by Rodgers and Hammerstein, based on the play *Liliom*, by Ferenc Molnar and adapted by Benjamin F. Glazer
The Eddy Duchin Story, Samuel Taylor, Leo Katcher
High Society, John Patrick, based on the play *The Philadelphia Story*, by Philip Barry
Meet Me in Las Vegas, Isobel Lennart

LAUREL AWARD

- Charles Brackett, Billy Wilder

ACADEMY AWARDS

Nominations were announced on February 18, 1957. Awards were presented on March 27 at the RKO Pantages Theater in Hollywood and the NBC Century Theater in New York. The ceremony was broadcast by NBC TV and radio.

BEST PICTURE

- *Around the World in 80 Days*
Friendly Persuasion
Giant
The King and I
The Ten Commandments

BEST DIRECTOR

- George Stevens, *Giant*
Michael Anderson, *Around the World in 80 Days*
Walter Lang, *The King and I*
King Vidor, *War and Peace*
William Wyler, *Friendly Persuasion*

BEST ACTOR

- Yul Brynner, *The King and I*
James Dean, *Giant*
Kirk Douglas, *Lust for Life*
Rock Hudson, *Giant*
Sir Laurence Olivier, *Richard III*

BEST ACTRESS

- Ingrid Bergman, *Anastasia*
Carroll Baker, *Baby Doll*
Katharine Hepburn, *The Rainmaker*
Nancy Kelly, *The Bad Seed*
Deborah Kerr, *The King and I*

BEST SUPPORTING ACTOR

- Anthony Quinn, *Lust for Life*
Don Murray, *Bus Stop*
Anthony Perkins, *Friendly Persuasion*
Mickey Rooney, *The Bold and the Brave*
Robert Stack, *Written on the Wind*

BEST SUPPORTING ACTRESS

- Dorothy Malone, *Written on the Wind*
Mildred Dunnock, *Baby Doll*
Eileen Heckart, *The Bad Seed*
Mercedes McCambridge, *Giant*
Patty McCormack, *The Bad Seed*

BEST WRITING (MOTION PICTURE STORY)

- Dalton Trumbo (originally identified as Robert Rich), *The Brave One*
Edward Bernds, Elwood Ullman, *High Society* (nomination withdrawn)
Leo Katcher, *The Eddy Duchin Story*
Jean Paul Sartre, *The Proud and the Beautiful*
Cesare Zavattini, *Umberto D*

BEST WRITING (SCREENPLAY—ADAPTED)

- S. J. Perelman, John Farrow, James Poe, *Around the World in 80 Days*
Norman Corwin, *Lust for Life*
Fred Guiol, Ivan Moffat, *Giant*
Tennessee Williams, *Baby Doll*
Friendly Persuasion (writer Michael Wilson declared uneligible for nomination)

BEST WRITING (SCREENPLAY—ORIGINAL)

- Albert Lamorisse, *The Red Balloon*
Federico Fellini, Tullio Pinelli, *La Strada*
Robert Lewin, *The Bold and the Brave*

William Rose, *The Ladykillers*
Andrew L. Stone, *Julie*

BEST SONG
- "Friendly Persuasion (Thee I Love),"
  Friendly Persuasion, Dimitri Tiomkin,
  Paul Francis Webster

"Julie," *Julie*, Tom Adair, Leith Stevens

"True Love," *High Society*, Cole Porter

"Whatever Will Be, Will Be (Que Sera,
  Sera)," *The Man Who Knew Too Much*,
  Ray Evans, Jay Livingston

"Written on the Wind," *Written on the
  Wind*, Sammy Cahn, Victor Young

BEST FOREIGN-LANGUAGE FILM
- *La Strada* (Italy)

The Captain of Kopenick (West Germany)

Gervaise (France)

Harp of Burma (Japan)

Qivitoq (Denmark)

Winners

BEST ART DIRECTION/SET DECORATION
(BLACK AND WHITE)
- Malcolm F. Brown, Cedric Gibbons, F.
  Keogh Gleason, Edwin B. Willis,
  Somebody up There Likes Me

(COLOR)
- John Decuir, Lyle R. Wheeler, Paul S.
  Fox, Walter M. Scott, *The King and I*

BEST CINEMATOGRAPHY
(BLACK AND WHITE)
- Joseph Ruttenberg, *Somebody up There
  Likes Me*

(COLOR)
- Lionel Lindon, *Around the World in 80
  Days*

BEST COSTUME DESIGN
(BLACK AND WHITE)
- Jean Louis, *The Solid Gold Cadillac*

(COLOR)
- Irene Sharaff, *The King and I*

BEST DOCUMENTARY
(FEATURE)
- *The Silent World*

(SHORT SUBJECT)
- *The True Story of the Civil War*

BEST FILM EDITING
- Gene Ruggiero, Paul Weatherwax,
  Around the World in 80 Days

BEST MUSIC
(SCORING OF A DRAMATIC OR COMEDY PICTURE)
- Victor Young, *Around the World in 80
  Days*

(SCORING OF A MUSICAL PICTURE)
- Ken Darby, Alfred Newman, *The King
  and I*

SCIENTIFIC OR TECHNICAL AWARDS
Class III (Certificate)
- Richard H. Ranger; Ted Hirsch, Carl
  Hauge, Edward Reichard; Technical
  Departments, Paramount Pictures;
  Roy C. Stewart and sons, C. R. Daily,
  transparency department, Paramount
  Pictures; construction department,
  MGM; Daniel J. Bloomberg, John
  Pond, William Wade, engineering
  and camera departments of Republic
  Studio

BEST SHORT SUBJECT
(CARTOON)
- *Mister Magoo's Puddle Jumper*

(ONE REEL)
- *Crashing the Water Barrier*

(TWO REEL)
- *The Bespoke Overcoat*

BEST SOUND RECORDING
- Carl Faulkner, *The King and I*

BEST SPECIAL EFFECTS
- John Fulton, *The Ten Commandments*

IRVING G. THALBERG MEMORIAL AWARD
- Buddy Adler

JEAN HERSHOLT HUMANITARIAN AWARD
- Y. Frank Freeman

HONORARY AWARD
- Eddie Cantor

· 1957 ·

Ink Battle over River Kwai

"Although it may be said in all fairness that the New York Film critics are a group of 16 rather stubborn individuals, it didn't take them long to agree that the best motion picture of 1957 was *The Bridge on the River Kwai*," reported Bosley Crowther of *The New York Times*. Crowther was among the seven crix who endorsed it on the first ballot, with four alternate votes going to *Twelve Angry Men*, three to *A Hatful of Rain* and two toward *Heaven Knows, Mr. Allison*. *Kwai* ultimately swept to victory with the necessary two-thirds tally on the second ballot.

Variety saluted the World War II military drama in its review, calling it "gripping, expertly put together and handled with skill in all departments." The $3 million pic was toplined by Alec Guinness giving "an unforgettable portrait," said *Variety*, of a strict British colonel who aims to prove his troops' mettle by forcing them to build a bridge benefiting their Japanese captors in Burma. *New York Post* critic Archer Winsten noted that the pic was more than two and a half hours long, but insisted that it "moves with such intensity of feeling and reality . . . that it seems to have been short." Crowther added: "No wonder (the crix) also voted its director, David Lean, as the year's best director and Alec Guinness, its bright, particular star, as the year's best actor. Mr. Lean was picked on the third ballot with 13 votes to 3 for Sidney Lumet's unimpeachable but limited direction of *Twelve Angry Men*. And Mr. Guinness was not selected as the best actor of the year until the sixth ballot when he won by a simple majority of 10 votes to 6 for Marlon Brando in *Sayonara*."

One week earlier, the National Board of Review had made the same three selections, but it broke with the crix when naming the year's best actress. The board opted for 28-year-old screen newcomer Joanne Wood-

Bridge on the River Kwai swept all four Best Picture kudos, but its two blacklisted scribes suffered humiliating defeats.

ward, who took on the role of a suburban housewife with a split personality in *The Three Faces of Eve* after the part was turned down by Jean Simmons, Judy Garland and Carroll Baker. Woodward received only one vote from the Gotham crix, then was dropped from consideration after the first ballot. The lead contenders were Deborah Kerr (*Heaven Knows, Mr. Allison*), Anna Magnani (*Wild Is the Wind*) and Eva Marie Saint (*A Hatful of Rain*). Kerr won on the fifth polling with 12 votes for her role as a nun who matches wits with a marine marooned on a Pacific atoll. "It was the one choice I didn't buy," harumphed the *Times*'s Crowther. He initially endorsed Audrey Hepburn (*Love in the Afternoon*), then switched his vote to Eva Marie Saint.

The crix dropped the award they added last year for best screenplay, no doubt in protest over a flap surrounding who actually wrote *The Bridge on the River Kwai*. The work was attributed to Pierre Boulle, the French author of the novel upon which the film was based, but Boulle didn't write in English and he confessed that he didn't pen the movie when he accepted the British Academy Award for Best Screenplay. *Kwai*'s script really had been written by blacklisted scribes Carl Foreman and Michael Wilson, the latter of whom was denied an Oscar bid last year for *Friendly Persuasion*.

When the screen writers' branch of the Writers Guild of America met to bestow their laurels this year, they refused to nominate *Kwai* and instead gave their prize for Best Written Drama to Reginald Rose, who recently adapted *Twelve Angry Men* for the silver screen after winning an Emmy for his TV version that aired on CBS's *Studio One* in 1954. John Patrick had been snubbed at the Oscars last year when *High Society* was wrongly attributed to the scribes of a Bowery Boys pic of the same name, but now he reaped the guild's kudos for *Les Girls* as Best Written Musical. No controversy surrounded the bestowal of the prize for Best Written Comedy, which went to Billy Wilder and I. A. L. Diamond for bringing Claude Anet's novel *Ariane* to the screen as *Love in the Afternoon*.

Reporting on the guild's awards dinner, *The New York Times* said, "The writers are the only persons in Hollywood who do not take themselves seriously while handing out awards. The principal skit was a travesty titled *Bridge on the River Burbank*. Jack L. Warner, president of Warner Brothers, was represented as the hostile commander (patterned after Sessue Hayakawa in *Bridge on the River Kwai*) of a studio exec who orders his writers to build a bridge so that theater operators who do not like the company's pictures can jump off of it."

The *Times* declared that "prizes went begging in a sense" when Hollywood's helmers gathered at the Biltmore Bowl for the Screen Directors Guild Awards. The *Times* noted that "none of the five principal winners was present" to receive their silver medallions as finalists—or the gold medallion as the year's top megger, which went to *Kwai*'s David Lean. Joviality reigned at this guild gathering, too, however, when past president Frank Capra defined the directors' traditional nemesis, the movie critic, as "a legless man who teaches running."

The Golden Globes had no problem with honoree turnout at their banquet, held at the Cocoanut Grove, which was "jampacked," reported *The Hollywood Citizen-News*, adding, "Everyone from those roving ambassadors, Mike and Liz Todd and their diamonds, to Red Buttons showed up. Red broke out some funny lines for the audience and Liz broke out a new Paris creation which had most of the women gasping. The bouffant of her glistening white gown ended where her knees began. A diamond tiara, genuine variety, glittered atop her dark tresses."

Also in attendance were Zsa Zsa Gabor, who was given a Globe as the most glamorous actress of 1957, plus the recipients of the Henriettas as World Film Favorites (reportedly based on a poll of movie fans in 58 countries)—Doris Day and Tony Curtis.

There were few surprises in the top award categories. *The Bridge on the River Kwai* claimed Best Drama Picture, Best Drama Actor for Alec Guinness and Best Director for David Lean. Joanne Woodward prevailed as Best Drama Actress for *The Three Faces of Eve*. The Globe for Best Actress in a Comedy or Musical went to Kay Kendall (*Les Girls*) as the wife of a British peer who recalls her early days as a member of a female song-and-dance troupe that once toured Europe. *Les Girls* beat *Pal Joey* and *Love in the Afternoon* as Best Comedy or Musical Picture. *Variety* had cheered the Cole Porter tuner in its review as "an exceptionally tasty musical morsel" worthy of "critical handstands."

> ## Sinatra's Rat Packers commandeered the Golden Globe gala.

Variety had also lauded the perf of the star who was on hand to claim his Globe as Best Actor in a Comedy or Musical. The tradepaper decreed that Frank Sinatra was "almost ideal" in *Pal Joey* "as the irreverent, free-wheeling, glib Joey" who croons what would become one of Ol' Blue Eyes's standards, "The Lady Is a Tramp." "Sinatra gives it powerhouse delivery," *Variety* said.

Onetime TV comic and Minsky's Burlesque jester Red Buttons earned kudos credibility as a screen star by claiming the prize for Best Supporting Actor in *Sayonara*. Buttons had wowed *Variety* by giving a "strong" perf as an Army sergeant in occupied Japan who opts to commit suicide rather than leave his Japanese bride behind when U.S. troops pull out. The 22-year-old Japanese actress who portrayed his wife, Miyoshi Umeki, was nominated in the supporting actress category, but she lost to Elsa Lanchester, who starred in Billy Wilder's adaptation of the Agatha Christie courtroom drama *Witness for the Prosecution*. Lanchester served as one of the Globe ceremony emcees, displaying "the brightest wit that brought down the house," the *Citizen-News* declared. "As Sinatra would phrase it, Elsa was a real gasser."

Lanchester was upstaged, however, by Sinatra and his Rat Pack members Dean Martin and Sammy Davis, who thought the fete was dragging on too long. They teamed up with Red Buttons and took charge of the ceremony, amusing the audience with the deft, quick way they bestowed the remaining awards.

Variety pegged Lanchester as one of the front-runners for the Oscars to be awarded a few weeks later. *Sayonara* led with the most noms (10), followed by nine for *Peyton Place*, but *Variety*'s industry poll foresaw a big night for *The Bridge on the River Kwai* (total bids eight), predicting it would sweep the prizes for best pic, director, actor and screenplay. *Variety* revealed, "*Kwai*, Best Picture favorite, garnered more votes than

Elizabeth Taylor was tragically widowed four days before the Oscars.

did all its opposition put together, and the same was true of Guinness, for best actor, and Lean, for director." The tradepaper believed that *Sayonara*'s one major trophy would go to Buttons. Joanne Woodward was cited as most likely to snatch the actress accolade.

For the first time since 1943, the films nominated for Best Director lined up exactly with the rivals for Best Picture. (The overlap happened often before that, when there were 10 candidates for best pic and only 5 for lead helmer.) Many award watchers attributed the sudden consistency to a recent rule change that made voting more consistent: nominees, just like winners in the past, were now chosen exclusively by the group's 1,700 members, thereby eliminating input from 15,000 union and guild members.

There was another key Oscar change this year: no more commercials in the Oscarcast. There were so many complaints in recent years about the long, dreary Oldsmobile plugs that the film academy persuaded the studios to pick up the $850,000 cost of televising the show to what *Variety* estimated would be a U.S. audience of 90 million. "For a change, filmdom itself was at the commercial wheel, with no shifts into low gear for the sponsor's message," *Variety* observed.

With Oldsmobile out, Chrysler pitchman Bob Hope returned as an Oscar emcee, although he shared the duty with several others. Hope was also back in top performance form, telling the audience at one point about his recent trip to the Soviet Union. "TV in every room," he boasted of his hotel, "only *it* watches *you!*"

There was less joviality among some nominees. Best Actress contender Lana Turner (*Peyton Place*) had just returned from a stressful vacation in Mexico with her mobster boyfriend Johnny Stompanato, so she refused to let him accompany her on awards night. She arrived at the ceremony late, looking rushed and flustered. "Lana

Turner, more nervous than usual, broke her shoe getting out of the car and also broke out in bumps—in places not associated with same," *Variety* columnist Archerd noted.

Another Best Actress candidate, Elizabeth Taylor (*Raintree County*), stayed at home where she broke out in tears throughout Oscar night. Four days earlier, her husband, Mike Todd—producer of last year's Best Picture *Around the World in 80 Days*—had died when his private plane crashed in New Mexico. Soon thereafter Archerd reported that the grieving Taylor, stunned by the news, "only kept repeating the fact that Todd didn't want her to take a chance by flying (with him) with a cold."

Last year Todd had boasted to friends that Taylor had an imminent date with Oscar— "She'll get it for *Raintree County!*" he promised. But Todd's film company had a guaranteed date with Oscar this year, since the academy had designated a special technical award to go to the engineers behind his widescreen film projection process called Todd-AO. Taylor remained calm during the early part of the kudocast as she viewed it with her brother and Todd's sister, but "broke up when the Todd-AO award was made," Archerd reported. "She could only watch the awards intermittently afterwards."

Variety's prediction about who'd win the actress gold came true: it went to Joanne Woodward, who'd become Mrs. Paul Newman only two months earlier. To claim her latest golden boy, she raced to the podium and said, "I can only say that I've been daydreaming about this since I was nine years old. I'd like to thank my parents for having more faith in me than anyone could." Her victory, *Variety* added, "brought the strongest ovation from the sell-out crowd." Backstage later, Archerd noticed: "Paul Newman was speechless with joy as he stood on the sidelines watching wife Joanne Woodward get the post-Oscar crush of press and fotogs."

Alec Guinness wasn't present to accept

An Oscar murder scandal plagued Lana Turner.

his Best Actor Oscar. The statuette was accepted on his behalf by Jean Simmons, who reminded the audience that she had starred with Guinness in David Lean's *Great Expectations* 13 years earlier.

Lean had been nominated for *Great Expectations* in 1946 and scored other bids for *Brief Encounter* (1946) and *Summertime* (1955), but he finally claimed his first victory for *Kwai*. In his thank-you remarks, he said, "Sweating away in the jungles of Ceylon, I never dreamed that the *Bridge* would bring me to Hollywood, much less to this stage for this award." He paid a hefty personal price for his gold-winning work, however. During the movie's lengthy production, his wife sued him for divorce on the grounds of desertion.

Kwai also earned the gold for best screenplay, but the novelist falsely listed as its screenplay scribe, Pierre Boulle, did now show up to accept the prize as he had the British Academy Award. Vixen Kim Novak stood in for him. Nearly 30 years later, the academy would acknowledge the pic's real authors and give statuettes to Michael Wilson's and Carl Foreman's widows.

Not only did *Variety*'s predictions for *Kwai* come true, but it was right about *Sayonara* nabbing the supporting actor laurels for Red Buttons. TV's former "Mr. Ho-Ho-Ho" cried as he accepted the tribute, saying, "I'm a very happy guy."

But *Variety* did not foresee the upset coming in the race for Best Supporting Actress. The paper didn't feel strongly about its projection, noting that Elsa Lanchester's "margin was very narrow, with Diane Varsi in *Peyton Place* and Carolyn Jones in *Bachelor Party* close contenders." When *Sayonara*'s Miyoshi Umeki prevailed, victory took her by surprise, too. "I wish someone would help me now," she said at the podium. "I have nothing in my mind. Thank all American people." The next day, *Variety* columnist Archerd noted, "Umeki, by the way, now plans to live in the USA." The 23-year-old TV, radio and film star of Japan only recently came to Americans' attention after a brief appearance on Arthur Godfrey's TV show. Soon after winning the Oscar, she married a TV producer and starred in such other screen works as *Flower Drum Song*.

But *Variety* did predict the winner of Best Picture correctly. The victory by *The Bridge on the River Kwai* marked the fourth consecutive year that an indie film won the top award and it also marked the second victory in four years by the same producer—Sam Spiegel, who oversaw 1954's best pic *On the Waterfront*. In his acceptance speech, he implored studio execs present to permit more films to be made outside Hollywood.

After the Oscar ceremony, the academy held its first-ever governors' ball, which was attended by Joanne Woodward, who received a kind tribute from a loser in the Best Actress race. *Variety*'s Archerd noted that Elizabeth Taylor sent a bouquet of white orchids to the fete at the Beverly Hilton Hotel with the following note: "I'm so happy and pleased for you. Love, Elizabeth Todd—and Mike, too."

When the ball at the Beverly Hilton was over, another Best Actress loser, Lana Turner, headed over to her suite at the Bel-Air Hotel where she was met by her mobster boyfriend Johnny Stompanato, who was furious that she didn't take him to the Oscars. In her memoirs, Turner reported that she received a "vicious beating at the hands of a madman."

A week and a half later, her daughter got even. When Stompanato attacked Turner during another argument, her daughter came to her rescue and stabbed him to death with a kitchen knife. She was tried for murder, but was acquitted.

▪ 1957 ▪

NATIONAL BOARD OF REVIEW

The board declared a best picture and foreign film of the year, then listed its remaining favorites according to highest scores. The vote results were announced in late December 1957.

BEST PICTURE
▪ *The Bridge on the River Kwai*
Twelve Angry Men
The Spirit of St. Louis
The Rising of the Moon
Albert Schweitzer
Funny Face
The Bachelor Party
The Enemy Below
A Hatful of Rain
A Farewell to Arms

BEST DIRECTOR
▪ David Lean, *The Bridge on the River Kwai*

BEST ACTOR
▪ Alec Guinness, *The Bridge on the River Kwai*

BEST ACTRESS
▪ Joanne Woodward, *The Three Faces of Eve, No Down Payment*

BEST SUPPORTING ACTOR
▪ Sessue Hayakawa, *The Bridge on the River Kwai*

BEST SUPPORTING ACTRESS
▪ Dame Sybil Thorndike, *The Prince and the Showgirl*

BEST FOREIGN FILM
▪ *Ordet* (Denmark)
Gervaise (France)
Torero! (Mexico)
The Red Balloon (France)
A Man Escaped (France)

SPECIAL CITATION
▪ For the photographic innovations in *Funny Face*

NEW YORK FILM CRITICS

Winners were announced on December 30, 1957.

BEST PICTURE
- *The Bridge on the River Kwai*

BEST DIRECTOR
- David Lean, *The Bridge on the River Kwai*

BEST ACTOR
- Alec Guinness, *The Bridge on the River Kwai*

BEST ACTRESS
- Deborah Kerr, *Heaven Knows, Mr. Allison*

BEST FOREIGN FILM
- *Gervaise* (France)

SCREEN DIRECTORS GUILD OF AMERICA

The initial list of nominees was narrowed down to a group of finalists who competed for the Best Director award, bestowed on February 8, 1958, at the Biltmore Hotel in Los Angeles.

BEST DIRECTOR
- David Lean, *The Bridge on the River Kwai*

Joshua Logan, *Sayonara* (finalist)
Sidney Lumet, *Twelve Angry Men* (finalist)
Mark Robson, *Peyton Place* (finalist)
Billy Wilder, *Witness for the Prosecution* (finalist)
George Cukor, *Les Girls*
Stanley Donen, *Funny Face*
José Ferrer, *The Great Man*
John Huston, *Heaven Knows, Mr. Allison*
Elia Kazan, *A Face in the Crowd*
Stanley Kramer, *The Pride and the Passion*
Anthony Mann, *Men in War*
Leo McCarey, *An Affair to Remember*
Robert Mulligan, *Fear Strikes Out*
John Sturges, *Gunfight at the O.K. Corral*
Billy Wilder, *Love in the Afternoon*
Fred Zinnemann, *A Hatful of Rain*

GOLDEN GLOBES

Nominations were announced on January 20, 1958. Awards were presented on Febru-

Two months after marrying Paul Newman, Joanne Woodward received a golden boy from John Wayne.

ary 22 at the Cocoanut Grove in the Ambassador Hotel in Los Angeles. The ceremony was telecast on L.A. station KTTV.

BEST DRAMA PICTURE
- *The Bridge on the River Kwai*

Sayonara
Twelve Angry Men
Wild Is the Wind
Witness for the Prosecution

BEST COMEDY OR MUSICAL PICTURE
- *Les Girls*

Don't Go Near the Water
Love in the Afternoon
Pal Joey
Silk Stockings

BEST MOTION PICTURE PROMOTING INTERNATIONAL UNDERSTANDING
- *The Happy Road*

BEST DIRECTOR
- David Lean, *The Bridge on the River Kwai*

Joshua Logan, *Sayonara*
Sidney Lumet, *Twelve Angry Men*

Billy Wilder, *Witness*
Fred Zinnemann, *A Hatful of Rain*

BEST ACTOR, DRAMA
- Alec Guinness, *The Bridge on the River Kwai*

Marlon Brando, *Sayonara*
Henry Fonda, *Twelve Angry Men*
Anthony Franciosa, *A Hatful of Rain*
Charles Laughton, *Witness for the Prosecution*

BEST ACTRESS, DRAMA
- Joanne Woodward, *The Three Faces of Eve*

Marlene Dietrich, *Witness for the Prosecution*
Deborah Kerr, *Heaven Knows, Mr. Allison*
Anna Magnani, *Wild Is the Wind*
Eva Marie Saint, *A Hatful of Rain*

BEST ACTOR, COMEDY OR MUSICAL
- Frank Sinatra, *Pal Joey*

Maurice Chevalier, *Love in the Afternoon*
Glenn Ford, *Don't Go Near the Water*
David Niven, *My Man Godfrey*
Tony Randall, *Will Success Spoil Rock Hunter?*

BEST ACTRESS, COMEDY OR MUSICAL
- Kay Kendall, *Les Girls*

Cyd Charisse, *Silk Stockings*
Taina Elg, Kay Kendall, *Les Girls*
Audrey Hepburn, *Love in the Afternoon*
Jean Simmons, *This Could Be the Night*

BEST SUPPORTING ACTOR
- Red Buttons, *Sayonara*

Lee J. Cobb, *Twelve Angry Men*
Sessue Hayakawa, *The Bridge on the River Kwai*
Nigel Patrick, *Raintree Country*
Ed Wynn, *The Great Man*

BEST SUPPORTING ACTRESS
- Elsa Lanchester, *Witness for the Prosecution*

Mildred Dunnock, *Peyton Place*
Hope Lange, *Peyton Place*
Heather Sears, The *Story of Esther Costello*
Miyoshi Umeki, *Sayonara*

Winners

MOST PROMISING NEWCOMER—MALE
- James Garner
- John Saxon
- Patrick Wayne

MOST PROMISING NEWCOMER—FEMALE
- Sandra Dee
- Carolyn Jones
- Diane Varsi

BEST FOREIGN FILMS
- *The Confessions of Felix Krull* (Germany)
- *Tizoc* (Mexico)
- *Woman in a Dressing Gown* (English language)
- *Yellow Crow* (Japan)

WORLD FILM FAVORITES
- Tony Curtis
- Doris Day

BEST FILM CHOREOGRAPHY
- Le Roy Prinz

CECIL B. DEMILLE AWARD
- Buddy Adler

SPECIAL ACHIEVEMENT AWARDS
- Zsa Zsa Gabor (Most Glamorous Actress)
- Hugo Friedhofer (For Bettering the Standard of Motion Picture Music)
- Bob Hope (Ambassador of Good Will)
- Jean Simmons (Most Versatile Actress)

WRITERS GUILD OF AMERICA

Nominations were announced on February 10, 1958. Awards were presented on March 12 at the Moulin Rouge restaurant in Los Angeles.

BEST WRITTEN DRAMA
- *Twelve Angry Men*, Reginald Rose

Heaven Knows, Mr. Allison, John Lee Mahin, John Huston, based on the novel by Charles Shaw
Paths of Glory, Stanley Kubrick, Calder Williamham, Jim Thompson, based on the novel by Humphrey Cobb

Peyton Place, John Michael Hayes, based
on the novel by Grace Metalious
Sayonara, Paul Osborn, based on the novel
by James A. Michener

BEST WRITTEN COMEDY

- *Love in the Afternoon*, Billy Wilder,
I. A. L. Diamond, based on the novel
Ariane by Claude Anet
Designing Woman, George Wells, based on
a suggestion by Helen Rose
Don't Go Near the Water, Dorothy
Kingsley, George Wells, based on the
novel by William Brinkley
Operation Mad Ball, Arthur Carter, Jed
Harris, Blake Edwards, based on the
play by Arthur Carter
Will Success Spoil Rock Hunter? Frank
Tashlin, based on the play by George
Axelrod

BEST WRITTEN MUSICAL

- *Les Girls*, John Patrick, story by Vera
Caspary
Funny Face, Leonard Gershe
The Joker Is Wild, Oscar Saul, based on the
book by Art Cohn about the life of Joe
E. Lewis
The Pajama Game, George Abbott, Richard
Bissell, based on the novel *7½¢* by
Richard Bissell
Pal Joey, Dorothy Kingsley, based on the
play by John O'Hara

LAUREL AWARD

- John Lee Mahin

ACADEMY AWARDS

Nominations were announced on February
18, 1958. Awards were presented on March
26 at the Pantages Theater in Hollywood.
The ceremony was telecast by NBC.

BEST PICTURE

- *The Bridge on the River Kwai*
Peyton Place
Sayonara
Twelve Angry Men
Witness for the Prosecution

BEST DIRECTOR

- David Lean, *The Bridge on the River
Kwai*
Joshua Logan, *Sayonara*
Sidney Lumet, *Twelve Angry Men*
Mark Robson, *Peyton Place*
Billy Wilder, *Witness for the Prosecution*

BEST ACTOR

- Alec Guinness, *The Bridge on the River
Kwai*
Marlon Brando, *Sayonara*
Anthony Franciosa, *A Hatful of Rain*
Charles Laughton, *Witness for the
Prosecution*
Anthony Quinn, *Wild Is the Wind*

BEST ACTRESS

- Joanne Woodward, *The Three Faces of
Eve*
Deborah Kerr, *Heaven Knows, Mr.
Allison*
Anna Magnani, *Wild Is the Wind*
Elizabeth Taylor, *Raintree County*
Lana Turner, *Peyton Place*

BEST SUPPORTING ACTOR

- Red Buttons, *Sayonara*
Vittorio De Sica, *A Farewell to Arms*
Sessue Hayakawa, *The Bridge on the
River Kwai*
Arthur Kennedy, *Peyton Place*
Russ Tamblyn, *Peyton Place*

BEST SUPPORTING ACTRESS

- Miyoshi Umeki, *Sayonara*
Carolyn Jones, *The Bachelor Party*
Elsa Lanchester, *Witness for the
Prosecution*
Hope Lange, *Peyton Place*
Diane Varsi, *Peyton Place*

BEST ADAPTED SCREENPLAY

- Pierre Boulle, Carl Foreman, Michael
Wilson, *The Bridge on the River Kwai*
John Michael Hayes, *Peyton Place*
John Huston, John Lee Mahin, *Heaven
Knows, Mr. Allison*
Paul Osborn, *Sayonara*
Reginald Rose, *Twelve Angry Men*

BEST ORIGINAL SCREENPLAY
- George Wells, *Designing Woman*

R. Wright Campbell, Ivan Goff, Ben Roberts, Ralph Wheelwright, *Man of a Thousand Faces*

Federico Fellini, Ennio Flaiano, Tullio Pinelli, *Vitelloni*

Leonard Gershe, *Funny Face*

Joel Kane, Dudley Nichols, Barney Slater, *The Tin Star*

BEST SONG
- "All the Way," *The Joker Is Wild*, Sammy Cahn, James Van Heusen

"An Affair to Remember," *An Affair to Remember*, Harold Adamson, Leo McCarey, Harry Warren

"April Love," *April Love*, Sammy Fain, Paul Francis Webster

"Tammy," *Tammy and the Bachelor*, Ray Evans, Jay Livingston

"Wild Is the Wind," *Wild Is the Wind*, Dimitri Tiomkin, Ned Washington

BEST FOREIGN-LANGUAGE FILM
- *The Nights of Cabiria* (Italy)

The Devil Came at Night (Germany)

Gates of Paris (France)

Mother India (India)

Nine Lives (Norway)

Winners

BEST ART DIRECTION/SET DECORATION
- Ted Haworth, Robert Priestly, *Sayonara*

BEST CINEMATOGRAPHY
- Jack Hildyard, *The Bridge on the River Kwai*

BEST COSTUME DESIGN
- Orry-Kelly, *Les Girls*

BEST DOCUMENTARY (FEATURE)
Albert Schweitzer, Jerome Hill

BEST FILM EDITING
- Peter Taylor, *The Bridge on the River Kwai*

BEST MUSIC SCORING
- Malcolm Arnold, *The Bridge on the River Kwai*

SCIENTIFIC OR TECHNICAL AWARDS
Class I (Statuette)
- Motion Picture Research Council, Todd-AO Corp., Westrex

Class II (Plaque)
- Société D'Optique et de Mecanique de Haute Precision; Harlan L. Baumbach, Lorand Wargo, Howard M. Little, Unicorn Engineering

Class III (Certificate)
- William B. Smith, Charles E. Sutter, General Cable, Paramount Pictures

BEST SHORT SUBJECT
(CARTOON)
- *Birds Anonymous*

(LIVE ACTION)
- *The Wetback Hound*

BEST SOUND RECORDING
- George Groves, *Sayonara*

BEST SPECIAL EFFECTS
- Walter Rossi, *The Enemy Below*

JEAN HERSHOLT HUMANITARIAN AWARD
- Samuel Goldwyn

HONORARY AWARDS
- Gilbert M. Anderson
- Charles Brackett
- B. B. Kahane
- Society of Motion Picture and Television Engineers

· 1958 ·

Defiant *Drama*, *Naughty* Gigi

The National Board of Review went right back to being stubborn. For the past four years it had agreed with the general kudos consensus over what the year's Best Picture was, but now it was behaving just as doggedly independent as it had throughout the 1940s and the early 1950s.

This year it hailed *The Old Man and the Sea* plus gave its Best Actor accolade to star Spencer Tracy for what *Variety* called his "distinguished and impressive performance" as Hemingway's fisherman hell-bent on catching a feisty marlin. Tracy's thesp accolade also cited his portrayal of a crusty Boston mayor in *The Last Hurrah*, which earned director John Ford his first tribute from the board. Two-time past honoree Ingrid Bergman returned as Best Actress for her role a maverick Christian missionary in *The Inn of the Sixth Happiness*.

The defiant board overlooked *The Defiant Ones*, which was the best-pic choice of both the New York Film Critics and the Golden Globes. The controversial drama starring Sidney Poitier and Tony Curtis as feuding black and white convicts chained together during an escape from prison was only the third movie produced by Stanley Kramer, but he already was a fave with the 15 crix who worked at eight Gotham newspapers. Kramer's *High Noon* had won their Best Picture plaque in 1952; this year they gave him their director's laurels, too. *The Defiant Ones* claimed Best Picture with 10 votes on the third ballot over *Separate Tables* (five votes).

Variety described *Separate Tables* as a "literate and absorbing" adaptation of Terrence Rattigan's play about the shenanigans at a British seaside boarding house. *Variety* said, "David Niven gives one of the best performances of his career" as a phony army major accused of deviant sex antics

Defiant Golden Globe and Gotham crix backed *The Defiant Ones*, starring Sidney Poitier and Tony Curtis, as Best Picture.

while wooing a virginal Deborah Kerr. "Voting for Best Actor was spirited," noted *The New York Times*, but the crix endorsed Niven over Alec Guinness (*The Horse's Mouth*) by an eight-to-seven score on the sixth and final ballot, when a majority vote determined the champ after no contender received a two-thirds tally earlier.

Deborah Kerr reaped one vote during the first round for Best Actress, then fell off the ballot as the race narrowed down to Susan Hayward (*I Want to Live!*), Elizabeth Taylor (*Cat on a Hot Tin Roof*) and Shirley Booth (*Hot Spell* and *The Matchmaker*). Hayward prevailed for her gritty portrayal of a convict who may have been wrongly executed for murder. "She has never done anything so vivid or shattering," said *The New York Times*.

The crix revived their award for best screenplay after nixing it last year when the producers of 1957's Best Picture *The Bridge on the River Kwai* refused to admit that it was penned by blacklisted scribes. Current Best Picture *The Defiant Ones* was co-written by blacklistee Nedrick Young, but he was identified by pseudonym Nathan E. Douglas. The Gotham crix had no problem with crediting him and partner Harold Jacob Smith as authors, but the crix believed that other blacklistees may have contributed to the script, too, so rather than cite any names, they announced that the prize heretofore would go to the motion picture, not the writers. Young and Smith were present at the kudos ceremony at Sardi's and nonetheless accepted the award—a plaque bearing the mastheads of the group's eight newspapers—themselves as representatives of the Writers Guild of America. Susan Hayward and David Niven were also present. The only absent winner was Stanley Kramer, who was in Australia making a new movie.

As the Oscars approached, leaders of the film academy got nervous; their two-year-old rule outlawing suspected Communists from competing was still on the books and certain to cause an uproar again now that it seemed likely that *The Defiant Ones* would be nominated. Two weeks after the crix's awards were announced, the academy declared that it was scrapping its ban because "experience has proven the bylaw to be unworkable."

Last year the Writers Guild of America refused to nominate *The Bridge on the River Kwai* when its blacklisted scribes weren't even cited with pseudonyms. This year the guild brazenly honored *The Defiant Ones*' "Douglas" and Smith as authors of the Best Written Drama and gave their laurel for Best Musical to Alan Jay Lerner for *Gigi*, which also won *Photoplay* magazine's Gold Medal.

Lerner and writing partner Frederick Lowe had won the Tony Award for Best Musical two years earlier for *My Fair Lady*. Their tuneful retelling of Bernard Shaw's twist on the *Pygmalion* myth was such a huge hit that it was considered untouchable as a film property as long as it ran on Broadway. Impatient MGM, eager for a similar success, hired the same creative team to write what *Variety* called "a French variation, by novelist Colette, of the Pygmalion legend." In its review of the result, the trade-paper noted that the duo's tunes "vie with and suggest their memorable *My Fair Lady* score" and applauded *Gigi* as "a nice romp of the hyper-romantic naughty '90's of Paris-in-the-spring, in the Bois, in Maxim's and in the boudoir."

Gigi claimed four awards at the Golden Globes: Best Musical (a new category separated from last year's prize for Best Comedy or Musical Picture), Best Director for Vincente Minnelli, Best Supporting Actress for Hermione Gingold and the special Cecil B. DeMille Award for Maurice Chevalier ("who well-nigh steals the picture," said *Variety*).

Gigi star Leslie Caron lost the Globe for Best Comedy or Musical Actress to Rosalind Russell, who was honored for her screen adaptation of the role she created on Broadway in *Auntie Mame*, which also won Best Comedy Picture.

The main drama awards reflected decisions made by the New York Film Critics: top pic *The Defiant Ones* and kudos to thesps David Niven and Susan Hayward. Hayward beat Deborah Kerr, who rebounded to claim the kudos, along with Rock Hudson, as World Film Favorites. "Miss Kerr, busy on a film abroad, cabled her thanks," noted *The Los Angeles Times*. Many other winners—including David Niven, Susan Hayward and Maurice Chevalier—were present among the 900 celebrants at the Cocoanut Grove gala.

What the *Times* didn't note was that Kerr was also busy overseas pursuing her

> # With nine wins, undefeated *Gigi* became Oscar's biggest champ.

romance with writer Peter Viertel, which shattered her longtime marriage and triggered such a scandal that it caused Kerr to lose custody of her children in the subsequent divorce suit. Nonetheless, she scored a respectable bid for Best Actress when the Oscar nominations were announced, pitting her against a star embroiled in one of the most notorious sex scandals in Hollywood history.

Soon after the death of producer Mike Todd, widow Elizabeth Taylor lost the public's sympathy when she found comfort in the arms of Todd's best friend, Eddie Fisher. General sentiment quickly sided with the woman that Fisher dumped for Taylor—his wholesome wife Debbie Reynolds, who was the mother of his two children. She was also America's favorite actress, according to *Photoplay*'s poll. "I thought we were happy," a bewildered Reynolds told the press, but *The New York Mirror* added, "The storybook marriage of Fisher and Reynolds skidded on a series of curves—Liz Taylor's."

Outraged columnist Hedda Hopper asked Taylor how she could do it.

"What do you expect me to do?" Taylor harrumphed. "Sleep alone?"

Taylor had been snubbed at the Golden Globes, but she competed at the Oscars for her saucy portrayal of Maggie the Cat in the screen adaptation of Tennessee Williams's Broadway hit *Cat on a Hot Tin Roof*. Her reviews were just as hot (*Variety* cheered Taylor for giving a "well-accented, perceptive interpretation"), but morally outraged movie-goers stayed away in droves. Taylor had been the number-two b.o. star in 1958. Soon thereafter she fell out of the top 10 and Debbie Reynolds zoomed up to fifth place.

On Oscar night, "The arrival of Elizabeth Taylor, squired by Eddie Fisher, brought forth the greatest acclaim of the evening," *Variety* reported on the outside crowd's response as the couple became the last stars to enter the Pantages Theater. Debbie Reynolds stayed away, choosing to watch the awards show on TV with Eva Gabor. "I felt this was Elizabeth's evening," she explained, graciously, to columnist Army Archerd.

DGA

Prexy George Sidney presents Vincente Minnelli with the directors' guild plaque for *Gigi*.

Variety called this year's Oscar derby a "toss up" as the paper finally appeased academy leaders and canceled its 11-year industry poll that forecasted winners. Best Picture rivals *Gigi* and *The Defiant Ones* led with the most bids—nine each. "The evening got off to a hot start when someone called the theater" with a bomb threat, *Variety* noted. "Extra fire detail searched the place from stem to stern and two fire trucks stood by" while the gala continued in the gutsy Hollywood tradition of "the show must go on." Meantime, TV viewership in the United States and Canada reached a record 100 million, according to Trendex.

Scandal-plagued Elizabeth Taylor and Deborah Kerr faced tough competish from screen newcomer Shirley MacLaine (*Some Came Running*), Globe and New York film crix champ Susan Hayward (*I Want to Live!*) and three-time past Oscar loser Rosalind Russell as gadfly Mame Dennis, a role she created on Broadway. *Auntie Mame* was the second-highest-grossing film of the year ($9 million) after *South Pacific* ($17 million), and also a contender for Best Picture.

The thesp winner turned out to be four-time past loser Susan Hayward, who, *Variety* noted, "garnered the heartiest ovation" on awards night "as she literally streaked down the right aisle to clutch an Oscar." Once she had it in hand and thanked her producer at the podium, Hayward headed backstage, where photographers asked her to kiss it. She laughed and replied, "I don't kiss anyone but my husband."

Much more agreeable was Best Supporting Actor winner Burl Ives, who "had no hesitancy about bestowing a healthy buss on his winning golden figurine," *Variety* observed when the champ arrived backstage. He was honored for his role as a gruff cattle baron in *The Big Country*, but also earned critical notice in 1958 as Big Daddy in *Cat on a Hot Tin Roof* and a domineering squire in *Desire under the Elms*. Feigning fatherhood, Ives cradled the Oscar in his arms and told the press, "It's the nicest baby in the world."

Missing on awards night was the winner of Best Supporting Actress, Wendy Hiller, who'd lost her previous Oscar bout as Best Actress in 1938 for *Pygmalion*. Now she was hailed for her role in *Separate Tables* as "the efficient hotel manager who finds her romance with Burt Lancaster shattered upon the arrival of his physically attractive and fashionable ex-wife," said *Variety*. Upon hearing the news that she'd reaped the gold, the noted British stage thesp told a London newspaper, "Never mind the honor, although I'm sure it's very nice of them. I hope this award means cash—hard cash."

Hiller's costar David Niven competed for Best Actor against two rivals—Paul Newman (*Cat on a Hot Tin Roof*) and Sidney Poitier (*The Defiant Ones*)—who claimed they couldn't be present on awards night due to Broadway obligations. But Niven was heavily favored to win after previously claiming the Golden Globe and New York film crix kudos, and he prevailed as expected. En route to claiming his Oscar, the excited champ stumbled on the stairs leading up to the stage. He excused himself at the podium, saying, "I'm so loaded down with good-luck charms I could hardly make the steps!"

Gigi had not been nommed for any acting honors, but it was up for Best Director. Vincente Minnelli had lost the prize once

Susan Hayward was hailed as Best Actress by the Oscars, Globes and N.Y. crix for her arresting portrayal of a death-row inmate in *I Want to Live!*

before, in 1951 to George Stevens (*A Place in the Sun*), even though his *An American in Paris* won Best Picture. This time Minnelli wasn't optimistic about his chances. "I almost didn't attend the ceremony, thinking they'll never give an Oscar to a musical," he remembered years later. "Then I heard my name called. It was miraculous." At the podium he said that receiving it was "just about the proudest moment of my life."

"To set up the drama of the evening, the acad had Ingrid Bergman do the honors" of bestowing the Best Picture trophy, *Variety* said, noting that it was "her first trip to Hollywood since 1949." Bergman presented it to the producers of *Gigi*, which had earlier won statuettes for writing, color cinematography, art direction, song, music score, film editing and costume design. Counting its triumph for direction, too, *Gigi* went undefeated all night, scoring nine wins for nine nominations, thus becoming the biggest champ in Oscar history after topping the previous record of eight victories held by *Gone With the Wind, From Here to Eternity* and *On the Waterfront*. *Gigi* also reaped a special award for star Maurice Chevalier.

Variety called the Oscar show "a topflight effort this time out—until it ran short. What might have been Hollywood's best Oscar production ended with an embarrassing thud as the two-hour production ran 20 minutes short" and cohost Jerry Lewis "tried valiantly to stretch, stretch, stretch." NBC finally pulled the plug and "the millions of television viewers watched a 15-minute sports film to fill."

Other cohost Bob Hope later called the finale snafu "the major goof of TV history."

▪ 1958 ▪

NATIONAL BOARD OF REVIEW

The board declared a best picture and foreign film of the year, then listed its remaining favorites according to highest scores. The vote results were announced in late December 1958.

BEST PICTURE
▪ *The Old Man and the Sea*
Separate Tables
The Last Hurrah
The Long Hot Summer
Windjammer
Cat on a Hot Tin Roof
The Goddess
The Brothers Karamazov
Me and the Colonel
Gigi

BEST DIRECTOR
▪ John Ford, *The Last Hurrah*

BEST ACTOR
▪ Spencer Tracy, *The Old Man and the Sea,*
The Last Hurrah

BEST ACTRESS
▪ Ingrid Bergman, *The Inn of the Sixth Happiness*

BEST SUPPORTING ACTOR
▪ Albert Salmi, *The Brothers Karamazov,*
The Bravados

BEST SUPPORTING ACTRESS
▪ Kay Walsh, *The Horse's Mouth*

BEST FOREIGN FILM
▪ *Pather Panchali* (India)
The Red and the Black (France)
The Horse's Mouth (U.K.)

My Uncle (France)
A Night to Remember (U.K.)

SPECIAL CITATION
▪ Robert Donat, *The Inn of the Sixth Happiness*

NEW YORK FILM CRITICS

Winners were announced on December 30, 1958. Awards were presented on January 24, 1959, at Sardi's restaurant in New York.

BEST PICTURE
▪ *The Defiant Ones*

BEST DIRECTOR
▪ Stanley Kramer, *The Defiant Ones*

BEST ACTOR
▪ David Niven, *Separate Tables*

BEST ACTRESS
▪ Susan Hayward, *I Want to Live!*

BEST SCREENPLAY
▪ *The Defiant Ones*

BEST FOREIGN FILM
▪ *My Uncle* (France)

SCREEN DIRECTORS GUILD OF AMERICA

The initial list of nominees was narrowed down to a group of finalists who competed for the Best Director award, bestowed on February 7, 1959, at the Beverly Hilton Hotel.

BEST DIRECTOR
▪ Vincente Minnelli, *Gigi*
Richard Brooks, *The Brothers Karamazov*

Richard Brooks, *Cat on a Hot Tin Roof*
(finalist)
Stanley Kramer, *The Defiant Ones* (finalist)
Delmer Daves, *Cowboy*
Stanley Donen, George Abbott, *Damn
Yankees*
Edward Dmytryk, *The Young Lions*
Richard Fleischer, *The Vikings*
Alfred Hitchcock, *Vertigo*
Martin Ritt, *The Long Hot Summer*
Mark Robson, *The Inn of the Sixth
Happiness* (finalist)
George Seaton, *Teacher's Pet*
Robert E. Wise, *I Want to Live!* (finalist)
William Wyler, *The Big Country*

D. W. GRIFFITH AWARD
■ Frank Capra

GOLDEN GLOBES

Nominations were announced on January
25, 1959. Awards were presented on March
5 at the Cocoanut Grove in the Ambassador
Hotel in Los Angeles. The ceremony was
telecast on L.A. station KTTV.

BEST DRAMA PICTURE
■ *The Defiant Ones*
Cat on a Hot Tin Roof
Home before Dark
I Want to Live!
Separate Tables

BEST COMEDY PICTURE
■ *Auntie Mame*
Bell, Book and Candle
Indiscreet
Me and the Colonel
The Perfect Furlough

BEST MUSICAL PICTURE
■ *Gigi*
Damn Yankees
South Pacific
Tom Thumb

BEST MOTION PICTURE PROMOTING
INTERNATIONAL UNDERSTANDING
■ *The Inn of the Sixth Happiness*
The Defiant Ones
Me and the Colonel

A Time to Live and a Time to Die
The Young Lions

BEST DIRECTOR
■ Vincente Minnelli, *Gigi*
Richard Brooks, *Cat on a Hot Tin Roof*
Stanley Kramer, *The Defiant Ones*
Delbert Mann, *Separate Tables*
Robert Wise, *I Want to Live!*

BEST ACTOR, DRAMA
■ David Niven, *Separate Tables*
Tony Curtis, *The Defiant Ones*
Robert Donat, *The Inn of the Sixth
Happiness*
Sidney Poitier, *The Defiant Ones*
Spencer Tracy, *The Old Man and the Sea*

BEST ACTRESS, DRAMA
■ Susan Hayward, *I Want to Live!*
Ingrid Bergman, *The Inn of the Sixth
Happiness*
Deborah Kerr, *Separate Tables*
Shirley MacLaine, *Some Came Running*
Jean Simmons, *Home before Dark*

BEST ACTOR, COMEDY OR MUSICAL
■ Danny Kaye, *Me and the Colonel*
Maurice Chevalier, *Gigi*
Clark Gable, *Teacher's Pet*
Cary Grant, *Indiscreet*
Louis Jordan, *Gigi*

BEST ACTRESS, COMEDY OR MUSICAL
■ Rosalind Russell, *Auntie Mame*
Ingrid Bergman, *Indiscreet*
Leslie Caron, *Gigi*
Doris Day, *Tunnel of Love*
Mitzi Gaynor, *South Pacific*

BEST SUPPORTING ACTOR
■ Burl Ives, *The Big Country*
Harry Guardino, *Houseboat*
David Ladd, *The Proud Rebel*
Gig Young, *Teacher's Pet*
Efrem Zimbalist, Jr., *Home before Dark*

BEST SUPPORTING ACTRESS
■ Hermione Gingold, *Gigi*
Peggy Cass, *Auntie Mame*
Wendy Hiller, *Separate Tables*
Maureen Stapleton, *Lonely Hearts*
Cara Williams, *The Defiant Ones*

MOST PROMISING NEWCOMER—MALE

- Bradford Dillmann
- John Gavin
- Efrem Zimbalist, Jr.

David Ladd
Ricky Nelson
Ray Stricklyn

MOST PROMISING NEWCOMER—FEMALE

- Linda Cristal
- Susan Kohner
- Tina Louise

Joanna Barnes
Carol Lynley
France Nuyen

Winners

WORLD FILM FAVORITES

- Rock Hudson
- Deborah Kerr

BEST FOREIGN-LANGUAGE FILMS

- *The Girl and the River* (France)
- *The Girl Rosemarie* (Germany)
- *A Night to Remember* (English language)
- *The Road a Year Long* (Yugoslavia)

SAMUEL GOLDWYN INTERNATIONAL AWARD

- *Two Eyes, Twelve Hands* (India)

CECIL B. DEMILLE AWARD

- Maurice Chevalier

SPECIAL ACHIEVEMENT AWARD

- David Ladd (Best Juvenile)

WRITERS GUILD OF AMERICA

Awards were presented on March 13, 1959, at the Moulin Rouge restaurant in Los Angeles.

BEST WRITTEN DRAMA

- *The Defiant Ones*, Harold Jacob Smith, Nathan E. Douglas (Nedrick Young)

Cat on a Hot Tin Roof, Richard Brooks, James Poe, based on the play by Tennessee Williams

I Want to Live! Nelson Gidding, Don Mankiewicz, based on articles by Ed Montgomery and the letters of Barbara Graham

The Long Hot Summer, Irving Ravetch, Harriet Frank, Jr., from the novel *The Hamlet* by William Faulkner

Separate Tables, Terence Rattigan, John Gay, based on the play by Terence Rattigan

BEST WRITTEN COMEDY

- *Me and the Colonel*, S. N. Behrman, George Froeschel, based on the play *Jacobowsky and the Colonel* by Franz Werfel

Houseboat, Melville Shavelson, Jack Rose

Indiscreet, Norman Krasna, based on his play *Kind Sir*

The Reluctant Debutante, William Douglas Home, Julius Epstein, from the play by William Douglas Home

Teacher's Pet, Fay and Michael Kanin

BEST WRITTEN MUSICAL

- *Gigi*, Alan Jay Lerner, based on the novel by Colette

Damn Yankees, George Abbott, based on the musical by George Abbott and Douglas Wallop and the novel by Douglas Wallop

The Girl Most Likely, Paul Jarrico, Devery Freeman, story by Paul Jarrico

South Pacific, Paul Osborn, adaptation of the Rodgers and Hammerstein musical, based on the collection of short stories *Tales of the South Pacific* by James A. Michener

Tom Thumb, Ladislas Fodor, based on the fairy tale by the Brothers Grimm

LAUREL AWARD

- Nunnally Johnson

ACADEMY AWARDS

Nominations were announced on February 23, 1959. Awards were presented on April 6 at the Pantages Theater in Hollywood. The ceremony was telecast by NBC.

BEST PICTURE

- *Gigi*

Auntie Mame
Cat on a Hot Tin Roof

The Defiant Ones
Separate Tables

BEST DIRECTOR

- Vincente Minnelli, *Gigi*
Richard Brooks, *Cat on a Hot Tin Roof*
Stanley Kramer, *The Defiant Ones*
Mark Robson, *The Inn of the Sixth
    Happiness*
Robert Wise, *I Want to Live!*

BEST ACTOR

- David Niven, *Separate Tables*
Tony Curtis, *The Defiant Ones*
Paul Newman, *Cat on a Hot Tin Roof*
Sidney Poitier, *The Defiant Ones*
Spencer Tracy, *The Old Man and the Sea*

BEST ACTRESS

- Susan Hayward, *I Want to Live!*
Deborah Kerr, *Separate Tables*
Shirley MacLaine, *Some Came Running*
Rosalind Russell, *Auntie Mame*
Elizabeth Taylor, *Cat on a Hot Tin Roof*

BEST SUPPORTING ACTOR

- Burl Ives, *The Big Country*
Theodore Bikel, *The Defiant Ones*
Lee J. Cobb, *The Brothers Karamazov*
Arthur Kennedy, *Some Came Running*
Gig Young, *Teacher's Pet*

BEST SUPPORTING ACTRESS

- Wendy Hiller, *Separate Tables*
Peggy Cass, *Auntie Mame*
Martha Hyer, *Some Came Running*
Maureen Stapleton, *Lonelyhearts*
Cara Williams, *The Defiant Ones*

BEST ADAPTED SCREENPLAY

- Alan Jay Lerner, *Gigi*
Richard Brooks, James Poe, *Cat on a Hot
    Tin Roof*
John Gay, Terence Rattigan, *Separate
    Tables*
Nelson Gidding, Don Mankiewicz, *I Want
    to Live!*
Alec Guinness, *The Horse's Mouth*

BEST ORIGINAL SCREENPLAY

- Harold Jacob Smith, Nathan E. Douglas
    (Nedrick Young), *The Defiant Ones*

William Bowers, James Edward Grant,
    The Sheepman
Paddy Chayefsky, *The Goddess*
Fay Kanin, Michael Kanin, *Teacher's Pet*
Jack Rose, Melville Shavelson,
    Houseboat

BEST SONG

- "Gigi," *Gigi*, Alan Jay Lerner, Frederick
    Loewe
"Almost in Your Arms," *Houseboat*, Ray
    Evans, Jay Livingston
"A Certain Smile," *A Certain Smile*,
    Sammy Fain, Paul Francis Webster
"To Love and Be Loved," *Some Came
    Running*, Sammy Cahn, James Van
    Heusen
"A Very Precious Love," *Marjorie
    Morningstar*, Sammy Fain, Paul Francis
    Webster

BEST FOREIGN-LANGUAGE FILM

- *Arms and the Man* (West Germany)
The Road a Year Long (Yugoslavia)
My Uncle (France)
The Usual Unidentified Thieves (Italy)
La Venganza (Spain)

Winners

BEST ART DIRECTION/SET DECORATION

- Preston Ames, William A. Horning,
    Keogh Gleason, Henry Grace, *Gigi*

BEST CINEMATOGRAPHY
(BLACK AND WHITE)
- Sam Leavitt, *The Defiant Ones*
(COLOR)
- Joseph Ruttenberg, *Gigi*

BEST COSTUME DESIGN
- Cecil Beaton, *Gigi*

BEST DOCUMENTARY
(FEATURE)
- *White Wilderness*, Ben Sharpsteen
(SHORT SUBJECT)
- *Ama Girls*, Ben Sharpsteen

BEST FILM EDITING
- Adrienne Fazan, *Gigi*

BEST MUSIC
(SCORING OF A DRAMATIC OR COMEDY PICTURE)
- Dimitri Tiomkin, *The Old Man and the Sea*

(SCORING OF A MUSICAL PICTURE)
- Andre Previn, *Gigi*

SCIENTIFIC OR TECHNICAL AWARDS
Class II (Plaque)
- Don W. Prideaux, Leroy G. Leighton, Lamp Division, General Electric; Panavision

Class III (Certificate)
- Willy Borberg, General Precision Lab; Fred Ponedel, George Brown, Conrad Boye, Warner Bros. Special Effects Dept.

BEST SHORT SUBJECT
(CARTOON)
- *Knighty Knight Bugs*

(LIVE ACTION)
- *Grand Canyon*

BEST SOUND
- Fred Hynes, *South Pacific*

BEST SPECIAL EFFECTS
- Tom Howard, *Tom Thumb*

IRVING G. THALBERG MEMORIAL AWARD
- Jack L. Warner

HONORARY AWARD
- Maurice Chevalier

· 1959 ·

Ben-Hur's *Miracle*

Ben-Hur's pursuit of the top film kudos looked a lot like its frenzied chariot race: alternately it led, fell behind, got bumped off track and finally sprinted to triumph.

MGM bet high stakes in this year's awards derby on the remake of its 1926 silent hit based on the 1880 bestseller by Civil War General Lew Wallace. The original had grossed $4.5 million and now, facing bankruptcy, the lion studio wagered that Cecil B. DeMille could duplicate the success he had with a previous biblical epic, *The Ten Commandments*, which grossed $34 million. DeMille filmed the new *Ben-Hur* in Rome over 10 months, building 300 sets and employing 8,000 actors in the most expensive production ever filmed. *Variety* cheered the 3-hour, 32-minute result: "The $15 million *Ben-Hur* is a majestic achievement, representing a superb blending of the motion picture arts by master craftsmen. Charlton Heston is excellent as the brawny yet kindly Ben-Hur, who survives the life of a galley slave to seek revenge on his enemy. His bitterness is exorcised only by a meeting with Christ on his way to Calgary."

Ben-Hur scored boffo b.o. when it opened in December 1959, and seemed to be miles out front in the race for the top awards. Then the National Board of Review released its vote results: *Ben-Hur* placed second behind another religiously inspired pic, *The Nun's Story*, which starred Audrey Hepburn as "a young Belgian woman struggling to be a successful member of an order of cloistered nuns," said *Variety*. "Fred Zinnemann's production is a soaring and luminous film."

A few days later, the New York Film Critics endorsed Zinnemann with its helmer's prize after voting described as "torrid" by *The New York Times*. Zinnemann tied *Ben-Hur*'s William Wyler on the first

Variety declared that N.Y. crix Best Actor James Stewart gave "the best perf of his career" in *Anatomy of a Murder* (with Ben Gazzara, right).

four ballots, then beat him on the sixth when a late-breaking rival railed into second place: Jack Clayton of *Room at the Top*.

While *Ben-Hur* and *The Nun's Story* reflected a new trend in virtuous movies, *Room at the Top* epitomized the sultry opposite. The British-made indie starred noted French thesp Simone Signoret as a mature married woman seduced by a young schemer (Laurence Harvey). Judges at Cannes were the first to get excited by it, giving Signoret their palm for Best Actress, but when critics hailed its arrival in the United States, religious leaders and Hays Office officials fumed. *Room at the Top* was banned in Atlanta and relegated to art houses in other cities after being denied the Production Code seal. Star Signoret was also denied the Best Actress accolade by the New York film critics when the same scribes who had embraced her so warmly in print opted for the saintly Audrey Hepburn on the sixth ballot by a narrow vote of eight to seven. (Her plaque would be accepted on her behalf by the less-than-saintly Elizabeth Taylor when Hepburn could not attend the kudos ceremony at Sardi's.)

Winner of the Venice Film Festival's Volpi Cup for Best Actor fared better with the same crix. James Stewart won their kudos on the fifth ballot by a 10-to-5 score over Paul Muni (*The Last Angry Man*) after trailing six to eight votes on the third tally. Stewart was hailed for what the *Times* called "probably the best performance of his career" as a scrappy defense attorney in Otto Preminger's *Anatomy of a Murder*, which also claimed the screenplay trophy. The crix had honored Stewart 20 years earlier with the same award for *Mr. Smith Goes to Washington*.

"No less than nine assorted pictures came in for at least one vote on the early ballots for the Best Picture award," observed the *Times*. *Ben-Hur* (five votes) led over *On the Beach* (three) and *Anatomy of a Murder* (two). Other rivals scoring one endorsement each included *Room at the Top*, which later rallied to second place during the fifth polling when *Ben-Hur* won.

WGA voters liked it *Hot*, picking Billy Wilder and I.A.L. Diamond.

Ben-Hur made up for its loss of the helmer's award by earning the equivalent kudos from the Directors Guild of America (which dropped "Screen" from its name this year). At the writers' guild awards, however, the pic lost the prize for Best Written Drama to *The Diary of Anne Frank*, no doubt due to a dispute over authorship. Five scribes reportedly worked on *Ben-Hur*'s script (Karl Tunberg, Christopher Fry, Maxwell Anderson, S. N. Behrman and Gore Vidal), but the guild decreed that only Tunberg deserved screen credit. Director Wyler protested, insisting that Fry be listed, too, but lost his case.

Winners of 1957's Best Written Comedy Award, Billy Wilder and I. A. L. Diamond, returned to reclaim the same category for *Some Like It Hot*, 1959's third-highest grosser ($7.2 million) featuring Marilyn Monroe in one of her steamiest roles and Jack Lemmon and Tony Curtis in drag. *The Five Pennies*, which starred Danny Kaye as jazz trumpeter Loring "Red" Nichols, reaped the prize for Best Written Musical over *Porgy and Bess* and *Li'l Abner*.

Hollywood stars went on strike in March 1960 to back up the Screen Actors Guild's demand that the television networks and studios pay actors residuals when their pics appear on TV. While the issue was being sorted out in private, there was some question whether the stars would appear in public at industry events like the Globes and Oscars. An additional controversy threatened to turn the Golden Globes into "the Golden Gloves" boxing match, according to *Variety*, when local station KTTV broadcast the gala but refused to pay stars for their appearances.

Execs from all three networks boycotted the gala, but only one star stayed away: Gina Lollobrigida. Twelve hundred showbiz leaders appeared for the event, including the notoriously aloof Bing Crosby, who made a special trip from Palm Springs to receive the Cecil B. DeMille Award, then left the party early.

Ben-Hur snagged the kudos for Best Drama Picture, Best Director and Best Supporting Actor (Stephen Boyd as Heston's nemesis Messala), but Heston lost the actor's race to Anthony Franciosa as a wanna-be Broadway star in *Career*.

Last year Elizabeth Taylor wasn't nommed for *Cat on a Hot Tin Roof* thanks to her scandalous affair with Eddie Fisher. Now that she and Fisher were wed, Taylor gained new respectability, which voters acknowledged by giving the onetime widow of Fisher's best friend their Best Actress trophy for her portrayal of a widow suspected of insanity in *Suddenly, Last Summer*. Taylor couldn't accept the trophy because she was laid up at home with a broken ankle, but her absence at the Globes meant that the coast was clear for the previous Mrs. Fisher, Debbie Reynolds, to show up, which she did, squired by Glenn Ford and besieged by paparazzi.

The press also pounced on the winner of Best Comedy Actress from *Some Like It Hot*, which won the added prizes of Best Comedy Picture and Best Comedy Actor for Jack Lemmon. "The seldom-seen-in-public-anymore Marilyn Monroe nearly stopped the show with her shoulder-shaking 'I want to thank you from the bottom of my heart,' " noted the *L.A. Daily Mirror*.

Monroe was snubbed when the Oscar noms were announced. The lineup for Best Actress included Taylor competing against two Hepburns: Katharine, her costar from *Suddenly, Last Summer*, and Audrey, winner of the New York film crix's plaque. They faced the National Board of Review's choice, Simone Signoret.

Taylor was also back on the list of Top 10 box office stars, apparently having been forgiven for her recent sins. A pious spirit pervaded this year's Oscar contest, too. "For the first time in the history of the Academy Awards, a majority of the films nominated for Best Picture are religious themed," *Variety* observed. They were *Ben-Hur* (12 noms), *The Diary of Anne Frank* (eight) and *The Nun's Story* (eight).

On awards night, *Variety* reported that "there seemed to be less electricity in the air than in previous years," no doubt due to a lack of suspense. Inside the theater, *Variety* said, "The runway was greased for the *Ben-Hur* chariot."

Ben-Hur charged through the early races, snagging laurels en route for special effects, costumes, film editing, music score, sound, art direction and cinematography. It also triumphed in the contest for Best Supporting Actor when Hugh Griffith prevailed for his role as a friendly sheik, beating Robert Vaughn (*The Young Philadelphians*), who'd campaigned vigorously to win, and crix darling George C. Scott (*Anatomy of a Murder*), who cared so little about the matchup that he stayed at home on Oscar night. Griffith cared, but he was also at home—far off in his native Britain.

Best Supporting Actress contender

Ben-Hur director William Wyler lost the N.Y. crix prize, but claimed the Globe (above), DGA and Oscar.

L.A. Herald

Thelma Ritter shunned the ceremony, too, assuming she'd lose for a fifth time. Shelley Winters had lost in 1951 for *A Place in the Sun*, but this year Winters was considered the front-runner for *The Diary of Anne Frank*. The former screen vixen not only gave a socko perf (*Variety* praised her for "a vivid characterization that scores on all levels"), but she gained 30 pounds to portray the whiny family friend who hides from the Nazis with the Frank brood. When she won, *Variety* described winters as "all jubilance, shouting, 'I've waited 15 years for this!' and stating her disbelief she'd actually won it."

Victory was also an emotional experience for the Best Actress champ, who confessed "great surprise" that her small indie film was a hit. When it earned Simone Signoret the Oscar over Taylor and the two Hepburns, she was ecstatic. "I can't say anything," she gasped at the podium. "I wanted to be dignified and all that, but I can't!"

In the actors' face-off, New York film crix champ Jimmy Stewart confronted Laurence Harvey, Charlton Heston, Paul Muni and Jack Lemmon. When Heston prevailed, he stumbled en route to the stage, just like last year's winner. "I feel like thanking the first secretary who let me sneak into a Broadway casting call," he said at the podium. Backstage later, he told the press, "Somebody just asked me what scene I enjoyed doing the most, and I told him that I didn't enjoy any of it. It was hard work."

Ben-Hur's awards chariot was back on track. Its next victory was for Best Director William Wyler, topping Billy Wilder (Some Like It Hot) and Fred Zinnemann, who had reaped the Best Director's prize for The Nun's Story one week earlier from the London Film Critics Circle. Variety noted

William Wyler's past Oscar wins for Mrs. Miniver and The Best Years of Our Lives, then declared that he "became the third megger in academy history to amass more than 2 of the cherished trophies. John Ford has won 4, Frank Capra 3. Wyler holds the nominations record, 11."

The next golden boy claimed by Ben-Hur—for Best Picture—brought its total to 11, which shattered Gigi's record for scoring the most wins in a single year. Its only loss was for the screenplay award, no doubt because of the hubbub surrounding the authorship of Ben-Hur's script. That prize went to Room with a View.

The Oscar ceremony was a standout for another reason: Variety declared that the evening was "without a flaw . . . brilliant with wit by emcee Bob Hope and glittering with high fashions of the day."

NBC experienced the opposite problem it had faced last year when the show ran 20 minutes short. This year it ran 20 minutes long, setting an ominous precedent for future years.

▪ 1959 ▪

NATIONAL BOARD OF REVIEW

The board declared a best picture and foreign film of the year, then listed its remaining favorites according to highest scores. The vote results were announced in late December 1959.

BEST PICTURE
▪ The Nun's Story
Ben-Hur
Anatomy of a Murder
The Diary of Anne Frank
Middle of the Night
The Man Who Understood Women
Some Like It Hot
Suddenly, Last Summer
On the Beach
North by Northwest

BEST DIRECTOR
▪ Fred Zinnemann, The Nun's Story

BEST ACTOR
▪ Victor Seastrom, Wild Strawberries

BEST ACTRESS
▪ Simone Signoret, Room at the Top

BEST SUPPORTING ACTOR
▪ Hugh Griffith, Ben-Hur

BEST SUPPORTING ACTRESS
▪ Dame Edith Evans, The Nun's Story

BEST FOREIGN FILM
▪ Wild Strawberries (Sweden)
Room at the Top (U.K.)
Aparajito (India)
The Roof (Italy)
Look Back in Anger (U.K.)

SPECIAL CITATIONS
▪ Ingmar Bergman

- Andrew Marton and Yakima Canut for their direction of the chariot race in *Ben-Hur*

NEW YORK FILM CRITICS

Winners were announced on December 28, 1959. Awards were presented on January 23 at Sardi's restaurant in New York.

BEST PICTURE
- *Ben-Hur*

BEST DIRECTOR
- Fred Zinnemann, *The Nun's Story*

BEST ACTOR
- James Stewart, *Anatomy of a Murder*

BEST ACTRESS
- Audrey Hepburn, *The Nun's Story*

BEST SCREENPLAY
- Wendell Mayes, *Anatomy of a Murder*

BEST FOREIGN FILM
- *The 400 Blows* (France)

DIRECTORS GUILD OF AMERICA

The initial list of nominees was narrowed down to a group of finalists who competed for the Best Director award, bestowed on February 6, 1960, at the Beverly Hilton Hotel in Los Angeles.

BEST DIRECTOR
- William Wyler, *Ben-Hur*

Charles Barton, *The Shaggy Dog*

Frank Capra, *A Hole in the Head*

Richard Fleischer, *Compulsion*

John Ford, *The Horse Soldiers*

Howard Hawks, *Rio Bravo*

Alfred Hitchcock, *North by Northwest*

Leo McCarey, *Rally 'Round the Flag, Boys!*

Otto Preminger, *Anatomy of a Murder* (finalist)

Douglas Sirk, *Imitation of Life*

George Stevens, *The Diary of Anne Frank* (finalist)

Billy Wilder, *Some Like It Hot* (finalist)

Fred Zinnemann, *The Nun's Story* (finalist)

D. W. GRIFFITH AWARD
- George Stevens

GOLDEN GLOBES

Nominations were announced on February 2, 1960. Awards were presented on March 10 at the Cocoanut Grove in the Ambassador Hotel in Los Angeles. The ceremony was telecast on L.A. station KTTV.

BEST DRAMA PICTURE
- *Ben-Hur*

Anatomy of a Murder
The Diary of Anne Frank
The Nun's Story
On the Beach

BEST COMEDY PICTURE
- *Some Like It Hot*

But Not for Me
Operation Petticoat
Pillow Talk
Who Was That Lady?

MGM LIONIZES OSCAR AS 'BEN-HUR' AMASSES RECORD 11; 20TH, 3

United Artists, Columbia Win 2 Each; One To UI

Ben-Hur's 11 Oscars topped *Gigi's* short-lived record of 9. Pic's only loss was in the screenplay race to *The Nun's Story*, which would lose WGA to *Anne Frank*.

BEST MUSICAL PICTURE
- *Porgy and Bess*
- *Li'l Abner*
- *Private Affair*
- *Say One for Me*
- *The Five Pennies*

BEST MOTION PICTURE PROMOTING INTERNATIONAL UNDERSTANDING
- *The Diary of Anne Frank*
- *The Nun's Story*
- *Odds against Tomorrow*
- *On the Beach*
- *Take a Giant Step*

BEST DIRECTOR
- William Wyler, *Ben-Hur*
- Stanley Kramer, *On the Beach*
- Otto Preminger, *Anatomy of a Murder*
- George Stevens, *The Diary of Anne Frank*
- Fred Zinnemann, *The Nun's Story*

BEST ACTOR, DRAMA
- Anthony Franciosa, *Career*
- Richard Burton, *Look Back in Anger*
- Charlton Heston, *Ben-Hur*
- Fredric March, *Middle of the Night*
- Joseph Schildkraut, *Diary of Anne Frank*

BEST ACTRESS, DRAMA
- Elizabeth Taylor, *Suddenly, Last Summer*
- Audrey Hepburn, *The Nun's Story*
- Katharine Hepburn, *Suddenly, Last Summer*
- Lee Remick, *Anatomy of a Murder*
- Simone Signoret, *Room at the Top*

BEST ACTOR, COMEDY OR MUSICAL
- Jack Lemmon, *Some Like It Hot*
- Clark Gable, *But Not for Me*
- Cary Grant, *Operation Petticoat*
- Dean Martin, *Who Was That Lady?*
- Sydney Poitier, *Porgy and Bess*

BEST ACTRESS, COMEDY OR MUSICAL
- Marilyn Monroe, *Some Like It Hot*
- Dorothy Dandridge, *Porgy and Bess*
- Doris Day, *Pillow Talk*
- Shirley MacLaine, *Ask Any Girl*
- Lilli Palmer, *But Not for Me*

BEST SUPPORTING ACTOR
- Stephen Boyd, *Ben-Hur*
- Fred Astaire, *On the Beach*
- Tony Randall, *Pillow Talk*
- Robert Vaughn, *The Young Philadelphians*
- Joseph Welch, *Anatomy of a Murder*

BEST SUPPORTING ACTRESS
- Susan Kohner, *Imitation of Life*
- Dame Edith Evans, *The Nun's Story*
- Estelle Hamsley, *Take a Giant Step*
- Juanita Moore, *Imitation of Life*
- Shelley Winters, *The Diary of Anne Frank*

MOST PROMISING NEWCOMER—MALE
- Barry Coe
- Troy Donahue
- George Hamilton
- James Shigeta
- Michael Callan

MOST PROMISING NEWCOMER—FEMALE
- Angie Dickinson
- Janet Munro
- Stella Stevens
- Tuesday Weld
- Dianne Baker
- Yvette Mimieux
- Cindy Robbins

Winners

BEST FOREIGN-LANGUAGE FILMS
- *Aren't We Wonderful* (Germany)
- *Black Orpheus* (France)
- *The Bridge* (Germany)
- *Odd Obsession* (Japan)
- *Wild Strawberries* (Sweden)

WORLD FILM FAVORITES
- Doris Day
- Rock Hudson

BEST ORIGINAL SCORE
- Ernest Gold, *On the Beach*

SAMUEL GOLDWYN INTERNATIONAL AWARD
- *Room at the Top*

SPECIAL JOURNALISTIC MERIT AWARD
- Hedda Hopper
- Louella H. Parsons

SPECIAL MERIT AWARD

- *The Nun's Story*

CECIL B. DEMILLE AWARD

- Bing Crosby

SPECIAL ACHIEVEMENT AWARD

- Ramon Novarro
- Francis X. Bushman
- Andrew Marton for directing chariot race in *Ben-Hur*

ACADEMY AWARDS

Nominations were announced on February 22, 1960. Awards were presented on April 4 at the RKO Pantages Theater, in Hollywood. The ceremony was telecast by NBC.

BEST PICTURE

- *Ben-Hur*

Anatomy of a Murder
The Diary of Anne Frank
The Nun's Story
Room at the Top

BEST DIRECTOR

- William Wyler, *Ben-Hur*

Jack Clayton, *Room at the Top*
George Stevens, *The Diary of Anne Frank*
Billy Wilder, *Some Like It Hot*
Fred Zinnemann, *The Nun's Story*

BEST ACTOR

- Charlton Heston, *Ben-Hur*

Laurence Harvey, *Room at the Top*
Jack Lemmon, *Some Like It Hot*
Paul Muni, *The Last Angry Man*
James Stewart, *Anatomy of a Murder*

BEST ACTRESS

- Simone Signoret, *Room at the Top*

Doris Day, *Pillow Talk*
Audrey Hepburn, *The Nun's Story*
Katharine Hepburn, *Suddenly, Last Summer*
Elizabeth Taylor, *Suddenly, Last Summer*

BEST SUPPORTING ACTOR

- Hugh Griffith, *Ben-Hur*

Arthur O'Connell, *Anatomy of a Murder*
George C. Scott, *Anatomy of a Murder*

Robert Vaughn, *The Young Philadelphians*
Ed Wynn, *The Diary of Anne Frank*

BEST SUPPORTING ACTRESS

- Shelley Winters, *The Diary of Anne Frank*

Hermione Baddeley, *Room at the Top*
Susan Kohner, *Imitation of Life*
Juanita Moore, *Imitation of Life*
Thelma Ritter, *Pillow Talk*

BEST ADAPTED SCREENPLAY

- Robert Anderson, *The Nun's Story*

I. A. L. Diamond, Billy Wilder, *Some Like It Hot*
Wendell Mayes, *Anatomy of a Murder*
Neil Paterson, *Room at the Top*
Karl Tunberg, *Ben-Hur*

BEST ORIGINAL SCREENPLAY

- Clarence Greene, Maurice Richlin, Russell Rouse, Stanley Shapiro, *Pillow Talk*

Ingmar Bergman, *Wild Strawberries*
Ernest Lehman, *North by Northwest*
Paul King, Maurice Richlin, Stanley Shapiro, Joseph Stone, *Operation Petticoat*
Marcel Moussy, Francois Truffaut, *The 400 Blows*

BEST SONG

- "High Hopes," *A Hole in the Head*, Sammy Cahn, James Van Heusen

"The Best of Everything," *The Best of Everything*, Sammy Cahn, Alfred Newman
"The Five Pennies," *The Five Pennies*, Sylvia Fine
"The Hanging Tree," *The Hanging Tree*, Mack David, Jerry Livingston
"Strange Are the Ways of Love," *The Young Land*, Dimitri Tiomkin, Ned Washington

BEST FOREIGN-LANGUAGE FILM

- *Black Orpheus* (France)

The Bridge (West Germany)
The Great War (Italy)
Paw (Denmark)
The Village on the River (Netherlands)

Winners

BEST ART DIRECTION
(BLACK AND WHITE)
- George W. Davis, Lyle R. Wheeler, Stuart A. Reiss, Walter M. Scott, *The Diary of Anne Frank*

(COLOR)
- Edward Carfagno, William A. Horning, Hugh Hunt, *Ben-Hur*

BEST CINEMATOGRAPHY
(BLACK AND WHITE)
- William C. Mellor, *The Diary of Anne Frank*

(COLOR)
- Robert L. Surtees, *Ben-Hur*

BEST COSTUME DESIGN
(BLACK AND WHITE)
- Orry-Kelly, *Some Like It Hot*

(COLOR)
- Elizabeth Haffenden, *Ben-Hur*

BEST DOCUMENTARY
(FEATURE)
- *Serengeti Shall Not Die*, Bernhard Grzimek

(SHORT SUBJECT)
- *Glass*, Bert Haanstra

BEST FILM EDITING
- John D. Dunning, Ralph E. Winters, *Ben-Hur*

BEST MUSIC
(SCORING OF A DRAMATIC OR COMEDY PICTURE)
- Miklos Rozsa, *Ben-Hur*

(SCORING OF A MUSICAL PICTURE)
- Ken Darby, Andre Previn, *Porgy and Bess*

SCIENTIFIC OR TECHNICAL AWARDS
Class II (Plaque)
- Douglas G. Shearer, MGM; Robert E. Gottschalk, John R. Moore, Panavision; Wadsworth E. Pohl, William Evans, Werner Hopf, S. E. Howse, Thomas P. Dixon, Stanford Research Institute, Technicolor Corp.
- Wadsworth E. Pohl, Jack Alford, Henry Imus, Joseph Schmit, Paul Fasshacht, Al Lofquist, Technicolor Corp.; Howard S.

Coleman, A. Francis Turner, Harold H. Schroeder, James R. Benford, Harold E. Rosenberger, Bausch & Lomb; Robert P. Gutterman, General Kinetics; Lipsner-Smith Corp.

Class III (Certificate)
- UB Iwerks, Walt Disney; E. L. Stones, Glen Robinson, Winfield Hubbard, Luther Newman, MGM

BEST SHORT SUBJECT
(CARTOON)
- *Moonbird*

(LIVE ACTION)
- *The Golden Fish*, Jacques-Yves Cousteau

BEST SOUND
- Franklin E. Milton, *Ben-Hur*

BEST SPECIAL EFFECTS
- Arnold Gillespie, Milo Lory, Robert MacDonald, *Ben-Hur*

JEAN HERSHOLT HUMANITARIAN AWARD
- Bob Hope

HONORARY AWARDS
- Lee De Forest
- Buster Keaton

WRITERS GUILD OF AMERICA

Awards were presented on May 6, 1960, at the Beverly Hilton Hotel in Los Angeles.

BEST WRITTEN DRAMA
- *The Diary of Anne Frank*, Frances Doogrich, Albert Hackett, based on the book *Anne Frank, the Diary of a Young Girl* and the play by Goodrich and Hackett

Anatomy of a Murder, Wendell Mayes, based on the novel by Robert Traver

Ben-Hur, Karl Tunberg, based on the novel *Ben-Hur (A Tale of Christ)* by General Lew Wallace

Compulsion, Richard Murphy, based on the novel by Meyer Levin

The Nun's Story, Robert Anderson, based on the book by Kathryn C. Hulme

BEST WRITTEN COMEDY

- *Some Like It Hot*, Billy Wilder, I. A. L. Diamond, suggested by a story by Robert Thoeren and M. Logan

A Hole in the Head, Arnold Schulman

North by Northwest, Ernest Lehman

Operation Petticoat, Stanley Shapiro, Maurice Richlin, story by Paul King and Joseph Stone

Pillow Talk, Stanley Shapiro, Maurice Richlin, story by Russell Rouse and Clarence Greene

BEST WRITTEN MUSICAL

- *The Five Pennies*, Melville Shavelson, Jack Rose, story by Robert Smith, based on the life of Loring "Red" Nichols

Li'l Abner, Norman Panama, Melvin Frank, based on their musical play by Al Capp

Never Steal Anything Small, Charles Lederer, based on the play *Devil's Hornpipe* by Maxwell Anderson and Rouben Mamoulian

Porgy and Bess, N. Richard Nash, based on the folk opera by George Gershwin, Ira Gershwin and DuBose Heyward and the play *Porgy* by DuBose Heyward and Dorothy Heyward

A Private's Affair, Winston Miller, based on a story by Ray Livingston Murphy

Say One for Me, Robert O'Brien

LAUREL AWARD

- Norman Krasna

· 1960 ·

Sons, Lovers, Lecherous Preachers and a Handy Manhattan Sex Pad

It was such a hot year for directors—with Billy Wilder exposing corporate sexcapades in *The Apartment* and Jack Cardiff revealing the fleshly obsessions of D. H. Lawrence in *Sons and Lovers*—that the excited New York crix couldn't decide on best pic or director.

The result was what *The New York Times* denounced as "a seeming embarrassment" that looked "foolish": they gave both films both awards. *The Apartment* had already earned high praise from *Variety* for being "high in comedy and wide in warmth (with Jack) Lemmon as a lonely insurance clerk with a convenient apartment that has become the rendezvous point for five of his bosses and their amours." *Variety* had also cheered Cardiff's "well-made and conscientious adaptation" of Lawrence's classic about the doomed romances of a British miner's son.

One week earlier, a much more decisive National Board of Review had embraced *Sons and Lovers* as best pic because of what its chairman Henry Hart called "some of the finest acting ever seen on the screen." Despite that praise, the board gave its performance honors to other thesps, declaring Greer Garson Best Actress for her toothy portrayal of Eleanor Roosevelt in *Sunrise at Campobello* and naming Robert Mitchum Best Actor for his dual roles as an Australian sheepherder in *The Sundowners* and as a studly Texas tycoon in *Home from the Hill*.

When the Gotham crix tried to pick the year's top actresses, Garson tied for second place on the first ballot behind the recent Best Actress sensation at Cannes—Melina Mercouri, who portrayed the big-hearted Greek hooker in *Never on Sunday*. On the last round, when only a majority of votes was needed instead of the two-thirds tally required earlier, Deborah Kerr finally

Variety said that Oscar, Globe and Gotham crix Best Picture *The Apartment* was "high in comedy and wide in warmth."

emerged the victor for portraying Mitchum's pioneer wife in *The Sundowners*. *Variety* had endorsed her star turn in its film review: "There is one fleeting eloquent scene at a train station, in which her eyes meet those of an elegant lady traveler, that ranks as one of the most memorable moments ever to cross a screen." It was third time that the crix had endorsed Kerr, who was now their most honored thesp.

Another past honoree, Burt Lancaster (*From Here to Eternity*), needed the same half-dozen tallies before he topped *Sons and Lovers*'s Trevor Howard for his latest Best Actor prize. Now he was hailed as a firebrand evangelist who indulges, noted *Variety*, "in the carnal pleasures he denounces vehemently from the pulpit" in the screen rendition of Sinclair Lewis's steamy bestseller *Elmer Gantry*, which Lancaster also produced. *Sons and Lovers* actually led the contests for best pic and best helmer on the first five ballots before one anti–*Sons and Lovers* critic surrendered his allegiance to *Elmer Gantry* and switched to *The Apartment* while settling for the two top ties.

Variety observed that the crix's recent choices for Best Picture had been "a pretty accurate barometer of the eventual Academy Award winner. Since 1944, the NY reviewers and the Academy members have differed only on four occasions, (but) the reviewers' vote to split the honors . . . will give the form sheet players some difficulty" in forecasting a champ this year.

The guilds' awards did a better job of pointing the way toward the eventual Oscar champs. The directors' and writers' groups both gave *The Apartment* high honors, although its helmer/writer Wilder missed the directors' bash because of a business trip to Europe. His absence was probably for the best, since the affair turned out to be a fiasco. Simultaneous ceremonies held in L.A. (from 10 to 11 P.M. at the Beverly Hilton Hotel) and New York (1 to 2 A.M. at the Waldorf-Astoria Hotel) were linked by a live phone hookup wired into loudspeakers. "It was a good idea," *Variety* said, "but AT&T's participation was somewhat lacking, and the (barely audible) telephone connection soon became more of a joke than a convenience."

Wilder managed to make it to the writers' gala, which went much more smoothly since it relied on live entertainment that Wilder helped to write and direct. More than a dozen other scribes also contributed to the savagely funny sketches that were by now popular hallmarks of the guild's annual banquets. This year the parodies were "the best and wittiest yet . . . penned with sword-sharp pencils," said *Variety*, which declared that the funniest one revealed how various directors would handle the same blackout scene: "Skit, depicting a husband saying goodbye to his wife while her lover hides in the closet, raked Hitchcock, Disney, Wilder,

> ## "Foolish" crix named both *The Apartment* and *Sons and Lovers* as best pic.

Skouras and Marlon Brando across the coals rollickingly."

As Wilder accepted the award for *The Apartment* as the year's Best Written Comedy, he told his peers, "Keep praying, cousins. We hope Oscar will say the right thing this year."

But Wilder's work hit an ominous snag when the Golden Globe noms came out. *The Apartment* was back in far-off fourth place for the most bids (four) behind *Spartacus* (six) and *Elmer Gantry* and *Sons and Lovers* (five each).

On awards night, *Spartacus* was declared Best Drama Picture and *Sons and Lovers*'s Cardiff claimed the helmer's globe, but *The Apartment* scored the most victories overall—three—including Best Comedy Picture. Last year's champ Jack Lemmon not only returned for the actor's Globe again, but he walked off with the actress prize, too, when he accepted for his absent costar Shirley MacLaine. It was MacLaine's second top honor for *The Apartment*; she'd been hailed as Best Actress at the Venice Film Fest six months earlier and would go on to win the British Academy Award soon after nabbing her Globe.

When a husband-wife team both netted Globes, they received one of the biggest laughs of the night. Not long after Janet Leigh reaped a trophy as Best Supporting Actress in *Psycho*, Tony Curtis accepted the Henrietta prize as a World Film Favorite. Curtis glared at his wife's costar in the audience and shouted, "Tony Perkins—get out of my wife's shower!"

One day after the Globe results were announced, the Academy of Motion Picture Arts and Sciences mailed out nominating ballots to its 2,300 members. When they were returned by April 3, all of the major Globe champs had scored Oscar bids, but not all of them were expected to prevail as winners on April 17.

At the Globes showdown, Elizabeth Taylor had lost for a movie she said "stinks"—

Butterfield 8. She'd accepted the role as a high-class hooker in the screen adaptation of John O'Hara's bestseller only because she was eager to wrap up her obligations to MGM and move on to her million-dollar paycheck for Twentieth Century-Fox's *Cleopatra.* Shortly before the Oscars, however, she was suddenly felled by a mysterious illness and admitted to a London hospital where doctors described her medical condition as "grave."

The tabloid media seized on the drama and portrayed Taylor as being near death as she battled what was soon described as pneumonia and surgeons performed a tracheotomy.

"There is no question about it now—Elizabeth Taylor will win the Oscar this year," columnist Sheilah Graham predicted. "Popular sentiment was against her because of her tie-up to the Eddie Fisher–Debbie Reynolds marital smash. Now everything is forgotten in the hope that this beautiful woman will regain her health and find a way of life that will bring her happiness."

Taylor recovered by Oscar night and vowed to attend the ceremony, which had to be moved to the Santa Monica Civic Auditorium this year after the Pantages Theater gave up too many seats during its renovation to show the widescreen *Spartacus.* "This is Hollywood's biggest night, so naturally we're holding it in Santa Monica," Bob Hope wisecracked. *Variety* thought that the switch of venue was appropriate since it was "here on the sand where Mack Sennett's bathing beauties romped in the early era of pix." The geographic move wasn't the only major change for the Oscar gala. ABC planned to broadcast the show after it outbid NBC for the rights.

Officials at the Santa Monica Civic Auditorium were not prepared for what followed, however. *Variety* described a "vast traffic snarl" that delayed the arrival of hundreds of stars, including Elizabeth Taylor, which outraged thousands of impatient fans

Two actresses scored Oscars for portraying hookers.

waiting outside. *Variety* noticed that one of the night's other top stars was virtually snubbed by the crowd after he climbed out of his limo: "Burt Lancaster was completely neglected until he got to the entrance."

When Taylor finally arrived, she was stormed by well-wishers who poured down from the bleachers. *Variety* columnist Army Archerd reported, "It took a flying wedge of friends, press and police to guide her—at painful snail pace, up the long red carpet to the theatre lobby where she had to take refuge in the rest room for 15 minutes."

Taylor competed against Greer Garson (*Sunrise at Campobello*), Deborah Kerr (*The Sundowners*), Shirley MacLaine (*The Apartment*) and Melina Mercouri (*Never on Sunday*), but her victory was considered such a foregone conclusion that none of her rivals bothered to attend, except for Garson, who was scheduled to present the Best Actor award.

When Taylor won as expected, her husband Eddie Fisher helped her to the stage where she spoke "a tone or two above a whisper," according to *Variety.* "I don't know how to express my gratitude for this and for everything," she said. "All I can say is thank you, thank you with all my heart."

Archerd spotted her a few minutes later: "She sat backstage immediately after being given the award, gasped for breath and cried. We were the only newsmen there to greet her. 'I didn't know I won,' she gasped."

Greer Garson appeared unruffled by her loss when she appeared at the podium to settle the actors' contest, which included Trevor Howard (*Sons and Lovers*), Globe and New York film crix honoree Burt Lancaster (*Elmer Gantry*), other Globe champ Jack Lemmon (*The Apartment*), Laurence Olivier (*The Entertainer*) and Spencer Tracy (*Inherit the Wind*).

Garson declared Lancaster the winner and smiled warmly as she handed him the statuette, saying, "So well earned."

"A lovely thing to say," Lancaster replied, smiling back. To the gathered crowd, he said, "I want to thank all who expressed this kind of confidence by voting for me. And right now I'm so happy that I want to thank all the members who didn't vote for me."

Lancaster's *Elmer Gantry* costar Shirley Jones was in a tight race for Best Supporting Actress against *Psycho*'s Janet Leigh. When Jones prevailed, it marked the second victory this year for an actress portraying a prostitute. The saucy role was a stretch for Jones since she originally gained fame as a blushing ingenue in Broadway's *Oklahoma!* and *Carousel*. In her acceptance speech, she thanked those shows' creators, Rodgers and Hammerstein, for giving her her first show-biz break.

In order to win the Oscar, Jones had mounted a hefty ad campaign, but it was a modest drive compared to how Chill Wills ambushed voters in order to win Best Supporting Actor for *The Alamo*. Wills went so far overboard that he was ultimately chided publicly by the pic's star and producer John Wayne, who wasn't shy about asking for Oscars—in fact, he spent $75,000 for *The Alamo*'s bigger campaign—but he was miffed by Wills's solo effort. In a letter to *Variety*, Wayne wrote, "I will refrain from using (strong) language because I am sure his intentions were not as bad as his taste."

Oscarcast emcee Bob Hope made a snide crack about the hubbub on awards night, saying, "I didn't know there was any campaigning until I saw my maid wearing a Chill Wills button."

Wills's chief rival was thought to be Sal Mineo (*Exodus*), who was so nervous about the match-up, he confessed to *Variety*, "I've been unable to sleep for days."

But an upset was scored in the race by *Spartacus*'s Peter Ustinov, who'd previously lost Oscar bouts for *Quo Vadis?* and *The Egyptian*. Now the victor said at the podium, "Having been educated in English schools, we were taught for at least 15 years of our lives how to lose gracefully and I've been preparing myself for that all afternoon. Now I don't know quite what to say."

The Alamo and *Elmer Gantry* were up for Best Picture, but they were considered long shots since they didn't receive bids for their directors. The remaining three rivals were given the best shot at the top two races: *The Apartment* (which led with the most nominations—10), *Sons and Lovers* (seven bids) and *The Sundowners* (five).

It was a rare occurrence in Oscar history, but a comedy ended up getting the last laughs.

The Apartment's producer, scribe and helmer earned a record tally of statuettes for one person in one year—three—when Billy Wilder claimed kudos for direction, writing and Best Picture.

"Thank you so much, you lovely, discerning people," he said at the podium.

After the ceremony concluded, Wilder took his golden booty to the Governors' Ball where he—and others—were startled to discover a suddenly revived Elizabeth Taylor, who celebrated her victory as Best Actress by dancing and drinking champagne.

▪ 1960 ▪

NATIONAL BOARD OF REVIEW

Winners were announced on December 22, 1960.

BEST PICTURE

▪ *Sons and Lovers*
The Alamo
The Sundowners
Inherit the Wind
Sunrise at Campobello
Elmer Gantry
Home from the Hill
The Apartment
Wild River
The Dark at the Top of the Stairs

BEST DIRECTOR
- Jack Cardiff, *Sons and Lovers*

BEST ACTOR
- Robert Mitchum, *The Sundowners,*
  Home from the Hill

BEST ACTRESS
- Greer Garson, *Sunrise at Campobello*

BEST SUPPORTING ACTOR
- George Peppard, *Home from the Hill*

BEST SUPPORTING ACTRESS
- Shirley Jones, *Elmer Gantry*

BEST FOREIGN FILM
- *The World of Apu* (India)
  General Della Rovere (Italy/France)
  The Angry Silence (U.K.)
  I'm All Right, Jack (U.K.)
  Hiroshima, Mon Amour (France/Japan)

NEW YORK FILM CRITICS

Winners were announced on December
29, 1960. Awards were presented on January
23, 1961, at Sardi's restaurant in New
York.

BEST PICTURE (TIE)
- *The Apartment*
- *Sons and Lovers*

BEST DIRECTOR (TIE)
- Jack Cardiff, *Sons and Lovers*
- Billy Wilder, *The Apartment*

BEST ACTOR
- Burt Lancaster, *Elmer Gantry*

BEST ACTRESS
- Deborah Kerr, *The Sundowners*

BEST SCREENPLAY
- Billy Wilder, I. A. L. Diamond, *The
  Apartment*

BEST FOREIGN FILM
- *Hiroshima, Mon Amour* (France/
  Japan)

Even though Elizabeth Taylor said *Butterfield 8* "stinks," she nabbed an Oscar for it after rallying from ill health and a scandalous affair with future hubby Eddie Fisher (left).

DIRECTORS GUILD OF AMERICA

The initial list of nominees was narrowed
down to a group of finalists who competed
for the Best Director award, bestowed on
February 4, 1961. Dual ceremonies were
held at the Beverly Hilton Hotel in Los
Angeles and the Waldorf-Astoria Hotel in
New York.

BEST DIRECTOR
- Billy Wilder, *The Apartment*
  Richard Brooks, *Elmer Gantry*
  Jack Cardiff, *Sons and Lovers* (finalist)
  Vincent J. Donehue, *Sunrise at Campobello*
  Lewis Gilbert, *Sink the Bismarck!*
  Alfred Hitchcock, *Psycho* (finalist)
  Walter Lang, *Can-Can*
  Delbert Mann, *The Dark at the Top of the
  Stairs*
  Vincente Minnelli, *Bells Are Ringing*
  (finalist)
  Vincente Minnelli, *Home from the Hill*
  Carol Reed, *Our Man in Havana*
  Alain Resnais, *Hiroshima, Mon Amour*
  Charles Walters, *Please Don't Eat the
  Daisies*
  Fred Zinnemann, *The Sundowners* (finalist)

D. W. GRIFFITH AWARD
- Frank Borzage

GOLDEN GLOBES

Nominations were announced on February
8, 1961. Awards were presented on March

16 at the Beverly Hilton Hotel in Los Angeles. The ceremony was telecast on L.A. station KTTV.

BEST DRAMA PICTURE

- *Spartacus*
Elmer Gantry
Inherit the Wind
Sons and Lovers
Sunrise at Campobello

BEST COMEDY PICTURE

- *The Apartment*
The Facts of Life
The Grass Is Greener
It Started in Naples
Our Man in Havana

BEST MUSICAL PICTURE

- *Song without End*
Bells Are Ringing
Can-Can
Let's Make Love
Pepe

BEST MOTION PICTURE PROMOTING INTERNATIONAL UNDERSTANDING

- *Hand in Hand*
Conspiracy of Hearts

BEST DIRECTOR

- Jack Cardiff, *Sons and Lovers*
Richard Brooks, *Elmer Gantry*
Stanley Kubrick, *Spartacus*
Billy Wilder, *The Apartment*
Fred Zinnemann, *The Sundowners*

BEST ACTOR, DRAMA

- Burt Lancaster, *Elmer Gantry*
Trevor Howard, *Sons and Lovers*
Laurence Olivier, *Spartacus*
Dean Stockwell, *Sons and Lovers*
Spencer Tracy, *Inherit the Wind*

BEST ACTRESS, DRAMA

- Greer Garson, *Sunrise at Campobello*
Doris Day, *Midnight Lace*
Nancy Kwan, *World of Suzie Wong*
Jean Simmons, *Elmer Gantry*
Elizabeth Taylor, *Butterfield 8*

BEST ACTOR, COMEDY OR MUSICAL

- Jack Lemmon, *The Apartment*
Dirk Bogarde, *Song without End*
Cantinflas, *Pepe*
Cary Grant, *The Grass Is Greener*
Bob Hope, *The Facts of Life*

BEST ACTRESS, COMEDY OR MUSICAL

- Shirley MacLaine, *The Apartment*
Lucille Ball, *Facts of Life*
Capucine, *Song without End*
Judy Holliday, *Bells Are Ringing*
Sophia Loren, *It Started in Naples*

BEST SUPPORTING ACTOR

- Sal Mineo, *Exodus*
Lee Kinsolving, *The Dark at the Top of the Stairs*
Ray Stricklyn, *The Plunderers*
Woody Strode, *Spartacus*
Peter Ustinov, *Spartacus*

BEST SUPPORTING ACTRESS

- Janet Leigh, *Psycho*
Ina Balin, *From the Terrace*
Shirley Jones, *Elmer Gantry*
Shirley Knight, *The Dark at the Top of the Stairs*
Mary Ure, *Sons and Lovers*

MOST PROMISING NEWCOMER—MALE

- Michael Callan
- Mark Damon
- Brett Halsey
Peter Falk
David Janssen
Robert Vaughan

MOST PROMISING NEWCOMER—FEMALE

- Ina Balin
- Nancy Kwan
- Hayley Mills
Jill Hayworth
Shirley Knight
Julie Newmar

Winners

BEST FOREIGN-LANGUAGE FILMS

- *The Man with the Green Carnation* (English language)

- *La Verité* (France)
- *The Virgin Spring* (Sweden)

BEST ORIGINAL SCORE
- Dimitri Tiomkin, *The Alamo*

WORLD FILM FAVORITES
- Tony Curtis
- Rock Hudson
- Gina Lollobrigida

SAMUEL GOLDWYN INTERNATIONAL AWARD
- *Never on Sunday* (Greece)

CECIL B. DEMILLE AWARD
- Fred Astaire

SPECIAL MERIT AWARD
- *The Sundowners*

SPECIAL ACHIEVEMENT AWARDS
- Cantinflas
- Stanley Kramer

WRITERS GUILD OF AMERICA

Awards were presented on March 26, 1961, at the Beverly Hilton Hotel in Los Angeles.

BEST WRITTEN DRAMA
- *Elmer Gantry*, Richard Brooks, based on the novel by Sinclair Lewis

Psycho, Joseph Stefano, based on the novel by Robert Bloch

Sons and Lovers, Gavin Lambert, T. E. B. Clarke, based on the novel by D. H. Lawrence

Spartacus, Dalton Trumbo, based on the novel by Howard Fast

The Sundowners, Isobel Lennart, based on the novel by Jon Cleary

BEST WRITTEN COMEDY
- *The Apartment*, Billy Wilder, I. A. L. Diamond

The Facts of Life, Norman Panama, Melvin Frank

North to Alaska, Martin Rackin, Lee Mahin, Claude Binyon, based on the

play *Birthday Gift* by Laszlo Fodor and an idea by Hans Kafka

Ocean's Eleven, Harry Brown, Charles Lederer, story by George Clayton Johnson and Jack Golden Russell

Please Don't Eat the Daisies, Isobel Lennart, based on the novel by Jean Kerr

BEST WRITTEN MUSICAL
- *Bells Are Ringing*, Betty Comden, Adolph Green

Can-Can, Dorothy Kingsley, Charles Lederer, based on the musical play by Abe Burrows

G.I. Blues, Edmund Beloin, Henry Garson

Let's Make Love, Norman Krasna, Hal Kanter

LAUREL AWARD
- George Seaton

ACADEMY AWARDS

Nominations were announced on February 27, 1961. Awards were presented on April 17 at the Santa Monica Civic Auditorium. The ceremony was telecast by ABC.

BEST PICTURE
- *The Apartment*
The Alamo
Elmer Gantry
Sons and Lovers
The Sundowners

BEST DIRECTOR
- Billy Wilder, *The Apartment*
Jack Cardiff, *Sons and Lovers*
Jules Dassin, *Never on Sunday*
Alfred Hitchcock, *Psycho*
Fred Zinnemann, *The Sundowners*

BEST ACTOR
- Burt Lancaster, *Elmer Gantry*
Trevor Howard, *Sons and Lovers*
Jack Lemmon, *The Apartment*
Laurence Olivier, *The Entertainer*
Spencer Tracy, *Inherit the Wind*

BEST ACTRESS
- Elizabeth Taylor, *Butterfield 8*
Greer Garson, *Sunrise at Campobello*

Deborah Kerr, *The Sundowners*
Shirley MacLaine, *The Apartment*
Melina Mercouri, *Never on Sunday*

BEST SUPPORTING ACTOR

■ Peter Ustinov, *Spartacus*
Peter Falk, *Murder, Inc.*
Jack Kruschen, *The Apartment*
Sal Mineo, *Exodus*
Chill Wills, *The Alamo*

BEST SUPPORTING ACTRESS

■ Shirley Jones, *Elmer Gantry*
Glynis Johns, *The Sundowners*
Shirley Knight, *The Dark at the Top of the Stairs*
Janet Leigh, *Psycho*
Mary Ure, *Sons and Lovers*

BEST ADAPTED SCREENPLAY

■ Richard Brooks, *Elmer Gantry*
T. E. B. Clarke, Gavin Lambert, *Sons and Lovers*
James Kennaway, *Tunes of Glory*
Isobel Lennart, *The Sundowners*
Harold Jacob Smith, Nedrick Young, *Inherit the Wind*

BEST ORIGINAL SCREENPLAY

■ I. A. L. Diamond, Billy Wilder, *The Apartment*
Mon Amour, Marguerite Duras, *Hiroshima*
Michael Craig, Bryan Forbes, Richard Gregson, *The Angry Silence*
Jules Dassin, *Never on Sunday*
Melvin Frank, Norman Panama, *The Facts of Life*

BEST SONG

■ "Never on Sunday," *Never on Sunday*, Manos Hadjidakis
"The Facts of Life," *The Facts of Life*, Johnny Mercer
"Faraway Part of Town," *Pepe*, Andre Previn, Dory Langdon
"The Green Leaves of Summer," *The Alamo*, Dimitri Tiomkin, Paul Francis Webster
"The Second Time Around," *High Time*, Sammy Cahn, James Van Heusen

BEST FOREIGN-LANGUAGE FILM

■ *The Virgin Spring* (Sweden)
Kapo (Italy)
Macario (Mexico)
The Ninth Circle (Yugoslavia)
La Verité (France)

Winners

BEST ART DIRECTION

(BLACK AND WHITE)
■ Alexander Trauner, Edward G. Boyle, *The Apartment*
(COLOR)
■ Alexander Golitzen, Eric Orbom, Russell A. Gausman, Julia Heron, *Spartacus*

BEST CINEMATOGRAPHY

(BLACK AND WHITE)
■ Freddie Francis, *Sons and Lovers*
(COLOR)
■ Russell Metty, *Spartacus*

BEST COSTUME DESIGN

(BLACK AND WHITE)
■ Edith Head, Edward Stevenson, *The Facts of Life*
(COLOR)
■ Bill Thomas, Valles, *Spartacus*

BEST DOCUMENTARY

(FEATURE)
■ *The Horse with the Flying Tail*, Larry Lansburgh
(SHORT SUBJECT)
■ *Giuseppina*, James Hill

BEST FILM EDITING

■ Daniel Mandell, *The Apartment*

BEST MUSIC

(SCORING OF A DRAMATIC OR COMEDY PICTURE)
■ Ernest Gold, *Exodus*
(SCORING OF A MUSICAL PICTURE)
■ Morris Stoloff, Harry Sukman, *Song without End*

SCIENTIFIC OR TECHNICAL AWARDS

Class II (Plaque)
■ Ampex Professional Products Co.
Class III (Certificate)
■ Arthur Holcomb, Petro Vlahos, Columbia Studio Camera Dept.; Anthony Paglia,

Twentieth Century-Fox Studio
Mechanical Effects Dept.; Carl Hauge,
Robert Grubel, Edward Reichard

BEST SHORT SUBJECT
(CARTOON)
- *Munro*

(LIVE ACTION)
- *Day of the Painter*

BEST SOUND
- Gordon E. Sawyer, Fred Hynes, *The Alamo*

BEST SPECIAL EFFECTS
- Tim Baar, Gene Warren, *The Time Machine*

JEAN HERSHOLT HUMANITARIAN AWARD
- Sol Lesser

HONORARY AWARDS
- Gary Cooper
- Stan Laurel
- Hayley Mills

▪ 1961 ▪

West Side *Glory*

The National Board of Review made a questionable pick for best pic— *Question 7*, a West German production described by *The New York Times* as "a propaganda film produced under the auspices of the Lutheran Church dealing with an East German youth torn between his religion and his desire for education in a Communist satellite." Board topper Henry Hart explained that it focused on "the most important theme of the twentieth century, to wit, the encroachment of the State into the realm of the individual."

The New York Film Critics also startled award watchers by naming, for the first time in the group's 27-year history, a musical— *West Side Story*. "To have done otherwise would have been criminal," insisted *Times* critic Bosley Crowther, who failed to report that a felony had nonetheless been committed by his peers in the New York Drama Critics Circle—plus the Tony Award voters—in 1957, when they snubbed the Broadway tuner in favor of *The Music Man*. But plaudits finally caught up with the show when the $6 million screen rendition was made in 1961—it was hailed by the *Times* as a "masterpiece" and by *Variety* as being "beautifully mounted, powerful, fascinating and impressive."

West Side Story's chief rival for top pic was *Judgment at Nuremberg*, scribe Abby Mann's big-screen adaptation of his TV drama about the trial of Nazis after World War II. *Variety* said the new version was "twice the size of the concise, stirring and rewarding production on television's *Playhouse 90* early in 1959." It featured three male leads—Maximilian Schell as a German defense attorney, Spencer Tracy as the postwar judge and Burt Lancaster as a Nazi—plus lots of satellite stars in cameos, including Judy Garland, Marlene Dietrich and Montgomery Clift. Crowther cheered

Sophia Loren's Italian-lingo role in *Two Women* was hailed by Cannes, N.Y. crix and Oscar voters.

Schell for doing "an absolutely gladiatorial job of projecting the skill, the passion and the courage of a strong, intensive man." *Variety* agreed: "Schell repeats the role he originated on TV with electric effect."

Schell led the crix's vote for Best Actor on the first ballot with four votes, followed by three for Paul Newman (*The Hustler*) and two for James Cagney (*One, Two, Three*). The National Board of Review's choice, Albert Finney (*Saturday Night and Sunday Morning*), scored only a single endorsement. Schell finally won on the sixth round when a simple majority of votes was needed instead of the two-thirds canvass required earlier.

Contacted afterward by the *Times*, Schell said, "I thought Spence (Spencer Tracy) would get the award." He admitted to being "scared" because winning the crix's honor "puts me on a peak and now I can only go down the mountain."

In the race for Best Actress, it also took six rounds for the journos to do what they'd never done before: hail the star of a foreign-language film. Sophia Loren had made many U.S. movies earlier in her career, but, tired of being regarded as a sex idol, she fled Hollywood for her native Italy in 1960 in order to do such serious work as Vittorio De Sica's *Two Women*, about a mother's failure to shield her daughter from the horrors of war. The film received wide release in the United States after Loren won the Best Actress laurel at Cannes and was quickly discovered by large audiences when it was denounced as "smut" by *The Saturday Evening Post* and other conservative voices. When the New York Film Critics honored the film for its artistic merits, Loren told the *Times* that her award was "the most exciting and wonderful news of my life."

Loren's toughest competish had been Geraldine Page (*Summer and Smoke*), who tied her with four votes on the first ballot, then trailed her by a score of 11 to 4 on the final round. "Not until after all the votes were counted did his colleagues learn that Joseph Mogenstern, film critic of the *Herald-Tribune*, who voted steadily for Piper Laurie as the best actress of the year, was engaged to her," the *Daily News* revealed. "They will be married Jan. 21, the day after the awards will be presented at a reception at Sardi's."

Two Women lost the kudos for Best Foreign Film by an overwhelming vote to Federico Fellini's *La Dolce Vita*, the art house sensation that had claimed the Palme d'Or at Cannes. Crowther called the crix's choice a "selection that could not conceivably have been avoided" since it was "one of the great films of all time."

In deciding the director's prize, the film crix leapt over *West Side Story*, no doubt because of the murky issue of who really helmed it. Several months after cameras started to roll, producer Robert Wise took over the megger's reins from Jerome Robbins, who'd originally staged it on Broad-

way. Crowther insisted that the crix "showed rare discrimination in voting the difficult award to Robert Rossen for *The Hustler*, although it was not even mentioned in the voting for the Best Picture award."

The Directors Guild of America didn't shy from embracing *West Side Story*, however, and the org bravely decreed that its prize should go to both Wise and Robbins. Luckily for the guild, it still had separate, simultaneous galas, which enabled Robbins to accept his kudos in New York—far away from the man who fired him, who took his bow in L.A.

The atmosphere was much more relaxed at the Writers Guild gala when *West Side Story* was proclaimed Best Written Musical. In fact, honoree Ernest Lehman helped to lighten the air by participating in the award show's bawdy entertainment. Several skits lambasted producers for lensing their pics overseas in order to avoid paying for union labor. The evening's finale was a song with the lyrics: "Spain is cheaper / The weather's sunny / Just bring Chuck Heston and money."

Attending the Golden Globes banquet was relatively cheap at $25 per couple. More than 1,000 people paid up in order to be in the ballroom at the Beverly Hilton Hotel for the program emceed by Steve Allen.

Judgment at Nuremberg led with the most bids (six), followed by *West Side Story* (five), but an upset was scored for Best Drama Picture by *The Guns of Navarone*, the year's top-grossing film, which earned Columbia $12.5 million in 1961 against the studio's $6 million investment. *Variety* approved of the celluloid result, calling the World War II cliffhanger a "winner" full of "nail-biting highlights." *Nuremberg*'s Stanley Kramer outgunned *Navarone*'s J. Lee Thompson for Best Director, however, and star Maximilian Schell reaped the accolade for Best Drama Actor.

A Majority of One claimed a trio of

> **West Side Story was the first musical named Best Picture by the N.Y. crix.**

awards: Best Comedy, Best Motion Picture Promoting International Understanding and Best Comedy/Musical Actress for Rosalind Russell as a Brooklyn widow who falls in love with a Tokyo widower during a trip to Japan. Accepting her fourth career Globe, Russell thanked the thesp who won a Tony Award for originating the role on Broadway, saying, "I share this award with Gertrude Berg."

West Side Story was the easy winner of Best Musical, but its stars scored mixed results. Richard Beymer, who portrayed Natalie Wood's forbidden Romeo, lost his bid for Best Actor in a Comedy or Musical to Glenn Ford (*Pocket full of Miracles*), but he beat costar George Chakiris to be named one of the year's Most Promising New Male Stars along with Warren Beatty and Bobby Darin. (George C. Scott was among the other losers.) Chakiris nonetheless prevailed as Best Supporting Actor for his cocky portrayal of a street gang leader in love with Best Supporting Actress champ Rita Moreno.

Moreno beat Judy Garland (*Judgment at Nuremberg*), who received the Cecil B. DeMille Award as a consolation prize. *Variety*'s reporter seemed irked that Garland took so long to claim it: "When her name was called, she bussed her hubby, then everyone along the path to the stage and it appeared for a time that she wouldn't make it." Part of her grandstanding was pure show: soon after the ceremony she announced that she and hubby Sid Luft were getting a divorce.

Garland's giddy display was upstaged by Marilyn Monroe, who was chosen a World Film Favorite by a poll of movie-goers for the second time in her career. *Variety* reported, "Monroe wafted onto the stage and, giggling, accepted her award in a manner that was more a burlesque of MM than the real thing. She was happy, happy, happy!"

The ceremony, broadcast by local station WTTV, was dismissed as "a night to forget"

West Side's two helmers accepted their guild kudos on different coasts.

by *Variety* even though the fete included the presentation of a special honorary award to *Variety* columnist Army Archerd. Other media denounced it so scathingly that the foreign press group's prexy, Swedish scribe Ingrid Clairmont, resigned the next day.

Controversy reigned at the Oscars, too, when "there was picketing by the Hollywood Race Relations Group, a minor disturbance which resulted in 10 arrests," *Variety* reported. "One picket bearing a sign, 'All Negroes Want a Break,' made a dash for the foyer as Johnny Mathis was entering, and was immediately surrounded by a dozen policemen and evicted."

There was little other excitement in front of the Santa Monica Civic Auditorium on Oscar night as most leading nominees arrived late—like Natalie Wood, who dashed inside on the arm of Warren Beatty—or didn't show up at all.

The most noisy no-show was George C. Scott, who dismissed the awards derby as "a weird beauty or personality contest" and asked the academy to withdraw his name as a Best Supporting Actor contender for *The Hustler*. The academy refused, informing Scott that it was his perf, not him, that was nommed. Oscarcast host Bob Hope referred to the hubbub in his intro remarks, asking the audience, "How 'bout that George C. Scott? He's sitting at home with his back to the TV set!"

Other top contenders were missing, too. *Variety* reported: "Audrey Hepburn, who was in from Switzerland, was bedded with flu in her BevHills Hotel room; Judy Garland also remained at the hotel with her son Joey, ill with an ear infection. Sophia Loren, who was expected, stayed in Rome with a case of nerves."

"I could not bear the ordeal of sitting in plain view of millions of viewers while my fate was being judged," Loren confessed in her memoirs years later. "If I lost, I might faint from disappointment. If I won, I would also very likely faint with joy. I decided it would be better to faint at home."

Loren had every reason to be jittery. No nominee had ever won for a non-English-speaking role and she was up against tough competish: past champ Audrey Hepburn (as bubbly bohemian Holly Golightly in Truman Capote's *Breakfast at Tiffany's*), her foe at the New York film crix vote Geraldine Page (as a tortured spinster in Tennessee Williams's *Summer and Smoke*), Piper Laurie (as Paul Newman's boozy bride in *The Hustler*) and Natalie Wood (as a Hispanic Juliet in modern-day New York in *West Side Story*).

Loren stayed up all night fretting about the outcome, then finally gave up on the race at dawn and went to bed, assuming she'd lost. Soon afterward she was wakened by a telephone call from Cary Grant, who told her she won.

"*Mama mia!* What a day!" Loren roared later when reporters besieged her with phone calls, but *Variety* missed witnessing her emotional response at the Oscar show, griping, "The audience was cheated of what is traditionally the show's most dramatic moment—the reaction of the winner of the Best Actress award."

Only two of the contenders for Best Actor were present, including Paul Newman, who was optimistic that he might prevail for portraying a savvy pool shark in *The Hustler*. His wife, Joanne Woodward, told *Variety*, "He feels it's the best thing he's ever done." Newman competed against the absent Spencer Tracy, who, according to *Variety*, was rooting for his *Judgment at Nuremberg* costar Maximilian Schell, an Oscar rookie. When Schell won, the Swiss-born thesp repeated the sentiments he had expressed after winning the New York film crix's tribute, saying, "This honors not only me, but the cast and that great old man who has been nominated for the eighth time now, Spencer Tracy." When the winner headed backstage, he looked stunned and told the press, "I thought Paul Newman would win!"

Judgment at Nuremberg tied *West Side Story* for having the most Oscar noms over all: 11. In addition to the actor's gold, it also scored the kudos for Best Screenplay, which was claimed by Gotham film crix honoree

Backstage at the Oscars, from left: champs George Chakiris, Greer Garson (accepting for Sophia Loren), Rita Moreno and Maximilian Schell.

Abby Mann, "who thanked producer Stanley Kramer and, by first name, each star of the cast of the film," *Variety* observed.

Judy Garland was expected to win Best Supporting Actress for her edgy role in *Nuremberg* as a gentile once jailed for the crime of befriending Jews. When Moreno pulled off an upset, *Variety* described the champ as being the night's "most emotional recipient" as she "floated down the aisle in a happy daze, and breathlessly told the audience, 'I can't believe it! Good lord! I leave you with that' . . . She came off stage muttering to herself, 'I still can't believe it. I thought Judy would win!'"

Moreno's and Chikiris's victories joined a string of other wins for *West Side Story* that included kudos for its musical score, cinematography, art direction, costume design, editing and sound. It looked like a sweep in the works, but the screen tuner faced a troubling omen looming over one of the upper races.

Several days before Oscar ballots were due, the academy's Board of Governors announced that *Nuremberg*'s helmer Stanley Kramer would receive the Irving Thalberg Award. Kramer was also a contender for Best Director and *Variety* said that the gesture "raises a basic question of ethics and, perhaps, even a suspicion that the Board of Governors is unwittingly misusing their influence."

Just in case the accusation proved true, the governors made a special point of bestowing a special honorary award upon Best Director contender Jerome Robbins, who helmed and choreographed the original Broadway show before being axed from the film by producer Robert Wise. It was an unnecessary precaution: Robbins and Wise both won the director's award—becoming the first co-champs in that category. Neither victor referred to the other in his acceptance speech.

Wise alone claimed the prize for Best Picture, saying, "It's been a wonderfully exciting evening for *West Side Story*." It was also nearly an historic evening in terms of its awards bounty. *West Side Story* took 10 competitive trophies in all—one short of the record held by *Ben-Hur*. The vote outcome was also noteworthy because it marked only the fourth time that the Academy Awards agreed with the New York film critics on the top three categories of Best Picture, Best Actor and Actress.

Variety groused about the movie's Oscar sweep: "The music drama dominated the awards to a degree that left little suspense. Vet press observers of Oscar events agreed this one was on the dull side. Only excitement was occasioned by the stage-crasher."

The excitement occurred when Shelley Winters and Vince Edwards were interrupted by a mysterious man as they presented the cinematography awards. "Wearing evening clothes befitting the occasion, he mumbled into the mike that he was the world's greatest gate-crasher and that he had a statuette for emcee Bob Hope, for a pic he made in 1938," *Variety* reported. "The uninvited guest had the presenters and everyone else so surprised nobody gave him the hook."

Soon after the hoaxer left the stage, Bob Hope told the audience, "Who needs Price Waterhouse? All we need is a doorman!" The Tony Awards would need one, too. The hoaxer—identified later as Brooklyn resident Stan Berman—would crash the Broadway kudofest next.

▪ 1961 ▪

NATIONAL BOARD OF REVIEW

Winners were announced on December 19, 1961.

BEST PICTURE
▪ *Question 7*
The Hustler
West Side Story
The Innocents
The Hoodlum Priest
Summer and Smoke
The Young Doctors
Judgment at Nuremberg
One, Two, Three
Fanny

BEST DIRECTOR
▪ Jack Clayton, *The Innocents*

BEST ACTOR
▪ Albert Finney, *Saturday Night and Sunday Morning*

BEST ACTRESS
▪ Geraldine Page, *Summer and Smoke*

BEST SUPPORTING ACTOR
▪ Jackie Gleason, *The Hustler*

BEST SUPPORTING ACTRESS
▪ Ruby Dee, *A Raisin in the Sun*

BEST FOREIGN FILM
▪ *The Bridge* (Federal Republic of Germany)
La Dolce Vita (Italy/France)
Two Women (Italy/France)
Saturday Night and Sunday Morning (U.K.)
A Summer to Remember (U.S.S.R.)

NEW YORK FILM CRITICS

Winners were announced on December 28, 1961. Awards were presented on January 20, 1962, at Sardi's restaurant in New York.

BEST PICTURE
▪ *West Side Story*

BEST DIRECTOR
▪ Robert Rossen, *The Hustler*

BEST ACTOR
- Maximilian Schell, *Judgment at Nuremberg*

BEST ACTRESS
- Sophia Loren, *Two Women*

BEST SCREENPLAY
- Abby Mann, *Judgment at Nuremberg*

BEST FOREIGN FILM
- *La Dolce Vita* (Italy)

DIRECTORS GUILD OF AMERICA

The initial list of nominees was narrowed down to a group of finalists who competed for the Best Director award, bestowed on February 10, 1962. Dual ceremonies were held at the Beverly Hilton Hotel in Los Angeles and the Waldorf-Astoria Hotel in New York.

BEST DIRECTOR
- Jerome Robbins, Robert E. Wise, *West Side Story*

Marlon Brando, *One-Eyed Jacks*
Frank Capra, *Pocketful of Miracles*
Jack Clayton, *The Innocents*
Blake Edwards, *Breakfast at Tiffany's* (finalist)
Peter Glenville, *Summer and Smoke*
John Huston, *The Misfits*
Elia Kazan, *Splendor in the Grass*
Henry Koster, *Flower Drum Song*
Stanley Kramer, *Judgment at Nuremberg* (finalist)
Philip Leacock, *Hand in Hand*
Mervyn LeRoy, *A Majority of One*
Joshua Logan, *Fanny*
Anthony Mann, *El Cid*
Robert Mulligan, *The Great Impostor*
Daniel Petrie, *A Raisin in the Sun*
Robert Rossen, *The Hustler* (finalist)
Robert Stevenson, *The Absent-Minded Professor*
J. Lee Thompson, *The Guns of Navarone* (finalist)
Peter Ustinov, *Romanoff and Juliet*
William Wyler, *The Children's Hour*

GOLDEN GLOBES

Nominations were announced on January 31, 1962. Awards were presented on March 5 at the Beverly Hilton Hotel in Los Angeles. The ceremony was telecast on L.A. station KTTV.

BEST DRAMA PICTURE
- *The Guns of Navarone*

El Cid
Fanny
Judgment at Nuremberg
Splendor in the Grass

BEST COMEDY PICTURE
- *A Majority of One*

Breakfast at Tiffany's
One, Two, Three
The Parent Trap
Pocketful of Miracles

BEST MUSICAL PICTURE
- *West Side Story*

Babes in Toyland
Flower Drum Song

BEST MOTION PICTURE PROMOTING INTERNATIONAL UNDERSTANDING
- *A Majority of One*

Bridge to the Sun
Judgment at Nuremberg

BEST DIRECTOR
- Stanley Kramer, *Judgment at Nuremberg*

Anthony Mann, *El Cid*
J. Lee Thompson, *The Guns of Navarone*
Robert Wise, Jerome Robbins, *West Side Story*
William Wyler, *The Children's Hour*

BEST ACTOR, DRAMA
- Maximilian Schell, *Judgment at Nuremberg*

Warren Beatty, *Splendor in the Grass*
Maurice Chevalier, *Fanny*
Paul Newman, *The Hustler*
Sidney Poitier, *Raisin in the Sun*

BEST ACTRESS, DRAMA
- Geraldine Page, *Summer and Smoke*

Leslie Caron, *Fanny*

Shirley MacLaine, *The Children's Hour*
Claudia McNeil, *Raisin in the Sun*
Natalie Wood, *Splendor in the Grass*

BEST ACTOR, COMEDY OR MUSICAL

- Glenn Ford, *Pocketful of Miracles*
Fred Astaire, *The Pleasure of His Company*
Richard Beymer, *West Side Story*
Bob Hope, *Bachelor in Paradise*
Fred MacMurray, *The Absent-Minded Professor*

BEST ACTRESS, COMEDY OR MUSICAL

- Rosalind Russell, *A Majority of One*
Bette Davis, *Pocketful of Miracles*
Audrey Hepburn, *Breakfast at Tiffany's*
Hayley Mills, *The Parent Trap*
Miyoshi Umeki, *Flower Drum Song*

BEST SUPPORTING ACTOR

- George Chakiris, *West Side Story*
Montgomery Clift, *Judgment at Nuremberg*
Jackie Gleason, *The Hustler*
Tony Randall, *Lover Come Back*
George C. Scott, *The Hustler*

BEST SUPPORTING ACTRESS

- Rita Moreno, *West Side Story*
Fay Bainter, *The Children's Hour*
Judy Garland, *Judgment at Nuremberg*
Lotte Lenya, *The Roman Spring of Mrs. Stone*
Pamela Tiffin, *One, Two, Three*

MOST PROMISING NEWCOMER—MALE

- Warren Beatty
- Richard Beymer
- Bobby Darin
George Chakiris
George C. Scott

MOST PROMISING NEWCOMER—FEMALE

- Ann-Margret
- Jane Fonda
- Christine Kaufmann
Pamela Tiffin
Cordula Trantow

Winners

BEST FOREIGN-LANGUAGE FILM

- *Two Women* (Italy)

SILVER GLOBES

- *Animas Tru Jano* (Mexico)
- *The Good Soldier Schweik* (Germany)

BEST ORIGINAL SCORE

- Dimitri Tiomkin, *The Guns of Navarone*

BEST SONG

- "Town without Pity," *Town without Pity*

WORLD FILM FAVORITES

- Charlton Heston
- Marilyn Monroe

SAMUEL GOLDWYN INTERNATIONAL AWARD

- *The Mark*

CECIL B. DEMILLE AWARD

- Judy Garland

SPECIAL MERIT AWARD

- Samuel Bronston, *El Cid*

SPECIAL JOURNALISTIC MERIT AWARD

- Army Archerd, *Daily Variety*
- Mike Connolly, *Hollywood Reporter*

WRITERS GUILD OF AMERICA

Awards were presented on March 15, 1962, at the Hollywood Palladium.

BEST WRITTEN DRAMA

- *The Hustler*, Sidney Carroll, Robert Rossen, based on the novel by Walter Tevis
Fanny, Julius Epstein, based on the play by S. N. Behrman and Joshua Logan, adapted from the plays of Marcel Pagnol
The Innocents, William Archibald, Truman Capote, based on William Archibald's dramatization of the novel *The Turn of the Screw* by Henry James
Judgment at Nuremberg, Abby Mann
A Raisin in the Sun, Lorraine Hansberry

BEST WRITTEN COMEDY

- *Breakfast at Tiffany's*, George Axelrod, based on the novella by Truman Capote
The Absent-Minded Professor, Bill Walsh,

based on the short story "A Situation of Gravity" by Samuel W. Taylor

A Majority of One, Leonard Spigelgass

One, Two, Three, Billy Wilder, I. A. L. Diamond, based on the play by Ferenc Molnar

The Parent Trap, David Swift, based on the novel *Das Doppelte Lottchen* by Erich Kastner

BEST WRITTEN MUSICAL

- *West Side Story*, Ernest Lehman, based on the musical by Arthur Laurents

Babes in Toyland, Ward Kimball, Lowell Hawley, based on the operetta by Victor Herbert and Glenn MacDonough

Blue Hawaii, Hal Kanter, story by Allan Weiss

Flower Drum Song, Joseph Fields, based on the novel by C. Y. Lee and the musical by Rodgers and Hammerstein

Snow White and the Three Stooges, Noel Langley, Elwood Ullman, story by Charles Wick

LAUREL AWARD

- Philip Dunne

VALENTINE DAVIES AWARD

- Mary McCall, Jr.

ACADEMY AWARDS

Nominations were announced on February 26, 1962. Awards were presented on April 9 at the Santa Monica Civic Auditorium. The ceremony was telecast by ABC.

BEST PICTURE

- *West Side Story*
Fanny
The Guns of Navarone
The Hustler
Judgment at Nuremberg

BEST DIRECTOR

- Jerome Robbins, Robert Wise, *West Side Story*
Federico Fellini, *La Dolce Vita*
Stanley Kramer, *Judgment at Nuremberg*
Robert Rossen, *The Hustler*
J. Lee Thompson, *The Guns of Navarone*

BEST ACTOR

- Maximilian Schell, *Judgment at Nuremberg*
Charles Boyer, *Fanny*
Paul Newman, *The Hustler*
Spencer Tracy, *Judgment at Nuremberg*
Stuart Whitman, *The Mark*

BEST ACTRESS

- Sophia Loren, *Two Women*
Audrey Hepburn, *Breakfast at Tiffany's*
Piper Laurie, *The Hustler*
Geraldine Page, *Summer and Smoke*
Natalie Wood, *Splendor in the Grass*

BEST SUPPORTING ACTOR

- George Chakiris, *West Side Story*
Montgomery Clift, *Judgment at Nuremberg*
Peter Falk, *Pocketful of Miracles*
Jackie Gleason, *The Hustler*
George C. Scott, *The Hustler*

BEST SUPPORTING ACTRESS

- Rita Moreno, *West Side Story*
Fay Bainter, *The Children's Hour*
Judy Garland, *Judgment at Nuremberg*
Lotte Lenya, *The Roman Spring of Mrs. Stone*
Una Merkel, *Summer and Smoke*

BEST ADAPTED SCREENPLAY

- Abby Mann, *Judgment at Nuremberg*
George Axelrod, *Breakfast at Tiffany's*
Sidney Carroll, Robert Rossen, *The Hustler*
Carl Foreman, *The Guns of Navarone*
Ernest Lehman, *West Side Story*

BEST ORIGINAL SCREENPLAY

- William Inge, *Splendor in the Grass*
Sergio Amidei, Diego Fabbri, Indro Montanelli, *General Della Rovere*
Grigori Chukhrai, Valentin Yoshov, *Ballad of a Soldier*
Federico Fellini, Ennio Flaiano, Tullio Pinelli, Brunello Rondi, *La Dolce Vita*
Paul Henning, Stanley Shapiro, *Lover Come Back*

BEST SONG

- "Bachelor in Paradise," *Bachelor in Paradise*, Mack David, Henry Mancini

"Love Theme from *El Cid* (The Falcon and the Dove)," *El Cid*, Miklos Rozsa, Paul Francis Webster

"Moon River," *Breakfast at Tiffany's*, Henry Mancini, Johnny Mercer

"Pocketful of Miracles," *Pocketful of Miracles*, Sammy Cahn, James Van Heusen

"Town without Pity," *Town without Pity*, Dimitri Tiomkin, Ned Washington

BEST FOREIGN-LANGUAGE FILM
- *Through a Glass Darkly* (Sweden)

Harry and the Butler (Denmark)
Immortal Love (Japan)
The Important Man (Mexico)
Placido (Spain)

Winners

BEST ART DIRECTION
(BLACK AND WHITE)
- Harry Horner, Gene Callahan, *The Hustler*

(COLOR)
- Boris Leven, Victor A. Gangelin, *West Side Story*

BEST CINEMATOGRAPHY
(BLACK AND WHITE)
- Eugen Shuftan, *The Hustler*

(COLOR)
- Daniel L. Fapp, *West Side Story*

BEST COSTUME DESIGN
(BLACK AND WHITE)
- Piero Gherardi, *La Dolce Vita*

(COLOR)
- Irene Sharaff, *West Side Story*

BEST DOCUMENTARY
(FEATURE)
- *Le Ciel et La Boue (Sky Above and Mud Beneath)*, Arthur Cohn, Rene Lafuite

(SHORT SUBJECT)
- *Project Hope*, Frank P. Bibas

BEST FILM EDITING
- Thomas Stanford, *West Side Story*

BEST MUSIC
(SCORING OF A DRAMATIC OR COMEDY PICTURE)
- Henry Mancini, *Breakfast at Tiffany's*

(SCORING OF A MUSICAL PICTURE)
- Saul Chaplin, Johnny Green, Irwin Kostal, Sid Ramin, *West Side Story*

SCIENTIFIC OR TECHNICAL AWARDS
Class II (Plaque)
- Sylvania Electric Products; James Dale, S. Wilson, H. E. Rice, John Rude, Laurie Atkin, Wadsworth E. Pohl, H. Peasgood, Technicolor Corp.; E. I. Sponable, Herbert E. Braff, Twentieth Century-Fox; F. D. Leslie, R. D. Whitemore, A. A. Alden, Endel Pool, James B. Gordon, Deluxe Laboratories

Class III (Certificate)
- Hurletron, Inc., Electric Eye Equipment Division; Wadsworth E. Pohl, Technicolor Corp.

BEST SHORT SUBJECT
(CARTOON)
- *Ersatz (The Substitute)*

(LIVE ACTION)
- *Seawards the Great Ships*

BEST SOUND
- Gordon E. Sawyer, Fred Hynes, *West Side Story*

BEST SPECIAL EFFECTS
- Vivian C. Greenham, Bill Warrington, *The Guns of Navarone*

IRVING G. THALBERG MEMORIAL AWARD
- Stanley Kramer

JEAN HERSHOLT HUMANITARIAN AWARD
- George Seaton

HONORARY AWARDS
- Fred L. Metzler
- Jerome Robbins
- William L. Hendricks

· 1962 ·

Lawrence *of Hollywood*

The Oscars and Golden Globes were on their own this year—they'd get no hints of what to pick as the best pics and perfs from the New York film critics. A Manhattan newspaper strike ended up pulling off what Hollywood studio execs never could: gagging movies' haughtiest opinion setters.

But that didn't stop scribe Bosley Crowther from ballyhooing his own choices in an article published in a strike-defying edition of *The New York Times*. "The best film of the year, in our opinion, was *A Taste of Honey*," he insisted, referring to the British drama about a lower-class white girl who gets pregnant by a black cook. "No doubt a few New York critics, to judge by their radiocast reviews, are going to show partiality towards *Lawrence of Arabia*," he growled, dismissing it as "a lot of sand and fury signifying little or nothing about Lawrence." But others disagreed, including *Variety*, which hailed the $15 million epic as "a king-size adventure yarn" about the campaign of British intelligence officer T. E. Lawrence to help the Arabs achieve independence from the Turks in World War I. Columnist Army Archerd cheered "a new star on the horizon—Peter O'Toole—and there's no question he's to be one!"

A rival, year-end blockbuster was the National Board of Review's choice for Best Picture—*The Longest Day*, described by *Variety* as "a stunning war epic. From personal vignettes to big battles, it details the first day of the D-Day landings by the Allies on June 6, 1944. The use of over 43 actual star names in bit and pivotal spots helps keep up the aura of fictionalized documentary." The $10 million production employed an additional 100 actors, 400 actual U.S. Army troops—and three directors hired and fired by maverick producer Darryl F. Zanuck, who ended up lensing much of the pic himself.

Variety predicted a bright future for Peter O'Toole, star of Oscar and Globe Best Picture *Lawrence of Arabia*.

The battle over who really helmed *The Longest Day* led to a sweep of kudos victories for its noncontroversial rival—*Lawrence*'s David Lean, who claimed the Directors Guild of America's top prize five years after being honored for *The Bridge on the River Kwai*. *Variety* noted that Lean confronted "much hardship and incredible logistics" over three years while battling the harsh sun and unruly sands of the Sudan and Saudi Arabia. *Lawrence*'s script, by Robert Bolt and Michael Wilson, wasn't nominated for a Writers Guild award, but the pic was nonetheless lampooned in a skit performed at the guild's kudos ceremony. *Lawrence* received a mock award for "stimulating Hollywood film production," which was accepted by José Ferrer portraying an emissary of Egyptian President Nasser. *Variety* reported that the emissary "remarked pic seen here is 'just the trailer . . . they're still shooting over there.'

Everybody is in the pic. It looked like Saturday night at P. J.'s,' cracked Ferrer. He ended with a mock message from Nasser: 'Come to our happy country on the banks of the Nile . . . all of you. But buy a one-way ticket. Your people have always walked home. Shalom.' "

Lawrence of Arabia was also the heavy favorite going into the Golden Globes, where it led with seven nominations. It reaped five wins: Best Drama Picture, Best Director, color cinematography and two golden orbs for its thesp hailed by Louella Parsons as "the new Valentino"—Omar Sharif, winner of Best Supporting Actor and Most Promising New Male Star.

In the race for Best Actor, Peter O'Toole's flashy perf was upstaged by the low-key screen work of Gregory Peck in *To Kill a Mockingbird*, a role described by *Variety* as "a wise, gentle, soft-spoken Alabama lawyer entrusted with the formidable dual chore of defending a Negro falsely accused of rape while raising his own impressionable, imaginative, motherless children."

Most surprising, though, was the outcome of the showdown over Best Drama Actress, which pitted two feisty veteran thesps against each other—Bette Davis and Katharine Hepburn—neither of whom had ever won a Globe.

Actually, Hepburn hadn't won any awards since her 1940 scroll from the New York Film Critics for *The Philadelphia Story* and her 1933 Oscar for *Morning Glory*. She'd been nominated for several Academy Awards and Golden Globes since, but when she recoiled from the races, she didn't receive what she obviously didn't want. Now she had her old awards appetite whetted, though, when her role as Eugene O'Neill's morphine-addicted mother in *Long Day's Journey into Night* was honored along with her costars' work at the Cannes Film Festival. As the Globe and Oscar races began, columnist Sheilah Graham was startled: "Hepburn, almost as much of a recluse

as Garbo, is almost as accessible as Zsa Zsa Gabor. She'd love to win!"

But no star wanted to win more than Bette Davis, whose career was suddenly resurrected by her gutsy portrayal of a grotesque ex-vaudeville star who, *Variety* noted, "runs unfettered through all the stages of oncoming insanity" in *What Ever Happened to Baby Jane? Variety* applauded Davis, but gave the film's best review to costar Joan Crawford, "who gives a quiet, remarkably fine interpretation" of the crippled sister tortured and taunted by Davis. Crawford failed to reap a Globe or Oscar bid, however. Rumors persisted that she was irked by the snubs, but Crawford denied it publicly while continuing to take playful swipes at Davis that extended their feud, which had began during filming.

While everyone awaited a fierce showdown between Davis and Hepburn at the Globes, a true shocker took place: an upset was scored by another veteran thesp, Geraldine Page, who was honored for her screen adaptation of the role she had originated on Broadway in Tennessee Williams's *Sweet Bird of Youth*. *Variety* praised her: "This is Page's picture. Her portrayal of the fading actress seeking substitute reality in drink and sex is a histrionic classic."

Gregory Peck claimed the actor's statuette for *To Kill a Mockingbird*. The equivalent kudos for comedy/musical thesps went to Marcello Mastroianni for what *Variety* called his "imaginative performance" as a man who murders his wife in *Divorce—Italian Style*. Rosalind Russell won her fifth career Globe as a stripper's controlling stage mom in *Gypsy*, which lost Best Musical Picture to the screen rendition of another Broadway tuner, *The Music Man*. Winner of Best Comedy was the same film honored by the writers' guild as top laffer—*That Touch of Mink*, described by *Variety* as "Cary Grant and Doris Day in coy he-she-nanigans."

> # There were no crix kudos due to a Gotham newspaper strike.

As the Oscar showdown loomed, a few top races already seemed locked up. *Lawrence of Arabia* led with the most noms—10—and looked like a cinch for Best Picture and Best Director, but awards watchers wondered: could Peter O'Toole pull off an upset over Gregory Peck for Best Actor if *Lawrence* sweeps the night? *Variety* columnist Army Archerd reported that *Lawrence* producer Sam Spiegel prepared for the possibility by trying to free O'Toole up from his commitment to do a play in the U.K. long enough to attend the Oscar show: "Sam Spiegel tried to buy out the London 'Baal' house to spring Peter O'Toole, but sez it was impossible to reach patrons to give 'em refunds. Spiegel sez, 'Peter is too conscientious to have walked out of the play for anything.' "

Another acting nominee who performed on a distant stage on Oscar night had no qualms about missing the awards show. Anne Bancroft was nommed for her role in *The Miracle Worker* as Annie Sullivan, the devoted mentor who tamed wild child Helen Keller and taught her how to communicate with a world she couldn't see or hear. On Oscar night, Bancroft appeared in *Mother Courage* on Broadway and felt no need to jilt her audiences to be with the same Hollywood crowd who'd previously denied her the screen role in *Two for the Seesaw* after she won a Tony Award for creating the role on stage. After she snagged another Tony for *The Miracle Worker*, she and costar Patty Duke managed to make the leap from Broadway to the screen at last only because the producers couldn't afford name stars.

Bancroft wasn't considered a serious contender against the big-name stars up for Best Actress. Bette Davis's toughest challenges seemed to come from Katharine Hepburn and Geraldine Page. Davis's *Baby Jane* costar Joan Crawford was snubbed by Oscar voters just as she'd been snubbed by Globe voters, but she was still poised to make trouble: She lined up commitments from the absent nominees to accept on their behalf in case any of them beat Davis.

Davis was skedded to present the writing awards on Oscar night and arrived at the Santa Monica Civic Auditorium long before the grandstands filled up outside. "Many fans loudly expressed disappointment that nominee Bette Davis had already been in the theater several hours," *Variety* reported. They apparently missed sight of her later as she occasionally stepped outside for fresh air after fainting backstage from what she insisted was the flu, not the jitters.

Back in 1945, Joan Crawford had claimed to suffer from the flu, too, when she accepted her Oscar for *Mildred Pierce* while remaining in bed at home. Seventeen years later she appeared calm and cool as she lingered on the red carpet outside the Oscar ceremony—dressed in a silver gown and what *Variety* called "her old diamonds of 20 years"—and signed autographs for eager fans. Like Davis, she was also an awards presenter, but Crawford arrived casually with the other stars close to the ceremony's starting time. In addition to Bancroft, Katharine Hepburn—who no longer seemed interested in the race—was also absent, but Crawford was ready to accept for either one of them in case of a surprise victory.

Later that night, when the Best Actress award was to be presented, both Crawford and Davis waited in separate backstage dressing rooms, smoking furiously. Then, *Variety* reported, "Anne Bancroft, not regarded as the hottest prospect to win, did it." *TV Guide* described the scene that followed: "Joan instantly stood erect—shoulders back, neck straight, head up. She stamped out her cigarette butt, grabbed the hand of the stage manager, who blurted afterward that she 'practically broke all my fingers with her strength.' Then she soared calmly on stage with that incomparable Crawford composure. Backstage, Bette bit her cigarette and seemed

> *Lawrence of Arabia* was snubbed (and skewered) by the writers' guild.

to stop breathing. Joan was out there; suddenly it was her night."

At the podium, Crawford read a note from Bancroft, who cited the names of *Miracle Worker*'s producer, director and writer: "Here's my little speech. Dear Joan: There are three reasons why I won this award—Fred Coe, Arthur Penn and William Gibson. Thank you."

Backstage, Crawford showed off the golden boy to the press as she hugged it, saying, "I wish I didn't have to give it up!" Later, Davis accused her of not giving up the statuette for a year. In fact, Crawford presented it to Anne Bancroft just a week later on the Broadway stage after a performance of *Mother Courage*.

Bancroft's costar Patty Duke had lost the Golden Globe to Angela Lansbury, who was now considered the Oscar front-runner as Best Supporting Actress for her portrayal of a scheming evil mother in *The Manchurian Candidate*. Sixteen-year-old Duke pulled off an upset, though, and became the youngest person ever to receive an Academy Award in a competitive race. As she accepted the honor, "Duke was choked with emotion," *Variety* noticed. "Clutching her Oscar, she uttered the briefest thanks of the evening, 'Bless you!' "

"Patty Duke sprang a surprise at the BevHilton party," columnist Archerd added. "She revealed her good luck charm, a chihuahua, Bambi, hidden during the evening's festivities in a bowling bag!" Duke's good luck would continue after the Oscars when she received her own self-titled TV series from ABC in the fall.

An equally startling upset occurred in the race for Best Supporting Actor, which was expected to go to recent Globe champ Omar Sharif. However, "Ed Begley, in a race against stiff odds, was a roundly applauded victor," *Variety* observed, adding that "he may have set a precedent" by becoming the first champion thesp to thank his agent. The agent would have missed the tribute if he planned to see it on TV—the set was stolen when his house was burgled early on Oscar day—but he told *Variety* "Thank God I had a ticket to the show!"

Considering that all of the other acting races went to first-time contenders, five-time nominee Gregory Peck must have felt nervous about his competish for Best Actor. In addition to *Lawrence of Arabia*'s Peter O'Toole, rivals included Marcello Mastroianni (*Divorce—Italian Style*), Jack Lemmon (*Days of Wine and Roses*), and Burt Lancaster, who'd taken top thesp honors at the Venice Film Festival for *Birdman of Alcatraz*. Peck was considered the front-runner, but he took no chances and carried a rabbit's foot to the showdown. When he became the first native Californian to win an Academy Award for acting, *Variety* said, "It was no surprise," and noted that his victory "was far and away the most popular choice of Hollywood's big night, receiving a tremendous ovation."

While *Lawrence of Arabia* was shut out of the acting races, it nonetheless took awards for its musical score, color cinematography, art direction, film editing, sound—and director. Accepting the latter prize, David Lean said, "This limey is deeply touched and gratefully honored."

When it also won Best Picture, producer Sam Spiegel thanked the "thousands who toiled in Arabia."

One of *Lawrence*'s few losers wasn't bitter about his defeat. Army Archerd reported, "Omar Sharif confided (in Arabic) to Danny Thomas at the post-Awards BevHilton party: 'It was best I didn't win for this wonderful role in such a great film—now I must prove myself. If I had won, I might not have the opportunity to pass this way again.' "

Joan Crawford wasn't nommed by the Globes or Oscars, but she still upstaged *Baby Jane* costar Bette Davis at the Academy Awards.

NEW YORK FILM CRITICS

There were no awards due to a newspaper strike in New York City.

NATIONAL BOARD OF REVIEW

Winners were announced on December 21, 1962.

BEST PICTURE
- *The Longest Day*
Billy Budd
The Miracle Worker
Lawrence of Arabia
Long Day's Journey into Night
Whistle down the Wind
Requiem for a Heavyweight
A Taste of Honey
Birdman of Alcatraz
War Hunt

BEST DIRECTOR
- David Lean, *Lawrence of Arabia*

BEST ACTOR
- Jason Robards, *Long Day's Journey into Night, Tender Is the Night*

BEST ACTRESS
- Anne Bancroft, *The Miracle Worker*

BEST SUPPORTING ACTOR
- Burgess Meredith, *Advise and Consent*

BEST SUPPORTING ACTRESS
- Angela Lansbury, *The Manchurian Candidate, All Fall Down*

BEST FOREIGN FILM
- *Sundays and Cybele* (France)
Barabbas (Italy)
Divorce—Italian Style (Italy)
The Island (Japan)
Through a Glass Darkly (Sweden)

DIRECTORS GUILD OF AMERICA

The initial list of nominees was narrowed down to a group of finalists who competed for the Best Director award, bestowed on February 9, 1963. Dual ceremonies were held at the Beverly Hilton Hotel in Los Angeles and the Waldorf-Astoria Hotel in New York.

BEST DIRECTOR
- David Lean, *Lawrence of Arabia*
Robert Aldrich, *Whatever Happened to Baby Jane?*
Morton DaCosta, *The Music Man*
John Frankenheimer, *Birdman of Alcatraz*
John Frankenheimer, *The Manchurian Candidate* (finalist)
Pietro Germi, *Divorce—Italian Style* (finalist)
John Huston, *Freud* (finalist)
Stanley Kubrick, *Lolita* (finalist)
Sidney Lumet, *Long Day's Journey into Night* (finalist)
Lewis Milestone, *Mutiny on the Bounty*
Robert Mulligan, *To Kill a Mockingbird*
Ralph Nelson, *Requiem for a Heavyweight*
Arthur Penn, *The Miracle Worker*
Tony Richardson, *A Taste of Honey*
Peter Ustinov, *Billy Budd* (finalist)
Bernhard Wicki, Ken Annakin, Andrew Marton, *The Longest Day* (finalists)

GOLDEN GLOBES

Nominations were announced on January 23, 1963. Awards were presented on March 5 at the Cocoanut Grove in the Ambassador Hotel in Los Angeles. The ceremony was telecast on L.A. station KTTV.

BEST DRAMA PICTURE
- *Lawrence of Arabia*
Adventures of a Young Man
The Chapman Report
Days of Wine and Roses
Freud
Lisa
The Longest Day

The Miracle Worker
Mutiny on the Bounty
To Kill a Mockingbird

BEST COMEDY PICTURE

■ *That Touch of Mink*
Best of Enemies
Boys Night Out
If a Man Answers
Period of Adjustment

BEST MUSICAL PICTURE

■ *The Music Man*
Girls! Girls! Girls!
Gypsy
Jumbo
The Wonderful World of the Brothers Grimm

BEST MOTION PICTURE PROMOTING INTERNATIONAL UNDERSTANDING

■ *To Kill a Mockingbird*
Best of Enemies
The Interns

BEST DIRECTOR

■ David Lean, *Lawrence of Arabia*
George Cukor, *The Chapman Report*
Morton DaCosta, *The Music Man*
Blake Edwards, *Days of Wine and Roses*
John Frankenheimer, *The Manchurian Candidate*
John Huston, *Freud*
Stanley Kubrick, *Lolita*
Mervyn LeRoy, *Gypsy*
Robert Mulligan, *To Kill a Mockingbird*
Martin Ritt, *Adventures of a Young Man*
Ismael Rodriguez, *Los Hermanos del Hierro*

BEST ACTOR, DRAMA

■ Gregory Peck, *To Kill a Mockingbird*
Bobby Darin, *Pressure Point*
Jackie Gleason, *Gigot*
Laurence Harvey, *The Wonderful World of the Brothers Grimm*
Burt Lancaster, *Birdman of Alcatraz*
Jack Lemmon, *Days of Wine and Roses*
James Mason, *Lolita*
Paul Newman, *Sweet Bird of Youth*
Peter O'Toole, *Lawrence of Arabia*
Anthony Quinn, *Lawrence of Arabia*

BEST ACTRESS, DRAMA

■ Geraldine Page, *Sweet Bird of Youth*
Anne Bancroft, *The Miracle Worker*
Bette Davis, *Whatever Happened to Baby Jane?*
Katharine Hepburn, *Long's Day Journey into Night*
Glynis Johns, *The Chapman Report*
Melina Mercouri, *Phaedra*
Lee Remick, *Days of Wine and Roses*
Susan Strasberg, *Adventures of a Young Man*
Shelley Winters, *Lolita*
Susannah York, *Freud*

BEST ACTOR, COMEDY OR MUSICAL

■ Marcello Mastroianni, *Divorce—Italian Style*
Stephen Boyd, *Jumbo*
Jimmy Durante, *Jumbo*
Cary Grant, *That Touch of Mink*
Charlton Heston, *The Pigeon That Took Rome*
Karl Malden, *Gypsy*
Robert Preston, *The Music Man*
Alberto Sordi, *The Best of Enemies*
James Stewart, *Mr. Hobbs Takes a Vacation*

BEST ACTRESS, COMEDY OR MUSICAL

■ Rosalind Russell, *Gypsy*
Doris Day, *Jumbo*
Jane Fonda, *Period of Adjustment*
Shirley Jones, *The Music Man*
Natalie Wood, *Gypsy*

BEST SUPPORTING ACTOR

■ Omar Sharif, *Lawrence of Arabia*
Ed Begley, *Sweet Bird of Youth*
Victor Buono, *Whatever Happened to Baby Jane?*
Harry Guardino, *The Pigeon That Took Rome*
Ross Martin, *Experiment in Terror*
Paul Newman, *Adventures of a Young Man*
Cesar Romero, *If a Man Answers*
Telly Savalas, *Birdman of Alcatraz*
Peter Sellers, *Lolita*
Harold J. Stone, *The Chapman Report*

BEST SUPPORTING ACTRESS

■ Angela Lansbury, *The Manchurian Candidate*

Patty Duke, *The Miracle Worker*
Hermione Gingold, *The Music Man*
Shirley Knight, *Sweet Bird of Youth*
Susan Kohner, *Freud*
Gabriella Pollotta, *The Pigeon That Took Rome*
Martha Raye, *Jumbo*
Kay Stevens, *The Interns*
Jessica Tandy, *Adventures of a Young Man*
Tarita, *Mutiny on the Bounty*

MOST PROMISING NEWCOMER—MALE

- Keir Dullea, *David and Lisa*
- Omar Sharif, *Lawrence of Arabia*
- Terence Stamp, *Billy Budd*
Peter O'Toole, *Lawrence of Arabia*
Paul Wallace, *Gypsy*

MOST PROMISING NEWCOMER—FEMALE

- Patty Duke, *The Miracle Worker*
- Sue Lyon, *Lolita*
- Rita Tushingham, *A Taste of Honey*
Dahlia Lavi, *Two Weeks in Another Town*
Janet Margolin, *David and Lisa*
Suzanne Pleshette, *Rome Adventure*

Winners

BEST FOREIGN-LANGUAGE FILM (TIE)

- *Best of Enemies* (Italy)
- *Divorce—Italian Style* (Italy)

BEST CINEMATOGRAPHY

(BLACK AND WHITE)
- *The Longest Day*
(COLOR)
- *Lawrence of Arabia*

BEST ORIGINAL SCORE

- Elmer Bernstein, *To Kill a Mockingbird*

WORLD FILM FAVORITES

- Doris Day
- Rock Hudson

SAMUEL GOLDWYN INTERNATIONAL AWARD

- *Sundays and Cybele* (France)

CECIL B. DEMILLE AWARD

- Bob Hope

ACADEMY AWARDS

Nominations were announced on February 25, 1963. Awards were presented on April 8 at the Santa Monica Civic Auditorium. The ceremony was telecast by ABC.

BEST PICTURE

- *Lawrence of Arabia*
To Kill a Mockingbird
The Longest Day
The Music Man
Mutiny on the Bounty

BEST DIRECTOR

- David Lean, *Lawrence of Arabia*
Pietro Germi, *Divorce—Italian Style*
Robert Mulligan, *To Kill a Mockingbird*
Arthur Penn, *The Miracle Worker*
Frank Perry, *David and Lisa*

BEST ACTOR

- Gregory Peck, *To Kill a Mockingbird*
Burt Lancaster, *Birdman of Alcatraz*
Jack Lemmon, *Days of Wine and Roses*
Marcello Mastroianni, *Divorce—Italian Style*
Peter O'Toole, *Lawrence of Arabia*

BEST ACTRESS

- Anne Bancroft, *The Miracle Worker*
Bette Davis, *What Ever Happened to Baby Jane?*
Katharine Hepburn, *Long Day's Journey into Night*
Geraldine Page, *Sweet Bird of Youth*
Lee Remick, *Days of Wine and Roses*

BEST SUPPORTING ACTOR

- Ed Begley, *Sweet Bird of Youth*
Victor Buono, *What Ever Happened to Baby Jane?*
Telly Savalas, *Birdman of Alcatrza*
Omar Sharif, *Lawrence of Arabia*
Terence Stamp, *Billy Budd*

BEST SUPPORTING ACTRESS

- Patty Duke, *The Miracle Worker*
Mary Badham, *To Kill a Mockingbird*
Shirley Knight, *Sweet Bird of Youth*
Angela Lansbury, *The Manchurian Candidate*
Thelma Ritter, *Birdman of Alcatraz*

BEST ADAPTED SCREENPLAY

- Horton Foote, *To Kill a Mockingbird*

Robert Bolt, Michael Wilson, *Lawrence of Arabia*

William Gibson, *The Miracle Worker*

Vladimir Nabokov, *Lolita*

Eleanor Perry, *David and Lisa*

BEST ORIGINAL SCREENPLAY

- Ennio De Concini, Pietro Germi, Alfredo Giannetti, *Divorce—Italian Style*

Ingmar Bergman, *Through a Glass Darkly*

Charles Kaufman, Wolfgang Reinhardt, *Freud*

Nate Monaster, Stanley Shapiro, *That Touch of Mink*

Alain Robbe-Grillet, *Last Year at Marienbad*

BEST SONG

- "Days of Wine and Roses," *Days of Wine and Roses*, Henry Mancini, Johnny Mercer

"Follow Me," *Mutiny on the Bounty*, Bronislau Kaper, Paul Francis Webster

"Second Chance," *Two for the Seesaw*, Andre Previn, Dory Langdon

"Tender Is the Night," *Tender Is the Night*, Sammy Fain, Paul Francis Webster

"Walk on the Wild Side," *Walk on the Wild Side*, Elmer Bernstein, Mack David

BEST FOREIGN-LANGUAGE FILM

- *Sundays and Cybele* (France)

Electra (Greece)

The Four Days of Naples (Italy)

Keeper of Promises (The Given Word) (Brazil)

Tlayucan (Mexico)

Winners

BEST ART DIRECTION

(BLACK AND WHITE)

- Henry Bumstead, Alexander Golitzen, Oliver Emert, *To Kill a Mockingbird*

(COLOR)

- John Box, John Stoll, Dario Simoni, *Lawrence of Arabia*

BEST CINEMATOGRAPHY

(BLACK AND WHITE)

- Jean Bourgoin, Henri Persin, Walter Wottitz, *The Longest Day*

(COLOR)

- Fred A. Young, *Lawrence of Arabia*

BEST COSTUME DESIGN

(BLACK AND WHITE)

- Norma Koch, *What Ever Happened to Baby Jane?*

(COLOR)

- Mary Wills, *The Wonderful World of the Brothers Grimm*

BEST DOCUMENTARY

(FEATURE)

- *Black Fox*, Louis Clyde Stoumen

(SHORT SUBJECT)

- *Dylan Thomas*, Jack Howells

BEST FILM EDITING

- Anne Coates, *Lawrence of Arabia*

BEST MUSIC

(MUSIC SCORE—SUBSTANTIALLY ORIGINAL)

- Maurice Jarre, *Lawrence of Arabia*

(SCORING OF MUSIC—ADAPTATION OR TREATMENT)

- Ray Heindorf, *The Music Man*

SCIENTIFIC OR TECHNICAL AWARDS

Class II (Plaque)

- Ralph Chapman; Albert S. Pratt, James L. Wassell, Hans C. Wohlrab; North American Philips Co.; Charles E. Sutter, William Bryson Smith, Louis C. Kennell, Paramount

Class III (Certificate)

- Electro-Voice, Louis G. MacKenzie

BEST SHORT SUBJECT

(CARTOON)

- *The Hole*

(LIVE ACTION)

- *Heureux Anniversaire (Happy Anniversary)*

BEST SOUND

- John Cox, *Lawrence of Arabia*

BEST SPECIAL EFFECTS
- Robert MacDonald, Jacques Maumont, *The Longest Day*

JEAN HERSHOLT HUMANITARIAN AWARD
- Steve Broidy

WRITERS GUILD OF AMERICA

Awards were presented on May 7, 1963, at the Beverly Hilton Hotel in Los Angeles.

BEST WRITTEN DRAMA
- *To Kill a Mockingbird*, Horton Foote, based on the novel by Harper Lee

Billy Budd, Peter Ustinov, DeWitt Bodeen, from the play by Louis O. Coxe, Robert H. Chapman, based on the novel by Herman Melville

Birdman of Alcatraz, Guy Trosper, based on the book by Thomas E. Gaddis

Freud, Charles Kaufman, Wolfgang Reinhardt

The Miracle Worker, William Gibson

BEST WRITTEN COMEDY
- *That Touch of Mink*, Stanley Shapiro, Nate Manaster

Mr. Hobbs Takes a Vacation, Nunnally Johnson, based on the novel by Edward Streeter

The Notorious Landlady, Larry Gelbart, Blake Edwards, based on a story by Margery Sharp

Period of Adjustment, Isobel Lennart, based on the play by Tennessee Williams

The Pigeon That Took Rome, Melville Shavelson, based on the novel *The Easter Dinner* by Donald Downes

BEST WRITTEN MUSICAL
- *The Music Man*, Marion Hargrove, based on the musical by Meredith Willson from a story by Meredith Willson and Franklin Lacey

Billy Rose's Jumbo, Sidney Sheldon, based on the musical and book by Ben Hecht and Charles MacArthur

Gypsy, Leonard Spigelgass, based on the musical play by Arthur Laurents and the memoirs of Gypsy Rose Lee

Hey, Let's Twist, Hal Hackady

State Fair, Richard Breen, from the novel by Phil Stong, the 1933 adaptation by Sonya Levien and Paul Green, and the 1945 screenplay by Oscar Hammerstein II

LAUREL AWARD
- Joseph L. Mankiewicz

VALENTINE DAVIES AWARD
- Allen Rivkin

SCREEN ACTORS GUILD

LIFETIME ACHIEVEMENT AWARD
- Eddie Cantor

· 1963 ·

Tom Jones, *You Rascal!*

After having no impact on the awards derby last year when its scribes were silenced by a newspaper strike, the New York Film Critics defined this year's race early on.

The crix shocked awards watchers by embracing *Tom Jones*, the same bawdy British farce chosen by the National Board of Review after the pic's savvy U.S. distributor, United Artists, gave both groups a private screening.

Jones was not the kind of movie that would normally claim lofty kudos. It may have been based on a classic 18th-century novel by Henry Fielding, but the pic focused mostly on the shameless bed-hopping of its smart-aleck hero (Albert Finney), who also flirted with movie-goers by winking at the camera. "Director Tony Richardson has occasionally pressed his luck with some over-deliberate arty camera bits," *Variety* warned, but the avant-garde helmer had staunch defenders among the Gotham scribes. Last year Bosley Crowther reported in *The New York Times* that he would've endorsed Richardson's *A Taste of Honey* as Best Picture if the crix had voted. This year New York newspaper writers were reminded of Richardson's talents at awards time just as his latest artistic endeavor debuted on Broadway to rave reviews—*Luther*, written by *Tom Jones* screenwriter John Osborne and starring Albert Finney.

Richardson's *Jones* had something else going for it among the Gotham scribes voting for Best Picture. It was a fun, fresh alternative to Hollywood's two biggest films in terms of screen size and box office: *How the West Was Won*, which opted for cinematic sprawl over adrenaline drama for 2½ hours, and *Cleopatra*, which failed to measure up to its early buzz and hype. *Cleopatra* was so expensive to produce ($44 million) that it nearly bankrupted Twentieth Century-Fox,

When Hollywood's $44 million *Cleopatra* tanked, all four kudos named Britain's risqué *Tom Jones* top pic.

and *Tom Jones*'s on-screen sexcapades were nothing compared to off-screen shenanigans that occurred on the *Cleopatra* set between Richard Burton and Eddie Fisher's wife, Elizabeth Taylor. *Variety*, however, hailed the final celluloid result as "a stunning achievement" and *The New York Times* proclaimed it "one of the great epic films of our day." Most other media crucified it.

The only film that posed a serious challenge to *Jones* in the critics' vote for Best Picture was *Hud*, which *Variety* described as "the story of a westerner (Paul Newman) who fights to come to terms with his embittered dad (Melvyn Douglas)." *Jones* led on the first ballot with seven votes to four, with scattered single votes going to *The Birds, It's a Mad, Mad, Mad, Mad World* and *To Kill a Mockingbird* (released in 1963 in New York).

In the race for Best Director, *Jones*'s Richardson led *Hud*'s Martin Ritt by only a narrow lead of six to five on the first polling, but then prevailed by a 10-to-4 score on the third round.

The crix's contest for Best Actor was its most dramatic. Prior to *Tom Jones*'s ambush of the early film awards, Paul Newman had been considered the front-runner for the year's male thesp honors. "The Academy may as well give him an Oscar right now and get it over with," *The New Yorker* sighed soon after the movie debuted. Newman only scored three votes on the crix's first ballot, however. Recent Venice film fest honoree Albert Finney led with five and picked up strength on subsequent ballots; Newman then fell behind Sidney Poitier, who *Variety* said gave a "standout performance" in *Lilies of the Field* "as a journeyman laborer who meets his match in five nuns from East Germany." Finney prevailed on the sixth ballot by an eight-to-six edge. His victory was noteworthy since *Tom Jones* was only Finney's third screen role, although he had received a few Best Actor votes from the crix in 1960 for *Saturday Night and Sunday Morning*.

Hud rallied to claim the Best Actress laurels for Patricia Neal, who *Variety* said "comes through with a rich and powerful performance as the housekeeper assaulted by Newman." She won the critics' vote by a landslide score of 11 to 3 over Leslie Caron in *The L-Shaped Room* on the first ballot. "Miss Neal's triumph in a small role was as unusual as Mr. Finney's victory in a comedy performance," the *Times*'s Crowther noted.

Hud also took the crix's laurel for Best Screenplay (beating *America, America* by a nine-to-four vote on the sixth ballot), a victory it later repeated at the writers' guild awards. The category for Best Written Musical was dropped this year. *Lilies of the Field* reaped the group's prize for Best Written Comedy over *Charade* and *Irma La Douce*.

One of the funniest skits performed at the guild's ceremony involved a film not even nominated by the scribes: Otto Preminger's *The Cardinal*, which starred Tom Tryon as an American priest aspiring to Rome's highest offices. In its sacrilegious send-up, actors portrayed a Protestant minister bestowing a plaque upon Preminger "in appreciation for his not having made a picture about us."

The Cardinal pulled off an upset at the Golden Globes to win Best Drama Picture over *Hud, Lilies of the Field* and *Cleopatra*, but the victory was just one of many jaw-droppers. Director John Huston was not known for his thesping skills, but his role as a prelate in *The Cardinal* topped critically hailed perfs by Roddy McDowall (*Cleopatra*), Melvyn Douglas (*Hud*) and Hugh Griffith (*Tom Jones*) for Best Supporting Actor. The New York crix's Best Actress Patricia Neal was nommed in the supporting category, but lost to Margaret Rutherford, the veteran British thesp who gave an inspired comic turn as a befuddled dowager in *The V.I.P.s*. Perhaps the biggest upset of all, however, was Tony Richardson's loss of the Best Director Award to Elia Kazan, who was hailed for *America, America*, his semi-autobiographical tale of a Greek boy who tries to immigrate to the United States.

Albert Finney lost the comedy actor's prize to Alberto Sordi (*To Bed or Not to Bed*) as an Italian businessman looking for thrills in Stockholm. But Finney was declared one of the Globes' Most Promising New Stars of the Year.

Globe leaders hoped to cope with a recent backlash against the success of British pics by creating a new category for Best English-Language Foreign Film, assuming it would go to *Tom Jones*. It did— in addition to the gold for the recently recombined categories for best musical and comedy movies (the two genres had had separate awards since 1958).

> ## The Cardinal pulled off a shocking Best Picture upset at the Golden Globes.

The ceremony was broadcast by the local L.A. NBC television affiliate and was hosted by Andy Williams. *Variety* praised it as "a bright TV spectacle and a challenge in terms of showmanship to its counterpart, the Oscarcast." There was one notable production snafu. When Shirley MacLaine accepted a statuette as Best Comedy/Musical Actress in *Irma La Douce*, her "thank you" was abruptly interrupted by a commercial break. "It was strange, as there was nothing offensive about her acceptance remarks other than humorous experiences in making the film," *Box Office* observed. Once off the air, MacLaine told the crowd that she had "researched" her role as a prostitute while in Paris.

Tom Jones led the Oscar derby with 10 nominations (followed by nine for *Cleopatra*) and was the clear front-runner for Best Picture since it had already won the directors' guild award and was only one of two contenders also nommed for Oscar's Best Director trophy. *Variety* noted that "major nominations are heavily represented by British entries," which included five of the 10 contenders for Best Actor and Actress and all of the candidates for Best Supporting Actress.

Best Actor "shoo-in" Albert Finney partied in Hawaii on Oscar night.

Few showed up on awards night, however—not even Albert Finney, who was considered a shoo-in for Best Actor. He'd recently quit his Broadway job and headed to Hawaii for fun. Fifty-six other nominees were also absent.

"There were fewer stars at this Academy Awards than at some of the town's top premieres, as forewarned and predicted, but the pea soup fog dramatically lifted in time for the TV curtain," *Variety* reported on awards night. "Fans in the stands were more vociferous than usual in appreciation of the stars that did show. The 3,000 fans squealed delightedly as their idols were introduced by emcee Army Archerd. There was enough paint and polish, Cadillacs, minks, gowns and glamour to satisfy them."

Finney was up against Paul Newman (*Hud*), Sidney Poitier (*Lilies of the Field*), Rex Harrison (as Caesar in *Cleopatra*) and Ireland's new 29-year-old star Richard Harris, who *Variety* said gave an "intelligent performance as the arrogant, blustering" football star in *This Sporting Life*.

When Poitier won, *Variety* called the victory "the biggest upset" among the awards and "the most popular choice of the night, without any doubt." The tradepaper observed that he received "a tremendous ovation" as "he became the first Negro to win this major recognition." Hattie McDaniel broke the color barrier to become the first African-American to win a thesping honor in 1939 when she was honored as Best Supporting Actress for *Gone With the Wind*, but no black actors had ever won in the lead categories. As Poitier headed to the podium, the orchestra chimed in with "Amen" (theme song to *Lilies of the Field*) and the audience cheered with near-religious fervor. He accepted the honor, saying, "It's been a long journey to this moment."

The next day New York City officials announced plans to give Poitier a hero's welcome with a ticker-tape parade.

"In the case of Rachel Roberts and Rex Harrison, the nominations mark only the second time in academy history that a husband and wife have been nominated in the acting ranks in the same year," *Variety* noted. "Alfred Lunt and Lynn Fontanne were in the running in 1932 for the same film, *The Guardsman*, although neither won." Roberts was up for her role as a repressed widow in *This Sporting Life* opposite Richard Harris.

But Roberts wasn't given much hope of beating Patricia Neal, who skipped the ceremony because she was pregnant and didn't want to fly from London. Neal was awakened at 6 A.M. with the news that she had won. "I was thrilled to hear the phone ringing," she told reporters. Army Archerd said the next day, "Femme winner Patricia Neal looms bigger today for the lead in *Who's Afraid of Virginia Woolf?*"

Variety noted the media's immediate response to the winners of Best Actor and Actress: "General press reaction was highly in approval of the Sidney Poitier and Patricia Neal awards, the backstage press losing their usual austerity to applaud soundly."

The winner of Best Supporting Actress was also in London when she heard the news of her victory. Margaret Rutherford (*The V.I.P.s*) issued a written statement the next day: "This Oscar is the climax of my career after 28 years of filming. This may sound presumptuous at my age—I'm 72 next month—but I like to feel that this will be the starting point of a whole new phase in films."

The winner of Best Supporting Actor was in Spain on Oscar night. Melvyn Douglas's award was accepted on his behalf by Brandon De Wilde, the only major *Hud* star who didn't get an Oscar bid. Douglas's victory was considered an upset over two rivals: Nick Adams, who starred in the courtroom drama *Twilight of Honor*, and Bobby Darin, who had recently made a career leap from

singing to acting and received critics' huzzahs for portraying a cowardly army corporal in *Captain Newman, M.D.* Columnist Sidney Skolsky reported that Adams did not take the news of his loss well: "He looked like Instant Murder."

Having been shut out of the acting races, *Tom Jones*'s chances looked slimmer for the top awards. "The sweep which had been predicted for the British contender in all pre-Academy polls failed to materialize," *Variety* reported, although *Tom Jones* pulled off victories for best adapted screenplay and music score.

It also broke loose on the last leg of the awards derby—displaying all the devilish spunk of its jaunty hero—and claimed the kudos for Best Director and Best Picture.

Variety called the Oscar gala "an efficiently executed, engagingly unpretentious affair. It was a lighthearted show in contrast to the defiantly defensive Oscarcast of last year." The reviewer particularly liked the deft handiwork of emcee Jack Lemmon: "With a twist of Lemmon, but not quite so many Limeys as some may have anticipated, the 130-minute telecast went off smoothly."

▪ **1963** ▪

NATIONAL BOARD OF REVIEW

Winners were announced on December 22, 1963.

BEST PICTURE
▪ *Tom Jones*
Lilies of the Field
All the Way Home
Hud
This Sporting Life
Lord of the Flies
The L-Shaped Room
The Great Escape
How the West Was Won
The Cardinal

BEST DIRECTOR
▪ Tony Richardson, *Tom Jones*

BEST ACTOR
▪ Rex Harrison, *Cleopatra*

BEST ACTRESS
▪ Patricia Neal, *Hud*

BEST SUPPORTING ACTOR
▪ Melvyn Douglas, *Hud*

BEST SUPPORTING ACTRESS
▪ Margaret Rutherford, *The V.I.P.s*

BEST FOREIGN FILM
▪ *8½* (Italy)
The Four Days of Naples (Italy)
Winter Light (Sweden)
The Leopard (Italy)
Any Number Can Win (France/Italy)

NEW YORK FILM CRITICS

Winners were announced on December 30, 1963. Awards were presented on January 18, 1964, at Sardi's restaurant in New York.

BEST PICTURE
- *Tom Jones*

BEST DIRECTOR
- Tony Richardson, *Tom Jones*

BEST ACTOR
- Albert Finney, *Tom Jones*

BEST ACTRESS
- Patricia Neal, *Hud*

BEST SCREENPLAY
- Irving Ravetch, Harriet Frank, Jr., *Hud*

BEST FOREIGN FILM
- 8½ (Italy)

DIRECTORS GUILD OF AMERICA

Awards were presented on February 22, 1964, at the Beverly Hilton Hotel in Los Angeles and the Waldorf-Astoria Hotel in New York.

BEST DIRECTOR
- Tony Richardson, *Tom Jones*

Federico Fellini, *8½*

Elia Kazan, *America, America*

Ralph Nelson, *Lilies of the Field*

Martin Ritt, *Hud*

HONORARY LIFETIME MEMBER
- Joseph C. Youngerman

WRITERS GUILD OF AMERICA

Awards were presented on March 9, 1964, at the Beverly Hilton Hotel in Los Angeles.

BEST WRITTEN DRAMA
- *Hud*, Harriet Frank, Jr., and Irving Ravetch, based on the novel *Horseman, Pass By* by Larry McMurtry

Anne Bancroft with Oscar and Globe Best Actor Sidney Poitier (*Lilies of the Field*): "It's been a long journey," he said.

America, America, Elia Kazan

The Balcony, Ben Maddow, based on the play by Jean Genet

Captain Newman, M.D., Richard L. Breen, Phoebe Ephron, Henry Ephron, based on the novel by Leo Rosten

The Great Escape, James Clavell, W. R. Burnett, based on the novel by Paul Brickhill

The Ugly American, Stewart Stern, based on the novel by William J. Lederer and Eugene Burdick

BEST WRITTEN COMEDY
- *Lilies of the Field*, James Poe, based on the novel by William E. Barrett

Charade, Peter Stone, story by Peter Stone and Marc Behm

Irma La Douce, I. A. L. Diamond, Billy Wilder, based on the musical play by Alexandre Breffort

Love with the Proper Stranger, Arnold Schulman

The Thrill of It All, Carl Reiner, story by Carl Reiner and Larry Gelbart

LAUREL AWARD
- John Huston

VALENTINE DAVIES AWARD
■ Morgan Cox

GOLDEN GLOBES

Nominations were announced on January 27, 1964. Awards were presented on March 11 at the Cocoanut Grove in the Ambassador Hotel in Los Angeles. The ceremony was telecast on L.A. station KTTV.

BEST DRAMA PICTURE
■ *The Cardinal*
America, America
Captain Newman, M.D.
The Caretakers
Cleopatra
The Great Escape
Hud
Lilies of the Field

BEST COMEDY OR MUSICAL PICTURE
■ *Tom Jones*
Bye Bye Birdie
Irma La Douce
It's a Mad, Mad, Mad, Mad World
A Ticklish Affair
Under the Yum Yum Tree

BEST MOTION PICTURE PROMOTING INTERNATIONAL UNDERSTANDING
■ *Lilies of the Field*
America, America
Captain Newman, M.D.
The Cardinal
A Global Affair

BEST DIRECTOR
■ Elia Kazan, *America, America*
Hall Bartlett, *The Caretakers*
George Englund, *The Ugly American*
Joseph L. Mankiewicz, *Cleopatra*
Otto Preminger, *The Cardinal*
Tony Richardson, *Tom Jones*
Martin Ritt, *Hud*
Robert Wise, *The Haunting*

BEST ACTOR, DRAMA
■ Sidney Poitier, *Lilies of the Field*
Marlon Brando, *The Ugly American*
Stathis Giallelis, *America, America*
Rex Harrison, *Cleopatra*

Steve McQueen, *Love with the Proper Stranger*
Paul Newman, *Hud*
Gregory Peck, *Captain Newman, M.D.*
Tom Tryon, *The Cardinal*

BEST ACTRESS, DRAMA
■ Leslie Caron, *The L-Shaped Room*
Polly Bergen, *The Caretakers*
Geraldine Page, *Toys in the Attic*
Rachel Roberts, *The Sporting Life*
Romy Schneider, *The Cardinal*
Alida Valli, *Paper Man*
Marina Vlady, *The Conjugal Bed*
Natalie Wood, *Love with the Proper Stranger*

BEST ACTOR, COMEDY OR MUSICAL
■ Alberto Sordi, *To Bed or Not to Bed*
Albert Finney, *Tom Jones*
James Garner, *Wheeler Dealers*
Cary Grant, *Charade*
Jack Lemmon, *Under the Yum Yum Tree, Irma La Douce*
Frank Sinatra, *Come Blow Your Horn*
Alberto Sordi, *To Bed or Not to Bed*
Terry Thomas, *Mouse on the Moon*
Jonathan Winters, *It's a Mad, Mad, Mad, Mad World*

BEST ACTRESS, COMEDY OR MUSICAL
■ Shirley MacLaine, *Irma La Douce*
Doris Day, *Move Over, Darling*
Audrey Hepburn, *Charade*
Ann-Margret, *Bye Bye Birdie*
Hayley Mills, *Summer Magic*
Molly Picon, *Come Blow Your Horn*
Jill St. John, *Come Blow Your Horn*
Joanne Woodward, *A New Kind of Love*

BEST SUPPORTING ACTOR
■ John Huston, *The Cardinal*
Lee J. Cobb, *Come Blow Your Horn*
Bobby Darin, *Captain Newman, M.D.*
Melvyn Douglas, *Hud*
Hugh Griffith, *Tom Jones*
Paul Mann, *America, America*
Roddy McDowall, *Cleopatra*
Gregory Rozakis, *America, America*

BEST SUPPORTING ACTRESS
■ Margaret Rutherford, *The V.I.P.s*
Diane Baker, *The Prize*

Joan Greenwood, *Tom Jones*
Wendy Hiller, *Toys in the Attic*
Linda Marsh, *America, America*
Patricia Neal, *Hud*
Lilo Pulver, *A Global Affair*
Lilia Skala, *Lilies of the Field*

MOST PROMISING NEWCOMER—MALE

- Albert Finney, *Tom Jones*
- Stathis Giallelis, *America, America*
- Robert Walker, *The Ceremony*
Alain Delon, *The Leopard*
Peter Fonda, *The Victors*
Larry Tucker, *Shock Corridor*

MOST PROMISING NEWCOMER—FEMALE

- Ursula Andress, *Dr. No*
- Tippi Hedren, *The Birds*
- Elke Sommer, *The Prize*
Joey Heatherton, *Twilight of Honor*
Leslie Paris, *For Love or Money*
Maggie Smith, *The V.I.P.s*

Winners

BEST FOREIGN-LANGUAGE FILM

- *Any Number Can Win* (France)

WORLD FILM FAVORITES

- Sophia Loren
- Paul Newman

SAMUEL GOLDWYN INTERNATIONAL AWARD

- *Yesterday, Today and Tomorrow*

CECIL B. DEMILLE AWARD

- Joseph E. Levine

ACADEMY AWARDS

Nominations were announced on February 24, 1964. Awards were presented on April 13 at the Santa Monica Civic Auditorium. The ceremony was telecast by ABC.

BEST PICTURE

- *Tom Jones*
America, America
Cleopatra
How the West Was Won
Lilies of the Field

BEST DIRECTOR

- Tony Richardson, *Tom Jones*
Federico Fellini, *8½*
Elia Kazan, *America, America*
Otto Preminger, *The Cardinal*
Martin Ritt, *Hud*

BEST ACTOR

- Sidney Poitier, *Lilies of the Field*
Albert Finney, *Tom Jones*
Richard Harris, *This Sporting Life*
Rex Harrison, *Cleopatra*
Paul Newman, *Hud*

BEST ACTRESS

- Patricia Neal, *Hud*
Leslie Caron, *The L-Shaped Room*
Shirley MacLaine, *Irma La Douce*
Rachel Roberts, *This Sporting Life*
Natalie Wood, *Love with the Proper Stranger*

BEST SUPPORTING ACTOR

- Melvyn Douglas, *Hud*
Nick Adams, *Twilight of Honor*
Bobby Darin, *Captain Newman, M.D.*
Hugh Griffith, *Tom Jones*
John Huston, *The Cardinal*

BEST SUPPORTING ACTRESS

- Margaret Rutherford, *The V.I.P.s*
Diane Cilento, *Tom Jones*
Dame Edith Evans, *Tom Jones*
Joyce Redman, *Tom Jones*
Lilia Skala, *Lilies of the Field*

BEST ADAPTED SCREENPLAY

- John Osborne, *Tom Jones*
Serge Bourguignon, Antoine Tudal,
  Sundays and Cybele
Richard L. Breen, Henry Ephron, Phoebe
  Ephron, *Captain Newman, M.D.*
James Poe, *Lilies of the Field*
Irving Ravetch, Harriet Frank, Jr., *Hud*

BEST ORIGINAL SCREENPLAY

- James R. Webb, *How the West Was Won*
Carlo Bernari, Pasquale Festa Campanile,
  Massimo Franciosa, Nanni Loy, Vasco
  Pratolini, *The Four Days of Naples*
Federico Fellini, Ennio Flaiano, Tullio
  Pinelli, Brunello Rondi, *8½*
Elia Kazan, *America, America*

Arnold Schulman, *Love with the Proper Stranger*

BEST SONG

- "Call Me Irresponsible," *Papa's Delicate Condition*, Sammy Cahn, James Van Heusen

"Charade," *Charade*, Henry Mancini, Johnny Mercer

"It's a Mad, Mad, Mad, Mad World," *It's a Mad, Mad, Mad, Mad World*, Mack David, Ernest Gold

"More," *Mondo Cane*, Norman Newell, Nino Oliviero, Riz Ortolani

"So Little Time," *55 Days at Peking*, Dimitri Tiomkin, Paul Francis Webster

BEST FOREIGN-LANGUAGE FILM

- *8½* (Italy)

Knife in the Water (Poland)

The Red Lanterns (Greece)

Los Tarantos (Spain)

Twin Sisters of Kyoto (Japan)

Winners

BEST ART DIRECTION

(BLACK AND WHITE)

- Gene Callahan, *America, America*

(COLOR)

- Herman Blumenthal, Hilyard Brown, John DeCuir, Boris Juraga, Maurice Pelling, Jack Martin Smith, Elven Webb, *Cleopatra*

BEST CINEMATOGRAPHY

(BLACK AND WHITE)

- James Wong Howe, *Hud*

(COLOR)

- Leon Shamroy, *Cleopatra*

BEST COSTUME DESIGN

(BLACK AND WHITE)

- Piero Gherardi, *8½*

(COLOR)

- Vittorio Nino Novarese, Renie, Irene Sharaff, *Cleopatra*

BEST DOCUMENTARY

(FEATURE)

- Robert Hughes, *Robert Frost: A Lover's Quarrel with the World*

(SHORT SUBJECT)

- Simon Schiffrin, *Chagall*

BEST FILM EDITING

- Harold F. Kress, *How the West Was Won*

BEST MUSIC

(MUSIC SCORE—SUBSTANTIALLY ORIGINAL)

- John Addison, *Tom Jones*

(SCORING OF MUSIC—ADAPTATION OR TREATMENT)

- Andre Previn, *Irma La Douce*

SCIENTIFIC OR TECHNICAL AWARDS

Class II (Certificate)

- Arnold Gillespie, Douglas G. Shearer, MGM

BEST SHORT SUBJECT

(CARTOON)

- *The Critic*

(LIVE ACTION)

- *An Occurrence at Owl Creek Bridge*

BEST SOUND

- Franklin E. Milton, *How the West Was Won*

BEST SOUND EFFECTS

- *It's a Mad, Mad, Mad, Mad World*, Walter G. Elliott

BEST SPECIAL EFFECTS

- Emil Kosa, Jr., *Cleopatra*

IRVING G. THALBERG MEMORIAL AWARD

- Sam Spiegel

SCREEN ACTORS GUILD

LIFETIME ACHIEVEMENT AWARD

- Stan Laurel

Two Fair Ladies

My *Fair Lady* certainly had to worry about *Dr. Strangelove or: How I Learned to Stop Worrying and Love the Bomb* when the New York Film Critics met to choose Best Picture. The conventional $17 million blockbuster led the wily *Strangelove* on the first ballot seven votes to three, but then fell behind by a six-to-five score on the second round. Bosley Crowther of *The New York Times* seemed to take *My Fair Lady*'s setback personally, huffing in his next-day report, "It only goes to show there are among us a few determinedly antagonist souls."

My Fair Lady reclaimed the lead on the next polling, but, as the tension intensified, nothing less than the fate of contemporary cinema seemed to hang in the balance. As the 13 crix sat silently in leather chairs in the conference room of the Newspaper Guild near Times Square, they smoked furiously and scribbled on tiny scraps of paper that they dropped into a paper box to be counted. Judith Crist of the *Herald Tribune* was among the crix who fought for *Strangelove* as a way of acknowledging the edgy new spirit of modern film, while the *Times*'s Crowther and Leo Mishkin of the *Morning-Telegraph* valiantly defended the classic virtues of *My Fair Lady*. The showdown went all the way to the sixth ballot, when a simple majority vote determined the champ instead of the two-thirds tally needed earlier. *My Fair Lady* ultimately declared victory by an eight-to-five edge—and *Strangelove*'s Stanley Kubrick was given the Best Director award as a consolation prize.

Strife over *My Fair Lady* was not unusual. The first hubbub broke out when Warner Bros. paid $5.5 million for the film rights to the Broadway hit and refused to take a chance on its unknown star. Previously, Julie Andrews had been snubbed

Julie Andrews (right) lost the *My Fair Lady* film role to Audrey Hepburn (left), but she bagged the Oscar for *Mary Poppins*.

L.A. Herald

when Tony Awards went to the tuner for Best Musical and to her costar Rex Harrison as Best Actor, but she lost out to Judy Holliday of *Bells Are Ringing*. The film role ended up going to Audrey Hepburn—who couldn't sing. Vocals had to be dubbed by Marni Nixon, who previously did ghost crooning for Deborah Kerr in *The King and I* and Natalie Wood in *West Side Story*. Columnist Sheilah Graham declared, "The criticism heaped upon Jack Warner for bypassing Julie has been like nothing I can remember in my years of reporting."

Warner would later be praised by *The New York Times* and other media for making the correct casting call, but, meantime, a cult of sympathy built up around Andrews, particularly when she starred in *Camelot* and lost the Tony Award *again*—this time to Elizabeth Seal for *Irma La Douce*. *Camelot* earned Andrews another prize, though—the attention of Walt Disney, who was so impressed by her performance that he offered her the lead role in his next movie, *Mary Poppins*, which he planned to lens in Hollywood at the same time as *My Fair Lady*. Gossip columnists smacked their lips and prepared for a battle between the two fair ladies, but both behaved graciously and remained mum.

When *Mary Poppins* premiered in September 1964, *Variety* hailed its star: "Julie Andrews's first appearance on the screen is a signal triumph." When *My Fair Lady* opened one month later, *Variety* called Audrey Hepburn "thoroughly beguiling— (even) though her singing is dubbed." When they squared off for Best Actress at the New York film crix vote, they tied for second place with two votes each, behind noted Broadway thesp Kim Stanley, who reaped nine endorsements for her role as a bogus psychic in *Seance on a Wet Afternoon*, her second feature film. Stanley won easily on the second ballot, mirroring her recent victory at the National Board of Review, and she impressed *Variety* columnist Sheilah Graham, who warned Hollywood: "Miss Stanley could walk away with the Oscar."

> ## The Servant's Dirk Bogarde lost the N.Y. crix Best Actor race by one vote.

The star of another art house hit, Dirk Bogarde of *The Servant*, made an impressive run for Best Actor "for his performance of the horrifying role of the evil genius," said *New York Times* scribe Bosley Crowther. "And he almost got it. He was beaten by one vote." Bogarde lost by a seven-to-six tally on the sixth ballot to British compatriot Rex Harrison. *The Morning-Telegraph*'s Leo Mishkin declared that Harrison was worthy of the win, but added, "There remains a suspicion that he was also being saluted for his Julius Caesar in *Cleopatra* last year." *The Servant* picked up the consolation prize of Best Screenplay for Harold Pinter.

Dr. Strangelove rallied at the writers guild awards to take a top prize as Best Written Comedy, but *My Fair Lady* lost to *Mary Poppins* as Best Written Musical. It wasn't until the Directors Guild of America awards that *Lady*'s helmer George Cukor received his first prize for what *Variety* called his "stunningly effective screen entertainment." Jack Warner would get his ultimate reward for *Lady* when it would go on to become his studio's top-grossing film ever, but meantime he also received an acknowledgment from the directors' guild, which embraced him as an honorary lifetime member.

When the Golden Globes took place two days later at the Cocoanut Grove, Warner also received acknowledgment from a curious source—the winner of the statuette for Best Comedy/Musical Actress. *Variety* reported, "Julie Andrews, in accepting her *Mary Poppins* award, broke long silence about hurt feelings over selection by Jack L. Warner of Audrey Hepburn for film version of *My Fair Lady*. She commented, 'and finally my thanks to the man who made all this possible, Jack Warner.'

"Warner, who followed Miss Andrews to pick up award to *Lady*, then referred to her observation by ad libbing, 'What's her name—Mary Poppins? Oh, yes, Andrews of Andrews Boulevard, Washington, D.C.'

"Host Andy Williams capped the episode and rocked Grove audience with wry comment that 'the voice of Jack Warner was dubbed by Marni Nixon.' "

After the ceremony, *Variety* asked Andrews whether her comment was planned or made on the spur of the moment. "Planned," she said, "but not for a long time. I hope it didn't sound bitchy." Andrews was especially sensitive to how it sounded, since the awards show was telecast nationally on NBC's *The Andy Williams Show*.

Audrey Hepburn may have lost her Best Actress bid to Julie Andrews, but *My Fair Lady* swept the Globes to take the prizes for

Best Picture (Comedy or Musical), Best Director (Cukor) and Best Actor (Rex Harrison). *Variety* noted that "*My Fair Lady* squeaked by *Becket* in the race for the top awards." The latter drama about the murder of the Archbishop of Canterbury (Richard Burton) by the barons of England's King Henry II (Peter O'Toole) had been voted Best Picture by the National Board of Review six weeks earlier. Now it claimed Globes for Best Drama Picture and Best Drama Actor Peter O'Toole, who beat his *Becket* costar Richard Burton, who was nommed for what *Variety* called his "superlative" perf as a defrocked American minister living in Mexico in Tennessee Williams's *The Night of the Iguana. Variety*'s initial review of the pic suggested why: "As Henry II, O'Toole makes of the king a tormented, many-sided baffled, believable human being."

A few weeks after the Globe gala, Oscar voters received their nomination ballots in the mail just as Julie Andrews's star appeal hit a new height with the release of *The Sound of Music.* When Oscar bids were announced, *Variety* reported, "Walt Disney's *Mary Poppins* leads the Oscar nomination race this year with 13 taps in what is expected to be the most hotly contested Academy Awards sweepstakes in years. Hal Wallis–Paramount's *Becket* and Warner Brothers' *My Fair Lady* are pressing hard with 12 apiece in spurts far-outdistancing any other nominated film." *Mary Poppins* was only one bid shy of the record held by *All about Eve.* "Julie Andrews fairly popped her buttons with excitement when told the news," *Variety* noted.

But Andrews proclaimed that she was "very sad" when she heard the shocking news of who wasn't nominated against her in the Best Actress race: Audrey Hepburn. *My Fair Lady* director George Cukor told Army Archerd, "I'm sick about it." *Variety* speculated over the Hepburn slight: "She did the acting, but Marni Nixon subbed for

> # Writers' guild voters preferred *Mary Poppins* to *My Fair Lady.*

her in the singing dept. and this is what undoubtedly led to her erasure."

Hepburn was nonetheless invited to participate in the Oscarcast to present the Best Actor prize as a stand-in for last year's Best Actress champ Patricia Neal, who had recently suffered three strokes. The non-nominee proved to be graciously eager to participate. Hepburn was the first star to arrive at the Santa Monica Civic Auditorium—or, considering the setting of the three top contending films, what gala host Bob Hope called "Santa Monica on the Thames."

Hepburn's costar Rex Harrison faced tough competish in the actor race, including both *Becket* stars. Some Oscar pundits pointed out that the last time two costars were nommed in the same top race—Katharine Hepburn and Elizabeth Taylor in *Suddenly, Last Summer* in 1959—both lost after their votes probably canceled each other out. Peter O'Toole's recent Golden Globe triumph over Richard Burton, however, proved that he was a serious contender. Also formidable in the race was Anthony Quinn, who played the title role in *Zorba the Greek* as a lusty, carefree peasant and Peter Sellers, who portrayed three loopy characters in *Dr. Strangelove.*

When Hepburn stood at the podium and opened the envelope to reveal the winner, *Variety* reported that she "literally screamed with delight to read that the decision went to Harrison. Harrison received a 40-second ovation, and in his acceptance remarks said he felt he should 'split it in half,' in obvious reference to Miss Hepburn."

Most of Julie Andrews's rivals didn't even bother to show up on Oscar night. New York film crix choice Kim Stanley remained in London, where she was starring in an Actors' Studio production of Chekov's *Three Sisters.* Sophia Loren (*Marriage, Italian Style*) was across town from her, being directed in a new film by Peter Ustinov, who was a contender for Best Supporting Actor. Also missing was

Anne Bancroft, who'd already received plenty of kudos for *The Pumpkin Eater*, including honors from the London Film Critics, the Cannes film fest and the Golden Globes. Debbie Reynolds was present in Hollywood on awards night, though, and had some reason for optimism. When gossip hen Louella Parsons saw her in *The Unsinkable Molly Brown*, she wrote, "Debbie Reynolds is a revelation and is certain to earn herself an Oscar nomination and perhaps an Oscar, too!"

Julie Andrews earned the Oscar, however, and said at the podium, "I know you Americans are famous for your hospitality, but this is really ridiculous." She gave Walt Disney "the biggest thank you" and expressed her appreciation to everyone else "for making me feel truly welcome in this country."

Globe Best Actor Peter O'Toole (right) with Richard Burton in Globe and NBR best pic *Becket*. Both thesps now reign as Oscar's biggest losers (seven defeats).

She then took her statuette backstage where she muttered, "I can't believe it! I can't believe it!" When a reporter asked Audrey Hepburn what she thought of Andrews's victory, Hepburn replied, "I'm thrilled for her, of course."

While British stars dominated the top thesp contests, an American was expected to prevail for Best Supporting Actress: Agnes Moorehead, who was best known for portraying a sly sorceress on TV, but was nommed for her role as a sassy housekeeper in *Hush . . . Hush, Sweet Charlotte*. *Variety* columnist Army Archerd reported that the bid shocked her: "Agnes Moorehead got her *Hush Hush* nomination news at home on a day off from *Bewitched*, and shouted with joy, 'I'm going to fall right outta bed!' "

But news of the eventual champ turned out to be even more shocking: a Russian-born, French-reared actress, who was honored for her role as an aging Greek courtesan. *Variety* reported, "Surprised came in Lila Kedrova's win as Best Supporting Actress for *Zorba the Greek* and crowd reaction indicated that this was possibly the most popular (or at least relaxed) win, although informal polls had placed her far down the line. Her reaction was one of genuine surprise and thrill, and applause literally carried her to the stage to receive her Oscar from Karl Malden."

An upset also occurred in the race for Best Supporting Actor, which was expected to go to either John Gielgud (*Becket*) or Stanley Holloway (*My Fair Lady*). Past Oscar champ Peter Ustinov claimed the race for his role in *Topkapi* as a dimwitted con man duped by shrewder thieves. Comedian Jonathan Winters, dressed in a dignified tuxedo, accepted on his behalf, saying, "I don't know whether Peter expected this or not. I certainly didn't or I would've been sure to wear black socks."

Despite *My Fair Lady*'s few losses, it carried the night. *Variety* noted, "In the nine categories in which *MFL* and *Poppins* were in direct competition, the former took seven, the latter one." One *Poppins* defeat was particularly noteworthy: Julie Andrews's husband Tony Walton lost the prize for best costumes to Cecil Beaton.

My Fair Lady claimed eight victories in all. In addition to the costume award and Rex Harrison's victory for Best Actor, it scored kudos for color cinematography, color art direction, sound, adapted musical scoring, Best Director and Best Picture.

George Cukor claimed his helmer's prize from Joan Crawford, saying, "I'm very grateful, very happy and very lucky." In past years, stars won Oscars for his films such as *The Philadelphia Story, Gaslight, Born Yesterday* and *A Double Life*, but *The New York Times* noted, "This was the first award for the veteran director known since 1930 as one of the best actors' directors in Hollywood."

Jack Warner thanked "those in the back lot, the front lot, upstairs, downstairs and everywhere."

The other big winner on Oscar night was the ceremony host. *Variety* said, "With the return of Bob Hope as emcee, the Academy Awards program regained some of its pep, vim and vigor noticeably absent when Hope was away."

Among his best jokes: "Julie Andrews is up for *Mary Poppins, or How I Learned to Stop Worrying and Love Jack Warner.*"

▪ 1964 ▪

NATIONAL BOARD OF REVIEW

Winners were announced on December 22, 1964.

BEST PICTURE
▪ *Becket*
My Fair Lady
The Girl with Green Eyes
The World of Henry Orient
Zorba the Greek
Topkapi
The Chalk Garden
The Finest Hours
Four Days in November
Seance on a Wet Afternoon

BEST DIRECTOR
▪ Desmond Davis, *The Girl with Green Eyes*

BEST ACTOR
▪ Anthony Quinn, *Zorba the Greek*

BEST ACTRESS
▪ Kim Stanley, *Seance on a Wet Afternoon*

BEST SUPPORTING ACTOR
▪ Martin Balsam, *The Carpetbaggers*

BEST SUPPORTING ACTRESS
▪ Edith Evans, *The Chalk Garden*

BEST FOREIGN FILM
▪ *World without Sun* (France/Italy)
The Organizer (France/Italy/Yugoslavia)
Anatomy of a Marriage (France/Italy)
Seduced and Abandoned (France/Italy)
Yesterday, Today and Tomorrow (Italy)

NEW YORK FILM CRITICS

Winners were announced on December 28, 1964. Awards were presented on January 23, 1965, at Sardi's restaurant in New York.

BEST PICTURE
▪ *My Fair Lady*

BEST DIRECTOR
▪ Stanley Kubrick, *Dr. Strangelove or: How I Learned to Stop Worrying and Love the Bomb*

BEST ACTOR
▪ Rex Harrison, *My Fair Lady*

BEST ACTRESS
▪ Kim Stanley, *Seance on a Wet Afternoon*

BEST SCREENPLAY
▪ Harold Pinter, *The Servant*

BEST FOREIGN FILM
▪ *That Man from Rio* (France/Italy)

DIRECTORS GUILD OF AMERICA

Awards were presented on February 6, 1965, at the Beverly Hilton Hotel in Los Angeles and the Waldorf-Astoria Hotel in New York.

BEST DIRECTOR
▪ George Cukor, *My Fair Lady*
Peter Glenville, *Becket*
John Huston, *The Night of the Iguana*
Stanley Kubrick, *Dr. Strangelove or: How I Learned to Stop Worrying and Love the Bomb*
Robert Stevenson, *Mary Poppins*

BEST HONORARY LIFETIME MEMBER
- Jack L. Warner

GOLDEN GLOBES

Nominations were announced on January 13, 1965. Awards were presented on February 8 at the Cocoanut Grove in the Ambassador Hotel in Los Angeles. The ceremony was telecast live on *The Andy Williams Show* on NBC.

BEST DRAMA PICTURE
- *Becket*

The Chalk Garden
Dear Heart
Night of the Iguana
Zorba the Greek

BEST COMEDY OR MUSICAL PICTURE
- *My Fair Lady*

Father Goose
Mary Poppins
The Unsinkable Molly Brown
The World of Henry Orient

BEST DIRECTOR
- George Cukor, *My Fair Lady*

Michael Cacoyannis, *Zorba the Greek*
John Frankenheimer, *Seven Days in May*
Peter Glenville, *Becket*
John Huston, *The Night of the Iguana*

BEST ACTOR, DRAMA
- Peter O'Toole, *Becket*

Richard Burton, *The Night of the Iguana*
Tony Franciosa, *Rio Conchos*
Fredric March, *Seven Days in May*
Anthony Quinn, *Zorba the Greek*

BEST ACTRESS, DRAMA
- Anne Bancroft, *The Pumpkin Eater*

Ava Gardner, *The Night of the Iguana*
Rita Hayworth, *Circus World*
Geraldine Page, *Toys in the Attic*
Jean Seberg, *Lilith*

BEST ACTOR, COMEDY OR MUSICAL
- Rex Harrison, *My Fair Lady*

Marcello Mastroianni, *Marriage, Italian Style*

Peter Sellers, *The Pink Panther*
Peter Ustinov, *Topkapi*
Dick Van Dyke, *Mary Poppins*

BEST ACTRESS, COMEDY OR MUSICAL
- Julie Andrews, *Mary Poppins*

Audrey Hepburn, *My Fair Lady*
Sophia Loren, *Marriage, Italian Style*
Melina Mercouri, *Topkapi*
Debbie Reynolds, *The Unsinkable Molly Brown*

BEST SUPPORTING ACTOR
- Edmond O'Brien, *Seven Days in May*

Cyril Delavanti, *The Night of the Iguana*
Stanley Holloway, *My Fair Lady*
Gilbert Roland, *Cheyenne Autumn*
Lee Tracy, *The Best Man*

BEST SUPPORTING ACTRESS
- Agnes Moorehead, *Hush . . . Hush, Sweet Charlotte*

Elizabeth Ashley, *The Carpetbaggers*
Grayson Hall, *The Night of the Iguana*
Lila Kedrova, *Zorba the Greek*
Ann Sothern, *The Best Man*

BEST MUSICAL SCORE
- Dimitri Tiomkin, *Fall of the Roman Empire*

Jerry Goldsmith, *Seven Days in May*
Laurence Rosenthal, *Becket*
Robert B. Sherman, Richard M. Sherman, *Mary Poppins*
Mikis Theodorakis, *Zorba the Greek*

BEST SONG
- "Circus World," *Circus World*, Dimitri Tiomkin, Ned Washington

"From Russia with Love," *From Russia with Love,* John Barry, Lionel Barr, Monty Norman
"Dear Heart," *Dear Heart*, Henry Mancini, Jay Livingston, Ray Evans
"Sunday in New York," *Sunday in New York,* Peter Nero, Carroll Coates, Roland Everett
"Where Love Has Gone," *Where Love Has Gone*, James Van Heusen, Sammy Cahn

Winners

MOST PROMISING NEWCOMER—MALE

- Harve Presnell
- George Segal
- Chaim Topol

MOST PROMISING NEWCOMER—FEMALE

- Mia Farrow
- Celia Kaye
- Mary Ann Mobley

BEST FOREIGN-LANGUAGE FILM (TIE)

- *The Girl with the Green Eyes* (England)
- *Marriage, Italian Style* (Italy)
- *Sallah* (Israel)

WORLD FILM FAVORITES

- Sophia Loren
- Marcello Mastroianni

CECIL B. DEMILLE AWARD

- James Stewart

WRITERS GUILD OF AMERICA

Awards were presented on March 17, 1965, at the Beverly Hilton Hotel in Los Angeles.

BEST WRITTEN DRAMA

- *Becket*, Edward Anhalt, based on the play by Jean Anouilh

The Best Man, Gore Vidal

The Night of the Iguana, Anthony Veiller, John Huston, based on the play by Tennessee Williams

One Potato, Two Potato, Raphael Hayes, Orville H. Hampton

Seven Days in May, Rod Serling, based on the novel by Fletcher Knebel and Charles W. Bailey II

BEST WRITTEN COMEDY

- *Dr. Strangelove or: How I Learned to Stop Worrying and Love the Bomb*, Stanley Kubrick, Peter George, Terry Southern

Father Goose, Peter Stone, Frank Tarloff, story by S. H. Barnett

The Pink Panther, Maurice Richlin, Blake Edwards

Topkapi, Monja Danischewsky, based on the novel *The Light of Day* by Eric Ambler

The World of Henry Orient, Nora Johnson, Nunnally Johnson

BEST WRITTEN MUSICAL

- *Mary Poppins*, Bill Walsh, Don Da Gradi, based on books by P. L. Travers

Kissin' Cousins, Gerald Drayson Adams, Gene Nelson

My Fair Lady, Alan Jay Lerner, based on the Lerner and Loewe musical and the play *Pygmalion* by George Bernard Shaw

Robin and the Seven Hoods, David Schwartz

Roustabout, Anthony Lawrence, Allan Weiss

The Unsinkable Molly Brown, Helen Deutsch, based on the musical by Richard Morris

LAUREL AWARD

- Sidney Buchman

VALENTINE DAVIES AWARD

- James R. Webb

ACADEMY AWARDS

Nominations were announced on February 23, 1965. Awards were presented on April 5 at the Santa Monica Civic Auditorium. The ceremony was telecast by ABC.

BEST PICTURE

- *My Fair Lady*

Becket

Dr. Strangelove or: How I Learned to Stop Worrying and Love the Bomb

Mary Poppins

Zorba the Greek

BEST DIRECTOR

- George Cukor, *My Fair Lady*

Michael Cacoyannis, *Zorba the Greek*

Peter Glenville, *Becket*

Stanley Kubrick, *Dr. Strangelove or: How I Learned to Stop Worrying and Love the Bomb*

Robert Stevenson, *Mary Poppins*

BEST ACTOR
- Rex Harrison, *My Fair Lady*
- Richard Burton, *Becket*
- Peter O'Toole, *Becket*
- Anthony Quinn, *Zorba the Greek*
- Peter Sellers, *Dr. Strangelove or: How I Learned to Stop Worrying and Love the Bomb*

BEST ACTRESS
- Julie Andrews, *Mary Poppins*
- Anne Bancroft, *The Pumpkin Eater*
- Sophia Loren, *Marriage, Italian Style*
- Debbie Reynolds, *The Unsinkable Molly Brown*
- Kim Stanley, *Seance on a Wet Afternoon*

BEST SUPPORTING ACTOR
- Peter Ustinov, *Topkapi*
- John Gielgud, *Becket*
- Stanley Holloway, *My Fair Lady*
- Edmond O'Brien, *Seven Days in May*
- Lee Tracy, *The Best Man*

BEST SUPPORTING ACTRESS
- Lila Kedrova, *Zorba the Greek*
- Gladys Cooper, *My Fair Lady*
- Dame Edith Evans, *The Chalk Garden*
- Grayson Hall, *The Night of the Iguana*
- Agnes Moorehead, *Hush . . . Hush, Sweet Charlotte*

BEST ADAPTED SCREENPLAY
- Edward Anhalt, *Becket*
- Michael Cacoyannis, *Zorba the Greek*
- Don Dagradi, Bill Walsh, *Mary Poppins*
- Peter George, Stanley Kubrick, Terry Southern, *Dr. Strangelove or: How I Learned to Stop Worrying and Love the Bomb*
- Alan Jay Lerner, *My Fair Lady*

BEST ORIGINAL SCREENPLAY
- S. H. Barnett, Peter Stone, Frank Tarloff, *Father Goose*
- Daniel Boulanger, Philippe de Broca, Ariane Mnouchkine, Jean-Paul Rappeneau, *That Man from Rio*
- Orville H. Hampton, Raphael Hayes, *One Potato, Two Potato*
- Mario Monicelli, Age Scarpelli, *The Organizer*
- Alun Owen, *A Hard Day's Night*

BEST SONG
- "Chim Chim Cher-Ee," *Mary Poppins*, Richard M. Sherman, Robert B. Sherman
- "Dear Heart," *Dear Heart*, Ray Evans, Jay Livingston, Henry Mancini
- "Hush . . . Hush, Sweet Charlotte," *Hush . . . Hush, Sweet Charlotte*, Mack David, Frank De Vol
- "My Kind of Town," *Robin and the Seven Hoods*, Sammy Cahn, James Van Heusen
- "Where Loves Has Gone," *Where Love Has Gone*, Sammy Cahn, James Van Heusen

BEST FOREIGN-LANGUAGE FILM
- *Yesterday, Today and Tomorrow* (Italy)
- *Raven's End* (Sweden)
- *Sallah* (Israel)
- *The Umbrellas of Cherbourg* (France)
- *Woman in the Dunes* (Japan)

Winners

BEST ART DIRECTION
(BLACK AND WHITE)
- Vassilis Fotopoulos, *Zorba the Greek*

(COLOR)
- Gene Allen, Cecil Beaton, George James Hopkins, *My Fair Lady*

BEST CINEMATOGRAPHY
(BLACK AND WHITE)
- Walter Lassally, *Zorba the Greek*

(COLOR)
- Harry Stradling, *My Fair Lady*

BEST COSTUME DESIGN
(BLACK AND WHITE)
- Dorothy Jeakins, *The Night of the Iguana*

(COLOR)
- Cecil Beaton, *My Fair Lady*

BEST DOCUMENTARY
(FEATURE)
- Jacques-Yves Cousteau, *World without Sun*

(SHORT SUBJECT)
- Charles Guggenheim, *Nine from Little Rock*

BEST FILM EDITING
- *Mary Poppins*, Cotton Warburton

BEST MUSIC

(MUSIC SCORE—SUBSTANTIALLY ORIGINAL)

- Richard M. Sherman, Robert B. Sherman, *Mary Poppins*

(SCORING OF MUSIC—ADAPTATION OR TREATMENT)

- Andre Previn, *My Fair Lady*

SCIENTIFIC OR TECHNICAL AWARDS

Class I (Statuette)

- Petro Vlahos, Wadsworth E. Pohl, UB Iwerks

Class II (Plaque)

- Pierre Angenieux; Carl W. Hauge, Edward H. Reichard, Job Sanderson, Sidney P. Solow

Class III (Certificate)

- Milton Forman, Richard B. Glickman, Daniel J. Pearlman, ColorTran; Steward Filmscreen Corp.; Anthony Paglia, Twentieth Century-Fox Studio Mechanical Effects Dept.; Edward H. Reichard, Carl W. Hauge, Leonard L. Sokolow; Nelson Tyler

BEST SHORT SUBJECT

(CARTOON)

- *Christmas Cracker*, National Film Board of Canada

The Pink Phink

(LIVE ACTION)

- *Casals Conducts: 1964*

BEST SOUND

- George R. Groves, *My Fair Lady*

BEST SOUND EFFECTS

- Norman Wanstall, *Goldfinger*

BEST SPECIAL VISUAL EFFECTS

- Peter Ellenshaw, Hamilton Luske, Eustace Lycett, *Mary Poppins*

BEST HONORARY AWARD

- William Tuttle

· 1965 ·

The Sound of Music *Ends on a High Note*

*T*he Sound of Music turned out to be more than just one of movie-goers' favorite things: it broke *Gone With the Wind*'s all-time b.o. record and rescued Twentieth Century-Fox from bankruptcy after its pyramid-high losses on *Cleopatra*. *Variety*'s reviewer heralded the sentimental songfest as "a warmly pulsating, captivating drama . . . magnificently mounted," but it was hardly in tune with the tastes of the notoriously edgy critics. Judith Crist blasted it in *The New York Herald Tribune*, Dwight MacDonald called it "The Sound of Mucus" in *Esquire* and Pauline Kael denounced it so vehemently in the pages of *McCall's* that the magazine fired her.

Therefore, the movie had dim prospects for kudos from the New York film critics, who became the first awards group to vote this year when the National Board of Review decided it needed more time to weigh the glut of films released in late December. *The Sound of Music* didn't reap even a single vote for Best Picture among the six pics proposed by the crix on the first ballot. Instead, one movie proved to be their literal darling in several categories: *Darling*.

The British indie helmed by John Schlesinger showcased a sexy new superstar hailed as the epitome of the free-spirited new woman of the sixties. While portraying a fashion model who ruthlessly bed-hops her way to the top, Julie Christie seduced most crix en route. "Christie almost perfectly captures the character of the immoral Diana, and very rarely misses her target," *Variety* said. Her free-spirited female fans admired her, too. Soon after Christie stripped off her miniskirt on screen, thousands of women donned the skimpy new garments off screen, sparking a fashion craze. Christie also reaped huzzahs for her other star turn in 1965. *Variety* called her "outstanding" as the

The critics' *Darling* won Best Picture, Director and Actress. *Variety* said star Julie Christie (above) was also "outstanding" in *Doctor Zhivago*.

mistress who inspires Omar Shariff to poetic heights in *Doctor Zhivago*.

In the crix's balloting for Best Picture, *Darling* led on the first polling with six votes, followed by four for *The Pawnbroker*, three for *Those Magnificent Men in the Their Flying Machines*, two for *Doctor Zhivago* and one each for *A Thousand Clowns* and *The Knack . . . and How to Get It*. It won on the sixth tally with eight votes out of 17. In the race for Best Director, Schlesinger led on the first round (five votes), but didn't prevail over David Lean (*Doctor Zhivago*) and Roman Polanski (*Repulsion*) until the sixth canvass.

Christie's contest for Best Actress pitted her against the year's other top Julie— Andrews. Christie led the *Sound of Music* star nine to two on the first polling, but then "won going away on the third ballot with a count of 11 votes to 4," noted *The New York Times.*

Reporting on the Best Actor race, Bosley Crowther of the *Times* boasted, "I was one of 11 of 17 critics who were in surprising accord on the third ballot that Oskar Werner gave the best performance as the spiritually exhausted ship's doctor in Stanley Kramer's *Ship of Fools.*" Werner topped Rod Steiger in *The Pawnbroker,* which had previously earned its star the Best Actor award at the 1964 Berlin Film Festival, and Werner's *Ship of Fools* costar Lee Marvin, who was voted Best Actor at the 1965 Berlin fest for portraying a drunken gunslinger and his evil twin in *Cat Ballou.*

Crowther did not agree with his peers on the issue of Best Screenplay, however. When they decided, after five voting rounds, not to bestow the prize this year, he blasted them for "shirking a valid responsibility."

Two weeks later the National Board of Review endorsed two of the crix's picks—Christie and Schlesinger—but opted for Marvin for Best Actor. Its choice for Best Picture was a surprising departure: *The Eleanor Roosevelt Story. Variety* described it as a nonfictional work "put together of stills, newsreel materials, TV kinescopes and other materials, plus a narration by Archibald MacLeish."

When the Directors Guild of America announced its nominees, there were two shocking omissions: David Lean (*Doctor Zhivago*) and William Wyler (*The Collector*). The guild made up for the latter snub by announcing that Wyler would receive its special D. W. Griffith Award, but there was no palm for Lean.

Future *Variety* editor Peter Bart, then a scribe for *The New York Times*, reported that further jolts awaited the "white-maned, tuxedo-glad guildsmen and their elegantly coiffed and bejeweled lady folks" when they arrived at the usually sedate awards banquet at the Beverly Hilton Hotel. The program opened with entertainment provided by a rock-and-roll band, "which brought forth a groan from some of the older, more austere guildsmen," Bart wrote. "At the end of the group's first number, two portly directors got to their feet and booed but the group had worked itself into a lather and glided irrevocably into another number, then another."

The Hollywood old guard struck back when the awards program began by declaring the one veteran helmer in the nominee lineup, *The Sound of Music*'s Robert Wise, the champ over four relative rookies (Sidney Furie, Sidney Lumet, John Schlesinger and Elliot Silverstein), as expected. Star Julie Andrews accepted on Wise's behalf, explaining that the honoree was directing a film in the Far East.

> ## *Zhivago* set a new record for the most Golden Globe wins: five.

Lean's snub was soon redressed by the Golden Globes when the foreign press gave him their helmer's prize over Wise, Wyler and Schlesinger. "This is the end of a hell of a suspenseful wait," Lean said with a smile when he accepted the statuette at the Cocoanut Grove ceremony.

Doctor Zhivago earned the most Globes in all, including additional trophies for Best Drama Picture, Best Original Score, Best Screenplay and Best Actor, setting a new record for reaping the most awards ever (five). "Biggest surprise of the evening was Omar Sharif's victory in the Best Actor category against the tremendous competition of Rex Harrison in *The Agony and the Ecstasy*, Sidney Poitier in *Patch of Blue*, Rod Steiger in *The Pawnbroker* and Oskar Werner in *Ship of Fools*," reported *The Hollywood Citizen-News*. The paper claimed Sharif was "shocked . . . and hadn't even given himself an outside chance of victory."

Werner rebounded to be named Best Supporting Actor for *The Spy Who Came in from the Cold,* but another front-runner suffered an upset when Julie Christie (*Darling*) lost to Samantha Eggar, who gave what *Variety* called "a remarkably restrained" perf as a kidnap victim in *The Collector.* Otherwise, favorites prevailed, with *The*

Sound of Music and star Julie Andrews being honored as Best Comedy or Musical Picture and best actress. Lee Marvin took a bow as best actor.

Best Supporting Actress Ruth Gordon (*Inside Daisy Clover*) gave the night's most amusing acceptance speech when the veteran thesp told the gathered crowd, "I'm a new girl in town and I am dying to be in pictures."

It was the second year that the gala was broadcast on NBC's *The Andy Williams Show. Variety* applauded the program for being "smooth and rapid and in color" and praised Williams for handling his hosting duties "professionally."

Less than one month later, there was an upset at the writers guild awards when the prize for Best Written Drama went to Morton Fine and David Friedkin, scribes of *The Pawnbroker*, which was described by *Variety* as "a painstakingly etched portrait of a man who survived the living hell of a Nazi concentration camp and encounters further prejudice when he runs a pawnshop in Harlem."

Woody Allen (*What's New, Pussycat?*) received his first WGA bid, but lost the award for Best Written Comedy to Herb Gardner, who was honored for *A Thousand Clowns,* the screen adaptation of his Broadway hit about a carefree nonconformist.

No upset was possible in the category of Best Written Musical, since *The Sound of Music* was the only nominee, resulting in Ernest Lehman's fourth WGA prize. The tuner was the target of one of the gala's customary spoof skits, which starred Mary Tyler Moore and Shelley Berman singing, "The hills are alive with the sound of music, and each singing nun is a brand new star!"

The Sound of Music entered the Oscar race tied with *Doctor Zhivago* with 10 noms each. Gossip columnists tried hard to heighten the rivalry between the pics' two Julies—Andrews and Christie—who were both up for Best Actress (Christie for *Darling*), but the stars didn't bite. Andrews told

Variety columnist Army Archerd, "It's funny. At last year's awards, everyone tried to make a feud between Audrey (Hepburn) and me—and now this." Actually, they were "chums," she insisted.

Both Julies planned to squash the rumors of bitterness between them by arriving together on Oscar night, but their studios split them up. Andrews received the bigger ovation of the two as she stepped onto the red carpet, which was seen in color by TV viewers for the first time.

Their competish for the actress laurels included Golden Globe champ Samantha Eggar (*The Collector*), past Oscar winner Simone Signoret as a faded Spanish countess in *Ship of Fools* and Elizabeth Hartman, who *Variety* said had "an excellent screen debut" as a woman blinded by a vicious mother (Shelley Winters), in *A Patch of Blue.*

"Miss Andrews says she doesn't think she can win," Archerd reported prior to the ceremony. *Variety* reported afterward, "Viewers saw Julie Christie breathless as they called her name for best actress of the year and the closeup of her in ecstasy and tears was a rare picture." The paper admitted that she had been "the expected winner, for those who hadn't seen *Darling* were generally enraptured by her showing in *Zhivago.*"

Lee Marvin (*Cat Ballou*) may have already won the Golden Globe plus kudos from the Berlin Film Fest and National Board of Review, but he was not considered a serious contender at the Oscars. He faced Rod Steiger (*The Pawnbroker*), Laurence Olivier (*Othello*), New York film crix champ Oskar Werner (*Ship of Fools*) and an overdue Richard Burton, who "fits neatly into the role of the apparently burned-out British agent" in *The Spy Who Came in from the Cold,* said *Variety.*

When Marvin prevailed for his tipsy gunslinger role, *Variety* observed that he "got the biggest ovation of the night for any winner" and noted that his "win breaks an

Zhivago's David Lean was snubbed by DGA.

Oscar bugagoo that comedy roles don't lead to awards." He said at the podium, "I think one half of this belongs to some horse somewhere in the Valley."

Best Supporting Actor nominee Martin Balsam was supposed to be somewhere out in Arizona shooting his new movie *Hombre* on Oscar night, but he slipped away without the director's permission. "Fortunately, he won," Army Archerd noted. Afterward, the relieved champ told *Variety*, "I doubt if I ever want to win again."

Shelley Winters certainly wanted to win again after having previously scored an Oscar for *The Diary of Anne Frank* in 1959. *Variety* lauded her courageous screen work as a "sleazy mother" in *A Patch of Blue*, but Winters worried that the role was too unsympathetic to win over voters. When she beat Globe champ Ruth Gordon (*Inside Daisy Clover*), she wept gratefully at the podium and told *Variety* backstage, "I hope I thanked everyone."

As Oscar night wound down, *The Sound of Music* team was worried, too. The pic had nabbed only three awards (film editing, music scoring and sound), compared to five for *Doctor Zhivago* (screenplay, music, cinematography, art direction and costume design). Then it suddenly rebounded when the prize for Best Director went to Robert Wise, who "was absent in Hong Kong," said *Variety*, "where *The Sand Pebbles* has run afoul of weather and street riots." Julie Andrews accepted the honor on Wise's behalf, then returned to her seat. When *The Sound of Music* was declared Best Picture a few minutes later, "she practically jumped out of her red dress, shouting, 'That's just great!' " *Variety* reported. "Robert Wise and his *Sand Pebbles* group were listening to the awards via Armed Forces Radio aboard their boat in the bay outside Hong Kong—but reception faded after the Best Scoring Award. A phone call brought 'em the news (2:30 P.M. H.K. time) and fireworks were set off aboard ship."

▪ 1965 ▪

NEW YORK FILM CRITICS

Winners were announced on December 27, 1965. Awards were presented on January 29, 1966, at Sardi's restaurant in New York.

BEST PICTURE
▪ *Darling*

BEST DIRECTOR
▪ John Schlesinger, *Darling*

BEST ACTOR
▪ Oskar Werner, *Ship of Fools*

BEST ACTRESS
▪ Julie Christie, *Darling*

BEST FOREIGN FILM
▪ *Juliet of the Spirits* (France/Italy/Federal Republic of Germany)

NATIONAL BOARD OF REVIEW

Winners were announced on January 9, 1966.

BEST PICTURE
▪ *The Eleanor Roosevelt Story*
The Agony and the Ecstasy
Doctor Zhivago
Ship of Fools
The Spy Who Came in from the Cold
Darling
The Greatest Story Ever Told
A Thousand Clowns
The Train
The Sound of Music

BEST DIRECTOR
▪ John Schlesinger, *Darling*

BEST ACTOR
▪ Lee Marvin, *Cat Ballou, Ship of Fools*

BEST ACTRESS

- Julie Christie, *Darling, Doctor Zhivago*

BEST SUPPORTING ACTOR

- Harry Andrews, *The Agony and the Ecstasy, The Hill*

BEST SUPPORTING ACTRESS

- Joan Blondell, *The Cincinnati Kid*

BEST FOREIGN FILM

- *Juliet of the Spirits* (France/Italy/Federal Republic of Germany)
The Overcoat (U.S.S.R.)
La Bohème (Switzerland)
La Tia Tula (Spain)
Gertrud (Denmark)

DIRECTORS GUILD OF AMERICA

Awards were presented on February 12, 1966, at the Beverly Hilton Hotel in Los Angeles and the Waldorf-Astoria Hotel in New York City.

BEST DIRECTOR

- Robert E. Wise, *The Sound of Music*
Sidney Furie, *The Ipcress File*
Sidney Lumet, *The Pawnbroker*
John Schlesinger, *Darling*
Elliot Silverstein, *Cat Ballou*

D. W. GRIFFITH AWARD

- William Wyler

GOLDEN GLOBES

Nominations were announced on January 5, 1966. Awards were presented on February 28 at the Cocoanut Grove in the Ambassador Hotel in Los Angeles. The ceremony was telecast live on *The Andy Williams Show* on NBC.

BEST DRAMA PICTURE

- *Doctor Zhivago*
The Collector
The Flight of the Phoenix
A Patch of Blue
Ship of Fools

Sound of Music didn't score a single vote for best pic from the Gotham crix, but won the Globe and Oscar. "That's just great!" roared star Julie Andrews (above).

BEST COMEDY OR MUSICAL PICTURE

- *The Sound of Music*
Cat Ballou
The Great Race
Those Magnificent Men in their Flying Machines
A Thousand Clowns

BEST DIRECTOR

- David Lean, *Doctor Zhivago*
Guy Green, *A Patch of Blue*
John Schlesinger, *Darling*
Robert Wise, *The Sound of Music*
William Wyler, *The Collector*

BEST ACTOR, DRAMA

- Omar Sharif, *Doctor Zhivago*
Rex Harrison, *The Agony and the Ecstasy*
Sidney Poitier, *A Patch of Blue*
Rod Steiger, *The Pawnbroker*
Oskar Werner, *Ship of Fools*

BEST ACTRESS, DRAMA

- Samantha Eggar, *The Collector*
Julie Christie, *Darling*
Elizabeth Hartman, *Ship of Fools*
Simone Signoret, *Ship of Fools*
Maggie Smith, *Othello*

BEST ACTOR, COMEDY OR MUSICAL

- Lee Marvin, *Cat Ballou*
Jack Lemmon, *The Great Race*
Jerry Lewis, *Boeing Boeing*

Jason Robards, *A Thousand Clowns*
Alberto Sordi, *Those Magnificent Men in Their Flying Machines*

BEST ACTRESS, COMEDY OR MUSICAL

■ Julie Andrews, *The Sound of Music*
Jane Fonda, *Cat Ballou*
Barbara Harris, *A Thousand Clowns*
Rita Tushingham, *The Knack*
Natalie Wood, *Inside Daisy Clover*

BEST SUPPORTING ACTOR

■ Oskar Werner, *The Spy Who Came in from the Cold*
Red Buttons, *Harlow*
Frank Finlay, *Othello*
Hardy Kruger, *The Flight of the Phoenix*
Telly Savalas, *Battle of the Bulge*

BEST SUPPORTING ACTRESS

■ Ruth Gordon, *Inside Daisy Clover*
Joan Blondell, *Cincinnati Kid*
Joyce Redman, *Othello*
Thelma Ritter, *Boeing Boeing*
Peggy Wood, *The Sound of Music*

MOST PROMISING NEWCOMER—MALE

■ Robert Redford
Ian Bannen
James Caan
James Fox
Tom Nardini

MOST PROMISING NEWCOMER—FEMALE

■ Elizabeth Hartman
Donna Butterworth
Geraldine Chaplin
Rosemary Forsythe
Maura McGiveney

BEST SCREENPLAY

■ Robert Bolt, *Doctor Zhivago*
Sterling Silliphant, *The Slender Thread*
Philip Dunne, *The Agony and the Ecstasy**
Guy Green, *A Patch of Blue*
John Kohn, Stanley Mann, *The Collector*
Philip Yordan, Milton Sperling, John Nielson, *Battle of the Bulge**

---

* HFPA's current records list the writer of *The Agony and the Ecstasy* as a screenplay nominee, but do not list the team behind *Battle of the Bulge*. *Variety*'s list, published on February 6, 1966, cities *Bulge* but not *Agony*.

BEST ORIGINAL SONG

■ "Forget Domani," *Yellow Rolls Royce*
"Ballad of Cat Ballou," *Cat Ballou*
"That Funny Feeling," *That Funny Feeling*
"The Shadow of Your Smile," *The Sandpiper*
"The Sweetheart Tree," *The Great Race*

BEST FOREIGN-LANGUAGE FOREIGN FILM

■ *Juliet of the Spirits* (Italy)
Circle of Love (La Ronde) (France)
Red Beard (Japan)
Tarahumara (Mexico)
The Umbrellas of Cherbourg (France)

BEST ENGLISH-LANGUAGE FOREIGN FILM

■ *Darling* (U.K.)
The Knack (U.K.)
The Leather Boys (U.K.)
90 Degrees in the Shade (Czechoslovakia)
Othello (U.K.)

Winners

BEST ORIGINAL SCORE

■ Maurice Jarre, *Doctor Zhivago*

WORLD FILM FAVORITES

■ Paul Newman
■ Natalie Wood

CECIL B. DEMILLE AWARD

■ John Wayne

WRITERS GUILD OF AMERICA

Awards were presented on March 23, 1966, at the Beverly Hilton Hotel in Los Angeles.

BEST WRITTEN DRAMA

■ *The Pawnbroker*, Morton Fine, David Friedkin, based on the novel by Edward Lewis Wallant
The Collector, Stanley Mann, John Kohn, based on the novel by John Fowles
A Patch of Blue, Guy Green, based on the novel *Be Ready with Bells and Drums* by Elizabeth Kata
Ship of Fools, Abby Mann, based on the novel by Katherine Ann Porter

The Spy Who Came in from the Cold, Paul Dehn, Guy Trosper, based on the novel by John Le Carré

BEST WRITTEN COMEDY
- *A Thousand Clowns*, Herb Gardner

Cat Ballou, Walter Newman, Frank R. Pierson, based on the novel *The Ballad of Cat Ballou* by Roy Chanslor

The Great Race, Arthur Ross, story by Arthur Ross and Blake Edwards

That Darn Cat!, Mildred Gordon, Gordon Gordon, Bill Walsh

What's New, Pussycat?, Woody Allen

BEST WRITTEN MUSICAL
- *The Sound of Music*, Ernest Lehman, based on the Rodgers and Hammerstein musical (no other nominees in this category)

BEST LAUREL AWARD
- Isobel Lennart

VALENTINE DAVIES AWARD
- Leonard Spigelgass

ACADEMY AWARDS

Nominations were announced on February 21, 1966. Awards were presented on April 18 at the Santa Monica Civic Auditorium. The ceremony was telecast by ABC.

BEST PICTURE
- *The Sound of Music*

Darling

Doctor Zhivago

Ship of Fools

A Thousand Clowns

BEST DIRECTOR
- Robert Wise, *The Sound of Music*

David Lean, *Doctor Zhivago*

John Schlesinger, *Darling*

Hiroshi Teshigahara, *Woman in the Dunes*

William Wyler, *The Collector*

BEST ACTOR
- Lee Marvin, *Cat Ballou*

Richard Burton, *The Spy Who Came in from the Cold*

Laurence Olivier, *Othello*

Rod Steiger, *The Pawnbroker*

Oskar Werner, *Ship of Fools*

BEST ACTRESS
- Julie Christie, *Darling*

Julie Andrews, *The Sound of Music*

Samantha Eggar, *The Collector*

Elizabeth Hartman, *A Patch of Blue*

Simone Signoret, *Ship of Fools*

BEST SUPPORTING ACTOR
- Martin Balsam, *A Thousand Clowns*

Ian Bannen, *The Flight of the Phoenix*

Tom Courtenay, *Doctor Zhivago*

Michael Dunn, *Ship of Fools*

Frank Finlay, *Othello*

BEST SUPPORTING ACTRESS
- Shelley Winters, *A Patch of Blue*

Ruth Gordon, *Inside Daisy Clover*

Joyce Redman, *Othello*

Maggie Smith, *Othello*

Peggy Wood, *The Sound of Music*

BEST ADAPTED SCREENPLAY
- Robert Bolt, *Doctor Zhivago*

Herb Gardner, *A Thousand Clowns*

John Kohn, Stanley Mann, *The Collector*

Abby Mann, *Ship of Fools*

Walter Newman, Frank R. Pierson, *Cat Ballou*

BEST ORIGINAL SCREENPLAY
- Frederic Raphael, *Darling*

Ken Annakin, Jack Davies, *Those Magnificent Men in Their Flying Machines*

Franklin Coen, Frank Davis, *The Train*

Jacques Demy, *The Umbrellas of Cherbourg*

Age Scarpelli, Suso Cecchi D'amico, Tonino Guerra, Mario Monicelli, Giorgio Salvioni, *Casanova '70*

BEST SONG
- "The Shadow of Your Smile," *The Sandpiper*, Johnny Mandel, Paul Francis Webster

"The Ballad of Cat Ballou," *Cat Ballou*, Mack David, Jerry Livingston

"I Will Wait for You," *The Umbrellas of Cherbourg*, Jacques Demy, Norman Gimbel, Michel Legrand

"The Sweetheart Tree," *The Great Race*, Henry Mancini, Johnny Mercer

"What's New, Pussycat?," *What's New, Pussycat?*, Burt Bacharach, Hal David

BEST FOREIGN-LANGUAGE FILM

- *The Shop on Main Street* (Czechoslovakia)

Blood on the Land (Greece)

Dear John (Sweden)

Kwaidan (Japan)

Marriage, Italian Style (Italy)

Winners

BEST ART DIRECTION
(BLACK AND WHITE)

- Robert Clatworthy, Joseph Kish, *Ship of Fools*

(COLOR)

- John Box, Terry Marsh, Dario Simoni, *Doctor Zhivago*

BEST CINEMATOGRAPHY
(BLACK AND WHITE)

- Ernest Laszlo, *Ship of Fools*

(COLOR)

- Freddie Young, *Doctor Zhivago*

BEST COSTUME DESIGN
(BLACK AND WHITE)

- Julie Harris, *Darling*

(COLOR)

- Phyllis Dalton, *Doctor Zhivago*

BEST DOCUMENTARY
(FEATURE)

- Sidney Glazier, *The Eleanor Roosevelt Story*

(SHORT SUBJECT)

- Francis Thompson, *To Be Alive!*

BEST FILM EDITING

- William Reynolds, *The Sound of Music*

BEST MUSIC
(MUSIC SCORE—SUBSTANTIALLY ORIGINAL)

- Maurice Jarre, *Doctor Zhivago*

(SCORING OF MUSIC—ADAPTATION OR TREATMENT)

- Irwin Kostal, *The Sound of Music*

SCIENTIFIC OR TECHNICAL AWARDS
Class II (Plaque)

- Arthur J. Hatch, Strong Electric Corp.; Stefan Kudelski

BEST SHORT SUBJECT
(CARTOON)

- Les Goldman, Chuck Jones, *The Dot and the Line*

(LIVE ACTION)

- Claude Berri, *The Chicken* (Le Poulet)

BEST SOUND

- Fred Hynes, James P. Corcoran, *The Sound of Music*

BEST SOUND EFFECTS

- Tregoweth Brown, *The Great Race*

BEST SPECIAL VISUAL EFFECTS

- John Stears, *Thunderball*

IRVING G. THALBERG MEMORIAL AWARD

- William Wyler

JEAN HERSHOLT HUMANITARIAN AWARD

- Edmond L. Depatie

HONORARY AWARD

- Bob Hope

SCREEN ACTORS GUILD

LIFETIME ACHIEVEMENT AWARD

- Bob Hope

· 1966 ·

Crix Blow-Up *in Gotham*

War broke out among the New York critics when a rebel faction created rival awards and fired its first salvo: *Blow-Up*.

The debut English-language film by Italian director Michelangelo Antonioni was hailed as Best Picture by the new group calling itself the National Society of Film Critics—even though its membership was composed, just like its foe, of Gothamites. The difference was that the new org contained magazine writers who'd been denied admission to the New York Film Critics, which was composed of newspaper scribes.

If the national society hadn't entered the awards derby, 1966 would've been one of those rare years when all the leading kudos agreed on one Best Picture. But its feisty 11 crix set out on a decidedly different path.

The new awards combined U.S. and foreign fare into one Best Picture race and non-Yankee movies ended up claiming all four kudos.

Blow-Up's Antonioni was named Best Director, which was the only race decided on the first ballot when a majority vote was needed for victory. If the showdown went to a second polling, winners were declared after adding up points scored by voters' first, second and third choices.

Sylvie was elected Best Actress for portraying a charming eccentric in *The Shameless Old Lady,* a French import based on a Bertolt Brecht short story. In second place was Britain's new breakout star Vanessa Redgrave, who had recently won Best Actress at the Cannes Film Festival for her role as a woman pursued by a wacky ex-husband in the U.K. production *Morgan!* In third place was Elizabeth Taylor, cited as a boozy faculty wife in *Who's Afraid of Virginia Woolf?* "Taylor earns every penny of her reported $1 million plus," *Variety* said in its review. "Her characterization is at once

David Hemmings and Vanessa Redgrave in *Blow-Up,* the first Best Picture of the new National Society of Film Critics, which was really comprised of New Yorkers.

sensual, spiteful, cynical, pitiable, loathsome, lustful and tender."

Variety said of Taylor's on- and off-screen husband, "Richard Burton delivers a smash portrayal," but he tied for second place in the Best Actor race with Paul Scofield as the martyred Sir Thomas More in *A Man for All Seasons*. The victor was Britain's Michael Caine, who *Variety* said gave "a powerfully strong performance as the woman-mad anti-hero" in *Alfie*.

Winners were determined during a vote conducted on January 2 and announced two days later at a cocktail party held at the Algonquin Hotel. Afterward, certificates of merit were mailed to the champs.

A few days later *Variety* commented on *Blow-Up*'s victories as Best Picture and Best Director: "The effect of the awards on pic's box-office performance should be worth watching." But *The New York Times* believed that two other factors might help the movie succeed even more: being condemned by the Catholic Church and denied a seal of approval from the Production Code. In the end, all three no doubt contributed toward *Blow-Up* becoming a long-running art house hit.

Runners-up for Best Picture at the society's vote were *A Man for All Seasons* and *Who's Afraid of Virginia Woolf?*—both of which faced off as the major contenders at the other kudos.

There was a curious coincidence dogging the pics' match-up at the New York Film Critics, which met at the newspaper guild's office in Manhattan's theater district. Both works were once performed nearby on Broadway stages, where they were declared Best Play in different years by both the Tony and New York Drama Critics Circle Awards.

At the New York Film Critics Awards, they were the two top vote-getters for Best Picture, although *A Man for All Seasons* won easily on the first ballot by a 10-to-3 score. *Blow-Up* was the only other contender, scoring one vote.

A real blow-up occurred soon afterward when *Times* critic Bosley Crowther insisted that his peers had "flipped their lids and voted like wild evangelists" by giving *A Man for All Seasons* more awards than any other in the crix group's history: four. Previously, seven films had earned three kudos each.

Variety had praised the drama about Catholic chancellor Thomas More's battle with his divorce-bent king, Henry VIII, as "excellent, handsome and stirring." Three of its awards were won on the first ballot, when it nabbed the requisite two-thirds vote needed from the 14 crix. In addition to its romp for Best Picture, it won the screenplay prize easily and Fred Zinnemann tied John Ford as the crix's most honored director by claiming his fourth laurel.

Paul Scofield faced tougher competish in the Best Actor race, leading Richard Burton by a 8–4 edge on the first round. Scofield triumphed on the second tally, 10 to 3, thereby winning his first screen prize for his first screen role. Years earlier he'd won a Tony Award for *A Man for All Seasons,* which featured him in his first role on an American stage.

It was in the actress showdown that things really "flared up," according to crix chief Judith Crist of *The World Journal Tribune. Virginia Woolf*'s Elizabeth Taylor led on the first polling with six votes, followed by Lynn Redgrave, who scored four votes as a pudgy ugly duckling in *Gregory Girl.* Redgrave pulled ahead seven votes to six on the third round, but then fell behind. On the sixth and final ballot, when only a simple majority vote was needed to determine the champ, the rivals "each had 7 votes and not one of the 14 critics was about to switch," Crist said. A tie was declared.

Redgrave was one of the few winners who showed up a month later at Sardi's restaurant to accept the crix's plaques, embossed with the logos of their publications. She happened to be in town rehearsing for her Broadway debut in *Black Comedy.* Zinnemann was also present.

Angry New York crix formed a rival National Society of Film Critics.

Otherwise, substitutes took bows. Marlon Brando flew in from Switzerland to accept for his *Reflections in a Golden Eye* costar Elizabeth Taylor. Angela Lansbury represented Paul Scofield. Myrna Loy stood in for an ailing Bette Davis, who'd been skedded to bestow special plaques to two retiring members of the crix group: Kate Cameron (*Daily News*) and Rose Pelswick (*Journal-American*). John Lindsay became the first Gotham mayor to participate in the kudos since Fiorello La Guardia caused a ruckus at the 1939 gala.

The National Board of Review made the same award choices, although Elizabeth Taylor claimed the actress honor solo.

Two Taylor movies competed for Best Written Drama at the Writers Guild awards: *Virginia Woolf* and *The Sand Pebbles. Virginia Woolf* won easily, giving Ernest Lehman his fifth guild win, a record. Past champs Billy Wilder and I. A. L. Diamond competed for Best Written Drama with *The*

Fortune Cookie, but lost to William Rose, author of *The Russians Are Coming, The Russians Are Coming,* which *Variety* described as "an outstanding Cold War comedy depicting the havoc created on a mythical Massachusetts island by the crew of a grounded Russian sub."

Between the two winners, it was *Virginia Woolf* that got torpedoed in this year's satiric skits performed before 2,500 industry leaders attending the gala at the Los Angeles Century Plaza Hotel. *Woolf* was combined with *The Sound of Music* into a farce titled "An Evening of Fun and Games with George and Martha von Trapp," starring Walter Matthau as *Virginia Woolf*'s George, Nanette Fabray as Martha and Tuesday Weld and Larry Hagman as their young victims.

Variety noted, "Prelude to skit explained that these days, to have a b.o. hit, you have to go to one extreme or the other. If *Woolf* had been a little cleaner or *Music* a little dirtier, Ernie Lehman, writer of both and producer of *Woolf*, would be a poor man today. Lyrics intertwined to the skit were to the tune of 'Music' but were not printable. Suffice it to say that sex, sex, sex and more sex interlarded the dialog and lyrics."

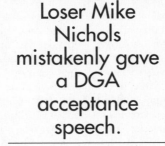

Loser Mike Nichols mistakenly gave a DGA acceptance speech.

As raunchy as the skit was, it sparked no protests. Another skit, depicting agents as insects and horned lizards, caused an uproar, however, when thin-skinned per-centers denounced it as "tasteless, childish, unprofessional and unfunny" and some agents even stormed out of the ceremony.

The mood was far more harmonious and upbeat when members of the directors' guild met at the Beverly Hilton Hotel. *Variety* reported: "A roar of approval greeted Fred Zinnemann's win. It was his second DGA victory, first time having been for *From Here to Eternity.* He now is the fifth two-time DGA winner, joining Joseph L. Mankiewicz, George Stevens, David Lean and Robert Wise.

"Danny Thomas was the local M.C. for the 80-minute presentation show, which also included entertainment digressions by presenters Edie Adams, Rowan & Martin and Polly Bergen."

NBC was pleased with the response the Golden Globes telecast had received when it was showcased on *The Andy Williams Show* for the past two years. Now the pea-cock web gave the kudos its own 90-minute special as part of a new, five-year deal that paid the Hollywood Foreign Press Associa-tion $70,000 annually in license fees.

Williams continued as host and prom-ised "a real suspense thriller," but, as *Variety* noted, "Winners generally paralleled the rumors circulating for many days."

A Man for All Seasons proved to be a movie for all awards when it claimed four Globes, including Best Drama Pic-ture, Best Director (Fred Zinnemann) and Best Screenplay (Robert Bolt). When the Best Actor nom-inees were announced sev-eral weeks earlier, *The Hollywood Citizen-News* promised "a knock-down and ring-a-ding battle" between Richard Burton, Michael Caine and Paul Scofield, but, on awards night, Scofield continued the romp he'd started with the New York Film Critics and National Board of Review.

Since Vanessa Redgrave and Lynn Red-grave were in the separate category for comedy/musical actresses, Gotham film crix and National Board of Review champ Elizabeth Taylor seemed to have a clear shot at Best Drama Actress. A reporter for the *Citizen-News* said, "I'd say that Elizabeth Taylor's performance in *Who's Afraid of Virginia Woolf?* puts her way out in front."

But a jaw-dropping upset occurred when that prize was claimed by Anouk Aimee as a widow who falls in love with a widower in *A Man and a Woman,* the popular art house hit from France that was also voted Best Foreign-Language Film.

Gossip wags stoked up sibling rivalry between the Redgrave sisters competing for

Best Comedy/Musical Actress. When Lynn was proclaimed the winner, *The London Evening Standard* reported, "The audience applauded wildly . . . then even more wildly as Vanessa stepped up to accept the award on Lynn's behalf. Lynn is starring in a Broadway play and couldn't be there for the occasion. Vanessa is in Hollywood filming *Camelot.*"

Winner of Best Comedy/Musical Picture, *The Russians Are Coming, The Russians Are Coming*, claimed the added prize of Best Actor for its rookie star, Alan Arkin. *Variety* had praised him in its review: "In his film bow, Arkin is absolutely outstanding as the courtly Russian who kisses a lady's hand even as he draws a gun."

The new Globes kudocast was "fast-moving," said *Variety*, but also "suspenseless."

Some critics fumed that *Who's Afraid of Virginia Woolf?* failed to win any awards despite having seven noms and they alleged that Elizabeth Taylor lost to Anouk Aimee because the latter agreed to be present at the gala. Hollywood Foreign Press Association prexy Herbert Luft denied the charge, insisting to *TV Guide,* "The Burtons couldn't have won because most of our members didn't like the picture. Of course, the Burtons could have been chosen World Film Favorites if they had announced they were coming to the awards." The latter admission shocked NBC execs, who had been assured by the HFPA earlier that the World Film Favorites were chosen by a poll of international movie-goers.

The Oscars faced the threat of not being telecast this year when the American Federation of Television and Radio Artists staged a strike against the TV networks. *Variety*'s Army Archerd reported, "At Oscar rehearsals, the tensionmeter hit the high mark as all awaited word from N.Y. 'It's like directing a Hitchcock movie,' admitted Acad show director Dick Dunlap, 'except the suspense is killing ME!' "

"What drama! What suspense!" gushed Bob Hope, who was set to emcee the gala for a thirteenth time. "And that's just wondering whether the show would go on!"

The 13-day strike dragged on all the way up to two hours before the Oscarcast,

The *N.Y. Times* said the Gotham crix "flipped their lids and voted like wild evangelists" by giving *A Man for All Seasons* a record-breaking four awards. It would also win four Globes and six Oscars.

then was settled. Meantime, an unprecedented crowd of 3,000 gawkers gathered outside the Santa Monica Civic Auditorium while the stars arrived early despite a light drizzle. Ronald Reagan received cheers and jeers from the crowd as he attended his first Oscar ceremony as governor of California.

"Backstage they say 'The Russians Are Coming, The Russians Are Coming,' " *Variety* noted, "but the British are already here!"

Five members of the Redgrave family hit the red carpet together: Sir Michael and his lady, Lynn, Vanessa and brother Corin. "To the Redgraves, all the world's a stage and they're acting all the parts," Bob Hope would josh later in his opening monologue.

Vanessa and Lynn were both nominated for Best Actress, marking the first sibling matchup at the Oscars since Joan Fontaine and Olivia de Havilland squared off in the same category in 1941. Academy officials thought it would be fun to have the older sisters back for the occasion and invited them to be presenters, but only de Havilland showed up. She arrived from Paris, where she left behind current nominees Elizabeth Taylor and Richard Burton. Taylor claimed that her husband was afraid of flying and she didn't want to leave him alone. The real reason was no secret: they were miffed that Burton, who'd lost four Oscar bouts in the past, was probably going to lose this time to Paul Scofield.

But Taylor was considered the odds-on favorite to claim her second career trophy. *Who's Afraid of Virginia Woolf?* led the year's Oscar derby with 13 nominations, followed by 8 each for *A Man for All Seasons* and *The Sand Pebbles* (the movie Robert Wise was filming in Hong Kong when he couldn't accept his Best Picture Oscar for *The Sound of Music*).

When Taylor won, the audience cheered wildly as Anne Bancroft headed to the podium to accept the statuette on her behalf. *Variety* reported that it was one of the most popular victories of the night, but its reporters were stunned to learn the next day that Taylor refused to issue a public statement of thanks.

The other most popular victory of the night was in the race for Best Supporting Actress, which was won by Taylor's costar Sandy Dennis, who was also not present. *Variety* reported, "She is in New York to shoot location scenes for a new film and, according to Mike Nichols, who accepted her award, was watching the proceedings on television at Frankie and Johnny's restaurant on West 45th Street in Manhattan." When a *Variety* reporter telephoned Dennis there, she referred to her Oscar statuette, saying, "This is the sort of doll a girl never gets too big to want to cuddle!"

Far less popular was the Best Supporting Actor champ, who was accused of competing out of category. Walter Matthau's comic portrayal of a sleazy lawyer had earned him over-the-title billing when *The Fortune Cookie* was released. At the Golden Globes, he'd been nominated in the lead-actor race, but then film academy officials made the controversial decision to list Matthau among the candidates for Best Supporting Actor at the Oscars. Protesters said he had an unfair advantage.

Matthau was not looking forward to Oscar night, especially since he had "suffered a broken arm and stitched-up face as a result of a bicycle accident on the Pacific Coast Highway," *Variety* reported. "Matthau's reluctance to be thus viewed: he hadn't as yet told his mother."

Richard Burton and Elizabeth Taylor gave career-capping perfs in *Who's Afraid of Virginia Woolf?* but boycotted the Oscar fete when it was clear Burton would lose. Victorious Taylor refused to thank the Acadmy. Pic suffered the biggest Golden Globe shut-out ever: 7 losses.

When he won, he mounted the stage cautiously and accepted the statuette from Shelley Winters, who observed, "You had a hard time getting here."

He replied, grinning, "The other day, as I was falling off my bike . . ."

Another male nominee was also not feeling well on Oscar night—Best Actor contender Steve McQueen (*The Sand Pebbles*), who told Army Archerd that he had a nervous stomach even though he believed he had little chance of winning. McQueen was so distraught that he left his Oscar tickets at home, "but had no trouble getting seated," said *Variety*.

McQueen agreed with fellow nominee Richard Burton that the champ would be Paul Scofield—who didn't show up for the Academy Awards either. He stayed at home in London with his wife while his *A Man for All Seasons* costar Wendy Hiller accepted the Oscar on his behalf. Hiller had been in London when she won her Oscar in 1958 as Best Supporting Actress in *Separate Tables*. When notified of her victory, she said back then, "I hope this award means cash—hard cash." Accepting the trophy on behalf of the absent Scofield, she was now far more high-minded, saying, "There is something very special in being recognized in a country by other than one's own."

A Man for All Seasons also claimed the laurels for best adapted screenplay ("You really are incredibly generous to aliens," said Robert Bolt) plus prizes for color cinematography and color costume design. Near evening's end, the royal costume drama added two more crowning victories—Best Director (Fred Zinnemann) and Best Picture—bringing its total tally to six.

Who's Afraid of Virginia Woolf? came close in the overall score, earning five: art direction, black-and-white costume design and black-and-white cinematography in addition to thesp honors for Elizabeth Taylor and Sandy Dennis.

Although most of the star honorees were absent, the presence of a few others redeemed the night. The most rousing ovation went to 1963 Best Actress Patricia Neal, who had recently rebounded from

three strokes. *The New York Times* reported: "Dressed in a multicolored silk gown which she said she bought in England for $37, Miss Neal received a minute-long standing ovation from the 2,500 people massed in the Santa Monica Auditorium. Visibly moved but in complete control of herself, the actress said quietly and in her familiarly throaty drawl, 'I thank you. I thank you. I'm sorry I've been away so long.' "

Another dramatic scene occurred when Ginger Rogers and Fred Astaire teamed up to present an award. As they stepped toward the podium, *Variety* noted, "They swept into a short, impromptu dance routine, their first since their last costarring assignment in the late 1940s in *The Berkleys of Broadway*."

▪ 1966 ▪

NEW YORK FILM CRITICS

Winners were announced on December 27, 1966. Awards were presented on January 29, 1967, at Sardi's restaurant in New York.

BEST PICTURE
▪ *A Man for All Seasons*

BEST DIRECTOR
▪ Fred Zinnemann, *A Man for All Seasons*

BEST ACTOR
▪ Paul Scofield, *A Man for All Seasons*

BEST ACTRESS (TIE)
▪ Lynn Redgrave, *Georgy Girl*
▪ Elizabeth Taylor, *Who's Afraid of Virginia Woolf?*

BEST SCREENPLAY
▪ Robert Bolt, *A Man for All Seasons*

BEST FOREIGN FILM
▪ *The Shop on Main Street* (Czechoslovakia)

NATIONAL SOCIETY OF FILM CRITICS

Winners were announced on January 4, 1967, at the Algonquin Hotel in New York.

BEST PICTURE
▪ *Blow-Up*

BEST DIRECTOR
▪ Michelangelo Antonioni, *Blow-Up*

BEST ACTOR
▪ Michael Caine, *Alfie*

BEST ACTRESS
▪ Sylvie, *The Shameless Old Lady*

NATIONAL BOARD OF REVIEW

Winners were announced on January 10, 1967.

BEST PICTURE
▪ *A Man for All Seasons*
Born Free
Alfie
Who's Afraid of Virginia Woolf?

The Bible
Georgy Girl
Years of Lightning, Day of Drums
It Happened Here
The Russians Are Coming, The Russians
   Are Coming
Shakespeare Wallah

BEST DIRECTOR
- Fred Zinnemann, *A Man for All Seasons*

BEST ACTOR
- Paul Scofield, *A Man for All Seasons*

BEST ACTRESS
- Elizabeth Taylor, *Who's Afraid of Virginia Woolf?*

BEST SUPPORTING ACTOR
- Robert Shaw, *A Man for All Seasons*

BEST SUPPORTING ACTRESS
- Vivien Merchant, *Alfie*

BEST FOREIGN FILM
- *The Sleeping Car Murders* (France)
The Gospel According to St. Matthew
   (France/Italy)
The Shameless Old Lady (France)
A Man and a Woman (France)
Hamlet (U.S.S.R.)

DIRECTORS GUILD OF AMERICA

Awards were presented on February 11, 1967, at the Beverly Hilton Hotel in Los Angeles and the Hilton Hotel in New York.

BEST DIRECTOR
- Fred Zinnemann, *A Man for All Seasons*
Richard Brooks, *The Professionals*
John Frankenheimer, *Grand Prix*
Lewis Gilbert, *Alfie*
James Hill, *Born Free*
Norman Jewison, *The Russians Are Coming, The Russians Are Coming*
Claude Lelouch, *A Man and a Woman*
Silvio Narizzano, *Georgy Girl*
Mike Nichols, *Who's Afraid of Virginia Woolf?*
Robert E. Wise, *The Sand Pebbles*

GOLDEN GLOBES

Nominations were announced on January 16, 1966. Awards were presented on February 15 at the Cocoanut Grove in the Ambassador Hotel in Los Angeles. The ceremony was telecast by NBC.

BEST DRAMA PICTURE
- *A Man for All Seasons*
Born Free
The Professionals
The Sand Pebbles
Who's Afraid of Virginia Woolf?

BEST COMEDY OR MUSICAL PICTURE
- *The Russians Are Coming, The Russians Are Coming*
A Funny Thing Happened on the Way to the Forum
Gambit
Not with My Wife, You Don't
You're a Big Boy Now

BEST DIRECTOR
- Fred Zinnemann, *A Man for All Seasons*
Lewis Gilbert, *Alfie*
Claude Lelouch, *A Man and a Woman*
Mike Nichols, *Who's Afraid of Virginia Woolf?*
Robert Wise, *The Sand Pebbles*

BEST ACTOR, DRAMA
- Paul Scofield, *A Man for all Seasons*
Richard Burton, *Who's Afraid of Virginia Woolf?*
Michael Caine, *Alfie*
Steve McQueen, *The Sand Pebbles*
Max von Sydow, *Hawaii*

BEST ACTRESS, DRAMA
- Anouk Aimee, *A Man and a Woman*
Ida Kaminska, *The Shop on Main Street*
Virginia McKenna, *Born Free*
Elizabeth Taylor, *Who's Afraid of Virginia Woolf?*
Natalie Wood, *This Property Is Condemned*

BEST ACTOR, COMEDY OR MUSICAL
- Alan Arkin, *The Russians Are Coming, The Russians Are Coming*
Alan Bates, *Georgy Girl*

Michael Caine, *Gambit*
Lionel Jeffries, *The Spy with a Cold Nose*
Walter Matthau, *The Fortune Cookie*

BEST ACTRESS, COMEDY OR MUSICAL
■ Lynn Redgrave, *Georgy Girl*
Jane Fonda, *Any Wednesday*
Elizabeth Hartman, *You're a Big Boy Now*
Shirley MacLaine, *Gambit*
Vanessa Redgrave, *Morgan!*

BEST SUPPORTING ACTOR
■ Richard Attenborough, *The Sand Pebbles*
Mako, *The Sand Pebbles*
John Saxon, *The Appaloosa*
George Segal, *Who's Afraid of Virginia Woolf?*
Robert Shaw, *A Man for All Seasons*

BEST SUPPORTING ACTRESS
■ Jocelyne LaGarde, *Hawaii*
Sandy Dennis, *Who's Afraid of Virginia Woolf?*
Vivien Merchant, *Alfie*
Geraldine Page, *You're a Big Boy Now*
Shelley Winters, *Alfie*

MOST PROMISING NEWCOMER—MALE
■ James Farentino, *The Pad*
Alan Arkin, *The Russians Are Coming, The Russians Are Coming*
Alan Bates, *Georgy Girl*
John Philip Law, *The Russians Are Coming, The Russians Are Coming*
Antonio Sabato, *Grand Prix*

MOST PROMISING NEWCOMER—FEMALE
■ Camilla Sparv, *Dead Heat on a Merry-Go-Round*
Candice Bergen, *The Group, The Sand Pebbles*
Marie Gomez, *The Professionals*
Lynn Redgrave, *Georgy Girl*
Jessica Walter, *Grand Prix*

BEST SCREENPLAY
■ Robert Bolt, *A Man for All Seasons*
Robert Anderson, *The Sand Pebbles*
Ernest Lehman, *Who's Afraid of Virginia Woolf?*
Bill Naughton, *Alfie*
William Rose, *The Russians Are Coming, The Russians Are Coming*

BEST ORIGINAL SONG
■ "Strangers in the Night," *A Man Could Get Killed*
"Alfie," *Alfie*
"Born Free," *Born Free*
"Georgy Girl," *Georgy Girl*
"A Man and a Woman," *A Man and a Woman*

BEST FOREIGN-LANGUAGE FOREIGN FILM
■ *A Man and a Woman* (France)
Hamlet (U.S.S.R.)
Impossible on Saturday (France/Israel)
Loves of a Blonde (Czechoslovakia)
Signore e Signori (Italy)

BEST ENGLISH-LANGUAGE FOREIGN FILM
■ *Alfie* (U.K.)
Blow-Up (Italy)
Georgy Girl (U.K.)
Morgan! (U.K.)
Royal Ballet's Romeo and Juliet (U.K.)
The Spy with a Cold Nose (U.K.)

Winners

BEST ORIGINAL SCORE
■ Elmer Bernstein, *Hawaii*

WORLD FILM FAVORITES
■ Julie Andrews
■ Steve McQueen

CECIL B. DEMILLE AWARD
■ Charlton Heston

WRITERS GUILD OF AMERICA

Awards were presented on March 28, 1967, at the Century Plaza Hotel in Los Angeles.

BEST WRITTEN DRAMA
■ *Who's Afraid of Virginia Woolf?*, Ernest Lehman, based on the play by Edward Albee
Harper, William Goldman, based on the novel *The Moving Target* by Ross MacDonald
The Professionals, Richard Brooks, based on the novel *A Mule for the Marquesa* by Frank O'Rourke

The Sand Pebbles, Robert Anderson, based on the novel by Richard McKenna

BEST WRITTEN COMEDY
- *The Russians Are Coming, The Russians Are Coming*, William Rose, based on the novel *The Off-Islanders* by Nathaniel Benchley

The Fortune Cookie, Billy Wilder, I. A. L. Diamond

How to Steal a Million, Harry Kurnitz, based on the story "Venus Rising" by George Bradshaw

Our Man Flint, Hal Fimberg, Ben Starr

You're a Big Boy Now, Francis Ford Coppola, from the novel by David Benedictus

LAUREL AWARD
- Richard Brooks

VALENTINE DAVIES AWARD
- Edmund H. North

FOUNDER'S AWARD
- Charles Brackett
- Richard Breen

ACADEMY AWARDS

Nominations were announced on February 20, 1967. Awards were presented on April 10 at the Santa Monica Civic Auditorium. The ceremony was telecast by ABC.

BEST PICTURE
- *A Man for All Seasons*

Alfie

The Russians Are Coming, The Russians Are Coming

The Sand Pebbles

Who's Afraid of Virginia Woolf?

BEST DIRECTOR
- Fred Zinnemann, *A Man for All Seasons*

Michelangelo Antonioni, *Blow-Up*

Richard Brooks, *The Professionals*

Claude Lelouch, *A Man and a Woman*

Mike Nichols, *Who's Afraid of Virginia Woolf?*

BEST ACTOR
- Paul Scofield, *A Man for All Seasons*

Alan Arkin, *The Russians Are Coming, The Russians Are Coming*

Richard Burton, *Who's Afraid of Virginia Woolf?*

Michael Caine, *Alfie*

Steve McQueen, *The Sand Pebbles*

BEST ACTRESS
- Elizabeth Taylor, *Who's Afraid of Virginia Woolf?*

Anouk Aimee, *A Man and a Woman*

Ida Kaminska, *The Shop on Main Street*

Lynn Redgrave, *Georgy Girl*

Vanessa Redgrave, *Morgan!*

BEST SUPPORTING ACTOR
- Walter Matthau, *The Fortune Cookie*

Mako, *The Sand Pebbles*

James Mason, *Georgy Girl*

George Segal, *Who's Afraid of Virginia Woolf?*

Robert Shaw, *A Man for All Seasons*

BEST SUPPORTING ACTRESS
- Sandy Dennis, *Who's Afraid of Virginia Woolf?*

Wendy Hiller, *A Man for All Seasons*

Jocelyne LaGarde, *Hawaii*

Vivien Merchant, *Alfie*

Geraldine Page, *You're a Big Boy Now*

BEST ADAPTED SCREENPLAY
- Robert Bolt, *A Man for all Seasons*

Richard Brooks, *The Professionals*

Ernest Lehman, *Who's Afraid of Virginia Woolf?*

Bill Naughton, *Alfie*

William Rose, *The Russians Are Coming, The Russians Are Coming*

BEST ORIGINAL SCREENPLAY
- Claude Lelouch, Pierre Uytterhoeven, *A Man and a Woman*

Michelangelo Antonioni, Edward Bond, Tonino Guerra, *Blow-Up*

Robert Ardrey, *Khartoum*

I. A. L. Diamond, Billy Wilder, *The Fortune Cookie*

Clint Johnston, Don Peters, *The Naked Prey*

BEST SONG

- "Born Free," *Born Free*, John Barry, Don Black

"Alfie," *Alfie,* Burt Bacharach, Hal David

"Georgy Girl," *Georgy Girl*, Jim Dale, Tom Springfield

"My Wishing Doll," *Hawaii,* Elmer Bernstein, Mack David

"A Time for Love," *An American Dream,* Johnny Mandel, Paul Francis Webster

BEST FOREIGN-LANGUAGE FILM

- *A Man and a Woman* (France)

The Battle of Algiers (Italy)

Loves of a Blonde (Czechoslovakia)

Pharaoh (Poland)

Three (Yugoslavia)

Winners

BEST ART DIRECTION
(BLACK AND WHITE)

- Richard Sylbert, George James Hopkins, *Who's Afraid of Virginia Woolf?*

(COLOR)

- Dale Hennesy, Jack Martin Smith, Stuart A. Reiss, Walter M. Scott, *Fantastic Voyage*

BEST CINEMATOGRAPHY
(BLACK AND WHITE)

- Haskell Wexler, *Who's Afraid of Virginia Woolf?*

(COLOR)

- Ted Moore, *A Man for all Seasons*

BEST COSTUME DESIGN
(BLACK AND WHITE)

- Irene Sharaff, *Who's Afraid of Virginia Woolf?*

(COLOR)

- Joan Bridge, Elizabeth Haffenden, *A Man for All Seasons*

BEST DOCUMENTARY
(FEATURE)

- Peter Watkins, *The War Game*

(SHORT SUBJECT)

- Edmond A. Levy, *A Year toward Tomorrow*

BEST FILM EDITING

- Henry Berman, Stewart Linder, Frank Santillo, Fredric Steinkamp, *Grand Prix*

BEST MUSIC
(ORIGINAL MUSIC SCORE)

- John Barry, *Born Free*

(SCORING OF MUSIC—ADAPTATION OR TREATMENT)

- Ken Thorne, *A Funny Thing Happened on the Way to the Forum*

SCIENTIFIC OR TECHNICAL AWARDS
Class II (Plaque)

- Mitchell Camera Corp.; Arnold & Richter KG

Class III (Certificate)

- Carroll Knudson, Panavision, Inc., Ruby Raksin

BEST SHORT SUBJECT
(CARTOON)

- *Herb Alpert and the Tijuana Brass Double Feature*

(LIVE ACTION)

- *Wild Wings*

BEST SOUND

- Franklin E. Milton, *Grand Prix*

BEST SOUND EFFECTS

- Gordon Daniel, *Grand Prix*

BEST SPECIAL VISUAL EFFECTS

- Art Cruickshank, *Fantastic Voyage*

IRVING G. THALBERG MEMORIAL AWARD

- Robert Wise

JEAN HERSHOLT HUMANITARIAN AWARD

- George Bagnall

HONORARY AWARDS

- Yakima Canutt
- Y. Frank Freeman

SCREEN ACTORS GUILD

LIFETIME ACHIEVEMENT AWARD

- Barbara Stanwyck

· 1967 ·

Bumping Off Bonnie and Clyde

Old Bosley Crowther was sick and tired of the brazen new films full of cheeky sex and flip violence being cheered by his peers. After 27 years as a member of—and often leading—the New York Film Critics, he was just days away from retirement and decided to take a parting shot. He stood up after the first ballot was tallied for Best Picture, took careful aim at the film that led the vote—*Bonnie and Clyde*—and blasted away at it verbally before a new count was taken.

His eloquence not only killed off its chances, but it persuaded his colleagues to endorse his favored alternative. Thus the gray-haired dandy who epitomized the white Yankee establishment caused the group to embrace a movie about racial prejudice against blacks as a Best Picture choice for the first time ever—thereby setting it up for future kudos, too. After winning the top trophy from the Gotham crix by an eight-to-five score on the sixth ballot, *In the Heat of the Night* would go on to claim the Golden Globe next—and, just six days after the assassination of Martin Luther King, Jr.— the Oscar.

Variety called *In the Heat of the Night* "an absorbing contemporary murder drama, set in the deep, red-necked South. Rod Steiger's transformation from a diehard Dixie bigot to a man who learns to respect Sidney Poitier stands out in smooth comparison to the wandering solution of the murder." The Gotham crix endorsed Steiger's perf, too, naming him Best Actor on the third ballot with 12 votes, followed by 2 for Yves Montand (*La Guerre est Finie*) and 1 for Spencer Tracy, who died 10 days after filming his last scene in *Guess Who's Coming to Dinner*, which also dealt seriously with black-white tensions.

Although *Who's Afraid of Virginia Woolf?* received several votes for Best Pic-

Retiring *Times* scribe Bosley Crowther launched *In the Heat of the Night* (starring Sidney Poitier and Rod Steiger) toward crix, Globe and Oscar victories.

ture at last year's crix pool, its rookie helmer Mike Nichols was snubbed in the competish for Best Director. This year the crix made it up to him with their helmer's prize for his second celluloid outing, *The Graduate*, which *Variety* described as "a delightful, satirical comedy-drama about a young man's seduction by an older woman and the measure of maturity which he attains from the experience." Nichols won on the sixth ballot with seven votes over Norman Jewison (*In the Heat of the Night*) and Arthur Penn (*Bonnie and Clyde*), who both earned four.

The actress prize was decided easily on the second canvass, with Dame Edith Evans receiving the backing of two-thirds of the 15 crix. *Variety* said of her perf in *The Whisperers:* "Her portrayal of the aging woman, now living on the near edge of insanity but unbowed by other physical hazards, makes the film."

Bonnie and Clyde did claim one prize— best screenplay—which caused Crowther some public embarrassment a few weeks later when he emceed the crix's awards ceremony at Sardi's restaurant. Crowther had to suffer giggles and guffaws from the audience as he was charged with the awkward task of introducing scribes David Newman and Robert Benton, who penned the romantic gangster hit. He deftly handled the task with humor, however, referring to the "highly *imaginative* and indisputably *original* script"—a comment *Variety* called "a lighthearted reminder of his published feelings that the film did not reveal the true Bonnie Parker and Clyde Barrow." As laughter grew, Crowther added, "I understand that they had trouble finding a producer for the film, but they stuck to their *guns*. And I hope we critics are understood when we stick to *our guns*." Crowther's peers cheered his stubbornness and, moments later, ambushed him with a surprise special award acknowledging his long service to the group. *Variety* noted that Crowther was "visibly moved."

The plaque for Best Picture was bestowed by Sen. Robert Kennedy, whom *Variety* called the gala's "surprise guest of honor." When he was off stage, the *Daily News* noted that the politico "stood shyly in the center of the room, like any other stargazer, unable to take his eyes off his dinner partner of the evening, Ingrid Bergman." Bergman presented the actress laurel to Anthony Quayle, accepting for the absent Evans. Albert Finney accepted on behalf of an absent Steiger. Mike Nichols accepted his own helmer's plaque, saying, "At the risk of demolishing the 'auteur' theory of directing, this film was made by a group of people"—many of whom he named, then added, "I can't really tell you who did what. I hope I did some of it."

Three weeks later Nichols did not make a speech at the New York gala for the directors' guild kudos, even though he won the top prize. He skipped the event after being embarrassed at last year's ceremony when his name was called as one of the finalists of the top prize and he mistakenly believed he won. "He gave a nice acceptance speech," noted *Variety*, which was followed by the

announcement of four more finalists—then the name of the actual winner, who turned out to be Fred Zinnemann. This year Nichols's award was accepted on his behalf by producer Laurence Turman, who told the crowd, "You already heard his acceptance speech."

The Graduate reaped huzzahs from the writers' guild, too, when scribes Calder Willingham and Buck Henry beat first-time nominee Neil Simon (*Barefoot in the Park*). *Bonnie and Clyde*'s David Newman and Robert Benton received two prizes: Best Written Drama plus a newly minted trophy for Best Written Original Screenplay.

The guild gala's stage show was a big disappointment. *Variety* reported, "There were occasional laughs, but too few for the long night. Perhaps the guild overreacted to the outburst of indignation which followed last year's awards show when a skit depicting agents as hideous insects infuriated the deal merchants. So this year the writers spent the night kidding about writers and, despite the contributions of 55—count them, 55—scripters, it wasn't amusing." Last year some agents stormed out of the gala in protest. This year scores of attendees left early due to boredom.

At the National Society of Film Critics Awards, *Bonnie and Clyde* also won a newly created accolade for Best Screenplay plus a new prize for Best Supporting Actor, which was awarded to Gene Hackman as one of the film's gang members. *Bonnie and Clyde* also came in second place for Best Picture, behind Ingmar Bergman's *Persona,* which swept two other categories. Bergman was cited as top helmer and star Bibi Andersson was named Best Actress for portraying a nurse tending to a noted stage thesp (Liv Ullmann) who suddenly and mysteriously refuses to speak. "Pic is hypnotic," *Variety* said, calling its direction and acting "perfection."

The system that the society used to select winners was changed this year to what *The*

Edith Evans won three Best Actress trophies for *The Whisperers.*

New York Times called an open "ballot voting procedure, which requires a simple majority on the first, second or third tally."

The Best Picture choice of the National Board of Review startled many observers because the film didn't get consistently good reviews. Variety thought the script for Far from the Madding Crowd suffered from a "basic banality" and followed Thomas Hardy's original novel too strictly.

Nevertheless, the pic was nominated for Best Drama Picture at the Golden Globes, competing against Bonnie and Clyde, Guess Who's Coming to Dinner, In Cold Blood— and eventual champ In the Heat of the Night, which also claimed laurels for its screenplay and Best Actor Rod Steiger.

In addition to endorsing the New York film crix's choices for top pic and actor, Hollywood Foreign Press Association voters also named the same Best Actress: Dame Edith Evans.

The Graduate won the most Golden Globes overall—Best Comedy/Musical Picture, Best Director (Nichols), Best Actress (Anne Bancroft) and both the male and female honors for Most Promising Newcomers (Dustin Hoffman and Katharine Ross). The Christian Science Monitor observed, "Hoffman brought down the Foreign Press house with his poker-faced remark, 'I'd like to thank the clappers.' "

Hoffman and Rod Steiger received the most enthusiastic ovations of the night, although Variety added, "Carol Channing was a popular win for Best Supporting Actress in Thoroughly Modern Millie."

Again the gala, hosted by Andy Williams, was broadcast nationally by NBC and reaped upbeat reviews despite the high number of victorious no-shows, which included Evans, Nichols, Richard Harris (Best Comedy/Musical Actor, Camelot) and Richard Attenborough (Best Supporting Actor, Doctor Dolittle). One notable guest scooted early. Producer/director Stanley Kramer left his dinner uneaten when Guess

Who's Coming to Dinner claimed no awards despite having six nominations.

Another pic with six bids also reaped no honors, but its stars scored lots of media notice at the bash. "Although Bonnie and Clyde won no awards, its stars Warren Beatty and Faye Dunaway received the most attention from photographers," observed the L.A. Times.

Hollywood Citizen-News columnist Sidney Skolsky was outraged at the kudos snub and was determined to get to the bottom of it. "Later, on the phone, a voting member of the Foreign Press told me they deliberately passed up Bonnie and Clyde because of its violence," he reported. "Since when did that outlaw a film? The movie that won, In the Heat of the Night, wasn't any shrinking violet in the violence department. I wager that the majority of the Foreign Press Awards will be foreign to the Academy Award winners on the night of April 8."

It looked as if Skolsky might be proved right when the Oscar nominations were announced and Bonnie and Clyde and Guess Who's Coming to Dinner led with 10 bids each. The Graduate was actually thought to be the frontrunner for Best Picture, though, since Nichols had already won the DGA prize; it tied In the Heat of the Night with a tally of seven noms. Dinner's topper Stanley Kramer told Variety columnist Army Archerd that he believed this year's race "was pretty wide open all the way."

Skolsky turned out to be wrong about the Oscar date, however. When the Rev. Martin Luther King, Jr., was assassinated four days before the ceremony, four African-American stars—Sammy Davis Jr., Diahann Carroll, Louis Armstrong and Beah Richards—notified the academy that they could not participate in the awards celebration. The academy's Board of Governors met in emergency session and ruled that the gala would be postponed for two days. A grateful Davis told Variety that black Americans, "from the most extreme militant to

> ## The Graduate was favored to win the Best Picture Oscar.

the most moderate, were thrilled that the picture industry finally did something for the black man as a whole."

On Oscar night, academy prexy Gregory Peck told the audience and TV viewers, "This has been a fateful week in the history of our nation and the two-day delay of this ceremony is the academy's way of paying our profound respect to the memory of Dr. Martin Luther King, Jr. Of the five films nominated for Best Picture, two dealt with the subject of understanding between the races. It was his work and his dedication that brought about the increasing awareness of all men that we must unite in compassion if we are to survive."

Emcee Bob Hope added, "The men who began our industry had at least one thing in common with the man from Atlanta. They had a dream."

As the award winners began to be revealed, *Variety* noticed, "no clear trend emerged until the final stretch. This served to create a tense atmosphere, engendered weeks ago by the number of hot-pic contenders and prolonged by the two-day postponement."

Prospects looked good for *The Graduate* early on when Mike Nichols won Best Director as expected. *The New York Times* noted that his victory "was obviously a very popular one, judging from the applause he received." Referring to the movie in his acceptance speech, Nichols said, "Until this moment, my greatest pleasure was making it," then added, "I'd like to wish my mother a happy birthday."

The Graduate's Dustin Hoffman was up for Best Actor, but he told reporters that he had voted for Steiger and said, "I hope to God I don't win. I really don't deserve it."

He and Steiger's toughest competish came from the late Spencer Tracy, who was considered a sentimental favorite. Tracy's widow was on hand to accept if he won and Steiger seemed resigned to lose, telling Archerd, "I've learned a lot about this business and that's not to stake one's life on awards." *Variety* added, "Rod Steiger still maintains he liked *The Pawnbroker* best. He was nominated for that film but lost out in the final balloting. Possibly because of that

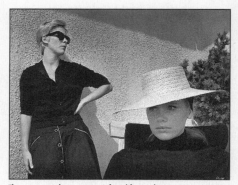

The new national crix society preferred foreign-lingo pix, citing Ingmar Bergman's *Persona*, which starred Best Actress Bibi Andersson (left) and Liv Ullmann. "Pic is hypnotic," *Variety* cheered.

he said that he didn't come to the awards expecting to win. 'Anybody who does better bring a gun with him,' he added."

Variety noted who was missing among the contenders: "Sidney Poitier, who was in three smash b.o. hits last year, two of which were in the Oscar running, said he was not disappointed at not having been nominated. 'To sit in that hall knowing full well that you'll be one of the four losers is not very pleasant,' he commented. 'I was secretly delighted I was not nominated.' "

Variety reported on the race's outcome: "Steiger never had won before, but his understanding eagerness, revealed in much recent publicity, was rewarded. The suspense over his acceptance speech was relaxed and included thanks to costar Sidney Poitier."

Steiger thanked "Mr. Sidney Poitier for the pleasure of his friendship, which gave me the knowledge and understanding of prejudice to enhance my performance. Thank you . . . and we *shall* overcome."

Tracy's longtime lover Katharine Hepburn, nominated for *Guess Who's Coming to Dinner,* stayed away from the ceremony out of deference to Tracy's widow, but still participated in the event. Dressed as Eleanor of Aquitaine, she appeared in a segment taped in France on the set of *The Lion in Winter*. As she introduced film clips of past winners on the occasion of the academy's 40th anniversary, *Variety* noted, "Miss Hepburn related how the awards came into being, explaining they first were given for achievements before 1929."

Hepburn's latest Oscar bid, her tenth, tied Bette Davis's record, but Hepburn was not expected to pull even with Davis's two past victories 34 years after her solo win for *Morning Glory*. Columnist Sheilah Graham was among the many media pundits rooting for *Bonnie and Clyde*'s Faye Dunaway. Globe champ Anne Bancroft and Globe and New York film crix victor Dame Edith Evans were also considered close rivals.

So when Hepburn won, the audience gasped. George Cukor accepted the honor on her behalf, acknowledging to the voters, "It was a very hard decision for you to make." The next day Hepburn sent a telegram to the academy, saying, "It was delightful, a total surprise. I feel I have received a big, affectionate hug from my fellow workers. They don't usually give these things to the old girls, you know."

George Kennedy didn't think that the academy's 3,009 voters would give him the trophy for Best Supporting Actor. *Variety* said he was "outstanding" as a chain gang leader in *Cool Hand Luke* and he campaigned vigorously for the honor (his ads in *Variety* showed him hauling a wounded Paul Newman on his shoulder; underneath was "George Kennedy—Supporting"), but he faced tough rivals. Among them was Globe champ Gene Hackman and another *Bonnie and Clyde* nominee who made Kennedy particularly nervous. *Variety* reported, "Kennedy stated he thought Michael J. Pollard would give him the most competition for Best Supporting Actor because of 'so many stories in the press about him.' Kennedy said he 'hoped' to win but didn't expect to. 'After all, the film is a year-and-a-half old and the incessant thinking about it can drive you out of your mind.' "

26 PICTURES

Writers Guild (Frightened Witless By Agents?) Stages Its Neuroses

By DAVE KAUFMAN

Hollywood, March 26. For their 20th annual awards dinner show, the Writers Guild on Saturday (23) offered a sharp and an unwelcome departure from their traditional rib roast of the industry's peculiarities, eccentricities, sacred cows. This time out, the sacred cows were treated with all the deference of those in India —they were spared the cutting barb, the irreverent gag, the witty comment on the foibles of the trade.

Perhaps the Guild "over-reacted," as they say in Washington, to the outburst of indignation which followed last year's awards show, when a skit depicting agents as hideous insects infuriated the deal merchants. So this year the writers spent the night kidding about writers, and despite the contributions of 55—count them, 55—scripters, it wasn't amusing.

ven when pix were the subject of skits, as were "Camelot" and "Guess Who's Coming To Dinner?" Guildsmen didn't really spoof the pix. Instead, those films served as a background for ribbing of writers. It all added up to his wife. There was a sly reference to agents' sensitivity to insects—a note on last year's indignation.

A brief film clip, material penned by George Seaton 15 years ago, was reprised. It showed the opening crawl of a film, in which a screen writer receives glowing credit. Bit was still good.

In a "Guess Who's Coming To Dinner" sketch were Sheldon Leonard as a writer-hating producer; Alice Ghostley, his wife; Greg Morris, a writer who is going to wed their offspring; Sidney Miller, a rabbi. Again, the focus was on the writer. Father is against the marriage because he is a producer, and his daughter wedding a writer would result in a "mixed marriage." But it all ends happily—at least for the couple, who are hitched. Again, there were a few good lines, but the concentration of emphasis on the writer as the real subject of the skit made it all a bit wearisome, coming in the shank of a long, long evening where writers had been the subject of just about every routine.

Writers were "witless" when they tweaked themselves during skits performed at the WGA ceremony, *Variety* said. Last year agents felt a painful sting.

When he won, Kennedy said, "I could cry. I have to thank the academy for the greatest moment of my life."

There was no front-runner in the race for Best Supporting Actress, which included Globe champ Carol Channing (*Thoroughly Modern Millie*), veteran thesp Mildred Natwick (*Barefoot in the Park*), Katharine Ross (*The Graduate*), Beah Richards (*Guess Who's Coming to Dinner*) and Estelle Parsons (*Bonnie and Clyde*).

A short time before the award was bestowed, Anne Bancroft shared some trivia with the audience: the Oscar statuette now weighed 11 pounds, but it weighed only 7 pounds when it was first minted in 1928. When Estelle Parsons was declared the victor and she held one in her hands, she exclaimed, "Boy, it's heavy!

"I have to thank David Merrick, who let me out of my Broadway play—*The Seven Descents of Myrtle*—so I could be here this evening," she continued. "Little did he know what it would mean to me, really. Thank you. It's really a great moment!"

"There was indeed something for everyone," *Variety* observed about how the awards were dispersed throughout the night, but added, "The most nominated films—*Bonnie and Clyde* and *Dinner*—wound up with but two awards."

"Although the awards to Mr. Steiger and Mr. Nichols had been expected, it was generally an evening of surprises," *The New York Times* added.

The biggest jaw-dropper occurred in the Best Picture race. The winner turned out to be *In the Heat of the Night,* which claimed the most total victories of the night—five—including best editing, sound and adapted screenplay in addition to the laurels for top pic and actor. Scribe Stirling Silliphant made the audience howl when he accepted his statuette, saying, "I really have no speech. The writers' guild doesn't allow us to do any speculative writing."

Newsweek reported that *Bonnie and Clyde* producer and star Warren Beatty growled "We waz robbed!" as he left the Santa Monica Civic Auditorium.

"Postmortems are likely to rage for a long time on this year's results," *Variety* said in its post-Oscars coverage. "*Bonnie* and *Dinner*, both b.o. successes, were mutually incompatible to respective partisans. Perhaps as in the case of the N.Y. crix awards, in which *Heat* finally won though *Bonnie* started as ballot winner, Acad voters were faced with an embarrassment of rich product.

"In any case, the possibility that older Acad members might make *Dinner* best pic, feared by some *Bonnie* supporters, did not materialize. *Heat* definitely was not a film likely to appeal to the complacent and elderly."

The elderly gent who was personally responsible for *Heat* winning its first of several Best Picture awards—Bosley Crowther—was supposed to be present on Oscar night in case it achieved its ultimate victory. Since retiring from *The New York Times*, Crowther had been hired as a creative consultant by Columbia Pictures, which invited him to be their V.I.P. guest at the awards show. But when Crowther arrived in town on the day of the ceremony, no one greeted him at the airport and he couldn't get a room at the Beverly Hills Hotel, where he'd been promised a reservation. Fellow critic Rex Reed reported that Crowther "ended up on top of his luggage at three o'clock in the morning looking for a place to stay."

▪ 1967 ▪

NEW YORK FILM CRITICS

Winners were announced on December 28, 1967. Awards were presented on January 28, 1968, at Sardi's restaurant in New York.

BEST PICTURE
▪ *In the Heat of the Night*

BEST DIRECTOR
▪ Mike Nichols, *The Graduate*

BEST ACTOR
▪ Rod Steiger, *In the Heat of the Night*

BEST ACTRESS
▪ Dame Edith Evans, *The Whisperers*

BEST SCREENPLAY
▪ David Newman, Robert Benton, *Bonnie and Clyde*

BEST FOREIGN FILM
▪ *La Guerre est Finie* (France)

NATIONAL BOARD OF REVIEW

Winners were announced on December 31, 1967.

BEST PICTURE
▪ *Far from the Madding Crowd*
The Whisperers
Ulysses
In Cold Blood

The Family Way
The Taming of the Shrew
Doctor Dolittle
The Graduate
The Comedians
Accident

BEST DIRECTOR
- Richard Brooks, *In Cold Blood*

BEST ACTOR
- Peter Finch, *Far from the Madding Crowd*

BEST ACTRESS
- Dame Edith Evans, *The Whisperers*

BEST SUPPORTING ACTOR
- Paul Ford, *The Comedians*

BEST SUPPORTING ACTRESS
- Marjorie Rhodes, *The Family Way*

BEST FOREIGN FILM
- *Elvira Madigan* (Sweden)
The Hunt (Spain)
Africa Addio (Italy)
Persona (Sweden)
The Great British Train Robbery (Federal Republic of Germany)

NATIONAL SOCIETY OF FILM CRITICS

Winners were announced on January 3, 1968, at the Algonquin Hotel in New York.

BEST PICTURE
- *Persona*

BEST DIRECTOR
- Ingmar Bergman, *Persona*

BEST ACTOR
- Rod Steiger, *In the Heat of the Night*

BEST ACTRESS
- Bibi Andersson, *Persona*

BEST SUPPORTING ACTOR
- Gene Hackman, *Bonnie and Clyde*

Thurs., April 11, 1968

KING TWICE TRIBUTED IN OSCARCAST

Two internationally broadcast tributes to the Rev. Dr. Martin Luther King Jr. gave a sobering note to the 40th Academy of Motion Picture Arts and Sciences awards festivities. Gregory Peck, prexy, spoke the formal Academy tribute in his opening remarks and Bob Hope concluded the night on a serious note of reflection and prom-

The postponed Oscar show saluted Martin Luther King, Jr., who was slain six days earlier.

BEST SUPPORTING ACTRESS
- Marjorie Rhodes, *The Family Way*

BEST SCREENPLAY
- David Newman, Robert Benton, *Bonnie and Clyde*

BEST CINEMATOGRAPHY
- Haskell Wexler, *In the Heat of the Night*

DIRECTORS GUILD OF AMERICA

The initial list of nominees was narrowed down to a group of finalists who competed for the Best Director award, bestowed on February 17, 1968. Dual ceremonies were held at the Beverly Hilton Hotel in Los Angeles and the Waldorf-Astoria Hotel in New York.

BEST DIRECTOR
- Mike Nichols, *The Graduate*
Robert Aldrich, *The Dirty Dozen*
Richard Brooks, *In Cold Blood* (finalist)
James Clavell, *To Sir, With Love*
Stanley Donen, *Two for the Road*
Norman Jewison, *In the Heat of the Night* (finalist)

Stanley Kramer, *Guess Who's Coming to Dinner* (finalist)
Arthur Penn, *Bonnie and Clyde* (finalist)
Stuart Rosenberg, *Cool Hand Luke*
Joseph Strick, *Ulysses*

D. W. GRIFFITH AWARD
- Alfred Hitchcock

HONORARY LIFETIME MEMBER
- Darryl F. Zanuck

GOLDEN GLOBES

Nominations were announced on January 21, 1968. Awards were presented on February 12 at the Cocoanut Grove in the Ambassador Hotel in Los Angeles. The ceremony was telecast by NBC.

BEST DRAMA PICTURE
- *In the Heat of the Night*
Bonnie and Clyde
Far from the Madding Crowd
Guess Who's Coming to Dinner
In Cold Blood

BEST COMEDY OR MUSICAL PICTURE
- *The Graduate*
Camelot
Doctor Dolittle
The Taming of the Shrew
Thoroughly Modern Millie

BEST DIRECTOR
- Mike Nichols, *The Graduate*
Norman Jewison, *In the Heat of the Night*
Stanley Kramer, *Guess Who's Coming to Dinner*
Arthur Penn, *Bonnie and Clyde*
Mark Rydell, *The Fox*

BEST ACTOR, DRAMA
- Rod Steiger, *In the Heat of the Night*
Alan Bates, *Far from the Madding Crowd*
Warren Beatty, *Bonnie and Clyde*
Paul Newman, *Cool Hand Luke*
Sidney Poitier, *In the Heat of the Night*
Spencer Tracy, *Guess Who's Coming to Dinner*

BEST ACTRESS, DRAMA
- Dame Edith Evans, *The Whisperers*
Faye Dunaway, *Bonnie and Clyde*
Audrey Hepburn, *Wait until Dark*
Katharine Hepburn, *Guess Who's Coming to Dinner*
Anne Heywood, *The Fox*

BEST ACTOR, COMEDY OR MUSICAL
- Richard Harris, *Camelot*
Richard Burton, *The Taming of the Shrew*
Rex Harrison, *Doctor Dolittle*
Dustin Hoffman, *The Graduate*
Ugo Tognazzi, *The Climax*

BEST ACTRESS, COMEDY OR MUSICAL
- Anne Bancroft, *The Graduate*
Julie Andrews, *Thoroughly Modern Millie*
Audrey Hepburn, *Two for the Road*
Shirley MacLaine, *Woman Times Seven*
Vanessa Redgrave, *Camelot*

BEST SUPPORTING ACTOR
- Richard Attenborough, *Doctor Dolittle*
John Cassavetes, *The Dirty Dozen*
George Kennedy, *Cool Hand Luke*
Michael J. Pollard, *Bonnie and Clyde*
Efrem Zimbalist, Jr., *Wait until Dark*

BEST SUPPORTING ACTRESS
- Carol Channing, *Thoroughly Modern Millie*
Quentin Dean, *In the Heat of the Night*
Lillian Gish, *The Comedians*
Lee Grant, *In the Heat of the Night*
Prunella Ransome, *Far from the Madding Crowd*
Beah Richards, *Guess Who's Coming to Dinner*

MOST PROMISING NEWCOMER—MALE
- Dustin Hoffman
Oded Kotler
Franco Nero
Michael J. Pollard
Tommy Steele

MOST PROMISING NEWCOMER—FEMALE
- Katharine Ross
Greta Baldwin
Pia Degermark
Faye Dunaway

Katharine Houghton
Sharon Tate

BEST SCREENPLAY
- Stirling Silliphant, *In the Heat of the Night*
- Robert Benton, David Newman, *Bonnie and Clyde*
- Lewis John Carlino, Howard Koch, *The Fox*
- Buck Henry, Calder Willingham, *The Graduate*
- William Rose, *Guess Who's Coming to Dinner*

BEST ORIGINAL SONG
- "If Ever I Should Leave You," *Camelot*
- "Des Ronds dans L'Eau," *Live for Life*
- "Please Don't Gamble with Love," *Ski Fever*
- "Talk to the Animals," *Doctor Dolittle*
- "Thoroughly Modern Millie," *Thoroughly Modern Millie*

BEST FOREIGN-LANGUAGE FOREIGN FILM
- *Live for life* (France)
- *The Climax* (France/Italy)
- *Closely Watched Trains* (Czechoslovakia)
- *Elvira Madigan* (Sweden)
- *The Stranger* (France)

BEST ENGLISH-LANGUAGE FOREIGN FILM
- *The Fox*
- *Accident*
- *The Jokers*
- *Smashing Time*
- *Ulysses*
- *The Whisperers*

Winners

BEST ORIGINAL SCORE
- Frederick Loewe, *Camelot*

WORLD FILM FAVORITES
- Julie Andrews
- Lawrence Harvey

CECIL B. DEMILLE AWARD
- Kirk Douglas

The directors guild's biggest loser (8 defeats) is Alfred Hitchcock, who received the special D. W. Griffith Award.

WRITERS GUILD OF AMERICA

Awards were presented on March 22, 1968, at the Beverly Hilton Hotel in Los Angeles.

BEST WRITTEN DRAMA
- *Bonnie and Clyde*, David Newman, Robert Benton
- *Guess Who's Coming to Dinner*, William Rose
- *In Cold Blood*, Richard Brooks, based on the book by Truman Capote
- *In the Heat of the Night*, Stirling Silliphant, based on the novel by John Ball
- *Up the Down Staircase*, Tad Mosel, based on the novel by Bel Kaufman

BEST WRITTEN COMEDY
- *The Graduate*, Calder Willingham, Buck Henry, based on the novel by Charles Webb
- *Barefoot in the Park*, Neil Simon
- *Divorce American Style*, Norman Lear, story by Robert Kaufman
- *The Flim-Flam Man*, William Rose, based on the novel by Guy Owen
- *A Guide for the Married Man*, Frank Tarloff

BEST WRITTEN MUSICAL

- *Thoroughly Modern Millie*, Richard Morris

Camelot, Alan Jay Lerner, based on his musical and the novel by T. H. White

Doctor Dolittle, Leslie Bricusse, based on the stories by Hugh Lofting

How to Succeed in Business without Really Trying, David Swift, based on the musical by Abe Burrows, Jack Weinstock and Willie Gilbert and the novel by Shepherd Mead

BEST WRITTEN SCREENPLAY

- *Bonnie and Clyde*, David Newman, Robert Benton

Guess Who's Coming to Dinner, William Rose

The President's Analyst, Theodore J. Flicker

LAUREL AWARD

- Casey Robinson

VALENTINE DAVIES AWARD

- George Seaton

ACADEMY AWARDS

Nominations were announced on February 19, 1968. Awards were presented on April 10 at the Santa Monica Civic Auditorium. The ceremony was telecast by ABC.

BEST PICTURE

- *In the Heat of the Night*

Bonnie and Clyde

Doctor Dolittle

The Graduate

Guess Who's Coming to Dinner

BEST DIRECTOR

- Mike Nichols, *The Graduate*

Richard Brooks, *In Cold Blood*

Norman Jewison, *In the Heat of the Night*

Stanley Kramer, *Guess Who's Coming to Dinner*

Arthur Penn, *Bonnie and Clyde*

BEST ACTOR

- Rod Steiger, *In the Heat of the Night*

Warren Beatty, *Bonnie and Clyde*

Dustin Hoffman, *The Graduate*

Paul Newman, *Cool Hand Luke*

Spencer Tracy, *Guess Who's Coming to Dinner*

BEST ACTRESS

- Katharine Hepburn, *Guess Who's Coming to Dinner*

Anne Bancroft, *The Graduate*

Faye Dunaway, *Bonnie and Clyde*

Dame Edith Evans, *The Whisperers*

Audrey Hepburn, *Wait until Dark*

BEST SUPPORTING ACTOR

- George Kennedy, *Cool Hand Luke*

John Cassavetes, *The Dirty Dozen*

Gene Hackman, *Bonnie and Clyde*

Cecil Kellaway, *Guess Who's Coming to Dinner*

Michael J. Pollard, *Bonnie and Clyde*

BEST SUPPORTING ACTRESS

- Estelle Parsons, *Bonnie and Clyde*

Carol Channing, *Thoroughly Modern Millie*

Mildred Natwick, *Barefoot in the Park*

Beah Richards, *Guess Who's Coming to Dinner*

Katharine Ross, *The Graduate*

BEST ADAPTED SCREENPLAY

- Stirling Silliphant, *In the Heat of the Night*

Richard Brooks, *In Cold Blood*

Fred Haines, Joseph Strick, *Ulysses*

Buck Henry, Calder Willingham, *The Graduate*

Donn Pearce, Frank R. Pierson, *Cool Hand Luke*

BEST ORIGINAL SCREENPLAY

- William Rose, *Guess Who's Coming to Dinner*

Robert Benton, David Newman, *Bonnie and Clyde*

Robert Kaufman, Norman Lear, *Divorce American Style*

Frederic Raphael, *Two for the Road*

Jorge Semprun, *La Guerre est Finie*

BEST SONG

- "Talk to the Animals," *Doctor Dolittle*, Leslie Bricusse

"The Bare Necessities," *The Jungle Book*,
   Terry Gilkyson
"The Eyes of Love," *Banning*, Quincy
   Jones, Bob Russell
"The Look of Love," *Casino Royale*, Burt
   Bacharach, Hal David
"Thoroughly Modern Millie," *Thoroughly
   Modern Millie*, Sammy Cahn, James
   Van Heusen

BEST FOREIGN-LANGUAGE FILM
- *Closely Watched Trains* (Czechoslovakia)
El Amor Brujo (Spain)
I Even Met Happy Gypsies (Yugoslavia)
Live for Life (France)
Portrait of Chieko (Japan)

Winners

BEST ART DIRECTION
- Edward Carrere, John Truscott, John W.
   Brown, *Camelot*

BEST CINEMATOGRAPHY
- Burnett Guffey, *Bonnie and Clyde*

BEST COSTUME DESIGN
- John Truscott, *Camelot*

BEST DOCUMENTARY
(FEATURE)
- *The Anderson Platoon*, Pierre
   Schoendoerffer
(SHORT SUBJECT)
- *The Redwoods*, Trevor Greenwood, Mark
   Harris

BEST FILM EDITING
- Hal Ashby, *In the Heat of the Night*

BEST MUSIC
(ORIGINAL MUSIC SCORE)
- Elmer Bernstein, *Thoroughly Modern
   Millie*

(SCORING OF MUSIC—ADAPTATION OR TREATMENT)
- Alfred Newman, Ken Darby,
   Camelot

SCIENTIFIC OR TECHNICAL AWARDS
Class III (Certificate)
- Electro-Optical Division, Kollmorgen
   Corp.; Panavision Inc.; Fred R. Wilson,
   Samuel Goldwyn Studio Sound
   Department; Waldon O. Watson,
   Universal City Studio Sound
   Department

BEST SHORT SUBJECT
(CARTOON)
- *The Box*
(LIVE ACTION)
- *A Place to Stand*

BEST SOUND
- Samuel Goldwyn Studio Sound
   Department, *In the Heat of the
   Night*

BEST SOUND EFFECTS
- John Poyner, *The Dirty Dozen*

BEST SPECIAL VISUAL EFFECTS
- L. B. Abbott, *Doctor Dolittle*

IRVING G. THALBERG MEMORIAL AWARD
- Alfred Hitchcock

JEAN HERSHOLT HUMANITARIAN AWARD
- Gregory Peck

HONORARY AWARD
- Arthur Freed

SCREEN ACTORS GUILD

LIFETIME ACHIEVEMENT AWARD
- William Gargan

· 1968 ·

Roaring Over Lion

"For the second consecutive year, the National Board of Review has selected a surprise entry as Best Picture," *Variety* reported. "Like *Far from the Madding Crowd*, last year's winner, *The Shoes of the Fisherman* received downbeat notices from most influential critics." Board chairman Henry Hart's defense of the pic was fishy: "Although I do not think Anthony Quinn is up to the impersonation of a Pope, the picture has two things going for it: a fairly intelligent, though not a realistic elucidation of the interplay of religion and politics in today's world"—and nifty Vatican sets.

But the grumbling over *Fisherman* was nothing compared to the roar over *The Lion in Winter*'s victory as Best Picture at the New York film crix powwow. *Lion* had actually been lionized by most reviewers. *Variety* lauded it as "an intense, fierce, personal drama" about the topsy-turvy marriage of England's bombastic King Henry II and his conniving Queen Eleanor. "Peter O'Toole scores a bull's-eye as the king," *Variety* added, "while Katharine Hepburn's performance is amazing."

Lion led throughout the first five rounds of the critics' vote, but failed to score a two-thirds majority over *Faces*, John Cassavetes's study of a marital bust-up that didn't get *Variety*'s endorsement (the trade-paper called it "an overblown opus").

On the sixth ballot, when a simple majority vote should have decided the victor, *Lion* led 12 to 10 (with one hold-out vote for *Oliver!*) and was about to be declared the winner when the meeting was suddenly interrupted by the late arrival of *Time* magazine's Stefan Kanfer. Kanfer was one of the half-dozen journalists recruited recently from magazines to join the group formerly composed only of newspaper scribes. The crix were eager to include his

Variety praised *The Lion in Winter*, starring Katharine Hepburn and Peter O'Toole, as "amazing," but when the Gotham crix named it Best Picture, some scribes revolted.

input, even though his vote was predictable: Kanfer had savaged *The Lion in Winter* in print. No one thought his vote would matter, though, since *Lion* had demonstrated a two-point lead earlier, so the crix voted to permit an "emergency" seventh ballot as a courtesy.

The results were surprising: the rival pics received 11 votes each, *Oliver!* took 1 and there was 1 abstention. The crix had accepted the tie and already moved on to decide another category when someone noted that, according to the group's bylaws, *Oliver!* should've been dropped from consideration on the last ballot. The judges then backtracked and conducted an eighth polling and *Lion* re-emerged the champ, 13 to 11.

That's when the meeting became "most heated" and "extremely acrimonious," according to later press reports. *Variety* reported that *Faces* advocates Renada Adler and Vincent Canby of the *Times* "staged a mutiny" and were joined by new recruit Richard Schickel of *Life,* who denounced the group's old members as "deadwood." The fight became so fierce that some members "had tears in their eyes," noted *Variety.* Four of the new members banded together and resigned.

The New York Times reported, "The resignations were withheld pending a meeting of the organization to discuss possible changes in voting procedure." Meantime, the rebels remained in the conference room of the New York Newspaper Guild and continued to vote in subsequent races.

The Lion in Winter's Peter O'Toole led the actors' race with 6 endorsements, followed by 4 for Alan Arkin *(The Heart Is a Lonely Hunter),* 3 for Per Oscarsson *(Hunger)* and 2 for George C. Scott *(Petulia).* By the sixth polling, O'Toole fell back to 2 votes, Scott climbed to second place with 8 and Arkin, with 13 votes, won for what *Variety* called his "erratic and mannered performance as a deaf-and-mute loner" in *The Heart Is a Lonely Hunter.*

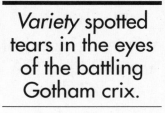

Variety spotted tears in the eyes of the battling Gotham crix.

The critics group's historical records are spotty about what happened next. Katharine Hepburn placed in the actress race with "either 3 or 4 votes" compared to "either 10 or 11" for Joanne Woodward in *Rachel, Rachel.* Woodward claimed victory with 18 votes on the third round over Tuesday Weld *(Pretty Poison),* who jumped to second place with 5.

Woodward's victory was a personal triumph, since *Rachel* was a small indie pic produced by her husband, Paul Newman, who also assumed the director's reins for the first time in his career. He was rewarded with the crix's helmer's prize, which he claimed on the sixth ballot over Cassavetes 11 to 9.

The Lion in Winter led the race for Best Screenplay on the first canvass, but lost to *Pretty Poison* on the sixth.

One month later, harmony was restored in the crix's group when the scribes gathered at the Rainbow Room to bestow their plaques. *Variety* reported, "To the photographers and cameramen present, greatest focus of interest, of course, was on husband-and-wife team of Joanne Woodward and Paul Newman. Maximilian Schell, in presenting the plaque to Newman, said the recipient had broken the ice for every actor who wanted to be a director." Schell, who had beat Newman for an Oscar in 1961, exulted in his old foe's victory for directing since Schell would soon helm his first picture, too.

At the directors' guild competish, Paul Newman made the cut that narrowed the race from 10 rivals to 5, but victory was claimed by another relative rookie, Anthony Harvey *(The Lion in Winter),* who'd helmed his first film only two years earlier. Now Harvey beat such veteran talent as William Wyler and Carol Reed, but he wouldn't get a chance to express his appreciation to guild voters. Acceptance speeches were eliminated at this year's banquet so the awards presentation could be kept to 40 minutes. It didn't matter to Harvey; he was "absent in London," *Variety* noted.

At the writers' guild honors, *The Lion in Winter*'s James Goldman was honored for adapting his Broadway play to the screen. Another stage scribe was also cited: Neil Simon, who had lost his bid last year for *Barefoot in the Park,* but now rallied for *The Odd Couple.*

"For the second year in a row, Swedish filmmaker Ingmar Bergman swept the awards of the National Society of Film Critics, the org of reviewers for weekly and monthly mags, some of the small-circulation 'highbrow' variety," reported *Variety.* Bergman reaped Best Picture and Best Director for *Shame,* which starred Liv Ullman and Max von Sydow as a refugee couple struggling to survive a war.

"Indeed, Scandinavia made an impressive

showing this year picking up all of the more important prizes as Denmark's Per Oscarsson was called top actor for *Hunger* and Norway's Liv Ullmann was voted foremost actress for *Shame*," the paper added. "She has previously picked up the award of the National Board of Review for work both in *Shame* and an earlier Bergman film *Hour of the Wolf*." All victors were chosen on the second ballot when members ranked their choices first, second and third after no winner claimed a majority on the first round, when voters were permitted only one choice each.

After broadcasting the Golden Globes last year as part of a five-year deal, NBC dropped the show when it was accused by the Federal Communications Commission of "substantially" misleading the public about the integrity of the awards process. Rumors persisted that winners were tipped off ahead of time in order to lure them to the ceremony, and there were questions about the scientific standards used in the poll that determined winners of World Film Favorites.

> ## *The Lion in Winter* reigned at the DGA, WGA and Golden Globes, too.

The awards gala went on anyway, with Dean Jones hosting, as 1,000 attendees supped on filet mignon and sipped French wines. Star presenters included Shelley Winters, Tony Curtis and Martin Landau. *The Los Angeles Herald Examiner* said, "It turned out to be a more intimate party with class like the old days before the TV cameras were hogging the spotlight. When Glenn Ford remarked to this effect on stage, he got a rousing ovation."

Drama was provided by some of the top award results. New York crix's Best Picture *The Lion in Winter* was crowned again and there was a surprise in the top category for comedies/musicals. *Funny Girl* and *The Odd Couple* were considered the early front-runners for that Best Picture kudo, but *Oliver!* pulled off an upset, claiming its first top-pic prize of the year—but not its last.

Most winners were absent, though, including *Rachel, Rachel*'s Best Director

and Actress Paul Newman and Joanne Woodward. So, too, were Best Actor Peter O'Toole (*The Lion in Winter*, also winner of Best Drama Picture), Best Supporting Actress Ruth Gordon (*Rosemary's Baby*), Most Promising New Stars (Leonard Whiting and Olivia Hussey of *Romeo and Juliet*), World Film Favorites Sidney Poitier and Sophia Loren, and *Oliver!* star Ron Moody, who won Best Comedy/Musical Actor, which was accepted by Cecil B. DeMille Award recipient Gregory Peck.

Present were such champs as Daniel Massey, who was declared Best Supporting Actor for portraying his godfather Noel Coward in *Star!*—plus sudden new star Barbra Streisand, who'd recently parlayed her Broadway success in *Funny Girl* to the screen, making, *Variety* noted, "a marked impact."

The outsized, Brooklyn-hewn personality made a notable impact at the Globes, too. "Barbra Streisand was the big event," the *Times* noted. "She wore a stunning coat-pants suit of brocade and fur that made her look exotically Mongolian." As she stood at the podium to collect her statuette for Best Musical/Comedy Actress, she said to the gathered members of the foreign press, "I hope I didn't get this award because I have an accent."

She added, coquettishly, "I don't think I would stand the Oscar thing!"

But Streisand had heard 12 hours earlier that she'd scored one of *Funny Girl*'s 8 Academy Award nominations. Only one pic nabbed more—*Oliver!*, with 11. Prior to the Globes, the only kudos group that had honored *Funny Girl* was the writers' guild, which voted it Best Written Musical. *Funny Girl* topped *Oliver!* at the box office—and some pundits even believed that it could triumph as Best Picture over *The Lion in Winter*, which had an obvious edge, since directors' guild champs had claimed Oscar's Best Picture trophy 15 out of the past 20 years.

Nominee oversights included *2001: A Space Odyssey,* which failed to score a Best Picture bid. Paul Newman wasn't nommed in the director's lineup, but he shrugged the snub off, telling *Variety* columnist Army Archerd, "I'm not competitive." His wife was furious, however, and she vowed to boycott the Oscars, telling Archerd, "I couldn't have been nominated for Best Actress or Estelle Parsons either without him being the director. I'm not going to go!" Later, when she calmed down, Newman persuaded her to attend since he was nominated as producer of Best Picture contender *Rachel, Rachel.*

This year the ceremony was moved to the Dorothy Chandler Pavilion, and *Variety* approved: "In all his 41 years, Oscar never found a more sumptuous home." There were nightmarish traffic problems outside, however, just as there were when the event was first held at the Santa Monica Civic Auditorium eight years earlier. "Many vehicles coming off the Santa Ana Freeway were caught in an almost inextricable mess," *Variety* observed. Admission prices ranged from $11 for seats in the second balcony to $2 in the loges.

"A crowd of about 3,000 was massed to ogle the famous," *The New York Times* noted. "The loudest outcries greeted the arrival of Miss Streisand as she arrived wearing a black see-through pants suit and escorted by her husband, Elliott Gould. Gasps, screams and other audible evidence of recognition also marked the arrival of three other best-actress nominees, Patricia Neal, Joanne Woodward and Vanessa Redgrave."

Missing among the night's top contenders was Cliff Robertson, who had previously vowed that, if he had to, he'd swim across the Pacific Ocean to be present at the Oscars. He was still in the Philippines filming *Too Late the Hero* on awards night, though, because director Robert Aldrich refused to let him leave despite Robertson's offer to pay $75,000 to cover the cost of production delays. Robertson's Oscar bid for *Charly* meant a lot to him. He initiated the role of a retarded man who becomes a genius after brain surgery in the TV drama

"Hello, gorgeous!" Barbra Streisand gasped as she admired her golden boy after tying Katharine Hepburn for Best Actress. Behind her: past Oscar champ Ingrid Bergman.

1968

The Two Worlds of Charlie Gordon. Earlier in his career, Robertson starred in *The Hustler* and *The Days of Wine and Roses* on TV, then lost the film roles to Paul Newman and Jack Lemmon. With *Charlie Gordon,* he took no chances, bought the screen rights and struggled for seven years to persuade Hollywood to let him make the movie. Once it was completed, he mounted an aggressive Oscar ad campaign in the trade press and scored an early victory by being named Best Actor by the National Board of Review.

Robertson faced tough challenges from Golden Globe champ Peter O'Toole and Gotham film crix choice Alan Arkin, but he prevailed on Oscar night.

When his *Hero* costar Michael Caine heard the news in the Philippines, he informed Robertson on the film set, where the actors cheered Robertson and hurled him into the air three times. "It's really hard to believe," Robertson told reporters who telephoned him moments later.

The press had anointed a favorite in the race for Best Supporting Actor—the 15-year-old thesp who played *Oliver*'s Artful Dodger "with knowing cunning and impudent self-confidence," said *Variety.* But Jack Wild got trumped by another Jack—Albertson, who was honored for reprising his Tony Award—winning role as the embittered father of an Army veteran returning from World War II in the Pulitzer champ *The Subject Was Roses*. The tough ex-vaudeville trouper cried at the podium and said, "I didn't expect to be this moved."

Another longtime star prevailed as Best Supporting Actress after having been nommed for her thesping skills once before (*Inside Daisy Clover*) and three times for writing with her husband Garson Kanin (*A Double Life, Adam's Rib* and *Pat and Mike*). Hailed finally for her role as a pushy witch-next-door in *Rosemary's Baby*, Ruth Gordon noted at the podium that she made her first film in 1915 and added, "I don't know why it took so long. My husband told me if I didn't win this time he wouldn't bring me again." The 72-year-old beamed and said, "I feel absolutely groovy!"

In the lead-actress race, Katharine Hepburn scored her eleventh nomination, thereby topping Bette Davis's old record. George Cukor, Gregory Peck and Anthony Harvey prevailed on her to attend this year's ceremony, but Hepburn stubbornly opted to stay at home and watch the gala on TV. She was pitted against three formidable foes: the popular favorite, Streisand; New York crix choice Joanne Woodward; and Patricia Neal (*The Subject Was Roses*), who may have been considered a sentimental favorite since she made, *Variety* noted, "a triumphant return to pix" after suffering three strokes.

Presenter Ingrid Bergman was charged with revealing the winner of the most closely watched race of the year. As she was ready to step out on stage, an accountant from Price Waterhouse told her to make sure she read "everything."

"I thought he was referring to all the names of the nominees," she later told Army Archerd.

When she opened the envelope, she announced, "It's a tie!" The 3,030 academy voters had split evenly between Hepburn and Streisand, causing the first tie ever in the actress race and the second in Oscar history. (Fredric March and Wallace Beery shared the gold in 1931–32.) Hepburn's back-to-back wins were the first consecutive victories in the category since Luise Rainer in 1936–37, and she set a new record

Globe champ *Oliver!* pulled off a shocking victory over *Lion in Winter* and *Funny Girl* for Oscar's Best Picture prize.

for total triumphs in the lead races: three. (Walter Brennan had claimed three in the supporting categories earlier.)

Variety noted that Streisand looked "a bit overwhelmed" when she arrived at the podium after ripping her bell-bottom pants on the stairs. She stood next to *Lion in Winter* director Anthony Harvey, who accepted for Hepburn.

"Hello, gorgeous!" Streisand gasped as she admired the statuette in her hands.

"I am very honored to be in such magnificent company as Katharine Hepburn," she added. "The first script of *Funny Girl* was written when I was only 11 years old. Thank God it took so long to get it right, you know?"

Backstage, a few minutes later, Streisand refused to go to the media rooms upstairs, exclaiming, "I can't go out and face those people!" Finally, *Variety* reported, she "reluctantly gave the press a few minutes. Her remarks were brief. She said winning the award was a 'wonderful thing' but 'not half as exciting as working on the film and seeing the finished product.' "

Considering Hepburn's victory, and earlier wins for best screenplay and musical score, *The Lion in Winter* seemed poised to pounce next on the best-director honor, which it had claimed at the directors' guild ceremony weeks earlier. But an upset gave the accolade to Sir Carol Reed (*Oliver!*), who'd lost previous Oscar bids for *The Fallen Idol* in 1949 and *The Third Man* in 1950.

"When director Reed accepted his Oscar, he pointed out that it was the first musical he had directed and he kept his thank you's brief and to the point," *Variety* said.

A few minutes later came the biggest upset of the night when *Oliver!* was proclaimed Best Picture.

The losers took the news in stride. After the Oscarcast, *Funny Girl*'s producer and director made a brief visit to the Governors' Ball, but then headed to Streisand's house for her private party, where they were joined by *The Lion in Winter* scribe James Goldman.

Streisand had good reason to be in a celebratory mood. It was a controversial decision, but the film academy had bent the rules and permitted her to become a member even before *Funny Girl* finished lensing. Assuming she voted for herself, Streisand could thank herself for victory.

The next day Streisand went to work on the set of *On a Clear Day You Can See Forever*, where she was confronted by cinematographer Harry Stradling, who demanded she pay up on a bet. He'd wagered $500 against her $100 that she'd win.

Archerd reported, "However, she paid him only $50—claimed it was a half-win."

▪ 1968 ▪

NEW YORK FILM CRITICS

Winners were announced on December 30, 1968. Awards were presented on January 26, 1969, at the Rainbow Room in New York.

BEST PICTURE
▪ *The Lion in Winter*

BEST DIRECTOR
▪ Paul Newman, *Rachel, Rachel*

BEST ACTOR
▪ Alan Arkin, *The Heart Is a Lonely Hunter*

BEST ACTRESS
▪ Joanne Woodward, *Rachel, Rachel*

BEST SCREENPLAY
▪ Lorenzo Semple, Jr., *Pretty Poison*

BEST FOREIGN FILM
▪ *War and Peace* (U.S.S.R.)

SPECIAL AWARD
▪ *Yellow Submarine* (for full-length animation)

NATIONAL BOARD OF REVIEW

Winners were announced on January 5, 1969.

BEST PICTURE
▪ *The Shoes of the Fisherman*
Romeo and Juliet
Yellow Submarine
Charly
Rachel, Rachel
The Subject Was Roses
The Lion in Winter
Planet of the Apes
Oliver!
2001: A Space Odyssey

BEST DIRECTOR
▪ Franco Zeffirelli, *Romeo and Juliet*

BEST ACTOR
▪ Cliff Robertson, *Charly*

BEST ACTRESS
▪ Liv Ullmann, *Hour of the Wolf, Shame*

BEST SUPPORTING ACTOR
▪ Leo McKern, *The Shoes of the Fisherman*

BEST SUPPORTING ACTRESS
- Virginia Maskell, *Interlude*

BEST FOREIGN FILM
- *War and Peace* (U.S.S.R.)
The Bride Wore Black (France/Italy)
Hagbard and Signo
    (Denmark/Iceland/Sweden)
Hunger (Denmark/Norway/Sweden)
The Two of Us (France)

NATIONAL SOCIETY OF FILM CRITICS

Winners were announced on January 6, 1969, at the Algonquin Hotel in New York.

BEST PICTURE
- *Shame*

BEST DIRECTOR
- Ingmar Bergman, *Shame, Hour of the Wolf*

BEST ACTOR
- Per Oscarsson, *Hunger*

BEST ACTRESS
- Liv Ullmann, *Shame*

BEST SUPPORTING ACTOR
- Seymour Cassel, *Faces*

BEST SUPPORTING ACTRESS
- Billie Whitelaw, *Charlie Bubbles*

BEST SCREENPLAY
- John Cassavetes, *Faces*

BEST CINEMATOGRAPHY
- William A. Fraker, *Bullitt*

SPECIAL AWARDS
(FEATURE-LENGTH DOCUMENTARY)
- Allan King, *Warrendale*
- Eugene S. Jones, *A Face of War*
(FEATURE-LENGTH ANIMATION)
- *Yellow Submarine*

DIRECTORS GUILD OF AMERICA

The initial list of nominees was narrowed down to a group of finalists who competed for the Best Director award, bestowed on February 22, 1969. Dual ceremonies were held at the Beverly Hilton Hotel in Los Angeles and the Waldorf-Astoria Hotel in New York.

BEST DIRECTOR
- Anthony Harvey, *The Lion in Winter*
Paul Almond, *Isabel*
Stanley Kubrick, *2001: A Space Odyssey*
    (finalist)
Jiri Menzel, *Closely Watched Trains*
Paul Newman, *Rachel, Rachel* (finalist)
Roman Polanski, *Rosemary's Baby*
Carol Reed, *Oliver!* (finalist)
Gene Saks, *The Odd Couple*
William Wyler, *Funny Girl* (finalist)
Franco Zeffirelli, *Romeo and Juliet*

GOLDEN GLOBES

Awards were presented on February 24, 1969, at the Cocoanut Grove in the Ambassador Hotel in Los Angeles.

BEST DRAMA PICTURE
- *The Lion in Winter*
Charly
The Fixer
The Heart Is a Lonely Hunter
The Shoes of the Fisherman

BEST COMEDY OR MUSICAL PICTURE
- *Oliver!*
Finian's Rainbow
Funny Girl
The Odd Couple
Yours, Mine and Ours

BEST DIRECTOR
- Paul Newman, *Rachel, Rachel*
Anthony Harvey, *The Lion in Wainter*
Carol Reed, *Oliver!*
William Wyler, *Funny Girl*
Franco Zeffirelli, *Romeo and Juliet*

BEST ACTOR, DRAMA
- Peter O'Toole, *The Lion in Winter*

Alan Arkin, *The Heart Is a Lonely Hunter*
Alan Bates, *The Fixer*
Tony Curtis, *The Boston Strangler*
Cliff Robertson, *Charly*

BEST ACTRESS, DRAMA
- Joanne Woodward, *Rachel, Rachel*

Mia Farrow, *Rosemary's Baby*
Katharine Hepburn, *The Lion in Winter*
Vanessa Redgrave, *Isadora*
Beryl Reid, *The Killing of Sister George*

BEST ACTOR, COMEDY OR MUSICAL
- Ron Moody, *Oliver!*

Fred Astaire, *Finian's Rainbow*
Jack Lemmon, *The Odd Couple*
Walter Matthau, *The Odd Couple*
Zero Mostel, *The Producers*

BEST ACTRESS, COMEDY OR MUSICAL
- Barbra Streisand, *Funny Girl*

Julie Andrews, *Star!*
Lucille Ball, *Yours, Mine and Ours*
Petula Clark, *Finian's Rainbow*
Gina Lollobrigida, *Buona Sera, Mrs. Campbell*

BEST SUPPORTING ACTOR
- Daniel Massey, *Star!*

Beau Bridges, *For Love of Ivy*
Ossie Davis, *The Scalphunters*
Hugh Griffith, *The Fixer*
Hugh Griffith, *Oliver!*
Martin Sheen, *The Subject Was Roses*

BEST SUPPORTING ACTRESS
- Ruth Gordon, *Rosemary's Baby*

Barbara Hancock, *Finian's Rainbow*
Abbey Lincoln, *For Love of Ivy*
Sondra Locke, *The Heart Is a Lonely Hunter*
Jane Merrow, *The Lion in Winter*

MOST PROMISING NEWCOMER—MALE
- Leonard Whiting, *Romeo and Juliet*

Alan Alda, *Paper Lion*
Daniel Massey, *Star!*
Michael Sarrazin, *The Sweet Ride*
Jack Wild, *Oliver!*

MOST PROMISING NEWCOMER—FEMALE
- Olivia Hussey, *Romeo and Juliet*

Ewa Aulin, *Candy*
Jacqueline Bisset, *The Sweet Ride*
Barbara Hancock, *Finian's Rainbow*
Sondra Locke, *The Heart Is a Lonely Hunter*
Leigh Taylor-Young, *I Love You, Alice B. Toklas*

BEST SCREENPLAY
- Stirling Silliphant, *Charly*

Mel Brooks, *The Producers*
James Goldman, *The Lion in Winter*
Roman Polanski, *Rosemary's Baby*
Dalton Trumbo, *The Fixer*

BEST ORIGINAL SONG
- "The Windmills of Your Mind," *The Thomas Crown Affair*

"Buona Sera, Mrs. Campbell," *Buona Sera, Mrs. Campbell*
"Chitty, Chitty, Bang Bang," *Chitty, Chitty, Bang Bang*
"Funny Girl," *Funny Girl*
"Star!," *Star!*

BEST FOREIGN-LANGUAGE FOREIGN FILM
- *War and Peace* (Russia)

The Bride Wore Black (France)
I Even Met Happy Gypsies (Yugoslavia)
Shame (Sweden)
Stolen Kisses (France)

BEST ENGLISH-LANGUAGE FOREIGN FILM
- *Romeo and Juliet*

Benjamin
Buona Sera, Mrs. Campbell
Joanna
Poor Cow

Winners

BEST ORIGINAL SCORE
- Alex North, *The Shoes of the Fisherman*

WORLD FILM FAVORITES
- Sophia Loren
- Sidney Poitier

CECIL B. DEMILLE AWARD
- Gregory Peck

WRITERS GUILD OF AMERICA

Awards were presented on March 23, 1969, at the Beverly Hilton Hotel in Los Angeles.

BEST WRITTEN DRAMA

- *The Lion in Winter,* James Goldman

The Heart Is a Lonely Hunter, Thomas C. Ryan, based on the novel by Carson McCullers

Petulia, Lawrence B. Marcus, based on the Barbara Turner adaptation of the novel *Me and the Arch Kook Petulia* by John Haase

Rachel, Rachel, Stewart Stern, based on the novel *A Jest of God* by Margaret Laurence

Rosemary's Baby, Roman Polanski, based on the novel by Ira Levin

BEST WRITTEN COMEDY

- *The Odd Couple*, Neil Simon

Hot Millions, Ira Wallach, Peter Ustinov

I Love You, Alice B. Toklas, Paul Mazursky, Larry Tucker

The Producers, Mel Brooks

Yours, Mine and Ours, Melville Shavelson, Mort Lachman, story by Madelyn Davis and Bob Carroll, Jr.

BEST WRITTEN MUSICAL

- *Funny Girl*, Isobel Lennart

Finian's Rainbow, E. Y. Harburg, Fred Saidy

Star! William Fairchild

LAUREL AWARD

- Carl Foreman

VALENTINE DAVIES AWARD

- Dore Schary

ACADEMY AWARDS

Nominations were announced on February 24, 1969. Awards were presented on April 14 at the Dorothy Chandler Pavilion in Los Angeles. The ceremony was telecast by ABC.

BEST PICTURE

- *Oliver*

Funny Girl

Rachel, Rachel

Romeo and Juliet

The Lion in Winter

BEST DIRECTOR

- Carol Reed, *Oliver!*

Anthony Harvey, *The Lion in Winter*

Stanley Kubrick, *2001: A Space Odyssey*

Gillo Pontecorvo, *The Battle of Algiers*

Franco Zeffirelli, *Romeo and Juliet*

BEST ACTOR

- Cliff Robertson, *Charly*

Alan Arkin, *The Heart Is a Lonely Hunter*

Alan Bates, *The Fixer*

Ron Moody, *Oliver!*

Peter O'Toole, *The Lion in Winter*

BEST ACTRESS (TIE)

- Barbra Streisand, *Funny Girl*
- Katharine Hepburn, *The Lion in Winter*

Patricia Neal, *The Subject Was Roses*

Vanessa Redgrave, *Isadora*

Joanne Woodward, *Rachel, Rachel*

BEST SUPPORTING ACTOR

- Jack Albertson, *The Subject Was Roses*

Seymour Cassel, *Faces*

Daniel Massey, *Star!*

Jack Wild, *Oliver!*

Gene Wilder, *The Producers*

BEST SUPPORTING ACTRESS

- Ruth Gordon, *Rosemary's Baby*

Lynn Carlin, *Faces*

Sondra Locke, *The Heart Is a Lonely Hunter*

Kay Medford, *Funny Girl*

Estelle Parsons, *Rachel, Rachel*

BEST ADAPTED SCREENPLAY

- James Goldman, *The Lion in Winter*

Vernon Harris, *Oliver!*

Roman Polanski, *Rosemary's Baby*

Neil Simon, *The Odd Couple*

Stewart Stern, *Rachel, Rachel*

BEST ORIGINAL SCREENPLAY

- Mel Brooks, *The Producers*

John Cassavetes, *Faces*

Arthur C. Clarke, Stanley Kubrick, *2001: A Space Odyssey*

Gillo Pontecorvo, Franco Solinas, *The Battle of Algiers*

Peter Ustinov, Ira Wallach, *Hot Millions*

BEST SONG

- "The Windmills of Your Mind," *The Thomas Crown Affair,* Alan Bergman, Marilyn Bergman, Michel Legrand

"Chitty Chitty Bang Bang," *Chitty Chitty Bang Bang,* Richard M. Sherman, Robert B. Sherman

"For Love of Ivy," *For Love of Ivy,* Quincy Jones, Bob Russell

"Funny Girl," *Funny Girl,* Bob Merrill, Jule Styne

"Star!" *Star!,* Sammy Cahn, Jimmy Van Heusen

BEST FOREIGN-LANGUAGE FILM

- *War and Peace* (U.S.S.R.)

The Boys of Paul Street (Hungary)
The Firemen's Ball (Czechoslovakia)
The Girl with the Pistol (Italy)
Stolen Kisses (France)

Winners

BEST ART DIRECTION

- John Box, Terence Marsh, Vernon Dixon, Ken Muggleston, *Oliver!*

BEST CINEMATOGRAPHY

- Pasqualino De Santis, *Romeo and Juliet*

BEST COSTUME DESIGN

- Danilo Donati, *Romeo and Juliet*

BEST DOCUMENTARY

(FEATURE)
- Bill McGaw, *Journey into Self*
(SHORT SUBJECT)
- Saul Bass, *Why Man Creates*

BEST FILM EDITING

- Frank P. Keller, *Bullitt*

BEST MAKEUP

- John Chambers, *Planet of the Apes*

BEST MUSIC

(ORIGINAL SCORE FOR A MOTION PICTURE [NOT A MUSICAL])
- John Barry, *The Lion in Winter*
(SCORE OF A MUSICAL PICTURE [ORIGINAL OR ADAPTATION])
- John Green, *Oliver!*

SCIENTIFIC OR TECHNICAL AWARDS

Class I (Statuette)
- Philip V. Palmquist, Minnesota Mining and Manufacturing Corp.; Dr. Herbert Meyer, Motion Picture and TV Research Center; Charles D. Staffell, Rank Organization; Eastman Kodak

Class II (Plaque)
- Donald W. Norwood, Eastman Kodak, Producers Service Co.; Edmund M. Di Giulio, Niels G. Peterson, Norman S. Hughes, Cinema Product Development; Optical Coating Laboratories; Eastman Kodak; Panavision; Todd-AO Co., Mitchell Camera Co.

Class III (Certificate)
- Carl W. Hauge, Edward H. Reichard, Consolidated Film Industries; E. Michael Meahl, Roy J. Ridenour, Ramtronics; Eastman Kodak, Consolidated Film Industries

BEST SHORT SUBJECT

(CARTOON)
- *Winnie the Pooh and the Blustery Day*
(LIVE ACTION)
- *Robert Kennedy Remembered*

BEST SOUND

- Shepperton Studio Sound Department, *Oliver!*

BEST SPECIAL VISUAL EFFECTS

- Stanley Kubrick, *2001:A Space Odyssey*

JEAN HERSHOLT HUMANITARIAN AWARD

- Martha Raye

HONORARY AWARDS

- John Chambers, *The Planet of the Apes*
- Onna White, *Oliver!*

SCREEN ACTORS GUILD

LIFETIME ACHIEVEMENT AWARD

- James Stewart

▪ 1969 ▪

Midnight Cowboy—*Classic Dark Horse*

The newspaper scribes of the New York Film Critics buckled quickly under pressure from the rival new National Society of Film Critics, composed of New York–based magazine writers.

The Gothamites squashed their old voting system, which required winners to receive a two-thirds edge on the first five ballots or a simple majority on the sixth. In its place it adopted the society's two-tier procedure: if no candidate received a majority on the first round, a winner was chosen on the second tally after the crix ranked their three favorite choices in descending order. New categories were added for supporting acting and the Gothamites' separate race for Best Foreign Film was dropped, allowing offshore fare to compete for Best Picture.

Now that they were using the same voting system, both crix groups elected the same foreign film as Best Picture—*Z*, which had also recently won the Jury Prize at Cannes. *Variety* called the French/Algerian thriller about a Greek political assassination "a punchy pic that mixes action, violence and conspiracy on a robust, lavish scale." National society member Arthur Schlesinger, Jr., of *Vogue* called *Z* "the most memorable political film of the decade."

Nearly all of the crix's decisions were made on second pollings. *Z* scored twice as many points for Best Picture as its nearest rivals, *Oh! What a Lovely War*, *The Damned* and *Midnight Cowboy*. The national society endorsed it by almost as wide a margin over *La Femme Infidèle* and *Stolen Kisses*. *Z*'s Henri Costa-Gavras claimed the Gothamites' helmer's prize (34 points) over Richard Attenborough (24 points for *Oh! What a Lovely War*), although he came in second (11 points) behind *Stolen Kisses*'s François Truffaut (12) at the national society vote.

Gotham scribes adopted the same voting system as the national society and named the same Best Picture—recent Cannes champ *Z*. Later, its producers became the first Globe champs to refuse that prize.

While the crix all rebelled against traditional Yankee fare for Best Picture and Director, they agreed on a Best Actor from a Hollywood film. Both groups endorsed Jon Voight as the naive wanna-be hustler in the first studio production to be slapped with an X rating after the old Production Code was replaced by a new ratings system. In 1969, X hadn't yet acquired its pornographic designation, but merely narrowed the movie's audience to viewers age 18 and older.

Nonetheless, *Midnight Cowboy* was called "shocking" by New York Film Critics member Wanda Hale of the *Daily News*. Despite its restrictive rating, it went on to become the year's third-highest-grossing movie and a classic studied in film schools, of course, but *The New York Times*'s Vincent Canby underestimated it at first, insisting, "It's not a movie for the ages."

Voight's closest competish was costar Dustin Hoffman, who appeared as the polar opposite of the preppie he'd portrayed in his last film outing, *The Graduate*. *Variety* sized him up as "a gimp-legged, always unshaven, cough-wracked petty chiseler who at first exploits and then befriends the stupid boy hustler from Texas."

Three thesps competed for both Best Actress laurels: Jane Fonda (*They Shoot Horses, Don't They?*), Vanessa Redgrave (*The Loves of Isadora*) and Maggie Smith (*The Prime of Miss Jean Brodie*). The Gothamites opted for Fonda, who *Variety* said gave a "dramatic and gripping" perf as "a hard-as-nails babe" hoofing it in a Depression-era dance marathon. The part was a career breakthrough for the one-time screen babe and it landed her on the cover of *Time* with her father, Henry, and brother Peter, whose own screen career had recently taken off on two speeding wheels in *Easy Rider*.

The national society, however, agreed with Cannes, honoring Vanessa Redgrave, whose grand portrayal of dance maverick Isadora Duncan was compared by *Variety* to Gloria Swanson's bravura screen mugging in *Sunset Boulevard*. Redgrave was Oscar- and Globe-nommed last year for the same role, but the 168-minute original *Isadora* was trimmed to 131 minutes this year, re-released as *The Loves of Isadora* and considered eligible anew by the same crix who initially overlooked it.

> WGA's tribute to Dalton Trumbo "buried past goblins," *Variety* said.

Both crix groups agreed on Best Supporting Actor on the first ballot—Jack Nicholson ("excellent as the articulate alcoholic" in *Easy Rider*, said *Variety*) and Best Screenplay on the second—*Bob & Carol & Ted & Alice*, which *Variety* hailed as an "almost flawless" exposé of the casual new morals of the wife-swapping sixties.

The National Board of Review didn't even list *Bob & Carol & Ted & Alice* on its list of Top 10 films. Its number-one pic was *They Shoot Horses, Don't They?* and, listed at number four, a movie that would also earn the board's Best Actor prize. *Variety* had called Peter O'Toole's perf as an eccentric British teacher in a musical version of *Goodbye, Mr. Chips* "a total departure" from his previous roles, but lauded him for crafting a character of "strength and dignity, whose tendency to appear ridiculous is endearing."

When the Golden Globe nominations came out, *Z* became embroiled in "a frenetic intrigue worthy of *Z* itself," *Variety* reported. Its U.S. distributor hoped to capitalize on *Z*'s crix kudos by positioning it as a contender for Best Picture at the Oscars, but when it was snubbed for the equivalent prize at the Globes, the distributor refused the nomination it received for Best Foreign Film. A New York attorney claiming to represent *Z*'s French producer denounced the distributor, flew to Los Angeles to accept the pic's nomination certificate from the Hollywood Foreign Press Association and announced, "If *Z* wins any picture awards, the producer will pick them up." A twist occurred a few weeks later when the French producer flew to L.A. and held a press conference with the distributor and lambasted the attorney as "an impostor." They reiterated their refusal to accept the bid, declared that they would not be present on awards night to accept the prize if it won and asked the press org's prexy to prevent the attorney from accepting it on their behalf.

Come awards night, *Z* did win Best Foreign Film, but "no one accepted the award, a first in Globe history," the *Times* noted.

The night's biggest champ was Best Drama Picture *Anne of the Thousand Days*, which *Variety* called "a stunningly acted, sumptuous, grand-scale wide-screen drama" starring Richard Burton as Henry VIII and Genevieve Bujold as his doomed bride Anne Boleyn. Bujold was named Best Actress, rookie helmer Charles Jarrott won Best Director and Richard Sokolove claimed script honors for adopting Maxwell Anderson's stage play.

Burton was nominated for Best Drama Actor against *Midnight Cowboy*'s Jon Voight and Dustin Hoffman, but an upset was scored by John Wayne, who was heralded for his comeback oater hit *True Grit*. In its review, *Variety* noted, "He towers over everything in the film—actors, script, even the magnificent Colorado mountains." He loomed large at the Globes gala, too. He was dogged by a horde of paparazzi from the moment he exited his fifth-floor suite at the Ambassador Hotel and headed down to the Cocoanut Grove for the ceremony, where he was greeted with two standing ovations. The first came when he pulled off a surprise win for Best Actor. As he received the statuette, he said, "Happiness just stepped up and greeted me."

A few minutes later, Wayne reaped another vertical ovation when he stepped up to the podium to bestow a special award. "Wayne reminisced about the old days at the Cocoanut Grove when you could get by on $5 with a bowl of spiked punch and watch Joan Crawford win a Charleston contest while Bing Crosby crooned from the stage," the L.A. Times reported. "Then he took the stage and presented Miss Crawford the Cecil B. DeMille Award for outstanding contributions to the entertainment field. 'She is the queen. Joan Crawford means motion pictures,' he said as Miss Crawford stepped on the stage, bare-shouldered and shapely."

Once-gritty John Wayne wept as he accepted his Oscar.

After Wayne's surprise victory for *True Grit,* other shocking wins included Patty Duke, who was proclaimed Best Musical or Comedy Actress as a lonely ugly duckling in *Me, Natalie.* The audience gasped when she triumphed over Barbra Streisand, Ingrid Bergman, Shirley MacLaine and Anna Magnani. Duke seemed stunned, too, and wept as she accepted the prize, saying, "This is insanity."

The biggest Globe surprise came in the race for Best Musical or Comedy Picture when *Cactus Flower, Paint Your Wagon, Hello, Dolly!* and *Goodbye, Columbus* lost to *The Secret of Santa Vittoria,* a humorous drama about the citizens of an Italian hill town trying to hide their wine supply from retreating Nazi soldiers.

Now that the Globes were no longer televised, HFPA leaders worried that atten-

dance might suffer, but the *L.A. Times* reported, "The list of absentees was small among the star-studded cast that filled the Cocoanut Grove to see and be seen, drink, dine and dance to the music of Freddy Martin's Orchestra."

Midnight Cowboy rebounded from its defeats at the Globes to win both guild honors, but neither winner showed up.

John Schlesinger was not present to accept his prize from the Directors Guild of America at the Beverly Hilton gala, which "would have been a sluggish affair if it wasn't for the spark-plug of the evening, emcee Hal Kanter," said *Variety.*

At the writers' guild gathering, scribe Waldo Salt wasn't present to claim his kudos for best adapted drama because he "had cold, was unable to attend," *Variety* reported. Also missing was William Goldman, whose *Butch Cassidy and the Sundance Kid* prevailed as best adapted drama over *Alice's Restaurant* (penned by Venable Herndon and Arthur Penn) and *Easy Rider* (ad-libbed by Peter Fonda, Dennis Hopper and Terry Southern). Present, though, was Arnold Schulman, who was honored for scripting the year's best comedy, *Goodbye, Columbus,* and Dalton Trumbo, who received the honorary Laurel Award. Trumbo had been blacklisted as one of the Hollywood 10 during the McCarthy era, which he referred to as he accepted his guild prize. "When you writers who are in your 40s or younger look back at that dark time, it will do no good to look for villains, heavies or saints," he said. "There were none. There were only victims." The Trumbo tribute, said *Variety,* "effected a kind of final burial to past goblins and hysteria."

The evening's mood was lifted by a stage spoof of a MGM props auction that included "shoulder pads worn by Jack Oakie and Joan Crawford in all of their pix, a stag film starring Lassie and Asta, and a gun taken from a stockholder after MGM announced it was going to remake *Four Horsemen of the Apocalypse,*" *Variety* said.

As the Oscar race neared, Universal hyped *Anne of the Thousand Days* with a blitz of tradepaper ads plus special screenings that lured academy members with the promise of free filet mignon and champagne. *Z* ads tubthumped its recent victories at the crix kudos and Cannes (but not the Golden Globes) as evidence that it was worthy of a Best Picture bid.

When the Oscar noms were announced, pundits were baffled over which film to cite as the Best Picture front-runner. Globes champ *Anne of the Thousand Days* led with the most bids (10), but it was widely believed to be doomed by weak b.o. and mixed reviews. *They Shoot Horses, Don't They?* nabbed the second most, but a nom for Best Picture was not among them. Next in the total tally with seven each were *Hello, Dolly!* (including Best Picture, but nothing for director Gene Kelly) and *Butch Cassidy and the Sundance Kid*, the year's top b.o. champ. *Butch* did score corresponding bids for Best Picture and Best Director, but its Oscar chances were considered dim since few reviewers considered it seriously as screen art. In fact, *Variety* called the entertaining western starring Paul Newman and Robert Redford a "near-comedy of errors."

Also up for Best Picture was a grateful *Z*, but it was considered most likely to win Best Foreign Film, since it was also nommed in that race. The last contender for the top prize was the recent recipient of the writers' and directors' guild awards—*Midnight Cowboy*. It only had six Oscar noms, though—which is not normally enough to pull off a Best Picture victory. Furthermore, it seemed impossible that the notoriously conservative voters would endorse an X-rated film as Best Picture. Academy prexy Gregory Peck bragged that he had recently brought in lots of new young blood, but there was still lots of old blood already in the august body and it

TOP DGA AWARD TO SCHLESINGER

Midnight Cowboy emerged as a serious rival late in the year's derby—at the DGA and WGA kudos after it was snubbed by the crix and Globes.

usually boiled at the sight of overt sexual film content.

When Oscar day came, suspense peaked.

Best Actress rival Jane Fonda broke off a cross-country trek through Indian reservations to be on hand for her first Oscar bout even though she knew her politics might hurt her chances. The New York film crix champ was still lambasted by conservatives as "Hanoi Jane" following her sympathetic visit to Vietnam's enemy capital.

Variety columnist Army Archerd noted where the other Fondas were (or weren't) on Oscar night: "Neither Peter nor papa Hank Fonda attended. Peter is off to location hunt. And Hank is outspoken in his objections to the awards—any awards—that pit actors' performances against each other. He fled to John Ford's boat in Mexico when nominated for *The Grapes of Wrath*."

Best Actress contender Liza Minnelli had recently been hurt in a motorcycle mishap with actor/writer/producer Tony Bill, but she made it to the awards gala. "It was a cuckoo accident!" she told Archerd. "We were only going 15 miles an hour. This is your friendly neighborhood Hell's Angel representative!" On Oscar night, her injuries were masked carefully by the same makeup artist who created the pronounced facial scars she bore the rest of the week while filming Otto Preminger's *Tell Me That You Love Me, Junie Moon*. She arrived at the awards ceremony telling reporters, "I'm lucky! I heal fast!" as she swept down the red carpet on the arm of her Oscar-winning father, Vincente. Her mother, Judy Garland, had died just months earlier and didn't live to see Liza became a film star.

The New York Times reported that "4,000 star-watchers occupied bleachers and stood behind police barricades outside" the Dorothy Chandler Pavilion as "3,000 dinner-jacketed and glittering-gowned movie colony notables" strolled past.

"They came to see John Wayne win," Army Archerd proclaimed later. "That was the unmistakable, overpowering feeling."

Wayne was the only front-runner on Oscar night. All other races were considered wide open—and even the Best Actor contest wasn't considered a lock. Some pundits insisted that the venerable old Hollywood cowboy could be upset by either of the brash *Midnight Cowboy* costars—or even Richard Burton, who was now up for his sixth career bid. Burton and wife Elizabeth Taylor had boycotted recent Oscar races when they felt that the feisty Welsh thesp didn't have a serious chance of winning. Taylor even missed her own victory for *Who's Afraid of Virginia Woolf?* in 1966. This year, however, she and Burton not only showed up, but they did so with Taylor brazenly showing off Burton's recent present to her—a $1 million diamond they had fashioned into a necklace just for the Oscar gala where Taylor was skedded to present Best Picture.

When the Best Actor winner was announced, the champ was frozen in disbelief. Wayne later told *Variety*, "I didn't know whether to just sit there or get up and run."

When he got up to the podium, *The New York Times* noted, "Mr. Wayne, unabashedly wiping his eyes, said, 'I feel very grateful, very humble.'" Then he made a playful reference to the one-eyed marshal he portrayed in *True Grit*: "Had I known (I'd win for this), I would've put that eye patch on 35 years earlier!"

Backstage afterward, he told the press, "It's ironic that I got the Oscar for a role that

Oscar Best Actress Maggie Smith (left) on the set of *The Prime of Miss Jean Brodie* with costars Robert Stephens and Celia Johnson: *Variety* called her perf a "triumph."

was the easiest of my career." He told Archerd that he thought his best career perf was actually in *She Wore a Yellow Ribbon,* which did not earn him an Oscar nom. His only previous bid was for *The Sands of Iwo Jima* in 1949.

Later that night, Duke claimed he didn't deserve to win. After the ceremony he joined the Burtons in their hotel room, where the three notorious revelers drank together till dawn. According to Burton biographer Melvyn Bragg, Wayne thrust his Best Actor statuette at Richard at one point and said, "You deserve this! Not me!"—but Burton declined the gift.

There were three front-runners in the race for Best Supporting Actor: Elliott Gould (*Bob & Carol & Ted & Alice*), recent Golden Globe champ Gig Young (*They Shoot Horses, Don't They?*) and crix groups' honoree Jack Nicholson (*Easy Rider*). Young triumphed for his role as "the promoter-emcee, the barker for a cheap sideshow attraction," said *Variety*. "Puffy-eyed, unshaven, reeking of stale liquor, sweat and cigarettes, Young has never looked older or acted better."

"I'm really quite speechless," he said in his acceptance speech. Backstage, he was asked by reporters whether Oscar victories by him and Wayne signaled a theme of Old Timers' Night. "It is as far as I'm concerned," he replied. "With pictures getting lewder and lewder, this is my last chance."

Young would make 12 more feature and TV films in his career, but only one hit—*Lovers and Other Strangers*—before the star of *They Shoot Horses, Don't They?* shot and killed his wife and himself in 1978.

Leaders in the race for Best Supporting Actress were Dyan Cannon (*Bob & Carol & Ted & Alice*) and Sylvia Miles (*Midnight Cowboy*), but the winner turned out to be another recent Globe grabber, Goldie Hawn (*Cactus Flower*). *The New York Times* described the victory as a "surprise," but that was an understatement. In its *Cactus Flower* review, *Variety* had said that Hawn "makes a credible screen debut" as the "Greenwich Village kook whom Walter Matthau contemplates marrying," but she was otherwise known chiefly as the ditzy babe covered in body paint on the quirky TV hit *Laugh-In*. She missed her big Oscar night, being in London filming *There's a Girl in My Soup* with Peter Sellers.

The winner of Best Actress turned out to be in London on Oscar night—and her victory was a far bigger upset than Hawn's. "An actress who wasn't considered a prime contender won her Best Actress Oscar in a triumph of artistry," *Variety* declared the next day when reporting on Maggie Smith's victory for *The Prime of Miss Jean Brodie*. Smith had scored a previous Oscar nomination for portraying Desdemona opposite Laurence Olivier in *Othello* in 1965. On Oscar night she was with him in Britain for the stage premiere of *The Beau Stratagem*.

It was Smith's recent turn on stage in Los Angeles that was credited with helping her pull off the Oscar shocker. *Jean Brodie* was old news as of Oscar time—it had played in movie theaters nearly a year earlier—but Smith dazzled local L.A. theatergoers during Oscar nomination season by starring in the Restoration comedy *The Beau Stratagem* and Chekov's *The Three Sisters*, two productions that marked the L.A. debut of Olivier's National Theatre of Britain. But her role in *Jean Brodie* also reaped huzzahs. *Variety* said, "Maggie Smith's tour-de-force performance as a schoolteacher slipping into spinsterhood is a triumph!"

The Fonda family turned out to have a

Crix Best Actor Jon Voight and Dustin Hoffman in *Midnight Cowboy*: its X rating prevented some newspapers from reporting its shocking Oscar upset. "The reverberations may last for years," said *Variety*.

bad Oscar night. Not only did Jane lose Best Actress, but her brother Peter lost the prize for original screenplay to William Goldman (*Butch Cassidy and the Sundance Kid*). Two writers' guild champs squared off over Best Adapted Screenplay—*Midnight Cowboy's* Waldo Salt and *Goodbye, Columbus's* Arnold Schulman. Salt won.

Prospects for other the major guild victor, *Midnight Cowboy's* John Schlesinger, to take the prize for Best Director improved dramatically when *Z* claimed the laurels for Best Foreign Film. *Z's* producer did not refuse the kudos, as he had at the Globes. "With this award, you help us," he told the audience, gratefully.

Schlesinger ended up prevailing for Best Director, although he was the night's third absent honoree who was in London. The statuette was claimed by Jon Voight, who told the audience, "John's shooting his next picture, *Sunday, Bloody Sunday*. I think he's on the phone in the back."

"By the time Elizabeth Taylor came forth to name the final winner, for Best Picture, it was a full and mostly interesting night," *Variety* proclaimed. "For TV viewers, it had all the elements of those daytime soapers—a degree of weeps, some suspense, yet even more, a tearful John Wayne. Can you top this?"

Oscar voters topped it with the biggest jaw-dropper of all: *Midnight Cowboy* won Best Picture. The Oscar audience gasped—and cheered—upon hearing the news.

"Paradox is that the film's X rating may keep a number of newspapers from reporting that *Midnight Cowboy* took so many Oscars," *Variety* noted. "A reporter for a paper of the Copley chain here said he is not allowed to give any editorial space to X-rated films.

Reporter for *The Oklahoma City Oklahoman*, apparently under the same restriction, said, 'Well, I'm glad *Midnight Cowboy* won, but, hell, I won't even be able to write about it.'

"The reverberations of the *Cowboy* wins may last on for years."

▪ 1969 ▪

NEW YORK FILM CRITICS

Winners were announced on December 29, 1969. Awards were presented on January 25, 1970, at Sardi's restaurant in New York.

BEST PICTURE
▪ *Z*

BEST DIRECTOR
▪ Costa-Gavras, *Z*

BEST ACTOR
▪ Jon Voight, *Midnight Cowboy*

BEST ACTRESS
▪ Jane Fonda, *They Shoot Horses, Don't They?*

BEST SUPPORTING ACTOR
▪ Jack Nicholson, *Easy Rider*

BEST SUPPORTING ACTRESS
▪ Dyan Cannon, *Bob & Carol & Ted & Alice*

BEST SCREENPLAY
▪ Paul Mazursky, Larry Tucker, *Bob & Carol & Ted & Alice*

NATIONAL BOARD OF REVIEW

Winners were announced on January 1, 1970.

BEST PICTURE
▪ *They Shoot Horses, Don't They?*
Ring of Bright Water
Topaz
Goodbye, Mr. Chips
The Battle of Britain

The Loves of Isadora
The Prime of Miss Jean Brodie
Support Your Local Sheriff
True Grit
Midnight Cowboy

BEST DIRECTOR
▪ Alfred Hitchcock, *Topaz*

BEST ACTOR
▪ Peter O'Toole, *Goodbye, Mr. Chips*

BEST ACTRESS
▪ Geraldine Page, *Trilogy*

BEST SUPPORTING ACTOR
▪ Philippe Noiret, *Topaz*

BEST SUPPORTING ACTRESS
▪ Pamela Franklin, *The Prime of Miss Jean Brodie*

BEST FOREIGN FILM
▪ *Shame* (Sweden)
Stolen Kisses (France)
The Damned (Italy)
La Femme Infidèle (France/Italy)
Adalen '31 (Sweden)

NATIONAL SOCIETY OF FILM CRITICS

Winners were announced on January 5, 1970, at the Algonquin Hotel in New York.

BEST PICTURE
▪ *Z*

BEST DIRECTOR
▪ François Truffaut, *Stolen Kisses*

BEST ACTOR
■ Jon Voight, *Midnight Cowboy*

BEST ACTRESS
■ Vanessa Redgrave, *The Loves of Isadora*

BEST SUPPORTING ACTOR
■ Jack Nicholson, *Easy Rider*

BEST SUPPORTING ACTRESS
■ Sian Phillips, *Goodbye, Mr. Chips*
■ Delphine Seyrig, *Stolen Kisses*

BEST SCREENPLAY
■ Paul Mazursky, Larry Tucker, *Bob & Carol & Ted & Alice*

BEST CINEMATOGRAPHY
■ Lucien Ballard, *The Wild Bunch*

SPECIAL AWARDS
■ Dennis Hopper, *Easy Rider*
■ Ivan Passer, *Intimate Lighting*

GOLDEN GLOBES

Nominations were announced on January 19, 1970. Awards were presented on February 2 at the Cocoanut Grove in the Ambassador Hotel in Los Angeles.

BEST DRAMA PICTURE
■ *Anne of the Thousand Days*
Butch Cassidy and the Sundance Kid
Midnight Cowboy
The Prime of Miss Jean Brodie
They Shoot Horses, Don't They?

BEST COMEDY OR MUSICAL PICTURE
■ *The Secret of Santa Vittoria*
Cactus Flower
Goodbye, Columbus
Hello, Dolly!
Paint Your Wagon

BEST DIRECTOR
■ Charles Jarrott, *Anne of the Thousand Days*
Gene Kelly, *Hello, Dolly!*
Stanley Kramer, *The Secret of Santa Vittoria*
Sydney Pollack, *They Shoot Horses, Don't They?*
John Schlesinger, *Midnight Cowboy*

BEST ACTOR, DRAMA
■ John Wayne, *True Grit*
Alan Arkin, *Popi*
Richard Burton, *Anne of the Thousand Days*
Dustin Hoffman, *Midnight Cowboy*
Jon Voight, *Midnight Cowboy*

BEST ACTRESS, DRAMA
■ Genevieve Bujold, *Anne of the Thousand Days*
Jane Fonda, *They Shoot Horses, Don't They?*
Liza Minnelli, *The Sterile Cuckoo*
Jean Simmons, *The Happy Ending*
Maggie Smith, *The Prime of Miss Jean Brodie*

BEST ACTOR, COMEDY OR MUSICAL
■ Peter O'Toole, *Goodbye, Mr. Chips*
Dustin Hoffman, *John and Mary*
Lee Marvin, *Paint Your Wagon*
Steve McQueen, *The Reivers*
Anthony Quinn, *The Secret of Santa Vittoria*

BEST ACTRESS, COMEDY OR MUSICAL
■ Patty Duke, *Me, Natalie*
Ingrid Bergman, *Cactus Flower*
Dyan Cannon, *Bob & Carol & Ted & Alice*
Kim Darby, *Generation*
Mia Farrow, *John and Mary*
Shirley MacLaine, *Sweet Charity*
Anna Magnani, *The Secret of Santa Vittoria*
Barbra Streisand, *Hello, Dolly!*

BEST SUPPORTING ACTOR
■ Gig Young, *They Shoot Horses, Don't They?*
Red Buttons, *They Shoot Horses, Don't They?*
Jack Nicholson, *Easy Rider*
Anthony Quayle, *Anne of the Thousand Days*
Mitch Vogel, *The Reivers*

BEST SUPPORTING ACTRESS
■ Goldie Hawn, *Cactus Flower*
Marianne McAndrew, *Hello, Dolly!*
Sian Phillips, *Goodbye, Mr. Chips*
Brenda Vaccaro, *Midnight Cowboy*
Susannah York, *They Shoot Horses, Don't They?*

MOST PROMISING NEWCOMER—MALE

- Jon Voight, *Midnight Cowboy*

Helmut Berger, *The Damned*

Glen Campbell, *True Grit*

Michael Douglas, *Hail Hero*

George Lazenby, *On Her Majesty's Secret Service*

MOST PROMISING NEWCOMER—FEMALE

- Ali MacGraw, *Goodbye, Columbus*

Dyan Cannon, *Bob & Carol & Ted & Alice*

Goldie Hawn, *Cactus Flower*

Marianne McAndrew, *Hello, Dolly*

Brenda Vaccaro, *Where It's At*

BEST SCREENPLAY

- John Hale, Bridget Boland, *Anne of the Thousand Days*

William Goldman, *Butch Cassidy and the Sundance Kid*

John Mortimer, *John and Mary*

Waldo Salt, *Midnight Cowboy*

David Shaw, *If It's Tuesday, This Must Be Belgium*

BEST ORIGINAL SONG

- "Jean," *The Prime of Miss Jean Brodie*

"Goodbye, Columbus," *Goodbye, Columbus*

"Raindrops Keep Fallin' on My Head," *Butch Cassidy and the Sundance Kid*

"Stay"

"The Time for Love Is Any Time"

"True Grit," *True Grit*

"What Are You Doing the Rest of Your Life," *The Happy Ending*

BEST FOREIGN-LANGUAGE FOREIGN FILM

- *Z* (Algeria/France) (award refused)

Adalen '31 (Sweden)

The Big Dig (Israel)

Fellini's Satyricon (Italy)

Girls in the Sun (Greece)

BEST ENGLISH-LANGUAGE FOREIGN FILM

- *Oh! What a Lovely War*

The Assassination Bureau

If

The Italian Job

Mayerling

Winners

BEST ORIGINAL SCORE

- Burt Bacharach, *Butch Cassidy and the Sundance Kid*

WORLD FILM FAVORITES

- Steve McQueen
- Barbra Streisand

CECIL B. DEMILLE AWARD

- Joan Crawford

DIRECTORS GUILD OF AMERICA

The initial list of nominees was narrowed down to a group of finalists who competed for the Best Director award, bestowed on February 14, 1970. Dual ceremonies were held at the Beverly Hilton Hotel in Los Angeles and the Waldorf-Astoria Hotel in New York.

BEST DIRECTOR

- John Schlesinger, *Midnight Cowboy*

Richard Attenborough, *Oh! What a Lovely War*

Costa-Gavras, *Z* (finalist)

George Roy Hill, *Butch Cassidy and the Sundance Kid* (finalist)

Dennis Hopper, *Easy Rider* (finalist)

Gene Kelly, *Hello, Dolly!*

Sam Peckinpah, *The Wild Bunch*

Larry Peerce, *Goodbye, Columbus*

Sydney Pollack, *They Shoot Horses, Don't They?* (finalist)

Haskell Wexler, *Medium Cool*

D. W. GRIFFITH AWARD

- Fred Zinnemann

WRITERS GUILD OF AMERICA

Awards were presented on March 13, 1970, at the Beverly Hilton Hotel in Los Angeles.

BEST DRAMA WRITTEN DIRECTLY FOR THE SCREEN

- *Butch Cassidy and the Sundance Kid*, William Goldman

Alice's Restaurant, Venable Herndon,
   Arthur Penn
Downhill Racer, James Salter
Easy Rider, Peter Fonda, Dennis Hopper,
   Terry Southern
Me, Natalie, A. Martin Zweiback, story by
   Stanley Shapiro and A. Martin
   Zweiback

BEST DRAMA ADAPTED FROM ANOTHER MEDIUM

- *Midnight Cowboy*, Waldo Salt, based on
   the novel by James Leo Herlihy
Anne of the Thousand Days, John Hale and
   Bridget Boland, adaptation by Richard
   Sokolove, based on the play by Maxwell
   Anderson
The Prime of Miss Jean Brodie, Jay
   Presson Allen, based on his play and the
   novel by Muriel Spark
They Shoot Horses, Don't They? James
   Poe, Robert E. Thompson, based on the
   novel by Horace McCoy
True Grit, Marguerite Roberts, based on
   the novel by Charles Portis

BEST COMEDY WRITTEN DIRECTLY FOR THE SCREEN

- *Bob & Carol & Ted & Alice*, Paul
   Mazursky, Larry Tucker
If It's Tuesday, This Must Be Belgium,
   David Shaw
Popi, Tina Pine, Lester Pine
Support Your Local Sheriff, William
   Bowers
Take the Money and Run, Woody Allen,
   Mickey Rose

BEST COMEDY ADAPTED FROM ANOTHER MEDIUM

- *Goodbye, Columbus*, Arnold Schulman,
   based on the novel by Philip Roth
Cactus Flower, I. A. L. Diamond, based on
   the play by Abe Burrows and the play
   by Pierre Barillet and Jean-Pierre Gredy
Gaily, Gaily, Abram S. Ginnes, based on
   the novel by Ben Hecht
John and Mary, John Mortimer, based on
   the novel by Mervyn Jones
The Reivers, Irving Ravetch, Harriet Frank,
   Jr., based on the novel by William
   Faulkner

LAUREL AWARD
- Dalton Trumbo

VALENTINE DAVIES AWARD
- Richard Murphy

MORGAN COX AWARD
- Barry Trivers

ACADEMY AWARDS

Nominations were announced on February
16, 1970. Awards were presented on April 7
at the Dorothy Chandler Pavilion in Los
Angeles. The ceremony was telecast by ABC.

BEST PICTURE
- *Midnight Cowboy*
Anne of the Thousand Days
Butch Cassidy and the Sundance Kid
Hello, Dolly!
Z

BEST DIRECTOR
- John Schlesinger, *Midnight Cowboy*
Costa-Gavras, *Z*
Arthur Penn, *Alice's Restaurant*
Sydney Pollack, *They Shoot Horses, Don't
   They?*
George Roy Hill, *Butch Cassidy and the
   Sundance Kid*

BEST ACTOR
- John Wayne, *True Grit*
Richard Burton, *Anne of the Thousand
   Days*
Dustin Hoffman, *Midnight Cowboy*
Peter O'Toole, *Goodbye, Mr. Chips*
Jon Voight, *Midnight Cowboy*

BEST ACTRESS
- Maggie Smith, *The Prime of Miss Jean
   Brodie*
Genevieve Bujold, *Anne of the Thousand
   Days*
Jane Fonda, *They Shoot Horses, Don't They?*
Liza Minnelli, *The Sterile Cuckoo*
Jean Simmons, *The Happy Ending*

BEST SUPPORTING ACTOR
- Gig Young, *They Shoot Horses, Don't
   They?*

Rupert Crosse, *The Reivers*
Elliott Gould, *Bob & Carol & Ted & Alice*
Jack Nicholson, *Easy Rider*
Anthony Quayle, *Anne of the Thousand Days*

BEST SUPPORTING ACTRESS
- Goldie Hawn, *Cactus Flower*
Catherine Burns, *Last Summer*
Dyan Cannon, *Bob & Carol & Ted & Alice*
Sylvia Miles, *Midnight Cowboy*
Susannah York, *They Shoot Horses, Don't They?*

BEST ADAPTED SCREENPLAY
- Waldo Salt, *Midnight Cowboy*
Bridget Boland, John Hale, Richard Sokolove, *Anne of the Thousand Days*
Costa-Gavras, Jorge Semprun, *Z*
James Poe, Robert E. Thompson, *They Shoot Horses, Don't They?*
Arnold Schulman, *Goodbye, Columbus*

BEST ORIGINAL SCREENPLAY
- William Goldman, *Butch Cassidy and the Sundance Kid*
Nicola Badalucco, Enrico Medioli, Luchino Visconti, *The Damned*
Peter Fonda, Dennis Hopper, Terry Southern, *Easy Rider*
Walon Green, Sam Peckinpah, Roy N. Sickner, *The Wild Bunch*
Paul Mazursky, Larry Tucker, *Bob & Carol & Ted & Alice*

BEST SONG
- "Raindrops Keep Fallin' on My Head," *Butch Cassidy and the Sundance Kid*, Burt Bacharach, Hal David
"Come Saturday Morning," *The Sterile Cuckoo*, Fred Karlin, Dory Previn
"Jean," *The Prime of Miss Jean Brodie*, Rod McKuen
"True Grit," *True Grit*, Elmer Bernstein, Don Black
"What Are You Doing the Rest of Your Life?" *The Happy Ending,* Alan Bergman, Marilyn Bergman, Michel Legrand

BEST FOREIGN-LANGUAGE FILM
- *Z* (Algeria/France)
Adalen '31 (Sweden)

The Battle of Neretva (Yugoslavia)
The Brothers Karamazov (U.S.S.R.)
My Night with Maud (France)

Winners

BEST ART DIRECTION
- Herman Blumenthal, John Decuir, Jack Martin Smith, Raphael Bretton, George Hopkins, Walter M. Scott, *Hello, Dolly!*

BEST CINEMATOGRAPHY
- Conrad Hall, *Butch Cassidy and the Sundance Kid*

BEST COSTUME DESIGN
- Margaret Furse, *Anne of the Thousand Days*

BEST DOCUMENTARY
(FEATURE)
- Bernard Chevry, *Arthur Rubinstein, The Love of Life*
(SHORT SUBJECT)
- Robert M. Fresco, Denis Sanders, *Czechoslovakia 1968*

BEST FILM EDITING
- Françoise Bonnot, *Z*

BEST MUSIC
(ORIGINAL SCORE FOR A MOTION PICTURE [NOT A MUSICAL])
- Burt Bacharach, *Butch Cassidy and the Sundance Kid*
(SCORE OF A MUSICAL PICTURE [ORIGINAL OR ADAPTATION])
- Lennie Hayton, Lionel Newman, *Hello, Dolly!*

SCIENTIFIC OR TECHNICAL AWARDS
Class II (Plaque)
- Hazeltine Corp.; Fouad Said; Juan de la Cierva, Dynasciences Corp.
Class III (Certificate)
- Otto Popelka, Magna-Tech Electronics; Fenton Hamilton, MGM; Panavision; Robert M. Flynn, B. Russell Hessy, Universal City Studios

BEST SHORT SUBJECT
(CARTOON)
- *It's Tough to Be a Bird*

(LIVE ACTION)
- *The Magic Machines*

BEST SOUND
- Jack Solomon, Murray Spivack, *Hello, Dolly!*

BEST SPECIAL VISUAL EFFECTS
- Robbie Robertson, *Marooned*

JEAN HERSHOLT HUMANITARIAN AWARD
- George Jessel

HONORARY AWARD
- Cary Grant

SCREEN ACTORS GUILD

LIFETIME ACHIEVEMENT AWARD
- Edward G. Robinson

· 1970 ·

Patton *Star Slaps Oscar*

Old Hollywood was crumbling in 1970. Only one of the original studio moguls—Darryl Zanuck—was still alive, the old star system was dead and, while indie and foreign pix prospered, Twentieth Century-Fox and MGM were so desperate for coin that they auctioned off Marilyn Monroe's bed from *Let's Make Love* and a pair of Judy Garland's ruby slippers from *The Wizard of Oz*.

Perhaps rallying to Tinseltown's defense, the National Society of Film Critics suddenly shrugged off its usual preference for foreign-lingo fare and named a Yankee studio production Best Picture for the first time in the five years of its existence: *M*A*S*H*.

Granted, the Twentieth Century-Fox co-production had already demonstrated a certain foreign sensibility by winning the Palme d'Or at Cannes. It also displayed a certain irreverent wit that's usually appreciated by edgy crix. Written by once-blacklisted scribe Ring Lardner, Jr., and directed by wunderkind Robert Altman, the tale of a U.S. Mobile Army Surgical Hospital (that is, M.A.S.H.) during the Korean war was called "a stomach-churning, gory, often tasteless, but frequently funny black comedy" by *Variety*. Runners-up for the top prize were *The Passion of Anna, The Wild Child, My Night at Maud's* and *Five Easy Pieces*. The crix stuck with a foreigner for Best Director—and the same foreigner no less that they'd chosen twice before: Ingmar Bergman (*The Passion of Anna*).

The New York Film Critics had chosen a foreign film last year (*Z*), but now embraced an American pic, too. *Variety* called *Five Easy Pieces* "an absorbing, if nerve-wracking, film" starring Jack Nicholson as a failed musician who hits the road in search of his past. It won on the second ballot with 27 points, followed by *The Passion of Anna*

Patton thesp George C. Scott bashed the Oscar as "barbarous" and "corrupt," but he accepted "the only award worth having" from the N.Y. crix. His wife, Colleen Dewhurst, attended the fete.

(12 points) and *M*A*S*H* (11). The Gotham crix also opted for an American helmer—Bob Rafelson (*Five Easy Pieces*).

Each crix group comprised 22 members. While only four scribes belonged to both (Pauline Kael of *The New Yorker*, Andrew Sarris of *The Village Voice*, Richard Schickel of *Life* and Hollis Alpert of *Saturday Review*), the orgs chose the same top thesps—and the same ones, curiously, who'd been cited by the National Board of Review. The year's consensus Best Actor was George C. Scott, who *Variety* said was "outstanding" as the bullheaded, sissy-slapping general in *Patton*. Best Actress was Glenda Jackson, who gave "a vital performance with punch and intelligence" as the sexually emancipated sculptress in *Women in Love*, said *Variety*. Throughout the voting period, Jackson was helped by having a high profile on TV as she reaped critics' huzzahs for her gutsy portrayal of England's Virgin Queen in the PBS miniseries *Elizabeth R.*

Both groups also chose the same Best Supporting Actor, Chief Dan George, who *Variety* said was "outstanding as an Indian chief who provides periodic inputs of philosophy" in the dramatization of Custer's last stand in *Little Big Man.* The orgs chose different supporting actresses from the same pic, *Five Easy Pieces*: the Gotham crix sided with the National Board of Review by embracing Karen Black as Nicholson's dumb, sex-crazed girlfriend; the national society opted for Lois Smith as his eccentric sister.

After sweeping up all the early kudos, George C. Scott seemed destined for the Golden Globe and Oscar next. But media pundits wondered: would he accept them? Back in 1961, he had denounced the Academy Awards derby as "a weird beauty or personality contest" when he refused his nomination for *The Hustler.* It didn't matter—he lost. This year, however, he looked invincible.

The first act in the drama was played out at the New York Film Critics Awards when Scott's wife, Colleen Dewhurst, showed up at the reception to accept his Best Actor plaque.

The media were stunned, but Dewhurst explained, "George thinks this is the only film award worth having." She apologized for his absence but said that he was in Spain filming *The Last Run.*

Also present at Sardi's restaurant was Glenda Jackson, who flew in from London for the awards reception. As she accepted her Best Actress honor from past champ Bette Davis, Jackson told the crowd, "Miss Davis should have this award in perpetuity."

Best Supporting Actor Chief Dan George "marched right into Sardi's in his celebration robes and had a ball," observed the *L.A. Times.*

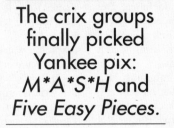

The crix groups finally picked Yankee pix: *M*A*S*H* and *Five Easy Pieces.*

The next day Scott barked at a Reuters reporter, "I will have nothing to do with the academy!" He was far more polite in a telegram he sent to the org, saying, "I simply do not want to get involved. Peculiar as it may seem, I mean no offense to the academy." He informed its leaders that he would not be present at the Oscar gala "nor will any legitimate representative of mine attend." The academy countered by informing the media, "There is no way the academy can strike Scott's nomination for Best Actor."

Scott was silent on the subject of the Golden Globes. When the nominations were released, he did not formally reject his bid for Best Drama Actor, nor did he announce that he'd accept the prize if he won it. The suspense lingered till Globes night.

In order to accommodate a larger crowd, this year's gala was moved to the Beverly Hilton Hotel from its former locale at the Cocoanut Grove. Jack Nicholson shocked the black-tie crowd by wearing patched blue jeans and sneakers. As the room filled up, *L.A. Herald Examiner* columnist James Bacon noticed the arrival of one of the recipients of the honorary award for World Film Favorite: "Barbra Streisand made her entrance through the rear door with her entourage and took the center table just like a superstar should." He also noticed a missing honoree: "Too bad Frank Sinatra didn't show up to receive his Cecil B. DeMille Award. It was Frank's kind of party. Every table had bottles on it and, by midnight, there were hundreds of empties."

Leading in total noms—seven—was *Love Story,* which starred Ryan O'Neal and Ali MacGraw as doomed Ivy League lovers in what would become 1971's top-grossing hit. Lots of critics lambasted the tearjerker—*New York Magazine* and *Today* show critic Judith Crist said it made her "reach for the barf bag instead of the Kleenex"—but *Variety* called it "an excellent film that's generally successful on all artistic levels."

O'Neal was nommed in the race for Best Drama Actor against George C. Scott. When Scott was declared the winner, the Hilton crowd was stunned to see Jane Wyman head to the podium to accept it. "I can't wait to hear his reaction," she said, smiling as she waved the statuette in the air. Later, she told the press that she was not acting officially on Scott's behalf.

DAILY *Variety* DAILY

Vol. 150   No. 44   Hollywood, California - 90028, Monday, February 8, 1971   15 Cents

'LOVE' GLOWS IN GOLDEN GLOBES

The Golden Globes turned into a lovefest for *Love Story*, which reaped a record-tying five awards: best drama pic, director, actress, script and music.

O'Neal's costar Ali MacGraw beat Glenda Jackson for the trophy for Best Drama Actress, which was accepted by Streisand. In the end, the Globes gala turned out to be a true lovefest for *Love Story*: The pic swept up five trophies, including Best Drama Picture, Best Director (Arthur Hiller), Best Screenplay (Erich Segal) and Best Musical Scoring (Francis Lai) in addition to the laurel for MacGraw.

A Copley newspaper columnist was among those who thought that *Love Story*'s John Marley was in a tight race with Chief Dan George to win Best Supporting Actor, but both contenders were upset by John Mills, who portrayed the misshapen mute in *Ryan's Daughter*. The scion of the noted British thesp family wasn't present, but the prize was accepted by his daughter Juliet.

Another daughter stood in for her famous father when it came time to bestow the Cecil B. DeMille Award. As Tina Sinatra accepted the statuette from Joan Crawford, "some hecklers started acting up," Bacon reported. "Joan told them off." What Crawford told them was so off-color that no newspaper could print it. Fortunately for the FCC-troubled Globes, the ceremony wasn't telecast again this year.

After *Love Story*, the only film to win more than one award was *Diary of a Mad Housewife,* which reaped Best Comedy/Musical Actress and Most Promising New Female Star for Carrie Snodgress, who was one of the year's breakout stars for her portrayal of a spiritually tortured suburban spouse. The Most Promising New Male Star was James Earl Jones, who'd lost his bout

for Best Drama Actor to Scott, but won plaudits for his portrayal of black heavyweight boxing champ Jack Johnson. "Jones' re-creation of his stage role in an eye-riveting experience," *Variety* cheered in its review of *The Great White Hope*.

M*A*S*H was named Best Comedy or Musical Picture, and there was an unprecedented tie in the match-up for Best Supporting Actress: Karen Black claimed her third kudos for *Five Easy Pieces*, while Maureen Stapleton was cited as the tearful wife of a beserk bomber in *Airport*.

M*A*S*H also proved to be a winner at the writers' guild awards when Ring Lardner, Jr., beat Mel Brooks (*The Twelve Chairs*), Renée Taylor, Joseph Bologna and David Zelad Goodman (*Lovers and Other Strangers*) and Buck Henry (*The Owl and the Pussycat*). Francis Ford Coppola and Edmund H. North took the drama category easily with *Patton*, but the two collaborators still had not met each other (North was hired to doctor Coppola's script after he wrote it). On awards night, Coppola was in New York working on *The Godfather*. He would miss his partner again at the upcoming Academy Awards.

Robert Anderson faced tough competish in the race for best adapted drama, but prevailed for *I Never Sang for My Father*.

Neil Simon had lost two previous guild bids (*Barefoot in the Park, The Odd Couple*), but now finally claimed his first kudos for *The Out-of-Towners*, which the playwright penned directly for the screen. Impressively, he beat such veteran scribes as the writing team of Billy Wilder and I. A. L. Diamond.

Variety reported "SRO 950–1,000 attending" the affair at the Beverly Hilton

Hotel. "Show was toplined by Allan Sherman, Jack Carter and Don Rickles with actor-writers also participating." The special Laurel Award honoring career achievement was presented to James Poe, author of *Around the World in 80 Days, Lilies of the Field* and *They Shoot Horses, Don't They?*

While Oscar's acting races appeared to be decided early this year, there was no front-runner for Best Picture prior to the directors' guild kudos, which usually forecasts the top Academy Award. Of the five directors nommed for the guild prize, only Arthur Hiller was written off, since *Love Story* had been blasted by most crix as lightweight. The other four rivals had viable chances: Robert Altman (*M*A*S*H*), David Lean (*Ryan's Daughter*), Bob Rafelson (*Five Easy Pieces*) and Franklin Schaffner (*Patton*).

When Schaffner won, *Variety* trumpeted the news under a page-one banner headline and its reporter reminded readers, "Schaffner's winning film was his second big artistic and commercial success in a limited 10-year screen career; he directed *Planet of the Apes,* a 1968 20th smash.

Patton's Franklin Schaffner topped veterans Altman and Lean at the DGA kudos.

"The awards and show portion of the dinner (at the Beverly Hilton Hotel) ran 65 minutes during which DGA prez Delbert Mann and m.c. Hal Kanter (latter consistently the best in these chores) joked nervously about the Hollywood depression but sounded an optimistic note for the future. Kanter saluted the feature and TV nominees for 'their unique ability—to find work.' "

When the Oscar nominations were announced, there were three surprises in the directors' lineup. Two DGA contenders were snubbed—Bob Rafelson (*Five Easy Pieces*) and David Lean (*Ryan's Daughter*)—and so was the man who helmed the movie that tied *Patton* for the most Oscar noms (10). *Airport's* George Seaton told *Variety* columnist Army Archerd that he wasn't upset. "It happened before with *Miracle on 34th Street*," he said, noting that

both of his pix had nonetheless received bids as Best Picture—plus nominations for his screenplays. Seaton won Best Adapted Screenplay in 1947. This year he had a hefty consolation prize ahead if he lost the scribe's prize and Best Picture bid. Archerd noted: "Seaton has a piece of the profits of *Airport*," which had already earned the Universal studio more than $40 million.

On Oscar day, *Variety* reported "slightly overcast skies," but there were greater storm clouds looming. George C. Scott was no longer being polite about what he thought of the Academy Awards, saying, "The ceremonies are a two-hour meat parade, a public display with contrived suspense for economic reasons." He dismissed the contest as "offensive, barbarous and innately corrupt."

Scott was just one of many no-shows. Best Actress contender Carrie Snodgress explained why she wouldn't attend: "I love my work, but I don't want to be 'a star' or 'best actress.' " When asked why she attended the recent Golden Globes, she said, "I went there because I thought I had to."

Ingmar Bergman, busy writing a script, sent his lover and lead star Liv Ullmann to accept his Irving Thalberg Award. A special prize was planned for Orson Welles, but he said couldn't accept it in person because he'd be in Brazil filming *The Other Side of the Wind*, a pic he'd never complete. He taped his acceptance speech for a segment to be shown during the Oscarcast, but he could've delivered the same words in person. He was actually in Hollywood when the presentation occurred, but he chose to snub the academy just as he had in 1941 when *Citizen Kane* was up for multiple awards. He wasn't alone in finding the current tribute odd. *The New York Times* called it a "contradiction," noting, "Welles has been virtually blackballed by the industry for years and finds it almost impossible to raise money to finance his pictures."

Best Actress front-runner Glenda Jackson wasn't at the Oscars because she said she couldn't afford the trip from London and she complained publicly that her studio, United Artists, didn't offer to pick up the tab. Some gossip columnists noted that she'd had enough money to attend the New York Film Critics Awards a few months earlier.

Soon after her Oscar victory, Jackson held a press conference and said, "I was amazed at how pleased I was" to win.

Also missing on Oscar night was the winner of Best Supporting Actress, who pulled off one of the year's two biggest upsets. Karen Black (*Five Easy Pieces*) and Sally Kellerman ("Hot Lips" in *M*A*S*H*) were thought to be the front-trunners, but a previous Best Actress champ came back to win another Oscar 39 years after her first. Helen Hayes was honored for portraying a spunky stowaway in *Airport*, but she wasn't on hand to accept it because she didn't think she'd win. The thesp widely known as "the First Lady of the American Stage" was on stage performing *Long Day's Journey into Night* at Catholic University in Washington, D.C. Army Archerd reached her by phone after her legit perf and Oscar victory and reported, "Miss Hayes was being partied in a dorm by the students serenading—and toasting—her."

Variety noted later: "Miss Hayes broke the jinx that two nominees in the same category from one film cancel each other out: Maureen Stapleton also was up for *Airport*."

The other big upset occurred in the race for Best Supporting Actor, which was expected to go to Chief Dan George, winner of two crix awards, but he turned out to be one of the night's "several front-runners who failed to last the course," *Variety* noted. "Instead, Metro's *Ryan's Daughter* was a surprise winner."

In his acceptance speech, previous Golden Globes champ John Mills referred to the emerald island where *Ryan's Daughter* was filmed: "I was speechless in Ireland and I'm speechless now." He was accompanied back to the press rooms by his daughter Juliet, who "was so happy when her father won, she cried," noted *Variety*.

Ring Lardner, Jr., gave one of the night's

Neil Simon finally won his first writers' guild prize (*The Out-of-Towners*), beating Billy Wilder and I.A.L. Diamond.

sassiest acceptance speeches when *M*A*S*H* won Best Adapted Screenplay. He referred to his previous Oscar win for *Woman of the Year* in 1942, saying, "At long last, a pattern has been established in my life. At the end of every 28 years I win one of these. So I will see you all again in 1999."

When *Patton* won Best Original Screenplay, Edmund H. North accepted the kudos solo. *Patton* also scored tech victories for editing, sound and art direction early in the evening, bringing its tally to four wins.

It picked up a fifth trophy when Franklin Schaffner prevailed, as expected, for Best Director. Archerd noted that the absent champ was in S'Agaro, Spain, "where he's winding down *Nicholas & Alexandra*. He was, needless to say, pleased with the news."

The audience at the Dorothy Chandler Pavilion buzzed with excitement as last year's winner of Best Supporting Actress, Goldie Hawn, approached the podium to bestow the prize for Best Actor. She giggled and said, "I can't wait!"—then ripped open the envelope and shrieked, "Oh, my God! The winner is George C. Scott!"

The audience gasped and an awkward moment followed as observers wondered if anyone would appear at the podium to claim the statuette.

Finally, *Patton*'s producer, Frank McCarthy, climbed the stage, took the trophy and thanked the academy audience.

Later on, when McCarthy climbed the stairs once more to claim the prize for Best Picture, the drama surrounding the biggest victory of all seemed almost anticlimactic.

The next day it was *Patton*'s win for Best Actor that had the media buzzing. Reporters tracked down Scott at Metropolitan Hospital in New York City, where he was filming *The Hospital*, and asked him if he'd seen the Oscarcast.

"No," he replied. He'd watched a hockey game on TV and gone to bed.

▪ 1970 ▪

NEW YORK FILM CRITICS

Winners were announced on December 28, 1970. Awards were presented on January 18, 1971, at Sardi's restaurant in New York.

BEST PICTURE
▪ *Five Easy Pieces*

BEST DIRECTOR
▪ Bob Rafelson, *Five Easy Pieces*

BEST ACTOR
▪ George C. Scott, *Patton*

BEST ACTRESS
▪ Glenda Jackson, *Women in Love*

BEST SUPPORTING ACTOR
▪ Chief Dan George, *Little Big Man*

BEST SUPPORTING ACTRESS
▪ Karen Black, *Five Easy Pieces*

BEST SCREENPLAY
▪ Eric Rohmer, *My Night at Maud's*

NATIONAL BOARD OF REVIEW

Winners were announced on January 3, 1971.

BEST PICTURE
▪ *Patton*
Kes
Women in Love
Five Easy Pieces
Ryan's Daughter

I Never Sang for My Father
Diary of a Mad Housewife
Love Story
The Virgin and the Gypsy
Tora! Tora! Tora!

BEST DIRECTOR
▪ François Truffaut, *The Wild Child*

BEST ACTOR
▪ George C. Scott, *Patton*

BEST ACTRESS
▪ Glenda Jackson, *Women in Love*

BEST SUPPORTING ACTOR
▪ Frank Langella, *Diary of a Mad Housewife*

BEST SUPPORTING ACTRESS
▪ Karen Black, *Five Easy Pieces*

BEST FOREIGN FILM
▪ *The Wild Child* (France)
My Night at Maud's (France)
The Passion of Anna (Sweden)
The Confession (France/Italy)
This Man Must Die (France/Italy)

NATIONAL SOCIETY OF FILM CRITICS

Winners were announced on January 10, 1971, at the Algonquin Hotel in New York.

BEST PICTURE
▪ *M*A*S*H*

BEST DIRECTOR
- Ingmar Bergman, *The Passion of Anna*

BEST ACTOR
- George C. Scott, *Patton*

BEST ACTRESS
- Glenda Jackson, *Women in Love*

BEST SUPPORTING ACTOR
- Chief Dan George, *Little Big Man*

BEST SUPPORTING ACTRESS
- Lois Smith, *Five Easy Pieces*

BEST SCREENPLAY
- Eric Rohmer, *My Night at Maud's*

BEST CINEMATOGRAPHY
- Nestor Almendros, *The Wild Child, My Night at Maud's*

SPECIAL AWARDS
- Donald Richie, MOMA's film department for Japanese retrospective
- Donald Talbot, New Yorker Theater

GOLDEN GLOBES

Nominations were announced on January 12, 1971. Awards were presented on February 5 at the Beverly Hilton Hotel in Los Angeles.

BEST DRAMA PICTURE
- *Love Story*
Airport
Five Easy Pieces
I Never Sang for My Father
Patton

BEST COMEDY OR MUSICAL PICTURE
- *M*A*S*H*
Darling Lili
Diary of a Mad Housewife
Lovers and Other Strangers
Scrooge

BEST DIRECTOR
- Arthur Hiller, *Love Story*
Robert Altman, *M*A*S*H*
Bob Rafelson, *Five Easy Pieces*

Ken Russell, *Women in Love*
Franklin Schaffner, *Patton*

BEST ACTOR, DRAMA
- George C. Scott, *Patton*
Melvyn Douglas, *I Never Sang for My Father*
James Earl Jones, *The Great White Hope*
Jack Nicholson, *Five Easy Pieces*
Ryan O'Neal, *Love Story*

BEST ACTRESS, DRAMA
- Ali MacGraw, *Love Story*
Faye Dunaway, *Puzzle of a Downfall Child*
Glenda Jackson, *Women in Love*
Melina Mercouri, *Promise at Dawn*
Sarah Miles, *Ryan's Daughter*

BEST ACTOR, COMEDY OR MUSICAL
- Albert Finney, *Scrooge*
Richard Benjamin, *Diary of a Mad Housewife*
Elliott Gould, *M*A*S*H*
Jack Lemmon, *The Out-of-Towners*
Donald Sutherland, *M*A*S*H*

BEST ACTRESS, COMEDY OR MUSICAL
- Carrie Snodgress, *Diary of a Mad Housewife*
Julie Andrews, *Darling Lili*
Sandy Dennis, *The Out-of-Towners*
Angela Lansbury, *Something for Everyone*
Barbra Streisand, *The Owl and the Pussycat*

BEST SUPPORTING ACTOR
- John Mills, *Ryan's Daughter*
Chief Dan George, *Little Big Man*
Trevor Howard, *Ryan's Daughter*
George Kennedy, *Airport*
John Marley, *Love Story*

BEST SUPPORTING ACTRESS (TIE)
- Karen Black, *Five Easy Pieces*
- Maureen Stapleton, *Airport*
Tina Chin, *The Hawaiians*
Lee Grant, *The Landlord*
Sally Kellerman, *M*A*S*H*

MOST PROMISING NEWCOMER—MALE
- James Earl Jones, *The Great White Hope*
Assaf Dayan, *Promise at Dawn*

Frank Langella, *Diary of a Mad Housewife*
Joe Namath, *Norwood*
Kenneth Nelson, *The Boys in the Band*

MOST PROMISING NEWCOMER—FEMALE
- Carrie Snodgress, *Diary of a Mad Housewife*

Jane Alexander, *The Great White Hope*
Lola Falana, *Liberation of L. B. Jones*
Anna Calder Marshall, *Pussycat, Pussycat, I Love You*
Marlo Thomas, *Jenny*
Angel Tompkins, *I Love My Wife*

BEST SCREENPLAY
- Erich Segal, *Love Story*

Leslie Bricusse, *Scrooge*
John Cassavetes, *Husbands*
Adrien Joyce, *Five Easy Pieces*
Ring Lardner, Jr., *M*A*S*H*

BEST SONG
- "Whistling Away the Dark," *Darling Lili*

"Ballad of Little Fauss and Big Halsey," *Little Fauss and Big Halsey*
"Pieces of Dreams," *Pieces of Dreams*
"Thank You Very Much," *Scrooge*
"Till Love Touches Your Life," *Madron*

BEST FOREIGN-LANGUAGE FOREIGN FILM
- *Rider in the Rain* (France)

Borsalino (Italy)
The Confession (France/Italy)
Investigation of a Citizen above Suspicion
The Traveller

BEST ENGLISH-LANGUAGE FOREIGN FILM
- *Women in Love*

Act of the Heart
Bloomfield
The Virgin and the Gypsy
The Walking Major

Winners

BEST ORIGINAL SCORE
- Francis Lai, *Love Story*

WORLD FILM FAVORITES
- Clint Eastwood
- Barbra Streisand

CECIL B. DEMILLE AWARD
- Frank Sinatra

DIRECTORS GUILD OF AMERICA

The award for Best Director was presented on March 12, 1971, at the Beverly Hilton Hotel in Los Angeles and the Waldorf-Astoria Hotel in New York.

BEST DIRECTOR
- Franklin Schaffner, *Patton*

Robert Altman, *M*A*S*H*
Arthur Hiller, *Love Story*
David Lean, *Ryan's Daughter*
Bob Rafelson, *Five Easy Pieces*

WRITERS GUILD OF AMERICA

Awards were presented on March 18, 1971, at the Beverly Hilton Hotel in Los Angeles.

BEST DRAMA WRITTEN DIRECTLY FOR THE SCREEN
- *Patton,* Francis Ford Coppola, Edmund H. North

Five Easy Pieces, Adrien Joyce, Bob Rafelson
Love Story, Erich Segal

BEST DRAMA ADAPTED FROM ANOTHER MEDIUM
- *I Never Sang for My Father,* Robert Anderson, based on his play

Airport, George Seaton, based on the novel by Arthur Hailey
Catch-22, Buck Henry, based on the novel by Joseph Heller
The Great White Hope, Howard Sackler, based on his play
Little Big Man, Calder Willingham, based on the novel by Thomas Berger

BEST COMEDY WRITTEN DIRECTLY FOR THE SCREEN
- *The Out-of-Towners,* Neil Simon

The Cheyenne Social Club, James Lee Barrett
The Private Life of Sherlock Holmes, Billy Wilder, I. A. L. Diamond, based on the novels by Sir Arthur Conan Doyle

Quackser Fortune, Gabriel Walsh
Start the Revolution without Me, Fred
    Freeman, Lawrence J. Cohen

BEST COMEDY ADAPTED FROM ANOTHER MEDIUM

- *M*A*S*H,* Ring Lardner, Jr., based on the novel by Richard Hooker
Lovers and Other Strangers, Renee Taylor, Joseph Bologna, David Zelad Goodman
The Owl and the Pussycat, Buck Henry, based on the play by Bill Manhoff
The Twelve Chairs, Mel Brooks, based on the novel by Ilya Ilf and Yevgeni Petrov
Where's Poppa? Robert Klane, based on his novel

LAUREL AWARD

- James Poe

VALENTINE DAVIES AWARD

- Daniel Taradash

MORGAN COX AWARD

- Leonard Spigelgass

FOUNDERS AWARD

- Lamar Trotti (posthumous)

ACADEMY AWARDS

Nominations were announced on February 22, 1971. Awards were presented on April 15 at the Dorothy Chandler Pavilion in Los Angeles. The ceremony was telecast by NBC.

BEST PICTURE

- *Patton*
Airport
Five Easy Pieces
Love Story
*M*A*S*H*

BEST DIRECTOR

- Franklin Schaffner, *Patton*
Robert Altman, *M*A*S*H*
Federico Fellini, *Fellini Satyricon*
Arthur Hiller, *Love Story*
Ken Russell, *Women in Love*

BEST ACTOR

- George C. Scott, *Patton*
Melvyn Douglas, *I Never Sang for My Father*
James Earl Jones, *The Great White Hope*
Jack Nicholson, *Five Easy Pieces*
Ryan O'Neal, *Love Story*

BEST ACTRESS

- Glenda Jackson, *Women in Love*
Jane Alexander, *The Great White Hope*
Ali MacGraw, *Love Story*
Sarah Miles, *Ryan's Daughter*
Carrie Snodgress, *Diary of a Mad Housewife*

BEST SUPPORTING ACTOR

- John Mills, *Ryan's Daughter*
Richard Castellano, *Lovers and Other Strangers*
Chief Dan George, *Little Big Man*
Gene Hackman, *I Never Sang for My Father*
John Marley, *Love Story*

BEST SUPPORTING ACTRESS

- Helen Hayes, *Airport*
Karen Black, *Five Easy Pieces*
Lee Grant, *The Landlord*
Sally Kellerman, *M*A*S*H*
Maureen Stapleton, *Airport*

BEST ADAPTED SCREENPLAY

- Ring Lardner, Jr., *M*A*S*H*
Robert Anderson, *I Never Sang for My Father*
Joseph Bologna, David Zelag Goodman, Renee Taylor, *Lovers and Other Strangers*
Larry Kramer, *Women in Love*
George Seaton, *Airport*

BEST ORIGINAL SCREENPLAY

- Francis Ford Coppola, Edmund H. North, *Patton*
Adrien Joyce [pseudonym of Carole Eastman], Bob Rafelson, *Five Easy Pieces*
Eric Rohmer, *My Night at Maud's*
Eric Segal, *Love Story*
Norman Wexler, *Joe*

BEST SONG

- "For All We Know," *Lovers and Other Strangers*, James Griffin, Fred Karlin, Robb Royer
- "Pieces of Dreams," *Pieces of Dreams,* Alan Bergman, Marilyn Bergman, Michel Legrand
- "Thank You Very Much," *Scrooge,* Leslie Bricusse
- "Till Love Touches Your Life," *Madron,* Arthur Hamilton, Riz Ortolani
- "Whistling Away the Dark," *Darling Lili,* Henry Mancini, Johnny Mercer

BEST FOREIGN-LANGUAGE FILM

- *Investigation of a Citizen above Suspicion* (Italy)

First Love (Switzerland)
Hoa-Binh (France)
Paix sur les Champs (Belgium)
Tristana (Spain)

Winners

BEST ART DIRECTION/SET DECORATION

- Urie McCleary, Gil Parrondo, Antonio Mateos, Pierre-Louis Thevenet, *Patton*

BEST CINEMATOGRAPHY

- Freddie Young, *Ryan's Daughter*

BEST COSTUME DESIGN

- Nino Novarese, *Cromwell*

BEST DOCUMENTARY

(FEATURE)
- Bob Maurice, *Woodstock*

(SHORT SUBJECT)
- Joseph Strick, *Interviews with My Lai Veterans*

BEST FILM EDITING

- Hugh S. Fowler, *Patton*

BEST MUSIC

(ORIGINAL SCORE)
- Francis Lai, *Love Story*

(ORIGINAL SONG SCORE)
- Beatles, *Let It Be*

SCIENTIFIC OR TECHNICAL AWARDS

Class II (Plaque)
- Edward H. Reichard, Leonard Sokolow, Consolidated Film Industries

Class III (Certificate)
- Eastman Kodak, Photo Electronics Corp.; Electro Sound Inc.; B. J. Losmandy; Sylvania Electric Products

BEST SHORT SUBJECT

(CARTON)
- *Is It Always Right to Be Right?*

(LIVE ACTION)
- *The Resurrection of Broncho Billy*

BEST SOUND

- Don Bassman, Douglas Williams, *Patton*

BEST SPECIAL VISUAL EFFECTS

- L. B. Abbott, A. D. Flowers, *Tora! Tora! Tora!*

IRVING G. THALBERG MEMORIAL AWARD

- Ingmar Bergman

JEAN HERSHOLT HUMANITARIAN AWARD

- Frank Sinatra

HONORARY AWARDS

- Lillian Gish
- Orson Welles

SCREEN ACTORS GUILD

LIFETIME ACHIEVEMENT AWARD

- Gregory Peck

▪ 1971 ▪

Late Connection *Stops* Clockwork

"It was largely a contest between *The Last Picture Show* and *A Clockwork Orange,*" reported *The New York Times* about the first bout of the year for Best Picture.

The showdown at the New York Film Critics pitted a quiet depiction of a dying Texas town against a shocking, X-rated vision of a future world besieged by rape and murder.

The Last Picture Show received high praise from *Variety,* which particularly liked the performance of "Ben Johnson, that old John Ford regular, as Sam the Lion, the owner of the picture show and pool room where the town boys hang out." Johnson received the crix's kudos as Best Supporting Actor. The supporting actress laurel went to costar Ellen Burstyn as "a tough, Dorothy Malone type of middle-aged beauty," said the *Times.*

Variety reserved greater praise for *A Clockwork Orange,* calling it "a brilliant nightmare," and the crix agreed with the higher assessment, endorsing it as Best Picture by a vote of 31 to 24 over *Picture Show.* Its helmer, Stanley Kubrick, was named Best Director—seven years after winning the same award for *Dr. Strangelove.*

The crix embraced another past champ when naming Best Actress—Jane Fonda, who was still infuriating America's conservatives with her anti–Vietnam war views while impressing movie critics with her blossoming acting skills. *Variety* declared her a "much-matured actress" when it saw her portray a hooker stalked by a killer in *Klute* and announced, "There is something great coming off the screen."

Fonda won with 38 points, followed by Gena Rowlands (*Minnie and Moskowitz,* 21 points) and Shirley MacLaine (*Desperate Characters,* 15 points).

The Best Actor race was a much closer

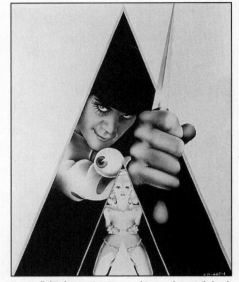

Variety called Gotham crix Best Picture and Director champ *A Clockwork Orange* "a brilliant nightmare."

match-up, with Gene Hackman (*The French Connection*) winning with 31 points over Peter Finch (*Sunday, Bloody Sunday,* 25 points) and Malcolm McDowell (*A Clockwork Orange,* 16 points). Steve McQueen and Jackie Gleason had both turned down the lead role in *Connection,* but Hackman, a noted character actor, saw the part as a chance for him to show off his full thesp chops while portraying the many facets of a tough New York narcotics cop hunting down heroin smugglers. He even did much of the stunt driving for the pic's climactic scene that had theater audiences gasping and roaring—"a great elevated train–automobile chase sequence that becomes almost too tense to be enjoyable," said *Variety.*

Hackman seemed laid back and grateful when he met the crix at their awards ceremony at Sardi's. "Hackman said it was the first time he had ever been to one of these events that he could get a seat," Rex Reed wrote in the *Daily News*. The Best Actor also seemed to be badly in need of a good script, fumbling as he spoke: "I'd like to say something special about William Friedkin, the director of *French Connection*—if I could think of something special to say about William Friedkin." Reed reported the crowd's response: "Nervous laughter."

Real wordsmiths—that is, crix—turned out to be the big winners at the crix gala. It was as if the pundit industry had decided to heed the recent advice of Jack Valenti, prexy of the Motion Picture Association of America. "The film industry spokesman described critics as physicians who should heal themselves—by making movies—if they wanted to be taken seriously as critics," reported the *Times*.

"For the first time in its history, the critics found themselves in the embarrassing position of giving a prize to a member of their own group—to Penelope Gilliatt of *The New Yorker*—for *Sunday, Bloody Sunday*," reported Reed on one of the recipients of the screenwriter's prize. Even more embarrassing was the choice of who would present the award to Gilliatt: screen scribe Eleanor Perry. "Penelope Gilliatt continually slaughters Mrs. Perry's writing talents in her reviews," Reed explained, observing that "a hush spread over the room" as Perry prepared to speak. She proved to be cordial and humorous, however, and "everyone breathed a sigh of relief, including Miss Gilliatt."

Gilliatt shared the prize with a former film critic as a result of *Sunday, Bloody Sunday* tying *The Last Picture Show* in the screenplay category. *Last Picture*'s co-writer and helmer Peter Bogdanovich informed the crowd that he used to be a critic, too, adding, "It's a particular honor to be honored by people who used to be one's peers."

The author of *A Clockwork Orange*, Anthony Burgess, who used to be a critic

> The N.Y. crix gave *New Yorker* critic Gilliatt their screenplay award.

for an English publication, *The Listener*, ended up "walking away with the affair," said *Variety*, when his "lightly irreverent but hilarious remarks put the shiv to films, film criticism, directors (no friend to Ken Russell) and kindred subjects." He accepted the award for his film's absent Best Director. Burgess explained: "He, God—I mean, Kubrick—doesn't fly."

Crix continued their kudos reign when awards were bestowed by the National Society of Film Critics at New York's Algonquin Hotel and Gilliatt won again—solo this time. She was one of five crix who belonged to both pundit groups, but she declined to participate at the voting conclave of either this year. The pollings were held just one day apart (compared to 10 days last year) while the national society aimed to jump ahead of the National Board of Review and steal some of its early thunder.

After choosing a U.S. film as Best Picture for the first time ever last year, the society now reverted to form and again embraced a foreign pic. Its choice was controversial: *Claire's Knee*, French filmmaker Eric Rohmer's exploration of a man's fetish for the leg of a teen girl he meets while vacationing at an Alpine lake. After viewing the movie, national society member Hollis Alpert warned in *Saturday Review*, "I'm going to have to toss that word 'masterpiece' around again!" But John Simon of *The New Leader* dismissed it as "a flimsy, dullish, trivial film enjoying an improbable popularity." For the Best Picture prize, *Claire's Knee* topped *The Conformist* and *A Clockwork Orange. The Conformist*, however, earned a consolation prize as Best Director for Bernardo Bertolucci.

Best Actor was Peter Finch as a middle-aged homosexual doctor in love with a young sculptor in *Sunday, Bloody Sunday*, beating Malcolm McDowell by almost twice as many points (33 to 17). Jane Fonda (*Klute*) took Best Actress by a wide margin, too, prevailing by a score of 27 to 15 over Bibi Andersson (*The Touch*).

The only Best Actress prize that Jane Fonda failed to win this year was from the National Board of Review, which bestowed its laurels on Irene Papas as Helen of Troy in an all-star, U.S.-Greece co-production of *The Trojan Women*. Gene Hackman was proclaimed Best Actor. An upset occurred in the Best Picture category when the board's prize went to *Macbeth*, Roman Polanski's rendition of the Shakespearean classic produced by Playboy Enterprises as its first feature film.

Macbeth wasn't among the Golden Globe nominations announced a few weeks later. That race was dominated by *The Last Picture Show,* which led with the most noms, followed by *The French Connection* and *Fiddler on the Roof* in second place.

But it was *Klute*'s solitary acting nom that proved to be the night's most dramatic category.

Variety columnist Army Archerd reported: "Jane Fonda stole the spotlight, although in absentia, at the Golden Globes, when Vietvet First Lt. Barry Romo accepted her Best Drama Actress Award 'on behalf of those of us who served in Vietnam.'" Fonda was in France filming *Tout Va Bien. Herald Examiner* columnist James Bacon observed that her stand-in was dressed oddly for a black-tie gala, wearing "an oversized Army tunic bedecked with medals" and scruffy, non-military blue jeans. "His acceptance speech, obviously inspired or approved by Miss Fonda, cast a tasteless political pall over an otherwise fun evening" and drew many boos, Bacon added.

Gene Hackman took the prize for Best Actor when *The French Connection* swept the top drama categories, including Best Picture and Director.

The new $9 million screen version of Broadway's longest-running hit, *Fiddler on the Roof,* won the comedy/musical awards for Best Picture, plus Best Actor for its star, Topol. The latter prize was a vindication for producer/director Norman Jewison, who had been criticized for passing over Broadway's Zero Mostel in favor of the little-

Jane Fonda earned most of the year's Best Actress trophies for portraying a stalked hooker in *Klute.* The only snub: National Board of Review. Her "tasteless" stand-in was booed at the Globes.

known Israeli who'd performed the role for a year on the London stage. The victory was also a salute to the judgment of Globe voters, who had hailed Topol seven years earlier as one of the foreign press's Most Promising New Male Stars. Topol mentioned his earlier Globe honor during his acceptance speech for his latest one, thanked the scribes for both and then, like his character Tevye in *Fiddler*, raised his eyes to heaven and said, "Thank you, God!" When Jewison accepted the prize for Best Picture, he thanked the movie's cast and crew, "who gave up two and a half years of their lives."

Another past recipient of a Globe for Most Promising Newcomer returned for a new honor, too—Ann-Margret. She was now hailed as Best Supporting Actress for her role in *Carnal Knowledge* as "a sexpot who really would like to get married and have kids," said *Variety*. The star got "very emotional" in her acceptance speech, the tradepaper added, as she insisted that the prize now established her as a serious actress, but the audience seemed to have trouble forgetting her erotic profile. She wore "a see-thru net floor-length cape over black tights clearly visible as she was spotlighted," Archerd observed.

This year's Most Promising New Stars included 18-year-old Desi Arnaz, Jr., who said in his acceptance speech, "I've lived here all my life—and I've been so close yet so far." Twiggy reaped a newcomer's prize, too, in addition to the accolade as Best Actress in a Comedy or Musical for her role as an ingenue in *The Boy Friend*. *Variety* had been dazzled by her in its review of the pic, citing her "unspoiled charm."

The Last Picture Show ended up with only one award—for Best Supporting Actor Ben Johnson, who thanked "John Ford for making it all possible." Johnson had starred in many old Ford-helmed westerns such as *Wagonmaster*. He had originally turned down the role in *The Last Picture Show*, but changed his mind when Ford intervened on behalf of director Bogdanovich and asked Johnson to take the part. Johnson's win and *The French Connection*'s triumph as Best Drama Picture were the most popular victories on Globes night, drawing hefty cheers from the crowd.

The crowd was composed of 1,000 Hollywood glitterati, who paid $50 per ticket and were entertained deftly by Steve Lawrence and Eydie Gormé. "Every star in town was there," insisted columnist Bacon. "I have always thought the Academy should hire these guys and gals from the Foreign Press to stage the Oscar show. They really get the turn-out. Too bad this show isn't on television."

As the honors approached from the Directors Guild of America, pundits seemed baffled over who the front-runner was. Friedkin had momentum following his recent Golden Globes sweep, but *The New York Times* noted that his "previous work (*The Birthday Party, The Night They Raided Minsky's*) may not have prepared anyone for the excellence of *The French Connection*." The 32-year-old unknown competed against a 32-year-old wunderkind who was being compared in the media to a young Orson Welles: Peter Bogdanovich (*The Last Picture Show*). Also in the running were John Schlesinger (*Sunday, Bloody Sunday*), who had already proved himself a champ with *Midnight Cowboy*, and Stanley Kubrick (*A Clockwork Orange*), who seemed overdue for a guild bow after previous losses for *Dr. Strangelove* and *2001: A Space Odyssey*. Missing from the competish was Norman Jewison (*Fiddler on the Roof*)—a snub that outraged many.

On awards night, when the nominees were hailed, Friedkin "ambled to the rostrum to get his finalist's plaque," *Variety* noted. Later, when his name was announced as the actual winner, he "streaked there to receive the top feature trophy."

Variety insisted that Friedkin's victory signaled the emergence of a larger industry trend, one projecting "some renaissance spirit . . .

"The tide has definitely turned back to American film forms," the tradepaper announced, and it saluted Friedkin for "explicitly making the points" in his acceptance speech.

At the kudos for the Writers Guild of America, *The French Connection* picked up a trophy as the year's Best Adapted Drama. The victory for scribe Ernest Tidyman, a former copy editor for *The New York Times*, seemed to confirm the movie's status as the

> ## Charlie Chaplin was "visibly moved" by his academy salute, said *Variety*.

1971

Oscar front-runner. When journalist Penelope Gilliatt reaped the prize as Best Original Drama, it was especially important to her since it was the first accolade she received for *Sunday, Bloody Sunday* beyond those given by her friends in the critics' groups.

The scribes' guild ceremony was dull. "Writers this year passed up its usual gridiron-type show and banquet such as they have had in the past," *Variety* noted. "Instead, awards were given at a cocktail reception at the BevHilton. About 400 turned out for the ceremony, below usual attendance."

There was nonetheless a great drama brewing around the ceremony that was related to a greater controversy beyond. Several weeks earlier, the Film Society of Lincoln Center had announced that Charlie Chaplin planned to break his 20-year, self-imposed exile from the United States and attend a special career tribute in New York. The news triggered mass excitement in showbiz circles.

But not in all political or business circles. Conservatives still refused to forgive Chaplin, now 82, for the leftist politics he embraced early in his film career and, when a proposal was made to the Hollywood Chamber of Commerce to give Chaplin a star in the Walk of Fame, its executive committee refused.

Outraged, stars such as Eddie Albert rallied to Chaplin's defense and fumed to *Variety* columnist Army Archerd, "Politics have no bearing on stars' talent!"

The Writers Guild of America agreed and announced that it was acknowledging Chaplin with an honor of its own—and one so new and special that it might never be given out again. Chaplin could not attend the ceremony to receive the new Medallion Award, but his son, actor Sidney Chaplin, appeared on his father's behalf.

The Academy Awards piped in next and decided to honor Chaplin, too. The film

The French Connection broke out of the derby pack at the Golden Globes, then sprinted to triumph at the guild kudos and Oscars.

academy had saluted him once before, at the very first Oscar ceremony in 1927–28, but it did so only to fend off outrage after academy leaders nullified his three nominations for *The Circus*. Chaplin didn't bother to show up to accept the resulting consolation prize back then, but when he was asked by the current academy leaders if he'd show up to accept a new tribute at the 1971 awards, he agreed.

The media buzzed with anticipation and delight. The Hollywood Chamber of Commerce panicked. Now that it was official that Chaplin was coming to town, the chamber didn't want to be embarrassed by its earlier decision to snub him. Its board of directors met to overrule its executive committee, and a star bearing Chaplin's name was installed promptly in the Walk of Fame.

"You think the Academy had troubles last year with George C. Scott refusing the Oscar?!" harrumphed *Herald Examiner* columnist James Bacon. This year, he warned, liberal politics promised to cause an even bigger hubbub. Not only would Chaplin be present, but Jane Fonda was certain to be nominated for *Klute*, and Vanessa Redgrave looked like a probable Best Actress rival for *Mary, Queen of Scots*. "Vanessa Redgrave is as much of a political activist for the same causes as Jane herself,"

Bacon reminded readers, citing the Black Panthers, the women's movement and anti-Vietnam war protests as the actresses' top political passions.

Previous to Oscar night, Fonda had told Bacon, "I don't care about the Oscars. I make movies to support my activist causes, not for any honors. I couldn't care less whether I win any awards or not."

But she certainly appeared eager on Oscar night as she swept down the red carpet in an informal pant suit instead of a formal dress.

Once again her father wasn't with her, which was last noticed in 1969 when she was nommed for *They Shoot Horses, Don't They?* Rumors flew about political tension between liberal Jane and conservative Henry, but some gossip wags claimed that Henry really shunned the Oscars because he was bitter that he'd never won one. Archerd noted, "He last attended an Academy Awards show 35 years ago. But he will cohost the upcoming Tony Awards."

Britain's Vanessa Redgrave was absent on Oscar night because the Nixon administration refused to give her a visa.

Variety felt another absence: "Once again George C. Scott was among the missing." Scott was nominated for *The Hospital*, although no one expected him to show up after the actor's vanishing act last year. Still, it struck some observers as curious that he didn't issue a public statement, as he had last year, refusing the nomination.

Three pix tied for the most noms (eight)—*The French Connection, The Last Picture Show* and *Fiddler on the Roof*—and Oscar watchers were pleased to note that among *Fiddler*'s bids was a Best Director mention for Jewison that made up for his DGA snub.

Half of *The Last Picture Show*'s bids were in the races for Best Supporting Actor and Actress. In the men's lineup, Ben Johnson competed against costar Jeff Bridges, the youngest member of the famed acting family and the first to score an Oscar nom. (Papa Lloyd told Archerd, "And we wanted him to be a doctor or a lawyer!") Both contenders faced *The French Connection*'s Roy Scheider, who reaped critics'

plaudits as Gene Hackman's police partner.

Following up on his previous kudos from the New York film crix, Golden Globes and National Board of Review, Johnson claimed the Oscar next. Holding the statuette in his hands at the podium, he said, emphasizing his Texas twang, "Boy, ain't that purty?!" Then he added: "What I'm about to say probably will stir up a lot of conversation all over the country. It's something I'd like to leave in everyone's mind." He grinned sheepishly and blurted out: "This couldn't have happened to a nicer fella!"

In the race for Best Supporting Actress, *The Last Picture Show*'s Ellen Burstyn seemed to be the front-runner after having won the kudos from both critics' groups, but awards prognosticators worried that she might lose votes to costar Cloris Leachman, who'd been honored by the National Board of Review for her portrayal of the adulterous wife of a football coach. Leachman benefited from being a popular sidekick character on *The Mary Tyler Moore Show*. It also seemed possible that Globe champ Ann-Margret could pull off an upset.

But an upset came from Leachman. *Variety* reported her response: "After racing to the stage breathlessly, she beamed at the audience giving her a big hand, and responded joyfully, 'I can't thank anybody. We all work together,' then proceeded to thank her piano teacher, dancing teacher, father ('he paid the bills') and her mom. Quipped Alan King after her departure, 'I had some funny jokes, but I've never been so moved by a family tree!' "

In the Best Actress race, Jane Fonda faced tough competish that included Janet Suzman, an esteemed member of Britain's National Theater, who portrayed the Russian czarina in *Nicholas and Alexandra*, and past champs Julie Christie (*McCabe & Mrs. Miller*) and Glenda Jackson (*Sunday, Bloody Sunday*). Overdue for the kudos was two-time past nominee Vanessa Redgrave, who was now cited as the title character in *Mary, Queen of Scots*.

Fonda, the only American in the lineup, prevailed. *Variety* reported that she "was glowing with happiness as she approached the stage. She received a big mitting, kept her thank you brief and remarked, 'There's a great deal to say and I'm not going to say it tonight.' "

Variety applauded her for displaying "good taste in her acceptance remarks."

Among the roles competing in the Best Actor race, *Variety* praised "Walter Matthau's terrific performance as an unwanted elderly parent who befriends a pregnant teenager" in *Kotch,* but the nominee considered himself a long shot. Columnist Army Archerd noted that Matthau was "well familiar with track odds" and calculated odds of 3–2 for both rivals Gene Hackman and Peter Finch.

"I hate to pick a winner," he told Archerd, "but, if forced to bet—Hackman."

Archerd reminded readers that Matthau proved a lousy Oscar seer in the past: "Matthau never thought he'd win for *The Fortune Cookie*." But Matthau turned out to be right this time. When Hackman won, the champ thanked "Billy Friedkin, who brought me through this one—I wanted to quit."

Friedkin and Peter Bogdanovich were the only two contenders for Best Director who'd never been nominated. Norman Jewison had been nommed for *In the Heat of the Night* and Stanley Kubrick and John Schlesinger were now both up for their third bids.

When Friedkin won, the 32-year-old became the youngest helmer ever to claim the prize. He celebrated after the Oscarcast by making good on a promise to a friend:

they headed to a sleazy strip club and drank champagne.

The French Connection also claimed the prize for Best Adapted Screenplay. In the end, it claimed five kudos—including Best Picture and the editing award, which was an acknowledgment of the pic's celebrated car-chase scene.

Oscar night's greatest triumph, though, belonged to Charlie Chaplin.

His tribute began with a short film bio, edited by Peter Bogdanovich, that showcased scenes from his classic films. Then academy president Daniel Taradash introduced him, saying, "Charlie Chaplin has made more people laugh than anyone in history." The film legend was greeted with one of the longest standing ovations in academy history.

"Visibly moved and shaking his head in near-disbelief, Chaplin composed himself sufficiently for a brief message of thanks," *Variety* reported.

"Words are so futile, so feeble," he said. "I can only say thank you for the honor of inviting me—all you wonderful, sweet people."

Jack Lemmon stepped out on stage with the Little Tramp's hat and cane. When Chaplin donned the hat, the crowd leaped to its feet again and the ceremony ended with the audience singing "Smile," a song written by Chaplin.

Variety declared, "The big winner of the key Academy Awards was the United States of America."

▪ 1971 ▪

NEW YORK FILM CRITICS

Winners were announced on December 29, 1971. Awards were presented on January 23, 1972, at Sardi's restaurant in New York.

BEST PICTURE
▪ *A Clockwork Orange*

BEST DIRECTOR
▪ Stanley Kubrick, *A Clockwork Orange*

BEST ACTOR
▪ Gene Hackman, *The French Connection*

BEST ACTRESS
▪ Jane Fonda, *Klute*

BEST SUPPORTING ACTOR
▪ Ben Johnson, *The Last Picture Show*

BEST SUPPORTING ACTRESS
▪ Ellen Burstyn, *The Last Picture Show*

BEST SCREENPLAY (TIE)
- Larry McMurtry, Peter Bogdanovich, *The Last Picture Show*
- Penelope Gilliatt, *Sunday, Bloody Sunday*

NATIONAL SOCIETY OF FILM CRITICS

Winners were announced on December 30, 1971. Awards were presented on January 30, 1972, at the Algonquin Hotel in New York.

BEST PICTURE
- *Claire's Knee*

BEST DIRECTOR
- Bernardo Bertolucci, *The Conformist*

BEST ACTOR
- Peter Finch, *Sunday, Bloody Sunday*

BEST ACTRESS
- Jane Fonda, *Klute*

BEST SUPPORTING ACTOR
- Bruce Dern, *Drive, He Said*

BEST SUPPORTING ACTRESS
- Ellen Burstyn, *The Last Picture Show*

BEST SCREENPLAY
- Penelope Gilliatt, *Sunday, Bloody Sunday*

BEST CINEMATOGRAPHY
- Vittorio Storaro, *The Conformist*

SPECIAL AWARD
- Marcel Ophuls, *The Sorrow and the Pity*

NATIONAL BOARD OF REVIEW

Winners were announced on January 6, 1972.

BEST PICTURE
- *Macbeth*
The Boy Friend
One Day in the Life of Ivan Denisovich
The French Connection
The Last Picture Show

Nicholas and Alexandra
The Go-Between
King Lear
Peter Rabbit and Tales of Beatrix Potter
Death in Venice

BEST DIRECTOR
- Ken Russell, *The Devils, The Boy Friend*

BEST ACTOR
- Gene Hackman, *The French Connection*

BEST ACTRESS
- Irene Papas, *The Trojan Women*

BEST SUPPORTING ACTOR
- Ben Johnson, *The Last Picture Show*

BEST SUPPORTING ACTRESS
- Cloris Leachman, *The Last Picture Show*

BEST FOREIGN FILM
- *Claire's Knee* (France)
Bed and Board (France/Italy)
The Clowns (Italy)
The Garden of the Finzi-Continis (Italy)
The Conformist (Italy)

GOLDEN GLOBES

Nominations were announced on January 12, 1972. Awards were presented on February 6 at the Beverly Hilton Hotel in Los Angeles.

BEST DRAMA PICTURE
- *The French Connection*
A Clockwork Orange
The Last Picture Show
Mary, Queen of Scots
Summer of '42

BEST COMEDY OR MUSICAL PICTURE
- *Fiddler on the Roof*
The Boy Friend
Kotch
A New Leaf
Plaza Suite

BEST DIRECTOR
- William Friedkin, *The French Connection*
Peter Bogdanovich, *The Last Picture Show*

Norman Jewison, *Fiddler on the Roof*
Stanley Kubrick, *A Clockwork Orange*
Robert Mulligan, *Summer of '42*

BEST ACTOR, DRAMA
■ Gene Hackman, *The French Connection*
Peter Finch, *Sunday, Bloody Sunday*
Malcolm McDowell, *A Clockwork Orange*
Jack Nicholson, *Carnal Knowledge*
George C. Scott, *The Hospital*

BEST ACTRESS, DRAMA
■ Jane Fonda, *Klute*
Dyan Cannon, *Such Good Friends*
Glenda Jackson, *Mary, Queen of Scots*
Vanessa Redgrave, *Mary, Queen of Scots*
Jessica Walter, *Play Misty for Me*

BEST ACTOR, COMEDY OR MUSICAL
■ Topol, *Fiddler on the Roof*
Bud Cort, *Harold and Maude*
Dean Jones, *Million Dollar Duck*
Walter Matthau, *Kotch*
Gene Wilder, *Willy Wonka and the Chocolate Factory*

BEST ACTRESS, COMEDY OR MUSICAL
■ Twiggy, *The Boy Friend*
Sandy Duncan, *Star-Spangled Girl*
Ruth Gordon, *Harold and Maude*
Angela Lansbury, *Bedknobs and Broomsticks*
Elaine May, *A New Leaf*

BEST SUPPORTING ACTOR
■ Ben Johnson, *The Last Picture Show*
Tom Baker, *Nicholas and Alexandra*
Arthur Garfunkel, *Carnal Knowledge*
Paul Mann, *Fiddler on the Roof*
Jan-Michael Vincent, *Going Home*

BEST SUPPORTING ACTRESS
■ Ann-Margret, *Carnal Knowledge*
Ellen Burstyn, *The Last Picture Show*
Cloris Leachman, *The Last Picture Show*
Diana Rigg, *The Hospital*
Maureen Stapleton, *Plaza Suite*

MOST PROMISING NEWCOMER—MALE
■ Desi Arnaz, Jr., *Red Sky at Morning*
Tom Baker, *Nicholas and Alexandra*
Timothy Bottoms, *Johnny Got His Gun*

Gary Grimes, *Summer of '42*
Richard Roundtree, *Shaft*
John Sarno, *Seven Minutes*

MOST PROMISING NEWCOMER—FEMALE
■ Twiggy, *The Boy Friend*
Sandy Duncan, *Million Dollar Duck*
Cybill Shepherd, *The Last Picture Show*
Janet Suzman, *Nicholas and Alexandra*
Dolores Taylor, *Billy Jack*

BEST SCREENPLAY
■ Paddy Chayefsky, *The Hospital*
John Hale, *Mary, Queen of Scots*
Andy Lewis, Dale Lewis, *Klute*
John Paxton, *Kotch*
Ernest Tidyman, *The French Connection*

BEST SONG
■ "Life Is What You Make It," *Kotch*
"Long Ago Tomorrow," *Long Ago Tomorrow*
"Rain Falls Anywhere It Wants To," *The African Elephant*
"Shaft," *Shaft*
"Something More," *Honky*

BEST FOREIGN-LANGUAGE FOREIGN FILM
■ *The Policeman* (Israel)
Claire's Knee (France)
The Conformist (Italy)
Tchaikovsky (Russia)
To Die of Love (France)

BEST ENGLISH-LANGUAGE FOREIGN FILM
■ *Sunday, Bloody Sunday*
The African Elephant
Friends
The Go-Between
Long Ago Tomorrow
The Red Tent

Winners

BEST ORIGINAL SCORE
■ Isaac Hayes, *Shaft*

WORLD FILM FAVORITES
■ Charles Bronson
■ Sean Connery
■ Ali MacGraw

CECIL B. DEMILLE AWARD
∎ Alfred Hitchcock

DIRECTORS GUILD OF AMERICA

The award for Best Director was presented on March 18, 1972, at the Beverly Hilton Hotel in Los Angeles and the Hilton Hotel in New York.

BEST DIRECTOR
∎ William Friedkin, *The French Connection*
Peter Bogdanovich, *The Last Picture Show*
Stanley Kubrick, *A Clockwork Orange*
Robert Mulligan, *Summer of '42*
John Schlesinger, *Sunday, Bloody Sunday*

WRITERS GUILD OF AMERICA

Awards were presented on March 21, 1972, at the Beverly Hilton Hotel in Los Angeles.

BEST DRAMA WRITTEN DIRECTLY FOR THE SCREEN
∎ *Sunday, Bloody Sunday,* Penelope Gilliatt
The Hellstrom Chronicle, David Seltzer
Klute, Andrew K. Lewis, David Lewis
Summer of '42, Herman Raucher

BEST DRAMA ADAPTED FROM ANOTHER MEDIUM
∎ *The French Connection,* Ernest Tidyman, based on the book by Robin Moore
A Clockwork Orange, Stanley Kubrick, based on the novel by Anthony Burgess
Johnny Got His Gun, Dalton Trumbo, based on his novel
The Last Picture Show, Larry McMurtry, Peter Bogdanovich, based on the novel by Larry McMurtry
McCabe & Mrs. Miller, Robert Altman, Brian McKay, based on the novel by Edmund Naughton

BEST COMEDY WRITTEN DIRECTLY FOR THE SCREEN
∎ *The Hospital*, Paddy Chayefsky
Bananas, Woody Allen, Mickey Rose
Carnal Knowledge, Jules Feiffer

Made for Each Other, Renée Taylor, Joseph Bologna
Taking Off, Milos Forman, Jean-Claude Carrière, John Guare, John Klein

BEST COMEDY ADAPTED FROM ANOTHER MEDIUM
∎ *Kotch,* John Paxton, based on the novel by Katharine Topkins
The Boy Friend, Ken Russell, based on the play by Sandy Wilson
Fiddler on the Roof, Joseph Stein, based on his play
Little Murders, Jules Feiffer, based on his play
A New Leaf, Elaine May, based on the short story "The Green Heart" by Jack Ritchie

LAUREL AWARD
∎ Ernest Lehman

VALENTINE DAVIES AWARD
∎ Michael Blankfort, Norman Corwin

MORGAN COX AWARD
∎ Allen Rivkin

MEDALLION AWARD
∎ Charles Chaplin

ACADEMY AWARDS

Nominations were announced on February 22, 1972. Awards were presented on April 10 at the Dorothy Chandler Pavilion in Los Angeles. The ceremony was telecast by NBC.

BEST PICTURE
∎ *The French Connection*
A Clockwork Orange
Fiddler on the Roof
The Last Picture Show
Nicholas and Alexandra

BEST DIRECTOR
∎ William Friedkin, *The French Connection*
Peter Bogdanovich, *The Last Picture Show*
Norman Jewison, *Fiddler on the Roof*
Stanley Kubrick, *A Clockwork Orange*
John Schlesinger, *Sunday, Bloody Sunday*

BEST ACTOR

- Gene Hackman, *The French Connection*

Peter Finch, *Sunday, Bloody Sunday*

Walter Matthau, *Kotch*

George C. Scott, *The Hospital*

Topol, *Fiddler on the Roof*

BEST ACTRESS

- Jane Fonda, *Klute*

Julie Christie, *McCabe & Mrs. Miller*

Glenda Jackson, *Sunday, Bloody Sunday*

Vanessa Redgrave, *Mary, Queen of Scots*

Janet Suzman, *Nicholas and Alexandra*

BEST SUPPORTING ACTOR

- Ben Johnson, *The Last Picture Show*

Jeff Bridges, *The Last Picture Show*

Leonard Frey, *Fiddler on the Roof*

Richard Jaeckel, *Sometimes a Great Notion*

Roy Scheider, *The French Connection*

BEST SUPPORTING ACTRESS

- Cloris Leachman, *The Last Picture Show*

Ann-Margret, *Carnal Knowledge*

Ellen Burstyn, *The Last Picture Show*

Barbara Harris, *Who Is Harry Kellerman and Why Is He Saying Those Terrible Things About Me?*

Margaret Leighton, *The Go-Between*

BEST ADAPTED SCREENPLAY

- Ernest Tidyman, *The French Connection*

Bernardo Bertolucci, *The Conformist*

Peter Bogdanovich, Larry McMurtry, *The Last Picture Show*

Vittorio Bonicelli, Ugo Pirro, *The Garden of the Finzi-Continis*

Stanley Kubrick, *A Clockwork Orange*

BEST ORIGINAL SCREENPLAY

- Paddy Chayefsky, *The Hospital*

Penelope Gilliatt, *Sunday, Bloody Sunday*

Andy Lewis, Dave Lewis, *Klute*

Elio Petri, Ugo Pirro, *Investigation of a Citizen above Suspicion*

Herman Raucher, *Summer of '42*

BEST SONG

- "Theme from *Shaft*," *Shaft*, Isaac Hayes

"The Age of Not Believing," *Bedknobs and Broomsticks*, Richard M. Sherman, Robert B. Sherman

"All His Children," *Sometimes a Great Notion*, Alan Bergman, Marilyn Bergman, Henry Mancini

"Bless the Beasts & Children," *Bless the Beasts & Children*, Perry Botkin, Jr., Barry Devorzon

"Life Is What You Make It," *Kotch*, Marvin Hamlisch, Johnny Mercer

BEST FOREIGN-LANGUAGE FILM

- *The Garden of the Finzi-Continis* (Italy)

Dodes'ka-Den (Japan)

The Emigrants (Sweden)

The Policeman (Israel)

Tchaikovsky (U.S.S.R.)

Winners

BEST ART DIRECTION

- Ernest Archer, John Box, Jack Maxsted, Gil Parrondo, Vernon Dixon, *Nicholas and Alexandra*

BEST CINEMATOGRAPHY

- Oswald Morris, *Fiddler on the Roof*

BEST COSTUME DESIGN

- Yvonne Blake, Antonia Castillo, *Nicholas and Alexandra*

BEST DOCUMENTARY

(FEATURE)

- Walon Green, *The Hellstrom Chronicle*

(SHORT SUBJECT)

- Robert Amram, Manuel Arango, *Sentinels of Silence*

BEST FILM EDITING

- Jerry Greenberg, *The French Connection*

BEST MUSIC

(ORIGINAL DRAMATIC SCORE)

- Michel Legrand, *Summer of '42*

(SCORING: ADAPTATION AND ORIGINAL SONG SCORE)

- John Williams, *Fiddler on the Roof*

SCIENTIFIC OR TECHNICAL AWARDS

Class II (Plaque)

- John N. Wilkinson, Optical Radiation Corp.

Class III (Certificate)

- Thomas Jefferson Hutchinson, James R. Rochester, Fenton Hamilton; Photo Research, Kollmorgen Corp.; Robert D. Auguste, Cinema Products; Producers Service Corp., Consolidated Film Industries; Cinema Research Corp., Research Products Inc.; Cinema Products Co.

BEST SHORT SUBJECT

(ANIMATED)

- *The Crunch Bird*

(LIVE ACTION)

- *Sentinels of Silence*

BEST SOUND

- David Hildyard, Gordon K. McCallum, *Fiddler on the Roof*

BEST SPECIAL VISUAL EFFECTS

- Danny Lee, Eustace Lycett, Alan Maley, *Bedknobs and Broomsticks*

HONORARY AWARD

- Charles Chaplin

SCREEN ACTORS GUILD

LIFETIME ACHIEVEMENT AWARD

- Charlton Heston

Kudos Can't Refuse The Godfather

"**I**f actor Stacy Keach can be heard muttering, 'I wuz robbed,' it's not because he's rehearsing for another sports role as a followup to his performance in *Fat City*," reported *Variety*.

In fact, Keach *wuz* robbed of the Best Actor award at the New York Film Critics vote when he won for his role as a small-town boxer, but then was dealt a sly left hook by a disgruntled critic "who perhaps not coincidentally had knocked Keach's *Fat City* performance in his published notice," *Variety* added.

Over the previous three years, the group had employed a two-ballot system to determine winners. The 20 members listed just one choice on the first ballot. If no candidate received a majority, then the victor was picked on a second polling after the crix ranked their three favorite candidates, granting three points to their top choice, two to their second and one to the third.

During the Best Actor vote this year, no winner emerged on the first canvass. Keach claimed the second round with a three-point edge over Marlon Brando (*The Godfather*).

"At this point a reviewer for a national magazine voiced the opinion that Keach's 20 points (out of a possible 60 from the 20 voting scribes) hardly constituted a group endorsement," *Variety* added. "He proposed that the rules be instantly amended to require 'at least 50 percent of the potential first-place points of the membership on all ballots.' There was some grumbling among the other reviewers that such last-minute rule changes were less than fair, but no one strongly opposed his insistence that the revised procedure be adopted immediately. As a result, three more ballots were held until the fifth-round tally resulted in the compromise choice of Laurence Olivier (30 points for *Sleuth*) over runners-up Brando (27), James Mason for *Child's Play* (20) and Peter

The national crix society made a surprising pick for Best Actor: supporting *Godfather* thesp Al Pacino (right). Costar Marlon Brando trounced Pacino at the Globes.

O'Toole for *The Ruling Class* (15). Fact that Keach failed even to place in the last balloting could well be explained by the pall that had been cast over his selection by the dissenting, rule-revising critic." Olivier scored low on the original vote, but later he "was apparently adjudged the safest and most widely acceptable choice," *Variety* said.

The same rule switch cost Eddie Albert (*The Heartbreak Kid*) the prize for Best Supporting Actor, which ended up going to *The Godfather*'s Robert Duvall.

For the first time since 1969, the Gotham crix cited a foreign-lingo film as Best Picture just as they had soon after the formation of the rival National Society of Film Critics, which preferred offshore pics—and usually ones by Sweden's Ingmar Bergman. This year the Gotham scribes chose Bergman's *Cries and Whispers* and gave him the additional awards for direction and screenplay for what *Variety* called his "bravado portrait of four women in a barren emotional landscape." When Star Liv Ullmann was named Best Actress, *Cries and Whispers* tied *A Man for All Seasons* (1966) as the crix's biggest champ.

Ullmann accepted her plaque in person when the crix gathered for their awards reception at Sardi's restaurant. She also accepted Bergman's kudos after explaining, noted *Variety*, "that the Swedish filmmaker had been fully prepared to attend the ceremony, but, at the last minute, backed down due to his fear of flying."

Variety called the event "a bland, quite distinguished affair" that received some "slight bite" by *Sleuth* director Joseph L. Mankiewicz, who was present to accept Laurence Olivier's plaque and couldn't resist tossing a barb at the choice of *Cries and Whispers* as best script. He asked the crix how they were "able to decide which film had the best screenplay through its subtitles."

The National Society of Film Critics agreed with the Gothamites on Bergman's screenplay and also cited the same Best Supporting Actress: Jeannie Berlin as a wacky newlywed in the screen adaptation of Neil Simon's play *The Heartbreak Kid* by Berlin's mother, director Elaine May. The society also endorsed, without flip-flopping, Berlin's costar Eddie Albert as Best Supporting Actor, although he shared the honor in a tie vote with Joel Grey, who'd previously won a Tony Award in 1967 for his Broadway turn as the devilish nightclub emcee in *Cabaret.* Society member Pauline Kael of *The New Yorker* sized his role up as "every tantalizingly disgusting show-biz creep one has ever seen."

The society crix did not choose Bergman's *Cries and Whispers* as Best Picture despite the strong preference they'd shown in the past toward works by the Swedish filmmaker. The pic ranked third in their vote behind *The Godfather* and, in first place—just as *Variety* had predicted two weeks earlier—*The Discreet Charm of the Bourgeoisie.* Society member Vincent Canby of *The New York Times* called *Discreet* a "brilliant new comedy" full of

When DGA picked Francis Ford Coppola, he looked like a cinch for the Oscar.

"mostly funny but sometimes somber thoughts on the French upper middle class" by Spanish helmer Luis Buñuel, who beat Bergman and Francis Ford Coppola (*The Godfather*) for Best Director.

The Godfather's Marlon Brando lost the Best Actor prize to costar Al Pacino, "thereby surprising many who had considered the young actor's performance to fall into the 'supporting' rather than 'leading' category,'" noted *Variety*.

The society agreed with the National Board of Review on Best Actress: Cicely Tyson as a sharecropper's wife battling the Depression in *Sounder*, which *Variety* praised as "an outstanding film" with "magnificent" performances by Tyson and Paul Winfield as her husband.

Weary of criticism that the critics' society wasn't truly national in scope, the group added 10 new members this year, although only 2 (Roger Ebert of *The Chicago Tribune* and Charles Champlin of *The Los Angeles Times*) lived outside New York City. Outraged, longtime members John Simon of *The New Leader* and Stanley Kauffmann of *The New Republic* quit, blasting some of the new blood's "lack of critical competence." *Variety* reported, "Simon and Kauffmann quit because they felt Champlin was too close to industry figures in Hollywood."

Variety also noted that 11 of the crix who now composed the 22-member society also belonged to the 20-member New York Film Critics, and the overlap was causing the leaders of both groups to hold behind-the-scenes talks about the possibility of a merger.

The society, however, had not been acting in a conciliatory way toward the Gothamites recently. In fact, this year it jumped ahead of them for the first time ever and announced its winners first. The National Board of Review, which used to pre-empt all other kudos, hadn't been out front since 1964, but this year it eclipsed both crix orgs thanks to the gumption of the new head of its Committee on Exceptional Films, book publisher Robert Giroux. The New York–based board chose the edgy screen adaptation of the New York stage hit *Cabaret* as Best Picture, which *Variety* had praised as "literate, bawdy, sophisticated, sensual, cynical, heart-warming and disturbingly thought-provoking."

Stacy Keach (*Fat City*) was voted Best Actor fairly and squarely by the Gotham crix, who then rescinded his prize to appease a "rule-revising critic," said *Variety*.

But *The New York Times* considered *The Godfather* higher art. Vincent Canby wrote, "Francis Ford Coppola has made one of the most brutal and moving chronicles of American life ever designed within the limits of popular entertainment."

When the Golden Globe nominations came out, *Cabaret* pulled off a big surprise: it outgunned *The Godfather* with the most bids—eight to seven—setting a new record for the most ever.

The tense showdown between the two pics promised to make the upcoming awards show dramatic—and this year millions of people could tune in to watch. The Hollywood Foreign Press Association announced that the ceremony would be back on TV for the first time since 1967. According to the terms of a five-year deal, the revived broadcast would be shown locally in Los Angeles on KTTV, which often aired ceremonies in the late 1950s and early 1960s, plus Metromedia stations in 25 other cities.

Just before the show, though, controversy erupted that threatened to spoil the celebratory occasion. Marlon Brando was not only up for Best Drama Actor (pitted against costar Al Pacino), but he was guaranteed a Globe as a World Film Favorite, having topped a survey conducted by the Reuters News Agency. He sent a telegram to the HFPA declaring that he would not be present at the Century Plaza Hotel gala to accept the trophy, however, and he did not want anyone else to accept it on his behalf. The wire cited "a lack of honor in this country today," considering the U.S. government's "imperialism and warlike intrusion in foreign countries, its treatment of the Indians and the blacks, the assault on the press and the rape of the ideals which were the foundation of this country. To accept an honor, however well intentioned, is to subtract from the meager amount left."

Tension built as the time came to bestow the award, but presenter Carol Burnett handled the situation deftly. As soon as Brando was declared the winner, she told the audience, "Marlon's in Tahiti and I'm going to take this to him *right now!*"

She grabbed the award and trotted off stage, flashing a mischievous smile.

Also absent was the female recipient of World Film Favorite—Jane Fonda. The audience was stunned to see her award accepted by her father, Henry, who had refused to attend recent Oscar ceremonies with her. As he accepted Jane's Globe, he said, "I'm proud of her for a lot of reasons. I'm particularly proud that she asked me to accept for her tonight."

Cabaret may have led with the most noms, but, *Variety* said, "not too surprisingly, Paramount's *The Godfather* was the big winner" with five Globes tying the record set by *Doctor Zhivago* in 1965. Its victories included Best Drama Picture, musical score, director (Francis Ford Coppola), screenplay (Coppola and Mario Puzo) and Best Drama Actor (Brando). No fuss or comment was made when no one appeared at the podium to accept Brando's second Globe.

Cabaret claimed three comedy/musical kudos: Best Picture, Best Supporting Actor (Joel Grey) and the Best Actress prize to the year's breakout thesp—Liza Minnelli. Minnelli had been Globe and Oscar nominated two years earlier for *The Sterile Cuckoo*, but *Cabaret* made her a film superstar, landing her on the covers of *Time, Newsweek* and *Life*. *The New York Times* declared that she "moves and sings with a strength, warmth, intelligence and sensitivity to nuance that virtually transfixes the screen."

Strangely, Diana Ross wasn't nominated opposite Minnelli for her film debut as songbird Billie Holiday in *Lady Sings the Blues*. Instead, Ross was up for Best Drama Actress, losing to Liv Ullmann as a 19th-century Swedish peasant who ventures to America in director Jan Troell's *The Emigrants*. (The New York film crix cited Ullmann for this role in addition to *Cries and Whispers* when hailing her as Best Actress.) Nonetheless, she won the consolation prize as Most Promising New Star in a motion picture. Desi Arnaz, Jr., who won the same prize last year, looked perplexed and shouted from the audience, "Is Diana Ross an up-and-coming newcomer?"

Obviously upset, Ross barked back from the podium, "Well, it's nice to be *somebody!*"

Best Comedy/Musical Actor was Jack Lemmon as an American tycoon who falls for the daughter of his late father's mistress while visiting Italy in Billy Wilder's *Avanti!*

The Godfather won easily at the writers' guild awards, while *Cabaret* emerged victorious in a close race with *The Heartbreak Kid, Butterflies Are Free* and *Avanti!* Peter Bogdanovich had lost a guild prize last year when *The Last Picture Show* was topped by *The French Connection,* but now he rallied by snagging a comedy prize with *What's Up, Doc?* co-writers Buck Henry (previous guild champ for *The Graduate,* 1967) and Robert Benton and David Newman, who both won two guild prizes for *Bonnie and Clyde* in 1967. Winner of best original drama was Jeremy Larner (*The Candidate*), a former speechwriter for Eugene McCarthy's 1968 presidential campaign. Larner penned the political satire *The Candidate*, starring Robert Redford as a gutsy political idealist.

"It was a gala night for writers, occurring in the midst of their industrywide strike, which didn't appear to dampen their

Natl. Bd. Of Rev. Again The Fustest With Year's Bests

For many years the first of the "year's best films" lists came from the National Board of Review of Motion Pictures. This is the or-

Variety noted that the board jumped back into the kudos derby lead for the first time since 1964.

enthusiasm," reported *Variety*. Part of the scribes' sunny mood no doubt had to do with the return of the gridiron-style stage show, which had been eliminated last year. After enduring much grousing, the guild reinstated it, but insisted that it would be the last performance.

When Coppola won the top prize from the Directors Guild of America, it appeared that *The Godfather*'s awards juggernaut was unstoppable. A curious victory occurred in the TV categories, however: Bob Fosse, a loser in the feature film lineup for *Cabaret*, was acknowledged for helming the TV variety special *Liza with a Z.* A few weeks later he won a Tony Award for directing *Pippin* on Broadway.

When the Oscar noms were announced, both Fosse and Coppola made the lineup, in addition to fellow DGA contender John Boorman (*Deliverance*). DGA rivals George Roy Hill (*Slaughterhouse-Five*) and Martin Ritt (*Sounder*) fell out, however, substituted by Joseph L. Mankiewicz (*Sleuth*) and Jan Troell (*The Emigrants*).

The Godfather seemed like the invincible frontrunner, with 11 noms. *Cabaret* followed with 10. The duo's Best Picture rivals were *Deliverance, The Emigrants* and *Sounder.*

The Best Actor category caused the most buzz, considering how Brando had spurned the Globe. Now pundits wondered: would he pull a George C. Scott at the Oscars? Unlike Scott two years ago, and unlike

Brando's recent action at the Globes, the *Godfather* star did not release a public statement declining the nomination.

Everything remained quiet up until Oscar day. Then, at 2:20 P.M., *Variety* columnist Army Archerd received a telephone call from a Brando representative, who said that the star would not attend the awards but that his girlfriend would be there, accompanied by an Apache Indian who would accept if he won.

One hour later, thousands of eager onlookers flanked the Oscar's red carpet. *The New York Times* reported, "The gaggle of superfans who crowded outside the music center shrieked for their favorites in true Hollywood fashion—Miss Minnelli, Mr. Grey. Jeannie Berlin, nominated as Best Supporting Actress for her role in *The Heartbreak Kid,* was clearly the most nervous contender. She almost fell off a stand where Army Archerd was introducing some of the guests before the ceremonies."

Once the awards showdown began, *The Godfather* started to take some early hits.

The National Society of Film Critics' Best Actor Al Pacino was considered an Oscar favorite when the film academy put him in the race for Best Supporting Actor. He faced tough competish from two costars, however, especially James Caan, who had recently starred in the highest-rated TV movie ever—*Brian's Song.*

Cabaret's Joel Grey wasn't optimistic. He told Archerd that he woke up in a cold sweat on Oscar day. "I went to the ceremony all but convinced that I wouldn't win," he added.

But when Grey ended up prevailing, he said at the podium, "Don't let anybody tell you that this isn't a terrific thrill!"

An even bigger upset occurred in the race for Best Supporting Actress, which contained no *Cabaret* or *Godfather* contenders. The two front-runners were Jeannie Berlin, who'd won dual crix honors, and Globe champ Shelley Winters, who'd been campaigning aggressively on the TV chat shows. The suddenly plump past Oscar champ was eager to tell America that she deliberately put on 40 pounds for her role in *The Poseidon Adventure.*

Globe and Oscar champ Liza Minnelli in *Cabaret*: the *N.Y. Times* said she "transfixes the screen."

The surprise victor turned out to be Eileen Heckart, hailed as the doting mother of a blind son who moves away from home in *Butterflies Are Free.* Heckart had initiated the role on London and New York stages.

In the Best Actress race, the only nominee who posed a challenge to Liza Minnelli was Diana Ross (*Lady Sings the Blues*), but the *Cabaret* star prevailed as expected. At the podium she saw her chance to shake the onslaught of recent parallels to her late mother, Judy Garland, and said, "Thank you for giving *me* this award. You've made *me* very happy!"

Cabaret swept up a surprising number of kudos all night. In addition to its two acting trophies, it also claimed statuettes for art direction, cinematography, film editing and musical score adaptation.

But no victory shocked awards-watchers more than *Cabaret*'s coup for the director's laurels. After his victory at the Directors Guild of America, Francis Ford Coppola was the clear front-runner. *Cabaret* helmer Bob Fosse told *Variety*'s Army Archerd before the ceremony, "I doubt if I have any chance to win tonight."

When Fosse won, Archerd reported "the biggest gasp from Academy members—and guests."

The Godfather finally stemmed its tide of losses by claiming the prize for Best

Adapted Screenplay. Coppola admitted at the podium, "I was beginning to think I wasn't going to get up here at all." The next day *The New York Times* gave him an additional prize—its Brightest Green Suit Award.

The Godfather's Brando was considered a shoo-in for Best Actor, but most pundits didn't know who'd appear at the podium if he won. The mystery was finally solved when presenters Roger Moore and Liv Ullmann opened an envelope and announced Brando's name.

A young woman dressed in Apache garb mounted the stage and brushed off Moore as he tried to give her the statuette.

"My name is Sacheen Littlefeather," she announced. "I'm Apache and I am president of the National Native American Affirmative Image Committee. I'm representing Marlon Brando, who, very regretfully, cannot accept this very generous award (because of) the treatment of American Indians today by the film industry."

Variety reported, "Some boos but more cheers greeted the Brando Oscar nix."

The New York Times declared that the snub "stunned the world and the film industry."

Backstage, Sacheen Littlefeather gave the press a 15-page statement from the star. "Perhaps you are saying to yourself, what the hell has all this got to do with the Academy Awards?" Brando's statement asked. "The motion picture community has been as responsible as any for degrading the Indian and making a mockery of his character, describing him as savage, hostile, evil. I think awards in this country at this time are inappropriate to be received or given until the condition of the American Indian is drastically altered."

Meantime, back out on stage, Clint Eastwood prepared to bestow the Best Picture prize and said, "I don't know if I should present this award on behalf of all the cowboys shot in John Ford westerns over the years."

When *The Godfather* won, producer Albert Ruddy referred to the *Cabaret* sweep earlier and said, "We were all getting nervous for a minute there."

Bogus Indian Sacheen Littlefeather said Marlon Brando declined the Oscar because of "the treatment of American Indians by the film industry." Brando refused his Globe for broader, wilder reasons.

The Godfather ended up with three Academy Awards. *Cabaret*'s tally of eight constituted the most wins any film ever scored without also winning Best Picture.

The Godfather's dramatic rally at the end of Oscar night ended up being dwarfed by the lingering buzz over Brando's action, which reverberated long after Oscar night.

Charleton Heston was among the stars who denounced it as "childish." Army Archerd was curious to learn Jane Fonda's reax since she chose to keep politics out of her own acceptance speech last year. When he phoned her the next day, she said, "I thought what he did was wonderful."

The controversy heightened when it was discovered that Sacheen Littlefeather was really a grade B actress named Maria Cruz, whose past gigs included a *Dark Shadows* promotional tour that billed her as Miss Vampire of 1970. After the Oscars, her biggest starring role would be turn out to be posing as a nude centerfold for *Playboy*.

The 1972 Oscar race may have contained eerie parallels to the awards two years earlier when George C. Scott raised a ruckus, but it also included an eerie reflection of last year's gala when Charlie Chaplin was given an honorary award, in part because he'd never received one in a competitive category.

This year Chaplin finally won an Oscar—for best musical score—and, oddly, it was for a film he made in 1952. *Limelight* was suddenly eligible now because of a technicality: it had never been shown in a Los Angeles theater prior to 1972.

▪ 1972 ▪

NATIONAL BOARD OF REVIEW

Winners were announced on December 14, 1972.

BEST PICTURE
▪ *Cabaret*
Man of La Mancha
The Godfather
Sounder
1776
The Effects of Gamma Rays on Man-in-the-Moon Marigolds
Deliverance
The Ruling Class
The Candidate
Frenzy

BEST DIRECTOR
▪ Bob Fosse, *Cabaret*

BEST ACTOR
▪ Peter O'Toole, *Man of La Mancha, The Ruling Class*

BEST ACTRESS
▪ Cicely Tyson, *Sounder*

BEST SUPPORTING ACTOR (TIE)
▪ Al Pacino, *The Godfather*
▪ Joel Grey, *Cabaret*

BEST SUPPORTING ACTRESS
▪ Marisa Berenson, *Cabaret*

BEST FOREIGN FILM
▪ *The Sorrow and the Pity* (Switzerland)
The Emigrants (Sweden)
The Discreet Charm of the Bourgeoisie (France)
Chloë in the Afternoon (France)
Uncle Vanya (U.S.S.R.)

NATIONAL SOCIETY OF FILM CRITICS

Winners were announced on December 27, 1972. Awards were presented on January 21, 1973, at the Algonquin Hotel in New York.

BEST PICTURE
▪ *The Discreet Charm of the Bourgeoisie*

BEST DIRECTOR
▪ Luis Buñuel, *The Discreet Charm of the Bourgeoisie*

BEST ACTOR
▪ Al Pacino, *The Godfather*

BEST ACTRESS
▪ Cicely Tyson, *Sounder*

BEST SUPPORTING ACTOR (TIE)
▪ Joel Grey, *Cabaret*
▪ Eddie Albert, *The Heartbreak Kid*

BEST SUPPORTING ACTRESS
▪ Jeannie Berlin, *The Heartbreak Kid*

BEST SCREENPLAY
▪ Ingmar Bergman, *Cries and Whispers*

BEST CINEMATOGRAPHY
▪ Sven Nykvist, *Cries and Whispers*

SPECIAL AWARDS
▪ Claude Jutra, *My Uncle Antoine*
▪ Ivan Passer, *Born to Run*; Robert Kaylor, *Derby*

NEW YORK FILM CRITICS

Winners were announced on January 3, 1973. Awards were presented on January 28 at Sardi's restaurant in New York.

BEST PICTURE
- *Cries and Whispers*

BEST DIRECTOR
- Ingmar Bergman, *Cries and Whispers*

BEST ACTOR
- Laurence Olivier, *Sleuth*

BEST ACTRESS
- Liv Ullmann, *Cries and Whispers, The Emigrants*

BEST SUPPORTING ACTOR
- Robert Duvall, *The Godfather*

BEST SUPPORTING ACTRESS
- Jeannie Berlin, *The Heartbreak Kid*

BEST SCREENPLAY
- Ingmar Bergman, *Cries and Whispers*

BEST DOCUMENTARY (SPECIAL AWARD)
- *The Sorrow and the Pity*

GOLDEN GLOBES

Nominations were announced on January 16, 1973. Awards were presented on January 28 at the Century Plaza Hotel in Los Angeles. The ceremony was telecast by Metromedia TV.

BEST DRAMA PICTURE
- *The Godfather*
Deliverance
Frenzy
The Poseidon Adventure
Sleuth

BEST COMEDY OR MUSICAL PICTURE
- *Cabaret*
Avanti!
Butterflies Are Free
Travels with My Aunt
1776

BEST DIRECTOR
- Francis Ford Coppola, *The Godfather*
John Boorman, *Deliverance*
Bob Fosse, *Cabaret*

Alfred Hitchcock, *Frenzy*
Billy Wilder, *Avanti!*

BEST ACTOR, DRAMA
- Marlon Brando, *The Godfather*
Michael Caine, *Sleuth*
Laurence Olivier, *Sleuth*
Al Pacino, *The Godfather*
Jon Voight, *Deliverance*

BEST ACTRESS, DRAMA
- Liv Ullmann, *The Emigrants*
Diana Ross, *Lady Sings the Blues*
Cicely Tyson, *Sounder*
Trish Van Devere, *One Is a Lonely Number*
Tuesday Weld, *Play It as It Lays*
Joanne Woodward, *The Effect of Gamma Rays on Man-in-the-Moon Marigolds*

BEST ACTOR, COMEDY OR MUSICAL
- Jack Lemmon, *Avanti!*
Edward Albee, *Butterflies Are Free*
Charles Grodin, *The Heartbreak Kid*
Walter Matthau, *Pete 'n' Tillie*
Peter O'Toole, *Man of La Mancha*

BEST ACTRESS, COMEDY OR MUSICAL
- Liza Minnelli, *Cabaret*
Carol Burnett, *Pete 'n' Tillie*
Goldie Hawn, *Butterflies Are Free*
Juliet Mills, *Avanti!*
Maggie Smith, *Travels with My Aunt*

BEST SUPPORTING ACTOR
- Joel Grey, *Cabaret*
James Caan, *The Godfather*
James Coco, *Man of La Mancha*
Alec McCowen, *Travels with My Aunt*
Clive Revill, *Avanti!*

BEST SUPPORTING ACTRESS
- Shelley Winters, *The Poseidon Adventure*
Marisa Berenson, *Cabaret*
Jeannie Berlin, *The Heartbreak Kid*
Helena Kallianiotes, *Kansas City Bomber*
Geraldine Page, *Pete 'n' Tillie*

MOST PROMISING NEWCOMER—MALE
- Edward Albert, *Butterflies Are Free*
Frederic Forrest, *When the Legends Die*
Kevin Hooks, *Sounder*

Michael Sacks, *Slaughterhouse-Five*
Simon Ward, *Young Winston*

MOST PROMISING NEWCOMER—FEMALE

- Diana Ross, *Lady Sings the Blues*

Sian Barbara Allen, *You'll Like My Mother*
Marisa Berenson, *Cabaret*
Mary Costa, *The Great Waltz*
Madeline Kahn, *What's Up, Doc?*
Victoria Principal, *The Life and Times of Judge Roy Bean*

BEST SCREENPLAY

- Mario Puzo, Francis Ford Coppola, *The Godfather*

Jay Allen, *Cabaret*
I. A. L. Diamond, Billy Wilder, *Avanti!*
James Dickey, *Deliverance*
Anthony Shaffer, *Frenzy*
Neil Simon, *The Heartbreak Kid*

BEST SONG

- "Ben," *Ben,* Walter Scharf, Don Black

"Carry Me," *Butterflies Are Free*, Robert Alcivar
"Dueling Banjos," *Deliverance*, Eric Weissberg
"Marmalade, Molasses and Honey," *The Life and Times of Judge Roy Bean*, Maurice Jarre, Marilyn Bergman and Alan Bergman
"Mein Herr," *Cabaret,* John Kander, Fred Ebb
"Money," *Cabaret,* John Kander, Fred Ebb
"The Morning After," *The Poseidon Adventure,* Al Kasha, Joel Hirschhorn
"Take Me Home," *Molly and Lawless John*, Johnny Mandel

BEST FOREIGN-LANGUAGE FOREIGN FILM

- *The Emigrants* (Part I), *The New Land* (Part II) (Sweden)

Cries and Whispers (Sweden)
The Discreet Charm of the Bourgeoisie (France)
Fellini's Roma (Italy)
Mirage (Peru)

BEST ENGLISH-LANGUAGE FOREIGN FILM

- *Young Winston*

Images
Living Free

The Ruling Class
X, Y & Zee

Winners

BEST ORIGINAL SCORE

- Nino Rota, *The Godfather*

WORLD FILM FAVORITES

- Marlon Brando
- Jane Fonda

CECIL B. DEMILLE AWARD

- Samuel Goldwyn

DIRECTORS GUILD OF AMERICA

The award for Best Director was presented on March 3, 1973, at the Beverly Hilton Hotel in Los Angeles and the Waldorf-Astoria Hotel in New York.

BEST DIRECTOR

- Francis Ford Coppola, *The Godfather*

John Boorman, *Deliverance*
Bob Fosse, *Cabaret*
George Roy Hill, *Slaughterhouse-Five*
Martin Ritt, *Sounder*

D. W. GRIFFITH AWARD

- William Wellman
- David Lean

HONORARY LIFE MEMBER

- David Lean

WRITERS GUILD OF AMERICA

Awards were presented on March 16, 1973, at the Beverly Hilton Hotel in Los Angeles.

BEST DRAMA WRITTEN DIRECTLY FOR THE SCREEN

- *The Candidate*, Jeremy Larner

Bad Company, David Newman, Robert Benton
The Culpepper Cattle Co., Eric Bercovici, Gregory Prentiss, story by Dick Richards

The Great Northfield Minnesota Raid,
   Philip Kaufman
Images, Robert Altman

BEST DRAMA ADAPTED FROM ANOTHER MEDIUM

- *The Godfather*, Mario Puzo, Francis Ford
   Coppola, based on the novel by Mario
   Puzo
Deliverance, James Dickey, based on his
   novel
Pete 'n' Tillie, Julius J. Epstein, based on
   the novel *Witch's Milk* by Peter De
   Vries
Slaughterhouse-Five, Stephen Geller, based
   on the novel by Kurt Vonnegut, Jr.
Sounder, Lonne Elder III, based on the
   novel by William H. Armstrong

BEST COMEDY WRITTEN DIRECTLY FOR THE SCREEN

- *What's Up, Doc?*, Buck Henry, David
   Newman, Robert Benton, Peter
   Bogdanovich
Get to Know Your Rabbit, Jordan
   Crittenden
Hammersmith Is Out, Stanford
   Whitmore
Minnie and Moskowitz, John Cassavetes
The War between Men and Women,
   Melville Shavelson, Danny Arnold

BEST COMEDY ADAPTED FROM ANOTHER MEDIUM

- *Cabaret*, Jay Presson Allen, based on the
   plays *Cabaret* by Joe Masteroff and *I
   Am a Camera* by John V. Druten and on
   the short story collection *Berlin Stories*
   by Christopher Isherwood
Avanti! Billy Wilder, I. A. L. Diamond,
   based on the play by Samuel Taylor
Butterflies Are Free, Leonard Gershe, based
   on his play
The Heartbreak Kid, Neil Simon, based on
   the short story "A Change of Plan" by
   Bruce Jay Friedman
Travels with My Aunt, Jay Presson Allen,
   Hugh Wheeler, based on the novel by
   Graham Greene

LAUREL AWARD
- William Rose

VALENTINE DAVIES AWARD
- William Ludwig

MORGAN COX AWARD
- David Harmon

ACADEMY AWARDS

Nominations were announced on February
12, 1973. Awards were presented on March
27 at the Dorothy Chandler Pavilion in Los
Angeles. The ceremony was telecast by
NBC.

BEST PICTURE
- *The Godfather*
Cabaret
Deliverance
The Emigrants
Sounder

BEST DIRECTOR
- Bob Fosse, *Cabaret*
John Boorman, *Deliverance*
Francis Ford Coppola, *The Godfather*
Joseph L. Mankiewicz, *Sleuth*
Jan Troell, *The Emigrants*

BEST ACTOR
- Marlon Brando, *The Godfather*
Michael Caine, *Sleuth*
Laurence Olivier, *Sleuth*
Peter O'Toole, *The Ruling Class*
Paul Winfield, *Sounder*

BEST ACTRESS
- Liza Minnelli, *Cabaret*
Diana Ross, *Lady Sings the Blues*
Maggie Smith, *Travels with My Aunt*
Cicely Tyson, *Sounder*
Liv Ullmann, *The Emigrants*

BEST SUPPORTING ACTOR
- Joel Grey, *Cabaret*
Eddie Albert, *The Heartbreak Kid*
James Caan, *The Godfather*
Robert Duvall, *The Godfather*
Al Pacino, *The Godfather*

BEST SUPPORTING ACTRESS
- Eileen Heckart, *Butterflies Are Free*
Jeannie Berlin, *The Heartbreak Kid*

Geraldine Page, *Pete 'n' Tillie*
Susan Tyrrell, *Fat City*
Shelley Winters, *The Poseidon Adventure*

BEST ADAPTED SCREENPLAY

- Francis Ford Coppola, Mario Puzo, *The Godfather*
Jay Allen, *Cabaret*
Lonne Elder III, *Sounder*
Julius J. Epstein, *Pete 'n' Tillie*
Bengt Forslund, Jan Troell, *The Emigrants*

BEST ORIGINAL SCREENPLAY

- Jeremy Larner, *The Candidate*
Luis Buñuel, Jean-Claude Carrière, *The Discreet Charm of the Bourgeoisie*
Chris Clark, Suzanne De Passe, Terence McCloy, *Lady Sings the Blues*
Carl Foreman, *Young Winston*
Louis Malle, *Murmur of the Heart*

BEST SONG

- "The Morning After," *The Poseidon Adventure*, Joel Hirschhorn, Al Kasha
"Ben," *Ben*, Don Black, Walter Scharf
"Come Follow, Follow Me," *The Little Ark*, Fred Karlin, Marsha Karlin
"Marmalade, Molasses & Honey," *The Life and Times of Judge Roy Bean*, Alan Bergman, Marilyn Bergman, Maurice Jarre
"Strange Are the Ways of Love," *The Stepmother*, Sammy Fain, Paul Francis Webster

BEST FOREIGN-LANGUAGE FILM

- *The Discreet Charm of the Bourgeoisie* (France)
The Dawns Here Are Quiet (U.S.S.R.)
I Love You, Rosa (Israel)
My Dearest Señorita (Spain)
The New Land (Sweden)

Winners

BEST ART DIRECTION

- Jurgen Kiebach, Rolf Zehetbauer, Herbert Strabel, *Cabaret*

BEST CINEMATOGRAPHY

- Geoffrey Unsworth, *Cabaret*

BEST COSTUME DESIGN

- Anthony Powell, *Travels with My Aunt*

BEST DOCUMENTARY
(FEATURE)

- Sarah Kernochan, Howard Smith, *Marjoe*
(SHORT SUBJECT)
- Charles Huguenot Van Der Linden, Martina Huguenot Van Der Linden, *This Tiny World*

BEST FILM EDITING

- David Bretherton, *Cabaret*

BEST MUSIC
(ORIGINAL DRAMATIC SCORE)

- Charles Chaplin, Raymond Rasch, Larry Russell, *Limelight* (1952)
(SCORING: ADAPTATION AND ORIGINAL SONG SCORE)
- Ralph Burns, *Cabaret*

SCIENTIFIC OR TECHNICAL AWARDS
Class II (Plaque)

- Joseph E. Bluth; Edward H. Reichard, Howard T. LaZare, Consolidated Film Industries; Edward Efron, IBM
Class III (Certificate)
- Photo Research, Kollmorgen Corp., PCS Technology Inc.; Carter Equipment Co., Ramtronics; David Degenkolb, Harry Larson, Manfred Michelson, Fred Scobey, Deluxe General; Jiro Mukai, Ryusho Hirose, Canon Inc.; Wilton R. Holm, Frank P. Clark, AMPTP Motion Picture and Television Research Center; Philip V. Palmquist, Leonard L. Olson, 3M; E. H. Geissler, G. M. Berggren, Wil-Kin Inc.

BEST SHORT SUBJECT
(ANIMATED)

- *A Christmas Carol*
(LIVE ACTION)
- *Norman Rockwell's World . . . An American Dream*

BEST SOUND

- David Hildyard, Robert Knudson, *Cabaret*

SPECIAL ACHIEVEMENT AWARD
(VISUAL EFFECTS)

- *The Poseidon Adventure*, L. B. Abbott, A. D. Flowers

JEAN HERSHOLT HUMANITARIAN AWARD

- Rosalind Russell

HONORARY AWARDS

- Charles S. Boren
- Edward G. Robinson

SCREEN ACTORS GUILD

LIFETIME ACHIEVEMENT AWARD

- Frank Sinatra

· 1973 ·

No Critical Difference

Adding "Circle" to the name of the New York Film Critics—which had used the term once before, briefly back in the early 1940s—did nothing to help round out the idea of what the group was all about.

The crix org, in fact, suddenly suffered from a severe identity crisis.

When the 1967 awards were decided, the Gotham group and the National Society of Film Critics had no members in common. By 1973, *Variety* noted, "Of the 19 voting members of the National Society, all but 4 are also members of the New York Film Critics Circle, so the voting similarity is not really surprising. The overlap has finally reached a point where two orgs' year-end honors may strike many as a bit redundant."

The vote outcomes were actually shockingly similar this year. Whereas last year the two groups agreed on two out of seven races, now six champs matched up. The only category they disagreed on was Best Actress. The Gothamites chose Joanne Woodward, whom *Variety* called "first rate" as the disillusioned wife facing middle age in *Summer Wishes, Winter Dreams.* The society picked Liv Ullmann for *The New Land,* the sequel to *The Emigrants,* for which the Gotham crix had lauded her last year.

The crix's consensus choices for Best Picture and Director were *Day for Night* and helmer François Truffaut. *Variety* described the pic as Truffaut's "love letter to the cinematic art" since it starred the avant-garde French megger as a director filming a movie. Best Supporting Actress was *Day*'s Valentina Cortese, whom *Variety* called "remarkable as an aging star who goes on despite a sick son."

Best Actor was the same thesp both crix groups had snubbed last year when he was honored with a Golden Globe and Oscar

French director François Truffaut (right) portrayed himself in *Day for Night,* which was named best pic by both crix orgs.

(both refused) for his career-resurrecting turn in the all-time b.o. champ *The Godfather.* The crix now caught up with Marlon Brando as an aging Lothario who has a kinky, hot-buttered affair with an anonymous young woman in *Last Tango in Paris.*

Best Supporting Actor was Robert De Niro, whom *Variety* called "outstanding" as a scrappy junior mobster in *Mean Streets.* Best Screenplay dramatized the lives of four misfit school pals in George Lucas's *American Graffiti.*

Considering the overwhelming redundancy between the two kudos, *Variety* said, "Merger of the groups now seems more logical than ever."

National society chairman Andrew Sarris of *The Village Voice* liked the idea and suggested a bold first step as a trial run: he asked the Gothamites if the two groups could hold their award ceremonies together.

The New Yorkers mulled over the offer for a few days, then turned it down on January 11. Sarris panicked. Since his group had voted on their awards first, he wanted to present them at a party before the circle's gala on January 27. The date that made the most sense was January 20, which meant he had only nine days to mount his ceremony.

Sarris not only got the fete organized in time, but his kudos upstaged its rival when the media prizes made headlines. A special cash award of $2,000 was skedded to be bestowed upon fledgling Cuban filmmaker Tomas Gutierrez Alea (*Memories of Underdevelopment*), but the U.S. State Department turned down his visa application. An official stated that "the denial represents a continuation of U.S. policy toward Cuba" and he warned that if anyone accepted the award on Alea's behalf, they would be in violation of the Trading with the Enemy Act.

Outraged, *The New York Times* and other media denounced the U.S. action. Writing in the *Voice,* Sarris marveled at the sudden attention his society was receiving: "All these years we have been giving out awards and no one paid much attention. Now the Cuban director of a good-to-middling movie is denied a visa by a stupid bureaucrat and we are on the front page."

When the society gathered with the winners at the Algonquin Hotel, Sarris fired back. He said that the award bestowed upon *Memories of Underdevelopment* didn't celebrate Cuban communism any more than an award bestowed upon *Day for Night* saluted French capitalism. But it was to no avail. Alea was not present to receive his honor and the society was forbidden by law to send it to him.

Day for Night was nommed as Best Foreign Film at the Golden Globes, but suffered one of the night's many upsets. "Biggest surprise among the 1973 winners, reflected in some audience gasps and mild applause, was choice of Maximilian Schell's *The Pedestrian* as Best Foreign Film," reported *Variety*. "Schell himself acknowledged the upset by paying tribute to François Truffaut, here from France and

The redundant crix groups now considered a merger.

generally regarded as a shoo-in for *Day for Night*."

Since *Day for Night* swept both crix's honors, there was no U.S. Best Picture front-runner heading into the Golden Globes. Many pundits were surprised by what pic snagged the most noms: *The Exorcist* (six).

The Exorcist, which was based on a 1949 case of demonic possession, was a b.o. blockbuster during awards season, but pundits were unsure how it would fare at the Hollywood showbiz awards. *Variety* had reviewed it respectfully, calling it "an expert telling of a supernatural horror story" that delivered "pure cinematic terror," but the pic's sensational subject matter and commercial success were considered drawbacks.

When the Globe results were in, *Variety* reported that *The Exorcist* copped the most trophies "and nary a soul retched, fainted or otherwise responded in exploitable fashion to pic's wins for best drama, director (William Friedkin), screenwriter (William Peter Blatty) and supporting actress (Linda Blair)."

Blatty said in his acceptance speech: "I suppose that the selection of *The Exorcist* will inspire a new devil theory to account for it."

When Linda Blair won, the overwhelmed 12-year-old lost emotional control at the podium, leading several reporters to claim that she looked as if she were truly possessed by a devil. Columnist Barney Glazer described the scene: "She tearfully and shriekingly came apart as if someone had poured molten lead into her ears. Which may be just one more valid reason to keep your children out of the entertainment world and let them enjoy a normal childhood."

Most of the other honorees were no-shows. George Segal and Glenda Jackson both won thesp laurels as the adulterous lovers in the romantic comedy *A Touch of Class*, but Segal stayed home because he didn't think he'd win and Jackson was busy in her native U.K.

New York film crix Best Actress Joanne Woodward lost to Marsha Mason, whom *Variety* had called "superb" as a prostitute who falls for a sailor in *Cinderella Liberty*. But Mason was A.W.O.L. at the kudos. Missing, too, was Best Drama Actor Al Pacino. *Variety* had hailed him as "outstanding as an honest New York policeman who helped expose corruption" in *Serpico*.

An upset occurred in the category of Best Comedy or Musical Picture, which was claimed by the small-budget teen hit *American Graffiti*.

The Globe gala was telecast live in L.A. and syndicated to 120 other urban markets in a 90-minute program aired the next day. Hosts again were Steve Lawrence and Eydie Gormé, who reaped crix huzzahs. Lawrence's best *Exorcist* joke: "The film is so frightening, even George Jessel is giving up 12-year-olds."

The Exorcist was nominated for Best Adapted Drama at the writers' guild awards, but lost to *Serpico*, penned by past guild honoree Waldo Salt (*Midnight Cowboy*, 1969) and Norman Wexler.

Paper Moon (Alvin Sargent) won as expected for best adapted comedy, but there was a mild surprise in the category for best original comedy when *A Touch of Class*'s Melvin Frank and Jack Rose prevailed over Woody Allen (*Sleeper*), Paul Mazursky (*Blume in Love*) and George Lucas (*American Graffiti*). The biggest surprise of the night was in the race for best original drama: Steve Shagan's *Save the Tiger* won out over Martin Scorsese's *Mean Streets*, Arthur Laurents's *The Way We Were* and David S. Ward's *The Sting*.

The upsets helped to provide some of the night's excitement since the standard entertainment was nixed. Many guests grumbled that they missed the satirical stage skits that were "in the past usually a highlight of Hollywood's awards season," said *Variety*. The

traditional dinner was replaced by a cocktail reception.

With *The Exorcist*'s defeat by the writers' guild, there was no clear front-runner heading into the showdown at the directors' guild. Helmer William Friedkin was a proven past winner for *The French Connection* in 1971, but no director had ever won for a horror movie. His competish: Bernardo Bertolucci (*Last Tango in Paris*), George Roy Hill (*The Sting*), George Lucas (*American Graffiti*) and Sidney Lumet (*Serpico*).

The winner turned out to be a real shocker: George Roy Hill. *The Sting* had won Best Picture from the National Board of Review, but the box office blockbuster starring Paul Newman and Robert Redford as 1930s Chicago con men wasn't taken seriously as an awards candidate afterward. It was ignored by the two crix groups and virtually snubbed at the Golden Globes, where it received only a single nomination—for best screenplay, which it lost—a fate similarly suffered at the Writers Guild of America.

Was *Exorcist* star Linda Blair possessed by a devil at the Golden Globes?

Variety reported, "Absent on Florida location filming, Hill was repped in acceptance by his wife, who at her husband's request specifically saluted Hill's directorial staff, and by Richard D. Zanuck who cracked that 'anyone who could work with five producers and still make a good picture deserves an award.' "

The entertainment at the banquet was lively and included a nudist fad just then spreading across America's college campuses: streaking.

"Emcee Ernest Borgnine set up an intro of visiting royalty (the Prince of Wales, he said), which turned out to be a streaker," *Variety* reported. "Streaking purists might disqualify the contender since he was, after all, wearing an athletic supporter."

When the Oscar noms were announced a few weeks later, one DGA contender—Sidney Lumet—was snubbed. In his place was

Ingmar Bergman for *Cries and Whispers,* which also scored a bid for Best Picture, which surprised many. *Cries* had won lots of critics' awards last year, but wasn't Oscar eligible until 1973, when it debuted in Los Angeles theaters.

Other Best Picture contenders were *American Graffiti, The Exorcist, The Sting* and *A Touch of Class.* Since *A Touch of Class* didn't snag a corresponding bid for Best Director, its chances looked slim. Front-runners were *The Exorcist* and *The Sting* with the most noms: 10.

On Oscar day, *Exorcist* director William Friedkin joined *Variety* columnist Army Archerd at his interviewers' stand on the red carpet and "observed that both the demonic thriller and his earlier Oscar-winning *The French Connection* were a bit ahead of their time, but hopefully not too much," Archerd reported.

Later, however, "producer-screenwriter William Peter Blatty said he was 'a little pessimistic,' " Archerd added. Blatty confessed that he was disappointed by the verdict at the directors' guild and perplexed by *Exorcist*'s defeat at the scribes' guild. "I couldn't understand the writers," he told Archerd. "They gave the picture a standing ovation at their screening."

When the Oscar ceremony began, Blatty turned out to have better luck with film academy voters, who gave him the award for Best Adapted Screenplay over the *Serpico* scribes who'd topped him at the guild laurels. Meantime, *The Exorcist*'s chief Oscar rival, *The Sting,* pulled even by taking the golden boy for Best Original Screenplay.

The Exorcist's defeat in the race for Best Supporting Actress was expected, since Linda Blair's chances were hurt by a controversy that broke soon after her Golden Globe win. Much of her performance's impact was due to the sacrilegious outbursts of the devil who possessed her. The voice was dubbed by Mercedes McCambridge, who wasn't given screen credit and was mouthing off about it in the press. Some pundits even thought that the past Oscar champ (1949 Best Supporting Actress, *All the King's Men*) should've shared in Blair's current Oscar nomination.

DGA champ George Roy Hill (center) chats with Paul Newman and Robert Redford on the set of the National Board of Review's and Oscar's Best Picture *The Sting.*

Also in the race were Candy Clark ("marvelous as the ditsy blonde" in *American Graffiti,* said *The New York Times*) and National Board of Review champ Sylvia Sidney ("first rate" as Joanne Woodward's dying mother in *Summer Wishes, Winter Dreams,* said *Variety*). They competed against two *Paper Moon* contenders: Madeline Kahn as a sassy carnival stripper and a 10-year-old moppet as an adorable flim-flam artist. In its review of *Paper Moon, Variety* announced, "Tatum O'Neal makes a sensational screen debut."

O'Neal's father, Ryan, couldn't escort her to the Oscars because he was working in London. When her name was announced as winner, her grandfather escorted her to the podium, where she said, "All I really want is to thank is my director Peter Bogdanovich and my father." She was suddenly the youngest star ever to win an Oscar, replacing Patty Duke, who was 16 when she was hailed for *The Miracle Worker.*

The Exorcist was repped in the race for Best Supporting Actor by Jason Miller as a devil-hunting priest, but the category had no front-runner. The winner turned out to be Golden Globe and National Board of Review champ John Houseman, who *Variety* said was "outstanding as the hard-nosed but urbane law professor in *The Paper Chase.*" Houseman was a renowned acting coach and one of the founders of the Mercury Theatre with Orson Welles, but he had little screen experience. "Almost for the first time in a long and tumultuous life, I am almost speechless," he said at the podium. He thanked his director for "the unspeakable gall to select this aging and obscure schoolmarm for this perfectly glorious part."

The biggest upset of the night occurred in the Best Actress race, which was considered a toss-up between New York film crix champ Joanne Woodward, Golden Globe victor Marsha Mason and Barbra Streisand, whom *Variety* lauded for showing "superior dramatic versatility" in the romantic megahit *The Way We Were*.

The winner turned out to be "long shot Glenda Jackson" for *A Touch of Class*, *Variety* noted. "Jackson's Best Actress Oscar is her second out of three nominations and surprising because she has previously not been considered a comedy actress."

Streisand's *The Way We Were* costar Robert Redford was nommed in the Best Actor race for *The Sting*, but one rival was "heavily favored," noted *Variety*. Jack Lemmon had been named Best Supporting Actor in 1955 for *Mr. Roberts,* but he still hadn't won a golden boy in the lead race despite nominations for *Some Like It Hot* and *The Apartment*.

When Lemmon finally prevailed this year for his perf as a distraught garment exec in *Save the Tiger, Variety* called him "perhaps the most popular winner of the night" and noted that he was "emotion-choked as he received his statue." He said, "I had a speech prepared—in 1959, but I've forgotten it."

Although *The Sting* scored no Oscars for acting, it reaped early wins for art direction, costumes (Edith Head) and music (two trophies for composer Marvin Hamlisch), in addition to its screenplay prize. Since it had previously claimed kudos from the directors' guild, it was considered likely to win the Oscar for Best Director next—and did. While claiming the statuette, George Roy Hill advised fellow directors how they could win an Oscar, too: hire the crew of *The Sting*. "It helps," he said. "Believe me."

David Niven was just about to introduce Elizabeth Taylor, who would reveal the Best Picture winner, when he was suddenly inter-

Presenter David Niven appeared nonplussed by the intrusion of a streaker at the Oscar show. A more modest nudist (wearing an athletic supporter) disrupted the DGA gala.

rupted by gasps and guffaws from the audience.

Behind him, a nude man ran past, flashing a peace sign.

The orchestra quickly struck up the tune "Sunny Side Up" while the TV camera switched to an angle that wouldn't reveal the man's genitals. David Niven grinned at the audience and said, "Ladies and gentlemen, that was bound to happen. Just think. The only laugh that man will probably ever get is for stripping and showing off his shortcomings."

Elizabeth Taylor stepped out on stage, looking flustered. "That's a pretty tough act to follow," she said. "I'm really nervous. That upset me."

Then she read off the nominees, opened the envelope and said, "Oh, I'm so glad. It's *The Sting*."

The Sting ended up with seven awards. "George Roy Hill expressed his surprise at the fuss made over the film," *Variety* noted afterward. Its helmer told the tradepaper backstage: "It was a fun picture to make, but I didn't think we would be doing what we are doing tonight."

The Exorcist ended up with only two awards, and its producer/scribe William Peter Blatty was furious. "Everything was 'Down with *The Exorcist*!'" he fumed at reporters backstage. "*The Exorcist* is head and shoulders the finest film made this year or in several years."

The pic's studio, Warner Bros., "will just have to settle for having one of the biggest-grossing films of all time," *Variety* shrugged.

Since the movie that claimed Best Picture at the two crix's awards wasn't up for Best Picture at the Oscars, it had to settle on Best Foreign Film, but its helmer François Truffaut seemed pleased. "Merci beaucoup!" he said to the voters. "I am very happy. Why? Because *Day for Night* is about show people."

One of the night's other notable champs was the recipient of the Irving Thalberg Award, Lawrence Weingarten, who had been one of the early sponsors of the award when it was created in 1937. Among the movies he produced were several Spencer Tracy–Katharine Hepburn classics, so the academy took a flier on inviting Hepburn to present it, even though Oscar's most-awarded actress had never before attended a ceremony. Surprisingly, she accepted.

The news was kept secret and, when the moment for her appearance came, it was staged in grand theatrical style. "To me, this is a star—Katharine Hepburn," David Niven announced as he gestured toward a high staircase. Oscar's queen appeared on top and, as she swept down the steps to approached the podium, the audience gasped, jumped to its feet and gave her a roaring ovation.

"Thank you very, very much," she said. "I am naturally deeply moved. I'm also very happy that I didn't hear anyone call out, 'It's about time!' I'm living proof that a person can wait 41 years to be unselfish."

Variety claimed that "Hepburn's past history of Oscar boycott was erased sentimentally and totally by her opening remarks."

Variety identified the streaker as "Robert Opel who runs an ad agency in Hollywood. He entered backstage with a press pass." Six years later, *Variety* would report on his tragic demise: Opel was murdered in a sex-gear shop he owned in San Francisco.

■ 1973 ■

NATIONAL BOARD OF REVIEW

Winners were announced on December 24, 1973.

BEST PICTURE
- *The Sting*
Paper Moon
The Homecoming
Bang the Drum Slowly
Serpico
O Lucky Man!
The Last American Hero
The Hireling
The Day of the Dolphin
The Way We Were

BEST DIRECTOR
- Ingmar Bergman, *Cries and Whispers*

BEST ACTOR (TIE)
- Al Pacino, *Serpico*
- Robert Ryan, *The Iceman Cometh*

BEST ACTRESS
- Liv Ullmann, *The New Land*

BEST SUPPORTING ACTOR
- John Houseman, *The Paper Chase*

BEST SUPPORTING ACTRESS
- Sylvia Sidney, *Summer Wishes, Winter Dreams*

BEST FOREIGN FILM
- *Cries and Whispers* (Sweden)
Day for Night (France)
The New Land (Sweden)
The Tall Blond Man with One Black Shoe (France)
Alfredo, Alfredo (Italy)
Traffic (France/Italy)

SPECIAL CITATIONS
- American Film Theatre, Ely Landau
- Woody Allen, *Sleeper*
- Walt Disney, *Robin Hood*
- Paramount, *Charlotte's Web*

NATIONAL SOCIETY OF FILM CRITICS

Winners were announced on January 5, 1974. Awards were presented on January 20 at the Algonquin Hotel in New York.

BEST PICTURE
- *Day for Night*

BEST DIRECTOR
- François Truffaut, *Day for Night*

BEST ACTOR
- Marlon Brando, *Last Tango in Paris*

BEST ACTRESS
- Liv Ullmann, *The New Land*

BEST SUPPORTING ACTOR
- Robert De Niro, *Mean Streets*

BEST SUPPORTING ACTRESS
- Valentina Cortese, *Day for Night*

BEST SCREENPLAY
- George Lucas, Gloria Katz, Willard Huyck, *American Graffiti*

BEST CINEMATOGRAPHY
- Vilmos Zsigmond, *The Long Goodbye*

SPECIAL AWARDS
- Tomas Gutierrez Alea, *Memories of Underdevelopment*
- Daryl Duke, *Payday*
- Robert Ryan, *The Iceman Cometh*

NEW YORK FILM CRITICS CIRCLE

Winners were announced on January 8, 1974. Awards were presented on January 27 at Sardi's restaurant in New York.

BEST PICTURE
- *Day for Night*

BEST DIRECTOR
- François Truffaut, *Day for Night*

BEST ACTOR
- Marlon Brando, *Last Tango in Paris*

BEST ACTRESS
- Joanne Woodward, *Summer Wishes, Winter Dreams*

BEST SUPPORTING ACTOR
- Robert De Niro, *Bang the Drum Slowly*

BEST SUPPORTING ACTRESS
- Valentina Cortese, *Day for Night*

BEST SCREENPLAY
- George Lucas, Gloria Katz, Willard Huyck, *American Graffiti*

GOLDEN GLOBES

Nominations were announced on January 9, 1974. Awards were presented on January 26 at the Beverly Hilton Hotel in Los Angeles. The ceremony was telecast live in Los Angeles on KTTV and syndicated to 120 Metromedia and other stations nationwide for broadcast one day later.

BEST DRAMA PICTURE
- *The Exorcist*
Cinderella Liberty
The Day of the Jackal
Last Tango in Paris
Save the Tiger
Serpico

BEST COMEDY OR MUSICAL PICTURE
- *American Graffiti*
Jesus Christ Superstar
Paper Moon
Tom Sawyer
A Touch of Class

BEST DIRECTOR
- William Friedkin, *The Exorcist*
Bernardo Bertolucci, *Last Tango in Paris*
Peter Bogdanovich, *Paper Moon*
George Lucas, *American Graffiti*
Fred Zinnemann, *The Day of the Jackal*

BEST ACTOR, DRAMA
- Al Pacino, *Serpico*
Robert Blake, *Electra Glide in Blue*
Jack Lemmon, *Save the Tiger*
Steve McQueen, *Papillon*
Jack Nicholson, *The Last Detail*

BEST ACTRESS, DRAMA

- Marsha Mason, *Cinderella Liberty*
Ellen Burstyn, *The Exorcist*
Barbra Streisand, *The Way We Were*
Elizabeth Taylor, *Ash Wednesday*
Joanne Woodward, *Summer Wishes, Winter Dreams*

BEST ACTOR, COMEDY OR MUSICAL

- George Segal, *A Touch of Class*
Carl Anderson, *Jesus Christ Superstar*
Richard Dreyfuss, *American Graffiti*
Ted Neely, *Jesus Christ Superstar*
Ryan O'Neal, *Paper Moon*

BEST ACTRESS, COMEDY OR MUSICAL

- Glenda Jackson, *A Touch of Class*
Yvonne Elliman, *Jesus Christ Superstar*
Cloris Leachman, *Charley and the Angel*
Tatum O'Neal, *Paper Moon*
Liv Ullmann, *Forty Carats*

BEST SUPPORTING ACTOR

- John Houseman, *The Paper Chase*
Martin Balsam, *Summer Wishes, Winter Dreams*
Jack Gilford, *Save the Tiger*
Randy Quaid, *The Last Detail*
Max von Sydow, *The Exorcist*

BEST SUPPORTING ACTRESS

- Linda Blair, *The Exorcist*
Valentina Cortese, *Day for Night*
Madeline Kahn, *Paper Moon*
Kate Reid, *A Delicate Balance*
Sylvia Sidney, *Summer Wishes, Winter Dreams*

MOST PROMISING NEWCOMER—MALE

- Paul Le Mat, *American Graffiti*
Carl Anderson, *Jesus Christ Superstar*
Robby Benson, *Jeremy*
Kirk Calloway, *Cinderella Liberty*
Ted Neely, *Jesus Christ Superstar*

MOST PROMISING NEWCOMER—FEMALE

- Tatum O'Neal, *Paper Moon*
Linda Blair, *The Exorcist*
Kay Lenz, *Breezy*
Michelle Phillips, *Dillinger*
Barbara Sigel, *Time to Run*

BEST SCREENPLAY

- William Peter Blatty, *The Exorcist*
Melvin Frank, Jack Rose, *A Touch of Class*
Darryl Ponicsan, *Cinderella Liberty*
Kenneth Ross, *The Day of the Jackal*
David S. Ward, *The Sting*

BEST SONG

- "The Way We Were," *The Way We Were*
"All That Love Went to Waste," *A Touch of Class*
"Breezy's Song," *Breezy*
"Lonely Looking Sky," *Jonathan Livingston Seagull*
"Rosa, Rosa," *Kazablan*
"Send a Little Love My Way," *Oklahoma Crude*

BEST FOREIGN FILM

- *The Pedestrian* (German)
Alfredo, Alfredo (Italy)
Day for Night (France)
Kazablan (Israel)
State of Siege (France)

Winners

BEST ORIGINAL SCORE

- Neil Diamond, *Jonathan Livingston Seagull*

WORLD FILM FAVORITES

- Marlon Brando
- Elizabeth Taylor

CECIL B. DEMILLE AWARD

- Bette Davis

DIRECTORS GUILD OF AMERICA

The award for Best Director was presented on March 16, 1974, at the Beverly Hilton Hotel in Los Angeles and the Hilton Hotel in New York.

BEST DIRECTOR

- George Roy Hill, *The Sting*
Bernardo Bertolucci, *Last Tango in Paris*
William Friedkin, *The Exorcist*
George Lucas, *American Graffiti*
Sidney Lumet, *Serpico*

WRITERS GUILD OF AMERICA

Awards were presented on March 21, 1974, at the Beverly Hilton Hotel in Los Angeles.

BEST DRAMA WRITTEN DIRECTLY FOR THE SCREEN
- *Save the Tiger*, Steve Shagan
Mean Streets, Martin Scorsese, Mardik Martin
Payday, Don Carpenter
The Sting, David S. Ward
The Way We Were, Arthur Laurents

BEST DRAMA ADAPTED FROM ANOTHER MEDIUM
- *Serpico*, Waldo Salt, Norman Wexler
Cinderella Liberty, Darryl Ponicsan, based on his novel
The Exorcist, William Peter Blatty, based on his novel
The Last Detail, Robert Towne, based on the novel by Darryl Ponicsan
The Paper Chase, James Bridges, based on the novel by John Jay Osborn, Jr.

BEST COMEDY WRITTEN DIRECTLY FOR THE SCREEN
- *A Touch of Class*, Melvin Frank, Jack Rose
American Graffiti, George Lucas, Gloria Katz, Willard Huyck
Blume in Love, Paul Mazursky
Sleeper, Woody Allen, Marshall Brickman
Slither, W. D. Richter

BEST COMEDY ADAPTED FROM ANOTHER MEDIUM
- *Paper Moon*, Alvin Sargent, based on a novel by Joe David Brown
Forty Carats, Leonard Gershe, based on a play by Jay Allen
Godspell, David Greene, John-Michael Tebelak, based on the play by John-Michael Tebelak and Stephen Schwartz

LAUREL AWARD
- Paddy Chayefsky

VALENTINE DAVIES AWARD
- Ray Bradbury
- Philip Dunne

MORGAN COX AWARD
- James R. Webb

FOUNDERS AWARD
- Ranald MacDougall

ACADEMY AWARDS

Nominations were announced on February 19, 1974. Awards were presented on April 2 at the Dorothy Chandler Pavilion in Los Angeles. The ceremony telecast by NBC.

BEST PICTURE
- *The Sting*
American Graffiti
Cries and Whispers
The Exorcist
A Touch of Class

BEST DIRECTOR
- George Roy Hill, *The Sting*
Ingmar Bergman, *Cries and Whispers*
Bernardo Bertolucci, *Last Tango in Paris*
William Friedkin, *The Exorcist*
George Lucas, *American Graffiti*

BEST ACTOR
- Jack Lemmon, *Save the Tiger*
Marlon Brando, *Last Tango in Paris*
Jack Nicholson, *The Last Detail*
Al Pacino, *Serpico*
Robert Redford, *The Sting*

BEST ACTRESS
- Glenda Jackson, *A Touch of Class*
Ellen Burstyn, *The Exorcist*
Marsha Mason, *Cinderella Liberty*
Barbra Streisand, *The Way We Were*
Joanne Woodward, *Summer Wishes, Winter Dreams*

BEST SUPPORTING ACTOR
- John Houseman, *The Paper Chase*
Vincent Gardenia, *Bang the Drum Slowly*
Jack Gilford, *Save the Tiger*
Jason Miller, *The Exorcist*
Randy Quaid, *The Last Detail*

BEST SUPPORTING ACTRESS
- Tatum O'Neal, *Paper Moon*
Linda Blair, *The Exorcist*
Candy Clark, *American Graffiti*

Madeline Kahn, *Paper Moon*
Sylvia Sidney, *Summer Wishes, Winter Dreams*

BEST ORIGINAL SCREENPLAY
- David S. Ward, *The Sting*

Ingmar Bergman, *Cries and Whispers*
Melvin Frank, Jack Rose, *A Touch of Class*
William Huyck, Gloria Katz, George Lucas, *American Graffiti*
Steve Shagan, *Save the Tiger*

BEST ADAPTED SCREENPLAY
- William Peter Blatty, *The Exorcist*

James Bridges, *The Paper Chase*
Waldo Salt, Norman Wexler, *Serpico*
Alvin Sargent, *Paper Moon*
Robert Towne, *The Last Detail*

BEST SONG
- "The Way We Were," *The Way We Were*, Alan Bergman, Marilyn Bergman, Marvin Hamlisch

"All That Love Went to Waste," *A Touch of Class*, George Barrie, Sammy Cahn
"Live and Let Die," *Live and Let Die*, Linda McCartney, Paul McCartney
"Love," *Robin Hood*, George Bruns, Floyd Huddleston
"Nice to Be Around," *Cinderella Liberty*, John Williams, Paul Williams

BEST FOREIGN-LANGUAGE FILM
- *Day for Night* (France)

The House on Chelouche Street (Israel)
L'Invitation (Switzerland)
The Pedestrian (West Germany)
Turkish Delight (Netherlands)

Winners

BEST ART DIRECTION
- Henry Bumstead, James Payne, *The Sting*

BEST CINEMATOGRAPHY
- Sven Nykvist, *Cries and Whispers*

BEST COSTUME DESIGN
- Edith Head, *The Sting*

BEST DOCUMENTARY
(FEATURE)
- Kieth Merrill, *The Great American Cowboy*

(SHORT SUBJECT)
- Julian Krainin, Dewitt L. Sage, Jr., *Princeton: A Search for Answers*

BEST FILM EDITING
- William Reynolds, *The Sting*

BEST MUSIC
(ORIGINAL DRAMATIC SCORE)
- Marvin Hamlisch, *The Way We Were*

(SCORING: ORIGINAL SONG SCORE AND/OR ADAPTATION)
- Marvin Hamlisch, *The Sting*

SCIENTIFIC OR TECHNICAL AWARDS
Class II (Plaque)
- Joachim Gerb, Erich Kaestner, Arnold and Richter Co.; Magna-Tech Electronic Co,; William W. Valliant, PSC Technology; Howard G. Ott, Eastman Kodak; Gerry Diebold, Richmark Camera Service; Harold A. Scheib, Clifford H. Ellis, Roger Banks, Research Products Inc.

Class III (Certificate)
- Rosco Laboratories; Richard H. Vetter, Todd-AO Corp.

BEST SHORT SUBJECT
(ANIMATED)
- Frank Mouris, *Frank Film*

(LIVE ACTION)
- William Fertik, Allan Miller, *The Bolero*

BEST SOUND
- Robert Knudson, Chris Newman, *The Exorcist*

IRVING G. THALBERG MEMORIAL AWARD
- Lawrence Weingarten

JEAN HERSHOLT HUMANITARIAN AWARD
- Lew Wasserman

HONORARY AWARDS
- Henri Langlois
- Groucho Marx

SCREEN ACTORS GUILD

LIFETIME ACHIEVEMENT AWARD
- Martha Raye

· 1974 ·

Coppola vs. Coppola

The National Board of Review was the first to declare 1974 the year of Francis Ford Coppola. At Christmastime, the hot helmer released *The Godfather, Part II*, which *Variety* insisted was "far from being a spinoff followup to its 1972 progenitor, but an excellent epochal drama in its own right." Coppola had won the Palme d'Or at Cannes a few months earlier for *The Conversation*, which starred "Gene Hackman as a professional surveillance expert whose resurgent conscience involves him in murder and leads to self-destruction," said *Variety*. When the board declared the latter Best Picture, chairman Robert Giroux noted that its success "is eminently fitting in the year of Watergate."

But the two critics' orgs continued to hail foreign fare for Best Picture, although this year at least they chose different pictures.

The New York Film Critics Circle "met in an airless conference room in midtown Manhattan," reported the *Daily News*. "They sat in big maroon, leather chairs and then scribbled their votes on scraps of paper which were collected in someone's orange rain hat.

"It was all amazingly calm, considering the egos present. There was no bloodshed, no violent explosions of temper."

The winner of Best Picture and Best Director was *Amarcord*, "Federico Fellini's reminiscences of boyhood in an Italian village" in the 1930s, said *Variety*. Its triumph was unexpected, according to *The Village Voice*'s Andrew Sarris, who credited "the considerable influence of *New York Magazine*'s Judith Crist" upon her peers. Runners-up for both laurels were *Godfather II* and Ingmar Bergman's *Scenes from a Marriage*. When the National Society of Film Critics voted one week later, "it went berserk," according to *Amarcord* booster

Scenes from a Marriage set a record for most awards (four) from the national crix society: Best Picture, Director and Screenplay (Ingmar Bergman) and Best Actress (Liv Ullmann, here with Erland Josephson). *Scenes* was declared ineligible at the Oscars.

Crist. The society embraced *Scenes from a Marriage*, Bergman's 2-hour, 48-minute drama about doomed lovers that he edited down from a 5-hour production aired originally on Swedish TV. Both crix orgs hailed Bergman for Best Screenplay and star Liv Ullmann as Best Actress. When the society also cited Bibi Andersson as Best Supporting Actress, *Scenes* set a record for most kudos (four) in the group's history.

There was also agreement between the groups on Best Actor: Jack Nicholson was cited for *The Last Detail* (for which he lost the Oscar in 1973—the year the pic was released in Los Angeles—then won Best Actor at Cannes in spring 1974) as well as Roman Polanski's *Chinatown*, in which Nicholson portrayed "a sort of low-key Raymond Chandler hero on a murder manhunt," said *Variety*.

This year the circle upstaged the rival society in two ways. It not only jumped ahead and voted first, but, after being snubbed by the society last year when it offered to stage a joint awards ceremony, the

Gotham group ended up with the only gala when the society couldn't afford its own.

But several top winners ended up snubbing the circle fete. "Jack Nicholson, Federico Fellini and Ingmar Bergman sent their regrets," noted Sarris. "Francis Ford Coppola was the soul of tact at Sardi's. Here he was patently a loser to Fellini (for Best Director) and Bergman (for Best Screenplay), and he not only accepted Fellini's award from Faye Dunaway, but he paid tribute to Fellini and Bergman as his mentors." Liv Ullmann was one of the few winners present. Sarris reported that she was dressed "in a strikingly dowdy outfit with ethnic overtones, but she was gracefully natural nonetheless."

Coppola had been shut out the night before, too, at the Golden Globes, where he competed against himself with dual bids for directing and writing *Godfather II* and *The Conversation*. *Godfather II* claimed no awards despite six noms.

Chinatown led with the most bids (seven) and ended up with the most wins—four: Best Drama Picture, Best Director (Roman Polanski), Best Actor (Jack Nicholson) and Best Screenplay (Robert Towne). Producer Bob Evans accepted most of the statuettes. Standing in for Polanski, who was in Paris directing a play, he said "that Polanski had had some hard personal times in Hollywood, but (on Globes night) he would have been 'the happiest Polack in the whole world,' " reported *Variety*. Immediately after the ceremony, Evans telephoned Nicholson on the set of *One Flew over the Cuckoo's Nest* and informed him that his victory had reaped rousing cheers from the audience.

Also receiving cheers was the Best Drama Actress win by Gena Rowlands, who'd come in second place at the New York crix vote, but now triumphed over crix champ Liv Ullmann for her perf as an anguished housewife in *A Woman under the Influence*. Rowlands didn't respond to the Globes news at first. *Variety*'s Army Archerd explained: "Reason for Gena Rowlands' delayed reaction to her win—hubby John Cassavetes had earlier told presenter (pal) Richard Harris, 'No matter whose name is on the winning card—read Gena's name.' She thought it was part of the gag."

When screen vixen Raquel Welch (*The Three Musketeers*) beat revered thesp Helen Hayes (*Herbie Rides Again*) for Best Comedy/Musical Actress, she accepted the victory as overdue validation of her serious acting chops. The Associated Press reported: "Miss Welch stood with tears streaming down her face and gulped, 'I'm awfully happy—I guess you can see that. I've been waiting for this since *One Million Years B.C.*' She referred to the film which she achieved her initial success as a semi-clothed sex symbol." As she took her bow, reporters noted that Welch was dressed in a slinky gown with a split skirt and plunging neckline revealing ample cleavage.

> Mel Brooks won his first WGA plaque for *Blazing Saddles*.

The *L.A. Times* noted that "the night's most popular award" went to Best Supporting Actor Fred Astaire as a con man in *The Towering Inferno*, the $14 million, star-studded blockbuster about a skyscraper blaze that *Variety* lauded as "one of the greatest disaster pictures ever made." He accepted the statuette with a grin, saying, "Show business is so wonderful. You never know what's going to happen to you next."

The winner of Best Comedy or Musical Picture was the prison football drama *The Longest Yard*. *Variety* questioned its classification: "The assignment of *The Longest Yard* to the comedy/musical category struck many as unusual from the day of the nominations; to be sure, there were moments of humor, but the ambiguity lingers on."

Producer Albert Ruddy accepted the honor by saluting star Burt Reynolds as "a really brilliant actor, who is better than he thinks he is, which is saying something."

Reynolds lost the matchup for Best

■ 365 ■

Actor to Art Carney, whom *Variety* praised in *Harry and Tonto* for being "excellent as an old N.Y. widower, who's evicted by force from a building being torn down and takes a cross-country trek with his pet cat named Tonto."

Globe voters rallied behind *Scenes from a Marriage* as Best Foreign-Language Picture soon after the news broke that the Oscars declared it ineligible for awards since its unedited version had been shown on Swedish TV in 1973. Hollywood stars and directors protested the decision in a letter-writing campaign that noted that *The Sorrow and the Pity* had been permitted to compete last year after it aired previously on French TV, but Oscar leaders refused to acquiesce.

The 90-minute Golden Globes ceremony was broadcast live by 67 stations via Metromedia's special "barbed wire" network; 61 more stations aired a taped version the next day. Gala emcee John Davidson earned high marks from crix, but the *L.A. Times* noted that the stars were upstaged by "Benji, the darling dog, who came on in the arms of *Benji*'s composer Euel Box," who won Best Song for "I Feel Love."

Godfather II made up for its snub at the Globes by rebounding at the Directors Guild of America. *Variety* reported, "Coppola, beating the handicap of a double nomination—for *The Conversation* and *Godfather II*—won for the latter, as he did for the original *Godfather*. Coppola had said he expected Roman Polanski to win."

Coppola not only topped Polanski for *Chinatown,* but also Bob Fosse for *Lenny,* the biopic of the controversial nightclub comic Lenny Bruce, portrayed by Dustin Hoffman. Coppola's DGA victory made him the front-runner to snag the Oscar next and he was listed among the nominees announced three weeks prior to the directors' gala. *Variety* cited ominous competition ahead: "It is remembered that

in 1972, Coppola won the DGA award but lost the directing Oscar to Fosse for *Cabaret*—only the second time a DGA win did not concur with the related Oscar—and this year they are up again for the same Oscar."

The Hollywood ceremony was emceed smoothly by Carl Reiner and featured entertainment by the Jimmy Henderson Band and comedy troupe Ace Trucking Company. DGA prexy Robert Wise began the evening with a tribute to two past guild leaders who had recently died—George Marshall and George Stevens. "A minute of standing silence was invoked for them," *Variety* reported.

Five days before the Oscars, Coppola scored another victory at the Writers Guild of America when he and Mario Puzo won the palm for best adapted screenplay for *Godfather II* over *Lenny* scribe Julian Barry. Coppola lost the contest for best original screenplay, however, when *The Conversation* bowed to *Chinatown* by Robert Towne.

Back in 1968, Mel Brooks lost his only previous bid for a guild prize (*The Producers*), but now he was part of the writing team claiming kudos for the bawdy Western spoof *Blazing Saddles*. Mordecai Richler shared the accolade for best adapted comedy with Lionel Chetwynd for the screen version of Richler's novel *The Apprenticeship of Duddy Kravitz* about "a nervy Jewish kid on the make in the 1940s," said *Variety*.

Variety noted that "the surprise of the night" was the bestowal of a special prize to Preston Sturges, marking "the first time the guild had ever given a posthumous Laurel Award." The honor acknowledged the Hollywood gadfly for his 26 screenplays, which included such classics as *The Miracle of Morgan's Creek* and *The Palm Beach Story*; it was accepted by his actor son Solomon.

> # Sinatra blasted Dustin Hoffman for calling the Oscars "an obscene evening."

On Oscar night, bad weather hit, dampening more than Hollywood stars' spirits.

"Dragging their hems and furs through the rain-wet walkways, they tried at first to pretend the sun was shining, but there were enough raindrops to sag hairdos and tuxedos creases," *Variety* reported. "With his usual sense of satire, Jack Nicholson alighted from his limo in black beret and dark sunglasses, Riviera-ready."

The reason Nicholson was in such a sunny mood was that the three-time past loser was now the front-runner to take Best Actor. "Not since Ray Milland guzzled his way to an Oscar in *The Lost Weekend* has an actor been such a sure bet as Jack Nicholson," insisted *The New York Daily News.*

The *Los Angeles Herald Examiner* agreed, and claimed that Nicholson's *Chinatown* was the Best Picture favorite, too. *Godfather II* suffered a severe drawback as a rival, according to columnist James Bacon: "Academy voters may figure the original won enough Oscars a few years ago—so give it to someone else." Bacon's Best Actress pick: Globe and crix champ Gena Rowlands.

Chinatown and *Godfather II*, both Paramount pix, were tied for the most nominations (11). Coppola's *The Conversation* was also up for Best Picture, marking the first time that a helmer had two works nommed for the top prize since John Ford pulled off the feat in 1940. Coppola copped just one bid for Best Director, though—*Godfather II*.

The pundits may have been betting on *Chinatown,* but Oscarcast cohost Bob Hope revealed his choice during the opening monologue: "I think *Godfather II* has an excellent chance of winning. Neither Mr. Price nor Mr. Waterhouse has been heard from in days. I'm wearing a tuxedo with a bulletproof cummerbund. Who knows what will happen if Al Pacino doesn't win?"

> ## "What's the matter, Ryan? Won't Tatum let you hold her Oscar?"

Godfather II scored early victories for art direction plus best musical score. The latter prize went to Nino Rota and Francis Ford Coppola's father, Carmine, causing Francis to hop up and down with joy when he heard the news. Carmine Coppola was obviously just as excited when he raced to the stage to claim the honor, thanked his son, returned to his seat—and dropped the statuette, breaking it.

Since three *Godfather II* stars were up for Best Supporting Actor, many pundits believed that they would cancel each other out. The sentimental favorite was Globe champ Fred Astaire, but a shocker occurred when the golden boy went to Robert De Niro for his Italian-speaking role as *Godfather II*'s young Don Corleone. The only other time that a foreign-language perf had been Oscar honored was Sophia Loren's 1961 Best Actress triumph for *Two Women.* De Niro's trophy was accepted by Francis Ford Coppola, who said, "I'm happy one of my boys made it. I think Robert De Niro is an extraordinary actor and he's going to enrich films that will be made in the years to come."

New York film crix champ Valerie Perrine (*Lenny*) and Diane Ladd (*Alice Doesn't Live Here Anymore*) were the faves to take Best Supporting Actress, but another upset occurred when a past Oscar victor returned for more gold. Two-time past Best Actress winner Ingrid Bergman (*Gaslight, Anastasia*) was lauded as a nerve-racked missionary in the Agatha Christie whodunnit *Murder on the Orient Express.* In her acceptance speech, Bergman revealed that she'd been rooting for *Day for Night*'s Valentina Cortese. "Please forgive me, Valentina," Bergman said. "I didn't mean to (win)."

It looked as if Best Actor contender Dustin Hoffman (*Lenny*) didn't want to win, considering some of his recent comments that had infuriated many Oscar fans, especially Frank Sinatra, who, with Hope, was one of the fete's four emcees. At one point in the evening, Sinatra let loose. *Variety* reported, "Sinatra gave the back of his hand publicly to Dustin Hoffman, who on a locally syndicated low-budget TV show had bum-rapped the Oscars. Sinatra said, 'Contrary to what Mr. Hoffman thinks, it is not an "obscene evening," it is not "garish" and it is not "embarrassing".' "

Hoffman stayed home on Oscar night, just like two other Best Actor contenders: three-time nominee Al Pacino (*Godfather II*) and Albert Finney (*Murder on the Orient Express*). Globe champ Art Carney showed up—the only rival who pundits thought could upset Jack Nicholson.

Carney had won five Emmys as Best Supporting Actor while portraying Jackie Gleason's goofy second banana on *The Honeymooners*. When he won the Oscar in a lead race for a serious dramatic role, he was hailed by his peers with a standing ovation. At the podium, the 55-year-old thesp confessed that he originally didn't want to take the part of a 72-year-old widower, but his agent yelled at him, "Do it! You're old!"

The actress who portrayed Carney's daughter in *Harry and Tonto*, Ellen Burstyn, was nommed in the lead actress contest for *Alice Doesn't Live Here Anymore*, the tale of a widow who chucks her old home life and hits the road with her young son. Burstyn was currently starring on Broadway in *Same Time, Next Year* (for which she'd win a Tony Award one week after the Oscars), but her producers agreed to let her scoot to L.A. for the Academy Awards. She ended up staying in New York, however, convinced that Gena Rowlands or Faye Dunaway (*Chinatown*) would strike gold.

When she won, Burstyn's director Martin Scorsese accepted the trophy, read off a list of people she wanted thanked, then added, "and she asked me to thank myself."

Also missing on awards night, was Coppola's old Best Director nemesis Bob Fosse, who was in Philadelphia opening his new stage show, *Chicago*. It didn't matter; Coppola finally prevailed.

He said at the podium: "I almost won

Francis Ford Coppola's *The Godfather, Part II* (starring Al Pacino, above) squared off against the helmer's Cannes champ *The Conversation* at the Golden Globes, guild awards and Oscars. Most kudos preferred the Mafia sequel, which *Variety* hailed as "an excellent epochal drama."

this a couple of years ago for the first half of the same picture, but that's not why we did part two." He paused to acknowledge applause and added, "Thanks for giving my dad an Oscar."

Coppola was backstage talking with the press when his name was called as co-winner, along with Mario Puzo, of Best Adapted Screenplay. It was his third Oscar victory as a screenwriter, following previous triumphs for *Patton* and *The Godfather*.

But Coppola was soon back in the main auditorium to claim the biggest victory of the night—Best Picture—marking the first and only time that a sequel took the honor.

Godfather II ended up with six trophies in all. *Chinatown*, despite 11 noms, claimed only one: Best Original Screenplay. The winner of Best Foreign-Language Picture was the Gotham crix's best pic, *Amarcord*, giving Federico Fellini his fourth Oscar.

After the ceremony, winners celebrated at the Governors' Ball at the Beverly Hilton Hotel. *Variety*'s Army Archerd reported some of the highlights: "A pooped pooch Benji sat at his table and wagged his tail affectionately as stars stopped by to pet him." The pooch truly put on the dog, considering his film's theme tune had lost Best Song to "We May Never Love Like This Again" from *The Towering Inferno*.

When paparazzi asked Carmine Coppola

to pose for photos with his trophy, he panicked, since his was broken. Archerd noticed: "He borrowed Ingrid Bergman's (she beat out his daughter Talia in Best Supporting performance) for still pix even though there were five Oscars on Coppolas' Ball table."

Art Carney danced till the last strands of the Tex Beneke Band stilled and the busboys cleared the tables. At one point, Ryan O'Neal approached him and asked Carney, "Can I hold your Oscar for a minute?"

"What's the matter, Ryan?" Carney asked. "Won't Tatum let you hold hers?"

▪ 1974 ▪

NATIONAL BOARD OF REVIEW

Winners were announced on December 25, 1974.

BEST PICTURE
▪ *The Conversation*
Murder on the Orient Express
Chinatown
The Last Detail
Harry and Tonto
A Woman under the Influence
Thieves Like Us
Lenny
Daisy Miller
The Three Musketeers

BEST DIRECTOR
▪ Francis Ford Coppola, *The Conversation*

BEST ACTOR
Gene Hackman, *The Conversation*

BEST ACTRESS
Gena Rowlands, *A Woman under the Influence*

BEST SUPPORTING ACTOR
▪ Holger Löwenadler, *Lacombe Lucien*

BEST SUPPORTING ACTRESS
▪ Valerie Perrine, *Lenny*

BEST FOREIGN FILM
▪ *Amarcord* (Italy)
Lacombe, Lucien (France)
Scenes from a Marriage (Sweden)
The Phantom of Liberty (France)
The Pedestrian (Federal Republic of Germany)

SPECIAL CITATIONS
▪ Special effects in *The Golden Voyage of Sinbad, Earthquake* and *The Towering Inferno*
▪ The film industry for more minority casting
▪ Robert G. Youngson

NEW YORK FILM CRITICS CIRCLE

Winners were announced on December 30, 1974. Awards were presented on January 26, 1975, at Sardi's restaurant in New York.

BEST PICTURE
▪ *Amarcord*

BEST DIRECTOR
▪ Federico Fellini, *Amarcord*

BEST ACTOR
▪ Jack Nicholson, *Chinatown, The Last Detail*

BEST ACTRESS
▪ Liv Ullmann, *Scenes from a Marriage*

BEST SUPPORTING ACTOR
▪ Charles Boyer, *Stavisky*

BEST SUPPORTING ACTRESS
▪ Valerie Perrine, *Lenny*

BEST SCREENPLAY
▪ Ingmar Bergman, *Scenes from a Marriage*

NATIONAL SOCIETY OF FILM CRITICS

Winners were announced on January 5, 1975. No awards ceremony was held.

BEST PICTURE
- *Scenes from a Marriage*

BEST DIRECTOR
- Francis Ford Coppola, *The Godfather, Part II; The Conversation*

BEST ACTOR
- Jack Nicholson, *Chinatown, The Last Detail*

BEST ACTRESS
- Liv Ullmann, *Scenes from a Marriage*

BEST SUPPORTING ACTOR
- Holger Löwenadler, *Lacombe Lucien*

BEST SUPPORTING ACTRESS
- Bibi Andersson, *Scenes from a Marriage*

BEST SCREENPLAY
- Ingmar Bergman, *Scenes from a Marriage*

BEST CINEMATOGRAPHY
- Gordon Willis, *The Godfather, Part II; Parallax View*

SPECIAL AWARD
- Jean Renoir

GOLDEN GLOBES

Nominations were announced on January 9, 1975. Awards were presented on January 25 at the Beverly Hilton Hotel in Los Angeles. The ceremony was telecast by Metromedia.

BEST DRAMA PICTURE
- *Chinatown*
  The Conversation
  Earthquake
  The Godfather, Part II
  A Woman under the Influence

Jack Nicholson (left) was on the set of *Cuckoo's Nest* when he got word of *Chinatown's* Golden Globe sweep, which included his trophy for Best Drama Actor. Both the star and pic were considered "sure bets" at the Oscars next.

BEST COMEDY OR MUSICAL PICTURE
- *The Longest Yard*
  The Front Page
  Harry and Tonto
  The Little Prince
  The Three Musketeers

BEST DIRECTOR
- Roman Polanski, *Chinatown*
  John Cassavetes, *A Woman under the Influence*
  Francis Ford Coppola, *The Conversation*
  Francis Ford Coppola, *The Godfather, Part II*
  Bob Fosse, *Lenny*

BEST ACTOR, DRAMA
- Jack Nicholson, *Chinatown*
  James Caan, *The Gambler*
  Gene Hackman, *The Conversation*
  Dustin Hoffman, *Lenny*
  Al Pacino, *The Godfather, Part II*

BEST ACTRESS, DRAMA
- Gena Rowlands, *A Woman under the Influence*
  Ellen Burstyn, *Alice Doesn't Live Here Anymore*
  Faye Dunaway, *Chinatown*
  Valerie Perrine, *Lenny*
  Liv Ullmann, *Scenes from a Marriage*

BEST ACTOR, COMEDY OR MUSICAL
- Art Carney, *Harry and Tonto*

James Earl Jones, *Claudine*

Jack Lemmon, *The Front Page*

Walter Matthau, *The Front Page*

Burt Reynolds, *The Longest Yard*

BEST ACTRESS, COMEDY OR MUSICAL
- Raquel Welch, *The Three Musketeers*

Lucille Ball, *Mame*

Diahann Carroll, *Claudine*

Helen Hayes, *Herbie Rides Again*

Cloris Leachman, *Young Frankenstein*

BEST SUPPORTING ACTOR
- Fred Astaire, *The Towering Inferno*

Eddie Albert, *The Longest Yard*

Bruce Dern, *The Great Gatsby*

John Huston, *Chinatown*

Sam Waterston, *The Great Gatsby*

BEST SUPPORTING ACTRESS
- Karen Black, *The Great Gatsby*

Beatrice Arthur, *Mame*

Jennifer Jones, *The Towering Inferno*

Madeline Kahn, *Young Frankenstein*

Diane Ladd, *Alice Doesn't Live Here Anymore*

MOST PROMISING NEWCOMER—MALE
- Joseph Bottoms, *The Dove*

Jim Hampton, *The Longest Yard*

Lee Strasberg, *The Godfather, Part II*

Steven Warner, *The Little Prince*

Sam Waterston, *The Great Gatsby*

MOST PROMISING NEWCOMER—FEMALE
- Susan Flannery, *The Towering Inferno*

Julie Gholson, *Where the Lilies Bloom*

Valerie Harper, *Freebie and the Bean*

Helen Reddy, *Airport 1975*

Ann Turkel, *99 and 44/100 Dead*

BEST SCREENPLAY
- Robert Towne, *Chinatown*

John Cassavetes, *A Woman under the Influence*

Francis Ford Coppola, Mario Puzo, *The Godfather, Part II*

Francis Ford Coppola, *The Conversation*

Stirling Silliphant, *The Towering Inferno*

BEST SONG
- "I Feel Love," *Benji*, Euel Box, Betty Box

"I Never Met a Rose," *The Little Prince*, Frederick Loewe, Alan Jay Lerner

"On and On," *Claudine,* Curtis Mayfield

"Sail the Summer Winds," *The Dove*, John Barry

"We May Never Love Like This Again," *The Towering Inferno*, Joel Hirschhorn, Al Kasha

BEST FOREIGN FILM
- *Scenes from a Marriage* (Sweden)

Amarcord (Italy)

The Apprenticeship of Duddy Kravitz (Canada)

Lacombe Lucien (France)

The Mad Adventures of "Rabbi" Jacob (France)

Winners

BEST ORIGINAL SCORE
- Alan Jay Lerner, Frederick Loewe, *The Little Prince*

WORLD FILM FAVORITES
- Robert Redford
- Barbra Streisand

CECIL B. DEMILLE AWARD
- Hal B. Wallis

DIRECTORS GUILD OF AMERICA

The award for Best Director was presented on March 15, 1975, at the Beverly Hilton Hotel in Los Angeles and the Hilton Hotel in New York.

BEST DIRECTOR
- Francis Ford Coppola, *The Godfather, Part II*

Francis Ford Coppola, *The Conversation*

Bob Fosse, *Lenny*

Sidney Lumet, *Murder on the Orient Express*

Roman Polanski, *Chinatown*

HONORARY LIFETIME MEMBER
- Charles Chaplin

WRITERS GUILD OF AMERICA

Awards were presented on April 3, 1975, at the Beverly Hilton Hotel in Los Angeles and the Time-Life building in New York.

BEST DRAMA WRITTEN DIRECTLY FOR THE SCREEN
- *Chinatown*, Robert Towne

Alice Doesn't Live Here Anymore, Robert Getchell

The Conversation, Francis Ford Coppola

Harry and Tonto, Paul Mazursky, Josh Greenfield

A Woman under the Influence, John Cassevetes

BEST DRAMA ADAPTED FROM ANOTHER MEDIUM
- *The Godfather, Part II*, Francis Ford Coppola, Mario Puzo, based on the novel *The Godfather* by Mario Puzo

Conrack, Irving Ravetch, Harriet Frank, Jr., based on the novel *The Water Is Wide* by Pat Conroy

Lenny, Julian Barry, based on his play

The Parallax View, David Giler, Lorenzo Semple, Jr., based on the novel by Loren Singer

The Taking of Pelham, One, Two, Three, Peter Stone, based on the novel by John Godey

BEST COMEDY WRITTEN DIRECTLY FOR THE SCREEN
- *Blazing Saddles*, Andrew Bergman, Mel Brooks, Norman Steinberg, Richard Pryor, Alan Uger

California Split, Joseph Walsh

Claudine, Tina Pine, Lester Pine

Phantom of the Paradise, Brian DePalma

Sugarland Express, Hal Barwood, Matthew Robbins, Steven Spielberg

BEST COMEDY ADAPTED FROM ANOTHER MEDIUM
- *The Apprenticeship of Duddy Kravitz*, Mordecai Richler, Lionel Chetwynd, based on the novel by Mordecai Richler

The Front Page, Billy Wilder, I.A.L. Diamond, based on the play by Ben Hecht and Charles MacArthur

Young Frankenstein, Gene Wilder, Mel Brooks, based on the novella *Frankenstein* by Mary Shelley

LAUREL AWARD
- Preston Sturges (posthumous)

VALENTINE DAVIES AWARD
- Fay Kanin

MORGAN COX AWARD
- Edmund H. North

ACADEMY AWARDS

Nominations were announced on February 24, 1975. Awards were presented on April 8 at the Dorothy Chandler Pavilion in Los Angeles. The ceremony was telecast by NBC.

BEST PICTURE
- *The Godfather, Part II*

Chinatown

The Conversation

Lenny

The Towering Inferno

BEST DIRECTOR
- Francis Ford Coppola, *The Godfather, Part II*

John Cassavetes, *A Woman under the Influence*

Bob Fosse, *Lenny*

Roman Polanski, *Chinatown*

François Truffaut, *Day for Night*

BEST ACTOR
- Art Carney, *Harry and Tonto*

Albert Finney, *Murder on the Orient Express*

Dustin Hoffman, *Lenny*

Jack Nicholson, *Chinatown*

Al Pacino, *The Godfather, Part II*

BEST ACTRESS
- Ellen Burstyn, *Alice Doesn't Live Here Anymore*

Diahann Carroll, *Claudine*

Faye Dunaway, *Chinatown*
Valerie Perrine, *Lenny*
Gena Rowlands, *A Woman under the Influence*

BEST SUPPORTING ACTOR
- Robert De Niro, *The Godfather, Part II*
Fred Astaire, *The Towering Inferno*
Jeff Bridges, *Thunderbolt and Lightfoot*
Michael V. Gazzo, *The Godfather, Part II*
Lee Strasberg, *The Godfather, Part II*

BEST SUPPORTING ACTRESS
- Ingrid Bergman, *Murder on the Orient Express*
Valentina Cortese, *Day for Night*
Madeline Kahn, *Blazing Saddles*
Diane Ladd, *Alice Doesn't Live Here Anymore*
Talia Shire, *The Godfather, Part II*

BEST ORIGINAL SCREENPLAY
- Robert Towne, *Chinatown*
Francis Ford Coppola, *The Conversation*
Robert Getchell, *Alice Doesn't Live Here Anymore*
Josh Greenfeld, Paul Mazursky, *Harry and Tonto*
Jean-Louis Richard, Suzanne Schiffman, François Truffaut, *Day for Night*

BEST ADAPTED SCREENPLAY
- Francis Ford Coppola, Mario Puzo, *The Godfather, Part II*
Julian Barry, *Lenny*
Mel Brooks, Gene Wilder, *Young Frankenstein*
Lionel Chetwynd, Mordecai Richler, *The Apprenticeship of Duddy Kravitz*
Paul Dehn, *Murder on the Orient Express*

BEST SONG
- "We May Never Love Like This Again," *The Towering Inferno*, Joel Hirschhorn, Al Kasha
"Benji's Theme (I Feel Love)," *Benji*, Euel Box, Betty Box
"Blazing Saddles," *Blazing Saddles*, Mel Brooks, John Morris
"Little Prince," *The Little Prince*, Alan Jay Lerner, Frederick Loewe
"Wherever Love Takes Me," *Gold*, Elmer Bernstein, Don Black

BEST FOREIGN-LANGUAGE FILM
- *Amarcord* (Italy)
Cats' Play (Hungary)
The Deluge (Poland)
Lacombe Lucien (France)
The Truce (Argentina)

Winners

BEST ART DIRECTION
- Angelo Graham, Dean Tavoularis, George R. Nelson, *The Godfather, Part II*

BEST CINEMATOGRAPHY
- Joseph Biroc, Fred Koenekamp, *The Towering Inferno*

BEST COSTUME DESIGN
- Theoni V. Aldredge, *The Great Gatsby*

BEST DOCUMENTARY
(FEATURE)
- Peter Davis, Bert Schneider, *Hearts and Minds*
(SHORT SUBJECT)
- Robin Lehman, *Don't*

BEST FILM EDITING
- Carl Kress, Harold F. Kress, *The Towering Inferno*

BEST MUSIC
(ORIGINAL DRAMATIC SCORE)
- Carmine Coppola, Nino Rota, *The Godfather, Part II*
(SCORING: ORIGINAL SONG SCORE AND/OR ADAPTATION)
- Nelson Riddle, *The Great Gatsby*

SCIENTIFIC OR TECHNICAL AWARDS
Class II (Plaque)
- Joseph D. Kelly, Glen Glenn Sound; Burbank Studio Sound Department; Quad-Eight Sound Corp.; Waldon O. Watson, Richard J. Stumpf, Robert J. Leonard, Universal City Studios Sound Department
Class III (Certificate)
- Louis Ami, Universal City Studios; Elemack Co.

BEST SHORT FILM

(ANIMATED)
- *Closed Mondays*

(LIVE ACTION)
- *One-Eyed Men Are Kings*

BEST SOUND

- Melvin Metcalfe, Sr., Ronald Pierce,
  Earthquake

SPECIAL ACHIEVEMENT AWARD (VISUAL EFFECTS)

- *Earthquake*
- Frank Brendel

- Glen Robinson
- Albert Whitlock

JEAN HERSHOLT HUMANITARIAN AWARD

- Arthur B. Krim

HONORARY AWARDS

- Howard Hawks
- Jean Renoir

SCREEN ACTORS GUILD

LIFETIME ACHIEVEMENT AWARD

- Walter Pidgeon

· 1975 ·

New L.A. Crix Group Goes Cuckoo

Gotham-based critics had recently ventured so far "downtown" with their award picks that some observers believed they'd lost their way—and possibly their minds. Neither the New York Film Critics Circle nor the National Society of Film Critics had chosen a mainstream American movie as Best Picture in several years, apparently concluding that foreign fare is better, absurdism is art, symbolism is required and dialogue is better read than heard.

The crix out in America's western chutzpah capital, meantime, decided to form a rival org that was closer to Hollywood in both geography and taste. Founded by *Free Press* critic Ruth Batchelor and *L.A. Times* reviewer Charles Champlin, the new Los Angeles Film Critics Association was formed because "the film capital of the world deserves to have awards from its own film critics," said Batchelor.

"The industry has been out here for 50 years and yet this is the first time the critics have united," she told the *L.A. Times*. Batchelor made a distinction between her org and the one in New York: "The critics there are only in print, but here we represent radio and television as well as newspapers, trade papers and magazines."

The crix voted on February 13 and gathered 11 days later at Pips, a Beverly Hills backgammon club, to announce their anointed. Due to a vote deadlock that Batchelor called "impossible to break," there was a tie for Best Picture.

One champ was *One Flew over the Cuckoo's Nest*, starring Jack Nicholson as a mental ward antihero ("either an illness faker or a free spirit," posited *Variety*) who leads his fellow patients in revolts against an iron-willed nurse, played by Louise Fletcher.

The co-winner was *Dog Day Afternoon*,

Dog Day Afternoon, starring Al Pacino as a crazed bank robber, tied *One Flew Over the Cuckoo's Nest* for the first Best Picture prize bestowed by the new Los Angeles Film Critics Association.

which *Variety* praised as "filmmaking at its best," starring Al Pacino as a desperate man who robs a bank so he can finance his boyfriend's sex-change operation. Pacino and helmer Sidney Lumet were named the crix's first Best Actor and Director.

Best Actress was Florinda Bolkan as "the heroine in Vittorio de Sica's portrait of escape from industrial life in *A Brief Vacation*," said the *L.A. Times*.

The choices were mostly in contrast to the typical picks of the East Coast crix, who surprised many observers this year by opting for a Yankee film—although, keeping with past preference, an indie with an arty feel. The two groups also opted for most of the same winners, just as they did two years ago.

Their mutual choice for Best Picture and Director was *Nashville* by Robert Altman, which tracked the lives of 24 characters over several days in the U.S. capital city of country music. Its success was credited to the Paulettes—the faithful disciples of *The New Yorker*'s Pauline Kael within the crix orgs. Kael got so excited when she saw a rough cut of *Nashville* and read an advance script that she published a review long before its premiere so she could drum up popular support, then she lobbied heavily on its behalf among her peers.

The National Society of Film Critics regained the lead over the Gotham crix and voted earlier, endorsing Jack Nicholson (*Cuckoo's Nest*) as Best Actor, just as both groups had done last year. When the Gotham crix voted this year, Nicholson topped himself, pulling 41 points for *Cuckoo's Nest* and 31 for *The Passenger*, with Al Pacino following in third place with 26.

In the race for the actress laurels, Florinda Bolkan placed behind Isabelle Adjani as an obsessed lover in François Truffaut's *The Story of Adele H*. The crix also agreed on Best Supporting Actress: Lily Tomlin as a gospel singer in *Nashville*.

But the two groups split on Best Supporting Actor, with the society siding with Henry Gibson as a tantrum-throwing crooner in *Nashville* and the Gotham circle picking Alan Arkin as a helmer of Hollywood westerns in the comedy *Hearts of the West*. Although the circle didn't give Truffaut its screenplay prize when it hailed his *Day for Night* as Best Picture two years ago, it gave him the prize this year for *Adele H*. The society made a surprise pick for Best Screenplay: *Shampoo* by Robert Towne and Warren Beatty.

Variety reported, "The circle also voted a resolution protesting the imprisonment of Soviet director Sergei Paradjanov (*Shadows of Our Forgotten Ancestors*) on charges of 'homosexualism.' The director had been sentenced to five years in a hard-labor camp."

Once again the society couldn't afford

The "Paulettes" rigged two Best Picture victories for *Nashville*.

an awards ceremony. The New York Film Critics Circle's bash went on as usual, with Andrew Sarris of *The Village Voice* calling it "the funniest and friendliest prize-giving jamboree I have ever witnessed"—even without the presence of that affable showbiz clown Jack Nicholson, whose plaque for Best Actor was accepted by Francis Ford Coppola.

Isabelle Adjani was present to claim her Best Actress honor, which was bestowed by Lillian Gish, who called attention to the victor's beauty, saying, "The camera fell in love with that face and what camera wouldn't?"

Sarris noted that Adjani "conveyed a torrential intelligence" in her acceptance speech, with "ideas and insights and impressions tumbling over each other in their haste to find expression." Afterward, when reporters asked Adjani if she thought her victory would help her win an Oscar next, she snapped back, "I care about my work and I'm not interested in becoming part of the Hollywood package!"

Sarris observed that Tomlin "never took off comically" as she accepted her thesp laurels. "She left us instead with a volatile mixture of wryness and shyness. She was certainly not in the mood to tell jokes for her supper."

Altman received his kudos for Best Picture and Director from two literary lions, E. L. Doctorow and Kurt Vonnegut, Jr. Sarris noted, "Altman ended the proceedings by congratulating us as critics for acting as a countervailing force to the bottom-line tendencies of the Hollywood Oscars and the Bankable Star System."

The National Board of Review agreed on the acting choices of Nicholson and Adjani—and also, in part, with the crix's pick for top pic. Even though board chairman Robert Giroux told *Variety* that 1975 was "a nearly disastrous year for quality," his group, like the Los Angeles crix org, named two Best Pictures. In the board's case, they were *Nashville* and *Barry Lyndon*, the latter of which *Variety* described as Stanley Kubrick's "most elegant and handsome adaptation" of William Makepeace Thackeray's 19th-century novel.

When the Golden Globe nominations came out, *Nashville* led with nine bids, setting a new record for the most in the awards history. On awards night, however, "The Globe dinner was clearly the time of the *Cuckoo*," *Variety* announced. It would end up tying the record for most victories (five).

Cuckoo's Nest went undefeated, claiming kudos for Best Drama Picture, Best Director (Milos Forman) and Best Screenplay. When it reaped the prizes for lead actors, too, it marked the first time that one film swept all top categories. Costar Brad Dourif also won the accolade for Best Movie Debut for portraying a man with a fatal mother's complex. (According to Globe scorekeeping, the rookie's prize is not credited to a film's tally.)

Jack Nicholson was away filming *Missouri Breaks,* but Best Actress Louise Fletcher was on hand to grasp her gold. Prior to *Cuckoo's Nest*, she hadn't worked for 10 years while raising two sons. Now that she was getting star treatment, she was overwhelmed. "I'd never been to a big Hollywood party, awards show or anything else until the foreign press awards," she said, marveling at how she now got "all expenses paid, the best hotels, restaurants—the works!"

When producer Michael Douglas accepted the top prize, he revealed the struggle behind getting the pic made. *Variety* reported, "Kirk Douglas, who starred in the 1963 Broadway production, tried for a dozen years to get it filmed, eventually yielding to his son Michael."

Neil Simon's laffer about sparring old vaudeville partners, *The Sunshine Boys*, claimed three kudos, including the top Globe as Best Comedy or Musical Picture. George Burns was nommed for his first

"Every film finished is a miracle," said DGA champ Milos Forman.

screen appearance in 36 years, but he lost Best Actor to costar Walter Matthau. *Variety* called the pair "the hit of the evening" when Burns followed Matthau to the stage and told the audience, "I just came up here to help him up, that's all." They received a standing ovation. Richard Benjamin won Best Supporting Actor for portraying the duo's peace-keeping agent/nephew.

Backstage, reporters asked Matthau if he thought the Globe victory would help his Oscar chances. "I don't think my shtick is strong enough for the academy," he replied. "This is going to be Jack Nicholson's year."

Variety said that Ann-Margret gave "the most enthusiastic and heart-felt speech of the evening" when she was named Best Comedy or Musical Actress for portraying the blind pinball wizard's mother in *Tommy*. She cried as she reminded the audience how she won a Globe as a Most Promising Newcomer in 1961, then reaped another for *Carnal Knowledge* in 1971.

Nashville, despite nine bids, claimed only one victory: Best Song for Keith Carradine's "I'm Easy."

"Steve Lawrence and Eydie Gormé hosted the televised part of the program," *Variety* reported. "The entire cast of *Shampoo* pulled out of the show two hours before air time, which left the Hollywood Foreign Press Association scrambling to fill their spots as presenters and their ringside table—directly in front of the camera." A bomb threat was called into the Beverly Hilton Hotel 20 minutes after the TV show began, but HFPA leaders refused to take it seriously, since they had received lots of prank calls earlier, including one that falsely reported that awards presenter Kate Jackson had been killed in a car crash.

Nashville continued its losing streak at the directors' guild kudos when Robert Altman lost to *Cuckoo's Nest*'s Milos Forman. *Variety* noted that he "concluded his brief thanks with an observation that anyone connected with film-making can readily dig: 'Every film finished is a miracle.' "

The Czechoslovakia-born helmer Forman told columnist Army Archerd that he was amazed by his victory: "I always heard that Hollywood was very chauvinistic—and full of surprises."

At the writers' guild honors, *Nashville*'s Joan Tewkesbury lost to *Dog Day Afternoon* scribe Frank Pierson in the race for best original drama, while the trophy for adapted drama was snagged by *Cuckoo's Nest*'s Lawrence Hauben and Bo Goldman. Neil Simon beat himself in the match-up for adapted comedies when *The Sunshine Boys* topped *The Prisoner of Second Avenue*, bringing Simon his third career prize from the guild.

After winning in the drama categories last year for *Chinatown*, Robert Towne was now hailed in the laffer lineup with co-writer Warren Beatty for *Shampoo*.

Gore Vidal stepped in as the guest speaker at the Los Angeles fete when Truman Capote canceled at the last minute, claiming illness. Alan King went on, as scheduled, in New York. A dinner dance followed the awards presentations instead of the traditional satirical stage skits.

Three days later, at the Oscars, there was no mystery about many of the top races. Voters had already shown that they were crazy about *Cuckoo's Nest*, giving it the most nominations—nine—followed by seven for *Barry Lyndon* and six for *Dog Day Afternoon*.

Most media predicted that *Cuckoo's Nest* would have a big night, at least sweeping the top prizes for Best Actor, Director and Picture.

As star Jack Nicholson arrived, it was clear that he had the fans' endorsement, too. They roared and cheered as he marched down the red carpet, and *Variety* observed that he "received a bouquet of tiny roses tossed from the crowd."

Cuckoo's Nest took one early prize—

best adapted screenplay—but then hit a snag in the race for Best Supporting Actor when Brad Dourif lost.

But the winner was no surprise. It turned out to be the sentimental favorite—80-year-old George Burns, who'd been placed in the supporting category by the academy and his studio, United Artists, after he lost to costar Matthau at the Golden Globes in the lead race.

As he clutched his Oscar, Burns told the crowd that this was his first film since 1939. "This is so exciting," he added. "I've decided to keep making one movie every 36 years. You get to be new again."

There was no front-runner in the race for Best Supporting Actress, so it was no surprise when Lee Grant prevailed for her role as a bored Beverly Hills housewife who has a fling with her hairdresser in *Shampoo*. What was a surprise was the outfit she wore to the podium: an old wedding dress. "It was an antique, picked up in a second-hand store, because she 'wanted to wear something that had roots,' " *Variety* reported. "Grant was a popular favorite, particularly because of sympathy over the cancellation of her *Fay* vidseries. She seemed to be alluding to the latter in her acceptance speech, thanking the artistic community for 'sustaining me through wins and losses.' "

There was no standout favorite for Best Actress either. *Cuckoo's Nest* was repped by Louise Fletcher, but some pundits claimed she really belonged in the supporting lineup and was only pushed up into the lead race because of what *Variety* called "a dearth of Hollywood candidates." Her strongest competish seemed to be crix pick Isabelle Adjani (*The Story of Adele H.*) and Globe champ Ann-Margret (*Tommy*).

When Fletcher won, *Variety* reported that her "acceptance speech was the emotional climax of the evening" as she used sign language to address her deaf parents watching on TV at home in Birmingham,

Oscar voters snubbed *Jaws* director Steven Spielberg.

Alabama. "I want to thank you for teaching me to have a dream," she said, crying. "You are seeing my dream come true."

There was no mystery about who'd win Best Actor, even though Jack Nicholson competed, for the third year in a row, against a thesp also considered overdue for the prize—Al Pacino (*Dog Day Afternoon*).

When he finally prevailed, *Variety* noted that the audience "jumped to its feet."

"I guess this proves that there are as many nuts in the academy as anywhere else," he said and then thanked his agent "who, about ten years ago, advised me that I had no business being an actor."

There was "one surprise among the nominees" for Best Director, *Variety* had noted when the contenders were announced weeks earlier: Federico Fellini, who was up for *Amarcord*, which won Best Foreign Film last year. "Steven Spielberg (*Jaws*) was the only director of a Best Picture contender who wasn't personally nominated," the paper added. "Only Forman is a first-time nominee."

In his acceptance speech on Oscar night, Forman "extended the compliment of being among such high-powered nominees as Sidney Lumet, Federico Fellini, Robert Altman and Stanley Kubrick," *Variety* added. He told the audience the secret of how he beat them: "I spent more time in mental institutions than the others."

When *Cuckoo's Nest* won Best Picture, producer Michael Douglas informed the audience that his pic was the first to sweep all top five categories of Best Actor, Actress, Director, Screenplay and Picture since *It Happened One Night*.

Walter Matthau (right) beat George Burns (left) for Best Actor at the Globes where *The Sunshine Boys* won best comedy pic, but Burns rallied at the Oscars in the supporting race.

Backstage later, Michael Douglas told *Variety*, "The best thing that could happen now is that some studio heads go back and reread some of the scripts they've turned down."

Douglas celebrated afterward at the Governors Ball, then headed over to La Scala restaurant, where he'd rented a private room for his cast and crew. Later, he invited friends and colleagues—including *Nashville*'s losing helmer Robert Altman—over to his house for a private party that finally ended at 4 A.M.

"I didn't want it to ever end," Douglas told Army Archerd.

The next day the writer who'd penned the novel that *Cuckoo's Nest* was based on, Ken Kesey, thought he had little reason to celebrate. He pointed out to reporters that none of the picture's winners mentioned him in their acceptance speeches.

▪ 1975 ▪

NATIONAL BOARD OF REVIEW

Winners were announced on December 23, 1975.

BEST PICTURE (TIE)
- *Nashville*
- *Barry Lyndon*

Conduct Unbecoming
One Flew over the Cuckoo's Nest
Lies My Father Told Me
Dog Day Afternoon
The Day of the Locust
The Passenger
Hearts of the West
Farewell, My Lovely
Alice Doesn't Live Here Anymore

BEST DIRECTOR (TIE)

- Robert Altman, *Nashville*
- Stanley Kubrick, *Barry Lyndon*

BEST ACTOR

- Jack Nicholson, *One Flew over the Cuckoo's Nest*

BEST ACTRESS

- Isabelle Adjani, *The Story of Adele H.*

BEST SUPPORTING ACTOR

- Charles Durning, *Dog Day Afternoon*

BEST SUPPORTING ACTRESS

- Ronee Blakley, *Nashville*

BEST FOREIGN FILM

- *The Story of Adele H.* (France)
A Brief Vacation (Italy)
Special Section (France)
Stavisky (France)
Swept Away (Italy)

SPECIAL CITATION

- *The Magic Flute*

NATIONAL SOCIETY OF FILM CRITICS

Winners were announced on December 29, 1975. No awards ceremony was held.

BEST PICTURE

- *Nashville*

BEST DIRECTOR

- Robert Altman, *Nashville*

BEST ACTOR

- Jack Nicholson, *One Flew over the Cuckoo's Nest*

BEST ACTRESS

- Isabelle Adjani, *The Story of Adele H.*

BEST SUPPORTING ACTOR

- Henry Gibson, *Nashville*

BEST SUPPORTING ACTRESS

- Lily Tomlin, *Nashville*

BEST SCREENPLAY

- Robert Towne, Warren Beatty, *Shampoo*

BEST CINEMATOGRAPHY

- John Alcott, *Barry Lyndon*

SPECIAL AWARD

- *The Magic Flute*

NEW YORK FILM CRITICS CIRCLE

Winners were announced on December 30, 1975. Awards were presented on January 25, 1976, at Sardi's restaurant in New York.

BEST PICTURE

- *Nashville*

BEST DIRECTOR

- Robert Altman, *Nashville*

BEST ACTOR

- Jack Nicholson, *One Flew over the Cuckoo's Nest*

BEST ACTRESS

- Isabelle Adjani, *The Story of Adele H.*

BEST SUPPORTING ACTOR

- Alan Arkin, *Hearts of the West*

BEST SUPPORTING ACTRESS

- Lily Tomlin, *Nashville*

BEST SCREENPLAY

- François Truffaut, Jean Gruault, Suzanne Schiffman, *The Story of Adele H.*

GOLDEN GLOBES

Nominations were announced on January 6, 1976. Awards were presented on January 24 at the Beverly Hilton Hotel in Los Angeles. The ceremony was telecast by Metromedia.

BEST DRAMA PICTURE

- *One Flew over the Cuckoo's Nest*
Barry Lyndon
Dog Day Afternoon
Jaws
Nashville

BEST COMEDY OR MUSICAL PICTURE

- ▪ *The Sunshine Boys*
- *Funny Lady*
- *The Return of the Pink Panther*
- *Shampoo*
- *Tommy*

BEST DIRECTOR

- ▪ Milos Forman, *One Flew over the Cuckoo's Nest*
- Robert Altman, *Nashville*
- Stanley Kubrick, *Barry Lyndon*
- Sidney Lumet, *Dog Day Afternoon*
- Steven Spielberg, *Jaws*

BEST ACTOR, DRAMA

- ▪ Jack Nicholson, *One Flew over the Cuckoo's Nest*
- Gene Hackman, *French Connection II*
- Al Pacino, *Dog Day Afternoon*
- Maximilian Schell, *The Man in the Glass Booth*
- James Whitmore, *Give 'Em Hell, Harry!*

BEST ACTRESS, DRAMA

- ▪ Louise Fletcher, *One Flew over the Cuckoo's Nest*
- Karen Black, *The Day of the Locust*
- Faye Dunaway, *Three Days of the Condor*
- Marilyn Hassett, *The Other Side of the Mountain*
- Glenda Jackson, *Hedda*

BEST ACTOR, COMEDY OR MUSICAL

- ▪ Walter Matthau, *The Sunshine Boys*
- Warren Beatty, *Shampoo*
- George Burns, *The Sunshine Boys*
- James Caan, *Funny Lady*
- Peter Sellers, *The Return of the Pink Panther*

BEST ACTRESS, COMEDY OR MUSICAL

- ▪ Ann-Margret, *Tommy*
- Julie Christie, *Shampoo*
- Goldie Hawn, *Shampoo*
- Liza Minnelli, *Lucky Lady*
- Barbra Streisand, *Funny Lady*

Cuckoo's Nest became the first film to sweep all the top Golden Globes and the second to snag all the leading Oscars. The latter sweep proved there were "nuts" in the academy, said Best Actor Jack Nicholson.

BEST SUPPORTING ACTOR

- ▪ Richard Benjamin, *The Sunshine Boys*
- John Cazale, *Dog Day Afternoon*
- Charles Durning, *Dog Day Afternoon*
- Henry Gibson, *Nashville*
- Burgess Meredith, *The Day of the Locust*

BEST SUPPORTING ACTRESS

- ▪ Brenda Vaccaro, *Once Is Not Enough*
- Ronee Blakley, *Nashville*
- Geraldine Chaplin, *Nashville*
- Lee Grant, *Shampoo*
- Barbara Harris, *Nashville*
- Lily Tomlin, *Nashville*

BEST ACTING DEBUT—MALE

- ▪ Brad Dourif, *One Flew over the Cuckoo's Nest*
- Roger Daltrey, *Tommy*
- Jeffrey Lynas, *Lies My Father Told Me*
- Chris Sarandon, *Dog Day Afternoon*
- Ben Vereen, *Funny Lady*

BEST ACTING DEBUT—FEMALE

- ▪ Marilyn Hassett, *The Other Side of the Mountain*
- Jeannette Clift, *The Hiding Place*
- Stockard Channing, *The Fortune*
- Barbara Carrera, *The Master Gunfighter*

Ronee Blakley, *Nashville*
Lily Tomlin, *Nashville*

BEST SCREENPLAY
- Laurence Hauben, Bo Goldman, *One Flew over the Cuckoo's Nest*
Peter Benchley, Carl Gottlieb, *Jaws*
Frank Pierson, *Dog Day Afternoon*
Neil Simon, *The Sunshine Boys*
Joan Tewkesbury, *Nashville*

BEST SONG
- "I'm Easy," *Nashville*, Keith Carradine
"How Lucky Can You Get," *Funny Lady,* John Kander, Fred Ebb
"My Little Friend," *Paper Tiger,* Roy Budd, Sammy Cahn
"Now That We're in Love," *Whiffs,* George Barrie, Sammy Cahn
"Richard's Window," *The Other Side of the Mountain,* Charles Fox, Norman Gibel

BEST FOREIGN FILM
- *Lies My Father Told Me* (Canada)
And Now My Love (France)
Hedda (England)
The Magic Flute (Sweden)
Special Section (Italy)

Winners
BEST ORIGINAL SCORE
- John Williams, *Jaws*

BEST DOCUMENTARY
- *Youthquake*

LOS ANGELES FILM CRITICS ASSOCIATION
Winners were announced on February 25, 1975, at the Pips club in Beverly Hills.

BEST PICTURE (TIE)
- *Dog Day Afternoon*
- *One Flew over the Cuckoo's Nest*

BEST DIRECTOR
- Sidney Lumet, *Dog Day Afternoon*

BEST ACTOR
- Al Pacino, *Dog Day Afternoon*

BEST ACTRESS
- Florinda Bolkan, *A Brief Vacation*

BEST SCREENPLAY
- Joan Tewkesbury, *Nashville*

BEST CINEMATOGRAPHY
- John Alcott, *Barry Lyndon*

BEST FOREIGN FILM
- *And Now My Love* (France), Claude Lelouch

SPECIAL AWARD
- *Love among the Ruins*, George Cukor

DIRECTORS GUILD OF AMERICA
The award for Best Director was presented on March 20, 1976, at the Beverly Hilton Hotel in Los Angeles and the Hilton Hotel in New York.

BEST DIRECTOR
- Milos Forman, *One Flew over the Cuckoo's Nest*
Robert Altman, *Nashville*
Stanley Kubrick, *Barry Lyndon*
Sidney Lumet, *Dog Day Afternoon*
Steven Spielberg, *Jaws*

HONORARY LIFE MEMBERSHIP
- Lew Wasserman

WRITERS GUILD OF AMERICA
Awards were presented on March 25, 1976, at the Beverly Hilton Hotel in Los Angeles and the Roosevelt Hotel in New York.

BEST DRAMA WRITTEN DIRECTLY FOR THE SCREEN
- *Dog Day Afternoon*, Frank Pierson, based on a magazine article by P. F. Kluge and Thomas Moore
French Connection II, Alexander Jacobs, Robert Dillon, Laurie Dillon
Nashville, Joan Tewkesbury
The Wind and the Lion, John Milius

BEST DRAMA ADAPTED FROM ANOTHER MEDIUM

- *One Flew over the Cuckoo's Nest*, Lawrence Hauben, Bo Goldman, based on the novel by Ken Kesey

Barry Lyndon, Stanley Kubrick, based on the novel by William Thackeray

Jaws, Peter Benchley, Carl Gottlieb, based on the novel by Peter Benchley

The Man in the Glass Booth, Edward Anhalt, based on his play

The Man Who Would Be King, John Huston, Gladys Hill, based on a story by Rudyard Kipling

BEST COMEDY WRITTEN DIRECTLY FOR THE SCREEN

- *Shampoo*, Robert Towne, Warren Beatty

Hearts of the West, Rob Thompson

The Return of the Pink Panther, Frank Waldman, Blake Edwards

Smile, Jerry Belson

BEST COMEDY ADAPTED FROM ANOTHER MEDIUM

- *The Sunshine Boys*, Neil Simon, based on his play

Hester Street, Joan Micklin Silver, based on the book *Yekl* by Abraham Cahan

The Prisoner of Second Avenue, Neil Simon, based on his play

LAUREL AWARD

- Michael Wilson

VALENTINE DAVIES AWARD

- Winston Miller

MORGAN COX AWARD

- William Ludwig

ACADEMY AWARDS

Nominations were announced on February 17, 1976. Awards were presented on March 29 at the Dorothy Chandler Pavilion in Los Angeles. The ceremony was telecast by ABC.

BEST PICTURE

- *One Flew over the Cuckoo's Nest*

Barry Lyndon

Dog Day Afternoon

Jaws

Nashville

BEST DIRECTOR

- Milos Forman, *One Flew over the Cuckoo's Nest*

Robert Altman, *Nashville*

Federico Fellini, *Amarcord*

Stanley Kubrick, *Barry Lyndon*

Sidney Lumet, *Dog Day Afternoon*

BEST ACTOR

- Jack Nicholson, *One Flew over the Cuckoo's Nest*

Walter Matthau, *The Sunshine Boys*

Al Pacino, *Dog Day Afternoon*

Maximilian Schell, *The Man in the Glass Booth*

James Whitmore, *Give 'Em Hell, Harry!*

BEST ACTRESS

- Louise Fletcher, *One Flew over the Cuckoo's Nest*

Isabelle Adjani, *The Story of Adele H.*

Ann-Margret, *Tommy*

Glenda Jackson, *Hedda*

Carol Kane, *Hester Street*

BEST SUPPORTING ACTOR

- George Burns, *The Sunshine Boys*

Brad Dourif, *One Flew over the Cuckoo's Nest*

Burgess Meredith, *The Day of the Locust*

Chris Sarandon, *Dog Day Afternoon*

Jack Warden, *Shampoo*

BEST SUPPORTING ACTRESS

- Lee Grant, *Shampoo*

Ronee Blakley, *Nashville*

Sylvia Miles, *Farewell, My Lovely*

Lily Tomlin, *Nashville*

Brenda Vaccaro, *Once Is Not Enough*

BEST ORIGINAL SCREENPLAY

- Frank Pierson, *Dog Day Afternoon*

Ted Allan, *Lies My Father Told Me*

Warren Beatty, Robert Towne, *Shampoo*

Federico Fellini, Tonino Guerra, *Amarcord*

Claude Lelouch, Pierre Uytterhoeven, *And Now My Love*

BEST ADAPTED SCREENPLAY
- Bo Goldman, Lawrence Hauben, *One Flew over the Cuckoo's Nest*

Gladys Hill, John Huston, *The Man Who Would Be King*

Stanley Kubrick, *Barry Lyndon*

Ruggero Maccari, Dino Risi, *Scent of a Woman*

Neil Simon, *The Sunshine Boys*

BEST SONG
- "I'm Easy," *Nashville*, Keith Carradine

"How Lucky Can You Get," *Funny Lady*, Fred Ebb, John Kander

"Now That We're in Love," *Whiffs*, George Barrie, Sammy Cahn

"Richard's Window," *The Other Side of the Mountain*, Charles Fox, Norman Gimbel

"Theme from *Mahogany* (Do You Know Where You're Going To)," *Mahogany*, Gerry Goffin, Michael Masser

BEST FOREIGN-LANGUAGE FILM
- *Dersu Uzala* (U.S.S.R.)

Land of Promise (Poland)

Letters from Marusia (Mexico)

Sandakan No. 8 (Japan)

Scent of a Woman (Italy)

Winners

BEST ART DIRECTION
- Ken Adam, Roy Walker, Vernon Dixon, *Barry Lyndon*

BEST CINEMATOGRAPHY
- John Alcott, *Barry Lyndon*

BEST COSTUME DESIGN
- Milena Canonero, Ulla-Britt Soderlund, *Barry Lyndon*

BEST DOCUMENTARY
(FEATURE)
- F. R. Crawley, James Hager, Dale Hartleben, *The Man Who Skied down Everest*

(SHORT SUBJECT)
- Robin Lehman, Claire Wilbur, *The End of the Game*

BEST FILM EDITING
- Verna Fields, *Jaws*

BEST MUSIC
(ORIGINAL SCORE)
- John Williams, *Jaws*

(SCORING: ORIGINAL SONG SCORE AND/OR ADAPTATION)
- Leonard Rosenman, *Barry Lyndon*

SCIENTIFIC OR TECHNICAL AWARDS
Class II (Plaque)
- Chadwell O'Connor, O'Connor Engineering Laboratories; William F. Miner, Universal City Studios; Westinghouse Electric Corp.

Class III (Certificate)
- Lawrence W. Butler, Roger Banks; David J. Degenkolb, Fred Scobey, Deluxe General Inc.; John C. Dolan, Richard Dubois, Akwaklame Co.; Joseph Westheimer; Carter Equipment Co., Ramtronics; Hollywood Film Co.; Bell & Howell; Fredrik Schlyter

BEST SHORT FILM
(ANIMATED)
- *Great*

(LIVE ACTION)
- *Angel and Big Joe*

BEST SOUND
- John Carter, Roger Heman, Robert L. Hoyt, Earl Madery, *Jaws*

SPECIAL ACHIEVEMENT AWARDS
(SOUND EFFECTS)
- *The Hindenburg*, Peter Berkos

(VISUAL EFFECTS)
- *The Hindenburg*, Glen Robinson, Albert Whitlock

IRVING G. THALBERG MEMORIAL AWARD
- Mervyn LeRoy

JEAN HERSHOLT HUMANITARIAN AWARD
- Dr. Jules C. Stein

HONORARY AWARD
- Mary Pickford

SCREEN ACTORS GUILD

LIFETIME ACHIEVEMENT AWARD
- Rosalind Russell

▪ 1976 ▪

Rocky *Comes Out Swinging*

One year after the Los Angeles critics got their own awards group up and running, they charged out of the gate to claim the early lead in the annual kudos derby.

They not only announced their winners first, beating out the other two crix orgs and even the National Board of Review, but again they topped the competish by naming two Best Pictures in a tie vote.

The first was *Rocky*, a David-versus-Goliath boxing tale starring Sylvester Stallone as what *Variety* called "a near-loser, a punchy reject" who gets his big chance to take on the heavyweight champ. The choice stunned awards-watchers: *Rocky*—written hastily in four days and filmed in just 28 days for only $960,000—had been dismissed as lightweight by some crix, but the L.A. org thought it was just the kind of American fable that was perfect to celebrate during the nation's bicentennial year. It was also the ideal counterpunch to the type of highbrow, foreign-lingo Best Picture choices that the eastern crix had been making lately.

Their second best pic aimed a knockout blow at the ethics of TV news execs in Los Angeles's rival media capital, New York City. *Variety* called *Network* "a bawdy, stops-out, no-holds-barred story of a TV network that will, quite literally, do anything to get an audience." They also acknowledged *Network*'s director Sidney Lumet and screenwriter Paddy Chayefsky.

Their Best Actor was Robert De Niro as a psychotic New York cabbie who goes berserk in *Taxi Driver*, which became a breakout critical hit after earning the Palme

ROCKY' BESTS: PIC, DIRECTION, EDITING

Dunaway, Finch, Straight, Robards, Avildsen, Chayefsky, Goldman In Winners' Circle

By A. D. MURPHY

After the L.A. crix picked *Rocky* as best pic to counter the highfalutin recent choices made by the N.Y. crix, it ended up slugging its way to the Oscars.

d'Or at Cannes. Their Best Actress choice proved that the crix were even open to the same kind of foreign fare that their East Coast peers usually prefer: Liv Ullmann was cited as a psychiatrist who suffers a nervous breakdown in Ingmar Bergman's *Face to Face*.

Being showbiz savvy, the L.A. crix put on a real show for the first time to present their second annual awards. Fifty guests were invited to join them at a cocktail party held in the grand hall of the former Doheny mansion, now the American Film Institute, where De Niro accepted his honor "with simple words of thanks," noted *Variety*. Ullmann's accolade was accepted by Carol Burnett, who said, "I can still see the tears on Ingmar Bergman's face when I turned down the role." A new prize for Best Documentary was accepted by producer Peter Bart, who stood in for the absent director of *The Memory of Justice*, which chronicled war atrocities from World War II to Vietnam.

If the choice of *Network* as Best Picture was a subtle slap at Gotham's media ethics, it's curious to note that the three New York–based awards groups responded by naming a Best Picture about media demonstrating the highest ethics—*All the President's Men*—based on the best-seller about *The Washington Post*'s investigation of Watergate.

The National Board of Review was the first to back it, ranking *Network* second on its list of 1976's Top 10 pix. The board agreed with the choice of Ullmann as Best Actress, but declared a different Best Actor: David Carradine as Woody Guthrie in *Bound for Glory*.

The New York Film Critics Circle and the National Society of Film Critics engaged in their usual calendar jockeying, with the circle jumping ahead of the society this year to name its choices first.

The Gothamites agreed with many of the L.A. crix picks: De Niro as Best Actor (topping Carradine, 33 points to 19), Ullmann as Best Actress (over *Network*'s Faye Dunaway, 41 points to 28) and Chayefsky for screenplay (over Harold Pinter's *The Last Tycoon*, 38 points to 20). The helmer of their Best Picture, *All the President's Men*, Alan J. Pakula, won Best Director (over Martin Scorsese, 37 points to 22). *Network* placed for Best Picture (with 26 points; *President* scored 40). *President* also earned the Best Supporting Actor prize for Jason Robards as *Washington Post* executive editor Ben Bradlee (over *Taxi Driver*'s Harvey Keitel, 37 points to 12).

All races were decided on two ballots, except for Best Supporting Actress, which needed a third canvass before Talia Shire prevailed for her role as Sylvester Stallone's plain-jane love interest in *Rocky*. She won with 41 points over Jodie Foster as a nymphet hooker in *Taxi Driver*.

After Jack Nicholson missed the past two awards galas when he was honored as the crix's Best Actor, he promised to show up this year to bestow the prize upon the newest champ. When he took his place on the podium at Sardi's restaurant, *The Village Voice* noted that he flashed "a mischievous grin that suggested he knew some incredible secret that we mere mortals could never be privy to. In whispery tones, he said that he was glad to present the Best Actor award to De Niro 'because Bobby is one of the few people who is less comfortable with public speaking than I am.' "

Another two-time past champ, Best Actress Liv Ullmann, tried to attend but was trapped in Toronto by a blizzard.

Best Supporting Actor Jason Robards received his award from the man he portrayed in real life—Ben Bradlee, who used a little "no-holds-barred newsroom banter," noticed *The New York Post*, when he thanked Robards for not making him "look like a horse's ass."

"Elizabeth Taylor, expressing tongue-in-cheek astonishment at being invited to anything by a group of film critics ('a first,' she said), gave the Best Picture award to *All the President's Men*, accepted by producer-actor Robert Redford," *Variety* reported. "Taylor couldn't resist congratulating Redford 'on behalf of all the women in America,' kissing him and then squealing like a schoolgirl as she returned to her seat.

"Redford, notoriously shy at media events, was not really expected to show. That he did was an indication of his pride in the pic and the status of the N.Y. critics prize. As it was, he managed the last entrance and the first exit."

Again, the National Society of Film Critics skipped holding a kudos fete. Certificates were mailed to the winners, several of whom turned out to be the same champs cited by the Gotham crix, including top actor De Niro and supporting thesp Robards. *The New York Times* noted the Best Actor's strong electoral pull: "De Niro won his award on the first ballot, an unusual event in the national society's voting procedure, receiving 16 of the 27 votes cast."

Strong support for *Taxi Driver* was evi-

> ## William Goldman beat himself at the WGA awards.

dent in other polling numbers: it came in second for Best Picture behind *All the President's Men* and earned the accolade for Best Director for Martin Scorsese over second-placed Alan J. Pakula. *Taxi Driver* also claimed the Best Supporting Actress trophy for Jodie Foster.

The society's Best Actress was Sissy Spacek (*Carrie*) as a nerdy girl who summons up telekinetic powers to wreak revenge on schoolmates who mocked her. Best Screenplay was a surprising choice: Alain Tanner's and John Berger's French-language script for the Swiss comedy *Jonah, Who Will Be 25 in the Year 2000*.

Taxi Driver hit a bump at the Golden Globes. It was not nominated for Best Drama Picture, which was considered a close race between *Network* and *All the President's Men*.

Network scored an early sweep of victories on gala night, claiming honors for Paddy Chayefsky's screenplay, Sidney Lumet's direction and Faye Dunaway's perf as a power-hungry, ratings-mad TV exec.

Lina Wertmüller became the first woman nommed by DGA and the Oscars.

When Peter Finch won Best Actor for his role as a TV anchor who freaks out during news broadcasts, the victory was greeted with cheers from the audience. Finch had died of a heart attack just two weeks earlier in the midst of a stressful publicity blitz for *Network*. After his widow accepted his statuette, smiling through a veil of tears, Finch was remembered by the foreign press with a moment of silence.

Just when it looked as if *Network* were certain to win Best Drama Picture, the audience gasped when the champ was revealed: *Rocky*. The *L.A. Times* noted that its producers were "jubilant," adding, "Like most viewers, they probably had given up in favor of *Network*." The *Times* noticed that the execs failed to mention Sylvester Stallone in their acceptance speech, which seemed strange since Stallone not only wrote the pic and starred in it, but struggled for years to get *Rocky* made.

The biggest Globe champ this year turned out to be Barbra Streisand's rock-music remake of *A Star Is Born* which went undefeated in five categories, tying the record for most Globe victories. It won best pic in the comedy/musical classification plus palms for Best Score (Paul Williams) and the perfs of Streisand and costar Kris Kristofferson. Streisand also claimed kudos for her debut as a tunesmith when "Evergreen" won Best Song. She accepted many of the statuettes with her ex-hairdresser/lover/co-producer Jon Peters at her side.

"Peters credited Streisand and Streisand credited Peters for their success and they hugged and kissed each other on and off camera," noticed the *Times*.

A Star Is Born was not nominated by the Directors Guild of America, and there was no clear front-runner for its helmer's prize when the dual-coast gala was staged six weeks after the Globes. Comedian Dick Martin hosted the fete at the Beverly Hilton Hotel in California, where entertainment was provided by sexpot singer Lola Falana.

Four of the five nominees were predictable: John Avildsen (*Rocky*), Sidney Lumet (*Network*), Alan J. Pakula (*All the President's Men*) and Martin Scorsese (*Taxi Driver*). One was a welcomed surprise: Lina Wertmüller (*Seven Beauties*).

The winner turned out to be a jaw-dropper: *Rocky*'s John Avildsen. His victory meant that the underdog movie about the triumph of underdogs was the front-runner to win the Best Picture Oscar.

Rocky was nominated at the writers' guild awards that took place two weeks later, but scribe Sylvester Stallone lost the race for best original drama to veteran scenarist Paddy Chayesfky (*Network*), who had won a guild prize five years earlier for *The Hospital*. As expected, past guild champ William Goldman (*Butch Cassidy and the Sundance Kid*, 1969) took the palm for best adapted drama for *All the President's Men*, beating his separate nomination for *Marathon Man*.

Blake Edwards and Frank Waldman (*The Pink Panther Strikes Again*) took the prize for best adapted comedy over Ernest Lehman (*Family Plot*) and Terrence McNally (*The Ritz*). The winner of best original comedy was Bill Lancaster (*The Bad News Bears*) over works by Neil Simon (*Murder by Death*), Mel Brooks (*Silent Movie*) and Paul Mazursky (*Next Stop, Greenwich Village*).

Neil Simon presented the honorary Laurel Award to Samson Raphaelson, author of *Heaven Can Wait, Suspicion* and *The Harvey Girls*. Cesare Zavattini—author of *The Bicycle Thief, Shoe Shine* and *Children of Sanchez*—was honored with the rarely bestowed Medallion Award, but he could not accept it in person due to illness.

Back by popular demand after an absence of several years was the gridiron-style entertainment featuring stage skits lampooning current Hollywood films and leaders. Thirty-four stars participated, including Bob Hope, Ed Asner, Jean Stapleton and Danny Kaye.

When the Oscars took place five days later, *Rocky* and *Network* led with the most nominations: 10. Two of *Rocky*'s bids belonged to Sly Stallone, making him only the third person—after Charlie Chaplin and Orson Welles—to be nominated for acting and writing in the same year.

Stallone arrived at the Dorothy Chandler Pavilion looking like a true heavyweight contender ready to grab the belt. As he swept down the red carpet, he charged up the cheering crowds around him by pumping his fists in air.

But once the ceremony began, things did not start well for *Rocky*.

All the President's Men garnered early kudos for sound, art direction and best adapted screenplay (William Goldman).

Then it pulled rank in the race for Best Supporting Actor. The two *Rocky* nominees

> ## "I thought *Rocky* would be the second half of a double bill at a drive-in."

(Burgess Meredith, Burt Young) knocked each other out, leaving Gotham crix honoree Jason Robards still standing. Robards thanked the man he portrayed on the screen, Ben Bradlee, "for being alive so I could come out and play with him."

Last year's winner of Best Supporting Actress was back in the race this year—Lee Grant (*Voyage of the Damned*). She faced two front-runners: National Society of Film Critics victor Jodie Foster (*Taxi Driver*) and Piper Laurie starring in her first film (*Carrie*) since being nommed for Best Actress in *The Hustler* (1961).

The winner turned out to be the upset of the night: Beatrice Straight (*Network*) as a wife who struggles to keep her dignity while her husband (William Holden) confesses to having an affair with a younger co-worker (Faye Dunaway). The two-scene, 10-minute role was the second shortest to win an Oscar, after the nine-minute record set by Anthony Quinn in *Lust for Life* (1956).

"I'm the dark horse," Straight acknowledged at the podium. "It's a great, great thrill and totally unexpected." She thanked scribe Chayefsky, "who writes what we all feel but cannot express."

Chayefsky prevailed over Sylvester Stallone in the contest for Best Original Screenplay, as expected. He thanked his wife and child, "two people who I could never really thank properly or enough."

Network had two nominees—Peter Finch and William Holden—in the Best Actor race, leading many pundits to believe that they'd split the pic's vote and hand victory to the star who'd swept the crix awards, Robert De Niro (*Taxi Driver*).

Finch was not expected to win, since the only other posthumous Oscar nominees in years past—Spencer Tracy and James Dean—both lost. Just in case Finch won, however, the telecast producers and director didn't want to risk having the ceremony becoming maudlin, so they asked Chayefsky to accept the statuette instead of Finch's widow.

When Finch won, Chayefsky appeared at the podium dutifully, but looked upset. Then he blurted out, "There's no reason for me to be here! There's only one person who should be up here and that's the person Finch wanted to accept his award. Are you in the house, Eletha?"

Finch's elegant, Caribbean-born wife came up on stage and said, "Before he died, Peter said to me, 'Darling, if I win I want to say thanks to my fellow actors who have given me encouragement over the years and thanks to Paddy Chayefsky for giving me the part.'"

Variety called her acceptance speech "most poignant" and "the emotional peak of the evening."

Network's Faye Dunaway was up for her third Best Actress nomination, but faced tough competish from another past Oscar contender, Liv Ullmann (*Face to Face*), the darling of the critics' orgs, who was also overdue to be embraced by the Hollywood crowd. Both rivals faced Sissy Spacek (*Carrie*), whom *Newsweek* hailed as "the most promising new actress in motion pictures."

When Dunaway prevailed, she said at the podium, "I didn't expect this to happen quite yet, but I thank you very much."

Dunaway's victory marked an Oscar milestone. By sweeping three thesp categories, *Network* tied *A Streetcar Named Desire*'s record for nabbing the most trophies for acting.

Near evening's end, *Rocky* seemed to be in serious trouble. Despite 10 nominations, it had scored only a single statuette—for film editing. If it was going to prove that it was a winner, it needed to pull off a real *Rocky*-style, come-from-behind rally.

It scored its first hit in the directors' race, which included a female nominee for the first time ever: Lina Wertmüller (*Seven Beauties*). When John G. Avildsen was proclaimed the victor, he hugged Sly Stallone in the audience and raced up to the podium.

"*Rocky* gave a lot of people hope," Avildsen said. "Stallone gave his guts and his heart and his best shot."

Peter Finch died of a heart attack just before his Globe and Oscar victories for *Network*, which tied *Rocky* for the best pic prize from the L.A. crix.

Then *Rocky* KO'd the competish and claimed the top prize: Best Picture.

Stallone joined his producers up on stage where they clasped their raised fists together in triumph—like prizefighters.

"To all the Rockys of the world, I love ya!" Stallone roared.

Earlier in the evening, Stallone had shone at the podium when he served as an awards presenter. *Variety* said that "the surprise appearance by Muhammad Ali (accusing Stallone of stealing the *Rocky* script from him) was a pleasant moment."

Another highlight of the Oscarcast occurred when *Rocky* lost Best Song despite a strong entry for "Gonna Fly Now," its hit tune that had been adopted by TV sports programs.

It lost to a song penned by a true heavyweight star, Barbra Streisand, who performed "Evergreen" during the ceremony, giving off "sheer star voltage," *Variety* said.

Claiming the statuette, the former Best Actress victor said, "In my wildest dreams, I never thought I'd win an Oscar for writing a song!" Her co-author, the vertically challenged Paul Williams, piped in, "I was going to thank all the little people, but then I remembered that I *am* the little people!"

Backstage after the ceremony, helmer John G. Avildsen revealed to the press how amazed he was that his movie defied the odds.

"I had no idea *Rocky* would be such a hit," he said. "I thought it was going to be the second half of a double bill at a drive-in."

LOS ANGELES FILM CRITICS ASSOCIATION

Winners were announced on December 21, 1976. Awards were presented on January 19, 1977, at the American Film Institute in Beverly Hills.

BEST PICTURE (TIE)
■ *Network*
■ *Rocky*

BEST DIRECTOR
■ Sidney Lumet, *Network*

BEST ACTOR
■ Robert De Niro, *Taxi Driver*

BEST ACTRESS
■ Liv Ullmann, *Face to Face*

BEST SCREENPLAY
■ Paddy Chayefsky, *Network*

BEST CINEMATOGRAPHY
■ Haskell Wexler, *Bound for Glory*

BEST MUSIC SCORE
■ Bernard Herrmann, *Taxi Driver*

BEST FOREIGN FILM
■ *Face to Face* (Sweden)

CAREER AWARD
■ Allan Dwan

NEW GENERATION AWARD
■ Martin Scorsese, Jodie Foster, *Taxi Driver*

SPECIAL AWARDS
■ Marcel Ophuls, *The Memory of Justice*
■ Max Laemmle

NATIONAL BOARD OF REVIEW

Winners were announced on December 22, 1976.

BEST PICTURE
■ *All the President's Men*
Network
Rocky
The Last Tycoon
The Seven-Per-Cent Solution
The Front
The Shootist
Family Plot
Silent Movie
Obsession

BEST DIRECTOR
■ Alan J. Pakula, *All the President's Men*

BEST ACTOR
■ David Carradine, *Bound for Glory*

BEST ACTRESS
■ Liv Ullmann, *Face to Face*

BEST SUPPORTING ACTOR
■ Jason Robards, *All the President's Men*

BEST SUPPORTING ACTRESS
■ Talia Shire, *Rocky*

BEST FOREIGN FILM
■ *The Marquise of O*
Face to Face
Small Change
Cousin, Cousine
The Clockmaker

NEW YORK FILM CRITICS CIRCLE

Winners were announced on January 3, 1977. Awards were presented on January 30 at Sardi's restaurant in New York.

BEST PICTURE
■ *All the President's Men*

BEST DIRECTOR
■ Alan J. Pakula, *All the President's Men*

BEST ACTOR
■ Robert De Niro, *Taxi Driver*

BEST ACTRESS
- Liv Ullmann, *Face to Face*

BEST SUPPORTING ACTOR
- Jason Robards, *All the President's Men*

BEST SUPPORTING ACTRESS
- Talia Shire, *Rocky*

BEST SCREENPLAY
- Paddy Chayefsky, *Network*

NATIONAL SOCIETY OF FILM CRITICS

Winners were announced on January 4, 1977. No awards ceremony was held.

BEST PICTURE
- *All the President's Men*

BEST DIRECTOR
- Martin Scorsese, *Taxi Driver*

BEST ACTOR
- Robert De Niro, *Taxi Driver*

BEST ACTRESS
- Sissy Spacek, *Carrie*

BEST SUPPORTING ACTOR
- Jason Robards, *All the President's Men*

BEST SUPPORTING ACTRESS
- Jodie Foster, *Taxi Driver*

BEST SCREENPLAY
- Alain Tanner, John Berger, *Jonah, Who Will Be 25 in the Year 2000*

BEST CINEMATOGRAPHY
- Haskell Wexler, *Bound for Glory*

GOLDEN GLOBES

Awards were presented on January 29, 1977, at the Beverly Hilton Hotel in Los Angeles.

BEST DRAMA PICTURE
- *Rocky*
All the President's Men

Feeling the punch from the L.A. crix, the Gothamites and national crix named a Yankee film best pic—*All the President's Men* (starring Robert Redford) after it was cited by the NBR.

Bound for Glory
Network
Voyage of the Damned

BEST COMEDY OR MUSICAL PICTURE
- *A Star Is Born*
Bugsy Malone
The Pink Panther Strikes Again
The Ritz
Silent Movie

BEST DIRECTOR
- Sidney Lumet, *Network*
Hal Ashby, *Bound for Glory*
John G. Avildsen, *Rocky*
Alan J. Pakula, *All the President's Men*
John Schlesinger, *Marathon Man*

BEST ACTOR, DRAMA
- Peter Finch, *Network*
David Carradine, *Bound for Glory*
Robert De Niro, *Taxi Driver*
Dustin Hoffman, *Marathon Man*
Sylvester Stallone, *Rocky*

BEST ACTRESS, DRAMA
- Faye Dunaway, *Network*
Glenda Jackson, *The Incredible Sarah*
Sarah Miles, *The Sailor Who Fell from Grace with the Sea*

Talia Shire, *Rocky*
Liv Ullmann, *Face to Face*

BEST ACTOR, COMEDY OR MUSICAL
■ Kris Kristofferson, *A Star Is Born*
Mel Brooks, *Silent Movie*
Peter Sellers, *The Pink Panther Strikes Again*
Jack Weston, *The Ritz*
Gene Wilder, *Silver Streak*

BEST ACTRESS, COMEDY OR MUSICAL
■ Barbra Streisand, *A Star Is Born*
Jodie Foster, *Freaky Friday*
Barbara Harris, *Family Plot*
Barbara Harris, *Freaky Friday*
Goldie Hawn, *The Duchess and the Dirtwater Fox*
Rita Moreno, *The Ritz*

BEST SUPPORTING ACTOR
■ Laurence Olivier, *Marathon Man*
Marty Feldman, *Silent Movie*
Ron Howard, *The Shootist*
Jason Robards, *All the President's Men*
Oskar Werner, *Voyage of the Damned*

BEST SUPPORTING ACTRESS
■ Katharine Ross, *Voyage of the Damned*
Lee Grant, *Voyage of the Damned*
Marthe Keller, *Marathon Man*
Piper Laurie, *Carrie*
Bernadette Peters, *Silent Movie*
Shelley Winters, *Next Stop, Greenwich Village*

NEW MALE STAR OF THE YEAR
■ Arnold Schwarzenegger, *Stay Hungry*
Lenny Baker, *Next Stop, Greenwich Village*
Truman Capote, *Murder by Death*
Jonathan Kahn, *The Sailor Who Fell from Grace with the Sea*
Harvey Stephens, *The Omen*

NEW FEMALE STAR OF THE YEAR
■ Jessica Lange, *King Kong*
Melinda Dillon, *Bound for Glory*
Mariel Hemingway, *Lipstick*
Gladys Knight, *Pipe Dreams*
Andrea Marcovicci, *The Front*

BEST SCREENPLAY
■ Paddy Chayefsky, *Network*
David Butler, Steve Shagan, *Voyage of the Damned*
William Goldman, *All the President's Men*
William Goldman, *Marathon Man*
Paul Schrader, *Taxi Driver*
Sylvester Stallone, *Rocky*

BEST SONG
■ "Evergreen," *A Star Is Born*, Barbra Streisand, Paul Williams
"Bugsy Malone," *Bugsy Malone*, Paul Williams
"Car Wash," *Car Wash*, Norman Whitfield
"Hello and Goodbye," *From Noon Till Three*, Elmer Bernstein
"I'd Like to Be You for a Day," *Freaky Friday*, Joel Hirschhorn, Al Kasha
"So Sad the Song," *Pipe Dreams*, Stephen Verona

BEST FOREIGN FILM
■ *Face to Face* (Sweden)
Cousin, Cousine (France)
Seven Beauties (Italy)
The Slipper and the Rose (U.K.)
Small Change (France)

Winners

BEST ORIGINAL SCORE
■ Kenny Ascher, Paul Williams, *A Star Is Born*

WORLD FILM FAVORITES
■ Sophia Loren
■ Robert Redford

CECIL B. DEMILLE AWARD
■ Walter Miris

DIRECTORS GUILD OF AMERICA

The award for Best Director was presented on March 12, 1977, at the Beverly Hilton Hotel in Los Angeles and the Tower Suite in New York.

BEST DIRECTOR
- John Avildsen, *Rocky*

Sidney Lumet, *Network*
Alan J. Pakula, *All the President's Men*
Martin Scorsese, *Taxi Driver*
Lina Wertmüller, *Seven Beauties*

WRITERS GUILD OF AMERICA

Awards were presented on March 24, 1977, at the Beverly Hilton Hotel in Los Angeles and the Essex House in New York.

BEST DRAMA WRITTEN DIRECTLY FOR THE SCREEN
- *Network*, Paddy Chayefsky

The Front, Walter Bernstein
The Omen, David Seltzer
Rocky, Sylvester Stallone
Taxi Driver, Paul Schrader

BEST DRAMA ADAPTED FROM ANOTHER MEDIUM
- *All the President's Men*, William Goldman, based on the book by Carl Bernstein and Bob Woodward

Bound for Glory, Robert Getchell, based on the autobiography by Woody Guthrie
Marathon Man, William Goldman, based on his novel
The Seven-Per-Cent Solution, Nicholas Meyer, based on his novel
The Shootist, Miles Hood Swarthout, Scott Hale, based on the novel by Glendon Swarthout

BEST COMEDY WRITTEN DIRECTLY FOR THE SCREEN
- *The Bad News Bears*, Bill Lancaster

Murder by Death, Neil Simon
Next Stop, Greenwich Village, Paul Mazursky
Silent Movie, Mel Brooks, Ron Clark, Rudy De Luca, Barry Levinson
Silver Streak, Colin Higgins

BEST COMEDY ADAPTED FROM ANOTHER MEDIUM
- *The Pink Panther Strikes Again*, Frank Waldman, Blake Edwards

The Bingo Long Traveling All-Stars and Motor Kings, Hal Barwood, Matthew

Robbins, based on the novel by William Brashler
Family Plot, Ernest Lehman, based on the novel *The Rainbird Pattern* by Victory Canning
The Ritz, Terrence McNally, based on his play
Stay Hungry, Charles Gaines, Bob Rafelson, based on the novel by Charles Gaines

LAUREL AWARD
- Samson Raphaelson

VALENTINE DAVIES AWARD
- Carl Foreman

MORGAN COX AWARD
- Herbert Baker

MEDALLION AWARD
- Cesare Zavattini

ACADEMY AWARDS

Nominations were announced on February 10, 1977. Awards were presented on March 29 at the Dorothy Chandler Pavilion in Los Angeles. The ceremony was telecast by ABC.

BEST PICTURE
- *Rocky*

All the President's Men
Bound for Glory
Network
Taxi Driver

BEST DIRECTOR
- John G. Avildsen, *Rocky*

Ingmar Bergman, *Face to Face*
Sidney Lumet, *Network*
Alan J. Pakula, *All the President's Men*
Lina Wertmüller, *Seven Beauties*

BEST ACTOR
- Peter Finch, *Network*

Robert De Niro, *Taxi Driver*
Giancarlo Giannini, *Seven Beauties*
William Holden, *Network*
Sylvester Stallone, *Rocky*

BEST ACTRESS
- Faye Dunaway, *Network*

Marie-Christine Barrault, *Cousin, Cousine*
Talia Shire, *Rocky*
Sissy Spacek, *Carrie*
Liv Ullmann, *Face to Face*

BEST SUPPORTING ACTOR
- Jason Robards, *All the President's Men*

Ned Beatty, *Network*
Burgess Meredith, *Rocky*
Laurence Olivier, *Marathon Man*
Burt Young, *Rocky*

BEST SUPPORTING ACTRESS
- Beatrice Straight, *Network*

Jane Alexander, *All the President's Men*
Jodie Foster, *Taxi Driver*
Lee Grant, *Voyage of the Damned*
Piper Laurie, *Carrie*

BEST ORIGINAL SCREENPLAY
- Paddy Chayefsky, *Network*

Walter Bernstein, *The Front*
Jean-Charles Tacchella, Daniele
    Thompson, *Cousin, Cousine*
Sylvester Stallone, *Rocky*
Lina Wertmüller, *Seven Beauties*

BEST ADAPTED SCREENPLAY
- William Goldman, *All the President's Men*

David Butler, Steve Shagan, *Voyage of the
    Damned*
Federico Fellini, Bernadino Zapponi,
    Fellini's Casanova
Robert Getchell, *Bound for Glory*
Nicholas Meyer, *The Seven-Per-Cent
    Solution*

BEST SONG
- "Evergreen," *A Star Is Born*, Barbra
    Streisand, Paul Williams

"Ave Satani," *The Omen*, Jerry Goldsmith
"Come to Me," *The Pink Panther Strikes
    Again*, Don Black, Henry Mancini
"Gonna Fly Now," *Rocky*, Carol Connors,
    Bill Conti, Ayn Robbins
"A World That Never Was," *Half a House*,
    Sammy Fain, Paul Francis Webster

BEST FOREIGN-LANGUAGE FILM
- *Black and White in Color* (Ivory Coast)

Cousin, Cousine (France)

Jakob, the Liar (German Democratic
    Republic)
Nights and Days (Poland)
Seven Beauties (Italy)

Winners

BEST ART DIRECTION
- George Jenkins, George Gaines, *All the
    President's Men*

BEST CINEMATOGRAPHY
- Haskell Wexler, *Bound for Glory*

BEST COSTUME DESIGN
- Danilo Donati, *Fellini's Casanova*

BEST DOCUMENTARY
(FEATURE)
- Barbara Kopple, *Harlan County, U.S.A.*

(SHORT SUBJECT)
- Lynne Littman, *Number our Days*

BEST FILM EDITING
- Richard Halsey, Scott Conrad, *Rocky*

BEST MUSIC
(ORIGINAL SCORE)
- Jerry Goldsmith, *The Omen*

(ORIGINAL SONG SCORE AND ITS ADAPTATION OR ADAPTATION SCORE)
- Leonard Rosenman, *Bound for Glory*

SCIENTIFIC OR TECHNICAL AWARDS
Class II (Plaque)
Barnebey-Cheney Co., Consolidated Film
    Industries; William L. Graham, Manfred
    G. Michelson, Geoffrey F. Norman,
    Siegfried Seibert, Technicolor
Class III (Certificate)
Fred Bartscher, Kollmorgen Corp.; Glenn
    Berggren, Schneider Corp.; Panavision;
    Hiroshi Suzukawa, Canon, Inc.; Wilton
    R. Holm, AMPTP Motion Picture and
    Television Research Center; Carl Zeiss
    Co.; Photo Research Division,
    Kollmorgen

BEST SHORT FILM
(ANIMATED)
- *Leisure*

(LIVE ACTION)
- *In the Region of Ice*

BEST SOUND
- Dick Alexander, Les Fresholtz, Arthur Piantadosi, Jim Webb, *All the President's Men*

SPECIAL ACHIEVEMENT AWARDS
(VISUAL EFFECTS)
- *King Kong*, Carlo Rambaldi, Glen Robinson, Frank van der Veer
- *Logan's Run*, L. B. Abbott, Glen Robinson, Matthew Yuricich

IRVING G. THALBERG MEMORIAL AWARD
- Pandro S. Berman

SCREEN ACTORS GUILD

LIFETIME ACHIEVEMENT AWARD
- Pearl Bailey

· 1977 ·

Woody Makes the Cut

Competition was so fierce between the awards groups to be the first out of the gate in the annual kudos derby that three of them announced their choices for the year's best films on the same day—12 days before the year was even over.

Given the timing, they couldn't be influenced by each other's choices, so it's not surprising that they picked three different Best Pictures.

Once again the Los Angeles Critics Association demonstrated that it was not afraid to embrace a commercial crowd-pleaser. In fact, it picked the biggest b.o. hit of all time—*Star Wars*, the sci-fi sensation hailed by *Variety* as "a magnificent film."

The National Board of Review cited *The Turning Point*, a ballet drama directed by former choreographer Herbert Ross, who conceived of the female-buddy story with his ex-ballerina wife plus scribe Arthur Laurents. *Variety* called it "one of the best films of its era" and, despite its arty subject, *The Turning Point* turned out to be a surprise financial success.

It was the Best Picture choice made by the National Society of Film Critics, though, that would end up having the most impact on the 1977 derby—Woody Allen's *Annie Hall*—which, curiously, hit this year's track just as last year's derby ended.

Variety's review of *Annie Hall* ran smack dab in the midst of its 1976 Oscar issue. It appeared on page two, right in between a list of the previous night's winners and Army Archerd's column announcing that a

Annie Hall was old news as of kudos season, but the National Society of Film Critics named it Best Picture and launched it toward the Oscars.

sequel to Best Picture champ *Rocky* was in the works.

Prior to *Annie Hall*, Woody Allen had been known chiefly for his knee-slapping laffers like *Sleeper, Bananas* and *Play It Again, Sam*. Now, *Variety* said, he had achieved his "most three-dimensional film to date. The gags still fly by in almost non-stop profusion, but there is an undercurrent of sadness and pain now, reflecting a maturation of style."

Variety also noted that it was Allen's "most overtly autobiographical film," since he starred opposite ex-lover Diane Keaton in a story line that obviously reflected their failed romance.

Since most of the members of the National Society of Film Critics were also members of the New York Film Critics Circle, it's not surprising that the circle also named *Annie Hall* Best Picture when it voted two days later. Its scores were similar, too. *Annie Hall* topped Luis Buñuel's *That Obscure Object of Desire* in the society vote

43 points to 27. It prevailed in the circle vote 41 to 28 against the same competish. Diane Keaton won thesp laurels from both groups over Shelley Duvall, who was the Best Actress choice of the L.A. film crix and Cannes film fest for her role as a ditsy spa worker in Robert Altman's *Three Women*. All of the circle's and society's races were decided in two or more ballots except the prize for Best Screenplay: Woody Allen claimed both orgs' kudos resoundingly on the first rounds.

While the Gotham crix named Allen Best Director by a 35-to-33 tally over Luis Buñuel, the society preferred Buñuel, giving him 31 points over Steven Spielberg (25 points for *Close Encounters of the Third Kind*) and Allen (24).

The two orgs also split over Best Actor. The society chose Art Carney as an aging private detective in *The Late Show* by a score of 25 to 19 over John Gielgud as a dying novelist in *Providence*. The circle opted for Gielgud by a 37-to-31 tally over Fernando Rey, who *Variety* said portrays "a sadomasochistic rich man who falls madly for his inept new maid" in *That Obscure Object of Desire*.

Woody snubbed the Oscars, Globes and Gotham crix, but showed up for the guilds' kudos.

The groups also disagreed in the lower acting contests. The society named Edward Fox Best Supporting Actor for his turn as a World War II U.S. military officer in *A Bridge Too Far*. Best Supporting Actress was Ann Wedgeworth as a two-timed wife in *Handle with Care*.

The circle embraced two *Julia* stars: Best Supporting Actor Maximilian Schell and Best Supporting Actress Vanessa Redgrave as underground agents in World War II.

In addition to casting ballots to decide award winners, the Gotham crix voted on a "motion to admit radio and television critics to its ranks, which presently include only writers from newspapers and magazines," *The New York Times* reported. "The motion was defeated."

The Gotham crix's awards party turned out to be dull thanks to how generous they were to Allen, who did not show up to express his thanks, even though *Annie Hall*'s four honors were historic. Only two other pix had scored four prizes from the circle in past years: *A Man for All Seasons* (1966) and *Cries and Whispers* (1972). Allen's costar and the crix's Best Actress Diane Keaton stood in for him, however, and brightened up the fete.

There was quite a lively awards presentation held on the opposite coast by the TV, radio, newspaper and magazine pundits belonging to the L.A. crix org. The crowd of 150 that gathered at Pips backgammon club in Beverly Hills included such honorees as Best Actress Shelley Duvall, Best Director Herbert Ross (*The Turning Point*) and the crix's choice for Best Actor, Richard Dreyfuss, who portrayed an aspiring New York thesp who sublets a room from a firebrand divorcée (Marsha Mason) in Neil Simon's *The Goodbye Girl*. It was a break-out year for Dreyfuss. He also starred in Spielberg's UFO hit *Close Encounters of the Third Kind*.

Jane Fonda did not win any prizes for her role in *Julia* as author Lillian Hellman coming to the rescue of a childhood friend who's become an anti-Nazi agent, but she showed up to collect plaques won by her absent costars. The role of her gal pal was portrayed by Vanessa Redgrave, who won the L.A. crix's Best Supporting Actress prize on top of the previous kudos she earned from the National Society of Film Critics. The L.A. crix's choice for Best Supporting Actor was Jason Robards as Hellman's lover, Dashiell Hammett.

The National Board of Review made some surprising picks for its thesp palms. Best Actor was John Travolta, whom *Variety* described as "an amiably inarticulate N.Y. kid who comes to life only in a disco" in *Saturday Night Fever*. Best Actress was *The Turning Point*'s Anne Bancroft "as a ballet star just reaching that uneasy age when a lot of Eve Harringtons (male and female) are beginning to move in," said *Variety*. Tom Skerritt won Best Supporting Actor for portraying the husband of Bancroft's best friend (Shirley MacLaine). The Board downgraded *Annie Hall*'s Diane Keaton to the supporting race, which she won.

Variety announced: "The Golden Globes Awards show has completed its nine-year off-network penance and will be back on NBC, which booted it off the air in 1968 after award procedures were blasted by the FCC as misleading." The ceremony was taped on Saturday night, January 28, and aired nationally one day later, expanded from its previous 90-minute length to a two-hour show. Despite the extra time, the Hollywood Foreign Press Association was asked to cut out some kudos, so it nixed the prizes for Most Promising Newcomer.

The night's big winner turned out to be Herbert Ross, director of *The Goodbye Girl* and *The Turning Point*. Both pix swept up. *The Turning Point* was declared Best Drama Picture and earned Ross the Globe for Best Director.

The Goodbye Girl nabbed trophies for Best Comedy or Musical Picture and Best Actor Richard Dreyfuss. Neil Simon was honored for his screenplay, too, while his wife, Marsha Mason, tied Diane Keaton (*Annie Hall*) for Best Actress.

In the drama races, Richard Burton received a rousing vertical ovation when he was hailed as top thesp for reprising the role he initiated before sellout crowds on Broadway as a psychiatrist trying to discover why a boy blinds horses in *Equus*. "When people stand up for you at an occasion like this, it really does something for you," he said, beaming at the podium. "I won this award 27 years ago for being the most promising actor and it's taken me 27 years to mature."

Also honored was *Equus* costar Peter

Firth, who won Best Supporting Actor for portraying the troubled boy that Burton tries to help.

Jane Fonda accepted two awards for *Julia*—her own as Best Drama Actress and one for absent costar Vanessa Redgrave as Best Supporting Actress. Accepting her own prize, Fonda said she shared it "with all the Julias everywhere who are challenged to make the world a better place." Fonda then addressed author Lillian Hellman in the audience, saying, "I'm so very proud to be able to portray you!"

The special Cecil B. DeMille Award was presented to Red Skelton, who accepted it, saying, "Who the hell is this guy DeMille?" Despite his joshing manner, Skelton was apparently nervous and tense. He clutched his statuette so hard that it snapped in two.

"I broke it!" he gasped. "I really did!"

At the Directors Guild of America awards six weeks later, the nominees represented "the best of the old and the best of the new school of directing," according to William Wyler, who had won the top prize in 1959 for *Ben-Hur*.

Variety interpreted Wyler's analysis thus: "Clearly, Herbert Ross (*The Turning Point*) and Fred Zinnemann (*Julia*) represent the old school and George Lucas (*Star Wars*) and Steven Spielberg (*Close Encounters*), both in their early 30s and with just three features apiece under their belts (albeit some of the most successful features in the history of the film industry), were the delegates from the new school. Appropriately enough, Woody Allen (*Annie Hall*) stands somewhere between the schools, both in age and experience."

After setting up the face-off, Wyler then opened the envelope to reveal the winner before the crowd of 1,200 gathered at the Beverly Hilton Hotel.

"*Monty Hall*," he said.

Luckily, Woody Allen wasn't present to hear the goof. He heard the news of his

> After 27 years, Richard Burton fullfilled his early Golden Globe promise.

victory at the DGA's New York ceremony at the St. Regis Hotel, where he accepted his plaque with a warm smile and few words.

Three weeks later, Woody Allen also showed up at the New York branch of the awards fete held by the Writers Guild of America. The four-time past loser (*What's New, Pussycat?*, *Take the Money and Run*, *Bananas*, *Sleeper*) now finally prevailed, beating Neil Simon (*The Goodbye Girl*) and George Lucas (*Star Wars*) for the prize for best original comedy, while the plaque for best adapted laffer went to Larry Gelbart (*Oh, God!*).

Old guild favorites triumphed in the drama categories: Arthur Laurents (previous guild honoree for *West Side Story*, 1961) won for best original drama (*The Turning Point*), and Alvin Sargent (previous champ for *Paper Moon*, 1973) won for best adapted drama (*Julia*). Only Laurents wasn't present to accept his laurels.

When the Oscars took place four days later, Woody Allen said he couldn't attend the gala because it fell on a Monday night, conflicting with his ongoing commitment to play clarinet in the New Orleans Marching and Funeral Band at Michael's Pub in New York City. He didn't seem to care that *Annie Hall* was the Best Picture front-runner after wining the DGA award—or that he himself was up for a triple-crown triumph in the other categories, being the first person since Orson Welles to snag simultaneous noms for acting, writing and directing. (Welles had scored one additional bid as a producer.)

One star who didn't miss the event was Vanessa Redgrave, who showed up despite the presence of pickets denouncing her outside the Dorothy Chandler Pavilion. They were militant members of the Jewish Defense League who'd been dogging her for weeks as part of a protest against a pro-Palestinian documentary that she produced. She ended up sneaking past them in an ambulance and entered the auditorium via a side door while they burned an effigy of her across the street.

Awards night marked the Oscar's golden anniversary, which was celebrated with a grand opening production number. As Debbie Reynolds sang "Look How Far We've Come," the stage behind her filled up with past Oscar champs such as Olivia de Havilland, Ernest Borgnine and Louise Fletcher.

"It looks like the road company of the Hollywood Wax Museum!" kidded emcee Bob Hope. "Good evening and welcome to the *real* star wars!"

One of the first award showdowns was for Best Supporting Actress, which pitted Redgrave against New York City Ballet dancer Leslie Browne (*The Turning Point*) and Quinn Cummings as Marsha Mason's precocious daughter in *The Goodbye Girl*.

When Redgrave won, she thanked her colleagues and said to the audience, "You should feel proud that in the last few weeks you've stood firm and you have refused to be intimidated by the threats of a small bunch of Zionist hoodlums whose behavior is an insult to the stature of Jews all over the world and their great and heroic record of struggle against fascism and oppression. I salute you and pledge to you that I will continue to fight against anti-Semitism and fascism."

Her speech was interrupted by outbursts of boos and cheers. After she left the stage, a moment of uneasy quiet followed.

Two *Julia* stars squared off in the race for Best Supporting Actor: Jason Robards and Maximilian Schell. They were pitted against ballet star Mikhail Baryshnikov in *The Turning Point*, Alec Guinness as a noble knight in *Star Wars* and Globe champ Peter Firth (*Equus*).

Last year's champ Jason Robards won again. Oscarcast emcee Bob Hope accepted the statuette for him, saying, "I think he's playing bridge with Marlon Brando and

> # Vanessa Redgrave caused an Oscar uproar blasting "Zionist hoodlums."

George C. Scott." In fact, Robards was starring in Eugene O'Neill's *A Touch of the Poet* on Broadway and he got miffed at Hope's joke because he had informed the academy why he couldn't be present on awards night.

Six-time loser Richard Burton (*Equus*) was favored finally to score his overdue Oscar for what the *L.A. Times* heralded as his "finest work since *Who's Afraid of Virginia Woolf?*" He ended up suffering an upset by Richard Dreyfuss, who looked stunned at the podium and confessed, "I didn't prepare anything . . ." At 29 years old, Dreyfuss was the youngest thesp to win Best Actor.

The Best Actress category featured three recent Golden Globe champs (Marsha Mason, Diane Keaton, Jane Fonda) plus the catfighting costars of the *Turning Point* (Anne Bancroft, Shirley MacLaine).

Keaton had the edge. Since winning kudos from the New York Film Critics Circle and the National Society of Film Critics for *Annie Hall*, she had also appeared to rave reviews in *Looking for Mr. Goodbar*. *Variety* described her role in *Goodbar* as "a girl who flees from a depressing home environment into the frantic world of singles bars and one-night physical gropings." Combined, her two featured roles made her, according to *The Village Voice*'s Andrew Sarris, "clearly the most dynamic woman star in pictures."

When Keaton won, *Variety* noted that she "accepted her Best Actress award with gracious mention of the other nominees."

Annie Hall's next best chance for victory was in the screenplay categories, but when scribe Paddy Chayefsky appeared at the podium to present them, he seemed perturbed. "Before I go on, there's a little matter I'd like to tidy up, at least if I expect to live with myself tomorrow morning," he said. "I would like to say—personal opinion, of course—that I'm sick and tired of people's exploiting the Academy Awards for the propagation of their own personal propaganda. I would like to suggest to Miss Redgrave that her winning an Academy Award is not a pivotal moment in history, does not require a

The new L.A. crix org took another commercial potshot at its snooty East Coast peers by declaring *Star Wars* Best Picture.

proclamation and a simple 'Thank you' would have sufficed."

He was cheered and booed simultaneously, just as Redgrave had been.

Then Chayesfky cited the winners: *Annie Hall* took the kudos for Best Original Screenplay and *Julia* claimed the laurels for Best Adapted Screenplay.

Considering *Annie Hall*'s victory at the Directors Guild of America, it was the front-runner for the helmer's Oscar, too. When Allen snagged it on top of the screenplay prize that he was awarded earlier, he became only the second person in Oscar history to earn both in the same year. Joseph L. Mankiewicz had pulled off the feat with *All about Eve* in 1950 and, before that, *A Letter to Three Wives* in 1949.

Since the director's prize usually lines up with Best Picture, *Annie Hall* was favored to score the top honor even though *The Turning Point* led with the most overall nominations (11). When *Annie Hall* prevailed, its victory marked the first time that the academy had given its top prize to a comedy since *Tom Jones* in 1963. *The Turning Point*'s defeat also marked a milestone. Failing to reap even a single win, it scored the biggest shutout in Oscar history.

Variety declared Allen's Oscar success a "near sweep." *Annie Hall*'s four victories—for writing, directing, Best Actress and Best Picture—precisely mirrored the kudos it had earned from the New York Film Critics

Circle. The movie backed by the circle's rival, the Los Angeles Film Critics Association—*Star Wars*—actually emerged with more honors in all when it garnered six tech awards.

Without Allen present to gush over, reporters chose to concentrate on the hoopla surrounding Vanessa Redgrave's acceptance speech.

"I am that Zionist hoodlum she was talking about," Alan King fumed to them back-stage. "It's just a pity I wasn't on the platform tonight. I would have gone for the jugular!"

"Jack Nicholson tried to sidestep the issue," *Variety* noted. "He quipped, 'I'm not very well read. What are Zionists? Are they Reds?' But he went on to observe that the Redgrave incident could establish a questionable precedent for using the Oscars to air views on other political donnybrooks around the world."

▪ 1977 ▪

NATIONAL BOARD OF REVIEW

Winners were announced on December 19, 1977.

BEST PICTURE
▪ *The Turning Point*
Annie Hall
Julia
Star Wars
Close Encounters of the Third Kind
The Late Show
Saturday Night Fever
Equus
The Picture Show Man
Harlan County, USA

BEST DIRECTOR
▪ Luis Buñuel, *That Obscure Object of Desire*

BEST ACTOR
▪ John Travolta, *Saturday Night Fever*

BEST ACTRESS
▪ Anne Bancroft, *The Turning Point*

BEST SUPPORTING ACTOR
▪ Tom Skerritt, *The Turning Point*

BEST SUPPORTING ACTRESS
▪ Diane Keaton, *Annie Hall*

BEST FOREIGN FILM
▪ *That Obscure Object of Desire* (Spain)
The Man Who Loved Women (France)
A Special Day (Italy)

Cria! (Spain)
The American Friend (Federal Republic of Germany)

SPECIAL CITATIONS
▪ Walt Disney Studios, *The Rescuers*
▪ Columbia Pictures for special effects in *Close Encounters of the Third Kind*

NATIONAL SOCIETY OF FILM CRITICS

Winners were announced on December 19, 1977.

BEST PICTURE
▪ *Annie Hall*

BEST DIRECTOR
▪ Luis Buñuel, *That Obscure Object of Desire*

BEST ACTOR
▪ Art Carney, *The Late Show*

BEST ACTRESS
▪ Diane Keaton, *Annie Hall*

BEST SUPPORTING ACTOR
▪ Edward Fox, *A Bridge Too Far*

BEST SUPPORTING ACTRESS
▪ Ann Wedgeworth, *Handle with Care*

BEST SCREENPLAY
▪ Woody Allen, Marshall Brickman, *Annie Hall*

BEST CINEMATOGRAPHY
- Thomas Mauch, Aguirre, *The Wrath of God*

LOS ANGELES FILM CRITICS ASSOCIATION

Winners were announced on December 19, 1977. Awards were presented on January 10, 1978, at the Pips club in Beverly Hills.

BEST PICTURE
- *Star Wars*

BEST DIRECTOR
- Herbert Ross, *The Turning Point*

BEST ACTOR
- Richard Dreyfuss, *The Goodbye Girl*

BEST ACTRESS
- Shelley Duvall, *Three Women*

BEST SUPPORTING ACTOR
- Jason Robards, *Julia*

BEST SUPPORTING ACTRESS
- Vanessa Redgrave, *Julia*

BEST SCREENPLAY
- Woody Allen, Marshall Brickman, *Annie Hall*

BEST CINEMATOGRAPHY
- Douglas Slocombe, *Julia*

BEST MUSIC SCORE
- John Williams, *Star Wars*

BEST FOREIGN FILM
- *That Obscure Object of Desire* (Spain), Luis Buñuel

CAREER ACHIEVEMENT AWARD
- King Vidor

NEW GENERATION AWARD
- Joan Micklin Silver, *Between the Lines*

SPECIAL AWARDS
- Charles Gary Allison, *Fraternity Row*
- Barbara Kopple

Shirley MacLaine (left) and Anne Bancroft squared off in Globe and NBR best pic *The Turning Point*, which suffered the biggest shut-out in Oscar history (11 losses).

NEW YORK FILM CRITICS CIRCLE

Winners were announced on December 21, 1977. Awards were presented on January 29, 1978, at Sardi's restaurant in New York.

BEST PICTURE
- *Annie Hall*

BEST DIRECTOR
- Woody Allen, *Annie Hall*

BEST ACTOR
- John Gielgud, *Providence*

BEST ACTRESS
- Diane Keaton, *Annie Hall*

BEST SUPPORTING ACTOR
- Maximilian Schell, *Julia*

BEST SUPPORTING ACTRESS
- Sissy Spacek, *Three Women*

BEST SCREENPLAY
- Woody Allen, Marshall Brickman, *Annie Hall*

GOLDEN GLOBES

Nominations were announced on January 10, 1978. Awards were presented on January 28 at the Beverly Hilton Hotel in Los Angeles. The ceremony was telecast by NBC.

BEST DRAMA PICTURE

- *The Turning Point*
Close Encounters of the Third Kind
I Never Promised You a Rose Garden
Julia
Star Wars

BEST COMEDY OR MUSICAL PICTURE

- *The Goodbye Girl*
Annie Hall
High Anxiety
New York, New York
Saturday Night Fever

BEST DIRECTOR

- Herbert Ross, *The Turning Point*
Woody Allen, *Annie Hall*
George Lucas, *Star Wars*
Steven Spielberg, *Close Encounters of the Third Kind*
Fred Zinnemann, *Julia*

BEST ACTOR, DRAMA

- Richard Burton, *Equus*
Marcello Mastroianni, *A Special Day*
Al Pacino, *Bobby Deerfield*
Gregory Peck, *MacArthur*
Henry Winkler, *Heroes*

BEST ACTRESS, DRAMA

- Jane Fonda, *Julia*
Anne Bancroft, *The Turning Point*
Diane Keaton, *Looking for Mr. Goodbar*
Kathleen Quinlan, *I Never Promised You a Rose Garden*
Gena Rowlands, *Opening Night*

BEST ACTOR, COMEDY OR MUSICAL

- Richard Dreyfuss, *The Goodbye Girl*
Woody Allen, *Annie Hall*
Mel Brooks, *High Anxiety*
Robert De Niro, *New York, New York*
John Travolta, *Saturday Night Fever*

BEST ACTRESS, COMEDY OR MUSICAL (TIE)

- Diane Keaton, *Annie Hall*
- Marsha Mason, *The Goodbye Girl*
Sally Field, *Smokey and the Bandit*
Liza Minnelli, *New York, New York*
Lily Tomlin, *The Late Show*

BEST SUPPORTING ACTOR

- Peter Firth, *Equus*
Mikhail Baryshnikov, *The Turning Point*
Alec Guinness, *Star Wars*
Jason Robards, *Julia*
Maximilian Schell, *Julia*

BEST SUPPORTING ACTRESS

- Vanessa Redgrave, *Julia*
Ann-Margret, *Joseph Andrews*
Joan Blondell, *Opening Night*
Leslie Browne, *The Turning Point*
Quinn Cummings, *The Goodbye Girl*
Lilia Skala, *Roseland*

BEST SCREENPLAY

- Neil Simon, *The Goodbye Girl*
Woody Allen, Marshall Brickman, *Annie Hall*
Arthur Laurents, *The Turning Point*
Alvin Sargent, *Julia*
Steven Spielberg, *Close Encounters of the Third Kind*

BEST SONG

- "You Light Up My Life," *You Light Up My Life*, Joseph Brooks
"Deep Down Inside," *The Deep*, John Barry
"How Deep Is Your Love," *Saturday Night Fever*, Robin, Barry and Maurice Gibb
"Nobody Does It Better," *The Spy Who Loved Me*, Marvin Hamlisch, Carole Bayer Sager
"Theme from *New York, New York*," *New York, New York*, John Kander, Fred Ebb

BEST FOREIGN FILM

- *A Special Day* (Italy)
Cria! (Spain)
A Life Ahead (France)
That Obscure Object of Desire (France/Spain)
Pardon Mon Affaire (France)

Winners

BEST ORIGINAL SCORE

- John Williams, *Star Wars*

WORLD FILM FAVORITES

- Robert Redford
- Barbra Streisand

CECIL B. DEMILLE AWARD
- Red Skelton

DIRECTORS GUILD OF AMERICA

The award for Best Director was presented on March 11, 1978, at the Beverly Hilton Hotel in Los Angeles and the St. Regis Hotel in New York.

BEST DIRECTOR
- Woody Allen, *Annie Hall*

George Lucas, *Star Wars*
Herbert Ross, *The Turning Point*
Steven Spielberg, *Close Encounters of the Third Kind*
Fred Zinnemann, *Julia*

WRITERS GUILD OF AMERICA

Awards were presented on March 30, 1978, at the Beverly Hilton Hotel in Los Angeles and the Essex House in New York.

BEST DRAMA WRITTEN DIRECTLY FOR THE SCREEN
- *The Turning Point*, Arthur Laurents

Close Encounters of the Third Kind, Steven Spielberg
The Late Show, Robert Benton
Saturday Night Fever, Norman Wexler, based on a story by Nik Cohn

BEST DRAMA ADAPTED FROM ANOTHER MEDIUM
- *Julia*, Alvin Sargent, based on the novel *Pentimento* by Lillian Hellman

I Never Promised You a Rose Garden, Gavin Lambert, Lewis John Carlino, based on the novel by Joanne Greenberg
Islands in the Stream, Denne Bart Petitclerc, based on the novel by Ernest Hemingway
Looking for Mr. Goodbar, Richard Brooks, based on the novel by Judith Rossner

BEST COMEDY WRITTEN DIRECTLY FOR THE SCREEN
- *Annie Hall*, Woody Allen, Marshall Brickman

The Goodbye Girl, Neil Simon
Slap Shot, Nancy Dowd
Star Wars, George Lucas

BEST COMEDY ADAPTED FROM ANOTHER MEDIUM
- *Oh, God!* Larry Gelbart, based on the novel by Avery Corman

Semi-Tough, Walter Bernstein, based on the novel by Dan Jenkins
The Spy Who Loved Me, Christopher Wood, Richard Maibaum, based on the novel by Ian Fleming

LAUREL AWARD
- Edward Anhalt

VALENTINE DAVIES AWARD
- Norman Lear

MORGAN COX AWARD
- John Furia, Jr.

ACADEMY AWARDS

Nominations were announced on February 21, 1978. Awards were presented on April 3 at the Dorothy Chandler Pavilion in Los Angeles. The ceremony was telecast by ABC.

BEST PICTURE
- *Annie Hall*

The Goodbye Girl
Julia
Star Wars
The Turning Point

BEST DIRECTOR
- Woody Allen, *Annie Hall*

George Lucas, *Star Wars*
Herbert Ross, *The Turning Point*
Steven Spielberg, *Close Encounters of the Third Kind*
Fred Zinnemann, *Julia*

BEST ACTOR
- Richard Dreyfuss, *The Goodbye Girl*

Woody Allen, *Annie Hall*
Richard Burton, *Equus*
Marcello Mastroianni, *A Special Day*
John Travolta, *Saturday Night Fever*

BEST ACTRESS
- Diane Keaton, *Annie Hall*

Anne Bancroft, *The Turning Point*
Jane Fonda, *Julia*
Shirley MacLaine, *The Turning Point*
Marsha Mason, *The Goodbye Girl*

BEST SUPPORTING ACTOR
- Jason Robards, *Julia*

Mikhail Baryshnikov, *The Turning Point*
Peter Firth, *Equus*
Alec Guinness, *Star Wars*
Maximilian Schell, *Julia*

BEST SUPPORTING ACTRESS
- Vanessa Redgrave, *Julia*

Leslie Browne, *The Turning Point*
Quinn Cummings, *The Goodbye Girl*
Melinda Dillon, *Close Encounters of the Third Kind*
Tuesday Weld, *Looking for Mr. Goodbar*

BEST ORIGINAL SCREENPLAY
- Woody Allen, Marshall Brickman, *Annie Hall*

Robert Benton, *The Late Show*
Arthur Laurents, *The Turning Point*
George Lucas, *Star Wars*
Neil Simon, *The Goodbye Girl*

BEST ADAPTED SCREENPLAY
- Alvin Sargent, *Julia*

Luis Buñuel, Jean-Claude Carrière, *That Obscure Object of Desire*
Lewis John Carlino, Gavin Lambert, *I Never Promised You a Rose Garden*
Larry Gelbart, *Oh, God!*
Peter Shaffer, *Equus*

BEST SONG
- "You Light Up My Life," *You Light Up My Life*, Joseph Brooks

"Candle on the Water," *Pete's Dragon*, Joel Hirschhorn, Al Kasha
"Nobody Does It Better," *The Spy Who Loved Me*, Marvin Hamlisch, Carole Bayer Sager
"The Slipper and the Rose Waltz (He Danced with Me/She Danced with Me)," *The Slipper and the Rose—The Story of Cinderella*, Richard M. Sherman, Robert B. Sherman

"Someone's Waiting For You," *The Rescuers*, Carol Connors, Sammy Fain, Ayn Robbins

BEST FOREIGN-LANGUAGE FILM
- *Madame Rosa* (France)

Iphigenia (Greece)
Operation Thunderbolt (Israel)
A Special Day (Italy)
That Obscure Object of Desire (Spain)

Winners

BEST ART DIRECTION
- John Barry, Leslie Dilley, Norman Reynolds, Roger Christian, *Star Wars*

BEST CINEMATOGRAPHY
- Vilmos Zsigmond, *Close Encounters of the Third Kind*

BEST COSTUME DESIGN
- John Mollo, *Star Wars*

BEST DOCUMENTARY
(FEATURE)
- *Who Are the DeBolts? And Where Did They Get 19 Kids?*, John Korty, Warren L. Lockhart, Dan McCann

(SHORT SUBJECT)
- *Gravity Is My Enemy*, John Joseph, Jan Stussy

BEST FILM EDITING
- Richard Chew, Paul Hirsch, Marcia Lucas, *Star Wars*

BEST MUSIC
(ORIGINAL SCORE)
- John Williams, *Star Wars*

(ORIGINAL SONG SCORE AND ITS ADAPTATION OR ADAPTATION SCORE)
- Jonathan Tunick, *A Little Night Music*

SCIENTIFIC OR TECHNICAL AWARDS
Class I (Statuette)
- Garrett Brown, Cinema Products Corporation Engineering staff, John Jurgens

Class II (Plaque)
- John Agalsoff, Emory M. Cohen, Barry K. Henley, Joseph D. Kelly, Hammond

H. Holt, Glen Glenn Sound; Eastman Kodak; N. Paul Kenworthy, Jr., William R. Latady; John Dykstra, Alvah J. Millers, Jerry Jeffress, Stefan Kudelski

Class III (Certificate)
- Ernest Nettman; Electronic Engineering Company of California; Dr. Bernard Kuhl, Werner Block, Osram; Panavision; Piclear

BEST SHORT FILM
(ANIMATED)
- *The Sand Castle*

(LIVE ACTION)
- *I'll Find a Way*

BEST SOUND
- Derek Ball, Don MacDougall, Bob Minkler, Ray West, *Star Wars*

SPECIAL ACHIEVEMENT AWARDS
(SOUND EFFECTS EDITING)
- Frank E. Warner, *Close Encounters of the Third Kind*

(SOUND EFFECTS)
- Benjamin Burtt, Jr., *Star Wars*

BEST VISUAL EFFECTS
- Robert Blalack, John Dykstra, Richard Edlund, Grant McCune, John Stears, *Star Wars*

IRVING G. THALBERG MEMORIAL AWARD
- Walter Mirisch

JEAN HERSHOLT HUMANITARIAN AWARD
- Charlton Heston

HONORARY AWARDS
- Margaret Booth
- Gordon E. Sawyer
- Sidney Paul Solow

SCREEN ACTORS GUILD

LIFETIME ACHIEVEMENT AWARD
- James Cagney

· 1978 ·

The Deer Hunter *Takes Early Aim at Gotham*

By 1978 it was common practice for a studio to open an Oscar-worthy film in Los Angeles during the last week of December so it could be eligible for Academy Awards, then delay its wider release for several weeks so it could be unveiled with appropriate ballyhoo while academy members inked their nomination ballots. But no studio had ever tried the trick in New York so that a pic could build early buzz while Gotham critics chose their anointed.

It was *Grease* producer Allan Carr who suggested the marketing scheme to Universal, which was worried about debuting *The Deer Hunter*. Only six years had passed since the end of America's involvement in the Vietnam war, the nation was still smarting from the tragedy and the pic's depiction of the conflict's impact on three soldiers who hail from the same Pennsylvania steel town was, warned *Variety*, "brutal."

But *Variety* also declared *The Deer Hunter* "powerful and fascinating" and it was clear to the suits at Universal that they might have Oscar's next Best Picture on the shelf.

A Universal marketing exec fessed up to *The New York Times* in late November that he'd soon be attempting the ploy. "He is aware that he is taking a risk," reported the *Times*, "that the New York critics may think he is trying to steamroll them and react negatively to the film."

The exec, however, said, "We are taking that chance. We have made a serious film about a subject that hasn't been successful at the box office before. The picture would die if we opened it cold in February. It must

Universal studio's risky marketing scheme paid off when The Deer Hunter *was voted Best Picture by the N.Y. crix, then Oscar voters.*

have awards to give it the stature it needs."

The Deer Hunter opened at New York's Coronet Theater on December 15 for only nine reserved-seat performances. Meantime, it was also premiered briefly in Los Angeles, where it could be viewed by invitation only. "We're showing it to publishers, editors, disk jockeys—anyone who attends parties and is likely to talk about the film," the exec added. "This is the sort of marketing that will kill you if you have a bad film." General release was planned for mid-February, just prior to the announcement of Oscar nominations.

But the Los Angeles Film Critics Association—the first crix org to announce its awards—snubbed *The Deer Hunter* as its Best Picture choice. The crix did name the film's helmer, Michael Cimino, as Best Director, but they opted to give their top kudos to another movie about Vietnam: *Coming Home.*

The L.A. crix also voted *Coming Home*'s stars Best Actor and Actress. In its review of the pic, *Variety* had lauded Jon Voight's return to the screen—"much more mature, assured and effective"—as a paraplegic veteran who falls in love with a former classmate doing volunteer work at the hospital where he's undergoing rehab. *Variety* had also praised Jane Fonda "in another memorable and moving performance," adding, "A sex scene between the two is a masterpiece of discreet romantic eroticism."

Fonda was also *Coming Home*'s producer. She commissioned the first script in 1973, supervised subsequent rewrites and hired its director (Hal Ashby) and her costar (Voight). She told reporters, "This movie means more to me than any movie I've done so far."

Runner-up for Best Actor was Gary Busey as the rock 'n' roll pioneer profiled in *The Buddy Holly Story*. Best Actress also-ran was Ingrid Bergman as a concert pianist battling her unruly daughter (Liv Ullmann) in Ingmar Bergman's *Autumn Sonata*. Woody Allen came in second place in the director's race for *Interiors*, which *Variety* said looks "like Ingmar Bergman's pictures." Allen also placed for the screenplay prize behind Paul Mazursky (*An Unmarried Woman*). Best Supporting Actor was Robert Morley as a flamboyant gourmand in *Who Is Killing the Great Chefs of Europe?* There was a tie for Best Supporting Actress between Mona Washbourne as the loyal aunt of poet Stevie Smith in *Stevie* and Maureen Stapleton, who wins the affections of a married E. G. Marshall in *Interiors*.

The kudos were presented at a ceremony taped for later telecast on the syndicated *Merv Griffin Show*.

The National Board of Review was the next group to sound off—and the next one to snub *The Deer Hunter*, not even listing it among its top 10 films of 1978. Its Best Picture choice was Terrence Malick's *Days of Heaven*, which *Variety* hailed as "one of the great cinematic achievements of the 1970s (about) a trio of nomads (whose) lives intersect with a wealthy wheat farmer" in 1916.

Two Vietnam-themed pix battled for the year's top kudos.

Ingmar Bergman was declared Best Director and Ingrid Bergman Best Actress. Jon Voight shared the Best Actor prize in a tie with Laurence Olivier as a Nazi hunter in *The Boys from Brazil*. Best Supporting Actor was veteran Hollywood stuntman Richard Farnsworth, who made his dramatic debut as a grizzled ranchhand in *Comes a Horseman*. Best Supporting Actress was Angela Lansbury as a romance novelist in Agatha Christie's whodunit *Death on the Nile*.

One day after the board released its awards rostrum came the good news that Universal hoped for—*The Deer Hunter* was voted top pic by the N.Y. crix, but only after it pulled ahead of *Days of Heaven* on the third ballot to claim victory by a score of 29 to 24. *Heaven*'s Terrence Malick nonetheless prevailed for the director's laurels, topping Paul Mazursky 29 points to 21. Mazursky's consolation prize was the screenplay award.

The Deer Hunter claimed one more accolade from the Gotham crix: Best Supporting Actor for Christopher Walken as a daredevil soldier who loses a round of Russian roulette while his hometown pals watch on in horror. He took the category with 35 points over Farnsworth (24). Maureen Stapleton won Best Supporting Actress (34 points) over Maggie Smith, who scored 26 points for her portrayal of a thesp who loses an Oscar in *California Suite*. Jon Voight (40) eclipsed Gary Busey (32) for Best Actor. All races were decided in two or more ballots, except Best Actress, which Ingrid Bergman snagged handily on the first tally with 14 points over distant rival Jill Clayburgh in *An Unmarried Woman* (4 points).

So that its 26 members would no longer be tempted to endorse the same foreign-lingo imports chosen as Best Picture by the rival National Society of Film Critics, the circle resurrected its old, separate award for Best Foreign Film, which went to Italy's *Bread and Chocolate*.

When the Gotham crix gathered at Sardi's for their awards party, *The Village Voice* noted that an eager "Michael Cimino clutched his Best Picture honor" proudly. Previous Best Actor champ Jon Voight seemed flip by comparison while "he discussed keeping one's head in place," the *Voice* added.

"Values get to be distorted," Voight said at the podium as he received his latest kudos. "Actors think about money. Actors think about too many silly things. It falls on the critics to get us on the path and encourage us to do it the right way."

Ingrid Bergman's Best Actress plaque was accepted by her daughter Isabella Rossellini, who had to suffer what the *Voice* called a "presumptuous" intro by acting coach Lee Strasberg.

"Young people do not see the love and romance of acting, but the weight and pressure of having to live up to the names of their famous parents," he said.

The *Voice* reported, "Rossellini replied that she was more than happy to have Ingrid and Roberto as mom and pop."

Paul Mazursky and Christopher Walken were on hand to take their turns at the podium next, while stand-ins included Colleen Dewhurst, who accepted for Maureen Stapleton, and *Days of Heaven* cast member Linda Manz, who claimed Terrence Malick's plaque.

Entertainment was provided by the comedy team of Monteith and Rand, who *Variety* said had "the hardbitten attending press in an uproar with their takeoff of critics at a screening of a sex film." The *Voice* noticed that the crix being lampooned "suspiciously resembled" two of its own scribes—Andrew Sarris and Molly Haskell—who laughed "at their own endearing idiosyncrasies."

When the National Society of Film Critics voted two weeks after the Gotham circle, it endorsed a few of the same honorees, including Best Actress Ingrid Bergman

(over Jane Fonda by a 45-to-30 count), Best Director Terrence Malick (25 to 19 over Bertrand Blier, *Get Out Your Handkerchiefs*) and Best Screenplay, with Paul Mazursky prevailing over Blier by a narrow 27-to-25 margin.

The society stuck by its renowned preference for foreign-lingo fare when it named Best Picture in a vote called "hotly contested" by *The New York Times*. Blier's raucous French social comedy *Get Out Your Handkerchiefs* finally won on the fourth ballot, but only after running substantially behind *Days of Heaven* and *The Deer Hunter* on the first three pollings.

"The group votes in much the same way as the New York organization," the *Times* explained. "On a first ballot, each member is allotted one vote. (If a film does not achieve a majority), each member makes three choices on subsequent ballots, awarding them three points, two points or one point.

"The voting rules, which stipulate that the winning film must appear on half of the members' ballots as well as receive a majority of points, can frequently lead to reversals. *Get Out Your Handkerchiefs* finally received 26 points with *The Deer Hunter* and *An Unmarried Woman* tied at 24. There were 22 points for *Days of Heaven*."

Richard Farnsworth and Robert Morley each scored 28 points to tie for Best Supporting Actor. Meryl Streep won Best Supporting Actress (over Maureen Stapleton, 24 to 20) for her portrayal of Christopher Walken's left-behind hometown lover in *The Deer Hunter*.

At the Golden Globes, *The Deer Hunter, Coming Home, Days of Heaven* and *An Unmarried Woman* squared off for Best Drama Picture, but none of them led with the most overall nominations. That distinction was held by the fifth contender, which led with six bids—*Midnight Express*, the tale of an American incarcerated in a brutal Turkish prison for trying to smuggle hashish.

> # Studios spent $500 per voter on Oscar campaigns.

Three weeks before the awards ceremony, there was more surprising Globe news: the gala would not be televised. The program's production company had failed to line up sponsorship in time. The firm asked the Hollywood Foreign Press Association to delay the ceremony until March, but the org refused.

When awards night came, the attendees who paid $100 per ticket to be at the Beverly Hilton Hotel didn't seem to mind. "The Golden Globes reveled in its return to television anonymity," *Variety* reported. "The bar opened at 5:30 P.M. The presentations did not get under way until after 8 P.M., following dinner during which wine and other libations flowed freely."

"This audience is loaded to the gills!" joked emcee Chevy Chase as he opened the ceremony, not realizing that the topic of substance abuse would soon become a serious issue.

The issue arose during the awards sweep of the movie about drugs—*Midnight Express*, which claimed four categories, including Best Drama Picture (a "surprise," said the Associated Press). It also earned kudos for its script, its music score and Best Supporting Actor John Hurt (as "a hard doper," said *Variety*). Best Film Debut champs were *Midnight* stars Brad Davis and Irene Miracle as the Yankee drug smuggler and his wife. (Ironically, in real life, Davis would end up dying from AIDS contracted as a result of actual drug abuse.)

The screenplay award went to Oliver Stone, who *Variety* said "did his best to snatch defeat from the jaws of victory."

While accepting his statuette, Stone "launched into a rambling polemic equating U.S. treatment of imprisoned drug users with the injustice depicted in *Midnight Express*," *Variety* added.

Stone said, "The United States can't point a finger at Turkey because we're putting people in jail for being high. Every person should have the right to pursue his own happiness!"

Stone's words were greeted with angry boos and catcalls from the audience, but he continued railing against "obscene and victimless drug charges." Irritated, Chevy Chase whispered loudly to him, "Just say 'thank you' and leave the stage." Stone refused and kept talking, even when the orchestra struck up loud music to drown him out. It was only when security guards approached the stage that he wrapped up quickly, flashed the audience a victory sign and trotted over to his seat.

"He's right," Chase said to the audience with a wry smile. "Of course, he's loaded."

A short while later, *Midnight Express*'s director, Alan Parker, "administered a final spanking to Stone" when he accepted the Best Picture award, *Variety* said.

"Oliver's very bright and very well meaning," Parker said. "He's also boring."

"Thank God we're not on television!" Chase roared when he resumed his emcee duties. The audience cheered.

Winners of the Best Drama Actor and Actress awards were far less dramatic. Jon Voight told the crowd, "The members of the foreign press represent to me the kind aunts and uncles of our industry." *Coming Home* costar Jane Fonda collected her Globe, saying, "I accept this for all the men in their wheelchairs and their lovers."

Chevy Chase's gumshoe laffer *Foul Play* led with the most noms in the comedy/music races, but lost the top prize for Best Picture to *Heaven Can Wait*, Warren Beatty's remake of *Here Comes Mr. Jordan*. Beatty even beat Chase for Best Actor soon after Chase lost the prize for Best Film Debut to Brad Davis. ("Here we go in the dumper again," Chase whined to the crowd.) Beatty was not present to accept his awards, but they were claimed by costar Dyan Cannon, who also reaped the Best Supporting

> The future Sundance film fest was launched as the Utah-U.S.A. Film Festival.

Actress honor for herself in an upset over Carol Burnett (*A Wedding*).

Ellen Burstyn (*Same Time, Next Year*) tied absent Maggie Smith for Best Actress. She accepted the Globe, saying, "When I was nominated for *The Exorcist* but didn't win, Billy Friedkin sent me his. Now that I've won, I can send it back."

Soon after its Globes romp, *Midnight Express* scored noms from the writers' and directors' guilds. At the scribes' kudos, Oliver Stone won Best Adapted Screenplay, but he did not make a fiery acceptance speech. The battle for best original drama spanned the writers of *Coming Home, The Deer Hunter, An Unmarried Woman, Interiors* and *Days of Heaven*. The victor was *Coming Home*, written in part by Waldo Salt, a two-time past guild winner for *Serpico* (1973) and *Midnight Cowboy* (1969).

Past guild champs took the other two races, too. Last year's honoree Larry Gelbart returned to reap the plaque for best original comedy for *Movie Movie*, his parody of the double features shown at theaters in the 1930s. 1975 guild winner Warren Beatty (*Shampoo*) was honored this year with co-writer Elaine May for *Heaven Can Wait*.

The writers' guild's drama winners *Coming Home* and *Midnight Express* both competed at the Directors Guild of America awards, where the pix's helmers Hal Ashby and Alan Parker, respectively, faced Paul Mazursky (*An Unmarried Woman*), Michael Cimino (*The Deer Hunter*) and the duo of Warren Beatty and Buck Henry (*Heaven Can Wait*).

When Cimino won, he gave what *Variety* called "an emotional acceptance speech," thanking his producer and distributor "for the courage to present a three-hour picture with subject matter that everyone thought was unacceptable to the American public."

Variety said of the victory, "Cimino's selection was not completely unexpected, as he had already copped similar nods from the L.A. film critics and the Golden Globes. *The Deer Hunter* thus takes a giant step toward the Oscar for best direction. Since the DGA awards were inaugurated in 1948, there have been only two exceptions to

A drama about a paraplegic Vietnam vet, *Coming Home*, was named Best Picture, Actor (Jon Voight) and Actress (Jane Fonda) by the L.A. crix, then won Oscars for its thesps.

identical choices by DGA members and voters from the Academy of Motion Picture Arts and Sciences."

As this year's Oscar derby heated up, Roger Ebert of *The Chicago Sun-Times* reported that the six major film studios each spent about $300,000 on campaigns that included private screenings for academy members and lots of ads in the trades. "That comes to $1.8 million—or $500 for every voting member of the academy," he pointed out.

Universal's tireless push behind *The Deer Hunter* paid off. It tied *Heaven Can Wait* for the most nominations—nine. *Coming Home* came in close behind with eight. Four of *Heaven Can Wait*'s bids were for Warren Beatty personally, making him the first person since Orson Welles to earn noms for writing, directing, acting and producing.

As the awards night began, host Johnny Carson promised the audience "two hours of sparkling entertainment spread out over a four-hour show."

When the award winners started to be revealed, neither nomination leader swept up. *The Deer Hunter* did nail trophies for sound and film editing and *Heaven Can Wait* copped the prize for art direction, but they both lost the screenplay races, one of which is usually claimed by the eventual Best Picture champ.

Heaven's Warren Beatty and Elaine May and *California Suite*'s Neil Simon lost the showdown for Best Adapted Screenplay to Oliver Stone, who appeared calm at the podium as he expressed his hope that the success of *Midnight Express* might help "all the men and women who are still in prison tonight." The quartet of *Deer Hunter* writers lost the race for Best Original Screenplay to the trinity of scribes behind *Coming Home*.

The three most-nominated films were repped in the race for Best Supporting Actor by Bruce Dern (*Coming Home*), Jack Warden (*Heaven Can Wait*) and Gotham crix champ Christopher Walken (*The Deer Hunter*), but some pundits predicted that the winner would be one of the other two candidates: John Hurt (*Midnight Express*) or National Society of Film Critics honoree Richard Farnsworth (*Comes a Horseman*). Walken prevailed.

There was no early leader in the race for Best Supporting Actress, which pitted the National Society of Film Critics champ (Meryl Streep) against the honoree of the Gotham and L.A. groups (Maureen Stapleton) and recent Globe grabbers Dyan Cannon and Maggie Smith.

When Smith won, she thanked her costar Michael Caine, claiming that he deserved half of her statuette: "It should be split down the middle."

Variety columnist Army Archerd noted, "It was ironic that Smith won for her *California Suite* role, part of which she filmed at last year's Oscars where she played a— loser!"

The Best Actor showdown seemed to be between the two stars of the two Vietnam-themed pix: Robert De Niro (*The Deer Hunter*) and Jon Voight (*Coming Home*). Voight had the early edge with endorsements from the Gotham and L.A. crix. When he triumphed, he wept as he thanked "the people in the chairs and the veterans."

Award forecasters split over who'd win Best Actress: Jane Fonda or Ingrid Bergman.

Variety said it was "ironic" that Maggie Smith won an Oscar for playing an Oscar loser opposite Michael Caine in *California Suite*.

When Fonda won, she expressed her thanks in words and in sign language. She explained why she used the latter form of communication: "While we were making the movie, we all became more aware of the problems of the handicapped. Over 14 million people are deaf. They are the invisible handicapped and can't share this evening, so this is my way of acknowledging them."

While she spoke, her father Henry watched the ceremony from a hospital room, where he was recovering from hip surgery.

The Deer Hunter rebounded from its losses in the races for writing and lead acting by striking gold for Best Director. As Michael Cimino clutched his statuette at the podium, he roared to the audience, "I love you madly!"

"A special moment was reserved for the climax when John Wayne came striding onto the stage of the Pavilion, one year after his open heart surgery, to present the Best Picture statuette," *Variety* reported. "Both he and Oscar, Wayne drawled, 'plan to be around a whole lot longer.'" (One would not be. Wayne died two months later.)

The night's big victor turned out to be *The Deer Hunter*—and the Universal studio for pursuing a risky awards strategy that proved to be a winner.

Warren Beatty proved to be a big loser when none of his four noms paid off.

The equivalent of an Oscar for small indie pix was created in 1978 when the Utah–U.S.A. Film Festival debuted. The future Sundance Film Festival was then small and based in Salt Lake City, but it had a big star behind it—Robert Redford, whose wife was a cousin of the festival's first prexy, Sterling Van Wagenen. Redford was involved only casually in the fest in the early days, but he served as its first chairman of the board and occasional spokesman. He was an earnest cheerleader, though, saying, "Utah is long overdue for cultural development in film art."

Local critics and professors screened 25 films to select six finalists. Each filmmaker received $1,000. The winner's prize: $5,000. All honorees were feted at an awards ceremony held at the Alta Club.

Org leaders claimed that 11,000 people participated in the fest, but *Variety* thought attendance seemed sparce, reporting, "The 800-seat 'big house' and twin 300-seaters at the new Trolley Corners complex were never totally filled despite the modest series ticket price of $12 and a single show charge of $3."

The winner of the Grand Jury Prize was *Girlfriends*, a comic drama about the split-up of two gal pals when one of them falls for a guy. A Special Jury Prize went to the runner-up, *The Whole Shootin' Match*, a tale of two Texas losers who try to strike it rich by going into the polyurethane business.

The festival also featured a retrospective roundup of classic films about the U.S. West and Southwest. There were panels featuring such Hollywood luminaries as Peter Bogdanovich and Mark Rydell discussing important showbiz subjects. An honorary prize was created in the memory of legendary director John Ford, who often filmed his westerns in Utah's Monument Valley. Its first recipient was one of Ford's favorite stars, John Wayne.

Out of all the fest's myriad attractions, the rookie events didn't seem to have the heft to steal the spotlight from the pros. Fest co-founder Lory Smith wrote years later in *Party in a Box*, however, "In wrapping up the festival, we were all astonished to discover, in reviewing the box-office figures, that these independent films were the most widely attended of the festival, an occurrence none of us had expected. We knew we were on to something."

▪ 1978 ▪

UTAH-U.S.A. FILM FESTIVAL

The festival was held September 6–12, 1978, at Trolley Corners Theaters in Salt Lake City, Utah.

GRAND JURY PRIZE
▪ *Girlfriends*, Claudia Weill

SPECIAL JURY PRIZE
▪ *The Whole Shootin' Match*, Eagle Pennel

JOHN FORD MEDALLION
▪ John Wayne

LOS ANGELES FILM CRITICS ASSOCIATION

Winners were announced on December 16, 1978. Awards were presented on January 19, 1979, on the syndicated TV series *The Merv Griffin Show*.

BEST PICTURE
▪ *Coming Home*

BEST DIRECTOR
▪ Michael Cimino, *The Deer Hunter*

BEST ACTOR
▪ Jon Voight, *Coming Home*

BEST ACTRESS
▪ Jane Fonda, *Coming Home, Comes a Horseman, California Suite*

BEST SUPPORTING ACTOR
▪ Robert Morley, *Who Is Killing the Great Chefs of Europe?*

BEST SUPPORTING ACTRESS (TIE)
▪ Maureen Stapleton, *Interiors*
▪ Mona Washbourne, *Stevie*

BEST SCREENPLAY
- Paul Mazursky, *An Unmarried Woman*

BEST CINEMATOGRAPHY
- Nestor Almendros, *Days of Heaven*

BEST MUSIC SCORE
- Giorgio Moroder, *Midnight Express*

BEST FOREIGN FILM
- *Madame Rosa* (France), Moshe Mizrahi

CAREER ACHIEVEMENT AWARD
- Orson Welles

NEW GENERATION AWARD
- Gary Busey, *The Buddy Holly Story*

NATIONAL BOARD OF REVIEW

Winners were announced on December 19, 1978.

BEST PICTURE
- *Days of Heaven*
Coming Home
Interiors
Superman
Movie Movie
Midnight Express
An Unmarried Woman
Pretty Baby
Girlfriends
Comes a Horseman

BEST DIRECTOR
- Ingmar Bergman, *Autumn Sonata*

BEST ACTOR (TIE)
- Jon Voight, *Coming Home*
- Laurence Olivier, *The Boys from Brazil*

BEST ACTRESS
- Ingrid Bergman, *Autumn Sonata*

BEST SUPPORTING ACTOR
- Richard Farnsworth, *Comes a Horseman*

BEST SUPPORTING ACTRESS
- Angela Lansbury, *Death on the Nile*

BEST FOREIGN FILM
- *Autumn Sonata* (Sweden)
Dear Detective (France)
Madame Rosa (France)
A Slave of Love (U.S.S.R.)
Bread and Chocolate (Italy)

NEW YORK FILM CRITICS CIRCLE

Winners were announced on December 20, 1978. Awards were presented on January 28, 1979, at Sardi's restaurant in New York.

BEST PICTURE
- *The Deer Hunter*

BEST DIRECTOR
- Terrence Malick, *Days of Heaven*

BEST ACTOR
- Jon Voight, *Coming Home*

BEST ACTRESS
- Ingrid Bergman, *Autumn Sonata*

BEST SUPPORTING ACTOR
- Christopher Walken, *The Deer Hunter*

BEST SUPPORTING ACTRESS
- Maureen Stapleton, *Interiors*

BEST SCREENPLAY
- Paul Mazursky, *An Unmarried Woman*

BEST FOREIGN FILM
- *Bread and Chocolate* (Italy)

NATIONAL SOCIETY OF FILM CRITICS

Winners were announced on January 3, 1979.

BEST PICTURE
- *Get Out Your Handkerchiefs*

BEST DIRECTOR
- Terrence Malick, *Days of Heaven*

BEST ACTOR
- Gary Busey, *The Buddy Holly Story*

BEST ACTRESS
- Ingrid Bergman, *Autumn Sonata*

BEST SUPPORTING ACTOR (TIE)
- Richard Farnsworth, *Comes a Horseman*
- Robert Morley, *Who Is Killing the Great Chefs of Europe?*

BEST SUPPORTING ACTRESS
- Meryl Streep, *The Deer Hunter*

BEST SCREENPLAY
- Paul Mazursky, *An Unmarried Woman*

BEST CINEMATOGRAPHY
- Nestor Almendros, *Days of Heaven*

GOLDEN GLOBES

Nominations were announced on January 9, 1979. Awards were presented on January 27 at the Beverly Hilton Hotel in Los Angeles. The ceremony was not telecast.

BEST DRAMA PICTURE
- *Midnight Express*
Coming Home
Days of Heaven
The Deer Hunter
An Unmarried Woman

BEST COMEDY OR MUSICAL PICTURE
- *Heaven Can Wait*
California Suite
Foul Play
Grease
Movie Movie

BEST DIRECTOR
- Michael Cimino, *The Deer Hunter*
Woody Allen, *Interiors*
Hal Ashby, *Coming Home*
Terrence Malick, *Days of Heaven*
Paul Mazursky, *An Unmarried Woman*
Alan Parker, *Midnight Express*

BEST ACTOR, DRAMA
- Jon Voight, *Coming Home*
Brad Davis, *Midnight Express*
Robert De Niro, *The Deer Hunter*
Anthony Hopkins, *Magic*
Gregory Peck, *The Boys from Brazil*

BEST ACTRESS, DRAMA
- Jane Fonda, *Coming Home*
Ingrid Bergman, *Autumn Sonata*
Jill Clayburgh, *An Unmarried Woman*
Glenda Jackson, *Stevie*
Geraldine Page, *Interiors*

BEST ACTOR, COMEDY OR MUSICAL
- Warren Beatty, *Heaven Can Wait*
Alan Alda, *Same Time, Next Year*
Gary Busey, *The Buddy Holly Story*
Chevy Chase, *Foul Play*
George C. Scott, *Movie Movie*
John Travolta, *Grease*

BEST ACTRESS, COMEDY OR MUSICAL (TIE)
- Ellen Burstyn, *Same Time, Next Year*
- Maggie Smith, *California Suite*
Jacqueline Bisset, *Who Is Killing the Great Chefs of Europe?*
Goldie Hawn, *Foul Play*
Olivia Newton-John, *Grease*

BEST SUPPORTING ACTOR
- John Hurt, *Midnight Express*
Bruce Dern, *Coming Home*
Dudley Moore, *Foul Play*
Robert Morley, *Who Is Killing the Great Chefs of Europe?*
Christopher Walken, *The Deer Hunter*

BEST SUPPORTING ACTRESS
- Dyan Cannon, *Heaven Can Wait*
Carol Burnett, *A Wedding*
Maureen Stapleton, *Interiors*
Meryl Streep, *The Deer Hunter*
Mona Washbourne, *Stevie*

BEST FILM DEBUT—MALE
- Brad Davis, *Midnight Express*
Chevy Chase, *Foul Play*
Harry Hamlin, *Movie Movie*
Doug McKeon, *Uncle Joe Shannon*
Eric Roberts, *King of the Gypsies*
Andrew Stevens, *The Boys in Company C*

BEST FILM DEBUT—FEMALE
- Irene Miracle, *Midnight Express*
Anne Ditchburn, *Slow Dancing in the Big City*
Annie Potts, *Corvette Summer*
Anita Skinner, *Girl Friends*
Mary Steenburgen, *Goin' South*

BEST SCREENPLAY

- Oliver Stone, *Midnight Express*

Woody Allen, *Interiors*

Colin Higgins, *Foul Play*

Robert C. Jones, Waldo Salt, Nancy Dowd, *Coming Home*

Paul Mazursky, *An Unmarried Woman*

Deric Washburn, *The Deer Hunter*

BEST SONG

- "Last Dance," *Thank God It's Friday*, Paul Jabara

"Grease," *Grease*, John Farrar

"The Last Time I Felt Like This," *Same Time, Next Year*, Marvin Hamlisch, Alan Bergman, Marilyn Bergman

"Ready to Take a Chance Again," *Foul Play*, Charles Fox, Norman Gimbel

"You're the One That I Want," *Grease*, John Farrar

BEST FOREIGN FILM

- *Autumn Sonata* (Sweden)

Death on the Nile (England)

Dona Flor and Her Two Husbands (Brazil)

A Dream of Passion (Greece)

Get Out Your Handkerchiefs (France)

Lemon Popsicle (Israel)

Winners

BEST ORIGINAL SCORE

- Giorgio Moroder, *Midnight Express*

WORLD FILM FAVORITES

- Jane Fonda
- John Travolta

CECIL B. DEMILLE AWARD

- Lucille Ball

DIRECTORS GUILD OF AMERICA

The award for Best Director was presented on March 10, 1979, at the Beverly Hilton Hotel in Los Angeles and the St. Regis Hotel in New York.

BEST DIRECTOR

- Michael Cimino, *The Deer Hunter*

Hal Ashby, *Coming Home*

Warren Beatty, Buck Henry, *Heaven Can Wait*

Paul Mazursky, *An Unmarried Woman*

Alan Parker, *Midnight Express*

WRITERS GUILD OF AMERICA

Awards were presented on April 5, 1979, at the Beverly Hilton Hotel in Los Angeles and the Sheraton Center in New York.

BEST DRAMA WRITTEN DIRECTLY FOR THE SCREEN

- *Coming Home,* Waldo Salt, Robert C. Jones, Nancy Dowd

Days of Heaven, Terrence Malick

The Deer Hunter, Michael Cimino, Deric Washburn, Louis Garfinkle, Quinn K. Redeker

Interiors, Woody Allen

An Unmarried Woman, Paul Mazursky

BEST DRAMA ADAPTED FROM ANOTHER MEDIUM

- *Midnight Express*, Oliver Stone, based on a book by William Hayes and William Hoffer

Blood Brothers, Walter Newman, based on a novel by Richard Price

Go Tell the Spartans, Wendell Mayes, based on a novel by Daniel Ford

Invasion of the Body Snatchers, W. E. Richter, based on a story by Jack Finney

Who'll Stop the Rain? Judith Rascoe, Robert Stone, based on a novel by Robert Stone

BEST COMEDY WRITTEN DIRECTLY FOR THE SCREEN

- *Movie Movie,* Larry Gelbart, Sheldon Keller

House Calls, Max Shulman, Julius J. Epstein, Alan Mandel, Charles Shyer

National Lampoon's Animal House, Harold Ramis, Douglas Kenney, Chris Miller

Once in Paris, Frank Gilroy

A Wedding, John Considine, Patricia Resnick, Allan Nicholls, Robert Altman

BEST COMEDY ADAPTED FROM ANOTHER MEDIUM

- *Heaven Can Wait*, Elaine May, Warren Beatty, based on a play by Harry Segall
California Suite, Neil Simon, based on his play
Same Time, Next Year, Bernard Slade, based on his play
Superman, Mario Puzo, David Newman, Leslie Newman, Robert Benton, based on the "Action Comics" by Jerry Siegel and Joe Shuster
Who Is Killing the Great Chefs of Europe? Peter Stone, based on a novel by Nan and Ivan Lyons

LAUREL AWARD

- Neil Simon

VALENTINE DAVIES AWARD

- Melville Shavelson

MORGAN COX AWARD

- George Seaton

ACADEMY AWARDS

Nominations were announced on February 20, 1979. Awards were presented on April 9 at the Dorothy Chandler Pavilion in Los Angeles. The ceremony was telecast by ABC.

BEST PICTURE

- *The Deer Hunter*
Coming Home
Heaven Can Wait
Midnight Express
An Unmarried Woman

BEST DIRECTOR

- Michael Cimino, *The Deer Hunter*
Woody Allen, *Interiors*
Hal Ashby, *Coming Home*
Warren Beatty, Buck Henry, *Heaven Can Wait*
Alan Parker, *Midnight Express*

BEST ACTOR

- Jon Voight, *Coming Home*
Warren Beatty, *Heaven Can Wait*
Gary Busey, *The Buddy Holly Story*

Robert De Niro, *The Deer Hunter*
Laurence Olivier, *The Boys from Brazil*

BEST ACTRESS

- Jane Fonda, *Coming Home*
Ingrid Bergman, *Autumn Sonata*
Ellen Burstyn, *Same Time, Next Year*
Jill Clayburgh, *An Unmarried Woman*
Geraldine Page, *Interiors*

BEST SUPPORTING ACTOR

- Christopher Walken, *The Deer Hunter*
Bruce Dern, *Coming Home*
Richard Farnsworth, *Comes a Horseman*
John Hurt, *Midnight Express*
Jack Warden, *Heaven Can Wait*

BEST SUPPORTING ACTRESS

- Maggie Smith, *California Suite*
Dyan Cannon, *Heaven Can Wait*
Penelope Milford, *Coming Home*
Maureen Stapleton, *Interiors*
Meryl Streep, *The Deer Hunter*

BEST ORIGINAL SCREENPLAY

- Nancy Dowd, Robert C. Jones, Waldo Salt, *Coming Home*
Woody Allen, *Interiors*
Ingmar Bergman, *Autumn Sonata*
Michael Cimino, Louis Garfinkle, Quinn K. Redeker, Deric Washburn, *The Deer Hunter*
Paul Mazursky, *An Unmarried Woman*

BEST ADAPTED SCREENPLAY

- Oliver Stone, *Midnight Express*
Warren Beatty, Elaine May, *Heaven Can Wait*
Walter Newman, *Bloodbrothers*
Neil Simon, *California Suite*
Bernard Slade, *Same Time, Next Year*

BEST SONG

- "Last Dance," *Thank God It's Friday,* Paul Jabara
"Hopelessly Devoted to You," *Grease,* John Farrar
"The Last Time I Felt Like This," *Same Time, Next Year*, Alan Bergman, Marilyn Bergman, Marvin Hamlisch
"Ready to Take a Chance Again," *Foul Play*, Charles Fox, Norman Gimbel

"When You're Loved," *The Magic of Lassie,* Richard M. Sherman, Robert B. Sherman

BEST FOREIGN-LANGUAGE FILM
- *Get Out Your Handkerchief* (France)

The Glass Cell (German Federal Republic)
Hungarians (Hungary)
Viva Italia! (Italy)
White Bim Black Ear (U.S.S.R.)

Winners

BEST ART DIRECTION
- Edwin O'Donovan, Paul Sylbert, George Gaines, *Heaven Can Wait*

BEST CINEMATOGRAPHY
- Nestor Almendros, *Days of Heaven*

BEST COSTUME DESIGN
- Anthony Powell, *Death on the Nile*

BEST DOCUMENTARY
(FEATURE)
- Arnold Shapiro, *Scared Straight!*

(SHORT SUBJECT)
- Ben Shedd, Jacqueline Phillips Shedd, *The Flight of the Gossamer Condor*

BEST FILM EDITING
- Peter Zinner, *The Deer Hunter*

BEST MUSIC
(ORIGINAL SONG SCORE AND ITS ADAPTATION OR ADAPTATION SCORE)
- Giorgio Moroder, *Midnight Express*

(ADAPTATION SCORE)
- Joe Renzetti, *The Buddy Holly Story*

SCIENTIFIC OR TECHNICAL AWARDS
(Academy Award of Merit—Film)
- Eastman Kodak Co.; Stefan Kudelski, Nagra Magnetic Recorders; Robert E. Gottschalk, Panavision Inc.

(Scientific and Engineering Award—Sound)
- Ioan R. Allen, Philip S. J. Boole, Ray M. Dolby, Stephen M. Katz, David P. Robinson, Dolby Laboratories

(Technical Achievement Award—Lenses and Filters)
- Karl Macher, Glenn M. Berggren, Isco Optische Werke; David J. Degenkolb, Arthur L. Ford, Fred J. Scobey, DeLuxe General; Kiichi Sekiguchi, CINE-FI; Leonard Chapman, Leonard Equipment; James L. Fisher, J. L. Fisher, Inc.; Robert Stindt, Production Grip Equipment

BEST SHORT FILM
(ANIMATED)
- Eunice Macaulay, John Weldon, *Special Delivery*

(LIVE ACTION)
- Taylor Hackford, *Teenage Father*

BEST SOUND
- Darin Knight, William McCaughey, Richard Portman, Aaron Rochin, *The Deer Hunter*

SPECIAL ACHIEVEMENT AWARD
(VISUAL EFFECTS)
- Les Bowie, Colin Chilvers, Denys Coop, Roy Field, Derek Meddings, Zoran Perisic, *Superman*

JEAN HERSHOLT HUMANITARIAN AWARD
- Leo Jaffe

HONORARY AWARDS
- Linwood G. Dunn
- Walter Lantz
- Museum of Modern Art Department of Film
- Laurence Olivier
- Loren L. Ryder
- King Vidor
- Waldon O. Watson

SCREEN ACTORS GUILD

LIFETIME ACHIEVEMENT AWARD
- Edgar Bergen

· 1979 ·

Kramer vs. Kramer Agreement Ends N.Y. vs. L.A. Crix Bouts

So far the L.A. and New York crix groups seemed to be 3,000 miles apart in their award choices. The Hollywoodites often favored lowbrow, high-adrenaline pop fare (*Star Wars, Rocky*) while the uppity Gothamites embraced works by Truffaut and Altman. This year, however, the two orgs not only named the same Best Picture for the first time yet—but they agreed on four other awardees.

The Hollywoodites voted first and backed Columbia's major Christmas release set in New York City—*Kramer vs. Kramer*, featuring Dustin Hoffman and Meryl Streep as divorcing yuppies who battle over custody of their young son (Justin Henry). *Variety* hailed it as "a perceptive, touching, intelligent film about one of the raw sores of contemporary America, the dissolution of the family unit."

The two crix orgs named Hoffman as Best Actor and Streep as Best Supporting Actress. Robert Benton earned *Kramer* additional kudos from the L.A. crix for directing and scripting, bringing its total tally to five—the most in the group's brief history.

When choosing Best Actress, the Hollywoodites proved once again that they weren't afraid of taking pop tastes seriously: they picked the perky ex-star of two lightweight TV series, *The Flying Nun* and *Gidget*. Sally Field had recently displayed her thesp skills by portraying 16 facets of a split personality in the TV movie *Sybil*— and won an Emmy as Best Actress—but she had trouble making the leap to feature films. When she finally got her first big break, playing a union rabble-rouser at a southern

DAILY | ***Variety*** | **DAILY**

VOL. 187 No. 39   74 Pages   Hollywood, California-90028, Tuesday, April 15, 1980   Newspaper Second Class P.O. Entry   25 Cents

'KRAMER' WINS FIVE-OSCAR JUDGMENT

Best Director and Best Screenplay Based On Material From Another Medium: Robert Benton for "Kramer Vs. Kramer" (left); Best Picture and Best Actor: Dustin Hoffman with Justin Henry in "Kramer Vs. Kramer" (center); Best Actress: Sally Field for "Norma Rae" (right). All three are first-time winners.

The N.Y. and L.A. crix finally agreed on the same Best Picture—*Kramer vs. Kramer*—which the Golden Globes and Oscars endorsed soon afterward.

textile factory in *Norma Rae*, the pic tanked at the box office. Determined to keep it alive, its savvy producers took it to the Riviera in May, where Field won Best Actress at Cannes. Field told the *L.A. Times* that she felt "like Princess Grace the night they showed my film, with people fighting to take my picture. They gave me a 10-minute standing ovation." That was just the kind of outside validation that made the L.A. crix feel comfortable with giving their highest acting honor to a former sitcom star who also happened to be one of their own. Field—the daughter of two grade B film thesps—had been raised in Hollywood.

The L.A. org's Best Supporting Actor plaque went to *Being There*'s Melvyn Douglas, who, *Variety* said, "just about steals the film with his spectacular performance as a dying financial titan" who mistakes a halfwit (Peter Sellers) for a genius.

Runners-up in the top categories included Francis Coppola's Vietnam opus *Apocalypse Now* (Best Picture and Director), Roy Scheider as a frazzled director and choreographer in Bob Fosse's autobiographical *All That Jazz* (Best Actor) and Mrs. Neil Simon, Marsha Mason, portraying herself as a newlywed whose hubby can't shake his first wife's death in Simon's autobiographical *Chapter Two* (Best Actress).

All of the winners except Melvyn Douglas showed up at the ceremony, taped for later broadcast on *The Merv Griffin Show*. "The laid-back atmosphere made the show more palatable than most award programs," said *Variety* of the 90-minute program.

When accepting the Best Actress honor, Sally Field revealed that *Norma Rae* director Marty Ritt warned her that crix might not take her seriously as a film actress, so he advised her not to take their future reviews too seriously either.

"Well, I want to take it *all* seriously tonight!" she roared to the L.A. crix.

When Dustin Hoffman thanked the group, he looked astonished, saying, "This is the first time I've been awarded by a body of critics—or a critical body."

> ## TV's ex-*Flying Nun*, Sally Field, took off at Cannes with *Norma Rae*.

Just four days after the L.A. crix voted, Hoffman won his second award from critics. He was such a popular choice for Best Actor with the Gotham circle that he won on the first ballot by 13 to three points over Peter Sellers (*Being There*). Sally Field won Best Actress on the second polling by 42 points to 34 over Bette Midler as rock tragedienne Janis Joplin in *The Rose*. Melvyn Douglas's nearest competish for Best Supporting Actor was Frederick Forrest as Joplin's lover in *The Rose* (46 to 17). When Meryl Streep's perf as a senator's mistress in *The Seduction of Joe Tynan* lost to her perf in *Kramer vs. Kramer* 33 to 32 points, the circle gave her the award for both roles.

Kramer was not the Gotham crix's first choice for Best Picture, however. The vote leader on the first two ballots was actually *Manhattan*, which *Variety* called Woody Allen's "familiar story of the successful but neurotic urban overachievers whose rela-

tionships always seem to end prematurely." *Manhattan* beat *Kramer* 29 points to 25 on the second tally, when a majority vote usually prevails, but it didn't meet the requirement of being listed on more than half of the 25 crix's ballots. The two pix tied on the third canvass, then *Kramer* pulled ahead on the fourth round, but it wasn't declared the winner until the fifth and final ballot. That's when *Manhattan* suddenly fell to third place and *Breaking Away*—a small pic about a Midwest bicycle race—zoomed ahead, finishing behind *Kramer* by just a single point: 30 to 29.

Consolation prizes went to the losers: Woody Allen nabbed the director's laurels over *Kramer*'s Benton (28 points to 23), and *Breaking Away* reaped Best Screenplay over *Manhattan* on the second tally 41 points to 38.

The Gotham crix's awards ceremony "was loads of fun, but Sardi's, as usual, was overcrowded and under-ventilated," griped *The Village Voice*. Robert De Niro made a rare public appearance in order to explain the absence of the Best Supporting Actress. "Something is wrong with Meryl's baby," he said about Streep. "She had to see the doctor." The three-month-old boy had an infection, but soon recovered.

Newsweek reported that "the notoriously temperamental Dustin Hoffman" pretended to take a "quick snooze" in the midst of the fete and then, when he took over the podium, "took the opportunity to rap the critics for their power." Hoffman accepted his plaque, saying, "It's a preposterous position to be named Best Actor—a bizarre situation to be in."

Best Actress Sally Field told *Newsweek*, "This is my first time up here, so I'm not going to knock anything."

In her acceptance speech, Field confessed, "The New York critics award is more important than anything except my children."

Voice columnist Arthur Bell responded

to the comment with a wisecrack about her boyfriend: "I wonder how I'd feel if I were Burt Reynolds."

After the presentation, "Paparazzi were allowed into the restaurant and behaved like animals," the *Voice* added. "There was a heated exchange between a freelance *Time* mag photographer and Dustin Hoffman's lawyer."

When the members of the National Society of Film Critics gathered to vote at the Algonquin Hotel in New York just four days after the Gotham crix held their election, they made a dramatic break from their past Best Pictures choices by backing *Breaking Away*. But the pic had irresistible winning qualities, according to Janet Maslin of *The New York Times:* "Here is a movie so fresh and funny it didn't even need a big budget or a pedigree. The bike race left at least one screening room audience cheering. Screening room crowds don't ordinarily cheer."

In the race for Best Picture, it scored 26 points, surpassing *Kramer vs. Kramer* (20) and *Manhattan* (17). *Breaking Away* also claimed the screenplay trophy with 46 points, followed by *Manhattan* (35) and *Kramer* (21). Robert Benton and Woody Allen tied for Best Director with 27 points each.

The other prizes mirrored the choices made by the other crix groups. Dustin Hoffman won Best Actor 53 to 30 over Peter Sellers. Sally Field (50) topped *The Marriage of Maria Braun*'s Hannah Schygulla (31). Frederick Forrest was named Best Supporting Actor over Melvyn Douglas, 36 to 23. Meryl Streep (52) won Best Supporting Actress over costar Jane Alexander and *Breaking Away*'s Barbara Barrie (24 points each)

The National Board of Review agreed on Sally Field as Best Actress and Meryl Streep for the supporting kudos, but cited different honorees in the other categories: *Manhattan* (Best Picture), Peter Sellers (Best Actor) and *Breaking Away*'s Paul Dooley, who was hailed as Best Supporting Actor for portraying a cyclist's father.

The board renamed its prizes the David Wark Griffith Awards ("in honor of the first poet of the American screen," said the press announcement) and presented them at a ceremony for the first time ever. The gala was held at Luchow's restaurant on Manhattan's 14th Street, just opposite the spot where D.W. Griffith's original Biograph Studio was once located.

"Every former movie actress over 60 in New York attended," observed *The Village Voice*, noting the presence of Joan Fontaine, Maureen O'Sullivan, Shelley Winters, Dina Merrill, Joan Bennett and Gale Sondergaard. Myrna Loy was given a special honor and, while she accepted it at the podium, made a confession about her early career as an actress: "I hated Irene Dunne. She got all the roles I wanted. I didn't know Joan Fontaine hated me and I'm happy to hear it."

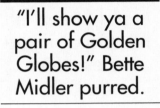

"I'll show ya a pair of Golden Globes!" Bette Midler purred.

One of Griffith's leading ladies, Lillian Gish, was in charge of bestowing the Best Picture prize. "Naturally, Woody Allen wasn't around to receive it," wisecracked *The Village Voice*. "The evening's nostalgia brought tears to the eyes of a hardened Paramount publicist and a former Oscar winner kept slugging down vodka to keep a lump from forming in her throat."

One of the winners who did show up to collect her kudos was Meryl Streep, who said that she was awed "at being in the presence of such illustrious peers."

At the Golden Globes, *Kramer* took the early lead with seven nominations. The divorce pic ended up claiming custody of four awards: best drama film, Best Actor (Hoffman), Best Supporting Actress (Streep) and Best Screenplay (Benton). Benton's loss in the director's race to Francis Coppola (who had recently dropped "Ford" as a middle name) shocked many observers, but it was *Kramer*'s defeat in another category that triggered a more hysterical response.

When its nine-year-old star Justin Henry lost the award for New Male Star of the Year to nine-year-old Ricky Schroeder (*The Champ*), he burst into tears. *The Philadelphia Journal* reported that Henry "just went crazy and threw a royal fit."

Schroeder acted like a wee gent by comparison when he accepted the trophy. "Even if you didn't vote for me, I still love you," he told the members of the foreign press.

Variety reported, "Dustin Hoffman created an uproar when he questioned the meaningfulness of such awards while accepting the Golden Globe as Best Drama Actor."

Hoffman said, "I think that awards are very silly. I think they pit talented people against each other and they hurt the hell out of the ones that lose."

"While Hoffman did not turn back his award, he told *Daily Variety* afterward that he had given his Golden Globe to *Kramer* producer Stanley Jaffe," the tradepaper reported.

Bette Midler created a bit of an uproar herself—a hilarious one—when she accepted two awards: Best Comedy/Musical Actress (*The Rose*) and New Female Star of the Year.

"As Joan Crawford once said, 'I'll show ya a pair of Golden Globes,' " she purred at the audience as she jiggled her breasts.

The gala was being broadcast nationally as a syndicated program, but the *L.A. Times* said, "Midler is not one to worry about the dignity of an awards show or the restraints of live television."

The self-proclaimed "trash with flash" queen added a serious note a few moments later: "This is the most wonderful thing that's ever happened to me."

The Dallas Morning News reported that Jane Fonda "planned to make a political speech" when she accepted a trophy for being the winner of Reuters's poll as World Film Favorite, "but at the last minute decided against it for fear that it would outshine her father, who was receiving an award on television."

Henry Fonda reaped the night's only standing ovation when he received the Cecil B. DeMille Award. "It's not how good you are," he told the crowd, "but how long you last."

Not present for the ceremony were Meryl Streep, Francis Coppola and the two victorious stars of *Being There*—Peter Sellers (Best Comedy/Musical Actor) and Melvyn Douglas (Best Supporting Actor). When Sally Field accepted her statuette as Best Drama Actress, she recounted how she had once broken up a Golden Globe ceremony at the Cocoanut Grove when one of her TV series was nominated. "Dressed in full *Flying Nun* regalia, she swooped down from the ceiling on wires and landed in the lap of John Wayne," *Variety* recalled.

Meryl Streep left her Oscar in the ladies' room.

At the kudos for the Directors Guild of America, Coppola, Woody Allen (*Manhattan*), James Bridges (*The China Syndrome*) and Peter Yates (*Breaking Away*) were among the contenders cited by the 5,900 voters, but Robert Benton won as expected, confirming *Kramer*'s status as the Oscar front-runner.

Benton also won the writers' guild award when *Kramer* beat *Norma Rae*, which was the sole other nominee up as best adapted drama.

There were also only two rivals for the prize as best original drama, which *China Syndrome*'s scribes copped over Coppola and his co-writers of *Apocalypse Now*. *Breaking Away*'s rookie scribe, Yugoslavian immigrant Steve Tesich, edged such established pros as Blake Edwards (*10*) and the writing team of Woody Allen and Marshall Brickman (*Manhattan*) to triumph as best original comedy. Veteran humorists James L. Brooks (*Starting Over*) and Allan Burns (*A Little Romance*) bowed to novelist Jerzy Kosinski (*Being There*) in the race for best adapted comedy.

The celebratory spirit of the writers' guild gala was marred by a serious accident when one of the night's speakers, Joshua Logan, was blinded by the lights at the

Wilshire Ebell Theater in Hollywood and "walked straight off the stage over a row of flowers into the orchestra pit," reported the *L.A. Times*. The noted 71-year-old legit director fell four feet, breaking an arm and cracking three ribs. "He was expected to be in the hospital for about a week," the *Times* added. "Aside from the Logan incident, the evening had a warm, witty and friendly tone."

When the Oscar nominations were announced, the contenders for Best Director did not line up with those up for the directors' guild award. Only three DGA rivals survived the cut—Benton, Coppola and Yates. James Bridges (*The China Syndrome*) and New York crix champ Woody Allen (*Manhattan*) were bumped by Bob Fosse (*All That Jazz*) and Edouard Molinaro (*La Cage aux Folles*). *Manhattan* and *The China Syndrome* had been favored for Best Picture bids, but were snubbed in that race, too. *Norma Rae* and *All That Jazz* took their places alongside the three expected rivals: *Breaking Away, Apocalypse Now* and *Kramer vs. Kramer*.

Kramer led with the most bids—nine—but it was tied by the late-rallying *All That Jazz*. Close behind was *Apocalypse Now*, with eight noms.

But *Variety* declared that *Kramer* was nonetheless "the favorite in all the pre-Oscar handicapping."

Since *Kramer* did not have a star up for Best Actress, that race appeared to be paced by Sally Field after she pulled off a triple crown sweep of the crix awards, plus nabbed the kudos of the National Board of Review and the Golden Globes. Her most serious competish seemed to be other Globe champ Bette Midler (*The Rose*) and last year's Oscar victor, Jane Fonda, who now competed as a TV reporter probing a nuclear power plant in *The China Syndrome*.

When Field prevailed, she warned at the podium, "I'm going to be the one to cry tonight, I'll tell you that right now." The former sitcom star said proudly as she clutched her statuette, "They said this couldn't be done!"

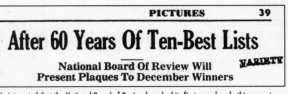

After 60 Years Of Ten-Best Lists

VARIETY

National Board Of Review Will Present Plaques To December Winners

Variety noted that the National Board of Review launched its first awards gala this year at Luchow's restaurant in New York.

After losing the Golden Globe, *Kramer*'s Justin Henry became the youngest nominee in Oscar history when he was nommed for Best Supporting Actor. He felt confident that he'd win this next race and even told *Variety* columnist Army Archerd that he'd prepared an acceptance speech. Archerd had also heard from veteran thesp Mickey Rooney, who'd recently become a born-again Christian. Commenting on his nom for portraying a retired racehorse trainer in *The Black Stallion*, he told Archerd, "My cup runneth over. I'm just so pleased!" Not so pleased to be in this race was the one contender who ended up winning—Melvyn Douglas, who snubbed the ceremony after telling reporters that he was miffed that he was competing against an eight-year-old.

As a consolation prize, Henry got a kiss blown to him from the stage by costar Meryl Streep when she reaped the trophy as Best Supporting Actress. "Holy mackerel!" she exclaimed as she took the statuette in hand. Catching her breath, she thanked costar Hoffman and writer/helmer Robert Benton, "to whom I owe this."

When it came time to unveil the Best Actor winner, suspense surrounded what Hoffman might say if he won, as was widely predicted despite formidable competish from Jack Lemmon (*The China Syndrome*), Roy Scheider (*All That Jazz*), Peter Sellers (*Being There*) and Al Pacino (*. . . And Justice for All*).

When Hoffman did prevail, *Variety* noted, "He refused to back off from previous criticism of acting competitions."

But he "was not really on the attack," *Variety* added, noting that Hoffman seemed much more conciliatory and positive than expected. In fact, he began his remarks with levity, thanking "my mother and father for not practicing birth control," and he singled out costar Justin Henry, saying, "If he loses again, we'll have to give him a lifetime achievement award."

Then Hoffman switched to a serious tone: "I'm up here with mixed feelings. I've criticized the academy before, with reason. I refuse to believe that I beat Jack Lemmon, that I beat Al Pacino, that I beat Peter Sellers. We are part of an artistic family. There are 60,000 members of the Screen Actors Guild who don't work. You have to practice accents while you're driving a taxi cab 'cause when you're a broke actor, you can't write and you can't paint. Most actors don't work and a few of us are so lucky to have a chance. And to that artistic family that strives for excellence, none of you have ever lost and I am proud to share this with you and I thank you."

"The audience loudly applauded," *Variety* noted.

Kramer vs. Kramer swept through the remaining top categories easily, next snatching up the laurels for Best Adapted Screenplay for Robert Benton, who crowed, "This really is one of the five best days of my whole life!" Francis Coppola and Bob Fosse squared off for a third time in the directors' race, but both lost to Benton.

When *Kramer* copped the top prize as Best Picture, too, its producer Stan Jaffe took it in hand and cheered, "Oh, boy!"

One other *Kramer* winner was far less appreciative of her own Oscar.

Soon after the ceremony, Meryl Streep left the statuette in the ladies' room. When a shocked woman found it there, she returned it to Streep immediately.

"Fear and Fantasy in Cinema" was the theme of this year's Utah–U.S.A. Film Festival, held in late October in Salt Lake City, where such showbiz heavyweights as Martin Sheen and helmer Sydney Pollack gathered to discuss the subjects on panels.

After losing the Gotham vote for Best Picture by a single vote, *Breaking Away* zoomed ahead at the national crix society race.

Winner of the Grand Jury Prize was *Spirit of the Wind*, a docudrama about the struggles of a family living in the Alaskan wilderness.

Special Jury Prizes went to two runners-up. One of them had won the Camera d'Or at Cannes five months earlier: *Northern Lights*, about a North Dakota farmer's crusade to stop bank foreclosures in 1915. The other honoree—*Over-Under, Sideways-Down*—chronicled the breakup of a marriage when a factory worker decides to become a professional baseball player.

Sydney Pollack made a news announcement during the fest that would affect its future greatly. He revealed that he and Robert Redford would "repay the business that's been so good to us for 20 years" by establishing a year-round Institute for Young Filmmakers at Redford's Sundance Resort near Provo. It would not compete with the festival, he said, nor would it be part of it—not yet.

▪ 1979 ▪

UTAH-U.S.A. FILM FESTIVAL

The festival was held October 26–30, 1979, at the Elks Building Cinemas and the Utah Media Center in Salt Lake City, Utah.

GRAND JURY PRIZE
▪ *Spirit of the Wind*, Ralph R. Liddle

SPECIAL JURY PRIZE
▪ *Northern Lights*, Rob Nilsson, John Hanson

- *Over-Under, Sideways-Down*, Steve Wax, Eugene Corr, Peter Gessner

LOS ANGELES FILM CRITICS ASSOCIATION

Winners were announced on December 15, 1979. Awards were presented on January 9, 1980. The ceremony was taped for broadcasting on *The Merv Griffin Show* on January 22.

BEST PICTURE
- *Kramer vs. Kramer*

BEST DIRECTOR
- Robert Benton, *Kramer vs. Kramer*

BEST ACTOR
- Dustin Hoffman, *Kramer vs. Kramer*

BEST ACTRESS
- Sally Field, *Norma Rae*

BEST SUPPORTING ACTOR
- Melvyn Douglas, *Being There, The Seduction of Joe Tynan*

BEST SUPPORTING ACTRESS
- Meryl Streep, *Kramer vs. Kramer, Manhattan, The Seduction of Joe Tynan*

BEST SCREENPLAY
- Robert Benton, *Kramer vs. Kramer*

BEST CINEMATOGRAPHY
- Caleb Deschanel, *The Black Stallion*

BEST MUSIC SCORE
- Carmine Coppola, *The Black Stallion*

BEST FOREIGN FILM
- *Soldier of Orange* (Netherlands), Paul Verhoeven

CAREER ACHIEVEMENT AWARD
- John Huston

NEW GENERATION AWARD
- John Carpenter, *Halloween*

NEW YORK FILM CRITICS CIRCLE

Winners were announced on December 19, 1979. Awards were presented on February 1, 1980, at Sardi's restaurant in New York.

BEST PICTURE
- *Kramer vs. Kramer*

BEST DIRECTOR
- Woody Allen, *Manhattan*

BEST ACTOR
- Dustin Hoffman, *Kramer vs. Kramer*

BEST ACTRESS
- Sally Field, *Norma Rae*

BEST SUPPORTING ACTOR
- Melvyn Douglas, *Being There*

BEST SUPPORTING ACTRESS
- Meryl Streep, *Kramer vs. Kramer, The Seduction of Joe Tynan*

BEST SCREENPLAY
- Steve Tesich, *Breaking Away*

BEST FOREIGN FILM
- *The Tree of Wooden Clogs* (Italy)

NATIONAL BOARD OF REVIEW

Winners were announced on December 21, 1979. Awards were presented on February 20, 1980, at Luchow's restaurant in New York.

BEST PICTURE
- *Manhattan*
Yanks
The Europeans
The China Syndrome
Breaking Away
Apocalypse Now
Being There
Time after Time
North Dallas Forty
Kramer vs. Kramer

BEST DIRECTOR
- John Schlesinger, *Yanks*

BEST ACTOR
- Peter Sellers, *Being There*

BEST ACTRESS
- Sally Field, *Norma Rae*

BEST SUPPORTING ACTOR
- Paul Dooley, *Breaking Away*

BEST SUPPORTING ACTRESS
- Meryl Streep, *Manhattan, The Seduction of Joe Tynan, Kramer vs. Kramer*

BEST FOREIGN FILM
- *La Cage aux Folles* (France/Italy)
The Tree of Wooden Clogs (Italy)
The Marriage of Marie Brown (Federal Republic of Germany)
Nosferatu the Vampyre (Federal Republic of Germany)
Peppermint Soda (France)

NATIONAL SOCIETY OF FILM CRITICS

Winners were announced on January 2, 1980.

BEST PICTURE
- *Breaking Away*

BEST DIRECTOR (TIE)
- Robert Benton, *Kramer vs. Kramer*
- Woody Allen, *Manhattan*

BEST ACTOR
- Dustin Hoffman, *Kramer vs. Kramer, Agatha*

BEST ACTRESS
- Sally Field, *Norma Rae*

BEST SUPPORTING ACTOR
- Frederic Forrest, *Apocalypse Now, The Rose*

BEST SUPPORTING ACTRESS
- Meryl Streep, *Manhattan, Seduction of Joe Tynan, Kramer vs. Kramer*

BEST SCREENPLAY
- Steve Tesich, *Breaking Away*

BEST CINEMATOGRAPHY
- Caleb Deschanel, *The Black Stallion, Being There*

GOLDEN GLOBES

Nominations were announced on January 8, 1980. Awards were presented on January 26 at the Beverly Hilton Hotel in Los Angeles. The ceremony was telecast nationally via syndication.

BEST DRAMA PICTURE
- *Kramer vs. Kramer*
Apocalypse Now
The China Syndrome
Manhattan
Norma Rae

BEST COMEDY OR MUSICAL PICTURE
- *Breaking Away*
Being There
Hair
The Rose
10

BEST DIRECTOR
- Francis Coppola, *Apocalypse Now*
Hal Ashby, *Being There*
Robert Benton, *Kramer vs. Kramer*
James Bridges, *The China Syndrome*
Peter Yates, *Breaking Away*

BEST ACTOR, DRAMA
- Dustin Hoffman, *Kramer vs. Kramer*
Jack Lemmon, *The China Syndrome*
Al Pacino, *And Justice for All*
Jon Voight, *The Champ*
James Woods, *The Onion Field*

BEST ACTRESS, DRAMA
- Sally Field, *Norma Rae*
Jill Clayburgh, *Luna*
Lisa Eichhorn, *Yanks*
Jane Fonda, *The China Syndrome*
Marsha Mason, *Promises in the Dark*

BEST ACTOR, COMEDY OR MUSICAL
- Peter Sellers, *Being There*

George Hamilton, *Love at First Bite*
Dudley Moore, *10*
Burt Reynolds, *Starting Over*
Roy Scheider, *All That Jazz*

BEST ACTRESS, COMEDY OR MUSICAL
- Bette Midler, *The Rose*
Julie Andrews, *10*
Jill Clayburgh, *Starting Over*
Shirley MacLaine, *Being There*
Marsha Mason, *Chapter Two*

BEST SUPPORTING ACTOR (TIE)
- Melvyn Douglas, *Being There*
- Robert Duvall, *Apocalypse Now*
Frederic Forrest, *The Rose*
Justin Henry, *Kramer vs. Kramer*
Laurence Olivier, *A Little Romance*

BEST SUPPORTING ACTRESS
- Meryl Streep, *Kramer vs. Kramer*
Jane Alexander, *Kramer vs. Kramer*
Kathleen Beller, *Promises in the Dark*
Candice Bergen, *Starting Over*
Valerie Harper, *Chapter Two*

NEW MALE STAR OF THE YEAR
- Ricky Schroeder, *The Champ*
Dennis Christopher, *Breaking Away*
Justin Henry, *Kramer vs. Kramer*
Dean-Paul Martin, *The Players*
Treat Williams, *Hair*

NEW FEMALE STAR OF THE YEAR
- Bette Midler, *The Rose*
Susan Anton, *Golden Girl*
Bo Derek, *10*
Lisa Eichhorn, *Yanks*
Lynn-Holly Johnson, *Ice Castles*

BEST SCREENPLAY
- Robert Benton, *Kramer vs. Kramer*
T. S. Cook, Mike Gray, James Bridges, *The China Syndrome*
Harriet Frank, Jr., Irving Ravetch, *Norma Rae*
Jerzy Kosinski, *Being There*
Steve Tesich, *Breaking Away*

BEST SONG
- "The Rose," *The Rose*
"Better Than Ever," *Starting Over*

"The Main Event," *The Main Event*
"Rainbow Connection," *The Muppet Movie*
"Through the Eyes of Love," *Ice Castles*

BEST FOREIGN FILM
- *La Cage Aux Folles* (France/Italy)
The Europeans (England)
The Marriage of Maria Braun (Germany)
Soldier of Orange (Holland)
Till Marriage Do Us Part (Italy)

Winners

BEST ORIGINAL SCORE
- Francis Coppola, Carmine Coppola, *Apocalypse Now*

WORLD FILM FAVORITES
- Roger Moore
- Jane Fonda

CECIL B. DEMILLE AWARD
- Henry Fonda

DIRECTORS GUILD OF AMERICA

The award for Best Director was presented on March 15, 1980, at the Beverly Hilton Hotel in Los Angeles and the Pierre Hotel in New York.

BEST DIRECTOR
- Robert Benton, *Kramer vs. Kramer*
Woody Allen, *Manhattan*
James Bridges, *The China Syndrome*
Francis Coppola, *Apocalypse Now*
Peter Yates, *Breaking Away*

WRITERS GUILD OF AMERICA

Nominations were announced on February 26, 1980. Awards were presented on April 3 at the Wilshire Ebell Theatre in Los Angeles and the McGraw-Hill Bali Room in New York.

BEST DRAMA WRITTEN DIRECTLY FOR THE SCREEN
- *The China Syndrome*, Mike Gray, T. S. Cook, James Bridges

Apocalypse Now, John Milius, Francis Coppola, Michael Herr

BEST DRAMA ADAPTED FROM ANOTHER MEDIUM

- *Kramer vs. Kramer*, Robert Benton, based on the novel by Avery Corman

Norma Rae, Irving Ravetch, Harriet Frank, Jr.

BEST COMEDY WRITTEN DIRECTLY FOR THE SCREEN

- *Breaking Away*, Steve Tesich

Manhattan, Woody Allen, Marshall Brickman

10, Blake Edwards

BEST COMEDY ADAPTED FROM ANOTHER MEDIUM

- *Being There*, Jerzy Kosinski, based on his novel

A Little Romance, Allan Burns, based on the novel $E = MC^2$, *Mon Amour* by Patrick Cauvin

Starting Over, James L. Brooks, based on the novel by Dan Wakefield

LAUREL AWARD

- Billy Wilder, I. A. L. Diamond

VALENTINE DAVIES AWARD

- David W. Rintels

MORGAN COX AWARD

- Fay Kanin

ACADEMY AWARDS

Nominations were announced on February 24, 1980. Awards were presented on April 14 at the Dorothy Chandler Pavilion in Los Angeles. The ceremony was telecast on ABC.

BEST PICTURE

- *Kramer vs. Kramer*

All That Jazz

Apocalypse Now

Breaking Away

Norma Rae

BEST DIRECTOR

- Robert Benton, *Kramer vs. Kramer*

Francis Coppola, *Apocalypse Now*

Bob Fosse, *All That Jazz*

Edouard Molinaro, *La Cage aux Folles*

Peter Yates, *Breaking Away*

BEST ACTOR

- Dustin Hoffman, *Kramer vs. Kramer*

Jack Lemmon, *The China Syndrome*

Al Pacino, *. . . And Justice for All*

Peter Sellers, *Being There*

Roy Scheider, *All That Jazz*

BEST ACTRESS

- Sally Field, *Norma Rae*

Jill Clayburgh, *Starting Over*

Jane Fonda, *The China Syndrome*

Marsha Mason, *Chapter Two*

Bette Midler, *The Rose*

BEST SUPPORTING ACTOR

- Melvyn Douglas, *Being There*

Robert Duvall, *Apocalypse Now*

Frederic Forrest, *The Rose*

Justin Henry, *Kramer vs. Kramer*

Mickey Rooney, *The Black Stallion*

BEST SUPPORTING ACTRESS

- Meryl Streep, *Kramer vs. Kramer*

Jane Alexander, *Kramer vs. Kramer*

Barbara Barrie, *Breaking Away*

Candice Bergen, *Starting Over*

Mariel Hemingway, *Manhattan*

BEST ORIGINAL SCREENPLAY

- Steve Tesich, *Breaking Away*

Woody Allen, Marshall Brickman, *Manhattan*

Robert Alan Arthur, Bob Fosse, *All That Jazz*

James Bridges, T. S. Cook, Mike Gray, *The China Syndrome*

Valerie Curtin, Barry Levinson, *. . . And Justice for All*

BEST ADAPTED SCREENPLAY

- Robert Benton, *Kramer vs. Kramer*

Allan Burns, *A Little Romance*

Francis Coppola, John Milius, *Apocalypse Now*

Marcello Danon, Edouard Molinaro, Jean Poiret, Francis Veber, *La Cage aux Folles*

Harriet Frank, Jr., Irving Ravetch, *Norma Rae*

BEST SONG
- "It Goes Like It Goes," *Norma Rae*, Norman Gimbel, David Shire

"I'll Never Say 'Goodbye'," *The Promise*, Alan Bergman, Marilyn Bergman, David Shire

"It's Easy to Say," *10*, Henry Mancini, Robert Wells

"The Rainbow Connection," *The Muppet Movie*, Kenny Ascher, Paul Williams

"Through the Eyes of Love," *Ice Castles*, Marvin Hamlisch, Carole Bayer Sager

BEST FOREIGN-LANGUAGE FILM
- *The Tin Drum* (Federal Republic of Germany)

The Maids of Wilko (Poland)
Mama Turns a Hundred (Spain)
A Simple Story (France)
To Forget Venice (Italy)

Winners

BEST ART DIRECTION
- Philip Rosenberg, Tony Walton, Gary Brink, Edward Stewart, *All That Jazz*

BEST CINEMATOGRAPHY
- Vittorio Storaro, *Apocalypse Now*

BEST COSTUME DESIGN
- Albert Wolsky, *All That Jazz*

BEST DOCUMENTARY
(FEATURE)
- *Best Boy*, Ira Wohl

(SHORT SUBJECT)
- *Paul Robeson: Tribute to an Artist*, Saul J. Turell

BEST FILM EDITING
- Alan Heim, *All That Jazz*

BEST MUSIC
(ORIGINAL SCORE)
- Georges Delerue, *A Little Romance*

(ORIGINAL SONG SCORE AND ITS ADAPTATION OR ADAPTATION SCORE)
- Ralph Burns, *All That Jazz*

SCIENTIFIC OR TECHNICAL AWARDS
(Academy Award of Merit)
- Mark Serrurier

(Scientific and Engineering Award)
- Mini-Micro Systems, Neiman-Tillar Associates

(Technical Achievement Award)
- Michael V. Chewey, Walter G. Eggers, Allen Hecht, MGM Laboratories; Irwin Young, Paul Kaufman, Frederik Schlyter, Du Art Film Labs; James S. Stanfield, Paul W. Trester; Zoran Perisic, Courier Films; A. D. Flowers, Logan R. Frazee; Photo research division, Kollmorgen Corp.; Bruce Lyon, John Lamb; Ross Lowell, Lowell-Light Manufacturing

BEST SHORT FILM
(ANIMATED)
- *Every Child*, Derek Lamb

(LIVE ACTION)
- *Board and Care*, Ron Ellis, Sarah Pillsbury

BEST SOUND
- Richard Beggs, Mark Berger, Nat Boxer, Walter Murch, *Apocalypse Now*

SPECIAL ACHIEVEMENT AWARD
(SOUND EDITING)
- Alan Splet, *The Black Stallion*

BEST VISUAL EFFECTS
- Nick Allder, Denys Ayling, H. R. Giger, Brian Johnson, Carlo Rambaldi, *Alien*

IRVING G. THALBERG MEMORIAL AWARD
- Ray Stark

JEAN HERSHOLT HUMANITARIAN AWARD
- Robert Benjamin

HONORARY AWARDS
- John O. Aalberg
- Charles G. Clarke
- Hal Elias
- John G. Frayne
- Alec Guinness

SCREEN ACTORS GUILD

LIFETIME ACHIEVEMENT AWARD
- Katharine Hepburn

▪ 1980 ▪

Extraordinary Star Lenses Ordinary People

It would soon be common-place for award groups to swoon over heartthrob male stars such as Kevin Costner, Warren Beatty, Clint Eastwood and Mel Gibson once they climbed into directors' chairs, but the phenomenon began with Robert Redford, who decided he wanted to call the shots because was tired of being fawned over by females.

"I've been grateful for a lot of it," Redford told writer James Spada about his sex-symbol status, "but I have felt reduced."

After reading a soon-to-be-published novel, *Ordinary People,* in galley form, Redford optioned the story of an affluent Chicago family haunted by the death of one son and the suicide attempt by another. He chose an atypical male lead, TV *Taxi* star Judd Hirsch, instead of himself and, in an inspired move of surprise casting, signed up perky TV icon Mary Tyler Moore to play the family's coldhearted mother. A tragic irony occurred just a month after the pic's release, however, when Moore's 24-year-old son Ritchy shot himself in the head with a pistol. UPI wrote that, suddenly, "there was an eerie feeling of reality surrounding the film."

Ordinary People reaped huzzahs from crix for its artistic content. *Variety* declared that Redford made "a remarkably intelligent and assured directorial debut in a powerfully intimate domestic drama."

The National Board of Review was the first to cite *Ordinary People* as Best Picture and Redford as Best Director. When the L.A. critics huddled to vote three days later at the Westwood Marquis Hotel, *The Los Angeles Herald Examiner* reported that they split into two camps. What the paper called "the Traditionalists" lobbied for both *Ordinary People* and *Tess*, a stylized retelling of the Thomas Hardy classic by director Roman Polanski, who had recently fled the United States when charged with having sex with a 13-year-old girl. The Traditionalists were opposed by "the Young Turks," who pressed forward on two fronts, too—splitting their votes between *Raging Bull*, Martin Scorsese's gritty portrayal of middleweight boxing champ Jake La Motta, and *The Stunt Man*, starring Peter O'Toole as a tyrannical film director who bullies a fugitive he's shielding from the law.

Raging Bull scored a KO punch as Best Picture, while Polanski prevailed as Best Director over Richard Rush (*The Stunt Man*) and Scorsese. *Raging Bull*'s Robert De Niro was hailed as Best Actor for portraying what *Variety* called "one of the most repugnant and unlikeable screen protagonists in some time." The runner-up was *The Elephant Man*'s John Hurt, who *Variety* said gave a virtuoso performance as "a hideously deformed man leading a perilous life in Victorian England."

Variety said Robert Redford made "a remarkably intelligent and assured directorial debut" in *Ordinary People*, which nabbed Best Picture trophies from NBR, N.Y. crix, Globes and Oscars.

Timothy Hutton, as *Ordinary People*'s suicidal teen, was named Best Supporting Actor over Joe Pesci as La Motta's seamy brother in *Raging Bull*, but costar Mary Tyler Moore lost out as Best Actress to a rival who would go on to become the second star after Sally Field to sweep all of the following top kudos: Oscar, Golden Globe, National Board of Review and the film crix trifecta (N.Y., L.A. and national society)— Sissy Spacek. In its review of *Coal Miner's Daughter, Variety* also endorsed Spacek for her "superb performance" as country music legend Loretta Lynn, adding, "Spacek deserves a special nod for doing all of her own singing with style and accuracy."

The crix's choice for Best Supporting Actress was Mary Steenburgen (*Melvin and Howard*) as the wacky first wife of real-life gas station jockey Melvin Dummar, who claimed that he once gave a lift to Howard Hughes and then ended up as one of the tycoon's chief heirs in the the controversial "Mormon will."

When the L.A. crix's awards were bestowed during a broadcast of *The Merv Griffin Show*, the usually reclusive De Niro showed up and thanked "Marty and Joe and Bob and Pete and Jake," referring to his helmer Scorsese, costar Pesci, producer Chartoff, producer Savage and the boxer he portrayed in *Raging Bull*— La Motta.

But the biggest surprise of the event was a live acceptance speech from Roman Polanski, who was beamed in via satellite from Paris.

"I thank you for this appreciation and I hope to see you soon," he said.

His award was accepted by *Tess* star Nastassja Kinski, age 17, who had been his lover a few years earlier.

"I can't believe he's not here," she said. "He's a great director and a great person. Everybody should see him the way he is."

Ten days after the L.A. crix voted, the New York pundits picked their winners—

> ## Sissy Spacek became the second star to sweep all the top modern kudos.

and picked three of the same honorees. Robert De Niro was named Best Actor (33 points) over *The Great Santini*'s Robert Duvall (29) and *The Stunt Man*'s Peter O'Toole (24). Sissy Spacek won Best Actress (37 points) over Mary Tyler Moore and *Private Benjamin*'s Goldie Hawn (20 each). Mary Steenburgen (31 points) topped *Urban Cowboy*'s Debra Winger (24) to be cited as Best Supporting Actress.

Melvin and Howard copped two other awards, including Best Screenplay for scribe Bo Goldman and Best Director for Jonathan Demme (27 points), who edged out Scorsese (25) and Redford (19).

But *Melvin and Howard* (22 points) was usurped for the Best Picture prize by *Ordinary People* (31) on the third ballot, when *Raging Bull* fell into in distant third place (12).

The fact that the prizes for Best Picture and Director went to different pix bothered legendary helmer George Cukor, who attended the Gotham crix's awards ceremony at Sardi's restaurant as a presenter. *Variety* noted that Cukor's comments were "a bit barbed" when he made a "tart rejoinder that, if *Ordinary People* deserved the Best Picture trophy, then its director should have also been accoladed. Robert Redford, in accepting, diplomatically smoothed things over, but the point merits consideration."

Cukor wasn't the only showbiz icon who appeared irked during the gala. "Ruth Gordon walked out in a huff," reported the *Daily News*, when she was told that she wouldn't be presenting the Best Supporting Actor award as previously planned. Best Supporting Actress Mary Steenburgen didn't show up at all because she had given birth to a daughter three days earlier.

Loretta Lynn turned down the crix's offer to bestow the Best Actress award to Spacek. Jake La Motta did show up, however, to present the Best Actor award upon the thesp who portrayed him on the screen. While reading from extensive notes, La

Motta said, "I wish I was more eloquent like Duskin—er, Dustin—Hoffman."

Variety fumed, "The ceremony has to go down as one of the dullest on record. Whose suggestion it was to ask Jake La Motta, he of the few thousand dull words, to make the Best Actor award to Robert De Niro, could not be ascertained. No one wanted to accept the blame."

Since 19 of the 25 members in the New York Film Critics Circle also belonged to the 37-member National Society of Film Critics, many observers expected similar honorees when the latter group voted one week after the Gothamites. The society agreed on only four out of seven races, however: Best Actress Spacek (over Mary Tyler Moore), Best Supporting Actor Pesci (over Timothy Hutton), Best Supporting Actress Steenburgen (over Debra Winger) and Best Screenplay *Melvin and Howard* (over *The Return of the Secaucus 7*, which had claimed the scribe's award from the L.A. crix).

"Chaos broke out" when Redford won the DGA prize.

Peter O'Toole ended up as Best Actor, beating De Niro by a single vote point. The society also chose different winners for Best Picture and Best Director and, just like the Gothamites, split the kudos between two pix. *Raging Bull*'s Scorsese claimed the helmer's laurels, while *Melvin and Howard* was hailed as 1980's top film. The *Daily News* commented on the latter victory: "The award could turn out to be a much-needed boost for a movie that has had such difficulty in attracting audiences that there have been rumors that Universal Pictures was going to remove it from circulation, re-edit the picture and re-release it under a new title."

Melvin and Howard was nominated for Best Comedy or Musical Picture at the Golden Globes, but it was up against tough competish, including *Coal Miner's Daughter, Fame* and *Airplane!*

The Associated Press predicted that a drama pic would end up striking the most gold on awards night. "*Ordinary People* is expected to be the big winner," the wire claimed when the bids were announced. Redford's pic led with seven nominations.

The Hollywood Foreign Press Association came out a winner early when CBS picked up the telecast for a five-year option, paying the org an annual license fee of $600,000. The *L.A. Times* cast a pall over the proceedings, however, when it investigated the press credentials of 15 out of the org's 78 voting members and reported that it couldn't locate 40 of the 60 publications that those members claimed to write for. "Four of the 15 members selected do work for the publications they list" with the Association of Motion Picture and Television Producers, the paper said.

But the kudocast still went on and *Ordinary People* pulled off an extraordinary sweep, copping five trophies, including Best Drama Picture, Best Director (Redford) and Best Drama Actress (Moore).

Moore thanked Redford "for his inspired and inspiring direction and for believing that there was a part of Beth (her film character) in me."

When Moore also accepted Redford's statuette on his behalf, she lost an earring while at the podium. Even a star-studded search party couldn't find it.

Reporters described Timothy Hutton as looking "bemused" when he won Globes for Best Film Debut and Best Supporting Actor. "This looks familiar," he said with a shrug when he accepted the second statuette. De Niro was not on hand to claim his trophy as Best Drama Actor.

Coal Miner's Daughter reaped honors for Best Comedy or Musical Picture and Best Actress Sissy Spacek, who said, "There's a cowboy named Jim Shoulders who once told me, 'I'd rather have a little luck than all the ability in the world.' I agree with him tonight."

The *L.A. Times* said the night's most popular winner was Best Comedy/Musical Actor Ray Sharkey, who portrayed a promoter of pop singers in *The Idolmaker*. Bounding up onto the stage while bursting with joy, he tossed off his tuxedo vest, held the Globe aloft and roared, "Look, ma!" Then he thanked "God, the whole world, the foreign press, my mother and my grandfather."

When William Peter Blatty won Best Screenplay for *Twinkle, Twinkle, "Killer" Kane*, he thanked "the foreign press and God with all my heart, though not necessarily in that order." His win ended up triggering what the *L.A. Times* called "a brouhaha" when *Killer* beat out *Ordinary People, Raging Bull* and *The Stunt Man*. The *L.A. Herald Examiner* described *Killer*'s script as "nothing but sophomoric claptrap," and the *L.A. Times* implied that voters picked it because they'd been won over by a savvy PR campaign that included two private screenings and a cocktail party at Blatty's Beverly Hills home.

As a crowd of 1,000 dined on prime rib at the Directors Guild of America gala, prexy George Schaefer promised that the event could be "the most painless, uncomplicated, relaxed awards dinner around," but chaos broke out when the winner was announced.

The *L.A. Times* reported that Robert Redford "had to fend off an unruly gang of photographers who closed in despite shouts from the audience of 'sit down!' as he made his way to the podium."

"Let me just thank everybody . . ." Redford began saying once he reached the stage, but he was distracted by an onslaught of camera flashes. "Will you please let me do this?! You can take pictures in the parking lot, OK?!" he barked at the shutterbugs.

The flashes ceased. He continued, speaking heartfelt words, "I am really shocked and very thrilled. This is a heavyweight crowd. I am honored."

Ordinary People continued its awards romp when members of the writers' guild gathered nine days afterward and Alvin Sargent claimed the prize for best adapted screenplay over the scribes of *Coal Miner's Daughter, The Stunt Man, The Great Santini* and *The Elephant Man*. Previously, Sargent had won guild honors for *Paper Moon* (1973) and *Julia* (1977).

Front-runners claimed the other races: Bo Goldman (*Melvin and Howard*, Best Original Drama), David and Jerry Zucker (*Airplane!*, Best Original Comedy) and Nancy Meyers, Charles Shyer and Harvey Miller (*Private Benjamin*, Best Adapted Comedy). Goldman had been hailed earlier, in 1975, for *One Flew over the Cuckoo's Nest*.

For only the second time in the guild's history, the career-saluting Laurel Award went to a posthumous recipient, Ben Hecht (*The Front Page, Twentieth Century*), who died in 1964.

After winning both guilds' awards plus Best Picture prizes from the New York Film Critics Circle, Golden Globes and National Board of Review, *Ordinary People* looked like the obvious Oscar front-runner, but it didn't fare well when the nominations were announced. It tied *Tess* for having only the fourth largest bids tally (six). The three leaders were *Raging Bull* (eight), *The Elephant Man* (eight) and *Coal Miner's Daughter* (seven).

Ten days before the ceremony, recently elected U.S. President Ronald Reagan taped an introductory segment for the broadcast, which marked only the second time that America's commander-in-chief would be involved in the kudocast—the first being Franklin Roosevelt, who addressed the Oscar crowd during a live radio broadcast in 1940.

One day before the telecast, however, Reagan was shot by a 25-year-old drifter who was trying to impress actress Jodie Foster by emulating what Robert De Niro did to win her affections in 1976 Best Picture nominee *Taxi Driver*: shoot a politician.

Oscar leaders put the ceremony on hold,

> "Once again a gunman's bullet" postponed the Oscar show.

then decided to stage it one night later once news spread that Reagan would survive. *Variety* reported, "Once again a gunman's bullet has forced the postponement of an Academy Awards show, ironically as the entertainment industry was basking in the honor of having a U.S. President from its ranks.

"Every day in history has at least one ironical footnote," the paper added. "In 1968, when the Martin Luther King assassination caused the postponement, the ultimate winner for Best Picture was *In the Heat of the Night*, produced by—Norman Jewison, producer of this year's postponed show."

On the eve of the reskedded gala, the White House informed Oscar leaders that Reagan and his wife Nancy planned to watch the ceremony from his hospital room and they hoped that it would include the segment he videotaped earlier.

Host Johnny Carson not only introduced the segment as planned, but he took a big gamble in his opening monologue by taking a humorous potshot at the president just two days after the real gunshots.

"The president has asked for severe cuts in aid to the arts and humanities," Carson said. "It's Reagan's strongest attack on the arts since he signed with Warner Brothers." Gasps erupted amongst the laughter in the audience.

Then Carson said, winking and smirking, "I'll bet he's up and around now!"

"Robert De Niro, a New Yorker who shuns Hollywood, looks like a sure bet to take the Best Actor Oscar, though he probably won't show," UPI reporter Vernon Scott predicted before the awards matchup. "De Niro refused to appear for his previous nominations (including his Best Supporting Actor victory for *The Godfather, Part II* in 1974) and the academy says he will snub the awards again this year."

But De Niro showed up, after all, and so did frequent loser Peter O'Toole, who was asked by *Variety* what he thought of his current chances. "I'd adore to win, wouldn't you?" he said. "The fact that I've lost five times intrigues me even more."

But De Niro prevailed, as forecast. At

The N.Y. and L.A. crix, Globes and Oscars all gave laurels to Robert De Niro in *Raging Bull*, the L.A. crix's choice for Best Picture.

the podium he said, "I'm a little nervous, I'm sorry. I forgot my lines, so the director wrote them down." He produced a list of colleagues that he thanked, including real-life boxer Jake La Motta "even though he's suing us."

De Niro tried to return to his seat, but presenter Sally Field steered him back to the press room, where reporters asked him about the link between Reagan's attempted assassination and *Taxi Driver*, which had earned him a nomination for Best Actor in 1976. "I don't want to discuss the matter now," he snapped back. "You're all nice, but that's it!" Then he darted out of the room.

"Best bet for supporting actor is Joe Pesci," UPI's Scott insisted when he sized up that race. "Timothy Hutton and Judd Hirsch will cancel each other out."

But Hutton won, and he was so excited when he heard the news that he tripped as he vaulted out of his seat. Robert Redford caught him. Once Hutton made it to the podium, he provided what *Variety* called one of the night's "sentimental highlights" when he said, "I would like to thank my father. I wish he was still here." His dad, actor Jim Hutton, died in 1979.

Variety claimed that the race for Best Supporting Actress was "handicapped as more of a toss-up because all five nominees were competing for the first time." The winner turned out to be the reaper of most of the year's kudos so far—Mary Steenburgen.

"Well, I'm gonna have to figure out something new to dream about, that's for sure!" she said at the podium. She thanked her "folks in Arkansas for always believing against the odds that something like this was going to happen. If anybody had a patron saint, it was me."

The thesp who had snagged every major award so far this year—Sissy Spacek—was expected to take one more. "Spacek is almost as strongly favored to win the Oscar for Best Actress as De Niro is for Best Actor," Vernon Scott forecast. "Mary Tyler Moore appears to be the second favorite."

When Spacek won, she thanked Loretta Lynn, "the lady who gave me all that hair."

Variety observed that both the Best Actress and Best Actor champs "each portrayed a living figure—Jake La Motta and Loretta Lynn—who were present in the audience, doubtlessly a first for the awards."

In the script categories, the writers' guild champs came through. When Bo Goldman accepted the kudos for Best Original Screenplay, he thanked Melvin Dummar "for sharing his life with me." Accepting the prize for Best Adapted Screenplay, Alvin Sargent described *Ordinary People* as "a film about all of us trying to understand all of us."

Roman Polanski was not on hand for the Best Director race, since the Los Angeles district attorney vowed to arrest him if he showed up at the Dorothy Chandler Pavilion. Vernon Scott didn't think Polanski had much of a chance, though. He sized up the race as being between two rivals: "Martin Scorsese is considered a close second to Redford in the balloting."

When Robert Redford won, *Variety* noted that he "joined a select circle. He's the first to win for his initial effort behind the camera since Delbert Mann for *Marty* (though Jerome Robbins shared codirecting

After previous wins for *Paper Moon* and *Julia*, Alvin Sargent was hailed by the WGA for his *Ordinary People* screenplay.

credit for *West Side Story* with veteran Robert Wise)."

Redford didn't bask in his victory, however. When he appeared at the podium, he just made a brief thank-you and scooted off stage.

A few minutes later, *Ordinary People* was declared Best Picture.

The usually shy Redford surprised many by showing up after the kudocast at the Governors Ball, where he huddled with *Variety*'s Army Archerd. "It's ironic I won for directing," said the thesp-turned-helmer, "but no less acceptable."

Robert Redford had been the first chairman of the board of directors of the U.S. Film Festival, which had recently dropped "Utah" from its name and moved from Salt Lake City to Park City. The new site was "30 miles distant, and several degrees frostier," noted *Variety,* explaining that organizers wanted to follow "the success of festivals in such nonmetropolitan centers as Cannes and Spoleto." The locale was close to Redford's Rocky Mountain home and to the Sundance Institute, which he had recently founded to give neophyte filmmakers "the chance to work without the pressure of commercial success," he said. Other than Redford's early part-time involvement as a member of the fest's board, there was no connection yet between the Sundance Institute and the indie U.S. Film Festival.

Eleven films vied for the fest's Grand Jury Prize, which was claimed by two pix. One champ, *Heartland*, had previously won the Golden Bear at the Berlin Film Festival and was described by the *L.A. Times* as capturing "the expanse of the wilderness and the lives of a couple who struggle to survive there."

The other victor was *Gal Young 'Un*, based on a short story about the plight of a wealthy old widow who marries a poor young schemer.

A Special Jury Prize went to the second-place contender, *The Return of the Secaucus 7*, which the *L.A. Times* described as "the story of seven old friends who reunite for a weekend of reminiscing and recounting of changes that have occurred since their polit-ically active college days. The jurors described the film as 'hysterically funny and incredibly perceptive.' "

Special Jury Prizes also were awarded to two documentaries. *The War at Home*, a 1979 Oscar nominee, chronicled the anti-Vietnam war protests in Madison, Wisconsin. Also cited was *The Day After Trinity*, a 1980 Oscar contender that examined the role of physicist J. Robert Oppenheimer in the development of the atom bomb. It was directed and produced by Jon Else, who accepted the award, saying, "All of us have to find some other way of coercing nations to stop dropping atomic bombs."

Redford's *Ordinary People* was not entered into awards competition, but it was shown as part of the indie festival's Directors Debut Showcase. Redford told the audience, "The chance to be totally responsible for my own vision was exciting. I have a lot of fool's courage. Despite people telling me to stop, it wouldn't work, I just plunged right in and kept going."

▪ 1980 ▪

NATIONAL BOARD OF REVIEW

Winners were announced on December 18, 1980. Awards were presented on January 26 at Luchow's restaurant in New York.

BEST PICTURE
▪ *Ordinary People*
Raging Bull
Coal Miner's Daughter
Tess
Melvin and Howard
The Great Santini
The Elephant Man
The Stunt Man
My Bodyguard
Resurrection

BEST DIRECTOR
▪ Robert Redford, *Ordinary People*

BEST ACTOR
▪ Robert De Niro, *Raging Bull*

BEST ACTRESS
▪ Sissy Spacek, *Coal Miner's Daughter*

BEST SUPPORTING ACTOR
▪ Joe Pesci, *Raging Bull*

BEST SUPPORTING ACTRESS
▪ Eva Le Gallienne, *Resurrection*

BEST FOREIGN FILM
▪ *The Tin Drum* (Federal Republic of Germany)
Kagemusha (Japan)
Knife in the Head (Federal Republic of Germany)
From the Life of the Marionettes (Federal Republic of Germany)
Eboli (Italy)

LOS ANGELES FILM CRITICS ASSOCIATION

Winners were announced on December 20, 1980. Awards were presented on January 9,

1981. The ceremony was telecast later by the syndicated *Merv Griffin Show*.

BEST PICTURE
- *Raging Bull*

BEST DIRECTOR
- Roman Polanski, *Tess*

BEST ACTOR
- Robert De Niro, *Raging Bull*

BEST ACTRESS
- Sissy Spacek, *Coal Miner's Daughter*

BEST SUPPORTING ACTOR
- Timothy Hutton, *Ordinary People*

BEST SUPPORTING ACTRESS
- Mary Steenburgen, *Melvin and Howard*

BEST SCREENPLAY
- John Sayles, *The Return of the Secaucus 7*

BEST CINEMATOGRAPHY
- Ghislain Cloquet, Geoffrey Unsworth, *Tess*

BEST MUSIC SCORE
- Ry Cooder, *The Long Riders*

BEST FOREIGN FILM
- *The Tin Drum* (Federal Republic of Germany), Volker Schlöndorff

BEST EXPERIMENTAL/INDEPENDENT FILM
- *Journey from Berlin* (1971), Yvonne Rainer
- *Demon Lover Diary*, Joel Demot

CAREER ACHIEVEMENT AWARD
- Robert Mitchum

NEW GENERATION AWARD
- Carroll Ballard, director, *The Black Stallion*

NEW YORK FILM CRITICS CIRCLE

Winners were announced on December 30, 1980. Awards were presented on January

25, 1981, at Sardi's restaurant in New York.

BEST PICTURE
- *Ordinary People*

BEST DIRECTOR
- Jonathan Demme, *Melvin and Howard*

BEST ACTOR
- Robert De Niro, *Raging Bull*

BEST ACTRESS
- Sissy Spacek, *Coal Miner's Daughter*

BEST SUPPORTING ACTOR
- Joe Pesci, *Raging Bull*

BEST SUPPORTING ACTRESS
- Mary Steenburgen, *Melvin and Howard*

BEST SCREENPLAY
- Bo Goldman, *Melvin and Howard*

BEST CINEMATOGRAPHY
- Geoffrey Unsworth, Ghislain Cloquet, *Tess*

BEST DOCUMENTARY
- *Best Boy*

BEST FOREIGN FILM
- *Mon Oncle d'Amerique*

NATIONAL SOCIETY OF FILM CRITICS

Winners were announced on January 6, 1981.

BEST PICTURE
- *Melvin and Howard*

BEST DIRECTOR
- Martin Scorsese, *Raging Bull*

BEST ACTOR
- Peter O'Toole, *The Stunt Man*

BEST ACTRESS
- Sissy Spacek, *Coal Miner's Daughter*

BEST SUPPORTING ACTOR
- Joe Pesci, *Raging Bull*

BEST SUPPORTING ACTRESS
- Mary Steenburgen, *Melvin and Howard*

BEST SCREENPLAY
- Bo Goldman, *Melvin and Howard*

BEST CINEMATOGRAPHY
- Michael Chapman, *Raging Bull*

U.S. FILM FESTIVAL

The festival was held January 12–18, 1981, at Park City, Utah.

GRAND JURY PRIZE
- *Heartland*, Richard Pearce
- *Gal Young 'Un*, Victor Nunez

SPECIAL JURY PRIZE
- *The Return of the Secaucus 7*, John Sayles
- *The Day After Trinity: J. Robert Oppenheimer and the Atomic Bomb*, Jon Else
- *The War at Home*, Glenn Silber, Barry Brown

SPECIAL JOHN FORD MEDALLION
- Henry Fonda

GOLDEN GLOBES

Nominations were announced on January 12, 1981. Awards were presented on January 31 at the Beverly Hilton Hotel in Los Angeles. The ceremony was telecast on CBS.

BEST DRAMA PICTURE
- *Ordinary People*
The Elephant Man
Raging Bull
The Stunt Man
Twinkle, Twinkle, "Killer" Kane

BEST COMEDY OR MUSICAL PICTURE
- *Coal Miner's Daughter*
Airplane!
The Idolmaker

Fame
Melvin and Howard

BEST DIRECTOR
- Robert Redford, *Ordinary People*
David Lynch, *The Elephant Man*
Roman Polanski, *Tess*
Richard Rush, *The Stunt Man*
Martin Scorsese, *Raging Bull*

BEST ACTOR, DRAMA
- Robert De Niro, *Raging Bull*
John Hurt, *The Elephant Man*
Jack Lemmon, *Tribute*
Peter O'Toole, *The Stunt Man*
Donald Sutherland, *Ordinary People*

BEST ACTRESS, DRAMA
- Mary Tyler Moore, *Ordinary People*
Ellen Burstyn, *Resurrection*
Nastassja Kinski, *Tess*
Deborah Raffin, *Touched by Love*
Gena Rowlands, *Gloria*

BEST ACTOR, COMEDY OR MUSICAL
- Ray Sharkey, *The Idolmaker*
Neil Diamond, *The Jazz Singer*
Tommy Lee Jones, *Coal Miner's Daughter*
Paul Le Mat, *Melvin and Howard*
Walter Matthau, *Hopscotch*

BEST ACTRESS, COMEDY OR MUSICAL
- Sissy Spacek, *Coal Miner's Daughter*
Irene Cara, *Fame*
Goldie Hawn, *Private Benjamin*
Bette Midler, *Divine Madness*
Dolly Parton, *9 to 5*

BEST SUPPORTING ACTOR
- Timothy Hutton, *Ordinary People*
Judd Hirsch, *Ordinary People*
Joe Pesci, *Raging Bull*
Jason Robards, *Melvin and Howard*
Scott Wilson, *Twinkle, Twinkle, "Killer" Kane*

BEST SUPPORTING ACTRESS
- Mary Steenburgen, *Melvin and Howard*
Lucie Arnaz, *The Jazz Singer*
Beverly D'Angelo, *Coal Miner's Daughter*
Cathy Moriarty, *Raging Bull*
Debra Winger, *Urban Cowboy*

BEST FILM DEBUT OF THE YEAR—MALE

- Timothy Hutton, *Ordinary People*

Christopher Atkins, *The Blue Lagoon*

William Hurt, *Altered States*

Michael O'Keefe, *The Great Santini*

Steve Railsback, *The Stunt Man*

BEST FILM DEBUT OF THE YEAR—FEMALE

- Nastassja Kinski, *Tess*

Nancy Allen, *Dressed to Kill*

Cathy Moriarty, *Raging Bull*

Dolly Parton, *9 to 5*

Debra Winger, *Urban Cowboy*

BEST SCREENPLAY

- William Peter Blatty, *Twinkle, Twinkle, "Killer" Kane*

Eric Bergren, Christopher DeVore, David Lynch, *The Elephant Man*

Lawrence B. Marcus, *The Stunt Man*

Mardik Martin, Paul Schrader, *Raging Bull*

Alvin Sargent, *Ordinary People*

BEST SONG

- "Fame," *Fame*, Michael Gore, Dean Pitchford

"Call Me," *American Gigolo*, Giorgio Moroder

"Love on the Rocks," *The Jazz Singer,* Neil Diamond

"9 to 5," *9 to 5*, Dolly Parton

"Yesterday's Dreams," *Falling in Love Again*, Michel Legrand

BEST FOREIGN FILM

- *Tess* (U.K.)

Breaker Morant (Australia)

Kagemusha Career (Japan)

The Last Metro (France)

My Brilliant Career (Australia)

Special Treatment (Yugoslavia)

Winners

BEST ORIGINAL SCORE

- Dominic Frontiere, *The Stunt Man*

CECIL B. DEMILLE AWARD

- Gene Kelly

WRITERS GUILD OF AMERICA

Nominations were announced on February 22, 1981. Awards were presented on March 24 at the Wilshire Ebell Theatre in Los Angeles and the McGraw-Hill building in New York.

BEST DRAMA WRITTEN DIRECTLY FOR THE SCREEN

- *Melvin and Howard*, Bo Goldman

Fame, Christopher Gore

My Bodyguard, Alan Ormsby

BEST DRAMA ADAPTED FROM ANOTHER MEDIUM

- *Ordinary People*, Alvin Sargent, based on a novel by Judith Guest

Coal Miner's Daughter, Tom Rickman, based on the book *Loretta Lynn: Coal Miner's Daughter* by Loretta Lynn with George Vecsey

The Elephant Man, Christopher Devore, Eric Bergren, David Lynch, based on the books *The Elephant Man and Other Reminiscenses* by Sir Frederick Treves and *The Elephant Man: A Study in Human Dignity* by Ashley Montagu

The Great Santini, Lewis John Carlino, based on a novel by Pat Conroy

The Stunt Man, Lawrence B. Marcus, Richard Rush, based on a novel by Paul Brodeur

BEST COMEDY WRITTEN DIRECTLY FOR THE SCREEN

- *Private Benjamin*, Nancy Meyers, Charles Shyer, Harvey Miller

9 to 5, Colin Higgins, Patricia Resnick

The Return of the Secaucus 7, John Sayles

Stardust Memories, Woody Allen

BEST COMEDY ADAPTED FROM ANOTHER MEDIUM

- *Airplane!* Jim Abrahams, David Zucker, Jerry Zucker

The Empire Strikes Back, Leigh Brackett, Lawrence Kasdan, George Lucas

Hopscotch, Brian Garfield, Bryan Forbes, based on a novel by Brian Garfield

1980

DIRECTORS GUILD OF AMERICA

The award for Best Director was presented on March 14, 1981, at the Beverly Hilton Hotel in Los Angeles.

BEST DIRECTOR
- Robert Redford, *Ordinary People*
Michael Apted, *Coal Miner's Daughter*
David Lynch, *The Elephant Man*
Richard Rush, *The Stunt Man*
Martin Scorsese, *Raging Bull*

D. W. GRIFFITH AWARD
- George Cukor

ACADEMY AWARDS

Nominations were announced on February 17, 1981. Awards were presented on March 31 at the Dorothy Chandler Pavilion in Los Angeles. The ceremony was telecast by ABC.

BEST PICTURE
- *Ordinary People*
Coal Miner's Daughter
The Elephant Man
Raging Bull
Tess

BEST DIRECTOR
- Robert Redford, *Ordinary People*
David Lynch, *The Elephant Man*
Roman Polanski, *Tess*
Richard Rush, *The Stunt Man*
Martin Scorsese, *Raging Bull*

BEST ACTOR
- Robert De Niro, *Raging Bull*
Robert Duvall, *The Great Santini*
John Hurt, *The Elephant Man*
Jack Lemmon, *Tribute*
Peter O'Toole, *The Stunt Man*

BEST ACTRESS
- Sissy Spacek, *Coal Miner's Daughter*
Ellen Burstyn, *Resurrection*
Goldie Hawn, *Private Benjamin*
Mary Tyler Moore, *Ordinary People*
Gena Rowlands, *Gloria*

BEST SUPPORTING ACTOR
- Timothy Hutton, *Ordinary People*
Judd Hirsch, *Ordinary People*
Michael O'Keefe, *The Great Santini*
Joe Pesci, *Raging Bull*
Jason Robards, *Melvin and Howard*

BEST SUPPORTING ACTRESS
- Mary Steenburgen, *Melvin and Howard*
Eileen Brennan, *Private Benjamin*
Eva Le Gallienne, *Resurrection*
Cathy Moriarty, *Raging Bull*
Diana Scarwid, *Inside Moves*

BEST ORIGINAL SCREENPLAY
- Bo Goldman, *Melvin and Howard*
Christopher Gore, *Fame*
Jean Gruault, *Mon Oncle d'Amerique*
Nancy Meyers, Harvey Miller, Charles Shyer, *Private Benjamin*
W. D. Richter, Arthur Ross, *Brubaker*

BEST ADAPTED SCREENPLAY
- Alvin Sargent, *Ordinary People*
Bruce Beresford, Jonathan Hardy, David Stevens, *Breaker Morant*
Eric Bergren, Christopher Devore, David Lynch, *The Elephant Man*
Lawrence B. Marcus, Richard Rush, *The Stunt Man*
Tom Rickman, *Coal Miner's Daughter*

BEST SONG
- "Fame," *Fame*, Michael Gore, Dean Pitchford
"9 to 5," *9 to 5*, Dolly Parton
"On the Road Again," *Honeysuckle Rose*, Willie Nelson
"Out Here on My Own," *Fame*, Lesley Gore, Michael Gore
"People Alone," *The Competition*, Wilbur Jennings, Lalo Schifrin

BEST FOREIGN-LANGUAGE FILM

- *Moscow Does Not Believe in Tears*
  (U.S.S.R.)
Confidence (Hungary)
Kagemusha (The Shadow Warrior) (Japan)
The Last Metro (France)
The Nest (Spain)

Winners

BEST ART DIRECTION

- Pierre Guffroy, Jack Stephens, Renn-
  Burrill, Société Francaise de
  Production, *Tess*

BEST CINEMATOGRAPHY

- Ghislain Cloquet, Geoffrey Unsworth,
  Tess

BEST COSTUME DESIGN

- Anthony Powell, *Tess*

BEST DOCUMENTARY

(FEATURE)
- *From Mao to Mozart: Isaac Stern in
  China*, Murray Lerner
(SHORT SUBJECT)
- *Karl Hess: Toward Liberty*, Roland Hallé,
  Peter W. Ladue

BEST FILM EDITING

- Thelma Schoonmaker, *Raging Bull*

BEST ORIGINAL SCORE

- Michael Gore, *Fame*

SCIENTIFIC OR TECHNICAL AWARDS

(Academy Award of Merit)
- Linwood G. Dunn, Cecil D. Love, Acme
  Tool and Manufacturing Co.
(Scientific and Engineering Award)
- Jean-Marie Lavalou, Alain Masseron,
  David Samuelson, Samuelson Film

Service; Edward B. Krause, Filmline
Corp.; Ross Taylor; Bernard Kuhl,
Werner Block, Osram GmbH; David
Grafton
(Technical Achievement Award)
- Carter Equipment Co.; Hollywood Film
  Co.; Andre DeBrie; Charles Vaughn,
  Eugene Nottingham, Cinetron
  Computer Systems; John W. Lang,
  Walter Hrastnik, Charles J. Watson, Bell
  and Howell Co.; Worth Baird, La Vezzi
  Machine Works; Peter A. Regla, Dan
  Slater, Elicon

BEST SHORT FILM

(ANIMATED)
- *The Fly*, Ferenc Rofusz
(LIVE ACTION)
- *The Dollar Bottom*, Lloyd Phillips

BEST SOUND

- Gregg Landaker, Steve Maslow, Peter
  Sutton, Bill Varney, *The Empire Strikes
  Back*

SPECIAL ACHIEVEMENT AWARD

(VISUAL EFFECTS)
- Richard Edlund, Brian Johnson, Dennis
  Muren, Bruce Nicholson, *The Empire
  Strikes Back*

HONORARY AWARDS

- Henry Fonda
- Fred Hynes

SCREEN ACTORS GUILD

LIFETIME ACHIEVEMENT AWARD

- Leon Ames

· 1981 ·

Chariots *Sweeps the Derby*

How did a little British indie about fleet-footed schoolboys end up winning the year's film-awards derby—even scoring the biggest upset in Oscar history?

It all started nearly a year earlier when Roger Ebert pushed *Chariots of Fire* out of the gate.

The critic for *The Chicago Sun-Times* was among those who gave *Chariots* a standing ovation when it debuted at the Cannes Film Festival in May 1981, but he became worried about its fate when the French crix savaged it in their reviews. The attacks not only ruined *Chariots*'s award chances, but threatened potential distribution deals that might be sealed at the fest. Ebert rallied to its defense, rounded up other American critics and pressed them to back *Chariots* for a new award he just invented—the American Critics' Prize—which would never again be bestowed at Cannes. Ebert got his way, but just barely: his fellow Yankee crix endorsed *Chariots* by a slim edge—six votes out of 11.

Happily, *Chariots of Fire* scored a U.S. distribution deal, too, and fared well when it opened in American theaters in late 1981, but it came to a crashing halt at the Los Angeles film crix awards. It failed to claim any kudos and even lost the prize for Best Foreign Film to *Pixote*, described by *Variety* as "a trenchant, uncompromising look at Brazilian juvenile delinquents."

The big winner turned out to be Louis Malle's indie *Atlantic City*, starring Burt Lancaster as an aging mobster who's smitten with a young vixen being hunted by the mafia (Susan Sarandon). Interestingly, the Hollywood crix named it Best Picture and Best Screenplay over *Reds*, a much-ballyhooed and well-reviewed opus by Hollywood kingpin Warren Beatty. *Variety* described *Reds* as "the story of American

Chariots of Fire tied *Reds* for the NBR's best pic prize, then fell behind. Late in the derby, it finally zoomed ahead to claim the top Oscar.

journalist-activist John Reed's stormy romantic career with writer Louise Bryant (Diane Keaton), a kinetic affair backdropped by pre–World War I radicalism and the Russian Revolution."

Lancaster won Best Actor over Henry Fonda, who teamed up with true 24-karat talent in *On Golden Pond*: his daughter Jane and fellow screen icon Katharine Hepburn. *Variety* cheered all the "meaty, major roles," especially the pairing of the senior Fonda with Hepburn: "They are miraculous together here, conveying heart-rending intimations of mortality which are doubly powerful due to the stars' venerable status."

The L.A. crix's choice for Best Actress was Meryl Streep, who gave what *Variety* called "strong" dual perfs as a mysterious nineteenth-century lover and a brusque 1980s actress in *The French Lieutenant's Woman*. Runner-up was Diane Keaton in *Reds*. Winner of Best Supporting Actor was John Gielgud as a caustic butler in *Arthur*, topping Jack Nicholson's portrayal of playwright Eugene O'Neill in *Reds*.

But *Reds* scored two notable victories. Maureen Stapleton was hailed as Best Supporting Actress for her role as anarchist

Emma Goldman, and Beatty claimed the director's laurels. Curiously, the runner-up in the helmer's race was not the director of the year's Best Picture, *Atlantic City*'s Louis Malle, but Lawrence Kasdan, who *Variety* said "makes an impressively confident directorial debut" in *Body Heat*.

The L.A. crix cut ties with *The Merv Griffin Show* this year and sold their broadcast rights to Metromedia, which syndicated the kudocast nationally as a stand-alone special, just as it had marketed the Golden Globes ceremony in the 1970s.

The cameras caught a warm sentimental moment at the fete when star Candice Bergen "glowed with pride," observed *Women's Wear Daily*, as she presented the Best Picture prize to hubby Louis Malle.

When Burt Lancaster accepted his accolade as Best Actor, he said, "We weren't thinking about awards while we were making this film, but I knew it was a fine film and a sensitive role for me, so I had a good time making it."

When Orson Welles stood in for the absent Warren Beatty, the message was clear: Beatty wanted to be perceived as the same wunderkind that Welles was when he started producing, writing, directing and starring in films all at once in the 1940s.

The National Board of Review not only agreed with Beatty as the year's Best Director, but also named *Reds* Best Picture—in a tie with *Chariots of Fire*, which suddenly zoomed into America's film-awards derby as a serious dark-horse contender.

Reds also scored the supporting actor prize for Jack Nicholson. Henry Fonda won Best Actor. A surprise occurred in the actress races when a three-year old pic claimed both contests. *Stevie* was originally released in 1978 in Los Angeles, where it snagged a L.A. film crix prize (Best Supporting Actress, Mona Washbourne) and reaped two Golden Globe nominations).

Now that *Stevie* had been released nationally, the board endorsed Washbourne's perf as the loyal aunt of poet Stevie Smith (Glenda Jackson) and cited Jackson as Best Actress.

One week later, Jackson and Washbourne also reaped kudos from the New York Film Critics Circle. Jackson won Best Actress with 36 points, followed by Faye Dunaway for her hanger-wielding portrayal of Joan Crawford in *Mommie Dearest* (34). Washbourne triumphed with 52 points over Maureen Stapleton (19).

Atlantic City garnered victories for Best Actor (Burt Lancaster prevailed with 58 points over Henry Fonda, with 27) and Best Screenplay (John Guare won with 48 points, surpassing Sidney Lumet and Jay Presson Allen, *Prince of the City*, with 25).

Lumet pulled off a huge upset by copping the prize for Best Director (33) over *Atlantic City*'s Louis Malle (26) and *Chariots of Fire*'s Hugh Hudson (25). *Variety* had lauded Lumet's "firm control of the sprawling canvas" that he unfurled in his exposé of New York police corruption.

Reds's Warren Beatty was only a distant also-ran in the helmers' race, but the movie rallied to win Best Picture on the second ballot with 37 points, followed by *Prince of the City* (25) and *Atlantic City* (22). In the match-up for Best Supporting Actor, *Reds*'s Jack Nicholson (29 points) lost to John Gielgud (36).

The Gotham crix were atypically decisive this year, according to *The New York Times*: "The group, meeting at the offices of the New York Newspaper Guild, arrived at each choice on the second ballot, though in past years it has usually required three, four or five ballots for agreement to be reached."

When the crix gathered for their awards presentation at Sardi's restaurant, "a good time was had by all," insisted the *Daily News*. "Even Warren Beatty, who seemed delighted that the scribes capable of saying so many mean, nasty things in print could turn out to be so nice in person."

When Beatty received the Best Picture

> "Awards are silly," said Gotham crix Best Actress Glenda Jackson.

prize for *Reds,* he said, "To get this recognition from such a mean, vitriolic, vituperative bunch is more than touching, it's paralyzing."

Burt Lancaster acknowledged the considerable clout of Pauline Kael within the crix's circle when he stopped to thank to her personally while en route to the podium to pick up his Best Actor plaque. He also acknowledged the esteem in which he held the crix award—the third of his career—by bringing along 10 of his family members to the ceremony or, as the *Daily News* wisecracked, "enough relatives to start his own repertory company. He said he wanted them to share in what he called one of the proudest moments of his career." *The Village Voice* called his acceptance speech "gracious" and noted that he cried as he introduced his family to the roomful of his film colleagues.

Glenda Jackson was far less appreciative of her accolade. When the *Voice* asked her if she'd ever dreamed that she'd win this award for *Stevie,* she snapped back: "I never dream about awards, but, if I did, the answer would be no. Awards are silly if you believe they mean more than they are. They're a nice reason to go out for an evening to a party."

John Gielgud couldn't attend, but he sent a telegram, which was read aloud by Liza Minnelli.

"*Atlantic City* pretty much swept the awards" from the National Society of Film Critics, reported *Variety* on the next batch of crix honors. Most curious: while a majority of the society's members may also have been members of the New York Film Critics Circle, its vote results came closer to mirroring the scribes on the Left Coast. Reported the *L.A. Herald Examiner:* "The society voting duplicated the Los Angeles Film Critics Association awards in four categories: Best Picture, Actor, Screenplay and Supporting Actress. All three critics' organizations have recognized Guare's script and Lancaster's performance, making *Atlantic*

"You should hear what they're saying about Pia Zadora!"

City the most heavily and consistently honored film in the year-end voting rituals."

Atlantic City won Best Picture by only a narrow edge, nabbing 33 points, followed by 30 for *Reds* and 24 for *Prince of the City.* Louis Malle won with 40 over Sidney Lumet (27). Lancaster prevailed with 76 points over Gene Hackman (32) as a married man who has an affair with neighbor Barbra Streisand in *All Night Long.*

Surprises among the votes included a Best Actress victory by Marilia Pera as a haggard prostitute in *Pixote* (37 points) over Faye Dunaway (29). Robert Preston was honored as Best Supporting Actor for his role as Doctor Feelgood in *S.O.B.* (50 points) over Jerry Orbach as a cop in *Prince of the City* (37).

Both the society and the Gotham crix circle adopted resolutions demanding that the Polish government release Andrzej Wajda "and all other Polish film directors, producers, screenwriters, actors and craftsmen who are currently being detained for their political beliefs and associations." Many of Poland's film artists were imprisoned as part of martial law imposed by Communist leaders aiming to squash the Solidarity union uprising.

When the Golden Globe nominations were announced, *Reds* led with seven noms, followed close behind a pic that hadn't figured strongly in the film-awards derby so far—*Ragtime*, described by *Variety* as "Milos Forman's superbly crafted screen adaptation" of E. L. Doctorow's novel about life in turn-of-the-century America.

Missing from the upper categories was *Atlantic City*, which was placed into the race for Best Foreign Film (opposite *Chariots of Fire*, which eventually won). Columnist Tom Bray fumed, "Of course, the only thing foreign about this film is its French-born director (who now resides in the U.S.). It's an American film, sponsored by American money, starring American actors and distributed by an American studio." Much of the pic was filmed in Canada, however, which may have explained its classification.

One of the highlights of the awards gala was Henry Fonda's victory for Best Drama Actor. Since he was still recovering from a near-fatal heart ailment, he watched the ceremony on TV at home while his daughter, Jane, accepted on his behalf, citing his "spirit and courage and determination.

"My dad doesn't believe in competing," she added, "but I'm so happy for him!"

Henry Fonda's nurse described his response as he watched: "I've never seen him grin so broadly."

Fonda beat Warren Beatty, who rebounded to claim the director's Globe, but otherwise *Reds* was shut out, even losing Best Drama Picture to *On Golden Pond*. Meryl Streep won Best Drama Actress for *The French Lieutenant's Woman*.

Arthur claimed the most kudos of the night—four: Best Comedy or Musical Picture, Best Song ("Best That You Can Do"), Best Supporting Actor (John Gielgud) and Best Comedy/Musical Actor for Dudley Moore as a perpetually pickled tycoon who falls for a hash-slinging waitress (Liza Minnelli).

A loser for Best Comedy or Musical Picture was *Pennies from Heaven*, Herbert Ross's esoteric tuner spoofing the fluffy Hollywood musicals of the Depression-plagued 1930s. However, star Bernadette Peters prevailed as Best Comedy/Musical Actress for portraying a virginal schoolteacher reduced to becoming a hooker.

Another upset occurred in the race for Best Supporting Actress when Maureen Stapleton (*Reds*) lost to Joan Hackett as a decaying Park Avenue diva in *Only When I Laugh*.

As shocking as many of the winners were on Globes night, none caused more jaws to drop than the prize for Best New Film Star.

Twenty-six-year-old Pia Zadora copped

the award for her debut screen role as a scheming nymphet in one of 1981's worst-reviewed pix, *Butterfly*. "It's truly terrible," insisted the *L.A. Times*, but *Playboy* called its star "Zadorable" and *Variety* offered a few kind words in its review, saying that the thesp "registers well with her little girl looks and Lolita sensuality." Prior to her screen bow, Zadora had toiled for 12 years on New York stages—including in a role opposite Tallulah Bankhead on Broadway in *Midgie Purvis*—but she had trouble being taken seriously as an artist after marrying an Israeli tycoon who shamelessly acted like her sugar daddy. Thirty years her senior, Mashulem Riklis produced *Butterfly* and showcased Zadora's concert act at his Las Vegas Riviera Casino. He finally went too far when he flew members of the Hollywood Foreign Press Association to Vegas to catch Zadora's singing act and to see an advance screening of *Butterfly*, which had not yet opened in theaters. It didn't matter that her recent album was charting well and had received socko reviews (even tough *L.A. Times* music critic Leonard Feather insisted, "She has it all—the range, the expert intonation") or that she received good reviews for a bad movie that also starred Orson Welles and Stacy Keach, who were not treated so kindly by crix. When the foreign scribes gave Zadora the Globe over Kathleen Turner, Elizabeth McGovern and Howard E. Rollins, the *Herald Examiner* shrieked, "*Quel scandal*! You should hear what they're saying!"

But foreign press prexy Judy Solomon tried to silence critics by speaking up in defense of the vote: "Her award was for 'new star.' Everyone reacts as if we called her Best Actress of the Universe. We didn't. I'm sure that when we gave the 'new star' award to Jessica Lange for *King Kong*, some people thought it was a joke."

No one was laughing weeks later, how-

> Matinee star Warren Beatty was embraced by the scribes' and helmers' guilds for *Reds*.

ever, when CBS announced that it would not broadcast the Golden Globes ceremony again next year.

"For the second year in a row, the Directors Guild of America gave its award as Best Director to an actor," observed *The New York Times* about the next set of kudos. When Warren Beatty accepted it, he said, "Only in America could a picture of this subject and this size be made without censorship from government or the people who put up the money." The *Times* pointed out that "the people who put up the money" were actually British, since *Reds* received its $33.5 million financing from a division of London's Barclay Bank. The bank got paid back quickly. As of March 3, *Variety* estimated that *Reds* had already reaped $12.7 million in U.S. domestic rentals.

According to the *L.A. Times*, Beatty was "mobbed by an insatiable horde of photographers and reporters" throughout the night as he tried to enjoy the dinner of prime rib, Caesar salad and string beans being served to the 2,000 guests at the Beverly Hilton Hotel. But he handled the frenzy gallantly. He even lingered after the banquet to give the paparazzi a private photo shoot, then signed an autograph for a little boy and scooted.

"The guild award now puts Beatty in the favorite's position to win the Oscar," announced the *L.A. Times*. "Only twice in 34 years has the guild recipient not also won the Academy Award."

Reds demonstrated further awards heft as it swept next through the writers' guild honors, which were decided this year by 1,500 voters weighing 121 eligible pix. Warren Beatty and Trevor Griffiths impressed pundits by beating *Atlantic City*'s John Guare for the prize as best original drama. Also surprising: how tame the paparazzi were when Beatty collected his latest guild kudos. The reason: guild leaders kept them corralled in a side room during the ceremony.

On Golden Pond's Ernest Thompson won a close race over the scribes of *Prince of the City* and *Ragtime*. *Arthur*'s Steve Gordon topped such stellar names as Blake Edwards (*S.O.B.*), Alan Alda (*The Four*

All three crix orgs named Burt Lancaster Best Actor for portraying an aging thug in *Atlantic City*, which was voted best pic by the L.A. crix and national society.

Seasons) and George Lucas and Philip Kaufman (*Raiders of the Lost Ark*).

An upset occurred in the match-up for best adapted comedy when noted Broadway playwrights Jerome Lawrence and Robert E. Lee (*First Monday in October*) lost to *Rich and Famous*'s Gerald Ayres.

When the Oscar nominations were announced, *Reds* was the clear front-runner with 12 bids, just two short of *All about Eve*'s record. Beatty scored noms as director, writer, actor and producer, thereby duplicating the milestone he achieved in 1978 with *Heaven Can Wait* when he tied Orson Welles's record grand slam for *Citizen Kane*.

In second place was *On Golden Pond*, with 10 bids. *Variety* columnist Army Archerd reported that star Henry Fonda, "who was not having one of his better weeks, was cheered enormously when wife Shirlee told him of *On Golden Pond*'s nominations. And when she said he was among them, Fonda yelled, 'Holy Mackeloney!' "

Even though Fonda faced Beatty and Burt Lancaster, winner of kudos from three crix orgs, *Variety* called Fonda "the odds-on-favorite to win this time."

When he prevailed, Jane appeared at the podium, looking ecstatic. "Oh, Dad, I'm so happy and proud for you!" she cheered. "I know he's watching and very, very happy and surprised and he probably said, 'Hey, ain't I lucky?!' as if luck had anything to do with it." She spoke for four minutes in all, ending with "Dad, me and the grandkids will be right over!"

The academy had a rule against proxies, but waived it so that Jane could stand in for her still-bedridden dad. *Variety* was grateful and didn't even mind her wordiness, saying, "Jane Fonda's thoughtful, warm acceptance on behalf of her father was what people tune in to see and hear."

In the race for Best Actress, pundits were outraged by the omission of Faye Dunaway from the nominees. The eventual winner was presumed to be either *Reds*'s Diane Keaton or *The French Lieutenant Woman*'s Meryl Streep. No one paid much attention to Katharine Hepburn's historic bid—her twelfth, setting a new record.

When Hepburn's name was announced as the winner, the audience gasped in shock. Presenter Jon Voight caught his breath and said, "I don't think there's anyone here or watching who doesn't appreciate the amount of love and gratitude represented by this Oscar selection tonight and we all send our love to Katharine." Like her nomination, her victory set a new Oscar record: with four wins for lead acting, Hepburn became the most honored thesp in academy history.

Reds was nommed in the race for Best Supporting Actor, too, but even contender Jack Nicholson dismissed his chances. "I'm pretty sure Sir John Gielgud will win and that's jake with me," he told Army Archerd. "I like a nice, relaxed evening. I'm hoping for a win for Warren." Gielgud took the category, as expected, but the 77-year-old thesp was in Munich filming *Wagner* with Richard Burton.

Reds rebounded in the contest for Best Supporting Actress when Maureen Stapleton beat Jane Fonda (*On Golden Pond*), Golden Globe champ Joan Hackett (*Only When I Laugh*) and Elizabeth McGovern as sex kitten Evelyn Nesbitt in *Ragtime*.

Stapleton said at the podium, "I'm thrilled, happy, delighted . . . sober! It is an evening for thanks. I want to thank everybody I ever met in my entire life and my inspiration, Joel McCrea."

Backstage later, she told *Variety* that she

Variety said Katharine Hepburn and Henry Fonda were "miraculous together" in *On Golden Pond*, which won Best Drama Picture at the Globes and reaped Oscars for both thesps.

expected to win "because I'm old and tired and I deserved it and I lost three times before. I hope this is only the beginning. Next I want to win as Best Actress, then Best Supporting Actor, Best Actor, all of it." She also revealed that she was disappointed in the personal life of the woman she portrayed in *Reds*. "Emma Goldman had no redeeming sexual features," she griped. "She beat up her lovers."

Reds won the prize for Best Cinematography next, and Warren Beatty was the heavy favorite to snag the director's honors since he had won the equivalent prize from the Directors Guild of America. When he prevailed, Beatty used much of the same acceptance speech he gave at the guild dinner, marveling at how he could make such a film without government censorship or meddling from investors.

Beatty was also up for the Best Original Screenplay award, which was bestowed next. That's when *Chariots of Fire* broke out of the pack.

Chariots scribe Colin Welland accepted the statuette, roaring his excitement, "What you've done for the British film industry! You may have started something. The British are coming!"

Soon thereafter *Chariots* beat *Reds* for the costume award, and the Oscarcast camera caught a closeup of the worried look on Warren Beatty's face. When *Chariots* also won the trophy for its hugely popular musical score, it tied *Reds*'s tally of three Oscars so far.

On Golden Pond pulled even with its own third victory when it won for best adapted screenplay, which was accepted by its jaunty scribe, Ernest Thompson. "See me later," he told the audience, tossing a kiss. "I would love to suck face with you all."

As all three pix headed into the last stretch of the Oscar derby, *Reds, On Golden Pond* and *Chariots of Fire* appeared to be neck and neck and neck.

Then *Chariots* breezed over the finish line.

Stunned, its producer David Puttnam said at the podium, "You are the most extraordinary, generous people on God's earth, not just the academy, to whom we are thankful, but as a country to have taken what is an absolutely Cinderella picture and awarded it this and come to it in droves!"

The next day, *Variety*'s editors seemed shocked by *Reds*'s failure to score its predicted sweep and observed, "The Oscars walked off the stage in all directions, nearly evenly spread over the major contenders."

Janet Maslin of *The New York Times* called this year's Oscar derby "the most exciting in recent years" since so many of the victories were unexpected.

Best Actress champ Katharine Hepburn told reporters soon afterward: "I was so dumbfounded. I'm so touched that my fellow actors cared to vote for me, a dear old thing."

She said of her equally old costar, Best Actor Henry Fonda, "I knew Hank would get it. He was amazing on that film. He wasn't feeling very well, you know, but you never would've known it." Fonda died five months later.

Still outside the big national film-awards derby this year was a smaller race, tailored specifically for indie horses, but one that was coming on fast. This year the U.S. Film Festival drew 20,000 attendees to snowy Park City, Utah, in late January, up 5,000 from last year.

Star judges included *Chicago Sun-Times* critic Roger Ebert and actress Lee Grant, who stunned festival-goers by declaring a three-way tie for the Grand Jury Prize.

Winners included *The Dozens*, a Boston-set docudrama about a woman who aims to start a new life after being sprung from prison for writing fraudulent checks. Sharing the laurels was *Street Music*, a wry drama about the wacky inhabitants of a shabby San Francisco hotel slated for demolition. The third champ was *Killer of Sheep*, a haunting look at black ghetto life in Central South Los Angeles, which was filmed for $13,000 over five years.

Director Francis Coppola didn't attend the festival to receive his special Video Award, but was beamed in via satellite hookup from his San Francisco office. Director Stanley Kramer was on hand to accept the John Ford Medallion, telling the audience, "I am your brother, you who use film as a weapon. I intend to be dangerous."

▪ 1981 ▪

LOS ANGELES FILM CRITICS ASSOCIATION

Winners were announced on December 14, 1981. Awards were presented on January 13, 1982, at the Beverly Wilshire Hotel in Los Angeles. The ceremony was telecast on L.A. station KTTV and aired nationally via syndication by Metromedia.

BEST PICTURE
▪ *Atlantic City*

BEST DIRECTOR
▪ Warren Beatty, *Reds*

BEST ACTOR
▪ Burt Lancaster, *Atlantic City*

BEST ACTRESS
▪ Meryl Streep, *The French Lieutenant's Woman*

BEST SUPPORTING ACTOR
▪ John Gielgud, *Arthur*

BEST SUPPORTING ACTRESS
- Maureen Stapleton, *Reds*

BEST SCREENPLAY
- John Guare, *Atlantic City*

BEST CINEMATOGRAPHY
- Vittoria Storaro, *Reds*

BEST MUSIC SCORE
- Randy Newman, *Ragtime*

BEST FOREIGN FILM
- *Pixote* (Brazil)

BEST EXPERIMENTAL/INDEPENDENT FILM
- *The Art of Worldly Wisdom*, Bruce Elder

CAREER ACHIEVEMENT AWARD
- Barbara Stanwyck

NEW GENERATION AWARD
- John Guare, *Atlantic City*

SPECIAL AWARD
- Kevin Brownlow, *Napoleon* (France, 1926)

NATIONAL BOARD OF REVIEW

Winners were announced on December 15, 1981.

BEST PICTURE (TIE)
- *Chariots of Fire*
- *Reds*
Atlantic City
Stevie
Gallipoli
On Golden Pond
Prince of the City
Raiders of the Lost Ark
Heartland
Ticket to Heaven
Breaker Morant

BEST DIRECTOR
- Warren Beatty, *Reds*

BEST ACTOR
- Henry Fonda, *On Golden Pond*

BEST ACTRESS
- Glenda Jackson, *Stevie*

BEST SUPPORTING ACTOR
- Jack Nicholson, *Reds*

BEST SUPPORTING ACTRESS
- Mona Washbourne, *Stevie*

BEST FOREIGN FILM
- *Oblomov* (U.S.S.R.)
The Boat Is Full (Switzerland)
The Last Metro (France)
Contract (Poland)
Pixote (Brazil)

SPECIAL AWARDS
- James Cagney
- Blanche Sweet
- Restoration of John Gance's *Napoleon*

NEW YORK FILM CRITICS CIRCLE

Winners were announced on December 21, 1981. Awards were presented on January 31, 1982, at Sardi's restaurant in New York.

BEST PICTURE
- *Reds*

BEST DIRECTOR
- Sidney Lumet, *Prince of the City*

BEST ACTOR
- Burt Lancaster, *Atlantic City*

BEST ACTRESS
- Glenda Jackson, *Stevie*

BEST SUPPORTING ACTOR
- John Gielgud, *Arthur*

BEST SUPPORTING ACTRESS
- Mona Washbourne, *Stevie*

BEST SCREENPLAY
- John Guare, *Atlantic City*

BEST CINEMATOGRAPHY
- David Watkin, *Chariots of Fire*

SPECIAL AWARDS
- *Napoleon* (France, 1926), Abel Gance, restored by Kevin Brownlow, David Gill
- Andrzej Wajda, Krzysztof Zanussi

NATIONAL SOCIETY OF FILM CRITICS

Winners were announced on January 3, 1982.

BEST PICTURE
- *Atlantic City*

BEST DIRECTOR
- Louis Malle, *Atlantic City*

BEST ACTOR
- Burt Lancaster, *Atlantic City*

BEST ACTRESS
- Marilia Pera, *Pixote*

BEST SUPPORTING ACTOR
- Robert Preston, *S.O.B.*

BEST SUPPORTING ACTRESS
- Maureen Stapleton, *Reds*

BEST SCREENPLAY
- John Guare, *Atlantic City*

BEST CINEMATOGRAPHY
- Gordon Willis, *Pennies from Heaven*

U.S. FILM FESTIVAL

This festival was held January 23–31, 1982, at Park City, Utah.

GRAND JURY PRIZE
- *The Dozens*, Christine Dall, Randall Conrad
- *Killer of Sheep*, Charles Burnett
- *Street Music*, Jenny Bowen

BEST DOCUMENTARY
(FILM)
- *Soldier Girls*, Joan Churchill, Nick Broomfield

(VIDEO)
- *Signed, Sealed and Delivered*, Erik Lewis, Don Gordon, Tami Gold

JOHN FORD MEDALLION
- Stanley Kramer

SPECIAL VIDEO AWARD
- Francis Ford Coppola

GOLDEN GLOBES

Nominations were announced on January 7, 1982. Awards were presented on January 30 at the Beverly Hilton Hotel in Los Angeles. The ceremony was telecast by CBS.

BEST DRAMA PICTURE
- *On Golden Pond*
  The French Lieutenant's Woman
  Prince of the City
  Ragtime
  Reds

BEST COMEDY OR MUSICAL PICTURE
- *Arthur*
  Four Seasons
  Pennies from Heaven
  S.O.B.
  Zoot Suit

BEST DIRECTOR
- Warren Beatty, *Reds*
  Milos Forman, *Ragtime*
  Sidney Lumet, *Prince of the City*
  Louis Malle, *Atlantic City*
  Mark Rydell, *On Golden Pond*
  Steven Spielberg, *Raiders of the Lost Ark*

BEST ACTOR, DRAMA
- Henry Fonda, *On Golden Pond*
  Warren Beatty, *Reds*
  Timothy Hutton, *Taps*
  Burt Lancaster, *Atlantic City*
  Treat Williams, *Prince of the City*

BEST ACTRESS, DRAMA
- Meryl Streep, *The French Lieutenant's Woman*
  Sally Field, *Absence of Malice*
  Katharine Hepburn, *On Golden Pond*
  Diane Keaton, *Reds*
  Sissy Spacek, *Raggedy Man*

BEST ACTOR, COMEDY OR MUSICAL
- Dudley Moore, *Arthur*

Alan Alda, *Four Seasons*

George Hamilton, *Zorro the Gay Blade*

Steve Martin, *Pennies from Heaven*

Walter Matthau, *First Monday in October*

BEST ACTRESS, COMEDY OR MUSICAL
- Bernadette Peters, *Pennies from Heaven*

Blair Brown, *Continental Divide*

Carol Burnett, *The Four Seasons*

Jill Clayburgh, *First Monday in October*

Liza Minnelli, *Arthur*

BEST SUPPORTING ACTOR
- John Gielgud, *Arthur*

James Coco, *Only When I Laugh*

Jack Nicholson, *Reds*

Howard E. Rollins, *Ragtime*

Orson Welles, *Butterfly*

BEST SUPPORTING ACTRESS
- Joan Hackett, *Only When I Laugh*

Jane Fonda, *On Golden Pond*

Kristy McNichol, *Only When I Laugh*

Maureen Stapleton, *Reds*

Mary Steenburgen, *Ragtime*

NEW FILM STAR OF THE YEAR—MALE OR FEMALE
- Pia Zadora, *Butterfly*

Elizabeth McGovern, *Ragtime*

Howard E. Rollins, *Ragtime*

Kathleen Turner, *Body Heat*

Rachel Ward, *Sharky's Machine*

Craig Wasson, *Four Friends*

BEST SCREENPLAY
- Ernest Thompson, *On Golden Pond*

Alan Alda, *The Four Seasons*

Warren Beatty, Trevor Griffiths, *Reds*

Kurt Luedtke, *Absence of Malice*

Harold Pinter, *The French Lieutenant's Woman*

BEST SONG
- "*Arthur*'s Theme (Best That You Can Do)," *Arthur*

"Endless Love," *Endless Love*

"For Your Eyes Only," *For Your Eyes Only*

"It's Wrong for Me to Love You," *Butterfly*

"One More Hour," *Ragtime*

BEST FOREIGN FILM
- *Chariots of Fire* (U.K.)

Atlantic City (Canada/France)

Das Boot (The Boat) (Germany)

Gallipoli (Australia)

Pixote (Brazil)

CECIL B. DEMILLE AWARD
- Sidney Poitier

DIRECTORS GUILD OF AMERICA

The award for Best Director was presented on March 13, 1982, at the Beverly Hilton Hotel in Los Angeles.

BEST DIRECTOR
- Warren Beatty, *Reds*

Hugh Hudson, *Chariots of Fire*

Louis Malle, *Atlantic City*

Mark Rydell, *On Golden Pond*

Steven Spielberg, *Raiders of the Lost Ark*

D. W. GRIFFITH AWARD
- Rouben Mamoulian

WRITERS GUILD OF AMERICA

Nominations were announced on February 23, 1982. Awards were presented on March 30 at the Wilshire Ebell Theatre in Los Angeles and the McGraw-Hill building in New York.

BEST DRAMA WRITTEN DIRECTLY FOR THE SCREEN
- *Reds*, Warren Beatty, Trevor Griffiths

Absence of Malice, Kurt Luedtke

Atlantic City, John Guare

Body Heat, Lawrence Kasdan

BEST DRAMA ADAPTED FROM ANOTHER MEDIUM
- *On Golden Pond*, Ernest Thompson, based on his play

Cutter's Way, Jeffrey Alan Fiskin, based on the novel *Cutter & Bone* by Newton Thornburg

Prince of the City, Jay Presson Allen, Sidney Lumet, based on a book by Robert Daley

Ragtime, Michael Weller, based on the
novel by E. L. Doctorow

BEST COMEDY WRITTEN DIRECTLY FOR THE SCREEN

- *Arthur*, Steve Gordon
The Four Seasons, Alan Alda
Raiders of the Lost Ark, George Lucas,
Philip Kaufman
S.O.B., Blake Edwards

BEST COMEDY ADAPTED FROM ANOTHER MEDIUM

- *Rich and Famous*, Gerald Ayres, based on
a play by John Van Druten
First Monday in October, Jerome
Lawrence, Robert E. Lee, based on their
play
For Your Eyes Only, Richard Maibaum,
Michael G. Wilson, based on the James
Bond books by Ian Fleming

LAUREL AWARD

- Paul Osborn

VALENTINE DAVIES AWARD

- Mort R. Lewis

MORGAN COX AWARD

- Brad Radnitz

ACADEMY AWARDS

Nominations were announced on February
11, 1982. Winners were announced on
March 29 at the Dorothy Chandler Pavilion
in Los Angeles. The ceremony was telecast
by ABC.

BEST PICTURE

- *Chariots of Fire*
Atlantic City
On Golden Pond
Raiders of the Lost Ark
Reds

BEST DIRECTOR

- Warren Beatty, *Reds*
Hugh Hudson, *Chariots of Fire*
Louis Malle, *Atlantic City*
Mark Rydell, *On Golden Pond*
Steven Spielberg, *Raiders of the Lost Ark*

BEST ACTOR

- Henry Fonda, *On Golden Pond*
Warren Beatty, *Reds*
Burt Lancaster, *Atlantic City*
Dudley Moore, *Arthur*
Paul Newman, *Absence of Malice*

BEST ACTRESS

- Katharine Hepburn, *On Golden Pond*
Diane Keaton, *Reds*
Marsha Mason, *Only When I Laugh*
Susan Sarandon, *Atlantic City*
Meryl Streep, *The French Lieutenant's
Woman*

BEST SUPPORTING ACTOR

- John Gielgud, *Arthur*
James Coco, *Only When I Laugh*
Ian Holm, *Chariots of Fire*
Jack Nicholson, *Reds*
Howard E. Rollins, Jr., *Ragtime*

BEST SUPPORTING ACTRESS

- Maureen Stapleton, *Reds*
Melinda Dillon, *Absence of Malice*
Jane Fonda, *On Golden Pond*
Joan Hackett, *Only When I Laugh*
Elizabeth McGovern, *Ragtime*

BEST ORIGINAL SCREENPLAY

- Colin Welland, *Chariots of Fire*
Warren Beatty, Trevor Griffiths, *Reds*
Steve Gordon, *Arthur*
John Guare, *Atlantic City*
Kurt Luedtke, *Absence of Malice*

BEST ADAPTED SCREENPLAY

- Ernest Thompson, *On Golden Pond*
Jay Presson Allen, Sidney Lumet, *Prince of
the City*
Harold Pinter, *The French Lieutenant's
Woman*
Dennis Potter, *Pennies from Heaven*
Michael Weller, *Ragtime*

BEST SONG

- "*Arthur*'s Theme (Best That You Can
Do)," *Arthur*, Peter Allen, Burt
Bacharach, Christopher Cross, Carole
Bayer Sager
"Endless Love," *Endless Love*, Lionel
Richie

"The First Time It Happens," *The Great Muppet Caper*, Joe Raposo
"For Your Eyes Only," *For Your Eyes Only*, Bill Conti, Mick Leeson
"One More Hour," *Ragtime*, Randy Newman

BEST FOREIGN-LANGUAGE FILM
- *Mephisto* (Hungary)
The Boat Is Full (Switzerland)
Man of Iron (Poland)
Muddy River (Japan)
Three Brothers (Italy)

Winners

BEST ART DIRECTION
- Leslie Dilley, Norman Reynolds, Michael Ford, *Raiders of the Lost Ark*

BEST CINEMATOGRAPHY
- Vittorio Storaro, *Reds*

BEST COSTUME DESIGN
- Milena Canonero, *Chariots of Fire*

BEST DOCUMENTARY
(FEATURE)
- Rabbi Marvin Hier, Arnold Schwartzman, *Genocide*
(SHORT SUBJECT)
- Nigel Noble, *Close Harmony*

BEST FILM EDITING
- Michael Kahn, *Raiders of the Lost Ark*

BEST MAKEUP
- Rick Baker, *An American Werewolf in London*

BEST ORIGINAL SCORE
- Vangelis, *Chariots of Fire*

SCIENTIFIC OR TECHNICAL AWARDS
(Academy Award of Merit)
- Fuji Photo Film Co.
(Scientific and Engineering Award)
- Nelson Tyler; Leonard Sokolow, Howard T. LaZare; Richard Edlund, Industrial

Light and Magic, Inc.; Edward Blasko, Roderick Ryan, Eastman Kodak
(Technical Achievement Award)
- Hal Landaker, Alan Landaker, Burbank Studios; Bill Hogan, Ruxton Ltd.; Richard Stumpf, Daniel R. Brewer, Universal City Studios; John DeMuth; Ernst Netmann, Continental Camera Systems; Bill Taylor, Universal City Studios; Peter D. Parks, Oxford Scientific Films; Louis Stankiewicz, H. L. Blachford; Dennis Muren, Stuart Ziff, Industrial Light and Magic

BEST SHORT FILM
(ANIMATED)
- *Crac*, Frédéric Back
(LIVE ACTION)
- *Violet*, Paul Kemp, Shelley Levinson

BEST SOUND
- Roy Charman, Gregg Landaker, Steve Maslow, Bill Varney, *Raiders of the Lost Ark*

SPECIAL ACHIEVEMENT AWARD
(SPECIAL EFFECTS)
- Richard L. Anderson, Ben Burtt, *Raiders of the Lost Ark*

BEST VISUAL EFFECTS
- Richard Edlund, Joe Johnston, Bruce Nicholson, Kit West, *Raiders of the Lost Ark*

GORDON E. SAWYER AWARD
- Joseph B. Walker

IRVING G. THALBERG MEMORIAL AWARD
- Albert R. Broccoli

JEAN HERSHOLT HUMANITARIAN AWARD
- Danny Kaye

HONORARY AWARD
- Barbara Stanwyck

· 1982 ·

Gandhi *Roughs Up* Tootsie, E.T.

The two big rivals for film kudos starred a quirky little gray space alien and, in the words of the second pic's director, "a funny little brown man dressed in a sheet and carrying a bean pole."

But *E.T. The Extra-Terrestrial* and *Gandhi* both turned out to be huge b.o. and critical hits. *E.T.*, in fact, became the biggest money-maker of all time, pulling in $187 million in domestic rentals to top the previous record set by *Star Wars* ($180 million). *The Los Angeles Times* cheered its creative success, too: "It may be the film of the decade and possibly the double decade." For a three-hour-plus movie about the nonviolent struggle to win India's independence from Britain, *Gandhi* scored impressive b.o., too—$24 million in U.S. rentals—and was hailed by *Variety* as "bold, sweeping and inspiring."

The L.A. crix were the first to name their winners and, just as they had bravely backed *Star Wars* as Best Picture in 1977, they also embraced the latest blockbuster from nearby Hollywood. *E.T.* and Spielberg beat *Gandhi* and its helmer Richard Attenborough handily for the pic and director's laurels, but *Gandhi*'s star Ben Kingsley prevailed as Best Actor over Peter O'Toole as a rowdy film star in *My Favorite Year*. The veteran of Britain's Royal Shakespeare Company was making his screen debut, but *Variety* insisted that Kingsley's portrayal was so "masterfully balanced and magnetic" that it seems "as though he has stepped through black-and-white newsreels into the present Technicolor reincarnation."

GANDHI' OSCAR'S MAN OF THE HOUR; KINGSLEY, STREEP, ATTENBOROUGH WIN

Lange And Gossett Capture Best Support Awards; 'E.T.' Takes Home Four Statuettes

By JIM HARWOOD

Columbia Pictures' "Gandhi" persevered against tough competition last night, taking eight Oscars — including best picture, actor and director — to overwhelm the opposition, challenged only by four below-the-line awards to "E. T. The Extra-Terrestrial."

Producer-director Richard Attenborough picked up his win on his first nomination by the Academy of Motion Picture Arts & Sciences, as did Ben Kingsley for his film debut in the title role.

In the other leading categories, Meryl Streep was named best actress for "Sophie's Choice," Jessica Lange for her supporting role in "Tootsie" and Louis Gossett Jr. for supporting actor in "An Officer And A Gentleman."

multiple winner, picking up one more for the original song "Up Where We Belong," music by Jack Nitzsche and Buffy Sainte-Marie; lyric by Will Jennings.

Interestingly, this is the third year in a row Award voters honored an actor-turned-director, with Attenborough following Warren Beatty and Robert Redford. This year's award also preserves the historic correlation between Oscar and the top Directors Guild of America honor, given to Attenborough last month.

"Gandhi" also bestowed honors on John Briley for original screenplay; Billy Williams and Ronnie Taylor for cinematography; John Bloom for editing; Stuart Craig, Bob Laing and Michael Seirton for art direction

Triumph of nonviolence: After early best-pic victories from the NBR and the Gotham circle, *Gandhi* rallied at the Oscars.

Co-founder of the crix's org, Charles Champlin of *The Los Angeles Times*, lauded the choice for Best Actress, calling Meryl Streep's turn as a Holocaust survivor in *Sophie's Choice* "the most moving performance by an actress, intellectually and emotionally, that I've seen in a very long time indeed." She topped Jessica Lange (*Frances*) as the rebellious actress Frances Farmer, who ended up in a mental asylum.

Best supporting thesps were both from George Roy Hill's adaptation of John Irving's novel *The World According to Garp*: John Lithgow as a football-jock-turned-transsexual (beating James Mason as Paul Newman's courtroom foe in *The Verdict*) and Glenn Close as a pioneering feminist (over Cher as a small-town clerk in *Come Back to the 5 and Dime, Jimmy Dean, Jimmy Dean*).

Barry Levinson's buddy pic *Diner* lost Best Screenplay to *Tootsie*, a comedy by Larry Gelbart and Murray Schisgal about an out-of-work thesp (Dustin Hoffman) who dresses in drag to land an acting gig on a soap opera.

Soon after the crix's awards telecast last year, *Times* scribes Charles Champlin and Sheila Benson resigned in protest. "I felt we had no business at all being in the entertainment business as a sort of fourth-rate competition to the Golden Globes," harrumphed Benson. The duo rejoined the group when the broadcast was scrapped this year.

Two days after the L.A. crix named their anointed, the National Board of Review sounded off. It agreed on the choices of Kingsley and Streep as Best Actor and Actress and Glenn Close as Best Supporting Actress, but disagreed over the other categories. *Gandhi* was voted Best Picture, Best Supporting Actor was Robert Preston as a gay cabaret star in *Victor/Victoria*, and Sidney Lumet was declared Best Director for his courtroom drama *The Verdict*.

Usually stodgy NSFC declared laffer *Tootsie* top pic.

The New York Film Critics Circle announced its winners one week after the board and picked several of the same champs. *Gandhi* won Best Picture with 36 points, edging out *Tootsie* (32) and *E.T.* (28). *The New York Times* described "this year's most hotly contested category" as Best Director when Spielberg and *Tootsie*'s Sydney Pollack tied at 33 points on the third ballot. "The group voted not to declare this a tie since its bylaws state that a winner must receive a plurality of points and must also appear on a majority of ballots," the paper added. "Pollack's name appeared on 14 ballots and Spielberg's on only 12. In a fourth ballot run-off vote, Pollack won 14 to 11."

The lead actors were both picked on a first polling when voters could cite only a single candidate. (On the second and third rounds, voters dispensed three, two and one points to their top three choices). Kingsley beat Dustin Hoffman 14 to 5. Streep claimed the Best Actress prize—the third of her career—with 14 votes over 3 each for Diane Keaton as a woman caught in a collapsing marriage in *Shoot the Moon* and

Jessica Lange as Hoffman's love interest in *Tootsie*. The scribes then decided that Lange's role was really a supporting one and named her Best Supporting Actress, with 39 points over Glenn Close in *Garp* (34). *Garp*'s Lithgow won Best Supporting Actor with 33 points over George Gaynes as a dimwitted soap star in *Tootsie* (21). *Tootsie* won Best Screenplay over *Diner* by a score of 42 to 31.

When the awards were bestowed at Sardi's a few weeks later, the event "unfurled with equal measures of high spirits and dignity," reported *Variety*. "Highlight of the evening was the Best Picture presentation to Sir Richard Attenborough's *Gandhi* by Coretta Scott King."

The widow of Martin Luther King "recalled and soundly trounced Sam Goldwyn's maxim that 'if you want to send a message, call Western Union,' " *Variety* added.

Mrs. King saluted the movie's theme of nonviolent protest, which was also her late husband's philosophy, and said, "Richard Attenborough's film defies Mr. Goldwyn's assertion and I believe the New York critics are sending that message to filmmakers everywhere."

Accepting the plaque as Best Actor, Ben Kingsley informed the crowd that the day marked the 35th anniversary of Gandhi's murder.

Jessica Lange uttered only a sheepish "thank you" as she accepted her kudos, but John Lithgow had the room howling when he received his plaque as Best Supporting Actor. "I have a bone to pick with the male critics," he growled. "They call Jessica Lange and Meryl Streep 'sensual,' 'alluring,' 'enticing.' They described me in *Garp* as 'hefty,' 'beefy,' 'gargantuan.' I began to feel like Wallace Beery. Only Pauline Kael called me pretty—*in italics*."

When *Sophie's Choice* novelist William Styron presented the cinematography award to his pic's lenser, he used the opportunity to take a potshot at the same scribe Lithgow had just thanked. *Variety* reported, "Styron leveled a broadside at *New Yorker* critic Pauline Kael (not by name) as someone 'plainly better suited to another line of work' for her 'ludicrous ill will' in slamming the pic."

Sophie's Choice's Meryl Streep took a dig at another scribe when she accepted the Best Actress laurels. *Variety* noted, "Streep reeled off a memorized list of the Gotham critics, intentionally mispronouncing *Sophie* debunker Andrew Sarris (*Village Voice*) as *Tsouris* (Yiddish idiom for 'aggravation'), then vouching that 'it's great to get your own back sometimes.' "

Considering the huge overlap in the membership between the Gotham circle and the National Society of Film Critics, it was surprising that the circle's Best Picture failed even to be a contender for the society's pic and helmer accolades. The society broke with both the Gotham and Los Angeles crix orgs and picked the Yankee laffer *Tootsie* as Best Picture, a radical departure from its notorious past preference for foreign art-house fare. *E.T.* came in second place.

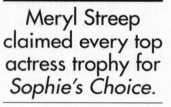

Meryl Streep claimed every top actress trophy for *Sophie's Choice*.

E.T.'s Spielberg took the prize for Best Director over *Tootsie*'s Pollack. *Gandhi*'s Ben Kingsley came close to snagging the Best Actor trophy, but lost to *Tootsie*'s Dustin Hoffman.

Meryl Streep continued her sweep of the lead actress kudos. Runner-up was Jessica Lange for both *Frances* and *Tootsie*. The crix then considered Lange's *Tootsie* role separately for Best Supporting Actress and she won over Glenn Close. And just as it had at the previous two crix's honors, *Tootsie* beat *Diner* for Best Screenplay. Tootie's four kudos tied it with *Nashville* and *Scenes from a Marriage* as the society's top champ. An upset occurred when Mickey Rourke was heralded as Best Supporting Actor for portraying a Romeo hairdresser in *Diner*, beating Bill Murray as Hoffman's best friend in *Tootsie*.

Meantime, as the major films were feted by the top kudos, the indies earned serious notice at the U.S. Film Festival, held high up in Utah's Rocky Mountains. Winner of the Grand Jury Prize was *Purple Haze*, which chronicled the struggles of a young man rebelling against his parents, college and the army draft in the summer of 1968. When it beat the pop cult hit *Eating Raoul*, impressed execs at Triumph Films offered *Purple Haze*'s producers a distribution deal.

CBS dropped its broadcast of the Golden Globe Awards following the Pia Zadora scandal last year. Dick Clark Productions picked up the TV rights, but failed to find any stations that could air the kudocast live, so it settled for preparing a taped presentation that would be shown nationally via syndication.

Military romance pic *An Officer and a Gentleman* led with the most nominations (six). It featured two hot stars—Richard Gere and Debra Winger—but *Variety* insisted that the pic "belongs to Louis Gossett, Jr., who takes a near-cliché role of the tough, unrelenting drill instructor and makes him a sympathetic hero without ever softening a whit." Gossett won the Globe for Best Supporting Actor, but wasn't on hand to accept. The only other trophy the pic claimed was for Best Song ("Up Where We Belong").

The biggest champ of the night was *Gandhi*, which, being a British production, was forced to compete for Best Foreign Film. When it claimed that prize plus Best Director, helmer Richard Attenborough said humbly at the podium, "We are merely chroniclers of a piece of history."

Gandhi also won the screenplay prize, plus two kudos for star Ben Kingsley— Best Drama Actor and New Male Star of the Year—leaving the pic undefeated. After the ceremony, Kingsley confided to the press, "I thought of my two nominations as a chance to lose twice," but when he snagged both victories, he told the audience, "I can't tell you how extraordinarily rejuvenating it is to be called a new star at 39."

Since *Gandhi* was out of the race for Best Drama Picture, *E.T.* claimed that Globe easily plus a prize for John Williams's popular music score.

Tootsie was named Best Comedy or Musical Picture and also copped kudos for Best Comedy/Musical Actor Dustin Hoffman and Best Supporting Actress Jessica Lange.

Tootsie's theme of cross-dressing was also reflected in the winner of Best Comedy/Musical Actress—Julie Andrews, who was honored for her role as a woman pretending to be a man in order to become a Parisian cabaret star in *Victor/Victoria*. Since the success of the pic recently revived Andrews's career, she told the crowd that her victory was "icing on the cake."

"The biggest ovation of the night went to Sir Laurence Olivier," Reuters reported. "The audience stood for more than a minute clapping and cheering before he could receive the Cecil B. DeMille Award. Introduced by Hoffman as 'the entertainer of our time,' Olivier told the audience, 'I worry a little that my cup is so full that it may shortly overflow—to your acute embarrassment."

But the Hollywood Foreign Press Association turned out to be embarrassed when Olivier threw his arms out while talking and broke off the top of his Golden Globe Award. "An unglued organizer hastily fixed the statuette just in time for Olivier's picture session," *People* magazine observed.

"The always generous foreign press managed to name not one, but three motion pictures as the best of the year," noted *The Los Angeles Herald Examiner* afterward. "By selecting *Tootsie* as best comedy, hailing *E.T.* as best drama, and by classifying *Gandhi* as a foreign film and then naming it best of its category, the foreign press managed, with Solomon-like ingenuity, to give a trophy to each of the three frontrunners in the current awards-season sweepstakes."

The paper added that one of the three pix was clearly far ahead in the year's awards derby: "If there was anything to learn from the Golden Globes, it is that *Gandhi* has a huge enthusiastic following. When the Academy Awards are handed out in April, *Gandhi* is in a position to claim the lion's share of the laurels."

Gandhi came closer to fulfilling that promise when Richard Attenborough was nominated by the Directors Guild of America, but he faced tough competish: Steven Spielberg had won the helmer's kudos from the L.A. crix and national society; Sydney Pollack had been the Gothamites' choice. Attenborough had been nommed by the DGA once before—in 1969 for *Oh! What a Lovely War.* When he finally prevailed this year, *Variety* noted that the guild was "again showing appreciation for the stewardship of a sprawling, complex, historical biodrama.

Attenborough told *Variety* he was "scared stiff" over the Oscar race.

"On his way to the stage, Attenborough paused to embrace Spielberg, whose box office magic is matched by his curse during awards season," *Variety* added. "A four-time DGA nominee and three-time Oscar nominee, Spielberg has yet to win either."

As he clutched his award, Attenborough said he accepted it as an expression of the same "hope, faith, love, compassion and tolerance demonstrated in the life of Mahatma Gandhi."

Being a foreign production, *Gandhi* was not eligible for honors from the Writers Guild of America, which celebrated its 50th anniversary this year. The prizes were swept up by other front-runners: *E.T.* (Best Original Drama), *Victor/Victoria* (Best Adapted Comedy) and *Tootsie* (Best Original Comedy). Larry Gelbart earned the third guild plaque of his career for *Tootsie*'s win. An upset occurred in the race for Best Adapted Drama when the scribes of *Sophie's Choice, The World According to Garp* and *The Verdict* were usurped by the authors of *Missing,* a b.o. disappointment that had played in theaters more than nine months earlier. The pic about American parents searching for their son killed during a Latin American coup was directed and co-written by Costa-Gavras, helmer and co-writer of the 1969 awards-sweeper *Z*.

When the Oscar nominations were announced, *Missing* pulled off its own coup by showing up on the Best Picture list, but it was snubbed in the director's lineup.

Variety reported, "For the third year in a row, members of the film academy have shown intense interest in biopix, handing *Gandhi* 11 Oscar nominations for a narrow lead over *Tootsie* with 10 and *E.T.* with 9. Last year it was *Reds* that led the pack with 12 and the year before *Raging Bull* and *The Elephant Man* tied with 8 each."

Among the stars in the running, Jessica Lange became the third actress to be nommed for both leading and supporting roles in the same year, following Fay Bainter (1938) and Teresa Wright (1942). Lange's sudden popularity marked a dramatic career comeback following a two-year drought after she starred in a remake of *King Kong*. She desperately wanted to shake off the memory of her hit monkey movie, but a rival network aired it on Oscar night, touting it as "starring double Oscar nominee Jessica Lange!"

Lucky for Lange, the votes were already cast and when the winner of Best Supporting Actress was announced, she claimed the kudos and said that she was grateful "to have had Dustin Hoffman as my leading lady" in *Tootsie*.

John Lithgow may have snagged laurels from the New York and L.A. crix, but Louis Gossett, Jr., seemed to be the Oscar front-runner after getting a boost from the Golden Globes. "This is a year when almost everyone except Lou Gossett was in drag—and that's why he will win," prophesied nominee Robert Preston, who turned out to be right. When Gossett became only the third African-American to win an Oscar and the first in 19 years, he told the audience, "I've got a spirit that guides me, starting from a great-grandmother who died at the age of 117."

Five years after the L.A. crix named all-time b.o. champ *Star Wars* best pic, they backed newest record-setter *E.T.*

UPI's Vernon Scott turned out to be right when he insisted that "Meryl Streep is an absolute shoo-in, dead-cinch lock to win the award for Best Actress." After Sally Field and Sissy Spacek, she became the third star to sweep all of the major kudos: Oscar, Globe and the crix awards trifecta (N.Y., L.A. and national society). Seven months pregnant, she waddled slowly up to the podium, dropped her written speech, awkwardly bent over to fetch it and then said, "Oh, boy! No matter how much you try to imagine what this is like, it's just so incredibly thrilling right down to your toes."

The Best Actor race pitted screen newbie Ben Kingsley against four Oscar-race veterans: five-time nominee (and onetime champ) Dustin Hoffman, eight-time contender (and two-time winner) Jack Lemmon, plus two serial losers. Paul Newman was up for his sixth bid and Peter O'Toole was up for his seventh. When they all lost to Kingsley, O'Toole became tied with Richard Burton for having the most nominations without a win.

Accepting the statuette, Kingsley announced, "This is an Oscar for vision, for courage, for acting and for peace."

Earlier, *Gandhi* picked up five tech awards: cinematography, art direction, costume design, editing and sound. When it copped the screenplay prize, too, it was clear that a sweep was in the works.

Richard Attenborough had admitted to *Variety* columnist Army Archerd that he was "scared stiff" of the director's show-down, but he won, as expected.

"I'm totally bowled over by this," he told the audience.

Variety observed, "This is the third year in a row that Acad voters honored an actor-turned-director, with Attenborough following Warren Beatty and Robert Redford."

Attenborough was also one of the pic's producers and had spent 20 years trying to bring the life of the Indian hero to the screen. Every Hollywood studio had turned it down, but he got it made by raising the financing himself.

He enjoyed his ultimate triumph when it won Best Picture. "It's not me you truly honor," he said humbly at the podium. "You honor Mahatma Gandhi and his plea to all of us to live in peace."

Meantime, watching from the audience was an unlikely Oscar attendee: George C. Scott, who'd refused his past Oscar nominations and the statuette he won in 1970 for *Patton*. He was now in town hyping interest in a *Patton* sequel and had called the film

Stage skits were once the toast of WGA galas. Here scribes croon "We're Still Here" at the fiftieth anniversary bash.

academy to see if he could rustle up some last-minute tix. He was given two seats in the back of the orchestra section.

Earlier that night, as Scott made his way into the Dorothy Chandler Pavilion, *Variety* columnist Army Archerd spotted him on the red carpet. "Your Oscar is waiting for you at the academy, Wilshire and Lapeer," Archerd shouted as Scott and his wife hurried past.

▪ 1982 ▪

LOS ANGELES FILM CRITICS ASSOCIATION

Winners were announced on December 11, 1982. Awards were presented in late January 1983 at Jimmy's restaurant in Beverly Hills. The ceremony was not telecast.

BEST PICTURE
- *E.T. The Extra-Terrestrial*

BEST DIRECTOR
- Steven Spielberg, *E.T. The Extra-Terrestrial*

BEST ACTOR
- Ben Kingsley, *Gandhi*

BEST ACTRESS
- Meryl Streep, *Sophie's Choice*

BEST SUPPORTING ACTOR
- John Lithgow, *The World According to Garp*

BEST SUPPORTING ACTRESS
- Glenn Close, *The World According to Garp*

BEST SCREENPLAY
- Larry Gelbart, Murray Schisgal, *Tootsie*

BEST CINEMATOGRAPHY
- Jordan Cronenweth, *Blade Runner*

BEST MUSIC SCORE
- James Horner and the Busboys, *48 Hours*

BEST FOREIGN FILM
- *The Road Warrior/Mad Max 2* (Australia)

BEST EXPERIMENTAL/INDEPENDENT FILM
- *Chan Is Missing*, Wayne Wang

CAREER ACHIEVEMENT AWARD
- Robert Preston

NEW GENERATION AWARD
- Melissa Mathison (screenwriter, *E.T. The Extra-Terrestrial*)

SPECIAL AWARD
- Carlo Rimbaldi (creator of E.T. puppet/costume)

NATIONAL BOARD OF REVIEW

Winners were announced on December 13, 1982. Awards were presented on February 14, 1983, at the Library for the Performing Arts at Lincoln Center in New York.

BEST PICTURE
- *Gandhi*

The Verdict
Sophie's Choice
An Officer and a Gentleman
Missing
E.T. The Extra-Terrestrial
The World According to Garp
Tootsie
Moonlighting
The Chosen

BEST DIRECTOR
- Sidney Lumet, *The Verdict*

BEST ACTOR
- Ben Kingsley, *Gandhi*

BEST ACTRESS
- Meryl Streep, *Sophie's Choice*

BEST SUPPORTING ACTOR
- Robert Preston, *Victor/Victoria*

BEST SUPPORTING ACTRESS
- Glenn Close, *The World According to Garp*

BEST FOREIGN FILM
- *Mephisto* (Federal Republic of Germany)

Das Boot (Federal Republic of Germany)
Three Brothers (France/Italy)
Yol (Turkey)
Siberiade (U.S.S.R.)

NEW YORK FILM CRITICS CIRCLE

Winners were announced on December 20, 1982. Awards were presented on January 30, 1983, at Sardi's restaurant in New York.

BEST PICTURE
- *Gandhi*

BEST DIRECTOR
- Sydney Pollack, *Tootsie*

BEST ACTOR
- Ben Kingsley, *Gandhi*

BEST ACTRESS
- Meryl Streep, *Sophie's Choice*

BEST SUPPORTING ACTOR
- John Lithgow, *The World According to Garp*

BEST SUPPORTING ACTRESS
- Jessica Lange, *Tootsie*

BEST SCREENPLAY
- Larry Gelbart, Murray Schisgal, *Tootsie*

BEST CINEMATOGRAPHY
- Nestor Almendros, *Sophie's Choice*

BEST FOREIGN FILM
- *Time Stands Still* (Hungary)

NATIONAL SOCIETY OF FILM CRITICS

Winners were announced on January 2, 1983.

BEST PICTURE
- *Tootsie*

BEST DIRECTOR
- Steven Spielberg, *E.T. The Extra-Terrestrial*

BEST ACTOR
- Dustin Hoffman, *Tootsie*

BEST ACTRESS
- Meryl Streep, *Sophie's Choice*

BEST SUPPORTING ACTOR
- Mickey Rourke, *Diner*

BEST SUPPORTING ACTRESS
- Jessica Lange, *Tootsie*

BEST SCREENPLAY
- Murray Schisgal, Larry Gelbart, *Tootsie*

BEST CINEMATOGRAPHY
- Philippe Rousselot, *Diva*

GOLDEN GLOBES

Nominations were announced on January 10, 1983. Awards were presented on January 29 at the Beverly Hilton Hotel in Los Angeles. The ceremony was taped for later broadcast via syndication by Dick Clark Productions.

BEST DRAMA PICTURE
- *E.T. The Extra-Terrestrial*
Missing
An Officer and a Gentleman
Sophie's Choice
The Verdict

BEST COMEDY OR MUSICAL PICTURE
- *Tootsie*
The Best Little Whorehouse in Texas
Diner
My Favorite Year
Victor/Victoria

BEST DIRECTOR
- Richard Attenborough, *Gandhi*
Costa-Gavras, *Missing*
Sidney Lumet, *The Verdict*
Sydney Pollack, *Tootsie*
Steven Spielberg, *E.T. The Extra-Terrestrial*

BEST ACTOR, DRAMA
- Ben Kingsley, *Gandhi*
Albert Finney, *Shoot the Moon*
Richard Gere, *An Officer and a Gentleman*
Jack Lemmon, *Missing*
Paul Newman, *The Verdict*

BEST ACTRESS, DRAMA
- Meryl Streep, *Sophie's Choice*
Diane Keaton, *Shoot the Moon*
Jessica Lange, *Frances*
Sissy Spacek, *Missing*
Debra Winger, *An Officer and a Gentleman*

BEST ACTOR, COMEDY OR MUSICAL
- Dustin Hoffman, *Tootsie*
Peter O'Toole, *My Favorite Year*
Al Pacino, *Author! Author!*
Robert Preston, *Victor/Victoria*
Henry Winkler, *Night Shift*

BEST ACTRESS, COMEDY OR MUSICAL
- Julie Andrews, *Victor/Victoria*
Carol Burnett, *Annie*
Sally Field, *Kiss Me Goodbye*
Goldie Hawn, *Best Friends*
Dolly Parton, *The Best Little Whorehouse in Texas*
Aileen Quinn, *Annie*

BEST SUPPORTING ACTOR
- Louis Gossett, Jr., *An Officer and a Gentleman*
Paul Julia, *Tempest*
David Keith, *An Officer and a Gentleman*
James Mason, *The Verdict*
Jim Metzler, *Tex*

BEST SUPPORTING ACTRESS
- Jessica Lange, *Tootsie*
Cher, *Come Back to the 5 and Dime, Jimmy Dean, Jimmy Dean*
Lainie Kazan, *My Favorite Year*
Kim Stanley, *Frances*
Lesley Ann Warren, *Victor/Victoria*

NEW MALE STAR OF THE YEAR
- Ben Kingsley, *Gandhi*
Eddie Murphy, *48 Hours*
David Keith, *An Officer and a Gentleman*
Kevin Kline, *Sophie's Choice*
Henry Thomas, *E.T. The Extra-Terrestrial*

NEW FEMALE STAR OF THE YEAR
- Sandahl Bergman, *Conan the Barbarian*
Lisa Blount, *An Officer and a Gentleman*
Katherine Healy, *Six Weeks*
Amy Madigan, *Love Child*
Aileen Quinn, *Annie*
Molly Ringwald, *Tempest*

BEST SCREENPLAY
- John Briley, *Gandhi*

Costa-Gavras, Donald Stewart,
Missing

Larry Gelbart, Murray Schisgal,
Tootsie

David Mamet, *The Verdict*

Melissa Mathison, *E.T. The Extra-Terrestrial*

BEST SONG
- "Up Where We Belong," *An Officer and a Gentleman*, Jack Nitzsche, Buffy Sainte-Marie, Will Jennings

"Eye of the Tiger," *Rocky III*, Jim Peterik, Frankie Sullivan III

"If We Were in Love," *Yes, Giorgio*, John Williams, Alan Bergman, Marilyn Bergman

"Making Love," *Making Love,* Leonard Rosenman

"Theme from *Cat People*," *Cat People,* David Bowie, Giorgio Moroder

BEST FOREIGN FILM
- *Gandhi* (U.K./India)

Fitzcarraldo (Germany)

The Man from Snowy River (Australia)

Quest for Fire (Canada/France)

La Traviata (Italy)

Yol (Switzerland/Turkey)

Winners

BEST ORIGINAL SCORE
- John Williams, *E.T. The Extra-Terrestrial*

CECIL B. DEMILLE AWARD
- Laurence Olivier

U.S. FILM FESTIVAL

The festival was held January 17–23, 1983, at Park City, Utah.

GRAND JURY PRIZE
- *Purple Haze*, David Burton Morris

BEST DOCUMENTARY
- *Dark Circle*, Judy Irving, Chris Beaver, Ruth Landy

SPECIAL JURY PRIZES
(FEATURE FILMS)
- *Dream On!*, Ed Harker
- *The Ballad of Gregorio Cortez*, Robert M. Young

(DOCUMENTARIES)
- *Coming of Age*
- *Fire on the Water*

MEDALLION AWARD
- Verna Fields

DIRECTORS GUILD OF AMERICA

Nominations were announced on January 30, 1983. Winners were announced on March 12 at the Beverly Hilton Hotel in Los Angeles.

BEST DIRECTOR
- Richard Attenborough, *Gandhi*

Taylor Hackford, *An Officer and a Gentleman*

Wolfgang Petersen, *Das Boot*

Sydney Pollack, *Tootsie*

Steven Spielberg, *E.T. The Extra-Terrestrial*

D. W. GRIFFITH AWARD
- John Huston

HONORARY LIFETIME MEMBERSHIP
- Elia Kazan
- Robert Wise

WRITERS GUILD OF AMERICA

Nominations were announced on February 15, 1983. Awards were presented on April 7 at the Beverly Hilton Hotel in Los Angeles and the McGraw-Hill building in New York.

BEST DRAMA WRITTEN DIRECTLY FOR THE SCREEN
- *E.T. The Extra-Terrestrial*, Melissa Mathison

An Officer and a Gentleman, Douglas Day Stewart

Shoot the Moon, Bo Goldman

BEST DRAMA ADAPTED FROM ANOTHER MEDIUM

- *Missing*, Costa-Gavras, Donald E. Steward, based on the novel *The Execution of Charles Horman* by Thomas Hauser

Sophie's Choice, Alan J. Pakula, based on the novel by William Styron

The Verdict, David Mamet, based on the novel by Barry Reed

The World According to Garp, Steve Tesich, based on the novel by John Irving

BEST COMEDY WRITTEN DIRECTLY FOR THE SCREEN

- *Tootsie*, Larry Gelbart, Murray Schisgal, Don McGuire

Diner, Barry Levinson

My Favorite Year, Norman Steinberg, Dennis Palumbo

BEST COMEDY ADAPTED FROM ANOTHER MEDIUM

- *Victor/Victoria*, Blake Edwards, based on the 1933 film *Viktor und Viktoria*

Fast Times at Ridgemont High, Cameron Crowe, based on his book

LAUREL AWARD

- Lamar Trotti

VALENTINE DAVIES AWARD

- Hal Kanter

MORGAN COX AWARD

- Irma Kalish

ACADEMY AWARDS

Nominations were announced on February 17, 1983. Awards were presented on April 11 at the Dorothy Chandler Pavilion in Los Angeles. The ceremony was telecast by ABC.

BEST PICTURE

- *Gandhi*

E.T. The Extra-Terrestrial

Missing

Tootsie

The Verdict

BEST DIRECTOR

- Richard Attenborough, *Gandhi*

Sidney Lumet, *The Verdict*

Wolfgang Petersen, *Das Boot*

Sydney Pollack, *Tootsie*

Steven Spielberg, *E.T. The Extra-Terrestrial*

BEST ACTOR

- Ben Kingsley, *Gandhi*

Dustin Hoffman, *Tootsie*

Jack Lemmon, *Missing*

Paul Newman, *The Verdict*

Peter O'Toole, *My Favorite Year*

BEST ACTRESS

- Meryl Streep, *Sophie's Choice*

Julie Andrews, *Victor/Victoria*

Jessica Lange, *Frances*

Sissy Spacek, *Missing*

Debra Winger, *An Officer and a Gentleman*

BEST SUPPORTING ACTOR

- Louis Gossett, Jr., *An Officer and a Gentleman*

Charles Durning, *The Best Little Whorehouse in Texas*

John Lithgow, *The World According to Garp*

James Mason, *The Verdict*

Robert Preston, *Victor/Victoria*

BEST SUPPORTING ACTRESS

- Jessica Lange, *Tootsie*

Glenn Close, *The World According to Garp*

Teri Garr, *Tootsie*

Kim Stanley, *Frances*

Lesley Ann Warren, *Victor/Victoria*

BEST ORIGINAL SCREENPLAY

- John Briley, *Gandhi*

Larry Gelbart, Don McGuire, Murray Schisgal, *Tootsie*

Barry Levinson, *Diner*

Melissa Mathison, *E.T. The Extra-Terrestrial*

Douglas Day Stewart, *An Officer and a Gentleman*

BEST ADAPTED SCREENPLAY

- Costa-Gavras, Donald Stewart, *Missing*

Blake Edwards, *Victor/Victoria*

David Mamet, *The Verdict*
Alan J. Pakula, *Sophie's Choice*
Wolfgang Petersen, *Das Boot*

BEST SONG

- "Up Where We Belong," *An Officer and a Gentleman*, Will Jennings, Jack Nitzsche, Buffy Sainte-Marie

"Eye of the Tiger," *Rocky III*, Jim Peterik, Frankie Sullivan III

"How Do You Keep the Music Playing?" *Best Friends*, Alan Bergman, Marilyn Bergman, Michel Legrand

"If We Were in Love," *Yes, Giorgio*, Alan Bergman, Marilyn Bergman, John Williams

"It Might Be You," *Tootsie*, Alan Bergman, Marilyn Bergman, Dave Grusin

BEST FOREIGN-LANGUAGE FILM

- *Volver a Empezar (To Begin Again)* (Spain)

Alsino and the Condor (Nicaragua)
Coup de Torchon (Clean Slate) (France)
The Flight of the Eagle (Sweden)
Private Life (U.S.S.R.)

Winners

BEST ART DIRECTION

- Stuart Craig, Bob Laing, Michael Seirton, *Gandhi*

BEST CINEMATOGRAPHY

- Ronnie Taylor, Billy Williams, *Gandhi*

BEST COSTUME DESIGN

- Bhanu Athaiya, John Mollo, *Gandhi*

BEST DOCUMENTARY
(FEATURE)

- *Just Another Missing Kid*, John Zaritsky

(SHORT SUBJECT)

- *If You Love This Planet*, Edward Le Lorrain, Terri Nash

BEST FILM EDITING

- John Bloom, *Gandhi*

BEST MAKEUP

- Michèle Burke, Sarah Monzani, *Quest for Fire*

BEST MUSIC
(ORIGINAL SCORE)

- John Williams, *E.T. The Extra-Terrestrial*

(ORIGINAL SONG SCORE AND ITS ADAPTATION OR ADAPTATION SCORE)

- Leslie Bricusse, Henry Mancini, *Victor/Victoria*

SCIENTIFIC OR TECHNICAL AWARDS
(Academy Award of Merit)

- August Arnold, Erich Kaestner, Arnold & Richter

(Scientific and Engineering Award)

- Colin F. Mossman, Rank Film Labs; Sante Zelli, Salvatore Zelli, Elemack Italia; Leonard Chapman; Dr. Mohammad S. Nozari, Minnesota Mining and Manufacturing; Brianne Murphy, Donald Schisler, Mitchell Insert Systems; Jacobus L. Dimmers, Teccon Enterprises

(Technical Achievement Award)

- Richard W. Deats; Constant Tresfon, Adriaan de Rooy, Egripment; Ed Phillips, Carlos de Mattos, Matthews Studio Equipment; Bran Ferren; Christie Electric; LaVezzi Machine Works

BEST SHORT FILM
(ANIMATED)

- *Tango*, Zbigniew Rybczynski

(LIVE ACTION)

- *A Shocking Accident*, Christine Oestreicher

BEST SOUND

- Gene Cantamessa, Don Digirolamo, Robert Glass, Robert Knudson, *E.T. The Extra-Terrestrial*

BEST SOUND EFFECTS EDITING

- Ben Burtt, Charles L. Campbell, *E.T. The Extra-Terrestrial*

BEST VISUAL EFFECTS

- Dennis Muren, Carlo Rambaldi, Kenneth F. Smith, *E.T. The Extra-Terrestrial*

GORDON E. SAWYER AWARD

- John O. Aalberg

JEAN HERSHOLT HUMANITARIAN AWARD
- Walter Mirisch

HONORARY AWARD
- Mickey Rooney

SCREEN ACTORS GUILD

LIFETIME ACHIEVEMENT AWARD
- Danny Kaye

Terms *Truly Endearing*

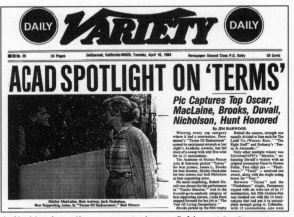

The film debut of writer/director James L. Brooks swept all of the year's Best Picture prizes (five) except the National Society of Film Critics.

The last time that the Oscars, Golden Globes, New York Film Critics Circle and the National Board of Review all agreed on a Best Picture, their choice was a haunting drama about a dysfunctional family (*Ordinary People*). This time the Los Angeles crix joined the others in embracing a dark pic about a twisted family—*Terms of Endearment*—that included a fun added twist: laughs.

Terms was written and directed by James L. Brooks, who had created the Emmy-winning TV comedies *The Mary Tyler Moore Show* and *Taxi*. Yearning to take on a bigger-screen medium, he decided to tackle a film adaptation of Larry McMurtry's novel about a shrewish mother (Shirley MacLaine) and her headstrong daughter (Debra Winger) who must put their petty fights aside in order to face a life-and-death battle together. MacLaine's character was such a hellcat that Brooks opted to warm her up by giving her a lover, so he created the role of a lecherous drunk who lives next door (Jack Nicholson).

"The teaming of MacLaine and Nicholson at their best makes *Terms of Endearment* enormously enjoyable," *Variety* cheered. Columnist Army Archerd added, "Oscar nominations are a cinch for Nicholson, Shirley MacLaine, Debra Winger and Brooks in his first outing as a director."

Prior to the Oscars, however, *Terms* had to pace the early film-awards derby. The National Board of Review was the first out of the gate and gave *Terms* its laurels for Best Picture, Director (Brooks), Actress (MacLaine) and Supporting Actor (Nichol-

son). *Terms* had to share the top pic prize, though, with *Betrayal*, a British screen adaptation of Harold Pinter's 1978 play about a ménage à trois. Tom Conti was named Best Actor for two roles—as a boozy Scottish poet in *Reuben, Reuben* and as a POW in a Japanese World War II camp in *Merry Christmas, Mr. Lawrence*.

Variety noted that *Terms* "monopolized the voting at the ninth annual L.A. Film Critics Association awards" by sweeping 5 of its 10 races, thereby tying *Kramer vs. Kramer* for reaping the most prizes in one year. It was named Best Picture over *Tender Mercies*, which snagged the Best Actor prize for star Robert Duvall as a has-been, drunken country crooner who straightens up when he falls in love. Best Actor runner-up was Tom Conti.

Terms's Brooks was hailed as Best Director over *Tender Mercies*'s Bruce Beresford. Shirley MacLaine was declared Best Actress over Jane Alexander as a survivor of a nuclear holocaust in *Testament*. In the race for Best Supporting Actor, Nicholson topped John Lithgow, who was cited for his roles as a bashful lover of Debra Winger in *Terms* and as a crazed airplane passenger in *Twilight Zone—The Movie*.

Best Supporting Actress was Linda Hunt, who was cast as a male Eurasian dwarf in *The Year of Living Dangerously*. Two thesps tied for second place: Cher as the lesbian roommate of the title character in *Silkwood* and Alfre Woodward as a novelist's housekeeper/confidante in *Cross Creek*.

Terms's fifth crix kudos was for Best Screenplay, beating Lawrence Kasdan and Barbara Benedek's drama *The Big Chill*, about 1960s radicals who have a heartfelt reunion at a 1980s funeral.

Winner of two awards was *Fanny and Alexander* (Best Foreign Film and Best Cinematography), which Ingmar Bergman declared would be his last film. *Variety* said that the semifictionalized memoir of the filmmaker's Swedish childhood "has everything to make it the Bergman feature film that could be remembered longest and most fondly by general audiences when his other, more anguished works are forgotten by all but the initiated."

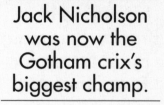

Jack Nicholson was now the Gotham crix's biggest champ.

When the New York Film Critics Circle voted four days after the Hollywoodites, *Fanny* was proclaimed Best Foreign Film and Bergman was named Best Director. Bergman took the latter prize with 38 points, surpassing Phil Kaufman, who earned 30 points for his adaptation of Tom Wolfe's book *The Right Stuff* about the early days of the U.S. space program.

Terms claimed the race for Best Picture with 35 points over *The Right Stuff* (19) and *Silkwood* (15). The choice marked only the second time that the Gotham group agreed with the L.A. crix org on the top prize during the nine years of their mutual existence. Previously, they had both picked *Kramer vs. Kramer* in 1979.

In the Best Actor race, Robert Duvall topped Gerard Depardieu, who was cited for two roles: as a leader of the French Revolution in *Danton* and as a peasant impostor in *The Return of Martin Guerre*.

The fiercest showdown was for Best Actress, which took five ballots before Shirley MacLaine (32 points) beat her *Terms* costar Debra Winger (30). An upset occurred for Best Screenplay when *Local Hero*, a comedy about a Scottish village, scored 35 points to triumph over *Terms* (30). Linda Hunt won a victory as Best Supporting Actress by only a single point over Cher (31 to 30). Nicholson won Best Supporting Actor easily on the first ballot (15 votes) over Ed Harris (4) as astronaut John Glenn in *The Right Stuff*. It was his fifth plaque from the Gotham crix, making him the biggest winner in the group's history.

When the Gotham crix and their honorees gathered at Sardi's restaurant for the awards presentation, Nicholson acknowledged that "no group has been so supportive of me and my work." He described *Terms* as "that rare thing, a completely happy creative experience." He also thanked "my leading lady," Shirley MacLaine.

MacLaine was generous in her praise of Nicholson when she took her turn at the podium, but she also was shockingly generous in her use of what *Variety* called "joyous four-letter expletives."

"I was scared shitless to come here," she said, "but it's really about time I got this award." She summed up the honor as "fan-fucking-tastic."

Mary Tyler Moore bestowed the plaque for Best Picture to her old colleague James L. Brooks. Ingmar Bergman dispatched his daughter by Liv Ullmann, Linn Bergman, to accept his third Gotham crix prize (he won two for *Cries and Whispers* in 1972). She read a telegram from him that said, "I am thrilled my youngest daughter can replace me at this very important moment marking the end of my filmmaking career."

When Linda Hunt accepted the honor as Best Supporting Actress, she saluted the courage of her director Peter Weir to believe that she could play a man convincingly.

"I feel very sorry for Peter, who's trying to do a film of Paul Theroux's *Mosquito Coast*, but can't get the money," she added. "Let's all find $13 million!"

Despite having such a huge overlap of members, the National Society of Film Critics mirrored only two of the Gotham circle's choices: Nicholson as Best Supporting Actor and underdog screenplay contender *Local Hero*.

Previous Best Actress favorite Shirley MacLaine was not a leading contender in this crix match-up. Costar Debra Winger (41 points) beat Joanna Cassidy (34) as a gutsy radio journalist covering the Nicaragua civil war in *Under Fire*. Sandra Bernhard scored an upset in the race for Best Supporting Actress for her role as a crazed fan who kidnaps her showbiz idol in *The King of Comedy*. She snagged 36 points, 14 more than Cher nabbed for *Silkwood*.

When the society reversed the Gothamites' vote results in the Best Actor contest, *Variety* didn't think the winner would jibe with future kudos: "The society's pick is unlikely to serve as a bellwether for the upcoming Oscar competition." Gerard Depardieu beat Robert Duvall by a 34-to-26 score.

The biggest surprise occurred in the top two races for Best Picture and Director where the society—one year after endorsing U.S. popcorn laffer *Tootsie* as top pic—reverted to its old preference for foreign-lingo art-house fare. Winner of both kudos was *Night of the Shooting Stars*, an import about the exploits of Italian villagers during World War II. Its 59 points beat two pix tied at 22 points each: Bergman's *Fanny and Alexander* and Rainer Werner Fassbinder's *Berlin Alexanderplatz*, which depicted German life in the 1920s. The brothers who helmed *Shooting Stars*, Paolo and Vittorio Taviana, prevailed by a score of 42 to 15 over Philip Kaufman (*The Right Stuff*).

There were so many comic dramas this year that the Hollywood Foreign Press Association had trouble classifying them for the Golden Globe Awards. The group ultimately concluded that *The Big Chill* should be in the comedy/musical categories and *Terms of Endearment* and *The Dresser* in the drama competish. The latter two had been submitted for the comedy races, but the producers did not protest the switches.

Terms of Endearment tied for the most nominations (six) with *Yentl*, Barbra Streisand's musical about a girl who disguises herself as boy so she can study Jewish law.

On awards night, the *L.A. Times* said that *Terms* "is beginning to look like a juggernaut as it plows through the award season toward Oscar." It copped four awards, including Best Drama Picture, Best Screenplay (Brooks), Best Actress (MacLaine) and Best Supporting Actor (Nicholson).

The *Times* described MacLaine as "the most exuberant winner of the night" and one who "had no pretentions to false modesty about her award."

"I did expect it and if I hadn't won it, I'd have cramped," she said, accepting it. "I sure deserve this. Thanks to the foreign press for being so brilliantly discerning!"

Soon after the gala, MacLaine headed to the airport so she could make it to the New York Film Critics Circle gala being held the next day. James L. Brooks and Jack Nicholson weren't up for the frenzied trip, though, so they skipped the Globes in favor of a making a more leisurely, advance trip to Gotham where their victories—unlike the Globes—were assured, since the winners had been announced earlier.

In the Globe race for Best Drama Actor, there was a tie between Robert Duvall (*Tender Mercies*) and Tom Courtenay, who portrayed a fawning backstage lackey to a fading stage star in *The Dresser*.

Educating Rita scored two kudos,

Streisand beat Brooks, Bergman, and Nichols for Best Director at the Globes.

including Best Comedy/Musical Actor for Michael Caine as a boozy professor who tutors a lower-class married woman with high ambitions (Julie Walters, who created the role on stage). The British Walters was co-host of the Golden Globes gala and when she won Best Actress, exclaimed, "Blimey! This looks like it's a fix! But you know it's not. They sent me my $2 back!"

When Caine claimed his Globe, he said, "The last time I won a Golden Globe was for the Most Promising Newcomer. I was beginning to feel I'd let the people who gave it to me down."

This year the Globes dropped the category for Best New Star while still suffering aftershocks from the Pia Zadora scandal of 1981. The gala was not being broadcast live by a major TV network, but Dick Clark Productions taped the show for later broadcast via national syndication.

The *L.A. Times* noted that "the night's most surprised winner" was Cher, who claimed the Best Supporting Actress Globe for *Silkwood*.

At the podium she was giddy, nervous, and dressed in a black leather miniskirt with a revealing upper-thigh slash.

"I don't have any speech prepared because I just didn't think I was going to win this!" she gasped. "Just look at my dress until I can think of something to say."

She pondered her victory for a moment and then thanked her mother, two children, former husband Sonny Bono and director Mike Nichols "for believing in me when all you moguls out there wouldn't give me a job."

When the Directors Guild of America nominees were announced one week prior to the Globes, an uproar occurred when Barbra Streisand wasn't listed for *Yentl*. Women's groups denounced the snub and Streisand's fans were furious.

The Golden Globes made it up to her, though. In addition to giving *Yentl* the top prize for Best Comedy/Musical Picture,

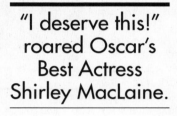

"I deserve this!" roared Oscar's Best Actress Shirley MacLaine.

Streisand beat James L. Brooks, Ingmar Bergman (*Fanny and Alexander*), Mike Nichols (*Silkwood*), Bruce Beresford (*Tender Mercies*) and Peter Yates (*The Dresser*) for Best Director.

When she accepted the prize, Streisand "appeared genuinely surprised," noted the *L.A. Times*. In her speech, she said that she hoped the victory represented "new opportunities for so many talented women who tried to make their dreams become realities, as I did."

In addition to Streisand, two other Globe contenders were also snubbed by the directors guild: Nichols and Yates. The nominees were all first-timers: Brooks, Beresford, Bergman, Philip Kaufman (*The Right Stuff*) and Lawrence Kasdan (*The Big Chill*). Brooks and Bergman were considered the front-runners, since both had won crix kudos.

When Brooks prevailed, he ambled up to the stage slowly, his hands in his pockets.

"The truth is this picture gave a lie to cynicism," he said at the podium, referring to the struggle he faced getting the picture made when most studios turned it down because the ending was downbeat. "What Paramount gave me was the opportunity to seek the best work I could do. We're all hungry for that."

After the ceremonies, Brooks said he had expected Ingmar Bergman to win, since he had announced that *Fanny and Alexander* would be his last film.

The guild bestowed the honorary D.W. Griffith Award upon Orson Welles, which "was particularly touching because he had withdrawn from the guild in 1949 to pursue his own movie projects independently," said the *L.A. Times*. "He recalled that when he first came to Hollywood, his most stalwart friends were movie directors such as Raoul Walsh, Howard Hawks and William Wellman."

At the Writers Guild of America awards, James L. Brooks entered *Terms of Endear-*

ment as a comedy and won the prize for adapted scripts. Accepting it, he said, "This is a room where you can count on someone to give you a joke whether you lose or win." Just then the fete's emcee, George Kirgo, reminded Brooks that they had worked together on the bomb TV series *My Mother the Car.*

Five-time past nominee Julius Epstein (*Reuben, Reuben*) finally won his first guild prize—the race for best adapted comedy (beating the scenarists of *The Right Stuff, The Year of Living Dangerously* and *Spofford*). The 74-year-old screen veteran thanked the seemingly unbeatable Brooks for not submitting *Terms* as a drama candidate.

"Is this award for literacy or longevity?" he asked the audience. "Either way, I'm very grateful and I leave you before you change your minds."

The *L.A. Herald Examiner* noted that "the younger writers prevailed" in the competish for best original comedy: Lawrence Kasdan and Barbara Benedek (*The Big Chill*) nailed Woody Allen (*Zelig*). Veteran scribe Horton Foote (1962 guild winner for *To Kill a Mockingbird*) beat Nora Ephron (*Silkwood*) to claim the kudos for best original drama (*Tender Mercies*).

Terms of Endearment had already earned an impressive $73 million in U.S. b.o. when James L. Brooks headed to London for its European premiere. That's where he was when UPI tracked him down for a reaction quote to the news that *Terms* had just scored the most Oscar nominations of the year: 11. Brooks expressed joy over his awards bounty, but also disappointment that he was "drinking flat champagne."

The Right Stuff's helmer/scribe Philip Kaufman had much more to be disappointed about. While his pic scored the second-most bids—eight, including one for Best Picture—he was snubbed for directing and writing kudos. *The Big Chill* was up for Best Picture, too, but its helmer, Lawrence Kasdan, was also overlooked. In their place were Mike Nichols (*Silkwood*) and Peter Yates (*The Dresser*), neither of whom had been nommed by the DGA.

On Oscar day, while holding forth from

Prexy Ernest Lehman, the writers guild's biggest champ (five wins), presides over the 1983 awards.

Writers Guild of America

his usual forecourt star-greeting stand, *Variety* columnist Army Archerd turned to the bleacher fans to learn who would win. *Variety* reported that he "conducted the customary voice vote to determine the audience's preference. Winners were Robert Duvall for Best Actor, Shirley MacLaine as Best Actress, Jack Nicholson as Best Supporting Actor and Cher as Best Supporting Actress. *Terms of Endearment* was the people's overwhelming choice for Best Picture."

Nicholson was an easy forecast since he had already won all other top kudos, including the Golden Globe, National Board of Review and the crix trifecta (N.Y., L.A. and the national society). When he nabbed the Oscar next, he became only the fourth thesp, after Sally Field, Meryl Streep and Sissy Spacek, to make the complete sweep. *Variety* noted another milestone: "For the record books, Nicholson fell in with Jack Lemmon and Robert DeNiro as the only actors to have won now in both categories, having taken Best Actor before for *One Flew over the Cuckoo's Nest.*"

Backstage, Nicholson told the media: "I

feel happy with this, but I'm going after a lot more. I want three or four more!"

Golden Globe champ Cher (*Silkwood*) might have been ahead in the outside fans' vote, but she was one of four neophytes in the Best Supporting Actress race. Glenn Close (*The Big Chill*) was the only rival who'd been nommed previously (last year for *Garp*) and she told Army Archerd, "For some reason, I'm more nervous this year."

The winner turned out to be the thesp chosen earlier by the L.A. and N.Y. film crix. Linda Hunt said at the podium, "There was an Indonesian phrase in the film that translates into English as 'water from the moon' and it means that which is unattainable. Making *The Year of Living Dangerously* was, to me, water from the moon."

When Best Actor front-runner Robert Duvall (*Tender Mercies*) sized up his competish for *The New York Daily News*, he said, "I guess it's me against the limeys!" Two of his British rivals (Caine and Courtenay) had earned Golden Globes just like Duvall, but Duvall also had snagged laurels from the New York and L.A. crix. Even Caine predicted to Army Archerd ahead of time that Duvall had it. When the three-time past loser finally proved himself a winner, Duvall said at the podium, "I'm very excited, very happy, very moved, very everything tonight."

Duvall's first film role was *To Kill a Mockingbird*, which had reaped an Oscar in 1962 for its scribe Horton Foote, who now shared in Duvall's night of triumph by winning Best Original Screenplay for *Tender Mercies*. When he won, Foote thanked "my old and dear friend Robert Duvall for his marvelous work which was the heart and soul of our film."

"Coming up to bat for the fifth time as Best Actress, MacLaine was a favorite to finally get her first win," reported *Variety*. The *L.A. Times* agreed, "barring an upset by Debra Winger or Meryl Streep." When MacLaine held the elusive Oscar in her hands at last, she said tearfully, "I have wondered for 26 years what this would feel like. Thank you for terminating the suspense." Then she added with sassy bravado, echoing her acceptance speech at the

Orson Welles was never nommed by the DGA, but received its special D. W. Griffith Award.

Golden Globes, "I deserve this!"

The rest of the top categories belonged to James L. Brooks.

Having been honored by the writers' guild, the L.A. film crix and the Golden Globes, he was the expected winner of the prize for Best Adapted Screenplay. Brooks faced formidable competish for Best Director ("some handicappers think Acad voters might hand Ingmar Bergman his first Oscar in seven nominations for *Fanny*," said *Variety*), but he prevailed just as he had at the directors' guild. "Brooks joined an elite group, becoming the fourth person to win an Oscar for his first feature," *Variety* noted.

"I feel like I've been beaten up," he said at the podium. "It's strange."

When he returned to the podium to claim the top trophy for Best Picture, he said, "This is an extraordinary evening for us. There's no way to express the gratitude."

In all, *Terms* claimed five victories, "winning every top category where it had a nomination," observed *Variety*.

Meantime, among the 10 small-pic contenders at the U.S. Film Festival, the Grand Jury Prize went to *Old Enough*, about the friendship between a rich girl and her poor gal pal. It was penned and helmed by 23-year-old Marisa Silver.

Eagle Pennell, a director who had won a special jury prize at the first festival in 1978, returned to claim the prize again, this time for *Last Night at the Alamo*, about the last round at a Houston saloon set for demolition. Another special prize was bestowed upon *Hero*, which depicts a wide spectrum of diverse Americans taking an absurdist taxi-ride-to-nowhere together.

Best Documentary champ was *Style Wars*, "a film about New York's grafitti artists and break dancers," said *Variety*. The Grand Jury Prize winners claimed $5,000 apiece. Other honorees received $1,000. The festival attracted about 15,000 people, many of whom arrived with their skis slung over their backs so they could hit the snowy slopes in between screenings at snug little theaters.

▪ 1983 ▪

NATIONAL BOARD OF REVIEW

The board declared a Best Picture and Foreign Film of the year, then listed its remaining favorites according to highest scores. The vote results were announced on December 14, 1983.

BEST PICTURE (TIE)
▪ *Terms of Endearment*
▪ *Betrayal*
Educating Rita
Tender Mercies
The Dresser
The Right Stuff
Testament
Local Hero
The Big Chill
Cross Creek
Yentl

BEST DIRECTOR
▪ James L. Brooks, *Terms of Endearment*

BEST ACTOR
▪ Tom Conti, *Reuben, Reuben; Merry Christmas, Mr. Lawrence*

BEST ACTRESS
▪ Shirley MacLaine, *Terms of Endearment*

BEST SUPPORTING ACTOR
▪ Jack Nicholson, *Terms of Endearment*

BEST SUPPORTING ACTRESS
▪ Linda Hunt, *The Year of Living Dangerously*

BEST FOREIGN FILM
▪ *Fanny and Alexander* (Sweden)
The Return of Martin Guerre (France)
Le Nuit de Varennes (France)
La Traviata (Italy)
The Boat People ((Hong Kong/China)

LOS ANGELES FILM CRITICS ASSOCIATION

Winners were announced on December 17, 1983.

BEST PICTURE
▪ *Terms of Endearment*

BEST DIRECTOR
▪ James L. Brooks, *Terms of Endearment*

BEST ACTOR
▪ Robert Duvall, *Tender Mercies*

BEST ACTRESS
▪ Shirley MacLaine, *Terms of Endearment*

BEST SUPPORTING ACTOR
▪ Jack Nicholson, *Terms of Endearment*

BEST SUPPORTING ACTRESS
▪ Linda Hunt, *The Year of Living Dangerously*

BEST SCREENPLAY
▪ James L. Brooks, *Terms of Endearment*

BEST CINEMATOGRAPHY
▪ Sven Nykvist, *Fanny and Alexander*

BEST MUSIC SCORE
- Philip Glass, *Koyaanisqatsi*

BEST FOREIGN FILM
- *Fanny and Alexander* (Sweden)

BEST EXPERIMENTAL/INDEPENDENT FILM
- *So Is This*, Michael Snow

CAREER ACHIEVEMENT AWARD
- Myrna Loy

NEW GENERATION AWARD
- Sean Penn

NEW YORK FILM CRITICS CIRCLE

Winners were announced on December 21, 1983. Awards were presented on January 29, 1984, at Sardi's restaurant in New York.

BEST PICTURE
- *Terms of Endearment*

BEST DIRECTOR
- Ingmar Bergman, *Fanny and Alexander*

BEST ACTOR
- Robert Duvall, *Tender Mercies*

BEST ACTRESS
- Shirley MacLaine, *Terms of Endearment*

BEST SUPPORTING ACTOR
- Jack Nicholson, *Terms of Endearment*

BEST SUPPORTING ACTRESS
- Linda Hunt, *The Year of Living Dangerously*

BEST SCREENPLAY
- Bill Forsyth, *Local Hero*

BEST CINEMATOGRAPHY
- Gordon Willis, *Zelig*

BEST FOREIGN FILM
- *Fanny and Alexander* (Sweden)

NATIONAL SOCIETY OF FILM CRITICS

Winners were announced on January 2, 1984.

BEST PICTURE
- *Night of the Shooting Stars* (Italy)

BEST DIRECTOR
- Paolo and Vittorio Taviani, *Night of the Shooting Stars*

BEST ACTOR
- Gerard Depardieu, *Danton, The Return of Martin Guerre*

BEST ACTRESS
- Debra Winger, *Terms of Endearment*

BEST SUPPORTING ACTOR
- Jack Nicholson, *Terms of Endearment*

BEST SUPPORTING ACTRESS
- Sandra Bernhard, *The King of Comedy*

BEST SCREENPLAY
- Bill Forsythe, *Local Hero*

BEST CINEMATOGRAPHY
- Hiro Norita, *Never Cry Wolf*

GOLDEN GLOBES

Nominations were announced on January 9, 1984. Awards were presented on January 28 at the Beverly Hilton Hotel in Los Angeles. The ceremony was broadcast nationally via syndication.

BEST DRAMA PICTURE
- *Terms of Endearment*
Reuben, Reuben
The Right Stuff
Silkwood
Tender Mercies

BEST COMEDY OR MUSICAL PICTURE
- *Yentl*
The Big Chill
Flashdance
Trading Places
Zelig

BEST DIRECTOR

- Barbra Streisand, *Yentl*

Bruce Beresford, *Tender Mercies*
Ingmar Bergman, *Fanny and Alexander*
James L. Brooks, *Terms of Endearment*
Mike Nichols, *Silkwood*
Peter Yates, *The Dresser*

BEST ACTOR, DRAMA (TIE)

- Tom Courtenay, *The Dresser*
- Robert Duvall, *Tender Mercies*

Tom Conti, *Reuben, Reuben*
Richard Farnsworth, *The Grey Fox*
Albert Finney, *The Dresser*
Al Pacino, *Scarface*
Eric Roberts, *Star 80*

BEST ACTRESS, DRAMA

- Shirley MacLaine, *Terms of Endearment*

Jane Alexander, *Testament*
Bonnie Bedelia, *Heart Like a Wheel*
Meryl Streep, *Silkwood*
Debra Winger, *Terms of Endearment*

BEST ACTOR, COMEDY OR MUSICAL

- Michael Caine, *Educating Rita*

Woody Allen, *Zelig*
Tom Cruise, *Risky Business*
Eddie Murphy, *Trading Places*
Mandy Patinkin, *Yentl*

BEST ACTRESS, COMEDY OR MUSICAL

- Julie Walters, *Educating Rita*

Anne Bancroft, *To Be or Not to Be*
Jennifer Beals, *Flashdance*
Linda Ronstadt, *The Pirates of Penzance*
Barbra Streisand, *Yentl*

BEST SUPPORTING ACTOR

- Jack Nicholson, *Terms of Endearment*

Steven Bauer, *Scarface*
Charles Durning, *To Be or Not to Be*
Gene Hackman, *Under Fire*
Kurt Russell, *Silkwood*

BEST SUPPORTING ACTRESS

- Cher, *Silkwood*

Barbara Carrera, *Never Say Never Again*
Tess Harper, *Tender Mercies*
Linda Hunt, *The Year of Living
    Dangerously*
Joanna Pacula, *Gorky Park*

BEST SCREENPLAY

- James L. Brooks, *Terms of Endearment*

Barbara Benedek, Lawrence Kasdan, *The
    Big Chill*
Julius J. Epstein, *Reuben, Reuben*
Ronald Harwood, *The Dresser*
Willy Russell, *Educating Rita*

BEST SONG

- "Flashdance . . . What a Feeling,"
    Flashdance, Giorgio Moroder, Keith
    Forsey, Irene Cara

"Far from Over," *Staying Alive,* Bee
    Gees
"Maniac," *Flashdance*, Michael Sembello,
    Dennis Matkosky
"Over You," *Tender Mercies*, Austin
    Roberts, Bobby Hart
"The Way He Makes Me Feel," *Yentl*, Alan
    Bergman, Marilyn Bergman, Michel
    Legrand

BEST FOREIGN FILM

- *Fanny and Alexander* (Sweden)

Carmen (Spain)
The Dresser (England)
Educating Rita (England)
The Grey Fox (Canada)

Winners

BEST ORIGINAL SCORE

- Giorgio Moroder, *Flashdance*

CECIL B. DEMILLE AWARD

- Paul Newman

U.S. FILM FESTIVAL

The festival was held January 23–29, 1984,
at Park City, Utah.

GRAND JURY PRIZE
(FEATURE FILMS)

- *Old Enough*, Marisa Silver

(DOCUMENTARIES)

- *Style Wars,* Tony Silver

SPECIAL JURY PRIZES
(FEATURE FILMS)

- *Last Night at the Alamo*, Eagle Pennell
- *Hero*, Alexandre Rockwell

(DOCUMENTARIES)
- *The Secret Agent,* Jackie Ochs
- *When the Mountains Tremble,* Pamela Yates, Thomas Sigel

DIRECTORS GUILD OF AMERICA

Nominations were announced on January 25, 1984. Awards were presented on March 10 at the Beverly Hilton Hotel in Los Angeles.

BEST DIRECTOR
- James L. Brooks, *Terms of Endearment*
Bruce Beresford, *Tender Mercies*
Ingmar Bergman, *Fanny and Alexander*
Lawrence Kasdan, *The Big Chill*
Philip Kaufman, *The Right Stuff*

ROBERT B. ALDRICH AWARD
- Robert E. Wise

D. W. GRIFFITH AWARD
- Orson Welles

WRITERS GUILD OF AMERICA

Awards were presented on April 5, 1984, at the Beverly Hilton Hotel in Los Angeles.

BEST ORIGINAL DRAMA
- *Tender Mercies,* Horton Foote
Silkwood, Nora Ephron, Alice Arlen
WarGames, Lawrence Lasker, Walter F. Parkes

BEST ADAPTED DRAMA
- *Reuben, Reuben,* Julius J. Epstein, based on the novel by Peter De Vries and the play *Spofford,* by Herman Shumlin
The Right Stuff, Philip Kaufman, based on the book by Tom Wolfe
The Year of Living Dangerously, David Williamson, Peter Weir, C. J. Koch, based on the novel by C. J. Koch

BEST ORIGINAL COMEDY
- *The Big Chill*, Lawrence Kasdan, Barbara Benedek
Risky Business, Paul Brickman
Zelig, Woody Allen

BEST ADAPTED COMEDY
- *Terms of Endearment*, James L. Brooks, based on the novel by Larry McMurtry
A Christmas Story, Jean Shepherd, Leigh Brown, Bob Clark, based on the novel by Jean Shepherd
To Be or Not to Be, Edwin Justus Mayer, based on a story by Melchoir Lengyel

LAUREL AWARD
- Melville Shavelson, Jack Rose, Norman Panama, Melvin Frank

VALENTINE DAVIES AWARD
- Jerome Lawrence, Robert E. Lee

MORGAN COX AWARD
- Nate Monaster

ACADEMY AWARDS

Nominations were announced on February 16, 1984. Awards were presented on April 9 at the Dorothy Chandler Pavilion in Los Angeles. The ceremony was telecast by ABC.

BEST PICTURE
- *Terms of Endearment*
The Big Chill
The Dresser
The Right Stuff
Tender Mercies

BEST DIRECTOR
- James L. Brooks, *Terms of Endearment*
Bruce Beresford, *Tender Mercies*
Ingmar Bergman, *Fanny and Alexander*
Mike Nichols, *Silkwood*
Peter Yates, *The Dresser*

BEST ACTOR
- Robert Duvall, *Tender Mercies*
Michael Caine, *Educating Rita*
Tom Conti, *Reuben, Reuben*
Tom Courtenay, *The Dresser*
Albert Finney, *The Dresser*

BEST ACTRESS
- Shirley MacLaine, *Terms of Endearment*
Jane Alexander, *Testament*
Meryl Streep, *Silkwood*

Julie Walters, *Educating Rita*
Debra Winger, *Terms of Endearment*

BEST SUPPORTING ACTOR

- Jack Nicholson, *Terms of Endearment*

Charles Durning, *To Be or Not to Be*
John Lithgow, *Terms of Endearment*
Sam Shepard, *The Right Stuff*
Rip Torn, *Cross Creek*

BEST SUPPORTING ACTRESS

- Linda Hunt, *The Year of Living Dangerously*

Cher, *Silkwood*
Glenn Close, *The Big Chill*
Amy Irving, *Yentl*
Alfre Woodard, *Cross Creek*

BEST ORIGINAL SCREENPLAY

- Horton Foote, *Tender Mercies*

Alice Arlen, Nora Ephron, *Silkwood*
Barbara Benedek, Lawrence Kasdan, *The Big Chill*
Ingmar Bergman, *Fanny and Alexander*
Lawrence Lasker, Walter F. Parkes, *War-Games*

BEST ADAPTED SCREENPLAY

- James L. Brooks, *Terms of Endearment*

Julius J. Epstein, *Reuben, Reuben*
Ronald Harwood, *The Dresser*
Harold Pinter, *Betrayal*
Willy Russell, *Educating Rita*

BEST SONG

- "Flashdance . . . What a Feeling," *Flashdance*, Irene Cara, Keith Forsey, Giorgio Moroder

"Maniac," *Flashdance,* Dennis Matkosky, Michael Sembello
"Over You," *Tender Mercies*, Bobby Hart, Austin Roberts
"Papa, Can You Hear Me?" *Yentl,* Alan Bergman, Marilyn Bergman, Michel Legrand
"The Way He Makes Me Feel," *Yentl*, Alan Bergman, Marilyn Bergman, Michel Legrand

BEST FOREIGN-LANGUAGE FILM

- *Fanny and Alexander* (Sweden)

Le Bal (Algeria)

Carmen (Spain)
Entre Nous (France)
Job's Revolt (Hungary)

Winners

BEST ART DIRECTION

- Anna Asp, *Fanny and Alexander*

BEST CINEMATOGRAPHY

- Sven Nykvist, *Fanny and Alexander*

BEST COSTUME DESIGN

- Marik Vos, *Fanny and Alexander*

BEST DOCUMENTARY

(FEATURE)

- *He Makes Me Feel Like Dancin'*, Emile Ardolino

(SHORT SUBJECT)

- *Flamenco at 5:15,* Cynthia Scott, Adam Symansky

BEST FILM EDITING

- Glenn Farr, Lisa Fruchtman, Tom Rolf, Stephen A. Rotter, Douglas Stewart, *The Right Stuff*

BEST MUSIC

(ORIGINAL SCORE)

- Bill Conti, *The Right Stuff*

(ORIGINAL SONG SCORE AND ITS ADAPTATION OR ADAPTATION SCORE)

- Alan Bergman, Marilyn Bergman, Michel Legrand, *Yentl*

SCIENTIFIC OR TECHNICAL AWARDS

(Academy Award of Merit)

- Kurt Larche, Osram GmgH

(Scientific and Engineering Award)

- Jonathan Erland, Roger Dorney, Apogee; Gerald L. Turpin, Lightflex; Gunnar P. Michaelson

(Technical Achievement Award)

- William G. Krokaugger, Mole-Richardson Co.; Jack Cashin, Ultra-Stereo Labs; Charles L. Watson, Larry L. Langrehr, John H. Steiner; Elizabeth D. de la Mare; Douglas Fries, John Lacey, Michael Sigrist; David J. Degenkolb

BEST SHORT FILM
(ANIMATED)
- *Sundae in New York*, Jimmy Picker

(LIVE ACTION)
- *Boys and Girls,* Janice L. Platt

BEST SOUND
- Mark Berger, David MacMillan, Tom Scott, Randy Thom, *The Right Stuff*

BEST SOUND EFFECTS EDITING
- Jay Boekelheide, *The Right Stuff*

SPECIAL ACHIEVEMENT AWARD
(VISUAL EFFECTS)
- Richard Edlund, Dennis Muren, Ken Ralston, Phil Tippett, *Return of the Jedi*

GORDON E. SAWYER AWARD
- John G. Frayne

JEAN HERSHOLT HUMANITARIAN AWARD
- M. J. Frankovich

HONORARY AWARD
- Hal Roach

SCREEN ACTORS GUILD

LIFETIME ACHIEVEMENT AWARD
- Ralph Bellamy

· 1984 ·

Vulgarian Rhapsody

According to Hollywood scuttlebutt, *Places in the Heart* was a cinch to sweep the upcoming kudos derby.

Variety called director-writer Robert Benton's depiction of his Texas hometown in the 1930s "flawlessly crafted" and *Places*'s upstart new studio, Tri-Star, backed it up with a massive marketing blitz when the pic premiered in September.

Come December, though, two pix by past Oscar-winning directors hit the track and suddenly looked like good bets, too.

One of the late-breaking front-runners was David Lean's first film in 14 years and "his best work since *The Bridge on the River Kwai* and *Lawrence of Arabia*," insisted *The New York Times*. *A Passage to India* was based on E. M. Forster's classic novel about the waning days of British rule over India and it featured three strong perfs "all played to near perfection," added the *Times*: Peggy Ashcroft as the wise mum of a British magistrate, Judy Davis as the magistrate's rigid fiancé and Victor Banerjee as a Muslim doctor who's punished for his overeagerness to please his overlords.

Neck and neck with Lean was Milos Forman, who had last pulled off a sweepstakes victory in 1975 with *One Flew over the Cuckoo's Nest*. Now he was in the running with his screen rendition of the 1980–1981 Tony Award–winning Broadway hit *Amadeus*, "a fictionalized account, based on well-informed speculation, of the relationship between Viennese court composer Antonio Salieri and Wolfgang Amadeus Mozart," said *Variety*, adding, "It is a caustic study of the collision between mediocrity and genius." A little-known legit thesp, F. Murray Abraham, took over the lead role of Salieri ("drawn as a character of Mephistophelian proportions," said *Variety*) that had earned Ian McKellen a Tony. Forman also recast the part of Mozart (origi-

The Gotham crix didn't give *Amadeus* a single vote for Best Picture, but it rallied at the Globes and Oscars.

nally played by Tim Curry), opting for the surprising choice of *National Lampoon's Animal House* star Tom Hulce, who Forman thought could do a socko job portraying the revered composer as a hyperactive vulgarian.

The Hollywood crix voted first and chose the movie with the vulgarian.

Amadeus had a hefty "For Your Consideration" ad campaign behind it in *Variety*, but its Best Picture victory at the Los Angeles Film Critics Association was still viewed as an upset. *A Passage to India* ended up with only a single award—Best Supporting Actress for Peggy Ashcroft, who beat Christine Lahti as Goldie Hawn's pal in *Swing Shift*.

Passage wasn't even a finalist for Best Picture or Director. *Amadeus* and Forman ended up edging out the Jewish-gangster drama *Once upon a Time in America* and its helmer Sergio Leone.

Amadeus also garnered kudos for F. Murray Abraham, who tied for the Best Actor laurels with Albert Finney (*Under the Volcano*) as a former British consul drinking himself to death in Mexico. *Amadeus* scribe Peter Schaffer won Best Screenplay for adapting his legitter to the screen, beating Alan Rudolph (*Choose Me*). Kathleen Turner was named Best Actress for two roles—as a fashion designer/hooker in *Crimes of Passion* and an adventure-craving romance novelist in *Romancing the Stone*. She topped Vanessa Redgrave as a 19th-century feminist in Henry James's *The Bostonians.*

Adolph Caesar was named Best Supporting Actor for the role he originated on stage as a martinet army sergeant in the Pulitzer Prize–winning *A Soldier's Story.* Runner-up was John Malkovich, who was cited for two perfs: as a blind man in *Places in the Heart* and a combat photographer in *The Killing Fields.*

When Forman traveled to L.A. for the crix's awards luncheon, which was held at the Westwood Marquis Hotel five weeks after the voting, he confessed to suffering from "an uncontrollable fear of flying and an even more uncontrollable fear of film critics."

> The Gotham crix kudos for *A Passage to India* were a "peace offering" to David Lean.

But Best Actress champ Kathleen Turner embraced the crix warmly when she accepted their kudo, calling it "very prestigious" and an award with "nice snob appeal to it." Adolph Caesar offered his "secret of being a good actor" when he claimed his prize: "Just say your lines and get off. This is not the biggest moment of your life." Peggy Ashcroft was not present, but costar Victor Banerjee stood in.

Two days after the L.A. crix votes were announced, the National Board of Review emphasized its disagreement by heaping the bulk of its kudos on *A Passage to India:* Best Picture, Director (Lean), Actor (Banerjee) and Actress (Ashcroft, upped from supporting status).

One day later, the New York Film Critics Circle endorsed many of the same choices while overtly snubbing *Amadeus.* In fact,

Amadeus didn't receive even a single vote in the Best Picture polling, which spanned 16 films, including such popcorn hits as *The Terminator, Purple Rain* and *Gremlins. A Passage to India* won on the second ballot with 42 points, followed by *The Killing Fields* (27), a drama about the Khmer Rouge's bloody takeover of Cambodia in the 1970s. In third place was *Stranger Than Paradise* (18), which *Variety* described as "a bracingly original avant-garde black comedy about a New York hipster being paid a surprise, and quite unwelcome, visit by a Hungarian cousin."

David Lean won Best Director with 41 points on the third canvass, beating Bertrand Tavernier, who scored 26 points for *A Sunday in the Country,* a French import about the reunion of a widowed painter and his children.

The Washington Post suggested that the high honors paid by the Gotham crix to David Lean were a peace offering since "Lean withdrew from the world of movies 14 years ago, in part due to the nasty reaction of the New York critics to his *Ryan's Daughter*."

In the supporting categories, Christine Lahti (*Swing Shift*) prevailed on the first ballot with 41 points over Melanie Griffith as a porno star in *Body Double* (27). The crix saluted recently deceased Ralph Richardson as a daffy, warm-hearted British earl in the $33 million *Tarzan* remake *Greystoke.* He polled 36 points versus 30 for John Malkovich (*Places in the Heart*). *Places* rebounded to claim Best Screenplay by a single point (31 to 30) over mermaid laffer *Splash.*

Vanessa Redgrave (*The Bostonians*) led the race for Best Actress on the first ballot, but Peggy Ashcroft finally declared victory on the fourth tally with 39 points, followed by 31 for Redgrave.

A similar flip-flop occurred in the race for Best Actor when Albert Finney (*Under the Volcano*) claimed an early lead, but then lost by a 46-to-31 score to Steve Martin, who was hailed as a divorce lawyer possessed by the spirit of a cranky heiress (Lily Tomlin) in *All of Me*. "The comic's victory here has to be regarded as coming out of left field," said *Variety,* since the win marked the first time in more than 20 years that the crix honored an overtly comedic perf. The last time was 1962—when Albert Finney was honored for *Tom Jones*. After this year's vote, Rex Reed griped about Martin's victory in *The New York Post:* "I'm still in shock over that one."

When the Gotham crix gathered at Sardi's in late January to dispense their laurels and to celebrate their 50th anniversary (just hours after the Golden Globes ceremony out in L.A.), it was "a fun-filled evening," reported *The New York Daily News*.

The fun began with Steve Martin's revenge. While claiming his plaque, he said, "It's a great honor to have been given this award by so many distinguished critics . . . and Rex Reed." Reed was not present for the ribbing.

The WGA trimmed its kudos to two categories, mirroring the Oscars.

Best Supporting Actress champ Christine Lahti thanked the crix for taking the beloved 75-year-old Dame Ashcroft out of her category and placing her in the race for Best Actress. "Of course, since the announcement of the awards, Peggy and I have both been asked to pose for *Playboy*," she wisecracked.

Overlapping membership between the New York Film Critics Circle and the Gotham-based National Society of Film Critics was still considerable—15 of the circle's 27 crix also belonged to the 32-member society—but the vote outcomes were dramatically different. In fact, the orgs agreed on only one award: Best Actor. Steve Martin scored 38 points to fend off challenges (25 points each) from Albert Finney (*Volcano*) and Robin Williams as a befuddled Soviet defector in *Moscow on the Hudson*.

The society disagreed with the circle over Peggy Ashcroft's classification and placed her in the race for Best Supporting Actress, which she lost to Melanie Griffith (*Body Double*) by a 19-to-36 score. Ralph Richardson earned only 26 points for *Greystoke*, thereby losing Best Supporting Actor to John Malkovich, who reaped 46 points for his roles in *Places in the Heart* and *The Killing Fields*. The L.A. crix's choice for Best Actress, Kathleen Turner, lost to Vanessa Redgrave by a 23-to-31 tally.

The biggest surprises were reserved for the top two awards. The *L.A. Herald Examiner* declared that the society "threw a monkey wrench into the movie-awards machinery" by naming *Stranger Than Paradise* as Best Picture (23 points). Runner-up was *A Sunday in the Country* (17). Best Director was Robert Bresson (30 points) for the French import *L'Argent*, "an austere tale of a robber who escapes jail and murders an old woman," said the *Herald Examiner*. Second place went to Bertrand Tavernier (*A Sunday in the Country*, 25 points). *Sunday*'s scribes lost the screenplay prize to the writers of *Splash*, 16 to 28.

Since the society "ignored the gathering consensus" and "struck out on its quixotic own" by opting for so many indie or foreign pix, the *Herald Examiner* said that the org's list of winners left "industry publicists wearing downcast faces." The reason: the results couldn't help them bolster their Golden Globe and Oscar campaigns.

When the Globe nominations were announced, the *Herald Examiner* pointed out a new concern: "The competitive element has been taken out of the best film contest because *A Passage to India*, the movie considered to be *Amadeus'* chief competition at the upcoming Oscars, has been nominated in a separate category—Best Foreign Film." *Passage* was considered a British movie, even though it was co-produced by a Hollywood studio, Columbia. In addition to its nom as best off-shore pic, it nabbed bids for Peggy Ashcroft (Best Supporting Actress), Maurice Jarre (Best Score), and David Lean (Best Director and screenplay scribe).

The biggest shocker among all the noms was in the directors' category. Although *Places in the Heart* was once considered the year's kudos front-runner, Robert Benton was snubbed for his work at the helm.

Amadeus was tied for the most bids with *The Killing Fields* (six each) and ended up with four victories.

Without *A Passage to India* as competish, *Amadeus* claimed Best Drama Picture easily. It also snagged Globes for Best Screenplay (Peter Shaffer) and Best Director (Milos Forman). Accepting the latter prize, Forman told the audience, "They love American movies in foreign countries, but they can be pretty funny about American movies *about* their countries."

When F. Murray Abraham beat costar Tom Hulce for Best Drama Actor, Hulce accepted the prize on behalf of the absent champ. "Well, after plaguing Salieri's life, I think it's only fitting that Mozart should accept his award," Hulce said.

Sally Field won Best Drama Actress for portraying a widow struggling to keep her farm and family intact during the Depression in *Places in the Heart.*

A Passage to India took the foreign film category easily, plus picked up honors for its musical score and star Peggy Ashcroft, who was in New York on Globes day accepting her honor from the Gotham crix.

A surprise occurred in the race for Best Comedy or Musical Picture when *Romancing the Stone* beat some of the year's top-grossing hits—including *Beverly Hills Cop, Ghostbusters* and *Splash.* Also honored was its star, Kathleen Turner, who accepted the Globe as Best Comedy/Musical Actress "sounding even more whiskey-voiced than usual because of the flu," observed the *Herald Examiner.*

"I lost to Pia Zadora three years ago in the best newcomer category," Turner reminded the audience. "This time it's obviously a lot more satisfying."

Steve Martin was voted Best Actor by the National Crix Society and N.Y. crix for *All of Me,* but failed to reap an Oscar nom.

The winner of the Best Actor trophy was "a genuine shock," said the *Herald Examiner* when Dudley Moore beat Eddie Murphy (*Beverly Hills Cop*), Steve Martin (*All of Me*), Robin Williams (*Moscow on the Hudson*) and Bill Murray (*Ghostbusters*). Moore was hailed for his role as a newscaster married to two pregnant women in *Micki and Maude.*

"I suppose Eddie, Steve, Robin and Bill just were not up to par this year," Moore said, accepting his Globe with a mischievous grin. "I mean, box office is one thing . . ."

L.A. film crix honoree Adolph Caesar (*A Soldier's Story*) and Richard Crenna as a scam artist in *The Flamingo Kid* were considered the favorites to win Best Supporting Actor, but an upset was scored by a non-thesp.

Before starring in *The Killing Fields*, 40-year-old Haing S. Ngor had been a doctor by profession in Cambodia. How he landed the film role was a fluke—by running into a casting agent at a wedding—but he no doubt was chosen to portray the real-life assistant of a reporter investigating the Cambodian war because he had experienced the conflict first hand. Ngor had been tortured and persecuted by the Khmer Rouge during his four years as a slave laborer, then escaped to the United States in 1980.

When he won the Globe, the *Herald Examiner* reported that "the audience responded with genuine emotion" by giving Ngor a standing ovation.

"I thank God and Buddha for allowing me the honor of telling the world what happened in my country," he said at the podium. "I accept not only on behalf of myself, but on behalf of all Cambodians around the world."

Also receiving a standing ovation was Elizabeth Taylor, who was honored with the Cecil B. DeMille Award after being introduced by Liza Minnelli as "just the biggest star in the world."

"It's incredible," Taylor said, hugging the statuette. "And to be given it by the press—that's really amazing! But I feel a sense of love and warmth in this room and it makes me feel that perhaps, after all, I have achieved something."

There was far less warmth waiting for her in the press room backstage later, however, when a cynical reporter plugged her with a touchy question about a recent death.

"A reporter asked Taylor if it was difficult watching film clips during the award presentation showing her with her late, ex-husband, Richard Burton," *USA Today* reported. "After an icy 'yes,' Liz left the press room."

Sizing up the overall award results, UPI declared, "The near sweep, along with earlier honors from several critics groups, establishes *Amadeus* as the film to beat in balloting for this year's Oscars."

But one week later, when the Oscar noms were unveiled, *Amadeus* suddenly had serious competish: it tied *A Passage to India* for the most bids—11.

The deadlock, some observers thought, might be broken early at the kudos bestowed by the Directors Guild of America.

The break occurred for *Amadeus* when

Frank Capra, Jack Lemmon and Robert Wise share a table at the directors' guild awards.

DGA/Nate Cutler

Milos Forman claimed his second DGA victory in nine years, after having been honored previously for *One Flew over the Cuckoo's Nest*.

"I thought I knew what I would say. . . . I was wrong," he said, accepting it. He paused for a moment, then added, "I'm thrilled."

Billy Wilder told a funny story as he accepted the honorary D.W. Griffith prize. *Variety* reported, "Wilder noted that an autograph hound recently asked him to sign three times; and when the veteran director asked why, he was told, 'For three Wilders, I can get one Spielberg.' "

The Writers Guild of America streamlined its kudos this year by combining the comedy and drama prizes. Now there were only two races—for adapted and original screenplays. Ballots were mailed to 8,100 members, who decided among 105 scripts.

One screenplay was overlooked: *Amadeus*.

The shocking omission was matched by a surprising result when one of the winners was announced. David Lean was nommed for *A Passage to India*, but lost the Best Adapted Screenplay accolade to Bruce Robinson for *The Killing Fields*.

Woody Allen had reaped nine nominations over the past 19 years, but scored only a single win—for *Annie Hall* (1977). Now he nabbed his second career victory for his

10th bid—*Broadway Danny Rose*, which starred Allen as "a small-time, good-hearted Broadway talent agent giving his all for a roster of hopeless clients," said *Variety.*

Oscars were presented five days after the writers' guild honors. Just behind the nominations leaders *Amadeus* and *A Passage to India* (11 each) were *The Killing Fields* and *Places in the Heart*, tied with 7 bids. Shocking oversights included Steve Martin, who wasn't up for Best Actor despite previous prizes from the New York Film Critics Circle and the National Society of Film Critics. Kathleen Turner might have been honored by the L.A. crix and Golden Globes, but Oscar voters snubbed her, too. *Variety* reported "considerable speculation" over which category Peggy Ashcroft might be listed in after she won kudos in both the lead and supporting races over the previous months. The suspense ended when she appeared in the academy's supporting lineup.

Ashcroft missed attending her first Oscar derby. Her friend and acting colleague Michael Redgrave died five days before the ceremony, so Ashcroft joined his daughter Vanessa (Best Actress nominee, *The Bostonians*) in heading to London for the funeral. Ashcroft missed the service due to a flu, but she won the Oscar, as was widely predicted.

Another of Britain's reigning stars who had died recently, Ralph Richardson, was among the contenders for Best Supporting Actor. The Gotham crix champ faced tough competish from L.A. crix winner Adolph Caesar, National Society of Film Critics honoree John Malkovich and Golden Globe victor Haing S. Ngor.

Ngor won, becoming only the second nonactor to earn a performance award since World War II amputee Harold Russell was named Best Supporting Actor for *The Best Years of Our Lives* (1946).

"This is unbelievable, but so is my entire life!" he roared. Soon afterward, he headed backstage and assumed a somber tone as he told reporters grotesque details of how he'd been tortured as a prisoner of the Khmer Rouge.

Ngor's victory, said *Variety,* "played out as one of the most dramatic in Academy Award history. The underdog—courtesy of the American Dream—could indeed come up a winner."

The day after his award triumph, Ngor went back to his regular job at an employment agency in Chinatown, but he left work early to sign up with an actors' agency. He made several more films after *The Killing Fields*, but his career was cut short in 1996 when he was murdered in his garage by a gang of drug dealers.

In the previous Best Actress races, Sally Field reaped no support from any of the three critics' orgs, but she gained such momentum after winning the Golden Globe that Knight Ridder and other media declared her to be the Oscar front-runner.

When she won, the previous Oscar champ (*Norma Rae*, 1979) gave one of the most memorable speeches ever. "I haven't had an orthodox career and I wanted more than anything to have your respect," she said. "The first time (that I won) I didn't feel it, but this time I feel it and I can't deny the fact you like me. Right now, *you like me!*"

The next day Field went back to work on her latest pic and *Variety* columnist Army Archerd reported: "Sally Field returned to the Florence, Ariz. (pop. 3,723) location of *Murphy's Romance* to find this banner across Main St.: 'You Found a Place in Our Hearts.' "

Places in the Heart scored a huge upset in the contest for Best Original Screenplay. The pic had lost the WGA palm to *Broadway Danny Rose* and the Golden Globe to *Amadeus,* but now scribe Robert Benton prevailed at the Oscars. Accepting it, he thanked the people in his hometown of Waxahachie, Texas, who cooperated with the film's production.

As expected, *Amadeus* copped the prize for Best Adapted Screenplay. Its star, F. Murray Abraham, was also "the outstanding favorite to win," according to UPI. When he triumphed as Best Actor, Abraham said at the podium, "It would be a lie if I told you I didn't know what to say. I've been working on this speech for about 25 years."

Amadeus snagged many of the crafts categories all night long, too, including makeup, sound, art direction and costumes. Its helmer, Milos Forman, may have faced formidable foes in the directors' race (three of his rivals were past winners), but he again scored the prize that he won for *One Flew over the Cuckoo's Nest* in 1975.

Amadeus's "sweep was so complete," said *Variety*, that Best Picture presenter Laurence Olivier "failed to even name the other nominees" before he opened the envelope and read off the title of the Mozart biopic as champ.

Forman claimed the high honor coolly while on stage, but when he got back to the press room he let loose, howling, "I love the Oscars!" His latest film had just won eight of them.

There was a lot to celebrate at the U.S. Film Festival, too: the debt-plagued indie event was rescued this year by Robert Redford's Sundance Institute. "It's a natural for Sundance to take over the festival's management," *Variety* said. "Both festival and institute are supportive of the independent filmmaker."

"We see ourselves at Sundance as the workplace and the festival as the showplace, and there is a very tight connection between the two," Redford said.

"While Redford has been the festival's honorary chairman in the past, he had very little to do with the event after its initial year," *Variety* noted. Redford said that he disdained festivals in general because they were generally nonproductive, but he was upbeat about the future possibilities of the Utah event.

This year's feature winner of the fest's Grand Jury Prize was *Blood Simple,* heralded by *Variety* as "an inordinately good low-budget film noir thriller" by Joel and Ethan Coen. The tale about a contract killer who double-crosses his client was produced for $1.5 million.

Among the recipients of the Special Jury Prizes bestowed upon the runners-up was *Stranger Than Paradise,* which the National Society of Film Critics had named Best Picture a few weeks earlier.

Immediately after the festival, Redford departed for Kenya to star opposite Meryl Streep in a new Sydney Pollack movie.

"It's a quality project," he told *Variety*. "It's a love story. Most of all it's intelligent." The pic was *Out of Africa*.

▪ 1984 ▪

LOS ANGELES FILM CRITICS ASSOCIATION

Winners were announced on December 15, 1984. Awards were presented on January 24, 1985, at the Westwood Marquis Hotel in Los Angeles.

BEST PICTURE
▪ *Amadeus*

BEST DIRECTOR
▪ Milos Forman, *Amadeus*

BEST ACTOR (TIE)
▪ F. Murray Abraham, *Amadeus*
▪ Albert Finney, *Under the Volcano*

BEST ACTRESS
▪ Kathleen Turner, *Crimes of Passion, Romancing the Stone*

BEST SUPPORTING ACTOR
▪ Adolph Caesar, *A Soldier's Story*

BEST SUPPORTING ACTRESS
▪ Peggy Ashcroft, *A Passage to India*

BEST SCREENPLAY
▪ Peter Shaffer, *Amadeus*

BEST CINEMATOGRAPHY
▪ Chris Menges, *The Killing Fields*

BEST MUSIC SCORE
▪ Ennio Morricone, *Once Upon a Time in America**

---

*Winner according to L.A.F.C.A. records. The *L.A. Times* reported on December 17, 1984 that Neville Marriner (*Amadeus*) won.

BEST FOREIGN FILM
- *The Fourth Man* (Netherlands)

BEST EXPERIMENTAL/INDEPENDENT FILM
- George Kuchar

SPECIAL AWARDS
- Andrew Sarris
- François Truffaut

NATIONAL BOARD OF REVIEW

The board declared a Best Picture and Foreign Film of the year, then listed its remaining favorites according to highest scores. The vote results were announced on December 17, 1984.

BEST PICTURE
- *A Passage to India*
Paris, Texas
The Killing Fields
Places in the Heart
Mass Appeal
Country
A Soldier's Story
Birdy
Careful, He Might Hear You
Under the Volcano

BEST DIRECTOR
- David Lean, *A Passage to India*

BEST ACTOR
- Victor Banerjee, *A Passage to India*

BEST ACTRESS
- Peggy Ashcroft, *A Passage to India*

BEST SUPPORTING ACTOR
- John Malkovich, *Places in the Heart*

BEST SUPPORTING ACTRESS
- Sabine Azema, *A Sunday in the Country*

BEST FOREIGN FILM
- *A Sunday in the Country* (France)
Carmen (Spain)
A Love in German (Federal Republic of Germany)
The Fourth Man (Netherlands)
The Basileus Quartet (France/Italy)

NEW YORK FILM CRITICS CIRCLE

Winners were announced on December 18, 1984. Awards were presented on January 27, 1985, at Sardi's restaurant in New York.

BEST PICTURE
- *A Passage to India*

BEST DIRECTOR
- David Lean, *A Passage to India*

BEST ACTOR
- Steve Martin, *All of Me*

BEST ACTRESS
- Peggy Ashcroft, *A Passage to India*

BEST SUPPORTING ACTOR
- Ralph Richardson, *Greystoke*

BEST SUPPORTING ACTRESS
- Christine Lahti, *Swing Shift*

BEST SCREENPLAY
- Robert Benton, *Places in the Heart*

BEST CINEMATOGRAPHY
- Chris Menges, *The Killing Fields*

BEST DOCUMENTARY
- *The Times of Harvey Milk*

BEST FOREIGN FILM
- *A Sunday in the Country* (France)

NATIONAL SOCIETY OF FILM CRITICS

Winners were announced on January 2, 1985.

BEST PICTURE
- *Stranger Than Paradise*

BEST DIRECTOR
- Robert Bresson, *L'Argent*

BEST ACTOR
- Steve Martin, *All of Me*

BEST ACTRESS
- Vanessa Redgrave, *The Bostonians*

BEST SUPPORTING ACTOR
- John Malkovich, *Places in the Heart, The Killing Fields*

BEST SUPPORTING ACTRESS
- Melanie Griffith, *Body Double*

BEST SCREENPLAY
- Lowell Ganz, Babaloo Mandel, Bruce Jay Friedman, *Splash*

BEST CINEMATOGRAPHY
- Chris Menges, *Comfort and Joy, The Killing Fields*

BEST DOCUMENTARY
- *Stop Making Sense*, Jonathan Demme

GOLDEN GLOBES

Nominations were announced on January 7, 1985. Awards were presented on January 27 at the Beverly Hilton Hotel in Los Angeles. The ceremony was broadcast nationally via syndication.

BEST DRAMA PICTURE
- *Amadeus*
The Cotton Club
The Killing Fields
Places in the Heart
A Soldier's Story

BEST COMEDY OR MUSICAL PICTURE
- *Romancing the Stone*
Beverly Hills Cop
Ghostbusters
Micki and Maude
Splash

BEST DIRECTOR
- Milos Forman, *Amadeus*
Francis Coppola, *The Cotton Club*
Roland Joffe, *The Killing Fields*
David Lean, *A Passage to India*
Sergio Leone, *Once upon a Time in America*

BEST ACTOR, DRAMA
- F. Murray Abraham, *Amadeus*
Jeff Bridges, *Starman*
Albert Finney, *Under the Volcano*
Tom Hulce, *Amadeus*
Sam Waterston, *The Killing Fields*

BEST ACTRESS, DRAMA
- Sally Field, *Places in the Heart*
Diane Keaton, *Mrs. Soffel*
Jessica Lange, *Country*
Vanessa Redgrave, *The Bostonians*
Sissy Spacek, *The River*

BEST ACTOR, COMEDY OR MUSICAL
- Dudley Moore, *Micki and Maude*
Steve Martin, *All of Me*
Eddie Murphy, *Beverly Hills Cop*
Bill Murray, *Ghostbusters*
Robin Williams, *Moscow on the Hudson*

BEST ACTRESS, COMEDY OR MUSICAL
- Kathleen Turner, *Romancing the Stone*
Anne Bancroft, *Garbo Talks*
Mia Farrow, *Broadway Danny Rose*
Shelley Long, *Irreconcilable Differences*
Lily Tomlin, *All of Me*

BEST SUPPORTING ACTOR
- Haing S. Ngor, *The Killing Fields*
Adolph Caesar, *A Soldier's Story*
Richard Crenna,*The Flamingo Kid*
Jeffrey Jones, *Amadeus*
Noriyuki "Pat" Morita, *The Karate Kid*

BEST SUPPORTING ACTRESS
- Peggy Ashcroft, *A Passage to India*
Drew Barrymore, *Irreconcilable Differences*
Kim Basinger, *The Natural*
Jacqueline Bisset, *Under the Volcano*
Melanie Griffith, *Body Double*
Christine Lahti, *Swing Shift*
Lesley Ann Warren, *Songwriter*

BEST SCREENPLAY
- Peter Shaffer, *Amadeus*
Bruce Robinson, *The Killing Fields*
David Lean, *A Passage to India*
Robert Benton, *Places in the Heart*
Charles Fuller, *A Soldier's Story*

BEST SONG

- "I Just Called to Say I Love You," *The Woman in Red*

"Against All Odds," *Against All Odds*
"Footloose," *Footloose*
"Ghostbusters," *Ghostbusters*
"No More Lonely Nights," *Give My Regards to Broad Street*
"When Doves Cry," *Purple Rain*

BEST FOREIGN FILM

- *A Passage to India* (U.K.)

Bizet's Carmen (France)
Dangerous Moves (Switzerland)
Paris, Texas (Germany, France)
A Sunday in the Country (France)

Winners

BEST SCORE

- Maurice Jarre, *A Passage to India*

CECIL B. DEMILLE AWARD

- Elizabeth Taylor

U.S. FILM FESTIVAL (SUNDANCE)

The festival was held January 18–27, 1985, at Park City, Utah.

GRAND JURY PRIZE
(FEATURE)

- *Blood Simple*, Joel Coen

(DOCUMENTARY)

- *Seventeen*, Joel De Mott, Jeff Kreines

SPECIAL JURY PRIZES
(FEATURE)

- *Almost You*, Adam Brooks
- *The Killing Floor*, William Duke
- *Stranger Than Paradise*, Jim Jarmusch

(DOCUMENTARY)

- *America and Lewis Hine*, Nina Rosenblum
- *In Heaven There Is No Beer*, Les Blank
- *Kaddish*, Steve Brand
- *Streetwise*, Martin Bell
- *The Times of Harvey Milk*, Robert Epstein

DIRECTORS GUILD OF AMERICA

Nominations were announced on February 1, 1985. Awards were presented on March 9 at the Beverly Hilton Hotel in Los Angeles.

BEST DIRECTOR

- Milos Forman, *Amadeus*

Robert Benton, *Places in the Heart*
Norman Jewison, *A Soldier's Story*
Roland Joffe, *The Killing Fields*
David Lean, *A Passage to India*

ROBERT B. ALDRICH AWARD

- Elliot Silverstein

D. W. GRIFFITH AWARD

- Billy Wilder

WRITERS GUILD OF AMERICA

Nominations were announced on February 14, 1985. Awards were presented on March 20 at the Beverly Hilton Hotel in Los Angeles.

BEST ORIGINAL SCREENPLAY

- *Broadway Danny Rose*, Woody Allen

El Notre, Gregory Nava, Anna Thomas
Places in the Heart, Robert Benton
Romancing the Stone, Diane Thomas
Splash, Lowell Ganz, Babaloo Mandel, Bruce Jay Friedman, based on a story by Brian Grazer

BEST ADAPTED SCREENPLAY

- *The Killing Fields*, Bruce Robinson, based on a *New York Times Magazine* article by Sydney Schanberg

Greystoke, P. H. Vazak, Michael Austin, based on the Tarzan books by Edgar Rice Burroughs
The Natural, Roger Towne, Phil Dusenberry, based on the book by Bernard Malamud
A Passage to India, David Lean, based on the book by E. M. Forster
A Soldier's Story, Charles Fuller, based on his play

MORGAN COX AWARD
- Edmund L. Hartmann

VALENTINE DAVIES AWARD
- Charles Champlin

FOUNDER'S AWARD
- Mary McCall, Jr.

LAUREL AWARD
- William Goldman

ACADEMY AWARDS

Nominations were announced on February 6, 1985. Awards were presented on March 25 at the Dorothy Chandler Pavilion in Los Angeles. The ceremony was telecast by ABC.

BEST PICTURE
- *Amadeus*
The Killing Fields
A Passage to India
Places in the Heart
A Soldier's Story

BEST DIRECTOR
- Milos Forman, *Amadeus*
Woody Allen, *Broadway Danny Rose*
Robert Benton, *Places in the Heart*
Roland Joffe, *The Killing Fields*
David Lean, *A Passage to India*

BEST ACTOR
- F. Murray Abraham, *Amadeus*
Jeff Bridges, *Starman*
Albert Finney, *Under the Volcano*
Tom Hulce, *Amadeus*
Sam Waterston, *The Killing Fields*

BEST ACTRESS
- Sally Field, *Places in the Heart*
Judy Davis, *A Passage to India*
Jessica Lange, *Country*
Vanessa Redgrave, *The Bostonians*
Sissy Spacek, *The River*

BEST SUPPORTING ACTOR
- Haing S. Ngor, *The Killing Fields*
Adolph Caesar, *A Soldier's Story*
John Malkovich, *Places in the Heart*

Noriyuki "Pat" Morita, *The Karate Kid*
Ralph Richardson, *Greystoke*

BEST SUPPORTING ACTRESS
- Peggy Ashcroft, *A Passage to India*
Glenn Close, *The Natural*
Lindsay Crouse, *Places in the Heart*
Christine Lahti, *Swing Shift*
Geraldine Page, *The Pope of Greenwich Village*

BEST ORIGINAL SCREENPLAY
- Robert Benton, *Places in the Heart*
Danilo Bach, Daniel Petrie, Jr., *Beverly Hills Cop*
Woody Allen, *Broadway Danny Rose*
Gregory Nava, Anna Thomas, *El Norte*
Bruce Jay Friedman, Lowell Ganz, Brian Grazer, Babaloo Mandel, *Splash*

BEST ADAPTED SCREENPLAY
- Peter Shaffer, *Amadeus*
Michael Austin, P. H. Vazak (pseudonym of Robert Towne), *Greystoke*
Bruce Robinson, *The Killing Fields*
David Lean, *A Passage to India*
Charles Fuller, *A Soldier's Story*

BEST SONG
- "I Just Called to Say I Love You," *The Woman in Red*, Stevie Wonder
"Against All Odds (Take a Look at Me Now)," *Against All Odds*, Phil Collins
"Footloose," *Footloose*, Kenny Loggins, Dean Pitchford
"Ghostbusters," *Ghostbusters*, Ray Parker, Jr.
"Let's Hear It for the Boy," *Footloose*, Dean Pitchford, Tom Snow

BEST FOREIGN-LANGUAGE FILM
- *Dangerous Moves* (Switzerland)
Beyond the Walls (Israel)
Camila (Argentina)
Double Feature (Spain)
Wartime Romance (U.S.S.R.)

Winners

BEST ART DIRECTION
- Patrizia Von Brandenstein, Karel Cerny, *Amadeus*

BEST CINEMATOGRAPHY
- Chris Menges, *The Killing Fields*

BEST COSTUME DESIGN
- Theodor Pistek, *Amadeus*

BEST DOCUMENTARY
(FEATURE)
- *The Times of Harvey Milk*, Robert Epstein, Richard Schmiechen,
(SHORT SUBJECT)
- *The Stone Carvers*, Marjorie Hunt, Paul Wagner

BEST FILM EDITING
- Jim Clark, *The Killing Fields*

BEST MAKEUP
- Paul Leblanc, Dick Smith, *Amadeus*

BEST MUSIC
(ORIGINAL SCORE)
- Maurice Jarre, *A Passage to India*
(ORIGINAL SONG SCORE AND ITS ADAPTATION)
- Prince, *Purple Rain*

SCIENTIFIC OR TECHNICAL AWARDS
(Scientific and Engineering Award)
- Donald A. Anderson, Diana Reiners, 3M Co.; Barry Stultz, Ruben Avila, Wes Kennedy, John Mosely, Film Processing Corp.; Kenneth Richter; Gunther Schaidt, Rosco Labs; John Whitney, Jr., Gary Demos, Digital Productions
(Technical Achievement Award)
- Donald Trumbull, Jonathan Erland, Stephen Fog, Paul Burk, Robert

Bealmear, Apogee; Howard Preston, Nat Tiffen

BEST SHORT FILM
(ANIMATED)
- *Charade*, Jon Minnis
(LIVE ACTION)
- *Up*, Mike Hoover

BEST SOUND
- Mark Berger, Todd Boekelheide, Chris Newman, Tom Scott, *Amadeus*

SPECIAL ACHIEVEMENT—SOUND EFFECTS EDITING
- Kay Rose, *The River*

BEST VISUAL EFFECTS
- George Gibbs, Michael McAlister, Dennis Muren, Lorne Peterson, *Indiana Jones and the Temple of Doom*

GORDON E. SAWYER AWARD
- Linwood G. Dunn

JEAN HERSHOLT HUMANITARIAN AWARD
- David L. Wolper

HONORARY AWARDS
- National Endowment for the Arts
- James Stewart

SCREEN ACTORS GUILD

LIFETIME ACHIEVEMENT AWARD
- Iggy Wolfington

▪ 1985 ▪

A Brazen Brazil Ploy

"The fame or infamy of the Los Angeles Film Critics Association rests on an incident that occurred in 1985," said the *N.Y. Times*. That's when the crix actually gave their Best Picture award to a film that wasn't scheduled for release.

Variety described the 2-hour, 17-minute *Brazil* as a "chillingly hilarious" fantasy about a future Orwellian world. Universal studio topper Sidney Sheinberg didn't get the joke, though, and pressed its creator—former Monty Python animator Terry Gilliam—to cut back the pic's length and give it an upbeat ending. Gilliam agreed to the trimming, but snipped out less than he promised—and he refused to budge at all over the finale. The duo deadlocked and the pic ended up on the shelf. Frustrated, Gilliam took out a full-page ad in *Variety* that read, "Dear Sidney, when are you going to release my film *Brazil*?" Sheinberg didn't write back.

Meantime, *L.A. Times* critic Jack Mathews, an ardent *Brazil* fan, arranged for fellow members of the crix org to see *Brazil* on the sly "not long before voting day," observed the *N.Y. Times*. The paper said that Mathews created "a swell of energy that he described as 'let's-do-something-important.' The group stunned the industry—and forced the movie's release—by giving *Brazil* awards for Best Picture, Best Director and Best Screenplay."

Soon thereafter, Universal execs, who had previously been hesitant about showing the pic to the public, were suddenly showing it to Oscar voters to woo awards.

"You gave us your stamp," acknowledged *Brazil*'s grateful producer when he accepted the Best Picture prize at the crix's awards luncheon weeks later. "For us, it made the difference between being dead or being alive."

The L.A. crix "stunned the industry" by naming *Brazil*, a film not skedded for release, as Best Picture.

Runner-up for Best Picture accolade was another Universal film, *Out of Africa*, described by *Variety* as "a sensitive, enveloping romantic tragedy" based on the life of Danish writer Isak Dinesen in British East Africa, circa World War I. Produced and directed by Sydney Pollack, it starred Meryl Streep as Dinesen and Robert Redford as her adventure-loving beau. Streep scored the Best Actress palm—her fourth from the L.A. crix, making her their most honored thesp. This year she edged out screen newcomer Whoopi Goldberg, who starred in Steven Spielberg's first serious dramatic outting, *The Color Purple*. *Variety* described the helmer's adaptation of Alice Walker's Pulitzer Prize–winning novel as "the story of a black family's growth and flowering over a 40-year period in the south," adding, "There is much to applaud (and cry about) here."

Another screen rookie—talk show host Oprah Winfrey—was up for Best Supporting Actress, but came in second behind Anjelica Huston as a monstrous mafia princess in *Prizzi's Honor*. Huston regarded the prize with awe when she accepted it at the crix luncheon, saying, "My first award ever! And in my own hometown, too!"

Prizzi was about the antics of a powerful crime family and *Variety* noted, "The pic itself was a family affair." It was directed by Huston's ailing 79-year-old-father John and starred her live-in lover Jack Nicholson as a slow-witted, tough-talking hit man. *Variety* said the pic had it all, packing "love, sex and murder—and dark comedy—into a labyrinthine tale." The critical huzzahs it reaped were enough to persuade Twentieth Century-Fox to give one more thing: a hefty Golden Globe/Oscar campaign.

Prizzi fared poorly with the rest of the L.A. crix kudos, though. William Hickey's perf as a mafia don placed second in the race for Best Supporting Actor. The winner was John Gielgud as an aging diplomat in *Plenty* and as an animal-rights crusader in *The Shooting Party*. *Prizzi* lost the screenplay laurels to *Brazil*, and Nicholson forfeited the Best Actor accolade to the artist who had recently snagged the equivalent prize at Cannes: William Hurt. Hurt became the hit of the art-house circuit in 1985 for portraying a flamboyant gay convict who entertains his cellmate (Raul Julia) by acting out movie melodramas in *Kiss of the Spider Woman*.

The runner-up for Best Director received a special Life Achievement Award—Akira Kurosawa, whose recent 16th-century epic *Ran*, a retelling of Shakespeare's *King Lear*, tied for Best Foreign Film with Argentina's *The Official Story*.

The National Board of Review gave Kurosawa its director's award, but opted for a different Best Picture—*The Color Purple*, which also earned the Best Actress laurels for Whoopi Goldberg. Costars of *Kiss of the Spider Woman* William Hurt and Raul Julia shared the Best Actor honors.

Four days after the L.A. crix shocked kudos watchers with their Best Picture choice, the Gotham crix met to ink their ballots. As the meeting convened, circle chairman Bruce Williamson of *Playboy* polled the 26 voting members to learn how many of them had seen *Brazil*. Twenty-five said

The "Paulettes" engineered *Ran's* best-pic victory at the crix society vote.

"yes." He then proceeded to conduct the Best Picture vote and was startled to see *Brazil* come in fourth place with only 17 points on the second ballot behind *Prizzi's Honor* (44), *The Purple Rose of Cairo* (22) and *Out of Africa* (19).

Prizzi scored an impressive sweep of four categories, tying it with *A Man for All Seasons* (1966), *Cries and Whispers* (1972) and *Annie Hall* (1977) as the biggest winner in the circle's history.

John Huston (42 points) beat Akira Kurosawa (25) on the second tally to claim the director's accolade. *Variety* noted, "Anjelica Huston won handily on the first ballot after facing little competition." When Jack Nicholson copped the actor's trophy over William Hurt by a 30-to-24 score on the third round, he increased his lead as the biggest winner in the award's history (six victories).

In the race for Best Actress, Meryl Streep led on the first ballot, but lost on the third polling by a 32-to-20 score to the Cannes recent Best Actress champ Norma Aleandro, who portrayed an uppercrust Argentinian caught in a political drama in *The Official Story*. John Gielgud (21 points) placed in the match-up for Best Supporting Actor behind Klaus Maria Brandauer (34) as Meryl Streep's philandering husband in *Out of Africa*. Winner of Best Screenplay was Woody Allen's *The Purple Rose of Cairo*, about a film character who steps off the screen and into real life. It beat Albert Brooks's whimsical road pic *Lost in America* 41 to 15.

"Every year the critics goof and schedule their bash on Super Sunday," harumphed *The New York Daily News*. But as the Chicago Bears and New England Patriots squared off at the Super Bowl, the circle's champs arrived dutifully at Sardi's, even sports nut Jack Nicholson, who chided his hosts for the skedding blunder. His plaque was bestowed by gracious Best Actress loser Meryl Streep, who called

Nicholson "the best I've ever worked with," handed him his kudos and then sneaked out of the restaurant via a back door in the kitchen.

Best Actress champ Norma Aleandro spoke next, saying, "I'm not sure if I'm dreaming, but that's OK because it's a beautiful dream."

Variety reported, "Funniest turn was provided by presenter Lily Tomlin, who called Anjelica Huston's performance a revelation and noted of her character in the film, 'Maerose is the kind of person I would have shoplifted with as a teenager.' "

Huston also accepted her father's plaque, reading a message from him that recalled his previous wins for *The Treasure of the Sierra Madre* (1948) and *Moby Dick* (1956). The note echoed his first acceptance speech, informing the crix, "You're still the conscience of the American film industry." He apologized for not being present, but blamed the "nebulizers, oxymeters and an array of oxygen tanks" that he was hooked up to.

Variety reported on the outcome of the National Society of Film Critics' voting: "Echoing other awards groups and most critics' Top 10 lists, *Prizzi's Honor* brought home the most gold." John Huston (44 points) won Best Director over Akira Kurosawa (34). Jack Nicholson (43) topped William Hurt (26) for Best Actor, and Anjelica Huston prevailed as Best Supporting Actress by a 48-to-38 tally over Mieko Harada as a scheming villainness in *Ran*. John Gielgud (27 points) eclipsed William Hickey (18) to win Best Supporting Actor.

Albert Brooks and partner Monica Johnson claimed revenge for their loss to Woody Allen (*Purple Rose*) at the Gotham crix kudos by besting Allen for the society's script laurels with 30 points to 27.

An upset occurred in the Best Actress contest when the national crix hailed a previously unconsidered role—Vanessa Redgrave as "a lonely Yorkshire schoolteacher

tormented by the memory of a teenage love affair" in *Wetherby*, said *Variety*. Her 21 points surpassed the 19 scored by Jessica Lange as lip-synching Patsy Cline in *Sweet Dreams*. *The New York Times* reported, "Many of those attending the National Society's meeting had the queasy feeling that the final choice was less a vote *for* Redgrave than *against* Meryl Streep."

The battle over Best Picture turned into a true clash between rival factions within the society: the Paulettes (disciples of *The New Yorker*'s Pauline Kael) and the Sarrisites (partisans of *The Village Voice*'s Andrew Sarris). The Sarrisites fought for *Shoah*, an eight-hour Holocaust documentary that Kael had panned in print weeks earlier, while the Paulettes pushed for *Ran*. Kael argued that *Shoah* belonged in the separate category for documentaries, but when the Sarrisites refused to back down, the Paulettes pressed on and eventually even threatened to throw their votes behind lowbrow kiddie laffer *Pee-Wee's Big Adventure*. Ultimately, *Ran* prevailed on the third ballot with 30 points, followed by 24 for *Purple Rose of Cairo*, 24 for *Prizzi's Honor* and 19 for *Shoah*. *Shoah* settled for the documentary award as a consolation prize.

Meantime, at the Golden Globes derby, three films tied for having the most nominations: *Out of Africa*, *Prizzi's Honor* and *Witness*, the latter described by *Variety* as "a gentle, affecting story of star-crossed lovers limited within the fascinating Amish community."

Prizzi's Honor knocked off the competish in four races: Best Comedy or Musical Picture, Best Director (John Huston), Best Actor (Jack Nicholson) and Best Actress (Kathleen Turner as a secret hired gun who has a dalliance with Nicholson). None of its victors was present, however.

Carl Reiner accepted on Nicholson's behalf, saying, "He's probably at a basketball game." In fact, Nicholson was en route

> # *Witness* scored a shocking triumph at the writers' guild.

to New York to accept his Best Actor award from the Gotham crix two days later.

The biggest champ among drama contenders was *Out of Africa*, which claimed three trophies, including Best Drama Picture, Best Supporting Actor (Klaus Maria Brandauer) and Best Score (John Barry). When accepting the top prize, producer/director Sydney Pollack thanked Universal for "the enormous courage it took to make this film." Backstage, he told the press that he was "flabbergasted" by the commercial success of the pic, which had already grossed $40 million.

Kiss of the Spider Woman's William Hurt was considered the front-runner for Best Drama Actor, but he was usurped by Jon Voight, who had recently scored a career comeback as an escaped convict in *Runaway Train*. Voight read from a prepared statement at the podium: "I am so humbly thankful that I can portray suffering souls in whom you can see a small light of God."

"Hattie McDaniel, here it is!" shrieked Whoopi Goldberg (*The Color Purple*) as she waved her Globe for Best Drama Actress in the air, thereby drawing a parallel to it and the Oscar won by the black supporting star of *Gone With the Wind* in 1939.

"This is the stuff you dream about," she added, then thanked Steven Spielberg for "pulling something out of me I didn't know I was capable of."

Whoopi Goldberg threw a hissy fit on Spielberg's behalf when the Oscar bids were announced and he wasn't listed among the 11 nominees for *The Color Purple*. She denounced academy voters as "a small bunch of people with small minds who chose to ignore the obvious." Others were outraged, too, and accused academy members of being jealous over Spielberg's financial success, which included producing 1985's top grosser *Back to the Future*. "Anyone who says that envy didn't affect Spielberg's chances would be crazy," Peter Bogdanovich said.

> ## *Variety* said Best Actress Geraldine Page gave "the perf of a lifetime" in *Bountiful*.

"Ironically, this has happened before," *Variety* noted, "in 1975 when *Jaws* was nominated for Best Picture but the young director was left out." Spielberg responded graciously, telling the *L.A. Times*, "I have no bone to pick with the academy. I support the nominations." Privately, however, he was reported to be crestfallen.

Spielberg wreaked his revenge at the directors' guild awards, where he was among the five contenders voted on by the org's 7,800 members, who ended up disagreeing with the 231 directors in the film academy.

When Spielberg won, the crowd at the Beverly Hilton gasped and he said at the podium, "I'm floored by this. If some of you are making a statement, thank God, and I love you for it. I never won anything before."

The *L.A. Times* called the victory "a direct slap at the academy," since guild members voted after the Oscar noms were announced.

The Color Purple's scribe Menno Meyjes was among the nominees competing for the Writers Guild of America awards held two weeks later, but the winners of the prize for Best Adapted Screenplay turned out, as predicted, to be Richard Condon and Janet Roach of *Prizzi's Honor*.

A shocker occurred in the race for Best Original Screenplay, however, when Woody Allen (*Purple Rose of Cairo*), Tom Benedeck (*Cocoon*) and Robert Zemeckis and Bob Gale (*Back to the Future*) lost to Earl W. Wallace (*Witness*).

Witness's surprising kudos strength was evidenced among the Oscar noms when it tied *Prizzi's Honor* for having the second most (8); *Out of Africa* tied *The Color Purple* for the lead (11). In addition to the Spielberg snub, other previous 1985 award champs were also overlooked: Vanessa Redgrave, Norma Aleando, John Gielgud and the *Lost in America* scribes.

"The guild's award to Mr. Spielberg makes the Oscar race more unpredictable," said *The New York Times*. "Only twice since the guild award was instituted in 1948 has the winner failed to collect the Oscar a few weeks later. Never before has the winner of the Directors Guild of America award failed to be nominated for an Oscar.

"This year there is consensus on only two likely winners," the paper added. "The 79-year-old director John Huston is the favorite for Best Director. He has been in frail health for several years, yet he managed to make a movie whose vitality was marveled at by critics. His daughter is far and away the front-runner for Best Supporting Actress." Most other award forecasters agreed, noting that dual Huston victories should prove irresistible to voters since the outcome would mirror the 1948 Oscars when Huston won Best Director for *The Treasure of the Sierra Madre* and another family member, his father—Anjelica's grandfather Walter—claimed a trophy as supporting actor.

The Wall Street Journal insisted that the two Hustons "can't lose," but cited suspense surrounding most other races: "Excitement is higher this year, mostly because it's simply harder to guess who will walk away with the golden statuettes that screenwriter Herman Mankiewicz once used as doorjambs."

After sweeping the crix awards trifecta, Anjelica Huston claimed Best Supporting Actress trophy easily, beating a rival that *Chicago Sun-Times* critic Roger Ebert thought might prove a spoiler—Oprah Winfrey—although he was betting on Huston, too. The victor accepted her statuette, saying, "This means a lot to me since it comes from a role in which I was directed by my father. And I know it means a lot to him."

In the race for Best Supporting Actor, Ebert wrote in *Movieline*, "Don Ameche will win for his high-spirited old guy in *Cocoon*. The role came in Ameche's 50th year as an active motion picture actor. If he doesn't, the dark horse is Klaus Maria Brandauer. In fact, both (rival nominees) Eric Roberts and William Hickey have predicted to me that Ameche will be the winner." *The*

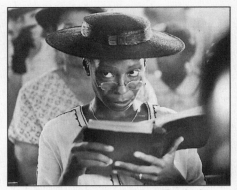

Globe champ Whoopi Goldberg denounced the "small minds" of Oscar voters for again snubbing Steven Spielberg, who was hailed by the DGA. *The Color Purple* ended up as Oscar's biggest loser.

Wall Street Journal disagreed, foreseeing a win for Gotham film crix and National Board of Review champ Klaus Maria Brandauer (*Out of Africa*).

When Ameche won, he was given a standing ovation as he headed to the stage where he addressed voters, saying, "You have given to me your recognition, you've given to me your love, you've given to me—and I hope I have earned—your respect. For all these, I am deeply grateful."

Backstage, *Variety* asked the champ about his plans, but he "admitted that since completing *Cocoon* more than a year and a half ago, he hasn't had another picture offer."

Suspense shrouded the Best Actor match-up, which pitted L.A. film crix honoree and first-time nominee William Hurt (*Kiss of the Spider Woman*) against Gotham crix and national society champ Jack Nicholson (*Prizzi's Honor*), who'd scored two previous Oscars over seven nominations. *The Wall Street Journal* said, "Nicholson is a slight favorite," but Roger Ebert was betting on Hurt, although warned, "The dark horse is James Garner as a crusty small-town pharmacist who falls in love with Sally Field in *Murphy's Romance*." Hurt didn't plan to attend the ceremony, but he told *Esquire* that Steven Spielberg "told me it was a big deal and I should go."

When he won, Hurt said at the podium,

"I didn't expect to be here, so I don't know what I'm going to say." He caught his breath, then added, "I'm very proud to be an actor."

With national society victor Vanessa Redgrave and Gotham crix champ Norma Aleandro out of the Best Actress contest, only National Board of Review winner Whoopi Goldberg and L.A. crix choice Meryl Streep were left among 1985 awardees. "The smart bet is Geraldine Page," insisted the *Journal*. *Variety* had praised Page for giving "the performance of a lifetime" in *The Trip to Bountiful*, which scribe Horton Foote had adapted from his 1953 Broadway play about an old woman who makes "a moving and memorable journey across the Gulf Coast to return to Bountiful, the town where she was born and raised." Roger Ebert went "out on a limb," however, and predicted Goldberg, saying, "My reason is a romantic one: I think audiences were genuinely moved, many of them to tears, by her performance."

If Page had lost her eighth career Oscar bid, she would have surpassed Peter O'Toole and Richard Burton as the biggest loser in the kudos' history, but she prevailed. The news caught her off guard, though. Out in the audience, she scrambled to find the shoes that she had kicked off earlier, then raced to the podium, where she thrust the statuette in the air and told the audience, "This is Horton Foote's fault!"

Meryl Streep's loss might have been an ominous omen for *Out of Africa*'s later chance at Best Picture, but the film did well in the crafts categories, claiming victories for cinematography, sound, art direction and music score. The *Journal* had said that the contest for Best Adapted Screenplay was "up for grabs," but *Out of Africa*'s Kurt Luedtke seized the trophy. In the showdown over Best Original Screenplay, the trio of *Witness* scribes repeated their writers' guild victory.

OUT OF AFRICA' LEADS OSCAR'S SAFARI

BEST PICTURE

Pic Bags 7 Awards; Hurt, Page, Pollack, A. Huston, Ameche Win; Indies Shine

Out of Africa was the runner-up for Best Picture at the L.A. crix vote, but emerged victorious at the Globes and Oscars.

When it came time to bestow the prize for Best Director, Oscarcast cameras showed a nervous John Huston seated in the audience with an oxygen tank. The cameras soon switched to Sydney Pollack, however, when he was declared the winner and raced toward the stage, stopping en route to shake Steven Spielberg's hand.

Variety declared the outcome "a shock," but, once revealed, it presaged *Out of Africa*'s next victory—Best Picture—bringing its kudos tally to seven. Producer/helmer Pollack returned to the podium to cop his second statuette and said, "This is a wonderful evening for all of us."

It turned out to be a terrible evening for *The Color Purple*. When it lost all of its 11 bids, it tied *The Turning Point* as the biggest loser in Oscar lore.

Backstage later, a reporter asked Pollack about *Purple*'s historic snub. "It's a difficult spot you've put me in," he confessed. "I don't want to put a damper on the evening by trying to speculate on an undiplomatic question with an undiplomatic answer." Instead, he addressed his own experience, adding, "It was a strange night. I didn't know what to expect. There was no consistency leading into the awards. It was a wide-open ball game. I thought Mr. Huston would get it."

When a victorious Geraldine Page bounded into the press room, she shouted,

"Yea for geriatrics!" Calming herself, she showed off her golden boy and said, "I don't know what made it slide into my welcoming arms this way, but I know what got me nominated. I did a damned good job. I don't want to stop now. It's just getting interesting."

A much more subdued William Hurt told the media that he was "surprised" that he, like Geraldine Page, had won an Oscar for an independent movie. *Variety* reported, "He stated that it was important that indies are going as far as they are, since it gives filmmakers a greater range of expression."

Indie pix gained a wider range of attention two days before the Oscars when the trade organization of the indie market, the Independent Feature Project/West, bestowed its first awards—the Independent Spirit prizes, which were voted on by the org's 800 members. At the debut presentation, the *L.A. Daily News* reported, "There was not just a certain spirit of satisfaction in the air, but more—an electric hum of excitement at a pitch not even reached two nights later at the Dorothy Chandler Pavilion."

Winner of the first Best Picture trophy was *After Hours*, Martin Scorsese's first film in a decade that didn't star Robert De Niro. Produced independently for $3 million and distributed by Warner Bros., it was described by *Variety* as "a nightmarish black comedy about one rough night in the life of a mild-mannered New York computer programmer (scrambling) through the anarchic, ever-treacherous streets of SoHo."

As a result of a tie vote, Scorsese shared the prize for Best Director with Joel Coen of *Blood Simple*, a Best Picture loser that had received the Grand Jury Prize at the U.S. Film Festival last year. (This year's fest champ *Smooth Talk* was an also-ran, too.) *Blood Simple* star M. Emmet Walsh was honored as Best Actor for his portrayal of a sleazy hit man who double-crosses his client.

The Trip to Bountiful made up for its defeat in the top race with two kudos, too:

The new Indie Spirits' first Best Picture champ was Martin Scorsese's *After Hours*, "a nightmarish black comedy," said *Variety*, starring Griffin Dunne and Teri Garr.

Best Actress for Geraldine Page and Best Screenplay for Horton Foote.

Kiss of the Spider Woman was bequeathed a Special Distinction prize for being the best feature of foreign origin or coproduction (U.S./Brazil).

The winner of the Grand Jury Prize at this year's U.S. Film Festival, *Smooth Talk*, was based on a Joyce Carol Oates story about a 15-year-old girl's sexual awakening and starred Laura Dern and Treat Williams. Recipient of the laurels for best documentary was *Private Conversations*, "a candid, behind-the-scenes glimpse of the making of Dustin Hoffman's TV version of *Death of a Salesman*," said *Variety*.

Winners claimed $2,500 and a Baccarat crystal obelisk plus 50,000 feet of 35mm film stock (best feature champ) and a Super 16mm camera (best documentary). Theater box office receipts grew 40 percent over last year, pooling $100,000.

"Films and skiing split the attention of many of the predominantly young visitors to this former mining town turned resort," *Variety* reported about the scene at Park City, Utah. "The intimate nature of the town, which basically consists of one main street and surrounding clusters of condominiums, lent itself to coincidental meetings, impromptu drinks and meals and plenty of new contacts."

LOS ANGELES FILM CRITICS ASSOCIATION

Winners were announced on December 14, 1985. Awards were presented on January 23, 1986, at the Westwood Marquis Hotel in Los Angeles.

BEST PICTURE
▪ *Brazil*

BEST DIRECTOR
▪ Terry Gilliam, *Brazil*

BEST ACTOR
▪ William Hurt, *Kiss of the Spider Woman*

BEST ACTRESS
▪ Meryl Streep, *Out of Africa*

BEST SUPPORTING ACTOR
▪ John Gielgud, *Plenty, The Shooting Party*

BEST SUPPORTING ACTRESS
▪ Anjelica Huston, *Prizzi's Honor*

BEST SCREENPLAY
▪ Terry Gilliam, Charles McKeown, Tom Stoppard, *Brazil*

BEST CINEMATOGRAPHY
▪ David Watkin, *Out of Africa*

BEST MUSIC SCORE
▪ Toru Takemitsu, *Ran*

BEST FOREIGN FILM (TIE)
▪ *Ran* (Japan)
▪ *The Official Story* (Argentina)

BEST EXPERIMENTAL/INDEPENDENT FILM
▪ *Fear of Emptiness*, Rosa Von Praunheim

NEW GENERATION AWARD
▪ Laura Dern

LIFETIME ACHIEVEMENT AWARD
▪ Akira Kurosawa

SPECIAL AWARD
▪ Claude Lanzmann, *Shoah*

NATIONAL BOARD OF REVIEW

The board declared a Best Picture and Foreign Film of the year, then listed its remaining favorites according to highest scores. The vote results were announced on December 16, 1985. Awards were presented on January 27, 1986, at the Japan Society in New York.

BEST PICTURE
▪ *The Color Purple*
Out of Africa
The Trip to Bountiful
Witness
Kiss of the Spider Woman
Prizzi's Honor
Back to the Future
The Shooting Party
Blood Simple
Dreamchild

BEST DIRECTOR
▪ Akira Kurosawa, *Ran*

BEST ACTORS
▪ Raul Julia, William Hurt, *Kiss of the Spider Woman*

BEST ACTRESS
▪ Whoopi Goldberg, *The Color Purple*

BEST SUPPORTING ACTOR
▪ Klaus Maria Brandauer, *Out of Africa*

BEST SUPPORTING ACTRESS
▪ Anjelica Huston, *Prizzi's Honor*

BEST FOREIGN FILM
▪ *Ran* (Japan)
The Official Story (Argentina)
When Father Was Away on Business (Yugoslavia)
La Chèvre (France)
The Home and the World (India)

NEW YORK FILM CRITICS CIRCLE

Winners were announced on December 18, 1985. Awards were presented on January 26, 1986, at Sardi's restaurant in New York.

BEST PICTURE
- *Prizzi's Honor*

BEST DIRECTOR
- John Huston, *Prizzi's Honor*

BEST ACTOR
- Jack Nicholson, *Prizzi's Honor*

BEST ACTRESS
- Norma Aleandro, *The Official Story*

BEST SUPPORTING ACTOR
- Klaus Maria Brandauer, *Out of Africa*

BEST SUPPORTING ACTRESS
- Anjelica Huston, *Prizzi's Honor*

BEST SCREENPLAY
- Woody Allen, *The Purple Rose of Cairo*

BEST CINEMATOGRAPHY
- David Watkin, *Out of Africa*

BEST DOCUMENTARY
- *Shoah*

BEST FOREIGN FILM
- *Ran* (Japan)

NATIONAL SOCIETY OF FILM CRITICS

Winners were announced on January 2, 1986.

BEST PICTURE
- *Ran* (Japan)

BEST DIRECTOR
- John Huston, *Prizzi's Honor*

BEST ACTOR
- Jack Nicholson, *Prizzi's Honor*

BEST ACTRESS
- Vanessa Redgrave, *Wetherby*

BEST SUPPORTING ACTOR
- John Gielgud, *Plenty, The Shooting Party*

BEST SUPPORTING ACTRESS
- Anjelica Huston, *Prizzi's Honor*

BEST SCREENPLAY
- Albert Brooks, Monica Johnson, *Lost in America*

BEST CINEMATOGRAPHY
- Takao Saito, Masaharu Ueda, Asakazu Nakai, *Ran*

BEST DOCUMENTARY
- *Shoah*, Claude Lanzmann

GOLDEN GLOBES

Nominations were announced on January 2, 1986. Awards were presented on January 24 at the Beverly Hilton Hotel in Los Angeles. The ceremony was broadcast nationally via syndication.

BEST DRAMA PICTURE
- *Out of Africa*
The Color Purple
Kiss of the Spider Woman
Runaway Train
Witness

BEST COMEDY OR MUSICAL PICTURE
- *Prizzi's Honor*
Back to the Future
A Chorus Line
Cocoon
The Purple Rose of Cairo

BEST DIRECTOR
- John Huston, *Prizzi's Honor*
Richard Attenborough, *A Chorus Line*
Sydney Pollack, *Out of Africa*
Steven Spielberg, *The Color Purple*
Peter Weir, *Witness*

BEST ACTOR, DRAMA
- Jon Voight, *Runaway Train*
Harrison Ford, *Witness*

Gene Hackman, *Twice in a Lifetime*
William Hurt, *Kiss of the Spider Woman*
Raul Julia, *Kiss of the Spider Woman*

BEST ACTRESS, DRAMA
- Whoopi Goldberg, *The Color Purple*
Anne Bancroft, *Agnes of God*
Cher, *Mask*
Geraldine Page, *The Trip to Bountiful*
Meryl Streep, *Out of Africa*

BEST ACTOR, COMEDY OR MUSICAL
- Jack Nicholson, *Prizzi's Honor*
Michael J. Fox, *Back to the Future*
Jeff Daniels, *The Purple Rose of Cairo*
Griffin Dunne, *After Hours*
James Garner, *Murphy's Romance*

BEST ACTRESS, COMEDY OR MUSICAL
- Kathleen Turner, *Prizzi's Honor*
Rosanna Arquette, *Desperately Seeking Susan*
Glenn Close, *Maxie*
Mia Farrow, *The Purple Rose of Cairo*
Sally Field, *Murphy's Romance*

BEST SUPPORTING ACTOR
- Klaus Maria Brandauer, *Out of Africa*
Joel Grey, *Remo Williams*
John Lone, *Year of the Dragon*
Eric Roberts, *Runaway Train*
Eric Stoltz, *Mask*

BEST SUPPORTING ACTRESS
- Meg Tilly, *Agnes of God*
Sonia Braga, *Kiss of the Spider Woman*
Anjelica Huston, *Prizzi's Honor*
Amy Madigan, *Twice in a Lifetime*
Kelly McGillis, *Witness*
Oprah Winfrey, *The Color Purple*

BEST SCREENPLAY
- Woody Allen, *The Purple Rose of Cairo*
Richard Condon, Janet Roach, *Prizzi's Honor*
William Kelley, Earl K. Wallace, *Witness*
Kurt Luedtke, *Out of Africa*
Robert Zemeckis, Bob Gale, *Back to the Future*

BEST SONG
- "Say You, Say Me," *White Nights*

"The Power of Love," *Back to the Future*
"Rhythm of the Night," *The Last Dragon*
"A View to a Kill," *A View to a Kill*
"We Don't Need Another Hero," *Mad Max: Beyond Thunderdome*

BEST FOREIGN FILM
- *The Official Story* (Argentina)
Colonel Redl (Hungary)
Ran (Japan)
When Father Was Away on Business (Yugoslavia)
A Year of the Quiet Sun (Poland)

Winners

BEST SCORE
- John Barry, *Out of Africa*

CECIL B. DEMILLE AWARD
- Barbara Stanwyck

U.S. FILM FESTIVAL (SUNDANCE)

The festival was held January 17–26, 1986, at Park City, Utah.

GRAND JURY PRIZE
(FEATURE)
- *Smooth Talk*, Joyce Chopra
(DOCUMENTARY)
- *Private Conversations*, Christian Blackwood

HONORABLE MENTION
(FEATURE)
- *Desert Hearts*, Donna Deitch
(YOUTH COMEDY)
- *Seven Minutes in Heaven*, Linda Feferman
(DOCUMENTARY)
- *Las Madres: The Mother of the Plaza de Mayo*, Susana Munoz, Lourdes Portillo

DIRECTORS GUILD OF AMERICA

Awards were presented on March 8, 1986, at the Beverly Hilton Hotel in Los Angeles.

BEST DIRECTOR
- Steven Spielberg, *The Color Purple*

Ron Howard, *Cocoon*

John Huston, *Prizzi's Honor*

Sydney Pollack, *Out of Africa*

Peter Weir, *Witness*

ROBERT B. ALDRICH AWARD
- George Sidney

GOLDEN JUBILEE AWARD
- Federico Fellini

D. W. GRIFFITH AWARD
- Joseph L. Mankiewicz

WRITERS GUILD OF AMERICA

Nominations were announced on February 9, 1986. Awards were presented on March 21 at the Beverly Hilton Hotel in Los Angeles and Hunter College in New York.

BEST ORIGINAL SCREENPLAY
- *Witness*, Earl W. Wallace, William Kelley

Back to the Future, Robert Zemeckis, Bob Gale

Cocoon, Tom Benedeck, story by David Saperstein

Mask, Anna Hamilton Phelan

The Purple Rose of Cairo, Woody Allen

BEST ADAPTED SCREENPLAY
- *Prizzi's Honor*, Richard Condon, Janet Roach, based on the novel by Richard Condon

Agnes of God, John Pielmeier, based on his play

The Color Purple, Menno Meyjes, based on the novel by Alice Walker

Out of Africa, Kurt Luedtke, based on books by Isak Dinesen, Judith Thurman, and Errol Trzebinski

The Trip to Bountiful, Horton Foote, based on his play

MORGAN COX AWARD
- Arthur Orloff

VALENTINE DAVIES AWARD
- Ronald Austin

LAUREL AWARD
- Waldo Salt

INDEPENDENT SPIRIT

Awards were presented on March 22, 1986, at the 385 North restaurant in Los Angeles.

BEST FEATURE
- *After Hours*

Blood Simple

Smooth Talk

The Trip to Bountiful

BEST DIRECTOR (TIE)
- Joel Coen, *Blood Simple*
- Martin Scorsese, *After Hours*

Joyce Chopra, *Smooth Talk*

Peter Masterson, *The Trip to Bountiful*

BEST ACTOR
- M. Emmet Walsh, *Blood Simple*

Ruben Blades, *Crossover Dreams*

Tom Bower, *Wildrose*

Treat Williams, *Smooth Talk*

BEST ACTRESS
- Geraldine Page, *The Trip to Bountiful*

Rosanna Arquette, *After Hours*

Laura Dern, *Smooth Talk*

Lori Singer, *Trouble in Mind*

BEST SCREENPLAY
- Horton Foote, *The Trip to Bountiful*

Joel Coen, Ethan Coen, *Blood Simple*

Tom Cole, *Smooth Talk*

Joseph Minion, *After Hours*

Winners

BEST CINEMATOGRAPHY
- Toyomichi Kurita, *Trouble in Mind*

REEL GOLD AWARD
- David Puttnam

SPECIAL DISTINCTION
- *Kiss of the Spider Woman*

ACADEMY AWARDS

Nominations were announced on February 5, 1986. Awards were presented on March 24 at the Dorothy Chandler Pavilion in Los Angeles. The ceremony was telecast by ABC.

BEST PICTURE
- *Out of Africa*
- *The Color Purple*
- *Kiss of the Spider Woman*
- *Prizzi's Honor*
- *Witness*

BEST DIRECTOR
- Sydney Pollack, *Out of Africa*
- Hector Babenco, *Kiss of the Spider Woman*
- John Huston, *Prizzi's Honor*
- Akira Kurosawa, *Ran*
- Peter Weir, *Witness*

BEST ACTOR
- William Hurt, *Kiss of the Spider Woman*
- Harrison Ford, *Witness*
- James Garner, *Murphy's Romance*
- Jack Nicholson, *Prizzi's Honor*
- Jon Voight, *Runaway Train*

BEST ACTRESS
- Geraldine Page, *The Trip to Bountiful*
- Anne Bancroft, *Agnes of God*
- Whoopi Goldberg, *The Color Purple*
- Jessica Lange, *Sweet Dreams*
- Meryl Streep, *Out of Africa*

BEST SUPPORTING ACTOR
- Don Ameche, *Cocoon*
- Klaus Maria Brandauer, *Out of Africa*
- William Hickey, *Prizzi's Honor*
- Robert Loggia, *Jagged Edge*
- Eric Roberts, *Runaway Train*

BEST SUPPORTING ACTRESS
- Anjelica Huston, *Prizzi's Honor*
- Margaret Avery, *The Color Purple*
- Amy Madigan, *Twice in a Lifetime*
- Meg Tilly, *Agnes of God*
- Oprah Winfrey, *The Color Purple*

BEST ORIGINAL SCREENPLAY
- William Kelley, Earl W. Wallace, Pamela Wallace, *Witness*
- Woody Allen, *The Purple Rose of Cairo*
- Aida Bortnik, Luis Puenzo, *The Official Story*
- Bob Gale, Robert Zemeckis, *Back to the Future*
- Terry Gilliam, Charles McKeown, Tom Stoppard, *Brazil*

BEST ADAPTED SCREENPLAY
- Kurt Luedtke, *Out of Africa*
- Richard Condon, Janet Roach, *Prizzi's Honor*
- Horton Foote, *The Trip to Bountiful*
- Menno Meyjes, *The Color Purple*
- Leonard Schrader, *Kiss of the Spider Woman*

BEST SONG
- "Separate Lives," *White Nights*, Stephen Bishop
- "Miss Celie's Blues (Sister)," *The Color Purple*, Quincy Jones, Lionel Richie, Rod Temperton
- "The Power of Love," *Back to the Future*, Johnny Colla, Chris Hayes, Huey Lewis
- "Say You, Say Me," *White Nights*, Lionel Richie
- "Surprise, Surprise," *A Chorus Line*, Marvin Hamlisch, Edward Kleban

BEST FOREIGN-LANGUAGE FILM
- *The Official Story* (Argentina)
- *Angry Harvest* (Federal Republic of Germany)
- *Colonel Redl* (Hungary)
- *Three Men and a Cradle* (France)
- *When Father Was Away on Business* (Yugoslavia)

Winners

BEST ART DIRECTION
- Stephen Grimes, Josie MacAvin, *Out of Africa*

BEST CINEMATOGRAPHY
- David Watkin, *Out of Africa*

BEST COSTUME DESIGN
- Emi Wada, *Ran*

BEST DOCUMENTARY
(FEATURE)
- *Broken Rainbow*, Maria Florio, Victoria Mudd

(SHORT SUBJECT)
- *Witness to War: Dr. Charlie Clements*, David Goodman

BEST FILM EDITING
- Thom Noble, *Witness*

BEST MAKEUP
- Zoltan Elek, Michael Westmore, *Mask*

BEST ORIGINAL MUSIC SCORE
- John Barry, *Out of Africa*

SCIENTIFIC OR TECHNICAL AWARDS
(Scientific and Engineering Award)
- IMAX Systems; Ernest Nettman, E. F. Nettman & Associates; Edward Phillips, Carlos de Mattos, Matthews Studio Equipment; Myron Gordin, Joe P. Crookham, Jim Drost, David Crookham, Musco Mobile Lighting

(Technical Achievement Award)
- Harrison and Harrison Optical Engineers; Larry Barton, Cinematography Electronics; Alan Landaker, Burbank Studios; David W. Spencer

BEST SHORT FILM
(ANIMATED)
- *Anna & Bella*, Cilia Van Dijk

(LIVE ACTION)
- *Molly's Pilgrim*, Jeff Brown, Chris Pelzer

BEST SOUND
- Gary Alexander, Peter Handford, Chris Jenkins, Larry Stensvold, *Out of Africa*

BEST SOUND EFFECTS EDITING
- Charles L. Campbell, Robert Rutledge, *Back to the Future*

BEST VISUAL EFFECTS
- David Berry, Scott Farrar, Ralph McQuarrie, Ken Ralston, *Cocoon*

JEAN HERSHOLT HUMANITARIAN AWARD
- Charles "Buddy" Rogers

HONORARY AWARDS
- Paul Newman
- Alex North
- John H. Whitney, Sr.

SCREEN ACTORS GUILD

LIFETIME ACHIEVEMENT AWARD
- Paul Newman, Joanne Woodward

▪ 1986 ▪

Platoon *Ambushes* Hannah

"*Hannah and Her Sisters* now has to be considered the year's front-runner for any and all available laurels," insisted the *L.A. Herald Examiner* soon after two crix groups announced their winners.

The Los Angeles Film Critics Association was the first to name it Best Picture. "*Hannah and Her Sisters* is one of Woody Allen's great films," declared *Variety*. "Indeed, he makes nary a misstep from beginning to end in charting the amorous affiliations of three sisters and their men over a two-year period. Its structure is a successful mixture of outright comedy, rueful meditations and sexual complications."

Helmer/scribe Oliver Stone was "shocked" by *Platoon's* sudden success at the Globes, DGA, Indie Spirits and Oscars after it was shunned by the crix kudos.

Allen reaped the additional prize of Best Screenplay, eclipsing David Lynch for *Blue Velvet*, but Lynch ended up claiming the Best Director accolade over Allen for his violent, quirky drama about a small-town do-gooder who tries to solve a murder mystery when he discovers a severed ear. The pic heralded the career comeback of *Easy Rider* star Dennis Hopper, who, said *Variety*, "creates a flabbergasting portrait of unrepentant, irredeemable evil" as a sadistic drug dealer. The crix named Hopper Best Supporting Actor, also citing his role as an alcoholic basketball fan in *Hoosiers*.

The crix's Best Actor choice was Bob Hoskins (*Mona Lisa*) as "an earnest, dumb ex-con who gets a job driving a tall, slender black whore (*Cathy Tyson*) to her various assignations and finds himself falling in love with her," said *Variety*. According to official crix org records, only Tyson was named Best Supporting Actress, but the *L.A. Times* article reporting on the vote outcome noted that she tied with Dianne Wiest, who portrayed a neurotic caterer in *Hannah*.

The *L.A. Times* said that "the biggest surprise in the major categories" occurred in the contest for Best Actress, which was claimed by Sandrine Bonnaire as a hitch-hiking drifter in the French import *Vagabond*, also winner of Best Foreign Film. Bonnaire beat out Marlee Matlin, a hearing-impaired actress making her film debut as a spunky deaf student in the screen adaptation of the 1980 Tony Award–winning play *Children of a Lesser God*.

The kudos were presented six weeks after the winners were announced and just one day after the unveiling of the Directors Guild of America nominees. In his acceptance speech for the crix's director prize, David Lynch "made a passing crack at the guild for leaving his name off the list," noted the *Herald Examiner*. New York–based Woody Allen skipped the luncheon, but apologized to the crix in a message relayed by *Hannah* star Barbara Hershey. "I don't go anywhere," Allen said. "I don't like hotels and strange showers scare me."

In past years when Allen was honored by the New York film critics, he usually snubbed their local fetes, too, but the Gothamites hailed him again anyway, endorsing *Hannah* as Best Picture nine years after they backed *Annie Hall*. *Hannah* won the vote resoundingly by a 50-to-27 score over *Platoon*, Oliver Stone's graphic depiction of the Vietnam War that was just then reaching theaters. Allen beat Stone for the director's palm, too (42 points to 30), earning his fifth career prize from the org as a helmer and scribe, thereby becoming the Gothamites' second biggest honoree, after Jack Nicholson. *Hannah* star Dianne Wiest won Best Supporting Actress (42 points), topping Cathy Tyson (*Mona Lisa*) and Mary Elizabeth Mastrantonio as the hyper-sexed girlfriend of an aspiring pool shark (Tom Cruise) in *The Color of Money* (14 points each).

The Color of Money marked the triumphant screen return of Paul Newman, who, *Variety* said, gave "an exceptional performance" while updating his 1961 role as a boozy pool shark in *The Hustler*. Newman lost the crix's Best Actor accolade to Bob Hoskins, however, by a narrow margin (35 to 41).

An even closer vote decided the Best Actress contest when Sissy Spacek (29 points) prevailed as a husband-shooting hothead in the film adaptation of the Pulitzer Prize–winning Broadway play *Crimes of the Heart*. Runner-up was Kathleen Turner (27), who gave "her richest performance yet," said *Vogue*'s Molly Haskell, as a housewife given the chance to redirect her life when she travels back in time.

Daniel Day-Lewis had a breakout year with critically lauded roles as a punk who has a steamy gay affair in *My Beautiful Laundrette* and as a snobbish aristocrat who has a detached heterosexual liaison in *A Room with a View*. He won Best Supporting Actor for both roles by a 33-to-16 tally over Andy Garcia as a chic cocaine dealer in *8 Million Ways to Die*. *Laundrette* (30 points) pulled off an upset for Best Screenplay over *Hannah* (28).

Village Voice gossipmeister Michael Musto reported on the awards presentation:

> ## Woody Allen skipped the L.A. crix homage to *Hannah* "because strange showers scare me."

"The New York Film Critics Circle shindig at Sardi's was such a tease, as most of the British winners didn't show, because they were in Britain, nor did Woody Allen, because he was uptown. Still, the usual perverse fun was had."

The perversity was championed by Best Actor presenter Lynn Redgrave, who "earned a place on the dais at a Friars Club," said *Variety*, when she let loose with a barrage of profanity as she reminded the audience that she had tied Elizabeth Taylor for the Best Actress award 20 years earlier. "She wasn't here—but fuck her, really!" Redgrave exclaimed, then thanked the crix on Bob Hoskins' behalf "because you haven't shat on his work—for very good reason." Broadway thesp Kate Nelligan stood in for the winner "and did a cute Cockney accent parodying how Hoskins' acceptance speech might have sounded," reported *Variety*.

Best Supporting Actress Dianne Wiest subbed for Woody Allen, noting that she had starred in four of his pix to date. "We have a few laughs and some great lunches," she recalled about their collaboration.

Other than Wiest, Sissy Spacek was the only other winner in attendance. *Variety* groused, "Scheduling the event for the second year in a row in conflict with the Super Bowl was a bad move, exacerbated by the New York Giants' presence this time in the big game."

Variety also griped about the awards gala held by the National Board of Review two weeks later. "Event was glamorous," the tradepaper admitted, "but the Whitney Museum basement locale proved an infelicitous choice (compared to last year's Japan House site), with overcrowding, difficult sight lines toward the dais and uncomfortable folding chairs in the too-small lobby."

Winner attendance was excellent, however, including Best Actress Kathleen

Turner and Best Supporting Actress Dianne Wiest, who used "much the same speech she delivered at the recent N.Y. film critics' awards," *Variety* observed.

The event's reigning star was Best Actor Paul Newman, who accepted his trophy from Career Achievement Award honoree Jack Lemmon. Bestowing the prize, Lemmon praised Newman's "simplicity, his economy" as an actor and his "personal grace" as a man.

Missing from the gala were Best Director Woody Allen ("a predictable no-show," said *Variety*) and Best Supporting Actor Daniel Day-Lewis (*My Beautiful Laundrette, A Room with a View*), who was in France filming *The Unbearable Lightness of Being*.

Winner of Best Picture was *A Room with a View*, which *Variety* called "a thoroughly entertaining screen adaptation of novelist E. M. Forster's comedy of manners about the Edwardian English upper class at home and abroad."

The National Society of Film Critics also passed up the *Hannah* bandwagon, giving it the sole prize of Best Supporting Actress, which was claimed by Dianne Wiest (43 points) over costar Barbara Hershey (16). The org agreed with the Gothamites on Best Screenplay (*My Beautiful Laundrette* beat *Hannah* 40 to 34) and with both the Gothamites and Hollywooders on Best Actor (Bob Hoskins bested *The Fly*'s Jeff Goldblum 42 to 33). A surprise occurred in the Best Actress match-up when Kathleen Turner and Sandrine Bonnaire (15 points each) were surpassed by dark horse Chloe Webb (34) as the real-life groupie murdered by boyfriend Sid Vicious of the Sex Pistols in *Sid and Nancy*.

Blue Velvet swept the other four categories to tie *Tootsie, Nashville* and *Scenes from a Marriage* as the society's all-time champ. It reaped kudos for cinematography, Best Supporting Actor Dennis Hopper (topping Daniel Day-Lewis 36 to 17) and Best Director David Lynch (35) over surprise

runner-up Andrei Tarkovsky (13 points for the late Russian's final film, *The Sacrifice*). The vote breakdown for Best Picture: *Blue Velvet* (40), *Hannah and Her Sisters* (28) and *Platoon* (18).

The society released its award results on January 4, 1987, two weeks after the *Herald Examiner* declared that Woody Allen's latest release suddenly seemed to have an inevitable future date with all of the year's top kudos. At that point the paper added, "With no mainstream Hollywood drama arriving at the last minute to eclipse *Hannah*'s sheen, Allen stands to repeat his 1977 Oscar sweep for *Annie Hall*." *Platoon* had just then arrived in movie houses, but it hadn't yet developed the groundswell of support that it would gain over the year-end holiday season and in early January. As a war veteran who'd witnessed the horrors of the Vietnam conflict first hand, director/writer Oliver Stone packed the pic with such unvarnished grittiness that it triggered a firestorm of debate nationwide—and a stampede to theaters. *Time* featured it on its cover in early 1987 and declared, "*Platoon* the picture is now *Platoon* the phenomenon."

But *Platoon* was still building its momentum when the Golden Globe nominations were announced the first week of January. It nonetheless scored an impressive four bids, although the tally was one shy of the number earned by the two front-runners: *Hannah and Her Sisters* and recent Cannes Palme d'Or champ *The Mission*, director Roland Joffe's $23 million drama about 18th-century Jesuit missionaries in South America. Some pundits griped that *Blue Velvet* wasn't nommed for Best Drama Picture or Director, but Lynch was nommed for Best Screenplay and Dennis Hopper was listed among the rivals for Best Supporting Actor, competing against himself in *Hoosiers*.

Hannah won Best Comedy or Musical Picture easily, beating box office titan *Croc-*

> Kathleen Turner appeared to be the Oscar front-runner for *Peggy Sue Got Married.*

odile Dundee, which rebounded with a victory—for Best Actor Paul Hogan as a gung-ho crocodile hunter in Australia.

The biggest upsets occurred in the races for Best Drama Actor and Actress. Harrison Ford, William Hurt and Paul Newman were usurped for the male laurels by Bob Hoskins (*Mona Lisa*). Marlee Matlin (*Children of a Lesser God*) didn't expect to win the actress contest, so the hearing-impaired star was confused when her name was announced. Only when the people at her banquet table gave her a standing ovation did she realize that she had won. Then she headed to the podium where she communicated in sign language, saying, "I can't believe it! I'm shaking!"

It was the showdown over Best Drama Picture that involved the most drama, though. *Platoon* faced just the kind of romantic, foreign-set film that Globe voters usually endorsed: *A Room with a View*.

When *Platoon* won, *Variety* reported that its victory was "a popular choice with the cheering Golden Globe audience and provided the emotional high point of the evening." The *Herald Examiner* recalled Stone's 10-year struggle to get the film made when the paper commented on the audience response, noting that "the loudest cheering came from the gathered film producers and studio executives, who, to a man, have slammed their doors in Stone's face for the past decade. Boy, you could drown in that teaspoonful of sincerity that engulfed the room."

Stone admitted that he was "shocked" when he won. "I really think that through this award you're acknowledging the Vietnam veteran," he said at the podium. "And I think what you're saying is that you now understand what happened over there and that it shouldn't happen again. This award really does belong to the Vietnam veterans, both living and dead."

Platoon ended up capturing the most

medals—three—including gold for Stone as Best Director. Its third accolade went to Best Supporting Actor Tom Berenger for portraying a menacing, scar-faced sergeant.

The next day the *L.A. Times* said, "If the Golden Globes are any sort of Oscar indicator, Oliver Stone better send his tuxedo straight back to the dry cleaners and start rehearsing his acceptance speech for the next round of awards."

The next round was actually the award bestowed by the Directors Guild of America, which had forecast the equivalent Oscar winner 35 times in the past 38 years. One of the few exceptions had occurred just last year when Steven Spielberg (*The Color Purple*) was awarded the DGA's top prize but wasn't even nommed at the Academy Awards, which ended up honoring Sydney Pollack (*Out of Africa*). This year observers wondered if the various directors' awards were out of whack again, since David Lynch scored helmer's prizes from both the L.A. crix and National Society of Film Critics, but wasn't even nommed by the guild.

> ## Four of the five films up for Best Picture at the Oscars were indies.

Variety reported, "While Stone was regarded as a DGA favorite going in, his triumph was not necessarily a *fait accompli*. Woody Allen had to be a strong contender. And not to be discounted was the depth of sentiment for Randa Haines (*Children of a Lesser God*) as the first American woman ever to achieve a nomination." The only other female nommed in the past was Italian helmer Lina Wertmüller (*Seven Beauties*), who had lost to John Avildsen (*Rocky*) in 1976.

Stone prevailed as the new winner and accepted his accolade "in a hushed voice," observed *Variety*.

"This is really a Cinderella story," Stone said of his victory, then described his awe at being in the same room with "the giants of my youth." Moments later two of those "giants" took over the stage as Joe Mankiewicz bestowed the special D.W.

Griffith Award upon Elia Kazan.

Platoon was nominated by the writers' guild, but Stone faced several formidable foes in the lineup for Best Original Screenplay. One of them was himself—he was up for *Salvador*, too—but he also faced Woody Allen (*Hannah*), Neil Jordan and David Leland (*Mona Lisa*) and David Lynch (*Blue Velvet*).

When Woody Allen won, it marked his third career victory (after *Annie Hall* and *Broadway Danny Rose*) over 13 nominations, but he wasn't present to receive the honor, even though it was announced ahead of time that he was guaranteed to get the separate, special Laurel Award for lifetime accomplishment. As expected, Ruth Prawer Jhabvala snagged Best Adapted Screenplay for *A Room with a View*.

Variety described the guild's simultaneous black-tie fetes on both coasts as "exuding equal measures of gravity and good spirits in light of the four week-old writers strike against CBS and ABC."

Oliver Stone was nominated against himself in three categories at the Independent Spirit Awards held two days later—and just two days before the Oscars. *Platoon* and *Salvador* were up for Best Picture, Director and Screenplay, competing against *Blue Velvet* and David Lynch.

Platoon and Stone ended up picking up what *Variety* called "a fresh burst of pre-Oscar momentum" by scoring four awards: Best Picture, Best Director, Best Screenplay and Best Cinematography.

In thanks, Stone told the crowd, "Independence is the greatest single treasure we have," then he became nostalgic. He recalled how he produced his first indie pic, *Seizure*, for $160,000 in 1972 and was "forced to flee creditors in Canada and to smuggle his master print out of the country in the dead of night," *Variety* said.

Stone's *Salvador* won Best Actor for star James Woods, whose victory didn't seem to bother loser Dennis Hopper, who was

DAILY **VARIETY** DAILY

215 No. 2   28 Pages   Hollywood, California 90028, Monday, March 9, 1987   Newspaper Second Class P.O. Entry   50 Cents

DGA FUELS STONE'S OSCAR DRIVE

FM Winds 7th Edition On High Note Thanks Largely Emerging HV Territories
By HY HOLLINGER

Pinsker's promotion becomes permanent as soon as formally approved by the UACI board.

Hussanein's resignation sent the weekend came as no surprise to the industry. He was reported ready in

HASSANEIN RESIGNS UACI CIRCUIT POST

Allen Pinsker has been named interim successor to Salah M. Hassanein as president of the 1795-screen theater division of United Artists Communications Inc., now controlled by Denver-based Tele-Communications Co.

Pinsker's promotion becomes permanent as soon as formally ap-

tional," "great," "record," "feverish," "phenomenal."

Realistically, however, some moderation could be detected — especially among the "theatrical-only" sellers who, although keeping to the

'Platoon' Director Captures Top Guild Award; ABC Wins Three Nods, Paces Networks
By WILL TUSHER

Oliver Stone, director and writer of the critically acclaimed and boxoffice smash "Platoon," was named top director of 1986 by the Directors Guild of America Saturday night.

nearly certain to win an Oscar in the same category.

Only three times in the 38-year history of the DGA awards has that recognition gone to a director who did not also earn an Oscar for his

Stone accepted his DGA prize "in a hushed voice," calling his victory for *Platoon* "a Cinderella story" as he addressed the "giants of my youth."

absorbed in watching a college basketball playoff game on a portable TV he brought to the ceremony.

Woods accepted his prize with a reference to the upcoming Oscar race in which he was pitted against a sentimental favorite. He said, "I'm so pleased that Paul Newman doesn't do independent films."

Blue Velvet star Isabella Rossellini wreaked revenge by claiming Best Actress over *Salvador* star Elpidia Carillo. When the daughter of triple Oscar champ Ingrid Bergman prevailed, *Variety* said that "the aura and imminence of the Academy Awards permeated the ceremony."

At the upcoming Oscars, four of the five pics up for Best Picture were indie productions: *Platoon, Hannah and Her Sisters, Children of a Lesser God* and *A Room with a View*. The only studio pic in the lineup was *The Mission* (Warner Bros.). "Small was in with academy voters this year," *Variety* observed when the noms were announced. *Platoon* and *A Room with a View* led with the most (eight), followed by *Hannah* and *The Mission* (seven).

Previous outrage over David Lynch not being nominated for Best Director at the Golden Globes now gave way to outrage that he did score an Oscar bid when *Blue Velvet* failed to make the Best Picture lineup. Lynch bumped out Randa Haines, whose *Children of a Lesser God* was up for top pic. Women's advocacy groups were furious.

Shortly before the Oscar ceremony approached, *Platoon* was clearly on the march. It blasted *Crocodile Dundee* out of its perch as the number-one box-office draw in America and its star Charlie Sheen made the cover of *People* magazine. *The New York Times* declared, "If the Hollywood grapevine is correct—and it usually is— *Platoon* will sweep the Oscars. *Blue Velvet*, the favorite 1986 movie of younger film critics, got only one Oscar nomination." *Platoon*'s chief competish was *Hannah and Her Sisters*, but the movie was already more than a year old. The last time that a pre-October release won Best Picture was nine years earlier—*Annie Hall*.

On Oscar night, Allen was exactly where he was when *Annie Hall* swept the awards in 1977: playing jazz clarinet at Michael's Pub in New York City. Also in the greater Gotham area was Paul Newman, who didn't want to face what might happen if he lost his seventh Best Actor bid: he'd tie Peter O'Toole and Richard Burton as the biggest loser in Oscar history. Newman told the Associated Press that his pursuit of the statuette was "like chasing a beautiful woman for 80 years. Finally, she relents and you say, 'I am terribly sorry. I'm tired.'

"I'm superstitious," he added. "I've been there six times and lost. Maybe if I stay away, I'll win."

Virtually all Oscar pundits declared that Newman had a lock on the race even though he'd lost all three critics' awards to Bob Hoskins and the Golden Globe to Harrison Ford (who didn't snag an Oscar bid). Only one pundit disagreed—*L.A. Times* critic Sheila Benson, who picked Indie Spirit victor James Woods.

"It would be just like the academy to give Newman a real award after they pensioned him off with a consolation prize last year," noted Andrew Sarris of *The Village Voice*. The 62-year-old Newman appeared grateful for the honorary 1985 Oscar, but said, "I'm certainly glad this didn't come wrapped in a gift certificate to Forest Lawn" and added his hope that "my best work is in front of me and not behind me."

When Newman won Best Actor this year, his award was accepted by producer/director Robert Wise, who never got to finish reading Newman's prepared

After six previous losses, Paul Newman (left, with Tom Cruise in *The Color of Money*) snubbed the Oscars, telling the AP, "I'm superstitious. Maybe if I stay away, I'll win."

statement because he was interrupted twice by award presenter Bette Davis. "I'd like to congratulate Paul," Davis said when she barged in the first time. "I'm sure he's listening. He's not here tonight. And this award, Paul, is long overdue."

Since Newman was married to past Best Actress winner Joanne Woodward (*The Three Faces of Eve*, 1957), he and his wife became only the second married couple to win Oscars as actors—after Laurence Olivier and Vivien Leigh.

A pair of lovers was about to become Oscar champs, too.

Best Actor loser William Hurt (*Children of a Lesser God*) was tapped to present this year's Best Actress award since he won the male honors last year. Among the contenders was his live-in lover and *Children* costar Marlee Matlin, who had pulled off a dramatic upset at the Golden Globes.

When the Oscar nominations came out in February, *New York Times* critic Vincent Canby said that he thought Kathleen Turner was out front, but warned about "a dark horse, Marlee Matlin." Few pundits thought that she had the inside track to win, but the *Voice*'s Andrew Sarris was one of the few who picked her as "a long shot" over front-runners Turner and Sissy Spacek.

When Hurt opened the envelope, he announced Matlin's name, smiled at her and signed the name of the winner for the TV camera. Her victory set a record: at age 21, she became the youngest winner of a top thesp award.

"I love you," she said to everyone, gushing and beaming at the podium.

Variety's Army Archerd called Matlin's victory "one of the most dramatic moments" that he had ever witnessed at the kudos and added, "The audience at home could not see the warm and long embrace she received from William Hurt off stage."

Backstage, she told reporters, "I feel that a lot of deaf people are jumping up and down. There are changes being made in society, not just for white Anglo-Saxons, but for everyone."

Platoon suffered no defeats in the top two acting races since it didn't have nominees there, but it did have two thesps in the ranks of contenders for Best Supporting Actor: Willem Dafoe and Tom Berenger as good and bad sergeants. Berenger had won the Golden Globe, but most Oscar oddsmakers—including editors of the *New York Times* and the *L.A. Times*—were betting on L.A. film crix and national society champ Dennis Hopper, who was up, surprisingly, for *Hoosiers*, not *Blue Velvet*. New York film crix honoree Daniel Day-Lewis was not nommed.

The winner turned out to be an upset— Michael Caine as Mia Farrow's philandering husband in *Hannah and Her Sisters*. Caine wasn't present to accept the kudos because he was in the Bahamas on the set of *Jaws IV*.

"Dianne Wiest seems to have the supporting actress category to herself," said *The New York Times*, noting her previous honors from the Gotham crix, the national society and the National Board of Review. The *Hannah* star's only competish seemed to be Maggie Smith who won the Golden Globe for portraying a bumbling chaperone in *A Room with a View*.

When Wiest won, she exclaimed, "Gee, this isn't like what I imagined it would be in the bathtub!" then thanked "my dearest friend"—agent Sam Cohn.

A few minutes later, as Wiest headed toward the media rooms backstage, she remembered someone she forgot to thank. *Variety* reported, "Before the crash of reporters was able to shout her a question, Dianne Wiest firmly put her statuette down and rushed to the mike to exclaim, 'I left Woody out of my speech!' "

Hannah pulled off a shocking victory next when it claimed the prize for Best Original Screenplay over *Platoon*, bringing its trophy tally to three. *Hannah* suddenly seemed to have a serious shot at Best Picture—along with *A Room with a View*, which copped Best Adapted Screenplay, Best Art Direction and Best Costumes. *Room*'s wins, insisted *Variety*, "kept the film in contention."

Meantime, *Platoon* reaped only two early wins: editing and sound.

"It was only in the waning minutes of the overtime three-hour and 20-minute show, that *Platoon* managed to nose out *Hannah* and *Room with a View*," observed *Variety*. That's when Oliver Stone won Best Director.

Stone repeated his Golden Globe speech on stage, but, once backstage, the former Viet vet elaborated, telling reporters that writing and directing *Platoon* was "a cathartic experience." He said that he felt sorry for other vets who "want to fight the war over, who want to revise it, who think we could have won if the politicians and the media hadn't sold us out. I don't agree with that at all."

A few moments later, *Platoon* won Best Picture, too.

Variety ran the banner headline the next day: "*PLATOON* COMES HOME A WINNER." The article noted that the independent film had come a long way, too, having "fought its way to the top of last night's Academy Awards" after a decade-long battle to reach the screen and early defeats at the critics' film awards.

A few months earlier, *Variety* reported, "With the increased attention and b.o. success that American indies have received over the past year, the buzz was obviously out in Hollywood that Park City was a scene to make."

"The U.S. Film Festival was more tightly packed than the white powder on the encircling hills" this year, said the *Herald Examiner*, describing the Rocky Mountains scene where 30,000 visitors arrived to view the 80 features and documentaries unspooled over ten days.

Winner of the Grand Jury Prize for features was *Waiting for the Moon*, billed by its director as "an imaginary biography" starring Linda Basset as Gertrude Stein and Linda Hunt as Alice B. Toklas. It shared the prize with *The Trouble with Dick*, which *Variety* described as "a sly sex comedy about a sci-fi novelist's writer's block." Best Documentary was *Sherman's March*, which *Variety* called the director/writer's "wry account of his search for women in the South."

Afterward, *Variety* added, "There was certainly no doubting the considerable success of the festival," which the tradepaper called "one of the most useful and impressively organized festivals going."

▪ 1986 ▪

NATIONAL BOARD OF REVIEW

The board declared a Best Picture and Foreign Film of the year, then listed its remaining favorites according to highest scores. The vote results were announced on December 11, 1986. Awards were presented on February 9, 1987, at the Whitney Museum in New York.

BEST PICTURE
▪ *A Room with a View*
Hannah and Her Sisters
My Beautiful Laundrette
The Fly
Stand by Me
The Color of Money
Children of a Lesser God
Round Midnight
Peggy Sue Got Married
The Mission

BEST DIRECTOR
▪ Woody Allen, *Hannah and Her Sisters*

BEST ACTOR
▪ Paul Newman, *The Color of Money*

BEST ACTRESS
▪ Kathleen Turner, *Peggy Sue Got Married*

BEST SUPPORTING ACTOR
▪ Daniel Day-Lewis, *My Beautiful Laundrette, A Room with a View*

BEST SUPPORTING ACTRESS
▪ Dianne Wiest, *Hannah and Her Sisters*

BEST FOREIGN FILM
▪ *Otello* (Italy)
Miss Mary (Argentina)
Ginger and Fred (Italy)
Ménage (France)
Men (Federal Republic of Germany)

CAREER ACHIEVEMENT AWARD
▪ Jack Lemmon

LOS ANGELES FILM CRITICS ASSOCIATION

Winners were announced on December 13, 1986. Awards were presented on January 29, 1987, at the Westwood Marquis Hotel in Los Angeles.

BEST PICTURE
▪ *Hannah and Her Sisters*

BEST DIRECTOR
▪ David Lynch, *Blue Velvet*

BEST ACTOR
▪ Bob Hoskins, *Mona Lisa*

BEST ACTRESS
▪ Sandrine Bonnaire, *Vagabond*

BEST SUPPORTING ACTOR
▪ Dennis Hopper, *Blue Velvet, Hoosiers*

BEST SUPPORTING ACTRESS
- Cathy Tyson, *Mona Lisa**

BEST SCREENPLAY
- Woody Allen, *Hannah and Her Sisters*

BEST CINEMATOGRAPHY
- Chris Menges, *The Mission*

BEST MUSIC SCORE
- Herbie Hancock, Dexter Gordon, *'Round Midnight*

BEST FOREIGN FILM
- *Vagabond* (France), Agnès Varda

BEST EXPERIMENTAL/INDEPENDENT FILM
- *Magdalena Criaga,* Nina Menkes
- *He Stands in the Desert Counting the Seconds of His Life,* Jonas Mekas

NEW GENERATION AWARD
- Spike Lee, *She's Gotta Have It*

LIFETIME ACHIEVEMENT AWARD
- John Cassavetes

SPECIAL AWARDS
- Rafigh Pooya, Fox International Theatre
- Chuck Workman, Directors Guild of America, *Precious Images*

NEW YORK FILM CRITICS CIRCLE

Winners were announced on December 15, 1986. Awards were presented on January 25, 1987, at Sardi's restaurant in New York.

BEST PICTURE
- *Hannah and Her Sisters*

BEST DIRECTOR
- Woody Allen, *Hannah and Her Sisters*

BEST ACTOR
- Bob Hoskins, *Mona Lisa*

---

*Winner according to L.A.F.C.A. records. The *L.A. Times* reported on December 15, 1986 that Dianne Wiest (*Hannah and Her Sisters*) also won in a tie vote.

BEST ACTRESS
- Sissy Spacek, *Crimes of the Heart*

BEST SUPPORTING ACTOR
- Daniel Day-Lewis, *My Beautiful Laundrette, A Room with a View*

BEST SUPPORTING ACTRESS
- Dianne Wiest, *Hannah and Her Sisters*

BEST SCREENPLAY
- Hanif Kureishi, *My Beautiful Laundrette*

BEST CINEMATOGRAPHY
- Tony Pierce-Roberts, *A Room with a View*

BEST DOCUMENTARY
- *Marlene*

BEST FOREIGN FILM
- *The Decline of the American Empire* (Canada)

NATIONAL SOCIETY OF FILM CRITICS

Winners were announced on January 4, 1987.

BEST PICTURE
- *Blue Velvet*

BEST DIRECTOR
- David Lynch, *Blue Velvet*

BEST ACTOR
- Bob Hoskins, *Mona Lisa*

BEST ACTRESS
- Chloe Webb, *Sid and Nancy*

BEST SUPPORTING ACTOR
- Dennis Hopper, *Blue Velvet*

BEST SUPPORTING ACTRESS
- Dianne Wiest, *Hannah and Her Sisters*

BEST SCREENPLAY
- Hanif Kureishi, *My Beautiful Laundrette*

BEST CINEMATOGRAPHY
- Fregderick Elmes, *Blue Velvet*

BEST DOCUMENTARY
- *Marlene*, Maximillian Schell

U.S. FILM FESTIVAL (SUNDANCE)

The festival was held January 16–25, 1987, at Park City, Utah.

GRAND JURY PRIZE
(FEATURE)
- *Waiting for the Moon*, Jill Godmilow
- *The Trouble with Dick*, Gary Walkow

(DOCUMENTARY)
- *Sherman's March*, Ross McElwee

SPECIAL JURY PRIZE
(FEATURE)
- *Working Girls*, Philip Hartman

(DOCUMENTARY)
- *Chile: When Will It End?*, David Bradbury

BEST CINEMATOGRAPHY
(FEATURE)
- *No Picnic*, Peter Hutton

(DOCUMENTARY)
- *Chile: When Will It End?*, David Bradbury

SPECIAL DISTINCTION
- *Sullivan's Pavilion*, Fred G. Sullivan

GOLDEN GLOBES

Nominations were announced on January 5, 1986. Awards were presented on January 31 at the Beverly Hilton Hotel in Los Angeles. The ceremony was broadcast nationally via syndication.

BEST DRAMA PICTURE
- *Platoon*

Children of a Lesser God
The Mission
Mona Lisa
A Room with a View
Stand by Me

BEST COMEDY OR MUSICAL PICTURE
- *Hannah and Her Sisters*

Crimes of the Heart

Crocodile Dundee
Down and Out in Beverly Hills
Little Shop of Horrors
Peggy Sue Got Married

BEST DIRECTOR
- Oliver Stone, *Platoon*

Woody Allen, *Hannah and Her Sisters*
James Ivory, *A Room with a View*
Roland Joffe, *The Mission*
Rob Reiner, *Stand by Me*

BEST ACTOR, DRAMA
- Bob Hoskins, *Mona Lisa*

Harrison Ford, *The Mosquito Coast*
Dexter Gordon, *'Round Midnight*
William Hurt, *Children of a Lesser God*
Jeremy Irons, *The Mission*
Paul Newman, *The Color of Money*

BEST ACTRESS, DRAMA
- Marlee Matlin, *Children of a Lesser God*

Julie Andrews, *Duet for One*
Anne Bancroft, *'night, Mother*
Farrah Fawcett, *Extremities*
Sigourney Weaver, *Aliens*

BEST ACTOR, COMEDY OR MUSICAL
- Paul Hogan, *Crocodile Dundee*

Matthew Broderick, *Ferris Bueller's Day Off*
Jeff Daniels, *Something Wild*
Danny DeVito, *Ruthless People*
Jack Lemmon, *That's Life!*

BEST ACTRESS, COMEDY OR MUSICAL
- Sissy Spacek, *Crimes of the Heart*

Julie Andrews, *That's Life!*
Melanie Griffith, *Something Wild*
Bette Midler, *Down and Out in Beverly Hills*
Kathleen Turner, *Peggy Sue Got Married*

BEST SUPPORTING ACTOR
- Tom Berenger, *Platoon*

Michael Caine, *Hannah and Her Sisters*
Dennis Hopper, *Blue Velvet*
Dennis Hopper, *Hoosiers*
Ray Liotta, *Something Wild*

BEST SUPPORTING ACTRESS
- Maggie Smith, *A Room with a View*

Linda Kozlowski, *Crocodile Dundee*

Mary Elizabeth Mastrantonio, *The Color of Money*

Cathy Tyson, *Mona Lisa*

Dianne Wiest, *Hannah and Her Sisters*

BEST SCREENPLAY
- Robert Bolt, *The Mission*

Woody Allen, *Hannah and Her Sisters*

David Leland, Neil Jordan, *Mona Lisa*

David Lynch, *Blue Velvet*

Oliver Stone, *Platoon*

BEST SONG
- "Take My Breath Away," *Top Gun*

"Glory of Love," *The Karate Kid, Part II*

"Life in a Looking Glass," *That's Life!*

"Somewhere Out There," *An American Tail*

"Sweet Freedom," *Running Scared*

"They Don't Make Them Like They Used to," *Tough Guys*

BEST FOREIGN FILM
- *The Assault* (Netherlands)

Betty Blue (France)

Ginger and Fred (Italy)

Otello (Italy)

Three Men and a Cradle (France)

Winners

BEST SCORE
- Ennio Morricone, *The Mission*

CECIL B. DEMILLE AWARD
- Anthony Quinn

DIRECTORS GUILD OF AMERICA

Nominations were announced on January 28, 1987. Awards were presented on March 7 at the Sheraton Premiere Hotel in Los Angeles.

BEST DIRECTOR
- Oliver Stone, *Platoon*

Woody Allen, *Hannah and Her Sisters*

Randa Haines, *Children of a Lesser God*

James Ivory, *A Room with a View*

Rob Reiner, *Stand by Me*

D. W. GRIFFITH AWARD
- Elia Kazan

WRITERS GUILD OF AMERICA

Awards were presented on March 26, 1987, at the Beverly Hilton Hotel in Los Angeles and the Saint nightclub in New York.

BEST ORIGINAL SCREENPLAY
- *Hannah and Her Sisters,* Woody Allen

Blue Velvet, David Lynch

Mona Lisa, Neil Jordan, David Leland

Platoon, Oliver Stone

Salvador, Oliver Stone, Richard Boyle

BEST ADAPTED SCREENPLAY
- *A Room with a View*, Ruth Prawer Jhabvala, based on the novel by E. M. Forster

Children of a Lesser God, Hesper Anderson, Mark Medoff, based on the play by Mark Medoff

Down and Out in Beverly Hills, Paul Mazursky, Leon Capetano, based on the film *Boudu Sauve des Eaux* by Rene Fauchois

Little Shop of Horrors, Howard Ashman, based on the play and previous film

Stand by Me, Raynold Gideon, Bruce A. Evans, based on the novella *The Body* by Stephen King

MORGAN COX AWARD
- Jean Butler

VALENTINE DAVIES AWARD
- William Froug

LAUREL AWARD
- Woody Allen

INDEPENDENT SPIRIT

Nominations were announced on February 19, 1987. Awards were presented on March 28 at the 385 North restaurant in Los Angeles.

BEST FEATURE

- *Platoon*
Blue Velvet
Down by Law
On Valentines Day
Salvador
Stand by Me

BEST FIRST FEATURE

- *She's Gotta Have It*
Belizaire the Cajun
A Great Wall
Hoosiers
True Stories

BEST DIRECTOR

- Oliver Stone, *Platoon*
Jim Jarmusch, *Down by Law*
David Lynch, *Blue Velvet*
Rob Reiner, *Stand by Me*
Oliver Stone, *Salvador*

BEST ACTOR

- James Woods, *Salvador*
Roberto Benigni, *Down by Law*
Willem Dafoe, *Platoon*
Dennis Hopper, *Blue Velvet*
Victor Love, *Native Son*

BEST ACTRESS

- Isabella Rossellini, *Blue Velvet*
Elpidia Carillo, *Salvador*
Patti Charbonneau, *Desert Hearts*
Laura Dern, *Blue Velvet*
Tracy Camila Johns, *She's Gotta Have It*

BEST SCREENPLAY

- Oliver Stone, *Platoon*
Raynold Gideon, Bruce Evans, *Stand by Me*
David Lynch, *Blue Velvet*
Oliver Stone, Richard Boyle, *Salvador*
Peter Wang, Shirley Sun, *A Great Wall*

Winners

BEST CINEMATOGRAPHY

- Bob Richardson, *Platoon*

SPECIAL DISTINCTION

- *A Room with a View*

ACADEMY AWARDS

Nominations were announced on February 11, 1986. Awards were presented on March 30 at the Dorothy Chandler Pavilion in Los Angeles. The ceremony was telecast by ABC.

BEST PICTURE

- *Platoon*
Children of a Lesser God
Hannah and Her Sisters
The Mission
A Room with a View

BEST DIRECTOR

- Oliver Stone, *Platoon*
Woody Allen, *Hannah and Her Sisters*
James Ivory, *A Room with a View*
Roland Joff, *The Mission*
David Lynch, *Blue Velvet*

BEST ACTOR

- Paul Newman, *The Color of Money*
Dexter Gordon, *'Round Midnight*
Bob Hoskins, *Mona Lisa*
William Hurt, *Children of a Lesser God*
James Woods, *Salvador*

BEST ACTRESS

- Marlee Matlin, *Children of a Lesser God*
Jane Fonda, *The Morning After*
Sissy Spacek, *Crimes of the Heart*
Kathleen Turner, *Peggy Sue Got Married*
Sigourney Weaver, *Aliens*

BEST SUPPORTING ACTOR

- Michael Caine, *Hannah and Her Sisters*
Tom Berenger, *Platoon*
Willem Dafoe, *Platoon*
Denholm Elliott, *A Room with a View*
Dennis Hopper, *Hoosiers*

BEST SUPPORTING ACTRESS

- Dianne Wiest, *Hannah and Her Sisters*
Tess Harper, *Crimes of the Heart*
Piper Laurie, *Children of a Lesser God*
Mary Elizabeth Mastrantonio, *The Color of Money*
Maggie Smith, *A Room with a View*

BEST ORIGINAL SCREENPLAY

- Woody Allen, *Hannah and Her Sisters*

Richard Boyle, Oliver Stone, *Salvador*

John Cornell, Paul Hogan, Ken Shadie, *Crocodile Dundee*

Hanif Kureishi, *My Beautiful Laundrette*

Oliver Stone, *Platoon*

BEST ADAPTED SCREENPLAY

- Ruth Prawer Jhabvala, *A Room with a View*

Hesper Anderson, Mark Medoff, *Children of a Lesser God*

Bruce A. Evans, Raynold Gideon, *Stand by Me*

Beth Henley, *Crimes of the Heart*

Richard Price, *The Color of Money*

BEST SONG

- "Take My Breath Away," *Top Gun*, Giorgio Moroder, Tom Whitlock

"Glory of Love," *The Karate Kid, Part II*, Peter Cetera, David Foster, Diane Nini

"Life in a Looking Glass," *That's Life*, Leslie Bricusse, Henry Mancini

"Me," *Little Shop of Horrors*, Howard Ashman, Alan Menken

"Somewhere Out There," *An American Tail*, James Horner, Barry Mann, Cynthia Weil

BEST FOREIGN-LANGUAGE FILM

- *The Assault* (Netherlands)

Betty Blue (France)

The Decline of the American Empire (Canada)

My Sweet Little Village (Czechoslovakia)

"38" (Austria)

Winners

BEST ART DIRECTION

- Brian Ackland-Snow, Gianni Quaranta, Elio Altamura, Brian Savegar, *A Room with a View*

BEST CINEMATOGRAPHY

- Chris Menges, *The Mission*

BEST COSTUME DESIGN

- Jenny Beavan, John Bright, *A Room with a View*

BEST DOCUMENTARY

(FEATURE)

- *Artie Shaw: Time Is All You've Got*, Brigitte Berman
- *Down and Out in America*, Joseph Feury, Milton Justice

(SHORT SUBJECT)

- *Women—For America, for the World*, Vivienne Verdon-Roe

BEST FILM EDITING

- Claire Simpson, *Platoon*

BEST MAKEUP

- Stephan Dupuis, Chris Walas, *The Fly*

BEST ORIGINAL MUSIC SCORE

- Herbie Hancock, *'Round Midnight*

SCIENTIFIC OR TECHNICAL AWARDS

(Scientific and Engineering Award)

- Bran Ferren, Charles Harrison, Kenneth Wisner, Associates and Ferren; Richard Bejamin Grant, Ron Grant, Auricle Control Systems; Anthony D. Bruno, John L. Baptista, MGM Laboratories; Manfred G. Michelson, Bruce W. Keller, Technical Film Systems; Robert Greenberg, Joel Hynek, Eugene Mamut, R/Greenberg Associates; Alfred Thumin, Elan Lipschitz, Darryl A. Armour, Richmark Camera Service; Richard Edlund, Gene Whiteman, David Grafton, Mark West, Jerry Jeffress, Bob Wilcox, Boss Film Corp.; William L. Fredrick, Hal Needham, Fritz Sennheiser

(Technical Achievement Award)

- Lee Electric; Peter D. Parks, Oxford Scientific Films; Matt Sweeney, Lucinda Strub; Alexander Bryce, Burbank Studios; John L. Baptista, MGM Laboratories; Hal Landaker, Alan Landaker, Burbank Studios; David W. Samuelson, William B. Pollard; Carl Holmes, Bran Ferren

BEST SHORT FILM

(ANIMATED)

- *A Greek Tragedy*, Willem Thijssen, Linda vagn Tulden

(LIVE ACTION)
- *Precious Images*, Chuck Workman

BEST SOUND
- Charles "Bud" Grenzbach, Simon Kaye, Richard Rogers, John K. Wilkinson, *Platoon*

BEST SOUND EFFECTS EDITING
- Don Sharpe, *Aliens*

BEST VISUAL EFFECTS
- Suzanne Benson, John Richardson, Robert Skotak, Stan Winston, *Aliens*

IRVING G. THALBERG AWARD
- Steven Spielberg

HONORARY AWARDS
- Ralph Bellamy
- E. M. (A1) Lewis

SCREEN ACTORS GUILD

LIFETIME ACHIEVEMENT AWARD
- Nanette Fabray

· 1987 ·

Late Reign for Last Emperor

It turned into a nail-biting, jaw-dropping race when virtually every kudos group bet on a different horse—and, in the end, the dark one came through.

But the 1987 derby began with "few surprises," said *Variety* when the paper reported on the historic breakthrough scored by *Broadcast News*, the newest movie from director/writer James L. Brooks, who had swept nearly all the top races in 1983 with *Terms of Endearment*.

Broadcast News reaped more awards than any movie in the history of the New York Film Critics Circle. Its five victories spanned all of the top categories: Best Picture, Director (Brooks), Actor (Jack Nicholson), Actress (Holly Hunter) and Screenplay (Brooks). Nicholson's latest honor was his seventh from the Gotham crix over 19 years—more than twice the number awarded to any other actor.

Variety hailed *Broadcast News* as "enormously entertaining." The sendup of TV news programs starred Holly Hunter and Albert Brooks as a neurotic producer and reporter who square off against a well-coiffed anchor played by recent Oscar champ William Hurt. Nicholson appeared in a cameo as the network's haughty national news star.

Broadcast News won Best Picture handily with 42 points on the second ballot. Its nearest rival was John Huston's last film *The Dead* (26), which was based on a *Dubliners* short story by James Joyce about an Irish holiday dinner in 1904. Huston trailed James L. Brooks with 23 points to 25 in the directors' race and Huston's son Tony, who had penned the script, lost the screenplay prize to Brooks 13 to 46.

Holly Hunter earned 35 points on the second Best Actress poll, topping Christine Lahti (28) as an eccentric aunt who raises two wily nieces in *Housekeeping*. Nichol-

With five victories, *Broadcast News* (starring William Hurt and Holly Hunter) became the biggest winner in Gotham crix history.

son was cited for two other roles in addition to his turn in *Broadcast News:* as a havoc-wreaking devil in *The Witches of Eastwick* and a Depression bum in *Ironweed*. The runner-up was Michael Douglas, who had two hit pix in 1987 (*Fatal Attraction* and *Wall Street*), but the crix only listed his role described by *Variety* as "a megalomaniacal arbitrageur" in Oliver Stone's *Wall Street*. He lost by a 20-to-25 score on the third ballot.

The supporting races "provided the most surprises," said *Variety*. Morgan Freeman (44 points) prevailed as a caustic pimp in *Street Smart* over Sean Connery (22) as an incorruptible Irish cop in *The Untouchables*. Vanessa Redgrave (35 points) was honored for portraying the literary agent of British playwright Joe Orton in *Prick Up Your Ears* over Anjelica Huston as a young Irish mother in *The Dead* (27).

When the awards were bestowed at Sardi's, James L. Brooks's historic day of triumph turned into what he called "a nightmare."

The fete began well when he received his Best Picture plaque from veteran CBS newsman Walter Cronkite, who said of the film, "I really see it mostly as the truth. It's one whale of a movie. Certainly, Jim Brooks knows the broadcast news business."

But when actor/playwright Wallace Shawn took the podium to bestow Brooks's screenplay prize, he prattled on, giving what *Variety* described as "a rambling political speech right out of a '60s protest march."

"Shut up, you fool!" shouted the notoriously outspoken critic John Simon of *New York Magazine.*

Newhouse Newspapers critic Richard Freeman shouted back at Simon, "Fuck off, you asshole!"

The room fell silent while "there was a lot of looking away," reported *The New York Post.*

Then Shawn resumed his political treatise, this time without interruption.

Usual bad boy Jack Nicholson was well behaved, by comparison. "He apologized for being the only actor not in a play this year," the *Post* reported. "Both Holly Hunter and Supporting Actress winner Vanessa Redgrave were unable to attend owing to stage commitments, Hunter in Los Angeles, Redgrave in London."

Best Supporting Actor Morgan Freeman was present, however, and "expressed his thrill at 'sitting at the same table with Jack Nicholson!' " noted the *Post.*

Nicholson was among the honorees hailed by the L.A. crix two days after the Gotham crix announced their winners. Only his roles in *The Witches of Eastwick* and *Ironweed* were listed—not *Broadcast News.* Due to a tie vote, he shared the honor with Steve Martin, who *Variety* described as "a wild and crazy guy with a big nose and gift for gab" in *Roxanne,* an update of *Cyrano de Bergerac.*

Another tie occurred in the race for Best Actress, when Holly Hunter (*Broadcast News*) shared the laurels with Sally Kirkland, who starred in *Anna* as a Czech actress struggling to make it in America.

The L.A. crix agreed with the choice of Morgan Freeman (*Street Smart*) as Best Supporting Actor and Sean Connery as runner-up, but they chose a different Best Supporting Actress. Winner was Olympia Dukakis as Cher's doting mama in *Moonstruck* over Vanessa Redgrave (*Prick Up Your Ears*).

The remaining top three categories— Best Picture, Director and Screenplay— were claimed by John Boorman and his latest film, which was suffering from limited release after a management changeover at Columbia studio. *Hope and Glory* was the director/writer's recollection of his childhood in Britain during World War II— a small film that didn't seem to have broad b.o. appeal, but the crix rallied behind it just as they had rescued *Brazil* in 1985. As soon as they declared it Best Picture, Columbia doubled the number of theaters where it played—from 50 to 100—and scheduled it for wide national release two days after the Oscar noms were set to be announced on February 19.

L.A. crix to Columbia studio: Rescue best pic *Hope and Glory*!

Hope and Glory pulled off a Best Picture victory over another Columbia production that was getting overlooked in the corporate shuffle, too: *The Last Emperor,* Bernardo Bertolucci's $25 million drama about the fall of China's Manchu dynasty ("an exquisitely painted mural of 20th century Chinese history," said *Variety*). John Boorman beat James L. Brooks for Best Director and *Moonstruck*'s John Patrick Shanley for Best Screenplay.

At the L.A. crix awards luncheon, Boorman thanked the scribes for their support, but only after he tweaked them by reading some of the bad reviews they had given him in years past. "It's rather like the cops and criminals," he said of their relationship. "You know, finally, at the end of the day, all we have is each other. Now that you've finally seen the light, I forgive you for all the false arrests and those beatings in the cell."

Steve Martin tweaked the management of *Roxanne*'s studio—Columbia—when he accepted his Best Actor prize. "I especially want to thank Guy McElwaine, the president of Columbia, who gave the project the go," he said. "I want to thank Steve Sohmer, the next president of Columbia, who oversaw (the project) during the casting phase. I want to thank David Puttnam, the next president of Columbia, who was behind us all the way. And Dawn Steel, the new president of Columbia, who supervised the release on cassettes. I just hope that each of *you* will be as supportive when you're president of Columbia."

"Even Dawn Steel laughed," the *L.A. Times* said of the audience reax.

Sally Kirkland's prize came at a crucial time—in the midst of the most aggressive one-person campaign in the history of film kudos. She had recently bought a blitz of ads in *Variety*, stormed the TV talk-show circuit and sent letters to every member of the film academy. Hollywood cynics snickered at her brazenness, but when she was validated by the local crix, "she had to compose herself a couple of times while thanking them," reported the *L.A. Times*. In her acceptance speech, she told the crix that their honor came after "26 films, 40 TV shows and 150 plays."

John Boorman repeated his victories for Best Director and Screenplay when the National Society of Film Critics voted in early January, but runner-up *The Dead* rallied to beat *Hope and Glory* as Best Picture by a 44-to-37 score.

Steve Martin won Best Actor with 47 points, beating Albert Brooks (30), who also placed third in the supporting actor race for *Broadcast News*. Morgan Freeman (62 points) took the latter category over Sean Connery (26).

Surprises occurred in the other matchups when Best Actress was claimed by Emily Lloyd as a rebellious 16-year-old girl ("played with exasperating charm," said

> ## N.Y. crix interrupted their gala, shouting, "You fool!" and "You asshole!"

Variety) in the British import *Wish You Were Here*. She won with 37 points, followed by Diane Keaton (24) as a power-mad career woman suddenly saddled with rearing a one-year-old relative in *Baby Boom*. Vanessa Redgrave lost Best Supporting Actress by one point (32 to 33) to Kathy Baker as a hooker in *Street Smart*.

Knight-Ridder news agency reported that the voting "was free of the rancor that often flavors the annual proceedings," but nonetheless reported on some ugly asides. When Lillian Gish (*The Whales of August*) was suggested as a Best Actress candidate, Morris Dickstein of *The Partisan Review* snarled, "Remind me. What has D.W. Griffith directed lately?"

Lillian Gish was set to be honored twice by the National Board of Review with D.W. Griffith Awards—named in honor of the man who had produced and directed most of Gish's early silent film classics. Gish tied Holly Hunter for the Best Actress prize and was also supposed to receive a Lifetime Achievement Award, but the 87-year-old thesp skipped the kudos ceremony in late February after suffering a fall one month earlier. Helen Hayes stood in for Gish and told the crowd, "Lillian was bullied into staying home tonight, and I'm sure that doctor has been dismissed."

Also absent from the fete were Holly Hunter ("stuck in L.A. working in a play," said *Variety*) and Best Supporting Actor Sean Connery ("a U.S. tax exile," explained *The New York Post*). Attendees included Best Actor Michael Douglas, Best Supporting Actress Olympia Dukakis and the night's biggest winner—Steven Spielberg, who snagged Best Picture and Director for *Empire of the Sun*, the tale of a British boy stranded in Japan-occupied China during World War II.

"China was great," he said at the podium. "We shot there three months."

The fete was held the night before the

announcement of Oscar nominations. When Spielberg was asked by reporters to predict how *Empire* would fare, he said, "I have a strong feeling I won't be nominated . . . just a hunch."

Empire had not done well at the Golden Globes a few weeks earlier. It won nothing, although it did score a nomination for Best Drama Picture. Spielberg wasn't nommed for Best Director.

What pix led the Globes race surprised observers. *Broadcast News* tied *The Last Emperor* and *Moonstruck* for the most bids: five. The National Society of Film Critics' choice for Best Picture, *The Dead*, received none.

The winners turned out to be even *more* shocking.

"*The Last Emperor* reigned over the foreign press corps' Golden Globes despite tough competish," reported the Associated Press. It was voted Best Drama Picture over *Empire of the Sun* and *Fatal Attraction*. Bertolucci topped James L. Brooks and John Boorman for Best Director and Best Screenplay. *Emperor* was also honored for Best Music Score.

> *Emperor* reigned undefeated at the Oscars with nine victories.

Bertolucci thanked a witch doctor in Zanzibar, who had recently told him to return to America because good news awaited him there.

There was good news for Michael Douglas (*Wall Street*) when he beat Jack Nicholson (*Ironweed*) for Best Drama Actor. The Best Actress front-runner was Glenn Close as a psychotic who stalks a married man she had a fling with in b.o. blockbuster *Fatal Attraction*. The winner, however, turned out to be tireless awards campaigner Sally Kirkland (*Anna*), who shrieked, "You made my day, my week, my month, my year, my lifetime!"

Broadcast News was considered a shoo-in as Best Comedy or Musical Picture, but lost in a startling upset to *Hope and Glory*. *Broadcast News* suffered another defeat when Holly Hunter lost Best Actress to Cher as an accountant who falls for her fiancé's brother in *Moonstruck*.

"Looking like a debutante in a black velvet gown with nary a hint of décolleté or belly button, Cher answered the crowd's huge roar of approval for her award by comparing her fans to those of the New York Jets football team," observed the *L.A. Times*.

"They've taken so much crap for being my fans," she said. "But you guys have hung in there—and here we are!"

She thanked *Moonstruck*'s helmer, Norman Jewison, whom she called "the grumpiest old director in the whole world" and also thanked her friends, "who have taken so much crap from me."

Moonstruck also claimed the Best Supporting Actress prize for Olympia Dukakis, whose cousin Michael, governor of Massachusetts, was running for U.S. President. Fighting back tears, she said, "I think this is the year for the Dukaki!"

Broadcast News's William Hurt and *Roxanne*'s Steve Martin both suffered upsets when the statuette for Best Comedy/Musical Actor went to Robin Williams as a manic military deejay in *Good Morning, Vietnam*. He was in New York City on Globes night, hosting TV's *Saturday Night Live*.

When five-time nominee *Broadcast News* was shut out, the *L.A. Times* reported, "Whispers spread through the International Ballroom of the Beverly Hilton that perhaps the Hollywood Foreign Press Association had not understood enough about the American TV news industry to appreciate Brooks' film—a charge that several of the journalists shrugged off.

"The Oscars are up for grabs!" the paper added, but the Associated Press suggested that the Globes might have established a new front-runner: "The four trophies give *The Last Emperor* hope as Hollywood prepares to cast ballots for Academy Award nominees. The ballots are arriving this week."

But *The Last Emperor* and *Broadcast News* both suffered setbacks at the writers' guild awards, which were held in February—a month earlier than usual. The winner of Best Original Screenplay turned out to be John Patrick Shanley's *Moonstruck*.

In the race for Best Adapted Screenplay, dramas usually have an edge, which boded well for *The Untouchables* (David Mamet), and *Full Metal Jacket* (Stanley Kubrick, Michael Herr, Gustav Hasford) over laffers like *The Princess Bride* (William Goldman). It was Steve Martin's comedy *Roxanne* that triumphed, however.

The suspense surrounding the award results was nothing compared to the drama hovering over all of the writers in the industry. They were in the throes of a month-long strike against the Alliance of Motion Picture and Television Producers and negotiations were not going well.

Guild fete emcee Hal Kanter lightened the mood of the evening by joking about some of the demands that the guild had recently put on the table. One of them, he said, was: "Directors must read the script before making changes."

He marveled at how arduous the job of writing can be for some.

"Sometimes it takes a writer two or three days to rewrite a single line of dialogue," he said. "An actor can do it in just a few moments."

When the nominees for the Directors Guild of America kudos were announced, the front-runners all made the cut: Bernardo Bertolucci (*The Last Emperor*), James L. Brooks (*Broadcast News*), Lasse Hallstrom (*My Life as a Dog*), Adrian Lyne (*Fatal Attraction*) and Steven Spielberg (*Empire of the Sun*).

The race looked close between Bertolucci and Brooks—until the Oscar nominations were released prior to the polls closing for the DGA award. Surprisingly, the academy snubbed two helmers: Brooks and Spielberg.

Bertolucci claimed the DGA prize eas-

Shanley, Martin Exhibit Write Stuff At WGA Nods
By DAVE KAUFMAN

John Patrick Shanley, for "Moonstruck," and Steve Martin, for "Roxanne," were the winners of Writers Guild of America bigscreen scripting nods at the 40th annual awards bash held Friday night at the BevHilton.

A concurrent event was held by WGA East in N.Y. at Windows on the World. Current WG strike

Variety reported on the upsets scored by WGA winners Steve Martin (Roxanne) and John Patrick Shanley (Moonstruck).

---

ily, probably as a result of diminished competish.

"This is a very nice welcome to a new member of the DGA," said the Italian helmer, who chose an international theme for his acceptance. "In the darkness of movie theaters, there are no more national identities. There are no more classes. Maybe I'm an idealist, but I still see movie theaters as big cathedrals where people come to dream the same dream together."

Variety declared, "The Italian director now moves far out in front in the Oscar race."

The Last Emperor was out front with the most total noms, too—nine—which meant it was now the Best Picture fave. *USA Today* was stunned: "Just two months ago, during a media blitz capped by *Newsweek*'s cover story, the betting was that *Broadcast News* would be this year's Oscar picture." *Broadcast News* had the second-most Oscar noms over all—seven—but a Best Picture victory seemed unlikely, considering it hadn't scored a corresponding bid for Best Director.

All of the categories were "riddled with surprises," said *Variety*. Brooks and Spielberg were replaced in the directors' lineup by Adrian Lyne (*Fatal Attraction*) and Norman Jewison (*Moonstruck*). Both of their movies made the cut for Best Picture. *Moonstruck* was even within striking distance of winning, according to *USA Today*.

The Best Picture choice of the National Society of Film Critics, *The Dead*, reaped only a single nom—Best Adapted Screenplay. Steve Martin was snubbed twice. Not only was he overlooked for a Best Actor bid just as in 1984 after two crix orgs named him Best Actor for *All of Me*, but he failed to score a screenplay nomination—even though *Roxanne* had won a writers' guild award.

Something else was odd about the screenplay categories. *The Last Emperor*, which competed for Best Original Screenplay at the WGA, was placed in the Oscar showdown for Best Adapted Screenplay. It turned out to be a fortunate switch. *Emperor* might have lost the guild trophy to *Moonstruck*, but it struck gold on Oscar night. *Moonstruck* did, too.

Moonstruck began way out front in the race for Best Supporting Actress since Gotham crix champ Vanessa Redgrave didn't make the lineup. "Everyone seems agreed on Olympia Dukakis," said the *L.A. Times* just prior to awards night. "The sentimental runner-up would be Ann Sothern (*The Whales of August*)."

But with previous honors from the L.A. crix, the Golden Globes and the National Board of Review, Dukakis won easily. In her acceptance speech, she referred to her cousin, who was also on a winning streak—sweeping through the Democratic primaries with seeming ease. Army Archerd noted, "Among the lines that will be quoted in future Oscar histories will undoubtedly be Olympia Dukakis' 'OK, Michael, let's go!' "

Backstage later, *Variety* noted, "Olympia Dukakis answered more questions about her famous cousin, Michael, than she did about her award." After the Oscarcast, she followed up on a prearranged date she had made with him to connect by phone. Michael was in New York campaigning for the state primary and received her call at the same Manhattan restaurant where she had filmed scenes in *Moonstruck*.

Moonstruck was also up for the Best Actress trophy, although pundits were split on whether or not Cher could prevail. "Cher will be allowed to come into her own as Best Actress at last," insisted the *L.A. Times*. "The only upset lurking might come from dark horse Sally Kirkland." But *USA Today* disagreed, claiming that Golden Globe victor Cher was in a close race with L.A. and

"I have no confidence!" Oscar's Best Actress Cher confessed backstage where she posed with Best Actor Michael Douglas.

N.Y. crix champ Holly Hunter, and asked: "Might the two actresses split the 'comedy' vote, enabling someone else to win?" The paper thought the answer was yes and bet on Glenn Close (*Fatal Attraction*), adding, "It's her fourth nom and it doesn't hurt that Close's performance is terrific."

But Cher proved to be triumphant, receiving, noted *Variety*, "the biggest ovation of all" as she headed to the stage while wearing "a nearly transparent gown."

"Though daring in dress as usual, Cher was modest in acceptance of her first Academy Award," reported *Variety*. She said, "I don't think this means I am somebody, but I guess I'm on my way."

Backstage, she was asked by reporters: Would she have more confidence now that she had won? "I have no confidence," she said. "It's not about having confidence. It's about doing your job."

In the race for Best Supporting Actor, Morgan Freeman might have swept the crix kudos trifecta, but Globe champ Sean Connery "is as sure a bet as you can find," claimed the *L.A. Times*.

When he won, Connery received one of the night's seven standing ovations. At the podium, he addressed "ladies, gentlemen, friends and a few enemies," saying, "This is the 60th anniversary of these Academy Awards and I realized just the other day that my first one and only attendance was 30 years ago. Patience truly is a virtue." Backstage later, reporters asked him if he'd ever play James Bond again. "I'm too old for that now," he said.

Kirk Douglas was too nervous to attend the Oscars this year. "I was afraid if I was there, I would jinx Michael," he told Army Archerd. The senior Douglas watched the show at his son Peter's house after giving a pep talk to his other, nominated son: "I forewarned Michael to be prepared for any eventuality. I reminded him that when I was up for *Lust for Life*, they said I was a shoo-in, but Yul Brynner won for *The King and I*."

Then, later that night, Michael won— and Kirk cried.

At the podium, Michael dedicated his award to "my father, who I don't think ever missed one of my college productions." He thanked him "for his continued support and for helping a son step out of a shadow. I'll be eternally grateful to you, dad!"

"For Michael Douglas, winning the Oscar last night for Best Actor was more rewarding than his gold statue 12 years ago as producer of Best Picture winner *One Flew Over the Cuckoo's Nest*," *Variety* reported. "This time out, he said, 'I was looking for credibility.' "

The Last Emperor had no noms in the acting categories. All night it marched steadily through the tech categories, however, claiming victories for cinematography, art direction, costumes, editing, sound and music score.

Then it faced the two top races. In the match-up for Best Director, some pundits thought Norman Jewison (*Moonstruck*) could prevail, making up for the embarrassing loss he suffered when *In the Heat of the Night* won Best Picture in 1967, but he lost the helmer's gold to Mike Nichols (*The Graduate*). Certainly, *Moonstruck* seemed to have momentum after its victories for screenplay, actress and supporting actress. Bertolucci also faced tough competish from L.A. and N.Y. crix honoree John Boorman.

As comic Robin Williams was about to reveal the winner, he noted that all of the contenders were non-Americans. "Along with the Oscars, the academy is giving out a green card," he said.

Then he opened the envelope and gave an Oscar statuette to Bertolucci, who accepted it, saying that he felt "one of the strongest emotions in my life." He thanked the Chinese "for allowing us to shoot in their beautiful country."

"With 8 wins out of 9 noms already in hand by the time the final award was announced, it was hardly a surprise that *The Last Emperor* would take the Best Picture Oscar and make it a clean sweep," *Variety* said, reporting on its next victory. "It was the first time a film won in every category it was competing in since *Gigi* also won 9 out of 9 in 1958. *Emperor*'s sweep was also the broadest since *West Side Story* won 10 Oscars in 1961."

Quite a few Oscar nominees weren't completely overlooked on academy weekend. Two days before the Oscarcast, the Independent Spirit Awards hailed four of them with kudos.

Variety noted that "one of the most emotional moments of the ceremony" was the victory of Sally Kirkland as Best Actress. *Variety* said, "Kirkland talked of the international collaboration in the making of *Anna* and how much it meant to her to finally be given a leading role in the cinema."

Morgan Freeman was declared Best Supporting Actor. Anjelica Huston won Best Supporting Actress and her recently deceased father, John, was named Best Director. *Variety* reported that the latter prize was accepted by Huston's son Tony, who wrote *The Dead*: "In an eerie echo of his father's trademark speech and accent, he said John Huston 'was indeed a most independent spirit—which we children quickly learned, to our profit and, sometimes, our dismay.' "

The winner of Best Picture was *River's Edge*, which *Variety* described as "a gritty and realistic tale of teenage murder." Best First Feature was the year's most commercially successful indie, *Dirty Dancing*, about teen mating antics during summer vacation in upstate New York.

"The Independent Feature Project helped Dennis Quaid celebrate his birthday by recognizing him as Best Actor for his role as the smart aleck New Orleans cop of *The Big Easy*," *Variety* reported. A grinning Quaid thanked ex-Columbia Pictures topper David Puttnam for "snatching it out of the jaws of death" after seeing *The Big Easy* "at a film festival in Park City."

The Park City fest was the U.S. Film Festival, where *The Big Easy* had been shown out of competition last year.

"This year's 10-day smorgasbord of indie films was the biggest ever," said the *L.A. Times*, "and, with about 33,000 tickets sold, the best attended."

Variety described the fest's closing-night event as so well attended that it was chaotic: "Several hundred guests competed for perhaps 200 chairs at a dozen tables. Appetizer-like food samples could be found on the periphery of the jam-packed room."

The winners being feted included Grand Jury Prize champ for Best Feature—*Heat and Sunlight. Variety* called it "an intense, brooding portrait of the last 16 hours of a romantic relationship, which scored points for bravery, integrity and overall risk-taking. Film faces a difficult future commercially." The prize was $2,500 and 100,000 feet of 35mm film processing.

Best Documentary was *Beirut: The Last Home Movie*, "about a Lebanese family that tries to maintain its Old World lifestyle in the war-torn city," said *Variety*.

A special honor was given to Viveca Lindfors for her performance as a senior Scandinavian-American farm wife in *Rachel River*.

"The festival's expanding profile was demonstrated during the awards party," the *L.A. Times* noted. "There was a cacophony of schmoozing that barely ebbed enough to acknowledge the winners of the film competition."

The winners compensated for the hubbub by shouting their brief acceptance speeches above the din. Rob Nilsson claimed his Grand Jury Prize for *Heat and Sunlight*, hollering, "All I can say is we gotta take risks! Go for it, you guys!"

Despite winning the top trophy, *Heat and Sunlight* didn't get a distribution deal at the fest. It took two more years before the pic was finally released commercially.

▪ 1987 ▪

NATIONAL BOARD OF REVIEW

The board declared a Best Picture and Foreign Film of the year, then listed its remaining favorites according to highest scores. The vote results were announced on December 15, 1987. Awards were presented on February 16, 1988, at Lincoln Center Library in New York.

BEST PICTURE
▪ *Empire of the Sun*
The Last Emperor
Broadcast News
The Untouchables
Gaby
Cry Freedom
Fatal Attraction
Hope and Glory

Wall Street
Full Metal Jacket

BEST DIRECTOR
▪ Steven Spielberg, *Empire of the Sun*

BEST ACTOR
▪ Michael Douglas, *Wall Street*

BEST ACTRESS (TIE)
▪ Lillian Gish, *The Whales of August*
▪ Holly Hunter, *Broadcast News*

BEST SUPPORTING ACTOR
▪ Sean Connery, *The Untouchables*

BEST SUPPORTING ACTRESS
▪ Olympia Dukakis, *Moonstruck*

OUTSTANDING JUVENILE PERFORMANCE
- Christian Bale, *Empire of the Sun*

BEST DOCUMENTARY
- *Chuck Berry: Hail! Hail! Rock 'n' Roll!* Taylor Hackford

BEST FOREIGN FILM (TIE)
- *Jean de Florette* (France)
- *Manon of the Spring* (France)
My Life as a Dog (Sweden)
Au Revoir les Enfants (France)
Tampopo (Japan)
Dark Eyes (Italy)

LIFETIME ACHIEVEMENT
- Lillian Gish

SPECIAL AWARD
- Frank Rowley, Regency Theater

NEW YORK FILM CRITICS CIRCLE

Winners were announced on December 17, 1987. Awards were presented on January 24, 1988, at Sardi's restaurant in New York.

BEST PICTURE
- *Broadcast News*

BEST DIRECTOR
- James L. Brooks, *Broadcast News*

BEST ACTOR
- Jack Nicholson, *Broadcast News, Ironweed, The Witches of Eastwick*

BEST ACTRESS
- Holly Hunter, *Broadcast News*

BEST SUPPORTING ACTOR
- Morgan Freeman, *Street Smart*

BEST SUPPORTING ACTRESS
- Vanessa Redgrave, *Prick Up Your Ears*

BEST SCREENPLAY
- James L. Brooks, *Broadcast News*

BEST CINEMATOGRAPHY
- Vittorio Storaro, *The Last Emperor*

BEST FOREIGN FILM
- *My Life as a Dog* (Sweden)

LOS ANGELES FILM CRITICS ASSOCIATION

Winners were announced on December 19, 1987. Awards were presented on January 21, 1988, at the Westwood Marquis Hotel in Los Angeles.

BEST PICTURE
- *Hope and Glory*

BEST DIRECÏOR
- John Boorman, *Hope and Glory*

BEST ACTOR (TIE)
- Steve Martin, *Roxanne*
- Jack Nicholson, *Ironweed, The Witches of Eastwick*

BEST ACTRESS (TIE)
- Holly Hunter, *Broadcast News*
- Sally Kirkland, *Anna*

BEST SUPPORTING ACTOR
- Morgan Freeman, *Street Smart*

BEST SUPPORTING ACTRESS
- Olympia Dukakis, *Moonstruck*

BEST SCREENPLAY
- John Boorman, *Hope and Glory*

BEST CINEMATOGRAPHY
- Vittorio Storaro, *The Last Emperor*

BEST MUSIC SCORE
- David Byrne, Ryuichi Sakamoto, Cong Su, *The Last Emperor*

BEST FOREIGN FILM
- *Au Revoir, Les Enfants* (France), Louis Malle

BEST EXPERIMENTAL/INDEPENDENT FILM
- *Mala Noche*, Gus Van Sant

NEW GENERATION AWARD
- Pedro Almodovar, *Law of Desire*

CAREER ACHIEVEMENT AWARD
- Samuel Fuller
- Joel McCrea

SPECIAL AWARD
- Pierre Sauvage, *Weapons of the Spirit*

NATIONAL SOCIETY OF FILM CRITICS

Winners were announced on January 3, 1988.

BEST PICTURE
- *The Dead*

BEST DIRECTOR
- John Boorman, *Hope and Glory*

BEST ACTOR
- Steve Martin, *Roxanne*

BEST ACTRESS
- Emily Lloyd, *Wish You Were Here*

BEST SUPPORTING ACTOR
- Morgan Freeman, *Street Smart*

BEST SUPPORTING ACTRESS
- Kathy Baker, *Street Smart*

BEST SCREENPLAY
- John Boorman, *Hope and Glory*

BEST CINEMATOGRAPHY
- Philippe Rousselot, *Hope and Glory*

SPECIAL AWARD
- Richard Roud

GOLDEN GLOBES

Nominations were announced on January 5, 1988. Awards were presented on January 23 at the Beverly Hilton Hotel in Los Angeles. The ceremony was telecast by ABC.

BEST DRAMA PICTURE
- *The Last Emperor*
La Bamba
Cry Freedom
Empire of the Sun
Fatal Attraction
Nuts

BEST COMEDY OR MUSICAL PICTURE
- *Hope and Glory*
Baby Boom
Broadcast News
Dirty Dancing
Moonstruck

BEST DIRECTOR
- Bernardo Bertolucci, *The Last Emperor*
Richard Attenborough, *Cry Freedom*
John Boorman, *Hope and Glory*
James L. Brooks, *Broadcast News*
Adrian Lyne, *Fatal Attraction*

BEST ACTOR, DRAMA
- Michael Douglas, *Wall Street*
John Lone, *The Last Emperor*
Jack Nicholson, *Ironweed*
Nick Nolte, *Weeds*
Denzel Washington, *Cry Freedom*

BEST ACTRESS, DRAMA
- Sally Kirkland, *Anna*
Glenn Close, *Fatal Attraction*
Faye Dunaway, *Barfly*
Rachel Levin, *Gaby*
Barbra Streisand, *Nuts*

BEST ACTOR, COMEDY OR MUSICAL
- Robin Williams, *Good Morning, Vietnam*
Nicolas Cage, *Moonstruck*
Danny DeVito, *Throw Momma from the Train*
William Hurt, *Broadcast News*
Steve Martin, *Roxanne*
Patrick Swayze, *Dirty Dancing*

BEST ACTRESS, COMEDY OR MUSICAL
- Cher, *Moonstruck*
Jennifer Grey, *Dirty Dancing*
Holly Hunter, *Broadcast News*
Diane Keaton, *Baby Boom*
Bette Midler, *Outrageous Fortune*

BEST SUPPORTING ACTOR
- Sean Connery, *The Untouchables*
Richard Dreyfuss, *Nuts*
Lee Ermey, *Full Metal Jacket*
Morgan Freeman, *Street Smart*
Rob Lowe, *Square Dance*

BEST SUPPORTING ACTRESS
- Olympia Dukakis, *Moonstruck*
Norma Aleandro, *Gaby*
Anne Archer, *Fatal Attraction*
Anne Ramsey, *Throw Momma from the Train*
Vanessa Redgrave, *Prick Up Your Ears*

BEST SCREENPLAY
- Bernardo Bertolucci, Mark Peploe, *The Last Emperor*
John Boorman, *Hope and Glory*
James L. Brooks, *Broadcast News*
David Mamet, *House of Games*
John Patrick Shanley, *Moonstruck*

BEST SONG
- "(I've Had) The Time of My Life," *Dirty Dancing*
"Nothing's Gonna Stop Us Now," *Mannequin*
"The Secret of My Success," *The Secret of My Success*
"Shakedown," *Beverly Hills Cop II*
"Who's That Girl," *Who's That Girl*

BEST FOREIGN FILM
- *My Life as a Dog* (Sweden)
Au Revoir les Enfants (Goodbye, Children) (France/Germany)
Dark Eyes (Italy/U.S.S.R.)
Jean de Florette (France)
Repentance (U.S.S.R.)

Winners

BEST SCORE
- Ryuichi Sakamoto, David Byrne, Cong Su, *The Last Emperor*

CECIL B. DEMILLE AWARD
- Clint Eastwood

U.S. FILM FESTIVAL (SUNDANCE)

The festival was held January 15–24, 1988, at Park City, Utah.

GRAND JURY PRIZE
(FEATURE)
- *Heat and Sunlight*, Rob Nilsson
(DOCUMENTARY)
- *Beirut: The Last Home Movie*, Jennifer Fox

SPECIAL JURY PRIZE
(FEATURE)
- *Lemon Sky*, Jan Egleson
(DOCUMENTARY)
- *Dear America*, Bill Couturie
- *Thy Kingdom Come, Thy Will Be Done*, Anthony Thomas

BEST CINEMATOGRAPHY
(FEATURE)
- *Rachel River*, Paul Elliott
(DOCUMENTARY)
- *Beirut: The Last Home Movie*, Alex Nepomniaschy

SPECIAL DISTINCTION: OUTSTANDING PERFORMANCE
- Viveca Lindfors, *Rachel River*

WRITERS GUILD OF AMERICA

Awards were presented on February 12, 1988, at the Beverly Hilton Hotel in Los Angeles and the Windows on the World restaurant in New York.

BEST ORIGINAL SCREENPLAY
- *Moonstruck*, John Patrick Shanley
Broadcast News, James L. Brooks
Hope and Glory, John Boorman
The Last Emperor, Mark Peploe, Bernardo Bertolucci
Radio Days, Woody Allen

BEST ADAPTED SCREENPLAY
- *Roxanne,* Steve Martin, based on the play *Cyrano de Bergerac* by Edmund Rostand
Fatal Attraction, James Dearden, based on his original screenplay *Diversion*
Full Metal Jacket, Stanley Kubrick, Michael Herr, Gustav Hasford, based on the novel *The Short-Timers* by Gustav Hasgford

The Princess Bride, William Goldman, based on his novel

The Untouchables, David Mamet, based on the TV series by Oscar Fraley and the works written by Oscar Fraley with Elliot Ness and Paul Robsky

MORGAN COX AWARD
- Daniel Taradash

VALENTINE DAVIES AWARD
- Lois Peyser

LAUREL AWARD
- Irving Ravetch and Harriet Frank, Jr.

DIRECTORS GUILD OF AMERICA

Awards were presented on March 12, 1988, at the Beverly Hilton Hotel in Los Angeles.

BEST DIRECTOR
- Bernardo Bertolucci, *The Last Emperor*
James L. Brooks, *Broadcast News*
Lasse Hallström, *My Life as a Dog*
Adrian Lyne, *Fatal Attraction*
Steven Spielberg, *Empire of the Sun*

ROBERT B. ALDRICH AWARD
- Sheldon Leonard

D. W. GRIFFITH AWARD
- Robert E. Wise

INDEPENDENT SPIRIT

Nominations were announced on February 11, 1988. Awards were presented on April 9 at Rosalie's 385 North restaurant in Los Angeles.

BEST FEATURE
- *River's Edge*
The Big Easy
Matewan
Swimming to Cambodia
Tough Guys Don't Dance

BEST FIRST FEATURE
- *Dirty Dancing*
Anna

Hollywood Shuffle
Siesta
Waiting for the Moon

BEST DIRECTOR
- John Huston, *The Dead*
Jonathan Demme, *Swimming to Cambodia*
Tim Hunter, *River's Edge*
Jim McBride, *The Big Easy*
John Sales, *Matewan*

BEST ACTOR
- Dennis Quaid, *The Big Easy*
Spalding Gray, *Swimming to Cambodia*
Terry O'Quinn, *The Stepfather*
Mickey Rourke, *Barfly*
James Woods, *Best Seller*

BEST ACTRESS
- Sally Kirkland, *Anna*
Lillian Gish, *The Whales of August*
Debra Sandlund, *Tough Guys Don't Dance*
Louise Smith, *Working Girls*
Joanne Woodward, *The Glass Menagerie*

BEST SUPPORTING ACTOR
- Morgan Freeman, *Street Smart*
Wings Hauser, *Tough Guys Don't Dance*
James Earl Jones, *Matewan*
Vincent Price, *The Whales of August*
David Strathairn, *Matewan*

BEST SUPPORTING ACTRESS
- Anjelica Huston, *The Dead*
Karen Allen, *The Glass Menagerie*
Kathy Baker, *Street Smart*
Martha Plimpton, *Shy People*
Ann Sothern, *The Whales of August*

BEST SCREENPLAY
- Neal Jiminez, *River's Edge*
Spalding Gray, *Swimming to Cambodia*
Agnieszka Holland, *Anna*
Tony Huston, *The Dead*
John Sales, *Matewan*

BEST FOREIGN FEATURE
- *My Life as a Dog* (Sweden)
Au Revoir, Les Enfants (France)
Hope and Glory (U.K.)
Prick Up Your Ears (U.K.)
Tampopo (Japan)

Winner

BEST CINEMATOGRAPHY
- Haskell Wexler, *Matewan*

ACADEMY AWARDS

Nominations were announced on February 17, 1988. Awards were presented on April 11 at the Shrine Auditorium in Los Angeles. The ceremony was telecast by ABC.

BEST PICTURE
- *The Last Emperor*
Broadcast News
Fatal Attraction
Hope and Glory
Moonstruck

BEST DIRECTOR
- Bernardo Bertolucci, *The Last Emperor*
John Boorman, *Hope and Glory*
Lasse Hallström, *My Life as a Dog*
Norman Jewison, *Moonstruck*
Adrian Lyne, *Fatal Attraction*

BEST ACTOR
- Michael Douglas, *Wall Street*
William Hurt, *Broadcast News*
Marcello Mastroianni, *Dark Eyes*
Jack Nicholson, *Ironweed*
Robin Williams, *Good Morning, Vietnam*

BEST ACTRESS
- Cher, *Moonstruck*
Glenn Close, *Fatal Attraction*
Holly Hunter, *Broadcast News*
Sally Kirkland, *Anna*
Meryl Streep, *Ironweed*

BEST SUPPORTING ACTOR
- Sean Connery, *The Untouchables*
Albert Brooks, *Broadcast News*
Morgan Freeman, *Street Smart*
Vincent Gardenia, *Moonstruck*
Denzel Washington, *Cry Freedom*

BEST SUPPORTING ACTRESS
- Olympia Dukakis, *Moonstruck*
Norma Aleandro, *Gaby*

Anne Archer, *Fatal Attraction*
Anne Ramsey, *Throw Momma from the Train*
Ann Sothern, *The Whales of August*

BEST ORIGINAL SCREENPLAY
- John Patrick Shanley, *Moonstruck*
Woody Allen, *Radio Days*
John Boorman, *Hope and Glory*
James L. Brooks, *Broadcast News*
Louis Malle, *Au Revoir, Les Enfants*

BEST ADAPTED SCREENPLAY
- Bernardo Bertolucci, Mark Peploe, *The Last Emperor*
Per Berglund, Brasse Brännström, Lasse Hallström, Reidar Jönsson, *My Life as a Dog*
James Dearden, *Fatal Attraction*
Gustav Hasford, Michael Herr, Stanley Kubrick, *Full Metal Jacket*
Tony Huston, *The Dead*

BEST SONG
- "(I've Had) The Time of My Life," *Dirty Dancing,* John Denicola, Donald Markowitz, Franke Previte
"Cry Freedom," *Cry Freedom*, George Fenton, Jonas Gwangwa
"Nothing's Gonna Stop Us Now," *Mannequin,* Albert Hammond, Diane Warren
"Shakedown," *Beverly Hills Cop II,* Harold Faltermeyer, Keith Forsey, Bob Seger
"Storybook Love," *The Princess Bride,* Willy Deville

BEST FOREIGN-LANGUAGE FILM
- *Babette's Feast* (Denmark)
Au Revoir, Les Enfants (France)
Course Completed (Spain)
The Family (Italy)
Pathfinder (Norway)

Winners

BEST ART DIRECTION
- Ferdinando Scarfiotti, Bruno Cesari, Osvaldo Desideri, *The Last Emperor*

BEST CINEMATOGRAPHY
- Vittorio Storaro, *The Last Emperor*

BEST COSTUME DESIGN
- James Acheson, *The Last Emperor*

BEST DOCUMENTARY
(FEATURE)
- *The Ten-Year Lunch: Wit and Legend of the Algonquin Round Table,* Aviva Slesin

(SHORT SUBJECT)
- *Young at Heart*, Pamela Conn, Sue Marx

BEST FILM EDITING
- Gabriella Cristiani, *The Last Emperor*

BEST MAKEUP
- Rick Baker, *Harry and the Hendersons*

BEST MUSIC SCORE
- David Byrne, Cong Su, Ryuichi Sakamoto, *The Last Emperor*

SCIENTIFIC OR TECHNICAL AWARDS
(Academy Award of Merit)
- Werner Block, Bernhard Kühl, Osram GmbH Research and Development Department

(Scientific and Engineering Award)
- Willi Burth, Kinotone Corp.; Ronald C. Barker, Chester L. Schuler, Montage Group; Colin F. Mossman, Rank Film Labs; Eastman Kodak; Fritz Gabriel Bauer; Zoran Perisic; Carl Zeiss Co.

(Technical Achievement Award)
- Ioan Allen, Dolby Labs; Joseph Eppolito, Wally Gentleman, William Mesa, Les Paul Robley, Geoffrey H. Williamson; Thaine Morris, David Pier; Tadeuz Krzanowski, Industrial Light and Magic; Dan C. Norris, Tim Cook, Jan Jacobsen

BEST SHORT FILM
(ANIMATED)
- *The Man Who Planted Trees*, Frédéric Back

(LIVE ACTION)
- *Ray's Male Heterosexual Dance Hall,* Jana Sue Memel, Jonathan Sanger

BEST SOUND
- Bill Rowe, Ivan Sharrock, *The Last Emperor*

SPECIAL ACHIEVEMENT—SOUND EFFECTS EDITING
- Stephen Flick, John Pospisil, *Robocop*

BEST VISUAL EFFECTS
- William George, Harley Jessup, Dennis Muren, Kenneth Smith, *Innerspace*

GORDON E. SAWYER AWARD
- Fred Hynes

IRVING G. THALBERG MEMORIAL AWARD
- Billy Wilder

SCREEN ACTORS GUILD

LIFETIME ACHIEVEMENT AWARD
- Red Skelton

▪ 1988 ▪

Rain Man *Makes "Big Splash"*

"A stunning surprise" is what *Variety* called the Best Picture choice of the Los Angeles Film Critics Association.

Prior to its selection, Oscar and Golden Globe voters had been looking eagerly to the crix for award guidance after a lackluster year dominated by popcorn pix like *Crocodile Dundee II, Die Hard* and *Three Men and a Baby*. "Given the lack of any clear-cut frontrunners, the competition seemed wide open," *Variety* reported.

But the crix's pick, *Little Dorrit*—a two-part, six-hour adaptation of the Charles Dickens classic that had grossed far less than $1 million in L.A. and New York theaters—had not been considered a contender.

Variety had hailed *Little Dorrit* in its review as "a remarkable achievement." Especially daring was how the film's two parts retold the same story of a young seamstress (Sarah Pickering) who looks after her father (Alec Guinness) in debtor's prison and falls in love with the good samaritan who tries to rescue them (Derek Jacobi). *Dorrit* also earned the prize of Best Supporting Actor for Guinness over second-place vote-getter Martin Landau as a crafty financier in *Tucker: The Man and His Dream*.

Best Picture runner-up was *Dead Ringers*, starring Jeremy Irons in the eerie dual roles of twin gynecologists who both fall in love with a famous actress (Genevieve Bujold). *Dead Ringers* rebounded from its loss to claim the director's laurels for David Cronenberg over Martin Scorsese, whose *The Last Temptation of Christ* was under attack by Christian fundamentalists for its depiction of Jesus' human weaknesses. Also honored was *Dead Ringers*'s Bujold as Best Supporting Actress over Miriam Margolyes as an aging chatterbox in *Dorrit*.

Jeremy Irons had been considered a

Little Dorrit, big surprise: The L.A. crix's choice for best pic spanned six hours of vintage Dickens and starred Sarrina Caruthers and Alec Guinness. It failed to be hailed by later kudos.

likely upcoming contender for Oscar's Best Actor prize, but the crix passed over his perf in favor of two roles by Tom Hanks, who was being cheered in packed theaters for his mischievous portrayal of a man who swaps bodies with a 13-year-old boy in *Big* and hailed by crix for his multi-faceted star turn in *Punchline*. In the latter role, *Variety* said Hanks "exhibits flashes of brilliance as a caustically tongued stand-up comic."

Christine Lahti won Best Actress as a secret anarchist wanted by the FBI in *Running on Empty*, eclipsing Diane Verona as the wife of sax legend Charlie Parker in the Clint Eastwood–helmed *Bird*. Best Screenplay was the baseball b.o. home-run *Bull Durham*, written by former minor-league player Ron Shelton. *Bull Durham* outscored *The Moderns*, a drama about an artists' community in 1920s Paris.

When Orion Pictures released *Mississippi Burning*, the studio ballyhooed it as a strong candidate for Best Picture kudos, which seemed to be supported by early reviews. *Variety* said it "captures much of the truth in its telling of the impact of a 1964 probe into the murders of three civil rights workers" in the Deep South, but warned that "its credibility is undermined by a fanciful ending." Civil rights groups soon attacked other aspects of its credibility, lambasting its producers for creating two fictitious white FBI agents as its central heroes. NAACP leader Benjamin Hooks said the pic "reeks with dishonesty, deception and fraud." As the controversy peaked, *Time* magazine insisted that "narrow historical criticism somehow seems irrelevant to a movie that so powerfully reanimates the past for the best of reasons," but most pundits dismissed its awards chances.

The National Board of Review was not dissuaded, however, and gave *Mississippi Burning* four kudos, including Best Picture and Director (Alan Parker). Star Gene Hackman had placed behind Tom Hanks when the L.A. crix voted, but the board named him Best Actor for a role that also impressed *Variety*, which said, "Hackman steals the picture as a messily sympathetic FBI man who connects keenly but briefly with the people" in a southern town. *Variety* also lauded the board's Best Supporting Actress choice, Frances McDormand, noting that she gave a "glowing performance as a deputy's wife who's drawn to Hackman." The winner of Best Supporting Actor was River Phoenix as Christine Lahti's musically gifted son in *Running on Empty*.

When naming Best Actress, the board became the first to heap laurels on a critically lauded perf by onetime child star Jodie Foster, who had recently returned to moviemaking after graduating from Yale. In *The Accused*, she took on the steamy role of a woman who's gang-raped at a roadside saloon and puts blame on the bystanders who egged on the assault. *The New York Times* praised Foster for giving "a splendid performance as a sexily dressed young

woman, not entirely sober and a little high on marijuana, who, as everybody says, 'asked for it.' "

Foster, Phoenix and McDormand were all present at the board's awards presentation held at Lincoln Center Library in New York, where José Ferrer presided as emcee for a fourth time. *Variety* reported that the occasion buzzed with "presenters and winners all stressing the importance of the discussion" surrounding *Mississippi Burning*.

Controversy also engulfed the Best Picture named by the New York Film Critics Circle just days after the L.A. crix and National Board of Review sounded off. Despite its victory, *The Accidental Tourist* did not have broad support within the circle and was chosen, said *The Village Voice*, "almost by accident."

Variety called *The Accidental Tourist* "a slow, sonorous and largely satisfying" love story about a dispirited travel writer (William Hurt) who falls for his feisty dog trainer (Geena Davis). But other media loathed it. "Everything about this glum and self-important adaptation of Anne Tyler's upper-cute novel is dim," insisted *Time*'s Richard Schickel. "Dim, too, is the judgment of the New York Film Critics Circle." The *L.A. Times* claimed that the org's selection as Best Picture "provoked loud 'huhs???' from coast to coast."

Schickel was obviously not among the 3 critics who endorsed the film on the first ballot when the 28 circle voters nominated 16 pix. Also receiving three votes—the most among contending films—was *A World Apart*, director Chris Menges's drama about South African apartheid as seen through the eyes of a 13-year-old girl (Jodhi May). *World* pulled ahead of *Tourist* on the second ballot by a score of 25 points to 24, but it tied its rival on the third and final tally when both films reaped 27 points. *Tourist* was declared the winner because it was listed in first, second or third place on at least half of the voters'

> # Gotham crix named *Accidental Tourist* best pic "almost by accident."

ballots, which was required by circle rules.

Other contests were equally heated. Menges and *Tourist*'s Lawrence Kasdan tied for second place on the first ballot for Best Director behind Wim Wenders, who was nommed for *Wings of Desire*, a whimsical tale of two angels who yearn to be human. Menges (27 points) finally prevailed on the third polling, however, when Kasdan (20) fell behind Clint Eastwood (24 points for *Bird*).

Dustin Hoffman's performance as an autistic savant in *Rain Man* led on the first canvass for Best Actor, followed by a tie for Gene Hackman (*Mississippi Burning*) and Tom Hanks (*Big*). Then Jeremy Irons (*Dead Ringers*) pulled even with Hoffman on the second tally (26 points each) and was declared the champ because he, like *The Accidental Tourist*, was listed on half of the ballots.

Further jockeying occurred in the race for Best Supporting Actor. Alec Guinness (*Little Dorrit, A Handful of Dust*) and Martin Landau (*Tucker*) tied for the lead on the first vote, followed by Dean Stockwell, who was cited for his roles as a Mafia don in *Married to the Mob* and as Howard Hughes in *Tucker*. Landau claimed a slim lead on the second round, but then scored only 19 points on the third and final tally, falling behind winner Stockwell (38) and runner-up Guinness (30).

The remaining two races were far less dizzying. Meryl Streep—who'd been hailed by the crix in years past for *Sophie's Choice* and *Kramer vs. Kramer*—claimed her third career prize for *A Cry in the Dark* as a real-life Australian convicted of killing her child despite her pleas that a wild dingo was to blame. *Variety* said Streep had "a stranglehold" on the category, beating Jodie Foster by a 41-to-24 score. Diane Venora (*Bird*) had an equally tight grip on Best Supporting Actress, edging out Jodhi May (*A World Apart*) 48 points to 22. Ron Shelton (*Bull Durham*) led all the way through the three-ballot race for Best Screenplay, but won by a mere point (33 to 32) over Shawn Slovo (*A World Apart*).

This year the crix moved up their awards ceremony by one week so it wouldn't compete with the Super Bowl, but it nonetheless ended up falling on an unfortunate day. Disgruntled circle member Janet Maslin of *The New York Times* thought it was a good time to publish her scathing review of *The Accidental Tourist*, which included a broadside at her peers for endorsing it. "I didn't mean to antagonize anybody," she told *Village Voice*'s Michael Musto, "but if you dish it out, you can take it."

The gala was abuzz with whispered gossip about the article, but *Tourist*'s director Lawrence Kasdan graciously chose not to mention it when he accepted the Best Picture plaque. He thanked his hosts for an award that encouraged "people to see a quiet movie that otherwise they might have missed."

Meryl Streep asked if Dustin Hoffman could present her with the Best Actress plaque, but he refused, telling circle leaders, "Look, I lost this year, by one point, to Jeremy Irons. And I once lost the Tony Award to Jeremy Irons. So he doesn't like me and I just can't see myself showing up there—as a loser." Instead, playwright Wendy Wasserstein stood in. As Streep accepted the prize, the *Voice* noticed she was "really shaking."

"You know me. I don't know you and we've had this relationship for years," she told the crix, looking "very nervous but grateful," reported *The New York Post*. Then Streep added, "It's because you are who you are that this means so much."

Throughout the first half of the fete, crix leaders were nervous, too, when their Best Actor honoree was nowhere in sight. He had been skedded to arrive on a Concorde flight from Europe, but, while the crowd waited, they were entertained by Best Supporting Actor Dean Stockwell singing his TV commercial jingle from *Married to the Mob*—"It's a Burger World Town." When

> The nat'l crix society embraced *Unbearable Lightness* quickly.

Irons finally appeared, he "proceeded to give a long, dry reflective speech no one understood but many enjoyed," said the *Voice*. Columnist Liz Smith reported that Irons had "paid for his own Concorde ticket because he feels the publicity and fallout from the event might influence Oscar voters later on when it comes to considering him as Best Actor for *Dead Ringers*." His expenditure would turn out to be for naught. Oscars voters did not nominate him one month later.

The National Society of Film Critics gathered to vote at the Algonquin Hotel three weeks after the Gotham circle announced its honorees, and it backed two of the same winners: Best Supporting Actor Dean Stockwell (45 points) over Alec Guinness (34) and Best Screenplay *Bull Durham* (47) over *Dead Ringers* (20).

But the society made radical departures in other categories, displaying its frequent fondness for arthouse hits when deciding Best Picture and director. "Best-film balloting was over quickly, an unusual occurrence," *Variety* reported. The winner was *The Unbearable Lightness of Being*, which *Variety* heralded as "a richly satisfying adaptation of Milan Kundera's 1984 bestseller of love and erotica set against the Russian invasion of Czechoslovakia." With 20 points, it just narrowly edged out *Women on the Verge of a Nervous Breakdown* (19), Pedro Almodovar's comedy about a pregnant woman (Carmen Maura) who unsuccessfully tries to commit suicide after being jilted by her married lover. *Unbearable* also claimed the director's laurels by a slim margin for Philip Kaufman (26 points) over Chris Menges (23 points for *A World Apart*).

Carmen Maura (13 points) lost the Best Actress contest to Judy Davis (19), whom *Variety* praised for exhibiting "great depth and subtlety" as a woman who encounters her long-lost daughter in Aussie import *High Tide*. The Best Actor choice was a shocker—Michael Keaton, who was cited

> ## sex, lies and videotape aroused the U.S. Film Festival.

for two roles: as a grotesque, havoc-wreaking spirit in *Beetlejuice* and as a cocaine addict in denial in *Clean and Sober*.

For Best Supporting Actress, the society preferred Mercedes Ruehl (21 points) as Dean Stockwell's jealous wife in *Married to the Mob* over Lina Olin as the curvy mistress of a Czech surgeon in *Unbearable* (20). Stockwell (45) pulled off a victory for Best Supporting Actor over Alec Guinness (34) after an unusually decisive one-ballot vote.

Sizing up all the crix's picks, *Variety* observed, "Group went against the grain by divvying out recognition to many films released early in the year rather than jumping on the late-1988 bandwagon."

But Golden Globe voters took a ride on mostly Christmas releases this year. Among them was the biggest noms bagger and the latest new leader of the Best Picture derby, *Working Girl* (six bids), starring Melanie Griffith as an ambitious secretary who outwits her boss-from-hell (Sigourney Weaver). *Running on Empty* scored the second-highest tally (five), followed by *A Cry in the Dark, Mississippi Burning* and *Rain Man* (four each).

"*Working Girl* broke away from the pack and broke the finish tape with the best numbers," a shocked *Variety* reported after awards night. *Working Girl* beat *Big, A Fish Called Wanda* and *Who Framed Roger Rabbit?* to win Best Comedy or Musical Picture and additional kudos for Best Song (Carly Simon's "Let the River Run") and the two women who portrayed the corporate catfighters.

"Here's to the working girls!" Griffith roared as she held her Best Actress statuette aloft at the ceremony, which was being broadcast by the cable channel TBS.

Weaver accepted her Globe as Best Supporting Actress, saying, "This is one for the bad girls, I guess!"

Weaver also received a Globe as Best Drama Actress for *Gorillas in the Mist* when an unprecedented three-way tie occurred. She was honored for portraying murdered anthropologist Dian Fossey, who had spent nearly 20 years studying wild gorillas in the Rwandan jungle.

When the winner claimed her second chunk of gold, UPI noted, "Weaver told the amused audience that the gorillas in her film really deserved the Golden Globe statuette, but, in as much as 'they can't eat it or make a nest of it, I think I'll keep it.' "

Sharing the victory with Weaver were Jodie Foster (*The Accused*) and Shirley MacLaine as a flamboyant piano teacher in *Madame Sousatzka*.

The winner of Best Drama Picture was the biggest Christmas b.o. hit, *Rain Man*, which starred Tom Cruise as a slick car salesman who tries to swindle his autistic brother (Dustin Hoffman) out of their father's $3 million estate. Hoffman ended up pulling off the real heist in this film, though—*The New York Times* said he stole the picture with a "remarkable performance of sustained virtuosity."

When Hoffman was hailed as Best Actor, "he wept through most of his speech," *Variety* noted. UPI described it as "a halting, stuttering expression of gratitude to his coworkers and the autistic people with whom he worked to perfect his role."

Backstage later, he told reporters, "The first time I was at the Globes it was 1967 and I won as Most Promising Newcomer for *The Graduate*. Sally Field, playing a Flying Nun at the time, dropped down on a wire to give it to me. I would give this back if that could happen again now."

Surprisingly, neither *Rain Man*'s helmer Barry Levinson nor *Working Girl*'s Mike Nichols was voted Best Director. The Globe ended up going to Clint Eastwood (*Bird*), who "was soft-spoken but obviously pleased" as he accepted it, observed the *Herald Examiner*. Voters agreed with the L.A. crix and named Tom Hanks Best Drama Actor for *Big*.

One film got noticeably burned—*Mississippi Burning*, which suffered a total shutout.

"Call it the year of no consensus," *The New York Daily News* said after the gala.

Best Drama Actor Dustin Hoffman (right, with Tom Cruise) wept at the Golden Globes when *Rain Man* was embraced after being shunned by the crix kudos.

"Now that the Golden Globes and every major critics' organization have given their blessing to film's best, there's one problem. They leave no clear consensus as to who and what will get Oscar nominations."

Variety disagreed, saying that *Rain Man* was now in the lead thanks to its Golden Globes success.

When the DGA contenders were announced three days after the Globes ceremony, *Rain Man*'s helmer Barry Levinson made the cut, as expected, but there were "a few surprises," according to press-conference emcee Steven Spielberg—and "a couple of happy ones, too."

Spielberg was pleased that his onetime protégé, Robert Zemeckis, was nommed for 1988's top-grossing pic, *Who Framed Roger Rabbit*, but disappointed that recent Globe champ Clint Eastwood (*Bird*) was snubbed. Also omitted: *The Accidental Tourist*'s Lawrence Kasdan. Controversy didn't hurt *Mississippi Burning*'s Alan Parker, as it turned out, but it was probably responsible for Martin Scorsese (*The Last Temptation of Christ*) being overlooked. Most surprising inclusion: 78-year-old veteran British helmer Charles Crichton for his comeback comic hit *A Fish Called Wanda*.

Two weeks later, Oscar nominees were unveiled and *Variety* declared in a banner headline: "*RAIN* MAKES BIG OSCAR SPLASH." *Rain Man* led with eight bids, followed by seven each for *Mississippi Burning* and *Dangerous Liaisons*.

Strangely, there was little overlap with the critics' kudos. Two out of the three crix's choices for Best Actor and Actress weren't even nommed, and none of the crix's Best Directors made the cut. Martin Scorsese bumped Zemeckis from the director's race, but neither Scorsese's *Last Temptation* nor Charles Crighton's *A Fish Called Wanda* was up for Oscar's Best Picture.

Rain Man's gathering support was seen next when the directors' guild results were in. "LEVINSON REIGNS AT DGA PARADE" declared the headline in *Variety*, which noted that "the enormously popular drama had previously received no other year-end honors" for helming.

"Levinson accepted his award modestly, marveling at how he became involved in *Rain Man* only a year ago," *Variety* reported. After several directors quit from the pic, Levinson pitched in to help and "suddenly ended up with the movie in my lap," he said.

Controversy caught up with *Mississippi Burning* again at the writers' guild awards when it failed to nab a nod. *Bull Durham* ended up scoring a grand slam after sweeping all three critics' awards.

In the match-up for Best Adapted Screenplay, voters endorsed *Dangerous Liaisons*, Christopher Hampton's adaptation of his legit hit *Les Liaisons Dangereuses*, which was based on the 1782 French novel chronicling "the cunning, cold-blooded sexual calculations of the French prerevolutionary upper class," said *Variety*.

Variety reported that the awards gala "was one of the liveliest in years." Naughty stage skits included a send-up of TV tabloid programs titled *Showbiz Hype Entertainment Enquirer Tonight* and a twist on *Rain Man* called *Writeman*, which *Variety* described as "a cleverly close spoof of Dustin Hoffman, this time as a writer savant whose brother is peddling him as a script doctor."

When the Laurel Award was bestowed

LEVINSON REIGNS AT DGA PARADE

After being snubbed at the Globes, *Rain Man* helmer Barry Levinson prevailed at DGA when Clint Eastwood (*Bird*) was shut out.

jointly on brothers Garson and Michael Kanin, *Variety* said they "were greatly affecting in their memories of growing up in Rochester, N.Y., fighting as kids, sustaining each other as struggling young writers."

Despite its setback at the WGA, *Rain Man*'s chances looked more and more sunny as the Oscars drew near and the race for Best Picture seemed to be limited to the three films nominated for both Best Picture and director. Of those, *Rain Man* stood out by default since it looked like *Mississippi Burning*'s chances were quickly going up in the flames of historical inaccuracy and *Working Girl* was in trouble thanks to the flip way that Oscar voters usually treat comedies.

Furthermore, Levinson's DGA victory virtually guaranteed his equivalent win at the Oscars, which meant that *Rain Man* would probably score Best Picture, too, since those two awards usually match up.

Nine weeks before the Academy Awards, *Rain Man* hadn't been considered a serious contender. Now, on Oscar eve, it looked invincible.

Writing in *TV Guide*, Kenneth Turan declared that "the feeling for *Rain Man* is so strong in Hollywood that it will likely bring the Best Director Oscar to Barry Levinson and the Best Actor Oscar to Dustin Hoffman, who won for *Kramer vs. Kramer* in 1979."

Pundits even wondered if it could pull off a complete sweep just as *The Last Emperor* had last year.

But then ominous dark clouds suddenly gathered overhead on Oscar day.

As the ceremony got under way at the Shrine Auditorium, *Rain Man* lost all of its showdowns in the crafts categories—for film editing, art direction, original score and cinematography. Its remaining four bids were all in the top races.

Dustin Hoffman's shot at Best Actor seemed secure, however. Pundits believed that Gene Hackman would suffer because of the *Mississippi Burning* flare-up and Tom Hanks (*Big*) could be hurt by Oscar's comedy curse. Furthermore, "there seems to be a readable groundswell for Hoffman this year," observed the *L.A. Times*.

That groundswell became dramatically apparent when the Oscar audience leapt to its feet in tribute as Hoffman was declared the winner.

Upon accepting his prize, he saluted his fellow nominees "even if they didn't vote for me," adding, "I didn't vote for you guys either." He then proceeded to ramble for so long that Liz Smith let him have it in her column the next day, blasting "his general egotism in thinking he never has to be prepared."

L.A. Times critic Sheilah Benson had "a hunch" that Jodie Foster (*The Accused*) would win Best Actress "based on the affection I've seen her generate in appearances at various awards groups. She's regarded as a real Hollywood product, as a veteran and even, as one friend suggested, as the prodigal daughter come home again" after attending college in the East.

But most other pundits backed Glenn Close as the malevolent marquise in *Dangerous Liaisons*. "Glenn Close has timing in her favor this year," insisted *TV Guide*. "She has been nominated five times, most spectacularly last year for *Fatal Attraction*, but has never won. That is the kind of morning-after grievance the academy most enjoys redressing."

What most pundits forgot, however, was that voters tend to favor victim roles over villains.

When Foster won, *Variety* columnist Army Archerd reported that she received "the biggest scream of surprise and approval from the audience."

"This is such a big deal and my life is so simple," she said, accepting her statuette. "There are very few things—there's love and work and family. And this movie is so special to us because it was all three of those things."

Variety called Foster's win "a mild surprise," which was nothing compared to the shocker that occurred in the contest for Best Supporting Actress.

Not one of the thesps honored by the three critics' groups made the cut. Of the actresses who did, there was one standout: double Globe champ Sigourney Weaver. She lost her bid for Oscar's Best Actress (*Gorillas in the Mist*), but most pundits believed she'd rebound with a victory for *Working Girl. Variety* noted the precedents: "In the previous four instances in Oscar history, when a performer was cited for both a leading and supporting performance in the same year, he or she has always won the supporting award."

Except this year. An anomaly finally occurred when Geena Davis prevailed over Weaver for her antics as a loopy lover and dog trainer in *The Accidental Tourist*.

An upset also occurred in the race for Best Supporting Actor, which included recent Globe victor Martin Landau (*Tucker*), National Board of Review honoree River Phoenix (*Running on Empty*), L.A. film crix champ Alec Guinness (*Little Dorrit*) and New York film crix and national society winner Dean Stockwell (*Married to the Mob*). *Entertainment Tonight* seemed to back Stockwell, as it followed him around all Oscar day with a camera crew. The *L.A. Times* bet that Landau would win "because it's a nice, safe, sentimental performance by a warmly regarded veteran."

The victor turned out to be the only contender who hadn't won a previous award, wasn't nominated by the Golden Globe and wasn't even considered by any of the critics kudos: Kevin Kline as an smug macho thug in *A Fish Called Wanda*.

Best Picture front-runner *Rain Man* had no stars up for supporting laurels, but it competed for Best Original Screenplay, which was expected to be a revealing match-up. *Rain Man* had lost the equivalent prize at the writers guild to *Bull Durham*. If its producers hoped to reverse the losing trend *Rain Man* was suffering early on Oscar night, they expected to see a dramatic win in this contest, since Oscar's Best Pictures usually claim a screenplay prize, too.

Then the skies opened for *Rain Man*, clearing the way for its victories as Best Director and Best Picture. For the fourth year in a row, Oscar voters endorsed a choice that had not been embraced by any of the top three crix orgs.

Variety proclaimed the next day that, by sweeping its top four academy races, *Rain Man* "emerged as Oscar's main man."

One man did not emerge from the night's ceremony with such a hearty embrace. The flamboyant producer of *Grease* and *You Can't Stop the Music* Allan Carr had taken over the Oscarcast this year, predicting, "The audience is going to be on its feet, screaming in the theater!" It turned out that TV critics led the screaming one day later.

Carr had promised that the opening number would be amazing, telling *Variety*, "You don't want to miss the beginning. When the curtain goes up, you want to be in your seat."

When the curtains opened, audience members couldn't believe their eyes. Carr had staged odd pairings of movie characters and settings that seemed to have no connection—and no theatrical payoff. The production number climaxed with Snow White teaming up with Rob Lowe to sing "Proud Mary."

The New York Times fumed in its review: "It deserves a permanent place in the annals of Oscar embarrassments."

Disney sure screamed loud and clear—claiming that the Oscars had violated its trademark of Snow White—and threatened to sue. "Because the academy did something kinda Dopey, Disney sure is Grumpy," said *Variety*.

The academy quickly issued a public apology and the issue was dropped.

While the award show for the big pix disappointed showbiz pros, the gala staged by the indies wowed 'em. This year the Independent Spirit Awards were moved from their 1987 restaurant location to the Blossom Room of the Roosevelt Hotel, site of the first Oscar banquet. Emcee Buck Henry noted that the Spirits seemed to be moving slowly "street by street, year by

year" closer to the Shrine Auditorium, where "ultimately this once small happy band will explode into national primetime prominence with an all-star show" like the Oscars.

A few Oscar contenders vied for Spirit honors, which were bestowed four days before the academy ceremony.

One of Oscar's Best Actor losers reaped a prize for *Stand and Deliver*—Edward James Olmos as a tough barrio teacher who inspires his rebellious students to succeed. The pic scored the biggest sweep in the kudos' brief history. *Stand and Deliver* nabbed six prizes in all, including Best Feature, Supporting Actor (Lou Diamond Phillips), Supporting Actress (Rosanna De Soto) and Director and Screenplay (Ramon Menendez).

Accepting his many trophies, producer Tony Musca recalled embarking on the project with Menendez. "We literally didn't have the dollar in our pocket to give Jaime Escalante to option the rights to his life story." *Variety* added, "He said he and Menendez used the hallway of a Sunset Boulevard building for their office and conducted their negotiations on the sidewalk."

Four days before she'd snag her first Oscar, Jodie Foster was hailed as the Indie Spirit's Best Actress for portraying a tough 1960s Catholic Bronx girl in *Five Corners*. Winner of the Best First Feature award was *Mystic Pizza*, which *Variety* lauded as "a genuine, moving and deftly told coming-of-age story about three young femmes."

Twenty-six-year-old Steven Soderbergh, a former volunteer driver for the U.S. Film Festival in Utah, returned this year with his own entry that not only won the newly created Audience Award—*sex, lies and videotape*—but dominated the buzz at the festival's post-screening parties.

sex had been hailed by *Variety* as "one of the best independent films in quite a long while." Production was financed using the monies pledged for worldwide videotape rights, but it had no theatrical distributor lined up before landing in Utah. *Variety* said, "Despite the limited rights available, theatrical distribs should be competing avidly for the film due to its promising potential on the upscale baby boomer circuit." The film was soon picked up by Miramax and went on to become the first debut film in more than 25 years to receive the Palme d'Or at the Cannes Film Festival, in addition to the Best Actor laurels for James Spader. Six months later, it picked up two acting kudos at the next voting conclave of the Los Angeles Film Critics Association and, three months after that, four trophies at the Independent Spirits gala, including Best Picture.

Curiously, however, *sex* did not win the U.S. fest's Grand Jury Prize of 1988, which went to *True Love*, "the story of the final weeks before the marriage of an Italian-American couple in the Bronx," said *Variety*. The paper called the victory "a mild surprise" since "most talk in the latter half of the festival had centered upon Soderbergh's startlingly fine psychological drama." *True Love*, however, created significant buzz, too, as did a loser, *Heathers*.

Hollywood hotshots soon took note and started to descend upon Sundance *en masse* in subsequent years in order to mine young talent between the Utah mountains where George Hearst, William Randolph's dad, had once unearthed a fortune in silver.

The New York Times noted, "Only 4 of the 17 fiction films had distributors when they reached the festival." Most left without same this year.

The winner of two documentary prizes was *For All Mankind*, which chronicled the Apollo moon missions. Recipient of the new Filmmaker's Trophy—which was voted on by the nominees attending the fest—was a production financed by ex-Beatle George Harrison's Handmade Films. *Powwow Highway* was described by *Variety* as "a buddy movie about two Cheyenne Indians trying to come to terms with their cultural heritage."

▪ 1988 ▪

LOS ANGELES FILM CRITICS ASSOCIATION

Winners were announced on December 10, 1988. Awards were presented on January 24 at the Bel Age Hotel in Los Angeles.

BEST PICTURE
▪ *Little Dorrit*

BEST DIRECTOR
▪ David Cronenberg, *Dead Ringers*

BEST ACTOR
▪ Tom Hanks, *Big, Punchline*

BEST ACTRESS
▪ Christine Lahti, *Running on Empty*

BEST SUPPORTING ACTOR
▪ Alec Guinness, *Little Dorrit*

BEST SUPPORTING ACTRESS
▪ Genevieve Bujold, *Dead Ringers, The Moderns*

BEST SCREENPLAY
▪ Ron Shelton, *Bull Durham*

BEST CINEMATOGRAPHY
▪ Henri Alekan, *Wings of Desire*

BEST MUSIC SCORE
▪ Mark Isham, *The Moderns*

BEST DOCUMENTARY
▪ *Hotel Terminus: The Life and Times of Klaus Barbie*, Marcel Ophuls

BEST FOREIGN FILM
▪ *Wings of Desire* (West Germany/France)

BEST EXPERIMENTAL/INDEPENDENT FILM
▪ *The Last of England*, Derek Jarman
▪ *Amerika*, Al Razutis

NEW GENERATION AWARD
▪ Mira Nair, director, *Salaam Bombay!*

CAREER ACHIEVEMENT AWARD
▪ Donald Siegel

SPECIAL AWARDS
- *Who Framed Roger Rabbit* (technical achievement)
- U.C.L.A. Film and Television Archive

NATIONAL BOARD OF REVIEW

The board declared a Best Picture and Foreign Film of the year, then listed its remaining favorites according to highest scores. The vote results were announced on December 13, 1988. Awards were presented on February 27, 1989, at Lincoln Center Library in New York.

BEST PICTURE
- *Mississippi Burning*
Dangerous Liaisons
The Accused
The Unbearable Lightness of Being
The Last Temptation of Christ
Tucker: The Man and His Dream
Big
Running on Empty
Gorillas in the Mist
Midnight Run

BEST DIRECTOR
- Alan Parker, *Mississippi Burning*

BEST ACTOR
- Gene Hackman, *Mississippi Burning*

BEST ACTRESS
- Jodie Foster, *The Accused*

BEST SUPPORTING ACTOR
- River Phoenix, *Running on Empty*

BEST SUPPORTING ACTRESS
- Francis McDormand, *Mississippi Burning*

BEST DOCUMENTARY
- *The Thin Blue Line*, Errol Morris

BEST FOREIGN FILM
- *Women on the Verge of a Nervous Breakdown* (Spain)
Pelle the Conqueror (Denmark)
Le Grand Chemin (France)

Salaam Bombay! (India)
A Taxing Woman (Japan)

CAREER ACHIEVEMENT
- Kirk Douglas

NEW YORK FILM CRITICS CIRCLE

Winners were announced on December 15, 1988. Awards were presented on January 15, 1989, at Sardi's restaurant in New York.

BEST PICTURE
- *The Accidental Tourist*

BEST DIRECTOR
- Chris Menges, *A World Apart*

BEST ACTOR
- Jeremy Irons, *Dead Ringers*

BEST ACTRESS
- Meryl Streep, *A Cry in the Dark*

BEST SUPPORTING ACTOR
- Dean Stockwell, *Married to the Mob, Tucker: The Man and His Dream*

BEST SUPPORTING ACTRESS
- Diane Venora, *Bird*

BEST SCREENPLAY
- Ron Shelton, *Bull Durham*

BEST CINEMATOGRAPHY
- Henri Alekan, *Wings of Desire*

BEST DOCUMENTARY
- *The Thin Blue Line*, Errol Morris

BEST FOREIGN FILM
- *Women on the Verge of a Nervous Breakdown* (Spain)

SPECIAL AWARD
- Tim Allen

NATIONAL SOCIETY OF FILM CRITICS

Winners were announced on January 8, 1989.

BEST PICTURE
- *The Unbearable Lightness of Being*

BEST DIRECTOR
- Philip Kaufman, *The Unbearable Lightness of Being*

BEST ACTOR
- Michael Keaton, *Beetlejuice, Clean and Sober*

BEST ACTRESS
- Judy Davis, *High Tide*

BEST SUPPORTING ACTOR
- Dean Stockwell, *Married to the Mob, Tucker: The Man and His Dream*

BEST SUPPORTING ACTRESS
- Mercedes Ruehl, *Married to the Mob*

BEST SCREENPLAY
- Ron Shelton, *Bull Durham*

BEST CINEMATOGRAPHY
- Henri Alekan, *Wings of Desire*

BEST DOCUMENTARY
- *The Thin Blue Line*, Errol Morris

SPECIAL AWARD
- Pedro Almodovar

GOLDEN GLOBES

Nominations were announced on January 4, 1989. Awards were presented on January 28 at the Beverly Hilton Hotel in Los Angeles. The ceremony was telecast by TBS.

BEST DRAMA PICTURE
- *Rain Man*
The Accidental Tourist
A Cry in the Dark
Gorillas in the Mist
Mississippi Burning
Running on Empty
The Unbearable Lightness of Being

BEST COMEDY OR MUSICAL PICTURE
- *Working Girl*
Big
A Fish Called Wanda
Midnight Run
Who Framed Roger Rabbit

BEST DIRECTOR
- Clint Eastwood, *Bird*
Barry Levinson, *Rain Man*
Sidney Lumet, *Running on Empty*
Mike Nichols, *Working Girl*
Alan Parker, *Mississippi Burning*
Fred Schepisi, *A Cry in the Dark*

BEST ACTOR, DRAMA
- Dustin Hoffman, *Rain Man*
Gene Hackman, *Mississippi Burning*
Tom Hulce, *Dominick and Eugene*
Edward James Olmos, *Stand and Deliver*
Forest Whitaker, *Bird*

BEST ACTRESS, DRAMA (TIE)
- Jodie Foster, *The Accused*
- Shirley MacLaine, *Madame Sousatzka*
- Sigourney Weaver, *Gorillas in the Mist*
Christine Lahti, *Running on Empty*
Meryl Streep, *A Cry in the Dark*

BEST ACTOR, COMEDY OR MUSICAL
- Tom Hanks, *Big*
Michael Caine, *Dirty Rotten Scoundrels*
John Cleese, *A Fish Called Wanda*
Robert De Niro, *Midnight Run*
Bob Hoskins, *Who Framed Roger Rabbit*

BEST ACTRESS, COMEDY OR MUSICAL
- Melanie Griffith, *Working Girl*
Jamie Lee Curtis, *A Fish Called Wanda*
Amy Irving, *Crossing Delancey*
Michelle Pfeiffer, *Married to the Mob*
Susan Sarandon, *Bull Durham*

BEST SUPPORTING ACTOR
- Martin Landau, *Tucker: The Man and His Dream*
Alec Guinness, *Little Dorrit*
Neil Patrick Harris, *Clara's Heart*
Raul Julia, *Moon over Parador*

Lou Diamond Phillips, *Stand and Deliver*
River Phoenix, *Running on Empty*

BEST SUPPORTING ACTRESS
- Sigourney Weaver, *Working Girl*
Sonia Braga, *Moon over Parador*
Barbara Hershey, *The Last Temptation of Christ*
Lena Olin, *The Unbearable Lightness of Being*
Diane Venora, *Bird*

BEST SCREENPLAY
- Naomi Foner, *Running on Empty*
Ronald Bass, Barry Morrow, *Rain Man*
Chris Gerolmo, *Mississippi Burning*
Fred Schepisi, Robert Caswell, *A Cry in the Dark*
Kevin Wade, *Working Girl*

BEST SONG (TIE)
- "Let the River Run," *Working Girl*
- "Two Hearts," *Buster*
"Kokomo," *Cocktail*
"Twins," *Twins*
"Why Should I Worry," *Oliver & Company*
"A Woman Loves a Man," *Bull Durham*

BEST FOREIGN FILM
- *Pelle the Conqueror* (Denmark)
Babette's Feast (Denmark)
Hanussen (Germany)
Salaam Bombay! (India)
Women on the Verge of a Nervous Breakdown (Spain)

Winners

BEST SCORE
- Maurice Jarre, *Gorillas in the Mist*

CECIL B. DEMILLE AWARD
- Doris Day

U.S. FILM FESTIVAL (SUNDANCE)

The festival was held January 20–29, 1989, at Park City, Utah.

GRAND JURY PRIZE
(DRAMATIC)
- *True Love*, Nancy Savoca
(DOCUMENTARY)
- *For All Mankind*, Al Reinert

FILMMAKER'S TROPHY
(DRAMATIC)
- *Powwow Highway*, Jonathan Wacks
(DOCUMENTARY)
- *John Huston*, Frank Martin

AUDIENCE AWARD
(DRAMATIC)
- *sex, lies, and videotape*, Steven Soderbergh
(DOCUMENTARY)
- *For all Mankind*, Al Reinert

DIRECTORS GUILD OF AMERICA

Nominations were announced on January 31, 1989. Awards were presented on March 11 at the Beverly Hilton Hotel in Los Angeles and the Plaza Hotel in New York.

BEST DIRECTOR
- Barry Levinson, *Rain Man*
Charles Crichton, *A Fish Called Wanda*
Mike Nichols, *Working Girl*
Alan Parker, *Mississippi Burning*
Robert Zemeckis, *Who Framed Roger Rabbit*

ROBERT B. ALDRICH AWARD
- Gilbert Cates

HONORARY LIFETIME MEMBER
- Sidney Lumet

WRITERS GUILD OF AMERICA

Awards were presented on March 20, 1989, at the Beverly Hilton Hotel in Los Angeles and the Windows on the World restaurant in New York.

BEST ORIGINAL SCREENPLAY
- *Bull Durham*, Ron Shelton
Big, Gary Ross, Anne Spielberg

A Fish Called Wanda, John Cleese, Charles Crichton
Rain Man, Ronald Bass, Barry Morrow
Working Girl, Kevin Wade

BEST ADAPTED SCREENPLAY

- *Dangerous Liaisons*, Christopher Hampton, based on his play and the novel *Les Liaisons Dangereuses* by Choderlos De Laclos
The Accidental Tourist, Frank Galati, Lawrence Kasdan, based on the book by Anne Tyler
Gorillas in the Mist, Anna Hamilton Phelan, Tab Murphy, based on the work by Dian Fossey and the article by Harold T. P. Hayes
The Unbearable Lightness of Being, Jean-Claude Carriere, Philip Kaufman, based on the novel by Milan Kundera
Who Framed Roger Rabbit, Jeffrey Price, Peter Seaman, based on the book *Who Censored Roger Rabbit* by Gary K. Wolf

MORGAN COX AWARD

- Robert I. Bolt

VALENTINE DAVIES AWARD

- Garson Kanin, Michael Kanin

LAUREL AWARD

- Ring Lardner, Jr.

INDEPENDENT SPIRIT

Awards were presented on March 25, 1989, at the Roosevelt Hotel in Los Angeles.

BEST FEATURE

- *Stand and Deliver*
Hairspray
Patti Rocks
The Thin Blue Line
Torch Song Trilogy

BEST FIRST FEATURE

- *Mystic Pizza*
Border Radio
The Chocolate War
Prince of Pennsylvania
The Wash

BEST DIRECTOR

- Ramon Menendez, *Stand and Deliver*
David Burton Morris, *Patti Rocks*
Errol Morris, *The Thin Blue Line*
Oliver Stone, *Talk Radio*
John Waters, *Hairspray*

BEST ACTOR

- Edward James Olmos, *Stand and Deliver*
Eric Bogosian, *Talk Radio*
Harvey Fierstein, *Torch Song Trilogy*
Chris Mulkey, *Patti Rocks*
James Woods, *The Boost*

BEST ACTRESS

- Jodie Foster, *Five Corners*
Ricki Lake, *Hairspray*
Nobu McCarthy, *The Wash*
Julia Roberts, *Mystic Pizza*
Meg Ryan, *Promised Land*

BEST SUPPORTING ACTOR

- Lou Diamond Phillips, *Stand and Deliver*
Ernest Borgnine, *Spike of Bensonhurst*
Divine, *Hairspray*
John Lone, *The Moderns*
John Turturro, *Five Corners*

BEST SUPPORTING ACTRESS

- Rosanna De Soto, *Stand and Deliver*
Bonnie Bedelia, *Prince of Pennsylvania*
Debbie Harry, *Hairspray*
Amy Madigan, *Prince of Pennsylvania*
Patti Yasutake, *The Wash*

BEST SCREENPLAY

- Ramon Menendez, *Stand and Deliver*
David Burton Morris, Chris Mulkey, John Jenkins, Karen Landry, *Patti Rcks*
Alan Rudolph, Jon Bradshaw, *The Moderns*
John Patrick Shanley, *Five Corners*
John Waters, *Hairspray*

BEST FOREIGN FILM

- *Wings of Desire* (West Germany/France)
Bagdad Cafe (West Germany)
Brightness (Mali)
The Kitchen Toto (U.K.)
A World Apart (U.K.)

Winner

BEST CINEMATOGRAPHY

■ Sven Nykvist, *The Unbearable Lightness of Being*

ACADEMY AWARDS

Nominations were announced on February 14, 1989. Awards were presented on March 29 at the Shrine Auditorium in Los Angeles. The ceremony was telecast by ABC.

BEST PICTURE

■ *Rain Man*
The Accidental Tourist
Dangerous Liaisons
Mississippi Burning
Working Girl

BEST DIRECTOR

■ Barry Levinson, *Rain Man*
Charles Crichton, *A Fish Called Wanda*
Mike Nichols, *Working Girl*
Alan Parker, *Mississippi Burning*
Martin Scorsese, *The Last Temptation of Christ*

BEST ACTOR

■ Dustin Hoffman, *Rain Man*
Gene Hackman, *Mississippi Burning*
Tom Hanks, *Big*
Edward James Olmos, *Stand and Deliver*
Max von Sydow, *Pelle the Conqueror*

BEST ACTRESS

■ Jodie Foster, *The Accused*
Glenn Close, *Dangerous Liaisons*
Melanie Griffith, *Working Girl*
Meryl Streep, *A Cry in the Dark*
Sigourney Weaver, *Gorillas in the Mist*

BEST SUPPORTING ACTOR

■ Kevin Kline, *A Fish Called Wanda*
Alec Guinness, *Little Dorrit*
Martin Landau, *Tucker: The Man and His Dream*
River Phoenix, *Running on Empty*
Dean Stockwell, *Married to the Mob*

BEST SUPPORTING ACTRESS

■ Geena Davis, *The Accidental Tourist*

Joan Cusack, *Working Girl*
Michelle Pfeiffer, *Dangerous Liaisons*
Frances McDormand, *Mississippi Burning*
Sigourney Weaver, *Working Girl*

BEST ORIGINAL SCREENPLAY

■ Ronald Bass, Barry Morrow, *Rain Man*
John Cleese, Charles Crichton, *A Fish Called Wanda*
Naomi Foner, *Running on Empty*
Gary Ross, Anne Spielberg, *Big*
Ron Shelton, *Bull Durham*

BEST ADAPTED SCREENPLAY

■ Christopher Hampton, *Dangerous Liaisons*
Jean-Claude Carrière, Philip Kaufman, *The Unbearable Lightness of Being*
Christine Edzard, *Little Dorrit*
Frank Galati, Lawrence Kasdan, *The Accidental Tourist*
Tab Murphy, Anna Hamilton Phelan, *Gorillas in the Mist*

BEST SONG

■ "Let the River Run," *Working Girl*, Carly Simon
"Calling You," *Bagdad Cafe*, Bob Telson
"Two Hearts," *Buster*, Phil Collins, Lamont Dozier

BEST FOREIGN-LANGUAGE FILM

■ *Pelle the Conqueror* (Denmark)
Hanussen (Hungary)
The Music Teacher (Belgium)
Salaam Bombay! (India)
Women on the Verge of a Nervous Breakdown (Spain)

Winners

BEST ART DIRECTION

■ Stuart Craig, Gerard James, *Dangerous Liaisons*

BEST CINEMATOGRAPHY

■ Peter Biziou, *Mississippi Burning*

BEST COSTUME DESIGN

■ James Acheson, *Dangerous Liaisons*

BEST DOCUMENTARY

(FEATURE)

- *Hotel Terminus: The Life and Times of Klaus Barbie*, Marcel Ophuls

(SHORT SUBJECT)

- *You Don't Have to Die, Malcolm Clarke*, William Guttentag

BEST FILM EDITING

- Arthur Schmidt, *Who Framed Roger Rabbit*

BEST MAKEUP

- Steve La Porte, Ve Neill, Robert Short, *Beetlejuice*

BEST MUSIC SCORE

- Dave Grusin, *The Milagro Beanfield War*

SCIENTIFIC OR TECHNICAL AWARDS

(Academy Award of Merit)

- Ioan Allen, Ray Dolby, Dolby Laboratories

(Scientific and Engineering Award)

- Roy W. Edwards, Photosonics; Arnold and Richter; Otto Blaschek, Arriflex Corp.; Bill Tondreau, Tondreau Systems; Alvah Miller, Paul Johnson, Lynx Robotics; Peter A. Regla, Elicon; Bud Elam, Joe Parker, Bill Bryan, Interactive Motion Control; Jerry Jeffress, Ray Feeney, Bill Holland, Kris Brown, Dan Slater

(Technical Achievement Award)

- Grant Loucks, Alan Gordon Enterprises; Geoffrey H. Williamson, Wilcam; BHP Inc.; Hollywood Film Co.; Bruce W. Keller, Manfred G. Michelson, Technical Film Systems; Antal Lisziewicz, Glenn M. Berggren, ISCO-OPTIC CmbH; James K. Branch, Spectra Cine; Bob Badami, Dick Bernstein, Bill Bernstein, Offbeat Systems; Gary Zeller, Emanuel Trilling; Paul A. Roos, Michael V. Chewey III, William L. Blowers, Nasir J. Zaidi

BEST SHORT FILM

(ANIMATED)

- *Tin Toy, John Lasseter*, William Reeves

(LIVE ACTION)

- *The Appointments of Dennis Jennings*, Dean Parisot, Steven Wright

BEST SOUND

- Dick Alexander, Willie D. Burton, Les Fresholtz, Vern Poore, *Bird*

BEST SOUND EFFECTS EDITING

- Charles L. Campbell, Louis L. Edemann, *Who Framed Roger Rabbit*

SPECIAL ACHIEVEMENT—ANIMATION DIRECTION

- Richard Williams, *Who Framed Roger Rabbit*

BEST VISUAL EFFECTS

- George Gibbs, Edward Jones, Ken Ralston, Richard Williams, *Who Framed Roger Rabbit*

GORDON E. SAWYER AWARD

- Gordon Henry Cook

HONORARY AWARDS

- Eastman Kodak
- National Film Board of Canada

SCREEN ACTORS GUILD

LIFETIME ACHIEVEMENT AWARD

- Gene Kelly

· 1989 ·

Late-Blooming Daisy

*D*riving Miss Daisy's trip to the Oscars—slow-chugging and meandering, as if it were out for a leisurely Sunday spin to the Piggly Wiggly—proved that tortoises win races.

Daisy got an early head start as the first film of 1989 to be declared Best Picture when it was hailed by the National Board of Review on December 13. *Variety* described *Daisy* as "a touching exploration of 25 years of change in Southern race relations (1948–73) as seen through the relationship of an elderly Jewish widow (Jessica Tandy) and her stalwart black chauffeur (Morgan Freeman)." Freeman won the board's Best Actor award, which he could place beside the Obie he earned for originating the role off Broadway. Tandy, however, lost the actress laurels to Michelle Pfeiffer, who, the *L.A. Times* said, "finally became a bankable star" as a sultry torch singer in *The Fabulous Baker Boys*. Tandy would wreak revenge later, but another oversight would go unredressed. *Variety* had cheered Bruce Beresford for his "sensitive direction" of *Driving Miss Daisy*, but the Yankee board snubbed the Aussie helmer—a decision that would prove to be an ominous foretelling of what was around the bend.

Three days after the board announced its champs, another movie about racial relations zoomed past *Daisy* when the L.A. crix seemed concerned about doing the right thing by Spike Lee's *Do the Right Thing*, which had recently lost the Palme d'Or at Cannes to last year's Sundance honoree *sex, lies, and videotape* amidst angry accusations of racism (mostly by Lee). The drama about a Brooklyn neighborhood engulfed by riots after cops kill a black man was voted Best Picture by the Hollywood crix over *Drugstore Cowboy,* which starred Matt Dillon as an addict who robs drugstores for drugs. *Cowboy* rebounded by roping the

The NBR picked *Driving Miss Daisy* as best pic early on, but the film fell far behind in the derby, then suddenly sped ahead at the Globes and Oscars. Not on board: its director, strangely, wasn't nommed.

screenplay award, while *Right Thing* copped two more prizes: Best Director for Lee (over Oliver Stone, *Born on the Fourth of July*) and Best Supporting Actor for Danny Aiello as a racist pizza-shop owner, topping Martin Landau as a married eye doctor with a roving eye in *Crimes and Misdemeanors*.

When he accepted the honors at the crix's gala, Lee was grateful, but obviously looking ahead to further kudos, saying his current wins "are going to help us definitely with the Oscar nominations (since) 85 percent of the academy voting members live here in the L.A. area."

As a result of a tie vote, the crix's Best Actress award was shared by Andie MacDowell as a frigid housewife in *sex, lies, and videotape* and Michelle Pfeiffer (*Baker Boys*). *Daisy*'s Morgan Freeman placed second in the match-up for Best Actor, losing to Daniel Day-Lewis, who *Variety* said, gave "a brilliant performance" in *My Left*

Foot as the Irish writer and artist Christy Brown, who had cerebral palsy. Brenda Fricker, as Brown's inspiring mum, won Best Supporting Actress over Anjelica Huston as a presumed-dead Holocaust survivor who catches up with her now-remarried husband in *Enemies: A Love Story*.

When the New York crix gathered to vote two days after their L.A. counterparts, the group no longer included journos from the *N.Y. Times*. The paper's management refused to let their employees lend the *Times*'s name to an org endorsing choices that often conflicted with its own annual top 10 list of the year's best pix. This year the *Times*'s list was topped by the French-lingo import *Chocolat*, about the memories of a young woman growing up in French West Africa in the late 1950s. When the crix org began voting, members skipped over it (not even picking it as Best Foreign Film) as well as the paper's second-ranked movie, *Crimes and Misdemeanors*, in favor of squaring off into rival camps over third-ranked *Do the Right Thing* and fourth-ranked *Enemies*. They'd end up settling on a compromise choice that was nowhere on the *Times*'s list.

Do the Right Thing "lunged out front" on the first ballot with six votes, followed by four for *Enemies* and one each for more than a dozen rival pix that included *My Left Foot*, according to *The Village Voice*'s Georgia Brown. It maintained its lead on the next round when the 29 voters added their second and third choices, granting three points to their favorite, two to their second and one to their third. Then, Brown noted, *Right Thing* stumbled: "On the third ballot, where the field narrows to five finalists, the game becomes Block the Other Camp. This is how *My Left Foot* won on a fourth ballot with 36 points," followed by 31 for *Enemies*. *Right Thing*—with 24—came in last.

"The pattern repeated in the voting for Best Director," Brown observed. "Spike Lee

The stalemated Gotham crix picked a compromise best pic: *My Left Foot*.

got the highest total (6) on ballot 1, and then finished last of the 5 on ballot 4, losing to Paul Mazursky (*Enemies*). Brian De Palma (*Casualties of War*) had 31, Bruce Beresford *Daisy*) 29."

My Left Foot's Day-Lewis claimed a rare, single-round victory for Best Actor over another thesp in a wheelchair—Tom Cruise, who was "stunning," said *Variety*, as a gung-ho army enlistee who becomes an anti-war fighter after being shot in Vietnam in *Born on the Fourth of July*, an adaptation of Ron Kovic's memoir that won the National Book Award in 1976. "Morgan Freeman, who redefines the word 'dignity' as *Daisy*'s long-suffering chauffeur (and who also starred this year in *Lean on Me* and supported in *Glory*) barely got a vote," Brown noticed.

Variety said that Freeman's *Glory* costar, Denzel Washington, gave "a great performance" as a runaway slave fighting for the Union army in the "eloquent, heart-tugging Civil War epic." He tied Alan Alda on the third ballot for Best Supporting Actor, but then lost by a single point (37 to 36) on the fourth polling. "Excuse me," Brown harrumphed, "but I felt a chill."

Racial prejudice wasn't the only charge Brown leveled against her peers. Since 21 of them were male out of the 29 voters, she accused them of being overly "red-blooded" when deciding Best Actress, bypassing 80-year-old Jessica Tandy (38 points) in favor of a seductive Michelle Pfeiffer (39), who wiggled seductively atop a piano as she warbled "Makin' Whoopee" in *Baker Boys*. The pattern was repeated in the race for Best Supporting Actress when the frumpy, middle-aged Brenda Fricker (24 points) lost to the curvy Lena Olin as a self-destructive lover in *Enemies* (40).

Brown's article received "coded nods" among those gathered at Sardi's for the awards ceremony, according to *The Village Voice*, but it was not discussed openly.

A nervous Pfeiffer accepted her prize, telling the crix, "I can't give a speech, but I can act."

Best Supporting Actor Alan Alda thanked Vincent Canby of *The New York Times* for calling him "priceless" in *Crimes* after labeling him "worthless" in a previous role.

Despite ending up a loser in all categories, good sport Spike Lee appeared at the gala to present the new award for Best New Director to British *wunderkind* Kenneth Branagh (*Henry V*), who wasn't on hand to accept.

"I'm happy to be here," Lee said, graciously, anyway.

A startled *Village Voice* whined, "Doesn't Spike realize he was ahead on the first ballot" for Best Picture and Director?

The National Society of Film Critics tried a new voting procedure on its own first ballots, suspending the rule of secrecy on the initial voting round only.

The switch didn't result in a significant change of outcome, according to most members, who still largely agreed with the Gotham crix.

Daniel Day-Lewis (53 points) repeated his previous victories as Best Actor by beating Morgan Freeman (36). Michelle Pfeiffer completed her sweep of the crix kudos, too, topping Jessica Tandy by a 37-to-31 score. *The Fabulous Baker Boys* snagged the additional prize of Best Supporting Actor for Beau Bridges as one of the two piano-playing Baker brothers (the "bubbly, ever-optimistic one," *Variety* noted) over Denzel Washington (*Glory*) by a 32-to-31 tally.

The Gotham crix's choice for Best Supporting Actress, Lena Olin (35 points), lost to her *Enemies* costar Anjelica Huston (43).

The biggest difference between the orgs' choices was in the top two races, which were both won by *Drugstore Cowboy*. It prevailed as Best Picture with 35 points over *Enemies* (20) and copped the Best

Director laurels for Gus Van Sant over Paul Mazursky (35 to 24).

Drugstore completed its sweep of the crix's screenplay awards by winning the society vote, too, 39 to 27.

While *Driving Miss Daisy* seemed to have wandered off on a side trip during the recent awards, the pic caught up with the competish by nabbing three nominations at the Golden Globes. Far ahead, though, with five bids each, were *Born on the Fourth of July, Glory* and *When Harry Met Sally* . . . (which *Variety* called "11 years of emotional foreplay between Billy Crystal and Meg Ryan (before) they realize they're perfect for each other"). *Do the Right Thing* had four. *Driving Miss Daisy* might have won a Pulitzer Prize as a stage play, but it wasn't up for the Globe's Best Screenplay trophy—and once again Bruce Beresford didn't make the directors' cut.

As a result, *Daisy* wasn't expected to do well, although all media, including the *L.A. Herald Examiner*, agreed that Jessica Tandy was "a sure shot" for Best Comedy/Musical Actress since her previous kudos nemesis, Michelle Pfeiffer, was placed in the separate drama lineup.

When Tandy prevailed as predicted, she told the crowd at the Beverly Hilton Hotel that she was "very proud and grateful."

The crowd was shocked a few minutes later when *Daisy* won Best Comedy or Musical Picture over *When Harry Met Sally* . . . , b.o. hit *The War of the Roses* and Disney's latest animated musical, *The Little Mermaid.*

Daisy star Morgan Freeman triumphed over equally tough competish for Best Comedy/Musical Actor, including Billy Crystal (*When Harry Met Sally* . . .), Steve Martin (as an unhinged dad in *Parenthood*), Michael Douglas (as an unhinged divorcé in *The War of the Roses*) and Jack Nicholson (as the Joker in *Batman*).

As he claimed his statuette, Freeman

Oscar front-runner *Born on the Fourth of July* swept the Globes and DGA.

assumed a serious tone, telling the crowd, "My mother used to say to me all the time, 'My boy, you're going to make it in Hollywood.' " He waved his Globe triumphantly in the air and shouted, "Well, Ma, look what they did!"

Although the crix kudos may have been guilty of an anti-black bias earlier, the same wasn't true of the Globes. Another big victor turned out to be Best Supporting Actor Denzel Washington (*Glory*), who told the crowd that he had a premonition he'd win.

"A few years ago, I was here for *Cry Freedom*, I was calm and I didn't feel I would win," he said. "But this year I *really* felt it."

The biggest champ of the night was *Born on the Fourth of July*, which snagged four wins out of its five noms.

Most poignant was its triumph for Best Screenplay, which was shared by helmer/producer Oliver Stone and the man upon whom the film was based: Ron Kovic.

Kovic appeared at the podium in his wheelchair and said, "Twenty-two years ago today, I was wounded in Vietnam. Lying in that field, I never I would have imagined that I would be before all of you tonight. This proves you *can* stand tall even if you're in a wheelchair."

When *Born* also snagged kudos as Best Drama Film and Best Director, Oliver Stone was asked by reporters how the pic's success compared to his *Platoon* awards sweep in 1986.

"Like getting a second daughter married off," he replied.

A dramatic triumph came in the race for Best Actor where Tom Cruise topped the crix's fave, Daniel Day-Lewis.

Cruise said that it was Kovic's "unrelenting quest for the truth that really drove this film," then headed backstage where he "jumped up and down like a chimp," said the *Herald Examiner*.

An equally jubilant Stone jumped on Spike Lee and gave him a bear hug while the latter tried to sneak out of the ceremony after failing to win any kudos. "Lee appeared embarrassed," noted *The Newark Star-Ledger.*

One day later, the *Herald Examiner* announced, "The Oscar nomination ballots go out today.

"Tom Cruise is now the favorite in the Best Actor Oscar category, suddenly jumping ahead of *My Left Foot* star Daniel Day-Lewis, who had won every other critics' award under the sun. Hollywood prefers a hometown boy.

"The Best Picture race now seems to be between *Born on the Fourth of July* and *Driving Miss Daisy.*"

But *Daisy* soon hit a bump in the road when the nominees were announced for the Directors Guild of America—and again Bruce Beresford wasn't nommed. This latest slap was the harshest yet, since only three DGA winners had ever failed to snag the equivalent Oscar—and the latter prize usually presaged the eventual Best Picture champ.

The producers' guild gave its new Zanuck award to two Zanucks.

Two weeks later, the Oscar noms were announced and Beresford was snubbed *again.*

The latest slight was especially strange considering how well *Daisy* did in other categories, scoring the most overall noms (nine), followed by eight for *Fourth of July*. Award pundits wondered: Could *Daisy* still win Best Picture? The film with the most noms usually does, but the last time a movie claimed the top prize without its director being nommed was *Grand Hotel* in 1931–1932.

This year's kudos derby was turning out to be one of the oddest ever.

Not only was Beresford missing from the list of DGA contenders, but the lineup failed to include *any* of the helmers honored already by the three crix orgs (Spike Lee, Paul Mazursky, Gus Van Sant) or the National Board of Review (Kenneth Branagh).

Instead, the contenders were Oliver Stone (*Born on the Fourth of July*), Woody Allen (*Crimes and Misdemeanors*), Rob Reiner (*When Harry Met Sally . . .*), Phil Alden Robinson (*Field of Dreams*) and Peter Weir (*Dead Poets Society*).

Previous champ Stone (*Platoon*, 1986) won easily, becoming only the seventh champ to claim the prize for a second time, following Joseph L. Mankiewicz, George Stevens, David Lean, Robert Wise, Fred Zinnemann and Francis Coppola.

"How sweet it is, and how fleeting," Stone told the crowd of 1,400 people gathered at the Beverly Hilton. "I always wanted to make movies and would give everything of myself when I had the chance. Nights like this were never expected and, when they came, they were that much sweeter."

One week later, just when *Born on the Fourth of July* looked like it was unstoppable on its drive toward an Oscar sweep, it lost the contest for Best Adapted Screenplay at the Writers Guild of America Awards. *Fourth of July* wasn't held up by *Drugstore Cowboy*, which had been unanimously embraced by the three crix orgs. *Cowboy*—based on an unpublished novel by James Fogle—wasn't even nommed. It was *Driving Miss Daisy*'s Alfred Uhry who rode triumphantly into the winner's circle.

When Uhry reached the podium at the Beverly Hilton—after a considerable trek from the back of the ballroom—he said, "My table was so far back I didn't think I had a chance." He confessed to being "really overwhelmed" and called himself "probably the luckiest writer who ever got to have a movie."

No-show Woody Allen won the prize for Best Original Screenplay for *Crimes and Misdemeanors*, following up on previous guild wins for *Annie Hall* (1977), *Broadway Danny Rose* (1984) and *Hannah and Her Sisters* (1986).

WGA prexy George Kirgo told the crowd, "Woody Allen has won three times before this and never showed up to receive our award. Does anybody here know Woody? Could you please tell him to come by and pick this stuff up? It's taking up a lot of room at the guild."

L.A. crix best pic *Do the Right Thing* (starring Spike Lee and Danny Aiello) led the early Gotham vote, but lost to *My Left Foot*.

The star attraction of the fete was Art Buchwald, who received honorary kudos after recently winning a lawsuit against Paramount Pictures for not compensating him after using his film treatment as a basis for the Eddie Murphy hit *Coming to America*. Buchwald and his producer were awarded $250,000 plus 19 percent of the pic's net profit, but they faced a new problem claiming their reward. *Coming to America* might have grossed $250 million, but Paramount said it didn't make a profit. Buchwald's attorneys were currently poring over the studio's ledgers to find out where the proceeds went.

"Buchwald confided that he had been 'nervous' about coming to L.A. for the guild ceremony because of the recent 5.5 earthquake in southern California," *Variety* reported. "He was 'about to cancel' his plans until he learned that Paramount was claiming it was only a 2.2."

On the eve of the Oscarcast, four crix at the *L.A. Times* posted their predix, revealing unanimous agreement over three top races: Best Actress (Jessica Tandy), Best Director (Oliver Stone) and Best Picture (*Born on the Fourth of July*). Fellow staffer Jack Mathews didn't participate in the 18-category breakdown, but noted elsewhere in the *Times* that he had "a buck in the office pool that *Driving Miss Daisy* will win both Best Adapted Screenplay and Best Picture."

As the Oscar show began, host Billy Crystal introduced a segment showcasing the year's top contenders, then said, "There are 330 pieces of film in that five-minute montage and what's amazing is that, according to Paramount, not one has yet to go into profits." The audience howled, then laughed even louder when he referred to *Driving Miss Daisy* as "the movie that apparently directed itself."

In the race for Best Supporting Actor, three out of the four *L.A. Times* crix picked Danny Aiello, previous winner of the L.A. film crix award for *Do the Right Thing*. One critic picked Marlon Brando as an outspoken South African judge in *A Dry White Season*. *Times* naysayer Mathews chose Golden Globe champ Denzel Washington (*Glory*), but warned that voters might opt for Martin Landau (*Crimes and Misdemeanors*) since he'd been passed over last year for *Tucker*.

Washington prevailed. At the podium he saluted "the black soldiers who helped to make this country free."

Backstage later, Washington told the press that *Glory* covered "a bit of history I knew nothing about before making the film. I was stunned that I wasn't taught this in school."

When sizing up the competish for Best Supporting Actress, the *L.A. Times* said, "Conventional wisdom has it that Lena Olin and Anjelica Huston, two of Ron Silver's three wives in *Enemies, A Love Story*, will cancel each other out in the voting and give Brenda Fricker (*My Left Foot*) a clear path. Others think that Huston will carry the day because she has done so much other good work lately."

This time the L.A. film crix champ did win—Fricker, an Irish thesp chiefly known for playing the lead on the popular BBC-TV medical soap opera series *Casualty*.

"I don't believe this!" she gasped, accepting the honor. She referred to her

Mon., March 26, 1990

'Cowboy,' 'sex,' 'Foot' Dance Away With Indie Spirit Nods

VARIETY (D)   By WILL TUSHER   MAR 2 6 1990

"Drugstore Cowboy" and "sex, lies, and videotape," ended up in a dead heat with four trophies each at the fifth annual Independent Spirit Awards of Independent Feature Project/West at the Hollywood Roosevelt Saturday, but "sex, lies, etc."

honored as best first feature.

Spike Lee, recipient of IFP's first annual Special Distinction Award, in recognition of "Do The Right Thing," sent a message vowing to keep on doing the right thing.

"Regardless of where I get my

National crix society best pic *Drugstore Cowboy* nabbed four Spirits, but lost the top prize to *sex, lies and videotape.*

real-life film character, saying, "I'd like to thank Mrs. Brown. Anybody who gives birth 22 times deserves one of these."

Fricker's costar Daniel Day-Lewis, who had previously swept all three crix awards, was the Best Actor choice of three of the four *L.A. Times* critics. The fourth pundit forecasted *Daisy*'s Morgan Freeman, who, Mathews agreed, "may have a slight edge." *Newsweek* bet on Globe champ Tom Cruise, who, at age 27, stood to become the youngest winner of the prize in Oscar history.

When Day-Lewis triumphed, *Variety* called him "an upset winner."

"You've just provided me with the makings of one hell of a weekend in Dublin!" he roared on stage as he acknowledged a standing ovation.

Backstage, he likened the shock of winning to "being involved in a major road accident—except the outcome is a bit more pleasurable."

Coincidentally, *Driving Miss Daisy* helmer Bruce Beresford had just survived a major road accident on the eve of the Oscarcast "and was thanking his lucky stars he was alive," noted *Variety*. "He and his daughter Tiffany were driving from the final location of *Mister Johnson* in Nigeria to the Kano airport when their car blew a tire, flipped four times and landed in a ditch. They miraculously escaped injury!"

Beresford made it to London that night, but, unfortunately, couldn't watch the Oscar telecast since it wasn't carried on his hotel TV. He ended up missing the drama that followed, which included the triumph of his star Jessica Tandy, who *Variety* had insisted was "a hands-down lock" for Best Actress.

"It's a miracle!" Tandy exclaimed when she accepted the prize. "I thank my lucky stars and (producers) Richard and Lili Zanuck, who had the faith to give me this wonderful chance and, also, most especially, to that forgotten man, my director, Bruce Beresford."

Variety added an historic observation: "An interesting footnote to Tandy's maiden nomination is that she was passed over for her stage-originated role of Blanche DuBois in the 1951 film version of *A Streetcar Named Desire*, which won an Oscar for Vivien Leigh. But for *Daisy*, Tandy was cast over other actresses who had played the role on stage.

"In winning the prize, she outdistanced George Burns, who was also 80, but 7 months younger when he won the Best Supporting Actor prize for *The Sunshine Boys* in 1975."

When she was informed backstage later that she was the oldest Oscar winner, Tandy gasped, "Am I? Well, good for me!"

An upset occurred in the match-up for Best Original Screenplay when writers' guild honoree Woody Allen (*Crimes and Misdemeanors*) lost to Tom Schulman of *Dead Poets Society*, a drama about an inspirational schoolteacher that was up for Best Picture, Best Director (Peter Weir) and Best Actor (Robin Williams).

As pundits wondered what would happen in the later showdown over Best Picture between *Born on the Fourth of July* and *Driving Miss Daisy*, the *L.A. Times* said, "We'll get our first clue when the award for Best Adapted Screenplay is presented. Uhry and Stone and Kovic are head to head in that category. Uhry has already won the award from the Writers Guild of America."

Uhry won, signaling what the *Times* called "the possibility of a *Daisy* coup."

Oliver Stone rebounded from his screenplay loss to claim the laurels for Best Director.

Stone thanked Oscar voters for "your acknowledgment that Vietnam is not over, although some people say it is." He also

thanked Kovic "for his largeness of heart" and star Tom Cruise "for making Ron's dream come true."

As the time soon drew near for revealing the winner of the Best Picture award, suspense peaked at the Dorothy Chandler Pavilion.

The outcome was a classic Oscar upset: *Driving Miss Daisy*.

Producers Richard and Lili Zanuck vaulted up to the stage. "We're up here for one very simple reason," Richard Zanuck said, "the fact that Bruce Beresford is a brilliant director."

Army Archerd said in his *Variety* column the next day, "As the academy audience applauded each time for 'the forgotten director' Bruce Beresford, one could not help but wonder where this audience of voters was when the nomination ballots went out."

A *Variety* reporter added, "The outcome of the Oscars is sure to raise the level of interest in Beresford's bypassing, for which no one has yet advanced a plausible theory."

Three days later, the Zanucks accepted a new award, which was named after Richard's father—former Warner Bros. production topper Darryl F.—and bestowed by the Producers Guild of America.

The new prize for Producer of the Year was presented by former U.S. president and Hollywood screen star Ronald Reagan. *Variety* reported, "Reagan noted that Richard Zanuck had a particularly difficult challenge to meet, following in the footsteps of his father, Darryl, who was honored in 1953 with the PGA's Milestone Award."

"I remember the award on the mantel at our home on the beach," the younger Zanuck said. "My father was a real producer in the real sense of the word. His creed was 'how to sell a good story.' I remembered that."

Drugstore Cowboy may have scored poorly at the Academy Awards, but the film that had been declared Best Picture by the National Society of Film Critics earned hefty consolation prizes just three days before the Oscarcast when the Independent Spirit Awards were bestowed.

Cowboy copped prizes for screenplay, cinematography, Best Actor (Matt Dillon) and Best Supporting Actor (Max Perlich), but it lost the top trophy for Best Picture.

In that race *Cowboy* "ended up in a dead heat," said *Variety*, with the film that caused maximum buzz at last year's U.S. Film Festival—Audience Award winner *sex, lies, and videotape*—and the pic that defeated *Sex* for the fest's 1988 Grand Jury Prize, *True Love*.

sex, lies, and videotape proved to be the Spirit winner, also garnering three other kudos: Best Director (Steven Soderberg), Best Actress (Andie MacDowell) and Best Supporting Actress (Laura San Giacomo).

The U.S. Film Festival added "Sundance" to its name this year, strengthening its connection to the indie institute that managed it. Fifteen pix were entered for dramatic competition, but jurors revealed that the race for the Grand Jury Prize came down to two rivals: *To Sleep with Anger*, which told the tale of what happens to a middle-class black family when a quirky friend (Danny Glover) of the father's moves in, and *Chameleon Street*, described by *The New York Times* as "the story of an uneducated black man who masquerades as a doctor, a lawyer and a Harvard student."

When *Chameleon* won, the *Times* noted that it had previously been "rejected by many distributors. Now the film's writer, director and star, Wendell B. Harris, Jr., is sorting through bids from casting agents interested in his acting, and his sales agency is screening the film for at least three major studios and an independent company, some of which passed on *Chameleon Street* the first time around."

To Sleep with Anger received the Special Jury Prize in consolation.

Winner of Best Documentary was *H-2 Worker*, which investigated the exploitation of Jamaican migrant workers in Florida. Recipient of the new Audience Award was *Longtime Companion*, which *Variety* described as "the first feature film to tell the story of how AIDS devastated and transformed the gay community." The new prize was added last year after John Waters's crowd-pleasing *Hairspray* failed to win any awards at Sundance in 1987 despite being a fest fave.

Two screenings had to be added to accommodate the demand to see the crowd-pleasing winner of the Filmmaker's Trophy, *House Party*, which *Variety* called a "fresh, commercial and very catchy" look at black teens' rap culture.

"No one could call the awards ceremony anything but understated," reported the *L.A. Times*. "The actor Willem Dafoe presented the prizes to the winners, many of whom wore jeans and snow boots.

"The ceremony's liveliest moment arrived when Mr. Harris, looking serene behind dark glasses, stepped up to accept his award for *Chameleon Street*.

" 'I want to show you what's really going on,' he said, and took off his glasses, gave an open-mouthed wide-eyed look of panic, then calmly replaced the glasses and his demeanor."

▪ 1989 ▪

NATIONAL BOARD OF REVIEW

The board declared a Best Picture and Foreign Film of the year, then listed its remaining favorites according to highest scores. The vote results were announced on December 13, 1989. Awards were presented on February 26, 1990, at Lincoln Center Library in New York.

BEST PICTURE
- *Driving Miss Daisy*
Henry V
sex, lies, and videotape
The Fabulous Baker Boys
My Left Foot
Dead Poets Society
Crimes and Misdemeanors
Born on the Fourth of July
Glory
Field of Dreams

BEST DIRECTOR
- Kenneth Branagh, *Henry V*

BEST ACTOR
- Morgan Freeman, *Driving Miss Daisy*

BEST ACTRESS
- Michelle Pfeiffer, *The Fabulous Baker Boys*

BEST SUPPORTING ACTOR
- Alan Alda, *Crimes and Misdemeanors*

BEST SUPPORTING ACTRESS
- Mary Stuart Masterson, *Immediate Family*

BEST DOCUMENTARY
- *Roger & Me*, Michael Moore

BEST FOREIGN FILM
- *The Story of Women* (France)
  Camille Claudel (France)
  La Lectrice (France)
  Chocolat (France/West Germany/Cameroon)
  The Little Thief (France)

SPECIAL AWARDS
- Robert Giroux
- Robert A. Harris
- Andrew Sarris, Molly Haskell

LOS ANGELES FILM CRITICS ASSOCIATION

Winners were announced on December 16, 1989. Awards were presented on January 16, 1990, at the Bel Age Hotel in Los Angeles.

BEST PICTURE
- *Do the Right Thing*

BEST DIRECTOR
- Spike Lee, *Do the Right Thing*

BEST ACTOR
- Daniel Day-Lewis, *My Left Foot*

BEST ACTRESS (TIE)
- Andie MacDowell, *sex, lies, and videotape*

- Michelle Pfeiffer, *The Fabulous Baker Boys*

BEST SUPPORTING ACTOR
- Danny Aiello, *Do the Right Thing*

BEST SUPPORTING ACTRESS
- Brenda Fricker, *My Left Foot*

BEST SCREENPLAY
- Gus Van Sant, Daniel Yost, *Drugstore Cowboy*

BEST CINEMATOGRAPHY
- Michael Ballhaus, *The Fabulous Baker Boys*

BEST MUSIC SCORE
- Bill Lee, *Do the Right Thing*

BEST ANIMATION
- *The Little Mermaid,* John Musker, Ron Clements

BEST DOCUMENTARY
- *Roger & Me*, Michael Moore

BEST FOREIGN FILM (TIE)
- *Distant Voices/Still Lives* (U.K.)
- *The Story of Women* (France)

BEST EXPERIMENTAL/INDEPENDENT FILM
- *The Long Weekend O' Despair*, Gregg Araki

NEW GENERATION AWARD
- Laura San Giacomo, *sex, lies, and videotape*

CAREER ACHIEVEMENT AWARD
- Stanley Donen

SPECIAL AWARD
- Margaret Herrick Library of the Academy of Motion Picture Arts and Sciences

NEW YORK FILM CRITICS CIRCLE

Winners were announced on December 18, 1989. Awards were presented on January 14, 1990, at Sardi's restaurant in New York.

BEST PICTURE
- *My Left Foot*

BEST DIRECTOR
- Paul Mazursky, *Enemies: A Love Story*

BEST NEW DIRECTOR
- Kenneth Branagh, *Henry V*

BEST ACTOR
- Daniel Day-Lewis, *My Left Foot*

BEST ACTRESS
- Michelle Pfeiffer, *The Fabulous Baker Boys*

BEST SUPPORTING ACTOR
- Alan Alda, *Crimes and Misdemeanors*

BEST SUPPORTING ACTRESS
- Lena Olin, *Enemies: A Love Story*

BEST SCREENPLAY
- Gus Van Sant, Daniel Yost, *Drugstore Cowboy*

BEST CINEMATOGRAPHY
- Ernest Dickerson, *Do the Right Thing*

BEST DOCUMENTARY
- *Roger & Me*, Michael Moore

BEST FOREIGN FILM
- *The Story of Women* (France)

NATIONAL SOCIETY OF FILM CRITICS

Winners were announced on January 7, 1990.

BEST PICTURE
- *Drugstore Cowboy*

BEST DIRECTOR
- Gus Van Sant, *Drugstore Cowboy*

BEST ACTOR
- Daniel Day-Lewis, *My Left Foot*

BEST ACTRESS
- Michelle Pfeiffer, *The Fabulous Baker Boys*

BEST SUPPORTING ACTOR
- Beau Bridges, *The Fabulous Baker Boys*

BEST SUPPORTING ACTRESS
- Anjelica Huston, *Enemies: A Love Story*

BEST SCREENPLAY
- Gus Van Sant, Daniel Yost, *Drugstore Cowboy*

BEST CINEMATOGRAPHY
- Michael Ballhaus, *The Fabulous Baker Boys*

BEST DOCUMENTARY
- *Roger & Me*, Michael Moore

GOLDEN GLOBES

Nominations were announced on December 27, 1989. Awards were presented on January 20, 1990, at the Beverly Hilton Hotel in Los Angeles. The ceremony was telecast by TBS.

BEST DRAMA PICTURE
- *Born on the Fourth of July*
Crimes and Misdemeanors
Dead Poets Society
Do the Right Thing
Glory

BEST COMEDY OR MUSICAL PICTURE
- *Driving Miss Daisy*
The Little Mermaid
Shirley Valentine
The War of the Roses
When Harry Met Sally . . .

BEST DIRECTOR
- Oliver Stone, *Born on the Fourth of July*
Spike Lee, *Do the Right Thing*
Rob Reiner, *When Harry Met Sally . . .*
Peter Weir, *Dead Poets Society*
Edward Zwick, *Glory*

BEST ACTOR, DRAMA
- Tom Cruise, *Born on the Fourth of July*
Daniel Day-Lewis, *My Left Foot*
Jack Lemmon, *Dad*
Al Pacino, *Sea of Love*
Robin Williams, *Dead Poets Society*

BEST ACTRESS, DRAMA

- Michelle Pfeiffer, *The Fabulous Baker Boys*

Sally Field, *Steel Magnolias*
Jessica Lange, *Music Box*
Andie MacDowell, *sex, lies, and videotape*
Liv Ullmann, *The Rose Garden*

BEST ACTOR, COMEDY OR MUSICAL

- Morgan Freeman, *Driving Miss Daisy*

Billy Crystal, *When Harry Met Sally . . .*
Michael Douglas, *The War of the Roses*
Steve Martin, *Parenthood*
Jack Nicholson, *Batman*

BEST ACTRESS, COMEDY OR MUSICAL

- Jessica Tandy, *Driving Miss Daisy*

Pauline Collins, *Shirley Valentine*
Meg Ryan, *When Harry Met Sally . . .*
Meryl Streep, *She-Devil*
Kathleen Turner, *The War of the Roses*

BEST SUPPORTING ACTOR

- Denzel Washington, *Glory*

Danny Aiello, *Do the Right Thing*
Marlon Brando, *A Dry White Season*
Sean Connery, *Indiana Jones and the Last Crusade*
Ed Harris, *Jacknife*
Bruce Willis, *In Country*

BEST SUPPORTING ACTRESS

- Julia Roberts, *Steel Magnolias*

Bridget Fonda, *Scandal*
Brenda Fricker, *My Left Foot*
Laura San Giacomo, *sex, lies, and videotape*
Dianne Wiest, *Parenthood*

BEST SCREENPLAY

- Oliver Stone, Ron Kovic, *Born on the Fourth of July*

Nora Ephron, *When Harry Met Sally . . .*
Kevin Jarre, *Glory*
Spike Lee, *Do the Right Thing*
Tom Schulman, *Dead Poets Society*
Steven Soderbergh, *sex, lies, and videotape*

BEST SONG

- "Under the Sea," *The Little Mermaid*

"After All," *Chances Are*
"The Girl Who Used to Be Me," *Shirley Valentine*

"I Love to See You Smile," *Parenthood*
"Kiss the Girl," *The Little Mermaid*

BEST FOREIGN FILM

- *Cinema Paradiso* (Italy)

Camille Claudel (France)
Jesus of Montreal (Canada)
My Uncle's Legacy (Yugoslavia)
The Story of Women (France)

Winners

BEST SCORE

- Alan Menken, *The Little Mermaid*

CECIL B. DEMILLE AWARD

- Audrey Hepburn

SUNDANCE U.S. FILM FESTIVAL

The festival was held January 19–29, 1990, at Park City, Utah.

GRAND JURY PRIZE

(DRAMATIC)
- *Chameleon Street*, Wendell B. Harris, Jr.

(DOCUMENTARY)
- *H-2 Worker*, Stephanie Black
- *Water and Power*, Pat O'Neill

FILMMAKER'S TROPHY

(DRAMATIC)
- *House Party*, Reginald Hudlin

(DOCUMENTARY)
- *Metamorphosis: Man into Woman*, Lisa Leeman

AUDIENCE AWARD

(DRAMATIC)
- *Longtime Companion*, Norman Rene, Craig Lucas

(DOCUMENTARY)
- *Berkeley in the Sixties*, Mark Kitchell

CINEMATOGRAPHY AWARD

(DRAMATIC)
- *House Party*, Peter Deming

(DOCUMENTARY)
- *H-2 Worker*, Maryse Alberti

SPECIAL JURY RECOGNITION

(DRAMATIC)
- *To Sleep with Anger*, Charles Burnett

(DOCUMENTARY)
- *Samsara: Death and Rebirth in Cambodia*, Ellen Bruno

DIRECTORS GUILD OF AMERICA

Awards were presented on March 10, 1990, at the Beverly Hilton Hotel in Los Angeles.

BEST DIRECTOR

- Oliver Stone, *Born on the Fourth of July*
Woody Allen, *Crimes and Misdemeanors*
Rob Reiner, *When Harry Met Sally . . .*
Phil Alden Robinson, *Field of Dreams*
Peter Weir, *Dead Poets Society*

ROBERT B. ALDRICH AWARD

- George Schaefer

D. W. GRIFFITH AWARD

- Ingmar Bergman

PRESTON STURGES AWARD

- Richard Brooks

HONORARY LIFE MEMBERSHIPS

- Barry Diller
- Sidney J. Sheinberg
- Elliot Silverstein

WRITERS GUILD OF AMERICA

Awards were presented on March 18, 1990, at the Beverly Hilton Hotel in Los Angeles and the Windows on the World restaurant in New York.

BEST ORIGINAL SCREENPLAY

- *Crimes and Misdemeanors*, Woody Allen
Dead Poets Society, Tom Schulman
The Fabulous Baker Boys, Steve Kloves
sex, lies, and videotape, Steven Soderbergh
When Harry Met Sally . . . , Nora Ephron

BEST ADAPTED SCREENPLAY

- *Driving Miss Daisy*, Alfred Uhry, based on his play

Born on the Fourth of July, Oliver Stone, Ron Kovic, based on the book by Ron Kovic
Field of Dreams, Phil Alden Robinson, based on the book *Shoeless Joe* by W. P. Kinsella
Glory, Kevin Jarre, based on the book *Lay This Laurel* by Lincoln Kirstein, the book *One Gallant Rush* by Peter Burchard and the letters of Robert Gould Shaw
My Left Foot, Shane Connaughton, Jim Sheridan, based on the book by Christy Brown

EVELYN F. BURKEY MEMORIAL AWARD

- Art Buchwald

MORGAN COX AWARD

- Oscar Saul

VALENTINE DAVIES AWARD

- John Furia, Jr.

LAUREL AWARD

- Donald Ogden Stewart

INDEPENDENT SPIRIT

Awards were presented on March 24, 1990, at the Roosevelt Hotel in Los Angeles.

BEST FEATURE

- *sex, lies, and videotape*
Drugstore Cowboy
Heat and Sunlight
Mystery Train
True Love

BEST FIRST FEATURE

- *Heathers*
84 Charlie Mopic
Powwow Highway
Sidewalk Stories
Talking to Strangers

BEST DIRECTOR

- Steven Soderbergh, *sex, lies, and videotape*
Jim Jarmusch, *Mystery Train*
Charles Lane, *Sidewalk Stories*
Nancy Savoca, *True Love*
Gus Van Sant, *Drugstore Cowboy*

BEST ACTOR

- Matt Dillon, *Drugstore Cowboy*

Nicolas Cage, *Vampire's Kiss*

Charles Lane, *Sidewalk Stories*

Randy Quaid, *Parents*

James Spader, *sex, lies, and videotape*

BEST ACTRESS

- Andie MacDowell, *sex, lies, and videotape*

Youki Kudoh, *Mystery Train*

Kelly Lynch, *Drugstore Cowboy*

Winona Ryder, *Heathers*

Annabella Sciorra, *True Love*

BEST SUPPORTING ACTOR

- Max Perlich, *Drugstore Cowboy*

Steve Buscemi, *Mystery Train*

Scott Coffey, *Shag*

Gary Farmer, *Powwow Highway*

Screamin' Jay Hawkins, *Mystery Train*

BEST SUPPORTING ACTRESS

- Laura San Giacomo, *sex, lies, and videotape*

Bridget Fonda, *Shag*

Heather Graham, *Drugstore Cowboy*

Mare Winningham, *Miracle Mile*

Mary Woronov, *Scenes from the Class Struggle in Beverly Hills*

BEST SCREENPLAY

- Gus Van Sant, Daniel Yost, *Drugstore Cowboy*

Steve De Jarnatt, *Miracle Mile*

Patrick Duncan, *84 Charlie Mopic*

Jim Jarmusch, *Mystery Train*

Daniel Waters, *Heathers*

BEST FOREIGN FILM

- *My Left Foot* (Ireland)

Distant Voices, Still Lives (U.K.)

Hanussen (West Germany, Hungary)

High Hopes (U.K.)

Rouge (Hong Kong)

Winners

BEST CINEMATOGRAPHY

- Robert Yeoman, *Drugstore Cowboy*

SPECIAL DISTINCTION AWARD

- Spike Lee

ACADEMY AWARDS

Nominations were announced on February 14, 1990. Awards were presented on March 26 at the Dorothy Chandler Pavilion in Los Angeles. The ceremony was telecast by ABC.

BEST PICTURE

- *Driving Miss Daisy*

Born on the Fourth of July

Dead Poets Society

Field of Dreams

My Left Foot

BEST DIRECTOR

- Oliver Stone, *Born on the Fourth of July*

Woody Allen, *Crimes and Misdemeanors*

Kenneth Branagh, *Henry V*

Jim Sheridan, *My Left Foot*

Peter Weir, *Dead Poets Society*

BEST ACTOR

- Daniel Day-Lewis, *My Left Foot*

Kenneth Branagh, *Henry V*

Tom Cruise, *Born on the Fourth of July*

Morgan Freeman, *Driving Miss Daisy*

Robin Williams, *Dead Poets Society*

BEST ACTRESS

- Jessica Tandy, *Driving Miss Daisy*

Isabelle Adjani, *Camille Claudel*

Pauline Collins, *Shirley Valentine*

Jessica Lange, *Music Box*

Michelle Pfeiffer, *The Fabulous Baker Boys*

BEST SUPPORTING ACTOR

- Denzel Washington, *Glory*

Danny Aiello, *Do the Right Thing*

Dan Aykroyd, *Driving Miss Daisy*

Marlon Brando, *A Dry White Season*

Martin Landau, *Crimes and Misdemeanors*

BEST SUPPORTING ACTRESS

- Brenda Fricker, *My Left Foot*

Anjelica Huston, *Enemies: A Love Story*

Lena Olin, *Enemies: A Love Story*

Julia Roberts, *Steel Magnolias*

Dianne Wiest, *Parenthood*

BEST ORIGINAL SCREENPLAY

■ Tom Schulman, *Dead Poets Society*
Woody Allen, *Crimes and Misdemeanors*
Nora Ephron, *When Harry Met Sally . . .*
Spike Lee, *Do the Right Thing*
Steven Soderbergh, *sex, lies, and videotape*

BEST ADAPTED SCREENPLAY

■ Alfred Uhry, *Driving Miss Daisy*
Shane Connaughton, Jim Sheridan, *My Left Foot*
Ron Kovic, Oliver Stone, *Born on the Fourth of July*
Paul Mazursky, Roger L. Simon, *Enemies: A Love Story*
Phil Alden Robinson, *Field of Dreams*

BEST SONG

■ "Under the Sea," *The Little Mermaid*, Howard Ashman, Alan Menken
"After All," *Chances Are*, Dean Pitchford, Tom Snow
"The Girl Who Used to Be Me," *Shirley Valentine*, Alan Bergman, Marilyn Bergman, Marvin Hamlisch
"I Love to See You Smile," *Parenthood*, Randy Newman
"Kiss the Girl," *The Little Mermaid*, Howard Ashman, Alan Menken

BEST FOREIGN-LANGUAGE FILM

■ *Cinema Paradiso* (Italy)
Camille Claudel (France)
Jesus of Montreal (Canada)
Waltzing Regitze (Denmark)
What Happened to Santiago (Puerto Rico)

Winners

BEST ART DIRECTION

■ Anton Furst, Peter Young, *Batman*

BEST CINEMATOGRAPHY

■ Freddie Francis, *Glory*

BEST COSTUME DESIGN

■ Phyllis Dalton, *Henry V*

BEST DOCUMENTARY
(FEATURE)

■ *Common Threads: Stories from the Quilt*, Bill Couturié, Robert Epstein

(SHORT SUBJECT)

■ *The Johnstown Flood*, Charles Guggenheim

BEST FILM EDITING

■ *Joe Hutshing, Born on the Fourth of July*, David Brenner

BEST MAKEUP

■ Lynn Barber, Kevin Haney, Manlio Rocchetti, *Driving Miss Daisy*

BEST MUSIC SCORE

■ Alan Menken, *The Little Mermaid*

SCIENTIFIC OR TECHNICAL AWARDS
(Scientific and Engineering Award)

■ James Ketcham, JSK Engineering; J. Noxon Leavitt; ISTEC; Geoffrey H. Williamson, Wilcam Photo Research; Klaus Resch, Erich Fitz, FGV Schmidle & Fitz; Robert D. Auguste; J. L Fisher

(Technical Achievement Award)

■ Dr. Leo Catozzo, Magna-Tech Electronic

BEST SHORT FILM
(ANIMATED)

■ *Balance*, Christoph Lauenstein, Wolfgang Lauenstein

(LIVE ACTION)

■ *Work Experience*, James Hendrie

BEST SOUND

■ Donald O. Mitchell, Gregg C. Rudloff, Elliot Tyson, Russell Williams II, *Glory*

BEST SOUND EFFECTS EDITING

■ Ben Burtt, Richard Hymns, *Indiana Jones and the Last Crusade*

BEST VISUAL EFFECTS

■ John Bruno, Dennis Muren, Dennis Skotak, Hoyt Yeatman, *The Abyss*

GORDON E. SAWYER AWARD

■ Pierre Angenieux

JEAN HERSHOLT HUMANITARIAN AWARD

■ Howard W. Koch

HONORARY AWARDS

■ Akira Kurosawa

- Society of Motion Picture and Television Engineers Engineering Committees

PRODUCERS GUILD OF AMERICA

Awards were presented on March 29, 1990, at the Regent Beverly Wilshire Hotel in Los Angeles.

DARRYL F. ZANUCK PRODUCER OF THE YEAR AWARD

- *Driving Miss Daisy*, Richard Zanuck, Lili Fini Zanuck

Born on the Fourth of July, A. Kitman Ho

Dead Poets Society, Steven Haft, Paul Junger Witt, Tony Thomas

Field of Dreams, Lawrence Gordon, Charles Gordon

Glory, Freddie Fields

Henry V, Bruce Sharman

My Left Foot, Noel Pearson

When Harry Met Sally, Rob Reiner, Andrew Scheinman

CHARLES B. FITZSIMONS HONORARY LIFETIME ACHIEVEMENT AWARD

- Charles B. FitzSimons

DAVID O. SELZNICK LIFETIME ACHIEVEMENT AWARD

- Hal Roach

SCREEN ACTORS GUILD

LIFETIME ACHIEVEMENT AWARD

- Jack Lemmon

· 1990 ·

Wolves *Devours the Mob*

For the first time ever, the three critics' groups endorsed the same Best Picture—just when the Oscars, Golden Globes and National Board of Review all backed a different choice.

Curiously, both pix were gun-slinging dramas—and the shoot-out between them starred trigger-happy gangsters, cops, soldiers and injuns.

The National Board of Review came out first with both barrels blazing—Best Picture and Best Director—for *Dances with Wolves* and helmer Kevin Costner, who also starred in the lead role as a U.S. Army officer who joins a Native American tribe. *Variety* said, "In his directorial debut, Costner brings a rare degree of grace and feeling to this elegiac tale of a hero's adventure of discovery among the Sioux Indians on the pristine Dakota plains of the 1860s."

The crix orgs endorsed Martin Scorsese's *GoodFellas*, which the *N.Y. Times* called "the most politically serious and most evilly entertaining movie yet made about organized crime."

The L.A. film crix were the first to name it Best Picture and Scorsese Best Director, topping second-place vote-getters *Dances with Wolves* and Costner. When *GoodFellas* claimed three additional prizes as well, it tied *Kramer vs. Kramer* and *Terms of Endearment* as the biggest winner in the L.A. group's history.

A standout among the cast members was Joe Pesci, who was voted Best Supporting Actor for portraying what *Variety* called a "short-fused psycho." He beat Bruce Davison as the doting lover of an AIDS victim in *Longtime Companion*.

Best Supporting Actress was Lorraine Bracco as the cocaine-addicted wife of a Mafia stoolpigeon. She beat Dianne Wiest as a perky Avon lady who adopts a razor-clawed freak in *Edward Scissorhands*.

All three crix orgs finally agreed on one best pic: the "evilly entertaining" *GoodFellas*, starring Robert De Niro (left) and Ray Liotta.

GoodFellas's fifth prize was for Best Cinematography.

The Best Actor nod went to Jeremy Irons (*Reversal of Fortune*), who *Variety* said gave "a memorable performance" as Claus von Bulow, the Newport socialite accused of trying to murder his wife. Irons beat a rival who would not show up in the vote tabs of any other kudos—Philippe Noiret as a post-war French army officer in *Life and Nothing But*. *Reversal* also won the screenplay prize.

The crix's Best Actress choice, Anjelica Huston, was cited for two roles: as a racetrack swindler in *The Grifters* and a child-hating sorceress in *The Witches*. She topped Joanne Woodward, who starred as a lonely Kansas City matron in *Mr. and Mrs. Bridge*.

When the awards were presented in mid-January, the celebratory spirit of the occasion was shattered by the breaking news that a U.S.-led coalition of nations had just launched an air and missile attack on Iraq in response to its recent invasion of Kuwait.

The *L.A. Daily News* noted, "Although events in the Middle East lent a somewhat somber tone to the usually festive event, many recipients managed to express some welcome humor."

"This must be the only profession in which I can be celebrated for being a bad girl," said a smirking Anjelica Huston, referring to her two dastardly, crix-honored roles.

Upon accepting his Best Actor plaque, Jeremy Irons revealed how he once was "dressed down" by a legit director on opening night after he took liberties with his stage role as a butler.

"I'm so glad that this time I've done my best and you tell me I've gotten it right," he said.

Martin Scorsese was in Florida filming *Cape Fear*, so he was not present to accept his Best Picture and Director plaques in person, but producer Irwin Winkler stood in and credited their film's success to its "wonderful critical reception."

The New York critics received it well, too, naming it Best Picture (47 points) over *Mr. and Mrs. Bridge* (19) and Scorsese as Best Director (16 votes) over Bernardo Bertolucci (*The Sheltering Sky*) and Barbet Schroeder (*Reversal of Fortune*), who each scored two votes on the first ballot.

"Oh, good, *Fellas*, ya won again!" cheered a headline in *The New York Post*.

Newsday noted that the crix experienced "relatively little trouble arriving at decisions in the two top categories" after a close vote last year that had been described by the *Post* as "combative." Perhaps it was the more agreeable ambience of the crix's new polling place. They met for their four-hour huddle at actor Patrick O'Neal's restaurant, the Ginger Man, instead of the usual stark boardroom of the newspaper guild. The meeting would be the last for a formidable member who was often accused of marshaling votes behind the scenes—Pauline Kael, who was retiring from *The New Yorker* after 24 years. Her parting shot may have been the poor showing of *Dances with Wolves*, which she'd attacked savagely in print as an

"epic made by a bland megalomaniac (the Indians should have named him Plays with Camera)."

GoodFellas scored the additional award of Best Actor for Robert De Niro, who was also hailed for portraying a man who emerges from a catatonic state after 30 years in *Awakenings*. It marked De Niro's fourth career award from the Gothamites, making him their second-most-honored thesp—after Jack Nicholson (seven wins). De Niro was acknowledged this time chiefly for his perf in *Awakenings*, but the crix voted to list his role in *GoodFellas*, too, after he beat Jeremy Irons on the third ballot by a 35-to-29 score.

The Gothamites reversed the results that the Hollywoodites arrived at in two categories. They gave the nod for Best Actress to Joanne Woodward (35 points) over Anjelica Huston (32) and Bruce Davison (48) was named Best Supporting Actor over Joe Pesci (34 points).

A crix first: the L.A. scribes and nat'l society agreed on every top race.

"Best Supporting Actress proved to be the most wide open category," reported *Newsday*. "Jennifer Jason Leigh, who portrayed prostitutes in *Last Exit to Brooklyn* and *Miami Blues*, received votes for her work in both films and finally prevailed on the fourth ballot. Her nearest competitor was Joan Plowright as the immigrant matriarch in *Avalon*." The score: 35 to 28.

The laurels for Best New Director were snagged by Whit Stillman for his ironic views of upperclass New Yorkers at Christmastime in *Metropolitan*. He won a decisive 12-to-3 victory on the first ballot over Aussie helmer Jane Campion (*Sweetie*), who had received the L.A. crix's New Generation Award. Stillman lost the prize for Best Screenplay, however, to Ruth Prawer Jhabvala (*Mr. and Mrs. Bridge*) by a 33-to-22 tally.

This year the Gotham crix moved their party from the restricted confines of Sardi's restaurant to the more spacious Pegasus Suite of the Rainbow Room atop Rockefeller Center. Not only did they need to accommodate a growing number of media heavyweights who wanted to attend, but Best Actor honoree Robert De Niro insisted on bringing 19 guests.

Variety noted that the event "took on some aspects of a roast" when circle chairman Rex Reed presided, "making often unprintable but amusing cracks." Reed saluted De Niro for "breaking our hearts in Awakenings and for being a quintessential scumbag in GoodFellas," but the Best Actor champ didn't respond in a gregarious way. He looked shy and nervous as he accepted his scroll with few words.

One of the fete's highlights occurred when Paul Newman introduced his wife and costar in the low-budget indie Mr. and Mrs. Bridge, Best Actress champ Joanne Woodward. He noted that it was "the first time I paid homage to my wife on my feet with my clothes on," then added that he felt uncomfortable "standing here in a suit."

Woodward told the crowd, "This suit is not only Mr. Bridge's suit, it is also Paul's salary."

Whereas Mr. and Mrs. Bridge challenged GoodFellas at the Gotham kudos and Dances with Wolves nipped at GoodFellas's heels when the L.A. crix voted, con artists took on the mobsters when the National Society of Film Critics convened. GoodFellas, however, beat The Grifters for Best Picture 43 votes to 23, while Scorsese prevailed as Best Director over The Grifters's Stephen Frears 49 to 21.

The society added a new category for Best Foreign-Language Film, but offshore non-English pix were still eligible to compete for the top prize. Winner of the new foreign-lingo kudo was Ariel, Aki Kaurismaki's dark comedy about an out-of-work miner who takes a road trip across Finland.

Among the various crix's choices for thesp laurels, the L.A. Times noted, "The critics groups have been doing flip-flops between Jeremy Irons and Robert De Niro

and Anjelica Houston and Joanne Woodward." The society ended up flipping for Huston (57 points) over Woodward (25) in the actress contest and flopping for Irons (53 points) as Best Actor over Danny Glover (20 points for To Sleep with Anger) and De Niro (19 for GoodFellas and Awakenings).

For the first time ever, the society's picks reflected all of the same choices made by the L.A. crix in the top categories. The differences occurred in the other races: Bruce Davison won Best Supporting Actor over Pesci by a 38-to-22 vote and Annette Bening (25) prevailed as Best Supporting Actress for portraying a curvy con in The Grifters. Runner-up was Uma Thurman, who scored 24 points in the dual roles as a homeless rich teen in Where the Heart Is and as the wife of writer Henry Miller in Henry and June. Best Screenplay was Charles Burnett's To Sleep with Anger, which had won a Special Jury Prize at last year's Sundance festival and now beat Tom Stoppard's espionage thriller The Russia House.

Just when it looked as if the crix awards had settled the issue of what film was out front for Best Picture in the annual kudos derby, a dark horse leapt onto the track and took the lead by scoring the most Golden Globe nominations (seven): The Godfather, Part III. Variety had cheered the pic in its review, saying that the $55 million production "matches its predecessors," the first part of which won the Golden Globe for Best Drama in 1972. Both parts had won Best Picture at the Oscars (1972, 1974).

But this year's Globes turned out to be a night of shocking upsets that resulted in Godfather III and GoodFellas suffering shutouts.

Dances with Wolves "mowed down both heavyweight gangland dramas," noted the L.A. Times. It won Best Drama Picture, Best Screenplay and Best Director. In the

> Green Card upset Pretty Woman and Home Alone at the Golden Globes.

helmer's race, Kevin Costner iced such formidable rivals as Francis Ford Coppola (*Godfather III*), Bernardo Bertolucci (*The Sheltering Sky*) and Martin Scorsese (*GoodFellas*), but he sounded humble as he accepted his Globe.

"One night doesn't make a career," he said. "But it feels as good as you might think it feels!"

Backstage, reporters besieged all the winners with questions about the growing conflict in the Persian Gulf, but Costner refused to comment, saying that he "didn't feel comfortable discussing the war while wearing a tuxedo."

Jeremy Irons's formal attire didn't hold the Best Drama Actor champ back from sounding off. "This is very serious business," he said. "If we'd spent all the billions that we're hurling at Iraq's Saddam Hussein on the new democracies in Eastern Europe, we'd all be sleeping better at night."

The race for Best Drama Actress had looked like a close contest between the thesp chosen by the Gotham crix, Joanne Woodward, and L.A. crix and national society champ Anjelica Huston. An upset, however, was scored by Kathy Bates as a psycho who kidnaps her favorite writer in *Misery*.

Other shockers occurred in the races for comedy/musical movies. It looked as if the Best Picture showdown was between two of 1990's biggest b.o. blockbusters—*Pretty Woman* and *Home Alone*—but *Variety* reported "a surprise outcome." The winner turned out to be *Green Card*, which *Variety* described as "a genial, nicely played romance about a French alien (Gérard Depardieu) who pairs up with a New Yorker (Andie MacDowell) in a marriage of convenience in order to remain legally in the U.S."

Variety described the pic's further awards luck: "And it was not Macaulay Culkin, the moppet star of *Home Alone*, but French actor Depardieu, making his Eng-lish-language film debut, who was declared Best Actor in a Comedy or Musical."

There was no surprise in the outcome of Best Comedy/Musical Actress. Julia Roberts was hailed for her perf in *Pretty Woman* as "a prostitute with a heart of gold who mellows a stuffy businessman," said *Variety*.

The race for Best Supporting Actress was thought to be between L.A. crix honoree Lorraine Bracco (*GoodFellas*), Shirley MacLaine as an alcoholic showbiz diva in *Postcards from the Edge* and Mary McDonnell, who *Variety* described as "an emotionally traumatized white woman adopted by the Sioux" in *Dances with Wolves*. The winner was an other-worldly choice: Whoopi Goldberg as a fake medium who encounters real spirits in *Ghost*.

"Damn, I'm glad I won this one!" Goldberg exclaimed when she clutched her Globe. "I really wanted it!"

There was another upset in the match-up for Best Supporting Actor when Bruce Davison (*Longtime Companion*) beat Joe Pesci (*GoodFellas*) and Al Pacino, who portrayed the explosive cartoon gangster Big Boy Caprice in *Dick Tracy*.

Sizing up all the Globe champs, *Variety* said, "The results could presage a strong night for sleepers at the March 25 Oscars."

The Golden Globes quickly reinvigorated *Dances with Wolves*'s Oscar chances, which were only enhanced when Kevin Costner won the top honor from the Producers Guild of America in early March.

"I feel like the new kid on the block," the *Wolves* co-producer said when he accepted it, "but you couldn't have a happier young man here tonight."

Eleven days later Costner faced the next major showdown—at the Directors Guild of America. Sentiment seemed to favor Martin Scorsese, though, since the two-time past loser (*Taxi Driver, Raging Bull*) was overdue for acknowledgment from his peers. Costner and Scorsese competed against

> *American Dream scored an unprecedented sweep at Sundance.*

Francis Ford Coppola (*The Godfather, Part III*), Barry Levinson (*Avalon*) and Guiseppe Tornatore (*Cinema Paradiso*).

When Costner prevailed, he told the crowd at the Beverly Hilton Hotel that the award "means a great deal to me, considering the men who were nominated in this category." Costner became only the fifth person to claim the prize for his first film.

The victory was also a vindication for him since so many Hollywood pundits had labeled the pic "Costner's Last Stand" after it was ambushed with problems during production, forcing Costner to contribute his $2 million salary to cover cost overruns. As of DGA awards night, *Dances with Wolves* had grossed an impressive $130 million at the U.S. box office.

It was well known that the DGA prize was a fairly reliable forecast of the eventual Oscar winner, since the two prizes had matched up every year except three since 1949. This year the Writers Guild of America touted its own powers of prognostication by issuing a notice boasting that 80 percent of Oscar scribes had previously been honored by their guild peers.

Dances with Wolves and *GoodFellas* faced off at the writers' guild just three days after they jockeyed at the directors' guild.

Wolves's Michael Blake triumphed in the race for Best Adapted Screenplay for successfully translating his novel to the screen. In his acceptance remarks, he blamed fellow writers for being "too often treated like employees rather than as creative partners" because they're such social recluses. He said that writers "don't take enough hand in the world around them."

Barry Levinson won Best Original Screenplay for *Avalon*, a drama about his family's struggles with assimilation as immigrant Jews in Baltimore. *Variety* reported, "Levinson briefly recalled how before shooting he gave his script to his father, who said, 'Well, it's not Academy Award material.' "

But when the Oscar nominations were announced, *Avalon* made the cut, *Dances with Wolves* led with 12—the most bids any pic had scored since *Reds* in 1981. *Godfa-*

National crix society Best Actress Anjelica Huston (left) and best supporting thesp Annette Bening costarred with John Cusack in *The Grifters*, the Indie Spirits' best pic.

ther III was far behind with 7 and *GoodFellas* followed with a good half dozen.

The only Oscar drama left looming was, according to the *L.A. Times*, "how big a sweep will develop for *Dances with Wolves?*"

While that question loomed over the major race, the indie horses hit the derby track with their own kudos.

Sixteen feature finalists competed for the Grand Jury Prize at the Sundance Film Festival, which dropped the "U.S." from its moniker of last year. *The New York Times* reported that the winner "was chosen with less pain and more unanimity than is usual," although response to the selection was quite the opposite. "Opinion on Todd Haynes' *Poison* had been sharply divided," *Variety* noted. "Its vociferous supporters extolled it as brilliant, while others considered it deplorable."

Variety's review called *Poison* "a conceptually bold, stylistically audacious first feature, a compelling study of different forms of deviance." Many audience members stormed out of the pic's screenings in response to "a scene in which convicts take turns spitting into a young boy's mouth," said the *Times*.

"I'm completely flabbergasted," Haynes said upon accepting the honor. "I was not expecting this at all. It's a difficult and complex film that not everyone could deal with. You're all the brave ones who weathered the film."

The Times reported on other races: "In contrast to the collegiality of the dramatic jury, a completely polarized documentary jury argued until 1:30 a.m. before splitting its grand prize between Barbara Kopple's *American Dream*, a political and social documentary about a strike at a Hormel meat-packing plant, and *Paris Is Burning*, a highly wrought tale of black and Hispanic homosexuals who sit at their sewing machines making gowns to wear at Harlem drag-queen balls."

American Dream also won the filmmakers' and audience prizes for documentaries, completing an unprecedented sweep of its categories. It would claim one more prize two months later—the Oscar for Best Documentary.

The filmmakers' drama trophy went to *Privilege*, "which mixes docu and dramatic techniques to explore the topic of menopause," said *Variety*. The Audience Award for features went to *One Cup of Coffee*, about a veteran white baseball player who adopts a young black rookie as a protégé.

Last year's winner of the Special Jury Prize at Sundance turned out to be the big champ at the Independent Spirit Awards— *To Sleep with Anger*, which earned Charles Burnett trophies for Best Director and Best Screenplay and also nabbed Best Actor (Danny Glover) and Best Supporting Actress (Sheryl Lee Ralph). Ralph triggered what *Variety* called "the most dramatic interval" of the kudofest by making "an emotional plea for an end to casting bias against women of color. Her remarks provoked a cheering ovation."

The Sleep with Anger lost the top race

After its NBR victory, *Dances with Wolves* got roughed up by *GoodFellas*, but then struck back at the Globes, WGA, DGA and Oscars.

for Best Picture to *The Grifters*, which, strangely, wasn't nominated in the directing and screenplay categories. *Grifters* also snagged the Best Actress laurels for star Anjelica Huston.

Best Supporting Actor was *Longtime Companion*'s Bruce Davison, previous choice of the Gotham crix and the National Society of Film Critics.

The biggest buzz of the event was caused by Kevin Costner, who received a Special Distinction Award while serving as the fete's keynote speaker. *L.A. Weekly* reported, "Costner unloaded a truly embarrassing speech, liberally sprinkled with 'fucks' and 'shits' (perhaps he thinks you have to talk ballsy to the independent crowd); rambled on about 'creativity' and 'individualism'; and injected some unnecessary, if accurate, disclaimers ('when I look at my own work I don't feel that I'm on the cutting edge of anything')."

On Oscar night "Kevin Costner was an early arrival—drawing predictably huge reaction" from the grandstands, reported *Variety*. The nominee had every reason to be eager and feel upbeat: all media forecasters, without exception, predicted that he and *Wolves* had a lock on Best Director and Best Picture.

Another forecasters' favorite, Best Supporting Actress nominee Whoopi Goldberg (*Ghost*), was actually the first to arrive, looking healthy and happy despite early reports that the pressure of being the frontrunner was taking its toll. A few days before the gala, *Variety*'s Army Archerd noted, "She's been suffering from a severe case of hives that had almost completely closed her eyes—and also caused her to gain weight. She's feeling better, not 100%."

Goldberg ended up feeling a whole lot better on Oscar night when she beat National Society of Film Critics champ Annette Bening (*The Grifters*) and L.A. crix honoree Lorraine Bracco (*GoodFellas*).

"Ever since I was a little kid, I wanted this," she said as she held the statuette, awestruck, in her grasp. "As a little kid I lived in the projects and you're the people I watched. You're the people who made me want to be an actor. I am proud to be an actor and I'm gonna keep on acting."

Ghost, a surprise nominee for Best Picture, also earned the trophy for Best Original Screenplay, beating writers' guild champ Barry Levinson (*Avalon*).

Variety reported on what the champ revealed backstage: "Bruce Joel Rubin said he owns 4 percent of *Ghost*. While he's yet to see a penny from the film, which has grossed about a half-billion dollars worldwide, he's 'hoping Paramount will be good to me.'"

Award seers were split on what would happen in the supporting-actor contest. Three out of four pundits at the *L.A. Times* foresaw a victory for Bruce Davison. The fourth pundit picked L.A. film crix and National Board of Review champ Joe Pesci, but *The New York Times*'s Chris Chase dismissed the good fella's chances, saying, "If you think they're going to give an Oscar to a psycho killer with a Napoleon complex who shoots (among 300 other people) an innocent bar boy, you're a harder case than I am." Chase bet on Al Pacino (*Dick Tracy*), who didn't score a Best Actor bid for *Godfather III*—"one of the year's major omissions," insisted *Variety*. Even Pesci told the press, "I kind of hope Al gets it."

Pesci put winning so far out of his head that he confessed to reporters that he didn't have an acceptance speech ready in case he was called to the podium.

When it happened, he looked frazzled, and simply said, "It's my privilege. Thank you."

Backstage, reporters grilled Pesci on

Variety called Sundance honoree *Poison* "a compelling study of different forms of deviance."

why his speech was so brief. "There were so many people to thank," he said, "I was afraid that, if I started, I couldn't stop and would get booed."

Prognosticators were also divided over who'd win Best Actress. Of the quartet of crix who sounded off in the *L.A. Times*, two bet on Gotham crix champ Joanne Woodward, one on L.A. crix and national society awardee Anjelica Huston and one on Golden Globe winner Kathy Bates.

When Bates won, she said in gratitude, "I'd like to thank the Academy. I've been waiting a long time to say that." She also thanked "my mom at home and my dad, who I hope is watching somewhere."

Backstage, she explained to reporters that her father had died two years earlier, but had been such an early supporter of her career goals that he paid for her first trip to New York so that she could pursue acting. "I just wish he could've been here tonight," she said, fighting off tears.

Even though *Dances with Wolves* was considered such a heavy favorite in the kudos sweepstakes, no forecasters picked star Kevin Costner to win Best Actor. Most bets were split between Jeremy Irons (L.A. crix, national society and Golden Globe champ) and Robert De Niro (Gotham crix and National Board of Review honoree). Three *L.A. Times* pundits backed Irons; one cited De Niro.

Irons prevailed. At the podium, he addressed his wife watching the gala on a London telly, saying, "I wish you were here to help me carry this because you helped me win it."

Backstage, reporters asked him if he thought the character he portrayed in *Reversal of Fortune*, Claus Von Bulow, was guilty or innocent of the attempted murder allegation. "Everything I think about him is on the screen," he replied.

Despite Kevin Costner's defeat for Best Actor, *Wolves* devoured the competish in numerous tech categories all night—including sound, film editing, cinematography and music score. If it was going to complete the sweep and claim Best Director and Picture, too, oddsmakers knew that it needed to claim the trophy for Best Adapted Screenplay earlier on in the night.

When the match-up came, *Wolves* was clearly out front, having already claimed the prize from the Writers Guild of America.

When *Wolves* won, *Variety* noted that the victory capped off an amazing rebound in the fortunes of writer Michael Blake, who, just "a few months ago was crashing alternately with Costner and producer Jim Wilson and, stone broke, was occasionally sleeping in his car. Now his novel from which the movie was drawn is atop the bestseller list and Blake is in some danger of ending up a fairly wealthy man."

But Blake was also a sick man who had Hodgkin's disease. "I'm in remission now and they expect me to recover fully," he told reporters, "but I live from blood test to blood test, like all cancer patients."

In the race for Best Director, Jack Mathews of the *L.A. Times* said, "Costner will probably win as Best Director, but there is sure to be a lot of support for Martin Scorsese (*GoodFellas*). Scorsese is the American director of the moment and has never won an Oscar."

But Costner won, as predicted. Once on stage, he said, "Everybody knows that you really don't make pictures yourself." He thanked the cast, the crew and his fellow producers, "who figured out through all my boyish enthusiasm that I was deadly serious about making this movie."

When it came time to reveal the Best Picture victor, there was no mystery what it would be. Upon hearing the news that *Wolves* had it, Costner reappeared at the podium and thanked "my Native American brothers and sisters, especially the Lakota Sioux."

The next day, *Variety* reported that "*Dances with Wolves* waltzed away with seven Oscars (and became) the first western to win Best Picture since *Cimarron* 60 years earlier."

▪ 1990 ▪

NATIONAL BOARD OF REVIEW

The board declared a Best Picture and Foreign Film of the year, then listed its remaining favorites according to highest scores. The vote results were announced on December 16, 1990. Awards were presented on March 4, 1991, at the Equitable Center in New York.

BEST PICTURE
▪ *Dances with Wolves*
Hamlet
GoodFellas
Awakenings
Reversal of Fortune
Miller's Crossing

Metropolitan
Mr. and Mrs. Bridge
Avalon
The Grifters

BEST DIRECTOR
▪ Kevin Costner, *Dances with Wolves*

BEST ACTOR (TIE)
▪ Robert De Niro, *Awakenings*
▪ Robin Williams, *Awakenings*

BEST ACTRESS
▪ Mia Farrow, *Alice*

BEST SUPPORTING ACTOR
▪ Joe Pesci, *GoodFellas*

BEST SUPPORTING ACTRESS
- Winona Ryder, *Mermaids*

BEST FOREIGN FILM
- *Cyrano de Bergerac* (France)

Jesus of Montreal (Canada)
The Nasty Girl (German)
Monsieur Hire (France)
Tie Me Up! Tie Me Down! (Spain)

CAREER ACHIEVEMENT AWARD
- James Stewart

LOS ANGELES FILM CRITICS ASSOCIATION

Winners were announced on December 16, 1990. Awards were presented on January 16, 1991, at the Bel Age Hotel in Los Angeles.

BEST PICTURE
- *GoodFellas*

BEST DIRECTOR
- Martin Scorsese, *GoodFellas*

BEST ACTOR
- Jeremy Irons, *Reversal of Fortune*

BEST ACTRESS
- Anjelica Huston, *The Grifters, The Witches*

BEST SUPPORTING ACTOR
- Joe Pesci, *GoodFellas*

BEST SUPPORTING ACTRESS
- Lorraine Bracco, *GoodFellas*

BEST SCREENPLAY
- Nicholas Kazan, *Reversal of Fortune*

BEST CINEMATOGRAPHY
- Michael Ballhaus, *GoodFellas*

BEST MUSIC SCORE
- Richard Horowitz, Ryuichi Sakamoto, *The Sheltering Sky*

BEST ANIMATION
- *The Rescuers Down Under*, Hendel Butoy, Mike Gabriel

BEST DOCUMENTARY (TIE)
- *Paris Is Burning*, Jenny Livingston, Barry Swimer
- *Pictures of the Old World*, Dusan Hanak

BEST FOREIGN FILM
- *Life and Nothing But* (France)

BEST EXPERIMENTAL/INDEPENDENT FILM
- *Tongues United*, Marlon Riggs

NEW GENERATION AWARD
- Jane Campion

CAREER ACHIEVEMENT AWARDS
- Chuck Jones
- Blake Edwards

SPECIAL AWARD
- Charles Burnett, *To Sleep with Anger*

NEW YORK FILM CRITICS CIRCLE

Winners were announced on December 18, 1990. Awards were presented on January 13, 1991, at the Pegasus Suite of the Rainbow Room in Rockefeller Center in New York.

BEST PICTURE
- *GoodFellas*

BEST DIRECTOR
- Martin Scorsese, *GoodFellas*

BEST NEW DIRECTOR
- Whit Stillman, *Metropolitan*

BEST ACTOR
- Robert De Niro, *GoodFellas, Awakenings*

BEST ACTRESS
- Joanne Woodward, *Mr. and Mrs. Bridge*

BEST SUPPORTING ACTOR
- Bruce Davison, *Longtime Companion*

BEST SUPPORTING ACTRESS
- Jennifer Jason Leigh, *Miami Blues, Last Exit to Brooklyn*

BEST SCREENPLAY
- Ruth Prawer Jhabvala, *Mr. and Mrs. Bridge*

BEST CINEMATOGRAPHY
- Vittorio Storaro, *The Sheltering Sky*

BEST FOREIGN FILM
- *The Nasty Girl* (Germany)

SPECIAL AWARDS
- Bruce Goldstein
- Karen Cooper
- Film Forum

NATIONAL SOCIETY OF FILM CRITICS

Winners were announced on January 6, 1991.

BEST PICTURE
- *GoodFellas*

BEST DIRECTOR
- Martin Scorsese, *GoodFellas*

BEST ACTOR
- Jeremy Irons, *Reversal of Fortune*

BEST ACTRESS
- Anjelica Huston, *The Grifters, The Witches*

BEST SUPPORTING ACTOR
- Bruce Davison, *Longtime Companion*

BEST SUPPORTING ACTRESS
- Annette Bening, *The Grifters*

BEST SCREENPLAY
- Charles Burnett, *To Sleep with Anger*

BEST CINEMATOGRAPHY
- Peter Suschitzky, *Where the Heart Is*

BEST DOCUMENTARY
- *Berkeley in the '60s*, Mark Kitchell

BEST FOREIGN-LANGUAGE FILM
- *Ariel* (Finland)

SPECIAL AWARDS
- Renee Furst
- Jean-Luc Godard

GOLDEN GLOBES

Nominations were announced on December 27, 1990. Awards were presented on January 19, 1991, at the Beverly Hilton Hotel in Los Angeles. The ceremony was telecast by TBS.

BEST DRAMA PICTURE
- *Dances with Wolves*
Avalon
The Godfather, Part III
GoodFellas
Reversal of Fortune

BEST COMEDY OR MUSICAL PICTURE
- *Green Card*
Dick Tracy
Ghost
Home Alone
Pretty Woman

BEST DIRECTOR
- Kevin Costner, *Dances with Wolves*
Bernardo Bertolucci, *The Sheltering Sky*
Francis Ford Coppola, *The Godfather, Part III*
Barbet Schroeder, *Reversal of Fortune*
Martin Scorsese, *GoodFellas*

BEST ACTOR, DRAMA
- Jeremy Irons, *Reversal of Fortune*
Kevin Costner, *Dances with Wolves*
Richard Harris, *The Field*
Al Pacino, *The Godfather, Part III*
Robin Williams, *Awakenings*

BEST ACTRESS, DRAMA
- Kathy Bates, *Misery*
Anjelica Huston, *The Grifters*
Michelle Pfeiffer, *The Russia House*
Susan Sarandon, *White Palace*
Joanne Woodward, *Mr. and Mrs. Bridge*

BEST ACTOR, COMEDY OR MUSICAL
- Gerard Depardieu, *Green Card*
Macaulay Culkin, *Home Alone*
Johnny Depp, *Edward Scissorhands*

Richard Gere, *Pretty Woman*
Patrick Swayze, *Ghost*

BEST ACTRESS, COMEDY OR MUSICAL
- Julia Roberts, *Pretty Woman*
Mia Farrow, *Alice*
Andie MacDowell, *Green Card*
Demi Moore, *Ghost*
Meryl Streep, *Postcards from the Edge*

BEST SUPPORTING ACTOR
- Bruce Davison, *Longtime Companion*
Armand Assante, *Q & A*
Hector Elizondo, *Pretty Woman*
Andy Garcia, *The Godfather, Part III*
Al Pacino, *Dick Tracy*
Joe Pesci, *GoodFellas*

BEST SUPPORTING ACTRESS
- Whoopi Goldberg, *Ghost*
Lorraine Bracco, *GoodFellas*
Diane Ladd, *Wild at Heart*
Shirley MacLaine, *Postcards from the Edge*
Mary McDonnell, *Dances with Wolves*
Winona Ryder, *Mermaids*

BEST SCREENPLAY
- Michael Blake, *Dances with Wolves*
Francis Ford Coppola, Mario Puzo, *The Godfather, Part III*
Nicholas Kazan, *Reversal of Fortune*
Barry Levinson, *Avalon*
Martin Scorsese, Nicholas Pileggi, *GoodFellas*

BEST SONG
- "Blaze of Glory," *Young Guns II*, Jon Bon Jovi
"I'm Checking Out," *Postcards from the Edge*, Shel Silverstein
"Promise Me You'll Remember," *The Godfather, Part III*, Carmen Coppola, John Bettis
"Sooner or Later," *Dick Tracy*, Stephen Sondheim
"What Can You Lose?," *Dick Tracy*, Stephen Sondheim

BEST FOREIGN FILM
- *Cyrano de Bergerac* (France)
Akira Kurosawa's Dreams (Japan)
The Nasty Girl (Germany)

Requiem for Dominic (Austria)
Taxi Blues (Russia)

Winners

BEST SCORE
- Richard Horowitz, Ryuichi Sakamoto, *The Sheltering Sky*

CECIL B. DEMILLE AWARD
- Jack Lemmon

SUNDANCE FILM FESTIVAL

The festival was held January 17–27, 1991, at Park City, Utah.

GRAND JURY PRIZE
(DRAMATIC)
- *Poison*, Todd Haynes
(DOCUMENTARY)
- *American Dream*, Barbara Kopple
- *Paris Is Burning*, Jennie Livingston

FILMMAKER'S TROPHY
(DRAMATIC)
- *Privilege*, Yvonne Rainer
(DOCUMENTARY)
- *American Dream*, Barbara Kopple

AUDIENCE AWARD
(DRAMATIC)
- *One Cup of Coffee*, Robin Armstrong
(DOCUMENTARY)
- *American Dream*, Barbara Kopple

WALDO SALT SCREENWRITING AWARD
- *Hangin' with the Homeboys*, Joseph Vasquez
- *Trust,* Hal Hartley

CINEMATOGRAPHY AWARD
(DRAMATIC)
- *Daughters of the Dust*, Arthur Jafa
(DOCUMENTARY)
- *Christo in Paris*, David and Albert Maysles

SPECIAL JURY RECOGNITION
- *Straight out of Brooklyn*, Matty Rich

PRODUCERS GUILD OF AMERICA

Winners were announced on February 18, 1991. Awards were presented on March 5 at the Regent Beverly Wilshire Hotel in Los Angeles.

DARRYL F. ZANUCK PRODUCER OF THE YEAR AWARD

- *Dances with Wolves*, Jim Wilson, Kevin Costner

Avalon, Mark Johnson, Barry Levinson

Awakenings, Penny Marshall, Elliot Abbott, Lawrence Lasker, Walter Parkes, Arne Schmidt

CHARLES B. FITZSIMONS HONORARY LIFETIME ACHIEVEMENT AWARD

- Stanley Rubin

DAVID O. SELZNICK LIFETIME ACHIEVEMENT AWARD

- Stanley Kramer

DIRECTORS GUILD OF AMERICA

Awards were presented on March 16, 1991, at the Beverly Hilton Hotel in Los Angeles.

BEST DIRECTOR

- Kevin Costner, *Dances with Wolves*

Francis Ford Coppola, *The Godfather, Part III*

Barry Levinson, *Avalon*

Martin Scorsese, *GoodFellas*

Giuseppe Tornatore, *Cinema Paradiso*

ROBERT B. ALDRICH AWARD

- Larry Auerbach
- Milt Felsen

PRESTON STURGES AWARD

- Billy Wilder

WRITERS GUILD OF AMERICA

Awards were presented on March 20, 1991, at the Beverly Hilton Hotel in Los Angeles and the Windows on the World restaurant in New York.

BEST ORIGINAL SCREENPLAY

- *Avalon*, Barry Levinson

Alice, Woody Allen

Ghost, Bruce Joel Rubin

Green Card, Peter Weir

Pretty Woman, J. F. Lawton

BEST ADAPTED SCREENPLAY

- *Dances with Wolves*, Michael Blake, based on his novel

Awakenings, Steven Zaillian, based on the book by Oliver Sacks

GoodFellas, Nicholas Pileggi, Martin Scorsese, based on the book *Wiseguy* by Nicholas Pileggi

The Grifters, Donald E. Westlake, based on the novel by Jim Thompson

Reversal of Fortune, Nicholas Kazan, based on the book by Alan Dershowitz

MORGAN COX AWARD

- Christopher Knopf

VALENTINE DAVIES

- Frank Pierson

LAUREL AWARD

- Alvin Sargent

ROBERT MELTZER AWARD

- Kirk Douglas

EDMUND H. NORTH FOUNDERS AWARD

- Daniel Taradash

INDEPENDENT SPIRIT

Nominations were announced on January 20, 1991. Awards were presented on March 23 at the Beverly Hilton Hotel in Los Angeles.

BEST PICTURE

- *The Grifters*

Henry, Portrait of a Serial Killer

The Plot against Harry

Pump Up the Volume

To Sleep with Anger

BEST FIRST FEATURE

- *Metropolitan*

House Party

Lightning over Braddock

The Natural History of Parking Lots
Twister

BEST DIRECTOR

- Charles Burnett, *To Sleep with Anger*
Reginald Hudlin, *House Party*
John McNaughton, *Henry, Portrait of a Serial Killer*
Allan Moyle, *Pump Up the Volume*
Michael Roemer, *The Plot against Harry*

BEST ACTOR

- Danny Glover, *To Sleep with Anger*
Martin Priest, *The Plot against Harry*
Chris Reid, *House Party*
Michael Rooker, *Henry, Portrait of a Serial Killer*
Christian Slater, *Pump Up the Volume*

BEST ACTRESS

- Anjelica Huston, *The Grifters*
Mary Alice, *To Sleep with Anger*
Eszter Balint, *Bail Jumper*
Carolyn Farina, *Metropolitan*
Joanne Woodward, *Mr. and Mrs. Bridge*

BEST SUPPORTING ACTOR

- Bruce Davison, *Longtime Companion*
Willem Dafoe, *Wild at Heart*
Robin Harris, *House Party*
Ben Lang, *The Plot against Henry*
Tom Towles, *Henry, Portrait of a Serial Killer*

BEST SUPPORTING ACTRESS

- Sheryl Lee Ralph, *To Sleep with Anger*
Tracy Arnold, *Henry, Portrait of a Serial Killer*
Ethel Ayler, *To Sleep with Anger*
Tisha Campbell, *House Party*
A. J. Johnson, *House Party*

BEST SCREENPLAY

- Charles Burnett, *To Sleep with Anger*
John McNaughton, Richard Fire, *Henry, Portrait of a Serial Killer*
Whit Stillman, *Metropolitan*
Michael Roemer, *The Plot against Harry*
Allan Moyle, *Pump Up the Volume*

BEST FOREIGN FILM

- *Sweetie* (Australia)

Black Rain (Japan)
City of Sadness (Taiwan)
The Cook, The Thief, His Wife, and Her Lover (France/Netherlands)
Freeze, Die, Come to Life (U.S.S.R.)

Winners

BEST CINEMATOGRAPHY

- Fred Elmes, *Wild at Heart*

SPECIAL DISTINCTION AWARD

- *Dances with Wolves*, Kevin Costner, Jim Wilson

JOHN CASSAVETES AWARD

- Edward R. Pressman
- Jon Jost

ACADEMY AWARDS

Nominations were announced on February 19, 1991. Awards were presented on March 25 at the Shrine Auditorium in Los Angeles. The ceremony was telecast by ABC.

BEST PICTURE

- *Dances with Wolves*
Awakenings
Ghost
The Godfather, Part III
GoodFellas

BEST DIRECTOR

- Kevin Costner, *Dances with Wolves*
Francis Ford Coppola, *The Godfather, Part III*
Stephen Frears, *The Grifters*
Barbet Schroeder, *Reversal of Fortune*
Martin Scorsese, *GoodFellas*

BEST ACTOR

- Jeremy Irons, *Reversal of Fortune*
Kevin Costner, *Dances with Wolves*
Robert De Niro, *Awakenings*
Gerard Depardieu, *Cyrano de Bergerac*
Richard Harris, *The Field*

BEST ACTRESS

- Kathy Bates, *Misery*
Anjelica Huston, *The Grifters*
Julia Roberts, *Pretty Woman*

Meryl Streep, *Postcards from the Edge*
Joanne Woodward, *Mr. and Mrs. Bridge*

BEST SUPPORTING ACTOR

- Joe Pesci, *GoodFellas*
Bruce Davison, *Longtime Companion*
Andy Garcia, *The Godfather, Part III*
Graham Greene, *Dances with Wolves*
Al Pacino, *Dick Tracy*

BEST SUPPORTING ACTRESS

- Whoopi Goldberg, *Ghost*
Annette Bening, *The Grifters*
Lorraine Bracco, *GoodFellas*
Diane Ladd, *Wild at Heart*
Mary McDonnell, *Dances with Wolves*

BEST ORIGINAL SCREENPLAY

- Bruce Joel Rubin, *Ghost*
Woody Allen, *Alice*
Barry Levinson, *Avalon*
Whit Stillman, *Metropolitan*
Peter Weir, *Green Card*

BEST ADAPTED SCREENPLAY

- Michael Blake, *Dances with Wolves*
Nicholas Kazan, *Reversal of Fortune*
Nicholas Pileggi, Martin Scorsese,
   GoodFellas
Donald E. Westlake, *The Grifters*
Steven Zaillian, *Awakenings*

BEST SONG

- "Sooner or Later (I Always Get My
   Man)," *Dick Tracy*, Stephen Sondheim
"Blaze of Glory," *Young Guns II*, Jon Bon
   Jovi
"I'm Checkin' Out," *Postcards from the
   Edge*, Shel Silverstein
"Promise Me You'll Remember," *The
   Godfather, Part III*, John Bettis,
   Carmine Coppola
"Somewhere in My Memory," *Home Alone*,
   Leslie Bricusse, John Williams

BEST FOREIGN-LANGUAGE FILM

- *Journey of Hope* (Switzerland)
Cyrano de Bergerac (France)
Ju Dou (Peoples's Republic of China)
The Nasty Girl (Germany)
Open Doors (Italy)

Winners

BEST ART DIRECTION

- Richard Sylbert, Rick Simpson, *Dick
   Tracy*

BEST CINEMATOGRAPHY

- Dean Semler, *Dances with Wolves*

BEST COSTUME DESIGN

- Franca Squarciapino, *Cyrano de
   Bergerac*

BEST DOCUMENTARY

(FEATURE)
- *American Dream*, Arthur Cohn, Barbara
   Kopple

(SHORT SUBJECT)
- *Days of Waiting*, Steven Okazaki

BEST FILM EDITING

- Neil Travis, *Dances with Wolves*

BEST MAKEUP

- John Caglione, Jr., Doug Drexler, *Dick
   Tracy*

BEST MUSIC SCORE

- John Barry, *Dances with Wolves*

SCIENTIFIC OR TECHNICAL AWARDS

(Academy Award of Merit)
- Eastman Kodak

(Scientific and Engineering Award)
- Bruce Wilton, Carlos Icinkoff,
   Mechanical Concepts; Arnold and
   Richter engineering department; Fuji
   Photo Film; Manfred G. Michelson,
   Technical Film Systems; John W. Lang,
   Walter Hrastnik, Charles J. Watson, Bell
   and Howell

(Technical Achievement Award)
- William L. Blowers, Belco Associates;
   Thomas F. Denove; Takuo
   Miyagishima; Panavision; Christopher
   S. Gilman, Harvey Hubert, Jr., Diligent
   Dwarves Effects Lab; Jim Graves, J&G
   Enterprises; Bengt O. Orhall, Kenneth
   Lund, Bjorn Selin, Kjell Hogberg, AB
   Film-Teknik; Richard Mula, Pete
   Romano, HydroImage; Paul Kiankhooy,
   Lightmaker Co.; All-Union Cinema and

Photo Research Institute; Iain Neil, Dedo Weigert, Paul Preo, Peter Baldwin, Fred Kolb, Jr.

BEST SHORT FILM
(ANIMATED)
- *Creature Comforts*, Nick Park

(LIVE ACTION)
- *The Lunch Date*, Adam Davidson

BEST SOUND
- Bill W. Benton, Jeffrey Perkins, Greg Watkins, Russell Williams II, *Dances with Wolves*

BEST SOUND EFFECTS EDITING
- Stephen H. Flick, *Total Recall*

SPECIAL ACHIEVEMENT AWARD—VISUAL EFFECTS
- Rob Bottin, Eric Brevig, Alex Funke, Tim McGovern, *Total Recall*

GORDON E. SAWYER AWARD
- Stefan Kudelski

IRVING G. THALBERG MEMORIAL AWARD
- David Brown
- Richard D. Zanuck

HONORARY AWARDS
- Sophia Loren
- Myrna Loy
- Roderick T. Ryan
- Don Trumbull
- Geoffery H. Williamson

SCREEN ACTORS GUIDE

LIFETIME ACHIEVEMENT AWARD
- Brock Peters

▪ 1991 ▪

Lambs: *First and Last Course*

When movie tix sales dropped 6.4 percent compared to last year, *Newsweek* blamed "grim" pix, insisting, "The big studio product, with few exceptions, was timid, unimaginative and dumb."

But most critics chose the grimmest film of the year when 81 of them were asked to name 1991's best pic in a nationwide poll conducted by the *L.A. Times.* They named *The Silence of the Lambs*, which starred Jodie Foster as a killer-hunting FBI agent who seeks advice from an incarcerated fiend (Anthony Hopkins) nicknamed Hannibal the Cannibal because he ate his murder victims— "with fava beans and a little Chianti," he noted. *Variety* said the pic "intelligently wallows in the fascination for aberrant psychology and perverse evil."

The selection of *Silence of the Lambs* was shocking for two reasons. Not only were the crix suddenly transcending their usual scorn for horror flicks, but also their usual avoidance of b.o. blockbusters. *Silence* was 1991's fifth top-grosser, earning more than $100 million.

Why?

Some pundits agreed with *Newsweek* that there were few alternatives. But *Silence* did face serious competish for kudos from new pics by past award magnets Oliver Stone and Warren Beatty.

While probing the assassination of President John F. Kennedy in *JFK,* Stone, said *Variety*, used "the sum of conspiracy theory points made by New Orleans d.a. Jim Garrison and others since to suggest as strongly as possible that Lee Harvey Oswald was a

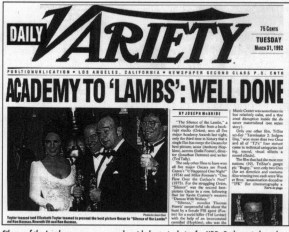

Silence of the Lambs was an uncommonly grisly best-pic choice for NBR, Gotham circle and Oscars. The year's fifth biggest grosser topped *Bugsy* and *JFK.*

patsy." Some observers thought Stone took too many theories too seriously, though, and ended up hurting his pic's credibility. Political columnists had a heyday taking potshots at it, and *Newsweek* declared on its cover, "The Twisted Truth of *JFK:* Why Oliver Stone's New Movie Can't Be Trusted." Nonetheless, *JFK* managed to stay in serious awards contention because some crix, like Roger Ebert of *The Chicago Sun-Times*, named it the best movie of the year.

Warren Beatty entered the year's kudos derby with *Bugsy,* which featured him as Benjamin "Bugsy" Siegel, the showbiz-loving gangster who invented Las Vegas. *The New York Times* hailed it as "smart and seductive" and *Variety* called it a "handsome pic," but the latter source also groused about "an unsatisfactory central romance." At the b.o., *Bugsy* performed only modestly well ($40 million) compared to Beatty's *Dick Tracy* last year ($120 million). Beatty told *Variety,* however, that he was "surprised at how well it has done" considering its dark view of America and a lead character who is "fairly nefarious."

When *Bugsy* hit the jackpot as the Best Picture selection of the Los Angeles Film Critics Association, the *L.A. Times* said, "The choice was seen by some as a minor surprise." One voter told the paper that *Bugsy* was "the one, major-studio, well-crafted entertainment that most critics could agree upon as being good. A lot of the other films that would be contenders have something in them that are objectionable to some of the critics."

Bugsy also claimed the kudos for Best Director Barry Levinson and Best Screenplay scribe James Toback. In all three categories, the second-placed pic was *The Fisher King*, the tale of a radio shock jock who's stopped from committing suicide by a wacky gadfly (Robin Williams) who's searching for the Holy Grail. Star Mercedes Ruehl—who had recently vaulted to stardom after giving a Tony-winning perf in Neil Simon's *Lost in Yonkers*—was named Best Actress for portraying the deejay's long-suffering girlfriend (she "sizzles," said *Variety*). Ruehl beat Geena Davis, who costarred with Susan Sarandon in *Thelma & Louise*, which *Variety* lauded as "a thumpingly adventurous road pic about two regular gals who shoot down a would-be rapist and wind up on the lam in their 1966 T-bird."

Warren Beatty lost Best Actor to Nick Nolte as an emotionally racked ex-teacher who falls in love with his sister's psychiatrist (Barbra Streisand) in *The Prince of Tides.*

Best Supporting Actor was Michael Lerner as a tyrannical film-studio mogul in *Barton Fink*. Runner-up was Robert Duvall as a southern gentleman who hires an unruly sexpot (Laura Dern) as a maid in *Rambling Rose.*

Best Supporting Actress was Jane Horrocks as a rebellious anorexic girl in *Life Is Sweet*. She beat Amanda Plummer as one of Robin Williams's eccentric disciples in *The Fisher King.*

Silence of the Lambs made a record sweep of the Gotham crix kudos.

When the crix gathered to bestow their kudos, the *L.A. Daily News* noted that "every presentation and acceptance speech was drenched with good cheer—a marked difference from last year's luncheon." As jovial as the comments were, many still had sting, such as Warren Beatty's reference to the event as a rare, cordial gathering of "those who make movies and those who complain about them."

Highlights of the gala included special career salutes to veteran horror thesp Vincent Price and composer Elmer Bernstein. New talent was also hailed when 23-year-old director John Singleton was honored for *Boyz N the Hood*, his "absorbing, smartly made dramatic encyclopedia of problems and ethics in the black community, 1991," said *Variety*. Singleton defined success to the crowd as "how long you stay around," and added, "You haven't seen the last of me!"

The luncheon dragged on for so long that the sun was starting to set as Beatty accepted his scroll for Best Picture. He cut his thank-you short, pointed to his new wife Annette Bening and reminded the audience that they had a hungry newborn daughter at home. "The person I'm with is a walking lunch for another small person," he said.

Beatty may have lost the crix's vote for Best Actor, but he reaped that honor from the National Board of Review two days later. The board also embraced the crix's second-place choice for Best Actress, but made Geena Davis share the accolade with *Thelma & Louise* costar Susan Sarandon.

Silence of the Lambs wasn't even considered for kudos by the L.A. crix, but it came roaring back at the board honors, snagging Best Picture and Best Director.

It scored an even bigger haul when the New York Film Critics Circle voted the next day. "It was the first time in the group's 56-year history that one film swept the major awards," reported *Variety*.

Silence snagged Best Picture, Director

(Demme), Actor (Anthony Hopkins) and Actress (Jodie Foster). In the first three races, *Silence* beat the same film—*My Own Private Idaho*, helmer Gus Van Sant's buddy pic about two gay hustlers. *Silence* claimed the top pic prize by a score of 36 to 11 points and Demme prevailed as Best Director 28 to 17. Hopkins (33 points) won the thesp race over the recent Best Actor champ at the Venice Film Festival, River Phoenix, who nabbed 16 points as "a believable, sometimes compelling figure of a young man urgently groping for definition in his life," said *Variety*. Best Actress Foster (30 points) survived a combined threat from Geena Davis and Susan Sarandon (25 each).

Considering *Silence*'s generous acknowledgment in the top four races, its performance in the Best Screenplay contest seemed odd: it came in distant fourth place with only 19 points—behind champ *Naked Lunch* (written by David Cronenberg, 27 points), *Thelma & Louise* (Callie Khouri, 20) and *Bugsy* (James Toback, 19).

"They shafted me!" fumed *Silence* scribe Ted Tally to *The Washington Post*. "They acted like this movie was born in a Federal Express envelope on the way to Jodie Foster's house."

The match-up for Best Supporting Actor took five ballots before the Gotham crix endorsed the same thesp honored recently at Cannes: Samuel L. Jackson as the lead star's drug-addicted brother in *Jungle Fever*.

He triumphed with 26 points over 23 scored by *Billy Bathgate*'s Steven Hill. Judy Davis was cited for two roles when named Best Supporting Actress: as a woman exterminated by her insect-exterminator husband in *Naked Lunch* and as a seductive secretary in *Barton Fink*. Her 24-point score topped the 20 earned by runner-up Juliette Lewis as a 15-year-old girl who gets involved with a psychopath in *Cape Fear*.

John Singleton (33) snagged the prize for Best New Director over Anthony Minghella, who reaped 18 points for his ghost drama *Truly, Madly, Deeply*.

When the Gotham crix gathered to bestow their laurels at the Pegasus Room at Rockefeller Center, one of the event's highlights was the presentation of the Best Actor plaque to Anthony Hopkins by an actor who portrayed one of his victims in the pic— Anthony Heald. Heald said, "My pleasure at being here was heightened when I found out my name was not on the menu."

All of the presentations were upstaged, however, by the sudden intrusion of nine members of a gay activist group "who ingeniously dressed in tuxes and passed out angry leaflets," noted *The Village Voice*. The leaflets fumed over the depiction of the serial killer in *Silence* as a gay man and chastised the Gotham circle "for honoring a film that feeds the myth that drag queens, since they wear dresses, must be sick." The pamphleteers escaped before security caught them and before they could hear the compliment they were paid by *Silence*'s helmer Demme.

"I thought that was exceptionally gracefully achieved," he told the crowd. "The information contained here in this leaflet is horrifying."

Silence of the Lambs may have been the top Best Picture choice of the crix polled nationally by the *L.A. Times*, but the film fared poorly in the voting held by the National Society of Film Critics.

Two pics dominated the kudos. Winner of Best Picture was *Life Is Sweet*, a quirky comic glimpse at a British working-class family by U.K. director Mike Leigh. In its review, *Variety* had called Leigh's real-life thesp wife Alison Steadman "superb" as a do-good suburban housewife. She won Best Actress by a score of 26 to 14 over Jodie Foster. Jane Horrocks (28 points) repeated her L.A. crix victory as Best Supporting Actress, beating Juliette Lewis (13).

Life Is Sweet prevailed as Best Picture by a close score of 21 to 17 over *Naked Lunch*. *Variety* had written of the latter pic that helmer/scribe "David Cronenberg has come up with a fascinating, demanding, mordantly

> ## L.A. crix's choice of *Bugsy* as best pic was "a minor surprise."

funny picture" while adapting William S. Burroughs's notorious novel about hedonists. The national crix made up for *Naked Lunch*'s loss in the top race by giving Cronenberg the prizes for Best Director (over Leigh, 18 to 14) and Best Screenplay (over *Bugsy*'s James Toback, 24 to 15).

River Phoenix avenged the loss he suffered at the Gotham crix vote by winning the national society's palm for Best Actor (26 points) over Warren Beatty (22). Best Supporting Actor was Harvey Keitel, who was cited for three roles: a wiseguy in *Bugsy* and a detective in *Thelma & Louise* and *Mortal Thoughts*. He beat *Billy Bathgate*'s Steven Hill 20 to 16.

When the Golden Globe nominations were announced, *Bugsy* led the pack with the most (eight), followed by five each for *Silence of the Lambs* and *The Fisher King*. The complete snubbing of *Boyz N the Hood*, which had grossed $55 million for Columbia, "brought a chorus of boos from several sectors," *Variety* noted.

When the winners were announced, *The New York Times* called the outcome "most curious."

Bugsy beat *Silence of the Lambs* and *JFK* for Best Drama Picture, but, strangely, it snagged no other kudos.

"Instead of cleaning up, *Bugsy* fell prey to a lone assassin: *JFK*, which won the Best Director Award for Oliver Stone—and thus elevated its chances in the Oscar derby," the *L.A. Times* said. "Stone told the audience he hopes his movie will prompt the government to open its secret files on the 1963 Kennedy assassination."

Stone also expressed his appreciation to the foreign press for their support: "At a time when so many media organizations are bashing this film, I really want to thank this one for being so generous."

The biggest Globe champ was actually Disney's musical cartoon version of *Beauty and the Beast*, which reaped three wins: Best Comedy or Musical Picture, Best Musical Score and Best Song (title tune).

Trumbo, Maltz widows thank WGA for honor

Continued from page 2

script of the ABC miniseries "Separate but Equal." He used the occasion to attack Oliver Stone's Kennedy assassination docudrama "JFK," whose script by Stone and Zachary Sklar was nominated for an adaptation award but lost to Ted Tally's "The Silence of the Lambs."

Stevens said he was accepting

Blacklisted writers' widows Esther Maltz and Cleo Trumbo with awards presenter Warren Beatty at WGA BevHills ceremony.

The widows of former blacklistees Dalton Trumbo and Albert Maltz accepted overdue WGA kudos from presenter Warren Beatty.

"The Globe show's most emotional moment came with composer Alan Menken paid tribute to his longtime writing partner, the lyricist Howard Ashman, who died from AIDS complications last year," the *L.A. Times* reported. "Thanking Disney for keeping the Hollywood musical alive, Menken said Ashman 'showed how it was done. All who worked with Howard know he is missed.' "

L.A. crix champ Nick Nolte (*Prince of Tides*) prevailed as Best Drama Actor even though he told the press that he expected *Silence*'s Anthony Hopkins to win. When *Silence*'s Jodie Foster followed up her accolade from the Gotham crix by earning a Globe for Best Drama Actress, she burst into giggles at the podium.

She later confessed to reporters backstage, "Whenever I win an award, I have this really annoying habit. I can't stop laughing."

The Fisher King snagged two kudos: Best Comedy or Musical Actor for Robin Williams and Best Supporting Actress Mercedes Ruehl.

Ruehl called her victory a "payback" for her years struggling as a rookie actress in New York and told the crowd, "I shall never waitress again and you are my witnesses!"

Far less cheerful was the winner of Best Comedy or Musical Actress—Bette Midler, who was honored as a cheeky USO diva who entertains U.S. troops during three wars in the b.o. flop *For the Boys*.

"I'm very touched," Midler told the crowd. "It makes me very happy that the Hollywood foreign press recognized our work when the American public dismissed us."

Midler confessed to reporters backstage that she was so depressed by the pic's "pathetic" performance that "I doubt everything now." When a reporter asked how she got through "this difficult period," she shot back, "What makes you think I'm through it?"

Since no one pic dominated the Golden Globes, the *L.A. Times* announced afterward, "The stage is set for the most wide open Oscar race for Best Picture in years."

A front-runner seemed to be firmly established with the Oscar noms were unveiled four weeks later and *Bugsy* led with the most bids—10. Warren Beatty had good reason to be optimistic. Over the previous 25 years of Oscar history, the noms leader had won Best Picture 23 times, but he also had cause to be especially nervous: the two exceptions were his own pics—*Bonnie and Clyde* and *Reds*.

Nomination runners-up behind *Bugsy* were *JFK* (eight bids) and seven each for *Silence of the Lambs* and *Prince of Tides*. All of them made the cut for Best Picture.

Noticeably missing from the *Tides* tally, though, was a shot at Best Director for Barbra Streisand, who'd been previously snubbed by Oscar voters in 1983 after the Golden Globes named *Yentl* Best Comedy/Musical Picture and Streisand was hailed as Best Director. She was the only DGA contender who didn't reap an Oscar bid.

"I'm trying not to take it personally," Streisand told *Variety* about the latest brushoff. "It's hard because I don't want to be bitter. I don't take it as a personal affront. I look at it as a larger problem." The problem was Oscar's historic disregard for women. Only once had a woman ever been nommed for the helmer's gold (Lina Wertmüller, 1976).

But Streisand did snag a bid from the Directors Guild of America, which had only considered women twice before in its history (Wertmüller plus Randa Haines, 1986). "Some think a sympathy backlash factor might propel her to a DGA victory," *Variety* surmised.

Septuagenarian Oscar champ Jack Palance (*City Slickers*) displayed his youthful vigor by doing one-handed push-ups.

On DGA awards night, Streisand joined L.A. crix champ Barry Levinson (*Bugsy*) and Globe victor Oliver Stone (*JFK*) at the Beverly Hilton gala in Los Angeles. The only absentee was Ridley Scott (*Thelma & Louise*), who was in Spain filming *1492*. Jonathan Demme was present at the guild's New York fete held at the United Nations.

Variety was not upbeat about Demme's chances, saying, "Conventional wisdom was that Demme had at least four strikes against him in the DGA and Oscar competitions: He is a first-time nominee with a film from a bankrupt studio (Orion) that was released early in 1991 and that deals with subject matter (serial murder and cannibalism) that could make many voters uneasy."

Silence of the Lambs had been honored one week earlier by the Producers Guild of America, but the awards gala had been besieged by gay-rights activists denouncing the pic for cashing in "on fear, hatred and misunderstanding." Leaflets distributed at the event asked, "Why else would audiences nationwide scream 'Kill the faggot!' in the big showdown shoot-out finale?!"

But Demme pulled off an upset victory at the DGA. Accepting the plaque, he roared, "This will show them out in La-La Land! If ever there was a group of people you can't fool, this is it!" Then he assumed a serious tone and noted that he was "the

44th white male to receive this award, which I have confused feelings about."

After *Silence*'s DGA victory, *Variety* reported that the pic "might be a more formidable (Oscar) contender than many thought," but some pundits predicted a backlash from West Coast industryites who might have been offended by Demme's dig at "La-La Land" when they watched his acceptance speech via satellite hookup at DGA's L.A. gala.

The New York Times reported the Demme had "plainly blundered," adding, "The folks in La-La Land were not amused. His remarks were seen as condescending and a little arrogant." Demme responded by issuing a three-page apology, admitting that his speech was "stupid" and "borne of the hometown euphoric frenzy that occurred in our room when a New Yorker actually got the nod." It was unclear how Demme's gaffe might impact Oscar voting, since ballots were due one week later and many voters no doubt had already sent theirs in before the hubbub.

> It was "the most wide open Oscar race for Best Picture in years."

Also a week after the DGA fete was the awards ceremony for the Writers Guild of America, where *Silence* completed its transguild sweep when Ted Tally won Best Adapted Screenplay over the scribes of *JFK* and *Prince of Tides*. A major upset occurred in the match-up for Best Original Screenplay when *Thelma & Louise*'s Callie Khouri triumphed over the scenarists of *Boyz N the Hood*, *Bugsy*, *The Fisher King* and *Grand Canyon*.

"Some of you may know this was my first attempt at screenwriting," she said, accepting her plaque. "And now I'm really seriously considering writing another one!"

Highlight of the ceremony was belated acknowledgment to two late veteran scribes who'd been slighted by the guild during the red scare days of the McCarthy era. Both members of the Hollywood 10 had been blacklisted and served jail time for their refusal to cooperate with the investigation by the House Committee on Un-American Activities. Frontman Michael Blankfort had assumed credit for Albert Maltz when the guild chose *Broken Arrow* as the Best Western of 1950, and Ian McLellan Hunter was credited with 1953's Best Comedy *Roman Holiday* instead of Dalton Trumbo.

Trumbo's widow Cleo Trumbo received a standing ovation after giving an emotional speech during which she said, "If there is anything to be learned from the Hollywood blacklist, it is that it need never have happened at all. I have every confidence that if this community is ever threatened again by repression, the writers' guild will be in the vanguard of the opposition."

Variety noted, "Her remarks were a subtle but pointed allusion to the fact that the Screen Writers Guild (predecessor of the WGA) abandoned the Hollywood 10 and cooperated with the film industry blacklist."

Maltz's widow, Esther, accepted her husband's overdue award and read from a speech he gave in 1948: "We preserve for ourselves the right to work free of censorship. That right also involves the right to be wrong."

As Oscar day approached, *Variety* sized up the derby as "the most wide-open race in years" and the *L.A. Times* agreed, adding, "All bets are off."

On Oscar morning, the *L.A. Times*'s Kenneth Turan sized up the latest thinking about the Best Picture match-up, noting that Disney's *Beauty and the Beast*—the first animated feature ever nommed for the top prize—was the most popular choice, but posited that it might be hurt by the thousand-plus actors who compose the academy's biggest voting bloc.

"*The Prince of Tides* was the pre-noms favorite and is the closest to the kind of big emotional picture the academy favors, but the snubbing of Streisand hurt the film's momentum," he said.

Bugsy "has demonstrated the across-the-board support essential to winning the top prize," he added, but warned that "its partisans tend to be more coolly admiring than passionate." Meantime, *Silence* "suffers from a grisly subject matter that is not keeping with the academy's more serene self-image."

Turan ended up betting on *Silence*, but four of his newspaper colleagues also piped in with their own predix. One agreed with Turan. The other three opted for disparate choices: *Bugsy, Beauty and the Beast* and *Prince of Tides.*

The Oscar ceremony opened with host Billy Crystal being wheeled out on a stretcher as he wore Hannibal the Cannibal's creepy mask. Crystal then stepped into the audience where he approached Hopkins and said, "I'm having some of the academy over for dinner. Care to join me?"

"Anytime!" Hopkins exclaimed.

Crystal's comic skills were soon tested when it time to bestow the first thesp award—for Best Supporting Actor.

Variety had reported that "veteran Jack Palance is seen by many as the sentimental favorite for his role as the prototypical cowboy in the contemporary comedy/western *City Slickers*," which was the year's fourth-highest grosser. All of the *L.A. Times* forecasters agreed except one, who rooted for L.A. crix awardee Michael Lerner (*Barton Fink*). When Palance won, he raced to the stage and gave what *Variety* called "a rowdy, off-color acceptance speech."

"You know, there's a time when you reach an age plateau where producers say, 'Well, what do you think? Can we risk it?' " he began. Then the 72-year-old thesp fell to the floor and started doing push-ups with both hands, then just one hand. "As far as the two-handed push-ups are concerned, you can do that all night," he added. "Doesn't make any difference if she's there or not. Besides, it's a hell of a lot less expensive."

Soon after Palance disappeared backstage, Crystal—his costar in *City Slickers*—fired off a string of jokes that he interjected throughout the night's Oscarcast.

"Jack is backstage on the StairMaster," he told the audience at one point.

Later, he said, "Jack Palance just bungee-jumped off the Hollywood sign," adding, "Try a little decaf, Jack!"

In the race for Best Supporting Actress, three of the five *L.A. Times* pundits bet on Golden Globe champ and L.A. crix honoree Mercedes Ruehl. Of the other two, one backed National Board of Review winner Kate Nelligan (*Prince of Tides*), the other Diane Ladd (*Rambling Rose*).

Ruehl ended up ruling, saying at the podium, "At this moment, dreadful memories have suddenly transformed themselves into nothing more than the sort of charming and amusing anecdotes for my memoirs."

Prior to awards night, *Variety* had noted that "Jodie Foster is generally expected to win." The previous Oscar winner (*The Accused*) had recently been heralded as "Entertainer of the Year" by *Entertainment Weekly* and was being widely lauded by crix for her successful debut as a director with *Little Man Tate.*

When she won, Foster said, "This has been such an incredible year! I would like to direct this to all the women who came before me who never had the chances that I've had and the survivors and the outcasts, my blood, my tradition."

Then she addressed her costar, Anthony Hopkins, in the audience by quoting a line from *Silence,* "*Quid pro quo,* Doctor."

But whether or not Hopkins could match her *quid pro quo* for Best Actor was in serious doubt. Some controversy surrounded his bid for Best Actor, since he had appeared on screen in *Silence* for only 22 minutes. While he'd been honored in the same category by the Gotham crix, the National Board of Review had named him Best Supporting Actor. Virtually all Oscar prognosticators—including the quintet at the *L.A. Times*—bet that the academy's choice would be Golden Globe champ and L.A. crix awardee Nick Nolte for *Prince of Tides.*

When Hopkins prevailed, *Variety* noted, "he seemed deeply moved" as he received a standing ovation while he headed to the stage.

"My God, I can't believe it!" he roared in triumph. "This is really unexpected. I am greatly honored."

Minutes later, when he greeted reporters backstage, he assumed Hannibal's voice and said, "If I hadn't won, you'd all be in trouble."

Prior to Hopkins's victory for *Silence*, no other pic had seemed to demonstrate noticeable momentum as the awards showdown headed toward the top kudos. *Bugsy* had earned two prizes—for costumes and art direction—and *JFK* claimed the laurels for editing and cinematography, but they both missed out in the script categories. *Bugsy* lost the race for Best Original Screenplay to *Thelma & Louise* and *JFK* bowed to *Silence* for Best Adapted Screenplay. Both pics' victories mirrored their success at the writers' guild.

When the time came to bestow the helmer's gold, it seemed clear that Jonathan Demme stood to repeat his directors' guild win even though he faced L.A. crix champ Barry Levinson, Golden Globe recipient Oliver Stone and *Boyz N the Hood*'s John Singleton, who made Oscar history by becoming the first African American and—at age 24—the youngest person ever to compete for the prize.

Demme won, confessing at the podium, "In the context of my movie-loving life, this is unanticipated." He directed thanks to his mother "for transferring your love of movies to me" and thanked his father "for making me think I could actually be a part of this industry."

His triumph was soon cut short backstage when the media ambushed him with questions about a ruckus that had taken place earlier outside the Dorothy Chandler Pavilion. A demonstration against *Silence* by more than 100 gay activists had resulted in 10 arrests.

"I endorse the protest," he replied, sympathetically, adding the admission, "My life is full of positive gay characters and yet my movies aren't."

Demme's night of triumph was completed, however, when *Silence* also nabbed the palm for Best Picture. The next day *Variety*'s headline cheered, "ACADEMY TO *LAMBS*: WELL DONE."

Silence's victories had defied Oscar's longstanding preference for pix released late in the calendar year. As of awards night, it was not only more than a year old, it had even been released commercially on videotape months before most of its rivals had premiered in theaters.

The pic's victories were also historic. *Silence* became only the third film in Oscar lore to claim all five top awards (picture, director, actor, actress and screenplay) after *It Happened One Night* and *One Flew over the Cuckoo's Nest*.

Variety added, "It was also the first film of its genre ever to be honored with a Best Picture Oscar."

Variety reported a breakthrough at the Sundance Film Festival a few months earlier when "competition outcome moved the fest back to a popular center after controversial choices last year."

Among the crowd-pleasing pix considered for the Grand Jury Prize for features were Quentin Tarantino's gritty *Reservoir Dogs,* but it was topped by *In the Soup,* which *Variety* described as "a big-hearted and loony comic noir about a struggling filmmaker taken under the wing of a magnanimous crook." The crook was portrayed by Seymour Cassel, who earned a special performance palm. The pic's grand jury victory marked a second Sundance kudo for filmmaker Alexandre Rockwell, who'd received a Special Jury Prize for *Hero* in 1983.

"It's very rare that a comedy wins a prize," noted one of the fest's jurors, *Newsweek*'s David Ansen, about Rockwell's latest winner, "but this was a comedy with soul, with extraordinary acting and a certain magic and poetry." *In the Soup* was not a pic with generous backing, however—it had been financed on credit cards.

Another double honoree was *The Waterdance*, which reaped the Audience Award for features plus the screenplay prize for co-director/writer Neil Jimenez, who dramatized his personal story of coping with becoming paralyzed by the waist down after an accident.

Also a double champ was *A Brief History of Time*, which won the Filmmaker's Trophy for documentaries and shared the Grand Jury Prize for same. It examined the life and scientific theories of disabled physicist Stephen Hawking.

The Filmmaker's Trophy for dramas went to *Zebrahead*, which *Variety* described as "a drama originated in Sundance workshops about a racially mixed group of high school students in search of community."

When *Zebrahead*'s director-screenwriter Anthony Drazan accepted his laurels at the fest's awards presentation, he told the crowd, "A year ago I was sitting here in the 12th row with a script in hand and I didn't know if I was going to be able to make it." Then he exclaimed, "To my fellow filmmakers— it can be done!"

The *L.A. Times* described the standing-room-only gala as "raucous" as participants roamed the room scouting for scarce hors d'oeuvres. Grand Jury Prize winner Rockwell roared to the crowd, "You guys can eat at my house anytime, anywhere! Don't worry about it!"

A winner of a Special Jury Prize at Sundance last year—*Straight out of Brooklyn*—returned for further kudos at this year's Independent Spirit Awards, where it was hailed as Best First Feature. The drama by 20-year-old filmmaker Matty Rich probed the lives of despair at Brooklyn's Red Hook Housing Project. *Variety* noted that Rich "delivered an acceptance speech that recounted the 'determination and perseverance' he needed to get his film made."

Rambling Rose was the top Spirit winner, scoring trophies for Best Feature, Best Director (Martha Coolidge) and Best Supporting Actress Diane Ladd as a matriarch of a family that takes in "an oversexed young woman (Ladd's real-life daughter Laura Dern) from the wrong side of the tracks," said *Variety*. Ladd was the only Spirit winner nommed in the same category at the Oscars.

Another triple champ was *My Own Private Idaho*, which lost its bids for Best Feature and Best Director but rebounded with victories for Best Actor River Phoenix, Best Music (a newly added award) and Best Screenplay. When Gus Van Sant accepted the latter palm, *Variety* reported, "He thanked William Shakespeare for the middle section of the movie and the studio musicians for contributing to the music." Keanu Reeves accepted for costar Phoenix, thanking voters for "recognizing an amazing performance in an amazing part."

Best Actress winner was Judy Davis, who *Variety* said was "terrific" as author George Sand as she "dresses mannishly, smokes cheroots and gets a maddening crush on composer Chopin" in *Impromptu*.

Writer Buck Henry was given a special kudo for hosting the awards gala for the seventh straight year. He acknowledged the honor, devilishly: "I'd say that I don't know what to say, but you'd know it was a lie."

▪ 1991 ▪

LOS ANGELES FILM CRITICS ASSOCIATION

Winners were announced on December 14, 1991. Awards were presented on January 21, 1992, at the Bel Age Hotel in Los Angeles.

BEST PICTURE
▪ *Bugsy*

BEST DIRECTOR
▪ Barry Levinson, *Bugsy*

BEST ACTOR
▪ Nick Nolte, *Prince of Tides*

BEST ACTRESS
▪ Mercedes Ruehl, *The Fisher King*

BEST SUPPORTING ACTOR
▪ Michael Lerner, *Barton Fink*

BEST SUPPORTING ACTRESS
▪ Jane Horrocks, *Life Is Sweet*

BEST SCREENPLAY
▪ James Toback, *Bugsy*

BEST CINEMATOGRAPHY
- Roger Deakins, *Barton Fink, Homicide*

BEST MUSIC SCORE
- Zbigniew Preisner, *The Double Life of Veronique; At Play in the Fields of the Lord; Europa, Europa*

BEST ANIMATION
- *Beauty and the Beast,* Gary Trousdale, Kirk Wise

BEST DOCUMENTARY
- *American Dream*, Barbara Kopple

BEST FOREIGN FILM
- *La Belle Noiseuse* (France)

BEST EXPERIMENTAL/INDEPENDENT FILM
- *All the Vermeers in New York,* Jon Jost

NEW GENERATION AWARD
- John Singleton, *Boyz N the Hood*

CAREER ACHIEVEMENT AWARDS
- Vincent Price
- Elmer Bernstein

SPECIAL AWARD
- National Film Board of Canada

NATIONAL BOARD OF REVIEW

The board declared a Best Picture and Foreign Film of the year, then listed its remaining favorites according to highest scores. The vote results were announced on December 16, 1991. Awards were presented on February 24, 1992, at the Equitable Center in New York.

BEST PICTURE
- *The Silence of the Lambs*
Bugsy
Grand Canyon
Thelma & Louise
Homicide
Dead Again
Boyz N the Hood
Rambling Rose
Frankie and Johnny
Jungle Fever

BEST DIRECTOR
- Jonathan Demme, *The Silence of the Lambs*

BEST ACTOR
- Warren Beatty, *Bugsy*

BEST ACTRESS (TIE)
- Susan Sarandon, Geena Davis, *Thelma & Louise*

BEST SUPPORTING ACTOR
- Anthony Hopkins, *The Silence of the Lambs*

BEST SUPPORTING ACTRESS
- Kate Nelligan, *Frankie and Johnny*

BEST FOREIGN FILM
- *Europa, Europa* (Germany/France)
The Vanishing (France/Netherlands)
La Femme Nikita (France)
My Father's Glory and *My Mother's Castle* (France)
Toto le Héros (Belgium)

CAREER ACHIEVEMENT AWARD
- Lauren Bacall

NEW YORK FILM CRITICS CIRCLE

Winners were announced on December 17, 1991. Awards were presented on January 12, 1992, at the Pegasus Suite of the Rainbow Room in Rockefeller Center in New York.

BEST PICTURE
- *The Silence of the Lambs*

BEST DIRECTOR
- Jonathan Demme, *The Silence of the Lambs*

BEST NEW DIRECTOR
- John Singleton, *Boyz N the Hood*

BEST ACTOR
- Anthony Hopkins, *The Silence of the Lambs*

BEST ACTRESS
- Jodie Foster, *The Silence of the Lambs*

BEST SUPPORTING ACTOR
- Samuel L. Jackson, *Jungle Fever*

BEST SUPPORTING ACTRESS
- Judy Davis, *Barton Fink, Naked Lunch*

BEST SCREENPLAY
- David Cronenberg, *Naked Lunch*

BEST CINEMATOGRAPHY
- Roger Deakins, *Barton Fink*

BEST DOCUMENTARY
- *Paris Is Burning,* Jennie Livingston

BEST FOREIGN FILM
- *Europa, Europa* (Germany)

NATIONAL SOCIETY OF FILM CRITICS

Winners were announced on January 5, 1992.

BEST PICTURE
- *Life Is Sweet*

BEST DIRECTOR
- David Cronenberg, *Naked Lunch*

BEST ACTOR
- River Phoenix, *My Own Private Idaho*

BEST ACTRESS
- Alison Steadman, *Life Is Sweet*

BEST SUPPORTING ACTOR
- Harvey Keitel, *Thelma & Louise, Bugsy, Mortal Thoughts*

BEST SUPPORTING ACTRESS
- Jane Horrocks, *Life Is Sweet*

BEST SCREENPLAY
- David Cronenberg, *Naked Lunch*

BEST CINEMATOGRAPHY
- Roger Deakins, *Barton Fink*

BEST DOCUMENTARY
- *Paris Is Burning,* Jennie Livingston

BEST FOREIGN FILM
- *The Double Life of Veronique* (France/Poland)

BEST EXPERIMENTAL FILM
- *Archangel,* Guy Maddin

SPECIAL CITATION
- Peter Delpeut, *Lyrical Nitrate*

GOLDEN GLOBES

Nominations were announced on December 29, 1991. Awards were presented on January 18, 1992, at the Beverly Hilton Hotel in Los Angeles. The ceremony was telecast by TBS.

BEST DRAMA PICTURE
- *Bugsy*
JFK
The Prince of Tides
The Silence of the Lambs
Thelma & Louise

BEST COMEDY OR MUSICAL PICTURE
- *Beauty and the Beast*
City Slickers
The Commitments
The Fisher King
Fried Green Tomatoes

BEST DIRECTOR
- Oliver Stone, *JFK*
Jonathan Demme, *The Silence of the Lambs*
Terry Gilliam, *The Fisher King*
Barry Levinson, *Bugsy*
Barbra Streisand, *The Prince of Tides*

BEST ACTOR, DRAMA
- Nick Nolte, *The Prince of Tides*
Warren Beatty, *Bugsy*
Kevin Costner, *JFK*
Robert De Niro, *Cape Fear*
Anthony Hopkins, *The Silence of the Lambs*

BEST ACTRESS, DRAMA
- Jodie Foster, *The Silence of the Lambs*

Annette Bening, *Bugsy*
Geena Davis, *Thelma & Louise*
Laura Dern, *Rambling Rose*
Susan Sarandon, *Thelma & Louise*

BEST ACTOR, COMEDY OR MUSICAL

- Robin Williams, *The Fisher King*
Jeff Bridges, *The Fisher King*
Billy Crystal, *City Slickers*
Dustin Hoffman, *Hook*
Kevin Kline, *Soapdish*

BEST ACTRESS, COMEDY OR MUSICAL

- Bette Midler, *For the Boys*
Ellen Barkin, *Switch*
Kathy Bates, *Fried Green Tomatoes*
Anjelica Huston, *The Addams Family*
Michelle Pfeiffer, *Frankie and Johnny*

BEST SUPPORTING ACTOR

- Jack Palance, *City Slickers*
Ned Beatty, *Hear My Song*
John Goodman, *Barton Fink*
Harvey Keitel, *Bugsy*
Ben Kingsley, *Bugsy*

BEST SUPPORTING ACTRESS

- Mercedes Ruehl, *The Fisher King*
Nicole Kidman, *Billy Bathgate*
Diane Ladd, *Rambling Rose*
Juliette Lewis, *Cape Fear*
Jessica Tandy, *Fried Green Tomatoes*

BEST SCREENPLAY

- Callie Khouri, *Thelma and Louise*
Lawrence Kasdan, Meg Kasdan, *Grand
  Canyon*
Oliver Stone, Zachary Sklar, *JFK*
Ted Tally, *The Silence of the Lambs*
James Toback, *Bugsy*

BEST SONG

- "Beauty and the Beast," *Beauty and the
  Beast*, Alan Menken, Howard Ashman
"Be Our Guest," *Beauty and the Beast*,
  Alan Menken, Howard Ashman
"Dreams to Dream," *An American Tail:
  Fievel Goes West*, James Horner, Will
  Jennings
"(Everything I Do) I Do It for You," *Robin
  Hood*, M. Kamen, B. Adams, R. J.
  Lange

"Tears in Heaven," *Rush*, Eric Clapton,
  Will Jennings

BEST FOREIGN FILM

- *Europa, Europa* (Germany)
The Double Life of Veronique
  (France/Poland)
La Femme Nikita (France)
High Heels (Spain)
Lost in Siberia (Russia)
Madame Bovary (France)

Winners

BEST SCORE

- Alan Menken, *Beauty and the Beast*

CECIL B. DEMILLE AWARD

- Robert Mitchum

SUNDANCE FILM FESTIVAL

The festival was held January 16–26, 1992,
at Park City, Utah.

GRAND JURY PRIZE

(DRAMATIC)
- *In the Soup*, Alexandre Rockwell
(DOCUMENTARY)
- *A Brief History of Time*, Errol Morris
- *Finding Christa*, Camille Billops, James
  Hatch

FILMMAKER'S TROPHY

(DRAMATIC)
- *Zebrahead,* Anthony Drazan
(DOCUMENTARY)
- *A Brief History of Time*, Errol Morris

AUDIENCE AWARD

(DRAMATIC)
- *The Waterdance,* Neal Jimenez, Michael
  Steinberg
(DOCUMENTARY)
- *Brother's Keeper,* Joe Berlinger, Bruce
  Sinofsky

WALDO SALT SCREENWRITING AWARD

- *The Waterdance,* Neal Jimenez

CINEMATOGRAPHY AWARD
(DRAMATIC)
- *Swoon,* Ellen Kuras

(DOCUMENTARY)
- *Shoot for the Contents,* Trinh T. Minh-ha, Kathleen Beeler

SPECIAL JURY RECOGNITION
- *The Hours and the Times*, Christopher Munch
- *My Crasy Life*, Jean-Pierre Gorin

OUTSTANDING PERFORMANCE
- Seymour Cassel, *In the Soup*

PRODUCERS GUILD OF AMERICA

Nominations were announced on January 28, 1992. Winners were announced on February 26. Awards were presented on March 4 at the Regent Beverly Wilshire Hotel in Los Angeles.

DARRYL F. ZANUCK PRODUCER OF THE YEAR AWARD
- *The Silence of the Lambs,* Ron Bozman, Edward Saxon, Kenneth Utt

At Play in the Fields of the Lord, Saul Zaentz

Boyz N the Hood, Steve Nicolaides

The Commitments, Roger Randall-Cutler, Lynda Myles

JFK, A. Kitman Ho, Oliver Stone

The Prince of Tides, Barbra Streisand, Andrew Karsch

NOVA AWARD
- Mattie Rich, *Straight out of Brooklyn*

DAVID O. SELZNICK LIFETIME ACHIEVEMENT AWARD
- Pandro S. Berman

DIRECTORS GUILD OF AMERICA

Awards were presented on March 14, 1992, at the Beverly Hilton Hotel in Los Angeles and the United Nations in New York.

BEST DIRECTOR
- Jonathan Demme, *The Silence of the Lambs*

Barry Levinson, *Bugsy*

Ridley Scott, *Thelma & Louise*

Oliver Stone, *JFK*

Barbra Streisand, *The Prince of Tides*

ROBERT B. ALDRICH AWARD
- Jack Shea

D. W. GRIFFITH AWARD
- Akira Kurosawa

HONORARY LIFE MEMBERSHIP
- Charles Champlin

WRITERS GUILD OF AMERICA

Awards were presented on March 22, 1992, at the Beverly Hilton Hotel in Los Angeles.

BEST ORIGINAL SCREENPLAY
- *Thelma & Louise*, Callie Khouri

Boyz N the Hood, John Singleton

Bugsy, James Toback

The Fisher King, Richard La Gravenese

Grand Canyon, Lawrence Kasdan, Meg Kasdan

BEST ADAPTED SCREENPLAY
- *The Silence of the Lambs*, Ted Tally, based on the novel by Thomas Harris

The Commitments, Dick Clement, Ian La Frenais, Roddy Doyle, based on the novel by Roddy Doyle

Fried Green Tomatoes, Fannie Flagg, Carol Sobieski, based on the novel by Fannie Flagg

JFK, Oliver Stone and Zachary Sklar, based on the books *On the Trail of the Assassins* by Jim Garrison and *Crossfire: The Plot That Killed Kennedy* by Jim Marrs

The Prince of Tides, Pat Conroy, Becky Johnston, based on the book by Pat Conroy

MORGAN COX AWARD
- Christopher Knopf

VALENTINE DAVIES AWARD
- Allan Burns

FOUNDER'S AWARD
- William Ludwig

LAUREL AWARD
- Frank Pierson

INDEPENDENT SPIRIT

Nominations were announced on January 13, 1992. Awards were presented on March 28 at Raleigh Studios in Los Angeles. Portions of the ceremony were broadcast later on Bravo.

BEST FEATURE
- *Rambling Rose*
City of Hope
Hangin' with the Homeboys
Homicide
My Own Private Idaho

BEST FIRST FEATURE
- *Straight out of Brooklyn*
Chameleon Street
Poison
The Rapture
Slacker

BEST DIRECTOR
- Martha Coolidge, *Rambling Rose*
Todd Hayes, *Poison*
Richard Linklater, *Slacker*
Gus Van Sant, *My Own Private Idaho*
Joseph B. Vasquez, *Hangin' with the Homeboys*

BEST ACTOR
- River Phoenix, *My Own Private Idaho*
Doug E. Doug, *Hangin' with the Homeboys*
Robert Duvall, *Rambling Rose*
Gary Oldman, *Rosencrantz and Guildstern Are Dead*
William Russ, *Pastime*

BEST ACTRESS
- Judy Davis, *Impromptu*
Patsy Kensit, *Twenty-One*
Mimi Rogers, *The Rapture*
Lili Taylor, *Bright Angel*

Lily Tomlin, *The Search for Signs of Intelligent Life in the Universe*

BEST SUPPORTING ACTOR
- David Strathairn, *City of Hope*
William H. Macy, *Homicide*
John Malkovich, *Queen's Logic*
George T. Odom, *Straight out of Brooklyn*
Glenn Plummer, *Pastime*

BEST SUPPORTING ACTRESS
- Diane Ladd, *Rambling Rose*
Sheila McCarthy, *Bright Angel*
Deidre O'Connell, *Pastime*
Emma Thompson, *Impromptu*
Mary B. Ward, *Hangin' with the Homeboys*

BEST SCREENPLAY
- Gus Van Sant, *My Own Private Idaho*
Floyd Byars, Fritjof Capra, *Mindwalk*
Lem Dobbs, *Kafka*
Michael Tolkin, *The Rapture*
Joseph B. Vasquez, *Hangin' with the Homeboys*

BEST FOREIGN FILM
- *An Angel at My Table* (New Zealand)
The Double Life of Veronique (France/Poland)
Life Is Sweet (U.K.)
Requiem for Dominic (Austria)
Taxi Blues (France/U.S.S.R.)

Winners

BEST CINEMATOGRAPHY
- Walt Lloyd, *Kafka*

BEST FILM MUSIC
- Bill Stafford, *My Own Private Idaho*

SPECIAL AWARD
- Buck Henry

ACADEMY AWARDS

Nominations were announced on February 19, 1992. Awards were presented on March 30 at the Dorothy Chandler Pavilion in Los Angeles. The ceremony was telecast by ABC.

BEST PICTURE
- *The Silence of the Lambs*
Beauty and the Beast
Bugsy
JFK
The Prince of Tides

BEST DIRECTOR
- Jonathan Demme, *The Silence of the Lambs*
Barry Levinson, *Bugsy*
Ridley Scott, *Thelma & Louise*
John Singleton, *Boyz N the Hood*
Oliver Stone, *JFK*

BEST ACTOR
- Anthony Hopkins, *The Silence of the Lambs*
Warren Beatty, *Bugsy*
Robert De Niro, *Cape Fear*
Nick Nolte, *The Prince of Tides*
Robin Williams, *The Fisher King*

BEST ACTRESS
- Jodie Foster, *The Silence of the Lambs*
Geena Davis, *Thelma & Louise*
Laura Dern, *Rambling Rose*
Bette Midler, *For the Boys*
Susan Sarandon, *Thelma & Louise*

BEST SUPPORTING ACTOR
- Jack Palance, *City Slickers*
Tommy Lee Jones, *JFK*
Harvey Keitel, *Bugsy*
Ben Kingsley, *Bugsy*
Michael Lerner, *Barton Fink*

BEST SUPPORTING ACTRESS
- Mercedes Ruehl, *The Fisher King*
Diane Ladd, *Rambling Rose*
Juliette Lewis, *Cape Fear*
Kate Nelligan, *The Prince of Tides*
Jessica Tandy, *Fried Green Tomatoes*

BEST ORIGINAL SCREENPLAY
- Callie Khouri, *Thelma & Louise*
Lawrence Kasdan, Meg Kasdan, *Grand Canyon*
Richard Lagravenese, *The Fisher King*
John Singleton, *Boyz N the Hood*
James Toback, *Bugsy*

BEST ADAPTED SCREENPLAY
- Ted Tally, *The Silence of the Lambs*
Pat Conroy, Becky Johnston, *The Prince of Tides*
Fannie Flagg, Carol Sobieski, *Fried Green Tomatoes*
Agnieszka Holland, *Europa, Europa*
Zachary Sklar, Oliver Stone, *JFK*

BEST SONG
- "Beauty and the Beast," *Beauty and the Beast*, Howard Ashman, Alan Menken
"Belle," *Beauty and the Beast*, Howard Ashman, Alan Menken
"Be Our Guest," *Beauty and the Beast*, Howard Ashman, Alan Menken
"(Everything I Do) I Do It For You," *Robin Hood: Prince of Thieves*, Bryan Adams, Michael Kamen, Robert John Lange
"When You're Alone," *Hook,* Leslie Bricusse, John Williams

BEST FOREIGN-LANGUAGE FILM
- *Mediterraneo* (Italy)
Children of Nature (Iceland)
The Elementary School (Czechoslovakia)
The Ox (Sweden)
Raise the Red Lantern (Hong Kong)

Winners

BEST ART DIRECTION
- Dennis Gassner, Nancy Haigh, *Bugsy*

BEST CINEMATOGRAPHY
- Robert Richardson, *JFK*

BEST COSTUME DESIGN
- Albert Wolsky, *Bugsy*

BEST DOCUMENTARY
(FEATURE)
- *In the Shadow of the Stars*, Allie Light, Irving Saraf
(SHORT SUBJECT)
- *Deadly Deception: General Electric, Nuclear Weapons and Our Environment*, Debra Chasnoff

BEST FILM EDITING
- Joe Hutshing, Pietro Scalia, *JFK*

BEST MAKEUP
- Jeff Dawn, Stan Winston, *Terminator 2: Judgment Day*

BEST ORIGINAL MUSIC SCORE
- Alan Menken, *Beauty and the Beast*

SCIENTIFIC OR TECHNICAL AWARDS
(Scientific and Engineering Award)
- Iain Neil, Albert Saiki, Panavision; Ray Feeney, Richard Keeney, Richard J. Lundell; Randy Cartwright, David B. Coons, Lem Davis, Thomas Hahn, James Houston, Mark Kimball, Peter Nye, Michael Shantzis, David F. Wolf, Walt Disney Feature Animation Dept.; George Worrall, Georg Thoma, Heinz Feierlein; Harry J. Baker, Guido Cartoni, Faz Fazakas, Brian Henson, Dave Housman, Peter Miller, John Stephenson, Mario Celso

(Technical Achievement Award)
- Dick Cavdek, Steve Hamerski, Otto Nemez International; Ken Robings, Clairmont Camera; Century Precision Optics; James Doyle, Robert W. Stoker, Jr.

BEST SHORT FILM
(ANIMATED)
- *Manipulation*, Daniel Greaves

(LIVE ACTION)
- *Session Man,* Rob Fried, Seth Winston

BEST SOUND
- Tom Johnson, Lee Orloff, Gary Rydstrom, Gary Summers, *Terminator 2: Judgment Day*

BEST SOUND EFFECTS EDITING
- Gloria S. Borders, Gary Rydstrom, *Terminator 2: Judgment Day*

BEST VISUAL EFFECTS
- Dennis Muren, Robert Skotak, Stan Winston, Gene Warren, Jr., *Terminator 2: Judgment Day*

GORDON E. SAWYER AWARD
- Ray Harryhausen

IRVING G. THALBERG MEMORIAL AWARD
- George Lucas

HONORARY AWARDS
- Pete Comandini
- Richard T. Dayton
- Donald Hagans
- Satyajit Ray
- Richard T. Ryan
- Richard J. Stumpf
- Joseph Westheimer
- YMC Laboratories

SCREEN ACTORS GUILD

LIFETIME ACHIEVEMENT AWARD
- Burt Lancaster

· 1992 ·

Eastwood Strikes Gold Out West

Clint Eastwood replayed the phone message left on his answering machine by a Warner Bros. exec five times before the news sank in: his newest pic, *Unforgiven*, had just been voted Best Picture by the L.A. film crix.

"It was unbelievable," he later recalled. "I didn't know when we started that it would have this impact."

Unforgiven had such a walloping impact on the crix that they gave it five awards—a tally that tied it with *Terms of Endearment, Kramer vs. Kramer* and *GoodFellas* as the most honored pic in the group's history. In addition to Best Picture, it reaped Best Director and Actor for Eastwood, Best Supporting Actor for Gene Hackman and Best Screenplay for David Webb Peoples.

Unforgiven, which had debuted four months earlier, was already a proven hit with the public, grossing $75 million by year's end. It was also a hit with the press. *Variety* heralded it as "a classic western for the ages," describing Eastwood's lead role as "a stubbly, worn-out, has-been outlaw" who goes after "the $1,000 reward posted for the hides of two men who gruesomely sliced up a prostitute." Hackman portrayed the town's sheriff, who's both a "folksy raconteur and a vicious sadist." Addressing his skills as a director, *Variety* cheered Eastwood for "crafting a tense, hard-edged, superbly dramatic yarn that is also an exceedingly intelligent meditation on the West, its myths and heroes."

The movie that placed behind it in the voting for top pic and director was *The Player*, recent winner of two prizes at Cannes—Best Director (Robert Altman) and Best Actor (Tim Robbins). *Variety*

CLINT CONQUERS DGA
First-time nominee wins feature helming prize
MAR 8   1993   VARIETY (3)

BY KATHLEEN O'STEEN

After 23 years as a member of the Directors Guild of America, Clint Eastwood attended his first DGA Awards banquet Saturday night and walked away with the evening's most coveted prize, being named best feature director of 1992 for Warner

Bros.' unconventional western drama "Unforgiven."

"I'm very flattered, very honored to be nominated in such distinguished company," Eastwood, a first-time nominee, told a ballroom packed with peers at the Beverly Hilton Hotel. "It was just one of those pictures that everything fell together."

Eastwood, a clear front-runner in the race with a Golden Globe already pocketed, is now within easy reach of adding an Oscar to his cache. He is only the fourth person to win a DGA award for a film in which he also starred.

Contending with Eastwood in the DGA race were Rob Reiner for
Turn to page 23

Clint Eastwood

"After 23 years as a member of the DGA, Clint Eastwood attended his first awards banquet and walked away" a champ, *Variety* said.

lauded it as "the deep dish on Hollywood," adding, "Mercilessly satiric yet good-natured, this enormously entertaining slam dunk quite possibly is the most resonant Hollywood saga since the days of *Sunset Boulevard* and *The Bad and the Beautiful*." The tale of a sleazy film studio exec (Robbins) who gets away with killing a down-and-out screenwriter was also noteworthy for featuring major stars portraying themselves in scattered cameos, including Anjelica Huston, Rod Steiger, Julia Roberts, Bruce Willis, Jack Lemmon, Nick Nolte and Cher. Veteran helmer Sydney Pollack, playing himself, was cited by the L.A. crix as the second-placed vote-getter in the race for Best Supporting Actor behind Gene Hackman, who was also listed his roles as a Beverly Hills doctor in *Death Becomes Her* and a blundering philanderer in Woody Allen's *Husbands and Wives*.

The crix's choice of Best Actress was Emma Thompson, whom *Variety* called "immensely sympathetic" as a high-spirited woman of no means who's seduced by a pernicious nobleman (Anthony Hopkins) in *Howards End*. Runner-up was Alfre Woodard as a headstrong nurse who takes on a crippled, booze-swilling ex-actress as a patient in *Passion Fish*.

In second place for Best Actor was Denzel Washington, who *Variety* said gave "a forceful, magnetic, mutilayered" perf in the title role of *Malcolm X.*

Variety called Judy Davis "incandescent" as a neurotic New Yorker busting up with hubby Sydney Pollack in *Husbands and Wives.* The L.A. crix voted her Best Supporting Actress over Miranda Richardson, who was considered for three roles: as the irate wife of a cheating politico in *Damage*, a lonely Brit who joins her gal pals for an extended stay in Italy in *Enchanted April* and a sex-charged terrorist in *The Crying Game.* *The Crying Game*'s Jaye Davidson took second place in the Best Supporting Actor race for the most talked-about film role of 1991—as a mysterious hairdresser with a secret. Produced in Ireland and the U.K., *The Crying Game* rebounded with a win as Best Foreign Film over *Raise the Red Lantern*, the tale of a concubine in 1920s China.

Crying Game's director/scribe Neil Jordan wasn't able to join the crix for their awards presentation when he missed his flight from New York, but *Variety* noted that, nonetheless, the "spirited and efficient luncheon at the Bel Age Hotel provided enough star power."

The event's reigning star, Clint Eastwood, took center stage to hail the crix for their courage in embracing a traditional western released months before the heavily hyped pix that angle for Oscars at year's end.

"The western is a true art form that is often unappreciated," he said. Now that *Unforgiven* was being touted as a serious Oscar contender thanks to the crix's nods, he saluted them as "the most sensitive and intelligent group of people in town" and gave them full credit, insisting, "You discovered this film."

Eastwood admitted that he was "overwhelmed," but added, "I'm the happiest guy around here!"

An equally buoyant Emma Thompson accepted her Best Actress plaque by thanking "the gravity-defying Merchant-Ivory" producer/helmer team. "Their gift to me was the role of a lifetime," she added.

Best Supporting Actress Judy Davis got an inadvertent laugh when she cited Woody Allen's "unique ability to understand women." She obviously hadn't considered how the comment would sound in light of the recent scandal surrounding Allen's bust-up with Mia Farrow when his affair with her adopted daughter was revealed. "You just can't say anything about him anymore!" she exclaimed, laughing, too.

Four days after the L.A. crix's vote, Judy Davis and Emma Thompson repeated their victories when the National Board of Board unveiled its anointed. The board opted for a different Best Picture and Director, however— *Howards End* and helmer James Ivory. Best Actor was Jack Lemmon, who had recently reaped the same honor at the Venice Film Festival for portraying an over-the-hill real-estate salesman desperate to score deals so he can keep his job in *Glengarry Glen Ross.* Winner of Best Supporting Actor was Jack Nicholson, whom *Variety* praised as "dynamite" in *A Few Good Men* as the martinet commander of a military base where two murders occurred.

> ## Scent of a Woman's Golden Globe victories smelled funny to some.

"An epidemic of no-shows by winners plagued the 75th annual D.W. Griffith Awards," *Variety* reported when the board bestowed its laurels at a fete held at New York's Equitable Center. Emma Thompson was homebound with the flu in London and James Ivory was filming in India, but the latter sent a videotape thank-you speech, and celebrity stand-ins did a crowd-pleasing job covering for the others. Matthew Broderick accepted on behalf of the absent Best Actor, saying, "I've never met Jack Lemmon, but I did talk to him on the phone and asked him what he would like me to tell you. He said, 'Tell them I think they made a brilliant choice.' "

Career Achievement Award honoree

Shirley Temple Black was on hand after recently returning from a four-year stint as Ambassador to Czechoslovakia. "Only the person who isn't working could come," she said, wryly. "I've been in between films for 44 years." *Variety* was "most disappointed" in the absence of the media-shy Jaye Davidson, who was awarded a special prize for making the year's Most Auspicious Debut in *The Crying Game.*

The New York film crix agreed with a number of the award choices made so far when they voted one day after the board and five days after their peers in L.A. Emma Thompson (40 points) topped Susan Sarandon (29 for *Lorenzo's Oil*) and Michelle Pfeiffer (14 points as a fed-up, abused wife in *Love Field*) for Best Actress. Miranda Richardson (32) prevailed over Judy Davis (27) as Best Supporting Actress and Gene Hackman (29) was voted Best Supporting Actor over last year's Sundance honoree Seymour Cassel (19 for *In the Soup*).

Gothamites opted for a different Best Actor, however, giving Denzel Washington (51 points, *Malcolm X*) a commanding victory over Harvey Keitel (17) as a corrupt, coke-snorting cop in *Bad Lieutenant.*

The Player and *Unforgiven* squared off in close contests for Best Picture and Best Director, with *The Player* claiming victory by a 37-to-35 vote for top pic and Altman prevailing over Eastwood 38 to 37. Both results were achieved on the second ballot, but a fourth ballot was needed before both pics' tangle with *The Crying Game* decided the winner of Best Screenplay. Final score: *Crying Game* 32, *Player* 27, *Unforgiven* 25.

"Now I have a real base of arrogance!" crowed Altman when he accepted his Best Director plaque at the awards gala held one month later. *The Player*'s critical and b.o. success marked a dramatic comeback for the helmer who had just endured a rocky decade following the disastrous reception of *Popeye*. "I'm gonna make the films I want

to make and you'll be able to rip me to shreds," he promised the crix.

Variety added, "Altman was in droll form, noting that the *N.Y. Times* did not allow its critics to vote. 'If you rescinded that rule, you could have prevented this,' he said, speculating that Clint Eastwood and *Unforgiven* would have won." *Times* critics Vincent Canby and Janet Maslin had been banned by their bosses from voting with any crix groups since 1989, but they remained as members of the circle.

Also raising eyebrows at the fete was Best Actor Denzel Washington. *Variety* reported, "Washington adopted a militant stance in accepting his kudos, noting the last three Best Actor Oscars went to British thesps."

The Oscar cliffhanger: "Can *The Crying Game* stop Clint?"

"In England, they prepare actors for the films in the theater," he said. "We have to support theater here, too, to get actors to show up on nights like this." Washington had originally portrayed Malcolm X on an off-Broadway stage in 1981.

When 25 crix belonging to the 35-member National Society of Film Critics met at the Algonquin Hotel in early January to choose their honorees, the balloting occurred in record time since all but one of the categories were decided in one voting round.

Even more surprising was the society's Best Picture choice. The org had been renowned for embracing small, edgy or artsy pix, opting only once in the past decade for a mainstream movie (*GoodFellas*). This year it gave *Unforgiven* a resounding victory with 47 points over *The Crying Game* (28) and *The Player* (23). Eastwood reaped Best Director with 43 points over Altman (28) and Jordan (23).

Eastwood, however, lost the contest for Best Actor by a narrow margin in the only polling that went to a second round. His 18-point score was topped by Stephen Rea (20) as a reluctant Irish Republican Army terrorist in *The Crying Game.*

Curiously, all of the society's top

awardees—except for Rea—mirrored the same decisions made three weeks earlier by the L.A. crix.

Best Actress Emma Thompson (41 points) beat Susan Sarandon (14), who was cited for the dual roles as a mother fighting to find a cure for her dying son in *Lorenzo's Oil* and as a cocaine addict in *Light Sleeper*. Judy Davis (36) claimed the supporting laurels over Miranda Richardson (23), who was in the running for all three of her 1992 roles. Gene Hackman (32) topped Jaye Davidson (13) for Best Supporting Actor. *Unforgiven*'s David Webb Peoples (40) won Best Screenplay over *The Crying Game*'s Jordan (31).

Sizing up the list of winners, *Variety* noted that "the organization came up with honorees that provide an unusual pre-Oscar consensus" when compared with the choices made by the other kudos and even the nominations just announced by the Hollywood Foreign Press Association.

Unforgiven scored four Golden Globe bids: Best Picture, Director (Eastwood), Supporting Actor (Hackman) and Screenplay (Peoples), although Eastwood did not make the cut for Best Drama Actor. Another snubbed notable was Neil Jordan, who failed to be listed in the director and screenplay races, although *Crying Game* did reap a bid for Best Drama Picture ("the only title that received a spontaneous round of applause when it was announced" at the nominations press conference, noted *Variety*). Two pix tied for the most bids (five)—*A Few Good Men* and Disney's latest animated release, *Aladdin*.

"I feel like I'm in my own movie!" Robert Altman gushed while walking among the galaxy of stars on the red carpet en route into the Globes ceremony at the Beverly Hilton Hotel. Once inside, he gushed again later on when *The Player* was voted Best Comedy or Musical Picture. Star Tim Robbins claimed the kudos as Best Actor, topping himself in a separate bid as a charismatic conservative Senatorial candidate in *Bob Roberts*, which marked his debut as a director and screenwriter.

Altman lost the nod for Best Director to Clint Eastwood, however, while *Unforgiven* also reaped the Globe for Best Supporting Actor. Victor Gene Hackman had looked noticeably glum and was grousing to colleagues, "I'd rather be home," but perked up once he heard the news of his victory—even though he now had to pay up on a $100 bet he made with a TV reporter that he'd lose.

Emma Thompson continued her recent winning streak by receiving the nod as Best Drama Actress. In her acceptance speech, she echoed the same plea she had made at the other kudos fetes. "If I have a wish left in the world," she said, "it's for the creation of more great female roles."

Enchanted April costars Miranda Richardson and Joan Plowright were hailed as Best Comedy/Musical Actress and Best Supporting Actress. The *L.A. Times* noted that Plowright "looked somewhat dazed" as she accepted the Globe for her role as a feisty widow. She called the occasion "the luckiest night of my life."

The biggest upset of the night was scored by *Scent of a Woman*, which featured Al Pacino in "a virtuoso star turn as a blind ex-military officer who introduces a greenhorn to the things of life," said *Variety*. Pacino was named Best Drama Actor over Denzel Washington, and *Scent* pulled off victories for Best Drama Picture and Best Screenplay over *Unforgiven, The Player* and *Howards End*.

When Pacino reached the podium, the *L.A. Times* noted, "He said he was unaccustomed to winning. He has been nominated for Oscars six times previously and nearly a dozen times for Globes, but had never won. The audience clearly showed its approval, rising to a standing ovation as Pacino took the stage."

Soon after the Globes ceremony, however, the media erupted in an outcry of dis-

The Indie Spirits were now held under a tent on Santa Monica Beach.

approval over *Scent*'s sweep. The *N.Y. Times* reported, "Hollywood is buzzing that numerous members of the foreign press group flew en masse (to New York) to see the film and to meet Al Pacino before the vote." Studio-sponsored junkets were becoming more and more common of late and were frequently attended by noted U.S. journalists, too, but this was the first year that HFPA members accepted producers' largesse. They also took junkets to see *Malcolm X, Bob Roberts, Batman Returns* and *Home Alone 2*, but gave those pix no awards. *Variety* added, "One member notes proudly that this year the HFPA nominated Michelle Pfeiffer for *Love Field*—'and she never cooperates at all.'" The HFPA took out an ad in *Variety* addressed as "An Open Letter to the Industry" in order "to refute strongly the suggestion that the win of *Scent of a Woman* had to do with anything but the merits of the film."

At the heart of the flapdoodle were the mixed reviews that *Scent* received when it premiered. Mostly, *Variety* had praised the pic, but added that it "indulgently stretches a modest conceit well past the breaking point." Pacino's perf had been in the running at earlier kudos. He had come in second place in the Best Actor polling by the National Board of Review and third place when the Gotham crix voted. The foreign press was vindicated a few weeks after its gala when *Scent*, Pacino and Martin Brest were nommed for top pic, actor and director at the Oscars.

But Brest did not nab a bid from the Directors Guild of America when the org announced its nominations one day after the Globes bash. *Variety* pegged the front-runners as Eastwood, James Ivory (*Howards End*) and Rob Reiner (*A Few Good Men*). Also nommed: Robert Altman (*The Player*) and Neil Jordan (*The Crying Game*). *The Crying Game* received a last-minute boost when Stephen Woolley took the top honor at the Producers Guild of America awards, held three days before the DGA ceremony. In the previous three years of its history, the PGA prize had correctly predicted the winner of Oscar's Best Picture.

Variety reported on the DGA outcome:

Variety called Gotham crix, Globes and Indie Spirit Best Picture *The Player* (starring Tim Robbins and Greta Scacchi) "the deep dish on Hollywood."

"After 23 years as a member of the DGA, Clint Eastwood attended his first awards banquet and walked away with the evening's most coveted prize. With a Golden Globe already pocketed, he is now within easy reach of adding an Oscar to his cache."

"I'm very flattered, very honored," he said at the podium. "It was just one of those pictures that everything fell together."

Seventy-seven adapted screenplays and 103 original scripts competed for the top prizes determined by the 3,054 voters belonging to the Writers Guild of America. A number of favorite past awardees scored new bids, including Woody Allen (*Husbands and Wives*), Bo Goldman (*Scent of a Woman*) and Ruth Prawer Jhabvala (*Howards End*).

"Two of the year's smallest and yet most controversial films turned out to be winners," *Variety* observed.

Neil Jordan made up for his loss at the directors' guild by prevailing over Woody Allen and David Webb Peoples for the original screenplay accolade.

Reporting on his acceptance speech, *Variety* said, "Jordan said that not only was his film initially turned down by every major studio in Hollywood, but that it also was turned down by 'every country in the world. So this award is particularly gratifying to me.'"

Michael Tolkin (*The Player*) won the prize for Best Adapted Screenplay over Goldman, Jhabvala and two-time past nominee David Mamet (*Glengarry Glen Ross*). When accepting his trophy, he referred to his father, Mel, a writer who had earned TV kudos from the guild for penning Sid Caesar's *Your Show of Shows* and other programs.

"My father was nominated five times by the WGA and he won four of those times," he said. "I didn't realize what an achievement that was until I joined the writers' guild 14 years ago."

Variety added, "Ironically, when he was asked by producer David Brown to adapt his novel, Tolkin said he agreed and was subsequently fired by his agent for accepting so little money."

The Player scored only one Independent Spirit nomination, but the savage send-up of the Hollywood system took its category—Best Picture—when the anti-Hollywood kudofest was held for the first time under a giant tent on the Santa Monica beach. *Variety* reported, "Many celebrities mused that they could think of no other Hollywood awards show where the guests had to wait in line for Porta Potties while facing hordes of autograph-seeking fans."

Although Robert Altman failed to be nommed for Best Director, Best Supporting Actress champ Alfre Woodard (*Passion Fish*) saluted the helmer she had worked with early in her career in *Health*, saying, "I run to catch your spirit."

The director's laurels were snagged by Carl Franklin for *One False Move*, a drama about savvy L.A. cops on the heels of fleeing drug thieves. He beat two formidable rivals—Allison Anders (*Gas Food Lodging*) and Quentin Tarantino (*Reservoir Dogs*). Three months earlier, Anders had been hailed as the year's Best New Director by the Gotham film crix in a close 28-to-27 vote over Tarantino.

Gas Food Lodging made up for its losses in the Best Picture and Best Director races with the Best Actress trophy for star Fairuza Balk as a self-conscious teenage girl living with her mom and sister. The film had lost out on kudos at last year's Sundance fest, but gained enough buzz to help it get a higher profile and better commercial distribution.

Best Actor was Harvey Keitel (*Bad Lieu-*

Neil Jordan (*The Crying Game*) followed up his screenplay victory at the Gotham circle with honors from the writers' guild (above) and Oscars.

tenant), who accepted his kudo telling the struggling indie filmmakers present, "If you want to do something bad enough, there's suffering we must endure."

The sole multiple winner was a pic that had reaped two kudos at last year's Sundance fest, *The Waterdance*, a drama about the rehab of a paraplegic. Paraplegic director/writer Neal Jimenez joked with the aud as he accepted his palms for Best First Feature and Best Screenplay, saying, "I guess we swept."

Two movies nominated for Best Picture at the upcoming Oscars had to square off in the Spirit's category for Best Foreign Film since they'd been produced in the U.K. When *The Crying Game* beat *Howards End*, Neil Jordan recalled his own "physical/aesthetic journey" as an indie filmmaker and insisted that if a space alien tried to understand human nature by studying current movies and TV, "It would learn sweet nothing of today."

Two days later, at the Oscars, many pundits called it Independents' Day since two indies—*The Crying Game* and *Howards*

WGA/Bonnie Clarke

End—made the race for Best Picture, but, oddly, not the film declared the year's best by both indie spirit voters and the Gotham crix: *The Player.* *Variety* editor-in-chief Peter Bart was outraged by the snub, writing about the pic, "It seems to me it may be the greatest send-up of Hollywood, and I'd hoped that Hollywood would get the joke."

Bob Altman made the cut for Best Director, but he bumped Rob Reiner, whose *A Few Good Men* took *The Player*'s place in the top pic lineup. Other notable oversights: no sign of Jack Lemmon or Tim Robbins in the actor's race or of Alfre Woodard among the rivals for supporting actress.

Howards End may have tied *Unforgiven* for the most noms—nine—but Kenneth Turan of the *L.A. Times* thought that the western's chief duelist was a pic that scored six.

"The Academy Awards come down to one simple question," he wrote. "Can *The Crying Game* stop Clint?"

By late March, *The Crying Game* had become an all-out art-house smash, causing stampedes to theaters by curious moviegoers eager to find out star Jaye Davidson's widely hushed secret. The *Times* thought that voters might choose *The Crying Game* because it's "a warmer picture than *Unforgiven* and one that has the possible advantage of being a spunky *Rocky*-type underdog." The director's award still seemed certain to go to Eastwood, but, the paper added, "It is worth noting that in two of the three years when the DGA winner did not win Best Picture, the Oscar went to *Chariots of Fire* and *Driving Miss Daisy*, both small films the academy took a definite shine to."

Nonetheless, Turan bet on *Unforgiven* winning Best Picture and was backed up by four of his *Times* colleagues who also published forecasts.

The first major showdown between the pix came in the category of Best Supporting Actor, where prognosticators were split between backing *Unforgiven*'s Gene Hackman and *Crying Game*'s Jaye Davidson. Three *L.A. Times* crix lined up behind the former, two the latter. The race was complicated by the inclusion of Al Pacino as a hotshot real-estate salesman in *Glengarry Glen Ross*. He was also up for Best Actor (*Scent of a Woman*). When other thesps had scored similar dual bids on six occasions in years past, they won in the supporting race five times.

But this time Hackman came through and dedicated his victory to his 88-year-old uncle, who had died the previous night. "He was a man who, years ago, was unconvinced acting would pay his nephew's bills," *Variety* noted. The win marked Hackman's second Oscar for playing a tough cop after previously being honored as 1971's Best Actor in *The French Connection*.

The *L.A. Times*'s Turan called the Best Supporting Actress lineup "one of the toughest categories to pick. Judy Davis is a consistently superior actress, but she may be hurt by the current uneasiness surrounding everything touching Woody Allen. Joan Plowright, the widow of Lord Olivier and all that, is a revered figure in the profession even though she has been selective in her film work." He picked Plowright, as did three of his colleagues. Davis got the stray vote.

Nowhere in the *Times*' appraisal of the category was any mention of Marisa Tomei, who, *Variety* said, "creates a buoyant chemistry as a kind of sexy hood ornament (for) a hopelessly inept lawyer" in *My Cousin Vinny.* *Variety* had pegged her nomination a surprise when it was announced since she was known mostly as a former soap opera and TV sitcom star. When she prevailed, *Variety* declared the upset "the biggest surprise of the night." Pundits surmised that she beat the odds because she was the only American in a race also including three Brits and one Aussie (Davis).

TV Guide and the dueling movie crix Roger Ebert and Gene Siskel thought that Susan Sarandon's Yankee blood might help her in the contest for Best Actress against veddy British Emma Thompson. But Thompson had not lost a single major awards race yet and had all five *L.A. Times* crix rooting for her.

"Good grief!" Thompson gasped when her name was called to claim the trophy, which she accepted thanking director James Ivory and producer Ismail Merchant "for paying me to play the part, which seems very unnecessary at the moment."

Backstage, she revealed to reporters that she had gotten nervous about her chances when Tomei won earlier. "I felt that this was going to be a real American night," said the thesp who now was only the fifth star in showbiz history to claim honors from the Oscars, Globes, National Board of Review and the top three crix orgs all in one year. Her predecessors: Meryl Streep (*Kramer vs. Kramer*), Sally Field *(Norma Rae),* Sissy Spacek (*Coal Miner's Daughter*) and Jack Nicholson (*Terms of Endearment*).

Howards End also scored the prize for Best Adapted Screenplay, giving scribe Ruth Prawer Jhabvala a matching bookend after the kudos she claimed in 1986 for *A Room with a View*.

When Al Pacino lost his bid for Best Supporting Actor, it marked his seventh Oscar defeat, tying him with Richard Burton and Peter O'Toole as the bigger loser in the award's history. He was considered the front-runner in the Best Actor race, though.

"There are so many factors in Al Pacino's favor that if he doesn't win for *Scent of a Woman*, his agent is likely to call for a recount," the *L.A. Times* said. "Not only has he been nominated eight times, but he plays a blind man who has both a drunk scene and a big crowd-pleasing oration at the film's close. Only Denzel Washington in *Malcolm X* has any hope of beating him."

Pacino had skipped most Oscarcasts in the past, but he was present this year. *Variety* columnist Army Archerd met him outside the Dorothy Chandler Pavilion before the ceremony and noted later, "Al Pacino was so nervous when I introduced him to the fans in the stands that he held tightly to my hand and couldn't think of any of his previous six nominations."

Pacino's dubious co-reign with Burton and O'Toole ended up lasting for only two hours. When he finally triumphed as Best Actor, he acknowledged a standing ovation from the crowd, saying, "You have broken my streak. This a proud and hopeful moment for me."

Pacino's victory marked a defeat for co-nominee Clint Eastwood, but since the latter

hadn't been expected to win, *Unforgiven's* boosters may not have been too disheartened about the pic's chances in other categories.

But *Unforgiven* also suffered losses for sound, art direction and cinematography early in the night, although it did win kudos for film editing and supporting actor Hackman.

Next came Best Original Screenplay, which was considered a crucial matchup since three-quarters of all past Best Picture champs had also garnered a script award.

All five *L.A. Times* pundits, however, predicted that *The Crying Game* would triumph. "*Unforgiven* supporters have other places to go," Turan reasoned. "*The Crying Game*'s partisans will feel this is its best chance for an Oscar."

Turan turned out to be right. When Neil Jordan won, he appeared breathless at the podium, saying, "Sorry. I didn't know these nominations were coming up. I was in the bathroom when I heard it."

Near evening's end, as time approached for the two top awards, Clint Eastwood had every reason for concern despite the *L.A. Times*'s forecast in the Best Director race. "Eastwood is a breeze, the one nomination in three he seems surest to walk home with," Turan insisted.

Indeed, Eastwood ended up taking the long stroll to the podium as predicted. When he took the statuette in hand, he said, "This is pretty good. This is all right."

Unforgiven faced only two serious rivals for the Best Picture prize: *The Crying Game* and *Howards End*. Pundits wrote off *Scent of a Woman*'s chances after the Golden Globe uproar, and *A Few Good Men* appeared to be out of the running since it didn't reap a corresponding Best Director bid for Rob Reiner. Reiner acknowledged his poor chances to Army Archerd prior to the Oscarcast, saying, "Look at the odds. Marisa Tomei has a better chance than we do."

Moments after Eastwood's victory for Best Director, he took another stroll to the podium to collect the top-pic statuette.

Backstage afterward, the 62-year-old champ sounded like a sage old-timer as he told reporters that winning means "more to me now" because "if you win early in your career, you might wonder, 'Where do I go from here?' Maybe at that time in life, you might not be mature enough. You might get carried away with yourself and start wearing a monocle and leggings and thinking you're a genius."

While the bigger independent pix did well at the Oscars with victories for Best Actress and Best Original Screenplay, the smaller indies continued to prosper at the Sundance Film Festival held far off in the Utah mountains, where this year more than 5,000 outsiders descended onto the snow-blanketed Park City, paying as much as $1,100 for the deluxe Fast Pass guaranteeing entry to any crowded screening.

Covering the award results, the *L.A. Times* reported, "The dramatic competition jury was nothing if not judicious, splitting the Grand Jury Prize between a veteran independent filmmaker and one of the 20-something newcomers whose presence dominated the 10-day event."

The young upstart, Bryan Singer, reaped the jury honor for his entry *Public Access*, described by the *Times* as "the portentous story of a mysterious young man who wreaks havoc in a bucolic small town. The talented 27-year-old director made the film in 18 days for $250,000 using short ends of leftover film stock from *Dracula* and *Hoffa*," two major studio releases. After getting discovered at Sundance, Singer would go on in his career to make such big-budget works as Oscar champ *The Usual Suspects*.

Singer shared the kudos with indie veteran Victor Nunez, who'd won the same prize at the fest in 1980 for *Gal Young 'Un*. Now he was honored for *Ruby in Paradise*, about a young Tennessee hills woman who settles in a redneck Florida resort community. *Variety* noted that it featured "a lovely central performance by newcomer Ashley Judd" and "was widely tipped for the top award," whereas *Public Access*'s co-victory as a "surprise." Nunez would go on in his career to surprise crix with such high-profile pix as *Ulee's Gold*, starring Oscar nominee Peter Fonda.

Two pix also split the Grand Jury Prize for best documentaries in addition to winning a second award each.

In *Children of Fate*, a young filmmaker ventured to the same ghetto in Sicily his father covered in a never-released documentary 30 years earlier and intercut his new color footage with what the *Times* called "the breathtakingly poetic original black-and-white shots." The result earned the father-son team the fest's accolade for best cinematography—and a nomination for Best Documentary at next year's Oscars.

Variety called grand jury co-winner *Silverlake Life* "a devastatingly intimate portrayal of the AIDS epidemic." It also garnered the fest's new Freedom of Expression Award.

Another double champ was *Something within Me*, which showcased children learning an uplifting curriculum of music while attending a rundown school in New York's impoverished South Bronx. It claimed both the filmmaker's and audience awards for best documentary.

Winner of the Filmmaker's Trophy for best dramatic feature was *Fly by Night*, a tale of New York City rap artists. The Audience Award for dramas went to *El Mariachi*, a Spanish-lingo pic shot in just two weeks for $7,000 about a mariachi performer mistaken for an escaped con.

Winners of the Grand Jury Prizes were awarded $2,500 each. Other honorees received plaques.

▪ 1992 ▪

LOS ANGELES FILM CRITICS ASSOCIATION

Winners were announced on December 12, 1992. Awards were presented on January 19, 1993, at the Bel Age Hotel in Los Angeles.

BEST PICTURE
▪ *Unforgiven*

BEST DIRECTOR
▪ Clint Eastwood, *Unforgiven*

BEST ACTOR
- Clint Eastwood, *Unforgiven*

BEST ACTRESS
- Emma Thompson, *Howards End*

BEST SUPPORTING ACTOR
- Gene Hackman, *Unforgiven*

BEST SUPPORTING ACTRESS
- Judy Davis, *Husbands and Wives*

BEST SCREENPLAY
- David Webb Peoples, *Unforgiven*

BEST CINEMATOGRAPHY
- Zhao Fei, *Raise the Red Lantern*

BEST MUSIC SCORE
- Zbigniew Preisner, *Damage*

BEST ANIMATION
- *Aladdin,* John Musker, Ron Clements, Douglas Edwards

BEST DOCUMENTARY
- *Black Harvest,* Bob Connolly and Robin Anderson
- *Threat,* Stefan Jarl

BEST FOREIGN FILM
- *The Crying Game* (Ireland), Neil Jordan

BEST EXPERIMENTAL/INDEPENDENT FILM
- *It Wasn't Love,* Sadie Benning

CAREER ACHIEVEMENT AWARD
- Budd Boetticher

NATIONAL BOARD OF REVIEW

The board declared a Best Picture and Foreign Film of the year, then listed its remaining favorites according to highest scores. The vote results were announced on December 16, 1992. Awards were presented on February 22, 1993, at the Equitable Center in New York.

BEST PICTURE
- *Howards End*
- *The Crying Game*
- *Glengarry Glen Ross*
- *A Few Good Men*
- *The Player*
- *Unforgiven*
- *One False Move*
- *Peter's Friends*
- *Bob Roberts*
- *Malcolm X*

BEST DIRECTOR
- James Ivory, *Howards End*

BEST ACTOR
- Jack Lemmon, *Glengarry Glen Ross*

BEST ACTRESS
- Emma Thompson, *Howards End*

BEST SUPPORTING ACTOR
- Jack Nicholson, *A Few Good Men*

BEST SUPPORTING ACTRESS
- Judy Davis, *Husbands and Wives*

MOST AUSPICIOUS DEBUT
- Jaye Davidson

BEST DOCUMENTARY
- *Brother's Keeper*

BEST FOREIGN FILM
- *Indochine* (France)
- *Raise the Red Lantern* (China/Taiwan/Hong Kong)
- *Tous les Matins du Monde* (All the Mornings of the World) (France)
- *Mediterraneo* (Italy)
- *Like Water for Chocolate* (Mexico)

CAREER ACHIEVEMENT AWARD
- Shirley Temple Black

SPECIAL AWARDS
- Robin Williams
- Ted Turner
- Beatrice Welles

NEW YORK FILM CRITICS CIRCLE

Winners were announced on December 17, 1992. Awards were presented on January 17, 1993, at the Pegasus Suite of the Rainbow Room in Rockefeller Center in New York. The ceremony was telecast by E! Entertainment Network.

BEST PICTURE
- *The Player*

BEST DIRECTOR
- Robert Altman, *The Player*

BEST NEW DIRECTOR
- Allison Anders, *Gas Food Lodging*

BEST ACTOR
- Denzel Washington, *Malcolm X*

BEST ACTRESS
- Emma Thompson, *Howards End*

BEST SUPPORTING ACTOR
- Gene Hackman, *Unforgiven*

BEST SUPPORTING ACTRESS
- Miranda Richardson, *The Crying Game, Damage, Enchanted April*

BEST SCREENPLAY
- Neil Jordan, *The Crying Game*

BEST CINEMATOGRAPHY
- Jean LePine, *The Player*

BEST DOCUMENTARY
- *Brother's Keeper*

BEST FOREIGN FILM
- *Raise the Red Lantern* (China/Taiwan/Hong Kong)

NATIONAL SOCIETY OF FILM CRITICS

Winners were announced on January 3, 1993.

BEST PICTURE
- *Unforgiven*

BEST DIRECTOR
- Clint Eastwood, *Unforgiven*

BEST ACTOR
- Stephen Rea, *The Crying Game*

BEST ACTRESS
- Emma Thompson, *Howards End*

BEST SUPPORTING ACTOR
- Gene Hackman, *Unforgiven*

BEST SUPPORTING ACTRESS
- Judy Davis, *Husbands and Wives*

BEST SCREENPLAY
- David Webb Peoples, *Unforgiven*

BEST CINEMATOGRAPHY
- Zhao Fei, *Raise the Red Lantern*

BEST DOCUMENTARY
- *American Dream*, Barbara Kopple

BEST FOREIGN-LANGUAGE FILM
- *Raise the Red Lantern* (China/Taiwan/Hong Kong)

SPECIAL CITATION
- *Another Girl, Another Planet,* Michael Almereyda

GOLDEN GLOBES

Nominations were announced on December 29, 1992. Awards were presented on January 24, 1993, at the Beverly Hilton Hotel in Los Angeles. The ceremony was telecast by TBS.

BEST DRAMA PICTURE
- *Scent of a Woman*
The Crying Game
A Few Good Men
Howards End
Unforgiven

BEST COMEDY OR MUSICAL PICTURE
- *The Player*
Aladdin
Enchanted April
Honeymoon in Vegas
Sister Act

BEST DIRECTOR
- Clint Eastwood, *Unforgiven*

Robert Altman, *The Player*
James Ivory, *Howards End*
Robert Redford, *A River Runs Through It*
Rob Reiner, *A Few Good Men*

BEST ACTOR, DRAMA
- Al Pacino, *Scent of a Woman*

Tom Cruise, *A Few Good Men*
Robert Downey, Jr., *Chaplin*
Jack Nicholson, *Hoffa*
Denzel Washington, *Malcolm X*

BEST ACTRESS, DRAMA
- Emma Thompson, *Howards End*

Mary McDonnell, *Passion Fish*
Michelle Pfeiffer, *Love Field*
Susan Sarandon, *Lorenzo's Oil*
Sharon Stone, *Basic Instinct*

BEST ACTOR, COMEDY OR MUSICAL
- Tim Robbins, *The Player*

Nicolas Cage, *Honeymoon in Vegas*
Billy Crystal, *Mr. Saturday Night*
Marcello Mastroianni, *Used People*
Tim Robbins, *Bob Roberts*

BEST ACTRESS, COMEDY OR MUSICAL
- Miranda Richardson, *Enchanted April*

Geena Davis, *A League of Their Own*
Whoopi Goldberg, *Sister Act*
Shirley MacLaine, *Used People*
Meryl Streep, *Death Becomes Her*

BEST SUPPORTING ACTOR
- Gene Hackman, *Unforgiven*

Jack Nicholson, *A Few Good Men*
Al Pacino, *Glengarry Glen Ross*
David Paymer, *Mr. Saturday Night*
Chris O'Donnell, *Scent of a Woman*

BEST SUPPORTING ACTRESS
- Joan Plowright, *Enchanted April*

Geraldine Chaplin, *Chaplin*
Judy Davis, *Husbands and Wives*
Miranda Richardson, *Damage*
Alfre Woodard, *Passion Fish*

BEST SCREENPLAY
- Bo Goldman, *Scent of a Woman*

Jerry Goldsmith, *Basic Instinct*

Ruth Prawer Jhabvala, *Howards End*
David Webb Peoples, *Unforgiven*
Aaron Sorkin, *A Few Good Men*
Michael Tolkin, *The Player*

BEST SONG
- "A Whole New World," *Aladdin*, Alan
  Menken, Tim Rice

"Beautiful Maria of My Soul," *The Mambo
  Kings*, Robert Kraft, Arne Glimcher
"Friend Like Me," *Aladdin*, Alan Menken,
  Howard Ashman
"Prince Ali," *Aladdin*, Alan Menken,
  Howard Ashman
"This Used to Be My Playground," *A
  League of Their Own*, Madonna, Shep
  Pettibone

BEST FOREIGN FILM
- *Indochine* (France)

Close to Eden (Russia)
Like Water for Chocolate (Mexico)
Schtonk (Germany)
Tous les Matins du Monde (France)

Winners

BEST SCORE
- Alan Menken, *Aladdin*

CECIL B. DEMILLE AWARD
- Lauren Bacall

SPECIAL ACHIEVEMENT AWARD
- Robin Williams, *Aladdin*

SUNDANCE FILM FESTIVAL

The festival was held January 21–31, 1993,
at Park City, Utah.

GRAND JURY PRIZE
(DRAMATIC)
- *Ruby in Paradise,* Victor Nunez
- *Public Access*, Bryan Singer

(DOCUMENTARY)
- *Children of Fate,* Andrew Young, Susan
  Todd, Robert Young, Michael Roemer
- *Silverlake Life: The View from Here,*
  Peter Friedman, Tom Joslin, Mark
  Massi

FILMMAKER'S TROPHY
(DRAMATIC)
- *Fly by Night,* Steve Gomer

(DOCUMENTARY)
- *Something within Me,* Emma Joan Morris

AUDIENCE AWARD
(DRAMATIC)
- *El Mariachi,* Robert Rodriguez

(DOCUMENTARY)
- *Something within Me,* Emma Joan Morris

WALDO SALT SCREENWRITING AWARD
- *Combination Platter,* Tony Chan, Edwin Baker

CINEMATOGRAPHY AWARD
(DRAMATIC)
- *An Ambush of Ghosts,* Judy Irola

(DOCUMENTARY)
- *Children of Fate,* Andrew Young, Robert Young

FREEDOM OF EXPRESSION AWARD
- *Silverlake Life: The View from Here,* Peter Friedman, Tom Joslin, Mark Massi

SPECIAL JURY RECOGNITION
(DRAMATIC—FIRST FEATURE)
- *Just Another Girl on the I.R.T.,* Leslie Harris

(SPECIAL DISTINCTION)
- *Lillian,* David Williams

(TECHNICAL ACHIEVEMENT)
- *Earth and the American Dream,* Bill Couturie

PRODUCERS GUILD OF AMERICA

Nominations were announced on February 3, 1993. Winners were announced on February 14. Awards were presented on March 3 at the Regent Beverly Wilshire Hotel in Los Angeles.

DARRYL F. ZANUCK PRODUCER OF THE YEAR AWARD
- *The Crying Game,* Stephen Woolley

A Few Good Men, David Brown, Rob Reiner, Andrew Scheinman
Howards End, Ismail Merchant
Scent of a Woman, Martin Brest
Unforgiven, Clint Eastwood, David Valdes

CHARLES B. FITZSIMONS LIFETIME MEMBERSHIP AWARD
- Leonard B. Stern

NOVA AWARD
- Laurie Park, *My Own Private Idaho*

DAVID O. SELZNICK LIFETIME ACHIEVEMENT AWARD
- David Brown, Richard Zanuck

DIRECTORS GUILD OF AMERICA

Nominations were announced on January 25, 1993. Awards were presented on March 6 at the Beverly Hilton Hotel in Los Angeles.

BEST DIRECTOR
- Clint Eastwood, *Unforgiven*

Robert Altman, *The Player*
James Ivory, *Howards End*
Neil Jordan, *The Crying Game*
Rob Reiner, *A Few Good Men*

ROBERT B. ALDRICH AWARD
- Gene Reynolds
- John Rich

D. W. GRIFFITH AWARD
- Sidney Lumet

PRESTON STURGES AWARD
- Blake Edwards

WRITERS GUILD OF AMERICA

Nominations were announced on February 22, 1993. Awards were presented on March 22 at the Beverly Hilton Hotel in Los Angeles.

BEST ORIGINAL SCREENPLAY
- *The Crying Game,* Neil Jordan

Husbands and Wives, Woody Allen
Lorenzo's Oil, George Miller, Nick Enright
Passion Fish, John Sayles
Unforgiven, David Webb Peoples

BEST ADAPTED SCREENPLAY
- *The Player,* Michael Tolkin, based on his novel

Enchanted April, Peter Barnes, based on the novel by Elizabeth von Arnim

Glengarry Glen Ross, David Mamet, based
  on his play
Howards End, Ruth Prawer Jhabvala, based
  on the novel by E. M. Forster
Scent of a Woman, Bo Goldman, suggested
  by a character from *Profumo di Donna*
  by Ruggero Maccari and Dino Risi and
  the novel *Il Buio e Il Miele* by Giovanni
  Arpino

AFRICAN-AMERICAN PIONEER AWARDS
- James Baldwin
- Ossie Davis
- Robert Goodwin
- Lorraine Hansberry
- Helen Thompson

MORGAN COX AWARD
- Irma Kalish

VALENTINE DAVIES AWARD
- True Boardman

LAUREL AWARD
- Horton Foote

INDEPENDENT SPIRIT

Nominations were announced on January
18, 1993. Awards were presented on March
27 in a tent on the Santa Monica beach. Portions of the ceremony were broadcast later
on Bravo.

BEST PICTURE
- *The Player*
Bad Lieutenant
Gas Food Lodging
Mississippi Masala
One False Move

BEST FIRST FEATURE
- *The Waterdance*
Laws of Gravity
My New Gun
Reservoir Dogs
Swoon

BEST DIRECTOR
- Carl Franklin, *One False Move*
Allison Anders, *Gas Food Lodging*
Abel Ferrara, *Bad Lieutenant*

Tom Kalin, *Swoon*
Quentin Tarantino, *Reservoir Dogs*

BEST ACTOR
- Harvey Keitel, *Bad Lieutenant*
Craig Chester, *Swoon*
Lawrence Fishburne, *Deep Cover*
Peter Greene, *Laws of Gravity*
Michael Rapaport, *Zebrahead*

BEST ACTRESS
- Fairuza Balk, *Gas Food Lodging*
Edie Falco, *Laws of Gravity*
Catherine Keener, *Johnny Suede*
Sheryl Lee, *Twin Peaks: Fire Walk with Me*
Cynda Williams, *One False Move*

BEST SUPPORTING ACTOR
- Steve Buscemi, *Reservoir Dogs*
William Forsythe, *The Waterdance*
Jeff Goldblum, *Deep Cover*
Wesley Snipes, *The Waterdance*
David Strathaim, *Passion Fish*

BEST SUPPORTING ACTRESS
- Alfre Woodard, *Passion Fish*
Brooke Adams, *Gas Food Lodging*
Sara Gilbert, *Poison Ivy*
Karen Silas, *Simple Men*
Denetra Vanese, *Jumpin' at the Boneyard*

BEST SCREENPLAY
- Neal Jimenez, *The Waterdance*
Allison Anders, *Gas Food Lodging*
Keith Gordon, *A Midnight Clear*
Paul Schrader, *Light Sleeper*
Billy Bob Thorton, *One False Move*

BEST FOREIGN FILM
- *The Crying Game* (U.K.)
Close to Eden (Russia)
Danzon (Mexico)
Howards End (U.K.)
Raise the Red Lantern
  (China/Taiwan/Hong Kong)

Winners

BEST CINEMATOGRAPHY
- Frederick Elmes, *Night on Earth*

JOHN CASSAVETES AWARD
- Ismail Merchant, James Ivory

SPECIAL DISTINCTION
- *The Hours and Times*, Chris Munch

ACADEMY AWARDS

Nominations were announced on February 17, 1993. Awards were presented on March 29 at the Dorothy Chandler Pavilion in Los Angeles. The ceremony was telecast by ABC.

BEST PICTURE
- *Unforgiven*
The Crying Game
A Few Good Men
Howards End
Scent of a Woman

BEST DIRECTOR
- Clint Eastwood, *Unforgiven*
Robert Altman, *The Player*
Martin Brest, *Scent of a Woman*
James Ivory, *Howards End*
Neil Jordan, *The Crying Game*

BEST ACTOR
- Al Pacino, *Scent of a Woman*
Robert Downey, Jr., *Chaplin*
Clint Eastwood, *Unforgiven*
Stephen Rea, *The Crying Game*
Denzel Washington, *Malcolm X*

BEST ACTRESS
- Emma Thompson, *Howards End*
Catherine Deneuve, *Indochine*
Mary McDonnell, *Passion Fish*
Michelle Pfeiffer, *Love Field*
Susan Sarandon, *Lorenzo's Oil*

BEST SUPPORTING ACTOR
- Gene Hackman, *Unforgiven*
Jaye Davidson, *The Crying Game*
Jack Nicholson, *A Few Good Men*
Al Pacino, *Glengarry Glen Ross*
David Paymer, *Mr. Saturday Night*

BEST SUPPORTING ACTRESS
- Marisa Tomei, *My Cousin Vinny*
Judy Davis, *Husbands and Wives*
Joan Plowright, *Enchanted April*
Vanessa Redgrave, *Howards End*
Miranda Richardson, *Damage*

BEST ORIGINAL SCREENPLAY
- Neil Jordan, *The Crying Game*
Woody Allen, *Husbands and Wives*
Nick Enright, George Miller, *Lorenzo's Oil*
John Sayles, *Passion Fish*
David Webb Peoples, *Unforgiven*

BEST ADAPTED SCREENPLAY
- Ruth Prawer Jhabvala, *Howards End*
Peter Barnes, *Enchanted April*
Richard Friedenberg, *A River Runs Through It*
Bo Goldman, *Scent of a Woman*
Michael Tolkin, *The Player*

BEST SONG
- "A Whole New World," *Aladdin*, Alan Menken, Tim Rice
"Beautiful Maria of My Soul," *The Mambo Kings*, Arne Glimcher, Robert Kraft
"Friend Like Me," *Aladdin*, Howard Ashman, Alan Menken
"I Have Nothing," *The Bodyguard*, David Foster, Linda Thompson
"Run to You," *The Bodyguard*, Jud Friedman, Allan Rich

BEST FOREIGN-LANGUAGE FILM
- *Indochine* (France)
Close to Eden (Russia)
Daens (Belgium)
A Place in the World (Uruguay)
Schtonk! (Germany)

Winners

BEST ART DIRECTION
- Luciana Arrighi, Ian Whittaker, *Howards End*

BEST CINEMATOGRAPHY
- Philippe Rousselot, *A River Runs Through It*

BEST COSTUME DESIGN
- Eiko Ishioka, *Bram Stoker's Dracula*

BEST DOCUMENTARY
(FEATURE)
- *The Panama Deception*, David Kasper, Barbara Trent

(SHORT SUBJECT)
- *Educating Peter*, Thomas C. Goodwin, Gerardine Wurzburg

BEST FILM EDITING
- Joel Cox, *Unforgiven*

BEST MAKEUP
- Michèle Burke, Greg Cannom, Matthew W. Mungle, *Bram Stoker's Dracula*

BEST ORIGINAL MUSIC SCORE
- Alan Menken, *Aladdin*

SCIENTIFIC OR TECHNICAL AWARDS
(Academy Award of Merit)
- Chadwell O'Connor, O'Connor Engineering Laboratories

(Scientific and Engineering Award)
- Claus Wiedemann, Robert Orban, Dolby Laboratories; Arriflex Corp., Otto Blaschek, engineering department of Arri; Loren Carpenter, Rob Cook; Ed Catmull, Tom Porter, Pat Hanrahan, Tony Apodaca, Darwyn Peachey; Ken Bates; Al Mayer; Iain Neil, George Kraemer; Hans Spirawski, Bill Eslick; Don Earl; Douglas Trumbull, Geoffrey H. Williamson, Robert D. Auguste, Edmund M. Di Giulio

(Technical Achievement Award)
- Robert R. Burton, Audio Rents; Tom Brigham, Douglas Smythe, computer graphics department, Industrial Light and Magic; Ira Tiffen; Iain Neil, Kaz Fudano

BEST SHORT FILM
(ANIMATED)
- *Mona Lisa Descending a Staircase*, Joan C. Gratz

(LIVE ACTION)
- *Omnibus*, Sam Karmann

BEST SOUND
- Doug Hemphill, Chris Jenkins, Simon Kaye, Mark Smith, *The Last of The Mohicans*

BEST SOUND EFFECTS EDITING
- Tom C. McCarthy, David E. Stone, *Bram Stoker's Dracula*

BEST VISUAL EFFECTS
- Doug Chiang, Ken Ralston, Doug Smythe, Tom Woodruff, Jr., *Death Becomes Her*

GORDON E. SAWYER AWARD
- Erich Kaestner

JEAN HERSHOLT HUMANITARIAN AWARD
- Audrey Hepburn
- Elizabeth Taylor

HONORARY AWARDS
- Federico Fellini
- Petro Vlahos

SCREEN ACTORS GUILD
LIFETIME ACHIEVEMENT AWARD
- Audrey Hepburn

▪ 1993 ▪

Schindler's *Historic Sweep*

*S*chindler's List made kudos history when it became the first pic to top every list of the current top awards.

But when its topper Steven Spielberg failed to be declared Best Director by two crix orgs for his three-and-a-half-hour Holocaust opus, a firestorm of controversy erupted.

In its review, *Variety* had cheered Spielberg's powerful demonstration of recent maturity at the helm: "This searing historical and biographical drama about a Nazi industrialist who saved some 1,100 Jews from certain death in the concentration camps, evinces an artistic rigor and unsentimental intelligence unlike anything the world's most successful filmmaker has demonstrated before."

The L.A. and Gotham crix bypassed him in favor of the first woman ever to win Best Director at Cannes, Jane Campion, "who now appears to be speaking a rich new cinema language" in her fourth career feature, *The Piano*, said the *N.Y. Times*. *Variety* lauded Campion for using "bold strokes" in "a visually sumptuous and tactile tale of adultery set during the early European colonization of New Zealand, with Harvey Keitel daringly cast in the role of a passionate lover, and Holly Hunter a knockout as a woman physically unable to articulate her feelings," being a mute. In addition to Cannes's director nod, *The Piano* claimed Best Actress for Hunter plus the highest honor, the Palme d'Or. Its kudos sweep triggered a seven-minute standing ovation at the fest.

Pundits posited that the reason that the crix snubbed Spielberg might be jealousy

Schindler's List became the only film in modern times to be named Best Picture by every leading awards group—from the National Board of Review to the Oscars.

over his recent b.o. success with summer dinosaur thriller *Jurassic Park*, which became the second-biggest grosser in U.S. film history—after Spielberg's *E.T. the Extraterrestrial*—and tops throughout the world. But critic Michael Medved threw gasoline on the firestorm by attributing the action to the crix's "feverish hunger to honor a woman—at all costs—despite the fact that their votes indicated they clearly liked Spielberg's movie better." Award groups had been accused of slighting women in the past when helmers like Barbra Streisand and Penny Marshall were overlooked despite receiving Best Picture bids at the Oscars.

"Hey, Steven: call a cop, 'cause you was robbed!" Medved cried in the *N.Y. Post*.

Gotham circle member Georgia Brown of *The Village Voice* was among those who shrieked "Bigotry!" in response. She claimed she'd voted for Mike Leigh (*Naked*) and "never considered that in not voting for Campion that I was failing to vote for a woman." L.A. crix prexy Henry Sheenan denounced Medved's accusation as "outrageously wrong, insensitive, insulting and demeaning."

Peter Rainer, prexy of the National Society of Film Critics—which had not yet picked its winners—piped in with a wisecrack: "If the critics associations were so determined to vote in a woman at all costs, how come Robin Williams did so poorly in the Best Actor voting for *Mrs. Doubtfire?*"

In fact, the L.A. crix's slight seemed to be directed more against Spielberg than men in general since Robert Altman (*Short Cuts*) placed second in the voting. *The Piano* was the runner-up behind *Schindler's List* for Best Picture, but, failing to prevail in either top two races, did earn Campion the screenplay laurels.

Piano star Holly Hunter was proclaimed Best Actress over Debra Winger, who was cited for two perfs: as the sad-sack sister of a dashing widow in *A Dangerous Woman* and as a Yankee poet who falls for noted British writer C. S. Lewis (Anthony Hopkins) in *Shadowlands*. *Variety* hailed Hopkins for "delivering a towering performance" in *Shadowlands*, one of the two roles that earned him the palm for Best Actor. He was also acknowledged for what *Variety* called his "superbly observed and nuanced" depiction of a proper British butler who secretly pines for a co-worker (Emma Thompson) in *Remains of the Day*.

Runner-up was Daniel Day-Lewis, who was considered for two movies, too. *Variety* praised him for "cutting an impressive figure" as a morally upright lawyer whose values are tested when he falls for his fiancé's sprightly cousin (Winona Ryder) in the screen adaptation of the Edith Wharton novel about 1870s New York society, *The Age of Innocence*. He was also cited for *In the Name of the Father*, in which he gave what *Variety* called a "first rate" perf as an Irish hippie who's thrown into a British jail after being wrongly accused of an IRA bombing.

The nod for Best Supporting Actor went to Tommy Lee Jones as a headstrong detective intent on catching an escacped convict who Jones doesn't know is innocent in *The Fugitive*, a feature adaptation of the hit 1960s TV series. *Variety* said, "It's another opportunity for Jones to remind us of his acting chops, a man part Mountie, part maniac, who loves his job, respects his team and thrives on the hunt."

Trailing behind him in the crix vote was Ralph Fiennes, whose role in *Schindler's List* was "as evil as any Nazi presented on screen over the past 50 years, but considerably more complex and human than most," said *Variety*.

As a result of a tie, the laurels for Best Supporting Actress were shared by Rosie Perez as a plane crash survivor in *Fearless* and Anna Paquin, an 11-year-old moppet who made her acting debut as Holly Hunter's daughter in *The Piano*. *Chicago Sun-Times* critic Roger Ebert saluted Paquin's screen bow as "one of the most extraordinary examples of a child's acting in movie history."

When the crix gathered to present their plaques, the kudos were bestowed in name only because the trophy shop failed to open on the day of the gala. Awardees proved to be good sports, though, particularly Spielberg, who acknowledged his Best Picture victory, saying, "It's a great honor standing in front of people I occasionally fear."

Buoyant Best Actress Holly Hunter said she was "so thrilled to be in the same room with people whose work is so honest."

Three days after the L.A. crix voted on their awards, the National Board of Review unveiled its champs, also citing *Schindler's List* as Best Picture, but dealing Spielberg yet another slap. For Best Director, it named Martin Scorsese, who'd reaped critical huzzahs for his sensitive—and meticulously accurate—portrayal of old-world manners in

---

Charges of "bigotry!" engulfed the Gotham crix vote.

The Age of Innocence after such previous gritty outings as *Taxi Driver* and *Raging Bull*.

The board agreed that Hopkins and Hunter were the year's Best Actor and Actress, but veered in the supporting races. It honored Leonardo DiCaprio, who had also received a special New Generation Award from the L.A. crix for portraying Johnny Depp's retarded younger brother in *What's Eating Gilbert Grape?*

The New York Film Critics Circle chose its winners one day after the board and four days after the L.A. crix. Its selection of *Schindler's List* for the top prize marked only the fifth time that the Gotham group had agreed with the L.A. crix org on Best Picture in the 19 years of their coexistence.

Schindler's List (34 points) didn't eclipse *The Piano* (31) in the Best Picture race until the fourth ballot after beating back a sudden come-from-behind rally by *Naked* on the third polling, when the dark horse suddenly leapt forward with the most first-placed votes, but then ended up with only 19 points over all. *Naked* nonetheless scored a Best Actor upset for recent Cannes champ David Thewlis, who *Variety* said pulls off "a tour-de-force as an unemployed philosopher-bum" who sets out on "a weird nocturnal odyssey through the streets of London." He beat Anthony Hopkins by the narrow margin of 39 to 37.

Jane Campion defeated Steven Spielberg for Best Director by a 34-to-31 score. When she also won Best Screenplay (30 points), the *N.Y. Times* spotted "an unlikely tie for second place" between the scenarist of *Schindler's List* (Steven Zaillian) and the scribes of the knee-slapping laffer *Groundhog Day* (Harold Ramis, Danny Rubin). Both pix garnered 22 points.

Holly Hunter (39) won Best Actress over Ashley Judd (25), who portrayed a sensitive young woman from the Tennessee hills who seeks a new life in Florida's "redneck Riv-

iera" in *Ruby in Paradise*, winner of last year's Grand Jury Prize at Sundance.

Ralph Fiennes (36 points) beat Leonardo DiCaprio (30) for Best Supporting Actor, while the femme laurels went to Gong Li as the ex-prostitute wife of a bisexual star of the Peking Opera in *Farewell, My Concubine*. She scored 38 points versus 23 for Rosie Perez.

USA Today noted that Steven Spielberg seemed to be "in a mellow, reflective mood" when he accepted his Best Picture plaque from the Gotham crix at the ceremony held in the Pegasus Room at Rockefeller Center.

"This movie has changed my life," he confesses. "I don't even know how, but I'm not the same person I was when I went to Poland in 1993."

Jane Campion was absent due to illness, but most other honorees were present. British thesp David Thewlis shared the fun he was experiencing while visiting America, particularly noting how much he enjoyed renting a white Mustang convertible. "A lot of British people do that," he insisted.

Ralph Fiennes thanked the winner of Best Cinematography, Polish-born Janusz Kaminski, "for lighting my nose." Kaminski lit up the festivities when he accepted his plaque and exclaimed, "I lost my virginity! This is my first award!"

The National Society of Film Critics announced its winners two and a half weeks after the Gothamites did so and gave *Schindler's List* four awards, thereby tying it with six other pix as the most honored film in the group's history. One of the kudos was Spielberg's first Best Director trophy of the year, which he finally snagged by surpassing Jane Campion, 46 points to 33. *Schindler's List* gave *The Piano* another pounding when it was voted Best Picture, 44 to 36. Its victory marked only the second time that the society agreed with the L.A. and N.Y. crix on the top prize, after previously joining them with kudos for *GoodFellas* in 1990. Ralph Fiennes (29) won Best

> An Altman pic (*Short Cuts*) was the Indie Spirits' big winner again.

Supporting Actor over Leonardo DiCaprio and Tommy Lee Jones (22 each). Its fourth victory was for Best Cinematography.

A grateful Spielberg didn't get the chance to thank society members in person since the group no longer held award ceremonies, but he acknowledged their largesse by sending them a letter: "From the bottom of my heart, and on behalf of thousands of survivors and six million spirits, thank you for bringing honor and attention to *Schindler's List*."

The society agreed with the Gotham circle on Best Actor—David Thewlis (45), who edged out Anthony Hopkins and Daniel Day-Lewis (25 each). Holly Hunter (52) continued her awards sweep by claiming Best Actress over Ashley Judd (28). In the screenplay match-up, Jane Campion (25) persisted undefeated by beating John Guare, who earned 17 points for the screen adaptation of *Six Degrees of Separation*, his Broadway hit about duped New York socialites that had been voted Best Play of 1990 by the New York Drama Critics Circle.

> Sundance honoree *Clerks* was financed on 10 credit cards for $27,575.

The society's only disagreement with previous kudos occurred in the race for Best Supporting Actress, which they decided in favor of Madeleine Stowe as a cheated-upon cop's wife who models nude for a female artist pal in *Short Cuts*. She won a narrow victory, 19 to 18, over Gwyneth Paltrow, "who steals every scene she's in as a bad girl" in *Flesh and Bone*, said *Variety*.

When *GoodFellas* reaped all three crix awards for Best Picture in 1990, it failed to be acknowledged by the National Board of Review. Considering that *Schindler's List* also snagged that prize this year, it thereby pulled off an unprecedented sweep of the four prizes. The accomplishment was particularly noteworthy in light of the fact that it didn't have one advantage enjoyed by its rivals in the award campaigns being mounted by studios and distribs. Spielberg refused to let Universal

Pictures send out videocassettes, insisting that viewers see the pic on a big screen in theaters.

Marketers, however, did not shrink from blitzing kudos voters with tapes of alternative choices as the year's campaigning reached a frenzied pitch. *The New York Times* reported, "Columbia Pictures has taken the lavish extra step of sending to each of the more than 4,500 members of the Academy of Motion Picture Arts and Sciences, via Federal Express, a custom-designed black box filled with video cassettes of nine films. Even by the normal standards of Hollywood excess, the black box startled many." The campaign cost "at least $300,000 (maybe even $400,000)," said the *Times*, and included tapes of *The Remains of the Day, The Age of Innocence, In the Line of Fire*—and even *Groundhog Day*. One Hollywood exec estimated that $4 million was being spent on ballyhoo industrywide.

Just as the kudos race heated up, Los Angeles got shook up by a major quake, which, curiously, didn't seem to distract attention from the next derby leg. The *N.Y. Times* noted, "Five days after a devastating earthquake struck Los Angeles, the folks in Hollywood did exactly what was expected of them: they put on their best clothes and went to an awards party."

Debra Winger and Tim Robbins didn't fly in from New York for the Golden Globes, but most other showbiz luminaries attended, albeit appearing a bit nervous.

"I thought of wearing a hard hat, but it wouldn't go with the clothes," Natasha Richardson told reporters on the red carpet.

Steven Spielberg revealed that he was worried about a new quake causing a blackout and displayed a small flashlight he was carrying "just in case."

"What'll I do if another one hits?" Robin Williams asked. "Stand near a lady who's had a face lift—because it won't fall."

Schindler's List tied *The Piano* for having the most Globe nominations—six—followed by five for *The Remains of the Day*.

Schindler was clearly the front-runner and "the sentimental favorite," said *Variety*, and it ended up with three wins: Best Drama Picture, Best Director and Best Screenplay.

When Spielberg accepted the helmer's prize, *Variety* noted, "It was the first time he has actually won one of Hollywood's major film prizes. In the past, he had been nominated for Globes and Oscars, but never took one home." The paper called his acceptance speech "one of the evening's two emotional high points."

"*Schindler's List* was my proudest moment as a filmmaker," he told the crowd that stood and cheered him. The Holocaust, he added, "is so painful to remember and so easy to forget. Thank God so many of you are remembering. This is dedicated to the survivors."

The night's other emotional high point was the appearance at the podium of Tom Hanks, who was nominated twice—as a recent widower who finds new love in *Sleepless in Seattle* (Best Comedy/Musical Actor) and as a lawyer with AIDS who sues his former law firm for firing him in *Philadelphia* (Best Drama Actor).

So far in his career, Hanks had achieved superstar rank after appearing in such 1980s popcorn hits as *Big* and *Splash*, but when he tried to make a major dramatic debut in *Bonfire of the Vanities* in 1990, the pic bombed. Undaunted, he rolled the dice on Jonathan Demme's *Philadelphia*, which was slated to be the first major studio movie dealing with the mounting AIDS epidemic and the first featuring a sympathetic gay character in a lead role. When it was released, the most shrill gay activists like writer Larry Kramer denounced it as tame, "inaccurate" and even "dishonest," but *Variety* was among the media rallying to its defense, praising Hanks for "a dynamite lead performance that constantly connects on the most basic human level." *Philadelphia* became a surprise hit, grossing $150 million.

The next surprise occurred when Hanks beat Daniel Day-Lewis and Anthony Hop-

The Piano's Holly Hunter won a Globe, Oscar and swept the crix trifecta. Costar Anna Paquin reaped an Oscar and L.A. crix trophy for a pic she was too young to see.

kins for the Best Drama Actor Golden Globe.

"It is odd and surreal for me to stand here and say that I feel lucky," he said solemnly while accepting it. "As a heterosexual man who does not have AIDS, to say I was lucky to play Andrew Beckett, a gay man who suffers from terminal AIDS. To stand here tonight after all we've been through as a city, to stand here today in the midst of all we're going through as a nation, as a people and as a society, in the face of the current holocaust that is taking several hundreds of thousands of lives. However, I have to say that I am a very lucky man."

"Hanks received a standing ovation as he left the stage," *Variety* observed.

Hanks lost his bid for Best Comedy/Musical Actor to Robin Williams, who starred as a divorced man so desperate to be with his estranged kids that he dons a wig and dress to sign on as their British nanny in *Mrs. Doubtfire*. The year's sixth-ranked hit, grossing $110 million, also won the Globe for Best Comedy/Musical Picture.

The ribald joker placed his thesp's statuette between his thighs when he accepted it and told the crowd, "I guess I am happy to be here."

When Angela Bassett was honored as Best Comedy/Musical Actress for portraying singer Tina Turner in *What's Love Got to Do with It*, *Variety* noted that the surprised champ "arrived on stage to whoops and cheers."

Holly Hunter continued her awards juggernaut by being named Best Drama Actress. Backstage, she told the press about her role in *The Piano*, "It's remarkable how much I didn't miss speaking. There's a magic—and a lot of economy in keeping things private."

The biggest upset of the night occurred when Winona Ryder (*The Age of Innocence*) beat Rosie Perez (*Fearless*) and Anna Paquin (*The Piano*) for Best Supporting Actress.

A few weeks later, Spielberg won top honors from the Producers Guild of America, then headed into the directors' guild kudos seemingly invincible against Jane Campion (*The Piano*), Martin Scorsese (*The Age of Innocence*), Andrew Davis (*The Fugitive*) and James Ivory (*The Remains of the Day*). He had received the guild's nod once before, for *The Color Purple* (1985), out of six previous bids and proved to be a champ again.

Accepting his latest accolade, he said, "I had a duty to do this movie as a filmmaker and as a Jew. It was a story that needed to be told."

He confessed to being overwhelmed by *Schindler*'s widespread acclaim and added, "I really thought I was making this film for third- and fourth-grade high school students as an educational film."

Schindler's List next topped the WGA list of contenders for Best Adapted Screenplay. *Variety* reported that scribe Steve Zaillian revealed "he and director Spielberg agreed that the film's imagery had to be horrific in a new way."

"There was a conscious choice to show it from a new perspective, to show things that haven't been seen before," Zaillian said.

Jane Campion picked up the screenplay prize, as expected. While suspense may have been missing from the gala, it turned out that drama was not. *Variety* reported "some technical difficulty" at the L.A. ceremony "when the large quill from the WGA's on-stage sign fell noisily to the floor, surprising presenters Ralph Fiennes and Angela Bassett. Fiennes deadpanned, 'This proves once again that the pen is mightier than the sword.'"

Variety said Tom Hanks (right, with Antonio Banderas) earned "validation as a dramatic actor" in addition to a Globe and Oscar for his daring role as gay man dying of AIDS in *Philadelphia*.

Soon after the Oscar nominations were announced, *Variety* columnist Army Archerd reported, "Spielberg was too nervous to watch the 5:30 ayem unveiling—even though he could not sleep and was wide awake. However, wife Kate went into an adjoining room and turned on the TV. She came back into their bedroom with both arms upright. Steven didn't know if she was just stretching to wake up or—. He was, natch, thrilled."

Schindler reaped 12 bids, just two short of the academy record. *The Piano* and *Remains of the Day* tied for second place (8), followed by *The Fugitive* and *In the Name of the Father* (7 each).

Surprisingly absent from all the top races was *The Age of Innocence*. Scorsese and fellow DGA nominee Andrew Davis (*The Fugitive*) got bumped from the director's race by Robert Altman (*Short Cuts*) and Jim Sheridan (*In the Name of the Father*). Altman, however, suffered the same schizophrenic fate he had endured last year when *The Player* wasn't up for Best Picture. This year *Short Cuts* didn't make the cut.

Also noteworthy: Jane Campion became only the second woman ever nommed for Best Director. The initial breakthrough was achieved by Lina Wertmüller for *Seven Beauties* (1976). An Oscar first occurred when two thesps reaped two noms each in one year: Holly Hunter and Emma Thompson.

On the eve of Oscar night, the *L.A. Times* declared, "The question is not if

Schindler's List will win, but how broad the victory will be."

But Miramax co-chairman and *Piano* producer Harvey Weinstein wasn't willing to concede. "I really sense something in the wind," he told *Variety*. "I predict there will be an upset in one of the two categories, either picture or the director. The race is far from over."

On Oscar night, *Schindler* won the first category it was nommed for—art direction—but its first big challenge lay ahead in the race for Best Supporting Actor.

Pundits were split on who'd win. This year the *L.A. Times* conducted a poll of 25 film pros to determine a "Hollywood Consensus" on all the top races. The results for supporting actor favored L.A. crix and Golden Globe champ Tommy Lee Jones. The *Times*'s own film reviewers, however, disagreed. Two picked Gotham crix and national society honoree Ralph Fiennes, one cited Jones and one backed Pete Postlethwaite, who portrayed Daniel Day-Lewis's dad in *In the Name of the Father*.

When Jones triumphed, he appeared at the podium sporting a shiny dome, having shaved his scalp for his latest role in *Cobb*. "The only thing a man can say at a time like this is 'I am not really bald,'" he said. *Variety* wrote of his victory over Fiennes: "It ended speculation of a sweep for *Schindler's List*."

Schindler had no thesps up for Best Supporting Actress. "This one is almost impossible to handicap," insisted the *L.A. Times*'s Kenneth Turan. "Rosie Perez and Winona Ryder are well liked actresses in not terribly popular films. Little Anna Paquin just might sneak in under the wire." He picked 11-year-old Paquin, bucking the "Hollywood Consensus" that favored Globe champ Ryder. Ryder was also the favorite of most Oscar seers nationwide. When she arrived at the Dorothy Chandler Pavilion, she told the press, "I'm very nauseous and dizzy and totally freaked out."

But it was Paquin who looked freaked out when her name was called as winner, a victory declared "the evening's biggest surprise" by *Variety*. "A clearly stunned Paquin was almost at a loss for words as she stood at

The L.A. and Gotham crix snubbed helmer Steven Spielberg in favor of Jane Campion (*The Piano*), but he received the DGA plaque from last year's champ Clint Eastwood.

the microphone, eventually thanking director Jane Campion and Hunter, among others."

The *L.A. Times* added, "When her speech was over, she clutched the statue to her chest like a treasured doll and broke tradition by running directly offstage to her seat. It was the performance of the evening."

Paquin also headed into the record books as the second-youngest Oscar champ. Although she and Tatum O'Neal were both 9 years old when they filmed their pix, O'Neal was 10 when she won the same prize in 1973 for *Paper Moon*.

Variety added, "Anna Paquin won for a film she hadn't seen yet, and her dad hinted it might be awhile, what with full-frontal Harvey Keitel and all. 'The film's an NC-16 in New Zealand,' said Brian Paquin. 'Let's just leave it at that.'"

Paquin beat her *Piano* costar Holly Hunter, but Hunter was the clear front-runner for Best Actress even though the *L.A. Times* warned that Golden Globe victor Angela Bassett was "a strong sentimental favorite."

But Hunter prevailed, making up for her loss in 1987 for *Broadcast News*. She now joined Sissy Spacek (*Coal Miner's Daughter*), Sally Field *(Norma Rae)*, Meryl Streep

(*Sophie's Choice*), Jack Nicholson (*Terms of Endearment*) and Emma Thompson (*Howards End*) as the only thesps to sweep all of the top film awards in one year.

She thanked her first piano teacher, adding, "And I need to thank my parents for letting me have those lessons."

The Piano claimed a third Oscar when Jane Campion reaped Best Original Screenplay. "I used to feel deeply cynical about award nights like this," she said, "but tonight I'm really overwhelmed. In fact, I've been close to tears several times."

"Steven Zaillian almost can't miss," the *L.A. Times* said of the race for Best Adapted Screenplay. When the *Schindler's List* scribe won, he said, "I owe this to my father, who believed in the thing that destroyed Oskar Schindler as a businessman—common decency."

The star who portrayed Schindler, Liam Neeson, and Daniel Day-Lewis were the only two nominees for Best Actor who seemed to have a chance of beating Globe champ Tom Hanks, who was favored by most forecasters.

Hanks lost his 1988 bid for *Big*, but when he won for *Philadelphia*, *Variety* noted that his victory "validates the star's successful transition from comedic to dramatic actor."

At the podium, he impressed Oscar watchers with a very dramatic acceptance speech in which he thanked "two of the finest gay Americans, two wonderful men, that I had the good fortune to be associated with, to fall under their inspiration at such a young age." One of them was a former classmate who'd died of AIDS, the other was "Mr. Rawley Farnsworth, who was my high school drama teacher, who taught me 'act well the part, there all the glory lies.' I wish my babies could have the same sort of teacher, the same sort of friends."

Prior to giving his speech, Hanks had called his now-retired, 69-year-old teacher to get his permission to mention his homosexuality. Farnsworth, who'd remained closeted all his life, told the press afterward that he was surprised Hanks knew he was gay.

Neeson's loss to Hanks was not an ominous sign for *Schindler*'s chances in the top two races, since the pic had picked up five other Oscars throughout the night. In addition to its laurels for screenplay and art direction, it also garnered honors for cinematography, music score and editing.

Even though Spielberg had lost previous Best Director bids for *Close Encounters of the Third Kind, E.T.* and *Raiders of the Lost Ark*, at last he was the front-runner. The *L.A. Times* said, "Biggest suspense of the night will be to see if Spielberg can come up with a new wrinkle for his acceptance speech."

When he finally won, he said, smiling, "I have never held one of these before!" then added, "This is the biggest drink of water after the longest drought in my life." He dedicated his win to "the six million who can't be watching."

Backstage later, he confessed to reporters that he had reconciled himself to losing, "but also admitted he might have gone home crushed without the statuette," *Variety* said.

But Spielberg also ended up with a second statuette in hand when *Schindler's List* was declared Best Picture, thus becoming the ninth film to win seven Oscars and the first black-and-white movie to claim the top prize since *The Apartment* in 1960.

"Hollywood's eternal little boy finally drew a man's respect," *Variety* announced the next day. "Spielberg, after years of disregard by academy voters, was vindicated. He showed Hollywood's toughest critics he could tackle greater themes than flying saucers and superhero archeologists, that he had a cinematic vision deserving of consideration."

While the Oscar ceremony was being telecast live on ABC, the Bravo cable channel hoped to catch viewers surfing during commercial breaks by airing segments of the Independent Spirit Awards gala held two days earlier. One of the pix competing for the Oscar's Best Director prize was also up for the same honor at the Spirits—*Short Cuts*, Robert Altman's adaptation of 10 Raymond Carver stories presenting "a bemused contemplation of the unaccountable way people behave when fate deals them unexpected hands," said *Variety*.

Short Cuts began the race with four noms—two less than front-runners *Ruby in Paradise* and *The Wedding Banquet*—but prevailed as the biggest winner, claiming three victories. *Short Cuts* was named Best Picture, in addition to reaping the director's palm for Altman and the screenplay award, which Altman shared with Frank Barhydt. Altman, who had also won Best Picture last year for *The Player*, was not on hand to accept his latest homage because he was in Paris shooting *Prêt-à-Porter*.

There was a notable number of other no-shows, too, including Best Actress Ashley Judd (*Ruby in Paradise*), who was away starring in a play. Also missing was Christopher Lloyd, who was hailed as Best Supporting Actor for portraying one of the many people who passes along the same scrap of currency in *Twenty Bucks*. Lili Taylor was not on hand to accept her Best Supporting Actress trophy as a girl obsessed with religion in *Household Saints*.

But Jeff Bridges was present to witness what *Variety* called the "thunderous ovation" he received upon being named Best Actor for portraying a man recently sprung from prison in *American Heart*, which he co-produced.

Variety noted that Robert Rodriguez received the same audience response when he was given the prize for Best First Feature for *El Mariachi*, a Spanish-lingo pic about a mariachi singer mistaken for a fleeing crook, which Rodriguez produced for only $7,000.

Variety reported that the winner seemed overwhelmed by the huzzahs and added, "Citing its flaws and his inexperience, he concluded that creativity, passion and hard work and not 'the wallet' were the vital difference for the films being honored."

Two Spirit champs had previously won kudos at last year's Sundance Film Festival, where *El Mariachi* took the Audience Award and *Ruby in Paradise* garnered the Grand Jury Prize.

This year 32 features and nonfiction works were angling for the accolades. "Surprise was the order of the evening," *Variety* noted when the winners were announced at the awards presentation ceremony.

"Although the voting by the five-member dramatic jury was unanimous, the decision on behalf of *What Happened Was . . .* came as quite a surprise to the crowd shoehorned into the Z Place club," the paper added.

The victor was the handiwork of Tom Noonan, an actor known for playing villains in *Manhunter* and *Last Action Hero*. The *L.A. Times* described *What Happened Was . . .* as "a two character, one-set drama detailing a painfully nervous first date between co-workers in a Manhattan law firm. Compellingly written and acted, it paints an achingly realistic picture of people desperately trying to connect." *What Happened Was . . .* also earned the script award for Noonan, which he could not claim in person because he was in New York appearing in a play. His co-producer, however, assured the crowd, "Tom's going to go nuts!"

"The Audience Award for *Spanking the Monkey* came as even more of a shock," *Variety* declared. Some offended viewers had stormed out of screenings of the dark comedy about a teen's sexually suggestive relationship with his mother, but the pic obviously impressed Hollywood honchos. It locked up a distribution deal with Fine Line just moments before it won the Audience Award as the filmmaker and the distrib exec stood in the back of Z Place while ignoring the order of an usher to take their seats.

The winner of the Filmmaker's Trophy for features also reaped the notice of honchos. *Clerks* told the tale of a New Jersey convenience-store attendant and his pushy pal who mans the video shop next door. The *L.A. Times* declared that its "odyssey from its festival-low $27,575 budget to a distribution deal with Miramax is Sundance's most unlikely success story." Winner Kevin Smith was a store clerk himself, who shot his pic, financed on 10 credit cards, at night when the shop was closed. According to Sundance co-founder Lory Smith, his rep "negotiated a distribution deal over three orders of potato skins at the Eating Establishment across the street from the Egyptian Theatre after the film's final performance." Smith accepted his Sundance accolade saying, "This is a really cool piece of glass!"

and departed the fest the next day to return to his clerk job.

Co-winner in the category, *Fresh*, was also picked up by Miramax. *Variety* described it as "a study of one boy's way out of the New York ghetto's drug environment." Its 13-year-old star was given a Special Recognition Award.

A standout among documentaries was *Hoop Dreams*, which chronicled the lives of two Chicago high-school basketball stars over four and a half years. It not only snagged an Audience Award, but created megawatt buzz throughout the fest—and beyond—when it would later be snubbed for Oscar consideration, triggering a national uproar that helped to turn it into a commercial hit. At the fest, its teary-eyed kudo recipient, Fred Mark, thanked the crowd, saying, "We poured so much of our lives into this film for so long, to see that what came from the bottom of our hearts touched your hearts is very gratifying."

But *Hoop Dreams* triggered a fest uproar when it failed to win the Grand Jury Prize for documentaries. That award went to *Freedom on My Mind*, described by the *L.A. Times* as "a vivid and informative evocation of the Mississippi Voter Registration Project of the early 1960s." *Freedom* would outscore *Hoop Dreams* again by snagging an Oscar nom.

▪ 1993 ▪

LOS ANGELES FILM CRITICS ASSOCIATION

Winners were announced on December 11, 1993. Awards were presented on January 18, 1994, at the Bel Age Hotel in Los Angeles.

BEST PICTURE
▪ *Schindler's List*

BEST DIRECTOR
▪ Jane Campion, *The Piano*

BEST ACTOR
▪ Anthony Hopkins, *Shadowlands, Remains of the Day*

BEST ACTRESS
▪ Holly Hunter, *The Piano*

BEST SUPPORTING ACTOR
▪ Tommy Lee Jones, *The Fugitive*

BEST SUPPORTING ACTRESS (TIE)
▪ Rosie Perez, *Fearless*
▪ Anna Paquin, *The Piano*

BEST SCREENPLAY
▪ Jane Campion, *The Piano*

BEST CINEMATOGRAPHY (TIE)
▪ Janusz Kaminski, *Schindler's List*
▪ Stuart Dryburgh, *The Piano*

BEST PRODUCTION DESIGN
▪ Allan Starski, *Schindler's List*

BEST SCORE
▪ Zbigniew Preisner, *Blue; The Secret Garden; Olivier, Olivier*

BEST ANIMATION
▪ *The Mighty River*, Frederic Back, Douglas Edwards

BEST DOCUMENTARY
▪ *It's All True*, Orson Welles, Myron Meisel, Bill Krohn, Richard Wilson

BEST FOREIGN FILM
▪ *Farewell, My Concubine* (Hong Kong)

BEST EXPERIMENTAL/INDEPENDENT FILM OR VIDEO
▪ *Silverlake Live: The View from Here*, Tom Joslin, Peter Friedman

NEW GENERATION AWARD
▪ Leonardo DiCaprio, *What's Eating Gilbert Grape?*

CAREER ACHIEVEMENT AWARD
▪ John Alton

NATIONAL BOARD OF REVIEW

The board declared a Best Picture and Foreign Film of the year, then listed its remaining favorites according to highest scores. The vote results were announced on December 14, 1993. Awards were presented on February 28, 1994, at the Equitable Center in New York.

BEST PICTURE
- *Schindler's List*
The Age of Innocence
The Remains of the Day
The Piano
Shadowlands
In the Name of the Father
Philadelphia
Much Ado about Nothing
Short Cuts
The Joy Luck Club

BEST DIRECTOR
- Martin Scorsese, *The Age of Innocence*

BEST ACTOR
- Anthony Hopkins, *The Remains of the Day, Shadowlands*

BEST ACTRESS
- Holly Hunter, *The Piano*

BEST SUPPORTING ACTOR
- Leonardo DiCaprio, *What's Eating Gilbert Grape?*

BEST SUPPORTING ACTRESS
- Winona Ryder, *The Age of Innocence*

BEST DOCUMENTARY
- *The War Room*

BEST FOREIGN FILM
- *Farewell, My Concubine* (Hong Kong)
El Mariachi (Mexico)
Un Coeur en Hiver (France)
The Story of Qui Ju (China)
The Accompanist (France)

HONORARY AWARDS
- Sean Connery
- Ruth Prawer Jhabvala
- Robert Rodriguez

NEW YORK FILM CRITICS CIRCLE

Winners were announced on December 15, 1993. Awards were presented on January 16, 1994, at the Pegasus Suite of the Rainbow Room in Rockefeller Center in New York.

BEST PICTURE
- *Schindler's List*

BEST DIRECTOR
- Jane Campion, *The Piano*

BEST ACTOR
- David Thewlis, *Naked*

BEST ACTRESS
- Holly Hunter, *The Piano*

BEST SUPPORTING ACTOR
- Ralph Fiennes, *Schindler's List*

BEST SUPPORTING ACTRESS
- Gong Li, *Farewell, My Concubine*

BEST SCREENPLAY
- Jane Campion, *The Piano*

BEST CINEMATOGRAPHY
- Janusz Kaminski, *Schindler's List*

BEST DOCUMENTARY
- *Visions of Light*

BEST FOREIGN FILM
- *Farewell, My Concubine* (Hong Kong)

NATIONAL SOCIETY OF FILM CRITICS

Winners were announced on January 3, 1994.

BEST PICTURE
- *Schindler's List*

BEST DIRECTOR
- Steven Spielberg, *Schindler's List*

BEST ACTOR
- David Thewlis, *Naked*

BEST ACTRESS
- Holly Hunter, *The Piano*

BEST SUPPORTING ACTOR
- Ralph Fiennes, *Schindler's List*

BEST SUPPORTING ACTRESS
- Madeleine Stowe, *Short Cuts*

BEST SCREENPLAY
- Jane Campion, *The Piano*

BEST CINEMATOGRAPHY
- Janusz Kaminski, *Schindler's List*

BEST DOCUMENTARY
- *Visions of Light*, Arnold Glassman, Todd McCarthy, Stuart Samuels.

BEST FOREIGN-LANGUAGE FILM
- *The Story of Qiu Ju* (China)

SPECIAL CITATION—EXPERIMENTAL FILM
- *Rock Hudson's Home Movies*, Mark Rappaport

SPECIAL CITATION
- *It's All True*, Richard Wilson, Myron Meisel, Bill Krohn, directors; Ed Marx, editor

GOLDEN GLOBES

Nominations were announced on December 22, 1993. Awards were presented on January 22, 1994, at the Beverly Hilton Hotel in Los Angeles. The ceremony was telecast by TBS.

BEST DRAMA PICTURE
- *Schindler's List*
The Age of Innocence
In the Name of the Father
The Piano
The Remains of the Day

BEST COMEDY OR MUSICAL PICTURE
- *Mrs. Doubtfire*
Dave
Much Ado about Nothing
Sleepless in Seattle
Strictly Ballroom

BEST DIRECTOR
- Steven Spielberg, *Schindler's List*
Jane Campion, *The Piano*
Andrew Davis, *The Fugitive*
James Ivory, *The Remains of the Day*
Martin Scorsese, *The Age of Innocence*

BEST ACTOR, DRAMA
- Tom Hanks, *Philadelphia*
Daniel Day-Lewis, *In the Name of the Father*
Harrison Ford, *The Fugitive*
Anthony Hopkins, *The Remains of the Day*
Liam Neeson, *Schindler's List*

BEST ACTRESS, DRAMA
- Holly Hunter, *The Piano*
Juliette Binoche, *Blue*
Michelle Pfeiffer, *The Age of Innocence*
Emma Thompson, *The Remains of the Day*
Debra Winger, *A Dangerous Woman*

BEST ACTOR, COMEDY OR MUSICAL
- Robin Williams, *Mrs. Doubtfire*
Johnny Depp, *Benny and Joon*
Tom Hanks, *Sleepless in Seattle*
Kevin Kline, *Dave*
Colm Meaney, *The Snapper*

BEST ACTRESS, COMEDY OR MUSICAL
- Angela Bassett, *What's Love Got to Do with It*
Stockard Channing, *Six Degrees of Separation*
Anjelica Huston, *Addams Family Values*
Diane Keaton, *Manhattan Murder Mystery*
Meg Ryan, *Sleepless in Seattle*

BEST SUPPORTING ACTOR
- Tommy Lee Jones, *The Fugitive*
Leonardo DiCaprio, *What's Eating Gilbert Grape?*
Ralph Fiennes, *Schindler's List*
John Malkovich, *In the Line of Fire*
Sean Penn, *Carlito's Way*

BEST SUPPORTING ACTRESS

- Winona Ryder, *The Age of Innocence*
- Penelope Ann Miller, *Carlito's Way*
- Anna Paquin, *The Piano*
- Rosie Perez, *Fearless*
- Emma Thompson, *In the Name of the Father*

BEST SCREENPLAY

- Steven Zaillian, *Schindler's List*
- Robert Altman, Frank Barhydt, *Short Cuts*
- Jane Campion, *The Piano*
- Ruth Prawer Jhabvala, *The Remains of the Day*
- Ron Nyswaner, *Philadelphia*

BEST SONG

- "Streets of Philadelphia," *Philadelphia*, Bruce Springsteen
- "Again," *Poetic Justice*, Janet Jackson, James Harris III, Terry Lewis
- "The Day I Fall in Love," *Beethoven's 2nd*, Carol Bayer Sager, James Ingram, Cliff Magness
- "Stay, Faraway," *So Close*, U2/Bono
- "You Made Me the Thief of Your Heart," *In the Name of the Father*, Bono/Friday/Seezer

BEST FOREIGN FILM

- *Farewell, My Concubine* (Hong Kong)
- *Blue* (Poland)
- *Flight of the Innocent* (Italy)
- *Justiz (Justice)* (Germany)
- *The Wedding Banquet* (Taiwan)

Winners

BEST SCORE

- *Heaven and Earth*, Kitaro

CECIL B. DEMILLE AWARD

- Robert Redford

SUNDANCE FILM FESTIVAL

The festival was held January 20–30, 1994, at Park City, Utah.

GRAND JURY PRIZE

(DRAMATIC)
- *What Happened Was . . .* Tom Noonan

(DOCUMENTARY)
- *Freedom on My Mind*, Connie Field, Marilyn Mulford

FILMMAKER'S TROPHY

(DRAMATIC)
- *Clerks*, Kevin Smith
- *Fresh*, Boaz Yakin

(DOCUMENTARY)
- *Theremin: An Electronic Odyssey*, Steven Martin

AUDIENCE AWARD

(DRAMATIC)
- *Spanking the Monkey*, David O. Russell

(DOCUMENTARY)
- *Hoop Dreams*, Steve James

CINEMATOGRAPHY AWARD

(DRAMATIC)
- *Suture*, Greg Gardiner

(DOCUMENTARY)
- *Colorado Cowboy: The Bruce Ford Story*, Morten Sandtroen

FREEDOM OF EXPRESSION AWARD

- *Dialogues with Madwomen*, Allie Light
- *Heart of the Matter*, Gini Reticker, Amber Hollibaugh

SPECIAL JURY RECOGNITION

(TECHNICAL ACHIEVEMENT)
- *Coming Out under Fire*, Arthur Dong

(TECHNICAL ACTING)
- Renee Humphrey, *Fun*
- Sean Nelson, *Fresh*
- Alicia Witt, *Fun*

(SHORTS)
- *Avenue X*, Leslie McCleave
- *Family Remains*, Tamara Jenkins

PRODUCERS GUILD OF AMERICA

Nominations were announced on January 19, 1994. Winners were announced on February 14. Awards were presented on March 2 at the Regent Beverly Wilshire Hotel in Los Angeles.

DARRYL F. ZANUCK PRODUCER OF THE YEAR AWARD

- *Schindler's List*, Steven Spielberg, Branko Lustig, Gerald R. Molen
The Fugitive, Arnold Kopelson
In the Name of the Father, Jim Sheridan
The Piano, Jan Chapman
The Remains of the Day, Mike Nichols, John Calley, Ismail Merchant

CHARLES B. FITZSIMONS LIFETIME HONORARY MEMBERSHIP AWARD

- Robert Finkel

NOVA AWARD

- Jan Chapman, *The Piano*

DAVID O. SELZNICK LIFETIME ACHIEVEMENT AWARD

- Saul Zaentz

DIRECTORS GUILD OF AMERICA

Awards were presented on March 5, 1994, at the Beverly Hilton Hotel in Los Angeles and the Russian Tea Room in New York.

BEST DIRECTOR

- Steven Spielberg, *Schindler's List*
Jane Campion, *The Piano*
Andrew Davis, *The Fugitive*
James Ivory, *The Remains of the Day*
Martin Scorsese, *The Age of Innocence*

ROBERT B. ALDRICH AWARD

- Burt Bluestein

D. W. GRIFFITH AWARD

- Robert Altman

WRITERS GUILD OF AMERICA

Awards were presented on March 13, 1994, at the Beverly Hilton Hotel in Los Angeles and the Tavern on the Green in New York.

BEST ORIGINAL SCREENPLAY

- *The Piano*, Jane Campion
Dave, Gary Ross
In the Line of Fire, Jeff Maguire

Philadelphia, Ron Nyswaner
Sleepless in Seattle, Nora Ephron, David S. Ward, Jeff Arch

BEST ADAPTED SCREENPLAY

- *Schindler's List*, Steven Zaillian, based on the novel by Thomas Keneally
The Fugitive, Jeb Stuart, David Twohy, based on the characters created by Roy Huggins
In the Name of the Father, Terry George, Jim Sheridan, based on the book *Proved Innocent* by Gerry Conlon
The Joy Luck Club, Amy Tan, Ronald Bass, based on the novel by Amy Tan
The Remains of the Day, Ruth Prawer Jhabvala, based on the novel by Kazuo Ishiguro

MORGAN COX AWARD

- Richard Powell

VALENTINE DAVIES AWARD

- Phil Alden Robinson

LAUREL AWARD

- Ruth Prawer Jhabvala

PAUL SELVIN AWARD

- Gary Ross, *Dave*

INDEPENDENT SPIRIT

Nominations were announced on January 16, 1994. Awards were presented on March 19 at the Hollywood Palladium in Hollywood. Portions of the ceremony were broadcast later on Bravo.

BEST FEATURE

- *Short Cuts*
Equinox
Much Ado about Nothing
Ruby in Paradise
The Wedding Banquet

BEST FIRST FEATURE

- *El Mariachi*
American Heart
Combination Platter
Mac
Menace II Society

BEST DIRECTOR
- Robert Altman, *Short Cuts*

Ang Lee, *The Wedding Banquet*
Victor Nunez, *Ruby in Paradise*
Robert Rodriquez, *El Mariachi*
John Turturro, *Mac*

BEST ACTOR
- Jeff Bridges, *American Heart*

Vincent D'Onofrio, *Household Saints*
Mitchell Lichtenstein, *The Wedding Banquet*
Matthew Modine, *Equinox*
Tyrin Turner, *Menace II Society*

BEST ACTRESS
- Ashley Judd, *Ruby in Paradise*

Suzy Amis, *The Ballad of Little Jo*
May Chin, *The Wedding Banquet*
Ariyan Johnson, *Just Another Girl on the I.R.T.*
Emma Thompson, *Much Ado about Nothing*

BEST SUPPORTING ACTOR
- Christopher Lloyd, *Twenty Bucks*

David Chung, *The Ballad of Little Jo*
Tate Donovan, *Inside Monkey Zetterland*
Todd Field, *Ruby in Paradise*
Edward Furlong, *American Heart*

BEST SUPPORTING ACTRESS
- Lili Taylor, *Household Saints*

Lara Flynn Boyle, *Equinox*
Ah-Leh Gua, *The Wedding Banquet*
Lucinda Jenney, *American Heart*
Julianne Moore, *Short Cuts*

BEST SCREENPLAY
- Robert Altman, Frank Barhydt, *Short Cuts*

Edwin Baker, Tony Chan, *Combination Platter*
Ang Lee, Neil Peng, James Schamus, *The Wedding Banquet*
Victor Nunez, *Ruby in Paradise*
Nancy Savoca, Richard Guay, *Household Saints*

BEST FOREIGN FILM
- *The Piano* (Australia/France)

Like Water for Chocolate (Mexico)

Naked (U.K.)
Orlando (U.K.)
The Story of Qui Ju (China)

Winners

BEST CINEMATOGRAPHY
- Lisa Rinzler, *Menace II Society*

FINDIE AWARD
- Robert Shaye

BRIAN GREENBAUM AWARD
- James Schamus, Ted Hope

SPECIAL AWARD
- Sandra Schulberg

ACADEMY AWARDS

Nominations were announced on February 9, 1994. Awards were presented on March 21 at the Dorothy Chandler Pavilion in Los Angeles. The ceremony was telecast by ABC.

BEST PICTURE
- *Schindler's List*

The Fugitive
In the Name of the Father
The Piano
The Remains of the Day

BEST DIRECTOR
- Steven Spielberg, *Schindler's List*

Robert Altman, *Short Cuts*
Jane Campion, *The Piano*
James Ivory, *The Remains of the Day*
Jim Sheridan, *In The Name of the Father*

BEST ACTOR
- Tom Hanks, *Philadelphia*

Daniel Day-Lewis, *In the Name of the Father*
Laurence Fishburne, *What's Love Got to Do with It*
Anthony Hopkins, *The Remains of the Day*
Liam Neeson, *Schindler's List*

BEST ACTRESS
- Holly Hunter, *The Piano*

Angela Bassett, *What's Love Got to Do with It*

Stockard Channing, *Six Degrees of Separation*
Emma Thompson, *The Remains of the Day*
Debra Winger, *Shadowlands*

BEST SUPPORTING ACTOR
- Tommy Lee Jones, *The Fugitive*

Leonardo DiCaprio, *What's Eating Gilbert Grape?*
Ralph Fiennes, *Schindler's List*
John Malkovich, *In the Line of Fire*
Pete Postlethwaite, *In the Name of the Father*

BEST SUPPORTING ACTRESS
- Anna Paquin, *The Piano*

Holly Hunter, *The Firm*
Rosie Perez, *Fearless*
Winona Ryder, *The Age of Innocence*
Emma Thompson, *In the Name of the Father*

BEST ORIGINAL SCREENPLAY
- Jane Campion, *The Piano*

Jeff Arch, Nora Ephron, David S. Ward, *Sleepless in Seattle*
Jeff Maguire, *In the Line of Fire*
Ron Nyswaner, *Philadelphia*
Gary Ross, *Dave*

BEST ADAPTED SCREENPLAY
- Steven Zaillian, *Schindler's List*

Jay Cocks, Martin Scorsese, *The Age of Innocence*
Terry George, Jim Sheridan, *In the Name of the Father*
Ruth Prawer Jhabvala, *The Remains of the Day*
William Nicholson, *Shadowlands*

BEST SONG
- "Philadelphia," *Philadelphia*, Neil Young

"Again," *Poetic Justice*, James Harris III, Janet Jackson, Terry Lewis
"The Day I Fall in Love," *Beethoven's 2nd*, James Ingram, Cliff Magness, Carole Bayer Sager
"Streets of Philadelphia," *Philadelphia*, Bruce Springsteen
"A Wink and a Smile," *Sleepless in Seattle*, Ramsey Mclean, Marc Shaiman

BEST FOREIGN-LANGUAGE FILM
- *Belle Epoque* (Spain)

Farewell, My Concubine (Hong Kong)
Hedd Wyn (U.K.)
The Scent of Green Papaya (Vietnam)
The Wedding Banquet (Taiwan)

Winners

BEST ART DIRECTION
- Allan Starski, Ewa Braun, *Schindler's List*

BEST CINEMATOGRAPHY
- Janusz Kaminski, *Schindler's List*

BEST COSTUME DESIGN
- Gabriella Pescucci, *The Age of Innocence*

BEST DOCUMENTARY
(FEATURE)
- *I Am a Promise: The Children of Stanton Elementary School*, Alan Raymond, Susan Raymond

(SHORT SUBJECT)
- *Defending Our Lives*, Margaret Lazarus, Renner Wunderlich

BEST FILM EDITING
- Michael Kahn, *Schindler's List*

BEST MAKEUP
- Greg Cannom, Ve Neill, Yolanda Toussieng, *Mrs. Doubtfire*

BEST ORIGINAL MUSIC SCORE
- John Williams, *Schindler's List*

SCIENTIFIC OR TECHNICAL AWARDS
(Academy Award of Merit)
- Manfred G. Michelson, Technical Film Systems; Panavision

(Scientific and Engineering Award)
- Fritz Gabriel Bauer, Les Dittert, George Joblove, Mark Leather, Douglas Smythe

(Technical Achievement Award)
- Harry J. Baker, William Blethen, David Degenkolb, Michael Dorrough, David Johnsrud, Wally Mills, Gary Nuzzi, Gustave Parada, Gary Stadler

BEST SHORT FILM

(ANIMATED)
- *The Wrong Trousers*, Nick Park

(LIVE ACTION)
- *Black Rider (Schwarzfahrer)*, Pepe Danquart

BEST SOUND

- Ron Judkins, Shawn Murphy, Gary Rydstrom, Gary Summers, *Jurassic Park*

BEST SOUND EFFECTS EDITING

- Richard Hymns, Gary Rydstrom, *Jurassic Park*

BEST VISUAL EFFECTS

- Michael Lantieri, Dennis Muren, Phil Tippett, Stan Winston, *Jurassic Park*

GORDON E. SAWYER AWARD

- Petro Vlahos

JEAN HERSHOLT HUMANITARIAN AWARD

- Paul Newman

HONORARY AWARD

- Deborah Kerr

SCREEN ACTORS GUILD

LIFETIME ACHIEVEMENT AWARD

- Ricardo Montalban

▪ 1994 ▪

Real Gumption vs. Pulp Fiction

Forrest Gump was like a box of chocolates: full of assorted sweet tales about a simple-minded hero who triumphs over a world gone mad. But critics often prefer their treats gritty and they smacked their lips loudly this year upon discovering the delights in *Pulp Fiction*. When the two pix squared off for the top kudos, the showdown did more than create an unlikely match-up between pix featuring an unflappable good samaritan and two heartless hit men—it was a classic example of the vast divide that sometimes forms between broad-popular and critical tastes.

"In 1994, it seemed, you might have been classified as either a *Forrest Gump* person or a *Pulp Fiction* person," the *L.A. Times* observed, "just as once upon a time you might have been asked whether you were a Beatles person or a Rolling Stones person."

But *Variety* bridged the gap between the samaritan and the contract killers by savoring both of their pix.

Variety called *Forrest Gump* "a technically dazzling film" that's "elegantly made (by director Robert Zemeckis) and winningly acted by Tom Hanks," who takes "a simpleton's charmed odyssey through 30 years of American history," encountering en route three U.S. presidents (Kennedy, Johnson and Nixon) and such stars as John Lennon and Elvis Presley.

Pulp Fiction starred John Travolta and Samuel L. Jackson as a bickering-buddy team of guns-for-hire, who *Variety* said give "superb performances" as they "bump off some kids who didn't play straight with a crime lord." The pic's excessive violence, rapid-fire profanity, overlapping plots and jumbled chronology put off many tradition-

'Pulp' prevails with L.A. crix

By TODD McCARTHY

HOLLYWOOD Quentin Tarantino's audacious crime drama "Pulp Fiction" strutted off with four top awards in voting by the Los Angeles Film Critics Assn. on Dec. 10, copping the prizes for best picture, director, screenplay and actor, John Travolta.

After "Pulp Fiction," the big-

Fine Line release had to be contented with the documentary award.

Along with Landau's, the other nods to "Ed Wood" went to the black-and-white cinematography of Stefan Czapsky and the musical score by Howard **TRAVOLTA**

the Palme d'Or at the Cannes Film Festival in May and went on to a successful domestic commercial run this fall. Along with winning the directing prize, he nabbed the screenplay award for the script he wrote based on stories by him and Roger Avary.

Despite being part of an ensemble cast, Travolta emerged victorious for the acting award for his performance as a small-time hood with eclectic tastes.

"This is really cool!" exclaimed "L.A. boy" Quentin Tarantino when the L.A. crix gave his *Pulp Fiction* four awards. The pic was disqualified at the WGA kudos.

ally minded movie-goers, but *Variety* echoed the critical consensus that the result was "spectacularly entertaining."

America's movie-going public clearly favored *Gump*, which became the fourth-highest-grossing film of all time ($300 million) despite frequent salvos from critics blasting it as saccharine schmaltz. But when *Pulp Fiction*'s Quentin Tarantino pulled off a shocking victory at Cannes and flashed his f-you finger at an outraged member of the audience, critics spotted their own horse and jumped on it.

The Los Angeles Film Critics Association began the year's derby by backing it first—and generously—giving it four awards. The crix hailed it as Best Picture and also gave Tarantino trophies for Best Director and Screenplay, the latter of which he shared with co-writer Roger Avary.

"This is really cool!" Tarantino exclaimed, accepting his bounty at the Bel Age Hotel luncheon. He said that he especially appreciated the L.A. kudos "because I'm an L.A. boy."

The fourth honor went to Best Actor John Travolta, who enjoyed a dramatic career resurrection thanks to *Pulp Fiction*'s widespread acclaim. The honoree confessed to the crix that he became so overjoyed after hearing the news that he won their award that he didn't sleep for three days.

"I was so excited," he said. "It had been so long since I had been honored as an actor on any level that I got confused. . . . It means a lot to me."

The crix org no longer disclosed its voting results, so it was not revealed what placed behind *Pulp Fiction* for Best Picture, but word leaked out about the Best Actor race. "*Cobb* star Tommy Lee Jones got close enough to prove the lead actor category at the Oscars could be a horse race," critic Todd McCarthy reported in *Variety*'s "Dish" column. " 'Dish' hears Jones was actually ahead after the first ballot. *Pulp Fiction* costar Samuel L. Jackson was a shade behind Travolta." The last tally was so close that four recounts had to be taken.

Tommy Lee Jones costarred in the film that won the Best Actress award for Jessica Lange, but the choice was a shocker because *Blue Sky* was a four-year-old work that had been stuck on the shelf during Orion's bankruptcy proceedings. But *Variety* was among the media that praised Lange's showy perf as a flipped-out army wife, saying that the role allowed her "almost unlimited opportunities to emote and strut her stuff, which she does magnificently and with total abandon."

In her acceptance speech, Lange paid tribute to the pic's late director, Tony Richardson, saying, "The plot could go to hell, and it did, but you never felt that he wasn't going to be vitally involved in and in love with his characters."

Variety also praised the winner of Best Supporting Actor, Martin Landau, for giving an "astonishing performance" as Bela Lugosi in *Ed Wood*. At the podium, Landau mused upon the revered *Dracula* star: "He was a morphine addict and an alcoholic at the same time, which is not an easy feat. He had a Hungarian accent, which is hard to

attain—and hard to lose, as witness the Gabor sisters."

Winner of Best Supporting Actress was away filming another movie: Dianne Wiest (*Bullets over Broadway*), who gave, said *The Wall Street Journal*, "an exquisitely flamboyant performance as a *grande dame* of the theater, who overacts just saying 'hello.' "

The National Board of Review couldn't decide between *Forrest Gump* and *Pulp Fiction* for Best Picture, so it gave the prize to both. Tarantino claimed the director's trophy solo, though, and *Gump* got the consolation prizes of Best Actor for Tom Hanks and Best Supporting Actor for Gary Sinise as a crippled Vietnam vet whose life was saved by Hanks.

The board's choice of Best Actress was Miranda Richardson as the haywire wife of poet T. S. Eliot in *Tom and Viv*, which also reaped Best Supporting Actress for Broadway veteran Rosemary Harris as Richardson's mother.

The highlight of the board's awards ceremony at New York's Tavern on the Green was the presentation of the Best Actor plaque to Hanks by David Letterman, who had just signed on to host the next Oscarcast. Letterman paid tribute to the champ as "a very considerate and very decent guy, and many times when he didn't really need to be that way to me or to anybody else. There ought to be a little bit more of that in show business." Letterman got blasted later by *USA Today* for being inconsiderate when he suddenly scooted out after his presentation, missing Hanks's acceptance speech.

A surprisingly strong opposition formed against *Pulp Fiction* when the Gotham crix gathered to vote five days after their L.A. peers and one day after the National Board of Review. *Pulp Fiction* led the race for Best Picture on the first ballot against scattered competition, but then a film that hadn't reaped a single vote on the first polling began to gain momentum. By the fourth

> "In 1994, you were either a *Forrest Gump* person or a *Pulp Fiction* person."

canvass, the two rivals were tied with 26 points each, followed by a surprising third-place entry: *Hoop Dreams* (16 points), the Sundance-honored basketball documentary that was suddenly being touted as a serious Oscar candidate for Best Picture after its distributors pushed the idea as a PR lark. *Hoop Dreams* was dropped on the fifth ballot, when circle rules require the top two vote-getters to face off in a final run-off election.

The winner turned out to be a startling choice: *Quiz Show*, Robert Redford's drama about the TV game show scandals of the 1950s, which had premiered to huge hype but then fared poorly at the b.o. when the pic itself suffered from scandalous accusations that it was historically inaccurate. *Variety* nonetheless applauded it as a "craftily done" work that was "strongly engrossing."

Just prior to the voting for Best Picture, Tarantino had achieved two victories: Best Screenplay over *Quiz Show* (circle records do not recall the score) and Best Director (32 points) over Krzysztof Kieslowski (22), who was nommed for the final installment of his "Three Colors" trilogy, *Red*—the pic that was *supposed* to beat *Pulp Fiction* at Cannes. *Red* took the crix's consolation prize as Best Foreign Film. Redford was not a leading candidate in the helmer's contest.

It was the second year in a row that the director and screenplay laurels didn't go to the Best Picture champ.

John Travolta was not a top contender for Best Actor, but his costar Samuel L. Jackson (26 points) lost the lead race on the third ballot by a mere point to Paul Newman (27), who "delivers one of his most engaging performances in years as the sort of old coot to be found in every small town," said *Variety*. The early leader in the voting was actually Tommy Lee Jones for his brazenly unflattering portrayal of baseball legend Ty Cobb in *Cobb*.

L.A. crix Best Actress Jessica Lange was not in the running at the Gotham vote either. The laurels were snagged by Linda Fiorentino as "a *femme fatale* who uses her beauty and her body to get what she wants without qualms" in *The Last Seduction,* said *Variety*. Her 29-point score eclipsed the 14 points reaped by Jennifer Jason Leigh, whom *Variety* heralded for giving a "striking performance" as tragic quipster Dorothy Parker in *Mrs. Parker and the Vicious Circle*.

But the Gotham crix embraced both of the L.A. crix's choices for the supporting honors. Dianne Wiest beat Uma Thurman as the sultry wife of a crime boss in *Pulp Fiction* by a narrow edge, 34 to 32. There is no surviving record of how Martin Landau scored against runner-up Paul Scofield as the father of the embattled contestant (Ralph Fiennes) in *Quiz Show*.

Robert Redford had lobbied his old *Butch Cassidy and the Sundance Kid* costar Paul Newman to take Scofield's part originally, but when Newman declined in favor of toplining *Nobody's Fool*, the latter made it up to Redford by agreeing to participate in a buddy swap of kudos at the Gotham crix awards gala. Each champ was skedded to present the other with his plaque, which meant that Redford had to leave his Sundance Film Festival two days after it opened.

Newman showed up early and started a betting pool on when his old pal would arrive. When Redford proved to be punctual, Newman groused, "I said he'd get here at 9:30. I lost. It's the second time he's been on time in seven years."

The men shared buddy tales with the audience when they took turns at the podium. "Redford praised Newman's generosity in getting him into *Butch Cassidy,*" *USA Today* reported. "Newman joshed about the time Redford left a wrecked, ribbon-tied Porsche in his driveway, saying, 'It had hit a telephone pole at about 90 miles an hour.' Newman had it compacted, sneaked all 1,900 pounds of it into Redford's house.

> ## *Quiz Show* had no initial votes, but won the Gotham crix's top prize.

But, Newman says: 'To this day, he has never admitted this Porsche was sitting in his vestibule. That's class!' "

When Tarantino accepted his plaque, *USA Today* made a snide observation: "We clocked 'y'know' a possible record seven times in a row." Fiorentino was absent, filming in San Francisco.

"The often idiosyncratic National Society of Film Critics was in uncommon accord with other film critics groups this season," *Variety* reported. "The only previously unanointed achievement cited was Jennifer Jason Leigh." The exception was noteworthy since Leigh portrayed Dorothy Parker, who once reigned as the ferocious queen of the famed literary roundtable at New York's Algonquin Hotel—where society members gather to vote. Thirty-four scribes participated this year out of the group's 42 members.

The only two pix that rivaled champ *Pulp Fiction* (41 points) for Best Picture were *Red* (28) and *Hoop Dreams* (25). *Gump* garnered merely 2 points. Tarantino beat Kieslowski by a close margin for Best Director (46 to 43) and trounced *Quiz Show*'s Paul Attanasio for Best Screenplay (66 to 26). Newman (33) won Best Actor over *Pulp* costars Jackson (26) and Travolta (22). Jackson was also nommed for *Pulp* in the Best Supporting Actor race, losing to Martin Landau, 65 to 36. Best Supporting Actress Dianne Wiest pulled off a huge lead over Uma Thurman, 52 to 21.

Forrest Gump (7 noms) held a slight edge over *Pulp Fiction* (6) when the Golden Globe bids were announced, but it achieved three decisive victories: Best Drama Picture, Best Director (Robert Zemeckis) and Best Drama Actor (Tom Hanks). *Pulp* received only the screenplay accolade for Tarantino and Avary. Since the Globe winners were announced one week after Oscar nomination ballots were mailed, *Variety* declared that *Gump* "seemed to be in an easy sprint toward the upcoming Oscar awards."

Slamdance, a rival fest, debuted during Sundance.

"We were all surprised by this," Hanks told reporters backstage about *Gump*'s romp. "After all, this movie has been out for a long time. I thought people would be tired of all the 'Gumpisms' by now."

Winner of Best Drama Actress, Jessica Lange, also professed to be surprised by being honored for an old pic. "I saw *Blue Sky* a couple of years ago," she said on stage. "I remember parts of it . . . a strange and peculiar little film."

The Lion King ruled the comedy/musical domain, winning Best Picture, Best Score and Best Song ("Can You Feel the Love Tonight"). *Variety* had lauded the jungle cub's coming-of-age tale for being "a dazzling—and unexpectedly daring—addition to the Disney canon."

The match-up for Best Comedy/Musical Actor featured such formidable competish as Terence Stamp as an aging drag performer in *The Adventures of Priscilla: Queen of the Desert* and Jim Carrey, who "exploded on the big screen with the unexpected hit *Ace Ventura: Pet Detective*," said the *L.A. Times*. But the champ turned out to be a foppish new British star, Hugh Grant, whose romantic and comic charms were being widely compared to Hollywood's earlier Grant— Cary.

When he was honored for his role as a persistent, bungling suitor in *Four Weddings and a Funeral,* he offered a classic example of wry British humor, saying, "It's tragic how much I'm enjoying this. Virtually uncool. It's with tremendous ill grace that I grudgingly acknowledge the contributions of a few other people. I *suppose* Mike Newell directed it quite well under difficult circumstances, though with tremendous bad temper." He then thanked "my girlfriend, Elizabeth Hurley, who put up with easily the nastiest, most ill-tempered, prima donna-ish actor in English cinema for six weeks—and then came back to me, which was really nice."

Tarantino displayed typical Yankee moxie when he took the podium to accept his screenplay trophy, saying, "Just as they were announcing (this award), I was, like, God, I hope I don't win and I have to go up there talk! I've just been sitting here getting hammered all night long. Oh, by the way, waiters! More wine at this table here!" Before scooting, he saluted himself and *Pulp*'s actors saying, "I really liked the script I wrote. They took it so far beyond that."

Jamie Lee Curtis won Best Comedy/ Musical Actress for portraying "the buttoned-up, soon-to-be awakened wife" of a secret agent in *True Lies*, said *Variety*. She thanked director James Cameron for "letting me hang from a helicopter on my 35th birthday."

Both Hanks and Lange were nominated for the new Screen Actors Guild Awards, which were telecast live by NBC from Universal Studios. *Variety* declared that the fledging kudocast went off "nearly without a hitch."

The highlight of the show occurred when Tom Hanks won Best Actor, pulled out his SAG card, kissed it and told the audience that he got it for doing the *Bosom Buddies* TV series. Then he pointed to the award statuette and noted that it includes the masks of comedy and tragedy. He added, "Both will make you lose sleep, question your motives, wonder why you are there, wonder why you are doing this in the first place. But if you are crazy enough, you can get one of these—a Screen Actors Guild card."

His speech was so enthusiastically received that it inspired a taped segment, which would be aired during subsequent ceremonies, featuring stars revealing how they got their own cards.

When Martin Landau was named Best Supporting Actor, he also impressed the assembled crowd of thesps with empathy, saying, "I know how tough it is out there, how hard it is to get a job and, after you get the job, to do the job well. A tough, tough life. Peaks and valleys, life and career. This is peak."

A peak of surprise occurred in the Best Actress race when the guild's 78,000 voters endorsed Jodie Foster (*Nell*) over L.A. crix

Dianne Wiest (left, with John Cusack) swept all the top kudos as a theater diva "who overacts just saying 'hello' " in Woody Allen's *Bullets over Broadway*.

honoree and Globe champ Jessica Lange as well as Meryl Streep (*The River Wild*), Meg Ryan (*When a Man Loves a Woman*) and Susan Sarandon (*The Client*). *Nell* had fared poorly at the b.o., but featured Foster in an outsize role as an untamed woman who grew up alone in an isolated backwoods cabin and speaks her own language. Dianne Wiest repeated her earlier victories in the supporting category for *Bullets over Broadway*.

Gump picked up another guild accolade one week later when it was backed by the Producers Guild of America awards, which had so far correctly predicted Oscar's Best Picture four times in the past five years. A first occurred, however, when all five PGA nominees lined up with films nommed by the Directors Guild of America.

At the DGA, front-runner Zemeckis faced off against Tarantino and Redford, in addition to Mike Newell (*Four Weddings and a Funeral*) and Frank Darabont for *The Shawshank Redemption*, a morality tale about prison buddies.

Redford stayed home, citing flu, but the other four rivals were all present when presenter Steven Spielberg announced the winner using words adapted from a line in *Gump*, saying, "I've got a box of chocolates for you, Bob!"

Variety reported the winner's response, "Zemeckis called it 'cosmic' that Spielberg presented the award because he had been the one who had convinced Sid Sheinberg at Universal to entrust $2 million to Zemeckis for *I Wanna Hold Your Hand*, his first feature."

Backstage, Zemeckis told reporters of *Gump*, "I had no idea it was going to become what it has."

Although *Pulp Fiction*'s scribes had won every screenplay prize to date, they weren't nommed by the Writers Guild of America because the pic was produced by a company (Jersey Films) that was not a guild signatory.

As a result, the contest for Best Original Screenplay was wide open, pitting together the scribes of *The Adventures of Priscilla, Queen of the Desert, Bullets over Broadway, Ed Wood, Four Weddings and a Funeral* and *Heavenly Creatures*. Richard Curtis triumphed for *Four Weddings*.

Considering *Gump*'s transguild sweep so far, scenarist Eric Roth pulled off an easy victory over the scribes of *Little Women, The Madness of King George, Quiz Show* and *The Shawshank Redemption*. When it prevailed, *Variety* reported that *Gump* "continued its awards season stampede."

Gump was not nommed at the Independent Spirit Awards, held two days before the Oscars, but other studio-produced pix such as Columbia's *I Like It Like That* did compete against traditional indies as a result of a change in eligibility that sparked controversy.

"The sources for financing for independent films have changed so dramatically," IFP/West topper Dawn Hudson explained in defense of the new rules. "It became really arbitrary." She defined the current criteria for eligibility as "economy of means, percentage of financing from independent sources, uniqueness of vision and original, provocative subject matter."

The latest Spirit contenders spanned productions made for $28,000 to $22 million. The nominees included such Oscar aspirants as *Pulp Fiction* and *Bullets over Broadway* as well as a crop of last year's Sundance awardees, including Grand Jury Prize winner *What Happened Was . . .*, Filmmaker's Trophy recipient *Clerks* and Audience Award champ *Spanking the Monkey*.

"If you are crazy enough, you can get one of these, a Screen Actors Guild card," said Best Actor Tom Hanks (*Forrest Gump*) at the new guild kudos. His speech inspired a segment used at future kudocasts.

The ceremony retained its anti-Oscar attitude, however, when it returned to a tent on the Santa Monica beach after suffering acoustics problems at the Hollywood Palladium last year. Tickets cost $210. Co-host Jodie Foster declared that the goal of the event was to "slag unmercifully those nasty studios!"

Studio-owned indies Miramax and Fine Line reaped the most prizes—eight and three, respectively. Four of the former's went to *Pulp Fiction*: Best Feature, Best Director, Best Screenplay and Best Actor (Samuel L. Jackson). Miramax positioned Jackson for the supporting category at the Oscars and costar Travolta for lead, so when Jackson won the Spirit in the top slot—which did not include costar Travolta—*L.A. Village View* called the win "redemptive."

Spanking the Monkey beat *Clerks* and *I Like It Like That* for Best First Feature and also was rewarded for Best First Screenplay. One of the Sundance fest champs from last year also scored a Spirit: Sean Nelson, who won Best Debut Performance for *Fresh*.

Dianne Wiest won Best Supporting Actress, while the trophy for supporting males went to *Bullets over Broadway* costar Chazz Palminteri as a thug who has the nerve to rewrite a play his gangster boss bankrolled.

Variety noted that the winner of Best Actress, Linda Fiorentino, "gave one of the more suggestive acceptance speeches" when she said that while *The Last Seduction* was a rewarding professional experience, it obviously had done nothing for her personal life considering she "hadn't been laid in three months." She asked if she could exchange her Spirit statuette for a date with presenter Gabriel Byrne.

Although Fiorentino also had been voted Best Actress by the New York Film Critics Circle, she was disqualified from Oscar consideration because her pic had been shown briefly on HBO while its frustrated producers continued their quest for a theatrical distributor.

Also missing from this year's lineup were Globe winners *The Lion King*, Hugh Grant and Jamie Lee Curtis. The ploy to get *Hoop Dreams* nommed for Best Picture flopped, but when the hugely popular docu also failed to make the cut for Best Documentary, the snub caused such an uproar that the academy agreed to reexamine its voting procedures in the future.

Gump, as expected, led with the most nominations (13), joining *Gone With the Wind, From Here to Eternity, Mary Poppins* and *Who's Afraid of Virginia Woolf?* for achieving a tally one shy of *All About Eve*'s record. *Bullets over Broadway, Pulp Fiction* and *The Shawshank Redemption* received seven bids.

DGA contenders Mike Newell (*Four Weddings and a Funeral*) and Frank Darabont (*The Shawshank Redemption*) got bumped from Oscar's director race by the surprising additions of Krzysztof Kieslowski (*Red*) and Woody Allen (*Bullets over Broadway*), but good sport Darabont told *Variety*, "I'm so delighted with seven nominations, there's no room for disappointment in that equation."

"This year's Oscar race can be summed up in six little words: When in doubt, go

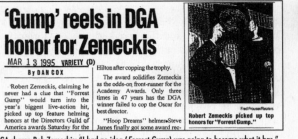

'Gump' reels in DGA honor for Zemeckis

MAR 1 3 1995   VARIETY (D)

By DAN COX

Robert Zemeckis, claiming he never had a clue that "Forrest Gump" would turn into the year's biggest live-action hit, picked up top feature helming honors at the Directors Guild of America awards Saturday for the

Hilton after copping the trophy.

The award solidifies Zemeckis as the odds-on front-runner for the Academy Awards. Only three times in 47 years has the DGA winner failed to cop the Oscar for best director.

"Hoop Dreams" helmer Steve James finally got some award rec-

Fred Prouser/Reuters

Robert Zemeckis picked up top honors for "Forrest Gump."

DGA champ Bob Zemeckis: "I had no idea (*Forrest Gump*) was going to become what it has."

with *Gump*," the *L.A. Times*'s Kenneth Turan declared. The only possible spoiler was not *Pulp Fiction*, he maintained, but *The Shawshank Redemption*: "Greeted with close to indifference by most critics and audiences, this film has nevertheless managed to arouse strong passion in the hearts of the Hollywood Establishment."

Gump's Gary Sinise and *Pulp Fiction*'s Samuel L. Jackson were both nommed in the male supporting race, but *Ed Wood*'s Martin Landau was endorsed by virtually all forecasters—including the contents of a fortune cookie that the star had opened recently in a San Fernando Valley restaurant and carried in his pocket afterward as a good-luck charm. "You will receive some high prize or reward," it promised.

"My God! What a night! What a life! What a moment! What everything!" he roared when he claimed the statuette, adding his thanks to Bela Lugosi, "wherever you are."

Backstage later, Landau confessed to reporters, "The fact that I kept hearing that I was a shoo-in made me nervous because I heard the same thing with *Crimes and Misdemeanors* and *Tucker* and I *did not* go home with the Oscar."

In the Best Supporting Actress race, oddsmakers backed Dianne Wiest even though she competed against *Bullets over Broadway* costar Jennifer Tilly. When Wiest prevailed eight years after winning the same kudo for *Hannah and Her Sisters,* she said, "This is as surprising and marvelous as it was the first time, although this time I need glasses." She pulled out her spectacles and read off a list of thank-yous.

Wiest and Landau were now only the seventh and eighth thesps to sweep the Oscars, the Globes and the crix kudos trifecta (L.A., N.Y. and national society).

The Best Actress match-up appeared to be narrowed down to Globe and L.A. crix champ Jessica Lange and SAG honoree Jodie Foster, with prognosticators split between them. Lange triumphed, saying, "This is such a wonderful honor, especially for a little film that seemed to have no future."

In the Best Actor contest, *Newsday* said "sentiment is on the side of John Travolta, who has miraculously risen from the ashes," but the *L.A. Times* disagreed. Turan noted, "History says that taking this Oscar two years running is quite a feat (only Spencer Tracy managed it, more than half a century ago), but Tom Hanks looks poised to do precisely that. For a while Paul Newman's career-defining work in *Nobody's Fool* seemed a strong contender, but Hanks appears to have outlasted him."

Upon winning, Hanks said, "I'm empowered to stand here thanks to the ensemble of actors who I shared the screen with, who made me a better actor."

Backstage, Hanks told reporters, "I think if I am nominated for anything next year, there will be a collective wave of suicide jumpers from the third tier of the Dorothy Chandler Pavilion. I don't think they'll allow it to happen."

After *Gump* also claimed the prize for Best Adapted Screenplay, Eric Roth told the media an anecdote about how one of its more popular aphorisms came to be: "The book said that being an idiot is no box of chocolates and I changed it to 'life is like a box of chocolates.' Bob Zemeckis said, 'What the hell does that mean?' and I said, 'You never know what you're going to get!' And that's how adaptations are done."

Despite forecasting a sweep for *Gump*, the *L.A. Times* offered hope to a rival in the race for original screenplays. "This is the category where the *Pulp Fiction* crowd will get what they came for," Turan pledged.

He proved right when Tarantino took the stage and acknowledged the *Gump* tide by saying, "I think this is probably the only award I'm going to win here tonight."

Gump also reaped awards for film editing and visual effects in addition to its victories for actor and screenplay. It would bring its total tally to six by claiming—to no one's surprise—the top two, too: Best Picture and Best Director.

When helmer Zemeckis appeared at the podium, *Variety* reported, "He was quick to thank Spielberg, who'd handed him the statuette, calling Spielberg his 'guiding influence.' He also thanked the audiences who 'in historic numbers embraced a film that, at its heart, offered a human, life-affirming story.' "

At this year's Sundance Film Festival, Robert Redford gave the welcoming address, crediting the event with "creating a sense of community" while hosting "a home crowd and a home game," then left the group and his nearby home to head to New York to accept *Quiz Show*'s Best Picture prize at the Gotham crix awards ceremony.

This festival's feature recipient of the Grand Jury Prize "proved a popular choice with the crowd" that Redford left behind, *Variety* noted. The winner was *The Brothers McMullen*, which was shot intermittently on weekends over eight months on a $28,000 budget by newbie filmmaker Edward Burns. Accepting the kudo for his tale of three Irish Catholic siblings who end up as roommates years after childhood, the shocked 26-year-old exclaimed, "This is too good to be true!" and thanked his mother, "who made me watch *Annie Hall*."

The winner of the Grand Jury Prize for documentaries, a category sponsored by Merecedes-Benz, was *Crumb,* director Terry Zwigoff's loopy look at the art and wacky life of illustrator Robert Crumb, which also won a cinematography award.

"I don't get a Mercedes with this, do I?" Zwigoff asked. "I'll take a used one."

Another double champ was *Angela,* which reaped the Filmmaker's Trophy for dramas plus a nod for its cinematographer. The *L.A. Times* called it a "beautifully made docu about a pair of little girls who have trouble separating fantasy from reality."

The recipient of the Filmmaker's Trophy

for docus was *Black Is . . . Black Was*, the last work of Marlon T. Riggs, who'd recently died of AIDS at age 37.

Picture Bride, the tale of a Japanese woman who moves to Hawaii in the early 1900s to marry a man she's never met, won the Audience Award for dramas. The equivalent accolade for docus hailed *Ballot Measure 9*, which chronicled the furor surrounding the 1992 drive to pass an anti-gay ordinance in Oregon. It tied with *Unzipped,* a glib and scathing look at the New York fashion industry as witnessed behind the scenes at an Isaac Mizrahi runway show. *Unzipped* was such a crowd pleaser at the fest that distribution rights were acquired by Miramax, which had previously picked up *Picture Bride*.

Sony Pictures Classics snagged the rights to the winner of the fest's screenwriting award, *Living in Oblivion,* "a dead-on and deft look at the worst day any independent director ever had," said the *L.A. Times*.

Several filmmakers who had their works rejected for fest competition created a concurrent, rival event called Slamdance for "filmmakers who begged for film stock, scoffed at permits, hired undiscovered actors and still owe their parents and friends thousands of dollars," they said.

▪ 1994 ▪

LOS ANGELES FILM CRITICS ASSOCIATION

Winners were announced in December 10, 1994. Awards were presented on January 17, 1995, at the Bel Age Hotel in Los Angeles.

BEST PICTURE
▪ *Pulp Fiction*

BEST DIRECTOR
▪ Quentin Tarantino, *Pulp Fiction*

BEST ACTOR
▪ John Travolta, *Pulp Fiction*

BEST ACTRESS
▪ Jessica Lange, *Blue Sky*

BEST SUPPORTING ACTOR
▪ Martin Landau, *Ed Wood*

BEST SUPPORTING ACTRESS
▪ Dianne Wiest, *Bullets over Broadway*

BEST SCREENPLAY
▪ Quentin Tarantino, Roger Avary, *Pulp Fiction*

BEST CINEMATOGRAPHY
▪ Stefan Czapsky, *Ed Wood*

BEST MUSIC
▪ Howard Shore, *Ed Wood*

BEST PRODUCTION DESIGN
▪ Dennis Gassner, *The Hudsucker Proxy*

BEST ANIMATION
▪ Roger Allers, Rob Minkoff, *The Lion King*

BEST DOCUMENTARY
▪ *Hoop Dreams*, Steve James, Peter Gilbert

BEST FOREIGN FILM
▪ *Red* (Switzerland/Poland/France)

BEST INDEPENDENT/EXPERIMENTAL FILM
▪ *Remembrance of Things Fast*, John Maybury

NEW GENERATION AWARD
▪ John Dahl, *The Last Seduction*

CAREER ACHIEVEMENT AWARD
▪ Billy Wilder

SPECIAL AWARD
▪ Pauline Kael

NATIONAL BOARD OF REVIEW

The board declared a Best Picture and Foreign Film of the year, then listed its remaining favorites according to highest scores. The vote results were announced on December 14, 1994. Awards were presented on February 27, 1995, at the Tavern on the Green in New York.

BEST PICTURE (TIE)
- *Forrest Gump*
- *Pulp Fiction*
Quiz Show
Four Weddings and a Funeral
Bullets over Broadway
Ed Wood
The Shawshank Redemption
Nobody's Fool
The Madness of King George
Tom and Viv
Heavenly Creatures

BEST DIRECTOR
- Quentin Tarantino, *Pulp Fiction*

BEST ACTOR
- Tom Hanks, *Forrest Gump*

BEST ACTRESS
- Miranda Richardson, *Tom and Viv*

BEST SUPPORTING ACTOR
- Gary Sinise, *Forrest Gump*

BEST SUPPORTING ACTRESS
- Rosemary Harris, *Tom and Viv*

BEST ENSEMBLE ACTING
- *Ready to Wear (Prêt-à-Porter)*

BEST FAMILY FILM
- *The Lion King*

BEST FOREIGN FILM
- *Eat Drink Man Woman* (Taiwan)
To Live (Hong Kong/China)
Strawberries and Chocolate (Cuba)
Red (Switzerland/Poland/France)
Queen Margot (France)

CAREER ACHIEVEMENT AWARD
- Sidney Poitier

NEW YORK FILM CRITICS CIRCLE

Winners were announced on December 15, 1994. Awards were presented on January 22, 1995, at the Pegasus Suite of the Rainbow Room in Rockefeller Center in New York.

BEST PICTURE
- *Quiz Show*

BEST DIRECTOR
- Quentin Tarantino, *Pulp Fiction*

BEST NEW DIRECTOR
- Darnell Martin, *I Like It Like That*

BEST ACTOR
- Paul Newman, *Nobody's Fool*

BEST ACTRESS
- Linda Fiorentino, *The Last Seduction*

BEST SUPPORTING ACTOR
- Martin Landau, *Ed Wood*

BEST SUPPORTING ACTRESS
- Dianne Wiest, *Bullets over Broadway*

BEST SCREENPLAY
- Quentin Tarantino, Roger Avary, *Pulp Fiction*

BEST CINEMATOGRAPHY
- Stefan Czapsky, *Ed Wood*

BEST DOCUMENTARY
- *Hoop Dreams*

BEST FOREIGN FILM
- *Red* (Switzerland/Poland/France)

SPECIAL AWARD
- Jean-Luc Goddard

NATIONAL SOCIETY OF FILM CRITICS

Winners were announced on January 3, 1995.

BEST PICTURE
- *Pulp Fiction*

BEST DIRECTOR
- Quentin Tarantino, *Pulp Fiction*

BEST ACTOR
- Paul Newman, *Nobody's Fool*

BEST ACTRESS
- Jennifer Jason Leigh, *Mrs. Parker and the Vicious Circle*

BEST SUPPORTING ACTOR
- Martin Landau, *Ed Wood*

BEST SUPPORTING ACTRESS
- Dianne Wiest, *Bullets over Broadway*

BEST SCREENPLAY
- Quentin Tarantino, Roger Avary, *Pulp Fiction*

BEST CINEMATOGRAPHY
- Stefan Czapsky, *Ed Wood*

BEST DOCUMENTARY
- *Hoop Dreams*, Steve James

BEST FOREIGN-LANGUAGE FILM
- *Red* (Switzerland/Poland/France)

SPECIAL CITATIONS
- *Satantango*, Bela Tarr
- *The Pharaoh's Belt*, Lewis Klahr

GOLDEN GLOBES

Nominations were announced on December 22, 1994. Awards were presented on January 21, 1995, at the Beverly Hilton Hotel in Los Angeles. The ceremony was telecast by TBS.

BEST DRAMA PICTURE
- *Forrest Gump*

Legends of the Fall
Nell
Pulp Fiction
Quiz Show

BEST COMEDY OR MUSICAL PICTURE
- *The Lion King*
The Adventures of Priscilla: Queen of the Desert
Ed Wood
Four Weddings and a Funeral
Ready to Wear (Prêt-à-Porter)

BEST DIRECTOR
- Robert Zemeckis, *Forrest Gump*
Robert Redford, *Quiz Show*
Oliver Stone, *Natural Born Killers*
Quentin Tarantino, *Pulp Fiction*
Edward Zwick, *Legends of the Fall*

BEST ACTOR, DRAMA
- Tom Hanks, *Forrest Gump*
Morgan Freeman, *The Shawshank Redemption*
Paul Newman, *Nobody's Fool*
Brad Pitt, *Legends of the Fall*
John Travolta, *Pulp Fiction*

BEST ACTRESS, DRAMA
- Jessica Lange, *Blue Sky*
Jodie Foster, *Nell*
Jennifer Jason Leigh, *Mrs. Parker and the Vicious Circle*
Miranda Richardson, *Tom and Viv*
Meryl Streep, *The River Wild*

BEST ACTOR, COMEDY OR MUSICAL
- Hugh Grant, *Four Weddings and a Funeral*
Jim Carrey, *The Mask*
Johnny Deep, *Ed Wood*
Arnold Schwarzenegger, *Junior*
Terence Stamp, *The Adventures of Priscilla: Queen of the Desert*

BEST ACTRESS, COMEDY OR MUSICAL
- Jamie Lee Curtis, *True Lies*
Geena Davis, *Speechless*
Andie MacDowell, *Four Weddings and a Funeral*
Shirley MacLaine, *Guarding Tess*
Emma Thompson, *Junior*

BEST SUPPORTING ACTOR

- Martin Landau, *Ed Wood*

Kevin Bacon, *The River Wild*

Samuel L. Jackson, *Pulp Fiction*

Gary Sinise, *Forrest Gump*

John Turturro, *Quiz Show*

BEST SUPPORTING ACTRESS

- Dianne Wiest, *Bullets over Broadway*

Kirsten Dunst, *Interview with the Vampire*

Sophia Loren, *Ready to Wear (Prêt-à-Porter)*

Uma Thurman, *Pulp Fiction*

Robin Wright, *Forrest Gump*

BEST SCREENPLAY

- Quentin Tarantino, Roger Avary, *Pulp Fiction*

Paul Attanasio, *Quiz Show*

Richard Curtis, *Four Weddings and a Funeral*

Frank Darabont, *The Shawshank Redemption*

Eric Roth, *Forrest Gump*

BEST SONG

- "Can You Feel the Love Tonight," *The Lion King*, Elton John, Tim Rice

"Circle of Life," *The Lion King*, Elton John, Tim Rice

"The Color of the Night," *Color of Night*, Jud J. Friedman, Lauren Christy, Dominic Frontiere

"Far Longer Than Forever," *The Swan Princess*, De Azevedo/Zippel

"I'll Remember," *With Honors*, Patrick Leonard, Madonna, Richard Page

"Look What Love Has Done," *Junior*, Carole Bayer Sager, James Ingram, James Newton Howard, Patty Smyth

BEST FOREIGN FILM

- *Farinelli* (Belgium)

Eat Drink Man Woman (Taiwan)

Queen Margot (France)

Red (Switzerland/Poland/France)

To Live (Hong Kong)

Winners

BEST SCORE

- Hans Zimmer, *The Lion King*

CECIL B. DEMILLE AWARD

- Sophia Loren

SUNDANCE FILM FESTIVAL

The festival was held January 19–29, 1995, at Park City, Utah.

GRAND JURY PRIZE
(DRAMATIC)
- *The Brothers McMullen*, Edward Burns

(DOCUMENTARY)
- *Crumb*, Terry Zwigoff

FILMMAKER'S TROPHY
(DRAMATIC)
- *Angela*, Rebecca Miller

(DOCUMENTARY)
- *Black Is . . . Black Was*, Marlon T. Riggs

AUDIENCE AWARD
(DRAMATIC)
- *Picture Bride*, Kayo Hatta

(DOCUMENTARY)
- *Ballot Measure 9*, Heather MacDonald
- *Unzipped*, Douglas Keeve

WALDO SALT SCREENWRITING AWARD
- *Living in Oblivion*, Tom DiCillo

CINEMATOGRAPHY AWARD
(DRAMATIC)
- *Angela*, Ellen Kuras

(DOCUMENTARY)
- *Crumb*, Maryse Alberti

FREEDOM OF EXPRESSION AWARD
- *When Billy Broke His Head . . . and Other Tales of Wonder*, Billy Golfus, David E. Simpson

SPECIAL JURY RECOGNITION
- *Jupiter's Wife*, Michel Negroponte

SPECIAL JURY AWARDS
(DIRECTING)
- Matthew Harrison, *Rhythm Thief*
- James Mangold, *Heavy*

(LATIN CINEMA)
- *Eagles Don't Hunt Flies*, Sergio Cabrera

(SPECIAL MENTION)
- *Strawberry and Chocolate*, Tomas Guitierrez Alea, Juan Carlos Tobio

(SHORT FILMMAKING)
- *The Salesman and Other Adventures*, Hannah Weyer
- *Tom's Flesh*, Jane Wagner, Tom diMaria

(SHORT FILMMAKING HONORABLE MENTION)
- *Nonnie and Alex*, Todd Field
- *Trevor*, Peggy Rajski

SCREEN ACTORS GUILD

Awards were presented on February 25, 1995, at Universal Studios in Los Angeles. The ceremony was telecast by NBC.

BEST ACTOR
- Tom Hanks, *Forrest Gump*

Morgan Freeman, *The Shawshank Redemption*

Paul Newman, *Nobody's Fool*

Tim Robbins, *The Shawshank Redemption*

John Travolta, *Pulp Fiction*

BEST ACTRESS
- Jodie Foster, *Nell*

Jessica Lange, *Blue Sky*

Meg Ryan, *When a Man Loves a Woman*

Susan Sarandon, *The Client*

Meryl Streep, *The River Wild*

BEST SUPPORTING ACTOR
- Martin Landau, *Ed Wood*

Samuel L. Jackson, *Pulp Fiction*

Chazz Palminteri, *Bullets over Broadway*

Gary Sinise, *Forrest Gump*

John Turturro, *Quiz Show*

BEST SUPPORTING ACTRESS
- Dianne Wiest, *Bullets over Broadway*

Jamie Lee Curtis, *True Lies*

Sally Field, *Forrest Gump*

Uma Thurman, *Pulp Fiction*

Robin Wright, *Forrest Gump*

LIFETIME ACHIEVEMENT AWARD
- George Burns

PRODUCERS GUILD OF AMERICA

Nominations were announced on January 26, 1995. Awards were presented on March 8 at the Regent Beverly Wilshire Hotel in Los Angeles.

DARRYL F. ZANUCK PRODUCER OF THE YEAR AWARD
- *Forrest Gump*, Steve Tisch, Steve Starkey, Wendy Finerman, Charles Newirth

Four Weddings and a Funeral, Duncan Kenworthy

Pulp Fiction, Lawrence Bender

Quiz Show, Robert Redford, Michael Jacobs, Julien Krainin, Michael Nozik

The Shawshank Redemption, Niki Marvin

CHARLES B. FITZSIMONS LIFETIME HONORARY MEMBERSHIP AWARD
- Joel Freeman

NOVA AWARD
- Bess O'Brien, Jay Craven, *Where the Rivers Flow North*

DAVID O. SELZNICK LIFETIME ACHIEVEMENT AWARD
- Howard Koch

SPECIAL MERIT AWARD
- Frederick Marx, Steve James, Peter Gilbert, Gordon Quinn, Catherine Allen, *Hoop Dreams*

DIRECTORS GUILD OF AMERICA

Awards were presented on March 11, 1995, at the Beverly Hilton Hotel in Los Angeles.

BEST DIRECTOR
- Robert Zemeckis, *Forrest Gump*

Frank Darabont, *The Shawshank Redemption*

Mike Newell, *Four Weddings and a Funeral*

Robert Redford, *Quiz Show*

Quentin Tarantino, *Pulp Fiction*

ROBERT B. ALDRICH AWARD
- Max A. Schindler

D. W. GRIFFITH AWARD
- James Ivory

WRITERS GUILD OF AMERICA

Awards were presented on March 19, 1995, at the Beverly Hilton Hotel in Los Angeles and the Tavern on the Green in New York.

BEST ORIGINAL SCREENPLAY

- *Four Weddings and a Funeral*, Richard Curtis
The Adventures of Priscilla, Queen of the Desert, Stephen Elliott
Bullets over Broadway, Woody Allen, Douglas McGrath
Ed Wood, Scott Alexander, Larry Karaszewski
Heavenly Creatures, Frances Walsh, Peter Jackson

BEST ADAPTED SCREENPLAY

- *Forrest Gump*, Eric Roth, based on the novel by Winston Groom
Little Women, Robin Swicord, based on the book by Louisa May Alcott
The Madness of King George, Alan Bennett, based on his play
Quiz Show, Paul Attanasio, based on *Remembering America: A Voice from the Sixties* by Richard N. Goodwin
The Shawshank Redemption, Paul Attanasio, based on the novella *Rita Hayworth and the Shawshank Redemption* by Stephen King

MORGAN COX AWARD

- Alfred and Helen Levitt

VALENTINE DAVIES AWARD

- Garry Marshall

IAN MCLELLAN HUNTER AWARD

- Robert Benton

RICHARD B. JABLOW AWARD

- Albert Ruben

LAUREL AWARD

- Charles Bennett

INDEPENDENT SPIRIT

Awards were presented on March 25, 1995, in a tent on the beach in Santa Monica. Portions of the ceremony were telecast by Bravo.

BEST FEATURE

- *Pulp Fiction*
Bullets over Broadway
Eat Drink Man Woman
Mrs. Parker and the Vicious Circle
Wes Craven's New Nightmare

BEST FIRST FEATURE

- *Spanking the Monkey*
Clean, Shaven
Clerks
I Like It Like That
Suture

BEST DIRECTOR

- Quentin Tarantino, *Pulp Fiction*
John Dahl, *Red Rock West*
Ang Lee, *Eat Drink Man Woman*
Roman Polanski, *Death and the Maiden*
Alan Rudolph, *Mrs. Parker and the Vicious Circle*

BEST ACTOR

- Samuel L. Jackson, *Pulp Fiction*
Sihung Lung, *Eat Drink Man Woman*
William H. Macy, *Oleanna*
Campbell Scott, *Mrs. Parker and the Vicious Circle*
Jon Seda, *I Like It Like That*

BEST ACTRESS

- Linda Fiorentino, *The Last Seduction*
Jennifer Jason Leigh, *Mrs. Parker and the Vicious Circle*
Karen Sillas, *What Happened Was . . .*
Lauren Velez, *I Like It Like That*
Chien-Lien Wu, *Eat Drink Man Woman*

BEST SUPPORTING ACTOR

- Chazz Palminteri, *Bullets over Broadway*
Gian Carlo Esposito, *Fresh*
Larry Pine, *Vanya on 42nd Street*
Eric Stoltz, *Pulp Fiction*
Nicholas Turturro, *Federal Hill*

BEST SUPPORTING ACTRESS
- Dianne Wiest, *Bullets over Broadway*

V. S. Brodie, *Go Fish*
Carla Gallo, *Spanking the Monkey*
Kelly Lynch, *The Beans of Egypt Maine*
Brooke Smith, *Vanya on 42nd Street*

BEST DEBUT PERFORMANCE
- Sean Nelson, *Fresh*

Jeff Anderson, *Clerks*
Jeremy Davies, *Spanking the Monkey*
Alicia Witt, *Fun*
Renee Zellweger, *Love and a .45*

BEST SCREENPLAY
- Quentin Tarantino, Roger Avary, *Pulp Fiction*

Woody Allen, Doug McGrath, *Bullets over Broadway*
John Dahl, Rick Dahl, *Red Rock West*
Alan Rudolph, Randy Sue Coburn, *Mrs. Parker and the Vicious Circle*
Hui-Ling Wang, James Schamus, Ang Lee, *Eat Drink Man Woman*

BEST FIRST SCREENPLAY
- David O. Russell, *Spanking the Monkey*

James Bosley, *Fun*
Tom Noonan, *What Happened Was . . .*
Kevin Smith, *Clerks*
Paul Zehrer, *Blessing*

BEST FOREIGN FILM
- *Red* (Switzerland/Poland/France)

Blue Kite (China)
The Boys of St. Vincent (Canada)
Ladybird, Ladybird (U.K.)
Thirty-Two Short Films About Glenn Gould (U.K.)

Winners

BEST CINEMATOGRAPHY
- John Thomas, *Barcelona*

FINDIE AWARD
- Samuel Goldwyn, Jr.

ACADEMY AWARDS

Nominations were announced on February 14, 1995. Awards were presented on March 27 at the Shrine Auditorium in Los Angeles. The ceremony was telecast by ABC.

BEST PICTURE
- *Forrest Gump*

Four Weddings and a Funeral
Pulp Fiction
Quiz Show
The Shawshank Redemption

BEST DIRECTOR
- Robert Zemeckis, *Forrest Gump*

Woody Allen, *Bullets over Broadway*
Krzysztof Kieslowski, *Red*
Robert Redford, *Quiz Show*
Quentin Tarantino, *Pulp Fiction*

BEST ACTOR
- Tom Hanks, *Forrest Gump*

Morgan Freeman, *The Shawshank Redemption*
Nigel Hawthorne, *The Madness of King George*
Paul Newman, *Nobody's Fool*
John Travolta, *Pulp Fiction*

BEST ACTRESS
- Jessica Lange, *Blue Sky*

Jodie Foster, *Nell*
Miranda Richardson, *Tom and Viv*
Winona Ryder, *Little Women*
Susan Sarandon, *The Client*

BEST SUPPORTING ACTOR
- Martin Landau, *Ed Wood*

Samuel L. Jackson, *Pulp Fiction*
Chazz Palminteri, *Bullets over Broadway*
Paul Scofield, *Quiz Show*
Gary Sinise, *Forrest Gump*

BEST SUPPORTING ACTRESS
- Dianne Wiest, *Bullets over Broadway*

Rosemary Harris, *Tom and Viv*
Helen Mirren, *The Madness of King George*
Uma Thurman, *Pulp Fiction*
Jennifer Tilly, *Bullets over Broadway*

BEST ORIGINAL SCREENPLAY
- Quentin Tarantino, Roger Avary, *Pulp Fiction*

Woody Allen, Douglas McGrath, *Bullets over Broadway*

Richard Curtis, *Four Weddings and a Funeral*

Peter Jackson, Frances Walsh, *Heavenly Creatures*

Krzysztof Kieslowski, Krzysztof Piesiewicz, *Red*

BEST ADAPTED SCREENPLAY

- Eric Roth, *Forrest Gump*

Paul Attanasio, *Quiz Show*

Alan Bennett, *The Madness of King George*

Robert Benton, *Nobody's Fool*

Frank Darabont, *The Shawshank Redemption*

BEST SONG

- "Can You Feel the Love Tonight," *The Lion King*, Elton John, Tim Rice

"Circle of Life," *The Lion King*, Elton John, Tim Rice

"Hakuna Matata," *The Lion King*, Elton John, Tim Rice

"Look What Love Has Done," *Junior*, James Newton Howard, James Ingram, Carole Bayer Sager, Patty Smyth

"Make Up Your Mind," *The Paper*, Randy Newman

BEST FOREIGN-LANGUAGE FILM

- *Burnt by the Sun* (Russia)
Before the Rain (Macedonia)
Eat Drink Man Woman (Taiwan)
Farinelli: Il Castrato (Belgium)
Strawberry and Chocolate (Cuba)

Winners

BEST ART DIRECTION

- Ken Adam, Carolyn Scott, *The Madness of King George*

BEST CINEMATOGRAPHY

- John Toll, *Legends of the Fall*

BEST COSTUME DESIGN

- Tim Chappel, Lizzy Gardiner, *The Adventures of Priscilla, Queen of the Desert*

BEST DOCUMENTARY

(FEATURE)

- *Maya Lin: A Strong Clear Vision,* Freida Lee Mock, Terry Sanders

(SHORT SUBJECT)

- *A Time for Justice,* Charles Guggenheim

BEST FILM EDITING

- Arthur Schmidt, *Forrest Gump*

BEST MAKEUP

- Rick Baker, Ve Neill, Yolanda Toussieng, *Ed Wood*

BEST ORIGINAL MUSIC SCORE

- Hans Zimmer, *The Lion King*

SCIENTIFIC OR TECHNICAL AWARDS

(Academy Award of Merit)

- Eastman Kodak, Paul Vlahos, Petro Vlahos

(Scientific and Engineering Award)

- Gary Demos, Dan Cameron, Information International; David DiFrancesco, Gary Starkweather, Pixar; Scott Squires, Lincoln Hu, Michael MacKenzie, Industrial Light and Magic; Ray Feeney, Will McCown, Bill Bishop, RFX; Les Dittert, Pacific Data Images; Glenn Kennel, Mike Davis, Eastman Kodak; Iain Neil, Al Saiki, Panavision International; James Ketcham, JSK Engineering; Paul Bamborough, Arthur Wright, Neil Harris, Duncan MacLean, George Sauve, Bill Bishop, Arpag Dadourian, Ray Feeney, Richard Patterson, William J. Warner, Eric C. Peters, Michael E. Phillips, Tom A. Ohanian, Patrick D. O'Conner, Joe H. Rice

(Technical Achievement Award)

- B. Russell Hessey, Special Effects Spectacular; Vincent T. Kelton, George Jackman, De La Mare Engineering; Emanuel Previnaire, Flying-Cam; Jacques Sax, Sonosax; Clay Davis, John Carter, Todd-AO; Stephen W. Potter, John B. Asman, Charles Pell, Richard Larson, LaTec Systems; Audio Tracks; Colin Broad, CB Electronics; Stephen Greenfield, Chris Huntley, Screenplay Systems; Art Fritzen, California Fritzen

Propeller; Mike Boudry, Computer Film; Mark R. Schneider, Herbert R. Jones, Christopher Conover, John R. B. Brown, Jack C. Smith, Michael Critchon, Emil Safier, Dieter Sturm, David A. Addleman, Lloyd A. Addleman, Frieder Hochheim, Gary Swink, Joe Zhou, Don Northrop

BEST SHORT FILM
(ANIMATED)
- *Bob's Birthday,* David Fine, Alison Snowden

(LIVE ACTION)
- *Franz Kafka's It's a Wonderful Life*, Peter Capaldi, Ruth Kenley-Letts
- *Trevor,* Peggy Rajski, Randy Stone

BEST SOUND
- Bob Beemer, Gregg Landaker, David R. B. Macmillan, Steve Maslow, *Speed*

BEST SOUND EFFECTS EDITING
- Stephen Hunter Flick, *Speed*

BEST VISUAL EFFECTS
- Allen Hall, George Murphy, Ken Ralston, Stephen Rosenbaum, *Forrest Gump*

IRVING G. THALBERG MEMORIAL AWARD
- Clint Eastwood

JEAN HERSHOLT HUMANITARIAN AWARD
- Quincy Jones

HONORARY AWARDS
- Michelangelo Antonioni
- John A. Bonner

▪ 1995 ▪

Leaving Sense *Behind—and Going Hog Wild*

Ironically, an awards derby that would end up making no sense at all—and one thrown into utter chaos by the late-breaking entry of a pic about a plucky pig—started out with a choice called *Sense and Sensibility*.

Sense was the first film named Best Picture when the National Board of Review jumped back into its old position as the first group to unveils its champs after having fallen behind the crafty L.A. crix in the past four years.

Sense and Sensibility—kudosed on its opening day at theaters nationwide—was a surprise choice, since most award watchers believed the board would take a flier on Ron Howard's summer blockbuster about America's ill-starred mission to the moon, *Apollo 13*, which was 1995's third-highest grosser ($92 million). *Sense*'s victory marked the first awards validation for the producers who backed an unlikely team to adapt a Jane Austen novel of manners: Oscar's 1992 Best Actress Emma Thompson (*Howards End*) penning her first screenplay and Ang Lee (*The Wedding Banquet, Eat Drink Man Woman*) directing his first non-Chinese movie. But "both potentially long-shot bets have paid off in spades," *Variety* declared in its review of the drama about two suddenly impoverished sisters in 18th-century England. *Apollo 13* ended up landing in second place on the board's list of the year's top 10 pix.

The board hailed Lee as Best Director and Thompson as Best Actress for two roles: as the sensible sibling in *Sense* and as British painter Dora Carrington in *Carrington*. Its pick for Best Actor was Nicolas Cage, who *Variety* said was in "top form" as a fired Hollywood agent who heads to Nevada's vice mecca to drink himself to death in *Leaving Las Vegas*, a $3.5 million indie funded by the French firm Lumiere

Nicolas Cage (with Elisabeth Shue) won six Best Actor trophies as a drunk with a death wish in *Leaving Las Vegas*, voted best pic by the Indie Spirits plus N.Y. and L.A. crix.

after scores of U.S. studios and production companies turned down the film's director/scribe/underscore composer Mike Figgis.

Just like its Best Actor choice, the board's decisions in the supporting-acting categories would turn out to be prescient once the year's derby was over.

Kevin Spacey had a breakout year reaping huzzahs for roles in four films: as John Doe in serial-killer thriller *Seven*, a mysterious thug who squeals on his cohorts in *The Usual Suspects*, a military medic tracking a deadly virus in *Outbreak* and a sadistic film-studio exec who gets kidnapped by a fed-up minion in *Swimming with Sharks*. The board honored him for *Seven* and *The Usual Suspects*. Best Supporting Actress was Mira Sorvino, who gave "a striking performance as a sweet-tempered hooker who gets a break from an unexpected source" in

Woody Allen's *Mighty Aphrodite*, said *Variety*.

Also of note—and curiously clairvoyant—was a special award bestowed by the board for career achievement to a heartthrob thesp who both starred in, and helmed, a gruesomely realistic battlefield saga about a 13th-century rebel who rallies fellow Scots against the British in *Braveheart*. *Variety* sized it up: "A huge, bloody and sprawling epic, Mel Gibson's second directing effort is the sort of massive vanity piece that would be easy to disparage if it didn't essentially deliver. Gibson's direction meanders at first, but takes hold once the fighting starts." *Braveheart* was ranked ninth on the board's top 10 list.

For the first time in eight years, the New York crix announced their honorees prior to their Left Coast peers. The Gothamites' three-hour voting powwow was especially heated while *Sense and Sensibility* took on challenges from *Leaving Las Vegas* and a surprise rival, Todd Haynes's *Safe*, about an L.A. housewife who suddenly registers allergic reactions to everyday substances. Final Best Picture score: *Leaving Las Vegas* 24 points, *Sense* 21 and *Safe* 17. Best Director outcome: Ang Lee 32 points, Mike Figgis 22 and Todd Haynes 17. Emma Thompson was a sixth-placed also-ran in the race for Best Actress, but she won the screenplay prize for *Sense* (30 points) over Amy Heckerling, who gave a different Jane Austen classic, *Emma*, a loopy, contemporary update in *Clueless* (18).

The actress accolade went to Jennifer Jason Leigh, who "plays a hard-drinking character on a downward slide as the drastically less talented of two singing sisters in *Georgia*," said the *N.Y. Times*. With 45 points, she outscored Elisabeth Shue (28), who *Variety* said did a "skillful" job portraying a hooker who harbors Cage during his final, booze-fueled descent in *Vegas*. Cage pulled off a decisive Best Actor victory (45 to 16) over Anthony Hopkins in the

Thesp Emma Thompson won six kudos for script writing.

title role as the fallen former U.S. president in Oliver Stone's *Nixon*.

Variety cheered Hopkins costar Joan Allen for displaying "surprising dimensionality and often touching humanity" as Richard Nixon's long-suffering wife Pat, but she lost the Best Supporting Actress race to Sorvino when the duo deadlocked with 27 points each and the latter was declared winner because her name appeared on more than half of the ballots (11).

It took three pollings before Kevin Spacey (27 points for all four of his pix) beat Don Cheadle (19) as a detective's quick-trigger sidekick in *Devil in a Blue Dress*.

"The biggest surprise from New York's toughest cineastes came from an endorsement of Chris Noonan's *Babe* as Best First Feature," gasped the *N.Y. Post*.

But the choice was no joke. *Variety* applauded *Babe* as "a dazzling family entertainment with enormous charm and breathtaking technical innovation. The Australia-set tale of a piglet who becomes a championship sheepdog is an unexpectedly enthralling story, relayed from the animals' perspective (and full of) plenty of comic relief."

Chris Noonan did not make the far trek from Down Under to accept his plaque, but a surprising number of winners showed up at the Rainbow Room gala despite a blizzard besieging Manhattan.

"We have the most spectacular view in the city and we can't see a thing!" griped crix chairman John Anderson of *Newsday* as he tried to peer out of the windows 46 stories above Rockefeller Center.

Nicolas Cage received the crix's present of a Best Actor plaque on his 32nd birthday. He accepted it gratefully by saluting the courage the crix showed in giving such generous acknowledgment to a small indie pic that was a risk for all concerned. His agent, he revealed, had urged him strongly not to take the role.

When Mike Figgis accepted the plaque

for Best Picture three weeks after the awards were decided, he noted that his film had since been cited for the same honor by another crix org in addition to receiving a Golden Globe nom for top drama film, but he credited the Gothamites with being the first to hail it in the top tier. He also revealed a special fondness for New York crix because they gave him his first thumbs-up reviews when he began his showbiz career as a performance artist in the 1970s.

"That response from New York gave me the strength to carry on," he insisted.

Jennifer Jason Leigh missed the fete when her flight from North Carolina was rerouted to Boston because of the blizzard. Emma Thompson sent word that she couldn't be present because she was "snowbound somewhere in Scotland."

The L.A. crix put their chips on *Vegas* next, marking only the sixth time in 21 years that they had backed the same Best Picture as their N.Y. colleagues. They also backed it up with twice as many awards, naming Mike Figgis as Best Director over Ang Lee, Nicolas Cage as Best Actor over Anthony Hopkins and Elizabeth Shue as Best Actress over Jennifer Jason Leigh.

The disclosure of runners-up marked a reversal of last year's policy to hush vote results. Award watchers were shocked when they learned what placed behind *Vegas* as Best Picture—*A Little Princess*, a whimsical tale about an orphaned girl that had bombed at the b.o. *Variety* lauded it as "an exquisite, perfectly played serious fantasy that movingly stresses the importance of magic and imagination in the scheme of things."

"The vote was very close," Susan King revealed in the *L.A. Times*. *A Little Princess* also garnered kudos for its music and production design.

The Hollywoodites reversed the order of the Gothamites' choices in the supporting

thesp races, opting for Don Cheadle over Kevin Spacey and Joan Allen over Mira Sorvino. Emma Thompson beat Mike Figgis for the screenplay plaque.

Thompson was the only top winner who wasn't present at the Bel Age Hotel luncheon when the plaques were bestowed one month after the voting. *Variety* reported, "*Vegas* players seemed genuinely thrilled" when they accepted their honors.

"Figgis thanked the scribes for helping push his small, low-budget pic beyond the realm of exclusive runs," *Variety* added. "Cage expressed delight at receiving his award from writers from his hometown, while a very emotional Shue confessed, 'I haven't won an award since seventh grade, for Most Improved Soccer Player—long haul!' "

Joan Allen said, "I hope this award will help dispel the rumor that Oliver Stone is not at his best when directing women."

Don Cheadle addressed *Devil in a Blue Dress* director Carl Franklin in the audience, saying, "I'd go through the fire for you, man—any time, any place, any project!"

Cheadle (34 points) repeated his victory over Kevin Spacey (16) and Joan Allen (55) again topped Mira Sorvino (28) when 17 members of the National Society of Film Critics gathered to vote at the Algonquin Hotel in New York. Twenty-two more crix voted by proxy, but, since their input was limited to first-ballot tallies, all 39 members determined only two races. Nicolas Cage won a commanding Best Actor victory (55 points) on the first polling over Sean Penn (26) as a death row inmate who accepts the friendship of a nun trying to save his soul in *Dead Man Walking*. All crix also chose Best Documentary, which agreed with the same selection made by the N.Y. and L.A. crix: last year's Sundance honoree *Crumb,* a portrait of underground comic artist Robert Crumb, who frequently uses his severely dysfunctional family for inspiration.

Sense and Sensibility was voted Best Picture by the new broadcast crix org.

When the races for top actress and screenplay stretched to second ballots, the 17 crix present chose Elisabeth Shue (47) over Jennifer Jason Leigh (26) and—in a major upset—Amy Heckerling (*Clueless*, 20 points) over André Téchiné, Gilles Taurand and Olivier Massart (*Wild Reeds*, 18 points). The latter vote was interpreted as a gesture by the oft-stodgy society to demonstrate that it has a sense of humor.

But if the screenplay results triggered snickers, the vote results for Best Picture could be said to have elicited squeals from stunned award watchers accustomed to the society embracing such esoteric fare as Akira Kurosawa's *Ran* and Ingmar Bergman's *Persona* and *Shame*.

Variety reported, "In a surprise pick by what some consider the most highbrow of the U.S. critics' groups, the Australian barnyard charmer *Babe* was named Best Picture." In fact, the society went hog-wild over *Babe*, giving it 30 points compared to 18 for *Crumb* and 14 for *Safe. Variety* added, "In an unusual occurrence, *Babe*'s Chris Noonan didn't even figure in the Best Director voting, while *Leaving Las Vegas*' Mike Figgis managed to cop the director prize even though his film didn't land in the top three (for Best Picture). But it was a narrow victory, with Figgis rating 17 points and *Safe*'s Todd Haynes right behind with 16."

This year a new crix group formed that comprised film reviewers working for TV, radio and computer online media—the Broadcast Film Critics Association. Its geographically dispersed 56 members voted via fax on the first ballot, then decided run-off contests by telephone.

Many of the results were eye-poppers, most notably the choice of *Braveheart*'s Mel Gibson as Best Director, followed by Ron Howard (*Apollo 13*) in second place. Although Ang Lee didn't land near the top of the helmer's list, his *Sense and Sensibility* won its first Best Picture prize since the National Board of Review hailed it three weeks earlier.

The new crix org also made a declaration of independence when it unveiled its top thesp winners: Nicolas Cage lost Best Actor to Kevin Bacon, who *Variety* said gave a "very impressive" perf as a convict suffering harsh conditions at Alcatraz in *Murder in the First*. Emma Thompson (*Sense and Sensibility, Carrington*) lost to Nicole Kidman (*To Die For*), who "displays great facility at conveying a winning personality, seductiveness, sincerity and utter ruthlessness as a modern monster who believes that something is important only if it's seen on the tube," said *Variety*.

Thesps with multiple pix tied for Best Supporting Actor. Kevin Spacey was cited for all four of his 1995 roles (*Seven, The Usual Suspect, Outbreak* and *Swimming with Sharks*), while Ed Harris was hailed for three: as a chain-smoking NASA flight director in *Apollo 13*, Watergate conspirator E. Howard Hunt in *Nixon* and a psychotic serial killer in *Just Cause*.

Mira Sorvino beat Joan Allen for Best Supporting Actress, and Emma Thompson reaped the screenplay laurels over Buck Henry (*To Die For*).

The broadcast crix's first awards ceremony was held at the Sofitel Hotel in L.A. Its most touching moment occurred when Mira Sorvino's father, teary-eyed thesp Paul, presented her with the Best Supporting Actress award after telling the crowd that he always knew his daughter was "the dancer, the jazz singer, the athlete . . . , but I never knew that she was funny."

Emma Thompson provided the gala's light-hearted highlight, addressing the crowd, "Dear, dear, dear, dear broadcasting critics: I can't tell you how much I would like to tell you that I did it all, and that I suffered." She acknowledged considerable help from producer Lindsay Doran, but added that she found it "appalling that I have to share the award with her."

"OK, it's a miracle!" said Golden Globe winner Sharon Stone.

Mel Gibson sent a videotaped message offering his thanks from the New York set of *Ransom*. He interrupted himself in mid-sentence to point at helmer Ron Howard, who was busy working in the background, and playfully blamed Howard for not being able to attend the kudofest.

After five years of being broadcast nationally via syndication and eight years on cable channel TBS, the Golden Globes returned to network TV this year for the first time since 1981, when NBC picked up the rights.

The fete promised to be dramatic, since so much suspense loomed over the award outcomes. *Sense and Sensibility* led with the most nominations (six), but in second place was a pic that hadn't been a player so far in the year's kudos derby: *The American President* (five noms), Rob Reiner's "romantic comedy about the dating problems of the world's most powerful man," said *Variety*. Tied with four noms each were *Apollo 13*, *Leaving Las Vegas* and *Braveheart*.

Variety reported on the result: "If anyone needed proof that this year's Oscar race is wide open, the Hollywood Foreign Press Association gave Golden Globes to 12 films and only *Sense and Sensibility* took home more than one award."

Sense's two victories were for Best Drama Picture and Best Screenplay. Emma Thompson amused the crowd by speaking as if she were Jane Austen as she accepted her statuette.

Sense's Ang Lee, however, lost the director's race in a major upset to Mel Gibson, who was cheered loudly by the crowd.

"I'm kind of tongue-tied," he admitted when he arrived at the podium. He then thanked his *Braveheart* colleagues and added as an afterthought, "And, oh, I better thank my wife. Otherwise, I'll have a Golden Globe mark on my head."

Nicolas Cage continued his unbeaten streak in the lead actor's category, but another Globe upset occurred in the Best Drama Actress race when Sharon Stone prevailed for her perf as a hooker-turned-gangster's-wife who helps to topple the Las Vegas mob in Martin Scorsese's *Casino*.

She accepted her trophy, laughing nerv-

The snooty national crix society named a funny best pic—*Babe*, which was later voted best laffer by the Globes.

ously, and said, "No one is more surprised than me. It's...uh...uh...OK, it's a miracle!"

But nothing seemed more miraculous to Globe watchers than the victory scored in the race for Best Comedy or Musical Picture, which included *The American President, Babe*, computer-animated blockbuster *Toy Story* and John Travolta's latest b.o. hit, *Get Shorty*.

The *L.A. Times* reported, "A great roar went up from the audience when *Babe* was selected." One of its producers, Don Miller, arrived on stage wearing a fake pig snout and said, "A lot of people helped bring this little pig to life. Universal said, 'A talking pig? Sure, why not!'"

John Travolta was proclaimed Best Actor in a Comedy or Musical for his widely cheered turn as a Miami loan shark who becomes a Hollywood producer in *Get Shorty*. Still glowing from his recent career resurrection after the success of *Pulp Fiction* last year, he said, thrusting his Globe in the air, "You've given me faith and, at the risk of sounding eliché, look at me!"

Nicole Kidman (*To Die For*) also

addressed her sudden acclaim when she received the Globe for Best Actress in a Comedy or Musical. "I don't feel I've changed," she said, "but my career has changed."

"In something of a surprise, Brad Pitt won Best Supporting Actor for his role as a crazed animal-rights activist in *Twelve Monkeys*," the *L.A. Times* reported. While accepting his Globe for pulling off a jaw-dropper over heavy favorite Kevin Spacey, Pitt mentioned a popular brand treatment for diarrhea, saying, "I'd like to thank the makers of Kaopectate. You know, they've done a great service for their fellow man."

Mira Sorvino mentioned *Mighty Aphrodite* filmmaker Woody Allen when she won Best Supporting Actress as expected, saying, "Woody told me about my character—not only is she cheap, but she's stupid."

The spirit of upsets that existed at the Globes continued through the guild awards that followed. At the Screen Actors Guild, Elisabeth Shue (*Leaving Las Vegas*), Emma Thompson (*Sense and Sensibility*) and Joan Allen (promoted from the supporting category for *Nixon*) were all usurped by a newbie in the Best Actress race: Susan Sarandon as the nun who tries to save Sean Penn's soul in *Dead Man Walking*.

With Joan Allen out of the supporting thesp lineup, Mira Sorvino looked like the clear favorite, but another awards rookie came through: Kate Winslet as Emma Thompson's reckless sister in *Sense and Sensibility*. Kevin Spacey (*The Usual Suspects*) and Don Cheadle (*Devil in a Blue Dress*) lost the matchup for Best Supporting Actor to Ed Harris (*Apollo 13*). *Apollo 13* also reaped the kudo for Best Cast Performance.

The only front-runner who came through was Nicolas Cage as Best Actor.

"I didn't go to college," he said, accepting the honor. "This is my university, and I'm going to consider this award to be my degree."

All three of the helmers who'd won trophies so far—Mike Figgis, Ang Lee and Mel Gibson—scored bids from the Directors Guild of America, which also nomi-

Ron Howard was "surprised and truly overwhelmed" when he won DGA after failing to be nommed for an Oscar.

nated Ron Howard (*Apollo 13*) and, surprisingly, British helmer Michael Radford for his Italian-language art-house hit *The Postman (Il Postino)*, about the friendship between a humble mail carrier and the great poet Pablo Neruda when the latter settles on a quiet Mediterranean island after being exiled from Chile.

The winner was a shocker—Ron Howard—a victory that drew shouts of surprise and a standing ovation.

"I didn't expect this at all," the stunned Howard said, accepting his plaque. "It's a weird business. I am surprised and truly overwhelmed."

Two days later, the Producers Guild of America gave its top prize to *Apollo 13*. Since the NASA space drama had won top prizes at three guild kudos so far, its prospects looked good at the Writers Guild of America. But its scribes—plus those behind *Babe, Leaving Las Vegas* and *Get Shorty*—all lost the race for Best Adapted Screenplay to Emma Thompson for *Sense and Sensibility*. The writers of *Clueless, Mighty Aphrodite, The American President* and *Muriel's Wedding* bowed to *Braveheart*'s Randall Wallace.

Suddenly, award forecasters were left scratching their noggins over what film could possibly be out front for the Best Picture Oscar.

Four different pix had been named Best Picture of the year so far: *Sense and Sensibility* (three times), *Leaving Las Vegas* (twice), *Babe* (twice) and *Apollo 13* (once). Applying past Oscar odds only confused the race further. It could be argued that *Sense and Sensibility* was the fave since, over the past 18 years, Oscar's Best Picture had reflected a Globe choice 15 times (*Babe* was written off this year, since academy voters usually scoff at laffers). *Apollo 13* had reason to be optimistic, too, however, since the PGA had correctly picked the eventual Oscar champ five times in the six years of its award's existence. Films honored by the WGA took Best Picture five times during the past decade, which was good news for *Braveheart* and *Sense and Sensibility*. Usually, the DGA could be counted on for the best omen of all. Since the guild's prize was first bestowed in 1948, its honoree had failed to win the equivalent Academy Award only three times. And the film that takes the helmer's golden boy usually wins Oscar's Best Picture: only five exceptions had occurred during the past 40 years. That meant that Ron Howard and *Apollo 13* were far out front and might be considered shoo-ins.

But then the biggest, most confounding surprise yet occurred when the Oscar bids were unveiled and Ron Howard and Ang Lee weren't nominated.

Making the cut were Mike Figgis (*Leaving Las Vegas*), Mel Gibson (*Braveheart*), Chris Noonan (*Babe*), Michael Radford (*The Postman*) and Tim Robbins (*Dead Man Walking*). *Leaving Las Vegas* and *Dead Man Walking*, however, were left out of the Best Picture lineup, having been bumped by *Apollo 13* and *Sense and Sensibility*.

Missing among the thesp nominees were past crix honorees Don Cheadle, Jennifer Jason Leigh, Nicole Kidman and Kevin Bacon. One contender who did make the list, Susan Sarandon, told *Variety*, "I'm just happy I'm not nominated with any pigs!"

"Surprise! Shock! Horror!" Those were the recurring words that greeted the Oscar announcements," *Variety* reported. *Braveheart* led with 10 noms, followed by *Apollo 13* with 9 and *Sense* and *Babe* with 7.

"The race for the 1995 statuette has been the despair of veteran Oscar watchers," Kenneth Turan sighed in the *L.A. Times* on Oscar morning. "The contest for Best Picture has proven fiendishly difficult to get a handle on. What it's finally come down to is whether the space shot has enough fuel left to hold off a fast-closing pig. *Apollo 13* has been a top contender since the day it came out, (but) there's no counting out the most determined of porkers, *Babe*. Its backers are the most passionate."

Turan and *Times* colleague Kevin Thomas bet on *Apollo 13*, which also got the endorsement of the paper's Hollywood Consensus poll of 50 top industryites.

Turan and Thomas backed *Apollo 13*'s Ed Harris to win Best Supporting Actor, too, although the Hollywood Consensus poll pointed to Kevin Spacey.

On Oscar night, the winner proved to be Spacey, who brought his mother along as his date to the ceremony. When he took the statuette in hand, he addressed her in the audience, saying, "Thank you so much for driving me to acting class on Ventura Boulevard when I was 16. I told you they would pay off, and here's the pudding."

The *Times* called the Best Supporting Actress race "a three-way toss-up" between Joan Allen, Mira Sorvino and Kate Winslet. Turan forecasted Winslet, co-worker Thomas picked Allen and the Hollywood Consensus poll endorsed Sorvino.

When Sorvino won, she became the eighth thesp honored for playing a hooker. She followed Spacey's lead by saluting a parent—her never-nominated dad, who burst into happy tears when he heard her name called.

"When you give me this award, you honor my father, Paul Sorvino, who taught me everything I know about acting," she said.

A sentimental favorite was nommed in the race for Best Actor—veteran thesp Massimo Troisi, who had died 12 hours after *The Postman* finished filming, but the *L.A. Times* insisted, "Nicolas Cage, who has won everything except the New Hampshire primary, is not going to be denied this year."

Turan was right. Soon after he received

his trophy, Cage met reporters backstage, where he discussed the choice he made not to portray his role as the classic, nasty sot. "A lot of alcoholics are very sweet people," he said. "I wanted to focus on the poetic and childlike qualities of being a drunk."

The Best Actress showdown included crix honoree Elisabeth Shue and Globe champ Sharon Stone, but the *Times* noted that they "both have to contend with Susan Sarandon, who is both a performer the academy likes a lot (four noms in the past five years) and someone who has never gone home a winner."

Sarandon received a standing ovation when she finally struck gold. She took the statuette in hand and said, "May all of us find in our hearts a way to nonviolently end violence."

Although past Best Actress victor Emma Thompson (*Howards End*) came out as loser in the current contest, she was heavily favored to become the first person to win Oscars for acting and writing. As predicted, she claimed the prize for Best Adapted Screenplay and said, "I went to visit Jane Austen's grave in Westminster Cathedral to pay my respects and tell her about the grosses. I don't know how she would actually react to an evening like this, but I do hope she knows how big she is in Uruguay."

The *Times* called the match-up over Best Original Screenplay "a two-film race," citing *The Usual Suspects* and *Braveheart* as front-runners. The paper's two pundits sided with *Suspects*, while the Hollywood Consensus poll favored *Braveheart*.

When *Suspects* won, scribe Christopher McQuarrie picked up on the night's earlier parental theme, saying, "Well, dad, I'm in the candy store. It's great!"

As the Oscar race approached the top kudo for Best Picture, suspense peaked since signs indicating a winner still pointed in so many different directions. In the past 20 years, the eventual Best Picture champ had claimed a screenplay award earlier in the night 16 times, but winner *Sense and Sensibility* failed to pick up any other kudos, indicating possible weakness. Therefore, *Apollo 13* and *Braveheart*—with two victories each in the craft categories—still appeared to be in the running and that plucky pig, who yearned to be a sheepdog, still threatened to be a dark horse.

Mel Gibson was heavily favored to become the fifth actor—after Warren Beatty, Clint Eastwood, Robert Redford and Kevin Costner—to win Best Director. The Golden Globe champ came through and revealed at the podium, "Now that I'm a bona-fide director with a golden boy, I suppose, like most directors, what I really want to do is act."

When the last envelope of the night was opened, the contents, said *Variety*, ended up making 1995 a "topsy-turvy year"—*Braveheart*.

The audience gasped and cheered the news.

Backstage, afterward, reporters asked Gibson how he felt about *Braveheart*'s dramatic double top victories. "It's like Oscar squared," he replied. "It's wonderful. I was mildly surprised (about the best pic victory). It was a crapshoot as far as I was concerned, but it just feels good to win."

In the end, *Babe* brought home the bacon, too, winning an Oscar for Best Visual Effects.

While *Leaving Las Vegas* was left out of Oscar's Best Picture race, it led the Independent Spirit competish with six bids. In second place, with five, was *Little Odessa*, a crime drama set in New York's Brighton Beach that had won the Silver Lion at the Venice Film Festival last year. Some of 1994's Sundance champs were in the running, too, including *Living in Oblivion, The Brothers McMullen* and *Picture Bride*. "Most obvious no-show in the noms was Woody Allen's *Mighty Aphrodite*," observed *Variety*.

Vegas swept the kudos with four victories: Best Feature, Director, Actress and Cinematographer. French producer Lila Cazes accepted the top prize by thanking the studios "for passing on the project so that I could produce it."

Director Mike Figgis revealed, "By making the film the way we made it, I threw myself into low-budget hell and turned down the James Bond movie (*Goldeneye*), which seemed like financial suicide at the time."

Variety credited Best Actress Elisabeth Shue with providing "the event's emotional high point" when she saluted a thesp she beat, Jennifer Jason Leigh, saying, "When I got the role, the first thing I watched was *Last Exit to Brooklyn*. That performance made me understand how much my character needed to be loved."

Mare Winningham also thanked Leigh when she won Best Supporting Actress for portraying Leigh's sister, a successful folk-rock singer, in *Georgia*. "You're the reason I'm up here," she said. "You're the heart and soul of *Georgia*."

Best Actor Sean Penn got the fete's top laugh when he addressed the audience with a variation on Sally Field's famous Oscar acceptance speech, saying, "You tolerate me, you really, really tolerate me!"

Best Supporting Actor was Benicio Del Toro, who portrayed one of the suspects accused of trying to hijack a gun-running truck in *The Usual Suspects*. The pic also claimed the screenplay prize, making Christopher McQuarrie the only honoree to win both a Spirit and an Oscar this year.

Although big features dominated the top races, *The Brothers McMullen* snagged the separate award for Best First Feature to add to the Grand Jury Prize it took at Sundance last year. Spirit voters gave their "Someone to Watch" Award to filmmaker Christopher Münch, who had just premiered his tribute to the dying Yosemite Valley Railroad, *Color of a Brisk and Leaping Day*, at Sundance, where it claimed the cinematography prize.

The winner of Sundance's Grand Jury Prize for features this year was *Welcome to the Dollhouse*, which had premiered to raves three months earlier at the Toronto Film Festival and snagged a distribution deal soon afterward. Director/writer Todd Solondz looked shocked when he was honored at Sundance for his dark comedy about an 11-year-old girl surviving the misfortunes of living in suburban New Jersey. He thanked "everyone who helped make something from truly the most unpromising of premises."

Husband-wife team Jeanne Jordan and Steve Ascher reaped both the Grand Jury Prize and Audience Award for documentaries for *Troublesome Creek*, which recorded the struggle of Jordan's family to hold onto their Iowa farm. Her father was with her when she accepted the kudos. "He felt sorry for us when we made this film," she said about him. "He didn't believe anyone would be interested in our story."

Another double champ was *Cutting Loose*, a view of New Orleans Mardi Gras as seen through the eyes of eight participants. It garnered the Filmmaker's Trophy for documentaries and a kudo for cinematography.

The *L.A. Times* described the recipient of the Filmmaker's Trophy for features, *Girls Town*, as "an intense, hard-edged examination of the lives of a trio of high school girls whose lives are wrenched by tragedy."

I Shot Andy Warhol created a sensation at the fest and earned a Special Jury Award for Lili Taylor as the late Valerie Solanas, who severely wounded the eccentric pop artist in 1968. Also recognized with special kudos was *When We Were Kings*, a documentary about Muhammad Ali and George Foreman's 1974 "Rumble in the Jungle" in Zaire that would go on to win an Oscar next year.

A noisy verbal fight broke out at a restaurant on Park City's Main Street when Miramax topper Harvey Weinstein and Pandora Cinema production chief Jonathan Taplin faced off in a late-night shouting match over distribution rights to some of the fest's hits. Weinstein won out by snatching some plums, paying $2.5 million for *Shine*, a film shown out of competition that would end up striking gold at next year's Oscars. He lost a bidding war, however, with Castle Rock, which paid $10 million for the world rights to the winner of the Audience Award, *The Spitfire Grill*, about a woman who tries to start a new life in a small Maine town after getting sprung from jail.

At the fest's awards ceremony, the room buzzed with chatter about all the big deals struck, which Sundance Institute prexy Robert Redford acknowledged by saying,

"We do very simple things to provide entertainment here. We leave it to the snow and to Harvey Weinstein."

Outside was 10 feet of snow that had fallen during three blizzards over the previous 10 days. Janet Maslin of the *N.Y. Times* spotted a thickly bundled filmmaker across the street from the gala that night who was undaunted by the elements, obviously fired by his burning desire to get his pic seen. Maslin noted that he operated "a tiny machine projecting the title of *Outside Looking In*, a 24-minute short (that he) offered to screen anytime, anywhere."

▪ 1995 ▪

NATIONAL BOARD OF REVIEW

The board declared a Best Picture and Foreign Film of the year, then listed its remaining favorites according to highest scores. The vote results were announced on December 13, 1995. Awards were presented on February 26, 1996, at the Tavern on the Green in New York.

BEST PICTURE
▪ *Sense and Sensibility*
Apollo 13
Carrington
Leaving Las Vegas
The American President
Mighty Aphrodite
Smoke
Persuasion
Braveheart
The Usual Suspects

BEST DIRECTOR
▪ Ang Lee, *Sense and Sensibility*

BEST ACTOR
▪ Nicolas Cage, *Leaving Las Vegas*

BEST ACTRESS
▪ Emma Thompson, *Sense and Sensibility, Carrington*

BEST SUPPORTING ACTOR
▪ Kevin Spacey, *Seven, The Usual Suspects*

BEST SUPPORTING ACTRESS
▪ Mira Sorvino, *Mighty Aphrodite*

BEST BREAKTHROUGH PERFORMER
▪ Alicia Silverston, *Clueless*

BEST ENSEMBLE ACTING
▪ *The Usual Suspects*

BEST DOCUMENTARY
▪ *Crumb,* Terry Zwigoff

BEST FOREIGN FILM
▪ *Shanghai Triad* (Hong Kong/ China)
Les Miserables (France)
The Postman (Il Postino) (Italy)
Farinelli (Belgium)
Lamerica (Italy)

FREEDOM OF EXPRESSION AWARD
▪ Zhang Yimou

BILLY WILDER AWARD
▪ Stanley Donen

CAREER ACHIEVEMENT AWARD
▪ Mel Gibson
▪ James Earl Jones

NEW YORK FILM CRITICS CIRCLE

Winners were announced on December 14, 1995. Awards were presented on January 7, 1996, at the Pegasus Suite of the Rainbow Room in Rockefeller Center in New York.

BEST PICTURE
▪ *Leaving Las Vegas*

BEST FIRST FEATURE
▪ *Babe*

BEST DIRECTOR
▪ Ang Lee, *Sense and Sensibility*

BEST ACTOR
- Nicolas Cage, *Leaving Las Vegas*

BEST ACTRESS
- Jennifer Jason Leigh, *Georgia*

BEST SUPPORTING ACTOR
- Kevin Spacey, *Seven, The Usual Suspects, Swimming with Sharks, Outbreak*

BEST SUPPORTING ACTRESS
- Mira Sorvino, *Mighty Aphrodite*

BEST SCREENWRITER
- Emma Thompson, *Sense and Sensibility*

BEST CINEMATOGRAPHER
- Lu Yue, *Shanghai Triad*

BEST DOCUMENTARY
- *Crumb*, Terry Zwigoff

BEST FOREIGN FILM
- *Wild Reeds* (France)

SPECIAL CITATION
- Fabiano Canosa, Joseph Papp Public Theatre film program

LOS ANGELES FILM CRITICS ASSOCIATION

Winners were announced on December 16, 1995. Awards were presented on January 17, 1996, at the Bel Age Hotel in Los Angeles.

BEST PICTURE
- *Leaving Las Vegas*

BEST DIRECTOR
- Mike Figgis, *Leaving Las Vegas*

BEST ACTOR
- Nicolas Cage, *Leaving Las Vegas*

BEST ACTRESS
- Elisabeth Shue, *Leaving Las Vegas*

BEST SUPPORTING ACTOR
- Don Cheadle, *Devil in a Blue Dress*

BEST SUPPORTING ACTRESS
- Joan Allen, *Nixon*

BEST SCREENPLAY
- Emma Thompson, *Sense and Sensibility*

BEST CINEMATOGRAPHY
- Lu Yue, *Shanghai Triad*

BEST MUSIC
- Patrick Doyle, *A Little Princess*

BEST PRODUCTION DESIGN
- Bo Welch, *A Little Princess*

BEST ANIMATION
- John Lasseter, *Toy Story*

BEST DOCUMENTARY
- *Crumb*, Terry Zwigoff

BEST FOREIGN FILM
- *Wild Reeds* (France)

BEST INDEPENDENT/EXPERIMENTAL FILM
- *From the Journals of Jean Seberg*, Mark Rappaport

NEW GENERATION AWARD
- Alfonso Cuaron, *The Little Princess*

CAREER ACHIEVEMENT AWARD
- Andre De Toth

NATIONAL SOCIETY OF FILM CRITICS

Winners were announced on January 3, 1996.

BEST PICTURE
- *Babe*

BEST DIRECTOR
- Mike Figgis, *Leaving Las Vegas*

BEST ACTOR
- Nicolas Cage, *Leaving Las Vegas*

BEST ACTRESS
- Elisabeth Shue, *Leaving Las Vegas*

BEST SUPPORTING ACTOR
- Don Cheadle, *Devil in a Blue Dress*

BEST SUPPORTING ACTRESS
- Joan Allen, *Nixon*

BEST SCREENPLAY
- Amy Heckerling, *Clueless*

BEST CINEMATOGRAPHY
- Tak Fujimoto, *Devil in a Blue Dress*

BEST DOCUMENTARY
- *Crumb,* Terry Zwigoff

BEST FOREIGN-LANGUAGE FILM
- *Wild Reeds* (France)

SPECIAL CITATION
- *Latcho Drom,* Tony Gatlif

SPECIAL ARCHIVAL PRIZE
- *I Am Cuba*, Mikhail Kalatozov

BROADCAST FILM CRITICS ASSOCIATION

Winners were announced on January 7, 1996. Awards were presented on January 22 at the Ma Maison Sofitel in Los Angeles.

BEST PICTURE
- *Sense and Sensibility*

BEST DIRECTOR
- Mel Gibson, *Braveheart*

BEST ACTOR
- Kevin Bacon, *Murder in the First*

BEST ACTRESS
- Nicole Kidman, *To Die For*

BEST SUPPORTING ACTOR (TIE)
- Kevin Spacey, *Swimming with Sharks, The Usual Suspects, Seven, Outbreak*
- Ed Harris, *Apollo 13, Nixon, Just Cause*

BEST SUPPORTING ACTRESS
- Mira Sorvino, *Mighty Aphrodite*

BEST SCREENPLAY
- Emma Thompson, *Sense and Sensibility*

BEST DOCUMENTARY
- *Crumb*, Terry Zwigoff

BEST FOREIGN FILM
- *The Postman (Il Postino)* (Italy)

FAMILY FILM AWARD
- *Babe*

GOLDEN GLOBES

Nominations were announced on December 21, 1995. Awards were presented on January 21, 1996, at the Beverly Hilton Hotel in Los Angeles. The ceremony was telecast by NBC.

BEST DRAMA PICTURE
- *Sense and Sensibility*
Apollo 13
Braveheart
The Bridges of Madison County
Leaving Las Vegas

BEST COMEDY OR MUSICAL PICTURE
- *Babe*
The American President
Get Shorty
Sabrina
Toy Story

BEST DIRECTOR
- Mel Gibson, *Braveheart*
Mike Figgis, *Leaving Las Vegas*
Ron Howard, *Apollo 13*
Ang Lee, *Sense and Sensibility*
Rob Reiner, *The American President*
Martin Scorsese, *Casino*

BEST ACTOR, DRAMA
- Nicolas Cage, *Leaving Las Vegas*
Richard Dreyfuss, *Mr. Holland's Opus*
Anthony Hopkins, *Nixon*
Ian McKellen, *Richard III*
Sean Penn, *Dead Man Walking*

BEST ACTRESS, DRAMA
- Sharon Stone, *Casino*
Susan Sarandon, *Dead Man Walking*
Elisabeth Shue, *Leaving Las Vegas*
Meryl Streep, *The Bridges of Madison County*
Emma Thompson, *Sense and Sensibility*

BEST ACTOR, COMEDY OR MUSICAL
- John Travolta, *Get Shorty*

Michael Douglas, *The American President*

Harrison Ford, *Sabrina*

Steve Martin, *Father of the Bride, Part II*

Patrick Swayze, *To Wong Foo, Thanks for Everything, Julie Newmar*

BEST ACTRESS, COMEDY OR MUSICAL
- Nicole Kidman, *To Die For*

Annette Bening, *The American President*

Sandra Bullock, *While You Were Sleeping*

Toni Collette, *Muriel's Wedding*

Venessa Redgrave, *A Month by the Lake*

BEST SUPPORTING ACTOR
- Brad Pitt, *Twelve Monkeys*

Ed Harris, *Apollo 13*

John Leguizamo, *To Wong Foo, Thanks for Everything, Julie Newmar*

Tim Roth, *Rob Roy*

Kevin Spacey, *The Usual Suspects*

BEST SUPPORTING ACTRESS
- Mira Sorvino, *Mighty Aphrodite*

Anjelica Huston,*The Crossing Guard*

Kyra Sedgwick, *Something to Talk About*

Kathleen Quinlan, *Apollo 13*

Kate Winslet, *Sense and Sensibility*

BEST SCREENPLAY
- Emma Thompson, *Sense and Sensibility*

Patrick Sheane Duncan, *Mr. Holland's Opus*

Scott Frank, *Get Shorty*

Tim Robbins, *Dead Man Walking*

Aaron Sorkin, *The American President*

Randall Wallace, *Braveheart*

BEST SONG
- "Colors of the Wind," *Pocahontas,* Alan Menken, Stephen Schwartz

"Have You Ever Really Loved a Woman?" *Don Juan DeMarco*, Bryan Adams, Michael Kamen, Robert John Lange

"Hold Me, Thrill Me, Kiss Me, Kill Me," *Batman Forever,* U2, Bono

"Moonlight," *Sabrina*, John Williams, Alan Bergman, Marilyn Bergman

"You've Got a Friend in Me," *Toy Story,* Randy Newman

BEST FOREIGN FILM
- *Les Miserables* (France)

Brother of Sleep (Germany)

French Twist (France)

Like Two Crocodiles (Italy)

Shanghai Triad (China)

Winners

BEST SCORE
- Maurice Jarre, *A Walk in the Clouds*

CECIL B. DEMILLE AWARD
- Sean Connery

SUNDANCE FILM FESTIVAL

The festival was held January 18–28, 1996, at Park City, Utah.

GRAND JURY PRIZE
(DRAMATIC)
- *Welcome to the Dollhouse*, Todd Solondz

(DOCUMENTARY)
- *Troublesome Creek*, Jeanne Jordan, Steve Ascher

FILMMAKER'S TROPHY
(DRAMATIC)
- *Girls Town,* Jim McKay

(DOCUMENTARY)
- *Cutting Loose*, Andrew Young, Susan Todd

AUDIENCE AWARD
(DRAMATIC)
- *The Spitfire Grill*, Lee David Zlotoff

(DOCUMENTARY)
- *Troublesome Creek,* Jeanne Jordan, Steve Ascher

WALDO SALT SCREENWRITING AWARD
- *Big Night*, Stanley Tucci, Joseph Tropiano

CINEMATOGRAPHY AWARD
(DRAMATIC)
- *Color of a Brisk and Leaping Day*, Rob Sweeney

(DOCUMENTARY)
- *Cutting Loose,* Andrew Young

FREEDOM OF EXPRESSION AWARD
- *The Celluloid Closet*, Robert Epstein, Jeffrey Friedman

SPECIAL JURY RECOGNITION
- *Girls Town,* Jim McKay
- *When We Were Kings*, David Sonnenberg, Leon Gast

(ACTING)
- Lili Taylor, *I Shot Andy Warhol*

(LATIN CINEMA)
- *Madagascar* (Cuba), Fernando Perez

(LATIN CINEMA HONORABLE MENTION)
- *Guantanamera*, Tomas Gutierrez Alea
- *Wild Horses*, Marcelo Pineyro

(SHORT FILMMAKING)
- *A Small Domain*, Britta Sjogren

(SHORT FILMMAKING HONORABLE MENTION)
- *Dry Mount*, Nichol Simmons
- *Pig*, Francine McDougall

CINEMA 100/SUNDANCE INTERNATIONAL AWARD
- Ciro Cappellari
- Tang Danian
- Chris Eyre
- Walter Salles
- Hirotaka Tashiro

SCREEN ACTORS GUILD

Awards were presented on February 24, 1996, at the Santa Monica Civic Auditorium. The ceremony was telecast by NBC.

BEST ACTOR
- Nicolas Cage, *Leaving Las Vegas*
Anthony Hopkins, *Nixon*
James Earl Jones, *Cry the Beloved Country*
Sean Penn, *Dead Man Walking*
Massimo Troisi, *The Postman (Il Postino)*

BEST ACTRESS
- Susan Sarandon, *Dead Man Walking*
Joan Allen, *Nixon*
Elisabeth Shue, *Leaving Las Vegas*
Meryl Streep, *The Bridges of Madison County*
Emma Thompson, *Sense and Sensibility*

BEST SUPPORTING ACTOR
- Ed Harris, *Apollo 13*
Kevin Bacon, *Murder in the First*

Kenneth Branagh, *Othello*
Don Cheadle, *Devil in a Blue Dress*
Kevin Spacey, *The Usual Suspects*

BEST SUPPORTING ACTRESS
- Kate Winslet, *Sense and Sensibility*
Stockard Channing, *Smoke*
Anjelica Huston, *The Crossing Guard*
Mira Sorvino, *Mighty Aphrodite*
Mare Winningham, *Georgia*

BEST CAST PERFORMANCE
- *Apollo 13*
Get Shorty
How to Make an American Quilt
Nixon
Sense and Sensibility

LIFETIME ACHIEVEMENT AWARD
- Robert Redford

DIRECTORS GUILD OF AMERICA

Awards were presented on March 2, 1996, at the Century Plaza Hotel in Los Angeles and the Russian Tea Room in New York.

BEST DIRECTOR
- Ron Howard, *Apollo 13*
Mike Figgis, *Leaving Las Vegas*
Mel Gibson, *Braveheart*
Ang Lee, *Sense and Sensibility*
Michael Radford, *The Postman (Il Postino)*

ROBERT B. ALDRICH AWARD
- Daniel Petrie

D. W. GRIFFITH AWARD
- Woody Allen

HONORARY LIFETIME MEMBERSHIP
- Chuck Jones

PRODUCERS GUILD OF AMERICA

Nominations were announced on January 18, 1996. Winners were announced on March 4. Awards were presented on March 6 at the Regent Beverly Wilshire Hotel in Los Angeles.

DARRYL F. ZANUCK PRODUCER OF THE YEAR AWARD

- *Apollo 13,* Brian Grazer, Todd Hallowell
The American President, Rob Reiner, Jeffrey Scott, Charles Newirth
The Bridges of Madison County, Clint Eastwood, Kathleen Kennedy
Dead Man Walking, Tim Robbins, John Kilik, Tim Bevan, Eric Fellner
Leaving Las Vegas, Lila Cazes, Annie Stewart, Stuart Reagen, Paige Simpson
The Postman (Il Postino), Mario Cecchi Gori, Vittorio Cecchi Gori, Gaetano Daniele, Albert Passone
Sense and Sensibility, Lindsay Doran, James Schamus, Sydney Pollack

CHARLES B. FITZSIMONS LIFETIME HONORARY MEMBERSHIP AWARD

- Robert B. Radnitz

NOVA AWARD

- Ed Burns, Dick Fisher, *The Brothers McMullen*

DAVID O. SELZNICK LIFETIME ACHIEVEMENT AWARD

- Walter Mirisch

SPECIAL AWARD

- Bonnie Arnold, Ralph Guggenheim, *Toy Story*

WRITERS GUILD OF AMERICA

Awards were presented on March 17, 1996, at the Beverly Hilton Hotel in Los Angeles and the Tavern on the Green in New York.

BEST ORIGINAL SCREENPLAY

- *Braveheart,* Randall Wallace
The American President, Aaron Sorkin
Clueless, Amy Heckerling
Mighty Aphrodite, Woody Allen
Muriel's Wedding, P. J. Hogan

BEST ADAPTED SCREENPLAY

- *Sense and Sensibility,* Emma Thompson, based on the novel by Jane Austen
Apollo 13, Al Reinert, William Broyles, Jr., based on *Lost Moon* by Jim Lovell, Jeffrey Kluger

Babe, George Miller, Chris Noonan, based on *The Pig Sheep* by Dick King-Smith
Get Shorty, Scott Frank, based on the novel by Elmore Leonard
Leaving Las Vegas, Mike Figgis, based on the novel by John O'Brien

MORGAN COX AWARD

- Mort Thaw

VALENTINE DAVIES AWARD

- Mike Farrell

LAUREL AWARD

- Daniel Taradash

INDEPENDENT SPIRIT

Nominations were announced on January 11, 1996. Awards were presented on March 23 in a tent on the beach in Santa Monica. Portions of the ceremony were telecast by Bravo.

BEST FEATURE

- *Leaving Las Vegas*
The Addiction
Living in Oblivion
Safe
The Secret of Roan Inish

BEST FIRST FEATURE

- *The Brothers McMullen*
Kids
Little Odessa
Picture Bride
River of Grass

BEST DIRECTOR

- Mike Figgis, *Leaving Las Vegas*
Michael Almereyda, *Nadja*
Ulu Grosbard, *Georgia*
Todd Haynes, *Safe*
John Sayles, *The Secret of Roan Inish*

BEST ACTOR

- Sean Penn, *Dead Man Walking*
Nicolas Cage, *Leaving Las Vegas*
Tim Roth, *Little Odessa*
Jimmy Smits, *My Family*
Kevin Spacey, *Swimming with Sharks*

BEST ACTRESS

- Elisabeth Shue, *Leaving Las Vegas*
Jennifer Jason Leigh, *Georgia*
Elina Lowensohn, *Nadja*
Julianne Moore, *Safe*
Lili Taylor, *The Addiction*

BEST SUPPORTING ACTOR

- Benicio Del Toro, *The Usual Suspects*
James Le Gros, *Living in Oblivion*
David Morse, *The Crossing Guard*
Max Perlich, *Georgia*
Harold Perrineau, *Smoke*

BEST SUPPORTING ACTRESS

- Mare Winningham, *Georgia*
Jennifer Lopez, *My Family*
Vanessa Redgrave, *Little Odessa*
Chloë Sevigny, *Kids*
Celia Weston, *Dead Man Walking*

BEST DEBUT PERFORMANCE

- Justin Pierce, *Kids*
Jason Andrews, *Rhythm Thief*
Lisa Bowman, *River of Grass*
Gabriel Casseus, *New Jersey Drive*
Rose McGowan, *The Doom
    Generation*

BEST SCREENPLAY

- Christopher McQuarrie, *The Usual
    Suspects*
Tom DiCillo, *Living in Oblivion*
Mike Figgis, *Leaving Las Vegas*
Todd Haynes, *Safe*
John Sayles, *The Secret of Roan Inish*

BEST FIRST SCREENPLAY

- Paul Auster, *Smoke*
Harmoney Korine, *Kids*
James Gray, *Little Odessa*
Steve McLean, *Postcards from America*
Kelly Reichardt, *River of Grass*

BEST FOREIGN FILM

- *Before the Rain* (Macedonia/U.K./France)
The City of Lost Children
    (France/Spain/Germany)
Exotica (Canada)
I Am Cuba (Russia/Cuba)
Through the Olive Trees (Iran)

"SOMEONE TO WATCH" AWARD

- Christopher Münch
Tim McCann
Jennifer Montgomery
Kelly Reichardt
Rafael Zelinsky

Winners

BEST CINEMATOGRAPHY

- Declan Quinn, *Leaving Las Vegas*

FINDIE AWARD

- Sony Pictures Classics

ACADEMY AWARDS

Nominations were announced on February 13, 1996. Awards were presented on March 25 at the Dorothy Chandler Pavilion in Los Angeles. The ceremony was telecast by ABC.

BEST PICTURE

- *Braveheart*
Apollo 13
Babe
The Postman (Il Postino)
Sense and Sensibility

BEST DIRECTOR

- Mel Gibson, *Braveheart*
Mike Figgis, *Leaving Las Vegas*
Chris Noonan, *Babe*
Michael Radford, *The Postman (Il Postino)*
Tim Robbins, *Dead Man Walking*

BEST ACTOR

- Nicolas Cage, *Leaving Las Vegas*
Richard Dreyfuss, *Mr. Holland's Opus*
Anthony Hopkins, *Nixon*
Sean Penn, *Dead Man Walking*
Massimo Troisi, *The Postman (Il Postino)*

BEST ACTRESS

- Susan Sarandon, *Dead Man Walking*
Elisabeth Shue, *Leaving Las Vegas*
Sharon Stone, *Casino*
Meryl Streep, *The Bridges of Madison
    County*
Emma Thompson, *Sense and Sensibility*

BEST SUPPORTING ACTOR

- Kevin Spacey, *The Usual Suspects*
James Cromwell, *Babe*
Ed Harris, *Apollo 13*
Brad Pitt, *Twelve Monkeys*
Tim Roth, *Rob Roy*

BEST SUPPORTING ACTRESS

- Mira Sorvino, *Mighty Aphrodite*
Joan Allen, *Nixon*
Kathleen Quinlan, *Apollo 13*
Mare Winningham, *Georgia*
Kate Winslet, *Sense and Sensibility*

BEST ORIGINAL SCREENPLAY

- Christopher McQuarrie, *The Usual Suspects*
Woody Allen, *Mighty Aphrodite*
Joel Cohen, Peter Docter, John Lasseter, Joe Ranft, Alec Sokolow, Andrew Stanton, Joss Whedon, *Toy Story*
Stephen J. Rivele, Oliver Stone, Christopher Wilkinson, *Nixon*
Randall Wallace, *Braveheart*

BEST ADAPTED SCREENPLAY

- Emma Thompson, *Sense and Sensibility*
William Broyles, Jr., Al Reinert, *Apollo 13*
Mike Figgis, *Leaving Las Vegas*
George Miller, Chris Noonan, *Babe*
Anna Pavignano, Michael Radford, Furio Scarpelli, Giacomo Scarpelli, Massimo Troisi, *The Postman (Il Postino)*

BEST SONG

- "Colors of the Wind," *Pocahontas*, Alan Menken, Stephen Schwartz
"Dead Man Walkin'," *Dead Man Walking*, Bruce Springsteen
"Have You Ever Really Loved a Woman," *Don Juan DeMarco*, Bryan Adams, Michael Kamen, Robert John Lange
"Moonlight," *Sabrina,* Alan Bergman, Marilyn Bergman, John Williams
"You've Got a Friend in Me," *Toy Story*, Randy Newman

BEST FOREIGN-LANGUAGE FILM

- *Antonia's Line* (Netherlands)
All Things Fair (Sweden)
Dust of Life (Algeria)
O Quatrilho (Brazil)
The Star Maker (Italy)

Winners

BEST ART DIRECTION

- Eugenio Zanetti, *Restoration*

BEST CINEMATOGRAPHY

- John Toll, *Braveheart*

BEST COSTUME DESIGN

- James Acheson, *Restoration*

BEST DOCUMENTARY

(FEATURE)
- *Anne Frank Remembered,* Jon Blair
(SHORT SUBJECT)
- *One Survivor Remembers*, Kary Antholis

BEST FILM EDITING

- Dan Hanley, Mike Hill, *Apollo 13*

BEST MAKEUP

- Lois Burwell, Peter Frampton, Paul Pattison, *Braveheart*

BEST MUSIC

(ORIGINAL DRAMATIC SCORE)
- Luis Enrique Bacalov, *The Postman (Il Postino)*
(ORIGINAL MUSICAL OR COMEDY SCORE)
- Alan Menken, Stephen Schwartz, *Pocahontas*

SCIENTIFIC OR TECHNICAL AWARDS

(Scientific and Engineering Award) [Camera]
- Digital Theater Systems; Dolby Laboratories; Sony; Colin Mossman, Joe Wary, Hans Leisinger, Gerald Painter, Deluxe Laboratories; David Gilmartin, Johannes Borggrebe, Jean-Pierre Gagnon, Frank Ricotta, Technicolor, Inc.; Ronald Goodman, Attila Szalay, Steven Sass, Spacecam Systems; Iain Neil, Rick Gelbard, Eric Dubberke, Panavision; Arnold and Richter Cine Technik, Alvy Ray Smith, Ed Catmull, Thomas Porter, Tom Duff, Martin Mueller, Howard Flemming, Ronald Uhlig
(Technical Achievement Award) [Sound]
- Al Jensen, Chuck Headley, Jean Messner, Hazem Nabulsi, CEI Technology; Peter Denz, Prazisions-Entwicklung Denz;

Gary Demos, David Ruhoff, Dan Cameron, Douglas Smythe, Lincoln Hu, Douglas S. Kay, Industrial Light and Magic; Institut National Polytechnique de Toulouse; Kodak Pathe CTP Cine; Eclair Laboratories; Martineau Industries; BHP; James Deas, Warner Bros.; Clay Davis, John Carter, Todd-AO; Computer Film Co.; Pascal Chedeville, Joe Finnegan; David Pringle, Yan Zhong Fang

BEST SHORT FILM
(ANIMATED)
- *A Close Shave,* Nick Park

(LIVE ACTION)
- *Lieberman in Love,* Christine Lahti, Jana Sue Memel

BEST SOUND
- Rick Dior, David Macmillan, Scott Millan, Steve Pederson, *Apollo 13*

BEST SOUND EFFECTS EDITING
- John Leveque, Bruce Stambler, *Batman Forever*

BEST VISUAL EFFECTS
- Scott E. Anderson, John Cox, Charles Gibson, Neal Scanlan, *Babe*

SPECIAL ACHIEVEMENT AWARD
- John Lasseter, *Toy Story*

GORDON E. SAWYER AWARD
- Donald C. Rogers

HONORARY AWARDS
- Kirk Douglas
- Chuck Jones

· 1996 ·

Independents' Year

Somebody should've called the kudos cops. It sure looked as if the early American award groups—apparently frustrated by a lack of worthy studio releases—had stolen their list of honorees from the Cannes Film Festival. Three of the pix taking top fest prizes would end up being named Best Picture stateside.

Cannes's Best Director accolade had been bestowed in May upon Joel Coen for *Fargo*, a quirky drama based on a 1987 case of kidnapping gone awry. *Variety* said *Fargo* rendered proper respect for crime-telling conventions at the same time "pushing them to an almost surrealistic extreme" in a pic that was also "very funny stuff." When the National Board of Review became the first Yankee kudos org to sound off, it hailed Coen as top helmer, too, and gave its Best Actress trophy to a standout in the *Fargo* cast—Frances McDormand as a pregnant sheriff who remains unflaggingly perky while facing down savage killers.

The board swiped a hit from another film fest, though, when choosing Best Picture—*Shine*, which had blazed so brilliantly at Sundance when it was shown out of competition last year that Miramax paid $2.5 million for the distrib rights after a heated bidding war broke out. *Shine* was based on the real-life story of Australian piano prodigy David Helfgott, who triumphed over madness to regain his former notoriety as a concert performer. Its star, Geoffrey Rush, would become the year's most-kudosed thesp for portraying the stammering, befuddled Helfgott, but the board opted for Tom Cruise as Best Actor instead. *Variety* said Cruise scored "one of his very best roles" in *Jerry Maguire* as a slick sports rep who quits his ruthless agency in order to pursue "his own Quixotic effort to be true to himself and stay in the game at the same time" while turning freelance. En route, he

Indie pix dominated the kudos, including *The English Patient* (voted tops by the Oscars, Globes and producers' guild) starring Ralph Fiennes and Kristin Scott Thomas.

falls in love with his awe-struck assistant, portrayed by Renee Zellweger, who was named the board's Breakthrough Performer.

Edward Norton was cited as Best Supporting Actor for his roles in three pix: as a dual-personality altar boy accused of butchering a bishop in *Primal Fear*, a smitten groom-to-be in *Everyone Says I Love You* and a lawyer defending the publisher of *Hustler* magazine in *The People vs. Larry Flynt*.

A tie was declared in the race for Best Supporting Actress between two costars of *The English Patient*: Juliette Binoche as a nurse who tends to a mysterious man burnt badly in a plane crash, and Kristin Scott Thomas as the dying lover he left behind before the plane went down.

"Gollee! I didn't know it was going to be this big!" Zellweger gasped when she arrived at New York's Tavern on the Green for the board's awards presentation.

Frances McDormand also seemed overwhelmed by the glitzy fete, confessing, "I'm not a glamour girl. I'm a funky girl."

The highlight of the bash was the acceptance speech of Edward Norton, who said, "This time two years ago, I tried to get a job waiting on tables at Tavern on the Green. I was turned down as talentless."

The New York Film Critics Circle announced its winners two days after the board. Voting records do not reflect the scores of contending pix, but they do reveal that the battle over Best Picture was heated. It took four ballots before *Fargo* finally prevailed as Best Picture. *The People vs. Larry Flynt* came in second place, followed by the Grand Prize winner at Cannes: *Breaking the Waves,* "a soaring story of love and devotion set in a remote, backward coastal village in north Scotland in the '70s," said *Variety. Waves* rebounded from the loss to snag the director's laurels for Lars Von Trier over past winner Jane Campion, who was now up for her adaptation of the Henry James classic *The Portrait of a Lady*, starring Nicole Kidman. *Waves* also won Best Actress for screen newcomer Emily Watson, whom *Variety* called "a major find, who gives an extraordinary performance . . . as a woman who talks to God and sleeps with other men at the behest of her paralyzed husband." Runner-up was Frances McDormand.

Geoffrey Rush was named Best Actor over Daniel Day-Lewis as a farmer who inadvertently triggers a witch hunt when he ends an illicit affair in *The Crucible*.

One of the victors in the supporting-thesp races was *Kansas City* star Harry Belafonte, "who invests his role as a slick gangster with a harsh toughness never before seen from the actor," said *Variety*. He topped Martin Donovan as Kidman's tubercular confidant in *The Portrait of a Lady*.

There was a surprising choice for the femme laurels—rock star Courtney Love, who *Variety* said "delivers an impulsive, nakedly emotional, quicksilver turn" as Flynt's drug-addled floozy wife in *The People vs. Larry Flynt*. She beat Barbara Hershey, who portrayed a grand lady who mentors the young Nicole Kidman in *The Portrait of a Lady*. Circle records don't disclose who placed behind the winner of Best Screenplay, which was claimed by Albert

Cannes and L.A. crix champ *Secrets and Lies* starred Cannes, Globe and L.A. crix Best Actress Brenda Blethyn (right) as a white British mum who discovers her long-lost daughter is black (Marianne Jean-Baptiste).

Brooks and Monica Johnson for their black comedy about a nagging parent, *Mother,* starring Debbie Reynolds in her first screen perf in 27 years.

Last year's screenplay champ at Sundance was declared Best First Feature: *Big Night,* which starred director/co-writer Stanley Tucci as one of two Italian immigrant brothers who face impossible odds while trying to open a restaurant.

Most of the winners gathered at the Rainbow Room restaurant in New York to receive their plaques. Courtney Love arrived with sometime boyfriend Edward Norton in tow in addition to an entourage that included director Oliver Stone. Stone was in a playful mood, at one point telling a bystander that Love was a hooker he met on the street, but he suddenly turned serious as he commandeered the podium to bestow her award. "Cherish this moment later when there are no awards," he told her somberly.

The *N.Y. Post* reported that the comment "raised more than a few eyebrows," but Love deflected the admonition jovially.

"Oliver! It's not so tragic!" she said. "I know you don't think I'm an actress!"

The *Post* said that "the best line of the evening came from actor/director Campbell Scott, who picked up an award with Stanley Tucci for their debut project *Big Night*. Said Scott, son of actor George C. Scott and the late Colleen Dewhurst, 'I grew up in a household where a nine-course meal was a carton of Virginia Slims.' "

Geoffrey Rush wasn't present, but he faxed his acceptance speech from Australia, where he was working on his next movie. It was read by *Shine* costar Lynn Redgrave, who shared a bawdy story about filming a scene in which Rush hops on a trampoline while wearing nothing but a Walkman and an open raincoat. Earlier, he had plucked flowers from the nearby garden and decorated his "glorious Australian crown jewels with every sort of bluebell and hyacinth," she said.

The *N.Y. Post* made a snide comment when reviewing the list of the circle's honorees, predicting that "a number of the films won't be setting any box office records in the near future." The reason: all of them, except for *Mother* and *The People vs. Larry Flynt,* were independent pix.

The pattern was repeated when the L.A. crix powwowed two days after the Gothamites, thereby marking the third year that both crix orgs gave high honors to indies.

But the L.A. crix embraced a different indie than the Gothamites this year and one totally ignored by them—*Secrets and Lies,* winner of the Palme d'Or at Cannes. "Mike Leigh's first film in three years has all the feel of a career-summarizing work," *Variety* cheered in its review of the tale of a professional black woman (Marianne Jean-Baptiste) who goes in search of her birth mother, who turns out to be a frumpy, working-class white woman (Cannes Best Actress Brenda Blethyn). Leigh and Blethyn won kudos as Best Director and Actress, too, beating out the helmer and star of *Fargo*, which also placed for Best Picture. *Fargo*, however, reaped the screenplay prize over *Big Night.*

Geoffrey Rush picked up one more Best Actor award when he narrowly defeated a surprising runner-up: Eddie Murphy, who not only reprised Jerry Lewis's 1963 role in *The Nutty Professor,* but also portrayed the title character's loopy mom and dad.

Edward Norton prevailed as Best Supporting Actor for all three of his 1996 pix

over Armin Mueller-Stahl as Rush's tyrannical father in *Shine.* The L.A. crix reversed the Gotham crix's preference for supporting actress candidates, choosing Barbara Hershey over Courtney Love.

Hershey's and Norton's acceptance speeches drew some of the liveliest audience response when they received their plaques from the L.A. crix at the Bel Age Hotel while a severe rainstorm raged outside. Hershey said that she felt she was putting her head in a guillotine every time she read a review of her films, but added, "every single atom of me is grateful for this award."

"Edward Norton regaled the crowd with near-perfect impersonations of directors Woody Allen and Milos Forman," *Variety* reported. "He recalled Forman calling him at his parents' home one year ago with an invitation to fly with him on Larry Flynt's private jet to the Bahamas. His sister summed his fortunes up aptly: 'Your life has taken a surreal turn.'"

Lynn Redgrave again stood in for Rush and relayed the trampoline story, while Emily Watson described how *Breaking the Waves* radically changed her life. As he accepted his Best Picture and Director plaques, British filmmaker Mike Leigh revealed, "I've always had good experiences with critics in L.A. I wish I could say the same about London."

The broadcast film crix jumped ahead of the National Society of Film Critics this year to announce their awardees next, agreeing with the Gotham crix on *Fargo* as Best Picture. *Fargo*'s closest competish was not a serious contender for the top prize at any of the other kudos, however— *The English Patient*, which nonetheless won Best Director and Screenplay for Anthony Minghella over Joel Coen (and co-writer/brother Ethan in the screenplay race). *Fargo* rebounded with a victory for Frances McDormand as Best Actress over

---

National Board of Review Best Picture *Shine* blazed at Sundance last year.

Diane Keaton, who portrayed a selfless woman stricken with leukemia in *Marvin's Room.*

Tom Cruise lost the Best Actor trophy to Geoffrey Rush, but the thesp who portrayed Cruise's top client in *Jerry Maguire* triumphed as Best Supporting Actor—Cuba Gooding, Jr., who played "a larger-than-life modern athlete with his strutting ego, showboating style and frank preference for money over the glory of the game," said *Variety.* The nonprint crix also gave a special Breakout Artist of the Year prize to costar Renee Zellweger and separate kudos, Best Child Performance, to Jonathan Lipnicki as her adorably precocious son.

Joan Allen was chosen as Best Supporting Actress as Daniel Day-Lewis's long-suffering wife in *The Crucible.* Runner-up was Courtney Love.

"We are in your debt," Anthony Minghella said to the crix at the awards gala. "Please keep on supporting independent films. They need your encouragement to reach the widest possible audience."

The Gotham crix, broadcast crix and Indie Spirits all named *Fargo* best pic.

Frances McDormand echoed his remarks by emphasizing that audiences need crix to guide them. Cuba Gooding, Jr., said that he had great respect for crix, adding, "I don't always like what you say, but I learn a lot."

Variety reported, "Much sport was made of the fact McDormand sleeps with *Fargo* director/co-writer Joel Coen, her husband. Coen said there wasn't much he could add now that his sexual escapades had been applauded."

Geoffrey Rush, finally appearing at a crix awards ceremony, seemed to disparage the whole idea of awards, saying, "I think to myself, 'That's not why we're in it,' but I find I've warmed to it more in the past couple of weeks."

Six-year-old Jonathan Lipnicki upstaged all his elders when he appeared at the podium and said, "I'd love to do *Jerry Maguire* all over again. This is the favorite day of my life. I love everybody!"

Cannes honoree *Breaking the Waves* became the fourth movie named Best Picture by American crix orgs when it was endorsed during a protracted, five-hour voting session of the National Society of Film Critics. It garnered the top award by a slim margin of 35 points to 31 over *Secrets and Lies,* although its helmer Lars Von Trier (36 points) achieved a slightly bigger edge over *Secrets*'s Mike Leigh (29) for Best Director. *Waves* took an additional prize when Emily Watson (40) pulled off a victory for Best Actress over Brenda Blethyn (30).

Martin Donovan (34 points) avenged his loss at the Gotham awards when he won Best Supporting Actor by tying Tony Shalhoub, who portrayed Stanley Tucci's restaurateur brother in *Big Night.* The film lost the screenplay laurels to *Mother* by a score of 22 to 26.

Barbara Hershey repeated her L.A. crix victory in the supporting-actress race by eclipsing *Jerry Maguire*'s Renee Zellweger.

Variety noted that the biggest surprise in the vote outcome was the Best Actor victory of *The Nutty Professor*'s Eddie Murphy. Two thesps tied for the runner-up position with 29 points each: Geoffrey Rush and Vincent D'Onofrio, who *Variety* said gave a "superb" perf as cocky *Conan the Barbarian* author Robert E. Howard in *The Whole Wide World.*

"Most would agree that this is a wide-open year," *Variety* declared when the Golden Globe nominations were announced. *The English Patient* led with the most bids (seven), followed by five each for *Shine, The People vs. Larry Flynt* and the much-anticipated screen adaptation of the hit Broadway musical *Evita,* starring Antonio Banderas and Madonna. Prior to *Evita*'s release, crix had been skeptical that the duo could pull off their all-singing roles as the fascist first couple of Argentina, but *Variety* later called Banderas "ideal" and said "Madonna gives her all to the title role and pulls it off superbly."

Fargo scored four noms, as did *The Mirror Has Two Faces*, a romantic tale of an ugly duckling–turned–swan directed by, and starring, Barbra Streisand. Missing from the nominee list were Gotham crix champ Henry Belafonte and national society honorees Martin Donovan and Tony Shalhoub.

Curiously, four of the five pix competing for Best Drama Picture were indies—*The English Patient, Breaking the Waves, Shine* and *Secrets and Lies*. Even more curious: the latter three were foreign productions. As the lone representative of traditional Hollywood studios, *The People vs. Larry Flynt*'s inclusion made the race look like Goliath versus four Davids.

When *The English Patient* won, it became the fifth Best Picture named in the year's kudos derby so far. A sixth addition occurred in the separate categories for musical/comedy pix when *Evita* took the Globe for top pic plus two more—for Best Song "You Must Love Me" (a popular Madonna radio hit) and Best Actress. Madonna's victory triggered the biggest audience cheers of the night and shocked pundits, who had pegged Frances McDormand and Debbie Reynolds as the actress category's front-runners.

For the first time since the 1950s, all DGA contenders were newbies.

"I feel like I'm dreaming right now!" Madonna gasped once she took the statuette in hand.

Evita costar Antonio Banderas was nommed for Best Comedy or Musical Actor opposite National Board of Review champ Tom Cruise and national society winner Eddie Murphy.

Tom Cruise ended up claiming the second top showbiz kudo of his career and thanked director Cameron Crowe for making *Jerry Maguire* "out of little moments."

Backstage, Cruise was ribbed by the press for wearing a regular suit to the black-tie gala. *Variety* noted that he sported "a bemused look" as he examined his attire, insisting, "This *is* a tuxedo."

The People vs. Larry Flynt took two consolation prizes after being shut out of the top race. Claiming the Globe for Best Screenplay, co-scribe Larry Karaszewski thanked his wife "for putting up with those boxes of *Hustler* magazine in the house." When he accepted the third Globe of his career (after previous victories for *One Flew over the Cuckoo's Nest* and *Amadeus*), Milos Forman addressed public objections being raised over his film's glamorization of a pornographer. He insisted that the movie's message was about the importance of the First Amendment's guarantee of free speech and added, "I never bought a copy of *Hustler* magazine, and I don't have any argument with people who think it's rather tasteless."

Geoffrey Rush was the clear favorite to prevail over *Larry Flynt*'s Woody Harrelson and *English Patient*'s Ralph Fiennes in the race for Best Drama Actor. When Rush was called to the stage as the winner, the *L.A. Times* reported, "He drew a laugh by thanking his newfound friends at Creative Artists Agency, then held his statue aloft with a broad smile and added, 'To all those people who were happy to bankroll the film as long as I wasn't in it!'"

New York crix Best Supporting Actress Courtney Love and National Board of Review supporting thesp Kristin Scott Thomas were promoted by the Globes to the lead actress category, where they competed against Brenda Blethyn, Emily Watson and Meryl Streep as Diane Keaton's hardhearted sister in *Marvin's Room*.

L.A. crix and Cannes champ Blethyn won and, once she got to the podium, admitted how "star-struck" she was to be among the Hollywood elite. She added, "I was so happy to be in the building, let alone standing here!"

One sudden star, Edward Norton, beat another, Cuba Gooding, Jr., for Best Supporting Actor, while a veteran thesp took the equivalent kudo for women.

"I'm flabbergasted!" exclaimed Lauren Bacall when she was hailed for her role as Streisand's hovering mother in *The Mirror Has Two Faces.*

Backstage, the 72-year-old star informed reporters that this was the first time she had ever won an award for a specific role in her 53-year career. "It just goes to show that if you live long enough and keep working, anything can happen," she added.

One month later, Bacall received the second competitive award of her career at the Screen Actors Guild fete, where she faced less heated competish without crix honorees Barbara Hershey, Joan Allen or Courtney Love in the race. With none of the crix picks nommed in the supporting male lineup, Cuba Gooding, Jr., triumphed easily.

Geoffrey Rush continued his march through the lead male races by taking another trophy. Compared to the other kudos, the SAG prize had special importance, he said, because it's bestowed by "a peer group from another country and that peer group is made up of some of my heroes of my childhood and my working life as an actor."

Gotham crix and national society Best Actress Emily Watson and Globe honoree Madonna failed to make the equivalent SAG match-up, so the race seemed to be between Globe and L.A. film crix awardee Brenda Blethyn and Frances McDormand, who'd been favored by the broadcast crix and National Board of Review.

"I'm unemployed for the moment, but this is really exciting," McDormand said upon winning. Once backstage, she addressed recent complaints about *Fargo* that were raised by Minnesotans who thought that McDormand's husband Joel and his co-writer/brother Ethan—both Minnesota natives—made fun of their mutual home state in the film. *Variety* noted that she triggered a "roar of laughs" among reporters when she said, "I don't think

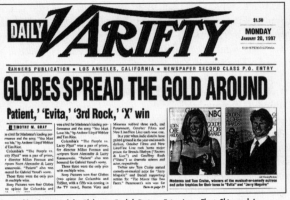

No one film dominated the Globes as *English Patient, Evita, Larry Flynt, Shine* and *Jerry Maguire* all claimed top statuettes.

they're mad at me. They're mad at Joel and Ethan."

Nathan Lane, Hank Azaria and Christine Baranski accepted the statuette for ensemble casts, which went to *The Birdcage,* an adaptation of the 1980 French gay cult hit *La Cage aux Folles.* After he and his costars beat the casts of *The English Patient* and *Shine,* a stunned Lane described how they felt when they heard the news: "It was pretty apparent you could knock us over with a feather."

For the first time since the 1950s, all of the DGA contenders were first-time nominees: Joel Coen *(Fargo),* Cameron Crowe *(Jerry Maguire),* Scott Hicks *(Shine),* Mike Leigh *(Secrets and Lies)* and Anthony Minghella *(The English Patient).* The one omission that surprised media pundits was Globe champ Milos Forman *(The People vs. Larry Flynt),* although the guild's failure to cite Lars Von Trier *(Breaking the Waves)* and Woody Allen *(Everyone Says I Love You)* also raised eyebrows.

The victor turned out to be Minghella, whose *English Patient* marked only his third outing at the helm.

"We are not horses," he said about all the nominees while accepting his plaque. "We are not in a race. We are all directors trying to survive and I am honored to be among them."

Four days later, the producers' guild acknowledged *English Patient* with its highest prize, which was accepted by producer Saul Zaentz, who also earned the new honorary Vision Award.

"This year is a madhouse of what can happen," he said at the podium.

English Patient's Anthony Minghella was the heavy favorite to take the laurels for adapted screenplays at the writers' guild fete held four days afterward, but Billy Bob Thornton (*Sling Blade*) pulled off an upset.

Controversy engulfed the showdown over Best Original Screenplay since it included *Secrets and Lies*, which was attributed to director Mike Leigh even though his actors improvised most of their dialogue. Category front-runners were thought to be Cameron Crowe (*Jerry Maguire*) and the team of Jan Sardi and Scott Hicks (*Shine*), but they were all usurped by Joel and Ethan Coen (*Fargo*). "The award is somewhat unexpected," *Variety* said, "if only because the movie was released more than a year ago."

Fargo led with the most nominations at the Independent Spirit Awards—six—and went undefeated in every race: Best Feature, Director (Joel Coen), Actor (William H. Macy), Actress (McDormand), Screenplay and Cinematography.

"Thanks," Ethan Coen said at the podium. "We deserve it."

McDormand said that the pic's overall success would not have been possible if *Fargo* had been made within the studio system. Referring to her character, she said, "Some studio executive would have said, 'Marge should be a little younger or maybe not so pregnant' or 'she should have a different accent.' I'm really happy for independents."

Bill Macy was not present to accept his trophy for portraying a sleazy car salesman who arranges to have his wife kidnapped.

Another Spirit champ, Elizabeth Peña, was busy having a baby, so she wasn't on hand to accept her accolade as Best Supporting Actress for portraying a small-town sheriff's wife in *Lone Star*, a losing Best Feature rival.

Last year's Best Supporting Actor Benicio Del Toro returned to reclaim the category for starring as the best friend of the title character—a celebrated graffiti artist— in *Basquiat*.

Sling Blade was proclaimed Best First Feature. When last year's Grand Jury Prize victor at Sundance, *Welcome to the Dollhouse*, entered the Spirit race, its 11-year-old star, Heather Matarazzo, was hailed for giving the year's Best Debut Performance. The "Someone to Watch" Award went to Larry Fessenden, the star-director-writer of vampire drama *Habit*.

Surprisingly, *Shine* was not up for Best Foreign Film, a category claimed by *Secrets and Lies*.

After the awards were bestowed, the *N.Y. Times* observed that husband and wife Joel Coen and Frances McDormand "swayed to a gospel choir and seemed relaxed and happy, though a tad sheepish over their embarrassment of riches."

Emcee Samuel L. Jackson warned the crowd that this year's crop of Spirit winners "could be a precursor to what's going to happen at the Oscars."

When the Academy Award race officially began, *Variety* announced, "The Oscar noms were so eclectic that everyone has a different theory on What This Year Means."

The English Patient led with 12 bids—two short of *All about Eve*'s record. *Fargo* and *Shine* scored 7 noms each and *Jerry Maguire* and *Secrets and Lies* followed with 5.

Jerry Maguire made the cut for Best Picture, but was slighted in the Best Director category. *Larry Flynt* experienced the reverse fate, although its Best Director nominee Milos Forman seemed less concerned about the top snub than he was about two others. He told *Variety* that he was sad Courtney Love and the pic's writers were overlooked. Globe champs *Evita* and Madonna were also shut out, as were crix honorees Martin Donovan, Tony Shalhoub and Harry Belafonte.

"*The English Patient*, which won nominations for almost every category, seems a cinch," *Entertainment Weekly* insisted, sizing up the race. "But either *Shine* or *Fargo*, riding a crest of emotion, could sneak in" for Best Picture. *TV Guide* and the *L.A. Times* agreed, but cited *Shine* alone as the possible spoiler.

As the Oscarcast began, host Billy Crystal joshed about the race being so dominated by indies when he referred to Hollywood as "Sundance by the Sea" and claimed that many of the acting nominees "had to show photo ID to get in here tonight."

Several unknowns were up for Best Supporting Actress, but all Oscar seers agreed that the never-before-nominated Lauren Bacall will, as *TV Guide* put it, "win in a walk." Only Barbara Hershey and Joan Allen were cited as possible dark horses. *English Patient*'s Juliette Binoche told *TV Guide*, "Lauren Bacall is going to win for sure, so I can go (to the Oscars) and feel safe."

But the 32-year-old, Paris-born thesp pulled off a jaw-dropper, causing a gasp from the audience.

"I'm so surprised!" said a shocked Binoche. "I didn't prepare anything. This is a dream, I think. A French dream."

Backstage, she told reporters, "I don't know why I got this. It's not my fault. I thought I was going to get the Oscar of chocolate Miramax gave us."

TV Guide called the match-up for Best Supporting Actor "one of the easiest picks of the night," naming Cuba Gooding, Jr. The *L.A. Times* concurred, but warned of a possible upset by the thesp honored by the Globes, the L.A. crix and the National Board of Review, noting, "The academy's weakness for new faces in the supporting categories could mean a move toward Edward Norton."

But it was the thesp who became famous for chanting "Show me the money!" in *Jerry Maguire* who saw Oscar gold. He was so excited over winning that he pranced around the stage and had trouble getting his thank-yous expressed in the time allotted for his acceptance speech. Oscarcast producer Gil Cates told *Variety,* "Then we started to sneak the orchestra in and he kind of rode the music like a guy out on the surf. It was spectacular. As the orchestra got louder, he got louder and he finished in time with the music as if it were planned." The audience stood and cheered.

Prior to the supporting races, *The Eng-lish Patient* snagged the laurels for art direction and costumes. Soon afterward, it proceeded to take the kudos for sound, editing, dramatic score and cinematography, "immediately establishing its dominance," *Variety* reported. By the time Andrew Lloyd Webber accepted a golden boy for Best Song ("You Must Love Me," *Evita*), he said, "Well, thank heavens there wasn't a song in *The English Patient*!"

But *The English Patient* juggernaut suddenly came to an abrupt halt in the category for Best Adapted Screenplay, where it was favored to win by two *L.A. Times* pundits plus the paper's Hollywood Consensus poll of 50 film industry insiders.

"Lord have mercy!" exclaimed Billy Bob Thornton when he prevailed for *Sling Blade,* "beating out adaptations from Arthur Miller and William Shakespeare," *Variety* noted. "Thornton's victory marks the first time since the category was created in 1956 that the winner of the race did not get a best-pic nomination."

Forecasters were divided over which pic would take the prize for original screenplays. The two *L.A. Times* pundits split between *Jerry Maguire* and *Shine,* while the paper's Hollywood Consensus poll and *Entertainment Weekly* backed *Fargo.*

Variety reported that "a big cheer went up when the Coen brothers" triumphed. The academy's two script choices mirrored the same selections made earlier by the writers guild.

Fargo got the endorsement of *Entertainment Weekly* and *TV Guide* in the Best Actress race when they picked SAG and National Board of Review honoree Frances McDormand. But the *L.A. Times* warned that she suffered from a disadvantage "since the award does not usually go to a comic performance." As a result, the paper's two pundits sided with Golden Globe and L.A. crix champ Brenda Blethyn.

When McDormand won, she thanked Ethan Coen, "who made an actor of me," his brother Joel, "who made a woman of me, and my son, Pedro, who has made a mother of me."

Virtually all Oscar handicappers picked Geoffrey Rush to score another Best Actor statuette after previous honors from the Globes, the Screen Actors Guild and the L.A., N.Y. and broadcast crix. He won easily, thanking, "the unstoppable David Helfgott—you truly are an inspiration." Earlier on Oscar night, Helfgott appeared on the kudocast and performed "The Flight of the Bumblebee" on a grand piano. Roger Ebert of *The Chicago Sun-Times* observed, "He talked to himself as he played, missing a few notes, but he was filled with energy—and with triumph as he finished with a flourish."

Considering the awards sweep it pulled off all night, *The English Patient*'s triumphs for Best Picture and Director came as no surprise. Its final tally of 9 kudos tied it with *The Last Emperor* and *Gigi* as the third-most-honored film in Oscar history behind *Ben-Hur* (11 wins) and *West Side Story* (10).

Roger Ebert wrote, "The awards for *The English Patient* must have been gut-wrenching for Twentieth Century-Fox, the film's original studio, which dropped it two weeks before shooting was set to begin. Miramax stepped in at the last moment and agreed to finance it." As its reward, Miramax earned its first Best Picture victory after previous bids for *The Crying Game, The Piano, Pulp Fiction* and *Il Postino (The Postman)*.

But *The English Patient*'s success was chiefly due to diehard producer Saul Zaentz, who had championed it through its many travails, just as he had two previous Oscar Best Picture victors *Amadeus* and *One Flew over the Cuckoo's Nest*. Only one other producer in Oscar history had ever pulled off three top wins—Sam Spiegel (*On the Waterfront, The Bridge on the River Kwai, Lawrence of Arabia*). On Oscar night, Zaentz became the first producer in 44 years to win the top trophy the same year he received the Irving Thalberg Award.

Additional Oscar drama occurred outside the feature categories when *When We Were Kings*—which recorded the dramatic "Rumble in the Jungle" bout between Muhammad Ali and George Foreman in 1974—was proclaimed Best Documentary.

The *L.A. Times* reported that one of the evening's most "moving moments occurred when Ali, who has Parkinson's disease, slowly walked to the stage with Foreman to a standing ovation."

When We Were Kings gained notoriety last year at Sundance, which was beset this year with what the *L.A. Times* called "relentlessly juvenile sensibility and subject matter." Perhaps that was because the young filmmakers didn't have Sundance Institute's elder topper present: an avalanche kept Robert Redford homebound.

Variety described the winner of the fest's Grand Jury Prize and screenwriter's award as far more "gritty," however—*Sunday*, which dramatized a brief affair between an actress and a homeless man she mistakes for a famous director.

The recipient of the Filmmaker's Trophy, voted on by the fest's participants, was *In the Company of Men*, "a dark tale about two corporate execs who intentionally hurt a vulnerable secretary," said *Variety*. The politically incorrect pic, produced for $25,000, also nabbed a distribution deal with Sony Pictures Classics and would end up on *Entertainment Weekly*'s and the *N.Y. Times*'s lists of the top 10 pix of 1997 despite a disappointing $3.5 million b.o. pay-off.

Hurricane (later renamed *Hurricane Streets*) reaped the most prizes, including the Audience Award for dramas plus accolades for directing and cinematography. The tale of a decent 15-year-old boy corrupted by ghetto life was the handiwork of first-time helmer Morgan J. Freeman. He accepted his kudos, saying, "I'm totally freaking out. I'm going to sit back down."

Hurricane tied for Audience Award with *love jones,* a drama about four African-Americans described as "over-educated and underemployed" by *Hurricane*'s filmmaker.

Licensed to Kill, which studied men convicted of murdering gays, pulled off two victories. After Arthur Dong claimed a director's prize, he was soon called to the podium to receive the Filmmaker's Trophy for documentaries. The *L.A. Times* reported, "He joked that he would've brought a change of clothes if he'd known, and settled for giving the crowd a brief look at his T-shirt, which said 'DYKE' in large capital letters."

Girls Like Us pulled off the biggest upset at the fest, snagging the Grand Jury documentary laurels for chronicling four years in the lives of four South Philadelphia teens. The Audience Award for documentaries went to a biopic, *Paul Monette*, about the National Book Award winner who died of AIDS in 1995.

Fest regular Parker Posey, who appeared in three pix shown at Sundance, received a special jury bow for portraying a wacky girl obsessed with Jacqueline Kennedy Onassis in the incest comedy *The House of Yes*, which Miramax aquired during Sundance for $1.5 million.

"I've never gotten an award," she said. "I've never even been at a podium. This is wild!"

▪ 1996 ▪

NATIONAL BOARD OF REVIEW

The board declared a Best Picture and Foreign Film of the year, then listed its remaining favorites according to highest scores. The vote results were announced on December 10, 1996. Awards were presented on February 24, 1997, at the Tavern on the Green in New York.

BEST PICTURE
- *Shine*
- *The English Patient*
- *Fargo*
- *Secrets and Lies*
- *Everyone Says I Love You*
- *Evita*
- *Sling Blade*
- *Trainspotting*
- *The People vs. Larry Flynt*
- *Breaking the Waves*
- *Jerry Maguire*

BEST DIRECTOR
- Joel Coen, *Fargo*

BEST ACTOR
- Tom Cruise, *Jerry Maguire*

BEST ACTRESS
- Frances McDormand, *Fargo*

BEST SUPPORTING ACTOR
- Edward Norton, *Primal Fear, Everyone Says I Love You, The People vs. Larry Flynt*

BEST SUPPORTING ACTRESS (TIE)
- Juliette Binoche, *The English Patient*
- Kristin Scott Thomas, *The English Patient*

BEST BREAKTHROUGH PERFORMER
- Renee Zellweger, *Jerry Maguire*

BEST ENSEMBLE PERFORMANCE
- *The First Wives Club*

BEST DOCUMENTARY
- *Paradise Lost: The Child Murders at Robin Hood Hills*, Joe Berlinger, Bruce Sinofsky

BEST FOREIGN FILM
- *Ridicule* (France)
- *Les Voleurs* (France)
- *Bitter Sugar* (Cuba)
- *La Ceremonie* (France)
- *Kolya* (Czech Republic)

SPECIAL ACHIEVEMENT AWARD
- Billy Bob Thornton, *Sling Blade*

CAREER ACHIEVEMENT AWARD
- Gena Rowlands

NEW YORK FILM CRITICS CIRCLE

Winners were announced on December 12, 1996. Awards were presented on January 5, 1997, at the Pegasus Suite of the Rainbow Room in Rockefeller Center in New York.

BEST PICTURE
- *Fargo*

BEST FIRST FEATURE
- *Big Night*

BEST DIRECTOR
- Lars von Trier, *Breaking the Waves*

BEST ACTOR
- Geoffrey Rush, *Shine*

BEST ACTRESS
- Emily Watson, *Breaking the Waves*

BEST SUPPORTING ACTOR
- Harry Belafonte, *Kansas City*

BEST SUPPORTING ACTRESS
- Courtney Love, *The People vs. Larry Flynt*

BEST SCREENWRITER
- Albert Brooks, Monica Johnson, *Mother*

BEST CINEMATOGRAPHER
- Robby Müller, *Breaking the Waves, Dead Man*

BEST DOCUMENTARY
- *When We Were Kings*, Leon Gast, David Sonenberg

BEST FOREIGN FILM
- *The White Balloon* (Iran)

MOST DISTINGUISHED REISSUE
- *Vertigo*

LOS ANGELES FILM CRITICS ASSOCIATION

Winners were announced on December 14, 1996. Awards were presented on January 15, 1997, at the Bel Age Hotel in Los Angeles.

BEST PICTURE
- *Secrets and Lies*

BEST DIRECTOR
- Mike Leigh, *Secrets and Lies*

BEST ACTOR
- Geoffrey Rush, *Shine*

BEST ACTRESS
- Brenda Blethyn, *Secrets and Lies*

BEST SUPPORTING ACTOR
- Edward Norton, *Everyone Says I Love You, The People vs. Larry Flynt, Primal Fear*

BEST SUPPORTING ACTRESS
- Barbara Hershey, *The Portrait of a Lady*

BEST SCREENPLAY
- Ethan Coen, Joel Coen, *Fargo*

BEST CINEMATOGRAPHY (TIE)
- Chris Menges, *Michael Collins*
- John Seale, *The English Patient*

BEST MUSIC SCORE
- Hal Willner and the Hey Hey Club Musicians, *Kansas City*

BEST PRODUCTION DESIGN (TIE)
- Brian Morris, *Evita*
- Janet Patterson, *The Portrait of a Lady*

BEST ANIMATION
- Nick Park, *Creature Comforts, A Grand Day Out, The Wrong Trousers, A Close Shave*

BEST DOCUMENTARY
- *When We Were Kings*, Leon Gast, David Sonenberg

BEST FOREIGN FILM
- *La Cérémonie* (France)

BEST INDEPENDENT/EXPERIMENTAL FILM
- *Sonic Outlaws*, Craig Baldwin

NEW GENERATION AWARD
- Emily Watson

CAREER ACHIEVEMENT AWARD
- Roger Corman

BROADCAST FILM CRITICS ASSOCIATION

Winners were announced on January 2, 1997. Awards were presented on January 20 at the Sofitel Hotel in Los Angeles.

BEST PICTURE
- *Fargo*

BEST DIRECTOR
- Anthony Minghella, *The English Patient*

BEST ACTOR
- Geoffrey Rush, *Shine*

BEST ACTRESS
- Frances McDormand, *Fargo*

BEST SUPPORTING ACTOR
- Cuba Gooding, Jr., *Jerry Maguire*

BEST SUPPORTING ACTRESS
- Joan Allen, *The Crucible*

BEST CHILD PERFORMANCE
- Jonathan Lipnicki, *Jerry Maguire*

BREAKOUT ARTIST OF THE YEAR
- Renee Zellweger, *Jerry Maguire*

BEST SCREENPLAY
- Anthony Minghella, *The English Patient*

BEST DOCUMENTARY
- *When We Were Kings*, Leon Gast, David Sonenberg

BEST FOREIGN FILM
- *Ridicule* (France)

LIFETIME ACHIEVEMENT AWARD
- Lauren Bacall

NATIONAL SOCIETY OF FILM CRITICS

Winners were announced on January 5, 1997.

BEST PICTURE
- *Breaking the Waves*

BEST DIRECTOR
- Lars von Trier, *Breaking the Waves*

BEST ACTOR
- Eddie Murphy, *The Nutty Professor*

BEST ACTRESS
- Emily Watson, *Breaking the Waves*

BEST SUPPORTING ACTOR (TIE)
- Martin Donovan, *The Portrait of a Lady*
- Tony Shalhoub, *Big Night*

BEST SUPPORTING ACTRESS
- Barbara Hershey, *The Portrait of a Lady*

BEST SCREENPLAY
- Albert Brooks, Monica Johnson, *Mother*

BEST CINEMATOGRAPHY
- Robby Muller, *Breaking the Waves, Dead Man*

BEST DOCUMENTARY
- *When We Were Kings*, Leon Gast, David Sonenberg

BEST FOREIGN-LANGUAGE FILM
- *La Cérémonie* (France)

SPECIAL CITATION
- James Katz, Bob Harris

GOLDEN GLOBES

Nominations were announced on December 19, 1996. Awards were presented on January 19, 1997, at the Beverly Hilton Hotel in Los Angeles. The ceremony was telecast by NBC.

BEST DRAMA PICTURE
- *The English Patient*
Breaking the Waves
The People vs. Larry Flynt
Secrets and Lies
Shine

BEST COMEDY OR MUSICAL PICTURE
- *Evita*
The Birdcage
Jerry Maguire

Everyone Says I Love You
Fargo

BEST DIRECTOR
- Milos Forman, *The People vs. Larry Flynt*
Joel Coen, *Fargo*
Scott Hicks, *Shine*
Anthony Minghella, *The English Patient*
Alan Parker, *Evita*

BEST ACTOR, DRAMA
- Geoffrey Rush, *Shine*
Ralph Fiennes, *The English Patient*
Mel Gibson, *Ransom*
Woody Harrelson, *The People vs. Larry Flynt*
Liam Neeson, *Michael Collins*

BEST ACTRESS, DRAMA
- Brenda Blethyn, *Secrets and Lies*
Courtney Love, *The People vs. Larry Flynt*
Kristin Scott Thomas, *The English Patient*
Meryl Streep, *Marvin's Room*
Emily Watson, *Breaking the Waves*

BEST ACTOR, COMEDY OR MUSICAL
- Tom Cruise, *Jerry Maguire*
Antonio Banderas, *Evita*
Kevin Costner, *Tin Cup*
Nathan Lane, *The Birdcage*
Eddie Murphy, *The Nutty Professor*

BEST ACTRESS, COMEDY OR MUSICAL
- Madonna, *Evita*
Glenn Close, *101 Dalmatians*
Frances McDormand, *Fargo*
Debbie Reynolds, *Mother*
Barbra Streisand, *The Mirror Has Two Faces*

BEST SUPPORTING ACTOR
- Edward Norton, *Primal Fear*
Cuba Gooding, Jr., *Jerry Maguire*
Samuel L. Jackson, *A Time to Kill*
Paul Scofield, *The Crucible*
James Woods, *Ghosts of Mississippi*

BEST SUPPORTING ACTRESS
- Lauren Bacall, *The Mirror Has Two Faces*
Joan Allen, *The Crucible*

Juliette Binoche, *The English Patient*
Barbara Hershey, *The Portrait of a Lady*
Marianne Jean-Baptiste, *Secrets and Lies*
Marion Ross, *The Evening Star*

BEST SCREENPLAY
- Scott Alexander, Larry Karaszewski, *The People vs. Larry Flynt*
Ethan Coen, Joel Coen, *Fargo*
Anthony Minghella, *The English Patient*
Jan Sardi, *Shine*
John Sayles, *Lone Star*

BEST SONG
- "You Must Love Me," *Evita*, Andrew Lloyd Webber, Tim Rice
"Because You Loved Me," *Up Close and Personal*, Diane Warren
"For the First Time," *One Fine Day*, Jud J. Friedman, James Newton Howard, Allan Dennis Rich
"I Finally Found Someone," *The Mirror Has Two Faces*, Barbra Streisand, Marvin Hamlisch, Robert "Mutt" Lange, Bryan Adams
"That Thing You Do!," *That Thing You Do!*, Adam Schlesinger

BEST FOREIGN FILM
- *Kolya* (Czech Republic)
The Eighth Day (Le Huitieme Jour) (Belgium)
Luna e L'Altra (Italy)
Prisoner of the Mountains (Russia)
Ridicule (France)

Winners

BEST SCORE
- Gabriel Yared, *The English Patient*

CECIL B. DEMILLE AWARD
- Dustin Hoffman

SUNDANCE FILM FESTIVAL

The festival was held January 16–26, 1997, at Park City, Utah.

GRAND JURY PRIZE
(DRAMATIC)
- *Sunday*, Jonathan Nossiter

(DOCUMENTARY)
- *Girls Like Us*, James C. Wagner, Tina DiFeliciantonio

FILMMAKER'S TROPHY
(DRAMATIC)
- *In the Company of Men*, Neil LaBute

(DOCUMENTARY)
- *Licensed to Kill*, Arthur Dong

AUDIENCE AWARD
(DRAMATIC)
- *Hurricane*, Morgan J. Freeman
- *love jones*, Theodore Witcher

(DOCUMENTARY)
- *Paul Monette: The Brink of Summer's End*, Monte Bramer

DIRECTING AWARD
(DRAMATIC)
- *Hurricane*, Morgan J. Freeman

(DOCUMENTARY)
- *Licensed to Kill*, Arthur Dong

WALDO SALT SCREENWRITING AWARD
- James Lasdun, Jonathan Nossiter, *Sunday*

CINEMATOGRAPHY AWARD
(DRAMATIC)
- *Hurricane*, Enrique Chediak

(DOCUMENTARY)
- *My America . . . or Honk If You Love Buddah*, Renee Tajima-Pena

FREEDOM OF EXPRESSION AWARD
- *Family Name*, Macky Alston
- *Fear and Learning at Hoover Elementary*, Laura Angelica Simon

LATIN AMERICAN CINEMA AWARD
- *Landscapes of Memory,* José Araujo

(HONORABLE MENTION)
- *Deep Crimson,* Arturo Ripstein

SHORT FILMMAKING AWARD
- *Man about Town*, Kris Isacsson

(HONORABLE MENTION)
- *Birdhouse,* Richard C. Zimmerman
- *Syphon-Gun*, K. C. Amos

SPECIAL JURY RECOGNITION
- *Sick: The Life and Death of Bob Flanagan, Supermasochist*
- Therese DePrez, *Going All the Way, Box of Moonlight*
- Parker Posey, *The House of Yes*

SCREEN ACTORS GUILD

Awards were presented on February 22, 1997, at the Shrine Auditorium in Los Angeles. The ceremony was telecast by NBC.

BEST ACTOR
- Geoffrey Rush, *Shine*
Tom Cruise, *Jerry Maguire*
Ralph Fiennes, *The English Patient*
Woody Harrelson, *The People vs. Larry Flynt*
Billy Bob Thornton, *Sling Blade*

BEST ACTRESS
- Frances McDormand, *Fargo*
Brenda Blethyn, *Secrets and Lies*
Diane Keaton, *Marvin's Room*
Gena Rowlands, *Unhook the Stars*
Kristin Scott Thomas, *The English Patient*

BEST SUPPORTING ACTOR
- Cuba Gooding, Jr., *Jerry Maguire*
Hank Azaria, *The Birdcage*
Nathan Lane, *The Birdcage*
William H. Macy, *Fargo*
Noah Taylor, *Shine*

BEST SUPPORTING ACTRESS
- Lauren Bacall, *The Mirror Has Two Faces*
Juliette Binoche, *The English Patient*
Marisa Tomei, *Unhook the Stars*
Gwen Verdon, *Marvin's Room*
Renee Zellweger, *Jerry Maguire*

BEST CAST PERFORMANCE
- *The Birdcage*
The English Patient
Marvin's Room
Shine
Sling Blade

LIFETIME ACHIEVEMENT AWARD
- Angela Lansbury

DIRECTORS GUILD OF AMERICA

Nominations were announced on January 21, 1997. Awards were presented on March 8 at the Century Plaza Hotel in Los Angeles and the Sheraton Hotel in New York.

BEST DIRECTOR
- Anthony Minghella, *The English Patient*
Joel Coen, *Fargo*
Cameron Crowe, *Jerry Maguire*
Scott Hicks, *Shine*
Mike Leigh, *Secrets and Lies*

ROBERT B. ALDRICH AWARD
- Delbert Mann

D. W. GRIFFITH AWARD
- Stanley Kubrick

PRODUCERS GUILD OF AMERICA

Nominations were announced on January 22, 1997. Awards were presented on March 12 at the Universal City Hilton Hotel in Los Angeles.

DARRYL F. ZANUCK PRODUCER OF THE YEAR AWARD
- *The English Patient*, Saul Zaentz
Fargo, Ethan Coen
Hamlet, David Barron
The People vs. Larry Flynt, Oliver Stone, Janet Yang, Michael Hausman
Shine, Jane Scott

CHARLES B. FITZSIMONS LIFETIME HONORARY MEMBERSHIP AWARD
- Norman Felton

NOVA AWARD
- Tom Cruise, Paula Wagner

DAVID O. SELZNICK LIFETIME ACHIEVEMENT AWARD
- Billy Wilder

VISION AWARD
- Saul Zaentz

WRITERS GUILD OF AMERICA

Nominations were announced on February 6, 1997. Awards were presented on March 16 at the Beverly Hilton Hotel in Los Angeles and the Tavern on the Green in New York.

BEST ORIGINAL SCREENPLAY
- *Fargo,* Joel and Ethan Coen
Jerry Maguire, Cameron Crowe
Lone Star, John Sayles
Secrets and Lies, Mike Leigh
Shine, Jan Sardi, Scott Hicks

BEST ADAPTED SCREENPLAY
- *Sling Blade,* Billy Bob Thornton, based on his play
The Birdcage, Elaine May, based on the play *La Cage aux Folles* by Jean Poiret and the screenplay by Francis Veber, Edouard Molinaro, Jean Poiret, Marcello Danon
Emma, Douglas McGrath, based on the novel by Jane Austen
The English Patient, Anthony Minghella, based on the novel by Michael Ondaatje
Trainspotting, John Hodge, based on the novel by Irvine Welsh

MORGAN COX AWARD
- Alan Mannings, Phil Fehrle, Rick Mittleman, Katherine Coker, Oliver Crawford, Dorothy C. Fontana, Michael A. Hoey, John Riley

VALENTINE DAVIES AWARD
- Jonathan Estrin, Shelley List

LAUREL AWARD
- Robert Towne

PAUL SELVIN AWARD
- Larry Karaszewski, Scott Alexander, *The People vs. Larry Flynt*

INDEPENDENT SPIRIT

Nominations were announced on January 9, 1997. Awards were presented on March 22 in a tent on the beach in Santa Monica. The ceremony was telecast by the Independent Film Channel. Portions were also telecast by Bravo.

BEST FEATURE

- *Fargo*
Dead Man
The Funeral
Lone Star
Welcome to the Dollhouse

BEST FIRST FEATURE

- *Sling Blade*
Big Night
I Shot Andy Worhol
Manny and Lo
Trees Lounge

BEST DIRECTOR

- Joel Coen, *Fargo*
Abel Ferrara, *The Funeral*
David O. Russell, *Flirting with Disaster*
Todd Solondz, *Welcome to the Dollhouse*
Robert M. Young, *Caught*

BEST ACTOR

- William H. Macy, *Fargo*
Chris Cooper, *Lone Star*
Chris Penn, *The Funeral*
Tony Shalhoub, *Big Night*
Stanley Tucci, *Big Night*

BEST ACTRESS

- Frances McDormand, *Fargo*
Maria Conchita Alonso, *Caught*
Scarlett Johansson, *Manny and Lo*
Catherine Keener, *Walking and Talking*
Rene Zellweger, *The Whole Wide World*

BEST SUPPORTING ACTOR

- Benicio Del Toro, *Basquiat*
Kevin Corrigan, *Walking and Talking*
Matthew Faber, *Welcome to the Dollhouse*

Gary Farmer, *Dead Man*
Richard Jenkins, *Flirting with Disaster*

BEST SUPPORTING ACTRESS

- Elizabeth Peña, *Lone Star*
Queen Latifah, *Set It Off*
Mary Kay Place, *Manny and Lo*
Lili Taylor, *Girls Town*
Lily Tomlin, *Flirting with Disaster*

BEST DEBUT PERFORMANCE

- Heather Matarazzo, *Welcome to the Dollhouse*
Jena Malone, *Bastard Out of Carolina*
Brendan Sexton, Jr., *Welcome to the Dollhouse*
Arie Verveen, *Caught*
Jeffrey Wright, *Basquiat*

BEST SCREENPLAY

- Joel Coen, Ethan Coen, *Fargo*
Jim Jarmusch, *Dead Man*
David O. Russell, *Flirting with Disaster*
Nicholas St. John, *The Funeral*
John Sayles, *Lone Star*

BEST FIRST SCREENPLAY

- Joseph Tropiano, Stanley Tucci, *Big Night*
Steve Buscemi, *Tree Lounge*
Lisa Krueger, *Manny and Lo*
Michael Scott Myers, *The Whole Wide World*
Suzan-Lori Parks, *Girl 6*

BEST FOREIGN FILM

- *Secrets and Lies* (U.K.)
L'America (Italy/France)
Breaking the Waves (Denmark)
Chungking Express (Hong Kong)
Trainspotting (U.K.)

"SOMEONE TO WATCH" AWARD

- Larry Fessenden, *Habit*
Joe Brewster, *The Keeper*
Chris Smith, *The Big One*

Winners

BEST CINEMATOGRAPHY

- Roger Deakins, *Fargo*

"TRUER THAN FICTION" DOCUMENTARY AWARD

- *When We Were Kings*, Leon Gast, David Sonenberg

ACADEMY AWARDS

Nominations were announced on February 11, 1997. Awards were presented on March 24 at the Shrine Auditorium in Los Angeles. The ceremony was telecast by ABC.

BEST PICTURE

- *The English Patient*
Fargo
Jerry Maguire
Secrets and Lies
Shine

BEST DIRECTOR

- Anthony Minghella, *The English Patient*
Joel Coen, *Fargo*
Milos Forman, *The People vs. Larry Flynt*
Scott Hicks, *Shine*
Mike Leigh, *Secrets and Lies*

BEST ACTOR

- Geoffrey Rush, *Shine*
Tom Cruise, *Jerry Maguire*
Ralph Fiennes, *The English Patient*
Woody Harrelson, *The People vs. Larry Flynt*
Billy Bob Thornton, *Sling Blade*

BEST ACTRESS

- Frances McDomand, *Fargo*
Brenda Blethyn, *Secrets and Lies*
Diane Keaton, *Marvin's Room*
Kristin Scott Thomas, *The English Patient*
Emily Watson, *Breaking the Waves*

BEST SUPPORTING ACTOR

- Cuba Gooding, Jr., *Jerry Maguire*
William H. Macy, *Fargo*
Armin Mueller-Stahl, *Shine*
Edward Norton, *Primal Fear*
James Woods, *Ghosts of Mississippi*

BEST SUPPORTING ACTRESS

- Juliette Binoche, *The English Patient*
Joan Allen, *The Crucible*
Lauren Bacall, *The Mirror Has Two Faces*
Barbara Hershey, *The Portrait of a Lady*
Marianne Jean-Baptiste, *Secrets and Lies*

BEST ORIGINAL SCREENPLAY

- Ethan Coen, Joel Coen, *Fargo*
Cameron Crowe, *Jerry Maguire*
Scott Hicks, Jan Sardi, *Shine*
Mike Leigh, *Secrets and Lies*
John Sayles, *Lone Star*

BEST ADAPTED SCREENPLAY

- Billy Bob Thornton, *Sling Blade*
Kenneth Branagh, *Hamlet*
John Hodge, *Trainspotting*
Arthur Miller, *The Crucible*
Anthony Minghella, *The English Patient*

BEST SONG

- "You Must Love Me," *Evita*, Andrew Lloyd Webber, Tim Rice
"Because You Loved Me," *Up Close And Personal*, Diane Warren
"For the First Time," *One Fine Day,* Jud J. Friedman, James Newton Howard, Allan Dennis Rich
"I Finally Found Someone," *The Mirror Has Two Faces*, Bryan Adams, Marvin Hamlisch, Robert "Mutt" Lange, Barbra Streisand
"That Thing You Do!," *That Thing You Do!*, Adam Schlesinger

BEST FOREIGN-LANGUAGE FILM

- *Kolya* (Czech Republic)
A Chef in Love (Georgia)
The Other Side of Sunday (Norway)
Prisoner of the Mountains (Russia)
Ridicule (France)

Winners

BEST ART DIRECTION

- Stuart Craig, Stephanie McMillan, *The English Patient*

BEST CINEMATOGRAPHY

- John Seale, *The English Patient*

BEST COSTUME DESIGN

- Ann Roth, *The English Patient*

BEST DOCUMENTARY
(FEATURE)
- *When We Were Kings*, Leon Gast, David Sonenberg

(SHORT SUBJECT)
- *Breathing Lessons: The Life and Work of Mark O'Brien*, Jessica Yu

BEST FILM EDITING
- Walter Murch, *The English Patient*

BEST MAKEUP
- David Leroy Anderson, Rick Baker, *The Nutty Professor*

BEST MUSIC
(ORIGINAL DRAMATIC SCORE)
- Gabriel Yared, *The English Patient*

(ORIGINAL MUSICAL OR COMEDY SCORE)
- Rachel Portman, *Emma*

SCIENTIFIC OR TECHNICAL AWARDS
(Academy Award of Merit)
- IMAX

(Scientific and Engineering Award)
- Jonathan Erland, Kay Beving Erland, Jim Hourihan, Zoran Kacic-Alesic, Brian Knep, William Reeves, John Schlag, Thomas Williams

(Technical Achievement Award)
- Nestor Burtnyk, Marceli Wein, National Research Council of Canada; David Benson, Dr. Garth A. Dickie, Craig Hayes, Florian Kainz, James Kajiya, Timothy Kay, Perry Kivolowitz, Brian Knep, Grant Loucks, William N. Masten, Ken Perlin, Richard A. Prey, Christian Rouet, Rick Sayre, Thomas Williams, Jeffrey Yost

BEST SHORT FILM
(ANIMATED)
- *Quest,* Tyron Montgomery, Thomas Stellmach

(LIVE ACTION)
- *Dear Diary,* David Frankel, Barry Jossen

BEST SOUND
- Mark Berger, Walter Murch, Chris Newman, David Parker, *The English Patient*

BEST SOUND EFFECTS EDITING
- Bruce Stambler, *The Ghost and the Darkness*

BEST VISUAL EFFECTS
- Volker Engel, Clay Pinney, Douglas Smith, Joseph Viskocil, *Independence Day*

IRVING G. THALBERG MEMORIAL AWARD
- Saul Zaentz

HONORARY AWARDS
- Volker W. Bahnemann
- Michael Kidd
- Joe Lombardi
- Burton "Bud" Stone

· 1997 ·

Titanic *Rises*

A movie about the biggest seafaring disaster of all time looked fated to become the biggest disaster in Hollywood history as the truly titanic production hit rough waters. Delays and cost overruns made the budget balloon from $100 million to $200 million-plus, gossip-meisters revealed fierce in-fighting on the set, stunt men shattered bones (rib, ankle, cheekbone) and the cast and crew were poisoned when they ate chowder spiked with angel dust.

But when the pic launched at theaters nationwide in mid-December, *Variety* declared, "This *Titanic* arrives at its destination. A spectacular demonstration of what modern technology can contribute to dramatic storytelling, James Cameron's romantic epic, the biggest roll of the dice in film history, will send viewers in search of synonyms for the title to describe the film's size and scope."

When kudos orgs starting sounding off, however, they literally missed the boat. Only once before had the first four awards of the year—National Board of Review and the three crix groups (N.Y., L.A. and national society)—ever agreed on one Best Picture: *Schindler's List*, which went on to snag the Golden Globe and Oscar next. This year, however, the kudos quartet all hopped aboard an alternative to *Titanic* that was fated to sink when it would collide with its hefty rival later on.

The National Board of Review was the first to back *L.A. Confidential*, giving accolades for Best Picture and Director (Curtis Hanson). *Variety* lauded the film in its review, too: "Drenched in the tawdry glamour of Hollywood in the early '50s and up to its ears in the delirious corruption of police and city politics, *L.A. Confidential* is an irresistible treat."

Two of the board's acting prizes went to the film that ranked second on its top 10 list

Initially, *L.A. Confidential*, starring Russell Crowe (center) and Guy Pearce (right), appeared invincible, being named best pic by the first five kudos groups.

of 1997 pix: *As Good As It Gets*, James L. Brooks's comedy about a curmudgeonly romance novelist (Best Actor Jack Nicholson) who ends up bonding with a gay-artist neighbor he detests (Best Supporting Actor Greg Kinnear) and a salty waitress he routinely taunts while dining at a neighborhood café (Helen Hunt).

Nicholson staged another comic performance at the board's awards gala at Tavern on the Green in New York when Rita Moreno gave him his Best Actor plaque. Noting that he was bored, Nicholson decided to spice up the proceedings by making oral-sex jokes while recounting—over Moreno's loud protests—how Moreno once starred as a hooker who serviced him often in *Carnal Knowledge*. When he refused to stop, "that provoked Moreno to go into spitfire mode and hurl a thick red binder of introductory remarks at the actor's skull," reported the *N.Y. Daily News*. "Nicholson was shaking off that missile when he was struck by Moreno's shoe."

The board's Best Actress plaque went to Helena Bonham Carter (*The Wings of the Dove*) as a young British aristocrat who plots to have her impoverished lover marry a dying American heiress so they can inherit her fortune.

Anne Heche was named Best Supporting Actress for two roles: as the wife of an FBI agent infiltrating the mafia in *Donnie Brasco* and as scheming White House advisor in *Wag the Dog*. When she accepted the prize, Heche said its value paled in comparison to her falling in love with TV star Ellen DeGeneres, which was "just the most brilliant thing I've ever done."

The board also gave an award for Best Ensemble Performance to a pic that had reaped the Grand Prize at Cannes—*The Sweet Hereafter*, starring Ian Holm as a big-city lawyer who arrives in a small town to launch a class-action suit in the aftermath of a school-bus crash that killed 14 children.

When the Gotham crix voted two days after the board, they were joined by two welcome additions to the circle: Janet Maslin and Stephen Holden of the *New York Times*. The duo's bosses at the paper had finally nixed a policy, enforced since 1989, that prohibited employees from voting in outside professional orgs. Now they joined their colleagues in backing *L.A. Confidential* for Best Picture, Director and Screenplay over *The Sweet Hereafter*, which placed second in all three match-ups. *Titanic* landed in third place in the top pic race, coming in "surprisingly strong in the voting," noted *The Village Voice*, "so much so that critics' head Thelma Adams (of the *N.Y. Post*) had a nightmare that it swept the awards and Billy Zane (the pic's villain) was sitting at the Rainbow Room with eyeliner and a whip."

The *Voice* claimed the crix's kudos gala at the Rainbow Room looked "like glorified lifetime achievement honors" since the top prizes went to so many veterans suddenly experiencing career rebounds.

Bridget Fonda surprised her father, Peter, by showing up to present him with the Best Actor plaque for *Ulee's Gold*, a pic

in which he gave such a powerful, smoldering perf as a repressed Florida beekeeper that the *L.A. Times* said he "wonderfully echoed his celebrated father, Henry." Fonda told *Entertainment Weekly*, "I understood the role so well because of the Henry Fonda you don't know, from our dining-room table." Peter was suddenly enjoying the most widespread acclaim he had received since 1969 when he was widely saluted as the pot-puffing biker Captain America in *Easy Rider*. Now he beat *The Sweet Hereafter*'s Ian Holm for the Gotham crix award.

During the Rainbow Room festivities, the crix fawned so shamelessly over Best Actress Julie Christie that her director/writer Alan Rudolph said later, "They were coming up to Julie like she was Elvis or something." The past Oscar champ (*Darling*, 1965) topped Helena Bonham Carter to snag the actress laurels for portraying an adulterous B-grade movie actress in *Afterglow*. *Variety* cheered her comeback pic, saying, "Christie dominates every scene she's in, rendering the witty, often wickedly funny lines with suave irony."

The N.Y. crix fawned over Best Actress Julie Christie "like she was Elvis."

Best Supporting Actor Burt Reynolds also experienced a dramatic career resurrection recently thanks to *Boogie Nights*, a racy exposé of cocaine-snorting porn makers in the 1970s. Prior to doing the film, 62-year-old Reynolds had been suffering from financial trouble, a messy public divorce and a string of bad movie choices that included *Cop and a Half* and *Striptease*, so he decided to roll the dice while taking on the role of a soft-hearted smut producer. He was so outraged later when he saw *Boogie Nights,* however, that he fired his agent.

When he accepted huzzahs from the Gotham crix, Reynolds referred to a famous effeminate exercise guru and a nonexistent sequel to one of his own earlier film flops, saying, "I thought the chances of my being here were the same as there being a Richard Simmons, Jr.—though it was very close with *Cannonball II*."

The Gotham crix named Joan Cusack Best Supporting Actress for her comic turn as an almost-bride-to-be who discovers, at the altar, that her fiancé's gay in *In & Out*. The org did not reveal who placed behind Cusack or Reynolds in the voting, nor did it disclose any ballot scores.

The L.A. crix agreed with their Gotham peers by hailing *L.A. Confidential* with kudos for Best Picture, Director and Screenplay over second-placed *The Sweet Hereafter.* Curtis Hanson accepted his triple honors at their awards luncheon, saluting them and their local environs, saying, "I grew up here. When I first got started in film, my dialogue was with critics. I learned a lot. It meant a lot."

The Los Angelenos also endorsed Best Supporting Actor Burt Reynolds, but he couldn't attend the gala due to a filming obligation. Reynolds won the prize over Kevin Spacey, whose role in *L.A. Confidential* was described by *Entertainment Weekly* as "a glory-hungry cop on the make (and the take)."

"I wish my dad were here tonight," said Globe champ Peter Fonda.

Best Actress Helena Bonham Carter couldn't join the crix either, but sent a note that read, "Those I live in dread of, I now love." She beat Helen Hunt (*As Good As It Gets*).

The crix's choice for Best Actor was Robert Duvall, who not only starred as a fiery Texas preacher on the lam from the law in his self-scripted *The Apostle,* but he also directed, produced and funded the movie after a fruitless, 13-year search to find a studio to pick it up. Duvall ended up pocketing a $1 million profit on the $5 million production when October Films bought the finished film. *Variety* noted that he received "one of the most enthusiastic responses from the crowd" at the Bel Age Hotel bash, adding, "He admitted it was nice to sweat out a contest and called the film and his role a career favorite." He beat Jack Nicholson for the honor.

Three weeks after the L.A. crix unveiled

their winners, the National Society of Film Critics embraced nearly all of the same choices. *L.A. Confidential* pulled off a resounding victory over *The Sweet Hereafter* for Best Picture, outscoring it by almost twice as many points on the first ballot (68 to 37). *L.A. Confidential* also surpassed *The Sweet Hereafter* for the director's kudo (60 points to 39) and script honor (71 to 33). First-ballot victories were claimed by Best Actress Julie Christie (over Helena Bonham Carter, 48 to 44) and Best Supporting Actor Burt Reynolds (over Kevin Spacey, 57 to 36). Best Actor Robert Duvall beat Peter Fonda on the second polling (28 to 18).

The society disagreed with the L.A. crix in only one category—Best Supporting Actress, giving the accolade to Julianne Moore (32 points) as a streetwise, coke-tooting porn actress and den mother to her costars in *Boogie Nights*. She beat Sarah Polley (21), who portrayed a paralyzed survivor of the bus crash in *The Sweet Hereafter.*

This year the Broadcast Film Critics Association announced a partial list of its winners in late December, but delayed the unveiling of its Best Picture choice till the awards dinner in January. The time split reflected a schizophrenic outcome between Best Picture and Director, with *L.A. Confidential* reaping the top pic prize and *Titanic*'s James Cameron snagging best helmer. The org also introduced a new kudo for Best Family Film, which went to the first production by the Fox studio's new animation division, *Anastasia*, a $50 million retelling of the fanciful myth about the Russian czar's daughter.

The org tapped Jack Nicholson as Best Actor, Helen Bonham Carter as Best Actress and Joan Cusack as Best Supporting Actress, but it made a departure from other crix in the Best Supporting Actor race, thereby stopping the sweep that Burt Reynolds had pulled off at the earlier reviewers' awards. The winner was Anthony Hopkins (*Amistad*) as former President John Quincy Adams, who once defended the case of a slave-ship rebellion all the way to the Supreme Court. *Amistad* was a lavish, $70 million production by Steven Spielberg that was expected to be a top rival for the year's film awards, but it ultimately failed to attract many kudos or film-goers.

The nonprint crix lauded another pic that had failed to reap any other trophies so far, too, although *Good Will Hunting* would mount a late rally afterward. It starred, and was written by, Matt Damon and Ben Affleck, two boyhood buddies from Boston who finally got their pic made after a five-year battle with Hollywood power moguls, resulting in what *Variety* called "an engaging and often quite touching" tale about two aimless, working-class pals. The crix gave *Good Will Hunting* their prize for Best Original Screenplay and bestowed separate laurels upon Damon as the year's Breakthrough Performer for his role as a university janitor and secret math prodigy.

When he accepted his plaques for Best Director and Adapted Screenplay, Curtis Hanson told the crix, "You have been very much the word-of-mouth for this picture. It's been in the theaters for four months, which is a very unusual thing for a movie these days."

Nicholson appeared groggy as he accepted his Best Actor award, but fessed up to the crix, saying, "I was running around all night. I hope I didn't offend anyone." Hopkins and Cusack dispatched stand-ins to claim their kudos and Helena Bonham Carter sent a videotaped thank-you speech that was shown to the crowd at the Sofitel Hotel.

After sailing with apparent ease through the first five sets of film kudos this year, *L.A. Confidential* at last hit an iceberg at the Golden Globes: *Titanic* led with a staggering tally of eight bids. *As Good As It Gets* placed second with six, followed by *L.A. Confidential* in the show position with five.

"This is a windfall day for the film!" *Titanic* director James Cameron cheered upon hearing the news. "It's a validation that there's something else important of substance here."

Missing from the lineup were a Best Drama Picture bid for *The Sweet Hereafter* or noms for two thesps who had been acknowledged generously by the crix: Robert Duvall and Julie Christie.

When awards day arrived, *Titanic*—which had already grossed $235 million domestically so far—cashed in on half of its Golden Globe bids, winning Best Drama Picture, Director, Music Score and Song ("My Heart Will Go On").

> *"Titanic got 14 Oscar nominations. One per lifeboat."*

As Cameron accepted the top prize, he asked the crowd, "So this does prove, once and for all, that size does matter?"

Backstage, reporters asked him if he was bitter about the early press reports that predicted *Titanic* would be a true disaster. "It's good to be gracious in victory," he answered. "Those people hadn't seen a foot of the film before writing about it."

A British indie nabbing only one nomination was considered a dark horse that could beat *As Good As It Gets* for Best Comedy or Musical Picture. *The Full Monty* had already beaten the odds at the b.o. The cheeky $3.5-million film about six out-of-work steelworkers who decide to put on a male-strip revue for coin had grossed a surprising $35 million domestically—and $150 million worldwide—to date.

But *As Good As It Gets* not only nabbed the top pic prize, it won two more. Helen Hunt was proclaimed Best Comedy or Musical Actress, which finally validated her talents as a serious screen thesp. The 34-year-old former child star had won two Emmys so far as Best Comedy Actress for her TV sitcom *Mad about You,* but her film roles were either too low-profile (starring in Sundance-hailed *The Waterdance*) or too thin (fleeing a pesky tornado in blockbuster *Twister*) for major notice.

When Jack Nicholson triumphed for the male thesp laurels, he mentioned the pic's co-producer/director/co-writer, saying, "I warned Jim (Brooks) this would give me another decade of not having to behave myself." He then mooned the audience—without dropping trou.

With Robert Duvall out of the race for Best Drama Actor, Gotham crix champ Peter Fonda prevailed easily, but not without irony. Back in 1963, he had lost the Golden Globe for Most Promising Male Newcomer to a trio of men that included the now-forgotten star of *America, America,* Stathis Giallelis.

"It's good to be back!" Fonda crowed at the podium as he clutched his long-elusive Globe. "I wish my dad were here tonight."

With New York and national society crix honoree Julie Christie out of the match-up for Best Drama Actress, pundits expected a victory by Helena Bonham Carter, but she was topped by Judi Dench, who portrayed a feisty Queen Victoria in *Mrs. Brown.*

Burt Reynolds faced tough competish for Best Supporting Actor from Anthony Hopkins (*Amistad*), Greg Kinnear (*As Good As It Gets*), three-time past Globe grabber Robin Williams (*Good Will Hunting*) and Rupert Everett (who reaped "the reviews of a lifetime as Julia Roberts' gay pal in *My Best Friend's Wedding,*" said *Variety*). But when Reynolds won, he said at the podium, "If you hang on to things long enough, they get back in style—like me. Remember that the old Stradivarius plays better than the new ones."

National Board of Review winner Anne Heche was not nommed for Best Supporting Actress, leaving the contest to two previous kudos honorees: New York and broadcast crix victor Joan Cusack (*In & Out*) and L.A. and national society champ Julianne Moore (*Boogie Nights*). An underdog pulled off an upset, however—Kim Basinger as a Veronica Lake look-alike hooker in *L.A. Confidential.* "The role and the reaction I've gotten to it have shocked

Best Supporting Actor (SAG and Oscar) Robin Williams (left) on the set of *Good Will Hunting* with director Gus Van Sant (center) and screenplay co-writer Matt Damon, who was hailed by Oscars, Globes and broadcast crix.

me completely," she told the press. "And to think I almost passed on it."

Another shocker occurred in the showdown over Best Screenplay. *L.A. Confidential* may have nabbed four of the crix groups' script kudos, but the foreign press preferred *Good Will Hunting* by Matt Damon and Ben Affleck. "We feel like impostors," Damon said backstage, "like the Milli Vanilli of screenwriters."

Damon and Affleck were up for a trophy at the writers' guild gala held one month later, but James L. Brooks and Mark Andrus (*As Good As It Gets*) rallied after their Globe loss to top the scribes of *Titanic, The Full Monty* and *Boogie Nights,* too. "There's a thing in Hollywood about always moving the finish line," Brooks said once he took the prize in hand. "Sometimes you just have to enjoy the moment."

The scenarists of *L.A. Confidential* (Curtis Hanson, Brian Helgeland) faced scribes of *Donnie Brasco, The Ice Storm, Wag the Dog, Hero* and *The Wings of the Dove* in the showdown for adapted works. After *L.A. Confidential* won, Helgeland told *Variety* privately, using a conspiratorial tone, "*L.A. Confidential* is the iceberg that's going to sink *Titanic.* They think they're going to take the Oscars, but we're waiting out here in the Atlantic for them."

But *Titanic* pulled ahead at the Producers Guild of America banquet one week later when Cameron took the top kudo over the producers of *Amistad, As Good As It Gets, Good Will Hunting* and *L.A. Confidential.*

"Someone said earlier that producing was about being on time and on budget," he said at the podium. "I guess that's not written in stone."

At the directors' guild bash four days later, Cameron faced his toughest kudos challenge yet if he expected to snag the top Oscars next, since the guild's lead honor had failed to line up with the academy's choice for Best Director only four times in the previous 50 years. All of the same pix nommed by the PGA made the DGA list, too.

When Cameron triumphed, he told the crowd at the Century Plaza Hotel in Los Angeles, "*Titanic* was a labor of love or, some might say, a crime of passion. Some nights I'd look up at the enormous set and say to myself, 'I must be out of my frigging mind!' "

Variety declared that *Titanic* was now out front, "sailing full-steam ahead toward the Oscars."

But *Titanic* first had to navigate the Screen Actors Guild awards, which took place one day after the directors' guild fete. The pic, however, suffered the same split fate in the nominations that it had at the Golden Globes when only one of its two lead stars—Kate Winslet—made the cut. Snubbed was Leonardo DiCaprio, who portrayed what *Variety* described as "a penniless, devil-may-care American" who falls for "a haughty society girl (Winslet) returning to Philadelphia to marry her rich snob fiancé (Billy Zane)."

Also overlooked by SAG was the same thesp slighted at the Globes: N.Y. and national society crix winner Julie Christie. That left Winslet facing off against Globe champs Helen Hunt and Judi Dench plus L.A. crix victor Helena Bonham Carter. Hunt triumphed, telling the audience that she found it "unfathomable" that she beat such talented rivals.

Hunt's costar and fellow Globe awardee Jack Nicholson prevailed for Best Actor,

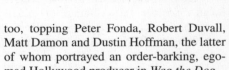

Titanic was snubbed by the crix kudos, but sailed off with four Globes and the DGA and PGA prizes. At the Oscars, the all-time b.o. champ tied the all-time Oscar record (11 wins).

too, topping Peter Fonda, Robert Duvall, Matt Damon and Dustin Hoffman, the latter of whom portrayed an order-barking, ego-mad Hollywood producer in *Wag the Dog*.

Nicholson ended up taking the statuette in hand, saying, "I love what I do and I love all the people I get to do it with."

An upset occurred in the race for Best Supporting Actor when Burt Reynolds and Anthony Hopkins lost to Robin Williams (*Good Will Hunting*).

A surprise occurred, too, in the match-up for Best Supporting Actress, which did not include Gotham and broadcast crix honoree Joan Cusack or National Board of Review champ Anne Heche. The odds favored L.A. and national society winner Julianne Moore and Globe recipient Kim Basinger.

Basinger won—but in a tie with *Titanic*'s Gloria Stuart, who was one of the founding members of the guild when she was a contract player for Fox and Paramount during the 1930s. Back then the now-87-year-old thesp had starred in such notable pix as *The Old Dark House* and *The Invisible Man*, but she hadn't acted in more than 50 years when Cameron tapped her to share Winslet's role, portraying the *Titanic* survivor as a 101-year-old who recalls the tragedy in flashback. When she was hailed by the guild with a standing ovation, Stuart confessed that she had dreamed of winning the award, but added, "I never thought it would happen. I'm so grateful. I'll never be able to tell you how grateful."

The striptease stars of *The Full Monty* won Best Cast Performance, but caused groans from the audience when thesp Mark Addy accepted the trophy, saying, "The clothes will stay on. Sorry to disappoint so many people."

"SHIP SHAPES OSCAR RACE," *Variety*'s headline declared when the Academy Award noms were unveiled. The paper added, "*Titanic* sailed into the Oscar record books with 14 nominations, tying *All about Eve* for most ever." *Entertainment Weekly*'s resident wag Jim Mullen made another observation, "*Titanic* got 14 nominations. One per lifeboat."

Titanic set another record when Gloria Stuart made the cut, becoming the oldest nominee in academy history. "When I started in the 1930s, I hoped for an Academy Award," the 87-year-old told *USA Today*. *L.A. Confidential* and *Good Will Hunting* reaped nine noms each, followed by seven for *As Good As It Gets.*

Missing from the lineup was a Best Director bid for James L. Brooks, who got bumped by *The Sweet Hereafter*'s Atom Egoyan even though *As Good As It Gets* snagged a Best Picture nom and *Hereafter* didn't.

But two other oversights caused more of a hubbub. Leonardo DiCaprio was a man overboard. He may have been the popular lead star of the biggest film of all time, but there was no sight of him in the Best Actor race. Just as curious: *Titanic* didn't get a screenplay bid. The snub was ominous. Not since *The Sound of Music* in 1965 had a film won Best Picture without its screenplay nominated. The issue heated up when Kenneth Turan of the *L.A. Times* infuriated *Titanic* fans by insisting that academy voters did "the sane thing by denying a nomination to James Cameron and his cobbled-together *Titanic* script. Any child would have no trouble pointing out the piece's flaws." Cameron fired back in a guest column published by the *Times* that really rocked Hollywood's boat.

But there were good omens ahead for

Titanic, too. The biggest Oscar drama looming was whether *Titanic* could break *Ben-Hur*'s record for the most wins: 11. Just like *Titanic, Ben-Hur* had been the most expensive pic of its day ($15 million) and was plagued by production ills, perhaps even more so since *Ben-Hur*'s producer died of a heart attack during filming.

On Oscar day, Turan rallied behind *Titanic*, writing, "Is anything out there going to sink that ship? Don't bet on it." Earlier in the month, the pic that Cameron had once called his "$200 million chick flick" became the first film ever to top $1 billion in worldwide ticket sales.

"I'm petrified," Cameron confessed to the *N.Y. Times* before the Oscarcast, but he arrived at the Shrine Auditorium, looking triumphant. Leonardo DiCaprio stayed home, however, disappointing his teen fans who howled for him from the bleachers, where many of them held up signs that declared "I Love You, Leo!"

Variety reported on the start of the Oscar show: "When host Billy Crystal entered on a set simulating the prow of the *Titanic*, it was clear which pic was the front-runner." A short time later, a brief film clip of *Titanic* was shown and Crystal quipped, "That cost $15 million." A TV camera zoomed in on Cameron in the audience, who was shown laughing and saying "That's about right!"

Titanic's initial big test came in the first awards category: Best Supporting Actress. *TV Guide* and two *L.A. Times* pundits picked Gloria Stuart, but *Entertainment Weekly* warned, "Kim Basinger may just edge Stuart."

When the latter forecast proved to be true, *Variety* wrote that *Titanic* "hit its first chunk of ice."

"Oh, my God, yes!" Basinger exclaimed when she received the statuette. "Wait a minute. We only get 30 seconds. I just want to thank everybody I've ever met in my entire life!"

The contest for Best Supporting Actor was considered a squeaker between SAG honoree Robin Williams and Burt Reynolds, who'd previously claimed the Golden Globe plus three crix prizes. The *L.A. Times*'s Turan and *Entertainment*

Weekly backed Williams. The *L.A. Times*'s Kevin Thomas and *TV Guide* endorsed Reynolds, "who will cry during his acceptance speech," *TV Guide* promised.

The champ was revealed to be three-time past loser Robin Williams, who gasped up on stage, "Oh, man! This may be the one time I'm speechless!" But that didn't turn out to be true as Williams went on to single out the twentysomething buddy team behind *Good Will Hunting*, saying, "Thank you, Ben and Matt. I still want to see some ID. . . . Most of all, I want to thank my father, up there, who, when I said, 'I want to be an actor,' he said, 'Wonderful, just have a backup profession, like welding.' "

Entertainment Weekly predicted Affleck and Damon would win Best Original Screenplay because they "will look so *cute* at the podium." The two *L.A. Times* pundits split, however, one picking the *Good Will Hunting* duo, the other citing writers guild champ James L. Brooks (*As Good As It Gets*).

When Affleck and Damon were named winners, Affleck revealed, "I just said to Matt, 'Losing would suck and winning would be really scary. And it is *really* scary.' " Their victory marked the third year in a row that actors took a screenplay prize, following earlier wins by Billy Bob Thornton (*Sling Blade*) and Emma Thompson (*Sense and Sensibility*).

After claiming kudos from four crix orgs and the writers guild, the scribes of *L.A. Confidential* received the backing of nearly all Oscar seers in the match-up for Best Adapted Screenplay. They won.

Entertainment Weekly sized up the Best Actor race as "a cockfight between the codgers," since it included Jack Nicholson (60 years old), Peter Fonda (57), Robert Duvall (67) and Dustin Hoffman (60). Billy Crystal said of the fifth contender, "Matt Damon must feel like he's playing on the seniors tour."

Forecasts were fractured over who'd prevail. The two *L.A. Times* crix split between Duvall and Fonda. *TV Guide* and *Entertainment Weekly* backed Nicholson.

"I dropped about three quarts of water the minute I heard my name," Nicholson told the press later. He was so shocked to hear the news that he even removed his ever-present sunglasses.

Once up on stage, Nicholson said, "I'd like to thank everybody here tonight for looking so good." Backstage later, he told the media that he'd forgotten to acknowledge his young children, who must be "having a ball" watching at home. "They don't know the difference between this and bowling, but they know dad won."

TV Guide sized up the Best Actress contest, saying, "This should be an easy category to handicap, but it isn't." Four of the rivals had received other kudos earlier this year: Helena Bonham Carter (three awards), Julie Christie (three), Helen Hunt (two) and Judi Dench (one). The only contender who hadn't been honored yet was considered a threat, too. "If *Titanic* sweeps the Oscars, Kate Winslet could win in an upset," warned the *N.Y. Times*.

But since the lineup included four British thesps and one American, *TV Guide* bet on "the only Yank at the tea party"— Helen Hunt. *Entertainment Weekly* and both *L.A. Times* crix picked her, too, noting that the last two times that a solo American had faced off against four foreigners at the Oscars, the Yanks won: Jane Fonda (*Klute*) and Marisa Tomei (*My Cousin Vinny*).

"I'm here for one reason—Jim Brooks," Hunt said when she accepted her golden boy. "I thank God for giving me a little piece of you." Hunt had struck further gold earlier that day when she renewed her *Mad about You* TV contract, which guaranteed her $1 million per episode. *Variety* observed, "She joins Goldie Hawn and Cloris Leachman as people who won an Oscar while simultaneously appearing in a TV series." The paper also pointed out that her and Nicholson's victories marked only the seventh time in 70 years of Oscar history that the two leading thesp trophies went to the same pic.

Titanic may have fared poorly in the acting races, but it swept through the crafts categories all night long, claiming nine wins: art direction, cinematography, costumes, editing, musical score, song, sound, sound editing and visual effects. It looked unstoppable as the Oscarcast headed toward the director's category next, which comprised five first-time nominees.

"I'm king of the world!" Cameron roared when he took the prize, quoting the most famous line of dialogue from his unnominated *Titanic* script. "I don't know about you, but I'm having a really great time!" he exclaimed to presenter Warren Beatty.

Earlier in the night, Cameron had won an Oscar for film editing, so when *Titanic* finally reaped Best Picture next, the producer/helmer/writer/editor received his third statuette. The last victory brought *Titanic*'s total tally to 11, thereby tying *Ben-Hur*'s record.

When he returned to the podium for Oscar's top kudo, Cameron assumed a serious demeanor and asked the audience to join him in a few seconds of silence in order to pay tribute to the more than 1,500 passengers who died on the luxury liner in 1912.

Then he added, joyously, "You've really made this a night to remember in every way. Now let's party till dawn!"

The overwhelming triumph of the Fox-Paramount co-production signaled that the studios had reclaimed Hollywood's highest honors after the domination of indies in recent years.

But the Oscar derby did include a number of indies that also were up for Independent Spirits, held two days earlier on the Santa Monica beach: *The Apostle, Ulee's Gold, Afterglow* and *The Sweet Hereafter.*

This year *Variety* said that the Spirits "got religion" when *The Apostle* led the race with six bids and pulled off victories for Best Feature, Director and Actor. All three kudos were claimed by Robert Duvall, since he wrote, produced, directed and funded the movie in addition to playing the lead role. He accepted them, saying, "This truly was an independent film. We made this under no one's auspices other than our own. It was a great experience and I hope we did justice to these good men—America's preachers."

A loser in the feature race rebounded with two wins—for Jason Lee as an abandoned best friend in *Chasing Amy*, written

and directed by Kevin Smith, who accepted a trophy for his screenplay about a comic-book artist who doggedly pursues a captivating woman even though she's gay. When Smith accepted his kudo, he opened his suit jacket to show off the Superman T-shirt he was wearing and said of his victory, "This makes up for every chick who ever told me I had a small dick."

The winner of Best First Feature was *Eve's Bayou,* a gothic drama about a Louisiana family's struggles to survive their father's infidelity. Acknowledging the victory, the relieved writer-director Kasi Lemmons confessed that he had been "smoking cigarettes bitterly in the parking lot all afternoon."

African-American thesp Debbi Morgan was hailed as Best Supporting Actress for portraying a psychic aunt in *Eve's Bayou.* She thanked Lemmon for creating "one of the most complex, colorful, bewitching characters an actress with the color of my skin has been able to play."

Variety noted that the award fete's "first awkward moment" occurred when the category came up for Best Debut Performance and the winner was nowhere in sight: Aaron Eckhart, who played a buff corporate yuppie who cruelly sets out to break the heart of a hearing-impaired co-worker in *In the Company of Men.* "As the presenters were about to exit, a flustered Eckhart arrived and accepted his prize with a terse 'thank you,'" *Variety* added. It was revealed later that Eckhart had been outside posing for photographers. The film was also honored with Best First Screenplay.

Not present at all to claim her laurels was Best Actress Julie Christie, but when one of *Afterglow*'s financial backers stood in for her, he amused the crowd by reading her thank-you message as if he were the actress.

Meantime, the Sundance Institute showed signs of growth by recently launching its own cable channel and announcing plans for a national network of theaters that would begin opening later in the year to showcase indie works.

The winner of the Sundance fest's Grand Jury Prize for features was *Slam,* a drama about a black poet incarcerated for minor drug charges. The *L.A. Times* griped that a loser in the race, *Next Stop, Wonderland,* had "probably ruined its chances for glory by being too accessible and getting a big-ticket distribution deal with Miramax" worth $6 million. Another widely touted also-ran, *High Art*, reaped the script award in consolation.

An additional loser was *Smoke Signals*, described by *Variety* as "the tale of a young Native American's struggle to ensure the body of his estranged father receives a proper burial." It made up for its jury defeat by nabbing both the Filmmaker's Trophy and Audience Award.

"The Audience Award was the one we really wanted," insisted screenwriter Sherman Lexie during the kudos ceremony.

The Audience Award for docus went to *Out of the Past*, a pic that hit close to home as Sundancers viewed it in screening rooms between the Utah mountains. It chronicled the battles faced by a lesbian who tries to form a gay-straight alliance at her Utah high school.

The jury documentary prize was split between two champs, including *The Farm*, a look inside the walls of the Angola maximum-security prison in Louisiana. The co-winner was *Frat House*, an exposé of the horrors of college fraternity hazing.

The Filmmaker's Trophy for docus was claimed by *Divine Trash*, about the making of John Waters's 1974 cult classic *Pink Flamingos*.

A new Director's Award was introduced this year. Feature champ was *Pi*, described by the *L.A. Times* as "an artistic and edgy piece of mystification about a young mathematician's attempt to bring order to the chaos of the stock market." Distrib rights were acquired during the fest by Live Entertainment. The victor among docus was *Moment of Impact,* which chronicled how its filmmaker and her family coped when her father became brain-damaged after a car accident.

The New York Times reported that fest harmony was shattered by "an unexpectedly discordant and angry note" when a docu about rock stars Kurt Cobain and Courtney Love was pulled from competish after lawyers alleged that it contained music that didn't have full legal clearances. Its producers denied the charge, but offered to cut out the controversial music sections in order to be included in the fest. Still-nervous Sundance leaders refused.

Further grousing occurred when a pic didn't make the cut for fest competition and was relegated to the second-tier American Spectrum screenings. Lions Gate execs checked it out and, four months later, ultimately closed a distrib deal. When the pic was released commercially seven months after that, the National Board of Review, L.A. crix and Oscar and Indie Spirit voters started to take notice, too, of *Gods and Monsters*.

▪ 1997 ▪

NATIONAL BOARD OF REVIEW

The board declared a Best Picture and Foreign Film of the year, then listed its remaining favorites according to highest scores. The vote results were announced on December 9, 1997. Awards were presented on February 9, 1998, at the Tavern on the Green in New York.

BEST PICTURE
▪ *L.A. Confidential*
As Good As It Gets

The Wings of the Dove
Good Will Hunting
Titanic
The Sweet Hereafter
Boogie Nights
The Full Monty
The Rainmaker
Jackie Brown

BEST DIRECTOR
▪ Curtis Hanson, *L.A. Confidential*

BEST DEBUT DIRECTOR
▪ Kasi Lemmons, *Eve's Bayou*

BEST ACTOR
- Jack Nicholson, *As Good As It Gets*

BEST ACTRESS
- Helena Bonham Carter, *The Wings of the Dove*

BEST SUPPORTING ACTOR
- Greg Kinnear, *As Good As It Gets*

BEST SUPPORTING ACTRESS
- Anne Heche, *Donnie Brasco, Wag the Dog*

BEST BREAKTHROUGH PERFORMER
- Bai Ling, *Red Corner*

BEST ENSEMBLE PERFORMANCE
- *The Sweet Hereafter*

BEST DOCUMENTARY
- *Fast, Cheap and Out of Control*, Errol Morris

BEST FOREIGN FILM
- *Shall We Dance?* (Japan)
Beaumarchais the Scoundrel (France)
Ma Vie en Rose (My Life in Pink) (Belgium)
La Promesse (Belgium)
Ponette (France)

FREEDOM OF EXPRESSION AWARD
- Richard Gere, Jon Avnet, *Red Corner*

SPECIAL ACHIEVEMENT AWARD
- Ben Affleck, Matt Damon, *Good Will Hunting*

CAREER ACHIEVEMENT AWARD
- Robert Duvall

NEW YORK FILM CRITICS CIRCLE

Winners were announced on December 11, 1997. Awards were presented on January 4, 1998, at the Pegasus Suite of the Rainbow Room in Rockefeller Center in New York.

BEST PICTURE
- *L.A. Confidential*

BEST FIRST FEATURE
- *In the Company of Men*

BEST DIRECTOR
- Curtis Hanson, *L.A. Confidential*

BEST ACTOR
- Peter Fonda, *Ulee's Gold*

BEST ACTRESS
- Julie Christie, *Afterglow*

BEST SUPPORTING ACTOR
- Burt Reynolds, *Boogie Nights*

BEST SUPPORTING ACTRESS
- Joan Cusack, *In & Out*

BEST SCREENWRITER
- Curtis Hanson, Brian Helgeland, *L.A. Confidential*

BEST CINEMATOGRAPHER
- Roger Deakins, *Kundun*

BEST DOCUMENTARY
- *Fast, Cheap and Out of Control*, Errol Morris

BEST FOREIGN FILM
- *Ponette* (France)

LOS ANGELES FILM CRITICS ASSOCIATION

Winners were announced on December 13, 1997. Awards were presented on January 14, 1998, at the Bel Age Hotel in Los Angeles.

BEST PICTURE
- *L.A. Confidential*

BEST DIRECTOR
- Curtis Hanson, *L.A. Confidential*

BEST ACTOR
- Robert Duvall, *The Apostle*

BEST ACTRESS
- Helena Bonham Carter, *The Wings of the Dove*

BEST SUPPORTING ACTOR
- Burt Reynolds, *Boogie Nights*

BEST SUPPORTING ACTRESS
- Julianne Moore, *Boogie Nights*

BEST SCREENPLAY
- Curtis Hanson, Brian Helgeland, *L.A. Confidential*

BEST CINEMATOGRAPHY
- Dante Spinotti, *L.A. Confidential*

BEST MUSIC
- Philip Glass, *Kundun*

BEST PRODUCTION DESIGN
- Peter Lamont, *Titanic*

BEST ANIMATION (TIE)
- *Hercules*
- *The Spirit of Christmas*

BEST DOCUMENTARY
- *Riding the Rails*, Michael Uys, Lexy Lovell

BEST FOREIGN FILM
- *La Promesse* (Belgium)

BEST INDEPENDENT/EXPERIMENTAL FILM
- *Finished*

NEW GENERATION AWARD
- Paul Thomas Anderson, *Hard Eight, Boogie Nights*

SPECIAL CITATION
- Peter Bogdanovich

NATIONAL SOCIETY OF FILM CRITICS

Winners were announced on January 3, 1998.

BEST PICTURE
- *L.A. Confidential*

BEST DIRECTOR
- Curtis Hanson, *L.A. Confidential*

BEST ACTOR
- Robert Duvall, *The Apostle*

BEST ACTRESS
- Julie Christie, *Afterglow*

BEST SUPPORTING ACTOR
- Burt Reynolds, *Boogie Nights*

BEST SUPPORTING ACTRESS
- Julianne Moore, *Boogie Nights*

BEST SCREENPLAY
- Curtis Hanson, Brian Helgeland, *L.A. Confidential*

BEST CINEMATOGRAPHY
- Roger Deakins, *Kundun*

BEST DOCUMENTARY
- *Fast, Cheap and Out of Control*, Errol Morris

BEST FOREIGN-LANGUAGE FILM
- *La Promesse* (Belgium)

SPECIAL CITATION
- *Nightjohn*, Charles Burnett

BROADCAST FILM CRITICS ASSOCIATION

Winners in all categories but Best Picture were announced on December 21, 1997. The top pic champ was revealed when the awards were presented on January 19, 1998, at the Sofitel Hotel in Los Angeles.

BEST PICTURE
- *L.A. Confidential*

BEST DIRECTOR
- James Cameron, *Titanic*

BEST ACTOR
- Jack Nicholson, *As Good As It Gets*

BEST ACTRESS
- Helena Bonham Carter, *The Wings of the Dove*

BEST SUPPORTING ACTOR
- Anthony Hopkins, *Amistad*

BEST SUPPORTING ACTRESS
- Joan Cusack, *In & Out*

BEST CHILD PERFORMANCE
- Jurnee Smollett, *Eve's Bayou*

BEST BREAKTHROUGH PERFORMER
- Matt Damon, *Good Will Hunting*

BEST ORIGINAL SCREENPLAY
- Matt Damon, Ben Affleck, *Good Will Hunting*

BEST ADAPTED SCREENPLAY
- Curtis Hanson, Brian Helgeland, *L.A. Confidential*

BEST DOCUMENTARY
- *Four Little Girls*, Spike Lee

BEST FOREIGN FILM
- *Shall We Dance?* (Japan)

BEST FAMILY FILM
- *Anastasia*

LIFETIME ACHIEVEMENT AWARD
- Robert Wise

GOLDEN GLOBES

Nominations were announced on December 18, 1997. Awards were presented on January 18, 1998, at the Beverly Hilton Hotel in Los Angeles. The ceremony was telecast by NBC.

BEST DRAMA PICTURE
- *Titanic*
Amistad
The Boxer
Good Will Hunting
L.A. Confidential

BEST COMEDY OR MUSICAL PICTURE
- *As Good As It Gets*
The Full Monty
Men in Black
My Best Friend's Wedding
Wag the Dog

BEST DIRECTOR
- James Cameron, *Titanic*
James L. Brooks, *As Good As It Gets*
Curtis Hanson, *L.A. Confidential*
Jim Sheridan, *The Boxer*
Steven Spielberg, *Amistad*

BEST ACTOR, DRAMA
- Peter Fonda, *Ulee's Gold*
Matt Damon, *Good Will Hunting*
Daniel Day-Lewis, *The Boxer*
Leonardo DiCaprio, *Titanic*
Djimon Hounsou, *Amistad*

BEST ACTRESS, DRAMA
- Judi Dench, *Mrs. Brown*
Helena Bonham Carter, *The Wings of the Dove*
Jodie Foster, *Contact*
Jessica Lange, *A Thousand Acres*
Kate Winslet, *Titanic*

BEST ACTOR, COMEDY OR MUSICAL
- Jack Nicholson, *As Good As It Gets*
Jim Carrey, *Liar Liar*
Dustin Hoffman, *Wag the Dog*
Samuel L. Jackson, *Jackie Brown*
Kevin Kline, *In & Out*

BEST ACTRESS, COMEDY OR MUSICAL
- Helen Hunt, *As Good As It Gets*
Joey Lauren Adams, *Chasing Amy*
Pam Grier, *Jackie Brown*
Jennifer Lopez, *Selena*
Julia Roberts, *My Best Friend's Wedding*

BEST SUPPORTING ACTOR
- Burt Reynolds, *Boogie Nights*
Rupert Everett, *My Best Friend's Wedding*
Anthony Hopkins, *Amistad*
Greg Kinnear, *As Good As It Gets*
Jon Voight, *The Rainmaker*
Robin Williams, *Good Will Hunting*

BEST SUPPORTING ACTRESS
- Kim Basinger, *L.A. Confidential*
Joan Cusack, *In & Out*
Julianne Moore, *Boogie Nights*
Gloria Stuart, *Titanic*
Sigourney Weaver, *The Ice Storm*

BEST SCREENPLAY

- Matt Damon, Ben Affleck, *Good Will Hunting*

Mark Andrus, James L. Brooks, *As Good As It Gets*

James Cameron, *Titanic*

Brian Helgeland, Curtis Hanson, *L.A. Confidential*

Hilary Henkin, David Mamet, *Wag the Dog*

BEST SONG

- "My Heart Will Go On," *Titanic*, James Horner, Will Jennings

"Go the Distance," *Hercules*, Alan Menken, David Zippel

"Journey to the Past," *Anastasia*, Stephen Flaherty, Lynn Ahrens

"Once upon a December," *Anastasia*, Stephen Flaherty, Lynn Ahrens

"Tomorrow Never Dies," *Tomorrow Never Dies*, Sheryl Crow, Mitchell Froom

BEST FOREIGN FILM

- *Ma Vie En Rose (My Life in Pink)* (Belgium)

Artemisia (France)

The Best Man (Italy)

Lea (Germany)

The Thief (Russia)

Winners

BEST SCORE

- James Horner, *Titanic*

CECIL B. DEMILLE AWARD

- Shirley MacLaine

SUNDANCE FILM FESTIVAL

The festival was held January 15–25, 1998, at Park City, Utah.

GRAND JURY PRIZE

(DRAMATIC)
- *Slam*, Marc Levin

(DOCUMENTARY)
- *The Farm: Angola, USA*, Jonathan Stack, Liz Garbus
- *Frat House*, Todd Phillips, Andrew Gurland

FILMMAKER'S TROPHY

(DRAMATIC)
- *Smoke Signals*, Chris Eyre

(DOCUMENTARY)
- *Divine Trash*, Steve Yeager

AUDIENCE AWARD

(DRAMATIC)
- *Smoke Signals*, Chris Eyre

(DOCUMENTARY)
- *Out of the Past*, Jeffrey Dupre

DIRECTOR'S AWARD

(DRAMATIC)
- *Pi*, Darren Aronofsky

(DOCUMENTARY)
- *Moment of Impact*, Julia Loktev

WALDO SALT SCREENWRITING AWARD

- *High Art*, Lisa Cholodenko

CINEMATOGRAPHY AWARD

(DRAMATIC)
- *2 by 4*, Declan Quinn

(DOCUMENTARY)
- *Wild Man Blues*, Tom Hurwitz

FREEDOM OF EXPRESSION AWARD

- *The Decline of Western Civilization, Part III*, Penelope Spheeris

LATIN AMERICAN CINEMA AWARD

- *¿Quién Diablos es Juliette?*, Carlos Marcovich

SPECIAL JURY AWARD

(ACTING)
- Andrea Hart, *Miss Monday*

SHORT FILMMAKING AWARD

- *Snake Feed*, Debra Granik

(HONORABLE MENTION)
- *Human Remains*, Jay Rosenblatt

WRITERS GUILD OF AMERICA

Nominations were announced on February 9, 1998. Awards were presented on February 21 at the Beverly Hilton Hotel in Los Angeles and the Roosevelt Hotel in New York.

BEST ORIGINAL SCREENPLAY

- *As Good As It Gets*, Mark Andrus, James L. Brooks
Boogie Nights, Paul Thomas Anderson
The Full Monty, Simon Beaufoy
Good Will Hunting, Matt Damon, Ben Affleck
Titanic, James Cameron

BEST ADAPTED SCREENPLAY

- *L.A. Confidential*, Brian Helgeland, Curtis Hanson
Donnie Brasco, Paul Attanasio, based on the book by Joseph D. Pistone and Richard Woodley
The Ice Strom, James Schamus, based on the novel by Rick Moody
Wag the Dog, Hilary Henkin, David Mamet, based on the book *American Hero* by Larry Beinhart
The Wings of the Dove, Hossein Amini, based on the novel by Henry James

MORGAN COX AWARD

- Melville Shavelson

VALENTINE DAVIES AWARD

- Gary David Goldberg

LAUREL AWARD

- Bo Goldman

PAUL SELVIN AWARD

- Frank Military, *Blind Faith*

PRODUCERS GUILD OF AMERICA

Nominations were announced on January 19, 1998. Awards were presented on March 3 at the Beverly Hilton Hotel in Los Angeles.

DARRYL F. ZANUCK PRODUCER OF THE YEAR AWARD

- *Titanic*, James Cameron, Jon Landau
Amistad, Steven Spielberg, Debbie Allen, Colin Wilson
As Good As It Gets, James L. Brooks, Bridget Johnson, Kristi Zea
Good Will Hunting, Lawrence Bender
L.A. Confidential, Arnon Milchan, Curtis Hanson, Michael Nathanson

MILESTONE AWARD

- Robert A. Daly, Terry Semel

NOVA AWARD

- Uberto Pasolini, *The Full Monty*

DAVID O. SELZNICK LIFETIME ACHIEVEMENT AWARD

- Clint Eastwood

VISION AWARD

- Steven Spielberg, Debbie Allen, Colin Wilson, *Amistad*

DIRECTORS GUILD OF AMERICA

Nominations were announced on January 26, 1998. Awards were presented on March 7 at the Century Plaza Hotel in Los Angeles and at the Windows on the World restaurant in New York.

BEST DIRECTOR

- James Cameron, *Titanic*
James L. Brooks, *As Good As It Gets*
Curtis Hanson, *L.A. Confidential*
Steven Spielberg, *Amistad*
Gus Van Sant, *Good Will Hunting*

ROBERT B. ALDRICH AWARD

- Martha Coolidge

D. W. GRIFFITH AWARD

- Francis Ford Coppola

PRESIDENT'S AWARD

- George Sidney

SCREEN ACTORS GUILD

Awards were presented on March 8, 1998, at the Shrine Auditorium in Los Angeles. The ceremony was telecast by TNT.

BEST ACTOR

- Jack Nicholson, *As Good As It Gets*
Matt Damon, *Good Will Hunting*
Robert Duvall, *The Apostle*
Peter Fonda, *Ulee's Gold*
Dustin Hoffman, *Wag the Dog*

BEST ACTRESS

- Helen Hunt, *As Good As It Gets*

Helena Bonham Carter, *The Wings of the Dove*

Judi Dench, *Mrs. Brown*

Pam Grier, *Jackie Brown*

Kate Winslet, *Titanic*

Robin Wright Penn, *She's So Lovely*

BEST SUPPORTING ACTOR

- Robin Williams, *Good Will Hunting*

Billy Connolly, *Mrs. Brown*

Anthony Hopkins, *Amistad*

Greg Kinnear, *As Good As It Gets*

Burt Reynolds, *Boogie Nights*

BEST SUPPORTING ACTRESS (TIE)

- Kim Basinger, *L.A. Confidential*
- Gloria Stuart, *Titanic*

Minnie Driver, *Good Will Hunting*

Alison Elliott, *The Wings of the Dove*

Julianne Moore, *Boogie Nights*

BEST CAST PERFORMANCE

- *The Full Monty*

Boogie Nights

Good Will Hunting

L.A. Confidential

Titanic

LIFETIME ACHIEVEMENT AWARD

- Elizabeth Taylor

INDEPENDENT SPIRIT

Nominations were announced on January 8, 1998. Awards were presented on March 21 in a tent on the beach in Santa Monica. The ceremony was telecast by the Independent Film Channel.

BEST FEATURE

- *The Apostle*

Chasing Amy

Loved

Ulee's Gold

Waiting for Guffman

BEST FIRST FEATURE

- *Eve's Bayou*

The Bible and Gun Club

Hard Eight

In the Company of Men

Star Maps

BEST DIRECTOR

- Robert Duvall, *The Apostle*

Larry Fessenden, *Habit*

Victor Nunez, *Ulee's Gold*

Paul Schrader, *Touch*

Wim Wenders, *The End of Violence*

BEST ACTOR

- Robert Duvall, *The Apostle*

Peter Fonda, *Ulee's Gold*

Christopher Guest, *Waiting for Guffman*

Philip Baker Hall, *Hard Eight*

John Turturro, *Box of Moonlight*

BEST ACTRESS

- Julie Christie, *Afterglow*

Stacy Edwards, *In the Company of Men*

Alison Folland, *All over Me*

Lisa Harrow, *Sunday*

Robin Wright Penn, *Loved*

BEST SUPPORTING ACTOR

- Jason Lee, *Chasing Amy*

Efrain Figueroa, *Star Maps*

Samuel L. Jackson, *Hard Eight*

Ajay Naidu, *Suburbia*

Roy Scheider, *The Myth of Fingerprints*

BEST SUPPORTING ACTRESS

- Debbi Morgan, *Eve's Bayou*

Farrah Fawcett, *The Apostle*

Amy Madigan, *Loved*

Miranda Richardson, *The Apostle*

Patricia Richardson, *Ulee's Gold*

BEST DEBUT PERFORMANCE

- Aaron Eckhart, *In the Company of Men*

Tyrone Burton, Eddie Cutanda, Phuong Duong, *Squeeze*

Lysa Flores, *Star Maps*

Darling Narita, *Bang*

Douglas Spain, *Star Maps*

BEST SCREENPLAY

- Kevin Smith, *Chasing Amy*

Robert Duvall, *The Apostle*

Christopher Guest, Eugene Levy, *Waiting for Guffman*
Paul Schrader, *Touch*
Victor Nunez, *Ulee's Gold*

BEST FIRST SCREENPLAY
■ Neil Labute, *In the Company of Men*
Paul Thomas Anderson, *Hard Eight*
Miguel Arteta, *Star Maps*
Daniel J. Harris, *The Bible and Gun Club*
Steven S. Schwartz, *Critical Care*

BEST FOREIGN FILM
■ *The Sweet Hereafter* (Canada)
Happy Together (Hong Kong)
Mouth to Mouth (Spain)
Nenette and Boni (France)
Underground (Bosnia)

"SOMEONE TO WATCH" AWARD
■ Scott Saunders, *The Headhunter's Sister*
Erin Digman, *Loved*
Tim Blake Nelson, *Eye of God*

Winners

BEST CINEMATOGRAPHY
■ Declan Quinn, *Kama Sutra*

"TRUER THAN FICTION" DOCUMENTARY AWARD (TIE)
■ *Soul in the Hole*, Danielle Gardner
■ *Fast, Cheap and Out of Control*, Errol Morris

ACADEMY AWARDS

Nominations were announced on February 10, 1998. Awards were presented on March 23 at the Shrine Auditorium in Los Angeles. The ceremony was telecast by ABC.

BEST PICTURE
■ *Titanic*
As Good As It Gets
The Full Monty
Good Will Hunting
L.A. Confidential

BEST DIRECTOR
■ James Cameron, *Titanic*
Peter Cattaneo, *The Full Monty*

Atom Egoyan, *The Sweet Hereafter*
Curtis Hanson, *L.A. Confidential*
Gus Van Sant, *Good Will Hunting*

BEST ACTOR
■ Jack Nicholson, *As Good As It Gets*
Matt Damon, *Good Will Hunting*
Robert Duvall, *The Apostle*
Peter Fonda, *Ulee's Gold*
Dustin Hoffman, *Wag the Dog*

BEST ACTRESS
■ Helen Hunt, *As Good As It Gets*
Helena Bonham Carter, *The Wings of the Dove*
Julie Christie, *Afterglow*
Judi Dench, *Mrs. Brown*
Kate Winslet, *Titanic*

BEST SUPPORTING ACTOR
■ Robin Williams, *Good Will Hunting*
Robert Forster, *Jackie Brown*
Anthony Hopkins, *Amistad*
Greg Kinnear, *As Good As It Gets*
Burt Reynolds, *Boogie Nights*

BEST SUPPORTING ACTRESS
■ Kim Basinger, *L.A. Confidential*
Joan Cusack, *In & Out*
Minnie Driver, *Good Will Hunting*
Julianne Moore, *Boogie Nights*
Gloria Stuart, *Titanic*

BEST ORIGINAL SCREENPLAY
■ Ben Affleck, Matt Damon, *Good Will Hunting*
Woody Allen, *Deconstructing Harry*
Mark Andrus, James L. Brooks, *As Good As It Gets*
Paul Thomas Anderson, *Boogie Nights*
Simon Beaufoy, *The Full Monty*

BEST ADAPTED SCREENPLAY
■ Curtis Hanson, Brian Helgeland, *L.A. Confidential*
Hossein Amini, *The Wings of the Dove*
Paul Attanasio, *Donnie Brasco*
Atom Egoyan, *The Sweet Hereafter*
Hilary Henkin, David Mamet, *Wag the Dog*

BEST SONG
■ "My Heart Will Go On," *Titanic*, James Horner, Will Jennings

"Go the Distance," *Hercules*, Alan Menken, David Zippel
"How Do I Live," *Con Air*, Diane Warren
"Journey to the Past," *Anastasia*, Lynn Ahrens, Stephen Flaherty
"Miss Misery," *Good Will Hunting*, Elliott Smith

BEST FOREIGN-LANGUAGE FILM
- *Character* (Netherlands)

Beyond Silence (Germany)
Four Days in September (Brazil)
Secrets of the Heart (Spain)
The Thief (Russia)

Winners

BEST ART DIRECTION
- Peter Lamont, Michael Ford, *Titanic*

BEST CINEMATOGRAPHY
- Russell Carpenter, *Titanic*

BEST COSTUME DESIGN
- Deborah L. Scott, *Titanic*

BEST DOCUMENTARY
(FEATURE)
- *The Long Way Home*, Rabbi Marvin Hier, Richard Trank

(SHORT SUBJECT)
- *A Story of Healing*, Donna Dewey, Carol Pasternak

BEST FILM EDITING
- Conrad Buff, James Cameron, Richard A. Harris, *Titanic*

BEST MAKEUP
- David Leroy Anderson, Rick Baker, *Men in Black*

BEST MUSIC
(ORIGINAL DRAMATIC SCORE)
- James Horner, *Titanic*

(ORIGINAL MUSICAL OR COMEDY SCORE)
- Anne Dudley, *The Full Monty*

SCIENTIFIC OR TECHNICAL AWARDS
(Academy Award of Merit)
- Guhnar P. Michelson

(Scientific and Engineering Award)
- Wilson H. Allen, Dominique Boisvert, Tom Duff, Réjean Gagné, John Gibson, Roy Hall, Kirk Handley, Chuck Headley, Al Jensen, Joel W. Johnson, William Kovacs, Rob Krieger, Daniel Langlois, Richard Laperrière, Samuel J. Leffler, Ray Meluch, Jean Messner, Hazem Nabulsi, John Neary, Milan Novacek, Eben Ostby, Glen Ozymok, Thomas Porter, William Reeves, Craig W. Reynolds, Scott Robinson, Richard Shoup, Alvy Ray Smith, Dave Springer

(Technical Achievement Award)
- Paul H. Breslin, Jack Cashin, Richard Chuang, Charles E. Converse, Philip C. Cory, Clark F. Crites, Kim Davidson, Mark Elendt, Glenn Entis, Monique C. Fischer, James F. Foley, Jim Frazier, F. Edward Gardner, Rick Gelbard, Greg Hermanovic, Roger Hibbard, Richard Hollander, Larry Jacobson, James J. Keating, Dan Leimeter, Iain Neil, Douglas W. Nishimura, James M. Reilly, Carl Rosendahl, Robert W. Stoker, Jr., Matt Sweeney, Michael Wahrman, Robert Weitz

BEST SHORT FILM
(ANIMATED)
- *Geri's Game*, Jan Pinkava

(LIVE ACTION)
- *Visas and Virtue*, Chris Donahue, Chris Tashima

BEST SOUND
- Tom Johnson, Gary Rydstrom, Gary Summers, Mark Ulano, *Titanic*

BEST SOUND EFFECTS EDITING
- Tom Bellfort, Christopher Boyes, *Titanic*

BEST VISUAL EFFECTS
- Thomas L. Fisher, Michael Kanfer, Mark Lasoff, Robert Legato, *Titanic*

GORDON E. SAWYER AWARD
- Don Iwerks

HONORARY AWARDS
- Pete Clark
- Stanley Donen

The year's awards battle was *supposed* to be a clash between war pix, but just when one of them conquered the other, slayed crix and seized the bulk of early kudos, the feathered pen of a bard proved mightier than any sword or bazooka.

Steven Spielberg took the early ground with summer release *Saving Private Ryan*, a graphic World War II drama about a small band of Yankee troops searching for a private who had parachuted behind enemy lines. Armed with a high-caliber cast that included Tom Hanks and Matt Damon, and reinforced by fawning reviews ("Magnificent!" gushed the *N.Y. Times*; "Brilliant!" cried *Time*), *Saving Private Ryan* was also cheered on by packed movie theaters that took in $190 million before year's end.

But come December, *Ryan*'s kudos chances were challenged by the long-awaited arrival of director Terrence Malick's first pic since *Days of Heaven* (1978). "*The Thin Red Line* has been the talk of film buffs since word leaked out in early 1996 that Malick had committed to filming James Jones' WWII novel about an army troop's rite of passage during the fierce battle of Guadalcanal," *Variety* reported. But when the movie finally premiered, *Variety* called it "a complex, highly talented work (that) may captivate some critics . . . but its abstract nature, emotional remoteness and lack of dramatic focus may frustrate mainstream audiences."

It suddenly looked as if *Saving Private Ryan* would have an easy time marching through the early awards.

But then the National Board of Review

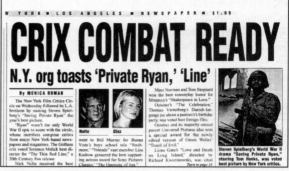

Spielberg's war epic looked Oscar bound when the N.Y. crix backed up the L.A. crix in naming *Saving Private Ryan* Best Picture.

released its list of victors and *Saving Private Ryan* was AWOL.

The board's surprising choice for Best Picture was *Gods and Monsters,* a poignant indie about the final, fade-out days of James Whale (Ian McKellen), the openly gay British director of *Frankenstein,* who lusts after a hunky heterosexual gardener despite the disapproval of his tut-tutting Hungarian housekeeper (Lynn Redgrave). "Better work by an actor will not be seen this year," insisted the *L.A. Times* about McKellen and the board agreed by declaring him Best Actor.

Gods and Monsters's helmer Bill Condon was passed over for Best Director in favor of Shekhar Kapur, whose *Elizabeth* reaped critical huzzahs for its literate and proto-feminist take on the life of England's 16th-century Virgin Queen.

The board also made a startling choice for Best Actress, naming noted Brazilian stage and TV thesp Fernanda Montenegro, winner of the same prize at the Berlin film fest for portraying a crusty con artist who begrudgingly helps a nine-year-old boy find his long-lost father in *Central Station*.

Supporting thesps were cited for multiple roles. Ed Harris was hailed as a godlike TV director in *The Truman Show* and as the boyfriend of the title character in *Stepmom*.

Christina Ricci had a standout year in three roles that included a spitfire tramp who swipes her gay brother's lover and $10,000 and hits the road in *The Opposite of Sex*. She was also acknowledged by the board for starring as the lead character's girlfriend in *Pecker* and a kidnap victim forced to pretend she's the wife of her abductor in *Buffalo 66*.

The board gave its plaque for ensemble acting to the cast of *Happiness*. Todd Solondz's shocking drama about pedophilia and other sexual shenanigans in suburbia that won the International Critics Prize at Cannes, but was considered so racy stateside that it was dropped by its initial distributor.

For the first time since 1994, the L.A. crix jumped ahead of their Gotham peers to announce their winners. The result: "*Saving Private Ryan* took its first critical beachhead," *Variety* reported. *Ryan* also scored kudos for director Spielberg and cinematography.

"I'm quitting while I'm ahead, so tonight I'm announcing my retirement," Spielberg joked when he accepted his laurels at the Bel Age Hotel gala, which was held for the first time at night.

Award watchers were surprised by what placed behind *Ryan* for top pic: *The Butcher Boy*, the tale of an emotionally disturbed Irish lad who discovers a love of violence when he becomes a butcher's assistant. The runner-up for Best Director was another unforeseen choice: John Boorman was hailed for *The General*, about the rise and bloody fall of an Irish crime boss.

Curiously, none of the pix competing for the top two kudos was a leading rival for the screenplay prize. That went to Warren Beatty and Jeremy Pisker for *Bulworth*. "a disarmingly blunt look at a U.S. Senator who suddenly starts speaking the truth about the day's important issues—in

rhyming rap cadences no less," said *Variety*.

What almost beat *Bulworth* for the script honor was a dark-horse pic that would suddenly break into a threatening trot later on in the year's awards derby: Marc Norman and Tom Stoppard's *Shakespeare in Love,* which *Entertainment Weekly* called "that rare thing, a literate crowd-pleaser. Yet it's also the richest and most satisfying romantic movie of the year."

Ian McKellen repeated his earlier victory for Best Actor, followed close behind by Nick Nolte, who portrayed what *Time* called "a part-time cop and fulltime burn-out" in *Affliction*.

After winning the Best Supporting Actress category three years ago as the presidential spouse in *Nixon.* Joan Allen now claimed the category again for playing a saccharine TV sitcom mom who discovers real feelings, including love, in *Pleasantville*. Runner-up was Kathy Bates as a gruff presidential campaign aid in charge of handling "bimbo eruptions" in *Primary Colors*.

The Gotham crix's award to Cameron Diaz caused an outcry.

Fernanda Montenegro tied for the lead actress accolade with Ally Sheedy as a lesbian drug addict who has an affair with her naive neighbor in *High Art*. Reviewers heralded the former Brat Packer's impressive perf as her career comeback, which Sheedy acknowledged when she accepted her award, saying, "Two years ago I could not get arrested!"

Another tie occurred among supporting male players, which included Billy Bob Thornton (*A Simple Plan*) as a backwoods loser who joins his buddies in swiping $4 million they discover in the wreckage of a plane crash. He shared the laurels with Bill Murray as a befuddled tycoon who matches wits with a crafty young nerd over the love of a schoolteacher in *Rushmore*.

An especially witty Murray had the crix howling when he accepted his plaque, at first pretending to be insulted by the tie, but then claiming it was obviously significant that he was called to the podium first. "I do not mind sharing the award because it's so goddamned close to second place," he added, then launched into a snit about the high price of drinks at the fete. He left a hundred-dollar bill on the podium and told the crix to use it toward having an open bar next year.

When he was honored next, Thorton fired back by recalling his early days in the music industry and said. "There were opening acts and then there were the headliners." The audience roared.

When the Gotham crix voted four days after their West Coast peers, they named *Saving Private Ryan* Best Picture (37 points) over *Affliction* (32) and *Happiness* (26). But *Variety* noted, "*Ryan* wasn't the only World War II epic to score with the circle."

The Thin Red Line's Terrence Malick (37 points) was named Best Director over Spielberg (32). *Happiness* came in second for the supporting male laurels when Dylan Baker, who portrayed the pic's controversial pedophile, lost to Bill Murray. *Affliction*'s Nick Nolte prevailed as Best Actor (47 points) over Ian McKellen (33) and the *Shakespeare in Love* scribes took Best Screenplay, but the other categories featured newcomers to the year's kudos derby.

The talent of the crix's supporting actress choice, Lisa Kudrow, may not have been widely appreciated in the past due to her role as a ditsy twentysomething in the TV sitcom *Friends,* but *Time* was so impressed with her star turn in *The Opposite of Sex* that it cheered, "What the heck, let's give a Nobel Prize to Lisa Kudrow as a twisted spinster looking for love!"

But when the Gotham crix gave their Best Actress trophy to Cameron Diaz as the flaky sexpot in *There's Something about Mary,* it triggered a media outcry.

"You know the planets are misaligned when the New York Film Critics Circle announces that 1998's master thespian was Cameron Diaz," fumed *Entertainment Weekly*.

"Those who oppose Diaz's win say it is just an example of how far the N.Y. critics' awards have fallen—that it's all about publicity," columnist Liz Smith wrote. "Those who approve of Cameron snatching the prize say criticism comes because she is so young, so beautiful, so sexy and because comedy is still considered less of an achievement than drama."

Diaz had not been a leading contender on the first two ballots, but rallied as a compromise choice later when the crix deadlocked between Fernanda Montenegro and Renee Zellweger, the latter of whom was considered for two roles: as a pouty daughter trying to cope with her mother's imminent death in *One True Thing* and as a young Jewish mother frustrated by conservative religious rules in *A Price above Rubies*. Diaz's victory, said circle chair Godfrey Cheshire, was "a case of the high-brow members teaming up with the low-brows against the middle brows." Final score on the fourth ballot: Diaz (32 points), Montenegro (28), Zellweger (28).

"The controversial, glamorous presence of Cameron Diaz was the *subject du jour* at the critics' gala," Smith reported about the event where Diaz "seemed to take pains to keep saying, 'I'm shocked, I'm shocked to get this award' to anyone who would listen." Diaz admitted to being "terrified" when she accepted her plaque.

When he took his Best Picture award for *Saving Private Ryan*, Spielberg, son of a World War II veteran, said, "I now understand what my dad went through."

Bill Murray chuckled and confessed what he was thinking privately when he reached the podium: "It's kind of funny to win something you didn't buy a chance on." Nick Nolte said that he was pleased to be acknowledged for one of those "films that we really love to do as artists."

When the National Society of Film Crit-

Spielberg's third victory made him DGA's all-time biggest champ.

ics unveiled its anointed three weeks after the Gothamites, *Entertainment Weekly* reported, "Observers scratched their heads." The society's choice for Best Picture, Director and Screenplay—Steven Soderbergh's *Out of Sight*—seemed to come right out of the blue.

Society exec director Liz Weis explained that *Saving Private Ryan* "was actually way ahead" in the voting with 47 points compared to 20 for *Sight* on the first ballot when members not present at New York's Algonquin Hotel were permitted to participate by proxy. She added, "It just wasn't on a majority of ballots," which was required by society rules. The same rules stipulated that proxies can't vote after the first polling, so when the top-pic race headed into second and third ballots, the outcome was left to the 22 members present out of the 51-person org. That's when *Sight* snagged 35 points, *Affliction* rallied to claim 25 and *Ryan* fell back to the rear position with 24. Soderbergh (28 points) won the helmer's battle over Malick and Spielberg (25 each). *Sight* scriptwriter Scott Frank topped *Shakespeare in Love*'s scribes, 27 to 26.

Although *Sight* shocked award watchers by being named Best Picture, *Variety* described it as "a sly, sexy, vastly entertaining film" starring George Clooney and Jennifer Lopez as a prison escapee and federal marshal who fall in love.

Nick Nolte (62 points) won a commanding first-ballot victory over Ian McKellen (45) for Best Actor. In the lead actress match-up, L.A. crix champ Ally Sheedy (27) beat Cate Blanchett (22), who gave a feisty portrayal of the title character in *Elizabeth*.

Last year noted British stage star Judi Dench won a Golden Globe as Queen Victoria in *Mrs. Brown*. Society crix hailed her this year as a no-nonsense Queen Elizabeth in *Shakespeare in Love*. Dench (28 points) beat Patricia Clarkson (26) as Ally Sheedy's heroin-addict roommate in *High Art*.

Bill Murray (33) continued his romp through the crix awards when he outdistanced Donald Sutherland (28), who starred as a wise track coach in *Without Limits*.

But Murray got stopped by the broadcast crix when they named Billy Bob Thornton as Best Supporting Actor. They also proved to be independently minded by declaring *Elizabeth*'s Cate Blanchett Best Actress.

Joan Allen and Kathy Bates tied for the supporting femme laurels, while Ian McKellen took another bow as Best Actor and Spielberg and *Ryan* reaped the Best Director and Picture honors.

When Spielberg accepted his trophies at the crix's bash, he mentioned how pleased he was to receive them from presenter Drew Barrymore, since he felt like her surrogate father after directing her in *E.T.* when she was six years old. McKellen thanked the nonprint reviewers for having the courage to hail a gay role and said that he considered their recognition further evidence that the world was "growing up."

When the Golden Globe nominations came out, *Saving Private Ryan* received five bids, but it was topped by *Shakespeare in Love* and *The Truman Show,* which both scored six. Surprisingly, *The Thin Red Line, Out of Sight, Pleasantville* and Ally Sheedy were shut out.

"All things being fair and equal in a battle of love and war, *Love* emerged numerically victorious at the Golden Globes," *Variety* reported with the results were in. "*Shakespeare in Love's* trophy tally came to three. *Ryan* took home two."

Shakespeare nabbed the screenplay accolade plus two kudos in the comedy/music categories: Best Picture and Actress. The latter prize went to Gwyenth Paltrow as an heiress smitten with the writings of the young Bard (Joseph Fiennes), who suffers from a bad case of writer's block till he falls for Paltrow and pens *Romeo and Juliet,*

Oscar upsetter *Shakespeare in Love* was "that rare thing, a literate crowd pleaser."

infusing it with tragic echoes of their doomed romance. Accepting her statuette, Paltrow thanked cast, crew, friends, family and Miramax's topper—"the Bomber Weinstein, my godfather."

"Who knew Harvey had a nickname?" *Variety* asked in its next-day report.

After claiming the script prize, Marc Norman told reporters backstage, "If Shakespeare was alive today, he'd be driving a Porsche, living in Bel Air and he'd have a deal with Paramount."

Saving Private Ryan garnered Best Drama Picture and Director. Spielberg told the media, "I made this film for my dad and all his combat friends. I hope this movie is a way of looking back to our fathers and grandfathers and saying, 'Thank you.' "

The Truman Show reaped honors for its music score and two thesps—Best Supporting Actor Ed Harris and Best Drama Actor Jim Carrey as the unknowing star of a 24-hour TV show that follows his seemingly perfect life in a sanitized small town.

Carrey's victory was a jaw-dropper since he was known chiefly as a slapstick comedian, but he trounced Tom Hanks, Ian McKellen and Nick Nolte. The *L.A. Times* said the upset "demonstrated that he now must be taken seriously as an actor."

"I'd like to thank the academy . . . oops, sorry," Carrey said when he took his Globe in hand. "This is serious. It's going to be so hard to talk out of my ass after this, but I'll manage. You know what this means, don't you? I'm a shoo-in for the Blockbuster award."

There was no front-runner in the race for Best Drama Actress, which pitted crix honorees Fernanda Montenegro and Cate Blanchett against Meryl Streep as Renee Zellweger's dying mom in *One True Thing* and Emily Watson (*Hilary and Jackie*) as celebrated British cellist Jacqueline du Pré, who died of multiple sclerosis at age 42 in 1987.

Soon after the stunned Blanchett prevailed, she met reporters backstage, saying, "I've been hugged more in the last four-and-a-half minutes than I have in the whole of my lifetime!"

Globe forecasters predicted that the match-up for Best Comedy or Musical

SAG victory is beautiful: *Shakespeare's* Gwenyth Paltrow bussed *Life's* Italian clown Roberto Benigni backstage.

Craig T. Mathew

Actor was between John Travolta for his savvy impersonation of President Bill Clinton in *Primary Colors* and Warren Beatty as the rapper senator in *Bulworth,* but Michael Caine pulled off an upset as a sleazy showbiz agent in *Little Voice.*

"My career must be slipping," Caine said at the podium. "This is the first time I've ever been available to pick up an award."

With *Pleasantville's* Joan Allen out of the contest for supporting actress, Caine's costar Brenda Blethyn, who portrayed a fun-loving working-class mum in *Little Voice,* was thought to be in a tight race with Judi Dench and Kathy Bates. But a star once honored for *Georgy Girl* usurped them all. Lynn Redgrave said, "I am a little overwhelmed because it has been 32 years since I stood one of these on the mantel and it's been calling for a friend ever since."

Central Station ended up snagging the Globe for Best Foreign Film after a ruckus broke out over the exclusion of a pic disqualified because it had been shown in Italy in 1997—*Life Is Beautiful,* which was suddenly emerging as a late-breaking dark horse in the year's kudos derby.

Life Is Beautiful—the handiwork of veteran Italian filmmaker Roberto Benigni—

had already endured enormous controversy for being a Holocaust comedy about a big-hearted clown who tries to shield his four-year-old son from the horrors of the concentration camp they're in by pretending it's all a game. But the *N.Y. Times* got the joke and insisted, "*Life Is Beautiful* plays by its own rules (and) effectively creates a situation in which comedy is courage." When the pic received the Grand Prize at Cannes, the flamboyant Benigni startled fest-goers by kissing the judges and throwing himself at the feet of jury prexy Martin Scorsese.

But being an offshore film, *Life* wasn't eligible for the writers' guild kudos. The race for Best Original Screenplay was left to the scribes of *Bulworth, The Opposite of Sex, Saving Private Ryan, Shakespeare in Love* and *The Truman Show.* When the Golden Globe victors ended up shining, *Shakespeare*'s Marc Norman said that he felt like a "hottie" and Tom Stoppard said, "I've been coming here for years, but I think it's only this movie that has enabled people to stop treating me as a visitor from the strange world of London theater."

In the category for adapted works, *Out of Sight*'s Scott Frank pulled off an upset over the scribes of *A Civil Action. Gods and Monsters, Primary Colors,* and *A Simple Plan.* Frank confessed that, when he first read the Elmore Leonard best-seller, he became concerned because it was "so good, all I can do is ruin it."

After suffering defeat at the writers guild, *Saving Private Ryan* ambushed the producers' guild and took the top prize, which previously had predicted the eventual Oscar champ 8 out of the past 10 years (80 percent). But the directors' guild had a slightly better forecasting score. Forty-one of the pix helmed by its top honorees had gone on to win the Best Picture Oscar over the past 51 years (80.4 percent). The guild's and Oscar's Best Directors lined up 47 times during that same period (92 percent).

The Oscar noms were already out when the DGA passed out its kudos and, happily, both lists of contenders matched up—a rare occurrence that happened last in 1981. But both lists contained a surprise: *Life Is Beautiful*'s Roberto Benigni filled the spot most

Don Roos scored twin Indie Spirits for his sassy directorial debut, *The Opposite of Sex:* Best First Feature and Best Screenplay.

pundits thought would be taken by *Elizabeth*'s Shekhar Kapur. *Variety* noted, "Of historical significance is the fact that this is Spielberg's ninth DGA nom, pushing him ahead of Alfred Hitchcock, Billy Wilder and Fred Zinnemann, who have eight each."

When Spielberg won, he emerged as the biggest champ in guild history after earlier victories for *The Color Purple* and *Schindler's List.* "I feel blessed and lucky that this project came to me," he said, accepting the plaque.

Saving Private Ryan may have earned a chestful of medals so far—including five Best Picture awards—but considerable forces were busy gathering over the next guild hill.

"*Shakespeare* Doth Nab 5 SAG Noms," *Variety* declared playfully in its headline when the Screen Actors Guild bids were announced. The pic scored one in every category ("*Shakespeare* couldn't have received any more," *Variety* observed), including one for a thesp overlooked at the Globes: Joseph Fiennes, who played the lovesick, Bambi-eyed bard. But the guild bypassed a huge number of thesps honored by other kudos earlier this year— Joan Allen, Jim Carrey, Michael Caine, Ed Harris, Lisa Kudrow, Bill Murray, Christina Ricci, Ally Sheedy and Fernanda Montenegro (whose name was not submitted for nomination—"presumably, an oversight," *Variety* said).

Ryan had two noms over all: one for lead star Tom Hanks and the other for the pic's whole battalion of thesps.

Primary Colors star Kathy Bates opened the ceremony with a tribute to the guild's actors, then took her seat in the audience only to be called back to the stage moments later when she won Best Supporting Actress. Appearing shocked, she said, "I didn't expect this. I thought, when they asked me to do the first thing, it meant I lost."

Also surprised by victory was Best Supporting Actor Robert Duvall, hailed for portraying a shifty corporate lawyer in *A Civil Action*, a role not previously singled out for kudos.

Prior to the SAG awards bash, Globe champ Gwyneth Paltrow told the media that she thought *Elizabeth*'s Cate Blanchett would prevail as Best Actress, so she looked stunned and unprepared when she was summoned to the podium. She rallied quickly and dedicated her award to "a brilliant, beautiful and profound actor, my mother, Blythe Danner." The Oscar race, she added, "was up to the gods." Soon thereafter, she returned to the podium as part of *Shakespeare*'s ensemble, which took the prize for Best Cast Performance.

But in a night of upsets, nobody expressed more amazement—or gratitude—than the recipient of Best Actor, Roberto Benigni. When he heard his name called, the overjoyed champ bounded up to the stage, picked up presenter Helen Hunt, spun her around and cried, "Mamma mia!" He then confessed—in his best broken Eng-

SUNSET IN UTAH
'Three Seasons' wins top fest kudos

By TODD McCARTHY

PARK CITY, Utah — "Three Seasons," Tony Bui's hauntingly poetic vision of contemporary Vietnam, was the big winner of the 1999 Sundance Film Festival, becoming the first film in fest history to snare both the grand jury prize and the audience award in the dramatic competition.

The October Films release, which is the first American picture to have been shot entirely in Vietnam, is also the first foreign-lingo film to have won either of Sundance's top two prizes. As the most artistically ambitious and stylistically accomplished picture in the dramatic competition, "Three Seasons" was widely deemed a worthy winner by critics and other festgoers. Pic is set for the competition at the Berlin Fest in February

"Three Seasons" is the first film to take both the grand jury prize and the audience award at the Sundance Film Festival.

and will open commercially in the U.S. in April.

The grand jury prize in the documentary competition, "American Movie," was also a well-received choice. Chris Smith's observant and often

Turn to page 32

A Sundance first: one feature (*Three Seasons*) won the Grand Jury and Audience Prizes.

lish—that he was so happy that "every organ in my body is moving in a very bad way!" The audience cheered wildly.

Benigni had another reason to be thrilled on SAG night. *Life Is Beautiful* had recently become so popular among movie-goers that, just a few months after its release, it was already the biggest foreign-lingo hit in American film history, grossing more than $30 million ($130 worldwide). The dark-horse pic was suddenly coming on so strong that it looked like a serious rival for top Oscars.

That suspicion was confirmed when Academy Award bids were unveiled and *Life Is Beautiful* reaped seven—the biggest tally among foreign-lingo films ever. Three were for Benigni (as director, actor, co-writer—putting him in the company of past triple contenders Orson Welles, Warren Beatty and Woody Allen). Two other noms were for Best Picture and Best Foreign Film—marking only the second time (after *Z* in 1969) that one movie made both races in one year. (*The Emigrants* was up for top foreign pic in 1971 and Best Picture in 1972.)

Shakespeare led with 13 bids, one short of *All about Eve*'s record. *Ryan* placed second with 11, and *Elizabeth* and *The Thin Red Line* tied *Life Is Beautiful* with 7. When

Variety spotted three World War II movies (*Ryan, Thin Red Line, Life Is Beautiful*) and two Elizabethan films (*Shakespeare, Elizabeth*) in the Best Picture showdown, it declared: "Oscar is wearing combat fatigues. And a codpiece."

But just like at the Globes, there were lots of people snubbed who'd won kudos earlier, including directors Steven Soderbergh, John Boorman and Shekhar Kapur plus thesps Jim Carrey, Cameron Diaz, Ally Sheedy, Joan Allen, Michael Caine, Lisa Kudrow, Christina Ricci and Bill Murray.

"Ever since *Private Ryan* opened last July, pundits have said it's the one to beat for the big prize," *Variety* reported. "The Oscar noms shift the odds a bit to *Shakespeare*'s advantage: in 14 of the past 15 years, the pic that grabbed the most nominations went on to win the Best Picture Oscar. It's hard to remember a year in which there were so many question marks and surprises."

More surprises would follow on awards night.

When the ceremony began, the first category to be decided was Best Supporting Actor. Two *L.A. Times* pundits picked L.A. and broadcast crix champ Billy Bob Thornton to win, while *TV Guide* and *Entertainment Weekly* endorsed Ed Harris. "He's got the Globe, but can you believe this guy's *never* won an Oscar?" *EW* asked about Harris, setting his odds at 5 to 2. In last place, with 10-to-1 odds, was veteran screen thesp James Coburn, who played Nick Nolte's tyrannical, alcoholic father in *Affliction*. The magazine said that Coburn may have "delivered a career-capping performance at age 70, (but) voters are no longer so inclined to use Oscars as *de facto* lifetime achievement awards—just ask Burt Reynolds and Lauren Bacall."

But Coburn beat the odds to claim the statuette, saying, "I've been doing this for over half my life. I finally got one right, I guess."

Entertainment Weekly, TV Guide and one *L.A. Times* pundit forecast that national crix society champ Judi Dench would take Best Supporting Actress, even though her role in *Shakespeare* was so brief (eight minutes)

that it would set a new record for the shortest Oscar perf. One other *Times* pundit, however, sided with SAG and broadcast crix honoree Kathy Bates, no doubt because she was the only American in the race. Whenever a similar match-up had occurred at Oscars past, the Yank always won. But not this time.

"I feel, for eight minutes on the screen, I should only get a little bit of him," Dench said when she was handed the golden boy.

Dench's win marked the second victory of the night for *Shakespeare,* which also took the prize for art direction early during the Oscarcast. *Saving Private Ryan* soon pulled even by nabbing the kudos for sound and sound effects.

The next race offered a glimpse at how formidable this year's wildcard—Roberto Benigni—might be, since *Life Is Beautiful* was up for Best Foreign Film.

When *Life* prevailed, Benigni proved to be truly wild. He danced on the back of seats in the audience and bounced up to the stage.

The *L.A. Times* reported, "He then threatened to kiss everyone for what he called 'a rainstorm of kindness.' " Benigni thanked his parents for giving him "the biggest gift—poverty" and dedicated his win to the Holocaust victims "who gave their lives in order that we could say 'life is beautiful.' " The audience gave him a cheery standing ovation.

"The cult of Terrence Malick wants to see its man take the stage for *The Thin Red Line*," *TV Guide* said when it sized up the contest for adapted works. *Entertainment Weekly* and one *L.A. Times* pundit also picked Malick, but the newspaper's other forecaster went out on a limb for *Gods and Monsters*—and proved to be right.

Ryan and *Shakespeare* squared off against *Life Is Beautiful* in the showdown over Best Original Screenplay, but all Oscar seers predicted an easy win for *Shakespeare. Entertainment Weekly* reasoned, "It's a movie about the genius of *writing,* which means voters will most likely pay tribute to it by rewarding the script."

They did. The trophy was claimed by *Shakespeare*'s co-writer, elegantly reserved

Tom Stoppard, who said with stoic aplomb, "I'm behaving like Roberto Benigni underneath."

SAG champ Benigni competed for Best Actor against two rivals who had been honored already by two crix orgs each—Ian McKellen and Nick Nolte—plus the hugely popular star of *Ryan,* Tom Hanks, a proven winner at two past Oscars.

Predix were scattered. The Las Vegas Hilton bet on Nolte, *Entertainment Weekly* backed Benigni, *TV Guide* and one *L.A. Times* pundit wagered on McKellen and the other *Times* prognosticator rooted for Hanks.

The audience ended up cheering Benigni when he was called to the stage for a second time. Obviously overwhelmed and giddy with excitement, he threw out his arms upon accepting the statuette and said, "This is a terrible mistake because I used up all my English! Now my body is in tumult because it's a colossal moment of joy. I would like to be Jupiter and kidnap everybody and lie down in the firmament making love to everybody!"

"Whatever this man is looped on, let's all get some," *Variety* said.

Benigni's triumph marked only the third time in Oscar history that a thesp was honored for a non-English role, following previous Italian-language wins by Sophia Loren in 1961 for *Two Women* and Robert De Niro in 1974 for *The Godfather, Part II.*

Another Oscar milestone was reached in the Best Actress competish when Meryl Streep (*One True Thing*) reaped her eleventh bid, which tied her with Jack Nicholson for having the second-most behind 12-time contender Katharine Hepburn.

But expert handicappers said the race was between two other rivals, splitting their endorsements between both Golden Globe champs: Cate Blanchett (*TV Guide,* one *L.A. Times* pundit) and Gwyneth Paltrow (*Entertainment Weekly,* Las Vegas Hilton, the other *L.A. Times* pundit).

When Paltrow won, she gave another Oscar-worthy perf at the podium as she wept with happiness while thanking a long list of family, friends and colleagues. Spy-ing the audience, the *L.A. Times* observed, "There was not a dry eye in the house."

When Paltrow got backstage, one reporter told her that she had triggered tears in the press room, too. "Come on, you all are a bunch of hardened, cynical journalists!" she exclaimed. "Don't try to pull that on me!"

Paltrow's win was the sixth of the night for *Shakespeare. Ryan* had claimed only four kudos when it came time to bestow Best Director, which all prognosticators agreed would go to Spielberg regardless of what film prevailed as best pic. When the forecast proved true, the previous awardee for *Schindler's List* became the seventeenth person in Oscar history to win more than one trophy for helming.

"Am I allowed to say I really wanted this?" he asked when he struck gold again. "I'd like to just thank—very, very sincerely—the families who lost sons in World War II."

Since the film that reaps the director's prize usually bags the Best Picture Oscar, too, *Ryan* seemed poised for ultimate conquest. *Variety* noted that it had a strategic advantage historically: "More than any other genre, war films have commanded their disproportionate share of Best Picture Oscars"—19 in the award's 70 years. *TV Guide, Entertainment Weekly* and both *L.A. Times* pundits were solidly in its camp. Only one prominent Oscar seer was fighting the good fight for *Shakespeare:* Roger Ebert of *The Chicago Sun-Times.*

When the last envelope was opened at the last Oscar ceremony of the century, its contents proved that all's well that ends well for *Shakespeare.*

Over all, it was night full of many surprises, but *Variety* noted, "Academy voters saved the biggest one for last."

Surprise reigned at the Independent Spirit awards, too. *Entertainment Weekly* reported, "Low key, yes, but the Spirits did offer vindication for those the academy forgot. Much-deserved statues went to Best Picture shut-out *Gods and Monsters, Rushmore* star Bill Murray, *The Opposite of Sex's* Don Roos and *High Art's* Ally Sheedy."

The big shocker was that the pix with the most bids did not snag the top kudos: *Affliction* led with six noms, followed by five for *High Art.*

But *Gods and Monsters,* which started with four chances, emerged with three wins: Best Feature, Actor and Supporting Actress.

Ian McKellen topped Nick Nolte for the male thesp's honor and saluted *Gods and Monsters*'s writer and director for championing a pic that "told the truth" about homosexuality and old Hollywood. "Have things changed?" he asked. "Well, an openly gay man is saying 'good morning' and 'thank you.' "

When his supporting costar Lynn Redgrave won, too, it was much appreciated by the screen veteran whose personal life was being rocked by scandal just when her professional career was experiencing an upswing. Two weeks before the awards gala, Redgrave split with her longtime husband and manager, who recently confessed that he had fathered an illegitimate child by his former assistant—who later married his son. When the love child officially entered her family, the clueless Redgrave helped to raise the boy as her adopted grandson.

"If you've been reading the tabloids, you know how very important this is to me," she said, accepting her trophy. "I went to my shrink first this morning. That was a great prep."

After penning such hits as *Boys on the Side* and *Single White Female*, Don Roos assumed the helm for the first time on his next project, *The Opposite of Sex*, and was rewarded with Spirits for Best First Feature and Best Screenplay. As he claimed the script prize, Roos thanked computer tycoon Bill Gates for creating the Microsoft program "or otherwise I'd be accepting this award with White-Out all over my fingers."

Strangely, neither Roos nor the helmer of *Gods and Monsters*, Bill Condon, were nommed for Best Director, which went to Wes Anderson (*Rushmore*) over such heavyweight rivals as Todd Solondz (*Happiness*), Paul Schrader (*Affliction*) and Todd Haynes (*Velvet Goldmine*).

Variety reported that the gala's "most emotional winner" was Best Actress Ally Sheedy (*High Art*), who warned the audience as she took the podium, "I'm not going to be quick. I don't care. I've never been nominated before and this may never happen again. I'm glad I wore my waterproof mascara."

Oscar-snubbed Bill Murray wasn't present to accept his prize for Best Supporting Actor, but sent a note, saying, "I'm still courting the academy."

A breakthrough occurred at the Sundance film fest when one pic claimed both the Grand Jury and Audience Prizes for features for the first time ever: *Three Seasons*, described by *Variety* as "a poetic vision of contemporary Vietnam." It also snagged a prize for cinematography.

"I'm completely blown away," said filmmaker Tony Bui as he reaped his kudos bounty. "This all feels like one big wonderful dream!"

American Movie, a wry look at the travails of a struggling Milwaukee filmmaker, not only claimed the Grand Jury Prize for docus, but also snagged a $800,000 distrib deal from Sony Pictures Classics. Its creator, Chris Smith, told the *N.Y. Times,* "I'm still going to try to borrow money off my dad. Otherwise, you get stuck having to use somebody's actress girlfriend in your movie."

An even bigger distrib deal was scored by *Tumbleweeds,* a mother-daughter road pic that lost the Grand Jury Prize for features, but rebounded with the Filmmaker's Trophy plus a plum contract with Fine Line. *Entertainment Weekly* said that director Gavin O'Connor "hammered out his reported $1 million to $1.5 million deal in a marathon 18-hour session during which he couldn't even leave to feed his dog." *Variety* said the deal was "north of $5 million." Next year, after the pic's release, O'Connor's film would strike gold at the foreign press and crix awards.

The Filmmaker's Trophy for docus went to *Sing Faster*, which offered a glimpse backstage at the San Francisco Opera. Winner of the Audience Award for docus was *Genghis Blues,* described by *Variety* as "an account of an American blues singer's absorption in Tuvan throat singing." A docu about American and Vietnamese women widowed by the war, *Regret to Inform*, was honored in the Director's Award lineup. Feature champ in that group was *Judy Berlin*, which spied a solar eclipse from the shores of Long Island, New York.

A tie occurred for the screenplay award between *Guinevere*, a drama about an innocent female student's affair with an older bohemian photographer, and *Joe the King*, "a study of an abused kid's traumatic life," said *Variety*.

The most notable fest entry was *Happy, Texas*, a Grand Jury Prize loser that earned a Special Jury Award for its star, Steve Zahn, as an escaped con who hides from the law by pretending to be a gay beauty-pageant judge. It became the target of a fierce bidding war between distributors, which Mira-

max ultimately won when it snatched the rights for a rumored $10 million.

Variety reported that Sundance was the setting for "one of the biggest shopping sprees of its 15-year history." Artisan Entertainment would turn out to get the biggest bargain when it paid $1.1 million for a "horror mockumentary" that won no awards, but was a big hit at midnight screenings: *The Blair Witch Project*, about three filmmakers who vanish in the woods after they set out to find a legendary sorceress. It was also destined to become a huge summertime hit, grossing more than $100 million within 30 days of its July 16 opening—and scaring up another $40 million by year's end. Filmed for $35,000 (plus $500,000 in post-production costs), *Blair* soon became, *Variety* noted, "in ratio to its original cost, the most profitable film ever made."

▪ 1998 ▪

NATIONAL BOARD OF REVIEW

The board declared a Best Picture and Foreign Film of the year, then listed its remaining favorites according to highest scores. The vote results were announced on December 8, 1998. Awards were presented on February 8, 1999, at the Tavern on the Green in New York.

BEST PICTURE
▪ *Gods and Monsters*
Saving Private Ryan
Elizabeth
Happiness
Shakespeare in Love
The Butcher Boy
Lolita
The Thin Red Line
A Simple Plan
Dancing at Lughnasa

BEST DIRECTOR
▪ Shekhar Kapur, *Elizabeth*

BEST ACTOR
▪ Ian McKellen, *Gods and Monsters*

BEST ACTRESS
▪ Feranda Montenegro, *Central Station*

BEST SUPPORTING ACTOR
▪ Ed Harris, *The Truman Show, Stepmom*

BEST SUPPORTING ACTRESS
▪ Christina Ricci, *The Opposite of Sex, Pecker, Buffalo 66*

BEST ENSEMBLE PERFORMANCE
▪ *Happiness*

BEST SCREENPLAY
▪ Scott B. Smith, *A Simple Plan*

BEST DOCUMENTARY
▪ *Wild Man Blues*, Barbara Kopple

BEST FOREIGN FILM
▪ *Central Station* (Brazil)
Life Is Beautiful (Italy)
The Thief (Russia)
Beyond Silence (Germany)
Men with Guns (U.S., Spanish language)

FREEDOM OF EXPRESSION AWARD
▪ Bernardo Bertolucci

BILLY WILDER AWARD
- Martin Scorsese

CAREER ACHIEVEMENT AWARD
- Michael Caine

SPECIAL ACHIEVEMENT AWARD
- Roberto Benigni, *Life Is Beautiful*

LOS ANGELES FILM CRITICS ASSOCIATION

Winners were announced on December 12, 1998. Awards were presented on January 20, 1999, at the Bel Age Hotel in Los Angeles.

BEST PICTURE
- *Saving Private Ryan*

BEST DIRECTOR
- Steven Spielberg, *Saving Private Ryan*

BEST ACTOR
- Ian McKellen, *Gods and Monsters*

BEST ACTRESS (TIE)
- Fernanda Montenegro, *Central Station*
- Ally Sheedy, *High Art*

BEST SUPPORTING ACTOR (TIE)
- Bill Murray, *Rushmore*
- Billy Bob Thornton, *A Simple Plan*

BEST SUPPORTING ACTRESS
- Joan Allen, *Pleasantville*

BEST SCREENPLAY
- Warren Beatty, Jeremy Pisker, *Bulworth*

BEST ANIMATION
- *A Bug's Life*
- *T.R.A.N.S.I.T.*

BEST CINEMATOGRAPHY
- Janusz Kaminski, *Saving Private Ryan*

BEST MUSIC
- Elliot Goldenthal, *The Butcher Boy*

BEST PRODUCTION DESIGN
- Jeannine Oppewall, *Pleasantville*

BEST DOCUMENTARY
- *The Farm: Angola, USA*, Jonathan Stack, Liz Garbus

BEST FOREIGN FILM
- *The Celebration* (Denmark)

BEST INDEPENDENT/EXPERIMENTAL FILM
- *Shulie*, Elizabeth Subrin

NEW GENERATION AWARD
- Wes Anderson, *Rushmore*

CAREER ACHIEVEMENT AWARD
- Julius Epstein
- Abraham Polonsky

SPECIAL AWARDS
- Rick Schmidlin, Walter Murch, Jonathan Rosenbaum, Bob O'Neil
- Barbara Zicka Smith

NEW YORK FILM CRITICS CIRCLE

Winners were announced on December 16, 1998. Awards were presented on January 10, 1999, at the Windows on the World restaurant in New York.

BEST PICTURE
- *Saving Private Ryan*

BEST FIRST FEATURE
- *Love and Death on Long Island*

BEST DIRECTOR
- Terrence Malick, *The Thin Red Line*

BEST ACTOR
- Nick Nolte, *Affliction*

BEST ACTRESS
- Cameron Diaz, *There's Something about Mary*

BEST SUPPORTING ACTOR
- Bill Murray, *Rushmore*

BEST SUPPORTING ACTRESS
- Lisa Kudrow, *The Opposite of Sex*

BEST SCREENWRITER
- Marc Norman, Tom Stoppard, *Shakespeare in Love*

BEST CINEMATOGRAPHER
- John Toll, *The Thin Red Line*

BEST DOCUMENTARY
- *The Farm: Angola, USA*, Jonathan Stack, Liz Garbus

BEST FOREIGN FILM
- *The Celebration* (Denmark)

SPECIAL AWARD
- Newly cut version of *A Touch of Evil*

NATIONAL SOCIETY OF FILM CRITICS

Winners were announced on January 3, 1999.

BEST PICTURE
- *Out of Sight*

BEST DIRECTOR
- Steven Soderbergh, *Out of Sight*

BEST ACTOR
- Nick Nolte, *Affliction*

BEST ACTRESS
- Ally Sheedy, *High Art*

BEST SUPPORTING ACTOR
- Bill Murray, *Rushmore*

BEST SUPPORTING ACTRESS
- Judi Dench, *Shakespeare in Love*

BEST SCREENPLAY
- Scott Frank, *Out of Sight*

BEST CINEMATOGRAPHY
- *The Thin Red Line*, John Toll

BEST DOCUMENTARY
- *The Farm: Angola, USA*, Jonathan Stack, Liz Garbus

BEST FOREIGN-LANGUAGE FILM
- *Taste of Cherry* (Iran)

SPECIAL CITATION
- *Mother and Son*

BROADCAST FILM CRITICS ASSOCIATION

Winners in all categories but Best Picture were announced on December 21, 1998. The top pic champ was revealed when the awards were presented on January 25, 1999, at the Sofitel Hotel in Los Angeles.

BEST PICTURE
- *Saving Private Ryan*

BEST DIRECTOR
- Steven Spielberg, *Saving Private Ryan*

BEST ACTOR
- Ian McKellen, *Gods and Monsters, Apt Pupil*

BEST ACTRESS
- Cate Blanchett, *Elizabeth*

BEST SUPPORTING ACTOR
- Billy Bob Thornton, *A Simple Plan, Primary Colors*

BEST SUPPORTING ACTRESS (TIE)
- Joan Allen, *Pleasantville*
- Kathy Bates, *Primary Colors*

BEST CHILD PERFORMANCE
- Ian Michael Smith, *Simon Birch*

BEST BREAKTHROUGH PERFORMER
- Joseph Fiennes, *Shakespeare in Love, Elizabeth*

BEST ORIGINAL SCREENPLAY
- Marc Norman, Tom Stoppard, *Shakespeare in Love*

BEST ADAPTED SCREENPLAY
- Scott A. Smith, *A Simple Plan*

BEST SCORE
- John Williams, *Saving Private Ryan*

BEST SONG
- "When You Believe," *The Prince of Egypt*, Stephen Schwartz

BEST ANIMATED FEATURE (TIE)
- *A Bug's Life*
- *The Prince of Egypt*

BEST DOCUMENTARY
- *Wild Man Blues*, Barbara Kopple

BEST FOREIGN FILM
- *Life Is Beautiful* (Italy)

BEST FAMILY FILM
- *A Bug's Life*

ALAN J. PAKULA AWARD
- John Travolta

GOLDEN GLOBES

Nominations were announced on December 17, 1998. Awards were presented on January 24, 1999, at the Beverly Hilton Hotel in Los Angeles. The ceremony was telecast by NBC.

BEST DRAMA PICTURE
- *Saving Private Ryan*
- *Elizabeth*
- *Gods and Monsters*
- *The Horse Whisperer*
- *The Truman Show*

BEST COMEDY OR MUSICAL PICTURE
- *Shakespeare in Love*
- *Bulworth*
- *The Mask of Zorro*
- *Patch Adams*
- *Still Crazy*
- *There's Something about Mary*

BEST DIRECTOR
- Steven Spielberg, *Saving Private Ryan*
- Shekhar Kapur, *Elizabeth*
- John Madden, *Shakespeare in Love*
- Robert Redford, *The Horse Whisperer*
- Peter Weir, *The Truman Show*

BEST ACTOR, DRAMA
- Jim Carrey, *The Truman Show*
- Stephen Fry, *Wilde*
- Tom Hanks, *Saving Private Ryan*
- Ian McKellen, *Gods and Monsters*
- Nick Nolte, *Affliction*

BEST ACTRESS, DRAMA
- Cate Blanchett, *Elizabeth*
- Fernanda Montenegro, *Central Station*
- Susan Sarandon, *Stepmom*
- Meryl Streep, *One True Thing*
- Emily Watson, *Hilary and Jackie*

BEST ACTOR, COMEDY OR MUSICAL
- Michael Caine, *Little Voice*
- Antonio Banderas, *The Mask of Zorro*
- Warren Beatty, *Bulworth*
- John Travolta, *Primary Colors*
- Robin Williams, *Patch Adams*

BEST ACTRESS, COMEDY OR MUSICAL
- Gwyneth Paltrow, *Shakespeare in Love*
- Cameron Diaz, *There's Something about Mary*
- Jane Horrocks, *Little Voice*
- Christina Ricci, *The Opposite of Sex*
- Meg Ryan, *You've Got Mail*

BEST SUPPORTING ACTOR
- Ed Harris, *The Truman Show*
- Robert Duvall, *A Civil Action*
- Bill Murray, *Rushmore*
- Geoffrey Rush, *Shakespeare in Love*
- Donald Sutherland, *Without Limits*
- Billy Bob Thornton, *A Simple Plan*

BEST SUPPORTING ACTRESS
- Lynn Redgrave, *Gods and Monsters*
- Kathy Bates, *Primary Colors*
- Brenda Blethyn, *Little Voice*
- Judi Dench, *Shakespeare in Love*
- Sharon Stone, *The Mighty*

BEST SCREENPLAY
- Marc Norman, Tom Stoppard, *Shakespeare in Love*
- Warren Beatty, Jeremy Pikser, *Bulworth*
- Andrew Niccol, *The Truman Show*
- Robert Rodat, *Saving Private Ryan*
- Todd Solondz, *Happiness*

BEST SONG

- "The Prayer," *Quest for Camelot*, David Foster, Carole Bayer Sager

"The Flame Still Burns," *Still Crazy*, Mick Jones, Marti Frederiksen, Chris Difford

"The Mighty," *The Mighty*, Trevor Jones, Sting

"Reflection," *Mulan,* Matthew Wilder, David Zippel

"Uninvited," *City of Angels*, Alanis Morissette

"When You Believe," *The Prince of Egypt*, Stephen Schwartz

BEST FOREIGN FILM

- *Central Station* (Brazil)

The Celebration (Denmark)

Hombres Armados (Men with Guns) U.S., Spanish language)

The Polish Bride (Netherlands)

Tango (Argentina)

Winners

BEST SCORE

- Burkhard Dallwitz, Philip Glass, *The Truman Show*

CECIL B. DEMILLE AWARD

- Jack Nicholson

SUNDANCE FILM FESTIVAL

The festival was held January 21–31, 1999, at Park City, Utah.

GRAND JURY PRIZE

(DRAMATIC)

- *Three Seasons*, Tony Bui

(DOCUMENTARY)

- *American Movie*, Chris Smith

FILMMAKER'S TROPHY

(DRAMATIC)

- *Tumbleweeds*, Gavin O'Connor

(DOCUMENTARY)

- *Sing Faster: The Stagehands' Ring Cycle*, Jon Else

AUDIENCE AWARD

(DRAMATIC)

- *Three Seasons*, Tony Bui

(DOCUMENTARY)

- *Genghis Blues*, Roko Belic

DIRECTOR'S AWARD

(DRAMATIC)

- *Judy Berlin*, Eric Mendelsohn

(DOCUMENTARY)

- *Regret to Inform*, Barbara Sonneborn

WALDO SALT SCREENWRITING AWARD

- *Guinevere*, Audrey Wells
- *Joe the King*, Frank Whaley

FREEDOM OF EXPRESSION AWARD

- *The Black Press: Soldiers without Swords*, Stanley Nelson

LATIN AMERICA CINEMA JURY AWARD

- *Santitos*, Alejandro Springall (Mexico)

WORLD CINEMA AUDIENCE AWARD

- *Run Lola Run*, Tom Tykwer (Germany)
- *Train of Life,* Radu Mihaileanu (France)

CINEMATOGRAPHY AWARD

(DRAMATIC)

- *Three Seasons*, Lisa Rinzler

(DOCUMENTARY)

- *Rabbit in the Moon, Regret to Inform*, Emiko Omori

SHORT FILMMAKING AWARD

- *More,* Mark Osborne

SPECIAL JURY AWARD

(COMEDIC PERFORMANCE)

- Steve Zahn, *Happy, Texas*

(DISTINCTIVE VISION IN FILMMAKING)

- Scott King, *Treasure Island*

(DOCUMENTARY)

- *On the Ropes*, Nanette Burstein, Brett Morgen

(LATIN AMERICAN CINEMA)

- *La Vida es Silbar (Life Is to Whistle)*, Fernando Pérez (Cuba)

(SHORT FILMMAKING)

- *Fishbelly White*, Michael Burke

(SHORT FILMMAKING HONORABLE MENTION)

- *Atomic Tabasco,* James Cox
- *Come unto Me: The Faces of Tyree Guyton*, Nicole Cattell
- *Devil Doll/Ring Pull*, Jarl Olsen

- *Pack of Gifts*, Corky Quakenbush
- *Stubble Trouble*, Philip Holahan

WRITERS GUILD OF AMERICA

Nominations were announced on February 3, 1999. Awards were presented on February 20 at the Beverly Hilton Hotel in Los Angeles and the Windows on the World restaurant in New York City.

BEST ORIGINAL SCREENPLAY
- *Shakespeare in Love*, Marc Norman, Tom Stoppard

Bulworth, Warren Beatty, Jeremy Pikser
The Opposite of Sex, Don Roos
Saving Private Ryan, Robert Rodat
The Truman Show, Andrew Niccol

BEST ADAPTED SCREENPLAY
- *Out of Sight*, Scott Frank, based on the novel by Elmore Leonard

A Civil Action, Steven Zaillian, based on the book by Jonathan Harr
Gods and Monsters, Bill Condon, based on the novel *Father of Frankenstein* by Christopher Bram
Primary Colors, Elaine May, based on the novel by Anonymous
A Simple Plan, Scott B. Smith, based on his novel

MORGAN COX AWARD
- Del Reisman

VALENTINE DAVIES AWARD
- Barry Kemp

FOUNDER'S AWARD
- Frank Pierson

LAUREL AWARD
- Paul Schrader

ROBERT MELTZER AWARD
- Paul Jarrico

EDMUND H. NORTH AWARD
- Frank Pierson

PAUL SELVIN AWARD
- Frank Military

PRODUCERS GUILD OF AMERICA

Nominations were announced on January 19, 1999. Awards were presented on March 3 at the Century Plaza Hotel in Los Angeles.

DARRYL F. ZANUCK PRODUCER OF THE YEAR AWARD
- *Saving Private Ryan*, Steven Spielberg, Ian Bryce, Mark Gordon, Gary Levinsohn, Bonnie Curtis, Allison Lyon Segan

Gods and Monsters, David Forrest, Beau Rogers, Stephen P. Jarchow, Clive Barker, Spencer Proffer, Sam Irvin, Valorie Massalas, Mark R. Harris, Gregg Fienberg, Paul Colichman
Life Is Beautiful, Elda Ferri, Gianluigi Braschi, Mario Cotone
Shakespeare in Love, Bob Weinstein, Julie Goldstein, David Parfitti, Donna Gigliotti, Harvey Weinstein, Edward Zwick, Marc Nerman
Waking Ned Devine, Alexandre Heylen, Stephen Margolis, Glynis Murray, Richard Holmes, Neil Peplow

MILESTONE AWARD
- Steven Spielberg

NOVA AWARD
- Peter Farrelly, Bobby Farrelly, *There's Something about Mary*

DAVID O. SELZNICK LIFETIME ACHIEVEMENT AWARD
- Ray Stark

VISION AWARD
- Gary Ross, *Pleasantville*

DIRECTORS GUILD OF AMERICA

Nominations were announced on January 25, 1999. Awards were presented on March 6 at the Century Plaza Hotel in Los Angeles.

BEST DIRECTOR
- Steven Spielberg, *Saving Private Ryan*

Roberto Benigni, *Life Is Beautiful*
John Madden, *Shakespeare in Love*
Terrence Malick, *The Thin Red Line*
Peter Weir, *The Truman Show*

ROBERT B. ALDRICH AWARD
- Arthur Hiller

SCREEN ACTORS GUILD

Nominations were announced on January 26, 1999. Awards were presented on March 7 at the Shrine Auditorium in Los Angeles. The ceremony was telecast by TNT.

BEST ACTOR
- Roberto Benigni, *Life Is Beautiful*

Joseph Fiennes, *Shakespeare in Love*
Tom Hanks, *Saving Private Ryan*
Ian McKellen, *Gods and Monsters*
Nick Nolte, *Affliction*

BEST ACTRESS
- Gwyneth Paltrow, *Shakespeare in Love*

Cate Blanchett, *Elizabeth*
Jane Horrocks, *Little Voice*
Meryl Streep, *One True Thing*
Emily Watson, *Hilary and Jackie*

BEST SUPPORTING ACTOR
- Robert Duvall, *A Civil Action*

James Coburn, *Affliction*
David Kelly, *Waking Ned Devine*
Geoffrey Rush, *Shakespeare in Love*
Billy Bob Thornton, *A Simple Plan*

BEST SUPPORTING ACTRESS
- Kathy Bates, *Primary Colors*

Brenda Blethyn, *Little Voice*
Judi Dench, *Shakespeare in Love*
Rachel Griffiths, *Hilary and Jackie*
Lynn Redgrave, *Gods and Monsters*

BEST CAST PERFORMANCE
- *Shakespeare in Love*

Life Is Beautiful
Little Voice
Saving Private Ryan
Waking Ned Devine

LIFETIME ACHIEVEMENT AWARD
- Kirk Douglas

INDEPENDENT SPIRIT

Nominations were announced on January 8, 1999. Awards were presented on March 20 in a tent on the beach in Santa Monica. The ceremony was telecast by the Independent Film Channel.

BEST FEATURE
- *Gods and Monsters*

Affliction
Claire Dolan
A Soldier's Daughter Never Cries
Velvet Goldmine

BEST FIRST FEATURE
- *The Opposite of Sex*

Buffalo 66
High Art
Pi
Slums of Beverly Hills

BEST DIRECTOR
- Wes Anderson, *Rushmore*

Todd Haynes, *Velvet Goldmine*
Lodge Kerrigan, *Claire Dolan*
Paul Schrader, *Affliction*
Todd Solondz, *Happiness*

BEST ACTOR
- Ian McKellen, *Gods and Monsters*

Dylan Baker, *Happiness*
Nick Nolte, *Affliction*
Sean Penn, *Hurlyburly*
Courtney B. Vance, *Blind Faith*

BEST ACTRESS
- Ally Sheedy, *High Art*

Katrin Cartlidge, *Claire Dolan*
Christina Ricci, *The Opposite of Sex*
Robin Tunney, *Niagara, Niagara*
Alfre Woodard, *Down in the Delta*

BEST SUPPORTING ACTOR
- Bill Murray, *Rushmore*

James Coburn, *Affliction*
Charles Dutton, *Blind Faith*
Gary Farmer, *Smoke Signals*
Philip S. Hoffman, *Happiness*

BEST SUPPORTING ACTRESS
- Lynn Redgrave, *Gods and Monsters*

Stockard Channing, *The Baby Dance*
Patricia Clarkson, *High Art*
Lisa Kudrow, *The Opposite of Sex*
Joely Richardson, *Under Heaven*

BEST DEBUT PERFORMANCE
- Evan Adams, *Smoke Signals*

Anthony R. Costanzo, *A Soldier's Daughter Never Cries*
Andrea Hart, *Miss Monday*
Sonja Sohn, *Slam*
Saul Williams, *Slam*

BEST SCREENPLAY
- Don Roos, *The Opposite of Sex*

Bill Condon, *Gods and Monsters*
David Mamet, *Spanish Prisoner*
Frank Military, *Blind Faith*
Paul Schrader, *Affliction*

BEST FIRST SCREENPLAY
- Darren Aronofsky, Eric Watson, Sean Gulette, *Pi*

Sherman Alexie, *Smoke Signals*
Lisa Cholodenko, *High Art*
Tamara Jenkins, *Slums of Beverly Hills*
Matthew Weiss, *Niagara, Niagara*

"SOMEONE TO WATCH" AWARD
- David Williams, *13*

Tony Barbieri, *One*
Lynn Herschman Leeson, *Conceiving Ada*
Eric Tretbar, *Snow*

PRODUCER'S AWARD
- Susan Stover, *High Art, Sticky Fingers of Time*

Margot Bridger, *The Delta*
Gill Holland, *Hurricane Streets*
Andrea Sperling, *Nowhere, Doom Generation*

BEST FOREIGN FILM
- *The Celebration* (Denmark)

Central Station (Brazil)
The Eel (Japan)
The General (Ireland)
Hana-Bi (Fireworks) (Japan)

Winners

BEST CINEMATOGRAPHY
- *Velvet Goldmine*, Maryse Alberti

"TRUER THAN FICTION" DOCUMENTARY AWARD
- *Regret to Inform*, Barbara Sonneborn

ACADEMY AWARDS

Nominations were announced on February 9, 1999. Awards were presented on March 21 at the Dorothy Chandler Pavilion in Los Angeles. The ceremony was telecast by ABC.

BEST PICTURE
- *Shakespeare in Love*

Elizabeth
Life Is Beautiful
Saving Private Ryan
The Thin Red Line

BEST DIRECTOR
- Steven Spielberg, *Saving Private Ryan*

Roberto Benigni, *Life Is Beautiful*
John Madden, *Shakespeare in Love*
Terrence Malick, *The Thin Red Line*
Peter Weir, *The Truman Show*

BEST ACTOR
- Roberto Benigni, *Life Is Beautiful*

Tom Hanks, *Saving Private Ryan*
Nick Nolte, *Affliction*
Edward Norton, *American History X*
Ian McKellen, *Gods and Monsters*

BEST ACTRESS
- Gwyneth Paltrow, *Shakespeare in Love*

Cate Blanchett, *Elizabeth*
Fernanda Montenegro, *Central Station*
Meryl Streep, *One True Thing*
Emily Watson, *Hilary and Jackie*

BEST SUPPORTING ACTOR
- James Coburn, *Affliction*

Robert Duvall, *A Civil Action*
Ed Harris, *The Truman Show*
Geoffrey Rush, *Shakespeare in Love*
Billy Bob Thornton, *A Simple Plan*

BEST SUPPORTING ACTRESS

- Judi Dench, *Shakespeare in Love*

Kathy Bates, *Primary Colors*

Brenda Blethyn, *Little Voice*

Rachel Griffiths, *Hilary and Jackie*

Lynn Redgrave, *Gods and Monsters*

BEST ORIGINAL SCREENPLAY

- Marc Norman, Tom Stoppard, *Shakespeare in Love*

Warren Beatty, Jeremy Pikser, *Bulworth*

Roberto Benigni, Vincenzo Cerami, *Life Is Beautiful*

Andrew Niccol, *The Truman Show*

Robert Rodat, *Saving Private Ryan*

BEST ADAPTED SCREENPLAY

- Bill Condon, *Gods and Monsters*

Scott Frank, *Out of Sight*

Terrence Malick, *The Thin Red Line*

Elaine May, *Primary Colors*

Scott B. Smith, *A Simple Plan*

BEST SONG

- "When You Believe," *The Prince of Egypt*, Stephen Schwartz

"I Don't Want to Miss a Thing," *Armageddon,* Diane Warren

"The Prayer," *Quest for Camelot*, David Foster, Tony Renis, Carole Bayer Sager, Alberto Testa

"A Soft Place to Fall," *The Horse Whisperer*, Allison Moorer, Gwil Owen

"That'll Do," *Babe: Pig in the City*, Randy Newman

BEST FOREIGN-LANGUAGE FILM

- *Life Is Beautiful* (Italy)

Central Station (Brazil)

Children of Heaven (Iran)

The Grandfather (Spain)

Tango (Argentina)

Winners

BEST ART DIRECTION

- Martin Childs, Jill Quertier, *Shakespeare in Love*

BEST CINEMATOGRAPHY

- Janusz Kaminski, *Saving Private Ryan*

BEST COSTUME DESIGN

- Sandy Powell, *Shakespeare in Love*

BEST DOCUMENTARY

(FEATURE)

- *The Last Days,* Ken Lipper, James Moll

(SHORT SUBJECT)

- *The Personals: Improvisations on Romance in the Golden Years,* Keiko Ibi

BEST FILM EDITING

- Michael Kahn, *Saving Private Ryan*

BEST MAKEUP

- Jenny Shircore, *Elizabeth*

BEST MUSIC

(ORIGINAL DRAMATIC SCORE)

- Nicola Piovani, *Life Is Beautiful*

(ORIGINAL MUSICAL OR COMEDY SCORE)

- Stephen Warbeck, *Shakespeare in Love*

SCIENTIFIC OR TECHNICAL AWARDS

(Academy Award of Merit)

- Avid Technology

(Scientific and Engineering Award)

- Richard Alexander, Arnold and Richter Cine Technik, Arri USA, Paul Bartlett, Dominique Boisvert, Ronan Carroll, Deluxe Laboratories, Eastman Kodak, Richard J. Federico, Roy B. Ference, Fred M. Fuss, Mohamed Ken T. Husain, Robert B. Ingebretsen, K-Tech Corporation, Stephen J. Kay, André LeBlanc, Hans Leisinger, Derek C. Lightbody, Michael E. McCrackan, Takuo Miyagishima, James A. Moorer, Colin Mossman, Iain Neil, Optex, Panavision, Philippe Panzini, Thomas F. Powers, Robert Predovich, Assaff Rawner, Mark Roberts, George John Rowland, Steven R. Schmidt, John Scott, Cameron Shearer, Michael Sorensen, Sorensen Designs, Thomas G. Stockham, Jr., Gary Tregaskis, Donald Trumbull, Ronald E. Uhlig, Simon Wakley, Rockwell Yarid, Carl Zeiss Co.

(Technical Achievement Award)

- Chris Barker, James Bartell, Trou Bayliss, Thaddeus Beier, Mitchell J. Bogdanowicz, Mike Bolles, James K. Branch, Garrett Brown, Dale

Brubacher-Cressman, Cablecam Systems, Cinema Products Co., David Cornelius, Mike Denecke, David DiFrancesco, Edmund M. Di Giulio, Eastman Kodak, Nick Foster, Joseph Fulmer, Frederick Gasoi, Carl F. Holtz, Jerry Holway, Carlos Icinkoff, Industrial Light and Magic, Manfred N. Klemme, David F. Kopperl, Ivan Kruglak, Mike Lazaridis, Michael Mackenzie, Bala S. Manian, Mechanical Concepts, Jim Meyer, Stan Miller, Takuo Miyagishima, National Film Board of Canada, Thomas L. Noggle, Udo Pampel, Panavision, Cary Phillips, A. Tulsi Ram, Research in Motion, Douglas R. Roble, James Rodnunsky, Rosco Laboratories, Albert K. Saiki, Bill Schultz, Richard C. Sehlin, Remy Smith, Sony Pictures Imageworks, Barry Walton, Bob Webber, James Webber, Donald E. Wetzel, Bruce Wilton, Nasir J. Zaidi, Ed Zwaneveld

BEST SHORT FILM
(ANIMATED)
- *Bunny,* Chris Wedge

(LIVE ACTION)
- *Election Night (Valgaften),* Anders Thomas Jensen, Kim Magnusson

BEST SOUND
- Ronald Judkins, Andy Nelson, Gary Rydstrom, Gary Summers, *Saving Private Ryan*

BEST SOUND EFFECTS EDITING
- Richard Hymns, Gary Rydstrom, *Saving Private Ryan*

BEST VISUAL EFFECTS
- Nicholas Brooks, Joel Hynek, Kevin Mack, Stuart Robertson, *What Dreams May Come*

IRVING G. THALBERG MEMORIAL AWARD
- Norman Jewison

HONORARY AWARDS
- David W. Gray
- Elia Kazan

1998

▪ 1999 ▪

A Rare Beauty Comes Up Roses

Two months after DreamWorks's *Saving Private Ryan* lost Best Picture at the 1998 Oscar derby, its still-smarting studio execs were watching a routine screening of one of their upcoming pix when they spotted their next horse and jumped on it.

The suits began spreading buzz on *American Beauty* so fast that the *N.Y. Times* called it "the most talked-about film of the moment" in July, two months before it was due to be released. One month later, the execs started placing ads in *Variety* that tickled industry interest by showing a photo of single rose petal resting lightly atop a girl's taut tummy. When *American Beauty* premiered at the Toronto film festival in September, their best hopes were confirmed as audiences cheered it wildly on the eve of its American debut.

"Unusually off-center for a major studio venture, this DreamWorks release will spark a raft of critical hosannas and play exceedingly well to sophisticated audiences attuned to its caustic wit and mischievous sensibility," *Variety* predicted. The tradepaper called the dark tale of a suburban couple's emotional meltdown "a real American original."

When the early awards derby began soon afterward, *Variety* noted, "*American Beauty* sounded the opening bell for the race, nabbing what is known as 'the *L.A. Confidential* slot': it's a mainstream-but-serious pic that critics have embraced as a signal that summer's over and thoughtful films have arrived." The comparison may have been apt, but it was also ominous considering

Early front-runner *American Beauty* was snubbed by the first three crix orgs after its NBR victory, then won kudos from the broadcast crix, Globes, PGA, WGA, DGA and, finally, the Oscars.

how poorly pix unveiled prior to December usually do in the derby. Autumn release *L.A. Confidential* swept virtually all of the early 1997 crix kudos, but then lost the Best Picture Oscar to *Titanic*. Mid-1998 release *Saving Private Ryan*—a "shoo-in" for the top prize, according to most pundits—was so old by the time the Oscars finally rolled around the following March that *Entertainment Weekly* said "we thought it won already"—just before it lost to *Shakespeare in Love*.

American Beauty outdistanced the competish for the first cup of the 1999 race when it was declared Best Picture by the National Board of Review. It also reaped Best Breakthrough Performance laurels for Wes Bentley as the suburban couple's pot-smoking, Peeping Tom neighbor who spies on their daughter with a camcorder. The latter award was shared by Hilary Swank (*Boys Don't Cry*), who had crix swooning over her raw perf as Teena Brandon, a young Nebraska woman who was raped and murdered for parading as a man. The helmer of the little-seen indie, Kimberly Peirce, was voted Best Debut Director.

American Beauty was helmed by red-hot British stage director Sam Mendes, who *Variety* said "displays a very sure hand in his first film." But the board gave its Best Director trophy to Anthony Minghella for his first outing since 1996 awards-sweeper *The English Patient—The Talented Mr. Ripley*, the tale of a social-climbing schemer (Matt Damon) who assumes the identity of his debonair idol (Jude Law) after murdering him. Prior to its release, the Miramax-Paramount co-production looked like the pic that could stop *American Beauty*'s march to the Oscars, but Minghella was so late putting the finishing touches on *Ripley* that it had to be shown to National Board of Review voters in rough form. The board should've waited for the last cut. *Variety* called the final result "a mostly intoxicating and involving tale of intrigue and crime that loses its stride somewhat in the home stretch." Other crix agreed and, although it was moderately successful ($40 million b.o. in its first month), *Ripley* failed to live up to its early hype.

The board's Best Actor was Russell Crowe, the 35-year-old New Zealand–born thesp who bulked up and donned a gray wig to play a frumpy 57-year-old tobacco exec in *The Insider*, a fact-based drama about a whistleblower who's double-crossed by *60 Minutes* when the show's producers kill the story they coaxed out of him. *Variety* called it "the best movie about the media since *All the President's Men*."

The Best Actress trophy went to Tony-winning British stage thesp Janet McTeer in *Tumbleweeds*, an indie discovered at Sundance last year about a wild, Southern single mom who uproots her daughter and hits the road in between disastrous serial romances.

> **"Don't wait to have a baby!" SAG's pregnant Best Actress Annette Bening said.**

Supporting players were honored for multiple roles. Philip Seymour Hoffman was hailed as a brash bohemian who tries to unmask Matt Damon in *The Talented Mr. Ripley* and as a male nurse who bonds with a dying old tycoon in *Magnolia*. Julianne Moore snagged the femmes' laurels for four perfs: as the tycoon's young wife in *Magnolia*, the mother of a drowned daughter in *A Map of the World*, a Southern woman coping with her eccentric family in *Cookie's Fortune* and a plotting troublemaker in *An Ideal Husband*.

Variety reported that there "were no clear-cut favorites going into the voting" session held by the L.A. crix, who were overwhelmed by "a great diversity in selections during the initial rounds." The paper also said that "voting in several categories couldn't have been closer," but the crix emerged from the conclave with a strong showing for *The Insider,* which reaped four kudos: Best Picture, Cinematography, Actor (Crowe) and Supporting Actor (Christopher Plummer as *60 Minutes* reporter Mike Wallace).

American Beauty placed second in the top pic race, but reaped Best Director when Sam Mendes edged out *Insider*'s Michael Mann. Crowe beat 80-year-old stuntman-turned-thesp Richard Farnsworth, who played a retiree who treks across Iowa on a lawn tractor in order to see his ailing brother in *The Straight Story*.

Hilary Swank earned one more Best Actress trophy when she received more crix votes than Reese Witherspoon as a high-school overachiever running for class president in *Election*. Chloë Sevigny, who portrayed Swank's lover in *Boys Don't Cry*, was named Best Supporting Actress over Samantha Morton as a shy mute who falls for a flashy jazz guitarist (Sean Penn) in *Sweet and Lowdown*.

Variety called *Beauty*'s script by playwright and TV scribe Alan Ball "as fresh and distinctive as any produced in the States in recent memory," but it lost the screenplay award to an absurdist pic about an unscrupulous trio who discover a magic portal into actor John Malkovich's head. Penned by another rookie film scribe, Charlie Kaufman, *Being John Malkovich* was hailed by *Entertainment Weekly* as "the most excitingly original movie of the year." Malkovich, portraying himself, placed behind Plummer in the Best Supporting Actor race.

When the honorees met the crix to accept their awards at the Bel Age Hotel gala, Kaufman thanked "the courageous John Malkovich for having a sense of humor about this."

The Insider was currently under attack by *60 Minutes* producers, who accused it of being factually inaccurate. While Michael Mann accepted its Best Picture plaque, he thanked his studio, Disney, for continuing to stand behind him.

Insider's supporting champ Christopher Plummer told his hosts, "The moment I left my mother's womb, she told me this: 'Always be nice to critics.' "

But it was *Insider*'s Best Actor who gave the Best Performance at a kudofest when he arrived, thirsty, from Australia and decided not to be nice. He echoed Bill Murray's complaint of last year when he groused, "It's bloody lovely to come flying all the way over here to a function with a cash bar!"

Soon after the L.A. crix gave it four awards, *Insider* looked as if it had the inside track on *Beauty* in the now-heated-up kudos race, but that was just when the oft-contrary-minded New Yorkers butted in and turned everything topsy-turvy.

Their Best Picture choice was ironic fair play, considering the Los Angelenos had named director Mike Leigh's *Secrets and Lies* top pic three years earlier—just days after the Gothamites backed *Fargo*. Leigh's latest, *Topsy-Turvy*, offered a backstage peek at how the busted-up British musical team of Gilbert and Sullivan reunited later in life to create one of their theatrical masterworks, *The Mikado*. The *N.Y. Times* called the movie "grandly entertaining—one of those films that creates a mix of erudition, pageantry and delectable acting as much as *Shakespeare in Love* did last year." *Topsy-Turvy* won with 40 points, topping *American Beauty, Being John Malkovich* and *The Straight Story*, which each earned 20 points.

"This was not a deliberate attempt to be different," crix topper Owen Gleiberman of *Entertainment Weekly* insisted to *Variety*. "This was an honest expression of how we felt."

Mike Leigh (35 points) also received the crix's director award (over *The Straight Story*'s David Lynch, 30 points) and expressed his delight to *Variety*, although he also cited a serious reservation: "I don't especially like that they pit us filmmakers in competition with each other, but it is awfully nice to have this double approbation."

Malkovich (46 points) beat *Boys Don't Cry* (44) to be named Best First Feature, a tribute to its 29-year-old director, Spike Jonze, who had recently graduated from doing TV commercials and music videos. Two of its supporting thesps claimed kudos, too. Catherine Keener was hailed as a conniving seductress, and John Malkovich became the first person in film awards history to be honored for playing himself. "They call that *acting?*" *Entertainment Weekly* whined.

The Gotham crix agreed with their L.A. peers in only one category, endorsing Hilary Swank as Best Actress (40 points) over Julianne Moore in *The End of the Affair* (29). For Best Actor, they chose the L.A. crix's runner-up Richard Farnsworth (43 points) over Russell Crowe (40) and made a surprising pick for Best Screenplay: the indie *Election,* written by Jim Taylor and Alexander Payne (44 points) over *Topsy-Turvy*'s Mike Leigh (26).

Election scored "upsets!" at the WGA and Indie Spirits.

"The National Society of Film Critics has a history of unorthodox votes," the *N.Y. Times* noted when reporting on the unprecedented outcome of the group's Best Picture vote. A tie occurred between *Topsy-Turvy* and *Malkovich* when both pix scored 29 points, followed by 19 for *Election*.

"The voting session was a long one, with numerous categories requiring several ballots before winners emerged," *Variety* said.

Best pic co-champ *Malkovich* also won Best Screenplay, topping *Election* 63 points to 48, but, strangely, it was not a leading contender for Best Director. Mike Leigh (36 points) won out over David O. Russell, helmer of *Three Kings*, a dark comedy about three American soldiers searching for gold after the Persian Gulf war.

Russell Crowe won Best Actor with 49 points, eclipsing Jim Broadbent (41) as the prudish William S. Gilbert in *Topsy-Turvy*. The *N.Y. Times* called Reese Witherspoon's victory as Best Actress "a small upset" when she outscored Hilary Swank, 33 to 29. Swank's costar Chloë Sevigny (27) prevailed as Best Supporting Actress over Julianne Moore (22), who was considered for four of her films.

Although Christopher Plummer and Philip Seymour Hoffman pulled even with 23 points each in the match-up for Best Supporting Actor, Plummer was proclaimed the winner because his name appeared on a plurality of the ballots.

At this point in the year's kudos derby, just as things started to look ugly for *Beauty*, the pic suddenly rallied to claim three trophies from the broadcast crix: Best Picture, Director and Original Screenplay.

The nonprint reviewers agreed with some their peers' earlier choices for Best Actor and Actress—tapping Russell Crowe and Hilary Swank—but they made two radical turns in the supporting categories. They backed Michael Clarke Duncan as a mysterious death-row inmate with magical pow-

ers in *The Green Mile* and they also gave the film its prize for Best Adapted Screenplay. Angelina Jolie was lauded as a mental-asylum rebel in *Girl, Interrupted*.

Beauty officially reclaimed its front-runner status when the Golden Globe nominations were unveiled and it led the pack with six. *Insider* and *Ripley* followed with five bids each and *Malkovich* scored four.

Topsy-Turvy and *Three Kings* reaped no noms at all, Spike Jonze failed to make the director's competish and Christopher Plummer, John Malkovich and Philip Seymour Hoffman were absent from the thesps' line-ups. Meantime, three films mostly overlooked by the crix kudos were coming on strong late in the year's derby and were all considered heavyweight Oscar contenders, but none of them received Globe bids for top pic: *The Sixth Sense* (1999's second-biggest hit, grossing $276 million, about a boy haunted by visions of dead people), *The Green Mile* (starring Tom Hanks as a prison guard who discovers Michael Clarke Duncan's secret powers) and *The Cider House Rules* (John Irving's screen adaptation of his best-selling novel about a Maine orphanage).

The Globes gala turned into what *Variety* called "a *Beauty* pageant" when the pic won three top prizes: Best Drama Picture, Director and Screenplay. The sweep had been foreseen by Steven Spielberg, who presented the helmer's prize to Sam Mendes after the two had chatted on the phone earlier in the week. Mendes thanked Spielberg "for telling me to wear comfortable shoes."

The race for Best Comedy or Musical Picture was considered a close contest between *Malkovich* and *Notting Hill*, which starred past Globe faves Julia Roberts and Hugh Grant in a romantic comedy that became the year's twelfth-highest grosser ($116 million). But they were both usurped by the year's third-biggest hit, *Toy Story 2* ($208 million), a sequel to the 1995 hit

Variety reported "an unprecedented number of film sales" at Sundance.

about a boy's playthings that come mysteriously to life when he's not looking. The victory was a shocker, considering that the original *Toy Story* lost to *Babe*.

Although *Insider*'s Russell Crowe had nabbed three out of the four crix's kudos so far, he faced formidable rivals for Best Drama Actor, including N.Y. film crix champ Richard Farnsworth and *Beauty*'s Kevin Spacey, who *Time* said gave "hands down the year's best performance" as a flipped-out, middle-aged man who quits his job, defies his wife, fires up marijuana joints and lusts after his daughter's nubile friend. All three thesps were all dealt a knockout punch, however, by Denzel Washington, who starred in *Hurricane* as real-life Rubin "Hurricane" Carter, a former middleweight boxer who spent two decades in prison for a murder he didn't commit.

Washington brought Carter up to the podium with him when he won, put his hand on Carter's shoulder and told the audience: "When I was a kid, we used to say grace to bless the table—the short version of 'God is love.' When we made this film, I really began to understand what 'God is love' means. This man right here is love."

Just like Crowe, the actress who swept three of the four crix awards, Hilary Swank, had reason to be concerned about winning, too, especially since the Best Drama Actress bout pitted her against a Hollywood heavyweight. Previous to *Boys Don't Cry*, the 25-year-old rookie had appeared for half of a TV season on *Beverly Hills, 90210* and had a supporting role in the film version of *Buffy the Vampire Slayer*. At the Globes, Swank ran into a veteran thesp—Annette Bening as Spacey's plastic wife who cracks up, too, when things get crazy in *Beauty*. Bening had been passed over for a Globe and Oscar in 1990, when the National Society of Film Critics honored her for *The Grifters*. Now, as Mrs. Warren Beatty, she was a showbiz insider who knew many of the Globe voters personally and she campaigned tirelessly in the media to win their favor despite being noticeably pregnant.

But Swank pulled off a dramatic victory nonetheless and dedicated her win to the

Topsy-Turvy scored Best Picture trophies from the Gotham crix and national society, but failed to be nommed in the top Globe, DGA, WGA, PGA or Oscar races.

memory of the victim she portrayed in *Boys Don't Cry*.

Last year Jim Carrey was denied an Oscar nomination after winning a Globe for *The Truman Show*. This year he was Globe-nominated for portraying late, oddball TV comic Andy Kaufman in *Man on the Moon*. He faced tough competish from two other past Globe victors—*Notting Hill*'s Hugh Grant and *Analyze This*'s Robert De Niro—but he prevailed.

"What's going on here, man?!" he gasped when he took the statuette in hand. "I'm the establishment I once rejected! I'm the Tom Hanks of the Golden Globes!"

Angelina Jolie had won two Globes in recent years for her work in TV movies, but she claimed her first for feature films when she was named Best Supporting Actress for *Girl, Interrupted* over Chloë Sevigny and Catherine Keener.

"You guys are so kind to me," she said to the members of the foreign press in the audience. "Like I must be paying you or something!"

The comment caused snickers back the press room, where reporters were reminded of recent accusations that a lead actress contender had tried to bribe Globe voters. *The Muse*'s Sharon Stone—and/or USA Films—sent all 82 members of the press org Coach watches valued at between $295 and $395 each. The HFPA sent the watches back immediately, but not before word leaked out and the news made national headlines.

The remaining front-runners in the race for Best Comedy or Drama Actress were national crix society winner Reese Witherspoon, National Board of Review honoree Janet McTeer and two-time past Globe champ Julia Roberts, who was the odds-on-favorite to win after having dominated the b.o. in 1999 with two huge hits—*Notting Hill* and *Runaway Bride*. McTeer, however, scored an impressive upset.

After starring as the frightened boy who sees ghosts in *The Sixth Sense*, 11-year-old Haley Joel Osment became one of the biggest breakout stars of 1999 and he was considered a strong rival for Best Supporting Actor. But he faced off against broadcast crix honoree Michael Clarke Duncan (*Green Mile*) and two other close rivals: last year's Globe winner for *Little Voice*, Michael Caine, as an ether-addicted abortionist who presides as a surrogate father over the orphans in *The Cider House Rules* and 1996 Globe-getter for *Jerry Maguire*, Tom Cruise, as a ferocious sex-advice guru in *Magnolia*.

Cruise sailed through, telling the audience, "I'm always surprised when I win stuff." Backstage, reporters asked him how he was able to rehearse for his raunchy *Magnolia* role while he was at home with his small children. "You get into a rhythm sometimes," he said. "You've got to make sure the doors are closed."

Beauty, Malkovich, Cider House, Hurricane and *Insider* all made the cut for the top prize bestowed by the producers' guild. When *Beauty* producers Bruce Cohen and Dan Jinks emerged as winners, Jinks said, "We're just a couple of guys who are doing what we want to do for a living."

Variety observed that "first-timers and hyphens dominated" the list of writers' guild rivals, spotting "only three WGA veterans among the 13 nominated feature scripts. Six of the contenders also directed the films for which they're cited." Only one past guild winner received a bid: *Insider*'s co-author Eric Roth, who had claimed a guild prize in 1994 for *Forrest Gump*.

Two first-time film scribes faced off in

Hilary Swank (*Boys Don't Cry*) gained the early Best Actress lead with kudos from the N.Y. and L.A. crix, Globes and Spirits. She stumbled at SAG, but rallied at the Oscars.

the race for Best Original Screenplay: Alan Ball (*Beauty*) and Charlie Kaufman (*Malkovich*). Considering *Beauty*'s recent kudos resurgence, its victory was predictable even if it did amaze its author, a TV sitcom scribe who began writing the pic in 1997 while working as a co-executive producer on *Cybill*. "This is all kind of overwhelming, because I never really expected my movie to get made," Ball told *Variety*.

But a huge upset was brewing in the category for adapted works, which was expected to go to John Irving, who had endured such a painful struggle to get his celebrated novel *The Cider House Rules* made into a movie—going through four directors and two producers in 13 years—that he wrote a whole, separate book about it (*My Movie Business: A Memoir*). *Election*'s Alexander Payne and Jim Taylor, however, ended up getting more guild votes despite that fact that their irreverent indie was such old news as of awards night that it was already out on videotape after grossing only $15 million in theaters.

Cider House suffered an even worse fate at the directors' guild awards: helmer Lasse Hallström didn't make the cut. Also snubbed were Norman Jewison (*Hurricane*), National Board of Review Best Director Anthony Minghella (*Ripley*) and Gotham crix and national society champ Mike Leigh (*Topsy-Turvy*). Four of the five nominees were 40 years old or younger: Spike Jonze (*Malkovich*), Michael Mann (*Insider*), Sam Mendes (*Beauty*) and M. Night Shyamalan (*Sixth Sense*). The fifth contender was Frank Darabont (*Green Mile*), who had been nominated in 1994 for *The Shawshank Redemption*. Mann won a guild kudo in 1979 for helming TV film *The Jericho Mile*.

When rookie Mendes won, as expected, he saluted DreamWorks, saying, "Thank you to the studio for giving a bloke from England a movie about the American suburbs and letting me make the movie I wanted to make."

The Screen Actors Guild awards were held one day later and, again, *Beauty* led the way—with nominations in every category but one.

Beauty's Kevin Spacey squared off against two recent Globe winners Denzel Washington and Jim Carrey, plus Russell Crowe (winner of three crix awards) and Philip Seymour Hoffman, who was snubbed by the guild in the supporting category but acknowledged for his lead star turn as a drag queen in *Flawless*.

Spacey won, telling the crowd at the Shrine Auditorium in Los Angeles that the message of *American Beauty* was that "sometimes we miss the things that are simple and clearly beautiful in our own heart."

Kudos handicappers were split over who'd prevail as Best Actress: Bening or Swank. When the very pregnant Bening was called to the podium, she said, "To all you actresses out there, don't wait to have a baby."

Beauty reaped a bid for Best Supporting Actor when Chris Cooper was hailed for portraying the martinet father of Spacey's Peeping Tom neighbor. The lineup also included Michael Caine, Haley Joel Osment, Globe champ Tom Cruise and broadcast crix honoree Michael Clarke Duncan. There was no clear front-runner. Ultimately, Caine pulled ahead to win.

The only category without a *Beauty* bid was Best Supporting Actress, which included two *Malkovich* stars, Catherine Keener and Cameron Diaz, plus Julianne Moore (National Board of Review champ), Angelina Jolie (broadcast crix and Globe) and Chloë Sevigny (L.A. crix and national society). Jolie triumphed—just as she had at last year's SAG kudos when she won a trophy for best perf in a telefilm (*Gia*).

Beauty emerged as the biggest SAG winner, garnering three accolades, including the prize for Best Cast Performance.

But just as the suddenly revived *Beauty* seemed poised to head into the Oscars and avenge the Best Picture loss its studio suffered in 1998, *Entertainment Weekly* declared, "Frankly, DreamWorks has reason to be concerned."

Last year's Best Picture spoiler, Miramax, had recently given up on its Paramount co-production *Ripley* and started marshaling its forces behind *Cider House*. "In *Variety* alone, Miramax bought 43 *Cider House* ads, 16 more than its nearest competitor," *Entertainment Weekly* observed.

The brazen ballyhoo paid off when nominations came out. *Cider House* may have been ignored by the Globes, crix and directors' guild kudos, but it scored seven bids, one less than *Beauty*. Even more surprising: Hollywood was suddenly reverberating with buzz that it could actually win.

Once-distant dark horses *Sixth Sense* and *Green Mile* now appeared at the front of the pack, too. Both scored Best Picture bids, although *Mile*'s Darabont failed to make the director's list, getting bumped by Spike Jonze, whose *Malkovich* was snubbed for a chance at top pic along with *Topsy-Turvy, Hurricane* and *Toy Story 2*. Overlooked thesps included Christopher Plummer, Chris Cooper, Seymour Philip Hoffman, Cameron Diaz, Reese Witherspoon, John Malkovich—and Jim Carrey. Last year Carrey could blame his failure to bag a bid on the fact that Oscar nomination ballots were due only five days after he won a Globe for *The Truman Show*. This year, however, there was plenty of time for the possibility of his *Man on the Moon* Globe victory to sink in—15 days—so the slap seemed deliberate.

But the Oscar ballots themselves—the second round, which determine winners—became a hot issue when four-fifths of voters didn't receive them in the mail. Careless postal authorities, it turns out, had accidentally routed them to a third-class shipping facility. While the mystery was still being sorted out, frantic academy leaders printed and shipped new ones and extended the deadline for their return. ("The Golden Globes never had this problem," *Variety* harrumphed.) Voters should have received the original ballots a week and a half before the SAG and DGA kudos were dispensed—while Denzel Washington and Hilary Swank were still glowing from their Golden Globe wins. But the new ballots arrived on the threshold of guild-kudos weekend, just when Washington's and Swank's front-runner status would be threatened by Spacey's and Bening's SAG victories. Meantime, *Hurricane*'s producers worried that the delay could hurt Washington the most since their pic was getting pummeled in the press by accusations that it took "poetic license" with facts of the real case.

Another fiasco followed when 55 Oscar statuettes disappeared shortly before the ceremony. Fifty-two were found a few days later in a Dumpster located in Los Angeles's Koreatown, and two men were arrested for the caper. The duo was booked on charges of grand theft since the missing statuettes had been valued at $18,000—which struck many observers as a paltry sum considering that Hollywood filmmakers spent a record $50 million to campaign for them this year.

Oscar leaders were already numb from the controversies erupting before the kudofest when they received more troubling news: reporters from *The Wall Street Journal* were canvassing academy members to discover how they had voted, the first time that the media had attempted such snooping since *Variety* abandoned its nine-year academy poll after the 1955 awards show (although the paper continued to make predictions based on canvassing industry pros

at large for two more years). Film academy prexy Robert Rehme denounced the effort as "a threat to the Academy Awards process," but Hollywood held its collective breath while waiting for the *Journal*'s Oscar-day edition to learn what its reporters unearthed.

Chicago Sun-Times critic Roger Ebert summed up the pending Oscar bout thus: "Will Miramax enforce the *Rules*? Or will DreamWorks gain revenge?" His answer: "My guess is that it will be an *American Beauty* evening." The *Journal* poll agreed, forecasting *Beauty* victories as Best Picture and Director, while holding out some slight hope for Spacey. Reporting on its Best Actor findings, the *Journal* revealed, "Washington squeaked ahead with less than a 7 percent lead—almost too close to call," but the paper still called him the likely winner anyway. It predicted victories for Hilary Swank, Michael Caine and Angelina Jolie with far more confidence.

All other media endorsed Jolie, too, with one exception: *Entertainment Weekly* reasoned that Toni Collette, who played Haley Joel Osment's mother, would win "based on *The Sixth Sense*'s popularity."

On kudos night, the young daughter of Jon Voight ended up being called to the stage where, appearing overwhelmed and dazzled, she said, "I'm surprised nobody ever fainted up here!" Jolie and Voight were now the second father-daughter team to claim Oscars after earlier wins by Jane and Henry Fonda.

"My dad said he was proud of me and that I was a good actress," Jolie told reporters backstage. "For him to think I'm a good actress is kind of a big deal!"

The match-up for Best Supporting Actor, said the *Journal*, "turned into a race between the oldest contender, Michael Caine, 67, and the youngest, Osment, 11." Caine had already proven himself a winner in the category in 1986 for *Hannah and Her Sisters*. Osment boosters were encouraged, however, by the fact that Oscar voters had previously embraced several children as champs, including Tatum O'Neal (*Paper Moon*), Patty Duke (*The Miracle Worker*) and Anna Paquin (*The Piano*). But all of them were girls. Past boy contenders had always struck out. Nonetheless, *Entertainment Weekly* stuck by Osment, while *TV Guide*, Roger Ebert and one *L.A. Times* pundit picked recent SAG champ Caine. The other *L.A. Times* pundit rooted for Tom Cruise.

Cider House's Caine proved to be the winner and also proved to be especially gracious toward his vanquished rivals, complimenting each one of them when he reached the podium. He addressed $20-million-per-pic superstar Cruise in the audience, saying, "Be happy you didn't win. If you had, your price would have gone down so fast. Have you any idea what supporting actors get paid?"

Cider House had another chance to prove its might in the race for Best Adapted Screenplay and meantime avenge the upset it suffered to *Election* at the writers' guild awards three weeks earlier.

All Oscar seers predicted it would rebound—and it did. Novelist-turned-screenwriter John Irving said in gratitude, "You must be trying to get me to reconsider my day job."

There was no mystery over the showdown for Best Original Screenplay, since *Beauty*'s Alan Ball had already claimed tributes from the writers' guild and Golden Globes. As expected, he came through and struck Oscar gold next.

How *Beauty* would fare in the two lead acting contests, though, remained the night's cliffhangers.

Before the *Journal* poll was published, *Entertainment Weekly*, Roger Ebert and E! Online bet on SAG champ Bening. *TV Guide* and the two *L.A. Times* pundits wagered on Swank.

The *Journal* reported, "Most academy members we contacted assumed Annette Bening would win—even though most of them didn't vote for her. Swank garnered nearly 43 percent of our interviewee's picks, almost double the number of votes as Bening."

When Swank prevailed, the victory was a personal triumph for the 25-year-old thesp and her mother. They had moved to Los Angeles from Iowa nine years earlier, arriving with only $75 between them and no place to stay, just so Swank could break into show business.

As she accepted her ultimate payoff, Swank shouted, "To my mom, who's up there (in the balcony) somewhere: it looks like living out of our car was worth it!"

Beauty had won only two awards (cinematography and original screenplay) when the time came to announce the winner of the Best Actor prize. Things looked grim for Spacey, since the *Journal* had reported that Washington had a narrow lead. Also, *TV Guide* and E! Online foresaw a Washington win. Spacey, however, did have the Associated Press, Roger Ebert, *Entertainment Weekly* and both *L.A. Times* pundits behind him.

Spacey ended up snatching the gold, becoming the only thesp to buck the *Journal* poll results.

"I rule!" he shouted from the podium, then added, wryly, "This is the highlight of my day." He thanked his friends "for pointing out my worst qualities. I know you do it because you love me."

In the directors' contest, *Entertainment Weekly* insisted, "Mendes' lead is as thin as a rose petal, but we're betting he takes it." The *Journal*'s poll discovered, in fact, that Mendes was ahead of his competish "by a margin of 21 percentage points, which was the widest lead of any contest in our survey."

After Mendes won, he told reporters backstage that he was so happy with *Beauty* that "I would've done this movie for free—and I practically did so. (DreamWorks exec) Steven Spielberg owes me a couple of quid." He was the sixth helmer to claim the category for his directorial debut.

After *Beauty*'s rally at the Golden Globes and its recent sweep of all four guild honors, there remained only one notable Oscar handicapper who believed that *Cider House* could sour its chances for Best Picture: Leonard Maltin of *Entertainment Tonight*. When *Beauty* plucked its fifth prize of the night, *Variety* declared, "DreamWorks achieved its *American* dream. This marks the first big win for the company after only two full years of distribution."

Variety also noted that it was huge victory for America's capital of filmmaking: "*Beauty* became the first Best Picture winner in 23 years—since the 1976's *Rocky*—to be majority-lensed in Hollywood."

"It's a Brit vs. the Brat," *Variety* reported when announcing the noms for the Independent Spirit awards. Two pix led with the most bids (five)—*Election* and *The Limey*, the latter described by *Variety* as "Steven Soderbergh's sleek detective yarn about a U.K. con on the hunt for his daughter's murderer in L.A." Soderbergh seemed like the front-runner, since he had proved himself a winner at the 1989 Spirits with *sex, lies and videotape* claiming Best Feature and Director.

But at this year's kudos, *Entertainment Weekly* reported, "The buzz word was *upset!*"

"*Election*'s wins for Best Feature, Director and Screenplay were big surprises," *Variety* noted. "As expected, *Boys Don't Cry*'s Hilary Swank and Chloë Sevigny walked away with prizes" in the lead and supporting actress categories.

Heeding pleas from small-budget producers who felt disadvantaged in the race for Best First Feature, *Spirit* leaders broke the category into separate awards for pix with coffers above and below $500,000. *Being John Malkovich*, produced for $12 million, took the top-dollar kudo in addition to the script award for newbies. Last year's Sundance standout *The Blair Witch Project*, lensed for $35,000 before post-production costs, copped the other trophy. Steve Zahn, who'd snagged a performance prize at Sundance last year for his role in *Happy, Texas*, reaped the Spirit for Best Supporting Actor.

"One of the afternoon's highlights came when the male lead award was presented to Richard Farnsworth for his performance in *The Straight Story*," *Variety* reported. "Farnsworth, who is nearing 80 and awaiting hip replacement surgery, hobbled onto the stage to a standing ovation. 'I hope this sets some sort of a trend for some of us older folk,' he said."

Winner of the "Someone to Watch" accolade was Cauleen Smith, whose first feature, *Drylongso*, followed a young woman as she took rapid-fire Polaroid pix of average young black men who the media said were "endangered" as a group due to urban ills.

At this year's Sundance fest, several pix turned out to be multiple winners.

Girlfight, which *Variety* called "a crowd-pleaser about a teenage girl's struggle to become a boxer," won the Grand Jury Prize for features in addition to a Director's Award. Screen Gems was apparently pleased by it, too, paying a reported $3 million for distrib rights.

Girlfight shared the jury feature prize with *You Can Count on Me*, a drama about a woman and her brother in a small town that also claimed the screenplay award. Its filmmakers were swamped with so many distrib offers that they postponed making a decision on what to do until after Sundance was over.

Winner of the jury's prize for documentaries was *Long Night's Journey into Day*, which *Variety* described as "an examination of the search for justice and healing in post-apartheid South Africa."

A film shown at the fest's sidebar American Spectrum screenings after it failed to make the cut for jury feature consideration scored a Sundance first by winning the Audience Award, helping it to nail a distrib deal from Lions Gate. *Entertainment Weekly* called *Two Family House* a "warmly and elegantly written and directed" portrait of an Italian-American family living in New York City in the 1950s.

The pic that won the Audience Award for documentaries turned out to be the fest's biggest winner numerically when it also received the Freedom of Expression Award and a prize for its black-and-white cinematography. *Dark Days*'s kudos were heady victories for its 26-year-old director Marc Singer, who had sold all his belongings to pay for film and camera equipment so he could spend two years living with, and filming, the homeless people who dwell in the rat-infested tunnels under New York City. When *Dark Days* became a fest hit, Singer told *Entertainment Weekly* that he was hearing applause in the strangest places around Park City, Utah. "I went to the supermarket and the checkout ladies started clapping," he said. "That was freaky."

Winner of the Audience Award for World Cinema was *Saving Grace*, described by *Variety* as an "oldsters-growing-marijuana comedy from Britain." The tradepaper added, "Fine Line Features $4 million purchase of *Saving Grace* was the highest for the fest."

There was "an unprecedented number of sales at this year's Sundance, bringing the total to nine with at least seven additional pacts likely in the coming weeks," *Variety* reported. "The Filmmaker's Awards, a fixture for years in which directors would vote for outstanding achievements in their own categories, were abandoned this year because things have gotten to the point where filmmakers are too busy with their own activities during the festival to see a sufficient number of other films."

▪ 1999 ▪

NATIONAL BOARD OF REVIEW

The board declared a Best Picture and Foreign Film of the year, then listed its remaining favorites according to highest scores. The vote results were announced on December 7, 1999. Awards were presented January 18, 2000, at the Tavern on the Green in New York.

BEST PICTURE
▪ *American Beauty*
The Talented Mr. Ripley
Magnolia
The Insider
The Straight Story
Cradle Will Rock
Boys Don't Cry
Being John Malkovich
Tumbleweeds
Three Kings

BEST DIRECTOR
▪ Anthony Minghella, *The Talented Mr. Ripley*

BEST DEBUT DIRECTOR
▪ Kimberly Peirce, *Boys Don't Cry*

BEST ACTOR
▪ Russell Crowe, *The Insider*

BEST ACTRESS
▪ Janet McTeer, *Tumbleweeds*

BEST SUPPORTING ACTOR
▪ Philip Seymour Hoffman, *Magnolia, The Talented Mr. Ripley*

BEST SUPPORTING ACTRESS
▪ Julianne Moore, *Magnolia, A Map of the World, An Ideal Husband, Cookie's Fortune*

BEST ENSEMBLE PERFORMANCE
▪ *Magnolia*

BEST BREAKTHROUGH PERFORMANCE
▪ Wes Bentley, *American Beauty*
▪ Hilary Swank, *Boys Don't Cry*

BEST SCREENPLAY
▪ John Irving, *The Cider House Rules*

BEST DOCUMENTARY
▪ *Buena Vista Social Club*, Wim Wender

BEST FOREIGN FILM
▪ *All about My Mother* (Spain)
Run Lola Run (Germany)
East-West (France)
Cabaret Balkan (France/Geece/Macedonia)
The Emperor and the Assassin (Japan/China/France)

OUTSTANDING INDIES
▪ *A Map of the World*
▪ *Election*
▪ *Go*
▪ *Limbo*
▪ *Lock, Stock and Two Smoking Barrels*
▪ *Man of the Century*
▪ *Stir of Echoes*

- *This Is My Father*
- *Twin Falls, Idaho*
- *A Walk on the Moon*

FREEDOM OF EXPRESSION AWARD
- *Tian Yu*, Joan Chen

BILLY WILDER AWARD
- John Frankenheimer

CAREER ACHIEVEMENT AWARD
- Clint Eastwood

SPECIAL ACHIEVEMENT AWARD
- Tim Robbins, *Cradle Will Rock*

LOS ANGELES FILM CRITICS ASSOCIATION

Winners were announced on December 11, 1999. Awards were presented on January 19, 2000, at the Bel Age Hotel in Los Angeles.

BEST PICTURE
- *The Insider*

BEST DIRECTOR
- Sam Mendes, *American Beauty*

BEST ACTOR
- Russell Crowe, *The Insider*

BEST ACTRESS
- Hilary Swank, *Boys Don't Cry*

BEST SUPPORTING ACTOR
- Christopher Plummer, *The Insider*

BEST SUPPORTING ACTRESS
- Chloë Sevigny, *Boys Don't Cry*

BEST SCREENPLAY
- Charlie Kaufman, *Being John Malkovich*

BEST CINEMATOGRAPHY
- Dante Spinotti, *The Insider*

BEST MUSIC
- *South Park: Bigger, Longer and Uncut*, Trey Parker, Marc Shaiman

BEST PRODUCTION DESIGN
- Rick Heinrichs, *Sleepy Hollow*

BEST ANIMATION
- *Iron Giant*, Brad Bird

BEST DOCUMENTARY
- *The Buena Vista Social Club*, Wim Wenders, Ry Cooder

BEST FOREIGN FILM
- *All about My Mother* (Spain)

BEST INDEPENDENT/EXPERIMENTAL FILM
- Owen Land

NEW GENERATION AWARD
- Alexander Payne, Jim Taylor, *Citizen Ruth, Election*

CAREER ACHIEVEMENT AWARD
- Dede Allen

SPECIAL AWARD
- Rick Schmidlin, Roger Mayre, Turner Classic Movies

NEW YORK FILM CRITICS CIRCLE

Winners were announced on December 16, 1999. Awards were presented on January 9, 2000, at the Windows on the World restaurant in New York.

BEST PICTURE
- *Topsy-Turvy*

BEST FIRST FEATURE
- *Being John Malkovich*

BEST DIRECTOR
- Mike Leigh, *Topsy-Turvy*

BEST ACTOR
- Richard Farnsworth, *The Straight Story*

BEST ACTRESS
- Hilary Swank, *Boys Don't Cry*

BEST SUPPORTING ACTOR
- John Malkovich, *Being John Malkovich*

BEST SUPPORTING ACTRESS
- Catherine Keener, *Being John Malkovich*

BEST SCREENWRITER
- Jim Taylor, Alexander Payne, *Election*

BEST CINEMATOGRAPHER
- Freddie Francis, *The Straight Story*

BEST ANIMATED FILM
- *South Park: Bigger, Longer and Uncut*, Trey Parker, Matt Stone

BEST DOCUMENTARY
- *The Buena Vista Social Club*, Wim Wenders

BEST FOREIGN FILM
- *All about My Mother* (Spain)

SPECIAL AWARD
- Manny Farber

NATIONAL SOCIETY OF FILM CRITICS

Winners were announced on January 8, 2000.

BEST PICTURE (TIE)
- *Being John Malkovich*
- *Topsy-Turvy*

BEST DIRECTOR
- Mike Leigh, *Topsy-Turvy*

BEST ACTOR
- Russell Crowe, *The Insider*

BEST ACTRESS
- Reese Witherspoon, *Election*

BEST SUPPORTING ACTOR
- Christopher Plummer, *The Insider*

BEST SUPPORTING ACTRESS
- Chloë Sevigny, *Boys Don't Cry*

BEST SCREENPLAY
- Charlie Kaufman, *Being John Malkovich*

BEST CINEMATOGRAPHY
- Conrad L. Hall, *American Beauty*

BEST DOCUMENTARY
- *Buena Vista Social Club*, Wim Wenders

BEST FOREIGN-LANGUAGE FILM
- *Autumn Tale*

EXPERIMENTAL FILM AWARD
- Robert Beavers

SPECIAL CITATION
- James Quandt

BROADCAST FILM CRITICS ASSOCIATION

Winners in all categories but Best Picture were announced on December 21, 1999. The top pic champ was revealed when the awards were presented on January 24, 2000, at the Sofitel Hotel in Los Angeles.

BEST PICTURE
- *American Beauty*

BEST DIRECTOR
- Sam Mendes, *American Beauty*

BEST ACTOR
- Russell Crowe, *The Insider*

BEST ACTRESS
- Hilary Swank, *Boys Don't Cry*

BEST SUPPORTING ACTOR
- Michael Clarke Duncan, *The Green Mile*

BEST SUPPORTING ACTRESS
- Angelina Jolie, *Girl, Interrupted*

BEST CHILD PERFORMANCE
- Haley Joel Osment, *The Sixth Sense*

BEST BREAKTHROUGH PERFORMER
- Spike Jonze, *Being John Malkovich, Three Kings*

BEST ORIGINAL SCREENPLAY
- Alan Ball, *American Beauty*

BEST ADAPTED SCREENPLAY
- Frank Darabont, *The Green Mile*

BEST SCORE
- Gabriel Yared, *The Talented Mr. Ripley*

BEST SONG
- "Music of My Heart," *Music of the Heart*, Diane Warren

BEST ANIMATED FEATURE
- *Toy Story 2*

BEST DOCUMENTARY
- *The Buena Vista Social Club*, Wim Wenders

BEST FOREIGN FILM
- *All about My Mother* (Spain)

BEST FAMILY FILM
- *October Sky*

GOLDEN GLOBES

Nominations were announced on December 20, 1999. Awards were presented on January 23, 2000, at the Beverly Hilton Hotel in Los Angeles. The ceremony was telecast by NBC.

BEST DRAMA PICTURE
- *American Beauty*
The End of the Affair
The Hurricane
The Insider
The Talented Mr. Ripley

BEST COMEDY OR MUSICAL PICTURE
- *Toy Story 2*
Analyze This
Being John Malkovich
Man on the Moon
Notting Hill

BEST DIRECTOR
- Sam Mendes, *American Beauty*
Norman Jewison, *The Hurricane*
Neil Jordan, *The End of the Affair*
Michael Mann, *The Insider*
Anthony Minghella, *The Talented Mr. Ripley*

BEST ACTOR, DRAMA
- Denzel Washington, *The Hurricane*
Russell Crowe, *The Insider*
Matt Damon, *The Talented Mr. Ripley*
Richard Farnsworth, *The Straight Story*
Kevin Spacey, *American Beauty*

BEST ACTRESS, DRAMA
- Hilary Swank, *Boys Don't Cry*
Annette Bening, *American Beauty*
Julianne Moore, *The End of the Affair*
Meryl Streep, *Music of the Heart*
Sigourney Weaver, *A Map of the World*

BEST ACTOR, COMEDY OR MUSICAL
- Jim Carrey, *Man on the Moon*
Robert De Niro, *Analyze This*
Rupert Everett, *An Ideal Husband*
Hugh Grant, *Notting Hill*
Sean Penn, *Sweet and Lowdown*

BEST ACTRESS, COMEDY OR MUSICAL
- Janet McTeer, *Tumbleweeds*
Julianne Moore, *An Ideal Husband*
Julia Roberts, *Notting Hill*
Sharon Stone, *The Muse*
Reese Witherspoon, *Election*

BEST SUPPORTING ACTOR
- Tom Cruise, *Magnolia*
Michael Caine, *The Cider House Rules*
Michael Clarke Duncan, *The Green Mile*
Jude Law, *The Talented Mr. Ripley*
Haley Joel Osment, *The Sixth Sense*

BEST SUPPORTING ACTRESS
- Angelina Jolie, *Girl, Interrupted*
Cameron Diaz, *Being John Malkovich*
Catherine Keener, *Being John Malkovich*
Samantha Morton, *Sweet and Lowdown*
Natalie Portman, *Anywhere but Here*
Chloë Sevigny, *Boys Don't Cry*

BEST SCREENPLAY
- Alan Ball, *American Beauty*
Charlie Kaufman, *Being John Malkovich*
John Irving, *The Cider House Rules*
Eric Roth, Michael Mann, *The Insider*
M. Night Shyamalan, *The Sixth Sense*

BEST SONG

- "You'll Be in My Heart," *Tarzan*, Phil Collins

"Beautiful Stranger," *Austin Powers: The Spy Who Shagged Me*, Madonna, William Orbit

"How Can I Not Love You," *Anna and the King*, Kenneth Edmonds, George Fenton, Robert Kraft

"Save Me," *Magnolia*, Aimee Mann

"When She Loved Me," *Toy Story 2*, Randy Newman

BEST FOREIGN FILM

- *All about My Mother* (Spain)

Aimee & Jaquar (Germany)

East-West (France)

Girl on the Bridge (France)

The Red Violin (Canada)

Winners

BEST SCORE

- *The Legend of 1900*, Ennio Morricone

CECIL B. DEMILLE AWARD

- Barbra Streisand

SUNDANCE FILM FESTIVAL

The festival was held January 20–30, 2000, at Park City, Utah.

GRAND JURY PRIZE
(DRAMATIC)

- *Girlfight*, Karyn Kusama
- *You Can Count on Me*, Kenneth Lonergan

(DOCUMENTARY)

- *Long Night's Journey into Day*, Frances Reid, Deborah Hoffmann

AUDIENCE AWARD
(DRAMATIC)

- *Two Family House*, Raymond De Felitta

(DOCUMENTARY)

- *Dark Days*, Marc Singer

(WORLD CINEMA)

- *Saving Grace*, Nigel Cole

DIRECTOR'S AWARD
(DRAMATIC)

- *Girlfight*, Karyn Kusama

(DOCUMENTARY)

- *Paragraph 175*, Robert Epstein, Jeffrey Friedman

WALDO SALT SCREENWRITING AWARD

- Kenneth Lonergan, *You Can Count on Me*

FREEDOM OF EXPRESSION AWARD

- *Dark Days*, Marc Singer

CINEMATOGRAPHY AWARD
(DRAMATIC)

- *Committed*, Tom Krueger

(DOCUMENTARY)

- *Americanos: Latino Life in the United States*, Andrew Young
- *Dark Days*, Marc Singer

JURY PRIZE IN LATIN AMERICAN CINEMA

- *Herod's Law*, Luis Estrada
- *No One Writes to the Colonel*, Arturo Ripstein

JURY PRIZE IN SHORT FILMMAKING

- *Five Feet High and Rising*, Peter Sollett

(HONORABLE MENTION)

- *The Bats*, Jim Trainor
- *Darling International*, Jennifer Todd Reeves, M. M. Serra
- *The Drowning Room*, Reynold Reynolds, Patrick Jolley
- *Friday*, Jodi Gibson
- *G.*, Rolf Gibbs
- *Hitch*, Bradley Rust Gray
- *Ice Fishing*, Alexandra Kondracke
- *This Is for Betsy Hall*, Hope Hall
- *Titler*, Jonathan Bekemeier

NHK SCREENPLAY AWARDS

- Carine Adler, *Finding Out*
- Jyunichi Mori, *Laundry*
- Randy Redroad, *Doe Boy*
- Dana Rotberg, *Ottila Ruada*

SPECIAL JURY AWARD
(ARTISTIC ACHIEVEMENT)

- *The Ballad of Ramblin' Jack*, Aiyana Elliott

(DOCUMENTARY WRITING)

- *George Wallace: Settin' the Woods on Fire*, Daniel McCabe, Paul Stekler, Steve Fayer

(PERFORMANCE)
- Donal Logue, *The Tao of Steve*

(ENSEMBLE PERFORMANCE)
- Janet McTeer, Aidan Quinn, Pat Carrollm Jane Adams, Gregory Cook, Iris DeMent, *Songcatcher*

PRODUCERS GUILD OF AMERICA

Nominations were announced on January 19, 2000. Awards were presented on March 2 at the Century Plaza Hotel in Los Angeles.

DARRYL F. ZANUCK PRODUCER OF THE YEAR AWARD
- *American Beauty*, Dan Jinks, Bruce Cohen

Being John Malkovich, Michael Stipe, Sandy Stern, Steve Golin, Vincent Landy

The Cider House Rules, Richard N. Gladstein

The Hurricane, Armyan Bernstein, John Ketcham, Norman Jewison

The Insider, Michael Mann, Jan Pieter Brugge

NOVA AWARD
- Gregg Hale, Robin Cowie, *The Blair Witch Project*

DAVID O. SELZNICK LIFETIME ACHIEVEMENT AWARD
- Jerry Bruckheimer

VISION AWARD
- Michael Stipe, Sandy Stern, Steve Golin, Vincent Landay, *Being John Malkovich*

WRITERS GUILD OF AMERICA

Nominations were announced on February 9, 2000. Awards were presented on March 5 at the Beverly Hilton Hotel in Los Angeles and the Plaza Hotel in New York.

BEST ORIGINAL SCREENPLAY
- *American Beauty*, Alan Ball

Being John Malkovich, Charlie Kaufman
Magnolia, Paul Thomas Anderson

The Sixth Sense, M. Night Shyamalan
Three Kings, David O. Russell, John Ridley

BEST ADAPTED SCREENPLAY
- *Election*, Alexander Payne, Jim Taylor, based on the novel by Tom Perrotta

The Cider House Rules, John Irving, based on his novel

The Insider, Eric Roth, Michael Mann, based on the article "The Man Who Knew Too Much" by Marie Brenner

October Sky, Lewis Colick, based on the book *Rocket Boys* by Homer H. Hickam, Jr.

The Talented Mr. Ripley, Anthony Minghella, based on the novel by Patricia Highsmith

MORGAN COX AWARD
- Ann Marcus

VALENTINE DAVIES AWARD
- Alan Alda

LAUREL AWARD
- Jean-Claude Carrier

PAUL SELVIN AWARD
- Michael Mann, Eric Roth, *The Insider*

DIRECTORS GUILD OF AMERICA

Nominations were announced on January 24, 2000. Awards were presented on March 11 at the Century Plaza Hotel in Los Angeles.

BEST DIRECTOR
- Sam Mendes, *American Beauty*

Frank Darabont, *The Green Mile*
Spike Jonze, *Being John Malkovich*
Michael Mann, *The Insider*
M. Night Shyamalan, *The Sixth Sense*

LIFETIME ACHIEVEMENT AWARD
- Steven Spielberg

SCREEN ACTORS GUILD

Nominations were announced on Feb. 1, 2000. Awards were presented on March 12 at the Shrine Auditorium in Los Angeles. The ceremony was telecast by TNT.

BEST ACTOR
- Kevin Spacey, *American Beauty*

Jim Carrey, *Man on the Moon*
Russell Crowe, *The Insider*
Philip Seymour Hoffman, *Flawless*
Denzel Washington, *The Hurricane*

BEST ACTRESS
- Annette Bening, *American Beauty*

Janet McTeer, *Tumbleweeds*
Julianne Moore, *The End of the Affair*
Meryl Streep, *Music of the Heart*
Hilary Swank, *Boys Don't Cry*

BEST SUPPORTING ACTOR
- Michael Caine, *The Cider House Rules*

Chris Cooper, *American Beauty*
Tom Cruise, *Magnolia*
Michael Clarke Duncan, *The Green Mile*
Haley Joel Osment, *The Sixth Sense*

BEST SUPPORTING ACTRESS
- Angelina Jolie, *Girl, Interrupted*

Cameron Diaz, *Being John Malkovich*
Catherine Keener, *Being John Malkovich*
Julianne Moore, *Magnolia*
Chloë Sevigny, *Boys Don't Cry*

BEST CAST PERFORMANCE
- *American Beauty*

Being John Malkovich
The Cider House Rules
The Green Mile
Magnolia

LIFETIME ACHIEVEMENT AWARD
- Sidney Poitier

INDEPENDENT SPIRIT

Nominations were announced on January 10, 2000. Awards were presented on March 25 in a tent on the beach in Santa Monica. The ceremony was telecast by the Independent Film Channel.

BEST FEATURE
- *Election*

Cookie's Fortune

The Limey
The Straight Story
Sugar Town

BEST FIRST FEATURE (OVER $500,000)
- *Being John Malkovich*

Boys Don't Cry
Three Seasons
Tian Yu
Twin Falls, Idaho

BEST FIRST FEATURE (UNDER $500,000)
- *The Blair Witch Project*

The City
Compensation
Judy Berlin
Treasure Island

BEST DIRECTOR
- Alexander Payne, *Election*

Harmony Korine, *Julien Donkey-Boy*
Doug Liman, *Go*
David Lynch, *The Straight Story*
Steven Soderbergh, *The Limey*

BEST ACTOR
- Richard Farnsworth, *The Straight Story*

John Cusack, *Being John Malkovich*
Terence Stamp, *The Limey*
David Strathairn, *Limbo*
Noble Willingham, *The Corndog Man*

BEST ACTRESS
- Hilary Swank, *Boys Don't Cry*

Diane Lane, *A Walk on the Moon*
Janet McTeer, *Tumbleweeds*
Susan Traylor, *Valerie Flake*
Reese Witherspoon, *Election*

BEST SUPPORTING ACTOR
- Steve Zahn, *Happy, Texas*

Charles Dutton, *Cookie's Fortune*
Clark Gregg, *The Adventures of Sebastian Cole*
Luis Guzman, *The Limey*
Terrence Dashon Howard, *The Best Man*

BEST SUPPORTING ACTRESS
- Chloë Sevigny, *Boys Don't Cry*

Barbara Barrie, *Judy Berlin*
Vanessa Martinez, *Limbo*

Sarah Polley, *Go*
Jean Smart, *Guinevere*

BEST DEBUT PERFORMANCE
- Kimberly Brown, *Tumbleweeds*
Jessica Campbell, *Election*
Jade Gordon, *Sugar Town*
Toby Smith, *Drylongso*
Chris Stafford, *Edge of Seventeen*

BEST SCREENPLAY
- Alexander Payne, Jim Taylor, *Election*
Lem Dobbs, *The Limey*
James Merendino, *S.L.C. Punk!*
Kevin Smith, *Dogma*
Audrey Wells, *Guinevere*

BEST FIRST SCREENPLAY
- Charlie Kaufman, *Being John Malkovich*
Kimberly Peirce, Andy Bienen, *Boys Don't Cry*
Anne Rapp, *Cookie's Fortune*
John Roach, Mary Sweeney, *The Straight Story*
Tod Williams, *The Adventures of Sebastian Cole*

"SOMEONE TO WATCH" AWARD
- Cauleen Smith, *Drylongso*
Dan Clark, *The Item*
Julian Goldberger, *Trans*
Lisanne Skyler, *Getting to Know You*

PRODUCERS AWARD
- Pamela Koffler, *I'm Losing You*
Eva Kolodner, *Boys Don't Cry*
Paul S. Mezey, *The City*
Christine Walker, *Backroads, Homo Heights*

BEST FOREIGN FILM
- *Run Lola Run* (Germany)
All about My Mother (Spain)
My Son the Fanatic (U.K.)
Rosetta (Belgium/France)
Topsy-Turvy (U.K.)

Winners
BEST CINEMATOGRAPHY
- Lisa Rinzler, *Three Seasons*

"TRUER THAN FICTION" DOCUMENTARY AWARD
- *Night Waltz: The Music of Paul Bowles*, Osley Brown

ACADEMY AWARDS

Nominations were announced on February 15, 2000. Awards were presented on March 26 at the Shrine Auditorium in Los Angeles. The ceremony was telecast by ABC.

BEST PICTURE
- *American Beauty*
The Cider House Rules
The Green Mile
The Insider
The Sixth Sense

BEST DIRECTOR
- Sam Mendes, *American Beauty*
Lasse Hallström, *The Cider House Rules*
Spike Jonze, *Being John Malkovich*
Michael Mann, *The Insider*
M. Night Shyamalan, *The Sixth Sense*

BEST ACTOR
- Kevin Spacey, *American Beauty*
Russell Crowe, *The Insider*
Richard Farnsworth, *The Straight Story*
Sean Penn, *Sweet and Lowdown*
Denzel Washington, *The Hurricane*

BEST ACTRESS
- Hilary Swank, *Boys Don't Cry*
Annette Bening, *American Beauty*
Janet McTeer, *Tumbleweeds*
Julianne Moore, *The End of the Affair*
Meryl Streep, *Music of the Heart*

BEST SUPPORTING ACTOR
- Michael Caine, *The Cider House Rules*
Tom Cruise, *Magnolia*
Michael Clarke Duncan, *The Green Mile*
Jude Law, *The Talented Mr. Ripley*
Haley Joel Osment, *The Sixth Sense*

BEST SUPPORTING ACTRESS
- Angelina Jolie, *Girl, Interrupted*
Toni Collette, *The Sixth Sense*
Catherine Keener, *Being John Malkovich*

Samantha Morton, *Sweet and Lowdown*
Chloë Sevigny, *Boys Don't Cry*

BEST ORIGINAL SCREENPLAY
- Alan Ball, *American Beauty*

Paul Thomas Anderson, *Magnolia*
Charlie Kaufman, *Being John Malkovich*
Mike Leigh, *Topsy-Turvy*
M. Night Shyamalan, *The Sixth Sense*

BEST ADAPTED SCREENPLAY
- John Irving, *The Cider House Rules*

Frank Darabont, *The Green Mile*
Alexander Payne, Jim Taylor, *Election*
Eric Roth, Michael Mann, *The Insider*
Anthony Minghella, *The Talented Mr. Ripley*

BEST SONG
- "You'll Be in My Heart," *Tarzan*, Phil Collins

"Blame Canada," *South Park: Bigger, Longer and Uncut*, Trey Parker, Marc Shaiman
"Music of My Heart" *Music of the Heart*, Diane Warren
"Same Me," *Magnolia*, Aimee Mann
"When She Loved Me," *Toy Story 2*, Randy Newman

BEST FOREIGN-LANGUAGE FILM
- *All about My Mother* (Spain)

Caravan (Nepal)
East-West (France)
Solomon and Gaenor (U.K.)
Under the Sun (Sweden)

Winners

BEST ART DIRCTION
- Rick Heinrichs, Peter Young, *Sleepy Hollow*

BEST CINEMATOGRAPHY
- Conrad L. Hall, *American Beauty*

BEST COSTUME DESIGN
- Lindy Hemming, *Topsy-Turvy*

BEST DOCUMENTARY
(FEATURE)
- *One Day in September*, Arthur Cohn, Kevin Macdonald

(SHORT SUBJECT)
- *King Gimp*, Susan Hannah Hadary, William A. Whiteford

BEST FILM EDITING
- Zach Staenberg, *The Matrix*

BEST MAKEUP
- Christine Blundell, Trefor Proud, *Topsy-Turvy*

BEST ORIGINAL MUSIC SCORE
- John Corigliano, *The Red Violin*

SCIENTIFIC AND TECHNICAL AWARDS
(Scientific and Engineering Award)
- Iain Neil, Rick Gelbard, Panavision; Nat Tiffen, Tiffen Manufacturing; Huw Gwilym, Karl Lynch, Mark Crabtree, James Moultrie, Mike Salter, Mark Craig Gerchman, Marlowe A. Pichel, L. Ron Schmidt, Nick Phillips, Fritz Gabriel Bauer

(Technical Achievement Award)
- Mitchell J. Bogdanowicz, Mary L. Schmoeger, Eastman Kodak; Hoyt H. Yeatman, Jr., Dream Quest Images; John C. Brewer, Eastman Kodak; Vivienne Dyer, Chris Woolf, Leslie Drever, Richard C. Sehlin

BEST SHORT FILM
(ANIMATED)
- *The Old Man and the Sea*, Alexander Petrov

(LIVE ACTION)
- *My Mother Dreams the Satan's Disciples in New York*, Barbara Schock, Tammy Tiehel

BEST SOUND
- John Reitz, Gregg Rudloff, David Campbell, David Lee, *The Matrix*

BEST SOUND EFFECTS EDITING
- Dane A. Davis, *The Matrix*

BEST VISUAL EFFECTS

- John Gaeta, Janek Sirrs, Steve Courtley, Jon Thum, *The Matrix*

GORDON E. SAWYER AWARD

- Roderick T. Ryan

IRVING G. THALBERG MEMORIAL AWARD

- Warren Beatty

HONORARY AWARD

- Andrzej Wajda

Derby Players

ACADEMY AWARDS

Hollywood's golden boy can turn struggling actors into superstars (Jack Lemmon, Kevin Spacey) and earn considerable more gold for sleeper pix ($100 million extra for *Shakespeare in Love*). The award can even make Hollywood's coolest cats cry. John Wayne never blinked when he faced down the Wild West's orneriest desperadoes on screen, but he fought back tears as he accepted a statuette near the end of his career for *True Grit*, saying, "I feel very humble."

The last leg of the year's awards derby can be exciting, too. Oscar fans may feel that they've been tipped off sufficiently about what film is out front for Best Picture, say, after the Golden Globes, guilds' and crix's kudos all sound off, but upsets happen all the time—as *Grand Hotel, The Greatest Show on Earth, Hamlet, An American in Paris, Casablanca, Oliver!, Chariots of Fire, The Silence of the Lambs, Braveheart* and *Shakespeare in Love* proved.

The world's most-watched telecast has been denounced as "a public hanging" by two-time champ Glenda Jackson and as "an obscene evening" by double champ Dustin Hoffman, but both stars seemed to enjoy themselves when they participated in the obscenity on air. Even crusty George C. Scott finally came around. He had trashed the kudofest as "a weird beauty or personality contest" when he refused his Best Actor trophy for *Patton* in 1970, but then, mysteriously, in 1972, Scott let it be known that he would not refuse an Oscar nomination for his directorial debut in *Rage*. None was forthcoming, but Oscar fans at last could see that the award's most strident critic was starting to crack. The opposition finally crumbled completely in 1982 when Scott actually purchased some last-minute tix to

Variety said that Oscar's first Best Picture winner, *Wings*, was full of "smashes and crashes of all types." The World War I aviation drama was the only silent film to claim the top prize.

the ceremony and tried to sneak into the Dorothy Chandler Pavilion with a minimum of fuss. *Variety* columnist Army Archerd spotted him on the red carpet, though, and yelled at Scott as he scooted by, "Your Oscar is waiting for you at the academy! Wilshire and Lampeer!"

Awards and nominations are decided by the 5,600 voting members of the Academy of Motion Picture Arts and Sciences based in Los Angeles, which has 6,300 total members. Annual dues are $250. Nominees are chosen by peer group—actors vote for actors, writers for writers—except in the Best Picture category, which all members can vote on. Most nominees are chosen by members who list their top five choices per category on a paper ballot (just three choices are listed in the categories for makeup, visual effects and sound effects editing). Screening panels, however, determine what gets nommed in the categories for documentaries, short subjects, foreign pix, makeup, visual effects and sound effects editing. The general membership decides who wins makeup, visual effects and sound effects editing, but members can vote on documentaries, short films and foreign pix only if they prove that they've attended screenings and seen all five nominees.

The academy's actors branch is the largest (1,321 voting members), followed by producers (460), executives (407), writers (404), members at large (402), sound (400), public relations (358) and directors (354). Some Oscar experts credit the large thesp voting bloc with triggering the upset scored by *Shakespeare in Love*—a pic about actors in Elizabethan England—over *Saving Private Ryan* in 1998. But those same voters didn't rally behind the showbiz-themed film that was named Best Picture one year later by the New York Film Critics Circle and the National Society of Film Critics: *Topsy-Turvy*. Mike Leigh's widely praised backstage peek into the lives of Gilbert and Sullivan didn't even get nominated for Best Picture at the Oscars, even though Leigh's *Secrets and Lies* made the cut in 1996 after reaping only a single Best Picture endorsement earlier from the crix groups (L.A.).

The film academy was founded in 1927, so says its original credo, to "promote harmony and solidarity among the membership" and to encourage "the interchange of constructive ideas" while also bestowing "awards of merit for distinctive achievement." It was created by MGM topper Louis B. Mayer, who came up with the idea one day when he was steaming mad about having been forced to sign a costly pact with industry unions. He envisioned a core Hollywood group that could act as a cross-industry union in the future and settle all conflicts amicably. Many of Hollywood's key players gave it a chance when he first trumpeted the idea, but it soon became apparent that Mayer and his studio-mogul cronies were calling all the shots at the new org.

Early academy president Frank Capra revealed later in Oscar's official history that, by 1935, directors, writers and stars were in open revolt and "the academy had become the favorite whipping boy of Hollywood. The odds were 10 to 1 (it) would fold and the Oscar would acquire the patina of a collector's item." Happily, Capra's leadership helped the academy to rediscover its initial, loftier vision of harmony and, by 1939, he said, "It was off and running!"

By the mid-1930s, however, separate guilds had also formed—and they soon got into the kudos game, too. In 1948, the directors' and writers' guilds both unveiled their own awards, meant to rival the prestige of the Oscars because they were also bestowed by peer groups. The new kudos never managed to achieve Oscar's luster, but they did end up spoiling some of Oscar's fun by foretelling many academy winners ahead of time. Most of Oscar's screenplay champs win a WGA trophy first. More than 90 percent of Oscar's Best Directors already have a guild kudo on the mantel at home when they take their golden boys in hand. The reason: the Oscars and the guilds share hundreds of the same voters. The guilds do have thousands of additional members who vote, too, but they are obviously like-minded.

Oscar voters love drunks, hookers and Brits.

Oscar victories aren't always about the best film work of the year, of course. Elizabeth Taylor reaped her first one for *Butterfield 8* (a movie she said "stinks") in 1960 because she nearly died of pneumonia. Jimmy Stewart won Best Actor for his supporting role in *The Philadelphia Story* in 1940 because voters had overlooked him one year earlier for *Mr. Smith Goes to Washington*. Nobody argues that *The Color of Money* (1986) is Paul Newman's best film to date, not even Paul Newman (who far prefers his perf in *Mr. and Mrs. Bridge*—but he'd already received his *Color of Money* consolation Oscar by the time he was nommed for *Bridge*, so he lost).

But the Oscars are still the most prestigious—and perhaps even the most accurate—of all the kudos, at least if final judgment is left to the 1,500 film pros who participated in a poll conducted by the

American Film Institute in 1996 to determine the 100 greatest movies ever made. Not one of the three crix orgs can claim that it has more entries on the list than the Oscars when counting up just the films that were made during the years that any one group has existed.

Oscar voters, however, do demonstrate obvious biases. For Best Picture, they like big-screen epics (*Titanic, The English Patient, Out of Africa, The Last Emperor*). They frown on comedies (rare exceptions include *Annie Hall, Tom Jones* and *The Apartment*). They're suckers for British accents (Michael Caine, Emma Thompson, Jeremy Irons, Daniel Day-Lewis). They also clearly like stars who take on handicapped roles (Dustin Hoffman, Cliff Robertson, Al Pacino) or salacious parts as hookers (Mira Sorvino, Jane Fonda, Julie Christie) or drunks (Nicolas Cage, James Coburn, Lee Marvin).

But no performances top those given on stage once awards night rolls around. That's when septuagenarian veterans drop to the floor to do one-handed push-ups, streakers fly by, stars give political tirades about "Zionist hoodlums" and fake injuns step up to the podium to refuse an award for an absent, angry star. Meantime, a billion people tune in to watch worldwide while advertisers pay $1.1 million for 30 seconds of commercial time. In 1999, the gala reaped the academy more than $29 million and broadcaster ABC $23 million in profits, according to *Variety*.

Oscar's biggest champ, Katharine Hepburn (four wins as Best Actress), says about the spectacle: "It's painful, but it's thrilling."

GOLDEN GLOBES

The Golden Globes are the second- or third-highest-rated awards show on TV, depending on how the Grammys do in a given year. The reason for their success: "The Golden Globes are fun," Warren Beatty once said. "The Oscars are business."

The Globe gala is the only time every year when Hollywood's film and TV titans get together for a party—and it's usually quite a loosey-goosey affair. Dinner and drinks are thrown in, just like the good old days when the Oscars, Emmys and Grammys used to be held at elegant banquets. The demon drink has caused its share of problems at Globes past, of course—at least it's what got blamed for obscenity-laced outbursts by stars such as Rita Hayworth (at her table, just having fun) and Joan Crawford (at the podium, defending Frank Sinatra from hecklers, doing it her way).

Spiritus fermenti has fomented some upbeat times, too. In the early years, the awards were bestowed by the journalist members of the Hollywood Foreign Press Association, but, in 1958, Rat Packers Frank Sinatra, Dean Martin and Sammy Davis, Jr., would have none of that. They ambushed the stage (whiskeys and cigarettes still firmly in hand) and started to dispense the kudos—sprinkled with lots of gags, of course—themselves. Their antics were such a hit that HFPA leaders invited them to come back and do it again the next year, which they did. From then on, stars have always reigned on stage. Many of them have been sober, too—as Bette Midler appeared to be when she accepted two statuettes in 1979, saying, "This is the most wonderful thing that's ever happened to me." "The last of the truly tacky ladies" looked genuinely humbled and grateful at first, but she didn't miss her chance to get down and dirty with the rowdy gang. Before taking her bow at the podium, she did a Marilyn Monroe–style shoulder shimmy and purred at the audience, "I'll show ya a pair of golden globes"—a joke first attributed to Joan Crawford at an earlier ceremony (not the Frank Sinatra outburst).

Considering how chummy the Hollywood crowd is with the foreign-press awards group, it's no surprise to discover what uncanny crystal balls the Globes can be when trying to predict the movie-industry Oscars.

Since their creation in 1943, the Globes have played a key role in the victories of at least 20 Oscar Best Pictures—and no doubt many more. But their impact can be seen best in the cases of those 20 films that did not receive a Best Picture laurel from any crix group prior to winning the Globe, then the Oscar. Many of the films were b.o. giants that the crix scorned because of their usual disregard for commercial success, so Oscar voters were well aware of those movies and may have named them Best Picture anyway. But certainly the Globes helped the pix along: *The Greatest Show on Earth, An American in Paris, Gigi, The Sound of Music, Lawrence of Arabia, Oliver!, The Godfather, The French Connection, One Flew over the Cuckoo's Nest* (it won the L.A. crix award after the Globe), *Platoon, Rain Man, Out of Africa, The Last Emperor, The English Patient, Titanic* and *Shakespeare in Love*. Four of the 20 Best Pictures spurned by the crix had been cited earlier by the National Board of Review: *Driving Miss Daisy, Dances with Wolves, Forrest Gump* and *American Beauty*.

Comparing Oscars to Globes is tricky since the Globes have twice as many awards, dispensing separate kudos for drama and comedy/musical races. The best way to measure the Globes' influence is probably to count up the number of Oscar Best Pictures that won one of the two (three, in some years) Globe Best Pictures first. It comes out to be an impressive number over the past 57 years: 41.

In the past 30 years, 23 of Oscar's Best Actors (77 percent) and 24 Best Actresses (80 percent) were previous Globe winners for the same roles. Some of the victors, such as Kathy Bates (*Misery*) and Sally Field (*Places in the Heart*), hadn't even been considered as candidates by the crix. The Globes have discovered lots of eventual Oscar champs in the supporting categories, too, including Louis Gossett, Jr. (*An Officer and a Gentleman*) and Haing S. Ngor (*The Killing Fields*). In the race for Best Director, the Globes were the first to endorse Mel Gibson (*Braveheart*) and others.

When the Globe voters strayed away from the Oscars and picked different Best Pictures, they still agreed with the New York crix on *The Defiant Ones*, the L.A. crix on *Bugsy,* the national society on *M*A*S*H*, the broadcast crix on *Sense and Sensibility* and the National Board of Review on *Sunset Boulevard*.

When they've gone their own way entirely in the Best Picture races, the choices were usually respectable (*East of Eden, The Turning Point, Midnight Express, On Golden Pond*), but sometimes criticized (*Scent of a Woman*). A few departures in the early years suggest that the HFPA membership might have been religious: *The Song of Bernadette, The Robe* and *The Cardinal*.

That's probably not the case nowadays—at least considering how some of the members behave when giving out awards. Since it's the job of the 90 foreign journalists who belong to the HFPA to pay special attention to breakout new stars and hot new movies while reporting for newspapers and other media back home, they often fawn over sexy megastars who've been ignored at the Oscars, such as Sharon Stone, Jim Carrey, John Travolta and Tom Cruise. Raquel Welch (*The Three Musketeers*) probably deserved to beat Helen Hayes (*Herbie Rides Again*) for Best Comedy/Musical Actress in 1974, but the critics howled anyway, just as they did in 1996 when Madonna (*Evita*) beat Frances McDormand (*Fargo*) in the same category.

The Globes have had a choppy TV history. The first telecasts covered the 1958 to 1963 award shows and were only seen locally in L.A. on KTTV. Then the fete got its first big national break when it was included as a special segment on *The Andy Williams Show* for two years. Broadcaster NBC was impressed enough by the response that it gave the Globes their own stand-alone show in 1966 and 1967, both hosted by Williams. When the show got axed after that, it didn't get back on the tube until it was shown in syndication starting in 1972. NBC did one more telecast in 1977 and CBS gave it a try in 1980 and 1981, but

Flowers for an early Globes gala came from Joan Bennett's garden.

it otherwise remained in syndication until 1987, when TBS aired the next eight galas. NBC picked up the show once again in 1995 and since then has been strict with HFPA about procedures. Members must now sign waivers attesting that they accepted no gifts from the studios other than customary promotional items. Also, they must submit at least four article clippings per year to the org's qualifications committee and HFPA must admit at least five new members every year. (There had been complaints about members' credentials and about HFPA behaving cliquishly.)

The group was founded in October 1943 by eight foreign journos who initially formed the Hollywood Foreign Correspondents Association. Since Twentieth Century-Fox's *The Song of Bernadette* swept their first awards, the presentations were made during a luncheon held on the studio lot. Winners were given scrolls. Sometime between 1945 and 1946, prexy Marina Cisternas dreamt up the idea of a golden statuette depicting the earth encircled by a strip of film. The early prizes were bestowed at ceremonies considered humble affairs by Hollywood standards. The 1944 fete was held at the Beverly Hills Hotel, but funds were so lean that flowers for the tables had to be provided by Joan Bennett's gardener.

In 1950, 12 dissidents broke away and formed the rival Foreign Press Association of Hollywood, which bestowed its own awards for a time, the Henriettas, named after their prexy, Henry Gris. The two orgs reunited under the new banner of the Hollywood Foreign Press Association in January 1954.

The Globes did not achieve the status they have today until 1972, when HFPA leaders moved the ceremony from February to the end of January so it would land close to the time when Oscar nomination ballots are due in. The ceremony was starting to be seen regularly on national TV by then, too. The Globes' prominence and influence increased again in 1989 when the nominations announcement was moved back from early January to late December (now usually the third Monday) so that Globe noms could be ballyhooed in newspaper ads for the big holiday movies. The ceremony was pulled back one week earlier, too—now usually falling on the third Sunday in January—so that it lands about a week to 12 days before Oscar nom ballots are due, thereby allowing more time for its award results to sink in. It hasn't helped Jim Carrey, though.

DIRECTORS GUILD OF AMERICA

Billy Wilder proved that he was Hollywood's greatest scripter (*Sunset Boulevard, Some Like It Hot*) when he set the record for the most writers' guild awards (six). But he once confessed before a directors' guild crowd, "I've always worried whether to a director, I am a director." Then in 1960, when he finally took a DGA plaque in hand for *The Apartment*—beaming with joy and bursting with excitement—he told his helming peers, "Well, this proves it."

The DGA award is Hollywood's most influential prize after the Oscar—for two reasons: directors are the reigning kings and queens of pix, so it matters a lot what their peers think, and, second, Oscar voters defer most often to the DGA's choices before inking their ballots.

In the past 52 years, the Oscars have embraced 48 of the guild's champs in the Best Director category. The only exceptions: the Oscars opted for Carol Reed (*Oliver!*) over DGA choice Anthony Harvey (*The Lion in Winter*) in 1968, Bob Fosse (*Cabaret*) over Francis Ford Coppola (*The Godfather*) in 1972, Sydney Pollack (*Out of Africa*) over Steven Spielberg (*The Color Purple*) in 1985, and Mel Gibson (*Braveheart*) over Ron Howard (*Apollo 13*) in 1995. That's an agreement rate of 92 percent. Forty-eight of the films that won the DGA prize were named Best Picture at the Oscars during those same 52 years—an overlap of 81 percent.

It's a bit surprising that the two groups think so similarly, considering the difference in their voting pools. There are 350 members of the film academy's directing branch, which determines Oscar nominees (all members vote on the winners). The

DGA contenders and winners are selected by its 11,000 members, many of whom are movie helmers, but many others work on TV series, commercials and music videos and are much younger than the typical academy demographic. Timing has a lot to do with the impact factor: DGA announces its nominees a week to 10 days before the first round of Oscar ballots are due; winners are declared 10 days to two weeks before the last round of Oscar ballots must be submitted. It's rare that the two lists of director nominees line up exactly, but the winners are uncannily similar.

The voting methods are similar: Members of both groups recommend five nominees during the first voting stage, ranking them according to preference, and then pick a winner from a list of five contenders.

The DGA's current coziness with the Oscars is ironic, considering that the two orgs started out at war with each other. The initial mission of the Academy of Motion Picture Arts and Sciences was to act as a cross-industry union, but when it became clear to directors, writers and stars that the org was merely a puppet of studio moguls, the latter groups bolted, formed their own guilds and tried to kill off the Oscars by declaring a boycott in 1935. Many of the top talent stayed home that year, but the academy survived primarily because a shrewd director, Frank Capra, served as its prexy at the same time he was helping to organize the helmers' guild. Although created a few years earlier, the Screen Directors Guild was formally inaugurated in 1936 and was later renamed the Directors Guild of America in 1960 when it merged with the Radio and Television Directors Guild.

Awards were first bestowed in 1948, the same year that the writers' guild got into the kudos game. Quarterly awards were given out in addition to the annual prize during the kudos' first eight years. Counting up the annual trophies from 1948 to today, Steven Spielberg reigns as the biggest champ, with three wins (*The Color Purple, Schindler's List, Saving Private Ryan*), and also holds the record for most bids (nine).

The DGA's prize is positioned after the

From left: Billy Wilder, George Sidney and George Seaton at a DGA awards gala in the 1950s.

critics and Golden Globes sound-off, so guild members often pick one of the many early Best Picture and Director choices to declare the Oscar front-runner. On two occasions, though, they didn't like any of the pix named to that point and went their own way—opting for John Schlesinger's *Midnight Cowboy* in 1969 and for Francis Ford Coppola's *The Godfather, Part II* in 1974, both of which went on to nab Best Director and Picture at the Academy Awards.

On two other occasions, they dismissed the choices made by the crix and Golden Globes in favor of films that showed early promise when they were cited by the National Board of Review, but then vanished from consideration: Franklin Schaffner's *Patton* in 1970 and George Roy Hill's *The Sting* in 1973. Ron Howard (*Apollo 13*, 1995) is the only DGA winner who failed to be nominated at the Oscars.

When *Variety* editor Peter Bart was still a scrappy cub reporter for *The New York Times* in 1964, he described the typical kudos ceremony: "The awards were presented amid the usual folderol of drum rolls, darting spotlights and sealed envelopes delivered by breathless aides." Two decades later, the *L.A. Times* observed, "There aren't a lot of stars in the crowd and speeches are generally shorter." The guild's then-prexy, Gil Cates, added, "This is really a family affair. Of course, it's quieter."

WRITERS GUILD OF AMERICA

The Writers Guild of America awards date back to 1948 when the org, founded in 1921, was still known as the Screen Writers Guild, but later morphed into its current name and setup by the mid-1950s.

Its awards ceremony was once considered "one of the toughest tickets to get in Hollywood," according to the *L.A. Times*. "The draw is the stage show during which writers get to howl back at Hollywood, and they do, in a show which is bawdy, irreverent and very often deftly devastating."

Hollywood agents didn't get the joke in 1966, though, when they were depicted on stage as insects and a horned lizard. Some stormed out and *Variety* reported that many more of "the percenters expressed anger and indignation" in a blitz of letters fired off to the guild the next day. But the skits often tweaked writers, too. The one that's most frequently reenacted is "Quizzically," I.A.L. Diamond's sendup of the frustrations experienced by two scribes who try to collaborate on a film script. (A fight breaks out between them when they can't think of a synonym for "quizzically"—a word they end up agreeing upon later once the heat of battle's over and they've forgotten that they dismissed the term earlier.) Unfortunately, skits are staged only occasionally today, having been bumped in favor of granting more time to bestow awards for the guild's members toiling in film, television and new media.

Winners are determined by the 12,000 members, who decide both nominees and winners. Unlike the directors' guild kudos, which uses a weighted ballot to determine

nominees, the writers' org merely has voters select five choices, without ranking them, from a long list of eligible pix.

Sixty-three of the movies that have won a WGA prize so far have also won one of the 116 screenplay awards presented by the Oscars during the same period (54 percent). But such a comparison is flawed because it wasn't until 1984 that the two orgs had parallel award categories. Since then, 19 WGA champs have won one of the 32 Oscars bestowed—an overlap of 59 percent.

When they were first introduced in 1948, the WGA awards covered five categories: musicals, dramas, comedies, westerns and "Screenplays Dealing Most Ably with Problems on the American Scene." By 1952, the guild apparently no longer cared about the American scene because it had narrowed down its contest to three races—for dramas, comedies and musicals. The musical slot got dropped a few times in the 1960s while the genre waned and rock 'n' roll roared, then was nixed completely in 1969 when the drama and comedy categories were split into separate races for original and adapted works. At that point, the guild had twice as many screenplay awards as the Oscars, but at least they were somewhat akin and would line up precisely 15 years later.

The guild's biggest kudos champs are Ernest Lehman and Billy Wilder (five each). Woody Allen actually holds the record for most noms (18), but he won only four times, tying Robert Benton for second place. (Wilder scored 15 noms, Lehman 10.)

Honored scripts span filmdom's finest: *Sunset Boulevard, All about Eve, On the Waterfront, Midnight Cowboy, Patton, The Hospital, The Godfather, Shakespeare in Love* and *Who's Afraid of Virginia Woolf?* But there were occasional choices that may be, depending on one's taste, considered dubious: *Me and the Colonel* topped *Indiscreet* (1958); *Dances with Wolves* devoured *Good-Fellas* and *The Grifters* (1990); *Braveheart* slayed *Mighty Aphrodite* and *Clueless* (1995).

> # Ernest Lehman and Billy Wilder are the WGA's biggest champs.

Yet some of the guild's choices may seem hipper with historic hindsight, too. Its 1964 victor *Dr. Strangelove* probably wears better today than the film that beat it at the Oscars—*Father Goose.*

What about oversights? Winners of Oscar's screenplay awards occasionally have failed to make the guild list. Some snubs may be due to a difference in taste (*How the West Was Won*, 1963), but there's no explaining how guild voters managed to overlook William Inge's *Splendor in the Grass* in 1961.

Some of Oscar's biggest champs (*Tom Jones, A Man for All Seasons, Gandhi, The Last Emperor, Chariots of Fire*) weren't nommed because they weren't eligible, being foreign productions. But even pureblood Yankee pix have had trouble making the cut. *Pulp Fiction* failed to snag a nom because its production company wasn't a guild signatory.

> The SAG kudo-cast has more heart than any other.

Only twice has the guild refused to nominate an eligible film that went on to claim Oscar's Best Picture trophy: *The Greatest Show on Earth* (probably because voters thought it was lightweight) and *The Bridge on the River Kwai* (for political reasons having to do with Hollywood blacklisting).

The blacklisting era is a touchy subject in guild history, since the org signed an agreement with the studios that permitted producers to omit screen credit if a scribe was a member of the Communist party or refused to deny any affiliation or sympathies.

But it was through the guild's awards process that its members rose up to denounce injustices when they occurred. Voters brazenly endorsed blacklisted scribe Michael Wilson for *A Place in the Sun* in 1951 and Carl Foreman for *High Noon* in 1952. It's unclear today how to interpret the results of the 1950 and 1953 races. Voters gave a kudo to Albert Maltz's frontman for *Broken Arrow* in 1950 and to Dalton Trumbo's stand-in for *Roman Holiday* in 1953, but it's possible that they were being naughty instead of patsies.

There's no disguising the fact, though, that the guild went along with listing the fictitious names on its ballot. The org eventually made up for it all in 1991 by giving the widows of Maltz and Trumbo retroactive awards in their husbands' names.

Also, in the end, the guild at least did not put up with the Red Scare as long at the Oscars did. In 1956, when Allied Artists studio refused to give Michael Wilson credit for *Friendly Persuasion*, the guild issued a ruling boldly declaring that Wilson was indeed its author and therefore eligible for a WGA award, which Wilson promptly won. At the Oscars, *Friendly Persuasion* was nommed without a name attached and lost.

One year later, Wilson and Carl Foreman were widely known to be the screenwriters of *The Bridge on the River Kwai*, but Columbia gave credit to Pierre Boulle, the author of the original French novel upon which the pic was based. Boulle, who didn't write in English, had admitted publicly that he didn't pen the movie, but this time the guild handled the hubbub simply by refusing to nominate *Kwai*. Several weeks later, when Boulle won the Oscar, he was not present to accept it. Anticipating his absence, the studio dispatched a stand-in, screen vixen Kim Novak, who said when she took the golden boy in hand, "This is the closest I'll ever come to one of these."

SCREEN ACTORS GUILD

SAG is the only guild with a televised awards ceremony, which is currently broadcast by TNT and previously by NBC (1994–1996). Its statuette is known simply as "The Actor" and has been bestowed since 1994. No star has won more than one trophy so far. Meryl Streep and Julianne Moore are tied for having the most noms (three).

The guild was founded in 1933 by a group of actors that included Boris Karloff.

It bestowed kudos for a short time in the 1930s, but on a monthly basis, and guild members quickly tired of them, so they were scrapped. Lifetime Achievement Awards have been given out since 1962. Today the annual competitive prizes have a distinct bias toward American actors (no foreigners at all were nommed in the kudos' first year), but occasional non-Yanks do sneak in and two have even won so far: Aussie Geoffrey Rush (*Shine*, 1996) and Italiano Roberto Begnini (*Life Is Beautiful*, 1998).

Film nominations are determined by a polling of 2,100 randomly selected SAG members who list five contenders in each category without regard to preference (just like writers' guild members; voters for the directors' guild honors and Oscars, however, rank their five choices by assigning point scores). The ballots are mailed out to the guild's 97,000 members close to the day in February when Oscar noms are announced, but the guild does not disclose how many ballots are returned. Winners are declared two weeks before the Oscars—or about 7 to 10 days before final Oscar ballots are due in.

In its brief six-year history, 10 of SAG's 12 Best Actor and Actress champs went on to win Oscars (83 percent). The two exceptions: SAG voters cited Jodie Foster for *Nell* in 1994 (Oscar picked Jessica Lange in *Blue Sky*) and Annette Bening for *American Beauty* in 1999 (Oscar chose Hilary Swank for *Boys Don't Cry*). The overlap is less impressive in the supporting categories and more difficult to tally, considering the 1997 SAG tie between Kim Basinger (*L.A. Confidential*) and Gloria Stuart (*Titanic*)—Basinger alone bagged the Oscar. But out of the 13 actors embraced by SAG in these races, 7 won Academy Awards (54 percent). The overall overlap for all races is 68 percent.

The SAG kudocast has more heart than any other because it showcases stars bonding closely with their peers. When Tom Hanks won Best Actor in 1994 for *Forrest Gump*, he pulled out his SAG card and recalled that he had earned the right to join the union by dressing in drag on the TV sitcom *Bosom Buddies*. Then he pointed to the guild's statuette, noted that it includes the masks of comedy and tragedy, and added,

"Both will make you lose sleep, question your motives, wonder why you are there, wonder why you are doing this in the first place. But if you are crazy enough . . . you can get one of these, a Screen Actors Guild card." The segment was such a hit that all ceremonies now include taped segments featuring stars talking about how they got their SAG cards.

PRODUCERS GUILD OF AMERICA

The Golden Laurel Awards are relatively new, but have correctly predicted the Oscar Best Picture champ nine times in 12 years. The three exceptions: PGA members chose *The Crying Game* in 1992 (Oscar picked *Unforgiven*). *Apollo 13* in 1995 (Oscar opted for *Braveheart*) and *Saving Private Ryan* in 1998 (*Shakespeare in Love* took the Academy Award).

The guild's top prize is called the Darryl F. Zanuck Producer of the Year award. Nominees are selected by a confidential committee of producers, and then a winner is chosen by the guild's 550 members, who are permitted to vote for a write-in candidate if they don't like the five pix cited by the PGA panel. The victor is announced about a week before the presentation ceremony, which is held at the Century Plaza Hotel in Los Angeles.

The PGA was founded in 1950 as the Screen Producers Guild, but then changed its name after merging with the Television Producers Guild in 1966. Although it's a guild, it is not recognized as an agent in collective bargaining with studios, but its guidelines and arbitration panels help to settle such hot industry issues as the current liberal use of producers' credits in film and TV.

NATIONAL SOCIETY OF FILM CRITICS

Society members include reviewers from print and online media, although TV and radio crix are permitted to join if they can survive the tough application procedure (none have recently). Some of the nation's big mags have made the cut, though (*Time, Entertainment Weekly, Vogue, Harper's Bazaar, New Yorker*), as well as big dailies (*N.Y. Times, L.A. Times, USA Today, Wall Street Journal*), big online players (MSNBC, Microsoft Slate) and smaller regional papers such as the *Village Voice, N.Y. Observer, Minneapolis City Pages, Chicago Reader* and *L.A. Weekly*.

"We have a tendency to want to be different," says prexy Peter Rainer of *New York Magazine* about their award choices. "It's a very unruly group. We don't run with the herd."

That's quite apparent from scanning a list of the group's past Best Pictures. Only rarely has the society embraced b.o. hits (*M*A*S*H, All the President's Men*), although it sometimes opts for mainstream works if they're macho (*Unforgiven, Pulp Fiction, GoodFellas, L.A. Confidential, Drugstore Cowboy, Blue Velvet, Breaking Away*) or— amazing many observers— funny (*Babe, Tootsie*). The fact that the group flashes an occasional sense of

---

10 of the national society's 34 best pics were foreign-lingo films.

---

humor shocks award watchers, since the society is renowned for favoring highbrow fare (*The Unbearable Lightness of Being, Nashville, Stranger Than Paradise, The Dead, Topsy-Turvy, Breaking the Waves, Blow-Up, Melvin and Howard*). Nearly a third of its Best Picture choices (10 out of 34) have even been foreign-lingo pix— three by Ingmar Bergman (*Persona, Shame, Scenes from a Marriage*). In 1990, the society created a separate category for foreign-language pix, but still permitted non-English fare to compete for the top award. In 1994, for example, Krzysztof Kieslowski's *Red* placed second in the voting for top pic behind *Pulp Fiction*, but it had to settle for the Best Foreign-Language Film award.

In its 34 years, the society has agreed with the Oscars on only three Best Pictures, but it can probably take credit for pushing one of them across the academy's finish

line—*Annie Hall*, an early spring release in 1977 that probably would've been forgotten by late December when other award groups seemed to be fawning over *Star Wars, Close Encounters of the Third Kind, The Turning Point* and *The Goodbye Girl*. Overall, the national crix have agreed with the Golden Globes (seven times) more often than the L.A. crix (six), but they're most in line with the Gothamites (eight).

No doubt the latter is true because the two groups have the biggest overlap of membership. Currently, 18 crix in the 31-member New York Film Critics Circle are also members of the 52-member national group (compared to 11 crix from the 53-member Los Angeles Film Critics Association). Still, Peter Rainer refers to the society as "a curmudgeonly alternative to the New York Film Critics Circle," primarily because the two Gotham-based orgs have always been at odds.

War was initially declared against the circle in 1966 by Hollis Alpert of *Saturday Review*, one of many magazine writers who had previously been denied membership in the newspaper-heavy org. Early that year, Alpert still held out hope of getting in if he could just land a job that had opened up at the *World-Journal-Telegram*. When he didn't get the post, though, he got sore enough to want to cause trouble. He decided to rough up the circle by calling together some of the other magazine malcontents to see if they wanted to form their own group. Quite a few heavyweights showed up at his apartment one night for the plotting session: Brendan Gill (*New Yorker*), Pauline Kael (*New Republic*), Joseph Morgenstern (*Newsweek*), Richard Schickel (*Life*), Andrew Sarris (*Village Voice*) and Sarris's future wife (and future critic) Molly Haskell, who was elected secretary. They decided to one-up the regional Gotham group by claiming national dominion even though their new society was composed exclusively of New York–based reviewers.

The Gothamites responded to the threat by suddenly admitting many of the society members who had previously been shut out. By 1973, 19 crix belonged to both the 22-member Gotham circle and the 23-member national society. Not surprisingly, the two groups agreed on six award categories that year, including Best Picture (*Day for Night*). There was lots of back-room discussion about merging the orgs for a while, but the society ultimately opted to remain independent. In the early 1970s, it started to reach out to critics in Chicago; Los Angeles; Boston; Washington, D.C.; and elsewhere in order to create a truly national membership base.

Today the group holds its business and voting meeting once a year in early January at New York's Algonquin Hotel (Brendan Gill's idea), where Dorothy Parker and other literary scalawags once sipped, quipped and savaged each other around the rim of the hotel's famed Round Table.

Only about half of the national members show up for the meeting, but the absentees are permitted to vote by proxy on the first ballot. After that, only attending members can participate. Sometimes that voting rule has affected the outcome radically. In 1998, for example, the first ballot tipped heavily toward *Saving Private Ryan* and *Shakespeare in Love*, but *Out of Sight* won when absent members were excluded on the second polling.

Balloting rules are virtually the same as those used by the Gotham circle. Voters list one candidate on the first round. If no film claims a majority, then voters rank their top three preferences, giving three points to their favorite, two points to their second choice, and so on. "It's open ballot so everyone knows who votes for whom," Rainer says, explaining that crix's names are revealed as their ballots are read off and tallied. (The Gothamites use a secret ballot.) Winners must not only score the most points, but must also be named on at least half of the ballots plus one.

Today the voting sessions last about three to four hours and are fairly civil, since little chatter is permitted. But that wasn't always so.

Andrew Sarris once wrote, "In those first years, we felt a genuine warming in our professional relationships, (but) it was only a matter of time before the lid would blow off." The org soon suffered from the same inner hostilities that tore at the seams of the Gotham circle. Things got so bad by the mid-1970s that member Judith Crist denounced the society as "a sour-grapes operation perpetrated by snobs." As late as 1988, *The Chicago Tribune* described the voting sessions as being "rowdy."

Things had calmed down by the 1990s, when a rule of relative quiet was enforced, but Janet Maslin and Stephen Holden still refused to join after the *N.Y. Times* lifted its ban against employees belonging to such orgs in 1997. They were hopping mad about how cliquishly the society was suddenly behaving, just as the circle used to. One of Maslin's and Holden's colleagues actually got turned down by the org after she followed the society's strict—and highly controversial—requirement forcing applicants to mail copies of past article clippings to every member. (The L.A. crix use the same admissions procedure, but it's less controversial because rejects tend to be freelancers, not full-time reviewers at major media.) Noted critic Jack Mathews of the *N.Y. Daily News* (formerly of *Newsday* and the *L.A. Times*) refuses to submit to the society's approval process, arguing that his professional credits speak for themselves. In 1999, a *Times* reviewer finally did join the group, but he was a new employee who happily agreed to do the copying-and-mailing duty—Elvis Mitchell, who was brought in from *The Fort Worth Star-Telegram* to replace Maslin when she retired.

Despite its occasional inner antics, the society has behaved quite heroically, too. When *Melvin and Howard* had a disastrous opening in five cities in 1980, Universal planned to pull it, re-edit it and retitle it before rolling out with a national release. The original version was saved, however, when the society named it Best Picture. The society has also taken on the Departments of State and Treasury on behalf of Soviet and Cuban filmmakers and has gotten involved in such hot-button issues as film ratings, colorization and preservation. The society is the nation's official critics' delegate to the National Film Registration Board of the Library of Congress.

In its first few years, the society held an awards gala, but doesn't anymore. Scrolls are mailed to the winners.

New York Film Critics Best Actress of 1944 Tallulah Bankhead (*Lifeboat*) wasn't nommed by Oscar voters.

NEW YORK FILM CRITICS CIRCLE

John Huston once called the New York Film Critics Circle "the conscience of the American film industry," but the group has also served as the industry's counterbalance—and even occasional inspiration, at least where the Oscars are concerned.

In the 65 years since the org was formed, it has agreed with Oscar voters only 27 times in the top category, but it can probably take credit for at least 13 Oscar Best Pictures: *The Lost Weekend, Gentleman's Agreement, All the King's Men, On the Waterfront, Marty, The Apartment, Tom Jones, A Man for All Seasons, In the Heat of the Night, The Deer Hunter, Ordinary People, Terms of Endearment* and *The Silence of the Lambs*. But most of that chumminess occurred during two spurts: 1944 to 1967 and 1977 to 1983. Outside of those periods, they've concurred only three times.

They agreed only once (*The Life of Emile Zola*, 1937) during the org's first nine years, in fact. The group set out to rebel against Hollywood tastes when it was formed hastily in 1935 soon after the New York Drama Critics Circle was created in October of that year. (The New York Film Critics didn't add "Circle" to its name officially until 1973, although the term was added and dropped occasionally during the early 1940s.) The first Best Picture that the group named—John Ford's gritty *The Informer*—was a deliberate mutiny against the Hollywood ballyhoo forming around Oscar's inevitable later choice—*Mutiny on the Bounty*. In subsequent years, the crix stuck to their artistic guns and backed *The Grapes of Wrath* over Oscar's Best Picture *Rebecca* in 1940 and then, one year later, showed their true fearlessness. They picked *Citizen Kane* even though it was in limited release (thanks to William Randolph Hearst's bully tactics) and even though one of the group's members, Rose Pelswick, worked at Hearst's *Journal-American* (no record of how she voted survives). Afterward, Howard Barnes of the *Herald-Tribune* said, "The mere fact that a dozen people have heckled me about our choice . . . makes me believe that we are exercising an important function."

Finally, in 1944, the crix sent Hollywood a peace overture in the form of a Best Picture plaque to a commercial pop hit (*Going My Way*) and immediately thereafter Oscar voters rubber-stamped 18 of the crix's 24 best pic selections. Their relationship after 1966 had less to do with their attitudes toward each other than with the Gothamites' attitude toward rival crix kudos groups that were then starting to form. The National Society of Film Critics came on the scene that year and decided to distinguish itself by picking highbrow, and often foreign-lingo, fare. Jealous Gothamites quickly started aping the society's tony tastes and, in the six-year span between 1969 and 1974, picked four offshore films as Best Picture: *Z, Cries and Whispers, Day for Night* and *Amarcord*.

Then the L.A. film crix organized in 1975 and refocused the Gothamites on Hollywood pix while seeming to challenge the East Coasters to a game of let's-see-who-can-push-the-most-ponies-through-to-the-Oscars. The Los Angelenos didn't play fair—they usually jumped ahead of the Gothamites to their announce their winners first—but the Gothamites won handily anyway, at least in the early years. In the eight years between 1977 and 1983, they launched seven Best Pictures that Oscar voters again rubber-stamped. In the subsequent 16 years, however, the Gothamites and Oscar voters split up again, agreeing only twice.

Hollywood nonetheless has such heartfelt respect and awe for the group that Sally Field actually said during her 1979 acceptance speech for *Norma Rae*: "The New York critics award is more important than anything except my children."

If only such lofty stars knew what went on behind the scenes in quirky Gotham.

When the crix org was formed in 1935, the *N.Y. Times* scoffed at the birth of "another 'kibitzer' prize committee" composed of "13 metropolitan cinema soothsayers" engaged in "star chamber proceedings." But the chamber's members were an impressive lot from the city's nine newspapers: *The American, Daily News, Herald Tribune, Journal, Mirror, Post, Times, Sun* and *World-Telegram*. No magazine writers were admitted (a policy that would backfire when the magazine scribes would later form a rival national society), but the group strained to prove how progressive it was by granting membership to a scribe from the Communist *Daily Worker* from 1936 to 1951. Early meetings were tense (*Times* writer Frank S. Nugent described "carbon monoxide in the air") and some members, like the crix from *The Sun*, quit in disgust, claiming the group lacked dignity.

> ## Gotham crix voting sessions have been full of screams, cheating and silliness.

Noted playwright and former *Post* and *Herald* staffer Robert Sherwood once called the Gothamites "the most intelligent and fairest group of critics in the world," but the notorious gadfly may have been joking. The best thing that its prexy, Bosley Crowther of the *N.Y. Times*, could say in 1940 about the typical voting conclave was that "never yet has there been the need for a riot call or a request for a doctor in the house." But in 1943, Crowther confessed, "Names have been called in brazen fashion, voices have been harshly raised and some rude reviewers have even offered to stand up for their candidates—outside. To put it bluntly, the voting sessions of the critics have sometimes been nigh unto brawls."

As early as the crix's second gathering in 1936, the *World-Telegram* reported "screams of dissenters" and "fierce laments" among voters. One year later, the *Post* noted that the voting "brought dissension, deadlock, attempts to trade votes, political maneuvers, cheating and charges of silliness." Part of the problem was due to the liberal imbibing of alcohol during the evening powwows, but that issue was eventually solved in the 1950s by skedding the meetings during morning hours. The rest of the problem, however, was due to the voting system in place: it sometimes took as many as two dozen ballots before a candidate could achieve the two-thirds majority needed to win. On more than one occasion, the crix ran out of scotch long before they got to go home, which only made the meetings testier.

Voting rules changed in 1941 so that winners were chosen on the sixth ballot by majority vote if no candidate received a two-thirds edge earlier. That system stayed in place through the infamous 1968 election, when *The Lion in Winter* was chosen Best Picture, creating an uproar described as being so "heated" and "acrimonious" that *Variety* reported that some crix even "had tears in their eyes." Knight-Ridder said that

Renata Adler of the *New York Times* "screamed her resignation from the group and announced, 'I'm going to call my shrink!'"

The next year the group adopted the same voting procedure used by the more civilized national society. Each critic now listed only one choice on the first ballot. If no pic or thesp received a majority, a second ballot ensued calling for crix to list their top three choices ranked best (three points) to third favorite (one point). The candidate with the most points won. In 1972, the latter rule was modified so that a candidate needed "at least 50 percent of the potential first-place points." Candidates were narrowed down to the top five vote-getters on the third ballot. If no winner emerged by the fourth ballot, then the two top vote-getters faced off in a final runoff polling. Unfortunately, this latter rule change was passed soon after Stacy Keach (*Fat City*) won Best Actor fairly and squarely at the 1972 meeting, then a revote was taken and he lost to Laurence Olivier (*Sleuth*). The rule was eventually modified so that the winner's name must appear on at least half of the ballots, not necessarily in first place.

The new voting procedures, daytime meetings and one more new dictum—minimal chatting and no debating—helped to quell overt hostilities to such an extent that Kathleen Carroll of the *Daily News* sighed after the 1974 conclave, "I, for one, am a little sad about the transformation of the group into a dull, respectable organization." But the changes didn't end in-fighting altogether. Olivier won Best Actor in 1972 only because he emerged as a compromise choice after the crix squared off into rival factions that couldn't resolve their battle over Marlon Brando (*The Godfather*) and Stacy Keach.

It's a nasty game called "Block the Other Camp," according to Georgia Brown of *The Village Voice*, and it resulted in the triumph of *My Left Foot* as Best Picture in 1989 after the crix couldn't decide between *Do the Right Thing* and *Enemies, A Love Story*. At least *My Left Foot* scored a few scattered points on the first ballot. *Quiz Show* reaped none during the first voting round in 1994,

but it won Best Picture after the two camps gave up their fights for *Forrest Gump* and *Pulp Fiction*. The game is also blamed for one of the more eyebrow-raising choices the circle's ever made: Cameron Diaz as Best Actress (*There's Something about Mary*) in 1998, when two camps couldn't decide between Fernanda Montenegro (*Central Station*) and Renee Zellweger (*One True Thing, A Price above Rubies*). The phenom is nothing new. In 1938, *Post* critic Archer Winsten wrote, "It often happens that you're voting more against someone you don't want than for someone you do." *Wuthering Heights* won Best Picture in 1939 on the 14th ballot after a deadlock could not be resolved between *Gone With the Wind* and *Mr. Smith Goes to Washington*.

The Gotham crix's award ceremonies are sometimes almost as lively as their voting sessions. The most explosive scene occurred at the 1989 fete when John Simon (*New York Magazine*) barked "Shut up, you fool!" to a rambling presenter and Richard Freeman (Newhouse newspapers) shouted back at Simon something Jimmy Stewart never said to Bob Hope at the Oscars: "Fuck off, you asshole!"

Sometimes the guests act up, too. When author William Styron presented an award at the 1982 ceremony, he was so upset about a recent review of the film version of his book *Sophie's Choice, Variety* reported, "Styron leveled a broadside at *New Yorker* critic Pauline Kael (not by name) as someone 'plainly better suited to another line of work' for her 'ludicrous ill will' in slamming the pic." When *Sophie's Choice* star Meryl Streep claimed her plaque as Best Actress, *Variety* said, "Streep reeled off a memorized list of the Gotham critics, intentionally mispronouncing *Sophie* debunker Andrew Sarris (*Village Voice*) as *Tsouris* (yiddish idiom for 'aggravation'), then vouching that 'it's great to get your own back sometimes.'"

But often the stars just seem to enjoy the chance to get down and dirty with the scrappy crix. When Paul Newman presented Joanne Woodward with a Best Actress plaque for *Mr. and Mrs. Bridge* in 1990, he confessed, "This is first time I paid homage to my wife on my feet with my clothes on." Shirley MacLaine said "I was scared shit-less to come here" in 1983, but she called her Best Actress victory for *Terms of Endearment* "fan-fucking-tastic."

The earliest galas were held at the Rainbow Room, then they were switched to Sardi's restaurant in the theater district till 1989. That's when they became so popular again—for the aforementioned entertainment reasons plus the fact that they're genuinely fun—that they had to be moved back to the Rainbow Room, albeit the Pegasus Suite this time.

Robert Sherwood attended the early soirées and became the first person to speak up about their obvious irony. He once told the crowd that this was the first time that "any group of critics has ever invited its victims to a cocktail party."

But they came gladly anyway and the earliest parties set the precedent for how much fun—and how glamorous—the event could be. During the late 1930s, the "fog-choked" Rainbow Room sparkled with such glitterati as Vivien Leigh, Laurence Olivier, Bette Davis, Kitty Carlyle, William Wyler, Ernst Lubitsch and Fritz Lang. Mary Pickford looked "slim and pretty in black and mink," said the *Post*, and Ethel Merman "stunning in silver fox." Gloria Swanson was spotted wearing "the cutest hat, making her appear like a Tibetan sorceress."

Entertainment included such amusing sights as an on-the-wagon John Barrymore slugging back ginger ales. But it also included a formal segment that was the highlight of every gala. For 30 minutes, the party was hooked up to a national audience via radio while distant voices were piped in from exotic places: Paul Muni from Budapest, Jean Renoir from Paris, Alfred Hitchcock and Robert Donat from London. Other A-list stars such as Orson Welles, Joan Fontaine, Henry Fonda and Ingrid Bergman would join the party from Hollywood and perform scenes from their award-winning movies.

But as classy as these affairs could be, sometimes things went haywire, too—as in 1939, when the Rainbow Room's circular

dance floor suddenly started spinning out of control. The *Herald-Tribune* reported that it "whirled around so briskly that numerous distinguished guests had to hang on to the bar for support," including Walter Huston, Shirley Booth and Joan Crawford.

The circle comprises 31 print crix. Unlike the L.A. crix org, it does not admit TV or radio reviewers. Circle members now gather at the Algonquin Hotel to vote (two to three weeks before their peers in the national society meet in the same locale). Prior to the 1990s, they huddled in a conference room at the *N.Y. Times* or newspaper guild.

LOS ANGELES FILM CRITICS ASSOCIATION

The laid-back Californians didn't get around to launching a crix org in America's movie capital until 1975, but the group has set off its share of earthquakes since.

Being far more hip to pop culture than its rivals, the association fearlessly picked *Star Wars* and *E.T. the Extra-Terrestrial* as the Best Pictures of 1977 and 1982 when the Gotham crix and Oscar voters went with *Annie Hall* and *Gandhi*.

"You discovered this film," Clint Eastwood told the crix in grateful acknowledgment in 1992 as he accepted one of the record-tying five awards they heaped upon his *Unforgiven* before it trotted off toward the Oscars. The group probably also launched *Kramer vs. Kramer* and *Amadeus* in that same direction.

It definitely did so for another pic in the org's second year when it first set off shock waves by unveiling a Best Picture that nobody had heard of—*Rocky*—and one that clearly came wrapped in a message. The message was the L.A. crix's favorite mantra to their peers in New York: popcorn pix can sometimes be yummy alternatives to the usual dry fare that wins awards. In 1976, the Gotham circle was still preoccupied with trying to pick snootier, more gourmet fare than the 10-year-old national society, but both latter groups certainly felt the punch when *Rocky* subsequently slugged its way through the Oscar match. Before that, *Rocky* had certainly looked like a lightweight awards contender, being a B-movie that was produced—for only $960,000—to be the late show at America's drive-in theaters.

Jessica Lange (*Blue Sky*), Sally Field (*Norma Rae*) and Mercedes Ruehl (*The Fisher King*) probably owe their Oscars to the L.A. crix, too, but the association has done lots more than just serve as a scouting agent for academy voters. It's frequently backed noncommercial pics that needed a deserved lift: *Atlantic City, Secrets and Lies, The Insider, Do the Right Thing, Little Dorrit* and *Hope and Glory*. Only some of those pix made it into the Oscar race later, but they all at least benefited from gaining wider theatrical release at the time and will be studied tomorrow by future film historians because they made the list.

The crix even once gave their Best Picture award to a film that wasn't skedded for release—*Brazil* (1985)—thereby forcing Universal execs to take it off the shelf and end their feud with director Terry Gilliam.

The 53-member group comprises newspaper, magazine, TV and online reviewers, including such notables as Leonard Maltin of *Entertainment Tonight*, Kenneth Turan and Kevin Thomas of the *L.A. Times*, Todd McCarthy and Emanuel Levy of *Variety* and Joe Morgenstern of *The Wall Street Journal*. It was founded in 1975 by now-retired *L.A. Times* critic Charles Champlin and *Free Press* scribe Ruth Batchelor.

It uses a simple voting system that doesn't seem to encourage the formation of the kind of factionalism that sometimes plagues the Gotham circle and national society voting sessions. Henry Sheehan of the *Orange County Register* explains the L.A. procedure thus: "We go around the room and everybody states their top three choices while someone keeps score. We take the top two vote-getters and decide the winner by a show of hands." That polling method has one drawback: Many members confess that if they're called upon late in the

Winners love to poke fun at the L.A. crix's cash bar.

polling process, they often switch their votes when it comes time for them to speak up and they notice that their original favorites aren't doing well. (Those same members say that they would prefer to use a secret ballot for the initial polling.) The voting conclaves are held at the home of one of the members.

The conclaves were tense and sometimes stormy in the early years, but they calmed down once discussion was no longer permitted. "The group has not been acrimonious," insists Kevin Thomas of the *L.A. Times*, who was one of the original members. "I've never seen any instance of arm twisting."

But the group's been rocked by criticism that it's too lax about membership rules, permitting occasional freelancers to join and then allowing them and retired crix to hang on. Onetime member Jack Mathews once fumed in the *L.A. Times* that "membership requirements are only slightly tighter than those for the Hertz No. 1 Club." Seven journos, however, were turned down among the nine who applied in June 2000 (applicants must send at least four article clippings to each current member and then submit to a group vote, just as in the national society). Kevin Thomas says, "I know I'll get in trouble for saying this, but things have gotten so loose through the years that I think we need to return to our original standards."

A past officer of the org will only speak anonymously about the reason for the lax rules: he says that tighter guidelines might force the ouster of the association's retired and beloved co-founder Chuck Champlin, who still keeps up on current movies, but writes only occasionally. "Nobody wants to see him defrocked by the group he founded, so they look the other way for now," he adds.

The crix's awards bash was televised as part of *The Merv Griffin Show* from 1978 to 1980, then was aired one year in national syndication, but the crix ultimately decided to keep their affair private. The event's relaxed atmosphere now allows for more informal give and take—and ribbing, usually from the stars. When *Bugsy*'s Warren Beatty accepted the Best Picture plaque in 1991, he confessed how strange he thought it was to be at a party for "those who make movies and those who complain about them."

The topic that seems to elicit the most grousing at the fetes is how liquid refreshments are served. When Russell Crowe arrived from Australia to receive his Best Actor prize for *The Insider* in 1999, he bellowed at the crix, "It's bloody lovely to come flying all the way over here to a function with a cash bar!" One year earlier, Best Supporting Actor Bill Murray (*Rushmore*) launched into a hilarious snit about the same issue and left a hundred-dollar bill on the podium, telling the crix to use it toward having an open bar the next year.

Stars love to act up—and open up—when huddling with the crix at the Bel Age Hotel ceremony. *Variety* observed in 1996, "Edward Norton regaled the crowd with near-perfect impersonations of directors Woody Allen and Milos Forman." When John Travolta accepted a Best Actor plaque for his career-comeback role in *Pulp Fiction* in 1994, he confessed to the crowd that he got so excited when he heard he won that he couldn't sleep for three days.

Helena Bonham Carter made a tender-hearted confession, too, after being voted Best Actress for *The Wings of the Dove* in 1997. She couldn't make the fete, but she sent a message that made the crix howl and whoop. Her note said, "Those I live in dread of, I now love."

BROADCAST FILM CRITICS ASSOCIATION

The Broadcast Film Critics Association is the biggest crix org in America (its 140 members dwarf the gang of 52 who belong to the National Society of Film Critics). Its ranks include *Good Morning America*'s Joel Siegel, *Rolling Stone*'s Peter Travers, ABC Radio's Bill Diehl, L.A. TV gadfly

Sam Rubin (KTLA) and New York's Dennis Cunningham (WCBS) and Jeffrey Lyons (WNBC). But there are also lots of lesser-knowns, of course, including reps from Uncle Ed's Entertainment Forum and If.com.

They all have one thing in common: they broadcast reviews via TV, radio or the Internet. The vast majority (60 percent) are local or national TV reviewers who are on the air "regularly," according to membership rules. Radio reviewers are permitted to join if they are based in New York or Los Angeles or else can be heard in 10 or more markets nationwide. "We decide who gets in from the Internet companies on a case-by-case basis," says org prexy and co-founder Joey Berlin of Celebrity Interviews.

"We're much more of a consensus, mainstream group," Berlin adds. "Our members aren't writing long think pieces. We're the what's-opening-this-Friday critics. We like to think of ourselves as those guys in the trenches, on the junkets, talking to directors and stars."

Their prize is officially called the Critics' Choice Award and is fairly new, being first bestowed in 1995. Winners are unveiled in two parts. All of them but one are announced around the third week of December, just when other crix orgs are sounding off. The big Best Picture champ, though, isn't revealed until the kudofest that's held at the Hotel Sofitel in Los Angeles in January. The bash usually takes place one day after the Golden Globes, since most of the group's nationally strewn membership happens to be in town then to cover the bigger, 24-karat event.

Winners are chosen using a one-round voting process. Members rank their five favorite films by granting five points to their top choice, four to their second, and so on. In all other categories, they rank only three choices in similar descending point-score order.

Of their five Best Picture pronouncements so far, most have reflected choices made by other crix orgs: *Fargo*, *L.A. Confidential* and *Saving Private Ryan*. In 1995, they agreed with the Globes and the National Board of Review on *Sense and Sensibility*. Only once, though, have they backed up Oscar voters: *American Beauty* (1999).

The Critics' Choice Awards are so new that they can't yet boast of having much impact on the year's overall film derby, but it's possible that they played a key role in Angelina Jolie's awards march in 1999. Prior to her nabbing a Globe, SAG honor and Oscar for *Girl, Interrupted*, Jolie was first heralded by the broadcast crix after being ignored by all other media kudos.

NATIONAL BOARD OF REVIEW

The National Board of Review is the New Hampshire primary of awards season—its small bloc of scrappy voters are heard first, usually around mid-December, and their voices echo far across the Globes and throughout Oscarland. The board began naming the year's best movies in New York soon after those Oscar voters did the same thing out west. Now the two oldest film contests start and end the yearly awards derby.

> The National Board of Review began as a censorship group.

The board is often confused with a critics' org, but it's really an old-fashioned, salon-styled, film appreciation society comprising diehard movie buffs, although not necessarily film professionals. Its core group of 13 members—those who sit on the Exceptional Photoplay Committee—include film teachers, book editors, a reviewer for Spanish-language newspapers and a First Amendment rights lawyer. "Everyone is involved in film or the arts in some way," insists executive director Lois Ballon, "and what we all share in common is a passionate love of movies."

Each member of the committee gets a full vote, then fractional votes are added in from screening committees comprising 90 additional judges, who pay $350 per year for membership. Studios often give members private viewings and let them linger when the lights go up so they can discuss the movies in depth. Sometimes the films' directors, stars or writers drop by to answer questions.

The board does not issue nominees. It produces its list of the year's best films, ranked from number 1 to 10. Winners are announced in December (sometimes too early; the board missed the opening of *Gone With the Wind* in 1939) and they're honored two months later at a dinner held at New York's Tavern on the Green, which glows amidst the snows of Central Park every February thanks to the considerable starlight emanating from the celeb-packed Crystal Room.

The board's influence has been considerable through the years. In 1934, it probably nudged the Oscars to notice *It Happened One Night*, which came close to being dismissed as a quickly lensed screwball comedy. When the New York Film Critics came on the scene one year later, the Gotham crix picked *The Informer* as Best Picture two weeks after the board did, but took full credit for championing a gritty small pic that didn't look like Oscar material. *Marty* snagged attention at Cannes earlier in 1955, but the board was the first to hail it stateside. The board was also the first to cite *Tom Jones* in 1963, but there's evidence to suggest that the Gotham crix probably would have done so a week later anyway.

Three of the board's Best Pictures—*Patton* (1970), *The Sting* (1973) and *Chariots of Fire* (1981)—were subsequently snubbed by the crix orgs and the Golden Globes, then resurfaced later at the tail end of the derby, at either the DGA kudos or the Oscars. Several others—including *Dances with Wolves* (1990), *Driving Miss Daisy* (1989) and *American Beauty* (1999)—were bypassed by the crix after they were endorsed by the board, only to resurface at the Golden Globes. The board clearly put *Gods and Monsters* on the derby track in 1998 and can take credit for trumpeting

Joan Crawford's comeback in 1945. When the board named its winners that year, *Variety* reported on the "the eye-opening selection of Joan Crawford as Best Actress" in *Mildred Pierce*. The feisty Crawford quickly hired a PR agent to handle her tub-thumping and she was off to snatch her overdue Oscar.

Several of the board's Best Picture choices have not worn well, including the "prematurely anti-Fascist" melodrama *Confessions of a Nazi Spy* (1939), West German/Lutheran Church propaganda pic *Question 7* (1961) and the poorly reviewed *Far from the Madding Crowd* (1967). When the board backed *The Shoes of the Fisherman* in 1968, its chairman issued a half-hearted explanation that sounded more like an apology. But the board's also made some courageous choices that never claimed another Best Picture prize, and perhaps unfairly so: *They Shoot Horses, Don't They?* (1969), *The Conversation* (1974), *Days of Heaven* (1978), *Manhattan* (1979), *The Color Purple* (1985), *Howards End* (1992) and *Shine* (1996). The board's kudos were known as the D.W. Griffith Awards until several years ago, when they were renamed the NBR Awards.

The board's beginnings date back to Christmas Eve 1908, when New York Mayor George B. McClennan shuttered 500 penny arcades and nickelodeons because "movies tend to injure the morals of the community." Films of the day were tame by modern standards, but their suggestive titles are evidence of how hard they tried to titillate film viewers: *The Bigamist, Old Man's Darling* and *Beware, My Husband Comes.*

Terrified that New York officials would censor films as the Chicago police had started doing one year earlier, the local People's Institute tapped 10 civic groups to form an org that would do the censoring itself—the National Board of Motion Picture Censorship. In 1916, the group got PR savvy and switched its name to the National Board of Review of Motion Pictures in an effort to emphasize its role as heralding movies' merits.

The board's Review Committee comprised 200 to 300 nonpaid reviewers who had no connection to the movie biz. The panel recommended its favorite choices to a smaller Exceptional Photoplays Committee, which issued the board's annual list of 10 best films. The board's overall motto was "Select the Best—Neglect the Rest" in order to emphasize that it was not really a censorship org. Its members screened hundreds of movies each year and endorsed most of them with viewing-age recommendations: "M" for mature audiences (18 years old and older), "F" for families (12 and up) and "J" for juvenile (under 12). Its legend—"Passed by the National Board of Review"—can still be seen in the opening credits of such classics as *Wuthering Heights* (1939).

In 1936, *The New York Times* noted that government officials in Providence, Rhode Island, and Boston relied on the board's recommendations when approving films that could be viewed locally. But most communities really only used the board's lists to weigh edgy independent films and imports shown by urban art houses. All Hollywood studio movies had to carry the seal of the Motion Picture Producers and Distributors of America (later renamed the Motion Picture Association of America), created in 1922 by former U.S. Postmaster General Will H. Hays, who forbade a screen kiss to last longer than a second and a half. By 1952, only two states—Florida and Rhode Island—and a few dozen municipalities nationwide had ordinances requiring the board's seal before a pic could be shown.

The board sustained itself by charging studios a fee to review their pix: $6.50 per reel (or 1,000 feet of celluloid), totaling $2,000 to $3,000 per studio per annum. The board also received income from publishing its *Weekly Guide to Selected Pictures, The Weekly Official Bulletin* and its monthly magazine, *Films in Review*, the latter of which still exists online today. Hollywood continued to back the board until 1951, when three studios cut their reviewing fees. MGM was next, yanking its funds in 1956, and the remainders (United Artists and Twentieth Century-Fox) quit a few years later. *Variety* reported, "There was a feeling that the NBR was duplicating the self-censoring activities of the Motion Picture Association of America."

While the group may have subsisted on Hollywood coin, it occasionally stressed its independence by flouting the big studios' clout. In 1941, the board did what the Oscars didn't have the guts to: it named *Citizen Kane* Best Picture even though the man the movie skewered, William Randolph Hearst, was in league with Louis B. Mayer, whose studio paid $2,500 to the National Board of Review that year.

INDEPENDENT SPIRITS

The purpose of the Independent Spirit award is to salute what past ceremony host Samuel L. Jackson once called "the strange, the weird, the eclectic, the visionary, the new blood."

Winners are chosen by the 8,000 members of the nationwide Independent Film Project after nominees are picked by an 11-member screening committee. Trophies are bestowed two days before the Oscars at a daytime bohemian bash held in a tent on the Santa Monica beach, where guests sip cosmopolitans, chow down goat-cheese eggplant baguettes and strut in ways that let them show off their tattoos to maximum effect while not having to shed too much leather. *Variety* once reported: "Many celebrities mused that they could think of no other Hollywood awards show where the guests had to wait in line for Porta-Potties while facing hordes of autograph-seeking fans."

It was also the setting for what has to be the most outrageous acceptance speech of all time, which was given by *Chasing Amy* writer-director Kevin Smith: "This makes up for every chick who ever told me I had a small dick."

The Spirits revealed a lot about themselves with their first Best Feature choice in 1985—Martin Scorsese's *After Hours,* described by *Variety* as "a nightmarish black comedy (in which) the cinema of paranoia and persecution reaches an apogee."

The award went mainstream the following year and opted for *Platoon,* then got giddy over *sex, lies and videotape* and gave old Hollywood a nasty slap with *The Player.* As expected, its edgy voters jumped on the *Pulp Fiction* bandwagon in 1994. After that point, all of its Best Feature prizes went to films that would be key players at the Oscars: *Leaving Las Vegas, Fargo, The Apostle, Gods and Monsters* and *Election.* Prior to that, most were not: *Short Cuts, Rambling Rose, Stand and Deliver* and *River's Edge.*

The Spirit was created as an offshoot of the original FINDIE ("Friends of Independents") award, which was first bestowed in 1984 by IFP and other groups. IFP took over the kudos in 1985 and staged them in a trendy restaurant. The new Spirits agreed with the Oscars on Best Actress of that year—Geraldine Page (*The Trip to Bountiful*)—but the two kudos went their separate ways for nearly a decade afterward. Then, in 1994, they both honored Quentin Tarantino's screenplay for *Pulp Fiction*, and it soon became common to see *Sling Blade* in both contests, even if slightly askew. The Spirits, for example, named *Sling Blade* Best First Feature of 1996, but didn't nominate Billy Bob Thorton for Best Actor (he made the Oscar competish) or screenplay (he won the golden boy).

The Spirit Award's recent lurch toward glam, high-profile indies put it at odds with its original goal—to be *anti*-Oscar—but the trend reflected what was happening in the movie biz. Not only were there more indie production companies than ever, but most big studios, through acquisition or development, sprouted indie offshoots and/or made partial investments in promising outside projects. "The sources for financing for independent films have changed so dramatically," confessed IFP/West topper Dawn Hudson in 1994. "It became really arbi-

> The Indie Spirit's aim is to "choke the establishment to death."

trary." The group's biggest challenge today is to define what the ever-changing indie is. Panels have to determine which films are eligible for awards based on a case-by-case study after weighing four criteria: uniqueness of vision; original, provocative subject matter; economy of means; and percentage of financing from independent sources.

Early on, IFP leaders were sensitive to giving edgy rookies a special boost by creating a separate category for Best First Feature in 1986. Lots of frontier films took the prize thereafter, including *Straight out of Brooklyn, El Mariachi, She's Gotta Have It, Spanking the Monkey* and *The Opposite of Sex*. But one sticky problem occurred that still plagues the kudos: seldom did the rookies get nommed for Best Director, which indicated that they weren't being taken as seriously as the Best Feature rivals in the over-all race. A few did win the main screenplay prize—including *The Waterdance* and *The Opposite of Sex*—but the Spirits still introduced a separate race for debut scripts in 1994 just to make sure they received their due. By 1999, the indie market had boomed so big that the Best First Feature category had to be split by dollar amount, separating films with budgets above $500,000 (winner was *Being John Malkovich*) and below (*The Blair Witch Project*).

Summing up the awards can best be done by counting up who's won the most. Among individuals, it's *Fargo's* Joel Coen with one award for writing (*Fargo*) and two for directing (*Blood Simple, Fargo*). Among pix, the two champs are *Fargo* and *Stand and Deliver* with six wins each. Together both pix are apt reflections of the prize's apparent goal to champion stories about little people coping with a big, often ugly world.

Voters proved that they like their Best Actors badder and meaner than the typical anti-hero when they opted for Sean Penn (*Dead Man Walking*) in 1995 over Nicolas Cage (*Leaving Las Vegas*). They also showed that they don't mind shameless tubthumpers when they picked Sally Kirkland (*Anna*) as top lead actress of 1987 over such reigning showbiz ladies as Lillian Gish (*The Whales of August*) and Joanne Woodward (*The Glass Menagerie*).

The bottom line: this is the only kufofest where Hollywood's inner brats at last get the big hug they have been crying for all over their 16-millimeter film.

The Spirit statuette was described best by scribe Buck Henry, who emceed many past fetes. He once noted that it features the abstract of a taloned bird clutching a thread of film. The bird, he said, is "circumventing the establishment, then choking it to death."

SUNDANCE FILM FESTIVAL

The Sundance Film Festival, lasting for 10 days in late January, is a great chance for Hollywood honchos to take a ski vacation and make the boss pay for it. They arrive in a snow-blanketed resort town called Park City, Utah (population 7,000), also to discover the latest gems amidst the indie pix unspooling between the craggy mountains where George Hearst, William Randolph's father, once made his fortune striking silver. Curiously, the film based on William's life, *Citizen Kane*, is considered the granddady of all indie pix.

And there are plenty of new treasures to find in the remote locale. Sundance is now the official Cinderella capital of showbiz, Schwab's drugstore moved a few hundred miles east into the Utah mountains. It's where a young New Jersey convenience store worker, Kevin Smith, showed off his $27,575 pic (*Clerks*), which he had financed on 10 credit cards, and snagged not only the Filmmaker's Trophy but a distribution deal with Miramax. It's where Victor Nunez, a two-time Grand Jury Prize winner (*Gal Young 'Un, Ruby in Paradise*) first gained notice, then moved on and up to create the pic that championed Peter Fonda's comeback, *Ulee's Gold*. Another Grand Jury Prize champ, Bryan Singer (*Public Access*) was discovered at Sundance and then went on to direct Oscar champ Kevin Spacey in *The Usual Suspects*.

Sundance is a place where both sides can strike it rich. Miramax picked up the distrib rights to *Shine* for $2.5 million at the fest when it was shown out of competition (it would gross $20 million domestically by Oscar time). Artisan Entertainment bagged the biggest bargain of all, though, buying *The Blair Witch Project*—initially shot for $35,000 before post-production costs—for $1.1 million, then watched it magically gross $140 million by year's end.

But it's also the scene of two notorious Big Deal fiascoes, both of which occurred when bidding wars got out of hand during the pitch of fest fever. Miramax paid $10 million for *Happy, Texas* and Castle Rock paid the kingly sum of $10 million for *The Spitfire Grill*—both of which turned out to be b.o. bombs.

"There's been a lot of talk about this festival becoming a meat market," fest topper Robert Redford once said, "but I'm fine with it being a market because it benefits the filmmakers."

Redford was the first chairman of the event when it started out as the Utah–U.S.A. Film Festival in Salt Lake City in September 1978, but he really had little to do with it. He took the job only because his wife, Lola, was a cousin of one of the fest founders, Sterling Van Wagenen. The event's goal was to promote Utah tourism and to draw filmmakers to the Beehive State.

Redford stepped back from his ceremonial lead role after the first year, but remained on the board, which also included Redford's business partner, producer-director Sydney Pollack, who ended up making his own pivotal contribution to the fest's eventual success when he told its cofounder Lory Smith in 1980: "You ought to move the festival to Park City and set it in the wintertime. You'd be the only film festival in the world held in a ski resort during ski season and Hollywood would beat down the door to attend."

Fest leaders knew a good idea when they heard it, so they transplanted the event to the then-idyllic little mountain village and made another savvy move, too: they dropped the "Utah" from the event's name

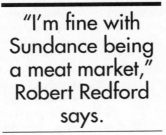

"I'm fine with Sundance being a meat market," Robert Redford says.

and simply called it—quite boldly—the U.S. Film Festival. The fest continued to grow steadily and even helped to hatch deals for a few of its scruffy young honorees. David Burton Morris reaped a distrib deal with Triumph Films right after his *Purple Haze* shocked fest-goers by winning the Grand Jury Prize over cult hit *Eating Raoul* in 1982.

Meantime, though, the fest was racking up debts it couldn't pay, so its leaders trekked a few mountains over, to Provo Canyon where Robert Redford lived and was setting up the Sundance Institute with Pollack in an effort to bring indie pros and neophytes together at a remote retreat where they could explore new ideas. Redford heard the fest leaders' pleas and agreed to have the institute assume control of the event.

When the merger was announced in 1984, *Variety* said, "It's a natural for Sundance to take over the festival's management. Both the festival and institute are supportive of the independent filmmaker." Immediately after Redford took the helm, a winner of the Grand Jury Prize, *Blood Simple*, became such a fest hit that Hollywood execs started taking serious notice and began trickling into town. In 1989, the U.S. Film Festival added "Sundance" to its name to become the Sundance U.S. Film Festival, then dropped the "U.S." one year later to assume its current moniker.

But Sundance didn't become the buzz-bursting, locust-besieged phenom it is today until after an event that occurred at the 1988 fest. That's when 26-year-old Steven Soderbergh, a former volunteer driver for the event, returned to town with his own amateur masterpiece in hand.

sex, lies and videotape rocked the Rocky Mountains enclave, won the Audience Award and got snatched up by Miramax, which took it to Cannes where it became the first debut film in more than 25 years to receive the Palme d'Or. When two other pix also emerged from Sundance in 1988 as pop hits as well—*Heathers* and *True Love*—there was no holding back the onslaught of Hollywood honchos who arrived the next year with blank contracts in hand and skis flung over their backs.

Many pix have been discovered at Sundance since—*Hoop Dreams, Gods and Monsters, Unzipped, Slacker, House Party* and *Reservoir Dogs*—but those examples are all indicative of an odd Sundance phenom. None of them won Grand Jury Prizes. Granted, the high jury award has hailed many esteemed pix in the past—*Welcome to the Dollhouse, Paris Is Burning, A Brief History of Time, Crumb, Slam, The Brothers McMullen*—but most of those films had distrib deals before they hit Park City, and only a few jury champs have experienced the Cinderella legend of the fest. Instead, many of the fairy-tale lucky ones were winners of an Audience Award (*sex, Unzipped, El Mariachi, Hoops*), the Filmmaker's Trophy (*House Party, In the Company of Men, Tumbleweeds*) or special laurels (*Straight out of Brooklyn; Happy, Texas; To Sleep with Anger; I Shot Andy Warhol*). *Heathers, Slacker, Reservoir Dogs* and *The Blair Witch Project* won nothing at all. *Gods and Monsters* didn't even make the cut for competition and had to be shown at the fest's sidebar screenings—where, luckily, it was discovered by an impressed distributor from Lions Gate.

Some pundits say that the phenom occurs because the five-member juries want to draw attention to worthy pix that might not be reaping the most buzz at the late-night, rented-condo after-parties. In short, the jury champs tend not to be the ones that Miramax topper Harvey Weinstein is screaming to get the distrib rights to during an after-midnight bidding war at the Barking Dog restaurant. If nothing else, the caliber of the grand jury winners has been steadily respectable, and many of them did go on to claim other high kudos later. One of the four pix tied as Sundance's biggest champ, *American Dream* (three awards), reaped accolades afterward from the National Society of Film Critics and the L.A. group. *Crumb* swept all four crix orgs after claiming the Grand Jury Prize for documentaries. Two more jury victors (*Paris Is Burning; The Farm: Angola, USA*) were later honored by two crix orgs each.

Sundance awardees in other categories have gone on to snag Oscars, including Special Jury Prize docu winners *The Times of Harvey Milk* and *When We Were Kings*. The winner of the 1998 Filmmaker's Award for features, *Tumbleweeds,* nabbed a Golden Globe for star Janet McTeer one year later and was nommed in Oscar's Best Actress race, too. Audience Award champ *Hoop Dreams* pulled off a slam dunk when it breezed the crix trifecta.

Variety's Todd McCarthy recently described the fest's stature: "Sundance ranks somewhere in the top five in importance worldwide."

Fest admission fees span $650 (Day-timer's Pass) to $4,000 (Eccles Pass).

Best Pictures

Awards are listed chronologically each year according to when winners were announced, not when the the statuettes were presented.

1927–1928
Academy Awards: *Wings* (Best Picture), *Sunrise* (Best Unique or Artistic Picture)

1928–1929
Academy Awards: *Broadway Melody*

1929–1930
Academy Awards: *All Quiet on the Western Front*

1930–1931
Academy Awards: *Cimarron*

1931–1932
National Board of Review: *I Am a Fugitive from a Chain Gang*
Academy Awards: *Grand Hotel*

1932–1933
National Board of Review: *Topaze*
Academy Awards: *Cavalcade*

1934
National Board of Review: *It Happened One Night*
Academy Awards: *It Happened One Night*

1935
National Board of Review: *The Informer*
New York Film Critics: *The Informer*
Academy Awards: *Mutiny on the Bounty*

1936
National Board of Review: *Mr. Deeds Goes to Town*
New York Film Critics: *Mr. Deeds Goes to Town*
Academy Awards: *The Great Ziegfeld*

1937
National Board of Review: *Night Must Fall*
New York Film Critics: *The Life of Emile Zola*
Academy Awards: *The Life of Emile Zola*

1938
National Board of Review: *The Citadel*
New York Film Critics: *The Citadel*
Academy Awards: *You Can't Take It with You*

1939
National Board of Review: *Confessions of a Nazi Spy*
New York Film Critics: *Wuthering Heights*
Academy Awards: *Gone With the Wind*

1940
National Board of Review: *The Grapes of Wrath*
New York Film Critics: *The Grapes of Wrath*
Academy Awards: *Rebecca*

1941
National Board of Review: *Citizen Kane*
New York Film Critics: *Citizen Kane*
Academy Awards: *How Green Was My Valley*

1942
National Board of Review: *In Which We Serve*
New York Film Critics: *In Which We Serve*
Academy Awards: *Mrs. Miniver*

1943
National Board of Review: *The Ox-Bow Incident*
New York Film Critics: *Watch on the Rhine*
Golden Globes: *The Song of Bernadette*
Academy Awards: *Casablanca*

1944

National Board of Review: *None But the Lonely Heart*
New York Film Critics: *Going My Way*
Golden Globes: *Going My Way*
Academy Awards: *Going My Way*

1945

National Board of Review: *The True Glory*
New York Film Critics: *The Lost Weekend*
Golden Globes: *The Lost Weekend*
Academy Awards: *The Lost Weekend*

1946

National Board of Review: *Henry V*
New York Film Critics: *The Best Years of Our Lives*
Golden Globes: *The Best Years of Our Lives*
Academy Awards: *The Best Years of Our Lives*

1947

National Board of Review: *Monsieur Verdoux*
New York Film Critics: *Gentleman's Agreement*
Golden Globes: *Gentleman's Agreement*
Academy Awards: *Gentleman's Agreement*

1948

National Board of Review: *Paisan*
New York Film Critics: *The Treasure of the Sierra Madre*
Golden Globes: (Tie) *Johnny Belinda, The Treasure of the Sierra Madre*
Academy Awards: *Hamlet*

1949

National Board of Review: *The Bicycle Thief*
New York Film Critics: *All the King's Men*
Golden Globes: *All the King's Men*
Academy Awards: *All the King's Men*

1950

National Board of Review: *Sunset Boulevard*
New York Film Critics: *All about Eve*
Golden Globes: *Sunset Boulevard*
Academy Awards: *All about Eve*

1951

National Board of Review: *A Place in the Sun*
New York Film Critics: *A Streetcar Named Desire*
Golden Globes: *A Place in the Sun* (drama), *An American in Paris* (comedy/musical)
Academy Awards: *An American in Paris*

1952

National Board of Review: *The Quiet Man*
New York Film Critics: *High Noon*
Golden Globes: *The Greatest Show on Earth* (drama), *With a Song in My Heart* (comedy/musical)
Academy Awards: *The Greatest Show on Earth*

1953

National Board of Review: *Julius Caesar*
New York Film Critics: *From Here to Eternity*
Golden Globes: *The Robe*
Academy Awards: *From Here to Eternity*

1954

National Board of Review: *On the Waterfront*
New York Film Critics: *On the Waterfront*
Golden Globes: *On the Waterfront* (drama), *Carmen Jones* (comedy/musical)
Academy Awards: *On the Waterfront*

1955

National Board of Review: *Marty*
New York Film Critics: *Marty*
Golden Globes: *East of Eden* (drama), *Guys and Dolls* (comedy/musical)
Academy Awards: *Marty*

1956

National Board of Review: *Around the World in 80 Days*
New York Film Critics: *Around the World in 80 Days*
Golden Globes: *Around the World in 80 Days* (drama), *The King and I* (comedy/musical)
Academy Awards: *Around the World in 80 Days*

1957
National Board of Review: *The Bridge on the River Kwai*
New York Film Critics: *The Bridge on the River Kwai*
Golden Globes: *The Bridge on the River Kwai* (drama), *Les Girls* (comedy/musical)
Academy Awards: *The Bridge on the River Kwai*

1958
National Board of Review: *The Old Man and the Sea*
New York Film Critics: *The Defiant Ones*
Golden Globes: *The Defiant Ones* (drama), *Auntie Mame* (comedy), *Gigi* (musical)
Academy Awards: *Gigi*

1959
National Board of Review: *The Nun's Story*
New York Film Critics: *Ben-Hur*
Golden Globes: *Ben-Hur* (drama), *Some Like It Hot* (comedy), *Porgy and Bess* (musical)
Academy Awards: *Ben-Hur*

1960
National Board of Review: *Sons and Lovers*
New York Film Critics: (Tie) *The Apartment, Sons and Lovers*
Golden Globes: *Spartacus* (drama), *The Apartment* (comedy), *Song without End* (musical)
Academy Awards: *The Apartment*

1961
National Board of Review: *Question 7*
New York Film Critics: *West Side Story*
Golden Globes: *The Guns of Navarone* (drama), *A Majority of One* (comedy), *West Side Story* (musical)
Academy Awards: *West Side Story*

1962
National Board of Review: *The Longest Day*
New York Film Critics: (no award)
Golden Globes: *Lawrence of Arabia* (drama), *That Touch of Mink* (comedy), *The Music Man* (musical)
Academy Awards: *Lawrence of Arabia*

1963
National Board of Review: *Tom Jones*
New York Film Critics: *Tom Jones*
Golden Globes: *The Cardinal* (drama), *Tom Jones* (comedy/musical)
Academy Awards: *Tom Jones*

1964
National Board of Review: *Becket*
New York Film Critics: *My Fair Lady*
Golden Globes: *Becket* (drama), *My Fair Lady* (comedy/musical)
Academy Awards: *My Fair Lady*

1965
New York Film Critics: *Darling*
National Board of Review: *The Eleanor Roosevelt Story*
Golden Globes: *Doctor Zhivago* (drama), *The Sound of Music* (comedy/musical)
Academy Awards: *The Sound of Music*

1966
New York Film Critics: *A Man for All Seasons*
National Society of Film Critics: *Blow-Up*
National Board of Review: *A Man for All Seasons*
Golden Globes: *A Man for All Seasons* (drama), *The Russians Are Coming, The Russians Are Coming* (comedy/musical)
Academy Awards: *A Man for All Seasons*

1967
New York Film Critics: *In the Heat of the Night*
National Board of Review: *Far from the Madding Crowd*
National Society of Film Critics: *Persona*
Golden Globes: *In the Heat of the Night* (drama), *The Graduate* (comedy/musical)
Academy Awards: *In the Heat of the Night*

1968
New York Film Critics: *The Lion in Winter*
National Board of Review: *The Shoes of the Fisherman*
National Society of Film Critics: *Shame*
Golden Globes: *The Lion in Winter* (drama), *Oliver!* (comedy/musical)
Academy Awards: *Oliver!*

1969

New York Film Critics: *Z*

National Board of Review: *They Shoot Horses, Don't They?*

National Society of Film Critics: *Z*

Golden Globes: *Anne of the Thousand Days* (drama), *The Secret of Santa Vittoria* (comedy/musical)

Academy Awards: *Midnight Cowboy*

1970

New York Film Critics: *Five Easy Pieces*

National Board of Review: *Patton*

National Society of Film Critics: *M*A*S*H*

Golden Globes: *Love Story* (drama), *M*A*S*H* (comedy/musical)

Academy Awards: *Patton*

1971

New York Film Critics: *A Clockwork Orange*

National Society of Film Critics: *Claire's Knee*

National Board of Review: *Macbeth*

Golden Globes: *The French Connection* (drama), *Fiddler on the Roof* (comedy/musical)

Academy Awards: *The French Connection*

1972

National Board of Review: *Cabaret*

New York Film Critics: *Cries and Whispers*

National Society of Film Critics: *The Discreet Charm of the Bourgeoisie*

Golden Globes: *The Godfather* (drama), *Cabaret* (comedy/musical)

Academy Awards: *The Godfather*

1973

National Board of Review: *The Sting*

National Society of Film Critics: *Day for Night*

New York Film Critics Circle: *Day for Night*

Golden Globes: *The Exorcist* (drama), *American Graffiti* (comedy/musical)

Academy Awards: *The Sting*

1974

National Board of Review: *The Conversation*

New York Film Critics Circle: *Amarcord*

National Society of Film Critics: *Scenes from a Marriage*

Golden Globes: *Chinatown* (drama), *The Longest Yard* (comedy/musical)

Academy Awards: *The Godfather, Part II*

1975

National Board of Review: (Tie) *Nashville, Barry Lyndon*

National Society of Film Critics: *Nashville*

New York Film Critics Circle: *Nashville*

Golden Globes: *One Flew over the Cuckoo's Nest* (drama), *The Sunshine Boys* (comedy/musical)

Los Angeles Film Critics Association: (Tie) *Dog Day Afternoon, One Flew over the Cuckoo's Nest*

Academy Awards: *One Flew over the Cuckoo's Nest*

1976

Los Angeles Film Critics Association: (Tie) *Network, Rocky*

National Board of Review: *All the President's Men*

New York Film Critics Circle: *All the President's Men*

National Society of Film Critics: *All the President's Men*

Golden Globes: *Rocky* (drama), *A Star Is Born* (comedy/musical)

Academy Awards: *Rocky*

1977

National Board of Review: *The Turning Point*

National Society of Film Critics: *Annie Hall*

Los Angeles Film Critics Association: *Star Wars*

New York Film Critics Circle: *Annie Hall*

Golden Globes: *The Turning Point* (drama), *The Goodbye Girl* (comedy/musical)

Academy Awards: *Annie Hall*

1978

Los Angeles Film Critics Association: *Coming Home*

National Board of Review: *Days of Heaven*

New York Film Critics Circle: *The Deer Hunter*

National Society of Film Critics: *Get Out Your Handkerchiefs*

Golden Globes: *Midnight Express* (drama), *Heaven Can Wait* (comedy/musical)

Academy Awards: *The Deer Hunter*

1979

Los Angeles Film Critics Association: *Kramer vs. Kramer*

New York Film Critics Circle: *Kramer vs. Kramer*

National Board of Review: *Manhattan*

National Society of Film Critics: *Breaking Away*

Golden Globes: *Kramer vs. Kramer* (drama), *Breaking Away* (Comedy/Musical)

Academy Awards: *Kramer vs. Kramer*

1980

National Board of Review: *Ordinary People*

Los Angeles Film Critics Association: *Raging Bull*

New York Film Critics Circle: *Ordinary People*

National Society of Film Critics: *Melvin and Howard*

Golden Globes: *Ordinary People* (drama), *Coal Miner's Daughter* (comedy/musical)

Academy Awards: *Ordinary People*

1981

Los Angeles Film Critics Association: *Atlantic City*

National Board of Review: *Chariots of Fire*

New York Film Critics Circle: *Reds*

National Society of Film Critics: *Atlantic City*

Golden Globes: *On Golden Pond* (drama), *Arthur* (comedy/musical)

Academy Awards: *Chariots of Fire*

1982

Los Angeles Film Critics Association: *E.T. The Extra-Terrestrial*

National Board of Review: *Gandhi*

New York Film Critics Circle: *Gandhi*

National Society of Film Critics: *Tootsie*

Golden Globes: *E.T. The Extra-Terrestrial* (drama), *Tootsie* (comedy/musical)

Academy Awards: *Gandhi*

1983

National Board of Review: (Tie) *Terms of Endearment, Betrayal*

New York Film Critics Circle: *Terms of Endearment*

Los Angeles Film Critics Association: *Terms of Endearment*

National Society of Film Critics: *The Night of the Shooting Stars*

Golden Globes: *Terms of Endearment* (drama), *Yentl* (comedy/musical)

Academy Awards: *Terms of Endearment*

1984

Los Angeles Film Critics Association: *Amadeus*

National Board of Review: *A Passage to India*

New York Film Critics Circle: *A Passage to India*

National Society of Film Critics: *Stranger Than Paradise*

Golden Globes: *Amadeus* (drama), *Romancing the Stone* (comedy/musical)

Academy Awards: *Amadeus*

1985

Los Angeles Film Critics Association: *Brazil*

National Board of Review: *The Color Purple*

New York Film Critics Circle: *Prizzi's Honor*

National Society of Film Critics: *Ran*

Golden Globes: *Out of Africa* (drama), *Prizzi's Honor* (comedy/musical)

Independent Spirit: *After Hours*

Academy Awards: *Out of Africa*

1986

National Board of Review: *Room with a View*

Los Angeles Film Critics Association: *Hannah and Her Sisters*

New York Film Critics Circle: *Hannah and Her Sisters*

National Society of Film Critics: *Blue Velvet*

Golden Globes: *Platoon* (drama), *Hannah and Her Sisters* (comedy/musical)

Independent Spirit: *Platoon*

Academy Awards: *Platoon*

1987

National Board of Review: *Empire of the Sun*

New York Film Critics Circle: *Broadcast News*

Los Angeles Film Critics Association: *Hope and Glory*

National Society of Film Critics: *The Dead*

Golden Globes: *The Last Emperor* (drama), *Hope and Glory* (comedy/musical)

Independent Spirit: *River's Edge*

Academy Awards: *The Last Emperor*

1988

Los Angeles Film Critics Association: *Little Dorrit*

National Board of Review: *Mississippi Burning*

New York Film Critics Circle: *The Accidental Tourist*

National Society of Film Critics: *The Unbearable Lightness of Being*

Golden Globes: *Rain Man* (drama), *Working Girl* (comedy/musical)

Independent Spirit: *Stand and Deliver*

Academy Awards: *Rain Man*

1989

National Board of Review: *Driving Miss Daisy*

Los Angeles Film Critics Association: *Do the Right Thing*

New York Film Critics Circle: *My Left Foot*

National Society of Film Critics: *Drugstore Cowboy*

Golden Globes: *Born on the Fourth of July* (drama), *Driving Miss Daisy* (comedy/musical)

Producers Guild of America: *Driving Miss Daisy*

Independent Spirit: *sex, lies, and videotape*

Academy Awards: *Driving Miss Daisy*

1990

National Board of Review: *Dances with Wolves*

Los Angeles Film Critics Association: *GoodFellas*

New York Film Critics Circle: *GoodFellas*

National Society of Film Critics: *GoodFellas*

Golden Globes: *Dances with Wolves* (drama), *Green Card* (comedy/musical)

Producers Guild of America: *Dances with Wolves*

Independent Spirit: *The Grifters*

Academy Awards: *Dances with Wolves*

1991

Los Angeles Film Critics Association: *Bugsy*

National Board of Review: *The Silence of the Lambs*

New York Film Critics Circle: *The Silence of the Lambs*

National Society of Film Critics: *Life Is Sweet*

Golden Globes: *Bugsy* (drama), *Beauty and the Beast* (comedy/musical)

Producers Guild of America: *The Silence of the Lambs*

Independent Spirit: *Rambling Rose*

Academy Awards: *The Silence of the Lambs*

1992

Los Angeles Film Critics Association: *Unforgiven*

National Board of Review: *Howards End*

New York Film Critics Circle: *The Player*

National Society of Film Critics: *Unforgiven*

Golden Globes: *Scent of a Woman* (drama), *The Player* (comedy/musical)

Producers Guild of America: *The Crying Game*

Independent Spirit: *The Player*

Academy Awards: *Unforgiven*

1993

Los Angeles Film Critics Association: *Schindler's List*

National Board of Review: *Schindler's List*

New York Film Critics Circle: *Schindler's List*

National Society of Film Critics: *Schindler's List*

Golden Globes: *Schindler's List* (drama), *Mrs. Doubtfire* (comedy/musical)

Producers Guild of America: *Schindler's List*

Independent Spirit: *Short Cuts*
Academy Awards: *Schindler's List*

1994

Los Angeles Film Critics Association: *Pulp Fiction*
National Board of Review: (Tie) *Forrest Gump, Pulp Fiction*
New York Film Critics Circle: *Quiz Show*
National Society of Film Critics: *Pulp Fiction*
Golden Globes: *Forrest Gump* (drama), *The Lion King* (comedy/musical)
Producers Guild of America: *Forrest Gump*
Independent Spirit: *Pulp Fiction*
Academy Awards: *Forrest Gump*

1995

National Board of Review: *Sense and Sensibility*
New York Film Critics Circle: *Leaving Las Vegas*
Los Angeles Film Critics Association: *Leaving Las Vegas*
National Society of Film Critics: *Babe*
Broadcast Film Critics Association: *Sense and Sensibility*
Golden Globes: *Sense and Sensibility* (drama), *Babe* (comedy/musical)
Producers Guild of America: *Apollo 13*
Independent Spirit: *Leaving Las Vegas*
Academy Awards: *Braveheart*

1996

National Board of Review: *Shine*
New York Film Critics Circle: *Fargo*
Los Angeles Film Critics Association: *Secrets and Lies*
Broadcast Film Critics Association: *Fargo*
National Society of Film Critics: *Breaking the Waves*
Golden Globes: *The English Patient* (drama), *Evita* (comedy/musical)
Producers Guild of America: *The English Patient*
Independent Spirit: *Fargo*
Academy Awards: *The English Patient*

1997

National Board of Review: *L.A. Confidential*

New York Film Critics Circle: *L.A. Confidential*
Los Angeles Film Critics Association: *L.A. Confidential*
National Society of Film Critics: *L.A. Confidential*
Broadcast Film Critics Association: *L.A. Confidential*
Producers Guild of America: *Titanic*
Golden Globes: *Titanic* (drama), *As Good as It Gets* (comedy/musical)
Independent Spirit: *The Apostle*
Academy Awards: *Titanic*

1998

National Board of Review: *Gods and Monsters*
Los Angeles Film Critics Association: *Saving Private Ryan*
New York Film Critics Circle: *Saving Private Ryan*
National Society of Film Critics: *Out of Sight*
Broadcast Film Critics Association: *Saving Private Ryan*
Producers Guild of America: *Saving Private Ryan*
Golden Globes: *Saving Private Ryan* (drama), *Shakespeare in Love* (comedy/musical)
Independent Spirit: *Gods and Monsters*
Academy Awards: *Shakespeare in Love*

1999

National Board of Review: *American Beauty*
Los Angeles Film Critics Association: *The Insider*
New York Film Critics Circle: *Topsy-Turvy*
National Society of Film Critics: (Tie) *Being John Malkovich, Topsy-Turvy*
Golden Globes: *American Beauty* (drama), *Toy Story 2* (comedy/musical)
Broadcast Film Critics Association: *American Beauty*
Producers Guild of America: *American Beauty*
Independent Spirit: *Election*
Academy Awards: *American Beauty*

Kudos Counts

Honorary awards are not included. TV awards are not included in the tallies for Golden Globes, directors' guild or writers' guild kudos. Awards for producing Best Picture are not included since they are usually awarded to the films and not the filmmakers. The New York Film Critics Circle list, for example, does not count Woody Allen's top prizes for *Annie Hall* and *Hannah and Her Sisters*.

ACADEMY AWARDS

MOST AWARDS: FILMS

Ben-Hur	11
Titanic	11
West Side Story	10
Gigi	9
The Last Emperor	9
The English Patient	9
Amadeus	8
Cabaret*	8
From Here to Eternity	8
Gandhi	8
Gone With the Wind	8
My Fair Lady	8
On the Waterfront	8

MOST NOMINATIONS: FILMS

All about Eve	14
Titanic	14
Forrest Gump	13
From Here to Eternity	13
Gone With the Wind	13
Mary Poppins*	13
Shakespeare in Love	13
Who's Afraid of Virginia Woolf?*	13
Becket*	12
Ben-Hur	12

*Did not win Best Picture

Dances with Wolves	12
The English Patient	12
Johnny Belinda*	12
Mrs. Miniver	12
My Fair Lady	12
On the Waterfront	12
Reds*	12
The Song of Bernadette*	12
A Streetcar Named Desire*	12

MOST ACTING NOMINATIONS: FILMS

All about Eve	5
Bonnie and Clyde*	5
From Here to Eternity	5
The Godfather, Part II	5
Mrs. Miniver	5
Network*	5
On the Waterfront	5
Peyton Place*	5
Tom Jones	5

MOST AWARDS: ACTORS

Katharine Hepburn (4 for Best Actress)
Walter Brennan (3 for Best Supporting Actor)
Ingrid Bergman (2 for Best Actress, 1 for Best Supporting Actress)
Jack Nicholson (2 for Best Actor, 1 for Best Supporting Actor)

MOST AWARDS: DIRECTORS

John Ford	4
Frank Capra	3
William Wyler	3

MOST NOMINATIONS: ACTORS

Katharine Hepburn	12
Meryl Streep	12
Jack Nicholson	11
Bette Davis	10
Laurence Olivier	10
Spencer Tracy	9

MOST NOMINATIONS: DIRECTORS
William Wyler (12)
Billy Wilder (8 for directing plus 12 for screenwriting)

TRIVIA
- Biggest Losers: The two films with the most nominations (11) that didn't result in a single win—*The Turning Point* and *The Color Purple*. Among actors, Richard Burton and Peter O'Toole never won despite earning seven nominations each.
- Walt Disney won the most Oscars: 26.
- Three films have won the top five awards (Best Picture, Director, Actor, Actress, Screenplay): *It Happened One Night* (1933–1934), *One Flew over the Cuckoo's Nest* (1975) and *The Silence of the Lambs* (1991).
- Sisters who've won: Olivia de Havilland and Joan Fontaine. Brothers: screenwriters William and James Goldman. Brother and sister: Lionel Barrymore and Ethel Barrymore. Husbands and wives: Vivien Leigh and Laurence Olivier, Paul Newman and Joanne Woodward. Fathers and daughters: Vincente and Liza Minnelli, Henry and Jane Fonda, Jon Voight and Angelina Jolie. Father, son and granddaughter: Walter, John and Anjelica Huston.
- Youngest winner among actors: Tatum O'Neal, *Paper Moon* (10 years old). Anna Paquin (*The Piano*) was the second-youngest (11). Both girls were 9 years old when they filmed their movies. Youngest Best Actor: Richard Dreyfuss (29), *The Goodbye Girl*. Youngest Best Actress: Marlee Matlin (21), *Children of a Lesser God*. Youngest nominee: Justin Henry (8), *Kramer vs. Kramer*. Oldest nominee: Gloria Stuart (87), *Titanic*.
- Oldest winner: Jessica Tandy, *Driving Miss Daisy* (80, seven months older than the also 80-year-old George Burns, *The Sunshine Boys*). Oldest Best Actor Winner: Henry Fonda (76), *On Golden Pond*. Oldest Best Supporting Actress: Peggy Ashcroft (77), *A Passage to India*.
- Youngest director to win: William Friedkin, 32 (*The French Connection*, 1971).
- First nominee to refuse an Oscar: Dudley Nichols for Best Screenplay *The Informer* (1935).

- Films that have won the most awards without winning Best Picture: *Cabaret* (eight, 1973), *A Place in the Sun* (six, 1951) and *Star Wars* (six, 1977).
- The only foreign-language films nominated for Best Picture were *Grand Illusion* (France, 1938), *Z* (France/Algeria, 1969), *The Emigrants* (Sweden, 1972), *Cries and Whispers* (Sweden, 1973), *The Postman (Il Postino)* (1995) and *Life Is Beautiful* (Italy, 1998).
- Hal Mohr, cinematographer of *A Midsummer's Night's Dream* (1935), is the only person to win an Oscar due to a write-in campaign. Studio exec Jack Warner pressed his employees to ignore the Oscar nominees that year and support company talent, but only Mohr prevailed.
- MGM mounted the first public campaign for Oscars by taking out ads in the tradepapers for *Ah, Wilderness!*, but the adaptation of Eugene O'Neill's Pulitzer Prize–winning comedy didn't win a single nomination.
- Only one thesp has ever won Best Actor for his film debut (Ben Kingsley), although several women reaped Best Actress for their first screen roles: Shirley Booth (*Come Back, Little Sheba*), Barbra Streisand (*Funny Girl*) and Marlee Matlin (*Children of a Lesser God*).
- The shortest perf to win an Oscar was Best Supporting Actress Judi Dench, who clocked only 8 minutes of screen time, thereby eclipsing Anthony Quinn (9 minutes in *Lust for Life*) and Beatrice Straight (10 minutes in *Network*).
- Directors who've won for their film debuts: Sam Mendes (*American Beauty*, 1999), Delbert Mann (*Marty*), Jerome Robbins (*West Side Story*), Robert Redford (*Ordinary People*), James L. Brooks (*Terms of Endearment*) and Kevin Costner (*Dances with Wolves*).
- John Barrymore was never even nominated, although his brother Lionel and sister Ethel both won awards. John once said, "This town is filled with hypocritical old biddies who are afraid that if I win, I'll show up drunk to accept it. And I just might."
- No one knows for sure who gave the academy's statuette the nickname of "Oscar," but there are three theories: (1) academy

librarian and future executive director Margaret Herrick named it after her uncle, Oscar Pierce; (2) showbiz columnist Sidney Skolsky borrowed the name from a vaudeville joke that began "Will you have a cigar, Oscar?"; (3) Bette Davis came up with it when aspects of the naked golden boy reminded her of her husband, Harmon Oscar Nelson, Jr.

■ Prior to the 1940s awards, word of the winners often leaked out early, usually because the academy tipped off reporters, who needed the information by 8:30 P.M. in order to make their deadlines. The announcements weren't made officially to the banquet guests until they finished dining at 11 P.M., but by then gossip about the winners had usually spread like wildfire. At the 1940 ceremony, the winners' names were kept secret until sealed envelopes were opened at the podium.

■ The Oscar statuette costs $400 to manufacture. But it can be worth lots to those who win it: Tom Hanks went from doing drag on a TV sitcom to making $20 million a pic thanks to those golden boys on his mantel for *Philadelphia* and *Forrest Gump*. If you count up all the money *Titanic* made after its Oscar bump (the pic had been released three months earlier) and divide by its 11 Oscars, the price comes to $24 million per win.

■ The most money ever paid for an Oscar statuette: $1.5 million was anted up at auction for *Gone With the Wind*'s Best Picture trophy. Only statuettes manufactured before 1950 can be sold legally today. All others are technically considered property of the film academy.

■ *Shakespeare in Love* earned an additional $64 million domestically ($100 million worldwide) at the box office as a result of winning Best Picture. *Braveheart*, however, reaped only an additional $2 million domestically.

■ Over the past 17 years, the movie with the most nominations has won Best Picture 16 times.

■ Since 1950, two-thirds of the winners for Best Picture have also been awarded one of the two screenplay awards.

■ Over the past 30 years only three films with a serious funnybone—*Annie Hall*,

Terms of Endearment and *Shakespeare in Love*—took the top prize.

■ The only stars to win an Oscar, Tony, Grammy and Emmy in competitive categories were Julie Harris and Rita Moreno. Barbra Streisand won an Emmy, Grammy and Oscar in the late 1960s, but got stopped at the Tonys by Carol Channing of *Hello, Dolly!* (Sweet revenge for Channing—since Streisand snatched the *Dolly!* movie role away from her.) Streisand does have an honorary Tony Award.

GOLDEN GLOBES

MOST AWARDS: FILMS

Tallies do not include awards and noms that films may have received in the Most Promising Newcomer categories. HFPA official records list the films along with the nominees in some years, but not others, reflecting a changing policy. They are eliminated here for consistency's sake.

Doctor Zhivago	5
The Godfather	5
Love Story	5
One Flew over the Cuckoo's Nest	5
A Star Is Born (1976)	5
All the King's Men	4
Amadeus	4
Anne of the Thousand Days	4
Chinatown	4
*Death of a Salesman**	4
The Exorcist	4
Gigi	4
The Goodbye Girl	4
Kramer vs. Kramer	4
A Man for All Seasons	4
Midnight Express	4
*Network**	4
Ordinary People	4
Prizzi's Honor	4
Sunset Boulevard	4
Terms of Endearment	4
Titanic	4

MOST NOMINATIONS: FILMS

*Nashville**	9
Bugsy	8

*Did not win Best Picture

Cabaret	8
Titanic	8
*America, America**	7
Anne of the Thousand Days	7
Chinatown	7
The English Patient	7
Forrest Gump	7
The Godfather	7
*The Godfather, Part III**	7
In the Heat of the Night	7
*Julia**	7
Kramer vs. Kramer	7
Lawrence of Arabia	7
Love Story	7
Ordinary People	7
*Reds**	7
*Who's Afraid of Virginia Woolf?**	7

MOST WINS: STARS, DIRECTORS, WRITERS

Tallies do not include wins for World Film Favorites because those victors were said to be determined by public polls, not HFPA members. The tallies do include bids for acting, directing, writing and Most Promising Newcomer, but not producing.

Francis Ford Coppola	5
Shirley MacLaine	5
Jack Nicholson	5
Rosalind Russell	5
Oliver Stone	5
Jane Fonda	4
Dustin Hoffman	4
Elia Kazan	4
Barbra Streisand	4
Warren Beatty	3
Ingrid Bergman	3
Tom Cruise	3
Milos Forman	3
Jessica Lange	3
Jack Lemmon	3
Tom Hanks	3
John Huston	3
Jessica Lange	3
Jon Voight	3
Billy Wilder	3
Robin Williams	3

---

*Did not win Best Picture

MOST NOMINATIONS: STARS, DIRECTORS, WRITERS

Jack Lemmon	15
Meryl Streep	15
Al Pacino	13
Shirley MacLaine	12
Jack Nicholson	12
Paul Newman	11
Warren Beatty	10
Dustin Hoffman	10

TRIVIA

■ The only Globe champ to win all of the top categories (picture, director, screenplay, actor and actress) is *One Flew over the Cuckoo's Nest* (1983).

■ Not only is Rosalind Russell tied for the most victories among thesps (five), but she never lost a Globe race (and never won an Oscar). One of Shirley MacLaine's five awards was for most Promising Newcomer, so that means Russell and Jack Nicholson actually have won the most Globes for individual performances.

■ Two films suffered the biggest shut-outs despite reaping seven noms each: *Who's Afraid of Virginia Woolf?* (1966) and *The Godfather, Part III* (1990).

■ Three pix are the biggest undefeated champs, all starting out with five noms each: *Doctor Zhivago* (1965), *One Flew over the Cuckoo's Nest* (1975) and *A Star Is Born* (1976).

■ The only three-way tie that's ever occurred in kudos history happened in 1988 when Jodie Foster (*The Accused*), Sigourney Weaver (*Gorillas in the Mist*) and Shirley MacLaine (*Madame Sousatzka*) all won Best Drama Actress.

■ Winners who refused a Globe included the producers of *Z*—Best Foreign-Language Foreign Film of 1969. They wanted *Z* to be included in the Best Picture races at the Globes and Oscars, but when it was nommed only in the Globe contest for offshore fare, they declined the prize. The controversy helped *Z* at the Oscars where it won Best Foreign Film. Marlon Brando refused a globe for *The Godfather* in 1972 because of U.S. "imperialism" and racism.

■ The youngest star to win a Globe was 9-year-old Ricky Schroeder (*The Champ*), who won Best New Star of the Year in 1979. Oldest winner: 80-year-old Best Actress Jessica Tandy (*Driving Miss Daisy*, 1989). Oldest Best Actor: 76-year-old Henry Fonda (*On Golden Pond*, 1981).

■ Sigourney Weaver is the only thesp to receive two acting awards for film work in one year (1988): Best Drama Actress (*Gorillas in the Mist*) and Best Supporting Actress (*Working Girl*).

■ The Globes dispense separate kudos for drama and comedy/musical races, which makes comparisons to the Oscars difficult, but in the past 57 years, the Oscars have validated one of the Globe top pics 41 times. In the past 30 years, 23 of Oscar's Best Actors (77 percent) and 24 Best Actresses (80 percent) were previous Globe winners for the same roles.

DIRECTORS GUILD OF AMERICA

BIGGEST WINNERS

Steven Spielberg	3
Francis Ford Coppola	2
Milos Forman	2
David Lean	2
Joseph L. Mankiewicz	2
Oliver Stone	2
Robert Wise	2
Fred Zinnemann	2

TRIVIA

■ Steven Spielberg has the most nominations: nine. In second place are Alfred Hitchcock, Billy Wilder and Fred Zinnemann with eight each. Since Hitchcock never won an annual kudo, that makes him the DGA's biggest loser.

■ Ron Howard (*Apollo 13*, 1995) was the only DGA winner who failed to be nominated at the Oscars.

■ On four occasions, the guild opted for the directors of films that failed to win any top Golden Globe or crix awards, but would go on to win the Oscar: John Schlesinger (*Midnight Cowboy*, 1969), Francis Ford Coppola (*The Godfather, Part II*, 1974), Franklin Schaffner (*Patton*, 1970) and George Roy Hill (*The Sting*, 1973). *Patton* and *The Sting* had been cited early on in the year's awards

derby by the National Board of Review, but then were snubbed by later kudos.

■ The only women nominated by the DGA were Randa Haines (*Children of a Lesser God*, 1986), Lina Wertmüller (*Seven Beauties*, 1976), Barbra Streisand (*The Prince of Tides*, 1991) and Jane Campion (*The Piano*, 1993).

WRITERS GUILD OF AMERICA

BIGGEST WINNERS

Ernest Lehman	5
Billy Wilder	5
Woody Allen	4
Robert Benton	4
Larry Gelbart	3
David Newman	3
Waldo Salt	3
Alvin Sargent	3
Neil Simon	3

MOST NOMINATIONS

Woody Allen	18
Billy Wilder	15
Ernest Lehman	10
Neil Simon	9
Robert Benton	8
Blake Edwards	7
Paul Mazursky	7
Joseph L. Mankiewicz	6

TRIVIA

■ Alvin Sargent is the only scribe to go undefeated with multiple nominations, scoring victories in 1973 (*Paper Moon*), 1977 (*Julia*) and 1980 (*Ordinary People*).

■ In the 52 years of the WGA's existence, Oscar voters bestowed 116 screenplay awards; 63 of them (or 54 percent) were WGA winners. The two kudos, however, did not have parallel categories until 1984. During the 16 years since then, 19 WGA champs won one of the 32 Oscars bestowed for scripts—or 59 percent.

■ In the past 52 years, 29 of Oscar's Best Pictures won a WGA award (55 percent). The overlap jumps considerably—to 70 percent—if the years are discounted when Oscar's Best Picture wasn't eligible for the WGA prize because it was foreign-made or produced by a firm that wasn't a guild signatory. Only twice did the WGA not nominate a film that went on to win Best Picture: *The Greatest Show on Earth* (probably because guild members thought it was lightweight) and *The Bridge on the River Kwai* (for political reasons). Only 12 Best Pictures lost their races at the WGA.

■ No writer has swept all of the top kudos in modern times. Emma Thompson nabbed the Oscar, Globe, WGA prize and laurels from three of the four crix orgs for *Sense and Sensibility* in 1995, but was denied a sweep by the National Society of Film Critics. Jane Campion's script for *The Piano* took all the top awards except the Globe in 1993. A consensus did occur in the 1950s over what the best screenplays of the year were, but there were far fewer kudos then and many of them refused to bestow a screenplay award while blacklisting went on. So the following scribes all pulled off sweeps even though they didn't take home all of the usual kudos: Paddy Chayefsky won the Oscar and WGA prize for *Marty* in 1955, but neither the Globes nor the New York film crix had a kudo for scripts. *Around the World in 80 Days* won the New York film crix prize, WGA and Oscar, but the Globes still didn't have a script competish. Billy Wilder and I. A. L. Diamond swept the Oscars, WGA and Gotham crix, but there was no Globe in 1960. Joseph L. Mankiewicz went undefeated for *All about Eve* in 1950, but the New York film crix had no category.

SCREEN ACTORS GUILD

TRIVIA

■ No star has won more than one trophy. Meryl Streep and Julianne Moore are tied for having the most noms (three).

■ *Shakespeare in Love* (1998) holds the record for most noms—five. *American Beauty* (1999) and *Good Will Hunting* (1997) both scored four.

■ In its six-year history, 10 of its 12 Best Actor and Actress champs went on to win Oscars (83 percent). Out of the 13 actors embraced by SAG in the supporting races, 7 won Academy Awards (54 percent). The total overlap rate for all races is 68 percent.

PRODUCERS GUILD OF AMERICA

TRIVIA

■ Steven Spielberg is the only multiple recipient of the relatively new Darryl F. Zanuck Producer of the Year Award, having won for *Schindler's List* (1993) and *Saving Private Ryan* (1998). The prize was created in 1989.

■ The PGA award has correctly predicted the Oscar Best Picture award nine times in the past 12 years. The exceptions: *The Crying Game* (1992), *Apollo 13* (1995) and *Saving Private Ryan* (1998).

NATIONAL SOCIETY OF FILM CRITICS

BIGGEST WINNERS: FILMS

Atlantic City	4
Blue Velvet	4
Breaking the Waves	4
Nashville	4
Tootsie	4
Scenes from a Marriage	4
Schindler's List	4
Unforgiven	4
Annie Hall	3
Breaking the Waves	3
Day for Night	3
Drugstore Cowboy	3
*Hope and Glory**	3
*Kramer vs. Kramer**	3
L.A. Confidential	3
*Leaving Las Vegas**	3
Life Is Sweet	3
Melvin and Howard	3
Out of Sight	3
Persona	3
*Prizzi's Honor**	3
Pulp Fiction	3
*Taxi Driver**	3

BIGGEST WINNERS: ACTORS, DIRECTORS, WRITERS

Ingmar Bergman**	5
Jack Nicholson	5
Anjelica Huston	3

---

*Did not win Best Picture
**Three awards for directing, two for screenwriting.

Vanessa Redgrave	3	*Schindler's List*	3
Martin Scorsese	3	*Terms of Endearment*	3
Liv Ullmann	3	*Tom Jones*	3
Woody Allen**	2	*Tootsie**	3
Bibi Anderson	2		
Albert Brooks	2		
Robert De Niro	2		

BIGGEST WINNERS: ACTORS, DIRECTORS, WRITERS

Curtis Hanson	2	Jack Nicholson	7
Dustin Hoffman	2	Woody Allen	5
Steve Martin	2	Robert De Niro	4
Paul Mazursky	2	John Ford	4
Vanessa Redgrave	2	Fred Zinnemann	4
Steven Spielberg	2	Ingmar Bergman	3
Meryl Streep	2	Ingrid Bergman	3
Quentin Tarantino	2	John Huston	3
François Truffaut	2	Elia Kazan	3
Gus Van Sant	2	Deborah Kerr	3
Diane Wiest	2	Burt Lancaster	3
		David Lean	3

NEW YORK FILM CRITICS CIRCLE

		Paul Mazursky	3
		Laurence Olivier	3
		Meryl Streep	3

BIGGEST WINNERS: FILMS

		Liv Ullmann	3
Broadcast News	5	Billy Wilder	3
Annie Hall	4	Joanne Woodward	3
Cries and Whispers	4		
A Man for All Seasons	4		

TRIVIA

Prizzi's Honor	4
Silence of the Lambs	4
All about Eve	3
All the President's Men	3
*Being John Malkovich**	3
*Breaking the Waves**	3
The Bridge on the River Kwai	3
Darling	3
Day for Night	3
Five Easy Pieces	3
From Here to Eternity	3
Going My Way	3
GoodFellas	3
Kramer vs. Kramer	3
L.A. Confidential	3
*The Last Picture Show**	3
The Lost Weekend	3
Melvin and Howard	3
Nashville	3
A Passage to India	3
*The Piano**	3
The Player	3

■ Only two races were ever decided by unanimous vote on the first ballot: *The Informer* won Best Picture in 1935 and Olivia de Havilland was voted Best Actress for *The Snake Pit* in 1948.

■ Charlie Chaplin is the only person who ever refused the award. He was upset that some members of the group initially panned *The Great Dictator* (1940), then gave him the Best Actor award because they wanted to resolve a 22-ballot deadlock and thought "he'll be a swell free attraction for us" at the Rainbow Room kudos ceremony. When Chaplin read about what happened at the crix powwow in the *N.Y. Mirror* (a disgruntled critic spilled the beans), Chaplin fired off a sternly stated no-thank-you note to the crix.

■ John Malkovich became the only person in the history of film awards to win a prize for portraying himself when the circle voted him 1999's Best Supporting Actor for *Being John Malkovich*.

■ Three months before George C. Scott refused the Best Actor Oscar for *Patton* (1970) his wife, Colleen Dewhurst,

*Did not win Best Picture
**One for directing, one for screenwriting.

accepted a New York Film Critics plaque on his behalf, saying, "George thinks this is the only film award worth having."

■ Stacy Keach (*Fat City*) was elected Best Actor during the 1972 voting session, but the crix decided to change their balloting procedure later during the same meeting. They took another Best Actor polling and gave the award to Laurence Olivier (*Sleuth*).

■ The number of award categories has grown significantly through the years. When *All about Eve* claimed three kudos in 1950, there were only four slots for American pix, so it therefore swept 75 percent of the prizes. Eight categories existed for Yankee pix when *Broadcast News* claimed five (62.5 percent) in 1987.

LOS ANGELES FILM CRITICS ASSOCIATION

BIGGEST WINNERS: FILMS

GoodFellas	5
Kramer vs. Kramer	5
Terms of Endearment	5
Unforgiven	5
Amadeus	4
Do the Right Thing	4
The Insider	4
L.A. Confidential	4
Leaving Las Vegas	4
*The Piano**	4
Pulp Fiction	4

BIGGEST WINNERS: ACTORS, DIRECTORS, WRITERS

Merly Steep	4
Jack Nicholson	3
Woody Allen	2
Warren Beatty	2
John Boorman	2
James L. Brooks	2
Daniel Day-Lewis	2
Robert De Niro	2
Clint Eastwood	2
John Gielgud	2
Gene Hackman	2
Holly Hunter	2
Anjelica Huston	2
Steven Spielberg	2

*Did not win Best Picture

Maureen Stapleton	2
Quentin Tarantino	2
Emma Thompson	2
Dianne Wiest	2

BROADCAST FILM CRITICS ASSOCIATION

The Critics' Choice award is only five years old, so it's difficult to compare or rank its winners. The biggest champs so far—

■ Among films: *American Beauty, Saving Private Ryan* and *Jerry Maguire* all scored three victories, although *Maguire* failed to be named Best Picture.

■ Among individuals: Curtis Hanson won two times, winning for both directing and writing *L.A. Confidential*.

NATIONAL BOARD OF REVIEW

BIGGEST WINNERS: FILMS

The Bridge on the River Kwai	4
A Man for All Seasons	4
Mississippi Burning	4
A Passage to India	4
All the President's Men	3
Cabaret	3
The Conversation	3
Empire of the Sun	3
Howards End	3
*Magnolia**	3
The Nun's Story	3
Reds	3
Sense and Sensibility	3
The Silence of the Lambs	3
*Terms of Endearment**	3
The Turning Point	3

BIGGEST WINNERS: STARS

Jack Nicholson	5
Ingrid Bergman	4
Ralph Richardson	4
Humphrey Bogart	3
James Cagney	3
Bing Crosby	3
Henry Fonda	3
Greta Garbo	3
Greer Garson	3
Gene Hackman	3

Laurence Olivier	3
Ginger Rogers	3

BIGGEST WINNERS: DIRECTORS

David Lean	4
Ingmar Bergman	2
John Huston*	2
Akira Kurosawa	2
John Schlesinger	2
William Wyler	2
Fred Zinnemann	2

INDEPENDENT SPIRIT

BIGGEST WINNERS: FILMS

Fargo	6
Stand and Deliver	6
*Drugstore Cowboy***	4
Leaving Las Vegas	4
Platoon	4
Pulp Fiction	4
sex, lies and videotape	4
*To Sleep with Anger***	4
The Apostle	3
Election	3
Gods and Monsters	3
*My Own Private Idaho***	3
Rambling Rose	3
Short Cuts	3

TRIVIA

■ *Drugstore Cowboy* holds the record for most noms (eight), followed by *Blue Velvet, House Party, Stand and Deliver* and *To Sleep with Anger* (seven each). Since *House Party* came up kudoless, it suffered the biggest shut-out in Spirit history.

■ Biggest undefeated champ: *Fargo* won all six awards for its six noms.

■ Joel Coen holds the record for winning the most among individuals (three), followed by Robert Altman, Robert Duvall, Anjelica Huston, Oliver Stone, Quentin Tarantino, Benicio de Toro and Gus Van Sant (two each). (Tally includes writing, directing and acting wins only, not victories for Best Picture or Best First Feature.)

---

*Huston also won a screenplay award.
**Did not win Best Feature or Best First Feature

SUNDANCE FILM FESTIVAL

TRIVIA

■ Four pix have won the most awards (three) at one fest: *American Dream* (1990), *Hurricane* (1996), *Three Seasons* (1998) and *Dark Days* (1999).

■ Two filmmakers have won the Grand Jury Prize twice: Eagle Pennell (1978, 1983) and Victor Nunez (1980, 1992).

■ Only one film has ever won both the Grand Jury Prize and Audience Award for features: *Three Seasons* (1998). Three pix in the Grand Jury documentary classification also won Audience Awards: *For All Mankind* (1988), *American Dream* (1990) and *Troublesome Creek* (1995).

COMPARING THE KUDOS

Jack Nicholson is the all-time king of most of the kudos. He is the biggest winner of awards from the Gotham crix (seven), national society (five) and National Board of Review (five). He has the most among male thesps at the Globes (five, tied for the most with Rosalind Russell), Oscars (tied with Walter Brennan, but one less than Katharine Hepburn) and L.A. film crix (four, one less than Meryl Streep).

STARS WHO WON NEW YORK FILM CRITICS AWARDS BUT NEVER WON OSCARS

Alan Arkin, Tallulah Bankhead, Charles Boyer, Ralph Fiennes, Albert Finney, Peter Fonda, Morgan Freeman, Greta Garbo, Arthur Kennedy, Deborah Kerr, Jennifer Jason Leigh, Ida Lupino, Steve Martin, Agnes Moorehead, Nick Nolte, William Powell, Burt Reynolds, Ralph Richardson, Kim Stanley, Margaret Sullavan, Liv Ullmann, Oskar Werner

DIRECTORS WHO WON NEW YORK FILM CRITICS AWARDS BUT NEVER WON OSCARS

Robert Altman, Ingmar Bergman, Federico Fellini, Alfred Hitchcock, Stanley Kramer, Stanley Kubrick, Gregory La Cava, Sidney Lumet, Terrence Malick, Paul Mazursky, Alan J. Pakula, Robert Rossen, Martin Scorsese, François Truffaut

STARS WHO WON OSCARS BUT NEVER WON NEW YORK FILM CRITICS AWARDS

Julie Andrews, Ethel Barrymore, Lionel Barrymore, Humphrey Bogart, Red Buttons, Cher, Joan Crawford, Clark Gable, Whoopi Goldberg, Tom Hanks, Goldie Hawn, Helen Hayes, Charleton Heston, Helen Hunt, Henry Fonda, Jack Lemmon, Fredric March, Walter Matthau, Al Pacino, Geraldine Page, Mary Pickford, Sidney Poitier, Cliff Robertson, Maggie Smith, Susan Sarandon, Frank Sinatra, Jessica Tandy, Spencer Tracy, John Wayne

DIRECTORS WHO WON OSCARS BUT NEVER WON NEW YORK FILM CRITICS AWARDS

Richard Attenborough, Bernardo Bertolucci, Frank Capra, Francis Ford Coppola, George Cukor, Michael Curtiz, Victor Fleming, Milos Forman, George Roy Hill, Barry Levinson, Lewis Milestone, Vincente Minnelli, Steven Spielberg, Oliver Stone, Robin Williams, Robert Wise

STARS WHO NEVER WON EITHER OSCARS OR NEW YORK FILM CRITICS AWARDS

Jean Arthur, Lauren Bacall, Alec Baldwin, John Barrymore, Richard Burton, Jim Carrey, Tom Cruise, Catherine Deneuve, Leonardo DiCaprio, Marlene Dietrich, Irene Dunne, Douglas Fairbanks, Sr., Douglas Fairbanks, Jr., Glen Ford, Harrison Ford, John Garfield, Judy Garland, Richard Gere, Lillian Gish, Cary Grant, Julie Harris, Leslie Howard, James Earl Jones, Elsa Lanchester, Angela Lansbury, Carole Lombard, John Malkovich, Marcello Mastroianni, Steve McQueen, Adolphe Menjou, Liam Neeson, Merle Oberon, Peter O'Toole, Sean Penn, Anthony Perkins, Tyrone Power, Vincent Price, Julia Roberts, Edward G. Robinson, Mickey Rooney, Gena Rowlands, Rosalind Russell, Meg Ryan, Winona Ryder, Peter Sellers, Jean Simmons, Barbara Stanwyck, Donald Sutherland, Gloria Swanson, Robert Taylor, Gene Tierney, John Travolta, Richard Widmark

DIRECTORS WHO NEVER WON EITHER OSCARS OR NEW YORK FILM CRITICS AWARDS

Clarence Brown, John Cassavetes, Cecil B. DeMille, Howard Hawks, Norman Jewison, James Ivory, Akira Kurosawa, Joshua Logan, Ernst Lubitsch, George Lucas, Arthur Penn, Roman Polanski, Otto Preminger, W. S. Van Dyke, Jean Renoir, Herbert Ross, King Vidor, Orson Welles

STARS WHO NEVER WON AN OSCAR

Alan Arkin, Jean Arthur, Lauren Bacall, Tallulah Bankhead, John Barrymore, Charles Boyer, Richard Burton, Jim Carrey, Glenn Close, Tom Cruise, Catherine Deneuve, Leonardo DiCaprio, Marlene Dietrich, Irene Dunne, Douglas Fairbanks, Sr., Douglas Fairbanks, Jr., Ralph Fiennes, Albert Finney, Peter Fonda, Glenn Ford, Harrison Ford, Errol Flynn, Morgan Freeman, Greta Garbo, Ava Gardner, John Garfield, Judy Garland, Richard Gere, Lillian Gish, Cary Grant, Bob Hope, Jean Harlow, Julie Harris, Rita Hayworth, Leslie Howard, Rock Hudson, James Earl Jones, Deborah Kerr, Jennifer Jason Leigh, Elsa Lanchester, Angela Lansbury, Myrna Loy, Ida Lupino, Carole Lombard, John Malkovich, James Mason, Marcello Mastroianni, Steve McQueen, Adolphe Menjou, Robert Mitchum, Marilyn Monroe, Agnes Moorehead, Liam Neeson, Nick Nolte, Merle Oberon, Maureen O'Hara, Peter O'Toole, Eleanor Parker, Sean Penn, Anthony Perkins, Michelle Pfeiffer, William Powell, Tyrone Power, Ronald Reagan, Burt Reynolds, Ralph Richardson, Julia Roberts, Edward G. Robinson, Mickey Rooney, Gena Rowlands, Rosalind Russell, Meg Ryan, Winona Ryder, Peter Sellers, Jean Simmons, Kim Stanley, Barbara Stanwyck, Donald Sutherland, Gloria Swanson, Robert Taylor, Gene Tierney, John Travolta, Kathleen Turner, Liv Ullmann

DIRECTORS WHO NEVER WON AN OSCAR

Robert Altman, Ingmar Bergman, Clarence Brown, John Cassavetes, Cecil B. De Mille, Federico Fellini, Howard Hawks, Alfred Hitchcock, Norman Jewison, James Ivory, Stanley Kramer, Stanley Kubrick, Akira Kurosawa, Gregory La Cava, Joshua Logan, Ernst Lubitsch, George Lucas, Sidney Lumet, Terrence Malick, Paul Mazursky, Alan J. Pakula, Arthur Penn, Roman Polanski, Otto Preminger, W. S. Van Dyke, Jean

Renior, Herbert Ross, Robert Rossen, Martin Scorsese, François Truffaut, King Vidor, Orson Welles

STARS WHO WERE NEVER NOMINATED FOR OSCARS

Tallulah Bankhead, John Barrymore, Dirk Bogarde, Beau Bridges, Jim Carrey, Joseph Cotten, Douglas Fairbanks, Sr., Douglas Fairbanks, Jr., Errol Flynn, Glenn Ford, Rita Hayworth, Bob Hope, Dennis Hopper, Peter Lorre, Ida Lupino, Marilyn Monroe, Tyrone Power, Vincent Price, Ronald Reagan, Robert Taylor, Bruce Willis

DIRECTORS WHO WERE NEVER NOMINATED FOR OSCARS

Tim Burton, Blake Edwards, D.W. Griffith, Howard Hawks, Ron Howard, John Landis, Fritz Lang, Spike Lee, Rouben Mamoulian, Penny Marshall, Paul Mazursky, Brian De Palma, Sam Peckinpah, George Sidney, Barbra Streisand (*Note*: Streisand won for acting and songwriting.)

STARS WHO NEVER WON GOLDEN GLOBES

Tallulah Bankhead, Ethel Barrymore, Lionel Barrymore, Humphrey Bogart, Kenneth Branagh, Jeff Bridges, Yul Brynner, James Cagney, Charlie Chaplin, Montgomery Clift, Claudette Colbert, Joan Crawford, Matt Damon, Bette Davis, Leonardo DiCaprio, Marlene Dietrich, Ralph Fiennes, Clark Gable, Greta Garbo, Mel Gibson, Cary Grant, Helen Hayes, Katharine Hepburn, William Holden, Anthony Hopkins, Anjelica Huston, Samuel L. Jackson, Vivien Leigh, Jennifer Jason Leigh, Karl Malden, John Malkovich, James Mason, Demi Moore, Eddie Murphy, Jason Robards, Susan Sarandon, Kevin Spacey, Jimmy Stewart, Christopher Walken, Orson Welles, Bruce Willis

DIRECTORS WHO NEVER WON GOLDEN GLOBES

Robert Altman, Michelangelo Antonioni, Ingmar Bergman, Peter Bogdanovich, Frank Borzage, Jane Campion, John Cassavetes, Brian De Palma, Blake Edwards, Federico Fellini, John Ford, Norman Jewison, James Ivory, Stanley Kubrick, Barry Levinson, David Lynch, George Lucas, Paul Mazursky, Sydney Pollack, Otto Preminger, Carol Reed, Jean Renoir, Tony Richardson, John Schlesinger, Martin Scorsese, George Stevens, Orson Welles, William Wellman, Robert Wise

BEST ACCEPTANCE SPEECHES

"Awards are nice, but I'd much rather have a job."

> —Jane Darwell, Best Supporting Actress Oscar, *The Grapes of Wrath*, 1940

"I'll just say what's in my heart: 'ba-bump, ba-bump, ba-bump.' "

> —Mel Brooks, Best Original Screenplay Oscar, *The Producers*, 1968

"I hope I didn't get this award because I have an accent."

> —Brooklyn-born, Golden Globe Best Actress champ Barbra Streisand to the Hollywood Foreign Press Association, *Funny Girl*, 1968

"I really have no speech. The writers' guild doesn't allow us to do any speculative writing."

> —Stirling Silliphant, Best Adapted Screenplay Oscar, *In the Heat of the Night*, 1967

"Well, I'm gonna have to figure out something new to dream about, that's for sure!"

> —Mary Steenburgen, Best Supporting Actress Oscar, *Melvin and Howard*, 1980

"I deserve this!"

> —Shirley MacLaine, Best Actress Oscar, *Terms of Endearment*, 1983

"The first time (that I won) I didn't feel it, but this time I feel it and I can't deny the fact you like me. Right now, *you like me!*"

> —Sally Field, Best Actress Oscar, *Places in the Heart*, 1984

"You tolerate me. You really, really tolerate me!"

> —Sean Penn, Independent Spirit Best Actor, *Dead Man Walking*, 1995

"A loaf of bread, two cans of tuna . . .
Oops, wrong sheet of paper!"
—Steve Martin, New York film crix Best
Actor, *All of Me*, 1984

"Gee, this isn't like what I imagined it
would be in the bathtub!"
—Dianne Wiest, Best Supporting Actress
Oscar, *Hannah and Her Sisters*, 1986

"I guess this proves that there are as many
nuts in the academy as anywhere else."
—Jack Nicolson, Best Actor Oscar,
*One Flew over the Cuckoo's
Nest*, 1975

"What I'd really like is a cigarette."
—Michelle Pfeiffer, Golden Globe Best
Actress, *The Fabulous
Baker Boys*, 1989

"This proves you *can* stand tall even if
you're in a wheelchair!"
—Ron Kovic, Best Screenplay Golden
Globe, *Born on the Fourth of July*, 1989

"I shall never waitress again and you are
my witnesses!"
—Mercedes Ruehl, Best Supporting
Actress Golden Globe, *The Fisher
King*, 1991

"I lost my virginity! This is my first award!"
—Janusz Kaminski, New York film crix
Best Cinematographer,
Schindler's List, 1993

"My God! What a night! What a life! What
a moment! What everything!"
—Martin Landau, Best Supporting Actor
Oscar, *Ed Wood*, 1994

"Now that I'm a bona-fide director with a
golden boy, I suppose, like most directors,
what I really want to do is act."
—Mel Gibson, Best Director Oscar,
Braveheart, 1995

"No one is more surprised than me. It's . . .
uh . . . uh . . . OK, it's a miracle."
—Sharon Stone, Golden Globe
Best Actress, *Casino*, 1995

"There's a thing in Hollywood about
always moving the finish line. Sometimes
you just have to enjoy the moment."
—James L. Brooks, writers guild Best
Original Screenplay, *As Good As
It Gets*, 1997

"I'd like to thank the academy . . . oops,
sorry. This is serious. It's going to be so
hard to talk out of my ass after this, but I'll
manage. You know what this means, don't
you? I'm a shoo-in for the Blockbuster
Award."
—Jim Carrey, Golden Globe Best
Drama Actor, *The Truman
Show*, 1998

"This is the highlight of my day."
—Kevin Spacey, Best Actor Oscar,
American Beauty, 1999

Journalists' Awards: Voters

HOLLYWOOD FOREIGN PRESS ASSOCIATION

Paoula Abou-Jaoude (Brazil), Vera Anderson (Mexico), Vivi Anderson (Sweden), Ray Arco (Romania), Rocio Ayuso (Spain), Ana Maria Bahiana (Brazil), Erwin Baker (Argentina), Anita Baum (Argentina), Michael Bayan (Mexico), Yani Begakis (Japan, Germany, Greece), Philip Berk (Portugal), Elmar Biebl (Germany), Silvia Bizio (Italy), Edmund Brettschneider (Germany), Kiki Brettschneider (Germany), Argentina Brunetti (Canada), Jorge Camara (Mexico, Latin America), Isabelle Caron (France), Jean-Paul Chaillet (France), Rui Henriques Coimbra (Portugal), Jenny Cooney Carrillo (Australia, New Zealand), Jean Cummings, (Finland, Netherlands, U.K.), Yola Czaderska-Hayek (Poland), Ersi Danou (Greece), Noel deSouza (India), Gabrielle Donnelly (U.K.), George Doss (Egypt), Mahfouz Doss (Egypt), Nick Douglas (Ireland), Maureen Dragone (Russia), Dagmar Dunlevy (Germany), B. J. Franklin (Germany, Austria, Switzerland, Japan), Armando Gallo (Italy, Finland), Gloria Geale, (U.K.), Avik Gilboa (Israel, Portugal), Mike Goodridge (U.K.), Andre Guimond (Canada), Algirdas Gustaitis (Australia, U.K.), John Hiscock (U.K.), Munawar Hosain (Bangladesh, Slovakia), Alan Hunter (New Zealand), Elisabeth Wille Jensen (Denmark), Yoram Kahana (Hungary), Erkki Kanto (Finland), Theo Kingma (Netherlands), Ron Krueger (Japan, Germany, Russia), Ahmed Lateef (Hong Kong), Kleo Lee (Japan, Greece), Elisa Leonelli (Italy), Lisa Lu (China), Howard Lucraft (U.K.), Helena Mar-Elia (Korea, Beirut, Lebenon), Karen Martin (U.K.), Lawrie Masterson (Australia, Singapore), Paz Mata (Spain), Peter McDonald (U.K.), Juliette Michaud (France), Max B. Miller (Germany), Aud Berggren Morisse (Norway), Yukiko Nakajima (Japan), Yoko B. Narita (Japan), Aniko Navai (Hungary), Sylvia Norris (U.K.), Yenny Nun-Katz (Chile), Scott Orlin (Germany), Ika Panajotovic (Yugoslavia), Mira Panajotovic (Yugoslavia), Alena Prime (France), Serge Rakhlin (Russia), J. Emilio Rondeau (Brazil), Patrick Roth (Germany), Mohammed Rouda (Kuwait), Frank Rousseau (France, Belgium), Marianne Ruuth (France, Mexico, Sweden), Sven Rye (Denmark), Frances Schoenberger (Germany), Elisabeth Sereda (Austria), Dierk Sindermann (Germany, Austria, Switzerland), Maria Snoeys-Lagler (Belgium, France), Judy Solomon (Israel), Lorenzo Soria (Italy), Hans J. Spurkel (Germany, Austria), Aida Takla O'Reilly (Egypt, France), Jack Tewksbury (France), Alessandra Venezia (Italy), Marlene von Arx (Switzerland), Helmut Voss (Germany), Jerry Watson (U.K.), Anita Weber (South Africa, France, Japan, Italy), Noemia Young (Canada)

NATIONAL SOCIETY OF FILM CRITICS

John Anderson, *Newsday*; David Ansen, *Newsweek*; Gary Arnold, *The Washington Times*; Jami Bernard, *The New York Daily News*; Jay Carr, *The Boston Globe*; Godfrey Cheshire, *New York Press*; Mike Clark, *USA Today*; Manohla Dargis, *Harper's Bazaar, L.A. Weekly*; David Denby, *The New Yorker*; Morris Dickstein, *The Partisan Review*; Roger Ebert, *The Chicago Sun-Times*; David Edelstein, *Microsoft Slate*; Joseph Gelmis, *Newsday*; Judy Gerstel, MSNBC; Owen Gleiberman, *Entertainment Weekly*; Hal Hinson, *Ifilm*; J. Hoberman, *The Village Voice*; Richard T. Jameson, *Film Comment*; Dave Kehr, *Citysearch*; Peter Keough, *The Boston Phoenix*; Stuart

Klawans, *The Nation*; Andy Klein, *New Times*; Emanuel Levy, *Variety*; Todd McCarthy, *Variety*; Elvis Mitchell, *The New York Times*; Joe Morgenstern, *The Wall Street Journal*; Rob Nelson, *City Pages*; Gerald Peary, *The Boston Phoenix*; John Powers, *Vogue*; Terrence Rafferty, *GO*; Peter Rainer, *New York Magazine*; Carrie Rickey, *The Philadelphia Inquirer*; Eleanor Ringel, *The Atlanta Journal*; Jonathan Rosenbaum, *The Chicago Reader*; Andrew Sarris, *The New York Observer*; Richard Schickel, *Time*; Lisa Schwarzbaum, *Entertainment Weekly*; Matt Zoller Seitz, *New York Press*; Henry Sheehan, *The Orange County Register*; Robert Sklar, *The Forward*; Michael Sragow, *Salon*; David Sterritt, *The Christian Science Monitor*; Chuck Stephens, *The San Francisco Bay Guardian*; Amy Taubin, *The Village Voice*; Ella Taylor, *L.A. Weekly*; Kevin Thomas, *The Los Angeles Times*; Peter Travers, *Rolling Stone*; Kenneth Turan, *The Los Angeles Times*; James Verniere, *The Boston Herald*; Armond White, *New York Press*, Liz Weis, executive director; Michael Wilmington, *The Chicago Tribune*; William Wolf, *Wolf Entertainment Guide*

NEW YORK FILM CRITICS CIRCLE

Thelma Adams, *New York Post*; John Anderson, *Newsday*; David Ansen, *Newsweek*; Jami Bernard, *New York Daily News*; Dwight Brown, *Emerge*; Bob Campbell, Newhouse News Service; Godfrey Cheshire, *New York Press*; Richard Corliss, *Time*; David Denby, *New Yorker*; Marshall Fine, Gannett Newspapers; Owen Gleiberman, *Entertainment Weekly*; J. Hoberman, *The Village Voice*; Stephen Holden, *New York Times*; Andrew Johnston, *Us Weekly*; Dave Kehr, *Film Comment*; Stuart Klawans, *The Nation*; Jack Mathews, *New York Daily News*; Joe Morgenstern, *Wall Street Journal*; Terrence Rafferty, *GQ*; Peter Rainer, *New York Magazine*; Rex Reed, *New York Observer*; Leah Rozen, *People*; Andrew Sarris, *The New York Observer*; Richard Schickel, *Time*; Lisa Schwarzbaum, *Entertainment Weekly*; Matt Zoller Seitz, *New York Press*;

John Simon, *National Review*; David Sterritt, *Christian Science Monitor*, Peter Travers, *Rolling Stone*; Amy Taubin, *The Village Voice*; Armond White, *New York Press*

LOS ANGELES FILM CRITICS ASSOCIATION

Robert Abele; David Ansen; Sheila Benson; Philip Berk; Jorge Camara; Charles Champlin; Dean Cohen; Manohla Dargis, *L.A. Weekly*; Alonso Duralde; David Ehrenstein; Harold Fairbanks; Stephen Farber; F. X. Feeney; Juan Rodriguez Flores; Brandon French; Steven Gaydos, *Variety*; James Greenberg; Ray Greene; Peter HennÉ; Kirk Honeycutt, *The Hollywood Reporter*; David Hunter; Leonard Klady; Andy Klein; Robert Koehler, *Variety*; David Kronke; Emanuel Levy, *Variety*; Lael Loewenstein; Rod Lurie; Leonard Maltin, *Entertainment Tonight*; Willard Manus; Joseph McBride; Todd McCarthy, *Variety*; Myron Meisel; Joe Morgenstern, *The Wall Street Journal*; Jean Oppenheimer; H. J. Park; John Powers; Peter Rainer, *New York Magazine*; Michael Rechtshaffen; Jerry Roberts; Harriet Robbins; Dorothy Rochmis; Robert Rosen; Dean Sander; David Sheehan; Henry Sheehan, *Orange County Register*; Charles Solomon; Bob Strauss; Ella Taylor, *L.A. Weekly*; Myra Taylor; Kevin Thomas, Kenneth Turan, *L.A. Times*; Glenn Whipp

BROADCAST FILM CRITICS ASSOCIATION

Brian Adams, KICU-TV, San Jose; Bob Aicardi, Weymouth Channel 10, Weymouth, MA; Mark S. Allen, KMAX-TV, Roseville, CA; Rick Anthony, Hard Radio.com; Raquel Bahamonde, WISH-TV, Indianapolis; Howard Benjamin, The Interview Factory; Sandy Benjamin, The Interview Factory; Joey Berlin, Celebrity Interviews; Anna Boiardi, TNT; Rich Borowy, Linear Cycle Productions; Bill Bregoli, Westwood One; Ron Brewington, ScreenScene.com; Anne Brodie, CTV/CFTO News, Ontario, Canada; Tom Brown, Turner Classic Movies; Dr. Joe Browne,

WOR, New York; Camara Jorge, Univision Network; Bill Carlson, WCCO-TV, Edina, MN; Mari Cartel, Channel Hollywood/ Celebrity Edge; Jimmy Carter, Nashville Network; Michael Cayer, Reviewers at Large/CFCF; Paul Chambers, CNN Radio; Chuck the Movieguy, WCWB/Pittsburgh; Bonnie Churchill, National News Syndicate/L.A. Times Syndicate; Mike Cidoni, WOKR, Rochester and WIXT, Syracuse, N.Y.; Paul Clinton, CNN; Cathy Cogan, MJI Broadcasting, Van Nuys, CA; Gary Cogill, WFAA-TV, Dallas; Linda Cook, KWQC-TV, Davenport, IA; Dennis Cunningham, WCBS-TV, New York; Sandi Davis, KRXO-FM, Norman, OK; Kirstie Day, The Movie Show, Calgary, Canada; Bob Denerstein, KMGH-TV, Denver; Bill Diehl, ABC Radio Network; Dan DiNicola, WRGB-TV, Niskayuna, N.Y.; John Di Simio, board of directors; Michael Doyle, Mike's Midnight Movie Reviews; Sara Edwards, WHDH, Boston; Ed Fairbanks, Cox Cable Orange County, CA; Cynthia Farah, KVIA, El Paso, TX; Jim Ferguson, Dish Network; Rosalie Fox, Associated Press; Jack Garner, WCMF, Rochester, N.Y.; Guy Giampapa, Walpole Community Television, East Walpole, MA; Suan Granger, SSG Syndicate; Mark Greczmiel, KCRA, Sacramento, CA; Laura Gross, LEG Productions; Stuart Halperin, Hollywood Online; Bill Harris, E! News Daily; Doug Harris, Connecticut Radio Network; Bob Healy, Satellite News Network; Dana Hersey, AMC; Devra Hill, KIEV-AM, Los Angeles; Lynda Hirsch, WKYC, Cleveland; Louis B. Hobson, CHFM, Calgary, Canada; Juliette Hohnen, Oxygen; Jeff Howard, The Movie Guys, KVVU-Fox, Las Vegas, NV; Terry Hunter, KGMB/Honolulu; Harlan Jacobson, WFUV-FM, WNYC-AM, New York; Andy Jones, E! Online; Diane Kaminsky; Lisa Karlin, Entertainment Weekly Radio; Steve Katinsky, Steve; Larry Katz, American Radio Networks; Kathryn Kinley, WPIX, New York; Bill Klein, WHAM/ WHEC-TV, Rochester, N.Y.; Craig Kopp, Startalk; Barry Krutchik, Premier Radio Networks; Dino Lalli, KOCO-TV, Edmond, OK; Joanna Langfield, Movie Minute; Mike LaSalle; Matt Levitz, LEG Productions; Joe Leydon, MSNBC.com; Ann Lieber, ET on the Radio; Rod Lurie, board of directors; Mary Lyon, HGTV; Jeffrey Lyons, WNBC, New York; Noel Manning, Cinema-scene; Fiore Mastracci, Outtakes with Fiore; Sean McBride, KFDM, Beaumont, TX; Holly McClure, Adrenaline Radio; Michael Medved, SRN Radio Network; Robin Milling, World Entertainment News Network; Shep Morgan, Jeanne Wolf's Hollywood; David Moss, WJW-TV, Cleveland; Terry David Mulligan, MovieTelevision; Jonathan Mumm, KXTV, Sacramento, CA; Gayl Murphy, ABC Radio; Greg Murray, Film Flix and Video Picks; Dave Neil, The Movie Guys, KVVU-Fox, Las Vegas; Steve Oldfield, WOFL, Orlando, FL; Kyle Osborne, NewsChannel 8, Springfield VA; Scott Patrick, One Starz!/Encore; Cindy Pearlman, WFLD-TV, Arlington Heights, IL; George Pennacchio, KABC-TV, Los Angeles; Mose Persico, CFCF-TV, Montreal, Canada; Jenny Peters; Bob Polunsky, KENS-TV, San Antonio; Leo Quinones, KLSX/KIIS, Los Angeles; Mark Ramsey, Movie Juice; Larry Ratliff, Larry, KABB-TV, San Antonio; Tim Reid, eyada.com; Mike Reynolds, AP Radio; Leslie Rigoulot, Movie Talk/Video Views and AOL: Film Scouts; Neil Rosen, New York 1; Sam Rubin, KTLA-TV, Los Angeles; Maria Salas, CBS-Telenoticias, Miami; Gino Salomone, WTMJ, Milwaukee; Gary Schendel, KGTV, San Diego; Melanie Seymour, Pentacom Productions; But Shapiro, WBJC, Baltimore; Bob Shaw, KTVU, Oakland, CA; David Sheehan, KCBS, Los Angeles; Jeffrey Shore, Zeal Media; Barbara Siegel, Siegel Entertainment Syndicate; Joel Siegel, *Good Morning America*; Scott Siegel, Siegel Entertainment Syndicate; Alan Silverman, Hollywood Bytes; Patty Spitler, WISH, Indianapolis; Greg Srisavasdi, E! Radio; James St. James, James St. James' Hollywood; Susan Stark, WWJ, Detroit; Patrick Stoner, WHYY, Philadelphia; Linda Stotter, Entertainment Time-Out; Jim Svejda, KNX-AM, Los Angeles; Roger Tennis, Clips; George Thomas, WELW-AM, Cleveland; Melissa Tong, International Channel; Peter Travers, *Rolling Stone*; John Urbancich,

SunNews.com; Sara Voorhees, Conus Communications; Jan Wahl, KRON, San Francisco; Chuck Walton, Hollywood.com; Dixie Whatley, WCVB-TV, Boston; James Wilson, KSDK-TV, University City, MO; Bill Wine, WTXF, Philadelphia; Jeanne Wolf, Jeanne Wolf's Hollywood; Paul Wunder, WBAI Radio; Bobbie Wygant, KXAS, Dallas, Ft. Worth; Paul Zimmerman, If.com; Bill Zwecker, WMAQ, Chicago

Index

Page numbers in italic indicate photographs.